A COMPANION TO LATE ANTIQUITY

BLACKWELL COMPANIONS TO THE ANCIENT WORLD

This series provides sophisticated and authoritative overviews of periods of ancient history, genres of classical literature, and the most important themes in ancient culture. Each volume comprises between twenty-five and forty concise essays written by individual scholars within their area of specialization. The essays are written in a clear, provocative, and lively manner, designed for an international audience of scholars, students, and general readers.

A COMPANION TO LATE ANTIQUITY

Edited by

Philip Rousseau
with the assistance of Jutta Raithel

WILEY-BLACKWELL

A John Wiley & Sons, Ltd., Publication

This paperback edition first published 2012
©2012 Blackwell Publishing Ltd

Edition history: Blackwell Publishing Ltd (hardback, 2009)

Blackwell Publishing was acquired by John Wiley & Sons in February 2007. Blackwell's publishing program has been merged with Wiley's global Scientific, Technical, and Medical business to form Wiley-Blackwell.

Registered Office
John Wiley & Sons Ltd, The Atrium, Southern Gate, Chichester, West Sussex, PO19 8SQ, United Kingdom

Editorial Offices
350 Main Street, Malden, MA 02148-5020, USA
9600 Garsington Road, Oxford, OX4 2DQ, UK
The Atrium, Southern Gate, Chichester, West Sussex, PO19 8SQ, UK

For details of our global editorial offices, for customer services, and for information about how to apply for permission to reuse the copyright material in this book please see our website at www.wiley.com/wiley-blackwell.

The right of Philip Rousseau to be identified as the author of the editorial material in this work has been asserted in accordance with the UK Copyright, Designs and Patents Act 1988.

Library of Congress Cataloging-in-Publication Data

A companion to late Antiquity/edited by Philip Rousseau; with the assistance of Jutta Raithel.
    p.   cm. — (Blackwell companions to the ancient world)
  Includes bibliographical references and index.
  ISBN 978-1-4051-1980-1 (hardcover : alk. paper) ISBN 978-1-118-25531-5 (pbk. : alk. paper)
1. Mediterranean Region—History—To 476.   2. Rome—History—Empire, 30 B.C.–476 A.D.
3. Civilization, Classical.   4. Hellenism.   I. Rousseau, Philip.   II. Raithel, Jutta.
  DE86.C63 2009
  937'.08—dc22

A catalogue record for this book is available from the British Library.

Set in 10/12.5pt Galliard by SPi Publisher Services, Pondicherry, India
Printed in Malaysia by Ho Printing (M) Sdn Bhd

1   2012

Contents

Figures

Maps

Notes on Contributors

CLIFFORD ANDO is Professor of Classics at the University of Chicago. He has recently published a book on religion in the Roman Empire, *The Matter of the Gods* (University of California Press, 2008), and is now working on a study of law and cultural change, to be published under the title *The Ambitions of Government*.

OLOF BRANDT is Secretary of the Istituto Pontificio di Archeologia Cristiana in Rome, and Assistant to the Chair of Early Christian Architecture at the same institute. He has excavated the early Christian baptistery of the church of San Lorenzo in Lucina in Rome, and is currently working on a new archaeological analysis of the Lateran baptistery.

PHILIP BURTON is Lecturer in New Testament Studies and Biblical Languages in the Department of Theology and Religion at the University of Birmingham. He is the author of The Old Latin Gospels: A Study of Their Texts and Language (Oxford University Press, 2000), of *Language in the* Confessions *of Augustine* (Oxford University Press, 2007), and has translated

Augustine's *Confessions* (Everyman, 2001). He is currently working on an edition of the Old Latin traditions of the Gospel according to John.

DANIEL F. CANER is Associate Professor in the Departments of History and Classics at the University of Connecticut, Storrs. He is the author of *Wandering, Begging Monks: Spiritual Authority and the Promotion of Monasticism in Late Antiquity* (University of California Press, 2002), and *History and Hagiography from the Late Antique Sinai* (Liverpool University Press, forthcoming). He is currently working on a book on monastic wealth and economy in the late antique east.

MALCOLM CHOAT is Lecturer in the Department of Ancient History at Macquarie University, Sydney. Most recently, he has published *Belief and Cult in Fourth Century Papyri* (Brepols, 2006). He is currently working on an edition of the bilingual papyrus archive of Apa Johannes.

DAVID COOK is Associate Professor of Religious Studies, specializing in Islam, at Rice University, Texas. He has published most recently *Understanding Jihad* (University of California Press, 2005) and *Martyrdom in Islam* (Cambridge University Press, 2007).

KATE COOPER is Senior Lecturer in Early Christianity at the University of Manchester and Director of its Centre for Late Antiquity. She is the author of *The Virgin and the Bride* (Harvard University Press, 1996), and joint editor (with Jeremy Gregory) of several Ecclesiastical History Society Meeting collections (Boydell Press, 2004, 2005, 2006). Her book *The Fall of the Roman Household* was published by Cambridge University Press in 2007, together with a collection edited with Julia Hillner, *Religion, Dynasty, and Patronage in Early Christian Rome, 300–900* (from the same publisher). She is now working on the first volume (250–500) of *The Oxford History of Medieval Europe*, and developing a more general book on early Christian women, aimed at disaffected female accountants and stockbrokers.

RAFFAELLA CRIBIORE is Professor of Classics at New York University. She is the author of *Writing, Teachers, and Students in Graeco-Roman Egypt* (Scholars Press, 1996), *Gymnastics of the Mind: Greek Education in Hellenistic and Roman Egypt* (Princeton University Press, 2001), *The School of Libanius in Late Antique Antioch* (Princeton University Press, 2007), and, with Roger Bagnall, *Women's Letters from Ancient Egypt, 300 BC–AD 800* (University of Michigan Press, 2006). She is currently working on the *Orations* of Libanius.

JAN WILLEM DRIJVERS is Lecturer in Ancient History in the History Department at the Rijksuniversiteit Groningen.

His latest book is *Cyril of Jerusalem: Bishop and City* (Brill, 2004), and he is coauthor of *Philological and Historical Commentary on Ammianus Marcellinus*, xxii–xxvi (Brill, 1995–2007). He coedited *Ammianus after Julian: The Reign of Valentinian and Valens in Books 26–31 of the Res Gestae* (Brill, 2007).

JENNIFER EBBELER is Assistant Professor of Classics at the University of Texas at Austin. She is the author of several articles on classical and late antique epistolography. Her first book, *Disciplining Christians: Correction and Community in Augustine's Letters*, is forthcoming from Oxford University Press.

JUDITH EVANS-GRUBBS is Professor in the Classics Department at Washington University in St. Louis. Author of *Law and Family in Late Antiquity: The Emperor Constantine's Marriage Legislation* (Clarendon Press, 1995), she has most recently published *Women and the Law in the Roman Empire: A Sourcebook on Marriage, Divorce, and Widowhood* (Routledge, 2002). Her current project is a book, *Children without Fathers in Roman Imperial Law*, to be published by Oxford University Press.

JAMES A. FRANCIS is Associate Professor of Classics in the Department of Modern and Classical Languages, Literatures, and Cultures at the University of Kentucky. He is author of *Subversive Virtue: Asceticism and Authority in the Second-Century Pagan World* (Pennsylvania State University Press, 1995). He is currently working on a book on visuality and verbal and visual representation in classical and late antiquity, tentatively titled *More than Meets the Eye: Image, Text, and Visuality in the Second to Fourth Centuries, CE.*

MICHAEL GADDIS is Associate Professor in the Department of History at Syracuse University. He is author of *There is No Crime for Those who Have Christ: Religious Violence in the Christian Roman Empire* (University of California Press, 2005) and (with Richard Price) *Acts of the Council of Chalcedon* (Liverpool University Press, 2005).

ANDREW GILLETT is Australian Research Council Queen Elizabeth II Fellow and Lecturer in Late Antiquity in the Department of Ancient History, Macquarie University, Sydney. His books include *Envoys and Political Communication in the Late Antique West, 411–533* (Cambridge University Press, 2003) and (as editor) *On Barbarian Identity: Critical Approaches to Ethnicity in the Early Middle Ages* (Brepols, 2002). His current research projects concern early medieval epistolary communication and late antique ethnography.

THOMAS GRAUMANN is Senior Lecturer in Early Church History at the University of Cambridge. His most recent major publication is *Die Kirche der Väter* (Mohr Siebeck, 2002), an analysis of the formation of patristic authority in theological discourse from the third to the fifth centuries. He is currently working on a new history of church councils in Late Antiquity.

KIM HAINES-EITZEN is Associate Professor of Early Christianity and Chair of the Department of Near Eastern Studies at Cornell University. She is author of *Guardians of Letters: Literacy, Power, and the Transmitters of Early Christian Literature* (Oxford University Press, 2000) and is working on a monograph that treats the intersection of gender and text transmission in early Christianity

(to be published by Oxford University Press), and on the forthcoming *Cambridge Companion to Christianity.*

GUY HALSALL is Professor in the Department of History at the University of York. His most recent book is *Barbarian Migrations and the Roman West, 376–568* (Cambridge University Press, 2007), and he collaborated with Wendy Davies and Andrew Reynolds in editing *People and Space in the Middle Ages, 300–1300* (Brepols, 2007). He is currently compiling a volume of his collected essays, and developing new thoughts on Merovingian cemeteries and social history (see his *Early Medieval Cemeteries*, Cruithne Press, and *Settlement and Social Organization*, Cambridge University Press, both 1995).

FELICITY HARLEY is Lecturer in Medieval Art History at the University of Melbourne and a Research Fellow at the Trinity College Theological School. She is currently completing a book on the emergence of Crucifixion iconography in Late Antiquity.

CAROLINE HUMFRESS is Reader in History in the School of History, Classics, and Archaeology at Birkbeck, University of London. She is the coauthor (with Peter Garnsey) of *The Evolution of Late Antiquity* (Orchard Academic, 2001; French tr. F. Regnot, Éditions La Découverte, 2004), and she is author of *Orthodoxy and the Courts in Late Antiquity* (Oxford University Press, 2007). She is currently working on a project exploring comparative ancient law and legal practice.

MARK HUMPHRIES is Professor of Ancient History in the Department of Classics, Ancient History, and Egyptology at

Swansea University. He has published various books and articles on ancient religions and Late Antiquity, notably *Communities of the Blessed: Social Environment and Religious Change in Northern Italy, 200–400* (Oxford University Press, 1999) and, most recently, *Early Christianity* (Routledge, 2006). He is currently working on usurpers and local politics in the late Roman world.

NAOMI KOLTUN-FROMM is Associate Professor in the Department of Religion, Haverford College. She has published most recently on Tatian, and is currently working on a book focusing on the connections made in early Jewish and Christian exegesis between holiness and sexuality in religious community formation, to be published under the title *The Hermeneutics of Holiness*.

BLAKE LEYERLE is the John Cardinal O'Hara Associate Professor of Early Christianity in the Department of Theology at the University of Notre Dame. She is the author of *Theatrical Shows and Ascetic Lives: John Chrysostom's Attack on Spiritual Marriage* (University of California Press, 2001), and is currently completing a book on early Christian pilgrimage.

CONRAD LEYSER is Fellow and Tutor in History at Worcester College, Oxford. Author of *Authority and Asceticism from Augustine to Gregory the Great* (Oxford University Press, 2000), he is reinventing himself as a historian of the late Carolingian and Ottonian episcopate, with articles on the Formosan Schism and Liudprand of Cremona either published or due to appear. He is coediting *England and the Continent in the Tenth Century*, to be published by Brepols; with Kate Cooper, he is co-editing a volume, *Making Early Medieval Societies: Conflict and Belonging in the Latin West, 400–1200*, to be published by Cambridge University Press.

RICHARD LIM is Professor of History at Smith College, responsible for teaching the history of the ancient Mediterranean, of Greece and Rome, and of Late Antiquity. Author of *Public Disputation, Power, and Social Order in Late Antiquity* (University of California Press, 1995), and joint editor (with Carole Straw) of *The Past before Us: The Challenge of Historiographies of Late Antiquity* (Brepols/Bibliothèque de l'Antiquité Tardive, 2004), he is currently working on a book about the reception of public spectacles and civic transformation in late Roman cities, as well as a volume on the social history of late antiquity and another on the historical interactions in premodern Eurasia.

RITA LIZZI TESTA is Professor of Roman History at the Università degli Studi, Perugia. Long noted for her work on both the eastern (*Il potere episcopale nell'Oriente romano: Rappresentazione ideologica e realtà politica nel IV–V secolo d. C.*, Edizioni dell'Ateneo, 1987) and the western episcopate (*Vescovi e strutture ecclesiastiche nella città tardoantica: L'Italia Annonaria nel IV–V secolo d. C.*, Edizioni New Press, 1989), she has published most recently *Senatori, popolo, papi: il governo di Roma al tempo dei Valentiniani* (Editrice Edipuglia, 2004), and has edited two important volumes: (with Jean-Michel Carrié) *Humana sapit: Études d'Antiquité tardive offertes à Lellia Cracco Ruggini* (Brepols, 2002), and *La trasformazioni delle élites in età tardoantica* (L'Erma di Bretschneider, 2006).

S. T. LOSEBY is Lecturer in Medieval History at the University of Sheffield. His most recent publications deal with urbanism in Gaul and exchange in the Mediterranean during Late Antiquity. He edited, with Neil Christie, *Towns in Transition: Urban Evolution in Late Antiquity and the Early Middle Ages* (Scolar Press, 1996), and is working on a book entitled *Marseille in Late Antiquity and the Early Middle Ages*, to be published by Oxford University Press.

NEIL MCLYNN is University Lecturer in Later Roman History in the Faculty of Classics at the University of Oxford and Fellow of Corpus Christi College. He has published widely in the field of Late Antiquity, including *Ambrose of Milan: Church and Court in a Christian Capital* (University of California Press, 1994). He is currently working on a study of the career of Gregory of Nazianzus.

ANDREW MARSHAM is Lecturer in Islamic History in the Department of Islamic and Middle Eastern Studies at the University of Edinburgh. He has published on rebellion and safe conduct in early Islam. His book, *Rituals of Islamic Monarch: Accession and Succession in the First Muslim Empire*, will be published by Edinburgh University Press in 2009.

WENDY MAYER is Research Associate in the Centre for Early Christian Studies at the Australian Catholic University. She has published most recently *The Homilies of St John Chrysostom – Provenance: Reshaping the Foundations* (Pontificio Istituto Orientale, Rome, 2005), and (with Bronwen Neil) *St John Chrysostom: The Cult of the Saints* (St Vladimir's Seminary Press, 2006). She is currently working on a critical analysis of the sources concerning John Chrysostom's life under the title *John Chrysostom: The Deconstruction of a Saint*, and with

Pauline Allen on a compendium and analysis of the sources concerning the churches of Antioch under the title *The Churches of Syrian Antioch (300–638 CE)*.

STRATIS PAPAIOANNOU is William A. Dyer Jr. Assistant Professor in the Humanities and Dumbarton Oaks Assistant Professor of Byzantine Studies in the Classics Department at Brown University. He has published widely on Byzantine Literature. Currently, he is completing a book-length study on autobiography and literary aesthetics in premodern Greek writing with a focus on Michael Psellos (provisional title: *Michael Psellos' Autography: A Study of Mimesis in Premodern Greek Literature*). He is also working on a critical edition of Psellos' letters.

KARLA POLLMANN is Professor of Classics at the University of St. Andrews. She has published most recently a commentary, with introduction and text, on Statius, *Thebaid* 12 (Ferdinand Schöningh, 2004), and has edited (with Mark Vessey) *Augustine and the Disciplines* (Oxford University Press, 2005). She is currently working on Augustine's *De Genesi ad litteram*, and is directing a major international and interdisciplinary project on the reception of Augustine through the ages. Her *Poetry and Exegesis in Premodern Latin Christianity* (edited jointly with Willemien Otten) was published by Brill in 2007.

STEFAN REBENICH is Professor of Ancient History and the Classical Tradition in the Department of History at the Universität Bern. He has published most recently *Jerome* (Routledge, 2002), following his major study *Hieronymus und sein Kreis* (Steiner, 1992), and *Theodor Mommsen: eine Biographie* (first published

Beck, 2002; 2nd edn., 2007). He is currently working on the correspondence between Theodor Mommsen and Friedrich Althoff, to be published by the Bavarian Academy.

ÉRIC REBILLARD is Professor of Classics and History at Cornell University. Author of *In hora mortis: évolution de la pastorale chrétienne de la mort aux IVe et Ve siècles dans l'Occident latin* (École Française de Rome, 1994), he has published most recently *Religion et sépulture: l'église, les vivants et les morts dans l'antiquité tardive (IIIe–Ve siècles)* (Éditions de l'École des Hautes Études en Sciences Sociales, 2003), of which an English translation will be published by Cornell University Press in 2008; and he has edited (with Michel Nancy) *Hellénisme et christianisme: questions de religion, de philosophie et d'histoire dans l'antiquité tardive* (Presses Universitaires du Septentrion, 2004). He is currently working on the interactions between Christians and non-Christians in Late Antiquity.

PHILIP ROUSSEAU is Andrew W. Mellon Professor of Early Christian Studies at The Catholic University of America. He has published most recently *The Early Christian Centuries* (Longman, 2002), and is working on a book tentatively entitled *The Social Identity of the Ascetic Master in Late Roman Christianity.*

CHRISTINE SHEPARDSON is Assistant Professor in the Department of Religious Studies at The University of Tennessee-Knoxville. Her first book is entitled *Anti-Judaism and Christian Orthodoxy: Ephrem's Hymns in Fourth-Century Syria* (Catholic University of America Press, 2008). Two recent articles study how religious authority relies on the manipulation of physical places in fourth-century Antioch (the theme of her next major study): "Controlling Contested Places: John Chrysostom's *Adversus Iudaeos* Homilies and the Spatial Politics of Religious Controversy," *Journal of Early Christian Studies* 15 (2007): 483–516, and "Burying Babylas: Meletius and the Christianization of Antioch," *Studia Patristica* 37, XV International Conference on Patristic Studies (forthcoming).

CLAIRE SOTINEL is Professor of Roman History in the Department of History at the Université Paris XII Val de Marne. Author of *Rhétorique de la faute et pastorale de la reconciliation dans la Lettre apologétique contre Jean de Ravenne* (École Française de Rome, 1994), she has published most recently *Identité civique et christianisme: Aquilée du IIIe au VIe siècle* (École Française de Rome, 2005). She is currently working on the role of information in Late Antiquity.

DENNIS E. TROUT is Associate Professor of Classical Studies at the University of Missouri-Columbia. He is author of *Paulinus of Nola: Life, Letters, and Poems* (University of California Press, 1999), and his recent publications include articles on Pope Damasus and Lombard Rome. He is currently preparing an annotated translation of the epigraphic poetry of Pope Damasus.

JOHN VANDERSPOEL is Professor of Late Antiquity in the Department of Greek and Roman Studies at the University of Calgary. He is author of *Themistius and the Imperial Court: Oratory, Civic Duty, and Paideia from Constantius to Theodosius* (University of Michigan Press, 1995). More recently, he coedited *The Cambridge Dictionary of Classical Civilization* (Cambridge University Press, 2006). He is currently preparing a book on the emperor

Julian and developing a project on the nature of the late antique west.

Mark Vessey is Principal of Green College and Professor of English at the University of British Columbia. He is author of *Latin Christian Writers in Late Antiquity and Their Texts* (Ashgate, 2005), and editor (with Karla Pollmann) of *Augustine and the Disciplines* (Oxford University Press, 2005). Current projects include a Blackwell Companion to Augustine and the translation and annotation of Erasmus' Annotations on Luke for the *Collected Works of Erasmus* (University of Toronto Press).

David Woods is College Lecturer in the Department of Classics at University College Cork. He has published numerous articles relating to the history of the late antique and early medieval periods, from the work of Ammianus Marcellinus to that of Adomnán of Iona. He is currently working on the relationship between, and reliability of, the surviving sources for the Arab–Byzantine wars of the seventh century.

Preface and Acknowledgments

The challenges we faced in creating this volume were considerable, the main consideration being a need to be different. Late Antiquity has recently attracted a new kind of interest, displayed precisely in the production of broad surveys like this one. The thirteenth and fourteenth volumes newly incorporated into the *Cambridge Ancient History* (Cameron and Garnsey 1998; Cameron et al. 2000), the compendium produced by Harvard University Press on the "postclassical world" (Bowersock et al. 1999), the volume *The Evolution of the Late Antique World* (Garnsey and Humfress 2001), and the collection of papers edited by Simon Swain and Mark Edwards (2004) are only the most obvious examples; there is more to come, notably in the relevant volumes of the *Cambridge History of Christianity.* A desire to sum up the scholarly achievements of a generation or more has, perhaps naturally, brought pressure to bear on potential editors and publishers alike.

In what way could we be different, therefore? My answer depended on a specific understanding of "Companion." Instead of drawing up a list of topics that I thought such a book should contain, and then asking potential contributors to write about one of them, I worked the other way around, approaching potential contributors, and then asking them what they would like to write about. My reasoning was that we would attract in that way well-documented essays that reflected what scholars working in the field found interesting and important; essays that would give some impression of how this or that topic was being defined and tackled. In a sense, therefore, the contributors designed the book. For reasons implicit in the scheme, I also tried to approach scholars who, while having proved themselves in early publications, still faced a substantial career of exploration in the period. Although that does not apply to every chapter, the number of younger scholars who have contributed gives the volume a special character.

There were predictable results. The first was an apparent selectivity; but that was also implicit in the scheme: for, there are aspects of Late Antiquity that nowadays attract less attention than they used to. The selectivity might reflect, therefore, new directions in which late antique studies are currently moving. Or one could put the matter another way and say simply that there are gaps. It is striking that no one saw fit to offer a chapter on the structure of the empire or on the way its government and administration functioned. Much is revealed when we compare the pattern here with the formalities of A. H. M. Jones's *Later Roman Empire* (Jones 1964) – a book we all grew up with (see Brown's review, Brown 1967b). So, while we have a perhaps predictable interest in families and monasticism, there is nothing on the army or on slavery. It remains true, nevertheless, that a treatment of more traditional topics is lodged within chapters ostensibly different in their focus. Government, for example, makes its appearance in the contexts within which it was applied. And one can also plead that the book as a whole gives a useful impression of what "late antique studies" meant to a significant cadre of its devotees in the early years of the twenty-first century.

But it is not, therefore, an exhaustive work of reference. We have taken the concept "Companion" seriously. Because we started out with authors rather than topics, the book presents itself as a potential journey in the company of enthusiasts and experts. Instead of examining a building, as it were, that conveniently stands still while we look it over, we set out across a landscape under the guidance of people who know it well, who have their favorite areas and landmarks, and can point them out with erudition and delight. Armed with such a gazetteer, readers can then make the journey over again by themselves, knowing what kinds of things they might look for and how to recognize their significance.

The model of a journey has other uses: for, if there is an overarching theme to the book, it consists in change and movement. Late Antiquity was a period in which little stood still (in spite of attempts to achieve the contrary). The men and women we observe in this exotic, distant setting were themselves in transit, displaced persons impelled by loyal or nostalgic recollections of their past, yet constantly stumbling upon unpredictable futures. That is no doubt true of every period of human experience. Yet, there is something specific about the combined uneasiness and inventive courage of late antique people – their "anxious" energy (see Dodds 1965, and Brown's review, Brown 1968a). They knew that the ground was shifting somewhat beneath their feet; but those who successfully mastered events were able to do so because they identified viable alternatives to their familiar habits of mind and culture.

So, what is Late Antiquity? It is not facetious to suppose that it is both antique and late. Equally to the point, it is not an entirely new concept. Those who study the late antique field today (and not only in the English-speaking world) feel naturally indebted to the work of Peter Brown, symbolized in what was an early and broad-ranging work, *The World of Late Antiquity* (Brown 1971b). Brown's point was in part to bridge a gap between studies of "the Later Roman Empire" and of "Byzantium," while paying due respect also to those cultures that lay to the east of the Greek world and to the west of Persia – cultures eventually brought under the sway of Islam.

To some extent, all scholars devoted to such a project are students of Gibbon (see Ando, ch. 5); and in his most famous work we see an unapologetic link between "late" and "decline." Among the finest analyses of our debt to Gibbon are the essays of Arnaldo Momigliano (a scholar to whom Peter Brown, by his own admission, owed a great deal: see his splendid obituary, Brown 1988a). One thinks especially of the papers collected in his *Studies in Historiography* (Momigliano 1966b). By the turn of the twentieth century, however, the later empire had already begun to acquire a more distinct and positive character in the eyes of historians, as we can see reflected in the work of, for example, J. B. Bury. His willingness to give independent definition to the period is reflected in a 1909 Creighton Memorial Lecture, "The Constitution of the Later Roman Empire" (Bury 1910). Twenty years before, he had published *A History of the Later Roman Empire, from Arcadius to Irene, 395 AD to 800 AD*, which he continued later with *A History of the Eastern Roman Empire, from the Fall of Irene to the Accession of Basil I, AD 802–867* (Bury 1889, 1912). His best-known summation of the period is probably his *History of the Later Roman Empire from the Death of Theodosius I to the Death of Justinian, AD 395 to AD 565* (Bury 1923), which he followed up five years later with a lecture series, *The Invasion of Europe by the Barbarians* (Bury 1928). Embedded in all those titles is a set of suppositions about the meaning of the late Roman period.

At the time Bury was developing his treatments of the theme, Ernst Stein was publishing (in 1928) his *Geschichte des spätrömischen Reiches* (familiar to most historians in its French translation by Jean-Rémy Palanque, *Histoire du Bas-Empire*, 1949–59). He had already published a volume on Byzantium in the later sixth century (Stein 1919). Meanwhile, on the basis of extensive scholarship toward the end of the nineteenth century, inspired by both Pan-Slavism and a burgeoning confidence in Greek self-identity, Norman Baynes was working on his *Byzantine Empire* (Baynes 1925). His earlier interest in the roots of that Byzantine tradition is demonstrated, for example, in his almost contemporary work *The Historia Augusta: Its Date and Purpose* (Baynes 1926), and by his Raleigh Lecture to the British Academy, "Constantine the Great and the Christian Church" (Baynes 1930). His understanding of the tradition was in some ways crowned by the book he edited with H. St. L. B. Moss, *Byzantium: An Introduction to East Roman Civilization* (Baynes and Moss 1948). (Moss himself had already published his *Birth of the Middle Ages, 395–814* (Moss 1935).) The overlap with Jones was now in place – the Jones who produced in the same period his wonderful volumes, *The Cities of the Eastern Roman Provinces* and *The Greek City from Alexander to Justinian* (Jones 1937, 1940). This is only to scratch the surface of late Roman scholarship between the two world wars; but it makes clear enough how firmly established the concept of Late Antiquity had become, in ways that broke barriers between Roman, Byzantine, and medieval history, well before 1971. (For further reflections, see Rebenich, ch. 6.)

Breaking the barriers was, however, a difficult task then and not markedly easier now. The different fields of inquiry – Roman, Byzantine, and medieval – are still often segregated into different departments in universities and entered upon under different banners, both conceptual and methodological (see Mayer, ch. 1). One complicating factor is the study of the "early Middle Ages." Just as we face here the question of how late is "late," so medievalists wonder how early is "early." One of the legacies of nineteenth-century nationalism was each nation's desire to have its own "heroic age," the supposed seedbed of its specific character. Franks, Lombards, and Anglo-Saxons had all been participants in the age of migration (more properly, perhaps, of immigration); and their descendants recognized their own *Volk* as essential to the *Völkerwanderung*. That momentous shift in populations sat squarely between familiar medieval developments and the more obviously Roman period; but it was always possible, furthermore – indeed, had been since the days of Jordanes and Gregory of Tours (Geary 1988, 2002; Goffart 1988, 2006) – to push back the specificity of "the people" to form a historical tradition at least parallel if not prior to that of Rome.

Similar problems attach to the notion of "Byzantium," for it is difficult to decide whether to start with Constantine and the building of his new capital in the AD 320s, or with later emperors like Justinian (AD 527–65), Heraclius (AD 610–41), or Basil I (AD 867–86). A lot depends on what one imagines such figures marked the beginning of; but it has always been difficult to present Constantine as a convincingly "Byzantine" figure (see Papaioannou, ch. 2).

A third difficulty arises in connection with Christianity. Here, for some historians, Constantine does mark a clear beginning, a break with the pagan past. Yet Christianity was established, obviously, long before Constantine, which makes it difficult to characterize that religion as another species of antiquity – as if to think that "late" antiquity means Christian antiquity. It is more convincing to think of "ancient Christianity" as a single historical unit, reaching from the first century AD; but that introduces the further difficulty of deciding when, if ever, that ancient Christianity could be said to have "ended" (Markus 1990). And the "novelty" of Constantine has long been hotly contested, especially if one brings into play factors other than the religious (Barnes 1981, 1982).

Lurking behind many of those difficulties and complexities is the notion that there *had* been a real divide, after which Roman government, culture, and religion took on markedly new forms; forms that were, nevertheless, neither Byzantine nor medieval. The divide took the form (in historians' minds) of a "third-century crisis," partly economic, partly political. The nature, indeed the reality, of the crisis has been endlessly debated in modern times; but, insofar as it existed (and there was obviously disruption of serious dimensions), it served to make any enduring antiquity seem "late." A major architect of the theory (somewhat in the spirit of Gibbon) was Michael Rostovtzeff, a Russian exile much embittered by the eventual outcome of the Revolution, which he saw as the destruction of the urban middle classes, the true guardians of both liberty and refinement. He detected a similar outcome in the third century, which ushered in (for him) an age of brutalism and ignorance (see especially Rostovtzeff 1926). Other writers have continued to refine the picture (Remondon 1964; MacMullen 1976). Rostovtzeff was only an extreme example of the disenchantment generated by the horrors of two world wars (another crucial exemplar was Henri Marrou: see Marrou 1938); a loss of faith in the achievements of both the Renaissance and the Enlightenment, each in their way the offspring of a "classical" mentality. To some degree, that correspondingly invited historians to think of later antiquity as more in accord with the spirit of Revolution and of Romanticism, not to say a demotic and progressive spirit. Such simplicities are impossible to sustain for long; but the rectification developed by a scholar like A. H. M. Jones gave Diocletian (the ostensible founder of the new order) a past that explained his propensities, defined his opportunities, encouraged his reactions, and inspired his reforms.

Jones was also confident in venturing at least to the lip of the Islamic era – another culture wedded to uncompromising monotheism and a politically inventive notion of the state and of civil society, both of them with ancient roots (Fowden 1993). So we are brought to Brown's subtitle (1971b), *From Marcus Aurelius to Muhammad*.

Late Antiquity is considered to be, therefore, after some things and before others. The polarities are significant, in that they conjure up slippage from state to state. One recalls both the anxiety and the speed of life in this period. It is no accident, perhaps, that many at the time felt that they were heading for the biggest ending of all, the end of the world; a moment of completion that would signal both the demise of Rome and the triumph of Christianity (Daley 1991). The finality was a sign that the future was hard to give a shape to: eschatology exhausted some people's capacity for optimism. Indeed, so confused was the vision of what was to come that dissent itself, especially theological dissent, became a hallmark of the Christianizing *mentalité* (see Graumann and Lim, chs. 36 and 33 respectively). One might almost argue that to be postclassical was to become theologically argumentative. Yet, the transformations envisaged by Augustine in his *City of God*, the inventive ambitions of new settler kings, and Justinian's ruthless desire to reinstate the glories of empire, all kept those with nerve and insight intent upon creating as well as salvaging. Antiquity for them was no longer a jewel to be preserved but a resource to be mined; a key not to escape or even to survival but rather to invention. Paradoxically, the apparent calm and confidence that we associate with the classical temper enabled the men and women of this more turbulent time to create the world in which we now live.

In conclusion, some brief but heartfelt words of gratitude: to the contributors, who have provided the most important ingredients of this volume (and have taught me to value colleagues who are accurate, patient, and prompt); to Jutta Raithel, for meticulous attention to detail in manuscripts and bibliographies; to my most recent collaborators at Blackwell – Barbara Duke, Janey Fisher, and Jacqueline Harvey – who aided the final dash to the finish (not forgetting the many others who encouraged and guided me at earlier stages, including Al Bertrand, Ben Thatcher, Rebecca du Plessis, and Hannah Rolls); and to my wife Thérèse, who steered me through many shoals of panic and despair, and without whose application the index would never have seen the light.

PHILIP ROUSSEAU

Abbreviations

Abbreviations used correspond to those adopted in *The Oxford Classical Dictionary* and *The Oxford Dictionary of the Christian Church*. Regularly referred to are:

ANRW   Hildegard Temporini (ed.), *Aufstieg und Niedergang der römischen Welt: Geschichte und Kultur Roms im Spiegel der neueren Forschung*, Berlin and New York, Walter de Gruyter (1972–)

CAH   *The Cambridge Ancient History*, Cambridge, Cambridge University Press. Many references will be to the recent new volumes:

          Bowman, Alan K., Cameron, Averil, and Garnsey, Peter (eds.), *The Cambridge Ancient History*, xii: *The Crisis of Empire, A.D. 193–337* (2005)

          Cameron, Averil, and Garnsey, Peter (eds.), *The Cambridge Ancient History*, xiii: *The Late Empire, A.D. 337–425* (1998)

          Cameron, Averil, Ward-Perkins, Brian, and Whitby, Michael (eds.), *The Cambridge Ancient History*, xiv: *Late Antiquity: Empire and Successors, A.D. 425–600*, Cambridge, Cambridge University Press (2000)

CC   *Corpus Christianorum* (normally the Series Latina), Turnhout, Brepols

CIL   *Corpus Inscriptionum Latinarum*, Berlin, Reimer/Walter de Gruyter (1863–)

CSEL   *Corpus scriptorum ecclesiasticorum latinorum*

ILS   H. Dessau (ed.), *Inscriptiones Latinae Selectae*, Berlin, Weidmann (1892–1916)

MGH	*Monumenta Germaniae Historica*
PG	J. P. Migne (ed.), *Patrologia Graeca*
PL	J. P. Migne (ed.), *Patrologia Latina*
PLRE	Jones, A. H. M., Martindale, J. R., and Morris, J. (eds.), *The Prosopography of the Later Roman Empire*, 3 vols., Cambridge, Cambridge University Press (1971–92)

CHAPTER ONE

Approaching Late Antiquity

Wendy Mayer

As we approach Late Antiquity in the first decade of the twenty-first century, a number of questions arise. We must ask ourselves not simply *what* is it that we see – that is, what does Late Antiquity look like, how do we define it, what shape does it currently take? – but also *why* do we see what we see? To what degree does the *way* in which we approach Late Antiquity shape the picture that we receive? This leads to a deeper question: what drives us to approach Late Antiquity in the particular ways that we do? What are the historical and ideological underpinnings of the approaches that were taken in the past or that we now exploit? These last two questions are explored at length in the chapters by Papaioannou, Leyser, Vessey, Ando, Rebenich, and Brandt (and touched on in Trout, Francis, Harley, Burton, Gillett, Halsall, Drijvers, and Lim). It is on the second question (how does the way in which we approach Late Antiquity shape the picture that we receive?) and its related issues that I want to focus here. My purpose is to raise awareness of how our approach to the field is a significant factor in shaping our perception, to learn what kinds of questions to ask of what we see, and to provide some understanding of the limitations of the methodologies, approaches, and theories that we apply. In this respect, the chapter is at its heart a consciousness-raising exercise, a warning to those about to enter the world of Late Antiquity that everything may not be as it at first appears.

Approaching the Evidence

As a first step in engaging with these particular issues, let us explore some of the problems that arise from the different types of evidence that are available to us, since the nature of the evidence itself and the methodological problems associated with interpreting it can significantly determine our approach. Essentially, the evidence available to scholars of Late Antiquity divides into two kinds: material sources (often derived from archaeological investigation, and here inclusive of art) and textual sources (that portion of evidence, of whatever kind, that comprises some form of written record). In this respect, we can already see some of the problems that arise, since, as Brandt and Francis point out, this dichotomy has been influential in establishing barriers between traditional disciplines. Scholars of art history or archaeology are often not skilled in interpreting textual evidence, while scholars skilled in the interpretation of textual evidence are often poorly trained, if at all, in the interpretation of archaeological or material remains. Furthermore, these classifications are in fact unhelpful in themselves, since textual evidence is often a subset of material evidence as presently defined. That is, the lines between the two can blur considerably, since much epigraphy is located on buildings, rock faces, caskets, gems, or other objects of interest in themselves, while mosaic-covered floors and walls, usually of interest for their pictorial or decorative elements, can contain names, dedications, and other forms of writing. Moreover, while the term "textual" implies that such evidence begins and ends in its present written form, this classification can in itself be misleading, since texts such as homilies or orations originated in an oral form and the written record can preserve in fossilization any one of a number of editorial layers. Letters likewise were communicated orally, usually being read aloud to the recipient or dictated in the first instance by the sender (Ebbeler, ch. 19), but at the same time the written letter as preserved can represent only a fraction of the actual communication (see Sotinel, ch. 9). The letter-carrier, an important link in the communicative act, as often as not delivered a report by word of mouth, which might represent the real content of the communication, the letter itself containing platitudes. That in Late Antiquity literary texts, too, should be seen as "performative" is a point raised in this volume by Haines-Eitzen (ch. 17) and Gillett (ch. 26).

This brings us to another issue. Traditionally, when we think of "textual," we tend to think of a particular kind of written evidence – namely that which is literary in form, such as historiographies, saints' lives, or philosophical treatises, with the concomitant effect that scholars who apply themselves to textual evidence often place less value on less literary textual forms, such as graffiti, epitaphs, or documentary papyri. In a similar fashion, the decorative arts – sculpture, painting, relief-carving, and the like; in reality a subset of material evidence – for historical reasons come with their own set of interpretive problems and ideological approaches (see Harley, ch. 21). As a result, the picture of Late Antiquity that we receive from any one scholar is in the first instance always going to be distorted, since it is a rare interpreter of the evidence who is skilled in every single problematic and every single kind of evidence. When we add to this the current tendency in Anglo-American scholarship to dismiss the political and administrative aspects of Late Antiquity in favor of the cultural and social (Ando, ch. 5), we (and here I mean as much "we the interpreters" as "we the viewers") need in addition to be wary both of the questions that have been asked of the evidence and of the landscape that we gaze upon in consequence.

These are simple problems, however, in relation to the difficulties that the evidence itself throws in our path, when we attempt to interpret it. A key theme in the chapters that follow is the fragility of evidence and its impermanence. There are salutary lessons to be learned in neglecting to take into account what has failed to survive when interpreting what is extant. In archaeology, bones, walls, coins, jewelry, tableware, and other durable artifacts are but a fragment of the entire picture. As Halsall (ch. 27) points out in regard to the territories that bordered the former Roman Empire, the very fact of finding Roman ware in these northern lands means that something that has left no trace in the archaeological record must have been traded in exchange, such as raw materials, slaves, or fabrics. The survival of textual evidence is equally quirky. As Choat (ch. 23) points out in regard to Coptic papyri in Egypt, the more humid climatic conditions in the Nile delta have meant that what must have been a large body of documentary evidence from a major urban center (Alexandria) has failed to survive, while the dry conditions further up the Nile insured that the documents of less significant settlements were preserved. Likewise, the simple decision to conduct an archaeological dig at Kellis (Ismant el-Kharab) in recent years, with its resultant corpus of finds, has demanded the adjustment of a range of assumptions about the rise of written communication in Egypt in Coptic. That is, before this additional body of evidence was recovered, it was assumed that there was a direct link between the use of Coptic and the rise of Egyptian monasticism. Now it can be seen that Coptic was more widely used, had connections with the domestic sphere, and was adopted by women more readily than Greek. New discoveries of doublets of already existing texts can also lead to dramatic reappraisal. In the case of the recently discovered "new" sermons of Augustine (Dolbeau 1996), some of those already known to us are proven now to have been severely shortened, due to editing. Dolbeau 23 is five-sixths longer than its counterpart, Sermon 374; and Dolbeau 26 contains more than 1,500 lines, compared to some sixty in Sermon 198 (Hill 2000). Much of the material that had been stripped out was topical and now helps us to understand better some aspects of the Donatist movement in North Africa. Or, as Trout (ch. 12) points out, the simple act of seeking out late antique material in a particular region (in this instance, Spain) can lead to the emendation of our picture of that territory as an epigraphic desert.

Failure to survive into the modern period, because of impermanence or fragility, or not failing to survive but existing undiscovered are, however, only two aspects of this problem. As Brandt (ch. 11) points out, the privileging of the classical era of Greece and Rome on ideological grounds often led in the past, in archaeological excavations, to the permanent destruction of late antique layers or architectural phases, in order to free that which was valued. Administrative and ideological decisions made in Late Antiquity itself can be equally responsible for the disappearance or suppression of sources. As Humfress (ch. 25) indicates in the case of Justinian's *Digest*, in the process of its assembly four centuries worth of jurisprudence was condensed from "more than three million lines … into roughly 150,000 lines, one twentieth of the original mass." Our reading of the contents of the *Digest* necessarily alters significantly when we understand, as Humfress goes on to explain, that the promulgation of the document was accompanied by the deliberate suppression of a vast quantity of purged material. Carolingian cultural imperialism, as Leyser (ch. 3) points out, is similarly responsible not only for the survival of Latin texts but also for their loss, just as the wilfulness of individual Carolingian scribes in copying nonapproved texts helped to reduce those losses. The point to be made here is that for a variety of reasons a large proportion of late antique evidence is always missing, and while sometimes parts of it will later be found, as in the examples of the dig at Kellis and the sermons of Augustine, more often than not it can never be recovered. The picture of Late Antiquity that we currently see, in consequence, is always subject to readjustment by the acknowledgment of gaps or by the appearance of new discoveries.

At the same time, gaps that appear to be gaps in the record can prove to be not gaps at all, but a failure in interpretive method. A case in point is the prevalent belief in a seventh-century "dark age" in the Near East as a consequence of the Islamic conquest. Where previously a theory of decline and impoverishment had been based on monumental architecture and site inscriptions, recent archaeological work in Jordan and Palestine has led to an improved coin record for the seventh to eighth centuries, which has in turn led to improved ceramic chronologies and typologies (Walmsley 2007). Where the seventh century had until recently been largely empty of pottery, that void is now being filled, with a resultant shift in the interpretation of the economic situation. This is due not only to freshly excavated material, the value of which can now be recognized, but also because the newly developed tools now permit retrospective identification. Brandt's Example 1 points to a similar reinterpretation of this period at Rome, likewise on the basis of an improved analysis of pottery. In another example, Trout points to a recent reframing of the apparent paucity of Latin epigraphy in the sixth and seventh centuries. Rather than positing a theory of decline, the suspicion has now been raised that in these centuries inscriptions were increasingly painted rather than incised, leading to a failure not in epigraphic habit, but in survival.

Awareness of gaps in the evidence, their possible causes, and the way in which they can distort our received picture of Late Antiquity, is only one aspect of which to be aware. Another, quite different point that we need to consider when approaching the evidence that does survive is the question of layers. As often as not, different types of evidence exist in multiple sets, or consist of a number of coexisting layers. Negotiating our way through those layers requires making value judgments and applying interpretive frameworks. The simple act of editing a text from a multitude of manuscripts, for instance, implies that we can recover the author's original version, that we can determine the precise relationship between the different versions of the text (as codified in the stemma), and even that the text has an author in the first instance. These assumptions and the resultant decisions that are made, problematic in themselves, dictate how we read the text and thus analyze the information that it contains. But, as we observed in the case of Augustine's sermons, the manuscripts on which an edition is based do not always lead back to the "original," but may represent instead an interim stage in the text. In that instance, the manuscripts known prior to the 1980s had all been copied from a version severely edited by medieval redactors, who had shaped the material to suit their own purposes. Multiple editions within the lifetime of an author are also not uncommon, leading to the coexistence of different "original" phases of a work, as Woods shows in the cases of the histories of Eunapius of Sardis and Malchus (ch. 24). In those instances, do we place priority on the most recent version, as being definitive, rather than privileging the original or first version as we would normally do, or do we value each version equally as having been produced at different times in the author's life with different agenda? What do we do, moreover, with works that fail to survive in their own right, but exist reshaped within a later work, such as Photius' ninth-century epitome of Philostorgius' *Ecclesiastical History*, or the *Chronicle* of Pseudo-Joshua the Stylite, an important sixth-century record of local events in Syria preserved entirely within the eighth-century *Chronicle* of Pseudo-Dionysius (Trombley and Watt 2000)? Editors who publish a document divorced from its context make decisions that permanently shape the reader's response. Or, what of texts such as the Jerusalem and Babylonian Talmuds, the Tosefta and Midrashim, or the Theodosian and Justinianic "law codes," which constitute the collation of multiple layers accrued over time? To talk of authorship is complicated and, in the case of the first four items, dates can be assigned only within a broad range. Even within the *Theodosian Code*, a legal opinion ascribed to a particular "author" is just as likely to have been drafted by a bureaucrat before being promulgated in the "author's" name. In the same way, letters that purport to be from a particular person's hand may in fact have been composed at that person's direction by a *notarius*, whose formulaic phrases, rather than the "author's," the letter conveys. When we make assumptions about authorship in those instances – that a particular rabbi spoke, that a particular consul or emperor promulgated a law, or that a particular individual wrote a letter – our approach to the texts might already be skewed.

The question of authorship itself can be problematic, and attribution, false or otherwise, can shift the context within which evidence is located and therefore interpreted. The late antique period is the golden age of pseudepigraphy, with many texts being passed down to the copyists of medieval times under false names. We have already encountered the case of Pseudo-Joshua and Pseudo-Dionysius within the genre of historiography. The homiletic genre is perhaps the most complex, but also serves to give an idea of the range of possibilities. In the case of John Chrysostom, while around 820 authentic sermons survive, another 3,000 or so are attributed to him in the manuscript tradition. In some cases (well over 1,000) the homilies contain genuine material from John's sermons, excerpted and combined with new material to create a text that suited the needs of audiences in the seventh, eighth, and ninth centuries. In the case of another 1,000 or so, the homilies were originally authored in their entirety by someone else. The corpora of a number of lesser-known preachers have survived in this manner, such as the sixth-century Leontius, a presbyter of Constantinople, and John's contemporary and enemy, Severian of Gabala. Similarly, in the case of Caesarius of Arles and Maximus of Turin, survival of many of their homilies has depended on attribution to Augustine. The case of Ephrem is even more complex. Works attributed to him survive in both Greek and Syriac, but the relationship between the two corpora is distant, and the biographies demonstrate two distinct personae (Griffith 1998). Identifying an "author" or even discussing authenticity in this instance is problematic, and so we talk of Ephrem Graecus and Ephrem Syrus to distinguish the two corpora. To further complicate matters, monks of the Greco-Syrian communities of the sixth century, in addition to transmitting the works of Ephrem Graecus in both Greek and Syriac, composed new poetic homilies and songs in his style and under his name (Griffith 1998). Gaddis (ch. 34) points to falsification of a quite different and more malicious kind in the case of conciliar Acts, particularly those of Chalcedon. There, language disparity enabled manipulation of translations of documents from the opposing sides to produce subtly altered texts that supported hostile propaganda.

In the case of art, architecture, and archaeological excavation, the impact upon interpretation of the way in which we handle layers (or phases) is just as profound. The church of Santa Maria Antiqua in the forum in Rome, which dates from the sixth century and is currently closed for study and restoration, is a case in point. The wall paintings, which date variously from the sixth to the late eighth century, present their greatest challenge on the wall to the right of the apse. There, seven separate layers of decoration can be identified: the earliest (marble tile) predates Christian use of the building (in the fourth and fifth centuries); the latest date to the time of the iconoclast controversy (www.archeorm.arti.benicultural.it/sma/eng). Each layer is significant in itself, each is only partially extant, and each is fragile. Recovery of any one layer is at the expense of another. Whatever decisions are made during the process of restoration will determine how the program of illustration inside the church is viewed for generations to come. The very phrase "pre-Christian use of the building" raises an issue discussed at length by Brandt in his chapter (11) on the archaeological record for Late Antiquity – namely, that buildings go through different phases of use or construction, of which any late antique phase may be only one of many. Do we analyze the late antique phases in the context of other late antique construction and building use, or do we also view the late antique phases of a particular building within the context of that same building's earlier and later use? Again, whatever decisions we make when analyzing these buildings do much to shape the picture that emerges. Brandt's discussion of the Harris stratigraphic method and its implications in this respect is particularly instructive. Reuse of building materials or of spolia from the classical period, as in the case of the Constantinian arch in Rome or the statuary relocated in the Constantinopolitan hippodrome by emperors from Constantine to Theodosius II (Bassett 2004), again present us with a diverse range of possibilities for interpretation. As Harley (ch. 21) also shows, whether we privilege the classical origins of the material or the way in which it is reframed and reshaped in Late Antiquity determines whether the late antique construction is viewed as symptomatic of transformation or decline. Whether we view the late antique result as an aesthetic object (in terms of visual reception) or as a political act (or in terms of its religious, social, or cultural function), our choice shapes the way in which we respond to it. Similarly, an art historian, an archaeologist, a political scientist, an anthropologist, a military or social historian will shape in their own way the questions that they ask. Understanding the multilayered nature of late antique evidence and the multiple contexts that consequently arise is an important part of approaching Late Antiquity.

A quite different theme that recurs throughout this volume is the at times contradictory nature of different types of evidence, and the problems this can pose for the interpreter. As we saw in the case of the seventh-century Near East, the evidence of monumental architecture and site inscriptions has been interpreted as pointing to economic decline and increasing impoverishment. Evidence from coins and pottery, on the other hand, now points on the contrary to an active monetary and trade economy, which displays little sign of major economic or organizational failure. In this case, the assumed "dark age" is dark only if we interpret monumental architecture and inscriptions as the chief signs of economic prosperity, and if we are unaware of the other type of evidence. Brandt's example of the *tituli* in Rome (where textual evidence – the *Liber Pontificalis* – claims that they were founded in the early second century, but the archaeological record shows no evidence of this) illustrates how conflict of this kind can lead to a variety of interpretations. It also shows the weight that tends to be placed on textual evidence, with the archaeological evidence being adduced to prove or disprove it: so, in this case, the assertion of the *Liber* that the *tituli* existed in some form is taken as reliable, even if its dating remains open to suspicion. Brandt's point is that such confidence can lead to overinterpretation of the evidence. The comparison with Jewish evidence of community organization also demonstrates how the location of evidence within a broader context can compel reinterpretation. As a final point, Brandt raises a more important question in regard to the handling of textual evidence: whether information from a sixth-century text should be read as anything other than evidence of a sixth-century preoccupation. Marsham (ch. 32) points to a less problematic case: the late seventh-century decree that Arabic be used as the official language for tax administration in the occupied territories in the east. Documentary papyri from Egypt show, on the contrary, that Greek and Coptic persisted alongside Arabic well into the ninth century, demonstrating a gap between official policy and actual practice. As Sotinel (ch. 9) shows, similar discrepancies existed between official and unofficial communication. In those instances, the contradictory evidence does not point to a problem in interpretation, but rather encourages us to look for the inconsistencies that could and did occur within late antique society.

Far simpler problems can cause the unwary to err, and thus reshape the picture. One of the most simple, yet most profound, is the question of date. The dating of late antique texts and material culture is often itself based on a series of assumptions (as in the case of seventh-century near eastern pottery above) and can be far less secure than one realizes. Since the discovery, for example, of the "dead cities" of the limestone massif in northwest Syria, the same coin, pottery, and architectural evidence has been dated variously on the basis of different sets of assumptions, giving rise to substantially different interpretations (Tchalenko 1953–8; Sodini et al. 1980; Tate 1992; Magness 2003; for an overview see Foss 1995 and Magness 2003: 195–9). The resultant variation in dating for the decline of the site spans the period between the sixth and tenth centuries, with profound implications for the thesis of Syrian decline in the sixth century prior to Umayyad rule. In another example, the dating of papyrological documents, spells, or amulets, in cases where no internal evidence for date exists, relies largely on the context of the find and the style of the script in which it is written. These criteria tend to offer no greater precision than a quarter or half century and can as often result in a range of several centuries, again with implications for interpretation. In cases where the *termini* of an author's career are known and provide a helpful *terminus ad* and *post quem*, our ability to pinpoint the date of texts that they are known to have authored tends to rest largely on a reading of internal evidence. In the case of Augustine's homilies, agreement on how to interpret the same internal evidence has shifted a number of times in the past few decades, with the result that even the latest dating system (Hombert 2000, who challenges La Bonnardière 1965) is now being overturned (Drobner 2000, 2003, 2004). Likewise, in the case of the largest surviving corpus of Greek homilies (John Chrysostom's), dates that had been established over three centuries of scholarship are now being overturned (Pradels et al. 2002; Mayer 1999, 2006). When it comes to the dating of a historical event referred to in texts, even when the date of the textual evidence itself is not in question, as often as not two interpreters who derive their evidence from the same texts will fail to agree. A compelling example is the date of the translation to Constantinople in the fourth century of the relics of Saints Andrew, Luke, and Timothy. Utilizing the same evidence, a variety of dates have been offered in recent decades, the latest diverging by some twenty years (Woods 1991; Burgess 2003).

The simple fact of how evidence is presented can also have a profound effect on how we approach a particular body of artifacts or texts. One negative example is the editions through which we access texts. Since the process of producing modern scientific editions is extremely slow, we are as often reliant on text editions produced in the early 1900s or even as far back as the 1700s. The way in which a group of documents is arranged in these instances consequently reflects scholarly opinion of the time of the edition, rather than the present. In the case of the letters of John Chrysostom, the current edition was produced by Bernard de Montfaucon in 1724, and the criteria according to which he arranged and numbered the letters are far from chronological. Recent scholarship has, moreover, completely overturned the received view of the chronology of the letters (Delmaire 1991), with the result that a person who reads them in their present sequence gains a far different picture when they reread them in the sequence proposed by Delmaire. Without the benefit of a reorganized edition, significant information is obscured from the reader, including a sense of how John's correspondence progressed as historical events related to his exile unfolded, of how different letter-bearers were utilized to deliver items to various locations in packets, and of who was writing to him and with what frequency. The positive impact of new technologies in terms of the way it presents evidence to us, on the other hand, cannot be overestimated. Three-dimensional imaging and computer graphics facilitate the reconstruction of buildings and sites, or the restoration of furnishings and interior decoration (see the computer-generated images of mosaics from Antioch and of the church at Seleucia Pierea in Kondoleon 2000), allowing the viewer to scan and interact with buildings and sites in ways that were impossible with photographs, drawings, or hand-constructed models. At the same time, the Internet is increasingly being utilized by archaeological teams to publish interim results in new ways and with unprecedented rapidity (e.g., www.sagalassos.be, which includes 360-degree scans of the site topography and summaries of current field notes). Only a small number of scholars of Late Antiquity currently utilize these technologies (for the more advanced resources available in classical antiquity see, e.g., www.stoa.org), but they are increasingly changing the way in which we approach and ask questions of the field, particularly in regard to material evidence.

While it may be exciting to apply novel approaches to the evidence, particularly those derived from other disciplines, it must also be recognized that each type of evidence has its limits. Asking new questions in order to expand our horizons and to look at the evidence in fresh ways may in fact produce false results (see Rebenich, ch. 6, on social Darwinism and evolutionary biology). While this should be no disincentive to approaching the evidence from new directions, since, as the other chapters show, significant reshaping of the picture of Late Antiquity can emerge, the same chapters as often as not demonstrate the problems that can occur when we push the evidence beyond its natural limits. Gillett (ch. 26), in particular, shows how the desire to read "barbarians" into late antique texts, driven by a late twentieth-century interest in ethnology and identity, is doomed to frustration. With only Greek and Roman texts in our possession, and in the total absence of "barbarian" ones, "we can look through Greco-Roman eyes to see how they perceived the Other and, therefore, themselves"; yet, no matter how much we want or try to, we cannot, via these same texts, recover "barbarian" self-identity. In a similar fashion, the feminist drive to recover late antique women from male-authored texts, which was prevalent in Anglo-American scholarship of the 1980s and 1990s, is now quietly being laid to rest, in recognition that such an endeavor is fraught with difficulty, if not impossible (Elizabeth Clark 1998). It remains to be seen whether the new tools currently being borrowed from other disciplines – discussion, for example, of "intertextuality" and the "linguistic turn" – further our knowledge of Late Antiquity or lead to distorted readings.

Other Considerations

Beyond the evidence itself, there are a number of other considerations that influence our approach to Late Antiquity. Several authors in this volume highlight the influence of definition or classification. Koltun-Fromm (ch. 37), for instance, points to the terms "Jews," "Judaism," "Christianity," "Christians," and demonstrates how a change in classification (with an attendant change in assumptions) can substantially alter the way that we read a text. She points to David Frankfurter's argument that "many of the texts that we think of as 'Christian' or even 'Jewish-Christian' are better understood as thoroughly Jewish texts when we redefine our 'Jewish' categories by late ancient standards." Moreover, a change in classification is itself most likely to result from a fundamental shift in scholarly conceptualization in the first instance. A single shift in the way we view Late Antiquity can thus have a ripple effect, resulting in further changes in perspective. Choat (ch. 23) points to similar difficulties with the definitions currently applied to Coptic culture, where Late Antiquity in Egypt is often identified as "the Coptic period." Not only is this term unhelpful, but terms such as "old Coptic" assume the existence of a "Coptic proper," while the label "magical papyri" likewise immediately places a group of texts, not always appropriately, within a particular context of meaning. Burton (ch. 22) points to a similar problem in regard to "late Latin," which we might also apply to the term "Late Antiquity." As he argues in the case of the former, it is aesthetic or confessional rather than linguistic considerations that condition its use. Koltun-Fromm in the end suggests that we would do better to stop worrying about how *we* define particular social and religious groups in Late Antiquity and ask instead how *they* defined *themselves*.

The question of whether a particular label that has meaning at one place or time is equally valid across the full geographic and chronological span of Late Antiquity is also significant. A case in point is the term "monk," which may have little validity in the third century and can mean quite different things in the fourth or sixth centuries, as well as describing a distinctly separate phenomenon in each of Egypt, Syria, Ireland, or Gaul. This in turn leads to the importance of sensitivity to regional variation within Late Antiquity, as Halsall (ch. 27) demonstrates when he defines three different trajectories of development and change among northern ethnic groups. The consideration of late Roman relations with ethnic groups beyond its borders calls for consciousness of yet another issue, raised by Humphries and Halsall – the Mediterranean-centered focus that has characterized until very recently the study of the late antique period. Why, Halsall ponders, does it sound right to talk of late antique Axum or Persia and yet odd to talk of late antique Ireland or Denmark? "Either," as he goes on to argue, "the 'late antique problematic' is specific to the history of the empire and its inhabitants, in which case *all* non-Roman lands should be excluded, or, which sounds more reasonable, any and all territories that came into contact with Rome and that therefore might (or might not) be affected by the west's political demise, or the longer-term changes around the Mediterranean, should be understood as encompassed within the notion of Late Antiquity." This same problematic highlights the influence of our textual sources for this period, which overwhelmingly view the world around them through a late Roman imperial lens (see Humphries, Gillett, Drijvers, and Vanderspoel). We rarely possess texts that were composed outside the empire looking in, such as the Sasanian *Book of Lords*. This point brings us to another element in Halsall's argument – the tendency of late antique scholarship to privilege textual evidence. We think more readily of a late antique Persia precisely because textual evidence concerning the region survives. In the case of regions and ethnic groups that habitually slip beneath our radar, there has been a heavy and influential reliance on material evidence.

If our view of the late antique ethnic groups has until recently been "Mediterraneanist," as Koltun-Fromm (ch. 37) and McLynn (ch. 38) demonstrate, our view of religious groups has until recently been "Christianist." "Paganism" and "Judaism," as those contributors demonstrate, are artificial constructs that arise from a Christian perspective. It can be instructive to observe the parallels between scholarly approaches to religious groups outside the boundaries of Christianity in Late Antiquity, and to the ethnic groups that bordered the late empire. Here once again, the "Christianist" lens is due as much to the bias of the surviving (textual) sources as the biases of the ideological approaches brought to bear in analyzing them. As many of the chapters in this volume show, paradoxically, it is important to resist (if we are to move beyond them) modes of viewing the late antique world that stem from the late antique world itself.

Definitions, distinctions, and biases within the field of late antique scholarship are not the only factors that shape the late antique world that we view. Ideological, political, and economic considerations beyond it have an influence, too. What we publish, and what we survey, dig, and analyze, and thus the picture that we derive, are to a degree directed, consciously or unconsciously, by governments, universities, and private foundations. In North America and Australia, new editions of late antique texts are produced slowly and infrequently, partly because in the first the definition of a research monograph usually does not include (for purposes of tenure decisions) an edited text, while in the second the government is reluctant to define a text edition as a research monograph for the purposes of allocating performance-based university research funding. In Australia, in the awarding of individual research grants, on the other hand, the editing of texts was until recently valued, but the current weight placed by assessors on the "innovation" of a proposal now makes the submission of such projects undesirable. In France, on the contrary, the editing of texts is actively assisted by the government and, in response to the government's ideological position, is actively pursued by senior scholars and their students, with the result that a large proportion of newly edited texts relevant to the field are produced in that country. A similar climate of encouragement prevails in Italy and existed until recently in Austria and Germany. The personal research choices of scholars from those countries exert in consequence a greater influence than might otherwise be the case on the particular texts that become available. In the field of archaeological excavation, well-known or major sites predominated until recent decades, in large part because these tended to yield spectacular finds and attract media attention along with government and private funding.

A different kind of influence is exemplified by the Turkish government's decision to build a new dam below Birecik on the Euphrates in 2000. This had the positive effect of stirring up international interest in Zeugma, which had hitherto been lackluster (Kennedy 2000), leading to the mounting of a "rescue mission" focused on its mosaics. William Frend documents a dramatic reorienting of our understanding of Nubia in Late Antiquity that occurred as the result of an international archaeological rescue mission mounted in the 1960s in response to the damming of the Nile to create Lake Nasser (Frend 1996: 298–313). Evidence that might otherwise be ignored gets explored as the result of such governmental decisions, as much as other evidence is removed, perhaps permanently, from the record. Unexpected changes in government itself can be equally influential, as exemplified by the annexation by Turkey in 1939 of the Syrian province now known as Hatay. Since all of the arrangements had been made with the French government, the excavations and surveys in Seleucia Pieria and Antioch by a Princeton University-led expedition, which largely dealt with the late antique phase of the site, were never completed. Half a century elapsed before archaeological survey work in that province resumed, following the establishment of a sound working relationship between western and Turkish archaeologists, local officials in Hatay, and the Turkish government. At a more basic level the ongoing needs of the local communities who live on or near late antique sites can have profound influence. The need to expand a field or orchard, the availability of ready-cut (antique) stone for a building project, or the pressures of population expansion can lead as much to fortuitous discovery as to the dismantling of a site over time and its dispersal. Regional politics and the value that local communities, governments, and institutions place on the exploration and preservation of late antique remains can have as much influence as the ideologies that underpin the pursuit of Late Antiquity by scholars.

Side by side with the current view of Late Antiquity as a period of transformation, the approach to Late Antiquity itself is in a state of transition. Archaeological excavation is moving from the investigation of monuments and major sites to a more holistic approach in which lesser sites, such as Sagalassos in Pisidia, are carefully explored layer by layer over a long period of time and examined not in isolation but within the context of the surrounding territory. Increased attention to dietary analysis based on animal bones and human feces recovered from middens, to regional flora via pollen studies, and to climatic change via the analysis of the growth rings in trees, are all part of this broader interest. The recent application of marine archaeology to the site of Aperlae in Lycia (www.sciencedaily.com/releases/2000/07/000727080709. htm) is another example of this changing focus. The increasing application of methodologies developed in other disciplines to the interpretation of texts is also characteristic. Identity theory, ethnology, intertextuality, gender theory, reception theory, the gaze, postcolonialism, Bourdieu's theory of *habitus*, to name but a few, increasingly shape our reading of texts. At the same time, there is a movement away from polarities such as Judaism/Christianity, magic/religion, philosophy/theology to a view, for instance, of philosophy and Christian theology as two different modes of spiritual discourse under the larger umbrella of religion. An accompanying distrust of traditional labels, definitions, and classifications now prompts instead the question: how did a person living in this particular late antique society view both the world around them and themselves? Terms such as "magic" are now avoided in favor of talking about the supernatural or the preternatural, a dimension that seamlessly meshes with the world with which a late antique person engaged. There is an increasing move to view belief systems, such as religions, no longer as monolithic but as multifaceted, such that "Judaism" no longer describes a single belief system but many interrelated belief systems that coexisted along a sliding scale. The previous focus on christianization is now yielding to an exploration of the dynamism within this period between Judaisms and Christianities on the one hand, and Greco-Roman religions, Christianities, and Judaisms on the other. Interest in the elites of late antique society is giving way to attempts to recover evidence about the poor and middling classes. The influence of postmodernity has given rise to a range of hitherto unexplored topics to do with the senses and the mind, such as memory, sight, and smell.

There remains one final reflection on how we approach Late Antiquity. In the early twenty-first century, scholars still largely approach the world of Late Antiquity after developing their linguistic and analytical skills in the fields of Classical or Medieval Studies (on the latter, see Leyser, ch. 3; on the exclusion of Oriental Studies, see Halsall (ch. 27) and Drijvers (ch. 29)). Each of these fosters a perspective that underpins the currently dominant paradigm of transformation, since the one encourages us to look at how the ancient world changed into something other than classical antiquity, the other at how the world after antiquity was transformed into something distinctly medieval. These two monolithic *termini* (the ancient and medieval worlds), traditionally accepted as two distinctive periods in history, leave Late Antiquity little space for existence as anything other than a bridge. This situation is perhaps itself only transitory. As the study of Late Antiquity consolidates as an academic field in its own right and future scholars begin to train primarily in this field, and as modernity with its Eurocentric viewpoint ceases to exert its hold – recent events in Afghanistan, Iraq, and Lebanon are stimulating a greater focus on Oriental and Islamic Studies even as I write – a final question comes to the fore. Will this volume itself become a relic of an approach to the field that follows the path of the paradigm of decline, as the next generation moves from a paradigm of transformation to an understanding of Late Antiquity as a discrete and distinctive historical period? Or will the periodization of history itself be cast aside, and will we see the rise of an entirely new paradigm that reframes these centuries in a radically different way? Whatever occurs, it is a sobering reflection that, as the twenty-first century draws to a close, the Late Antiquity with which the new generation engages (if, that is, "Late Antiquity" as a concept still exists) may well look significantly different from the Late Antiquity with which we engage now in this first decade of the same century. In the end, Koltun-Fromm points in her chapter (37) to a fundamental truth: Late Antiquity is in essence whatever we construct of it, with the question of why we shape it the way we do being of almost as much interest as trying to retrieve Late Antiquity itself.

BIBLIOGRAPHICAL NOTE

Stimulation for this chapter arises from a number of conferences that have reflected on Late Antiquity or on methodologies relevant to it in the past few years: the conference "The World of Late Antiquity: The Challenge of New Historiographies" (Smith College, Massachusetts, 1999; see Straw and Lim 2004); the biennial conferences "Ancient Studies – New Technology: The World Wide Web and Scholarly Research, Communication, and Publication in Ancient, Byzantine, and Medieval Studies" (initiated at Salve Regina University, Newport, RI in 2000 and held most recently at James Madison University, Harrisonburg, VA in 2004); and most recently the 2005 Dumbarton Oaks Symposium, "Urban and Rural Settlement in Anatolia and the Levant 500–1000 CE: New Evidence from Archaeology" (Washington, DC, April 21–4, 2005), and "Early Christian Studies and the Academic Disciplines" (Center for the Study of Early Christianity, Catholic University of America, Washington, DC, June 5–8, 2005). Many of the questions raised here reflect or owe their origin to ideas put forward by the speakers at those conferences and the debates that ensued. For the English-speaking scholar, the conferences, "Shifting Frontiers in Late Antiquity" (held biennially within the US: www.sc.edu/ltantsoc) and "Late Antique Archaeology" (held annually in Britain and other European countries: www.lateantiquearchaeology.com) are important venues for focused reflection on the field. The proceedings of both conferences are published regularly (*Shifting Frontiers* by various publishers, most recently Ashgate; *Late Antique Archaeology* by Brill).

PART I

The View from the Future

Any period as remote as Late Antiquity we see through a thick haze of memory and interpretation. What meaning we decide to attach to the phrase "Late Antiquity" will be governed not only by our own interests and prejudices but also by the account of the period we have received from more recent observers. The same will have been true of those observers themselves; observers who, in the case of Late Antiquity, are scattered across more than fifteen centuries.

Those observers are part of Late Antiquity's future. They thought of the late Roman centuries in ways that the people of the period itself could rarely have imagined. What must fascinate the historian is the variety of viewpoints that were thus established, to all of which we stand as heirs. A moment's reflection will confirm that such an outcome is hardly surprising; but it remains easy to forget how differently the same series of events could seem to people in changed circumstances – leaving aside, for the moment, the fact that more was discovered or remembered as time passed.

The five chapters that follow, therefore, present us with two sets of data: first, the shifting viewpoints of those who came later; and second, the accumulated judgments that we must now come to terms with in making our own historical assessments.

Men and women of the Byzantine period, right down to the fifteenth century, seem to have been content to imagine that they were part of what we now think of as late Roman history. What Stratis Papaioannou helps us to see, however, is the conceit, perhaps even the illusion, that informed that view; and his account reminds us how easily nostalgia and traditional affirmations can overlook or occlude deep change (ch. 2). In the medieval west, by contrast, there was a readiness to reform and restore; but Conrad Leyser's most telling point, perhaps, is that the appeal to ancient models could be an instrument of transformation: one had to adjust one's view of the past, if one wished to put it to the service of a contemporary agenda (ch. 3).

The restoration of the past took on a different complexion in the Renaissance. Mark Vessey reminds us that there was considerable tension between an admiration for what had been "lost" in medieval darkness and a loyalty to elements of Christian culture that were precisely what the "Middle Ages" had preserved: one suspects that applause for "rebirth" was often designed to assuage the sense that one was not as novel as one might have wished (ch. 4). With the Enlightenment comes, in Clifford Ando's chapter, a more disengaged sense that the Roman world really had collapsed, and that modernity, whether of ideas or technologies, represented a more honest sense of progress (ch. 5). That confidence would be modified during the Romantic period; but Stefan Rebenich (ch. 6) presents us with a vivid description of scholarly enthusiasms, which provided (on the basis, to be fair, of exhaustive learning in the sixteenth and seventeenth centuries) not only an inconceivably richer database than even Gibbon could marshal but also fuel for the emotional and constitutional needs of the nation-state (feelings and institutions that would eventually undermine all taste for empire).

Memory, however, is never content with what is recent; and we are not merely creatures of the nineteenth century. All contemporary accounts of the Late Antiquity have their Byzantine, medieval, Renaissance, or Enlightenment layers. The long process of recollection and analysis is, even yet, inescapable – indeed, we should not feel obliged to escape it. Few of our judgments would be intelligible or convincing if we did not acknowledge how much our legacy sustains, without compromising, the freshest account of scholarly inquiry.

CHAPTER TWO

The Byzantine Late Antiquity[1]

Stratis Papaioannou

One could begin this chapter by claiming that there never was a Byzantine Late Antiquity. The people we now call the Byzantines would most likely have felt puzzled by such a suggestion. The myth of a continuous and relatively unchanged Christian empire from the fourth century through to the fifteenth century was fundamental for Byzantium, as it has been fundamental for Byzantine Studies as well. In the first grand narratives of Byzantine historiography and historiography *about* Byzantium, the distinction between "Late Antiquity" and "Byzantium" is hardly ever made.

While, from a modern perspective, this myth of monolithic continuity has been dismantled, it is another matter altogether to locate the consciousness of a break with Late Antiquity *within* Byzantine culture. Not that the Byzantines were insensitive to change or discontinuity (see Magdalino 1999). We can demarcate, for instance, Byzantium's Hellenism or, even, Byzantium's *romanitas*, for those were categories from which people in Byzantium could distance themselves. Yet, the sense of continuity with much of what we now call Late Antiquity – its discourse and institutions – was for Byzantine culture absolutely rudimentary, an almost biological necessity. Byzantium recognized in the Christian Late Antiquity its fathering past, a past that was most ancient (*archaiotaton*) and yet its true origin. It was a past performed anew in imperial and ecclesiastic ceremony, remembered in feasts throughout the annual calendar, experienced in various places and spaces, viewed in images, rehearsed in public and private readings, narrated in hagiography and history. It was a past to which one gained access primarily by perception (Spiegel 1983) and memory (Klein 2000), rather than by cognition or critique. To perceive and to remember is to evoke a presence. To evoke a presence is to seek identity. Thus to write about Byzantium's Late Antiquity is to write about Byzantium itself.

[1] This essay was written while in residence at the Freie Universität, Berlin with the support of a Fellowship from the Alexander von Humboldt Foundation. I am indebted to both institutions. I also wish to thank Diether R. Reinsch and Athanasios Markopoulos.

The overwhelmingly subjective relation to the past that Byzantium projects may obscure the fact that, like any other "past," Late Antiquity was for Byzantium not only a reality but also a construction. On a closer look, it is possible to detect several Byzantine versions of Late Antiquity, which were fashioned and refashioned in order to serve various ideologies of power and technologies of culture – imperial, ecclesiastical, and personal. I wish here to make the case that the study of Byzantine Late Antiquity pertains not simply to the study of Byzantium. In its continuous as well as fragmented – in a word, dialogical – relation to the late antique past, Byzantium can indeed tell us something about *that* past. Historians of Late Antiquity cannot afford to ignore Byzantium – not only because much of the late antique material and discursive evidence depends upon the cultural choices made by generations of Byzantine individuals and institutions, but also because Byzantium's continuity (or discontinuity) with Late Antiquity unfolds a historical hermeneutics that derived from the very same culture that we strive to interpret. The cultural processes that Byzantine society developed over time can tell us something about the cultural dynamics of Late Antiquity itself.

What follows is one possible example of such a historical hermeneutic. It pertains specifically to late antique discourse as received by Byzantium and to the ways in which this reception influenced Byzantine historiography about Late Antiquity. I will examine two separate layers of Byzantine writing: (1) metahistory (White 1973, 1987; Barthes 1981), namely Byzantine statements about the aesthetic principles that govern narratives about the past, and (2) literary criticism, namely aesthetic readings of late antique texts. One can trace a significant development in Byzantine metahistory and literary criticism. From an initial emphasis on the ability of discourse to mediate content – truth in general, but especially historical truth – Byzantine authors moved toward an increasing appreciation of form itself. This development influenced the ways in which Byzantine authors wrote about their late antique past. While initially Late Antiquity was regarded as a historical past immediately *present* in Byzantine historiography, gradually Byzantine authors became aware of how their writing about the past was mediated through form, and of how the past could therefore be creatively constructed to meet the demands or tastes of the present. What I wish to argue is that this development from valuation of content to valuation of form, and the parallel change from a *perceived* late antique presence to a *constructed* late antique tradition, represent the unfolding over time of a dynamic within Byzantium that was already inherent in late antique discourse itself. For, while the dominant view of discourse in Late Antiquity stressed the importance of content, in practice late antique authors pursued modes of writing that aspired to and were founded in the powers of form, the powers of rhetoric. By looking at Byzantine conceptions of how to write about the past and how to read texts from the past, I wish to argue that Byzantine discourse unravels the discursive contradictions and the variety of aesthetic potentials existent in Late Antiquity.

Some limitations are necessarily imposed upon this examination. Due to the constraints of space, I can only look here at a few Byzantine authors, a group of authors that date from the eighth through the early thirteenth century. They were united not so much by their social background or ideological standpoint as by their aspirations and their cultural context. They were monks and clerics, scholars and intellectuals, who strove for authority within their society and shared a culture that displayed cohesion, albeit subject to change (a culture dating from *c.* AD 750 to 1204: from iconoclasm to the capture of Constantinople by the Crusaders). After AD 1204, that cohesion was substantially altered by a new European order. I shall also confine myself to a segment of late antique discourse that remained dominant in Byzantium – namely, patristic writing of the fourth and early fifth centuries. Authors like Gregory of Nazianzus and John Chrysostom were copied, read, imagined, and imitated in Byzantium. They were truly the fathers of a massive cultural production. Finally, a note about my theoretical presuppositions is in order. My approach is inspired by what has been termed "philologically grounded eclecticism" (Ziolkowski 1996: 530), especially by readings of premodern texts that treat their metarhetorical assumptions as indices and repositories of cultural tensions and negotiations. (Examples of such readings: Goldhill 1986; Winkler 1990; Halperin 1992; Spence 1996; Zeitlin 1996; and Bynum 2001.)

Content 1: Looking at the Past at the End of Antiquity

Let me begin with a short tale from a Byzantine text that records the cultural achievements of Late Antiquity. In a brief narrative from the *Parastaseis Syntomoi Chronikai*, an anonymous collection of descriptions of Constantinopolitan monuments written in the eighth or early ninth century (Mango 1963; Cameron and Herrin 1984; Dagron 1984: 29–48; Ševčenko 1992: 289–93; James 1996), we find what we may regard as the encapsulated completion of the cultural workings of Late Antiquity; a Byzantine review of the ways in which Late Antiquity reacted to its own classical and Greco-Roman heritage (for which see Averil Cameron 1996). In this tale (*Parastaseis* 27–8), two friends – one of whom is the narrator – visit an abandoned part of the city in order to, as the narrator claims, narrate and explain (*historein*) the statues that exist there. Coming to a late antique statue, they stop and marvel at it (*thaumazein*). Suddenly, the statue falls and kills the narrator's friend. Entirely shocked, the narrator first tries to hide the body, then declares the event to the authorities. People gather amazed at the miraculous event (again, *thaumazein*). A "philosopher" divines that, according to a text of the past, the statue's fall was the work of divine providence, and the emperor orders the statue to be buried, "for it was impossible for it to be destroyed." The narrator concludes with an exhortation to his reader: "Studying these things in truth [*alêtheia*], pray not to fall into temptation, and beware when you behold the old statues, especially the pagan ones."

As the story suggests, what collapses upon the head of the unfortunate Byzantine viewer is not simply a statue. It is also a system of knowledge that collapses, a method of viewing, and a mode of representation. By the end of the story, explanatory narrative (*historia*) has been replaced by truth (*alêtheia*); truth that is now based on textual authority from the past, to be interpreted by an authority in the present and enforced by imperial power. Aesthetic marvel has been displaced by miraculous wonder. And an awesome materiality (the statue is *pachys*, heavy and thick) has been hidden – buried, as it were – under a prescriptive discourse of moral imperative and perfect clarity. The narrator tells us that he has studied with precision (*akribeia*) and is making visible (*phaneroun*) that which he is narrating. This movement from the old to the new, as thematized by this short tale, implies the completion of a cultural project. It is as if the ambiguous and dangerous world of antiquity was safely buried, Late Antiquity had completed its work, and the Byzantine Middle Ages could begin.

Content 2: Byzantine Chronicles and Late Antique Theological Transparency

The story of a collapsing statue summarizes the epistemic, moral, and aesthetic imperatives that Late Antiquity bequeathed to Byzantine discourse, especially with respect to the manner in which Byzantium was to look at, and consequently speak about, its past. The chroniclers of the ninth century knew these imperatives well. When they come to narrate their historical past, they define clearly their metahistory, the presuppositions that govern their writing of history. Theophanes the Confessor (*c.* AD 760–817/18), one of the first medieval Byzantine chroniclers who devotes his narrative to Late Antiquity, speaks in the introduction to his *Chronographia* of the precision (*akribeia*) with which he composed his work (Theophanes, *Chronikon* 3–4). Precision means here absence of mediation. Theophanes claims that all events are presented in their correct order (*taxis*) without any interpretive rearrangement. Similarly, Georgios the Monk (in the second half of the ninth century), author of a universal chronicle that begins from the creation of the world and ends in the year AD 842, declares that his narrative presents "the entire truth" (*alêtheia*) without any exterior cover but with "most transparent clarity" (*saphêneia enargestatê*). His discourse is "plentiful of content" and void of "fashioned words and artistic constructions." It is written without hiding falsehood behind a "most forceful method of construction." His is a discourse, he tells us, that will narrate a past in which pagan idols, fictions, and myths are overthrown and that will thus teach salvation; a discourse, as Georgios implies, of direct vision (*theôria*) that does not alter or deceive the senses (*aisthêseis*) (*Chronikon* 1–5; with Karpozilos 2002: 233–42).

Such metahistory is reflected in the historical narrative itself: these chronicles are full of visible signs, *sêmeia*, that make the presence of both God and the past directly accessible to the reader. The reader can see, hear, and perceive the very texture of past events: heretics suffering terrible deaths, the sign of the cross appearing time and again, fires that destroy, physical objects that obey the metaphysical order. Furthermore, the history of Late Antiquity is presented as a competition of signs – that is, the emergence of new Christian signs and the destruction of pagan ones. For instance, Constantine's mother, Helen, finds the Holy Cross under a temple and statue of the "demon" Aphrodite in Jerusalem. Then, through the power of the Holy Cross, the body of a sick woman who had been rendered "breathless and immovable" is revived. Later in Constantinople, Constantine erects his own statue, as part of the construction of his new city; but Julian, soon after Constantine's death, installs there idols of himself and other pagan Gods. Julian's idols are then superseded by a discovered statue of Christ. Julian also attempts to converse with an idol of Apollo, who is silenced, however, by the holy relics of a Christian martyr. So the story continues (Theophanes, *Chronographia* 25–6, 28, 49–50). These narratives are structured around "perceptual grids" (Spiegel 1983: 46). They show little interest in comprehending the past per se or historicizing it. Representation supersedes explanation, cognition, and critique. The reader is confronted with a series of narratives that are intended to function as direct and transparent *images* of the past.

What is at work in both the metanarrative theory and the narrative practice of these chronicles is a dominant theoretical stance adopted in late antique discourse: the pursuit of clarity and utter transparency (*saphéneia* and *enargeia*), the suppression or erasure of the surface of discourse; in short, the valuing of truth over discursive form. Eusebius, Athanasius, Basil of Caesarea, Gregory of Nazianzus, Gregory of Nyssa, John Chrysostom, Theodoret of Cyrrhus, all speak out repeatedly against discursive form, deceitful appearance, and rhetorical hypocrisy, and in favor of transparent and clear signs, presences, and truth. This is a transparency quite different from the aesthetic principles of *enargeia* or *akribeia* that defined much of Greco-Roman, Hellenistic, and imperial aesthetics; the transparency that Lucian, for instance, demands of history writing or that such historians as Dionysius of Halicarnassus and Plutarch pursued (Walker 1993). In the Greco-Roman theory of writing, transparency is appreciated not merely for the representation of truth, but also for the very artistry involved in producing a transparent representation. Greco-Roman aesthetics, therefore, which forms the background to late antique patristic aesthetics, values clarity and truth *as well as* the artistic ability to make the content of discourse available to the senses. In the late antique version of transparency, the one that Byzantines later inherit, artistry is to accede entirely to the moral demands of authenticity, according to which transparency does not carry even a hint of artificiality. Discourse is intended to let the listener or reader hear or (primarily) *see through* it; to bestow upon its content an unmediated presence. In late antique aesthetics, veracity replaces verisimilitude and theology replaces rhetoric.

This theoretical development marked a significant stage in the history of late antique discourse: the gradual disappearance of the conscious and acknowledged production of fiction. By the fifth century, fictional narratives – most notably the Greco-Roman novel – gradually disappear from cultural production and are replaced by hagiographical narratives that never acknowledge their fictionality (Bowersock 1994a). In cultural terms, such a disappearance is an inseparable feature of the gradual decline in and ultimate ending of the production of new, free-standing sculpture (the last recorded new statue during the Late Antiquity was made in the seventh century: Mango 1986). This suppression of fiction and "burying" of statues – those inescapably *material* artistic signs – are related symptoms of the theoretical stance against rhetorical and aesthetic appearance that Late Antiquity bequeathed to Byzantium.

Byzantine writers knew well that this theoretical attitude was late antique. Georgios the Monk, for instance, repeatedly invokes the authority of Gregory of Nazianzus and other patristic authors in support of his historical writing. In John of Damascus' eighth-century *Sacra Parallela*, a slightly earlier systematization of late antique knowledge, late antique texts are excerpted and codified under such headings as "On truth and trustworthy testimony," "On external beauty and the good appearance of the body," "On those who keep silence," "On hypocrisy, and irony, and feigned piety." Evident in the *Parallela* is a fear of words as mere ornamentation, forgery, and simulation; a fear of the surface of discourse and the aesthetics of mere appearance. Late antique texts are paraded one after the other precisely to reinforce that fear. What is interesting here is that the late antique theory of discourse and its fear of discursive *form* is adopted by those who in Byzantium write the history of Late Antiquity. The late antique past is thus determined by an aesthetics propagated during that past. For it is *theological* transparency, namely the necessity for an uninterrupted continuity of content and form, that defines the Byzantine perception of Late Antiquity. Byzantine historiography, it appears, is absolutely entangled in Late Antiquity. It can only view the late antique past through late antique eyes.

Form 1: Ninth-Century Literary Criticism and the Appreciation of Form

A monumental literary critical work of the mid ninth century – the *Bibliothêkê* of the patriarch Photius (*c.* AD 810–after 893) – presents a more nuanced approach. (The exact date of the *Bibliothêkê* remains a matter of debate: Treadgold 1980; Markopoulos 2004.) Photius reviews 386 books, works written mostly by late antique authors. Indeed, we know about some of these authors only through the *Bibliothêkê*. Photius is particularly fascinated with history (Kustas 1953; Mendels 1986; Efthymiadis 2000). Late antique authors are, for him, primarily a source for establishing the historiography of Christian dogmatic precision, *akribeia*. Photius is ambivalent about all Christian authors working before the establishment of Nicene orthodoxy – from Justin to Origen, from Clement to Eusebius. Photius is even more fascinated with style. Most of the authors that he discusses are placed under close stylistic scrutiny. He considers few of them perfect: only the historians Arrian and Malchus, and the theologians Basil of Caesarea and Germanos, patriarch of Constantinople (Phot. *Bibl.* 92, 78, 233). While Photius' stylistic criteria derive some of their force from Greco-Roman rhetorical theory (Orth 1928, 1929; Hartmann 1929; Kustas 1962; Afinogenov 1995), his most important stylistic principle is a late antique one, transparency. He insists on the ideal of an unbroken link between content and form. He employs a variety of Greek terms: clarity (*saphêneia*), purity (*katharotês*), transparency (*to dieides*), and precision (*akribeia*). In accord with those principles, he thinks of authorship as akin to fatherhood, as offering a genealogical clarity. The discursive form or style must present, therefore, both its content and its author's signature.

Consistent as it may be with late antique aesthetics, Photius' emphasis on transparency is, nevertheless, marked by a subversive undercurrent that surfaces in his reviews. By insisting on the description of style, and not merely of content, Photius grants style a significant autonomy. For instance, he occasionally finds fault with revered Christian authors who deviate from the norms of style and *genre* (*Bibl.* 86 on John Chrysostom as epistolographer; 195 on Maximus the Confessor and dialogue writing). More importantly, he does not refrain from reviewing books that are purely and expressly fictional (from Lucian's satire to Heliodorus' novel: *Bibl.* 128, 73). He admires the style of those texts, which do not dress themselves up as truth, and he finds some moral value in their fictional imitation of reality. Indeed, what seems to bother Photius most are texts that pretend to be truthful while being purely fictional, namely "heretical" texts (*Bibl.* 114 on the early Christian author Leucius Charinus; 189 on Akestorides). He thus marks a shift in emphasis. While late antique aesthetics demanded transparency in representation, in order to guard the moral superiority of content, Photius, by appreciating transparency, begins to see the value of discourse as such. It is no coincidence, for instance, that he is unenthusiastic about such late antique allegorical theology as that of Maximus the Confessor (*Bibl.* 192). For Photius, allegorical theology demands a search for meaning *behind,* and *regardless* of, textual form.

Photius' evaluation of discourse brings to the fore a consciousness of form that is absent from the historiography of his own day; but he is not alone in his project. He has to be placed in the wider context of discussions of form in the eighth and ninth centuries. This is the period of iconoclasm (Brubaker and Haldon 2001) – that is, a period of discussion that focused precisely on form and representation. Such authors as John of Damascus, Theodore of Stoudios, and Photius himself construct highly complex theories of the image. The question that these authors go to great pains to answer is how images can afford their viewer a relation with, perception or cognition of, the persons depicted *in* iconic representation. For them, the question is about form, the material side of representation (Barber 2002). Not surprisingly, these authors approach the debate by turning to late antique theological aesthetics (Demoen 1998, 2000; Louth 2006). They trawl late antique theology for definitions of the terms "image" (*eikôn*), "imprint" (*typos*), and "shape" (*morphê*). These terms were used in Late Antiquity primarily in a metaphorical way, in order to describe, for example, the genealogical relationships within the Christian Trinity. In the new Byzantine context, the terms are used to evaluate material representations. What are *metaphors* of truth in late antique discourse (that is, discursive functions that enable one to imagine truth) become *images* in Byzantine iconophile language (that is, material representations of truth). By returning in this way to late antique theology, the writers of the later period make form more than content the matter for discussion. In this light, we can understand Photius' approach to discourse. As in iconophile arguments, he builds his aesthetics upon late antique principles, yet this aesthetics is simultaneously a departure from the traditional emphasis. Byzantine discourse has moved from late antique *theories of truth* and is now engaged in *theories of representation.*

Form 2: Eleventh-Century Readings
of Late Antique Texts

The next significant step in the Byzantine theory of discursive representation is marked by attempts to establish a rhetorical canon, which was crystallized in the eleventh century. Ioannes Sikeliotes (early eleventh century), Ioannes Mauropous (*c.* AD 1000–after 1075), Ioannes Doxapatres (mid eleventh century), and Michael Psellos (AD 1018–78) are rhetoricians who rewrite Greco-Roman rhetorical theory by substituting new authors for the literary canon of the past (which had consisted of such authors as Demosthenes, Plato, and Homer). This is the period when Basil of Caesarea, Gregory of Nazianzus, and John Chrysostom are combined as the preeminent authorities on dogma, morality, and (more importantly) style (Mauropous, *Discourse on the Three Holy Fathers and Teachers, Basil the Great, Gregory the Theologian, and John Chrysostom*; Michael Psellos, *Styles of the Fathers*; see Agapitos 1998b). Eleventh-century theoreticians value style more intensely than did Photius. They invent such questions as "does rhetoric exist?" and "was there a time when rhetoric did not exist?" They answer the former with an affirmative and the latter with a negative (Doxapatres, *Prolegomena* 83. 1–93. 15). These questions are framed in a late antique theological manner; they are reminiscent of such questions as "was there a time when the *Logos* (Christ) did not exist?" (Athanasius, *De decretis Nicaenae synodi, passim*). This substitution of rhetoric for the divine Logos is a telling symptom of the shift in the appreciation of discourse.

In these eleventh-century writings, discourse is not merely granted autonomous value (as we saw in Photius), but is increasingly appreciated in itself. For Photius, form is important; yet more important remains the content to which form must be wedded. By comparison, in the eleventh century (especially in the writings of Michael Psellos), the reader is allowed some indulgence with regard to the surface of the text. Psellos remarks, for example, that when he reads Gregory of Nazianzus he is quite often captivated by the exterior beauties of the text; he forgets the intended meaning (*nous*), and is upset when he is forced to return to an understanding of the text's content (*Discourse Improvised on the Style of the Theologian*). Here, form does not merely come to the fore, but becomes indeed the only thing visible. Notably, Gregory's discourse is imagined in the same text by Psellos as an ancient statue like that of Aphrodite, well fashioned and full of material brilliance. Late antique discourse has regained its materiality. Its exterior form is no longer buried under the weight of meaning, but has acquired an appearance that draws to itself readers with desires for aesthetic pleasure.

Form 3: Twelfth-Century Writings about
the Late Antique Past

By the twelfth century, such sentiments are commonplace. For instance, Theodoros Prodromos (*c.* AD 1100–*c.*1170) admits that pure meaning ("mind": *nous*) may be of some value for its unmediated contemplation (*theôria*) of "naked" things (*Letter 7, PG* 133: 1261b–5b); but rhetorical language (the "tongue": *glôtta*) is equally if not more valuable, with its swift movement, multiplicity, and mediation of sight. Such views generate a variety of remarkable literary phenomena in the twelfth century. That century is, after all, the time when the conscious production of fiction and interest in sculpture are revived in premodern Greek culture, after a silence of several centuries (Beaton 1996, Agapitos and Reinsch 2000, and Roilos 2005; Mango 1963 and Grabar 1976). What pertains to my discussion here is that such views enabled a new understanding of historiography and a new writing of the past (Macrides and Magdalino 1992; Agapitos 2004; and, for comparison, Spiegel 1993). Four illustrative examples are texts by Ioannes Zonaras (late eleventh century AD–after 1159?), Eustathius, bishop of Thessalonike (*c.* AD 1115–95/6), Konstantinos Manasses (*c.* AD 1130–*c.*1187), and Niketas Choniates (AD 1155/7–1217).

Ioannes Zonaras composed a universal chronicle sometime after AD 1118 (see Grigoriadis 1998). In his introduction, he surprisingly declares that his historiography will *not* be characterized by precision (*akribeia*); rather, his text will be varied, while its author (whom Zonaras calls "its father") will assume the voices and styles of others (*Epitomê Historiôn* 1–6). By such a statement, Zonaras wishes to ward off the possible criticism that his work is not precisely truthful by pointing out that the truth of his history depends upon the truth of his sources. Simultaneously, however, such a statement asserts Zonaras' consciousness of the unavoidable discursive qualities and likely fictionality of his creation. He knows – or says that he knows – that his text does not make the past transparent.

This consciousness allows Zonaras to criticize both his sources and the past itself (Magdalino 1983). Neither the past nor the sources are presented as a series of unmediated images. Zonaras' history has characteristics often markedly different from earlier Byzantine chronicles. Like Theophanes the Confessor, he mentions the statue that Constantine erected during the foundation of Constantinople (ed. Büttner-Wobst, pp. 17–18); but here, the statue is not inscribed within the context of a competition of signs, as in Theophanes, but is exhibited, rather, as a beautiful product of Greco-Roman culture. The statue is originally a depiction of Apollo, brought from Ilion, the ancestral city of ancient Rome. Most importantly, it is a statue that "displayed the precision (*akribeia*) of an ancient hand, that creates objects that are almost breathing." *Akribeia* here is restored to its original, Hellenistic, meaning. Zonaras stresses the artistry and verisimilitude of a Greco-Roman and late antique object. It is no coincidence that this statue also falls, killing several Constantinopolitan pedestrians. This collapse, however, which happens during Zonaras' lifetime, is not a sign of a mysterious force, as in the *Parastaseis*, but functions, rather, as a metaphor for Zonaras' fierce critique of contemporary imperial power.

A similar awareness of the discursive qualities of historical discourse is expressed by Eustathius, bishop of Thessalonike, an author most famous for his extensive commentaries on the Homeric epics. Eustathius wrote a historical narrative *On the Capture of Thessalonike* sometime after AD 1185. In the *prooimion* (3–4), Eustathius distinguishes at the practical level between the narration of past events and the narration of contemporary ones. The historian of the past, according to Eustathius, often theologizes, expands his discourse, and unsparingly applies cosmetics to his expression for the sake of beauty. He becomes infatuated with descriptions, and presents much for the sake of pleasure. He might even "behave like a dancer," and he places in the foreground "strange stories," while he artistically contrives discourses for "showing off." Eustathius, being a historian of the present, will do something different. For him, the history of the present is to be a mixture of styles, ranging from simplicity to elaborate rhetoric. That the historian of the past is charged with profuse rhetoricality may be equally a rhetorical gesture by Eustathius himself. It is founded, nevertheless, upon the same notion that we encountered in Zonaras: history writing cannot but be affected by rhetoric's ornate and varied forms.

It is in the context of such metahistorical consciousness that a new late antique past is produced in the twelfth century. In Konstantinos Manasses' universal chronicle, the *Chronikê Synopsis* (see Jeffreys 1979; Reinsch 2002; Nilsson 2006), late antique theological signs, *sêmeia*, have receded (the word *sêmeion* is virtually absent). They are replaced by the distinctive ingredients of premodern fiction: heroic acts, statuesque bodies, powerful men who express their suffering and emotions, beautiful and attractive women, women actively involved in the making of history, dialogues, dreams, love stories, poisonous apples, terrible eunuchs. The chronicle also displays the distinctive stylistic devices of contemporary fiction (it should be remembered that Manasses is the author of one of four fictional romances produced in the twelfth century). The chronicle is written in verse, like the majority of the novels in this period. It also contains elaborate Homeric-like metaphors, several short digressive narratives, *encomia*, rhetorical addresses, and evocations of the audience (a marker of likely public performance). Furthermore, with several maxims of timeless morality that usually conclude the narration of an event (*sententiae*), Manasses enters the fabric of his history, expresses his opinion, and allows his audience to distance themselves from the past by looking at their own present condition. With such themes and rhetorical techniques, the historian exposes the rhetorical character of his historical work. Manasses turns the past, Late Antiquity included, into a stage for rhetoric.

My final example is Niketas Choniates' *Chronikê Diêgesis*, a history of the twelfth-century Byzantine Empire and its collapse. This history includes a description of several statues of Constantinople's late antique past in an appendix to the main narrative also known as *De Signis* (647–55; see Cutler 1968; Saradi 2000). The statues that Choniates describes could still be seen at the end of the twelfth century, but were destroyed by the crusaders, "people ignorant and untouched by beauty," in Choniates' words. A remarkable distance separates Choniates' narrative from the story of the *Parastaseis* with which I began. Choniates' statues are not inhabited by miraculous powers and awesome materiality, in need of control by moral methods of viewing. Rather, his statues display an aesthetic variety (*poikilia*); perform (*hypokrinesthai*) beauty; they evoke pleasure at their sight and sorrow at their destruction. These are artistic objects that should invite the amazement (*thauma*) and the softening (*malthattein*) of their viewers. The signs of Late Antiquity are here fully transformed or, as it were, exhumed and restored.

Conclusions

Here, our brief survey of the Byzantine Late Antiquity comes to a close. By following Byzantine historiographical writing, we traced the application of late antique aesthetic principles to the Byzantine construction of its past; authors such as Theophanes and Georgios the Monk write the past as a series of signs immediately available to the reader. We then noted, within Byzantine literary criticism of late antique texts, the shift toward an expansion and renegotiation of those aesthetic principles. Photius and later authors such as Michael Psellos advance an appreciation of form and style besides and, often, *despite* content and meaning. Finally, we detected a Byzantine rewriting of the history of the late antique past, a rewriting that was based on the new methods of reading the texts of the past. In Konstantinos Manasses or in Niketas Choniates, the past is aestheticized. It is to be narrated in an ostensibly rhetorical mode, or to be appreciated for its full aesthetic value. The original late antique projection of theology was gradually replaced in Byzantium by a consciousness of discursive aesthetics and an appreciation of form.

This change may appear at first glance to mark a radical break from Late Antiquity, a break from its critique of fiction and appearance. Yet, at every moment in this gradual development, Byzantine authors deliberately present their approaches, whether traditional or innovative, as being firmly established in the late antique tradition. From the author of the *Parastaseis Chronikai* to Choniates and from Photius to Psellos, the writing of the late antique past and the reading of late antique discourse is imagined as a continuation of late antique precepts. The Byzantines are not mistaken in that claim. Their approaches, varied as they may be, are all different threads of a complex texture already inherent in late antique discourse itself. For what the Byzantine dialogue with its past reveals is the dialogical nature of Late Antiquity itself. It reveals tensions, open-ended structures, and unspoken conditions of a highly discursive culture. For is not the late antique aversion to rhetoric also a rhetorical pose? Is not the patristic appetite for metaphors also a concession to discourse? Is not the claim that one is telling the truth simultaneously an attempt to silence the fiction involved in the telling? As the Byzantine reading of late antique texts and the writing of late antique history suggests, theology may be the most explicit statement of Late Antiquity, yet aesthetics is the tacit knowledge that conditions its cultural dynamics.

BIBLIOGRAPHICAL NOTE

No comprehensive treatment of Byzantium's relation to its late antique past exists. Nevertheless, most studies about middle and late Byzantine culture deal with the reception of Late Antiquity in one fashion or another. A good starting point for the study of the Byzantine Late Antiquity are several items in *The Oxford Dictionary of Byzantium* (Kazhdan 1991), where one can also find further information and bibliography on Byzantine authors and topics mentioned above;

see also Beck 1959; Hunger 1978; and Kazhdan 1999. For the Byzantine view of the past in general, see Beck 1978; Jeffreys 1979; Mango 1980: 189–200; Dagron 1984; Kazhdan and Epstein 1985; Lemerle 1986; Kazhdan 1987; Ševčenko 1992; Magdalino 1992 (with Spiegel 1994); Magdalino 1994 (with Clarke 1990 and Averil Cameron 1996); Kazhdan 1995; Speck 1998; and especially Magdalino 1999. See also Vryonis 1978; Adler 1989; Gray 1989; Stolte 1991; Macrides 1991; Koder 1991–2; Maas 1992; and T. S. Brown 1993. For the Byzantine view of the Hellenic and Roman past in particular, see Irmscher 1973; Mullett and Scott 1981; Garzya 1985; Baldwin 1988; Macrides and Magdalino 1992 (with Magdalino 1983); Mosshammer 1998; and Markopoulos 2006. On Byzantine historiography, see Karpozilos 1997–2002; Odorico and Agapitos 2006 with further bibliography. Byzantine chronicles were translated into other pre-modern languages (for example, Church Slavonic), and so influenced the construction of the past in later premodern cultures as well (Sorlin 1973; Franklin 1992). For the textual transmission of late antique texts, see Hunger et al. 1961 and *Byzantine Books and Bookmen* 1975. Ground-breaking work has been produced on Gregory of Nazianzus: see http://nazianzos.fltr.ucl.ac.be. Byzantine manuscripts often reveal a fascinating reading of late antique discourse through their mere selection, arrangement, or illustration of texts: see, for examples, Wilson 1978 and Pontikos 1992 (on a thirteenth-century manuscript aligning late antique with Byzantine rhetorical production), and Brubaker 1999 (on a ninth-century illustrated manuscript of Gregory of Nazianzus' *Homilies*). From the numerous studies on Byzantine reception of specific aspects of the late antique world, three examples may suffice here: Angelidi 1991 (the hagiographical refashioning of a late antique woman); Agapitos 1998a (the reading of late antique fiction); and Lauxtermann 2003 (the formation of Byzantine poetry in response to late antique reading and writing poetic habits). Some of the themes presented above are further elaborated in Papaioannou 2004, 2006a, and 2006b.

CHAPTER THREE

Late Antiquity in the Medieval West[1]

Conrad Leyser

As a child, she tells us, Teresa of Avila used to read the *Lives of the Saints* with her brother. Together they would discuss how they might become martyrs: "We settled to go together to the country of the Moors, begging our way for the love of God, that we might be there beheaded." When the improbability of this scheme dawned on them, they developed an alternative: "My brother and I set about becoming hermits and in an orchard belonging to the house we contrived, as well as we could, to build hermitages, by piling up small stones one on the other, which fell down immediately; and so it came to pass that we found no means of accomplishing our wish." So Teresa had to settle for life as a nun – but she continued, so she says, to model her life on early Christian texts. In her novitiate, suffering from physical and nervous collapse, Teresa recalls, "It was a great help to my patience that I had read the story of Job in the *Morals* of St Gregory, which the Lord seems to have used to prepare me for this suffering" (Cohen 1957: 43).

In the *Life of Teresa of Avila by Herself*, we see the strange shape and formidable power of Late Antiquity across the west in the medieval period. Our task is to explain how a woman in sixteenth-century Spain could have taken texts written a millennium previously as a direct template for her life (Weber 1990). That the world of the Later Roman Empire should have come to mean "monasticism, the cult of the saints, the texts of the Fathers," has been for some a cause of grief. For Edward Gibbon, notoriously, the sight of bare-footed friars in the Capitol at Rome was the inspiration for his *History of the Decline and Fall of the Roman Empire*, or so he later claimed (Gibbon 1907: 160; see Ando, ch. 5). The modern study of Late Antiquity has tended to react against Gibbon's claim that it was Christian "superstition" that sapped imperial vigor and opened the way to the barbarian invasions. Peter Brown's *The Rise of Western Christendom*, in particular, argues for Christianity as part of the

[1] My thanks to Richard Corradini, Maximilian Diesenberger, Henrietta Leyser, and in particular to Kate Cooper, Helmut Reimitz, and Mark Vessey.

solution to late Roman problems, not their cause (Brown 2003). In a further twist, some scholars have recently made the case that, as a field, Late Antiquity airbrushes out the catastrophe of collapse as seen by Gibbon (Liebeschuetz 2001a; Heather 2005; Ward-Perkins 2005). Here, I would simply point out that scholars on all sides of this debate must acknowledge (more than hitherto) that our access to Late Antiquity is hugely mediated by the medieval west, and specifically the institutional structures of the medieval church. This mediation cannot simply be bypassed: it needs to be understood if we are to move forward. A study of the cultural memory of Late Antiquity as a subject in its own right has much to offer both medievalists and late antiquarians.

A word of caution, however. No one in the period AD 200–1500 thought of themselves as living in either "Late Antiquity" or "the medieval west." These labels are the creations of what we regard as the modern era (Delogu 2002: 13–57). To ask about the reception of Late Antiquity in the medieval west is therefore to risk posing an entirely artificial question – one anachronism compounding another. The challenge, then, is to approach the question of the uses of the past across at least a millennium of western European history without imposing a conventional periodization on segments of that past.

If we adopt contemporary periodization, we find that "modernity" dawns in the sixth century (Cassiodorus is the first Latin writer to use the term *modernus*), but does not begin in earnest until the ninth (Freund 1957; Vessey and Halporn 2004: 6). In the self-consciously revived Roman Empire of Charlemagne and his successors, we may recognize a decisive phase in the commodification of the past. The more the Carolingians sought to preserve and define "things Roman," the greater the transformation they wrought, turning their ancient inheritance into a modern fetish. Scholars will continue to debate to what extent Carolingian intervention made a lasting difference to the infrastructure of the Latin west: here, more perhaps than elsewhere, ambitions and rhetoric exceeded what was possible (e.g., Sullivan 1989; Fouracre 1995; Nelson 2002). But in the history of cultural memory, the ninth century represents a clear break. In what follows, I shall consider how the Carolingians inaugurated the era of "mechanical reproduction" in the history of the Latin book. I shall then consider the three building blocks of Teresa of Avila's subjectivity as a child and a young woman: the cult of the saints, the institution of monasticism, and the texts of the Fathers, in particular of Gregory the Great.

Letters and the Renewing of Memory: The Carolingian Renaissance

Charlemagne, we are told by one of his son's courtiers, moved the statue of Theoderic the Ostrogoth from Ravenna to his palace at Aachen (*MGH, Poetae* ii: 370–8; for places mentioned in this chapter see Map 1). It is not as easy as we might think imaginatively to move it back. The revival of the Roman Empire in the west by Charlemagne and his family did not represent the interposition of a pious fiction that we can simply brush away. Our access to "Late Antiquity" is irreversibly refracted through the Carolingian prism. In the Latin world at least, almost every stone and every

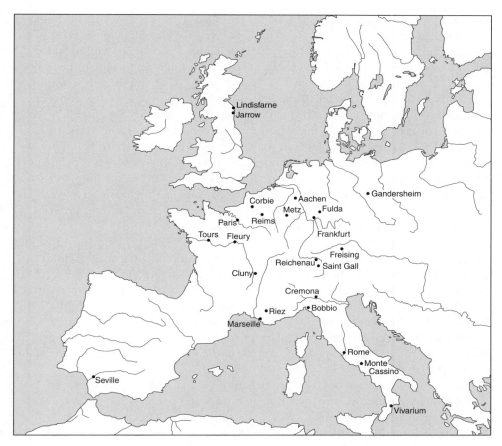

Map 1 Late Roman Learning in the West: Preservation and Transmission.

word from the Later Roman Empire owes its survival to decisions taken in the eighth and ninth centuries. Fewer than 2,000 Latin manuscripts survive from the period before AD 800; from the century after AD 800, we have over 7,000. For every eighth-century copy of a text that has survived, we have ten copies from the ninth century (Lowe 1937–71; Bischoff 1998, 2004; Ganz 2004). Every serious student of Latin Late Antiquity must at some point acknowledge their dependence on Carolingian scribes and their masters, and reckon with the consequences. Traditionally, the story of the textual production of the Carolingian Renaissance, or more precisely its program of reform (*correctio*), is told in a spirit of celebration; we give thanks, for example, for the preservation of Ammianus and Boethius. But empires, as Charlemagne knew from experience and from his favorite book, the *City of God*, are not built without loss, and we must also assess the cost of Carolingian cultural imperialism (Nelson 2006: 12).

The premise of *correctio* was a bold and self-conscious development in script and in language. Crudely put, before the Carolingian revolution, the Latin world knew a diversity of scripts, fundamentally based in late Roman upper-case lettering (uncial and rustic capitals). Around this had developed regional variations and systems of cursive script and shorthand (such as the so-called Tironian notes to be found in Merovingian manuscripts, a system itself subject to Carolingian *correctio*: Ganz 1991). From the late eighth century, having acquired the largest empire since the fall of Rome in the west, the Franks sought to impose a new uniformity in Latin book culture. Carolingian minuscule was a regular script that imposed not only new standards with regard to letter formation and conjunction but also new conventions on the page – the practices of word separation and punctuation, for example – which we moderns take for granted, but which were unknown in the Later Roman Empire (Parkes 1992; Ganz 1995). Words in the Carolingian empire were to be seen as well as heard. An oral culture was not enough to guarantee the persistence of memory. "For what purpose were letters invented? For the renewing of memory so that all you wish may be said; because of the variety of language memory grew weak and letters were invented": so a Carolingian grammar book (Berlin, Stiftung Preussischer Kulturbesitz, Diez B. Sant. 66: 345–6, cited by Ganz 1995: 796).

In this new age of facilitated *Reproduzierbarkeit*, a new literary language came into being. Although the matter remains open to debate, an influential analysis holds that, in "correcting" for what they saw to be the corrupted Latin of the texts they received, and in restoring what they presumed to be classical purity, the Carolingians instituted a decisive break with the living Latinity of the late Roman period (Wright 1982; Banniard 1992). Henceforward, there was a divide between the high literary language of the court and the vernaculars spoken around the empire. Here, perhaps most clearly, we see that the price of *correctio* in the name of preservation is inevitably to change the character of the thing so "preserved."

What, in terms of texts, did the Carolingians copy and what, can we guess, has been lost? Classicists, of course, owe their Roman history and poetry – Virgil, Livy, Caesar – to Carolingian scribes (Reynolds 1983). The expansion of Greek learning at St. Gall, for example, is often celebrated (Herren 1988). But we are entitled to guess at what has not come down to us. A large part of the story here (in particular with regard to municipal archives) doubtless has to do with the poor capacity of papyrus to survive the conditions of the Latin west. Also, of course, we must reckon with the predilection for Christian sources over non-Christian. But it is not just the secular inheritance that may have been impoverished (for example, the opening books of Ammianus, not transmitted in the one surviving ninth-century copy, Reynolds 1983: 6–8). Those Christian texts that were most in demand have suffered in the process: new copies have superseded old ones, leaving us little trace of what came before. Hence we have no copies of the *Rule of St. Benedict* prior to the eighth century, because Charlemagne was confident (or put it about that he was confident) that he had received the autograph direct from Montecassino (Zelzer 1989). Similarly, once Pope Hadrian II had made his edition of the *Register* of Pope Gregory the Great, compressing many thousands of letters on papyrus into two parchment volumes, this seems to have sapped the will of even the papal chancery to preserve the whole archive (Castaldi 2004).

Correctio involved canon formation. The Carolingians were largely (although not solely) responsible for the construction of the Latin patristic tradition. The four Latin Fathers – Ambrose, Jerome, Augustine, and Gregory the Great – emerge clearly in the library catalogs of the ninth century (McKitterick 1989). If we scan backwards, we can see this canon taking shape in Bede, Isidore of Seville, Gregory, and before him, in the late Roman period itself, in Gennadius of Marseille and in Jerome (Vessey 1989). The antiquity of the canon was crucial for the Carolingians – more so, in fact, than its content. Take for example the pseudo-Gelasian decree regarding approved and non-approved Christian reading (*De libris recipiendis et non recipiendis*). This is found first in late eighth-century copies, and then in abundance. Clearly, its systematic listing appealed to the Carolingian program of *correctio*, even though its prescriptions were not in fact followed. If they had been, we would know about the Roman cult of the martyrs only through hearsay. Scribes in fact cheerfully ignored the authority of Gelasius, even as they copied what they presumed to be his decree: in Fulda Bonifatius 2, the very earliest copy, the decree is followed by a work of Faustus of Riez, who is squarely on the pseudo-Gelasian list of "nonapproved" authors (Dobschütz 1912).

Such wilfulness could surely cut both ways. In other contexts, the Carolingians were ruthless in implementing what they took to be the guidelines of the tradition they received. Let us take the case of Jerome, revered by the Carolingians for his *correctio* of the Bible. Every year, for over fifty years, the scriptorium at Tours produced two complete copies of Jerome's Vulgate (Ganz 1995: 799–800). What were the consequences of this extraordinary effort for the copying of the correspondence and the controversies of Jerome? It is tempting to suppose that the letters of Paula, Eustochium, and Demetrias fell by the wayside here – although we should remember that it was in Jerome's interest, as the literary client of these great patrons, to preserve his writings: the great could secure a record for themselves in the more durable medium of stone (Brubaker 1997). It is likely, however, that Jerome's opponents were consigned to oblivion by Carolingian scribes. We know of Jovinian and Vigilantius only through Hieronymian polemical attack; but we know enough to see that these men themselves enjoyed exalted backing from the later Roman aristocracy. It has been shown, in fact, that the majority supported their position, and we should not be surprised by Jerome's disgrace in the AD 380s (Hunter 1987; Cooper 1996). Voluble as he remained in exile in Bethlehem, he cut an increasingly isolated figure. The evidence suggests, for example, that the virgin Demetrias and her kin paid more attention to Augustine than to Jerome when defining her profile as a patron (Kurdock, forthcoming). Only in the ninth century did Jerome emerge as the victor in his debates, and as an authority figure in his own right, as opposed to a decorative "ear-tickler" of Roman *matronae* (Fontaine 1988, on Jerome's patron Pope Damasus).

Carolingian *scriptoria* determined not only the content of what has been passed on, but also its form. The idea of *correctio* involved generic principles of ordering. Sometimes those principles were inherited, as in the case of Gregory's *Register*, where Hadrian followed long established chancery practice in dating the letters to indictions. Similarly, the emperor Charles the Bald, taking the *Theodosian Code* as his model, oversaw the fashioning in the Edict of Pitres (AD 864) of "the most remarkable piece of legislation between Justinian's Novels and the twelfth century" (Nelson 1996: 93). But in other contexts, the Carolingians created their own genres. The most important of these, perhaps, was the historical annal. Annals ordered and recorded contemporary events according to the Incarnational dating system developed by Dionysus Exiguus in the fifth century, deployed first in historical writing by

Bede, and then taken over by myriad and unknown Carolingian compilers. A similar passion for order and system is displayed in the legendary of saints' lives, and in Benedict of Aniane's intervention in the tradition of the monastic Rule – both topics that I consider further below.

We can overestimate Carolingian textual uniformity. Sometimes, in fact, the uniformity is in the eye of later beholders. With regard to the annalistic tradition, we have recently begun to perceive the extent to which the procedures of nineteenth-century editors have suggested a degree of organization that was not in fact there (Reimitz 2004; Corradini, forthcoming). Thus, the so-called "Royal Frankish Annals" or the "Annals of Fulda" represent a bundle of traditions, the synoptic version of which was the creation of Georg Pertz in his edition for the *Monumenta Germaniae Historica*. The most recent scholarship on Carolingian manuscript assembly has emphasized its profoundly improvised and provisional quality. For example, an anatomy of an imposing Carolingian history book containing the Royal Frankish Annals, Einhard's *Life of Charlemagne*, the *Liber Pontificalis*, and an account of the martyrdom of St. Stephen plausibly relates the assemblage to a specific moment in September AD 869, the imperial coronation of Charles the Bald staged by Hincmar of Reims at St. Stephen's in Metz, following the death of Charles's nephew Lothar II (Reimitz 2000b). Although the codex endured, doubtless to be used by later generations of readers, its particular configuration of Frankish history, to celebrate the conjunction of the West Frankish and the Middle Kingdoms, was somewhat outmoded by August of the following year, when Charles and his brother Louis the German redivided the Frankish heartlands between them. Five years later, Charles's coronation at Rome at the hands of Pope John VIII rendered the earlier coronation, and the commemorative manuscript that accompanied it, entirely obsolete.

Put another way, the Carolingian project of *correctio* and the ordering of tradition was an attempt to harness powers that they knew to be quite beyond their control. These empire builders and makers of memory were well versed in the frailty of institutional procedures, their liability to be disrupted and subverted. In the AD 820s, a monk at Reichenau experienced a terrifying vision of the emperor Charlemagne in hell, his genitals gnawed at by beasts for sins unspecified (Dutton 1994). A poor woman at Laon was recorded as experiencing a similar vision. It took another monk (possibly also from Reichenau) to experience the reassuring vision that everything was in order, and that the emperor had been spared the pains of hell, thanks to the prayers of the living. In recording these visions, Carolingian authors reached for late antique apocalyptic literature such as the *Apocalypse of Paul* and (in the same tradition) the fourth book of the *Dialogues* of Gregory the Great. The otherworldly landscape evoked by these texts was a space in which it was possible to meditate on Augustine's grim pronouncements on the costs of empire, and on its fragility (e.g., August. *De civ. D.* 19. 7).

What these stories also point to is the prime mover of the ninth-century cultural memory in the Latin west: the greatness of Charlemagne. The first layman to receive biographical treatment in the post-Roman west, Charles was "magnus" in the eyes of his contemporaries (Lehmann 1929). He was a man who never slept, whose death was almost impossible to apprehend (Dutton 1994). Here was a mortal who had apparently managed to lift himself out of the temporal ebb and flow, to invite comparison with the fabled greatness of Rome. Charlemagne was of course to die, and his empire was to prove pitiably short-lived. Already in the AD 830s, as disputes between Louis the Pious and his sons spiraled out of control, Carolingian intellectuals were asking themselves where it had all gone wrong. But they continued to do so in the language of ancient and late antique Rome excited by Charlemagne's monumental stature (Ganz 1987).

"Greatness," then, was abroad. It was a cultural good mediating the relation between the past and the present. By the end of the century, greatness was bestowed on others, notably, as we shall see, Gregory the Great. And while the political superstructures of the Carolingian empire collapsed, its religious and cultural base structures, set up for the recall and organization of the late Roman past, endured. To two such structures we now turn: the cult of the saints, and the monastic tradition.

Sites of Memory: Monasticism and the Cult of the Saints

The debate about whether Christianity was the cause of or the solution to the Fall of Rome has centered, above all else, on the cult of the saints. For Gibbon, there was perhaps no clearer index of the rising tide of superstition; for Peter Brown, no clearer example of the creativity of late Roman religious culture (Brown 1982; Hayward 1999). In the present context, we must ask whether this debate has been accurately founded, or whether our view of the cult of the saints in Late Antiquity has been skewed by our unwitting adoption of Carolingian perspectives and assumptions about sainthood.

Saints were central to the Carolingian project. The late eighth-century preface to the Salic Law grounds the Carolingian claim to empire in the blood of the Roman martyrs: the Franks were better placed to protect the shrines of Rome than were the Romans themselves (Nelson 1995: 424). This claim was not simply a statement of military fact: it was also an ideological pronouncement about the relation between sanctity and temporal power, and about the canon of sainthood. At the Synod of Frankfurt in AD 794, Charlemagne announced that there were to be no more new saints: his goal was to focus attention on the special relationship between his family and the Roman martyrs (Fouracre 1999). So enthusiastic were the Franks in appropriating relics of the martyrs, that the pope insisted, at the end of the eighth century, that there should be a moratorium on relic translations. It was to last a generation – before the floodgates opened again in the AD 820s, as memorably recorded by Einhard in his account of his acquisition of the relics of Marcellinus and Peter (Smith 2000c).

Relics needed narrative in order to acquire durable meaning (Geary 1978). If we turn from relics to the texts that storied them, we find one of the few contexts where manuscript evidence survives in enough density from before and after the AD 800 preservation watershed for us to be able to see clearly what the effect of the Carolingian intervention was. As far as we can tell, the earliest saints' lives originate as pamphlet literature, whether in North Africa around the shrines of Stephen at Uzalis and Hippo, or in Rome at the behest of specific neighborhoods and aristocratic networks (Delehaye 1910; Cooper 1999). Very few examples of these *libelli* survive: the vast majority of saints' lives are transmitted to us in large Carolingian lectionaries (Poulin 2006; Pilsworth, forthcoming). These collections, as has been shown with reference to Bavarian hagiography, are structured according to classic Carolingian principles of standardization (Diesenberger 2006). Jumbled local collections of *Lives* are replaced with an ordered sequence that follows the sequence of the liturgical year rather than idiosyncratic patterns of narrative affiliation.

To assess the transmission and use of saintly tradition across and beyond the Carolingian period, let us take the *Passion* of SS. John and Paul (*Bibliotheca Hagiographica Latina* 3242). We have, unusually, a *libellus* copy of the text in a manuscript now preserved in St. Petersburg (St. Petersburg Q v I 5, to which was joined *Par. Lat.* 12634; see Poulin 2006: 107). The text, which is explicitly entitled the *Passio Iohannis et Pauli*, tells the story of two palace eunuchs martyred under the emperor Julian. This is clearly a foundation myth for the basilica of SS. Giovanni e Paolo (see Brandt, ch. 11), at the foot of the Caelian Hill in Rome, a "big and beautiful church" according to the description in a pilgrim's guide dated to the early seventh century (but transmitted, inevitably, in a late eighth-century Carolingian copy; see Leyser 2000b and Diesenberger 2005). In its Roman context, the *passio* should be seen in the context of intra-urban burial in Rome (Costambeys 2001). In defiance of imperial prescription, the city filled up with the community of the dead, even as its living population was drastically and horrifically depleted across the fifth and sixth centuries (see Rebillard, ch. 15). The church of SS. Giovanni e Paolo (as also of S. Bibiana) represents the efforts of urban dynasties, incorporating both laymen and clerics, to shore up urban property in the context of this depletion.

In the context, however, of its being copied around AD 600 and subsequently transmitted north of the Alps, the text moves from this late antique urban and ecclesial context out into the countryside and into a specifically monastic institutional context (Leyser 2007). The *passio* was copied most probably in Campania in circles familiar with the monastic teachings of Augustine and with the *Rule of the Master* tradition and possibly associated with Eugippius of Lucullanum; and from there it moved north to Corbie, where it joined another codex probably produced in the same Campanian milieu, displaying similar interest in Augustine and the *Rule of the Master* (*Par. Lat.* 12205; see Masai and Vanderhoven 1953). In these contexts, reaching from Campania to Corbie, the "House of John and Paul" became a symbol for the monastery. The story of the martyrdom becomes in spiritual terms a lesson for the monks in preparation for death. On this earth, meanwhile, the defying of the emperor by the martyrs may have served as a symbol of monastic immunity claimed by houses like Corbie. Dedicated to SS. Peter and Paul, Corbie claimed to be a new Rome.

Meanwhile, great interest was shown by Carolingian copyists in another, longer version of the story of John and Paul, in which the figure of the emperor appeared in a more flattering light (*Bibliotheca Hagiographica Latina* 3636, 3638). In this account, which may in fact predate the *Passion of John and Paul* found in the Corbie codex, the story of John and Paul is a coda to the *Passion of Gallicanus*, a Roman general serving under the emperor Constantine (or Constantius: the tradition is characteristically uncertain). In this version, prior to the accession of Julian the Apostate, there is a halcyon period when Gallicanus conquers the known world as the emperor's general, before forswearing the hand of his daughter, Constantia (or Constantina). While the *Passion of John and Paul* presents an institutional face-off between the state and its citizens, the *Passion of Gallicanus* is a family drama, offering an insider's view of how the state can function. The appeal of this version to the Carolingian world may readily be understood. By the same token, in the following century, and in the Roman Empire of the Ottonians, we find the Gallicanus story retold by Hrosvitha of Gandersheim, who did not hesitate to draw parallels between Gerberga, the abbess of Gandersheim, and Constantia, the imperial princess sworn to continence (Wailes 2001).

From Campania to Corbie and on to Gandersheim: all these were monastic contexts, very different from the original urban setting of the martyr piety in which all these houses partook. But these monastic contexts were very different from each other. The "development of the western monastic tradition" is a story that may productively be retold under the heading "Late Antiquity in the medieval west."

In a very traditional perspective, the appeal of which is still strong, the "Benedictine" tradition is formed immediately in the sixth century. The *Rule of St. Benedict*, composed around AD 540, is brought to Rome by Benedict's disciples after the sack of Monte-cassino. Pope Gregory writes the *Life* of Benedict in the *Dialogues*, and the combination of this text with the *Rule*, according to the classic account of Jean Leclercq, establishes the matrix of monastic life (Leclercq 1957). The *Rule* institutes a framework for the daily encounter with the word of God, the contemplative fruits of which are articulated in the *Life*, and in Gregory's other writings. While this may work as a theology of the monastic life, it is not a historical account of the formation of the tradition.

The *Rules* of the Master and of Benedict, produced in Italy in the middle of the sixth century, were the works of authors who wished to present monasticism as an ancient craft, like medicine or law, involving mastery of a tradition and a set of techniques These *Rules* were in fact practical handbooks and as such were presented anonymously. When Gregory selected Benedict as the central figure of Italian holy men and women, he endowed with a personality and a history a figure whose own authorial strategy had been as unobtrusive as possible, and whose teachings were of a piece with this reticence (Leyser 2000a). The *Rule* recommended that monks remain for a while in a community, following a shared routine, before striking out on their own. The Benedict of the *Dialogues* is a young man who, disenchanted with his studies at Rome, heads straight for the wilderness as a hermit. He attracts followers, but also enemies: he abandons his first set of communities at Subiaco, to set up another at Montecassino. It is here, according to Gregory, that he finally acquires the stability recommended in the *Rule*. In other words, the *Rule of St. Benedict* and the account of Benedict in the *Dialogues* are at cross purposes, and their conjunction to form "the Benedictine tradition" was by no means a self-evident or self-explanatory process. At Rome, in particular, the fact that Gregory took an interest in Benedict seems to have retarded the development of the city's monastic culture, given Gregory's unpopularity with the Roman clergy (Llewellyn 1974).

Across eighth-century Europe, however, there were readers of the *Rule* and the *Dialogues* who saw ways to assimilate them. We might pick out three in particular. Firstly, the Anglo-Saxon Wynfrith – better known as Boniface, the name he assumed in honor of the Roman martyr (Lifshitz 2006) – made it his business to bring the

English enthusiasm for Gregory and for the *Rule of St. Benedict* to the continent. In the following generation, further out toward the missionary frontier in Bavaria and Austria, Arbeo of Freising expertly assimilated the *Dialogues* to the *Rule* in his *Life of Corbinian* (although it is now clear that both Boniface and Arbeo were further from the missionary frontier than has traditionally been thought: Wood 2001: 57–73, 150–60; for Arbeo's connections in Italy, Reimitz 2000a). Finally, and perhaps most importantly, we have the Lombard writer Paul the Deacon, author of a biography of Gregory the Great and himself a monk at Montecassino, who awaits his historian as the maker of the Benedictine tradition. (It should be noted, however, that Paul is not the author of a commentary on the *Rule*: this attribution has long been exposed as a piece of tenth-century sleight of hand by the then abbot of Montecassino: Pohl 2001).

Nonetheless, an element of tension between the institutional Benedict of the *Rule* and the charismatic figure of Gregory's making remained in play in the ninth century. On the one hand, we have the main architect of the Benedictine tradition, Benedict of Aniane. His two massive compendia, the *Concordia Regularum*, composed at some point in the AD 780 s, and the *Codex Regularum*, composed AD 816–17, were classics of Carolingian canon formation, which have conditioned the way we think about monasticism ever since (Semmler 1983). With these compilations, Benedict of Aniane remade the *Rule* of his namesake in a Carolingian image. The *Rule* presents itself as an introductory handbook to the monastic tradition, for beginners. The collections of Benedict drove this humility trope into reverse. The *Rule of St. Benedict* was the summation of all existing monastic tradition. Benedict had gathered into "a single sheaf the sheaves of his predecessors" (Benedict of Aniane, *Concordia Regularum*, *praef.*, *PL* 103: 15), and this work of synthesis was what Benedict of Aniane hoped to achieve across the empire with the standardization of monastic observance.

Such a synthesis remained a dream, but the dream was enough in itself to universalize the criteria by which monastic life was assessed. Coupled with the imperial reach of Louis the Pious, Benedict of Aniane's promotion of the *Rule of St. Benedict* served to constitute what was subsequently thought of as "western monastic culture." Such a thing had not existed before. Later on, after the millennium, monasteries in France would start to claim Charlemagne as their legendary founder (Remensnyder 1994): the truth that these legends express is that it was the Carolingian idea of empire that gave to the various local traditions descended from late Roman monasticism a name and a shape.

That said, Benedict of Aniane did not have a monopoly on Benedict of Nursia. The monks of S. Benoit sur Loire at Fleury saw themselves as the guardians of the "Gregorian" Benedict of the *Dialogues* – the apocalyptic holy man, not the anonymous legislator. According to Paul the Deacon, the relics of Benedict and Scholastica had been taken from Montecassino to Fleury and Le Mans in the seventh century. Paul's account is sketchy in the extreme, but it seems to have been enough to provide a foundation for an entire tradition (indeed, debate still rages as to the reliability of Paul's testimony). Across the ninth century, as Fleury witnessed the translation north of the relics of Roman martyrs, one inmate of the community, Adrevald, decided the story of Benedict's earlier translation needed to be properly told. In a triptych of related works, Adrevald described in detail how the body of Benedict had come from Montecassino north to Fleury, the vicissitudes it had undergone, and the unstoppable flow of miraculous power from its new location (Vidier 1965; Head 1990).

When, in the tenth century, Odo of Cluny, the "Benedictine" house *sans pareil*, came to reform Fleury, he met with strenuous resistance: the monks met him on the ramparts with weapons (John of Salerno, *Vita Odonis* 3. 8, *PL* 133: 80–1). In the tension here we can see the continuation of the ninth-century debate between Adrevald and Benedict of Aniane, between charisma and institution as forms of cultural memory. This conflict between the local and the multinational brand was to continue in the monastic tradition deep into the twelfth and thirteenth centuries (Henrietta Leyser 1984).

The Making of Gregory "the Great"

It is a commonplace among scholars, whether friends or enemies of the patristic tradition, that Augustine, of the four Latin Fathers, stands head and shoulders above the other three in terms of his influence and importance; but it is a fallacy. A recent study shows that our view of Augustine's importance is based on a very narrow selection of medieval library catalogs (Turcan-Verkerk, forthcoming). If our sample is the eighty or so well-known catalogs, then Augustine indeed appears to be most copied and most read, although Gregory the Great is not far behind (thirty-three catalogs for Augustine, twenty-six for Gregory). But this represents about a quarter of the 350 or so extant Latin medieval library catalogs. In a complete survey, the picture changes entirely. The dominant presence by far is Gregory (111:59 in Gregory's favor). Augustine may have been favored by elite libraries – or by those with strident aspirations, like the small abbey of Nogent in northern France, where Guibert presented his personal story of thwarted ambition as a recasting of Augustine's *Confessions* – the ground bass of medieval libraries according to the catalog record was Gregory. The same conclusion is suggested by the biographical tradition: Augustine received one early medieval biographical treatment; Ambrose and Jerome two, but Gregory four free-standing lives, plus three treatments in the course of other works (the *Liber Pontificalis*, Gregory of Tours, and Bede; see Boesch Gajano 2004b).

That Augustine is the preserve of elite libraries may have the unfortunate effect of confirming a well-established modern prejudice that Gregory was not a thinker of the same caliber. But the secret of Gregory's appeal was not that he was suitable for a middlebrow audience. The reasons were surely simpler: Gregory had been bishop of Rome, not of an obscure town in North Africa few had ever heard of; and he had lived more recently and in more familiar circumstances. In terms of space and time, he was an altogether more accessible figure than Augustine, or Jerome, or Ambrose. In other words, something of the modern image of Gregory – that he was a liminal figure, on the border between the ancient and the medieval worlds – was already taking shape in the early medieval commemoration (Boesch Gajano 2004a: 15–18). Gregory was both a figure of venerable authority, whose texts could be excerpted in canonical collections or devotional *florilegia*, and, at the same time, a wonder-worker, sometimes a shockingly real *praesentia* in the here and now. Gregory embodied the two faces of the Carolingian commemoration of Late Antiquity: the ordered alignment of tradition, and the stunning deployment of power, miraculous or otherwise.

The paradox of Gregory's distance and proximity was most clearly stated, perhaps, by his most famous biographer, John the Deacon, writing in the mid AD 870s. John was acutely conscious of the irony that no Roman life of Gregory had been produced, whereas all the peoples of Latin Europe – the Franks, the Anglo-Saxons, and the Lombards – had all produced their own *vitae*. John's response was to produce the longest saint's life in early medieval Europe. But the comparison with other *vitae* is unfair, in that John's text is a hybrid. Within the frame of a biographical narrative, it is a canonical collection, plundering the *Register* of Gregory's letters (in the two-volume edition of Pope Hadrian, leaving untouched the papyrus originals: see Castaldi 2004). John risked alienating readers, not only because he wrote at such length, but also because he presented Gregory as an authority figure, whose every pronouncement was law.

In his fourth and final book, therefore, John attempts to counteract the alienating effect of his own monumentalizing strategy. He tells a number of miracle stories based at Gregory's monastery of St. Andrew's, including his own cure by touching one of Gregory's garments; he describes Gregory and his parents as depicted on the walls of the monastery; and, at the very end, he stages a remarkable *pièce justificatif* (Devos 1964). A figure appears to John in a dream, and reproaches him for spending so long on the life of one long dead. The horrible apparition is answered by Gregory himself, who appears in the company of Pope Nicholas I to put the ghostly figure to flight. Now, part of John's purpose here is purely circumstantial polemic: this is a tract against Formosus, the great rival of John's patron Pope John VIII, who was chased from the city in AD 876 (Leyser 2003). But it is also a serious reckoning with the issue of temporality. Gregory, John was arguing, was both ancient and modern; to his true heirs, he was a source not only of *auctoritas* but also of immediate *virtus*.

John's work, and that of his fellow biographers (in particular, an unknown mid ninth century interpolator of Paul the Deacon's *Life of Gregory*: see Leyser, forthcoming), had the same effect on Gregory as Benedict of Aniane had on the reputation of Benedict. Gregory became the gold standard for a newly internationalized and professionalized episcopate. For example, Hincmar of Reims reproaches his nephew Hincmar of Laon for having failed to do his duty (or having failed to do his bidding). At his consecration, the uncle recalls, he had presented his nephew with a copy of Gregory's *Pastoral Rule* (Hincmar of Reims, *Opusculum LV capitulorum*, praef., *MGH Conc.* IV Supp. II, 146). How had the younger Hincmar failed to follow its directives? This was evidently not a special transaction between family members: Gregory's manual for all those in power – the *rectores*, by which he had not meant only bishops – had become part of the liturgy of episcopal consecration. It was the exercise of power that had preoccupied Gregory when he wrote the treatise; but the restriction of his message to the episcopacy was not what he had wanted at all (Markus 1986). Gregory, an eschatological prophet, had sought to address all those in power, as Hincmar's contemporary Alfred the Great appreciated when he commissioned an English translation of the text.

Once begun, however, the process of clerical professionalization across Latin Europe under the aegis of a memory of Gregory could not be halted. The issue is clearest if we stay focused on the so-called Formosan Schism. Returned to Rome after his exile by John VIII, but hardly as a commander of consensus, Formosus became pope in AD 891. But he had previously been bishop of the suburbicarian see of Porto. After his death, his opponents staged the notorious Synod of the Corpse, where his body was put on trial and his ordinations invalidated – because of his transfer from Porto. Transfer had been outlawed by the Council of Nicaea, argued Formosus' accusers, with a measure of justification. With no less plausibility, the defenders of Formosus, on the other hand, argued that there were precedents for valid transfer. Some were reflected in clerical careers during the Later Roman Empire; other key examples were taken from Gregory's *Register* – instances where he had suppressed a see that was no longer viable after the Lombard invasion of Italy (Scholz 1992; Sommar 2002).

The dangers of this line of argument, as Liudprand of Cremona saw very vividly, was that, if the legitimacy of transfer were upheld, being a bishop would become a job for careerists rather than a sacred trust between a shepherd and his flock. Even while defending Formosus vehemently and vividly against the desecration that had been wrought on his body, Liudprand railed against bishops who prostituted themselves (literally, according to Liudprand) for the sake of advancement, in particular to the see of Peter (*Antapodosis* 1. 2). By the end of the tenth century, however, episcopal transfer was normal, in particular to Rome (Goez 1970). It also became normal for popes to assume new names when they took office. Gerbert of Reims, tutor of the emperor Otto III, moved to Rome without a murmur of dissent. His papal name, fittingly, was Silvester. There could be no mistaking the fact that, whatever the particular political infrastructure, there was now a Latin Europe, in which powerful patrons, both lay and ecclesiastical, sought to move their protégés around, as they had done in the Roman world.

By the turn of the eleventh century, then, your bishop was not necessarily someone you knew: he might well be a career bishop, who filled the post for as long as it suited him or his patron. To defend themselves against the abuse of power by such men and their backers, local churches and monasteries developed job specifications. In the process of professionalization, a whole new set of criteria were set in place by which bishops could be assessed. How to judge the likely quality of an episcopal candidate? The main answers provided by the reformers were: his celibacy, and his dealings with money. It is no accident that the Roman deacon Hildebrand, who was to preside over and direct this reforming movement, assumed as pope the name Gregory.

Conclusion

Modern scholarship, it is often said, begins with the critical study of late antique sources in the medieval west. In AD 1443 the Florentine scholar Lorenzo Valla released to the public his treatise on the *Donation of Constantine*, which purported to represent the gratitude of the emperor Constantine to Pope Sylvester. This document, on which claims to temporal power had been based by the medieval papacy, was, argued Valla, nothing but a forgery. The claims built around it had rested on sand. Together with his humanist contemporaries, Valla did not hesitate to reach the wider conclusion that there was a line to be drawn between their own times, based on the rediscovery of antiquity as it had actually been, and the false conscious-ness of the "Middle Ages," the period between the ancient world and their own self-styled "Renaissance" (see Vessey, ch. 4). That these terms are still with us is a testament to the persuasiveness of Valla and his contemporaries. For all that the development of Late Antiquity as a field in the past two generations has dispelled the image of the Dark Ages, the suspicion lingers in even the very best modern Anglo-American scholarship that the story of "Late Antiquity in the medieval west" is a story of reduction, diminishment, and the wilful obscurantism of the ecclesiastical hierarchy (Clark 1992).

Systematic study of Late Antiquity's standing in the medieval west can help to move the discussion forward, and Valla's treatise is, ironically, a good place to start. What has come to be commemorated as "Valla's discovery" was a complex and long drawn-out process, of which his treatise was a midway point. First, as Valla well knew, the conclusion that the *Donation* was a forgery had already been reached by Nicholas of Cusa and Reginald Peacock. (The former, it should be noted, was a cardinal, which immediately complicates the picture conventionally drawn of a medieval obscurantist hierarchy and a lay humanism of the future.) Second, the public impact of Valla's findings was felt only some two generations after his death, when his treatise fell into the hands of the printer Ulrich von Hutton, who did not hesitate to stage its publication as a media event.

If we look afresh at Valla's claim – to have recaptured antiquity in a way unknown to previous generations – we can see that it is a familiar trope, well worn since the Carolingian period that had produced the forged *Donation* in the first place. From this perspective, it is hard to see the difference between the "medieval" and the "early modern" approach to the past. The spurious *Donation* and Valla's critique of it surely have much in common: both texts claim privileged access to a "Late Antiquity" of their own making. Both were tendentious pieces, but both were to enjoy remarkable success, thanks in no small part to new technologies for the diffusion of text (Caroline minuscule, printing). To the forger(s) of the *Donation*, and the scholar who exposed it, "Late Antiquity" was, like the Roman Empire itself in the post-Constantinian period, a zone of opportunity, to be exploited with enthusiasm. The energetic modern study of Late Antiquity lies squarely within a great tradition.

BIBLIOGRAPHICAL NOTE

The uses of the late antique past in the Middle Ages have long been a subject of study (see, e.g., Munier 1957), but "cultural memory in the Middle Ages" as a self-conscious topic is a relatively recent development (see Geary 1994b; Remensnyder 1994). Working initially on questions of ethnic identity in the early Middle Ages, scholars in Vienna have come to show what may be done with manuscripts in the field of cultural memory: see Reimitz 2000b, 2004; Pohl 2001; Diesenberger 2006; and Corradini, forthcoming. A primary goal of this chapter is to encourage students of Late Antiquity to appreciate the interest and importance of issues of manuscript transmission. In English, see McKitterick 2004; on the Carolingians, see McKitterick 1995; on the later Middle Ages, see Sansterre 2004. Dijkstra and van Dijk 2006 came out too late for me to be able to take account of it. The best account of how "Late Antiquity" and the "Middle Ages" join is Peter Brown 2003.

CHAPTER FOUR

Cities of the Mind: Renaissance Views of Early Christian Culture and the End of Antiquity

Mark Vessey

A Science of Antiquities

A century and a half after *The Decline and Fall of the Roman Empire*, Freud began *Civilization and Its Discontents* with a vision like that vouchsafed to Gibbon as he sat "amidst the ruins of the Capitol," listening to vespers being sung in the church of Santa Maria in Ara Coeli or, as he calls it in his *Memoirs*, "the temple of Jupiter" (Gibbon 1907: 160):

> Now let us, by a flight of imagination, suppose that Rome is not a human habitation but a psychical entity with a similarly long and copious past – an entity, that is to say, in which nothing that has once come into existence will have passed away and all the earlier phases of development continue to exist alongside the latest ones. This would mean that in Rome the palaces of the Caesars and the Septizonium of Septimius Severus would still be rising to their old heights on the Palatine ... [and] the same piece of ground would be supporting the church of Santa Maria sopra Minerva and the ancient temple over which it was built. (Freud 1930: 7)

Freud and Gibbon are as one in their response to Rome as a city perfect in "the art of growing old by playing on all its pasts" (Certeau 1984: 91). Both play on our archaeological awareness that the City of the Popes was no longer the City of the Caesars. As the survival of structures from earlier periods licenses the psychological analogy, so the disappearance of others guarantees that it will be abandoned. Cities do not endure like the individual psyche. Classical archaeology is a science of ruins and remains taken for monuments and documents, data for the construction of narratives of continuity that reconcile our collective experience in the present with our conviction of belonging to a species with a "long and copious past."

Foucault acknowledged the power of "archaeology" when he used the term to unsettle the very idea of a continuous narrative of "humanity" (Foucault 1972: 7–10).

Historical research had lately turned away from "the general model of a consciousness that acquires, progresses, and remembers," to concentrate instead either on long-term interactions between human beings and their environments or on local patterns of thought and behavior. There had been a shift from transcribing "documents" for the sake of a narrative to describing "monuments" in order to make a map. The "notion of discontinuity," once regarded as an obstacle to historical synthesis, had "become one of the basic elements of historical analysis."

In recalling a past time "when archaeology . . . aspired to the condition of history," Foucault looked back toward Gibbon. The modern science of archaeology grew out of an older study of "antiquities" (Momigliano 1966b: 1–39; 1990: 54–79). Ancient Graeco-Roman thought distinguished between "history" as the chronological narration of public (political, military) events and "antiquities" as the systematic treatment of particular aspects of culture (language and literature, religion, social customs). The clarity of the distinction and the option of purposefully combining the two modes of inquiry were lost sight of in the Middle Ages, to be grasped again in the Renaissance as part of a general discovery of "Antiquity" (Jacks 1993). Later, in response to an Enlightenment ideal of "philosophic history," antiquarian research was exploited for large-scale narrative history, and modern historiography was born (Momigliano 1966b: 40–55; but see Phillips 1996).

Judged after the event, Renaissance antiquarianism missed its rendezvous with history writ large (Cochrane 1981: 423–44). Instead, it shaped forms of historical consciousness that found expression in narratives of long-term *discontinuity*. This chapter will suggest how an archaeological perception of the cultural specificity of a remote age made possible the initial discernment of a unity approximating to "Late Antiquity." To appreciate the difference that made, we must first reenter a world in which there was no science for turning memorials of the past into "documents" or "monuments" in the modern sense.

The Translation and Revision of St. Jerome

Early in the fourteenth century, clergy of Santa Maria Maggiore determined that their most precious relic, the Holy Crib, would acquire greater luster if reunited with the remains of St. Jerome, buried in the Cave of the Nativity in Bethlehem (Rice 1985: 49–63). An account was produced, describing how, centuries earlier, the saint appeared to a monk "dwelling in foreign lands" and told him to exhume his body for reburial next to the Chapel of the Presepio in the church of the Blessed Virgin at Rome. The *Translation*, reproduced among testimonies to Jerome in Migne (*PL* 22: 238–40), is accompanied by three letters. The first, containing an account of Jerome's death, purports to come from his friend, Eusebius of Cremona. The second, written in the name of Augustine of Hippo to Cyril of Jerusalem, tells how Jerome's departing soul appeared to several persons, including the writer. The third, Cyril's reply, relates miracles that then occurred and how, despite efforts to rehouse the saint's remains in a marble tomb, the corpse kept returning to the trench where it had been laid. Jerome told Cyril in a vision, "My body will never be moved by so much as an inch from the pit in which it lies until the city of Jerusalem has been captured by infidels, when it will be taken to Rome where it will repose for a long time."

These texts were circulated to insure that Jerome's person would be forever linked with Santa Maria Maggiore. "I was by myself in my cell at Hippo," writes "Augustine" to "Cyril." "I had pen, papyrus and writing-tablet in hand, and was on the point of writing a letter to the most holy Jerome, . . . because I knew that no one living could give me clearer instruction . . . I had barely inscribed the words of the initial greeting 'to Jerome,' when suddenly the room where I was standing was filled with a light and a fragrance such as our time has never known and which it is beyond my power to express" (*PL* 22: 283–4). The emphasis on the epistolary-scribal situation betrays the technology of the whole dossier. Classical epistolary theory held that letters were a medium for the communion of separated souls. Christian letter-writers of the Later Roman Empire spiritualized the convention. That Jerome could still seem vividly present centuries later was attributable in part to his own ingenious use of the epistolary form. Since the accessibility of this monastic teacher outside his cell had always been a textual artifice, one way of reading him faithfully in later times was to reembody him in writings that would keep his person alive, not least at the claimed site of his tomb. The Roman "forger" took a leaf from the master's book.

For his fourteenth-century votaries, Jerome belonged to the same time as themselves, imagined as the last of the world eras prophesied in *Daniel*, or as the sixth "day" in an Augustinian week of ages. By the first reckoning, the present age was as old as the Roman Empire, the dominion of which had been inherited by popes and Holy Roman Emperors (Goez 1958). By the second, it began with the Incarnation, dated to the reign of Augustus. Either way, it had so far run without a break for over 1,300 years and would end only with the end of time itself, foretold in *Revelation*. No consistent stress was placed on the phenomena that we, following Gibbon and Renaissance precedent, take to signify the transition from an ancient Roman to a medieval, Christian world: the documents or monuments of that transition were not yet visible as such. "In the writings of the Middle Ages, the Fall of Rome is scarcely noticed, and nowhere felt to be a puzzle in need of explanation" (Demandt 1984: 89). Changes perceived to have occurred in the centuries since Christ and Augustus could be articulated in terms of "translation" or "revision." Writing – often, rewriting – was instrumental to the process. The translation and revision of Jerome belong to hagiography. The same function characterized other genres, including universal history or chronicle, biblical exegesis, and the bio-bibliographical compendium of "Famous Men" (*De viris illustribus*). All were extensible, uninterrupted, encompassing forms: textual instantiations of a continuity of culture subject to the unity of divinely created Nature transfigured by Dante as the Book of the Universe (*Paradiso* 33. 85–6).

If contemporaries expressed surprise at the new proofs of Jerome's return to Rome, their scruples have gone unrecorded. The authenticity of the letters of "Eusebius," "Augustine," and "Cyril" was not seriously questioned until Erasmus denounced them as fictions in his landmark edition of the *Opera Hieronymi* in 1516. Erasmus treated the contents of the dossier as documents and monuments in the modern historical sense: as cultural artifacts with a specific relation to their time and place of production, rather than as elements of a timeless re-presentation of "Jerome." He had no way of proving that the dust preserved in the Roman basilica was not Jerome's. The exclusive objects of his "archaeology" were the verbal forms that we now call "texts," specifically those bearing the higher knowledge that he and others of like mind called *bonae litterae*. These men were philologists – editors, textual critics, commentators – whose application to texts reflected a broader interest in the survivals of an ancient culture: "Philology and antiquarianism had been inseparable in antiquity; they were again inseparable in the Renaissance" (Momigliano 1990: 71). Renaissance "humanism" favored types of discourse for which there were classical models, known as "humane studies" (*studia humanitatis*): grammar, rhetoric, poetry, history, and moral philosophy. But it was not only the humanists' choice of models that set them apart from, and in some cases against, their equally learned contemporaries. Far more radical and disruptive was their claim to restore a lost culture.

The tale of how long-standing habits of transhistorical "presentism" gave way in western Europe to the collective consciousness of the ancient past as something cut off from the present, recoverable only with the greatest difficulty, has been told many times – usually as the invention of the "Middle Ages" and the "Renaissance." We shall now consider whether it may not also include the discovery of "Late Antiquity."

Petrarch in Double Time: Dilemmas of a Poet-Historian

Francesco Petrarca (1304–74) is the acknowledged pioneer of the modern historical imagination of Rome. He visited the city for the first time in 1337 and went back in 1341 to be crowned with laurels as "poet and historian" in a ceremony on the Capitoline. His description of Roman promenades in the company of his friend Giovanni Colonna combines elements of personal observation with data from ancient (including early Christian) sources:

> You and I took our walks in that city, . . . at every step happening on something to stir our thoughts and words. Here was the residence of Evander, here the house of Carmenta, here the cave of Cacus, here the nursing she-wolf . . . And here Christ came to find his fleeing lieutenant; here Peter was crucified, Paul beheaded, Lawrence grilled . . . here Silvester hid, Constantine was healed of his leprosy, Calixtus mounted his glorious bier. But why continue? Can I fix Rome for you on this poor sheet of paper? (*Familiarium rerum libri* (hereafter *Fam.*) 6. 2. 5–14, tr. Bishop 1966: 63–5)

Petrarch relied on a twelfth-century handbook for pilgrims, the *Mirabilia urbis Romae*, which mingled topographical and legendary information from all periods; but it was a qualified reliance. Recent Italian taste for precise imitation of ancient Latin authors had bred in him a reverence for old texts, which he now turned into a new kind of historical criticism. When Colonna identified part of the monastery of

San Gregorio on the Caelian as a ruined temple of the sun-god, Petrarch pointed to a passage in Jerome's translation of Eusebius' *Chronicle* and reclaimed the edifice (incorrectly) as the Septizonium of Septimius Severus (Weiss 1969: 33).

Historians of scholarship concede that Petrarch's achievement was more than scholarly (e.g., Pfeiffer 1976: 8). His feats as a discoverer and collator of codices of classical Latin authors were impressive (Reynolds and Wilson 1991: 128–34), but it was a particular quality of affective imagination that enabled him to summon the Roman past in a way that would shape the vision of later generations. In a verse-epistle to Virgil he describes how he walked around Mantua in search of places known to the poet. The modern tourist recognizes the mood but, as Thomas Greene points out, "in Petrarch's century it was a momentous acquisition." He was "the first to notice that classical antiquity was very different from his own ... world, and the first to consider antiquity more admirable" (Greene 1982: 90). This admiration entailed an intuition of "the possibility of a cultural alternative": the prospect of reconfiguring the relationship between past and present so that the former surfaced within the latter. Hence the prominence in Petrarch's writings of a particularly tendentious idiom of "archaeology," applicable equally to objects, texts, and cultures. Its key metaphor is one of disinterment, "a digging up that was also a resuscitation" (Greene 1982: 92).

What place did Petrarch assign to early Christianity or "Late Antiquity" in his scheme of cultural renovation? There is a telling passage in his account of conversations that he and Colonna used to have on the roof of the Baths of Diocletian:

> When we had clambered on the walls of the crumbling city, we had the broken ruins under our eyes. We talked long of the city's history. We seemed to be divided; you seemed better informed in modern, I in ancient history, if we call "ancient" [*antiquum*] whatever preceded the celebration of Christ's name at Rome and its veneration by Roman emperors, "modern" [*novum*] everything from then until our own day. (*Fam.* 6. 2. 16, tr. Bishop 1966: 66, modified)

The distinction between "ancient" and "modern" – which here excludes any "middle" age – would be conventional, but for the lateness and sharpness of the caesura. The reference to Christian emperors dictates a Constantinian date for the start of the modern age. Instead of a single era dating from the Incarnation, Petrarch imagines an ancient Roman time that would end with the onset of imperial Christianity. From their Tetrarchic belvedere, Francesco and Giovanni have seen the shadow of a new historiography.

For Petrarch, "Late Antiquity" would have comprised the period from Augustus to Constantine. As a historian, he did not venture far into it. "What else, then, is all history if not the praise of Rome?" he once famously asked; but his chief historical work, a *De viris illustribus*, begins with Romulus and breaks off with Cato. Challenged to justify the omission of famous men of recent generations, he replied that he did not wish to "drive his pen so far and through such regions of darkness' (*Fam.* 20. 8. 11). This "darkness" first of all enshrouded Rome. In Petrarch's incomplete epic the *Africa*, the elder Scipio carries his prophecy of Rome's future greatness no further than the emperor Titus, because he cannot bear to relate how rule passed later into the hands of men of African and Spanish descent (2. 274–8). Not for this Roman poet and patriot the comfortable myth of the empire's successive "translations" into more recent polities. The second century already announced a Dark Age. "[I]t is clear," wrote the grandson of the Roman historian Theodor Mommsen, "that Petrarch discarded the whole history of the Roman Empire during Late Antiquity and the Middle Ages because within that age, everywhere in the western world, had come into power 'barbarous' nations which brought even Rome and the Romans under their domination" (Mommsen 1942: 236). In Petrarch, we trace the origins of the modern consciousness of Rome's fall and its cultural consequences: "By setting up the 'decline of empire' as a dividing point and by passing over the traditional marks either of the foundation of the Empire or of the birth of Christ, [he] introduced a new chronological demarcation in history" (Mommsen 1942: 239). In so doing, he gave the cue to a tradition of Italian humanist historiography that began with Flavio Biondo's *Historiae ab inclinatione romani imperii* (completed in 1453), which in its turn paved the way for Gibbon (D'Elia 1967: 35–40; Demandt 1984: 96–7).

This attachment to a remote Roman past came at a price:

> I devoted myself especially to the study of antiquity [Petrarch writes], for I always disliked our own age – so much so, that had it not been for the love of those dear to me [*amor carorum*], I would have preferred to have been born in any other time than our own. In order to forget my own times, I have always tried to place myself mentally in another age. (*Letter to Posterity*, Musa 1985: 3)

In the same breath he recalls how belatedly he had come to a true appreciation of "sacred [i.e., biblical and Christian] literature." There is a tension between the equally stylized confessions of a youthful passion for pagan poetry and an unnatural passion for antiquity. Petrarch's "antiquity" predated imperially sanctioned Roman Christianity. How did he retain his affection for *that* past while turning to a "sacred literature" that he associated with the writings of the church Fathers, especially Augustine (Trinkaus 1970: 565–8)? Was it love for certain *early Christian* authors, considered by him as contemporaries, that kept him from migrating forever into an imaginary old Roman world? The ambivalence at the heart of such passages reflects a conflict between two imaginations of time. While his major works project a public, secular, Roman, historiographical scheme of time, Petrarch reserved for himself a private, Christian, nonhistorical sphere. According to Ronald Witt, the "single-minded secularism of Petrarch's conception of public time" created "an enormous and persistent contradiction" that ran throughout his life; by excluding most of Christian history it "robbed him of any way to interpret Jerome or his beloved Augustine as anything beyond participants in a world in decline." Those Christian giants "appeared in his writings . . . in a private time without continuity with its past" (Witt 2000: 282).

Witt's hypothesis of Petrarchan double time is borne out by the difference in literary genres chosen by this writer for communion with his most cherished ancient pagan authors and with Augustine. In the final book of his *Letters on Familiar Matters*, he addresses himself in verse or prose to (among others) Cicero, Seneca, Livy, Horace, Virgil, and Homer. Several of the letters are subscribed from a place in

Italy "here above [*apud superos*]" and dated from the Incarnation. Whereas Dante could still imagine himself conversing with pagan *auctores* in a shared landscape ("there below") and a unitary, Christian era, Petrarch uses the act of epistolography to mark the historical and cultural distance separating him from his illustrious predecessors. These are truly *epistolae*, tokens of longing and lack. "I have spoken of many things as if to one present," he confides at the end of a letter to Homer, "but as I step back from the ardour of my fancy I realize how far away you are and fear that you may have trouble reading so much in that place of darkness" (*Fam.* 24. 12. 42).

With his favorite Christian authors it is otherwise. None receives a familiar letter and, when Petrarch does commune with one of them in a text of his own, it is a dialogue ostensibly for his eyes only. This is the *Secretum*, in which "Franciscus" confers with a man whom he instantly recognizes as Augustine. Here the genre serves to erase rather than to emphasize the textual medium. The *Secretum* is a fictive record of conversation in a shared present, the opposite of epistolary encounter: Franciscus and Augustinus are no more separated by history than the conversation partners of Augustine's *Soliloquia*. Since it is a new understanding of the distinctness of the past that makes Petrarch's letters to classical authors poignant, we should not simply equate his relationships with them and the "conjuring up [*sic*] of Augustine in the *Secretum*" (Gouwens 1998: 65). The imputation of necromancy is false. When Petrarch raises the dead, he gives his revenant a ghostly visage (*Africa* 9. 169). Augustinus, however, walks into Franciscus' waking life, looking as of old in Hippo; the Renaissance tropes of disinterment and resuscitation do not apply. This saintly father appears neither as a spirit nor in a resurrection body but as an old man (*grandaevus*), as if transported directly from the 430s to the 1340s. We are not far from the miraculous world of letters in which "Jerome" could drop in on "Augustine" to explain an awkward point in theology.

Admittedly, the *Secretum* is an isolated work, and even there the ambitions of humanist philology are exhibited in ways completely alien to the medieval hagiographical tradition (Quillen 1998: 182–216). The illusions of dialogue aside, Petrarch communes with Augustine through the books that transmitted his works. In the celebrated account of the ascent of Mont Ventoux (*Fam.* 4. 1), he has the *Confessions* in hand. Books are the indispensable, corporeal medium both of his perception and of his possession of "famous men" from earlier centuries; at times they are surrogates for their authors (Findlen 1998: 92–3). Titles of works by Augustine (alone of the church Fathers) appear on the list of Petrarch's "Favorite Books [*Libri mei peculiares*]" with those of works by Cicero, Seneca, Virgil, and others (Ullman 1955: 117–37). Yet Augustine is never straightforwardly of the latter company, never "classical" in the historically articulated sense in which those writers represented for Petrarch the culture of antiquity (*pace* Rabil 1988a). Not only are Augustine's works ranked apart in the list of "Favorite Books": the list itself appears on the flyleaf of a codex containing his *De vera religione*. Petrarch's intimacy with Augustine was of a more everyday kind than the strange familiarity that he sought to establish, through his own texts as much as theirs, with the great literary exemplars of a lost Roman past. Pierre de Nolhac devoted a chapter, after others on Petrarch's knowledge of ancient Greek and Latin authors, to his acquaintance with "The Fathers of the Church and Modern Authors." The conjunction is still good. However pregnant with future worlds of feeling and expression Petrarch's readings of Augustine may be, the latter still stood inside Petrarch's inherited culture, in the shared "unhistorical" time of what we now call the western Middle Ages (compare Bergvall 2001: 33–69; Stock 2001: 71–85; Fubini 2003: 43–65).

After Petrarch: New Literary Histories

What was lost to the Middle Ages and restored in the Renaissance, according to Momigliano, "was the Varronian idea of 'antiquitates' – the idea of a civilization recovered by systematic collection of the relics of the past" (Momigliano 1966b: 5). Before Petrarch, the last exponents of that Varronian project were "late antique" authors like Servius, Macrobius, and Symmachus and, with a difference, Augustine in the *City of God* (Momigliano 1990: 69–70). Servius and Macrobius were two of Petrarch's most prized sources. Marginalia show him using the *City of God* as he did those pagan authorities, as a guide to *pre-Christian* Roman culture (Nolhac 1907, i: 197–8). The same goes for other Latin Fathers. Thus a passage from Jerome's *Chronicle* contributes to a "field survey" of Rome. Petrarch also used the *Chronicle* for reconstructing Latin *literary* history: "Within the encyclopaedia of the *Chronicle*, [he] discovered a complete epitome of the history of ['classical'] Latin literature. Indeed, this was the only manual of literary history available to him" (Billanovich 1954: 17).

Although the *Chronicle* was not Petrarch's only source for Latin literary history, it was his only substantial source for the history of *pre-Christian* Latin "letters," and that – rather than any body of Christian writing or "sacred literature" – was the main focus of his literary-historical interest. Varro's *Imagines*, an illustrated directory of eminent Greeks and Romans, had laid the basis for the bio-bibliographical compendia of such later Latin writers as Suetonius (Blum 1983: 55–80). That genre was still alive in the schools and salons of the fourth century, when it furnished Jerome with many of the supplementary "Roman" notices in the *Chronicle*. Then, shortly before Augustine (in the *City of God*) revived the Roman antiquarian tradition in order to bury it, Jerome gave the *coup de grâce* to the "classical" bio-bibliographical tradition in his catalogue of "Ecclesiastical [i.e., Christian] Writers," also known as *De viris illustribus*. This summary chronological account of Christian authors and their works – from St. Peter to Jerome himself – set the pattern of Christian literary history and bibliographical reference for the Latin Middle Ages (Blum 1983: 79–130; Rouse and Rouse 1991: 469–94; Sharpe 2003: 117–18, 281–3). It was being reworked as late as the thirteenth century, following the principle of continuous accommodation that we have noted as a feature of medieval Latin culture. Petrarch broke with that principle, composing a *De viris illustribus* that had nothing to do with Christian writers, and going back to Jerome's *Chronicle* to excavate the records of a Latin literary history that no one in almost a millennium had considered in its own right (see also Witt 2000: 282–6).

As Augustine's *City of God* aided Petrarch in an archaeological enterprise that bypassed the "late antique" levels of Roman civilization, Jerome encouraged him and his successors in a literary-historical enterprise from which Christian authors *as such* were practically excluded. After Petrarch, pursuing the path he had marked, the Paduan humanist Sicco Polentone (1376–1447) produced a massive synthesis of Latin literary history from Livius Andronicus to the present. Ecclesiastical writers of Late Antiquity and the Middle Ages are nearly invisible in his *Scriptorum illustrium linguae latinae libri XVIII*. The only ones cited with any regularity (Jerome, Augustine, Isidore) appear solely as authorities on earlier – i.e., "classical" – literary history, alongside Quintilian, Aulus Gellius, and Macrobius (Ullman 1928; Vessey 2004).

That was not, however, Petrarch's only legacy. Spurred by his example, the next few generations of Italian humanists returned with new eyes to the ancient Christian texts that, in one form or another (frequently abbreviated, excerpted, misattributed, or interpolated), had long been part of the common stock of Latin learning. Recent scholarship has made much of this "patristic humanism." "Reinvigorated study of the Church Fathers formed an integral part of the humanists' overall agenda to revivify the ancient world," writes Charles Stinger. No less than their pagan counterparts, ancient Christian authors were regarded "as individual sources of experiences or interpretations whose meaning and significance needed to be historically constructed and critically assessed" (Stinger 1997: 473–5; see also Stinger 1977). Another modern historian claims that "[t]he discovery, rediscovery, and reevaluation of Christian antiquity was an integral part of the more general humanist rediscovery and reevaluation of ancient art and letters" (Rice 1988: 17).

Such statements are useful antidotes to the old view of Italian humanism as a "pagan" movement. Yet we should be wary of crediting humanists after Petrarch with too clear-sighted a view of "Christian antiquity." Petrarch's immediate followers were no more successful than he had been in reconciling a "modernist" narrative of the decline of the Roman Empire with traditional belief in the continuity of Roman Christianity from the time of Augustus. New historiography and old providentialism remained on separate planes. Meanwhile, the main tendency of early humanist reappropriation of the Fathers was to emphasize the latter's solidarity with "classical" values, especially in the use of rhetoric and literary fictions. So much is clear from the repeated attempts to explain away Jerome's vision of a conflict between Christianity and Ciceronianism (Jerome, *Ep.* 22. 30; Rice 1985: 85–7; Lardet 2000: 220–6). The humanists' objective was to make good "classicists" of the Fathers, against the norms of Scholastic theology, rather than (in antiquarian mode) to reconstitute anything like an "ancient Christian" culture from extant materials.

From Roman Empire to Republic of Letters: Lorenzo Valla

Generalizations about the Renaissance discovery of "Christian antiquity" rely heavily on the least representative, most controversial of Quattrocento humanists, Lorenzo Valla. Valla (*c.* 1406–57) is remembered chiefly for a bravura demonstration of the inauthenticity of the *Donation of Constantine*, a fictitious record of that emperor's transfer of ecclesiastical primacy and temporal dominion over Italy and the western provinces to Pope Sylvester and his successors (Setz 1975). Others had called the genuineness of the *Donation* in question, but it was left to Valla to expose the flimsiness of the tradition, the anachronistic assumptions behind the supposed grant, and the impossibility that the Latin in which it was cast could have been drafted in a fourth-century imperial chancellery. Only "some fool of a priest" (Coleman 1922: 133), writing long after the events he claimed to describe, trained in an unclassical Latin, could have produced such nonsense. Similar philological methods were applied by Valla to other pseudepigrapha, "classical" and "patristic," and to the *textus receptus* of the New Testament in the translation attributed to Jerome. "If any one man is of crucial importance in the development of awareness of literary evidence and criticism of documents, that man is Valla" (Burke 1969: 58; see Gaeta 1955: 143).

The *Declamation* on the *Donation of Constantine* went off like a time bomb. Little known (and never printed) in the fifteenth century, it was used as an engine of antipapal propaganda by both Continental and English Reformers (Setz 1975: 151–82; Waswo 1987: 91; Camporeale 2002: 576–9). That it was Valla, among Quattrocento humanists, who appealed to Protestant Reformers may be put down to his skill in evoking the early Christian past as a foil to the current state of Christendom. The figure of apostolic simplicity that he creates for Pope Sylvester was meant to pose a moral alternative to the worldly pontiffs of his own day. And yet this "historical" Christian antiquity was at most a hypothesis, which Valla made little attempt to impress upon his contemporaries (Gray 1965: 40–2). The real force of his *Declamation* as the charter for a new kind of history lies elsewhere.

Toward the end of his discourse, Valla launches a fresh train of thought. If Constantine *had* made this donation, and if Pope Sylvester or one of his successors had then lost control of the lands in question, what right would a later Roman pontiff have to repossess them? No better, asserts Valla, than any party has to reclaim territory originally obtained by conquest. Nations made subject by Roman arms could as legitimately overthrow their oppressors as the citizens of old Rome had slain Julius Caesar. In the name of the political freedoms of the former Roman Republic, Valla, who liked to style himself a *civis Romanus*, insisted upon the inalienable right of the "new peoples" of former Roman lands to enjoy their possessions without fear of papal or other encroachment. He even added a special claim on behalf of "Goths" and other nations who had never submitted to Rome's imperial might in the first place (*Declamation*, ed. Setz, 44*–46*). These paragraphs of the *Declamation* go beyond critique of the *Constitutum Constantini*. By its rejection of Roman state aggression, Valla's argument undercut a millennial tradition of Christian providential politics, which interpreted Rome's conquests as part of God's plan for disseminating the gospel. The triumphalist, imperial form of that doctrine was manifestly excluded, but so was the more circumspect "republican" version devised by Augustine (*City of God* 5) after the Gothic sack of Rome in AD 410 and widely assimilated in the political thought of the western Middle Ages. Augustine had desacralized the history of Rome (see now Markus 2006: 31–48). Valla desacralizes that of "Roman" Christianity (Camporeale 2002: 557–75).

The postcolonial turn in Valla's *Declamation* is complemented by the preface to his most deeply meditated work, the *Elegantiae Latini sermonis*. The *Elegantiae* describes the grammar, diction, and stylistic graces of "classical" Latin, as attested by authors from Cicero to Quintilian. Formalizing what for Petrarch and others had been little more than a practical consensus, the work became an influential textbook of humanist Latinity (Moss 2003: 35–57). Valla held that the cultural achievement of the ancient Romans far outdistanced, as it had long outlasted, their feats of military conquest. Nations subdued by Roman arms might feel deprived of their natural liberty, but those who received the gift of Latin were ennobled by it.

> It is thus a great sacrament of the Latin language [he writes] and truly a sign of its divine power, that it has been piously and reverently preserved for so many centuries by foreigners, barbarians and enemies . . . We have lost Rome, lost kingship and dominion, albeit by fault of the times, not of our own. Yet in virtue of this more magnificent dominion we still reign over a large part of the world . . . For wherever the Roman language rules, there is Roman empire [*ibi . . . romanum imperium est ubicumque romana lingua dominatur*]. (*Eleg.* 1, *praef.*, Garin 1977: 596)

Latin is the language of the intellectual disciplines – philosophy, oratory, law, and every kind of literary endeavor. At this point, Valla's tone changes abruptly: what lover of learning or the public good will not weep to see the state of the Latin language now reduced to that of Rome at the time of its capture by the Gauls? "Everything has been turned upside down, burned, ruined . . . [I]t is much if the Capitol survives." Valla makes the fall of Rome a figure for the general wrack of Latin as the universal language of learning. The "Gauls" in this case are the abusers of Latin. In the preface to a later section, Valla calls them "Goths" and "Vandals," adding a more concretely historical dimension to his rhetorical figure of thought. These people "again and again poured into Italy and captured Rome," confusing both the genealogy of the peninsula and its language. Books in "Gothic" hands were still extant. "When a people could debase the Roman script like that, what might they not do to the language? . . . Just see what a decline there is of Roman learning [*litteratura romana*]!" (*Eleg.*, Garin 1977: 610).

The "Goths" of foremost concern here are latter-day jurists guilty of corrupting legal Latin. Valla's historical analogy nonetheless assumes a general outline of western history marked by the ascendancy, decline (after the fifth century), and longed-for revival of Latin learning. He may defend the rights of Goths and other non-Roman peoples to freedom from Roman (including papal) tyranny, but never doubts the cultural supremacy of Latin in its "classical" form. The main preface to the *Elegantiae* ends with a clarion call for a new Camillus, who will emulate his ancient namesake and refound Rome, this time as an international republic of letters.

Among the provinces to be recovered for the new republic, Valla includes theology (Camporeale 1993). Pure Latin was as much a prerequisite for divinity as for truthful and effective discourse in other disciplines. "A person who, without knowing how to speak clearly [*eleganter*], sets down his thoughts in writing, in theology above all, is quite without shame; and if he admits to doing so by design, he is quite demented" (*Eleg.*, Garin 1977: 620). The only available models for good Latin in the service of theology are those pioneer Christian "classicists," the Latin church Fathers. Jerome's "dream" is no argument against taking pagan authors as exemplars of Latin eloquence (*Eleg.* 4, *praef.*). Exalting the Fathers for their Latinity, Valla disparages theologians of more recent date: the former were like bees collecting nectar from distant fields (i.e., pagan authors) to lay up stores of honey; the latter are like ants stealing grains of wheat from nearby, only to bury them. "I would rather be a foot-soldier of the king-bee," says the martial Valla, "than lead a whole army of ants' (ibid. 622). He took the same position in a speech that he gave for the feast of St. Thomas Aquinas in 1457, in the Roman church of Santa Maria sopra Minerva (Gray 1965; Camporeale 1993: 105–9).

Classical or Christian, the ancient past imagined by Valla and most other Quattrocento humanists was conceived "in terms of its literary productions" (Gray 1965: 41). Their antiquarianism – like Varro's, Augustine's, and in large measure Petrarch's – was primarily *textual*. Applied to individual documents or literary works, it manifested itself as philology, chiefly in annotated editions of ancient authors, both classical and patristic. The steady march of editions of and commentaries on Cicero, Quintilian, Seneca, Augustine, Ambrose, and Jerome (and, not far behind them, their Greek counterparts) is one of the clearest indices of the Renaissance "recovery" of an ancient Mediterranean culture. Harder to discern are the underlying assumptions of humanist editors and commentators about the lower chronological limit of that culture. This difficulty is integral to the history of antiquarian thought. The sole medieval descendant of the Roman, Varronian tradition of "archaeology" was the Christian catalogue of authors modeled after Jerome's *De viris illustribus.* By design, such intellectual histories presented a single, homogeneous ecclesiastical culture, composed of texts from the whole Christian era. The genre was spectacularly revived in print by Johannes Trithemius with his *Liber de scriptoribus ecclesiasticis,* which once more brought the history down to the present (Basel, 1494). Meanwhile, as we have seen, Petrarch had cleared the way for a classicizing literary historiography that left out early Christian authors, with the partial exception of those who composed in classical meters. The print-age career of this narrower literary history can be dated from the *De poetis latinis* of Petrus Crinitus (Florence, 1505). Such, then, were the alternatives: an *ecclesiastical history of letters* without internal articulation because coextensive with Christianity, and a *history of Latin literature* based on a Renaissance scheme of postclassical decline and modern revival, without any significant Christian reference. Valla's tendentious sketch of a history of western culture as the quasi-political history of Latin learning in *all* disciplines, including theology (and canon law), could be claimed in retrospect as the blueprint for a more comprehensive narrative of discontinuity and change. Before such a narrative could become current, however, there had to be a fresh reckoning with the antiquarian and philological legacy of Jerome.

Living Monuments: Erasmus on the Christian Classics

Our story ends with Erasmus' monumental edition of the works of Jerome (Basel, 1516). Neither this enterprise nor the edition of the New Testament that he produced in the same year would have been conceivable without the teaching and example of Valla. Erasmus (1466–1536) came early to the *Elegantiae* and swallowed it whole. He took Valla not only as an arbiter of Latinity but also as a guide to the cultural history of the west. "Who is so small-minded," he asked in a letter of 1490, "as not to accord generous praise and the warmest possible affection to Valla, who bestowed such intense industry, application, and exertion in combating the follies of the barbarians and rescuing literature [*litterae*] from extinction?" (*Ep.* 26, ed. Allen, i. 115; Mynors and Thomson 1974: 48). Following Valla's lead, Erasmus diagnosed a disastrous falling-off in Latin "letters" after the fifth century, adopted "barbarian" as a smear-term for Scholastic theologians and anyone else who failed to meet humanist standards, promoted the church Fathers – with Jerome first – as exemplars of theological discourse, and dedicated himself to the restoration of a lost *Christian* culture of texts (Camporeale 1972: 283 and *passim*; 2002: 48; Rummel 1986: 85–8; 1995: 84–6 and *passim*; Jardine 1993: 66–7; Bejczy 2001: 2–4).

Erasmus' Valla is the refounder of a commonwealth of letters (*res litteraria*). If he never calls him Camillus, it is only because his patience with anachronistic analogies was shorter than his hero's. Erasmus was far less an antique Roman republican than either Valla or Petrarch. The city of Rome, to which he made just one unhappy visit, held no magic for him; he would have been the last man on earth to dream of raising its ancient walls and buildings again. When Erasmus laments the ruin of a once great literary republic, the polity that he has in mind is one in which the revealed truth of the Christian religion had already consummated all that was morally, intellectually, and rhetorically beneficial in classical culture (Bolgar 1954: 336–41). His encyclopedic collection of ancient proverbs, the *Adagia*, stockpiles classical assets for ready use; his rhetorical manual, *De copia*, shows how they are to be deployed. These and other "literary and educational" works for which classicists still honor Erasmus are strictly cognate with his editions of Jerome and the New Testament. As the unique medium of the life-giving word of Christ, the Greek New Testament needed to be conveyed to Latin readers – always Erasmus' main constituency – in the most faithful and expressive terms possible, and these would not necessarily be Jerome's, since neither Valla nor Erasmus considered much if any of the *textus receptus* to be attributable to that church Father. Conversely, the authentic literary *œuvre* of Jerome represented the nearly perfect fusion of classical eloquence and erudition with God-given wisdom – Christianity with the priceless advantage of Ciceronianism. Whereas Valla felt obliged to justify Jerome's continued classical readings, Erasmus (in the *Life of Jerome* prefixed to his edition) went out of his way to defend him against humanist critiques of his Latinity (Brady and Olin 1992: 54–61).

The aims of Erasmus' edition of Jerome have been well explored in recent scholarship (Rice 1985: 116–36; Jardine 1993; Clausi 2000; Pabel 2004). What needs underlining here is its role in establishing an Erasmian literary history. In the preface addressed to Archbishop Warham, Erasmus develops Valla's sketch of the decline and fall of the Roman state and of the Latin language into a pathetic narrative of the demise of Latin Christian literary culture under late Roman emperors and their successors. The "character of princes had quite degenerated into a barbaric form of tyranny and bishops had come to love their lay lordships more than the duty of teaching." The task of instruction was abandoned to monks unworthy of the name.

Bonae litterae were neglected, Greek and Hebrew scorned, and Latin "so much contaminated with an ever-changing barbarism that Latin by now was the last thing it resembled." The art of eloquence was despised; history, geography, and *antiquitates* were no longer studied. The common stock of letters, *res litteraria*, "was reduced to a few sophistic niceties" or confined to summaries and excerpts. As a result, the "old authors [*veteres scriptores*]" all but disappeared in a "holocaust of humane literature" and any who showed interest in "the better kind of learning [*litteratura melior*]" were "expelled from the ranks of the learned" (Allen, ii. 214; Brady and Olin 1992: 6, modified).

The "holocaust" (Gk. *panolethria*) of humane learning is one of *early Christian* texts. Though Erasmus yields to no one in his qualified regard for classical (i.e., pagan) literature, his sole concern here is with Christian writers, beginning with Clement of Rome. They are the *veteres scriptores* (translated by Brady and Olin as "classic authors"); the church Fathers acquire at Erasmus' hands a new kind of "classic" status (Pfeiffer 1976: 84 and n. 4; Boeft 1997; Sider 1998). They exhibit classical rhetorical values and so license humanist practice, and they come as close as anyone to combining classical and Christian learning in due proportion (Bejczy 2001: 24–32).

The ultimate sources for this Erasmian understanding of a "classical Christian" culture are Jerome's letter to the Roman orator Magnus (Jerome, *Ep. 70*) and the latter part of Book 2 of Augustine's *De doctrina christiana*, with its residually Varronian disquisition on the liberal and other arts (Béné 1969; Shanzer 2005). Where Erasmus goes beyond his predecessors is in the literary history that corroborates his theory. Jerome's *De viris illustribus* was another touchstone, already prominent in *The Antibarbarians*, a humanist manifesto begun while the author was still an Augustinian novice. Erasmus read Jerome's polemical preface as a vindication of the humanist educational program. He then drew the lower temporal limit of ancient Christian wisdom, eloquence, and learning just below the point where Jerome ended – which had been with Jerome. (Only Bede among later writers is regularly spared by Erasmus.) The full import of this restriction is revealed by the architecture of the *tomus primus* of the 1516 edition of Jerome (Vessey 2005b). Having begun by bewailing the "holocaust" of ancient Christian writings, Erasmus closes with Jerome's catalogue, framed by a preface on the same theme. The work is a painful reminder of how few of those "outstanding monuments [*egregia monumenta*]" now remain, unless "maimed, corrupted and adulterated." Such a tragic loss should "provoke all who favour good authors to read the more eagerly what has survived, since so little has been left us by the ruin of the ages" (fo. 138^r).

A Renaissance without Rome; or, The Prospect of Late Antiquity

Temporum ruina: that is the keynote of Erasmus' philology and the trope that keeps him shoulder to shoulder with earlier Renaissance restorers of ancient culture.

Now, however, the culture is both specifically Christian in content and clearly demarcated in time. Reading Jerome after Petrarch and Valla, Erasmus made a gap in the history of western Christianity that had never loomed so large before. The theological and ecclesiastical consequences were momentous. Even if Erasmus is rarely taken for an ecclesiastical historian, his schemes undoubtedly influenced the historical consciousness of such Protestant reformers as Melanchthon and Flacius, as well as that of their Roman Catholic opponents, including the great Baronius (Ferguson 1948: 39–46; Backus 2003: 326–91). That a later historian like Tillemont should have confined himself to the ecclesiastical history of *les six premiers siècles* may also be set down partly to Erasmus' account: it was he who entrenched the division between the Age of the Fathers and what followed. The formidable patristic scholarship of the Benedictines of St. Maur, which Tillemont exploited and Gibbon admired, likewise drew much of its inspiration from Erasmus' work as an editor of the Fathers.

Erasmus also holds in suspense for a while the nostalgia for ancient Rome. Unlike Petrarch, Valla, or Gibbon, he has no vision of the Capitol. The objects left behind by time's ruin he sees as *monumenta* in an exclusively textual sense: monuments of human learning and divinely derived wisdom made available once more through the medium of pure and eloquent Latin "letters." His work on Jerome and the New Testament is exemplary. Both sets of texts were to be made to speak again with the accents of their authors, in spite of the hazards of transmission; but they could speak only as *texts*. When Erasmus writes of bringing "Jerome" to life again, he has no thought of summoning a ghost: his "Jerome" is a creation of the written and printed page. And even there, "Hieronymus" is not a living person in the way "Augustinus" could be imagined by a reader of Petrarch. Master of the dialogue, Erasmus never represents himself in conversation with a church Father. Nor, as theorist and practitioner of the familiar letter, has he any time for the impersonations of "Eusebius," "Augustine," and "Cyril" that had kept Jerome's presence alive at Santa Maria Maggiore.

Erasmus' return *ad fontes* is largely free of nostalgia for lost worlds and of the ordinary delusions of the "metaphysics of presence." Jerome belonged to a time and culture long gone and now wholly inaccessible. What contemporaries still had, Erasmus insisted, were the texts – tools for a modern transformation of Christendom. His ideal city was not a reborn Rome or any other fantasy of the "archaeological" imagination, but a Christian community of letters. We glimpse it in his colloquy on "The Religious Feast" (Boyle 1977: 129–41). "What is a state [*civitas*]," he asks a Benedictine monk, "but a huge monastery?" (*Ep.* 858, Allen, iii. 376; O'Malley 1988: 97). He explained in the edition of Jerome that the uncorrupted monastic ideal of civilization was now represented solely by Christian writings from the fourth and early fifth centuries. These were products of a short-lived late Roman environment, which Henri-Irénée Marrou would one day call "the culture of the Theopolis" (Marrou 1949: 694–5; Vessey 1998: 388–90). As first surveyor of the (Christian) monuments of that always unreal city, Erasmus has the best claim of any Renaissance or "early modern" man to have anticipated our latter-day science of "Late Antiquity."

BIBLIOGRAPHICAL NOTE

The mid- to late twentieth-century rise of "Late Antiquity" as, in part, a replacement formula for "the decline and fall of the Roman Empire" runs parallel with a critique of "the Renaissance" that has led to the rise of "early modernity" as a cross-disciplinary concept. Any approach to these periodizations must still take account of such classics as Ferguson 1948, Panofsky 1960, Weiss 1969, and, in smaller compass, Burke 1969. Renaissance visions of the end of Rome and the later period of ancient culture are finely if cursorily treated in the longer surveys of D'Elia 1967 and Demandt 1984. The present essay owes much to the spirit of recent, conservatively revisionist work on early modern cultivations of a "classical" past, as represented by Grafton 1992, 2001, Barkan 1999, and the 1998 *American Historical Review* forum on "The Persistence of the Renaissance" (here Findlen 1998 and Gouwens 1998). For the patristic or early Christian literary dimension of the relationship, Jardine 1993 blazes a trail that others have just begun to follow.

CHAPTER FIVE

Narrating Decline and Fall

Clifford Ando

As a field of study, Late Antiquity is largely the product of Anglo-American scholarship, and it is perhaps two generations old (Ando 2001: 371–5; see Rebenich, ch. 6). It came into existence in part through the discovery of new subjects for inquiry and in part through the rejection of earlier preoccupations. Thus Peter Brown, in his remarkable review of A. H. M. Jones's *Later Roman Empire*, simultaneously applauds its erudition in matters of law and government and removes those topics from the nascent field of Late Antiquity altogether: Jones, Brown suggests, had provided "not a complete social history of the Later Roman Empire, but the first, irreplaceable chapter in the history of the Byzantine state" (Brown 1972a: 73). The discovery of Late Antiquity also sets Anglophone scholarship of the last four decades apart from historiographic traditions in Germany, France, and Italy, in each of which the end of Antiquity is attributed to a variety of causes and made the antecedent of eras marked, in the eyes of historians, by radically different characteristics (Marrou 1938: 658–702; Momigliano 1963a; Hübinger 1968, 1969; Cracco Ruggini 1988; Brown et al. 1997; Carrié 2001).

Even so, all these varied traditions take their cue from Edward Gibbon's *History of the Decline and Fall of the Roman Empire*, the first volume of which was published in 1776. A French translation was started in the same year; and German and Italian translations began to follow in 1779. Publication of the complete work in English was achieved in 1788, and it has remained in print ever since. The life of its text and the responses it has generated have been the subject of two works of reference and a recent monograph (Norton 1940; Craddock 1987; Womersley 2002). Yet, the nature of Gibbon's influence consists neither in his overall periodization – no one has followed him in dating the fall of Rome to 1453 – nor in his specific arguments, which are often unexpected and have just as often been misread. Rather, it rests upon the language and form he gave to the trope of "fall"; upon the power of his portrait of Antonine Rome, which emerges as a simulacrum of Enlightenment Europe *avant la lettre*; and upon the strength of his conviction not only that Rome fell but also that its fall mattered, that it was "a revolution which will ever be remembered, and is still felt by the nations of the earth" (Gibbon 1994 (hereafter *DF*), i. 31), "the greatest, perhaps, and most awful scene in the history of mankind" (*DF* iii. 1024).

I highlight the notion of "decline and fall," not only because Gibbon gave near final form to a dominant preoccupation of European historiography, for which that phrase might serve as token (Pocock 2003), but also because it is precisely in its evaluation and consequent rejection of that tradition that modern historiography diverges from Gibbon's own. Preferring to live in a world transformed rather than fallen, modern scholars of Late Antiquity have focused on a set of phenomena – ceremony and asceticism, poverty and *paideia* – analyzed in such a way as not only to suggest the contours of an age but also to assign to them heuristic value in the interests of a new periodization. The axes along which earlier generations charted decline – those of law and government, political culture and civic institutions – have been either superseded or ascribed to periods of history not denominated "late antique."

But, if our modern preoccupations were not Gibbon's, he did not ignore them. In his view, monks and eunuchs were not agents or engines of social change: they were, rather, symptomatic: if not accidental then incidental consequences of other movements in culture, society, and politics. Writing of eunuchs, for example, Gibbon believed that "the use and value of those effeminate slaves gradually rose with the decline of the empire" (*DF* i. 182); and on monks, "If it be possible to measure the interval, between the philosophic writings of Cicero and the sacred legend of Theodoret, between the character of Cato and that of Simeon, we may appreciate the memorable revolution which was accomplished in the Roman empire within a period of five hundred years" (*DF* ii. 429). Reading Gibbon thus confronts us with a periodization that subordinates our interests to another narrative, and it behooves us to ask what changes in culture and society that greatest of historians privileged in narrating and explaining both decline and fall and, necessarily, the start and end of Late Antiquity. In that task we are at the very outset doubly confounded, first by that sleight of hand with which Gibbon several times identifies the reign of Augustus as a turning point in the fortunes of the empire, even though he commences his narration more than two centuries after Augustus reorganized the government (*DF* i. 211–12; see also 127–8 and 611–12), and, second, by his endpoint. For if his choice of AD 1453 requires his process of "decline and fall" to include what we now think of as Late Antiquity, we have to acknowledge that choice problematic. Not only was it not a canonical date for the fall of Rome: Gibbon failed to make it so, one obvious reverse in the pervasive influence of this most canonical text.

If Gibbon's Late Antiquity is not quite ours – despite its remaining the sole great narrative of that period in any language – it was not the one expected by his contemporaries either. To understand why, we need to appreciate the historical and historiographic contexts in which Gibbon worked. As a historian, he drew upon four bodies of work in crafting his text. First, Enlightenment histories of manners aimed above all to explain the progress of human society, along axes both moral and economic, toward a condition in which the ability of citizens to exercise their virtue and maintain their station was grounded positively in commerce and property and, more distantly, in systems of law, and then, more negatively, in their freedom from confessional interference (Womersley 1988; Pocock 1999b). Second, Gibbon rested his narrative upon the extraordinary chronological spadework achieved in ecclesiastical historiography. Third, remarkable efforts to recover nonliterary evidence, undertaken by the Académie des Inscriptions as the champion of a more scientific history, were making possible new forms of historical writing (Kelley 1970; Pocock 1999a: 137–68, 207–39, 261–74). Fourth, and more remotely, there was by Gibbon's day a long tradition of both writing about and questioning the reality of the fall of Rome (Pocock 2003). Those responsible for these separate schools of thought and bodies of work found much to admire in Gibbon's account; but they were also both astonished and dismayed by his forging of a new genre based upon their own approaches but reaching well beyond them.

It was clerics – ecclesiastical historians, whom Gibbon dubbed "the watchmen of the Holy City" – who felt most aggrieved, and whose attacks he countered with a lengthy essay, "A Vindication of some passages in the fifteenth and sixteenth chapters of the History of the Decline and Fall of the Roman Empire" (1779). The exchange did not end there (Womersley 2002). Their sense that all was not right in Gibbon's *History* was correct; but his errors were not those they identified, nor did they characterize his argument correctly. Although he would not excuse its sordid past, Gibbon did not blame the Church for the fall of Rome. Yet, in an important sense, the reaction of the ecclesiastical establishment confirmed Gibbon in two crucial convictions, one historiographic, the other political: first, that "in the relation of religious events" few "deserved the singular praise of holding a steady and equal hand" (*DF* iii. 1171); and, second, that while "the operation of … religious motives was variously determined by the temper and situation of mankind" (*DF* ii. 416), established religions had their own recursive power over the societies in which they worked. For though they might once have been products of societal forces, the institutions of utopian and scriptural religions in particular, ascribing their own legitimacy to extra-human powers, come inevitably to exercise an autonomous influence upon those societies. This had been the most pernicious effect of the credulity of some Christians, among whom miracle tales "debased and vitiated the faculties of the mind; they corrupted the evidence of history; and superstition gradually extinguished the hostile light of philosophy and science" (*DF* ii. 428).

Against those backdrops – the one sketching Gibbon's context, the other our own – I shall begin to explore the unfolding of Gibbon's Late Antiquity. What understanding of society and of social change made Antonine, or even Augustan, Rome the starting point for decline, and what were the devices whereby Gibbon so famously made Christianity the handmaid of politics? In what might decline and fall consist, and what can it tell us about Late Antiquity?

Christianity and Barbarism

It might seem dangerous, faced with so artful and ironic an author as Gibbon, to begin by recounting what he himself says. I shall attempt later to isolate some features of his irony and its analytical import. It seems worth emphasizing, nevertheless, that Gibbon identifies three causes of the empire's decline and excuses two more. The two factors absolved are the barbarians and Christianity. In both cases, Gibbon addresses an audience that expects him to argue the contrary, namely, that the barbarian invasions caused the collapse of Roman government in the west, and that conversion to Christianity corrupted the culture and weakened the discipline of the Roman state. In both cases he effects his absolution by arguing that the agency and efficacy of one party of historical actors depended upon the actions and condition of others. So, for example, he believed that barbarians outside the empire were able to surmount its defenses and wreak havoc upon its interior only when they "discovered [its] decline" already far advanced (*DF* i. 212). At other times, stability within the empire allowed the emperor to project strength without. Such had been the case during the first two centuries of the imperial era, when "the enemies of Rome were in her bosom" (*DF* i. 213); and it was a significant index of Diocletian's achievement that such was the case again under the Tetrarchy (*DF* i. 368).

I list Gibbon's causes separately at the risk of diminishing or effacing the complex relations between them. First, the Romanization of provincial populations, particularly those in the west, failed at precisely the time when the population of Italy was itself ceasing to be Roman. Second, the "nice frame of civil policy instituted by Augustus" was subverted by Severus, and its dissolution ushered in a period of political anarchy that brought enormous social and economic devastation (*DF* i. 147; see 267, 290, and 312). Third, each successive governing class of the early and high empire experienced a failure of nerve, a loss of virtue, and so abdicated to successive groups of non-Romans the role of defending Rome.

In relation to those causes, I shall explore, first, some of the historiographic and literary devices that Gibbon deployed – both those he inherited and those he invented – in order to elaborate the causes individually while binding them together in a single argument; second, the effect Gibbon assigns to changes in Roman political culture of the early and high empire – namely, a loss of liberty entailed by the acquisition of empire itself; and third, the place Gibbon assigns to Christianity, within his narrative and within the history of decline and fall.

A historical process that unfolded over 1,500 years can scarcely have been visible to contemporaries and must pose multiple challenges to the historian, at the level of argument, analysis, and narrative. Gibbon acknowledges this difficulty most explicitly in describing eras that will have seemed to contemporaries ones of stability and strength. For example, the "long peace and uniform government of the Romans" under the Antonines – precisely that era, Gibbon famously suggests, that another would identify without hesitation as the period during which the condition of the human race was most happy and prosperous (*DF* i. 103) – introduced "a slow and secret poison into the vitals of the empire," but it "was scarcely possible that the eyes of contemporaries should discover in the public felicity the latent causes of decay and corruption" (*DF* i. 83). Likewise, after describing how "the arduous work of rescuing the distressed empire from tyrants and barbarians had ... been completely achieved" by that group of emperors whom he calls "a succession of Illyrian peasants," Gibbon undertook to explain why a portrait of "the complicated system of policy introduced by Diocletian, improved by Constantine, and completed by his immediate successors, [will] not only amuse the fancy by [providing a] singular picture of a great empire, but will [also] tend to illustrate the secret and internal causes of its rapid decay" (*DF* i. 384; see also 386–7 and 602–3).

The existence of "latent" and "secret" causes presents the historian with several hurdles, of which I single out three: first, the need to describe social change, when the evidence provided by contemporaries largely fails to address it; second, the need to relate the actions of individuals who experienced but did not perceive that change; and third, the need to situate analysis of unperceived change within narrative. What events constituted the change at issue, and how and when to tell its story, and the story of its causes and effects?

Gibbon surmounted the first of these hurdles, that of describing social change using contemporary evidence, in part by recourse to a classical trope, namely the vocalizing, through collective speakers, of sentiments both opportune, in that they seem apposite to the situation, and anachronistic, in providing an analysis useful to posterity, with its different awareness and interests. For example, during the early centuries of the Roman Empire, people within its borders had been distinguished according to juridical rank; but ideally, provincials might become more Roman even as the Romans maintained their status and their virtue. The ideal, however, was not realized, for reasons I shall shortly attempt to untangle. The consequences of that failure Gibbon describes thus:

> But when the last enclosure of the Roman constitution was trampled down by Caracalla, the separation of professions gradually succeeded to the distinction of ranks. The more polished citizens of the internal provinces were alone qualified to act as lawyers and magistrates. The rougher trade of arms was abandoned to the peasants and barbarians of the frontiers, who knew no country but their camp, no science but that of war, no civil laws, and scarcely those of military discipline. (*DF* i. 186)

That long-term change then impinged upon the world of politics when the army, and in particular the Praetorian Guard, discovered its power to select and impose an emperor:

> The advocates of the guards endeavoured to justify by arguments the power which they asserted by arms; and to maintain that, according to the purest principles of the constitution, *their* consent was essentially necessary in the appointment of an emperor. The election of consuls, of generals, and of magistrates, however it had been recently usurped by the senate, was the ancient and undoubted right of the Roman people. But where was the Roman people to be found? Not surely amongst the mixed multitude of slaves and strangers that filled the streets of Rome; a servile populace, as devoid of spirit as destitute of property. The defenders of the state, selected from the flower of the Italian youth, and trained in the exercise of arms and virtue, were the genuine representatives of the people, and the best entitled to elect the military chief of the republic. (*DF* i. 129)

As Gibbon tells it, "the advocates of the guards" staked their claim in the terms later used by Augustine, rewriting Cicero: "What was a city, except its people?" But however ancient the question, it highlights here the distance that separates this moment from any time when the Roman people might meaningfully have been identified either with its army or with an electorate.

Gibbon understood the violence of that contrast to exist in two distinct arenas: first, as a function of the language through which contemporaries both perceived and endlessly reconstituted their political reality and, second, as a tool by which later readers might assess those ancient illusions. As regards the first, Gibbon was no less sensible than Augustus "that mankind is governed by names"; nor, in Gibbon's view, was that prince "deceived in his expectation, that the senate and people would submit to slavery, provided they were respectfully assured that they still enjoyed their ancient freedom" (*DF* i. 96). The ancients' use of language and ideas that they failed to recognize as anachronistic constitutes an important category of action that Gibbon needed to narrate; and that was the second of the hurdles set in place by his appeal to "latent" and "secret" causes. Perhaps the most conspicuous early example of such action is Decius' attempt to revive the office of censor. That effort followed upon an "investigat[ion of] the more general causes, that, since the age of the Antonines, had so impetuously urged the decline of the Roman greatness. [Decius] soon discovered that it was impossible to replace that greatness on a permanent basis, without restoring public virtue, ancient principles and manners, and the oppressed majesty of the laws" (*DF* i. 262).

Though Gibbon allowed that the censorship, "as long as it had subsisted in its pristine integrity, had so much contributed to the perpetuity of the state," and though he commended Decius for his goodwill (*DF* i. 262, 263), he condemned the office as obsolete and the project as impracticable:

> A censor may maintain, he can never restore, the morals of a state. It is impossible for such a magistrate to exert his authority with benefit, or even with effect, unless he is supported by a quick sense of honour and virtue in the minds of the people, by a decent reverence for the public opinion, and by a train of useful prejudices combating on the side of national manners. In a period when these principles are annihilated, the censorial jurisdiction must either sink into empty pageantry, or be converted into a partial instrument of vexatious oppression. It was easier to vanquish the Goths than to eradicate the public vices; yet even in the first of these enterprises, Decius lost his army and his life. (*DF* i. 264)

Gibbon's evaluation of Decius' abortive revival of the censorship operates in three distinct registers of his text. First, it accords with his sense that the laws and policies of government can direct, but not contradict, the state of manners in society more generally, a principle that receives further illustration in the reigns of Tacitus and Jovian. The former's attempt "to heal the wounds" inflicted on the state in the course of the third century and "to restore, at least, the image of the ancient Republic," is labeled an impossibility (*DF* i. 331–2); the latter had "the good fortune to embrace the religious opinions which were supported by the spirit of the times," illustrating thereby that the "slightest force, when it is applied to assist and guide the natural descent of its object, operates with irresistible weight" (*DF* i. 961; see also 439).

The second register evoked by the reforms of Decius is one of theme, that of belatedness. Decius failed, according to Gibbon, for two related reasons: he was attempting to impose upon his modern world a classical solution or, perhaps, to recreate some classical reality in a context in which it could not but be incoherent (compare *DF* ii. 799, where Gibbon assesses Justinian's revival of classical Roman law); and he failed to apprehend correctly his present situation and what was possible within it. Such failures of apprehension on the part of historical agents are often wedded to a confidence on their part that they do, in fact, perceive and can, in fact, control the evolution of manners. Gibbon expresses the gap between such confidence and its outcomes by the use of irony, which constitutes his third register. Indeed, irony serves throughout the *History* as a device both rhetorical and analytic. It is one Gibbon wields with surprising sympathy, and rarely with condescension.

Operating beyond the awareness of the actors on his stage, Gibbon's "secret and internal causes" also lay outside his narrative. That is to say, insofar as his narrative pursued the thought and action of ancients, it could not accommodate analysis of causation and change outside their awareness, except through some structural departure from narrative itself. So, for example, he introduced his "distinct view of the complicated system of policy" implemented by Diocletian, Constantine, and his successors, with a set of programmatic remarks on the proper balance to be maintained between the history of law and society on the one hand, and of those individuals who wrote the laws on the other:

> In the pursuit of any remarkable institution, we may be frequently led into the more early or the more recent times of the Roman history; but the proper limits of this inquiry will be included within a period of about one hundred and thirty years, from the accession of Constantine to the publication of the Theodosian Code ... This variety of objects will suspend, for some time, the course of the narrative; but the interruption will be censured only by those readers who are insensible to the importance of laws and manners, while they peruse, with eager curiosity, the transient intrigues of a court, or the accidental event of a battle. (*DF* i. 602–3)

This disdain for political narrative, and the corresponding privileging of social-historical analysis, are constantly reflected not only in Gibbon's occasional and ostentatious withholding of detail but also in his multiple systems for interrupting, exploding, and collapsing the insistent logic of chronology. It is not, of course, that rulers of great empires could not deeply affect the lives of their subjects: it was precisely their power to do so, through the "artificial powers of government," that aroused Gibbon's horror at monarchy as a political system (*DF* i. 120). But there were limits to the apprehension as also the agency even of despots, and so, in Gibbon's view, "to illustrate the obscure monuments of the life and death of each individual, would prove a laborious task, alike barren of instruction and of amusement" (*DF* i. 288; cf. 303). He similarly eschewed the compiling of biographical details when he drew to a close his account of the Severan dynasty and turned his attention to the effects of the *Constitutio Antoniniana*:

> The dissolute tyranny of Commodus, the civil wars occasioned by his death, and the new maxims of policy introduced by the house of Severus, had all contributed to increase the dangerous power of the army, and to obliterate the faint image of laws and liberty that was still impressed on the minds of the Romans. The internal change, which undermined

the foundations of the empire, we have endeavoured to explain with some degree of order and perspicuity. The personal characters of the emperors, their victories, laws, follies, and fortunes, can interest us no farther than as they are connected with the general history of the Decline and Fall of the monarchy. (*DF* i. 178)

Gibbon likewise deplored the impossibility of narrating the chaotic movements of barbarian peoples and the instability of their internal arrangements (*DF* i. 252). His solution was to "consult order and perspicuity, by pursuing, not so much the doubtful arrangement of dates, as the more natural distribution of subjects" (*DF* i. 268; cf. 988–9), a device to which he had recourse also when confronting the "very doubtful chronology" of Diocletian's reign (*DF* i. 362–3), or the "number and variety" of important events in the reign of Constantine, "by which the historian must be oppressed ... unless he diligently separates from each other the scenes which are connected only by the order of time" (*DF* i. 585).

Virtue and Despotism

I must leave aside any consideration of the classical roots of this aspect of Gibbon's art: I content myself with the suggestion that he owes more to Thucydides, and even to Tacitus, than is generally recognized. And I set aside for the moment the most famous of those historical phenomena that Gibbon divorced from "the natural order of events" (*DF* i. 363), namely the rise of Christianity, whose existence (but not whose name) is acknowledged and dismissed first in a footnote, as being "well known," but whose importance, he concedes in a later note, "will require a distinct chapter of this work" (*DF* i. 53 n. 83; 57 n. 3). For it is my contention that the pattern set by Gibbon in his first volume, of segregating and then postponing inquiry into Christianity, established a paradigm that he followed throughout – in separating Constantine's and Licinius' meeting in Milan from any mention of their famous "Edict" by 299 pages, in his treatment of Constantine's conversion, and in his study of monasticism. I also contend that Gibbon so treated Christianity for two reasons. First, thus separating its history from that of the empire allowed him both to respect and to upend two distinct traditions within ecclesiastical historiography: that developed between the time of Origen and the time of Augustine, both of whom saw the Christian community as a separate polity; and that represented by Protestants of Gibbon's own day, who believed the Church to have been corrupted by its association with the world in the aftermath of Constantine's conversion (*DF* i. 732). Second, by construing the Christian community of that period as a polity, Gibbon was able to invite his readers to see its history as analogous to that of the empire itself, even in the period of its persecution. We therefore have to appreciate the relationship Gibbon posits between political form and political virtue, insofar as these are connected in the history of decline and fall, before we can see how that relationship structured his account of both the intrinsic character and the historical development of Christianity.

Gibbon animates his account of political virtue and its fortunes under the empire using a set of polarities that are both structural and historical: contrasts between east and west, center and periphery, past and present, freedom and despotism. I call these *both* structural and historical, because Gibbon describes events and eras in which Asia and Europe collide, for example, but the polarity between the characters of Europe and Asia informs his depiction of Roman manners even when no conflict with Parthia or Islam is involved. The constituents that animate that contrast between east and west receive their clearest articulation at the close of chapter 2, in which Gibbon attempted to explain "in what manner the most civilized provinces of Europe, Asia, and Africa were united under the dominion of one sovereign, and gradually connected by the most intimate ties of laws, of manners, and of language" (*DF* i. 499):

> Domestic peace and union were the natural consequences of the moderate and comprehensive policy embraced by the Romans. If we turn our eyes towards the monarchies of Asia, we shall behold despotism in the centre, and weakness in the extremities; the collection of the revenue, or the administration of justice, enforced by the presence of an army; hostile barbarians established in the heart of the country, hereditary satraps usurping the dominion of the provinces, and subjects inclined to rebellion, though incapable of freedom. But the obedience of the Roman world was uniform, voluntary, and permanent. The vanquished nations, blended into one great people, resigned the hope, nay, even the wish, of resuming their independence, and scarcely considered their own existence as distinct from the existence of Rome. (*DF* i. 70)

But the unification of the Roman Empire, which might be qualified as a good when contrasted with the mere dominion over unwilling subjects exercised by "the monarchies of Asia," occupied a rather different position in the history of Roman manners, internally regarded. In that story, "in proportion as the public freedom was lost in extent of conquest, war was gradually improved into an art, and degraded into a trade" (*DF* i. 38).

Gibbon here alludes to events and changes outside the scope of his work, to the replacement of citizen legionaries by mercenaries from the provinces and, beyond that, to the professionalization of the citizen army in late republican Rome. "In a civilized state," such as Rome of the mid-republic may have been, "every faculty of man is expanded and exercised; and the great chain of mutual dependence connects and embraces the several members of society" (*DF* i. 237; cf. 240). The virtue of the citizen at such a time consisted above all in service to the commonwealth, by the common man in the army or "in constant and useful labour," and by "the select few, placed by fortune above that necessity" (*DF* i. 237), "in the offices of the state, and the ceremonies of religion" (*DF* i. 607). Moreover, as Gibbon understood it, Rome of the mid-republic had succeeded in overthrowing the dominance of blood and the institutions of vassalage "so incompatible with the spirit of a free people" (*DF* i. 607). Those institutions had maintained the privileges of the patricians, and so had come as close as might be to rely on "distinctions of personal merit" (*DF* i. 603). But Gibbon's interest in republican citizenship went further still. For, though his topic required him repeatedly to contrast the loyalty of "legionaries, who enjoyed the title and privileges of Romans [and] were enlisted for the general defence of the republic," with that of "mercenary troops, [who] heard with cold indifference the antiquated names of the republic and of Rome" (*DF* i. 832), he crucially understood legionaries to have been citizens too: "That public virtue, which among the ancients was denominated patriotism, is derived from a strong sense of our own interest in the preservation and prosperity of the free government of which we are members" (*DF* i. 39). One privilege and consequence of membership in a commonwealth was "some share in enacting those laws, which it was their interest as well as duty to maintain" (*DF* i. 38). Not for nothing did Gibbon liken the study of Roman law to "breath[ing] the pure and invigorating air of the republic" (*DF* ii. 779). Precisely because he understood the law to condition and express a society's manners in accordance with the wishes of its sovereign members, he declared "the laws of a nation [to] form the most instructive portion of its history" (*DF* ii. 779).

But an empire could not be a republic. "There is nothing perhaps more adverse to nature and reason than to hold in obedience remote countries and foreign nations, in opposition to their inclination and interest" (*DF* iii. 142). Roman policy may have aimed to make Romans of their subjects, and indeed, "as long as Rome and Italy were respected as the centre of government, a national spirit was preserved by the ancient, and insensibly imbibed by the adopted, citizens" (*DF* i. 186). But this system proved impossible to sustain. There was first the problem, apparent already in antiquity and stated clearly by Ammianus (19. 11. 7), "that [citizens] will pay dearly to spare their bodies" from military service, "which ambition has often harmed the Roman state." Even then, for so long as "the principal commands of the army were filled by men who had received a liberal education, were well instructed in the advantages of laws and letters, and who had risen, by equal steps, through the regular succession of civil and military honours," the legions displayed a "modest obedience" (*DF* i. 186). But this system rested on an unsustainable paradox: Romans and Italians who ceased to serve defaulted on their claim to "the national spirit"; but it was not clear how barbarian subjects could form a citizen army (*DF* i. 345). If, at one time, "Spain, Gaul, Britain, and Illyricum [had] supplied the legions with excellent soldiers, and constituted the real strength of the monarchy," their populations as a whole "no longer possessed that public courage which is nourished by the love of independence, the sense of national honour, the presence of danger, and the habit of command. They received laws and governors from the will of their sovereign, and trusted for their defence to a mercenary army" (*DF* i. 83). Citizens of a republic, with the capacity for virtue, do not so much receive as enact laws; in that respect, and in others, the Romanization of provinces could only remain partial. "[T]he sovereignty of the capital was gradually annihilated in the extent of conquest; the provinces rose to the same level, and the vanquished nations acquired the name and privileges, without imbibing the partial affections, of Romans" (*DF* i. 384).

For Ammianus, who knew only monarchs, the unwillingness of provincial citizens to bear arms was a moral failure and required no further explanation. For Gibbon, however, that loss of virtue had a history that reached back into the republic, one that could not be told apart from the history of politics. For as service in arms was a preeminent expression of patriotism, so, Gibbon implies, the end of republican government will have dissolved that sense of membership that "rendered the legions of the Republic almost invincible" (*DF* i. 39). Gibbon did not tell that story, though he famously repented "not hav[ing] given the history of that fortunate period that was interposed between the two Iron ages" or having "deduced the decline of the Empire from the civil Wars, that ensued after the fall of Nero or even from the tyranny which succeeded the reign of Augustus" (marginalia to Gibbon's copy of vol. 1, p. 1; reprinted in *DF* iii. 1093). To do so would have required him to explain how the exercise of republican virtue had acquired for Rome an empire by which the liberty of its citizens was threatened and its virtue corrupted, and to sustain which the Roman republic was obliged to transform itself into a monarchy and so to surrender its freedom and virtue altogether. But if Gibbon did not relate the causes why Rome became "an absolute monarchy disguised by the forms of a commonwealth," he worked assiduously to explain the effects of that transformation, in which "the distinctions of personal merit and influence, so conspicuous in a republic, so feeble and obscure under a monarchy, were abolished by the despotism of the emperors" (*DF* i. 603).

Gibbon's history of monarchy at Rome develops in two directions at once: it charts the irrational character of authoritarian power and studies the way in which the loss of freedom and the consequent inability to exercise civic virtue affected Roman society. Gibbon knew that there had been good kings, but he could not define monarchy without imagining its corruption:

> The obvious definition of a monarchy seems to be that of a state, in which a single person, by whatsoever name he may be distinguished, is intrusted with the execution of the laws, the management of the revenue, and the command of the army. But, unless public liberty is protected by intrepid and vigilant guardians, the authority of so formidable a magistrate will soon degenerate into despotism. (*DF* i. 85)

Gibbon's concern derived from the pattern of history. In his view, "[t]he true interest of an absolute monarch generally coincides with that of his people. Their numbers, their wealth, their order, and their security are the best and only foundations of his real greatness; and were he totally devoid of virtue, prudence might supply its place, and would dictate the same rule of conduct" (*DF* i. 144); but the "united reigns" of Nerva, Trajan, Hadrian, and Marcus were "possibly the only period in history in which the happiness of a great people was the sole object of government" (*DF* i. 101–2). At other times, the effect of monarchy was to concentrate power in the hands of individuals, even the most able of whom could not have "subdue[d] millions of followers and enemies by their own personal strength" (*DF* i. 139). At the death of Commodus, for example, Gibbon remarks, "Such was the fate of the son of Marcus, and so easy was it to destroy a hated tyrant, who, by the artificial powers of government, had oppressed, during thirteen years, so many millions of subjects, each of whom was equal to their master in personal strength and personal abilities" (*DF* i. 120). Likewise, "the most important care of [Julia] Mamaea and her wise counsellors, was to form the character of the young emperor," Alexander Severus, "on whose personal qualities the happiness or misery of the Roman world must ultimately depend" (*DF* i. 172). Nor was an emperor's capacity to work harm limited by his caprice. Whether by mere proximity or by delegation, under the empire all manner of individuals came to wield derivative and "arbitrary" power (*DF* i. 161). And indeed, Gibbon's remarks on one such office, the praetorian prefecture – that it was originally found to be "incompatible with public freedom," but "as the sense of liberty became less exquisite, the advantages of order were more clearly understood" – are the closest he comes to explaining the end of democracy at Rome (*DF* i. 611–12).

In Gibbon's view, the success of the Augustan system rested on its employment of the Senate as an "intermediate power, however imaginary, between the emperor and the army" (*DF* i. 147; see also 93, 96), and so long as it persisted, "princes were in some measure obliged to assume the language and behavior suitable to the general and first magistrate of the republic" (*DF* i. 387). The system was unsustainable, on two grounds. First, the stationing of an elite corps in the capital "taught them to perceive their own strength, and the weakness of the civil government; to view the vices of their masters with familiar contempt, and to lay aside that reverential awe, which distance only, and mystery, can preserve towards an imaginary power" (*DF* i. 128); and second, removed from any meaningful opportunity to exercise traditional forms of elite virtue, the would-be governing class in Rome and Italy dissipated its strength and sank into torpor. Their decline was made most manifest when the emperor Gallienus, in fear that the Senate might one day "rescue the public from domestic tyranny as well as foreign invasion," published an edict prohibiting senators from military commands and even from approaching legionary camps. His fear that the senators would object was, according to Gibbon, groundless. "The rich and luxurious nobles, sinking into their natural character, accepted, as a favour, this disgraceful exemption from military service; and as long as they were indulged in the enjoyment of their baths, their theatres, and their villas, they cheerfully resigned the more dangerous cares of empire to the rough hands of peasants and soldiers" (*DF* i. 273).

But the collapse of the empire's governing class had begun much earlier, and took place on two levels. One was that of culture, and derives (like the "imaginary" powers of government) from some failure of correspondence between action, ability, apprehension, and reality. For the educated class in the provinces, like that of Italy, looked ever to the literary models generated in a world unlike their own. "[T]rained by a uniform artificial foreign education, [they] were engaged in a very unequal competition with those bold ancients, who, by expressing their genuine feelings in their native tongue, had already occupied every place of honour" (*DF* i. 84). It was this system of education that inspired the culture of belatedness that Gibbon so often described and deplored. The other level is that of virtue, and on that level the collapse had advanced far already in the second century, and is clearly visible even in Gibbon's most famous panegyric to the Antonine empire:

> If a man were called to fix the period in the history of the world, during which the condition of the human race was most happy and prosperous, he would, without hesitation, name that which elapsed from the death of Domitian to the accession of Commodus. The vast extent of the Roman empire was governed by absolute power, under the guidance of virtue and wisdom. The armies were restrained by the firm but gentle hand of four successive emperors, whose characters and authority commanded involuntary respect. The forms of the civil administration were carefully preserved by Nerva, Trajan, Hadrian, and the Antonines, who delighted in the image of liberty, and were pleased with considering themselves as the accountable ministers of the laws. Such princes deserved the honour of restoring the republic, had the Romans of their days been capable of enjoying a rational freedom. (*DF* i. 103)

In their incapacity for freedom, the Romans of the second century resemble none so much as the provincial subjects of the monarchies of Asia (see *DF* i. 70, quoted above). Such was the power of government, so high the price of empire.

The Christian Republic

Thus far I have followed Gibbon in "adopt[ing] the division unknown to the ancients of civil and ecclesiastical affairs' (*DF* i. 585), and I have already suggested what two of his motives for so doing might have been. I wish now to outline what this division enabled him to say, both about the history of Christianity and about the place of Christianity within the history of the declining monarchy.

Gibbon opens chapter 15 by declaring the object of his inquiry to be not Christianity as a religion, "as she descended from Heaven, arrayed in her native purity," but rather "the imperfections of the uninspired teachers and believers of the gospel," and "the inevitable mixture of error and corruption, which she contracted in a long residence upon earth, among a weak and degenerate race of beings" (*DF* i. 446). Chapters 15 and 16 then cover much of the same chronological ground twice: chapter 15 considers five "secondary causes of the rapid growth of the Christian church" (*DF* i. 447), 16 the relations between that Church and the Roman government. I have suggested that, in so organizing his material, Gibbon followed those ancients who construed the place of the Christian community in the world by using metaphors of statecraft and politics. But a human society of sufficient size, complexity, and geographic extent must needs take on the characteristics of a political collectivity, and in so doing it would expose itself to the same processes of change, corruption, and decay as any other. It was thus that Gibbon could deploy against the early Church the same analytical tools he brought to bear against the empire, and could claim for that project the implicit endorsement of the Church itself.

Like Rome itself, whose growth Gibbon charted from its early kings to the third century AD (*DF* i. 211–12), the "Christian republic" only "gradually formed an independent and increasing state in the heart of the Roman empire" (*DF* i. 447). In this it resembled any other human society, which, as Gibbon knew, had to achieve a certain size and productivity before it could support an army or an educated elite (*DF* i. 127, 237 and especially 508, where the analogy between earthly and religious societies is made explicit). And like Rome, the Christian community passed in history through a period as a "commonwealth" (*DF* i. 482), during which its members felt their interest to lie "in the preservation and prosperity of their government" (*DF* i. 39), and "conceived [themselves] obliged to submit [their] private opinions and actions to the judgment of the greater number of [their] associates" (*DF* i. 240).

> The safety of that society, its honour, its aggrandizement, were productive, even in the most pious minds, of a spirit of patriotism, such as the first of the Romans had felt for the republic, and sometimes of a similar indifference, in the use of whatever means might probably conduce to so desirable an end. (*DF* i. 482–3)

Unfortunately, "in the church as well as in the world" (*DF* i. 483), the increasing complexity of a society places stress on its internal orderings, not least on its ability to afford all individuals an equal chance to exercise their civic virtue. "The ecclesiastical governors of the Christians" – the wording is not innocent – "were taught to unite the wisdom of the serpent with the innocence of the dove; but as the former was refined, so the latter was insensibly corrupted, by the habits of government" (*DF* i. 483). And as the individual leaders of the Christian community came to resemble the earthly politicians who ordered the cities of the empire, so they organized themselves as a governing class and institutionalized their authority by "adopt[ing] the useful institutions of the provincial synods," which "they may justly be supposed to have borrowed" from the provincial councils of their own country: "the Amphictyons, the Achaean league, or the assemblies of the Ionian cities" (*DF* i. 486).

"In the church as well as in the world," it is the tendency and inclination of governing elites to enhance and retain such power as they have, and the role of institutions of government to make and enforce the law.

> [The bishops and martyrs] were destitute of any temporal force, and they were for a long time discouraged and oppressed, rather than assisted, by the civil magistrate; but they had acquired, and they employed within their own society, the two most efficacious instruments of government, rewards and punishments; the former derived from the pious liberality, the latter from the devout apprehensions, of the faithful. (*DF* i. 490)

There is, furthermore, an enduring tension within republican government, because of which "nobilities see liberty as the power to rule, peoples as the freedom from being ruled by others" (Pocock 2003: 209). When once the people surrender in any degree their law-making capacity, they shall discover their liberty forever compromised.

> As the legislative authority of the particular churches was insensibly superseded by the use of councils, the bishops obtained by their alliance a much larger share of executive and arbitrary power; and as soon as they were connected by a sense of their common interest, they were enabled to attack with united vigour, the original rights of their clergy and people. (*DF* i. 487)

In their exercise of legislative authority, and executive and arbitrary power, the bishops of the early Church remind readers of Septimius Severus.

> His haughty and inflexible spirit could not discover, or would not acknowledge, the advantage of preserving an intermediate power, however imaginary, between the emperor and the army. He disdained to profess himself the servant of an assembly that detested his person and trembled at his frown; he issued his commands, where his requests would have proved as effectual; assumed the conduct and style of a sovereign and a conqueror, and exercised, without disguise, the whole legislative, as well as the executive power. (*DF* i. 147)

"Posterity, who experienced the fatal effects of his maxims and example, justly considered him as the principal author of the decline of the Roman empire" (*DF* i. 148).

It is not, of course, that the Church failed or even faltered under such leaders. Nevertheless, they were men, and "of all our passions and appetites, the love of power is of the most imperious and unsociable nature" (*DF* i. 109). Thus, though the bishops and martyrs "concealed from others, and perhaps from themselves, the secret motives of their conduct" (*DF* i. 483), they could not but work for the aggrandizement of their power and the dominion of their Church. In Gibbon's words,

> Their mutual hostilities sometimes disturbed the peace of the infant church, but their zeal and activity were united in the common cause, and the love of power, which (under the most artful disguises) could insinuate itself into the breasts of bishops and martyrs, animated them to increase the number of their subjects, and to enlarge the limits of the Christian empire. (*DF* i. 490)

So it was, even in the age of persecution, that "the Church still continued to increase its outward splendour as it lost its internal purity" (*DF* i. 510). "The limits of the Roman empire still extended from the Western Ocean to the Tigris, and from Mount Atlas to the Rhine and the Danube. To the undiscerning eye of the vulgar, Philip appeared a monarch no less powerful than Hadrian or Augustus. The form was still the same, but the animating health and vigour were fled" (*DF* i. 212). Christian society thus came ever more to resemble that other empire, from whose opposition it derived new vigor (*DF* i. 446), and whose growth had been purchased with the virtue and liberty of its members. It was, one might argue, not so much their collision as their union that was inevitable.

When Gibbon first lists the five causes of "the rapid growth of the Christian church," he names the fourth "the pure and austere morals of the Christians" (*DF* i. 447). But when he comes to that cause in the course of his fuller exposition, he speaks instead of "the virtues of the first Christians" (*DF* i. 475). The new wording involves a paradox that Gibbon is at pains to resolve. In his view, "there are two very natural propensities which we may distinguish in the most virtuous and liberal dispositions, the love of pleasure and the love of action" (*DF* i. 478). If the former is properly refined, "it is productive of the greatest part of the happiness of private life." "The love of action," on the other hand, "is a principle of a much stronger and more doubtful nature. It often leads to anger, to ambition, and to revenge; but when it is guided by the sense of propriety and benevolence, it becomes the parent of every virtue" (*DF* i. 478). By "virtue," Gibbon means the virtue of the citizen – so much is clear from the distinction he draws between happiness as a quality of private life, on the one hand, and states and empires (as well as families) as the beneficiaries of virtuous action, on the other. That he and his intended readers might share a metaphysical view different from that of the early Christians, who confounded morals with virtues, drives the seeming irony of his conclusion:

> The character in which both the one and the other should be united and harmonized, would seem to constitute the most perfect idea of human nature. The insensible and inactive disposition, which should be supposed alike destitute of both, would be rejected, by the common consent of mankind, as utterly incapable of procuring any happiness to the individual, or any public benefit to the world. But it was not in this world, that the primitive Christians were desirous of making themselves either agreeable or useful. (*DF* i. 478)

But residents of this world they were, and to the extent that the primitive Christians paid attention to their conduct in it, they avowed, and indeed generally yielded, "the most passive obedience to the laws" (*DF* i. 514; see also 732). Gibbon devotes chapter 16 to the question how so pure a religion could have provoked such anger, not least in a culture that so valued tolerance. One answer must surely be that the Christians "declined the active cares of war and government" (*DF* i. 514), and so removed themselves from membership in civil society. Nor was Gibbon alone in finding the Christians out of place in the world, and strangers even in a declining empire (see Euseb. *Hist. eccl.* 1. 1. 1).

> But while they inculcated the maxims of passive obedience, they refused to take any active part in the civil administration or the military defence of the empire. Some indulgence might, perhaps, be allowed to those persons who, before their conversion, were already engaged in such violent and sanguinary occupations; but it was impossible that the Christians, without renouncing a more sacred duty, could assume the character of soldiers, of magistrates, or of princes. This indolent, or even criminal disregard to the public welfare, exposed them to the contempt and reproaches of the Pagans who very frequently asked, what must be the fate of the empire, attacked on every side by the barbarians, if all mankind should adopt the pusillanimous sentiments of the new sect. (*DF* i. 482)

Framed in terms of Gibbon's concern for republican citizenship, the pagans might be understood to ask what sort of citizen a Christian could be. Had Rome been a republic, the answer would have been none, none at all.

But the magistrates who persecuted the Christians in the first three centuries did not govern a republic, but merely behaved as if they did. In so restating the pagans' question, we indulge ourselves in that nostalgia that led Decius, Tacitus, and later Justinian in different ways to misapprehend their world; and in apprehending that indulgence, we perceive Gibbon's artistry and argument anew. The ruthless cunning of Constantine, who so esteemed, protected, and promoted the Christians of his era, is perhaps a better guide (*DF* i. 730). Framed in light of his policy, the postulates of the pagans' question should be reversed: in what sort of society would a Christian be an ideal citizen? The answer is clear: a despotic one.

> The passive and unresisting obedience, which bows under the yoke of authority, or even of oppression, must have appeared, in the eyes of an absolute monarch, the most conspicuous and useful of the evangelic virtues. The primitive Christians derived the institution of civil government, not from the consent of the people, but from the decrees of heaven. The reigning emperor, though he had usurped the sceptre by treason and murder, immediately assumed the sacred character of viceregent of the Deity. To the Deity alone he was accountable for the abuse of his power; and his subjects were indissolubly bound, by their oath of fidelity, to a tyrant, who had violated every law of nature and society. (*DF* i. 731)

The policy of Constantine, and particularly its success, thus reveals him to be the true heir to Severus, and Christianity to be an essentially Asian religion – for it had been Severus who first filled the Senate "with polished and eloquent slaves from the eastern provinces, who justified personal flattery by speculative principles of servitude. These new advocates of prerogative were heard with pleasure by the court, and with patience by the people, when they inculcated the duty of passive obedience, and descanted on the inevitable mischiefs of freedom" (*DF* i. 147–8).

The thematic and verbal echoes that tie Constantine to Severus reveal several truths, not least that Christianity was not the cause of decline, but symptomatic of it. Gibbon had warned that this was so. At the close of his narrative of the rise of Constantine, he termed the reunification of the empire under that ruler a "revolution," of which "the foundation of Constantinople, and the establishment of the Christian religion, were the immediate and memorable consequences" (*DF* i. 445). For, while "readers who are insensible to the importance of laws and manners" might have thought the foundation of a capital on the Bosphorus, on the borders of Asia, a turning point in the history of the empire, Gibbon regarded it only as an illustration of "the secret and internal causes of its rapid decay" (*DF* i. 602). Like "the fatal though secret wound inflicted upon the Senate from the hands of Diocletian and Maximian" – namely, "the inevitable operation of their absence" (*DF* i. 386) – momentous political acts like "the foundation of Constantinople and the establishment of the Christian religion" achieve their status as turning points by virtue of their narratibility, and Gibbon's art was governed essentially by the ambition to restore them to their proper place in history.

For Gibbon, then, Christianity as a force in Roman history serves as handmaid to historical changes that were already operative in the empire prior to Constantine – changes that were also unfolding within the Christianity community itself. It became the religion of the empire at that moment when the character of its citizens had assimilated to the virtues required of subjects of despotic rule; while the union of ecclesiastical with imperial authority produced a relation of codependence that could "only be compared to the respect with which the senate had been treated by the Roman princes who adopted the policy of Augustus" (*DF* i. 765). Of the empire in the second century, Gibbon had written: "[t]he obedient provinces of Trajan and the Antonines were united by laws, and adorned by arts." Those emperors "knew and valued the advantages of religion, as it is connected with civil government. They encouraged the public festivals which humanize the manners of the people" (*DF* i. 59). It is a measure of the change in Rome from the second to the fourth century, and of the distance between civil and despotic government, that Gibbon found Constantine's policy appropriate to its context:

> But the operation of the wisest laws is imperfect and precarious. They seldom inspire virtue, they cannot always restrain vice. Their power is insufficient to prohibit all that they condemn, nor can they always punish the actions which they prohibit. The legislators of antiquity had summoned to their aid the powers of education and of opinion. But every principle which had once maintained the vigor and purity of Rome and Sparta, was long since extinguished in a declining and despotic empire. (*DF* i. 730)

BIBLIOGRAPHICAL NOTE

Interested readers should turn first to Gibbon himself. The *History* is available in several editions, but the best is that by David Womersley (Gibbon 1994), who scrupulously restores Gibbon's punctuation, spelling, and notes, and adds an index of sources. Of Gibbon's other writings, the most important to the present study is the response he addressed to critics of the treatment afforded Christianity in his first volume – "A Vindication of some passages in the fifteenth and sixteenth chapters of the History of the Decline and Fall of the Roman Empire" – originally published in 1779, and reproduced in Patricia Craddock's edition of Gibbon's *English Essays* (Craddock 1972: 229–313) and in David Womersley's edition of the *History* (*DF* iii. 1106–84). Gibbon's autobiography (Gibbon 1984) is justly famous. Further biographical information is available in the journal he kept from August 4, 1761, when he was a captain in the Hampshire militia, until his arrival in Rome on October 2, 1764 – the visit that inspired him to write the *History* (Low 1929; Bonnard 1945, 1961).

Studies of the *History* abound. Much modern criticism derives from the work of Italian scholars of the Enlightenment, produced in the middle years of the twentieth century. That tradition, in its English form, is represented above all by Arnaldo Momigliano, who recognized in Gibbon's work an attempt to reconcile three quite distinct modes of historical inquiry (Momigliano 1966a, 1980). But by far the most ambitious study of Gibbon and of the intellectual contexts in which he worked is J. G. A. Pocock's *Barbarism and Religion*, of which four volumes are now in print (1999a, 1999b, 2003, 2005), and two more are due to appear. A brief essay (Pocock 1996), drafted as an introduction to his second volume, offers an exciting précis of European historiography down to the eighteenth century. Among single-volume studies, Porter 1988 offers a general survey, while Womersley 1988 attempts to trace Gibbon's evolving understanding of his own project. Others have approached Gibbon from a literary perspective: Braudy 1970 reads Gibbon alongside Hume and Fielding; Carnochan 1987 contains a set of related essays; and Bond 1960 provides a valuable study of Gibbon's language.

Finally, after a lull, historians of Late Antiquity are returning to the question of whether "decline" is an apposite term. Matthews (1997) does so through Gibbon's own eyes, while Liebeschuetz (2001a), Heather (2005), and Ward-Perkins (2005) all look again at issues that preoccupied him – the sheer weight of empire, on the one hand, and the violence wreaked on social and economic life by the barbarian invasions on the other.

CHAPTER SIX

Late Antiquity in Modern Eyes

Stefan Rebenich

On September 12, 1921, during an autumn colloquium on the arts and sciences, Ernst Kornemann (1868–1946) gave a lecture in Kiel on the decline of the ancient world. He described the topic of his address as "the problem of problems" in historiography. Then he proposed a possible solution: he suggested that the prosperity at the time of imperial rule had generated decadence everywhere, paralyzed social cohesion, destroyed the military masculine morale that had once made Rome great, and led the emperors to pursue an illusory policy of peace. In consequence, cultural life had come under the detrimental influence of a collectivist religiosity of eastern provenance (Kornemann 1922).

That was not an original view. In the humanities, the problem formulated by Kornemann had been an enigma for centuries – and it still is. The discussion centered on two questions: why did the Roman Empire decline; and when did this decline occur?

Let us first address the associated division of history into periods. Italian scholars of the Renaissance thought in terms of antiquity, the Middle Ages, and the modern age – a model still familiar today. This model, which displaced the universal historical periodization characteristic of the Christian tradition – especially the theory of the four empires – was based on the assumption that the so-called Middle Ages had been a 1,000-year-long period of decline. That decline had to be overcome by bringing about a new epoch, one that would be connected to the period these scholars regarded as their norm: pagan and Christian antiquity.

After the sixteenth century, numerous authors tried to define more precisely the nature and date of the transition from antiquity to the Middle Ages. Their suggestions included the coming to power of Diocletian (AD 284); the era of Constantine, in particular his accession (AD 306), his victory at the Milvian Bridge (AD 312), or the beginning of his autocratic rule (AD 324); and the crossing of the Danube by the Goths (AD 376), the Battle of Hadrianople (AD 378), and the settlement of the Goths within the empire (AD 382). These events, they argued, while not constituting the boundary between antiquity and the Middle Ages themselves, prepared the ground for an event that actually signaled that antiquity had ended – namely the loss of the unity of the empire, following the death of Theodosius I (AD 395), the sack of Rome by Alaric (AD 410), or (most often mentioned) the deposition of Romulus Augustulus (AD 476) – an event that even contemporaries like Eugippius, Count Marcellinus, and Procopius considered a turning point. All of these suggestions were based on the assumption that there had been a sudden change in historical circumstances, triggered either by internal developments or by such external catastrophes as the triumph of the Christian faith or invasion by barbaric hordes.

In the nineteenth century, historians discarded that view: the notion of a gradual change replaced the idea of an abrupt transition. Scholars no longer considered the break between antiquity and the Middle Ages as clear-cut as their predecessors had, and, influenced by the classic work of the Austrian historian Alfons Dopsch (1868–1953), *Wirtschaftliche und soziale Grundlagen der europäischen Kulturentwicklung* (1918–20), many emphasized the continuity rather than the discontinuity between antiquity and the Middle Ages. As a result, the boundary between antiquity and the Middle Ages clearly shifted to later periods: among the proposals were now the invasion of Italy by the Lombards (AD 568), the reigns of the emperors Justinian (AD 527–65) or Heraclius (AD 610–41), or the pontificate of Pope Gregory the Great (AD 590–604). The Belgian economic historian Henri Pirenne (1862–1935) even advocated the thesis that Islam alone – or, more precisely, the advance of the Arabs in North Africa and Spain – had brought about the epochal change (Pirenne 1937). This notion of a successive transformation lasting several centuries established Late Antiquity as an epoch *sui generis*. The concept of a "long" Late Antiquity that lasted from the third century to the seventh proved not only extremely rewarding for political, but also for ecclesiastical, cultural, economic, social, and literary history.

As to the causes of the decline of the Roman Empire, it must be kept in mind that, ever since the age of humanism, Late Antiquity has been regarded as an era of decline, thought to have begun with Constantine, with the soldier emperors, with Commodus, or even with Augustus. Numerous explanations for the supposed fall of the *Imperium Romanum* and the ancient world have been given (D'Elia 1967; Demandt 1984). Frequently, individual accounts have revealed more about the ideological and political position of their authors than about the historical patterns they claim to portray. The most prominent of the critical internal and external events that have been suggested are the rise of Christianity, the division between rich and poor, the spread of the Germanic peoples, exhausted sources of subsistence – through deterioration of the climate, soil erosion, and depopulation – as well as lead poisoning and hypothermia, racial interbreeding and biological degeneration: all of these possibilities have been considered by various authors. Views that are diametrically opposed to each other can also be found: for some, the Germans are destructive, while others regard them as protectors and revivers of ancient culture; here the end of Greco-Roman paganism is mourned, there the birth of Christian Europe is welcomed. Authors like Oswald Spengler (1880–1936) and Arnold Toynbee (1889–1975) attempted to derive from the decline of the Roman world a theory of change, a notion of cultural cycles that would explain the emergence of new patterns of social, political, and cultural organization. Representatives of the materialistic view of history – which is now obsolete – portrayed Late Antiquity as a transitional period between ancient slave-owning society and the feudalism of the Middle Ages (Heinen 1980). In recent decades, however, the perception of Late Antiquity has significantly changed: the period is no longer seen as an era of decline and crisis but as an epoch of metamorphosis in the Mediterranean region (Liebeschuetz 2001b).

A Positive View of Late Antiquity

An enumeration of individual positions and concepts (such as I have provided above) can be only a starting point for a critical history of earlier and contemporary studies in Late Antiquity. To provide a necessary corrective to current research and an incentive to examine the discipline itself more critically, we have to identify the historical circumstances that influenced the historiography on Late Antiquity. Over the centuries, both humanism and Protestantism impeded a positive view of Late Antiquity as an epoch in its own right, and scholars thought of it as a transitional period between antiquity and the Middle Ages, and judged it unfavorably as an era of decline. Still, the production of the great editions of texts composed by Christian authors and other writers of Late Antiquity that was characteristic of this phase was of vital importance for subsequent research into the later period. Thus, in the seventeenth and eighteenth centuries, scholars from the Netherlands and France, Italy and Germany, England and the Scandinavian countries succeeded the humanists and emerged as literary critics and editors. A multitude of late classical and Byzantine works were printed for the first time – in some instances supplemented by brilliant conjectural emendations and profound annotations. The Huguenot and lawyer Jacobus Gothofredus (Jacques Godefroy, 1587–1652) deserves a special mention here: even today, his commentary on the *Codex Theodosianus* (1665) is indispensable. Moreover, a wealth of antiquarian literature was devoted to the late Roman Empire and the early Church.

Catholic scholars had always been eager, since the Counter-Reformation, to present the foundation of the Roman Church as a feature of Christian antiquity. From 1643 onward, the Jesuit Bollandists edited and commented on hagiographic texts. For over two generations, from the late 1660s, the Benedictine congregation of St. Maur (the "Maurists," such as Jean Mabillon, Bernard de Montfaucon, and Thierry Ruinart) published editions of numerous "Fathers of the Church" that in many respects have not been surpassed to the present day. The French cleric Jacques-Paul Migne (1800–75) reprinted a large number of the texts in his extensive and still widely consulted editorial enterprise, the *cursus completus* of early ecclesiastical and medieval writings of the Fathers (the *Patrologia Latina* and the *Patrologia Graeca*, known universally as "Migne"). Meanwhile, Louis Sébastien Le Nain de Tillemont (1637–98), having made extensive use of primary sources, had published two general accounts of the imperial and ecclesiastical history of the (late) Roman Empire: *Mémoires pour servir à l'histoire ecclésiastique des six premiers siècles* (sixteen volumes,

1693–1712), and *Histoire des empereurs* (six volumes, 1690–1738), the latter covering the period from Augustus to Anastasius, 31 BC–AD 518. Up to the end of the nineteenth century, both works had a lasting effect on the scholarly perception and study of Late Antiquity.

The secularized historiography of the Enlightenment likewise put greater emphasis on the decline of the Roman Empire than on the rise of the Roman republic. Gibbon was not in this regard the only figure of importance. In his *Considérations sur les causes de la grandeur des Romains et de leur décadence* (1734), Montesquieu had already shown how ingenious legislation had made Rome great, but also how, with law-governed necessity, the cost of Rome's triumph was its decline, as the temptations of power destroyed the virtues of the Roman people and the principles of Roman politics. With the French Revolution, however, the Roman republic became once again the focus of scholarly and public interest all over Europe.

An Authority for the Present

From the eighteenth to the nineteenth centuries, antiquity was reinterpreted in Europe in historical, political, and aesthetic terms. The enthusiasm for "classical" Greek art and literature – a marked development in Germany toward the end of the eighteenth century – hastened a tendency to separate pagan from Christian antiquity. The idealization of Greece had already acquired a contemporary political dimension: in accordance with the liberating traditions of the Enlightenment, Johann Joachim Winckelmann (1717–68) and his contemporaries saw Athens as not only a center of artistic and humane ideals, but also a seat of political freedom. By restoring to the center of inquiry this more loosely structured history of ancient Greece, the German *Bürgertum* discovered a welcome alternative to the cultural hegemony of the French.

But German neohumanism did not by any means lead inevitably to a diminution of interest in Late Antiquity. On the contrary: from the French Revolution on, a positive view of this epoch spread throughout Europe. The decline of the Roman Empire, it was believed, affected only paganism, which had outlived its use and had to make way for Christianity and the Germanic kingdoms. The experience of political and social revolutions in Europe between 1789 and 1848 established Late Antiquity as an epoch in its own right, characterized by changes and reassessments that were, in turn, compared to phenomena of the present. The present, in other words, was historicized, and the past acquired a controlling authority in contemporary debate (Herzog 1987b). In the previous generation Gibbon had never harnessed Late Antiquity in this way to a new view of the European future, since he had never envisaged that a catastrophe comparable to the decline of the ancient world would happen in his own time. During the first half of the nineteenth century, however, a range of scholars and *littérateurs* in France (Herzog 1987a) and England (DeLaura 1969), as well as Germany – liberals, absolutists, and ultramontanists – projected their respective political expectations (and disappointments) onto Late Antiquity. The Left celebrated a "radical" early Christianity, welcomed the industrial workers as new "invaders," and condemned the "bourgeois" conformity of the Constantinian era. The failure of the Revolution of 1848 inspired yet another interpretation that transformed the positive political manipulation of Late Antiquity and relegated it once more to the past. The barbarians were now no longer seen as bearers of an ancient legacy but as founders of early nationalism. Authors inspired by neohumanism (not only in Germany) once more idealized Greco-Roman antiquity, while clearly distinguishing it from the late empire.

After the mid-nineteenth century, the Rome of Late Antiquity was rediscovered by the literary avant-garde. European intellectuals like Flaubert and Mallarmé, Walter Pater and Oscar Wilde transformed a decadent Late Antiquity without future prospects into a model epoch for the *fin de siècle*. They claimed to have recognized there (although they distorted it in many ways) what they thought of as the predecessor of the "modern" author. The experience of living themselves in what they saw as a "late" period distanced them from at least some of the realities of that past, and fostered a melancholic modernity that took pleasure in death and decline. This nineteenth-century aesthetic pessimism favored in particular the use of subjects relating to Late Antiquity. Thus, the first stanza of the sonnet *Langueur* by Paul Verlaine (1844–96), published in 1883, reads:

> Je suis l'Empire à la fin de la décadence,
> Qui regarde passer les grands Barbares blancs
> En composant des acrostiches indolents
> D'un style d'or où la langueur du soleil danse.

And the English literary critic Arthur Symons (1865–1945) ascribed to the literature of Late Antiquity "an intense self-consciousness, a restless curiosity in research, an over-subtilising refinement upon refinement, a spiritual and moral perversity" (Fletcher 1979: 24).

Late Antiquity and German *Altertumswissenschaft*

In the nineteenth century, the German program of *Altertumswissenschaft* had a lasting influence on classical studies throughout the western world, representing a profound break in the exploration not only of Late Antiquity but of antiquity as a whole (Rebenich 2000a). Independent scholarly methods and enterprises that had been pursued in the Netherlands, France, England, and Italy up till then were abandoned. Within a few decades, the *Altertumswissenschaft*, established by Christian Gottlieb Heyne (1729–1812) at the University of Göttingen, had succeeded in transforming an aristocratic hobby into an academic discipline and promoting a new professorial elite. The interpretation of written records, based on a thorough survey of the sources, now became the cognitive process crucial to historical research. The fundamental principle of this research was objectivity; but belief in the inherent significance of historical events was also important, as was the role of the individual. Following the lead of Barthold Georg Niebuhr (1776–1831) and August Boeckh (1785–1867), many authors of the period saw the central responsibility of the scientific disciplines relating to antiquity as *cognitio totius antiquitatis*, that is, as an understanding of the classical heritage in its entirety: pagan as well as Christian; of the early Greek period just as much as of the late Roman period. Prodigious joint productions – *Corpora*, *Monumenta*, and *Thesauri* – made the legacy of the ancient world more accessible (Rebenich 1999). Scholars adopted with fresh confidence an empirical style of historical analysis. Faith in progress and scientific optimism characterized this new professional study of antiquity in universities and academies. The work of Theodore Mommsen (1817–1903), who demanded that scholars "organize the archives of the past" according to a detailed program of his own devising, provides the best-known example (Rebenich 2002). A large-scale enterprise emerged, devoted to the study of antiquity, that impressively confirmed the efficiency of *Quellenforschung* but also encouraged a division between the editing and the interpretation of sources, thus turning many scholars into mere laborers. The historicization of the ancient world necessarily implied the rejection of an earlier view – that antiquity represented some sort of norm, or that it validated a contemporary aestheticism. The unique position of antiquity, especially that of the Greeks, was sacrificed.

The ideal of totality regarding the study of antiquity implied the collecting, critical editing, and historical evaluation of Christian and late antique evidence. Consequently, the *hêrôs ktistés* of modern Roman classical studies, Theodor Mommsen, had already, at the beginning of his academic career, dealt with questions about the history and chronology of the written records of the Later Roman Empire, especially Roman law and its sources. His understanding of constitutional law made him presume a clear division between the early and high empire and Late Antiquity. Mommsen contrasted the principate of Augustus with the "dominate" of the late empire, a period that, as he argued, began with Diocletian and was characterized by an excessive veneration of the emperor as *dominus* in a supposedly "oriental" (that is, predominantly Persian) style.

For many different disciplines the historico-critical method now formed the basis for their examination of Late Antiquity. The central task, for those who adopted this approach, was the editing of the relevant sources. The editions thus created formed a reliable basis for all historical reconstructions of Late Antiquity (and continue to do so). In 1828, Niebuhr created the *Bonner Corpus der byzantinischen Geschichtsschreiber*, from 1866 onward the *Corpus scriptorum ecclesiasticorum latinorum* was published in Vienna; and from 1928 onward Eduard Schwartz (1858–1940) set about editing the *Acta conciliorum oecumenicorum*. In 1891, the committee on the fathers of the church was founded at the Academy in Berlin, where historians, theologians, and classicists together edited the *Griechische christliche Schriftsteller der ersten (drei) Jahrhunderte*. This venture demonstrates how textual criticism historically surmounted the paradigm of decline: the theologians regarded the edition of the fathers as a vital instrument for the historically reliable reconstruction of the dogmatic conditioning of early Christianity; the historians wanted to reconstruct the history of Christianity in the Roman state; and the philologists intended to write a history of the literature of both the high and the later empire (Rebenich 2001).

Ancient writers were now published who had previously been ignored, either because their subjects did not coincide with popular taste, or because scholars schooled in the Latin of Cicero took exception to their barbaric style. With his great editions for the *Monumenta Germaniae historica*, Mommsen made accessible the history of Late Antiquity (Croke 1990b). He himself edited the *History of the Goths* by Jordanes, the *Variae* of Cassiodorus, and the *Chronica minora*; and he energetically assisted with other editions. Additionally, there are his great patristic editions: the *Life of Severin* by Eugippius, the *Liber pontificalis*, and Rufinus' translation of Eusebius' *Historia ecclesiastica*. Mommsen also made outstanding contributions to the collections of legal texts of Late Antiquity. He published between 1868 and 1870, with the help of Paul Krüger, the vast two-volume edition of the *Digesta*, followed in 1872 by a more concise volume that was part of the *Corpus iuris civilis*. He did extensive preliminary work for the edition of the *Codex Theodosianus*, published posthumously in 1904. These editions of Christian and late classical texts formed the basis for linguistic discussions about "vulgar" Latin and a distinctively Christian Latin ("eine christliche Sondersprache") that prompted an intensive debate in the twentieth century (Mohrmann 1977: 111–40).

Mommsen had intended to create, in collaboration with the Protestant ecclesiastical historian Adolf Harnack (1851–1930), a prosopography of Late Antiquity. But this large-scale interdisciplinary project, which sought to create a fundamental prosopographical reference work for secular and ecclesiastical historians, as well as for theologians and philologists, failed – its objective was too broad – and it was finally abandoned in the 1930s. The materials collected, however, served as a basis for the *Prosopography of the Later Roman Empire* and the *Prosopographie chrétienne du bas-empire* (Rebenich 1997a; 1997b: 247–326).

Dissenting Perspectives on Late Antiquity

In the second half of the nineteenth century, an awareness of an impending crisis spread through the world of classical studies – just as it did in other disciplines. Criticism focused on a scholarship that threatened to fall apart and produce only imitators. The watchword "historicism" appeared with increasing frequency in contemporary discussions; and soon the phrase "crisis of historicism" became popular (Rebenich 2000a). Critics denounced the relativism of values that had come to characterize historically oriented inquiries – which they accused of being out of touch with everyday life – and condemned the sterile objectiveness of antiquated research. Under the influence of Jacob Burckhardt (1818–97) and Friedrich Nietzsche (1844–1900), as well as of earlier conceptions, scholars argued over the problematic correlation of scholarship and life. They questioned the legitimacy of a classical scholarship that concentrated on positivist results and whose historical relativism undermined any normative understanding of antiquity.

Intellectual dissidents now searched for new concepts and explanations, which prompted the reconstruction of the history of early Christianity and Late Antiquity.

Jacob Burckhardt opted for a historical understanding of the past and rejected theological explanations. He explained the triumph of Christianity in Late Antiquity as the result of developments within paganism. In his first work, *Die Zeit Constantins des Grossen*, published in 1853, he described the Roman emperor as "a brilliant man, whose ambition and thirst for power afforded him no rest"; a calculating politician, in other words, in respect of whom "there could be no talk of Christianity and paganism, conscious religiousness and an absence of religion." "Such a person," Burckhardt declared, "is essentially unreligious, even if he should imagine himself as standing at the center of a church community."

Friedrich Nietzsche attacked those of his colleagues who attempted to understand the present by studying the past but effectively destroyed in this process all historical norms. He distanced himself from the relativizing examinations of Late Antiquity and boldly blamed the Christians for the fall of Rome. In the fourth part of *Thus Spake Zarathustra* (1885), he wrote,

> It was once – methinks year one of our blessed Lord –
> Drunk without wine, the Sybil thus deplored,
> "How ill things go! Decline! Decline!
> Ne'er sank the world so low!
> Rome now hath turned harlot and harlot-stew,
> Rome's Caesar beast, and God – has turned Jew!"

In his *Antichrist*, published in 1894, he described Christianity as the "vampire" of the Roman Empire. Christians, "these holy anarchists," had destroyed the empire, "until no stone was left standing on top of another – until even the Germanic peoples and other boors were able to take it under their control." In this way, he had rejected all those who, like Hegel (1770–1831), regarded Christians and Germanic peoples as the pioneers of progress.

The Challenge of Evolutionary Biology

Otto Seeck (1850–1921), a pupil of Mommsen, tried to offer a new explanation for the fall of Rome. His six-volume *Geschichte des Untergangs der antiken Welt*, stands out in particular for its close adherence to the sources, its impressive wealth of detail, and its superior control of the subject matter. Seeck aspired to make it more than just a summary of what had happened: he aimed to introduce the reader to "the laws governing historical processes of formation and decline" (Seeck 1897–1920, i: preface). The thematically oriented chapters of the first few volumes were especially devoted to that objective: Seeck constructed an impressive scenario of decline that culminated in "the elimination of the best" ("die Ausrottung der Besten": i. 269–307). The notion of "Ausrottung" referred to a series of negative choices, the beginning of which Seeck dated back to the time of the Gracchi. The ancient world, he argued, need not have come to an end. The collapse occurred only when, because of failures internal to Rome, the most industrious people had become a small minority, and when, because of the laws of heredity, "inherited cowardice" and "moral weakening" had emerged as dominant characteristics of society.

Seeck's ideas were shaped by the evolutionary biology of the nineteenth century. Today, these theories may seem strange, occasionally even repulsive, but they are representative of the period. An entire generation of scholars tried to transfer the discoveries made by the natural sciences – more precisely, the theory of heredity – to the cultural evolution of mankind. Evolutionary biology turned into a paradigm of historical discovery. If individual humans could be seen as belonging to a more general chain of being, scholars were suddenly able to ask how important a role evolution and selection played in society. At the end of the nineteenth and the beginning of the twentieth centuries, Darwin's theory of the descent of man was equally popular among left-wing politicians, liberal intellectuals, and conservative philosophers. The theory of the heredity of acquired characteristics brilliantly justified the middle-class ideology of achievement. A number of different, partly contradictory, theories were published, now usually classified as "social Darwinism." These theories were combined with eugenic considerations, scientific reflections on population, racial deliberations, and ideas about social hygiene. Seeck's *Geschichte* can be understood only if one keeps this in mind. He combined and adapted individual pieces of research he came across in biology and related sciences and transferred them to the history of Late Antiquity. His account combines biological theory with a detailed event-oriented history based on a meticulous critical assessment of the sources (Rebenich 2000b).

Seeck's *Geschichte*, reprinted several times in quick succession – which indicates wide appreciation by a large audience – remained, however, the work of an outsider. His main thesis, "die Ausrottung der Besten," met with disapproval among scholars. They only praised his adherence to the sources in describing political history. Most historians of antiquity in Germany, and also in other European countries, continued to make use of the concept of "decline" when interpreting Late Antiquity; but they thought of this decline as a complex process of political, social, and religious disintegration that had already started in the time of the empire itself, or even in the time of the republic. The process was often described in terms of denationalization, proletarianization, and orientalization. Many thought that the hostility of the Christians toward the state had been one of the causes of the crisis. Not only the Germanic peoples, but also the Catholic Church were regarded as the legitimate heirs to the Roman Empire. In an essay from 1885, for example, Harnack emphasized that "it [the Church] is indeed nothing else than the universal Roman Empire itself, but in the most wonderful and beneficent metamorphosis, built upon the Gospel as a kingdom of Jesus Christ: Christus vincit, Christus regnat, Christus triumphat" (Harnack 1906: 233).

A "Long" Late Antiquity

In 1901, the Viennese art historian Alois Riegl (1858–1905) published his *Spätrömische Kunstindustrie*, a work in which he first harnessed the aesthetics of the *fin de siècle* to the historical understanding of early Christian and late antique art. The distinction between prosperity and decline, between the beautiful and the hideous, was abolished; the artistic style of the epoch was understood not as the product of a universal culture but as an autonomous phenomenon. Riegl did not regard the architecture and sculpture, painting and craftwork of the late empire as evidence for a barbaric style or a cultural decline, but as proof of a specific "artistic will." This artistic will, which constituted a separate epochal style that continued to reflect its classical legacy, originated from a conviction directed toward the afterlife, and manifested itself in Christianity (Elsner 2002). Riegl defined Late Antiquity as an epoch delimited by the Edict of Milan (AD 313) and the accession of Charles the Great (AD 768). Students of the Later Roman Empire now began to adopt this periodization from art history. Seeck had thought of antiquity as ending with the political demise of the Western Roman Empire in AD 476. Eduard Meyer (1855–1930), however, defined Late Antiquity (in the second edition of his *magnum opus*, the *Geschichte des Altertums*) in a manner comparable to that of Riegl: as the transitional period between Diocletian and Charles the Great (Meyer 1910: 249). Similarly, Matthias Gelzer (1886–1974) described Late Antiquity in his programmatic lecture on "Classical Studies and Late Antiquity" (1926) as reaching from the third to the sixth centuries (Gelzer 1963: 387–400). Thus the notion of a "long" Late Antiquity had come into being, and the term "Late Antiquity" entered other European languages ("bas-empire," "antiquité tardive," "basso impero," and "bajo imperio").

From the turn of the century, representatives of the so-called "school of religious history" (*religionsgeschichtliche Schule*) consistently divorced ancient Christianity from the Christianity of other periods and described in more particular terms first the interaction of various forms of religious belief and practice in the ancient Mediterranean world, and second the earliest phases of the dissemination of the Christian message. Hermann Usener (1834–1905) had already recognized the significance of late classical lives of the saints for the study of both Christian and pagan antiquity. Shortly afterward, the so-called "Cambridge Ritualists" investigated (partly under the influence of Sir James Frazer, 1854–1941) the social function of religious rituals and their significance for the formation of group cohesion and group identity. The circle included Francis Cornford (1874–1943, married to Charles Darwin's granddaughter) and Arthur B. Cook (1868–1952, author of *Zeus: A Study of Ancient Religion*, 1914–40), together with the Oxford scholar Gilbert Murray (1866–1957). Similar lines of inquiry had been pursued in France by Émile Durkheim (1858–1917). The Belgian Franz Cumont (1868–1947) and, slightly later, the English scholar Arthur Darby Nock (1902–63) contributed with exceptional distinction to the study of late antique religion (Bonnet 2005). One cannot overestimate the extent to which this research into religious history helped to overcome traditional denominational notions of ancient religions in general and of Christianity in particular (Graf 2002).

The Impact of Social and Economic History

In the twentieth century, the concept of Late Antiquity as a self-contained epoch was revised and, once again, utilized to cope with the crises of the time. The Protestant theologian Ernst Troeltsch (1865–1923) compared the culture toward the end of antiquity to the neohumanist movement at the time of Goethe, and demanded an intensive historical study of Late Antiquity in order to reestablish, in present-day Europe, the teachings of early Christianity and thereby to overcome the crisis of historicism (Troeltsch 1925: 65–121). With his extensive research program on the interaction between antiquity and Christianity, the Catholic religious historian Franz Josef Dölger (1879–1940) attempted to counter contemporary movements that rejected all adjustment of Christian tradition to modern times. After World War II, the Dölger-Institute – named after him – was founded in Bonn. Since 1950, it has been responsible for publishing the *Reallexikon für Antike und Christentum* (Schöllgen 1993).

During the conflicts, controversies, and convulsions of the first half of the twentieth century, Late Antiquity was frequently referred to, both inside and outside the humanities, as providing an analogy to contemporary events. The epoch stood in the eyes of some as an admonition to the present. Manifest social contrasts in the nineteenth century and the ideas of historical materialism made various scholars more sensitive to aspects of social and economic history. The works of Max Weber (1864–1920) were of special significance for the analysis of the structure of late classical society (Nippel 2000). In an 1896 lecture on "The Social Reasons for the Decline of the Roman Empire" (Weber 1988: 289–311), and in his study on "Agrarian Conditions in Antiquity" (first published in the *Handwörterbuch der Staatswissenschaften* of 1909; see Weber 1988: 1–288), Weber identified, among other factors, the following reasons for the crisis: the equal status of slaves and free small-scale tenants; the decline of the cities and of the empire's financial apparatus; the rise of a barter economy and the rapid bureaucratization of the administration; and the restriction of private economic initiative. He thus addressed several topics that were to be discussed in detail by scholars over the following years – some of them taking account of Weber's position, others not. In his early writings, Weber had avoided any tendency to make the study of antiquity part of an analysis of current experience; but by 1909 he had come to regard the late Roman state as a frightening totalitarian vision of the future: "In all likelihood the bureaucratization of society will at some stage take control of capitalism in our civilization as it did in antiquity" (Weber 1988: 278). The pessimistic view of the epoch held during the second half of the nineteenth century had caught up with the social sciences of the twentieth century.

The Russian historian of antiquity Michael Iwanowitsch Rostovtzeff (1870–1952) also regarded Late Antiquity as a reflection of the present. The October Revolution of 1918 had forced him to flee first to Sweden and then to Oxford. In 1920 he accepted a professorship at the University of Wisconsin, Madison; and in 1925 he moved to Yale. His personal experiences as an immigrant influenced his epochal *Social and Economic History of the Roman Empire* (1926). This work is a passionate plea for the social and political significance of a prosperous urban middle class that had provided the *Imperium Romanum* with its visible splendor and had indeed ruled it. According to Rostovtzeff, the period of crisis for the Roman Empire began in the third century and was accompanied by a decline of the traditional urban economy and a leveling of social classes. The idealization of the Roman "bourgeoisie" not only advanced the historical study of the classical era and its political economy but also reflected the political anti-Bolshevism of the Russian bourgeoisie (Marcone 1999).

Late Antiquity and the Decline of Cultures

World War I and the Russian October Revolution intensified the atmosphere of desolation that had been spreading throughout the middle-class elite of Europe since the turn of the century. Many contemporaries believed that their own armed conflicts and ideological disputes marked the end of global hegemony for Europe, and they tried to come to terms with this realization by bringing once more to the fore a cyclical interpretation of history, for which the fall of Rome stood as a historic paradigm. The most important and influential work of this sort was Oswald Spengler's (1880–1936) *Der Untergang des Abendlandes* (1918–22), which was influenced by Seeck's *Geschichte* as well as by the research of the *religionsgeschichtliche Schule*. Spengler interpreted Germany's military defeat as a symptom of the defeat of Europe as a whole. No more than a gentleman scholar, he based his interpretation of world history on the assumption that every culture, in accordance with some natural law, advanced through the ages of man and underwent three phases: development, prosperity, and decline. Spengler regarded the Battle of Actium in 31 BC as the event that marked the end of antiquity. After that came an intermediate period of 1,000 years without any development, which Spengler saw characterized by a "magic" or "Arabian" culture. The structure of this culture was still organized as it had been in antiquity; its nature was, according to Spengler, the product of a supposedly "oriental" influence. The fate of the empire, the crisis of Late Antiquity, and the turmoil of the *Völkerwanderung* were consequences of the ossification of a once lively ancient culture – a process that had begun under Augustus. Spengler's pseudo-scientific theory of the decline of cultures gave the past a modern touch, in order to aid the analysis of the political present. In the 1920s and 1930s, his absurd and offensive speculations fascinated not only sectors of the conservative and culturally pessimistic middle classes but also some students of the ancient world, who felt insecure due to the waning significance of their disciplines and the challenge presented by established scientific and political systems and who, consequently, wanted to restore to antiquity a forceful historical significance.

Some Italian and German scholars went on to support the fascist and National Socialist states, and individual ancient historians such as Wilhelm Weber (1882–1948) continued to interpret Late Antiquity by utilizing racist categories (Christ 1982: 210–21; 2006: 69–74). Outside Italy and Germany, however, the image of the late empire was very much governed by the then current experience of violence, occupation, and expulsion. Ernst Stein (1891–1945) published the first volume of his famous *Geschichte des spätrömischen Reiches* in Vienna in 1928. After World War II, the work was translated into French, and a second volume was written in French (Stein 1949–59), for this highly esteemed liberal Jewish patriot of the Habsburg monarchy categorically refused to continue publishing in German after 1933.

In 1948, Pierre Courcelle (1912–80) published his *Histoire littéraire des grandes invasions germaniques*, in which numerous passages implied, or depended upon, reflection on the recent past. The account is divided into *invasion, occupation*, and *libération*. The Vandal Huneric sets up a "concentration camp [*camp de concentration*]" for rebellious Catholics (1948: 183), and Hilderic pursues intermittently a "policy of appeasement [*politique d'appaisement*]" (1948: 195). In his book *L'Empire chrétien*, written during the German occupation of France and first published in 1947, André Piganiol (1883–1968) disputed the theory of decadence and reestablished the disaster theory of the Italian humanists, who had considered the Germanic peoples as the destructive element responsible for the decline of the Roman Empire. Piganiol distanced himself from the National Socialist *Germanenverklärung*, the romanticization of the Germanic peoples, and made the famous point, "Roman civilization did not die of its own accord: it was assassinated" (1947: 422; 1972: 466). Arnaldo Momigliano aptly referred to this statement as the "*cri de coeur* of a valiant Frenchman against *boches* and collaborationists" (Momigliano 1969: 646).

New Paths to Late Antiquity

After the end of World War II, the decisive driving force behind research into Late Antiquity was supplied by English and French scholars. Henri-Irénée Marrou (1904–77) published his *Retractatio* in 1949, which exerted considerable influence. In it, he "retracted" (echoing Augustine himself) the central claim of his book *Saint Augustin et la fin de la culture antique*, published a decade earlier (Riché 2003). Previously, Marrou had described the culture of Late Antiquity as decadent, ailing, and weak and had made Augustine into a *lettré de la décadence*. Now he openly declared that his former position had been wrong, and he acknowledged the cultural achievements of the epoch as innovative and trendsetting. He put aside the idea of a distinct break-up of – or an abrupt end to – the ancient world: instead, he preferred to speak of "internal changes that were in fact signs of that civilization's vigour and vitality" (1949: 690). As a result, the way was made clear for a new evaluation of the cultural achievements and literary style of Late Antiquity, an evaluation echoed later in the work of Pierre Courcelle and Jacques Fontaine (Vessey 1998).

In England, a new era of research into Late Antiquity began in the late 1950s and early 1960s. It is closely linked with the names of A. H. M. Jones (1904–70), Arnaldo Momigliano (1908–87), and Peter Brown (b. 1935). In 1964, having studied the period for many years, Jones published his three-volume work *The Later Roman Empire, 284–602: A Social, Economic and Administrative Survey*, which still provides the most reliable general account of the epoch (Gwynn, forthcoming). Jones had an excellent command of previous research and possessed an extensive knowledge of the sources; he painted a very diverse picture, distanced himself from monocausal attempts at explanation, examined a number of interacting factors that had, in his opinion, caused the decline of the Roman Empire, and helped to overcome the popular notion that the late empire was governed by coercion and despotism

(Meier 2003). He took into account the crisis of the economy and the tax burden, the decrease in population and the shortage of workers, the orientation of Christian teaching toward the afterlife and the bureaucratization of the administration, the barbarization of the army and the invasions by the Germanic tribes. Chiefly, however, it was "the increasing pressure of the barbarians, concentrated on the weaker western half of the empire, which caused the collapse" (Jones 1966: 370). Jones, like Marrou, also supported prosopographical research into Late Antiquity, an approach inspired to an important degree by Sir Ronald Syme's studies of the early and high principate. Syme (1903–89) achieved for Roman history what Lewis Namier (1888–1960) had achieved in his studies of eighteenth-century Britain.

Equally momentous was a series of lectures held at the Warburg Institute in London in late 1958 and early 1959, on the initiative of Arnaldo Momigliano. In 1963, these lectures were published under the title *Conflict between Paganism and Christianity in the Fourth Century.* In his programmatic opening essay, Momigliano (1963a) discussed the controversial relationship between Christianity and paganism, demonstrated what a fertile field the period of Late Antiquity could be, questioned the traditional notion of the decline of the Roman Empire, and argued against the conventional dichotomy between secular and ecclesiastical history.

In 1971, building upon the accomplishments of more recent English and French works, and taking into account both anthropological research (such as that of Edward Evans-Pritchard and Mary Douglas) and the historiography of the *Annales* school (exemplified not least by Evelyne Patlagean), Peter Brown, who had previously become well known for his biography of Augustine (1967a), published his small but exceptionally popular book, *The World of Late Antiquity* (1971b). This work dramatically affected how a whole generation on both sides of the Atlantic perceived Late Antiquity (*Symbolae Osloenses* 1997: 5–90). Brown's Late Antiquity extended from the third into the seventh century and embraced both the western provinces of the Roman Empire and Sasanian Iran. The periodization, "from Marcus Aurelius to Muhammad," called to mind the subtitle of Roger Rémondon's *Crise de l'empire romain* (1964) but deliberately covered a longer period and dispensed with much of the *crise*. Brown did not talk about decline, and his Roman Empire did not collapse with the deposition of the last emperor in AD 476. Instead, he offered the impression of an intellectually, artistically, and religiously productive epoch, characterized by change, diversity, and creativity. The influence of the postwar Marrou is evident. Brown's article "The Rise and Function of the Holy Man in Late Antiquity" (1971a), published in the same year, strengthened an already existing scholarly interest in the cults of saints and martyrs (deeply rooted in the Bollandist tradition represented by Hippolyte Delehaye, 1859–1941) and in the ascetic practice and religious experience of Late Antiquity (Elm 1998: 343–4; see Rousseau 1978, MacCormack 1981, and Stancliffe 1983).

The impact of these new approaches on both British and international research were profound (Averil Cameron 2002: 166–7; Liebeschuetz 2004: 260–1). In Britain, an older Oxbridge tradition of classical education was challenged; a tradition the representatives of which had not considered Late Antiquity to be part of classical antiquity and – under the influence of Gibbon – had dismissed the period as decadent.

For a while, in the British university system, the Late Roman Empire had been regarded as part of "modern" history. As early as 1889, J. B. Bury (1861–1927) had written a study of "the Later Roman Empire" from the reign of Arcadius to that of Irene. Shortly afterward, he also began to edit anew Gibbon's masterpiece. By the time he published (1923) his influential *History of the Later Roman Empire from the Death of Theodosius I to the Death of Justinian*, he was Regius Professor of Modern History at Cambridge. But the first edition of the *Cambridge Ancient History*, in which Bury had an important hand, ended at AD 324.

In Britain, a complex interweaving of historiographical trends characterized the intervening period since the late 1880s, featuring (for example) Sir Samuel Dill (1844–1924; see Dill 1899, 1926), W. P. Ker (1855–1923; see Ker 1904), T. R. Glover (1869–1943; see Glover 1901), and Hector Munro Chadwick (1870–1947; see Chadwick 1912). Almost any attempt at periodization has been challenged or abandoned for one reason or another, especially by those who wanted to retain Late Antiquity as part of classical studies (but see Stevens 1933), as can be deduced not only from lecture timetables at several British universities but also from the second edition of the *Cambridge Ancient History*, which contains two extensive volumes devoted to Late Antiquity that cover the period AD 337–600.

It is, however, not only in the English-speaking world that Late Antiquity has become a popular subject of a historical research that is characterized by a wide variety of methods and a paradigm shift. French, Italian, Greek, Austrian, Hungarian, and German scholars – for example, Andreas Alföldi, André Chastagnol, Evangelos Chrysos, Lellia Cracco-Ruggini, Alexander Demandt, Jean Gaudemet, Santo Mazzarino, Walter Pohl, Johannes Straub, Karl Friedrich Stroheker, and Herwig Wolfram – have also fostered our understanding of the Later Roman Empire. They have contributed over the past decades to what Andrea Giardina has described as a general "explosion" in late antique studies (Giardina 1999). The research into a "long" Late Antiquity has for the most part superseded the previous discourse on when and why the Roman Empire declined. Transformation, change, transition, and evolution are the favored epithets to apply to the epoch. Instead of a *caesura*, the historical continuum, the *longue durée*, is stressed. Cooperation between various disciplines has proven fruitful, with the consequence that sociological, anthropological, and gender-focused methodologies have successfully been applied to Late Antiquity. Marxist concepts, by contrast, have become less popular, following the perceived bankruptcy of some forms of socialism. The religious persuasion of a historian plays an insignificant role in what is now largely secularized research: an emphasis on cultural history considers religion as a cultural factor. Scholars are searching for the construction of "identities" and "ethnicities." Even in a newly unified Europe, regional history is emphasized. In North America, where Brown eventually moved (first to Berkeley and then to Princeton) and where Late Antiquity is a focus of interest for scholars like Alan Cameron, John Matthews, Glen Bowersock, and Timothy Barnes, a multicultural and postcolonial discourse has dominated the study of the late empire. As a result, topics in institutional and administrative history are scarcely pursued, political history is not very popular, and even economic history interests only a few – Peter Garnsey (Garnsey 1998) and Chris Whittaker (Whittaker 1994) being notable exceptions.

The late twentieth century may come to be considered the heyday of late antique studies. Old certainties have been dislodged but, thanks in part to the very vividness of description involved, a path has also been left open to an enduring debate about the relevance of that remote era to an understanding of our modern world.

BIBLIOGRAPHICAL NOTE

At present, a comprehensive, methodically reflective, and current account of the history of research into Late Antiquity is not available. Liebeschuetz 2004 gives a first introduction to the topic in English. The preface in Herzog 1989: 38–44 is stimulating and informative. D'Elia 1967 and Demandt 1984 provide important summaries.

PART II

Land and People

The notion that a sense of geography is essential to historical understanding will be neither strange nor disturbing. In relation to Late Antiquity, as to any historical period, a knowledge of where human beings were settled, of where they forged their aspirations and experienced their hopes and failures, of how their setting affected their cast of mind, is an inescapable concomitant of historical inquiry.

The Later Roman Empire was an empire of the sea, or rather of seas, for it was not just a matter of the Mediterranean, important though that may have been (Ahrweiler 1966; Rougé 1975; Horden and Purcell 2000): the Black Sea, the Red Sea, and the Persian Gulf were all part of the picture (see Map 2). And these seas were complex in their shapes, and provided access not only over a wide area but to a great variety of terrains. The Mediterranean had its natural division between east and west, running down the Italian peninsula and across to North Africa: an unequal division, moreover, in that the eastern portion was much larger than the western. The eastern was also characterized by what we may think of as its great inlets: the Ionian and Adriatic Seas, dividing Italy from the Balkans, and the Aegean Sea, running north to the crucial straits of the Dardanelles. One has to remind oneself also of the great bight that runs to the south of Turkey, making Antioch, for example, so much further east than Ephesus. Finally, this was a sea of islands. In the west lay Corsica, Sardinia, and the Balearics; Sicily and Malta were part of the divide; the Aegean was a great mass of islands, guarded as it were to the south by Crete; and Cyprus nestled below the coast of Turkey. This was no open or high sea and, even if one left its thousands of miles of indented coastline, one was never far from land. All these features become immediately evident when one consults a map; but in one's imagination it is easy to think of a single and empty stretch of water.

The Red Sea was different in being long and narrow. True, one could usefully sail north and south, between Egypt and the open water that led to the further coasts of Africa and of India; but the Red Sea was also a sea to cross, making the ancient kingdoms of Axum, Meroe, and Ethiopia almost the natural neighbors of Arabia and

Map 2 Land and People: The Roman World in Late Antiquity.

the Yemen. The effect upon trade, politics, and ideas was never insignificant. And it was natural to hug the coast around into the Persian Gulf, with its further concentrations of settlement and commerce, and eventual access to the southern reaches of the Persian Empire.

Finally, there was the Black Sea. Access, then as now, depended upon the control of narrow waters; but, once gained, access guaranteed both expanse and variety. It was as far from Constantinople to the Caucasus as it was from Greece to the Levant. The southern coast was imperial territory, but then merged into potential points of contact with Armenia and with Persia beyond. To the north, however, a longer coast-line reached into wilder country, rich in timber, hides, and slaves; and the venturesome could take advantage not only of the Danube basin but also of the great rivers west and east of Crimea, the Dnieper and (in the Sea of Azov) the Don – an area long colonized by the Greeks.

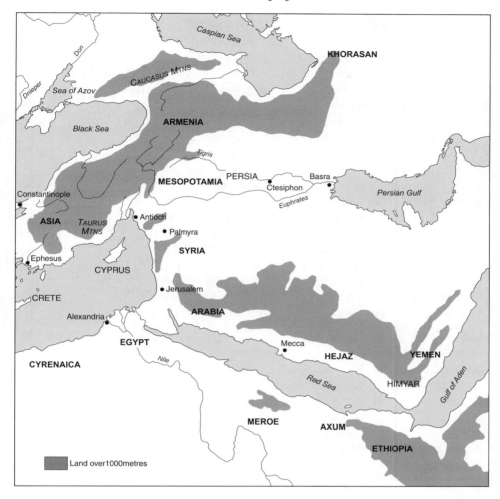

Map 2 (cont.)

Into seas, of course, rivers flowed, and in many cases provided further access inland. It is always worth bearing in mind where those rivers lay. In the western Mediterranean, pride of place goes to the Rhône, which created an important corridor to Lyon and beyond – the route to Trier and the Moselle, and from there to the middle Rhine. Into the eastern Mediterranean flowed the Nile, another gateway – to Egypt, Sudan, and the mountains of Africa. Both the Danube and the Rhine we have mentioned, rising close to one another, passing through broad plains as often as narrow gorges, uniting peoples on both banks and in themselves immensely long channels of communication. Into the Persian Gulf flowed the rivers of Mesopotamia, the Euphrates and the Tigris, a long and densely populated path from Armenia to the eastern seas. But smaller rivers had their significance: the steep waterways that flowed from Turkey into the Black Sea; the similar defiles that ran north from Greece toward the Danube, inviting intrusion southward.

And the flow of water was, of course, from mountain to plain. The mountains were as crucial a feature of the late Roman scene as any other. They formed boundaries, marked the limits of dense settlement and agriculture, set off the farmer from the herdsman, and gave shelter to bandits and misanthropes. It is an easy matter to run through their names: the Atlas, the Pyrenees, the Alps, the Carpathians, the Caucasus, the highlands of Armenia, the Iranian plateau. Each in their way affected the fortunes of those who did not live in them, either as a challenge or an impediment.

Such were the defining elements of settlement and mobility (explored further particularly in the chapters by Humphries (7), Leyerle (8), and Sotinel (9)); but we are concerned here with "people" as well as with "land." What physical traces can we discern that offer clues to the human adaptation and development of this wide territory? Here, cities and sites and inscriptions play their part. They also occupy what we think of as landscape: they are visible, they have survived, they have names and places on our maps (as described here by Loseby (ch. 10), Brandt (ch. 11), and Trout (ch. 12)). And with the inscribed word we begin to touch the human beings themselves, their self-image, their pride, belief, and hope. This land that we look at was occupied by people born, married, parents as well as governors and governed, and eventually remembered in their death. Before we think of politics, we think of the hierarchies, the industries, the swift uncertainty of ordinary life (the task begun by Cooper (ch. 13), Evans-Grubbs (ch. 14), and Rebillard (ch. 15)).

CHAPTER SEVEN

The Shapes and Shaping of the Late Antique World: Global and Local Perspectives

Mark Humphries

The Shape of the World: Eternal Rome and Its Rivals

In the autumn of AD 417, the Gallic aristocrat and former prefect of the city of Rome, Rutilius Namatianus (*PLRE* ii: 770–1), set sail from Ostia, heading home to his estates in southern Gaul. He later described his journey in a pleasant elegiac poem called *On His Return* (*De redito suo*). It began with verses reflecting upon Roman greatness and imperial destiny, stating that Rome "had made a city out of what had once been a world" (*De redito suo* 1. 66). By Rutilius' day, that was a well-worn theme. A similar witty play on the Latin words for world (*orbis*) and city (*urbs*) had been made in the age of the emperor Augustus (27 BC–AD 14) by the poet Ovid, when he said that the space allotted to the city of Rome was the same as that of the world (*Fasti* 2. 683–4). So confident an assertion might well be expected of the Augustan age, given the recent startling expansion of Roman territorial power. It might seem less obvious for Rutilius to have reprised it, given that he was writing only seven years after a Gothic army had sacked Rome, and at a time when the unity of the western empire was being eroded by barbarian tribes. Yet his reiteration of the theme shows the persistence into Late Antiquity of a long established tradition about the shape of the world and the central place of Rome within it.

A comparable reflection of that tradition was to be found in the work of another author who spent time at Rome, some twenty-five years before Rutilius. The historian Ammianus Marcellinus' description of the Huns emphasized their almost bestial barbarity, and implicitly linked their lack of civilized habits (such as urban living, agriculture, and even cooking) to the fact that they lived far beyond the empire's frontiers, "near the frozen ocean" (Amm. Marc. 31. 2. 1; see Wiedemann 1986).

In terms of both culture and habitation, the Huns were remote from the civilized world of Rome. Ammianus' geographical vision was one that could trace its heritage back to late-archaic Greece. Its basic conception was of an inhabited world, the *oikoumenē*, surrounded by an ocean; at the center lay the Mediterranean, where civilization was to be found; and the further one moved from this center, the more barbaric the world became (Romm 1992). At first, the civilized center was the Greek world around the Aegean, but in time, with the rise of Roman power, Rome and Italy came to constitute the center (Plin. *HN* 3. 1. 1–5; 3. 5. 39). Such a conception, as the remarks of Ammianus and Rutilius show, remained influential in Late Antiquity (Humphries 2007c; see Inglebert 2001: 27–192).

Just as views of the center of the world had shifted from Greece to Rome, however, there were signs in Late Antiquity that alternative conceptions of the shape of the world and the location of its center were taking form. Rome's status as the center of the empire was undermined in various ways. The tendency of emperors, from the late second century onward, to reside for strategic reasons in cities close to the frontiers meant that Rome itself was no longer the center of imperial power and patronage (Millar 1992: 28–53). Constantine's creation of Constantinople exacerbated the trend. Initially, Rome's superior status was maintained by, for example, according to senators of the old capital higher rank than that enjoyed by senators of the new city on the Bosphorus (Heather 1998: 185). Indeed, Ammianus could still refer to Rome as the eternal city (*urbs aeterna*) sixty years after Constantinople's foundation (16. 10. 14; see 14. 6. 3–6). It would be unwise, therefore, to see the foundation of Constantinople as marking a swift eclipse of Rome's ancient ideological significance, even if, already in the fourth century, some authors were extolling the advantages of the new capital over the old (Them. *Or*. 6. 83c–d). Nevertheless, Constantinople's priority was firmly established by the seventh century, when the local *Chronicon Paschale* asserted that Constantine intended from the outset that his new city should be a second Rome and endowed it with institutions that reflected that aspiration (*Chron. Pasch.* s.a. 330). While even at this late stage Rome could still be regarded as an imperial city (Humphries 2007a), its dilapidation and increasing identification with the emerging institution of the papacy left Constantinople's elevated status within the empire unrivaled.

Such factors hint at an eastward shift in the geopolitical focus of Late Antiquity. But the development of Constantinople was only one reason for this. Another was the growing significance of Jerusalem, and the Holy Land generally, in an empire that was becoming increasingly Christian (Wilken 1992). Constantine himself expended much patronage in endowing Jerusalem with church buildings that reflected its importance in the Christian worldview as the site of Christ's passion and resurrection, and this activity was to foster an upsurge in Holy Land pilgrimage (Hunt 1982). As a result, Jerusalem was on its way to becoming the conceptual center of the world for medieval Christendom (Wilken 1992: 230).

Those changes were not unrelated to political developments between the third century and the seventh. A worldview that emphasized the centrality of the Mediterranean world under Roman rule was harder to maintain as the empire's dominance was undermined, first by the establishment of barbarian kingdoms in the west, and later by the emergence of the Islamic caliphate in the east (Olster 1996). Where once there had been a single state, now there was a multiplicity of polities. Thus the shape of the world in Late Antiquity underwent profound changes, not only conceptually but also in terms of the lived experience of the inhabitants of that world.

A Fragile Unity

In the late fourth century, before the onslaughts that would lead to its dismemberment, the Roman Empire still stretched from northern Britain to the Sahara desert in Africa, and from Europe's Atlantic shores to Syria. Most of the empire's inhabitants, lowly farmers and artisans, would never see much of the world beyond their own immediate environs; but for those with talent, connections, and privilege it was possible to pursue a career that would bring appointments across the length and breadth of the empire (Marcone 1998).

Consider, for example, the case of Nummius Aemilianus Dexter (*PLRE* i: 251). He was governor of Asia in the AD 380s, when, on the main street of the province's metropolis of Ephesus, he erected a statue, known from the commemorative inscription on its base, in honor of the deceased father of the reigning eastern Augustus, Theodosius I (AD 379–95). In AD 387 he served as *comes rerum privatarum* (controller of the emperor's private finances) at Constantinople. Later still, in AD 395, we find him mentioned in a number of imperial laws as praetorian prefect of Italy. Dexter, however, hailed from the far west of the empire, from Barcelona in Spain, where his father, Pacianus, had been bishop. It was there that the provincials of Asia paid for the erection of a statue of him, with an inscription on its base recording that this gift sought to honor him for good deeds performed by him during his governorship. Through his term of office in Asia, Dexter forged a link between the cities of Ephesus and Barcelona. By the standards of the Roman elite in the age of Theodosius, his career was by no means unique. Several other Spaniards are known to have filled important positions in the eastern administration of Theodosius, himself a Spaniard (Matthews 1975: 108–12). Through such appointments, the unity of the empire was articulated by personal connections and obedience to the emperor (Kelly 2004: 192–203).

That unity, moreover, was self-consciously promoted by the state, even when (as was customary from the late third century onward) more than one emperor ruled concurrently. The effective separation of the empire into eastern and western halves after Theodosius' death in AD 395 did little to undercut those ideals. Imperial unity was the theme of a series of events orchestrated by the eastern emperor Theodosius II in the middle years of his long reign (AD 408–50). In AD 437, his daughter Eudoxia was married to the western emperor Valentinian III (AD 425–55) amid splendid pomp in Constantinople. Around the same time occurred the publication of his great compendium of fourth- and fifth-century imperial law, the *Theodosian Code* (*Codex Theodosianus*). Copies of this were then given to the senator Anicius Acilius Glabrio Faustus (*PLRE* ii: 452–4), who had traveled from Rome to attend the imperial wedding. On returning to Rome the following year, Faustus convened a special meeting of the senate at which, amid chanted acclamations celebrating the virtues of imperial government, the law code was promulgated for the western empire. In a variety of ways, then, the events of AD 437–8 sought to emphasize that the parts of the empire, east and west, were inextricably bound together (Matthews 2000: 1–9, 31–49).

By the middle of the fifth century, such assertions of unity were almost poignantly optimistic. Already by this stage, several western provinces had fallen out of imperial control into the hands of barbarian overlords. As the senators of Rome were acclaiming the *Theodosian Code*, a bitter struggle for the mastery of Roman Africa was coming to a close; within a year, that region and its greatest city, Carthage, would fall under the sway of the Vandals. Within forty years, moreover, there would not even be an emperor in the west. Hence the events of AD 437–8 give a striking indication of how the unity of a divided empire, however much it might have formed the bedrock of imperial aspirations, was confounded by the harsh realities of fragmentation.

Intimations of that fragility, moreover, were already apparent in the days of Dexter and Theodosius I. Behind the facade of unity suggested by the presence of a Spanish emperor and Spanish officials in the late-fourth-century east lay a real tension. While the proconsulship of Asia was given to other men from the west like Dexter, the presence of westerners throughout the east was, for the most part, limited. Instead, most administrative posts in the eastern provinces went to men from those regions themselves (Matthews 1975: 114–15). What we are presented with, then, is something of a dichotomy between a strong western presence at Theodosius' imperial court in Constantinople and in a few other posts (such as the governorship of Asia), and an administration of the eastern provinces that relied heavily on local grandees (Heather 1998: 204–8). The ties of unity that linked Ephesus and Barcelona through the figure of Dexter were perhaps exceptional rather than customary.

Unity and Diversity in the Roman Empire: Land, Economy, Culture, Power

It is all too easy to be beguiled by the careers of men like Dexter and the evidence they provide for the apparent unity of the vast territory that Rome held under its sway. Of course, the empire was held together by networks other than political ones. Inter-regional trade was a powerful contributor to creating a single Roman world (Greene 1986; Ward-Perkins 2005: 87–104). But by concentrating above all on the unity of the empire, we miss the essential diversity of the various elements of which it was composed. Indeed, the apt remark has been made that "the Roman Empire is too *often* seen as a whole, too *seldom* as a collection of provinces" (Wickham 2005: 3). Such factors often recede from view when emphasis is placed on the shared political and cultural experiences of the empire's social elite, based mostly in cities (Garnsey and Saller 1987: 178–95).

Examination of the individual territories that made up the Roman Empire presents a picture of astonishing diversity. That was in part the product of geography. The empire comprised various ecological zones, ranging from the areas of arid semi-desert in the Near East and Africa to the climatic extremes of hot summers and bitterly cold winters found, for example, in much of Continental Europe and central Asia Minor. Even this distinction is quite crude. Within individual regions and provinces there could be stark differences of landscape and ecology, which in turn could give rise to divergent economic structures. In Italy, for example, the upland areas in the Apennines and the Alps were best suited to pastoral economies, although the scale of activity varied in different parts of the peninsula (Frayn 1984: 11–27). More lowland regions were better suited to arable crops, although again regional variation existed: the volcanic soils of Campania were ideal for growing vines and olive trees; the latter, however, did not grow in the Po valley, where crops such as grain and rice flourished (Wickham 2005: 33–4).

Such variety – which can be mirrored in provinces throughout the empire – had ramifications for the imperial economy, a feature often trumpeted as symbolic of the unity and sophistication of the Roman world (see Schiavone 2000). There can be little dispute that there had been a considerable volume of long-distance trade under the early empire, and that this suffered disruption and retraction during Late Antiquity (McCormick 2001: 25–119; Ward-Perkins 2005: 123–36). But we must also recognize that, even during the early imperial centuries, such interregional exchanges were liable to seasonal variation (Duncan-Jones 1990: 7–29; see McCormick 2001: 444–68), were limited by quite basic sailing technologies (Horden and Purcell 2000: 123–72), and existed side by side with more local patterns of production and redistribution that were, perhaps, more characteristic of the patterns of ancient trade generally (Woolf 1992; see Morony 2004: 175–6).

In addition to differences of ecology and economy, there was considerable cultural diversity within the empire. At a basic level, this was related to ecological factors, and was manifested, for example, in the consumption of different animal products in different regions: zooarchaeological remains imply a predilection for pork in Italy and southern Gaul, beef in northern Gaul, and lamb and goat in Libya (Dyson 2003: 66). Diversity was visible too in linguistic terms, with a division between the use of Latin as the major public language (used, for instance, in inscriptions) in the western provinces and Greek in the east – although Latin was the official language of Roman law throughout the empire (Millar 1999: 105–8). It should be noted, however, that Latin was phased out as the language of governance and law in the east under Justinian. By then, the east constituted the core of imperial territory, and Latin would likely have been incomprehensible to the larger part of its inhabitants; thus Justinian's decision was a tardy recognition of everyday realities by the slow-moving engines of the administration (Croke 2005: 73–4).

Those distinctions become more complex when considered at a more local level. Various languages had survived in spoken form throughout earlier centuries of Roman rule (Mitchell 2000: 120–1), and some – such as Punic and Libyan in North Africa and the Palmyrene dialect of Aramaic in the Near East – had also been used in public documents (W. V. Harris 1989: 175–90; Millar 1968). Late Antiquity, however, saw the emergence of a variety of vernaculars – such as Armenian, Syriac, and, to a lesser extent, Coptic – as literary languages, particularly in the service of Christian discourse (Jones 1964: 991–7; Bowersock 1990: 29–35, 57–8; Thomson 2000: 667–71). Those linguistic divergences mirrored other cultural peculiarities that might be manifested, for example, in religious terms. In Syria and Armenia, hostility to the authority of Constantinople perhaps accounts for the adherence of both areas to Monophysite Christianity (Fowden 1993: 104–9; Hugh N. Kennedy 2000: 599; but see Jones 1959).

Such diversity should not occasion a great deal of surprise, given that the empire had been assembled from a variety of cultural zones, each of which interacted with Roman culture in its own peculiar ways (useful syntheses in Ball 2000 and Wells 1999 on east and west respectively). As the example of local vernaculars shows, such diversity persisted into Late Antiquity, and whatever elements contributed toward unity occurred within that context of variety. It should be remembered, however, that those various manifestations of diversity were not necessarily coterminous. Nor were they continuous throughout the early and late Roman periods, as culture, society, and economy were constantly developing and reshaping. In particular, the empire's Levantine provinces seem to have undergone a process of considerable economic expansion during the fifth and sixth centuries that contrasted markedly with retraction elsewhere (Morony 2004: 168–83; Ward-Perkins 2005: 123–6).

In such circumstances, we might think of the political unity of the empire as being maintained only by keeping in check various tendencies that might lead it to spring apart. That was, indeed, apparent in the very foundations of the empire, which rested on the incorporation of communities, mainly cities, that were largely left to run their own affairs. So long as various dues were paid – either tangibly as taxes or compulsory services, or symbolically in terms of allegiance and imperial service – direct interference from the imperial authorities occurred only to insure the smooth operation of the state's administrative and legal apparatus or to settle problems whose resolution confounded the abilities of local elites (Garnsey and Saller 1987; Moralee 2004). Such a policy suited elites across the length and breadth of the empire since, through their participation in imperial government, they were able to maintain their social preeminence within their communities (Veyne 1976; Heather 1994a; Lendon 1997). Intervention by the imperial authorities was probably more intrusive after the provincial reforms of Diocletian, which saw an increase in the number of governors and other bureaucrats, and a gradual erosion of the administrative autonomy formerly enjoyed by civic elites (Jones 1964: 737–66; Liebeschuetz 2001a: 104–36). Even then, there was still a degree of tension between the aspirations of central government and the limitations imposed by time, distance, and noncompliance (Kelly 2004: 114–29).

Furthermore, the empire encompassed within its boundaries societies whose integration was, in many respects, quite minimal. Beyond the cities, there was often considerable continuity of patterns of land use and settlement from pre-Roman times (Dyson 2003: 42–5, 75–6), suggesting that, in some places (although certainly not all), integration into the empire had a minimal impact on the everyday experiences of peasant farmers. The backwardness of country folk was a common literary trope throughout antiquity; but the assertion of Bishop Synesius of Ptolemais that a peasant in his native Cyrenaica thought that the ruler of the world in the early fifth century was the Homeric king Agamemnon implies a world outside the cities where the high politics of the Roman Empire mattered little (Synesius, *Ep.* 148; Bregman 1982: 19). The limits of Roman power were not only cultural, but political also. For example, the tribes living in the mountains of Cilicia in southeastern Asia Minor constituted a society over which Roman rule had little direct influence, and they are recorded as launching attacks – variously categorized as banditry and rebellion – on the settlements of the coastal plains from the first century until the fifth (Hopwood 1989). Outbreaks of disorder in other provinces occurred throughout the empire's existence, suggesting that the image of the Roman Empire as all-powerful needs to be tempered by frank acknowledgment of its many failures even within its territorial limits (Shaw 1984a; Nippel 1995: 100–12; Grünewald 2004). It ought to be borne in mind, for instance, that the evidence for the workings of imperial administration in the provinces – whether inscriptions or law codes – represents its response to failings within the system and, as such, might be better regarded as a guide to the aspirations of government rather than its actual achievements (Harries 1999: 77–98).

From the foregoing, it could be argued that what was truly remarkable about the Roman Empire was not that it fell, but that it should have lasted so long in an age when communications, through which its unity might be secured, were limited (Kelly 2004: 115–17). In fact, before the collapse that overcame the west in the fifth century, there were hints that different regions might pursue their own destinies, if strong, central authority were undermined. Thus the political upheavals of the third century yielded clear signs that the empire might fracture, with a breakaway empire in Britain, Gaul, and Spain (AD 259–74) and another in the Middle East ruled from the Syrian city of Palmyra (AD 260–72) (Drinkwater 1987; Millar 1993: 159–73). Other instances can be found of those tendencies, notably the various usurpers who emerged during the late third, fourth, and early fifth centuries in, particularly, the northwestern provinces (Casey 1994; Paschoud and Szidat 1997; Kulikowski 2000). In each of those cases, however, the secessionist regimes conceived of their authority in legitimate imperial terms, as can be seen from coins and inscriptions (Long 1996). That was also the case, albeit in different ways, for the various successor kingdoms that replaced the Roman Empire in the west in the fifth century. Thus in AD 500, the Ostrogothic king of Italy, Theoderic, visited Rome in the time-honored manner of a Roman emperor, performing a ceremonial arrival (*adventus*), addressing the senate, hosting games in the circus, and staying in the old imperial palace on the Palatine hill (Vitiello 2004). Similarly, the Frankish kings of Gaul hosted chariot races in circuses at Paris and Soissons, apparently in imitation of practice at Constantinople (McCormick 1986: 332–4). For all its limitations, the image of imperial authority was so potent that it was the most natural means of expressing legitimacy even for elites that sought to secede from or replace it.

Grand Narratives and Regional Perspectives

It is important to keep those tensions between cohesion and fragmentation in view if we are not to arrive at a simplistic account of the events that constitute the traditional grand narrative of Late Antiquity, in which the Roman Empire is dismembered by foreign invaders. Some efforts to comprehend that process have tended to emphasize the homogeneity of the Roman Empire in cultural, economic, and political terms (Heather 2005: 15–45; Ward-Perkins 2005: 87–168); there is a risk here, however, in making its disintegration seem excessively cataclysmic. It is clear that the strains placed on the Late Roman Empire could engender (or exacerbate) local and regional rivalries, particularly by encouraging competition for political authority and resources. That was particularly the case, for example, in the west in the middle of the fifth century, when, after the murder of Valentinian III in AD 455, there came a swift succession of short-lived emperors (Harries 1994). Although the prize in those conflicts was the imperial throne, the motives were indicative of rival regional interests. By that stage, Gaul had long suffered invasions, and its defense had been a priority during the long period when western affairs had been dominated by the *magister militum* Aëtius (AD 433–54) (O'Flynn 1983). At the same time, Italy was also falling prey to attacks, not only from the north but also from the south by the Vandals in Africa. It is possible to discern a vigorous debate over how best to defend the empire, with candidates for the throne – the Gauls Avitus and Majorian, and the Italians Libius Severus and Olybrius – representing the interests of different regional elites (Humphries 2000: 526–8).

Such regional concerns can be discerned also among the peoples living along the empire's frontiers, particularly in the east, where we can often observe local interests in great detail, thanks to a vigorous source tradition in Armenian and Syriac (see "Bibliographical note" below, s.v. al-Tabari, *Chronicle of Zuqnîn*; Faustus of Byzantium; Pseudo-Joshua; and Sebeos). Here, both Roman emperors and Persian shahs sought to influence local potentates living in the zone between their two empires (Isaac 1992: 229–49; Parker 1986; see Drijvers, ch. 29, in this volume). That did not prevent power-brokers along the frontiers from seeking to pursue policies independent of their nominal overlords. Thus, for instance, the Armenian king Pap (AD 368–75), who was installed with Roman help, sought to balance the Roman influence over his kingdom by negotiating with Persia – an act of independence for which he paid a heavy price, when Valens, his Roman overlord, had him assassinated (Blockley 1992: 34–6). Similarly, the emperor Anastasius I's war against Persia in AD 502–6 caused widespread upheavals along the frontier that were exploited as opportunities for raiding and gathering booty by the Arab allies of both Rome and Persia (Pseudo-Joshua the Stylite, *Chron.* 80).

The behavior of those Armenians and Arabs indicates that any consideration of the late antique grand narrative needs to construct an account of events that does not simply prioritize the unity of the Roman Empire. Some further examples show how the upheavals of Late Antiquity were experienced in different parts of the empire, often in ways that confound expectations based on the frameworks that underpin traditional narratives. The Spanish chronicler Hydatius of Lemica wrote an account that stretches from AD 378 to 468, and therefore covers many of the key events that saw the western provinces dismembered and displaced by barbarian kingdoms. Yet his attitude in such matters is insistently local (Gillett 2003: 54). He recounts in great detail the invasions of Spain by Goths, Vandals, and Sueves, and, in particular, diplomatic exchanges that had a major impact on his home province of Gallaecia in northwestern Spain. By contrast, events that modern historians would regard as pivotal in any narrative of the fall of the Roman Empire often receive rather perfunctory treatment at his hands. For example, he dispenses with the sacks of Rome by the Goths in AD 410 and the Vandals in AD 455 in just a few lines (Hydatius, *Chron.* 35, 160). In both cases, those events are overshadowed by Hydatius' more detailed account of contemporary events in Gallaecia. For Hydatius, then, the activities that impinged on conditions of life in northwestern Spain counted for more than events in the ancient heart of the empire. This parochial vision was emulated by later Spanish chroniclers, such as John of Biclaro and Isidore of Seville (see Wolf 1990).

A similar example is provided by the retirement forced upon the emperor Romulus Augustulus by the warlord Odoacer in AD 476. In traditional histories, that event has sometimes been regarded as marking not just the end of Roman rule in the west, but the end of the ancient world *tout court*. Most immediate contemporaries seem not to have viewed it that way: by AD 476, after all, the western empire had been reduced to a rump in Italy, with other regions already firmly under the sway of barbarian kings. The events of that year took on greater significance only in the sixth century in the lead-up to the emperor Justinian's reconquest of Italy (Croke 1983): then, for the first time, the deposition of Romulus Augustulus was presented as marking the demise of the Roman Empire in the west (Marcellin. *comes, Chron.* s.a. 476. 2).

The Geopolitics of the Late Antique World

The emphasis on barbarian invasions of the empire in both traditional and recent interpretations of Late Antiquity reflects the preeminence of a scheme of historical analysis that places the Mediterranean heartland of the Roman Empire at the center of things. As a result, the invasions of foreign peoples can – as has been stated by an anthropologist investigating the relationship of imperial China with its nomadic neighbors – "consist of seemingly random events presented chronologically, with one obscure tribe following another" (Barfield 1989: 1). Both ancient sources and modern analyses often adopt that point of view, relegating the history of the invading peoples to the margins (in every sense) and giving little consideration to their concerns. To proceed in that way is to risk diminishing the barbarian peoples to mere stereotypical marauders bent on destruction (Ward-Perkins 2005: 1–10; see Gillett, Halsall, and Vanderspoel, chs. 26–8, in this volume). If, however, we attempt to comprehend the barbarian invasions not only from the perspective of the invaded, but also from that of the invaders, it is important to attempt to see the Roman Empire as part of an interlocking system of regions encompassing Eurasia (and parts of Africa) as well as the Mediterranean. After all, the political displacement of the Roman Empire by a number of successor states suggests a narrative in which the histories of the Roman and non-Roman worlds not only collided, but also overlapped and intersected.

Any attempt to elucidate non-Roman perspectives on the history of Late Antiquity is fraught with difficulty, above all on account of the sources. The Romans themselves grant occasional glimpses of the world beyond the frontiers. In AD 356, for example, the eastern praetorian prefect Musonianus sought to gain diplomatic advantage over the Persians when he learned that Shah Shapur II was beleaguered by troubles on his distant, central Asian frontiers (Amm. Marc. 16. 9. 2–3). Our sources are sometimes very detailed indeed: for instance, Priscus of Panium's account of his journey to the court of Attila the Hun, located beyond the Danube frontier (Priscus, fr. Blockley 1981: 11. 2), or, more than 100 years later, Menander the Guardsman's reports of Constantinopolitan diplomatic exchanges with peoples living north of the Black Sea and the Caucasus, such as the emerging Turks (e.g., Menander Protector, fr. Blockley 1985a: 10. 1). While such notices show that the Romans were aware that the peoples beyond the imperial frontiers had their own complex political concerns, the very fact that much of our understanding of the non-Roman peoples is often limited to accounts handed down by writers from within the empire presents several problems. For instance, we must be on guard against the sort of aloof Roman cultural bias that we saw in Ammianus' account of the Huns (Heather 1999). More importantly, however much detail imperial sources might give on particular incidents, the overall picture of the non-Roman peoples that they present is generally fragmentary (on the Huns, see Sinor 1990).

Archaeology can provide some help, but presents its own problems. It is very difficult indeed – and some would argue flatly that it is impossible – to deduce not only political history but also ethnic identity from material remains alone (see Brandt, ch. 11, in this volume). In addition, modern scholarship is currently deeply divided on issues of what theoretical models to apply to the development of barbarian societies in Late Antiquity (Gillett 2002b; Noble 2006). That leaves us with numerous unanswered questions. Roman sources, for example, suggest that the Germanic tribes east of the Rhine underwent some process of confederation into larger units during the third century. Archaeology, however, sheds little light on that development (Elton 1996: 15–16; Todd 1998: 461–3). It is likely, nevertheless, that traffic to and fro across the frontiers of the empire – which were always as much zones of communication as of demarcation (Whittaker 1994) – meant that peoples outside the empire were strongly influenced by aspects of Roman culture (Heather 2005: 84–94). In some cases, we are left groping for answers about how the mechanisms of interaction worked. Excavations of a settlement at Gudme on the Danish island of

Funen yielded a hoard of 285 Roman silver coins of mid-fourth-century date, all but one of which came not from across the nearby Rhine frontier, in the Roman west, but from mints located in the eastern provinces (Hamerow 2002: 157–9). The reason for their presence is not easy to determine, even at a site that had long-standing contacts with the Roman world (Wells 1999: 247–52).

There is one frontier where it is possible to examine in detail Roman action in a broader geopolitical context: namely, that of the east. We have already noted how Roman sources acknowledged that Sasanid Persia, a realm that stretched deep into central Asia, was often beleaguered by problems on frontiers other than the one it shared with Rome. By exploiting sources other than traditional classicizing histories (for example, ecclesiastical sources, numismatics, and writings in Syriac, Armenian, and Arabic), we can get a sense of the broader geographical arena within which Romano-Persian relations were played out (Fowden 1993; Humphries 2007b). For instance, the long succession of wars fought between the emperor Constantius II (AD 337–61) and Shah Shapur II (AD 309–79), involved not only conflict along the frontier in northern Mesopotamia, but also diplomatic exchanges with polities in other regions such as Himyar in southern Arabia and Axum in the Ethiopian high-lands (Thélamon 1981: 47–9, 72–5). We also know that the Roman Empire was not the only foe that Shapur had to contend with, even along his western frontier. Thanks to a detailed (if somewhat tendentious) account preserved by the medieval Arab al-Tabari, which can sometimes be supported by archaeology, we know that early in his reign he launched a series of punitive expeditions into the Arabian peninsula (al-Tabari 1. 836–9, tr. Bosworth 1999: 54–6; see Potts 1990: 239–41; Hoyland 2001: 27–30). Such episodes from the age of Shapur II can be reduplicated for much of Late Antiquity, when we see Romans and Persians jostling for influence throughout a region stretching from the Caspian Sea and Caucasus mountains in the north to the Gulf of Aden at the southern end of the Red Sea (Fowden 1993: 100–37). Occasionally, our geographic horizons can stretch even further, such as when we read (again in al-Tabari) of the last Sasanid shah, Yazdgerd III (AD 632–51) seeking help from the Chinese emperor against the Arabs (al-Tabari 1. 2683, 2688–9, 2690–2, tr. Smith 1994: 54–62).

It is clear that reverberations of Romano-Persian interaction were felt far beyond the immediate frontier zone. It was a conduit rather than a barrier for trade networks linking the Mediterranean world with regions producing silk and spice in central Asia, India, and the Far East (Miller 1969). Other exchanges, particularly cross-cultural ones, piggy-backed on that trade (Bentley 1993: 29–110; Foltz 1999; Ball 2000: 106–48). Religious history yields striking examples. Manichaeism, which originated in Mesopotamia in the third century, reached as far west as North Africa and Italy, and spread eastward, along the silk routes of central Asia, to China (Lieu 1992). So-called "Nestorian" Christianity, which was effectively banished from Roman soil after the council of Ephesus in AD 431, also spread through Asia (Foltz 1999: 62–73) as well as into Arabia (Potts 1990: 241–7). Occasionally, too, there are hints that events in one part of Eurasia could have ramifications in another. It has been suggested, for example, that an upsurge in

Romano-Persian hostilities in the sixth and seventh centuries caused such disruption in trade routes crossing through Mesopotamia that there was a consequent upsurge in trade across Arabia, as well as in the Persian Gulf and the Indian Ocean (Daryaee 2003; Morony 2004: 184–8).

Such interactions show that the Mediterranean world of Late Antiquity was part of a larger cultural and economic zone. Indeed, interesting light can be shed on the fortunes of the Later Roman Empire by looking at it from such a broader geopolitical point of view. Population movements that, when portrayed as barbarian invasions or viewed from within the narrow confines of the Roman world, often seem singularly cataclysmic, were experienced in different although equally disruptive ways by communities in central Asia (Christian 1998: 209–43). Just as the Roman Empire was assaulted by nomadic Huns in the fifth century, so too Sasanid Persia faced invasions by Hunnic Hephthalites through the Caucasus and Khorasan mountains flanking the Caspian Sea (Bivar 1983: 211–14), while a related tribe, the Hunas, launched attacks through the Hindu Kush on the Gupta kingdom in India (Chakrabarti 1996: 187–8; Litvinsky 1996b: 141–3). The Persian shahs Kavad I (AD 488–96, 499–531) and Khusro I (AD 531–79) recognized that such invasions were a common threat and suggested to the Romans that they mount a joint defense of the mountain passes in the Caucasus (Blockley 1985b).

These last examples provide a striking indication of how adoption of a different geographical perspective can shed new light on the accepted grand narrative of late antique history. All too often, the focus of discussions of the late antique world is the Mediterranean, with occasional glances to more far-flung regions (particularly in Europe). Recent studies have emphasized that a focus on the Mediterranean as a basic unit for analysis is not entirely satisfactory (Malkin 2005). By looking for common features, it tends to overshadow the local peculiarities that can be identified, as we have seen, in late antique economic life, political actions, and historical narratives. Moreover, a focus on the Mediterranean serves to downplay the links particular regions within it had with neighboring areas of Eurasia (and Africa). There is plainly a need to think of the shape of the late antique world in ways that allow for an intersection between local and global perspectives, in addition to Mediterranean ones. There are already signs that scholars are beginning to break free of the tyranny of "Mediterraneanism." Inspired by the letter of Shah Khusro II to the emperor Maurice, in which Persia and the Roman Empire (based at Constantinople) are described as the two eyes of the world (Theophylact Simocatta 4. 11. 2–3), Garth Fowden has written of a "Mountain Arena," stretching from the Bosphorus to Afghanistan, and from the Caucasus to Ethiopia and southern Arabia, as the crucible within which the political ramifications of monotheism were worked out in Late Antiquity (Fowden 1993). Similarly, Barry Cunliffe has suggested a coherent history for communities stretching along the Atlantic littoral from Iceland to Morocco (Cunliffe 2001). One value of using these different geographical categories is that they allow us to consider comparative material that can help us to refine our analyses of accepted grand narratives (Little 2004: 920–6). But their utility is greater than just that. As this chapter has suggested, part of the challenge facing those who wish to interpret the world of Late Antiquity is the need not only to acknowledge those features that highlight its unity or diversity but also to appreciate how developments in the Mediterranean intersect with those over a wider geographical area.

BIBLIOGRAPHICAL NOTE

Any study of the issues addressed in this chapter must now begin with *CAH* xii–xiv and the masterly synthesis of Wickham 2005. For political cohesion and its limits, see especially Millar 1992, Lendon 1997, Kelly 2004: all usefully examine continuities and discontinuities between the early and late empire. There is likely to be much debate about the coherence of the late Roman world as a result of Heather 2005 and Ward-Perkins 2005, both of which (but especially the latter) may be read as a counterblast to Brown 1971b. Regional diversity is discussed not only by Wickham 2005, but also in the relevant chapters in *CAH* xiv and, from the perspective of urban history, Liebeschuetz 2001a. Interactions between the Mediterranean world and the wider Eurasian land mass are most easily accessed through Fowden 1993; in addition, Bentley 1993, Litvinsky 1996a, and Christian 1998 provide useful overviews, while Elizabeth Key Fowden 1999 offers a perceptive case study of the world between Rome and Persia. For questions of methodological paradigms, see Little 2004 and Malkin 2005.

I append full references to some of the less familiar sources I have referred to.

al-Tabari (1999), *The History of al-Tabari*, v: *The Sasanids, the Byzantines, the Lakmids, and Yemen*, tr. C. E. Bosworth, Albany, State University of New York Press.

al-Tabari (1994), *The History of al-Tabari*, xiv: *The Conquest of Iran*, tr. G. Rex Smith, Albany, State University of New York Press.

Chronicle of Zuqnin (1999), *The Chronicle of Zuqnin*, iii and iv: AD 488–775, tr. Amir Harrak, Toronto, Pontifical Institute of Mediaeval Studies.

Faustus of Byzantium (1989), *The Epic Histories attributed to P'awstos Buzand (Buzandaran Patmut'wnk)*, tr. Nina G. Garsoïan, Cambridge, MA, Harvard University Press.

Pseudo-Dionysius (1996), *The Chronicle of Pseudo-Dionysius of Tel-Mahre*, tr. W. Witakowski, Liverpool, Liverpool University Press.

Pseudo-Joshua (2000), *The Chronicle of Pseudo-Joshua the Stylite*, tr. Frank R. Trombley and John W. Watt, Liverpool, Liverpool University Press.

Sebeos (1999), *The Armenian History attributed to Sebeos*, tr. R. W. Thomson and James Howard-Johnson, Liverpool, Liverpool University Press.

Wolf, Kenneth Baxter (1990), *Conquerors and Chroniclers of Early Medieval Spain*, Liverpool, Liverpool University Press.

CHAPTER EIGHT

Mobility and the Traces of Empire

Blake Leyerle

In the late fourth century, John Chrysostom was moved to reflect on how travel conditions had changed since the time of the patriarchs. Abraham's faithful reaction to God's command to go to a place he did not know was all the more impressive since "traveling was so unpleasant at that time: it was not possible then, as it is now, to mingle with others safely and to travel abroad without apprehension" (*Hom. in Gen.* 31. 17). Chrysostom's world was one in which people undertook extensive journeys for a variety of reasons with striking matter-of-factness (see Map 3, p. 124). Evidence from Egypt suggests that even quite humble people traveled (Adams 2001: 157–9). Those who did not themselves travel, would have met travelers and known others who had gone on journeys. One of the most distinctive features of the Roman Empire was the fluidity of people, goods, and capital (Horden and Purcell 2000). The infrastructure that permitted this ease of travel reveals not only rich data about the technological achievement and daily life of Late Antiquity, but also a compelling set of cultural meanings. Roads and the promotion of travel were a central mechanism for the invention and advertisement of imperial power; "romanization" can, indeed, be understood as a change in mobility and interconnectivity (Laurence 2001: 91).

A Culture of Movement

The affairs of empire were responsible for the bulk of traffic on the road in Late Antiquity. The state and fiscal bureaucracy, as well as the military, were dependent upon communication, and communication rested entirely upon the movement of bodies. Couriers and lesser officials crossed the empire bearing letters, decrees, reports, and gifts (Bagnall 1993: 162–3). The army's constant need for communication insured that, at any given time, several soldiers in every military unit would be away serving as couriers (Sherk 1974; Austin and Rankov 1995; Kolb 2001: 98–9).

Members of the governing elite traveled to take up positions in the military and in the provinces. Emperor and governors oversaw campaigns, inspected cities, and met with subjects.

Legal business often necessitated travel. Manumitted slaves had to present themselves before the provincial governor to receive their official grant of freedom. Every petition had to be hand-delivered (J. L. White 1986: 194–6, 215–18). When summoned, a person had to travel to the place of the assizes. By the later third century, the imperial law courts were no longer stationed in Rome, but had become roving entourages (Salway 2001: 59–60). It is indeed possible that the traveler we know as the Bordeaux pilgrim undertook the bulk of his journey for legal reasons: that he traveled to Constantinople, where the emperor Constantine was in residence from October AD 332 to May AD 333, before embarking on his religiously motivated journey to Jerusalem (Salway 2001: 36).

The most conspicuous group of travelers was undoubtedly the military, and every major road was engineered to accommodate personnel and baggage wagons. The deployment of troops entailed mass movement. Wherever the military went, fleets of vehicles and pack animals followed as well as crowds of servants, grooms, porters, and women. Careful planning was required to supply the needs of troops on the move. An often quoted passage from the *Historia Augusta* suggests that an itinerary, complete with dates and stopping places, was published two months ahead of time to insure adequate provisioning (*SHA, Alex. Sev.* 45. 2–3; see Ambrose, *Exp. Ps.* 118. 5. 2). Army recruits journeyed to Rome for induction and assignment to their individual units (Adams 2001: 146–52). Even when not on active duty, individual soldiers traveled and arranged for family members to visit. Tariff inscriptions indicate that soldiers' wives and prostitutes paid higher tolls for their road use, presumably because the state wanted to profit from this group of regular travelers (Philostr. *VA* 1. 20).

Business affairs spurred other travelers. While large-scale importers and exporters preferred to use shipping routes, given the crushing cost of moving goods overland, small merchants shuttled between their sources of supply and their markets. According to Apuleius, trade "in honey, cheese, and other foodstuffs of that kind used by innkeepers," kept one man traveling through Thessaly, Aetolia, and Boeotia (Apul. *Met.* 1. 5). Tollbooth receipts show that donkey and camel caravans regularly traveled through the western and eastern deserts in Egypt (Adams 2001: 150; see Salway 2001: 26, 59). Effective agricultural exploitation demanded mobility as well as the use of migrant labor (Suet. *Vesp.* 1; Horden and Purcell 2000: 385–6). Wealthy landlords like Pliny, or his delegates, needed to visit their distant estates on a regular basis (Pliny, *Ep.* 3. 19. 4; 1. 3. 2; 9. 15. 3; 4. 14. 8). Artisans and entertainers traveled throughout the empire to ply their distinctive trades (Laurence 2001: 169; Grey 2004). Other mobile specialists included mercenaries, pirates, and robbers (Horden and Purcell 2000: 387–8). Severe economic pressure also fed population redistribution through the practices of tax evasion and slavery (De Ste Croix 1981: 216).

Family matters often prompted travel. Letters from the period suggest that the presence of a large number of expatriates in an area insured a steady flow of potential couriers (Llewelyn 1994: 26–9). The notes they carried back and forth often contained requests for further travel: that relatives come to celebrate birthdays and festivals, to attend funerals, or to look after the sick (Adams 2001: 148–50).

For the sake of higher education, elite students traveled to centers of learning like Athens, Antioch, or Beirut (Llewelyn 1998: 117–21; Watts 2004; see Cribiore, ch. 16). Many of these students would later travel to lecture or to take up positions. Augustine, for example, went first to Rome and then to Milan (August. *Conf.* 5. 8; 5. 13). Research interests prompted Galen to travel to the Greek island of Lemnos to investigate a particular kind of soil (Gal. *De simplicium medicamentorum temperamentis* 9). Sightseeing was another educational enterprise enjoyed by the moneyed (Lucian, *Peregrinus* 35; Apul. *Met.* 2. 21; Aelius Aristides, *Or.* 36; Chevallier 1976: 147; Salzman 2004).

Religion also fostered mobility. From its foundation, travel was one of the hallmarks of Christianity. Individual churches were founded by itinerant preachers and depended upon subsequent visits for material and ideological support (*Didachē* 11–15; Llewelyn 1998: 54–7). Even after ecclesiastical authority became vested in local bishops and deacons, clergy still traveled on missionary voyages as well as to church synods and councils and, upon occasion, to disciplinary hearings (Wood 2001; Euseb. *Vit. Const.* 3. 6; see Sotinel 2004; Palladius, *Dial.* 7. 87–9; Socrates, *Hist. eccl.* 6. 15; Sozomen, *Hist. eccl.* 8. 16). The press of ecclesiastical travel provoked Ammianus Marcellinus' complaint about the "throngs of bishops hastening hither and thither on the public mounts" (Amm. Marc. 21. 16. 18).

In Egypt, the practice of "cutting loose and taking off" (*anachōrēsis*) was so common that it became the technical term for religious withdrawal. Recent studies have sharpened our awareness of monastic mobility, identifying travel as a widespread ascetic practice (Caner 2002; Dietz 2005).

Among the reasons for Christian travel, pilgrimage merits particular attention. Not that it was unknown in the ancient world: hope had long urged the sick to make their way to healing shrines and pilgrims to holy sites (Kötting 1950: 33–53). Arguably the most famous of these, Aelius Aristides, traveled to various Asclepian shrines in search of "comfort" from his multiple afflictions – a concept that combined the hope of healing with that of religious experience (*Sacred Discourses* 2. 49–50; 3. 6–7; 4. 83; 6. 1; see Pliny, *Ep.* 5. 19). In the wake of Constantine's ambitious building program, however, the phenomenon of Christian pilgrimage grew tremendously in scope and importance.

While a few pilgrims had come to Palestine "for prayer and investigation" in the third century (Euseb. *Hist. eccl.* 6. 11. 12; Wilken 1992: 109), it was the lure of being "on the very spot" that brought Egeria to the Holy Land in the following century, and caused John Chrysostom to wish for the leisure and bodily strength to travel to Philippi to kiss the chains that had imprisoned Paul (Egeria, *It.* 4. 6; Chrysostom, *Hom. in Ep. ad Ephes.* 8. 2). So powerful was this sense of place that Jerome could promise Marcella that if she came to Palestine she would see not simply the sites of scriptural stories, but the actual events themselves. Together, he assures her, they will "see Lazarus come forth tied up in winding bands ... and perceive the prophet Amos sounding the shepherd's horn upon his mountain" (*Ep.* 46. 13; see

Ep. 108. 10). To be in the place of revelation was to be in the time of revelation (Wilken 1992: 120).

For others, the goal of pilgrimage was a person rather than a place (Frank 2000). So many visitors traveled to hear "a word" from the solitaries of Egypt that Apa Arsenius feared that the sea would become a highway (*Apophthegmata Patrum*, Arsenius 28). Other monks, however, welcomed these visitors, and monastic houses sprang up at convenient intervals along the main pilgrim routes precisely in order to supply the needs of pilgrims (Hunt 1982: 62–6; Hirschfeld 1992: 55–6). Along with food and lodging (for up to a week, according to Palladius, *Hist. Laus.* 7), they provided a certain amount of tour guidance. Their confidence in being able to identify the places where scriptural events had occurred rested, according to Egeria, upon a "tradition … handed down to them by their predecessors" (Egeria, *It.* 12. 2–4). Their hospitality was not wholly disinterested, as pilgrimage had become an increasingly common prelude to entering the monastic life. Certainly, the record of people who passed through Jerome's monastery in Bethlehem constitutes a virtual *Who's Who* of the late fourth-century Christian world (Clark 1992: 28–33).

Not all early Christian travel was voluntary. Both Paul and Ignatius were compelled by the state to go to Rome and their death. During the Decian persecution, Cyprian, along with other clergy, went into exile. His place of exile was no more remote than the suburbs of Carthage, but from that remove he penned (in his *De lapsis*) a defense of flight that contained the seeds of a theology for refugees. Others had to travel much farther. When Constantine banished Athanasius from Alexandria, he sent him to Gaul, in what was to be only the first of five exiles (Brakke 1995: 8). Banished from Gaul, Hilary traveled east to Constantinople.

In the face of the Germanic migrations of the fifth and sixth centuries, many were forced to take to the road. The sack of Rome in AD 410 initiated waves of migration to Africa and the eastern provinces (Jerome, *Ep.* 128. 5). And in the sixth century, Africans fled to Spain from their Vandal-occupied homeland (Dietz 2005: 22–3).

In sum, Late Antiquity was an astonishingly mobile society, profoundly marked by displacement. Soldiers, government officials, and the well-to-do, as well as artisans, entertainers, pilgrims, Christian clergy, and small merchants, readily undertook long-distance travel. Regional travel was regularly undertaken by farmers, pastoralists, and migrant workers. Ascetics were often wanderers. Litigation, persecution, and social unrest compelled rich and poor alike to engage in evasive behavior. But, no matter what the circumstances or motivation, all travelers used the same network of roads and shipping routes that spanned the empire. To the details of this impressive infrastructure we now turn.

Mobility's Infrastructure

At the height of the empire, some 300,000 kilometers of graveled or paved highways linked the disparate provinces to Rome (Forbes 1955: 138). The width and quality of these roads varied tremendously. The majority of routes were simply graveled paths.

Under dry conditions, these were perfectly adequate, but in poor weather they might turn into "deep impassable mud" (Procop, *Aed.* 5. 3. 12–13). Routes such as these have not withstood the passage of time. What remains today are stretches of premier roadway, the result of skilled engineering and considerable monetary outlay.

First a bed was dug and leveled. On all but the flattest terrain, absolute straightness was abandoned in favor of following the contours of the land. In rugged terrain, routes usually followed older paths, skirting mountains and avoiding defiles. But, if the need were great enough, Roman engineers were prepared to bore through mountains or cantilever a roadway along the side of a cliff (Forbes 1955: 150; Chevallier 1976: 104–6). Even when tunneling through solid rock, military routes had to be at least 8 feet wide to accommodate heavy baggage wagons. But the most typical road width was 10 Roman feet, a span only slightly narrower than a modern lane (Casson 1988: 354).

Once the roadbed was prepared, it was filled with a foundation mixture of broken pottery, small stones, and usually some waterproofing material. Heavy rollers were used to flatten this mixture to prevent heaving and cracking. Finally, flat paving stones were fitted closely together to form an unbroken surface (Forbes 1955: 146–7; Casson 1988: 354). The surface was slightly crowned and ditches were dug on either side to facilitate drainage. The result of this labor was a road some 100 to 140 centimeters (39–55 inches) deep, or three to four times the depth of a modern roadbed (Forbes 1955: 148). Roads built over unstable ground might require even more elaborate construction techniques (Chevallier 1976: 89–90).

This impressive technology gave Roman roads exceptional durability: they could sustain the wear of iron wheels for seventy to a hundred years before needing thorough reconstruction, though high-traffic stretches might need servicing every thirty to forty years. Even relatively simple cobble roads, in which cobbles were embedded in a 10-centimeter (3.9 inch) sand bed, probably had a life of ten to fifteen years (Forbes 1955: 148–9). In the northern parts of the empire, however, where frost caused cracks and potholes, roads needed more frequent repair. Funding for road works was initially raised through direct taxation, though private benefaction also played a role. Within Italy, the maintenance of the road system gradually devolved upon specially appointed officials; in the provinces it remained a duty of the governor (Ramsay 1904: 392).

The Speed of Travel

The speed of travel along these well-engineered roads strikes us as almost unbelievably slow. Casson estimates that a person, traveling by foot on level ground, would go on average fifteen to twenty miles (24–32 km) per day (Casson 1974: 188). Thus, on his forced march from Antioch to Rome, Ignatius would have spent eighty-six days walking and nine days aboard ship (Ramsay 1904: 384–6). In a carriage, one could reasonably expect to cover twenty-five to thirty miles a day (40–48 km) at a rate of four miles (6.5 km) an hour. Under duress, this rate might increase to as much as forty or forty-five miles (65 or 72.5 km) per day, but not for long (Chevallier 1976: 188). While horses were the swiftest means of conveyance, they were costly to purchase and maintain. Donkeys were useful, especially in mountainous regions, but the load they could carry was significantly less than that of a horse (K. D. White 1984: 129). By far the most popular animal for traveling was the mule, a cross between a horse and a donkey that combined the best features of both. In the eastern provinces, dromedaries were also used (Egeria, *It.* 6. 1–2; Casson 1988: 356; Bagnall 1993: 38–40). They could carry twice as much as a mule and at greater speed (Coulston 2001: 112).

While a variety of vehicles were available, a number of technological problems slowed their progress. Traction was generally poor without "dished" wheels that could grip the crowned road surface (Chevallier 1976: 89; Forbes 1955: 138). A fixed front axle demanded a slow, wide arc on every turn. Without ball or roller bearings, or cost-effective lubrication, wheel hubs were vulnerable to friction from the axle (Harris 1974; Casson 1988: 356). Steep gradients posed a real danger for heavily laden wagons, since neither efficient bits nor brakes had been invented. There was the further danger of an animal slipping on slick sections of the stone-paved road (Polge 1967: 28–34). Horse "shoes" were first designed to improve traction rather than to protect sensitive hooves (Apul. *Met.* 4. 4, 9. 32; Green 1966). Finally, none of the wheeled conveyances had any suspension system. Given the bone-jarring prospect of long-distance driving, most people preferred to walk.

The laborious difficulty of travel over land is graphically summed up in the prices for conveyance of goods. From Diocletian's Price Edict of AD 301, A. H. M. Jones has calculated that a wagonload of wheat doubled its price every 300 miles (482 km) (Jones 1964, ii: 841; see Yeo 1946). At such a rate, it was far cheaper to bring wheat to Rome from Egypt by ship than to carry it even seventy-five miles (120 km) by road. Personal travel was also costly. Apuleius writes that the outlay necessary for Lucius' trip from Corinth to Rome "melted away his humble inheritance" (Apul. *Met.* 11. 28). For the nonelite, travel also meant time away from land and livelihood (Adams 2001: 147).

To the expected difficulties and delays of travel, we must add the danger of bandits. Suetonius and Strabo praise Augustus for suppressing brigandage (Suet. *Aug.* 32; Strabo, *Geograph.* 4. 6. 6), but Luke's story of the Good Samaritan takes for granted the likelihood of robbers setting upon travelers on deserted stretches of road (Luke 10:30; see 2 Cor. 11: 26; Plin. *HN* 6. 25; Artemidorus, 3. 5; Apul. *Met.* 1. 7; Adams 2001: 154; Isaac 1984). In AD 296, a soldier wrote to his wife: "Bring your gold jewellery with you, but don't wear it!" (*P. Mich.* 214). Poorer travelers were always more vulnerable to assault than the rich who typically traveled with a retinue and might have the resources to hire a military escort (Lucian, *Alex.* 55). Some routes were best avoided altogether; Basil of Caesarea was astonished that no one had warned the priest Dorotheus about the road to Rome from Constantinople (Basil, *Ep.* 215; see August. *Conf.* 3. 8. 16, 7. 21. 27; Tert. *De resurr.* 43). In addition to bandits, drunks could be a problem (Adams 2001: 154). Other perils included roving packs of wolves or fierce dogs (Apul. *Met.* 8. 15–17; 9. 36), bridges in ruinous disrepair (Procop. *Aed.* 5. 5), and avalanches (Strabo, *Geograph.* 4. 6. 6).

The Courier Service

In order to insure a reliable, steady flow of information to the government, the emperor Augustus developed the *cursus publicus* or state courier service (see Sotinel, ch. 9). At first, a series of runners brought dispatches, but this system was soon abandoned in favor of a relay of vehicles. The latter system, in which a single courier traveled the whole distance on a series of light wagons, ferries, and sailing ships, sacrificed speed for the sake of the more detailed information that could be obtained by questioning the messenger (Suet. *Aug.* 49. 3). The *cursus* was originally an infrastructure for use solely by designated state officials (*Supplementum epigraphicum Graecum* 26. 1392: 13 ff.), but because vehicles could accommodate additional people and baggage, it quickly devolved into a transportation system and remained thus throughout Late Antiquity (Kolb 2001: 95–6; see August. *Conf.* 5. 13. 23; Chrysostom, *Hom. in Ep. ad Hebr.* 2. 5).

The average speed of the *cursus* was perhaps five Roman miles an hour, or fifty Roman miles a day (approximately 75 km) (Ramsay 1904: 387–8; Forbes 1955: 154; Chevallier 1976: 194). In a pinch, dispatch bearers occasionally covered twice or even three times the distance (Procop. *Anecdota* 30. 1). Speed always depended upon the season, the quality of the road, and the density of the traffic (Libanius, *Or.* 21, 15–16; Aelius Aristides, *Sacred Discourses* 2. 60–2; Chevallier 1976: 193). In the late fourth century, a special section of the *cursus* was established for express service, the so-called *cursus velox.*

Only designated officials had the right to use this relay system (Llewelyn 1995); to prove entitlement, they were required to carry a *diploma/evectio* sealed by the governor of the province, authenticating their business and stipulating the type of transport to which they were entitled (Chevallier 1976: 182). An edict of Constantine makes it clear that travelers had to furnish their own drivers (*Cod. Theod.* 8. 5. 2, AD 316; Kolb 2001: 101). Initially, the government reimbursed these services but, by Late Antiquity, the economic burden fell entirely upon the local inhabitants (Kolb 2001: 97–8). Despite the fact that penalties attached to those found abusing the system, legal and epigraphic evidence suggests that fraud was common (Forbes 1955: 153; Chevallier 1976: 182–4, 188).

Orientation Devices

When pondering the question of how travelers planned their routes and made their way across the empire, scholars have long assumed that the Romans had scale maps (Sherk 1974: 559; Dilke 1985: 244; Harvey 1987: 466). But Kai Brodersen has now convincingly shown that simple lists of stations along a route (*itineraria adnotata*), like that found in the Bordeaux itinerary or inscribed on a variety of surfaces, served as the most common means of orientation in antiquity (Brodersen 2001; Salway 2001: 48–54). "Illustrated" maps (*itineraria picta*) were also available, of which the best known, as well as the most beautiful, is the Peutinger Table, a twelfth-century copy of a Roman civilian map. In brilliant colors, it traces the main routes of the empire, depicts major topographical features, and indicates resting stops, towns, and cities (Bosio 1983). While the sequence of stations and the distances between them are fairly accurate, there is no concern for scale or even geographical accuracy. As Brodersen comments, its utility, like that of a modern subway map, lies in the clarity with which it presents a network of roads that facilitates route selection (Brodersen 2001: 18; see Veg. *Mil.* 3. 6; Salway 2001: 28–32, 43–7).

Once on a main road, progress could be measured by counting off milestones, of which about 4,000 examples survive from across the empire. These were columnar markers set at intervals along the road and readily visible from a distance, since they stood some six to eight feet (2–4 m) above the ground. Inscribed with the distance to or from a perceived end point of the road, they helped travelers calculate their progress as well as plan overnight stops. Wall plaques, or *tabellaria*, listing distances along several routes radiating from a central point, were often positioned at major nodes (Salway 2001: 54–8). In desert regions, piles of small stones were used to mark the edges of the roadway (Adams 2001: 141; see Egeria, *It.* 6).

Inns

Inns were typically located a day's journey, or twenty-five miles (40 km), along all the main routes, unless difficult terrain demanded closer placement (Casson 1988: 354). Hostelries were needed not only for the refreshment of travelers, but also for the regular exchange of horses and vehicles for those using the *cursus*. Stops made simply for fresh equipment were originally called *mutationes* (changes), whereas overnight stays were termed *mansiones* (rest stops), but by the time of the *Theodosian Code*, these terms were used interchangeably (Chevallier 1976: 185). A typical daily ration for a man traveling with the right of requisition (*annona*) was one-sixth of a *modius* of bread, one *sextarius* of wine, and half a *litra* of meat (Adams 2001: 142). From one rest stop to another, two changes seem to have been typical. The Bordeaux pilgrim, for example, records that he covered the 2,221 miles from Bordeaux to Constantinople with 230 changes and 112 rest-stops: an average rate of travel of about 19.8 miles, or just under 32 km per day. Occasional difficult stretches demanded three or even four changes of equipment a day.

Facilities at *mansiones* varied considerably. Traveling in northern Greece, Lucius complained that his bed, "besides being a bit too short and missing a leg, was rotten" (Apul. *Met.* 1. 11; see Aelius Aristides, *Sacred Discourses* 2. 61). In Palestine, Paula refused invitations to lodge at official *mansiones*, preferring to stay at what Jerome terms "miserable inns" (*Ep.* 108. 7, 9, 14; Kleberg 1957: 91–6). But where travelers had a choice in accommodation, quality tended to improve (Plut. *Mor.* 532B–C). In Asia Minor, Epictetus suggests that a traveler might be tempted to linger in a luxurious inn (*Discourses* 2. 23. 36); in that same region Aelius Aristides preferred to stay at an inn rather than at the house of a friend (*Or.* 27).

While the facilities at inns undoubtedly varied, church leaders uniformly bemoaned their moral laxity. Gregory of Nyssa sternly warns Christians against undertaking pilgrimages on the grounds that "the inns and hostelries and cities of the East present many examples of license and indifference to vice" (*Or.* 2; see Plin. *HN* 36. 5; Ulp. *Dig.* 3. 2. 4. 2; 23. 2. 43. 1 and 9; *Cod. Theod.* 4. 56. 3). The sixth-century *Life* of Theodore of Sykeon takes the association of inns with prostitution utterly for granted (Nicephorus, *Encomium in S. Theodorum Siceotam* 3). For this reason, churches and monasteries often founded hospices for travelers (Basil, *Ep.* 94; Gregory of Nazianzus, *Or.* 43. 63; Palladius, *Hist. Laus.* 7).

Travel by Sea

Compared to the grinding tedium of travel overland, travel by water, if the winds were favorable, seemed almost immediate. Thus, while the Greeks had many words for the sea, their favorite term was *pontos*, a word that never entirely severed its connotation of a bridge.

As there were no dedicated passenger boats, those wishing to travel by sea booked passage aboard merchant vessels destined, ideally, for the same port. The largest of the grain ships might take on 600 passengers (Joseph. *Vit.* 15); but on Paul's ship to Rome, there were 276 people in all, of which perhaps 260 were passengers (Acts 27: 37). Synesius tells us that he traveled with about fifty other passengers, a third of whom were women (*Ep.* 4). Those desiring to go from Rome to Alexandria were the most fortunate. The capital city's constant need for wheat insured a steady stream of huge cargo ships. These freighters offered no special amenities for travelers, but typically made good time. Those wishing to go to less frequented destinations had to resign themselves to several layovers and the use of progressively smaller vessels. A passenger heading to Palestine from Rome was well advised to board a grain ship for Alexandria and proceed from there to Palestine (Philo, *In Flacc.* 5. 26).

During the summer months, when the so-called "yearly" or "etesian" winds blew steadily from the northwest, the run from Rome to Alexandria was relatively speedy, with two weeks being average. But the return voyage was a laborious affair; boats skirted the coast of Roman Palestine until they could cross on the leeward side of the island of Rhodes. From there, they sailed to Crete, before striking across to Malta and on to Sicily. Only then could they make their way up the western side of Italy into the harbor at Puteoli or Ostia (Ramsay 1904: 379–81). This circuitous route usually took about two months, but might be longer. When Gregory of Nazianzus sailed from Alexandria to Greece, he reached Rhodes only on the twentieth day (*Or.* 18. 31). Even with a favorable wind, ancient ships probably averaged no more than 4 to 6 knots, and against the wind, half of that or less.

Unlike modern sailing craft, which are more at risk when sailing close to land, ancient ships were most vulnerable on the open sea. Sudden strong gusts of wind brought pressure to bear on the huge central sail, causing the central mast to work like a giant lever and splinter the ship's hull (Ramsay 1904: 399; Acts 27; Achilles

Tatius, *Leucippe and Cleitophon* 3. 3. 1–5. 5). In addition to the danger of storms and pirates (Achilles Tatius 5. 7; Chrysostom, *De virg.* 24. 2), travelers had to contend with the inevitable bouts of seasickness (Oldelehr 1977).

Most people who wished to travel by sea simply walked the quays asking where ships were bound, as Libanius did in AD 340 when looking for passage from Constantinople to Athens (*Or.* 1. 31). But in Rome's great port city of Ostia, a square directly inland from the harbor held the offices of all the merchants plying trade overseas. A prospective traveler might simply make a round of the square to book passage on any ship (Casson 1988: 361). Because ships did not sail on a schedule, passengers were then compelled to linger about the waterfront until a herald announced their ship's departure (August. *Conf.* 5. 8; Philostr. *VA* 8. 14).

As the hold was mostly reserved for cargo, ballast, and packing material, there was limited room for passengers below board. A few might travel down by the bilge water in the ancient equivalent of steerage. Lucian's characters describe these quarters as so cramped and uncomfortable that they were fit only for criminals (*Jupp. trag.* 48; see Athenaeus, *Learned Banquet* 5. 207–8). Most passengers camped out on the open deck, either setting up temporary shelters or simply rolling out bedding (Achilles Tatius, 2. 33. 1; Petron. *Sat.* 100. 6; Lucian, *Toxaris* 20; Pachomius, *Reg.* 119). Well-to-do travelers brought on board an impressive array of creature comforts with a corps of servants to deploy them but, for the majority, few amenities were available. Fresh drinking water was provided from a specially lined tank located either in the hold or on deck (Gregory of Nazianzus, *Poemata* 11. 145–7; Casson 1971: 177). In boats equipped with a galley, passengers might make use of it once the crew had been fed (Van Doorninck 1972: 137–44). The only other convenience may have been a latrine. Some relief sculptures show a small covered structure perched over the water on the stern directly behind the steering apparatus, but this is only a guess (Casson 1971: 180).

Having discovered a kind of concrete capable of setting under water, Roman engineers were able to construct breakwaters to insure calm harbors. In Alexandria, the first lighthouse was acclaimed as one of the seven wonders of the world. Like all lighthouses in antiquity, it served to guide boats into the harbor rather than to warn them of dangerous rocks or reefs (Casson 1988: 362). This function is clear in Chrysostom's praise of monastic life: "There is a calm port. [Monks] are like beacons sending forth their light from a high point to those sailing in from afar. Stationed in the harbour, drawing all people to their own tranquility, they preserve from shipwreck those who look to them" (*Hom. in Ep. 1 ad Tim.* 14. 3).

Having arrived in port, passengers headed further inland might reembark, as did Lady Poemenia, on smaller vessels designed to travel along rivers (Palladius, *Hist. Laus.* 35; Hunt 1982: 76–7). Traveling upstream on rivers such as the Danube, Rhône, or Seine, often demanded towing, which was effected usually by humans but sometimes by animals. For this reason, towpaths were a common feature along both sides of the riverbanks.

Travel by sea, potentially so swift, was available only part of the year. From November 10 until March 10, the sea was "closed." During the winter season, only vessels constrained by need, such as the Roman grain ships and military craft, plied the waters (Rougé 1966: 32–3). Travel was restricted not only because of the risk of storms but also because of the increased cloud cover that precluded navigation (Casson 1988: 357).

Even this brief overview of the infrastructure of travel by land and by sea in Late Antiquity reveals its extraordinary scope. As impressive as the monumentality of the system is the mobility that it insured. Both of these aspects, I suggest, were always about power. The long reach of the road and water transport system was synonymous with the grasp of Rome; and the mobility it fostered was fundamental to the creation of imperial subjects.

The Traces of Empire

As the military conquered new territory, they laid down roads and built bridges (Hunt 1982: 52–8; Coulston 2001: 127). For the protection of travelers, the roadbeds were laid slightly below the crest of hills and away from densely wooded areas (Chevallier 1976: 114). Roads were one of the most visible signs of Roman occupation.

Provincial roads were built to improve trade as well as security. Services sprang up along the major routes to provide infrastructural support. The movement of goods and people, in turn, fostered urbanization (Isaac and Roll 1982: 90–2), with the result that vanished roadways can often be reconstructed from patterns of human settlement (Chevallier 1976: 43, 117). According to Tacitus, roads and the Roman style of urban living were key elements in the subjugation of Britain (*Agr.* 31; Laurence 2001: 74–88).

On the perimeter of the empire, gravel roads were typical. These marked a contrast with the stretches of premier roadway that characterized the Mediterranean core (Laurence 1999: 58–77; 2001: 82). Technically, these latter were over-engineered, their excessive durability proven by their existence nearly two millennia later. This monumentality was intentional; it asserted the irresistible power of Rome. Bridges were even more impressive. Caesar's successful bridging of the Rhine on two occasions was an engineering triumph. According to Pliny, the building of bridges was one of the suitable topics in a literary celebration of war (Pliny, *Ep.* 8. 4. 2). Although Apollodorus of Damascus' bridge over the Danube was dismantled by Hadrian in the second century, it was still worthy of praise four centuries later (Dio Chrys. *Or.* 68. 13. 1–6; Procop. *Aed.* 4. 6. 11–16; Coulston 2001: 124).

The construction of transportation routes was inseparable from imperial propaganda. Scenes on Trajan's column depicting the clearing of forests and the graveling of roads trumpet the Roman virtues of discipline and control over natural resources, in contrast to barbarian disorganization and panic (Coulston 2001: 123, 126–9; see Salway 2001: 56). By slicing across "established field networks for mile after mile, slighting pre-existing boundaries, political groupings and patterns of kinship," Roman roads proclaimed "the domination of Rome and the inadequacy of indigenous arrangements" (Muir 2000: 100); they expressed in material form the relationship between the colonizing and the colonized societies (Howe 2005: 29). Perhaps especially in those places where the military was absent, the road averred the proximity of Roman power, the real possibility that the army could arrive at any time, at a moment's notice.

The contribution of roads to imperial propaganda is particularly visible in the milestones that punctuated the routes. These were not simply markers of distance. If they had been, they would have been stationed at roughly equal intervals along all major thoroughfares. But in Palestine, as Isaac and Roll have shown, milestones were clustered in inhabited areas and almost entirely absent in deserted regions, where, one might have thought, they would have been especially needed (Isaac and Roll 1982: 91–8). Their inscriptions explain this puzzle. In the early empire, in addition to providing the distance to or from the closest major city, they typically recorded the name of the ruling emperor as well as some action he had effected to improve the road: that he had, for example, paved or restored it. In the later empire, milestones are still inscribed to the emperor. But they credit him with restoring not the road, but peace to the empire. Milestones, like coins, played an ideological role. In times of political unrest, they were used by the military to express their allegiance; in times of political calm, they were employed by the central authorities to assert stability (Laurence 2004: 45–53).

Roads, like maps, mark boundaries and articulate degrees of belonging. By allowing for the measurement of distance between places, they gave geographical unity to the province and, eventually, to the empire as a whole. On that great schematic diagram of routes known as the Peutinger Table, the centrality of Rome is intentionally marked horizontally as well as vertically (Salway 2001: 22–6). The long reach of the empire is registered in the image of a small temple at the western edge of India identified as a *templum Augusti*. The public recording of intercity distances invited a sense of regional interconnection. It was no longer sufficient to think of oneself only in terms of one's immediate locale: identity came to be articulated more broadly, even as wider notional entities like Roman Italy or Britannia were formed (Laurence 2001: 90–1). What we customarily term "romanization," might then, as Laurence suggests, be better understood as a change in the nature of mobility (Laurence 1999; 2001: 67). In a very real sense, the movement not only of diplomats, troops, and officials but also of ordinary people like artisans, agriculturalists, merchants, and ascetics "performed" the empire.

The performance of empire is given unlikely expression in the work known to us as the *Bordeaux Itinerary*. Many scholars believe that the anonymous pilgrim author wrote down his itinerary simply to facilitate the future travel of others (Hunt 1982: 55; Dietz 2005: 18–19). Given what we know of the itinerary form, such later use is probable. But it is also quite possible that ideology – both Christian and imperial – prompted his hand. As a record of travel over thousands of miles, the Bordeaux pilgrim's narrative iterates the empire; it affirms the interconnection of parts, that no region is isolated or inaccessible to the traveler (Laurence 1999; 2001: 80–1; Elsner 2000). Yet despite the extraordinary distance traveled, the itinerary remains strikingly static. Instead of verbs, noun follows noun; and nomination, as David Spurr has suggested in a different colonial context, is a strategy of appropriation (Spurr 2001: 31–2). By listing the cities passed and stops made, the pilgrim possesses them. Even the exotic locales and events mentioned in the biblical record are claimed as part of his quotidian world "back home" (Leyerle 1996). The primacy of connection champions the historicity of the biblical record: the place where Elisha miraculously purified a fountain is as evidently "genuine" as an area known for the breeding of curule horses; similarly, the place where Jesus taught his disciples and the region where the Jura mountains rise. As Jaś Elsner has noted, the grand summaries of his travel (which occur four times in the text) re-form the empire in Christian terms. To the expected *metropoleis* of Rome and Milan are added the recently dedicated city of Constantinople and the noncity of Jerusalem, important for no other reason than as the site of Jesus' Passion. In a remarkably economic fashion, the *Bordeaux Itinerary* maps the ideology of a Christian empire (Elsner 2000: 188–9; Jacobs 2004: 104–5).

Conclusion

John Chrysostom's admiration for the patriarch's willingness to travel, alluded to at the beginning of this essay, thus depends upon a prior acknowledgment of the effects of empire. Wherever the Romans went, they built roads and established shipping routes to secure access to outlying areas and to encourage mobility. The twin themes of dominion and travel are strikingly linked in Aelius Aristides' fulsome praise of the second-century Roman emperor, Antoninus Pius:

> Now it is possible for both Greek and barbarian, with his possessions or without them, to travel easily wherever he wishes, quite as if he were going from one country of his to another. And he is frightened neither by the Cilician Gates [a mountain pass in southern Turkey], nor by the sandy, narrow passage through Arabia to Egypt, nor by impassable mountains, nor by boundless, huge rivers, nor by inhospitable barbarian races. But it is enough for his safety that he is a Roman, or rather one of those under you. And what was said by Homer, "The earth was common to all," you have made a reality, by surveying the whole inhabited world, by bridging the rivers in various ways, by cutting carriage roads through the mountains, by filling desert places with post stations, and by civilizing everything with your way of life and good order ... And now, indeed, there is no need to write a description of the world, nor to enumerate the laws of each people, but you have become universal geographer for all men by opening up all the gates of the inhabited world and by giving to all who wish it the power to be observers of everything ... and by organizing the whole inhabited world like a single household. (Aelius Aristides, *Or.* 26. 100–2, tr. Behr 1981–6, ii: 95–6)

Not just a happy result of empire, mobility was its main building block. By moving across the empire, late antique travelers created its unity and were, in turn, romanized.

BIBLIOGRAPHICAL NOTE

To learn more about the essential connectivity and fluidity of the Mediterranean region, see Horden and Purcell's groundbreaking and immensely learned study (2000).

For details about the infrastructure of overland travel in Late Antiquity, Casson's works remain indispensable (1974, 1988). The older, technical, studies of Forbes (1955) and Chevallier (1976) continue to illuminate, as does William Ramsay's astonishingly comprehensive encyclopedia article (1904). Casson (1969, 1971) and Rougé (1966) should be consulted for issues pertaining to maritime travel. Dilke remains the classic study of maps and mapmaking (1985); for newer, theoretical perspectives and helpful correctives, see Salway (2001), Brodersen (2001), and Ray Laurence (2001, 2004). More recent bibliography is abundantly available in Horden and Purcell (2000).

For reevaluations of travel in Late Antiquity, especially as it related to imperial ideology, see the work of Ray Laurence (1999, 2001) and the volumes of essays collected by Adams and Laurence (2001) and by Ellis and Kidner (2004).

To learn more about Christian pilgrimage in Late Antiquity, one can turn to the magisterial works of B. Kötting (1950), E. D. Hunt (1982) and R. Wilken (1992). These should be supplemented by Frank's study of pilgrimage to living people, especially to "holy men" (2000), and by Elsner's and Jacobs' illuminating application of postcolonial criticism (Elsner 2000; Jacobs 2004). See Hirschfeld (1992) for the material contribution of monasticism to pilgrimage. For a new appreciation of the extent of ascetic mobility, see Caner (2002) and Dietz (2005).

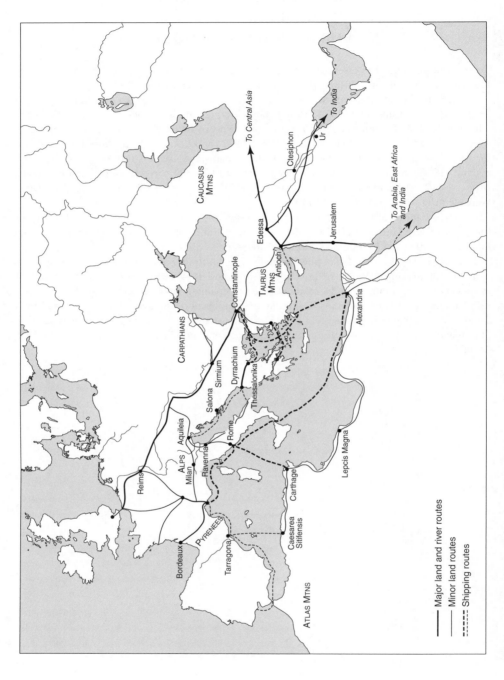

Map 3 Travel and Communication in the Late Empire.

Major land and river routes
Minor land routes
Shipping routes

To Central Asia

To India

Ctesiphon

Ur

Edessa

Jerusalem

To Arabia, East Africa and India

CAUCASUS MTNS

Constantinople

TAURUS MTNS
Antioch

Alexandria

CARPATHIANS

Salona
Sirmium

Dyrrachium

Thessalonika

Aquileia

ALPS
Milan

Ravenna

Rome

Lepcis Magna

Reims

Carthage

PYRENEES

Bordeaux

Tarragona

Caesarea Stifiensis

ATLAS MTNS

CHAPTER NINE

Information and Political Power

Claire Sotinel

Introduction

The idea of information is not an easy one to define, partly because it is so familiar, partly because it is at the core of a wealth of scientific and sociological research unrelated to ancient history. We are living in an information age, which began, according to some historians, at the earliest with the invention of printing and the dissemination of cheaper books, or, according to others, later with the invention of the telegraph – which gave information a speed "essentially separated from the speed of human travel" (Brown and Duguid 2000: 17) – or even with the invention of the computer. Antiquity was not an information age, but this does not mean that information is in itself a modern idea. Information, in the sense (as the *Oxford English Dictionary* puts it) of "communication of the knowledge or 'news' of some fact or occurrence," or of "new information about a subject of some public interest that is shared with some portion of the public" (Stephens 1997: 4), existed long before any age of information. The questions I raise in this chapter are concerned with how much information mattered in the Roman world and how much it changed in Late Antiquity. Although studies on information in premodern societies have interested mainly medievalists (Mostert 1999; Gauvard 2004), ancient historians have not been entirely indifferent to it. Many studies have been devoted to the history and organization of the *cursus publicus*, a sophisticated system of imperial post allowing official messengers to circulate at high speed and in safety throughout the empire (Naudet 1858; Pflaum 1940; Di Paola 1999; Kolb 2000); to the *frumentarii* and *agentes in rebus*, administrative agencies whose specific purpose was to circulate information (Giardina 1977; Carrié 1999); to military intelligence (Lee 1993; Austin and Rankov 1995), diplomatic relations (Gillett 2003) and archives (Demougin 1994). The proceedings of two conferences on information in the ancient world have been recently published (Andreau and Virlouvet 2002; Capdetrey and Nelis-Clément 2006). Moatti 2006 considers the same range of questions for an earlier period. A recent "Shifting Frontiers in Late Antiquity" meeting was focused on "Travel, Communication and Geography in Late Antiquity" (Ellis and Kidner 2004). But to my knowledge, there is only one book specifically devoted to the question of information in all its different aspects. Sian Lewis's work, *News and Society in the Greek Polis*, when it was published in 1996, opened a new field of investigation, and it is surprising that no similar work has been done on the Roman world, for the transformation of City into Empire changed dramatically the function and the conditions of information.

This chapter is no substitute for such a study, and not just because it concerns only developments in Late Antiquity. I aim to show, rather, how interesting and fruitful it would be to undertake serious work on the subject. I am mainly concerned here with political information. In the first part, I shall investigate the possible role played by political information in the Late Roman Empire. Then I shall expound the changes in information control during the period: the increasing sophistication, the concurrence of new nonofficial systems of information, and the emergence of new, more fragmented, information patterns. In conclusion, two questions will be addressed: how are the changes in information related to the political changes of the empire, including the creation of separate kingdoms in the west? How can the history of information in the ancient world contribute to the history of information in general?

Information and Politics in the Roman World

There is no political power without information; spreading news and exercising political control are closely related (see Map 3 on travel and communication in the late empire). The emperor must know and must inform. He must know about his potential resources in order to be able to spend them and, what is perhaps more important in the Roman Empire, to avoid fraud. He must know as much as possible about his entourage, in order to prevent plots and other political threats. He must also know something about the opinion of the citizens, in order to avoid revolts and all kinds of unrest that might challenge his power. He must know about the policies of foreign countries, naturally in time of war, but also in peacetime, to prevent or prepare for conflict. In addition, the emperor must publicize his decisions, so that they can acquire the force of law governing the whole empire. The larger the empire, the more crucial it is for the central power to know what happens in its territory and to be able to circulate its decisions. The larger the empire, the more difficult the task. We have plenty of documents about public information, made necessary not only by the need for "disseminating the knowledge of Roman rules and Roman procedures," but also to inspire the "provincial loyalty" required for the survival of the empire (Ando 2000: 78). For a long time, the well-known imperial policy of leaving as much autonomy as possible to the cities helped to limit the need for exchanging information between center and periphery. The delicate balance between central power and local autonomy was one of the keys to Roman success, and it is certainly one of the most fascinating objects of study in political history. Nevertheless, imperial power took care to improve the traditional ways of transmitting information. Much work has been devoted to the *cursus publicus*, which is often seen as emblematic of Roman control over the territory. The *cursus publicus* was a sophisticated system of *relais de postes* under the care of the imperial authorities. The faster system, the *cursus velox*, allowed official envoys (so the evidence of the *Theodosian Code* suggests) to travel anything between 50 and 80 km per day (Stoffel 1994: 163; see Ramsay 1925). Such speed would seem slow nowadays, but it was superior by far to any other means of communication, and that is precisely what mattered: the important point in matters of political information is not so much absolute but relative speed; to be the first to know is the key to efficiency (Van Creveld 1985: 22, quoted in Lee 1993: 163).

Ancient historians were very conscious that relative speed was important. Let us examine a significant example of political information, related by Ammianus: the double announcement of Julian's death and of the peace of Nisibis in AD 363 (Amm. Marc. 25. 8–10; see Zos. *Hist. eccles.* 3. 33. 1; 3. 35. 1–2 ; Chauvot 1988: 133–5). From Ur, in Chaldea, the newly elected emperor Jovian sent the military tribune Memoridus and the *notarius* Procopius to Illyricum and Gaul to announce the death of Julian, and the elevation of Jovian to the rank of Augustus (Amm. Marc. 25. 8. 8; all translations by John C. Rolfe). First, they were to go to Sirmium to meet Lucillianus, Jovian's stepfather, to bring him the official documents (*codicilles*) that would give him new authority as *magister equitum et peditum*, and to ask him to go to Milan to "attend to any difficulties there, or if ... any new dangers should arise, to resist them" (25. 8. 9).

Beside these official instructions and documents, the messengers had also been given a secret letter (*secretiores ... litteras*) to be given to Lucillianus, carrying more complex instructions: he was to organize a group of trustworthy people who might work for the emperor, to avoid any movement of protest against him. The two messengers had their own "secret mission" too: they were expected to "set the course of events in a favourable light, and wherever they went, to agree with each other in spreading the report that the Parthian campaign had been brought to a successful end [*extollere seriem gestorum in melius, et rumores quaqua irent, uerbis diffundere concinentibus, procinctum Parthicum exitu prospero terminatum*]" (25. 8. 12).

Speed was decisive for the success of the mission. The emissaries were to "hasten their journey by adding night to day, to put into the hands of the governors and the military commanders of the provinces the messages of the new emperor, to secretly sound the sentiments of all of them, and to return speedily with their replies, in order that as soon as it was learned how matters stood in the distant provinces, timely and careful plans might be made for safeguarding the imperial power" (25. 8. 12). According to Ammianus, they fulfilled their mission in four months – that is, they covered an average of 65 km per day: not much less than the maximum speed of the *cursus velox*; and the difference can easily be explained by the fact that the same men did the whole journey, without relays, and that they had to stop in Illyricum (Chauvot 1988: 133; Stoffel 1994: 163). And yet, even at such a speed, they were too slow, since "meanwhile rumour, the swiftest messenger of sad events, outstripping these messengers, flew through provinces and nations" (25. 8. 13).

This story tells us much about the importance of information in the Roman political world. Political allegiance in the provinces – essential to the unity of the empire – depended on the capacity of the imperial authorities to control the spreading of news. To succeed, the emperor had to be able to convey his decisions at a distance (here, the appointment of new officers, precise orders given to Lupicinus), to control the quality of the news (here, to give a positive interpretation of the military situation, a goal he can reach only, in this case, through manipulation), and to get reliable information in order to make wise political decisions. If any one of the three conditions was lacking, the power of the emperor was under threat.

Actually, not all three of the tasks given to the messenger were fulfilled in our example with the same success. The performative information was dutifully and efficiently transmitted: Lupicillus did indeed become *magister militum*, he did indeed go to Milan and settle things there. The propaganda information did not go as well: not only does Ammianus note that rumor was swifter than official messengers but, when Lucillianus arrived in Rheims to take control of the army (Amm. Marc. 25. 10. 6–7), a subordinate official who had cause to fear the new general "falsely asserted that Julian was still alive and that a man of no distinction had raised a rebellion; in consequence of his falsehoods a veritable storm broke out among the soldiery and Lucillianus and Seniauchus were killed." This episode suggests that the two imperial envoys had failed in spreading the news of Jovian's legitimacy, to say nothing of alleged success in Persia. It suggests, too, that neither the rumor of the disaster endured by the Roman army in its war with Persia, correct as it was, nor the official news brought by the messengers, had reached the Gallic army. Finally, the gathering of information was only partially successful. Indeed, the two messengers could transmit the "sad news" of Lupicinus' ultimate failure, but they did not know that "the Gallic army embraced with favour the rule of Jovian"; it took other imperial messengers to carry this message to the emperor, more or less at the same time (Amm. Marc. 25. 10. 8).

Such an episode demonstrates how important and complex a role information played in political matters. Did this role change in Late Antiquity? The reorganization of the imperial administration in the late third and fourth centuries certainly increased the need for political information but, in many respects, continuity is more striking than change. We do not know of any particular technical or institutional innovation: the *cursus publicus* was organized in the reign of Augustus and the new body of *agentes in rebus*, created at the beginning of the fourth century (Seeck 1901; Reincke 1935), was the direct successor of the *frumentarii* known in the High Empire. Yet the Late Roman Empire improved its control of information, while the pattern of news spreading changed mainly under the influence of the political fragmentation of the empire. A third change in the field was the birth of a new information network between Christian churches, which sometimes interfered with other channels of communication. But this is too vast a subject to be addressed in this chapter (see Leyerle (ch. 8), Haines-Eitzen (ch. 17), and Lim (ch. 33)).

An Increasing Need for Circulation of News

There is no doubt that Late Antiquity saw reinforced political control of communication and serious improvement in the circulation of news. This was true everywhere in the empire in the fourth century, and was still true in the east until the sixth century and later. A larger and more centralized administration, a characteristic feature of the Later Roman Empire, developed an "enhanced ability to collect, collate, and retrieve information, by the use of skilled personnel primarily dedicated to specialist administrative tasks" (Kelly 2004: 1). A good impression of the changes in this matter is given by a law of AD 321: "On account of the remissness of the judges who delay the execution of the imperial orders, We have dispatched various men to the different provinces to report to Our knowledge the matters which they see have been promoted by diligence and those that they blame on the ground that they are ruined by sloth" (*Cod. Theod.* 15. 1. 2). It is here a matter of public building, but the process of centralization is clearly defined, as well as the key role played by information in this process: because the emperor cannot trust the local people in charge, he sends envoys whose only task is to gather information, which can lead to political action. Though Roman centralization was never as complete as used to be thought, whatever effort was made in that direction needed more information. Army, administration, and taxes were of course the most demanding areas. Justinian's law settling the fiscal system in AD 545 gives a striking image of a centrally controlled empire (Justinian, *Nov.* 223):

> Every year, the praetorian prefects worked out the global tax sum to be required for the year, taking into account, above all, the costs of war, the main variable in the budget. These sums had a basic stability, but the presupposition that tax levels could change regularly is assumed by a wide range of sources, and was a consistent feature of Roman and indeed post-roman tax system. The rates, set out in great detail, were communicated to provincial governors and thence, by formal proclamation, to cities, whose councillors had the task of ensuring collection, overseen by other councillors and/or by central government officials, in an ever-changing set of institutional protocols, as *curiales* or officials thought out new loopholes or abuses, which were corrected by later legislation. (Wickham 2005: 71)

Wickham's impressive summary might exaggerate slightly the efficiency of the imperial system of taxation, but it rightly stresses the importance of information in such a sophisticated tributary empire.

Another reason why the need for information increased in Late Antiquity was the fact that, for most of the time between the reign of Diocletian and the end of the Western Roman Empire, there was more than one emperor. Portraits of emperors, painting or statues, had always been widespread in the empire; but only with the fourth century do we have evidence of a systematic policy of sending portraits at the beginning of a reign (Zanker 1983; Ando 2000: 228–32). During the last years of the Tetrarchy, when Constantine was hailed emperor by his troops in Britain in 306, he sent his laureate portrait to Galerius, then the senior Augustus. After some hesitation, Galerius accepted Constantine as his junior colleague and sent him the imperial *insignia*. At a distance, tokens of power had been exchanged, as a substitute for an actual meeting (Lactant. *De mort. pers.* 25; Bruun 1976: 124). In this case, news was part of a political action: by sending the *insignia*, Galerius had not simply expressed an opinion but had made Constantine a legitimate emperor. The use of a medium (the laureate image or the imperial *insignia*) was made necessary by the distance between the two emperors. We do not know that Galerius sent the portrait of Constantine on to the provinces, but that was still the rule.

In the late fifth century, when Anthemius became emperor in the west, he sent a legation to Constantinople to meet the eastern emperor Leo. After having received the embassy and accepted the laureate image of the new emperor, Leo commanded "that this portrait of his, joined with ours, shall share the same honours as our portrait to the delight of all our people, so that all the cities joyfully shall realize that the rulers of both parts of the empire act in concert and that we have been united into one with His Indulgence." The fact is recorded as part of imperial protocol in Constantine VII Porphyrogennetos' tenth-century work *On the Administration of the Empire* (*De administrando imperio* 1, quoted by Bruun 1976: 124). (Although this passage is a later interpolation, suppressed in the most recent edition of the text, it probably reflects a contemporary source.) Here, the dissemination of imperial images was clearly a way of asserting the unity of the empire, precisely at a time when the threat of division is high.

We hear from Theophilus, bishop of Alexandria at the end of the fourth century, that imperial portraits were "painted and set up in the midst of the marketplace"; and these images were used as substitutes for the actual presence of the emperor. They were to be treated with great respect and were displayed in the place of honor during spectacles (Ando 2000: 212; see *Cod. Theod.* 8. 11. 3, "if by chance We display the sacred imperial countenances to the eager multitude"). Such portraits were part of the display of imperial authority and, in this area as in many, the late empire was a time of both continuity and creative innovation. While imperial portraits were no less ubiquitous than in earlier periods (Ando 2000: 232–45), the semantics of imperial imagery changed in a remarkable way, stressing the superiority of the emperor over other men, his privileged link with the divinity. Moreover, at the end of the fourth century, Christian symbols were included in the representation of power (on statues, on coins, and on mosaic portraits), and new opportunities for display were seized upon – for example, in churches (Elsner 1998: 53–87).

Using the same language as emperors, the Ostrogoth Theoderic, king in Italy AD 493–526, had his image depicted on a mosaic in the church of S. Vitale in Ravenna. As soon as the Byzantines regained control over Italy, after twenty years of war against the Goths, Justinian had this image replaced by his own, so communicating in a lavish way his legitimate authority to the Christian population of the city, which was at the time the capital of Italy.

A Permanent Search for Political Control

To meet such an increasing need for information, the imperial government never ceased to improve its courses of action to secure it. Even if the *cursus publicus* did not improve its speed, it was carefully kept under imperial control. Both its functions, carrying goods directed to the *fiscus* or the *res privata* and transmitting information, were of crucial importance for the emperor. The many texts of the *Theodosian Code* dealing with this matter repeat that the provinces were responsible for the expenses of maintaining the *cursus publicus* (paying for the animals, their food, probably the buildings) – and a heavy responsibility it was – but it remained strictly under imperial control, run and controlled by imperial agents, all its employees, mule drivers, wagoners, or veterinarians paid by the emperor (*Cod. Theod.* 8. 5. 31). Even more important, the emperor was careful to control the quality and the number of people allowed to use the *cursus*. Warrants could be given only by imperial authority, under the control of *agentes in rebus* specially charged with this task. If there was any doubt about the authenticity of a warrant, only judges could decide (*Cod. Theod.* 8. 5. 8, AD 354; 8. 5. 8, AD 357; 8. 5. 12, AD 362; 8. 5. 22, AD 365; 8. 5. 32, AD 371). One obvious goal of such a policy was to spare the resources of the state, but another, no less important, was to authenticate the messengers as representing the emperor.

The techniques of administration became more sophisticated, but in practice, much depended on the local political situation. In the east, the *cursus publicus* underwent many reforms during the reign of Leo and Justinian, mostly aimed at reducing the cost (Leo: *Cod. Just.* 12. 50. 22;[1] Justinian: *Nov.* 17. 9; 134. 1; see Stoffel 1994: 159–60). The historian Procopius of Caesarea disapproved greatly of Justinian's reform:

> For the Roman Emperors of earlier times, by way of making provision that everything should be reported to them speedily and be subject to no delay, – such as the damage inflicted by the enemy upon each several country, whatever befell the cities in the course of civil conflict, or of some unforeseen calamity, the acts of the magistrates and of all others in every part of the Roman Empire – and also, to the end that those who conveyed the annual taxes might reach the capital safely and without delay or risk, had created a swift public post extending everywhere, in the following manner. (Procop. *Anecdota*, 30. 2)

In this passage, Procopius clearly underlines the link between the *cursus uelox* and the *cursus clabularius* devoted to heavy transports of goods. The link between taxation and information was more than the sharing of the same postal system.

---

[1] Political information (which is what I have concentrated on) is only part of the story. On several occasions, we have observed the role played by the spreading of Christianity and the expansion of the church through the redirection of interest toward religious matters, or the role played by bishops in the spreading of news or the writing of history. These are only a few aspects of a much wider history that has still to be written. Another feature is the role that information played in everyday life, especially for those who were not news-hungry by profession, as were historians, administrators, or bishops. What did others expect in the matter of speed, accuracy, and frequency? When the holy Mary the Egyptian, whose life was written in the sixth century, was discovered by the monk Zosima after forty-two years of solitary life in the desert, she began to flee to avoid the meeting; but when the monk at last caught up with her, she said: "Man, why did you come to see a sinful woman? Why did you want to see a poor woman bare of any virtue? However, as the Holy Spirit has guided you up to this point, so that you can do something for me in my old age, tell me: what is happening among the Christian people? How are the kings? How is the business of the Church going?" (*Vit. S. Mariae Aegyptiae* 2. 14). Even one so lowly and remote could not shake off entirely a need to be informed.

In the west, local situations were more varied. In Britain, according to archaeo-logical evidence, the post stations were abandoned already at the end of the third century, and only a few were restored in the fourth century (Black 1995: 76–88). In Italy, the *cursus publicus* is often said to have collapsed at the end of the fifth century but, if this was the case, it was restored by the Gothic king Theoderic, who was well aware of its importance: "Thanks to it both the efficiency of the embassies and the speed of our decisions are secured: it supplies efficiency to our royal power through various orders; it enriches our treasure by frequent collections" (Cassiod. *Var.* 5. 5; see Stoffel 1994: 157–9). In Africa, the Vandals made some use of it after they conquered Proconsularis, as did the Visigoths in Spain and the Burgundians in Gaul (Africa: Diesner 1968; Spain: Arce 1990; Burgundy: Ganshof 1928: 81 n. 6). It would be misleading to say that the collapse of the *cursus publicus* disrupted the flow of information. As we shall see later, it was rather the change of interest in news – what specialists in information sciences sometimes call "newsworthiness" – that lay behind that collapse.

The centralized organization of the *cursus publicus* went hand in hand with the development of the body known as the *agentes in rebus*. Probably created under the Tetrarchy to replace the hated *frumentarii*, their functions were complex, but most often related to political control: junior agents served as horseback couriers; they could then serve in almost all the major offices of the empire; they depended on the *magister officorum* and were renowned for their efficiency, their *esprit de corps*, and their corruption (Stoffel 1994: 135–7; Carrié 1999). Ammianus paints a dark picture of them as people always involved in political plots and other intrigues (Amm. Marc. 14. 11; 15. 3; 15. 5). The emperor Julian disliked them and reduced their number, but it grew again after his death. Recent historical research has proved that they were not "secret agents," as old translations often call them, being much more versatile civil servants; but their nickname of *curiosi* proves how important gathering infor-mation was among their other tasks (Giardina 1977; Carrié 1999).

A law of AD 430 reduced their number to 1,174, possibly both for east and west (*Cod. Theod.* 6. 27. 23), but another under the reign of Leo (AD 457–74) set it at 1,248 (*Cod. Iust.* 12. 20. 3) for the east only (they didn't exist any more in the west). Their increasing number and importance is inseparable from the permanent effort to improve the administration that is so characteristic of the Late Roman Empire. A. H. M. Jones considered such a feature one of the major causes of the decline of the Roman Empire: it is now often seen as one of its major achievements (Jones 1964: 401–10; 601–6; Kelly 2004: 1–7).

On the other hand, information probably remained a more basic element in the conduct of foreign relations. Foreign embassies were sent only on specific occasions, to prevent war or to negotiate some isolated problem; being a diplomat was not a profession, not even a recognized specific skill (Lee 1993: 32–48). Interior embassies from cities to the imperial court were still paid for by municipal authorities, and were usually forbidden to use the *cursus publicus*: the emperor preferred to rely on the reports of imperial officers rather than having to deal directly with provincials. This did not prevent provincials sending petitions, either to the governor or, less often, directly to the emperor. Such a course of action was not always successful, as the famous affair of the count Romanus suffices to demonstrate. When Lepcis Magna was attacked by nomadic tribes in AD 363 and could not get the help of the Roman army led by the *comes per Africam* Romanus, the provincial council sent two legates to the emperor Valentinian, then in Trier, "to tell him fearlessly of the lamentable ruin of the province," bring a complaint against the *comes*, and ask for help. This first embassy only launched an inquiry. A second one, sent in AD 365, when the first legates had yet to return home, fared even worse: one of the legates died in Trier, and two others were condemned to have their tongues cut out. Even though they managed to flee in time to avoid the terrible penalty, their failure was patent (Amm. Marc. 28. 6. 5–28; see Coşkun 2004). At the same period, however, petitions were common and imperial legislation was often an answer to letters or *suggestiones* from officials or sometimes from private persons (Millar 2002a). In this last case, especially in the east, the author of the petition was most often an ecclesiastical figure, bishop or holy man, who was able to inform the emperor directly of local problems. The case of Appion, bishop of Syene in Upper Egypt, is well known: he asked Theodosius II to place more troops in southern Egypt, and obtained direct satisfaction when the *dux* of the Thebaid received orders as Appion had asked (Millar 2002a).

Political fragmentation in the west had other consequences for patterns of political information. We know very little of their inner organization during Late Antiquity; what had previously come within the scope of ordinary administrative business (like reports from governors to the emperor, petitions, etc.) became, instead, a matter of diplomatic relations. Andrew Gillett has recently stressed the similarities between internal and external embassies, suggesting that the latter were actually not very different from the former (Gillett 2003: 6). But even if the vocabulary and the procedures stayed more or less unchanged, their incidence changed, as well as the occasions and the level of decision. As Gillett writes, "Embassies and envoys were important during the fragmentation of the West because disunity gives rise not only to conflict but also to communication" (Gillett 2003: 3). Instead of a centralized pattern of information, to and from the capital, a pattern of multilateral communication emerged, probably much nearer to the modern concept of diplomacy than foreign embassies in the Roman Empire.

Information and Public Opinion

The imperial regime of Late Antiquity used no less propaganda than the less authoritarian Augustan regime of the first two centuries, and this propaganda was addressed not only to the highest groups of the society – for example, the privileged group of citizens inhabiting the city of Rome – but also to a wider range of the population.

As we have seen, the attitude of Jovian at the beginning of his reign shows that propaganda and rumor mattered almost as much as the spreading of imperial orders or the gathering of information for the emperor. This was true not only in periods of political or military crisis. The care the imperial administration took to inform the population of the Roman world of the laws of the empire, the name and image of the rulers, or the fate of the army, though no novelty in Late Antiquity, tended to increase.

As Ammianus bitterly notes, all victories were imperial, even when the emperor had not been present at the action. It was not really an "arrogant lie," as Ammianus claims, when Constantius celebrated Julian's victories in Gaul on his own behalf (Amm. Marc. 16. 12. 69) or, if it was a lie, it was no more than all emperors had done since Augustus. But the practice may have become more systematic and more sophisticated than it had ever been before. Ammianus speaks of the *laureatae litterae*, the letters wreathed in laurel, which were sent to the provinces to proclaim imperial victory. Such letters were occasions of public celebration and had become so frequent and so expensive that at least two laws were published to control these excesses (*Cod. Theod.* 8. 11. 2, AD 365; 12. 13. 4, AD 379). A Greek inscription in Rome dating from the fourth century probably offers testimony to such a celebration, in this case over the announcement of a victory by an *angelliaphoros*, a "bearer of news" (Mazzarino 1974; inscription *IGRom.* 69; see Herodian 8. 6. 6–8).

The accession of new emperors or the gaining of military victories were not the only occasions for the central power to send information to the population of the empire. The promulgation of the new consuls is compared in texts of law to other "auspicious announcements," such as victories or triumphs; the main difference is that it happened at regular intervals, every year, and was announced, in the words of a law of AD 365, "throughout the Empire" (*Cod. Theod.* 8. 11. 1, AD 364; 8. 11. 2, AD 365; 8. 11. 3, AD 369; Bagnall et al. 1987: 26). The consular system was used by the emperors to date their laws, edicts, letters of all sorts and, in most of the provinces of the empire, it was used to date contracts, testaments, or other private acts with legal force, and quite often, especially in the fourth century, funerary inscriptions (Bagnall et al. 1987: 58–84, also 28–9). The dissemination of the official formula, which was used with a remarkable uniformity, is attested by Egyptian papyri and tells a lot about the capacity of the Later Roman Empire to control massive diffusion of information on a regular basis (Bagnall et al. 1987: 26, 67–9). In the same way, the imperial law had to be disseminated in all provinces, as is expressly stated in the first book of the *Theodosian Code*: "We do not permit any person either to be ignorant of or to pretend ignorance of the constitutions which have been carefully weighed with long deliberation by Our Serenity" (*Cod. Theod.* 1. 1. 2). The correct dissemination of the law was even more important in a divided empire. To insure that "any law in one part of this very closely united Empire [shall] be valid in the other part, on condition that it does not rest upon doubtful trustworthiness or upon a private assertion," "from that part of the Empire in which it will be established, it shall be transmitted with the sacred imperial letters, it shall be received in the bureaus of the other part of the Empire also, and it shall be published with the due formality of edicts" (*Cod. Theod.* 1. 1. 5). We should remember that the imperial law expresses an ideal image of the empire rather than a realistic one, but the principle of law itself rests on an efficient network of communication (see Humfress, ch. 25). The *Theodosian Code* itself was promulgated in Constantinople on October 29, AD 437, was presented to the Roman Senate on December 25, AD 438, and was due to go into effect on January 1, AD 439, a very short delay indeed (*Nov. Theod.* 1).

It was not only new information that was disseminated all over the empire. The emperor used various kinds of media to convey what he wanted the people to know or to believe. Coins or milestones were used as support for basic imperial messages. In Late Antiquity, the legends and images on coins or medallions systematically advertised imperial ideology – genealogical claims, religious affiliation, affirmation of power over barbarians (Ando 2000: 215–28). Milestones also served as a common medium for propaganda. The name of the emperor who had ordered the construction or the repair of the road, which was usually inscribed on these markers, became more and more important. In the classical period, the main inscription was the distance to the nearest city; in Late Antiquity, it was formulaic praise of the emperor. Systematic studies of milestones have been carried out in Italy and Africa; in both cases, there are peaks in their production during the reign of Maxentius (AD 294–306) and of Magnus Maximus (AD 383–8). It has been noted that in the reign of Magnus Maximus, the inscriptions are almost completely uniform, with expressions also used on coins (Italy: Laurence 2004; Africa: Salama 1987). This suggests that these emperors, who both had great difficulty in asserting their legitimacy (they are both labeled "tyrant" by official historiography), worked out new ways to make their claims known to as many inhabitants of the empire as possible. To put it simply, they had a policy of communication.

It is difficult to understand why such an authoritarian regime was so eager to advertise its virtues. Clifford Ando does not hesitate to speak of "mass communication," "public opinion," and "consensus" in his analysis of provincial loyalty in the Roman Empire (Ando 2000). I am more hesitant. We need to be sure of who the actual addressees of such sophisticated political communication were. All the sources we have, including inscriptions, can only testify to the reaction of an urban elite of literate men, who were, as members of the local *curiae*, personally involved in the administration of the empire; their loyalty was indeed necessary to its survival. Some sources occasionally mention more ordinary people, like the crowds gathered to listen to imperial announcements. But did the imperial power care about their reactions? I would not exclude the possibility that the main recipient of all the ideological discourse was the imperial administration itself, and that it is all a question of self-justification and self-perception (for the earlier period, see Eck 1998).

Information and the Political Fragmentation of the Empire

For all the efforts made, the late Roman Empire was never in complete control of the spreading of news. Every political crisis brought problems of communication, of which both imperial authorities and public opinion were well aware. At the end of the fourth century, at a time of crisis between the two *partes imperii*, the Greek historian Eunapius complained about the difficulty of gathering reliable news:

> During the time of Eutropius the eunuch (AD 395–399) it was impossible to include in a history an accurate account of events in the West. For the length and duration of the sea-voyage made the reports late and useless because they were out of date, as if they had fallen into some chronic and long-drawn-out illness. If any officials or soldiers had access to information on political activity, they related it as they wished, biased by friendship or hostility or a desire to please someone. And if you brought together three or four of them with conflicting versions as witnesses, there would be a great argument which would proceed from passionate and heated interjections to a pitched battle. They would say: "Where did you get this from?" "Where did Stilicho see you?" "Would you have seen the eunuch ?" so that it was quite a task to sort out the tangle. From the merchants there was no reasonable information, since they either told many lies or said what they wished to profit from. (Eunap. *Hist.* 56, fr. Blockley 1981: 74)

This is sometimes read as an indication of growing difficulties arising from the political division of the empire (Chauvot 1988), but it says even more about the difference between official and unofficial communication.

A few years later, when Alaric and the Goths were threatening Rome and the emperor Honorius, Theodosius II published a law attempting to block all circulation of information between the west and the east, specifying that "It must be overseen with the same diligence that if the intruder should say that he has messages from the aforesaid Emperor to any other person than Me, the bearer shall be detained, and the sacred imperial letter, with all the documents, shall be sealed and transmitted to My Clemency" (*Cod. Theod.* 7. 16. 2). According to Fergus Millar, it would be misleading to think that the emperor was able to have such an extended control over information: the decision was directly caused by the usurpation of Attalus (Millar 2002a: 581). This is certainly true, but the text shows how much the imperial power was aware of the importance of information. The usurper and the Goths left Italy in AD 412, and the blockade was probably lifted at the time, but the text was considered important enough to be collected among the laws of the *Theodosian Code*. According to the fifth-century church historian Socrates, "When the Emperor Honorius died, Theodosius – now sole ruler – having received the news, concealed the truth as long as possible, misleading the people sometimes with one report, and then with another. But he privately dispatched a military force to Salonae, a city of Dalmatia, that in the event of any revolutionary movement in the West there might be resources at hand to check it" (Socrates, *Hist. eccl.* 7. 22). Manipulating information clearly was a response to political crisis and, at the same time, a crisis in information was considered as a symptom of political crisis.

Much of our evidence about crisis in information is linked to the division of the empire into two parts run by two distinct administrations. How much this division affected the patterns of information in the Roman world and to what extent these changes in the spreading of news and information contributed to the political fragmentation of the west are questions too important to be addressed in such a brief essay. It will be enough to raise some important questions.

We have already seen that the division of the empire created new needs in communication, as well as new formal channels of communication like, for example, the announcement of new reigns. At the same time, some traditional channels of communication became less efficient. The most eloquent sign of this is the transformation of the use of the consulate in administrative documents. In AD 411, the name of the western consul (no less than the emperor Honorius himself) was for the first time not correctly quoted in administrative documents in the east. "It seems clear that they did not receive the usual notification from the western court (presumably because of the dislocation in Italy), and, rather than guess, they took the unprecedented step of proclaiming the eastern consul alone, adding the cumbersome saving formula 'and whoever shall have been announced' " (Bagnall et al. 1987: 17). What could have been an accident, due to the specific situation of Italy at the time, was actually the first step in a continuing evolution. The systematic study of the use of consular dating has shown that "as the fifth century progressed, the dissemination of the new consular names took longer and longer not only between the East and the West, but even within the two halves of the Empire" (Bagnall et al. 1987: 33). This is probably more important as a symptom of information crisis than a instance of an emperor's attempt to block or distort information. It was due less to any sort of actual difficulty of communication (the intensity of clerical communication at the same time shows that there was no problem in traveling: Sotinel 2004 and forthcoming) than to a change of newsworthiness. It reveals a loss of interest in what happens in the other part of the empire.

The tendency became more marked in the west because of political fragmentation. Some of the new kingdoms were rather isolated and their inhabitants had little possibility of gathering news. This is the case in the Galician kingdom, where Hydatius wrote his *Chronicle* in AD 469, "at the edge of the entire world" (Hydatius, *Chron.*, *praef.* 1). There is something moving in the scrupulous way he stresses his lack of information and his desire to gather more. Clearly in his case, gaps in his account of contemporary events have two different explanations: a selective interest that gave priority to ecclesiastical matters, and the difficulty of gathering news. This latter difficulty may explain in part why he names only one embassy to an eastern emperor, or why he ignores the diplomatic activity preceding Attila's invasion of Gaul (Gillett 2003: 54); but selective interest can be the only explanation for his ignorance of the name of some bishops of Jerusalem or Alexandria. As he himself plainly notes, "Who had been the successors of the aforementioned Arians and the predecessors of John as bishops of Jerusalem, Hydatius, who is writing this, had no way of knowing," and "the author of this work did not know who presided over the church of Alexandria after Theophilus" (Hydatius, *Continuatio Chron.* 296, 299: see Gillett 2003: 50–3).

Hydatius is probably more explicit about the state of his knowledge than other chroniclers, but the double tendency toward a more circumscribed horizon (especially in terms of geography) and a lack of reliable sources of information can be observed in all western historians after the fourth century. It would be worth while taking a fresh look at their work in this light (see Woods, ch. 24).

Interestingly enough, the same evolution can be observed in eastern chronicles, in areas where centralized imperial communication is still working perfectly well. The *Chronicle* of Pseudo-Joshua the Stylite, written at the very end of the fifth century, depicts a society where all the traditional tools of imperial communication are still functioning. The entry of the new governor and the presentation of imperial edicts regulated the public life of Edessa, the capital city. For example, the author describes the arrival of an edict of the emperor Anastasius remitting the *chrysargyron*: "This edict did not go only to Edessa but to all cities of the Roman domain. [In Edessa] the whole city rejoiced. They all dressed up in white, from the greatest to the least, and carrying lighted candles and burning censers, to the accompaniment of psalms and hymns, they went out to the *martyrion* of Mar Sergius and Mar Simon, thanking God and praising the emperor" (Trombley and Watt 2000: 30). At the time of the chronicler, Edessa was involved in war with Persia, and the text is rich in data on the matter, but the interest of the author lies exclusively in his hometown. Such a change of interest from imperial to local history, even in works claiming to be universal histories, have been noticed in the works of many late antique chroniclers (Bagnall et al. 1987: 47–57; Muhlberger 1990: 267–78). It reveals both a change in the technology of information and in newsworthiness; a change that needs to be investigated as an important part of the transformation of the Roman world (see Humphries, ch. 7).

BIBLIOGRAPHICAL NOTE

There is no general survey of this chapter's subject, but the theme of the circulation of information is touched on in all works concerning the political history of the Roman Empire. It is particularly well covered in Ando 2000 and Millar 2006. For a special discussion of method and the importance of the subject, see Lewis 1996, which is concerned with the Greek city, or Mostert 1999, which provides a systematic methodological treatment for the Middle Ages. Kolb 2000 is a recent discussion of the important subject of the *cursus publicus*. No progress in the study of the subject can be expected except through archaeological discoveries. For Late Antiquity, foreign relations with Eastern neighbors of the empire have been the subject of a magisterial study by Lee 1993, while Gillett 2003 offers interesting views on the transformations that affected political communication at the end of Late Antiquity.

CHAPTER TEN

Mediterranean Cities

S. T. Loseby

When Procopius declared the Romans to be the most city-loving (*philopolides*) of all peoples (*Goth.* 8. 22. 5), it was in the particular context of their preservation of the monuments of the Eternal City despite the vicissitudes of barbarian rule. But the phrase could be said more generally to encapsulate the centrality of the city to Roman conceptions of civilization and culture. The Romans took the city-state model, projected it across their empire, and used it to sustain a world-system. That came about in part because they inherited Greek ideals of the city as a political community, and absorbed into their control a host of cities that were already functioning along such lines. But government through the cities also afforded an immensely practical and inexpensive solution to a problem that perennially confronted the rulers of premodern societies as soon as their polities had expanded beyond a certain point, that of exercising power over distance. The devolution of a substantial degree of autonomy to the level of the city limited the administrative, financial, and military obligations of the Roman state. Meanwhile, it satisfied the political and social aspirations of provincial elites who, in exchange for the regular forwarding of taxes and routine maintenance of order, could initially be left largely to their own devices, retaining their local power within a context defined and secured by Rome.

The ideological attractions and functional advantages of cities as interfaces between central and local authority were perceived to be such that where urbanism did not already exist, it was deemed necessary to invent it. The standard organizational unit of the Roman Empire thus came to be the *civitas* or *polis*, terms that denoted the city itself, but also the surrounding territory for which it was administratively responsible. Every citizen of the empire belonged to one such community, and we might reasonably assume that, for most of them, their city was the effective as well as the conceptual limit of their horizons. Members of the elite might have both the desire and the opportunity to play their part on a wider imperial stage, but in so doing they maintained a lifelong devotion to their *patria*. Where Rome demanded awe, one's hometown inspired love (e.g., Ausonius, *Ordo nob. urb.* 20. 38–40).

The criteria for defining a community as "urban" have been endlessly debated by historians, but civic status was, within the Roman Empire, an essentially juridical category. No comprehensive list of cities exists, but one might crudely estimate that there were perhaps a little under 2,000 communities in and around the late antique Mediterranean that fulfilled the requisite administrative functions. Their distribution was erratic. The urban network in each region had generally been established upon its incorporation into the empire. Since the Romans usually aimed to uphold the social and political status quo in the territories they conquered or absorbed, they tended at that stage to recognize as cities all the communities that had suitable pretensions, so perpetuating the regional settlement hierarchy in its existing evolutionary state. Consequently, there was little uniformity between regions, either in the distribution of cities or in the extent of their dependent territories, which bore no necessary or consistent relationship to their agricultural potential. Rarely was this pattern fundamentally transformed in later centuries. Even after some unusually sustained efforts at administrative rationalization, the late antique diocese of Asiana still contained hundreds of cities, with commensurately small territories. To judge by the number of communities that had bishops, the African urban network was even denser. In Spain and southern Gaul, by contrast, cities could be numbered in the dozens, and those were comparatively few and far between (Jones 1964: Map V, 1064–5).

The persistence of this inconsistent overall pattern did not mean that the urban network was altogether fossilized. Emperors were at liberty to make or break cities, and, because their creation was an acknowledged attribute of good rulership, they liked to be seen to do the former. They might, for example, respond favorably to persons petitioning for the promotion of village communities, who shrewdly tailored their claims to the priorities of the ruler concerned. Both Orcistus in Asia Minor and Maiuma, Gaza's port, owed their elevation under Constantine in part to their professed enthusiasm for the emperor's Christian religion; Julian predictably reversed the latter decision, when Gaza opportunistically appealed (*ILS* 6091; Sozom. *Hist. eccl.* 5. 3. 8–9). Justinian, also no stranger to gesture politics, elevated the headland of Caputvada in Byzacena to civic status to commemorate the fact that his troops had landed there before proceeding to the reconquest of Africa (Procop. *Aed.* 6. 6; see *Vand.* 3. 14. 17). Whether those communities made play of their prior possession of some of the political or architectural trappings of Roman urbanism, or were endowed with them retrospectively, their claim to be cities was in the imperial gift.

In terms of legal status, the Mediterranean cities of Late Antiquity were more equal than before; the subtler gradations of colonial or municipal standing that had existed in earlier periods survived in residual form as matters of civic pride, but had lost their formal significance (Kotula 1974; Lepelley 1992). In practice, of course, they were as diverse as ever. Their infinite variety was generated by the interaction of the economic, topographical, and historical circumstances peculiar to each individual city, the effects of which were only superficially overridden by their incorporation within the Roman Empire. Take, for example, the question of their populations. This is at best an exercise in educated guesswork, but the range of possibility was clearly immense. At the handful of Mediterranean "*mégapoles*" (Nicolet et al. 2000) – Rome, Constantinople, Alexandria, Antioch, and perhaps Carthage – it could run comfortably into six figures. We generally lack any viable data for communities at the other end of the spectrum, but there were certainly micropoles with permanent populations that may never have exceeded a few hundred. In Egypt, where papyrological evidence for private housing provides at least some basis for numerical extrapolation, one recent estimate has postulated fifty major cities with an average population of 25,000 (Bagnall and Frier 1994: 55; see Bagnall 1993: 53; Alston 2002: 331–4). The proportion of the Egyptian population resident in cities is likely to have been particularly high, so urban communities elsewhere in the empire may typically have had rather fewer inhabitants; but this is already to venture into the realm of speculation.

Since they were defined in juridical terms, late antique cities and their territories could therefore be variously large or small, rich or poor, bustling or somnolent, in combinations that exhibit consistency only at the regional level, and then only to a limited extent. Some of them had longer histories than Rome herself, with fully elaborated urban layouts and monumental landscapes that asserted as much; others owed their very existence to imperial fiat and their street-grids to the efforts of Roman surveyors. A buzzing metropolis like Antioch had twenty-four-hour shopping and street lighting (Lib. *Or.* 11. 255–67); lesser cities, then as now, went to sleep at sunset. But, despite their boundless diversity, the majority of Mediterranean cities did share some basic similarities, in both political organization and physical appearance, that allow them to be treated as an analytical category. What is more, their superficial homogeneity in those respects had increased over time as they conformed ever more closely, both by their own volition and in response to official encouragement, to the norms and expectations of the imperial framework within which they were operating.

Constitutionally, Roman cities were governed by an aristocratic city council (the *curia* or *boulê*), a self-selecting body whose members (the "decurions") held office by virtue of a property qualification, for life, and in practice by hereditary right. Architecturally, every self-respecting city needed to look the part; a conventional urban landscape would feature an array of public monuments, amenities, and open spaces, harmoniously assembled within a coherent and, where possible, orthogonal layout. The creation, maintenance, and celebration of this canonical urban aesthetic were in large measure the responsibility of the decurions; for much of the first two centuries AD, they embraced it with great gusto. In the process of competing both individually (for local office and prestige) and collectively (against their peers in neighboring cities), they spent lavishly on buildings and entertainments for their fellow citizens, and made sure to leave a public record of their munificence in thousands of inscriptions. Where cities already existed, they embellished them further; where they did not, they invested massively in their creation. The city thereby became both the quintessential manifestation of Roman civilization and the ultimate symbol of its success in persuading local elites throughout the empire to buy into a shared set of political and cultural values.

Cities can usefully be regarded as "fields of action integral to some larger world ... within which the interactions and contradictions of that larger world are displayed with special clarity" (Abrams and Wrigley 1978: 3). Their representative potential is especially apparent in Late Antiquity. Firstly, because cities were absolutely central to the established dynamics of Roman society, any changes taking place within them were particularly responsive to and constructive of more general political or cultural trends. Second, because Roman urbanism carried such a pronounced visual and monumental identity, the study of cities allows us to appreciate the material as well as the conceptual consequences of such developments, and in turn to explore the further layer of "interactions and contradictions" that emerge when surviving literary or artistic representations of late antique urban life are considered alongside its archaeological realities. Finally, because cities existed everywhere within the empire, and because they all enjoyed some basic features in common, their fortunes can be discussed comparatively within the context of the late antique reformation and subsequent disintegration of the Roman world-system.

To keep this overview within manageable bounds, I shall limit myself thematically to late antique developments within the common urban constitutional and architectural frameworks outlined above, chronologically to the period between the fourth century and the reign of Justinian, and geographically to the cities of the Mediterranean world (excluding Rome and Constantinople, both *sui generis*). Classical urbanism in northwestern Europe and the Danubian provinces had originally been the product of a more artificial and less intensive pattern of development. Although late antique cities here were susceptible to many of the trends prevailing elsewhere, the urban histories of the regions within and behind those frontier zones were conditioned by specific sets of influences that retain a more distinctively regional flavor throughout (Esmonde Cleary 1989: 64–85; Poulter 1992; Loseby 2000, 2006; see Halsall, ch. 27). However, the Mediterranean world sustained a common economic and cultural heritage in Late Antiquity, and Justinian's reconquests fleetingly restored to nine-tenths of it a political integrity from which only the shores of Gaul and much of Spain were excluded. Until the middle of the sixth century, therefore, its cities can be said to have developed within a context that allows broad-brush comparisons to be made, the enormous extent of regional and local variation notwithstanding. Beyond that, however, the regional trajectories of urbanism diverge too far to be contained within an overarching framework.

The reshaping of the late antique city as a political community was the product of the intersection of two parallel trends, neither of which could be said to have caused the other directly, though each of them was intensified by their interdependence. The first of these brought change to cities from without. The reform of the administrative machinery of the Roman state in and after the third century was probably essential to its continued survival, but it undermined the established ethos of civic government in a number of interconnected ways. The centralization of power within a significantly enlarged and more meddlesome imperial bureaucracy left the cities with less freedom to manage their own affairs. The absorption of civic lands and taxes into central coffers similarly deprived them of a regular revenue stream. Although in AD 374 it was enacted that the cities should once again receive a third of their own taxes and of the rents on their former lands, even this partial concession remained at the mercy of imperial financial control (*Cod. Theod.* 4. 13. 7; 15. 1. 18; Jones 1964: 732–4). Meanwhile, the empire continued to rely on the cities for the local operation of the tax system, but monitored their efforts more closely than before. The increase in both the tax burden and the government's determination to realize it made the role of the decurions in its collection and redistribution less appealing, because potentially the financial liabilities were heavy and the personal consequences of failure painful and humiliating (Brown 1992: 53–7). Civic power, in relation to the imperial bureaucracy, was thus declining in status and autonomy, even as the state ratcheted up the demands it made upon its holders.

There are also signs that the political culture of the cities was already changing from within, even before the impact of those developments had begun to bite. The competitive munificence that had contributed so heavily to "the grandeur that was Rome" was less enduring than much of its awesome monumental legacy. The erection of all those buildings and statues, the upkeep of the public cityscape, and the provision of the more evanescent entertainments, feasts, and distributions of food and money that brought it all to life, were the fruit of thousands of grandiose gestures from benefactors, whose displays of pride in their city and goodwill toward their fellow citizens guaranteed them prestige in their lifetime and commemoration after death. In a vivid depiction of the fulsome, formalized expressions of communal gratitude with which such generosity was received, John Chrysostom (*De inani gloria* 4–5; Brown 1992: 83) has the people of Antioch hail a patron of the city "the Nile of gifts"; the preacher's aim was to emphasize the vanity of such moments in a city where his audience could still be dazzled by their glory. By the late fourth century, however, Antioch was exceptionally wealthy and fortunate in its benefactors. The regular (and sometimes superfluous) inundation of the empire's cities with structures and amenities had already slowed to a trickle in many regions, as the flood of benefactions was either cut off at source or diverted into new, Christian channels. Our best indication of the generalized nature of this development, and to some extent of the regional variations in its chronology, is the plummeting in the number of inscriptions that eloquently catalogued such munificence alongside the holding of the civic offices with which it was customarily associated. Such inscriptions tail off as early as the later second century in some areas, only shortly after classical urbanism had been fully realized. The trend becomes increasingly widespread thereafter, and, although bound up with the more general decline of the so-called "epigraphic habit" (MacMullen 1982; see Trout, ch. 12), it is nevertheless symptomatic of the sea-change taking place in the attitudes of the elite to their cities. Before Late Antiquity had even begun, the undertaking of curial office and its associated expenditures had in many communities become a source of resentment rather than of pride (Garnsey 1974; Brown 1978: 27–53).

The structural reforms of the later third century tended in general to consolidate rather than reverse existing trends, and the reformers' approach to civic government was no exception. By then, greater centralization had become not only administratively desirable, but also culturally feasible. By formally reducing the financial resources and political autonomy available to the decurions, imperial policy encouraged the nascent shift in attitudes, pushing up the costs of civic office-holding while further diminishing its already dwindling prestige. The parallel proliferation of posts within government service offered an alternative outlet for personal ambition. Those posts provided an entrée to the charmed circles of imperial power that had largely been denied to earlier generations of provincial elites, and held out the enticing prospect of lifelong escape from the curial cul-de-sac, thanks to the immunity that government service conferred upon its officials. The enthusiastic pursuit of such opportunities by the decurions amply confirms their prevailing mood of disenchantment.

Although some voluntary spending on traditional civic amenities continued to be commemorated in familiar style in the economically flourishing and culturally conservative African provinces of the fourth century (Lepelley 1979–81), epigraphic evidence of such expenditure elsewhere in the west had virtually disappeared by that date, notably in Italy itself (Ward-Perkins 1984: 14–37). In the late antique east, meanwhile, such euergetism did persist, but on a scale significantly reduced by comparison with earlier centuries (Roueché 1989: xix–xxvii). The provision and maintenance of public monuments and amenities became instead part of the competence of provincial governors (*Cod. Theod.* 15. 1, *passim*). They duly dominate the continuing epigraphic record of such activity, and even in Africa, where old habits of munificence died hardest, they take precedence in inscriptions over the civic dignitaries who had actually paid for the works. One such inscription from Lambaesis in Numidia, erected between AD 379 and 383, records the repair of the city's aqueduct and its *curia*, and punningly describes how the latter was thereby rescued from the ravages of time and the unconcern (*incuria*) of older generations (*ILS* 5520; Lepelley 1979–81, ii: 420–1). In other regions, however, it seems the decurions were past caring. For their part, governors were much keener to carry out prestigious new building than humdrum repairs, and they were not shy of stripping lesser cities of their statues and marbles in order to concentrate their efforts on the provincial capitals in which they resided (*Cod. Theod.* 15. 1. 14, AD 365).

Our best evidence for the late antique interaction of those trends derives from the insistent but inconsistent efforts of the imperial government to restrain or to manage their effects. No fewer than 192 laws dating from between AD 315 and 436 are preserved in the *Theodosian Code* under the rubric "concerning the decurions" (*Cod. Theod.* 12. 1), and this legislation was consolidated and further expanded by Justinian a century later (e.g., *Cod. Iust.* 10. 32). Much of it was designed either to narrow the numerous avenues of escape from curial office – via promotion to senatorial rank, the performance of civil or military service to the state, or membership of the clergy – or, since this often proved impracticable or undesirable, to limit the impact of such flight upon the human or financial resources of the cities (Jones 1964: 737–57). The multifarious edicts flit between hard-line and more flexible approaches, but their reiteration of similar themes confirms that their effectiveness was limited and, as usual, their implementation was spasmodic. Some effort was occasionally made to alleviate curial burdens, clearly but fleetingly in the nostalgic reign of Julian, but also under Valentinian I and Valens, when the aforementioned restoration of a proportion of civic revenues was made for the maintenance of public works (*Cod. Theod.* 15. 1. 18, AD 374; 4. 13. 7, AD 375; see 15. 1. 32, AD 395). The considerable routine costs to cities of maintaining the urban landscape were subsequently further reduced by the enactment of legislation permitting the alienation of public buildings, but only if they were redundant or ruined (e.g., *Cod.*

Theod. 15. 1. 40, AD 398). Here again, the state was rationalizing a development that was already under way (see below). But a more radical attempt to transfer responsibility for tax collection from the decurions to the *honorati* (former officials of senatorial rank) never got off the ground, and appears to have been driven more by distrust of the city councillors than by sympathy for their supposed plight (*Cod. Theod.* 12. 6. 9; 12. 6. 5, AD 365). Such radical innovations were in any case exceptional; the state's relentless tinkering with the cogs made only minor adjustments to the operation of the machinery. The basic structural relationship between the imperial and the civic administrations was therefore sustained through to the reigns of Anastasius and Justinian, and its perceived deficiencies provided an ongoing stimulus to the reconfiguration of urban political culture.

The perceptions of the civic leaders alternately coerced or cajoled by this legislation are not widely recorded, unless by a resounding epigraphic silence. But they were much too resourceful simply to accept the burdens thrust upon them by the late antique state. Their machinations are perhaps best brought out in the orations of Libanius, professor of rhetoric at Antioch in the later fourth century, precisely because of an affected reluctance to move with the times that made him seem "tiresome" to contemporaries (*Or.* 2; but see also Cribiore, ch. 16). The old-school virtues of civic government were close to Libanius' heart – and the council house at Antioch within earshot of his classroom (*Or.* 46. 16) – but even as a passionate defender of the councils and an apologist for their members, he was well aware that the latter were complicit in their supposed suffering.

The richer decurions adopted one of two strategies (Jones 1964: 740–57; Liebeschuetz 1972: 174–86). The more obvious was to secure immunity, ideally by using their wealth or influence to obtain one of the numerous real or honorary positions in the imperial service that carried senatorial rank. Their prime motivation in this was probably not money, but status. As *honorati*, they enjoyed significant legal and social privileges and, having successfully leapt the divide between central and local power structures, they ranked above the decurions in civic society. They could enjoy a high political profile wherever they were domiciled, without the expense and tedium of curial obligations. The alternative approach, for those unable to escape altogether, was not simply to shoulder the necessary minimum, but to shift the weight of curial obligations to their advantage. Hierarchies had always existed within the city councils, whether official or informal. The former derived from progress through the sequence of leading civic magistracies and priesthoods and the acquisition of seniority thereby, the latter from advantages of birth, wealth, or connection. Not surprisingly, those two sources of superiority overlapped. When curial office was still something to be desired, the fault-lines inherent within the councils could be concealed beneath the cloak of competition and collective interest. The leading decurions would generally get their way, but there were few real losers as long as playing the game was in itself beneficial. The more that liability for civic liturgies was seen as discreditable, however, the more valuable became their ability to manipulate the allocation of curial responsibilities to their advantage.

The state acknowledged the supremacy of those *principales* in its legislation, but was uncomfortably aware of their oppressive tendencies (Jones 1964: 731 n. 41).

In Antioch, for example, the council was formally divided into three groups, the first of which came to lord it over the others. To Libanius, wedded to traditional ideals of mutual curial interest, this was like rams butting lambs (Lib. *Or.* 48. 40–1). To the *prôtoi* of the council, who retained for themselves such roles as were financially or personally profitable while dumping the more crippling burdens onto their less wealthy or influential colleagues, it was a matter of insuring that the exercise of civic leadership was still worth their while. Weeping crocodile tears about the head-long decline in curial numbers, they obstructed imperial attempts to reverse it. Their active collusion in the escapes of their peers into government service could be motivated by money or the promise of future favors, or, more cynically still, because the withdrawal of their more powerful rivals enabled them to snap up more of the remaining perks of curial office for themselves (Lib. *Orr.* 48–9). From the perspective of the tax-paying peasant, all decurions were tyrants because they ruthlessly exploited their fiscal authority (Salvian, *De Gub.* 5. 18); but some were in a position to be more tyrannical than others, because they were capable of driving their fellows to ruin as well. The superficial unity of the decurions as a caste conceals the substantial inequalities in wealth and power prevalent among them (Lepelley 1983).

The *curia* therefore became an increasingly dysfunctional and anachronistic institution. Its numbers were steadily eroded as the powerful climbed out and the hapless went under, and they were not replenished from below. Its members worked against each other as well as together. Its leaders still had powers worth exploiting, but those were distinctly second-best to the real status that now lay elsewhere. The average decurion became decidedly ordinary; in a sliding scale of fines for Donatists, he is classed alongside the tradesmen and plebs (*Cod. Theod.* 16. 5. 52, AD 412). The emperors still needed the city councils, *faute de mieux*, to underwrite the tax system at the local level, but civic leadership came to devolve upon persons of superior social standing: those of senatorial rank, the handful of centrally appointed local officials, and a new urban potentate in the person of the bishop (Liebeschuetz 2001a: 104–68; see Lizzi Testa, ch. 35). This reconfiguration of civic power was an organic rather than an institutionalized development, its evolution was gradual and varied, and the new ruling bodies it created were never legally or terminologically formalized (Laniado 2002). But such coteries of "leaders," "notables," or "elders" joined the bishops at the head of urban societies throughout the Mediterranean in the fifth and sixth centuries and predictably drew the leading city councillors, in their guise as the major local landowners (*possessores*), into their informal nexus. The Roman state finally caught up with this development, when Anastasius and Justinian assigned legal responsibility for the appointment of leading civic magistrates to this group (*Cod. Iust.* 1. 4. 19, AD 505; 1. 4. 17, AD 491–505; Justinian, *Nov.* 128. 16, AD 545). Meanwhile, Anastasius had stripped the decurions of their tax-allocating powers (and, in a visible assertion of their reduction to the ranks, their formal dress), and instead entrusted that role to centrally appointed *vindices*. Our historical sources retrospectively observe that this move marked the effective end of the councils as organs of urban government (Evagr. *Hist. eccl.* 3. 42; Malalas, *Chron.* 16. 400; Lydus, *Mag.* 3. 49; 1. 28). If Justinian's legislation remained anxious to sustain the decurions thereafter, it was in the derisory capacity of minor urban functionaries.

In the west, political crisis and fragmentation complicated matters immensely, but similar underlying trends are nevertheless apparent. Here too, by the sixth century, city councillors were forfeiting their local political dominance to notables, while the rulers of the emerging successor states often preferred to rely on directly accountable nominees to insure the loyalty and good government of the cities. That resulted in the diffusion of an administrative innovation with its origins in the twilight years of the western empire, namely the appointment of counts to run individual cities (Claude 1964). The *comes civitatis* took over former curial responsibilities for taxation and the maintenance of local order, and administered new military burdens such as troop levies; it was his tricky task to bridge a divide between court and city that was no longer mediated by multiple layers of bureaucracy. The system was much less elaborate than the one that had operated before, but it was still grounded in the existing framework of cities and their dependent territories (Loseby 2006: 83–93). In some Gallic, Spanish, and Italian cities, the city councils did retain a residual function alongside the count, the bishop, and the "magnates" (or some similar social group); but from the mid sixth century onward they fade steadily if erratically from view (Liebeschuetz 2001a: 124–36).

In the fifth and sixth centuries, it was still possible to describe the decurions as the "sinews of the state and the vital organs of the cities" (Majorian, *Nov.* 7, AD 458; see Cassiod. *Var.* 9. 2). Both of those pieties were becoming anachronistic, but especially the latter. Mediterranean cities were able to survive their late antique evisceration because they remained the power bases of a resident elite of serving, former, or honorary officials, and the fiscal system continued to be administered through them. Nor did the end of the curial system of government make any necessary difference to their more general social and economic functions (Whittow 1990). Indeed, the role of the city as the center of its dependent territory had meanwhile been newly and powerfully revitalized by the triumph of Christianity. The mapping of the organization of the Church onto the cellular framework of the empire was still in a formative state in our period, and it would never be wholly or perfectly achieved. Its structure nevertheless conformed, *grosso modo*, to the established pattern of city and territory, so the *civitas* became a pastoral as well as a political and fiscal unit. The bishop oversaw its spiritual life from the city, assisted in his ministrations by a socially privileged and sometimes substantial clerical establishment. He offered a new source of urban-based power and patronage deriving from a familiar combination of financial muscle and social standing, but his judicial and spiritual authority lent them new and significant weight (Rebillard and Sotinel 1998; Rapp 2005a).

The ideal and reality of episcopal behavior, the impact of the Church on public life, and the more general dynamics of the relationship between secular and ecclesiastical power are specifically addressed in other contributions to this volume (see, in addition to Lizzi Testa (ch. 35), Lim and Gaddis, chs. 33 and 34 respectively), so the implications of those developments for cities need be considered here only briefly. It would be simplistic to suggest that bishops filled a power vacuum in urban communities, because the powerful still lived in them. Even so, the role of the bishop did grow into the spaces created by the ongoing reconfiguration of the urban political community. The late antique state was constantly in search of city-based functionaries who might absorb some of the duties of recalcitrant decurions and overburdened governors and their staffs, while at the same time monitoring their abuses of power; but its attempts to square those circles through the agency of secular officials such as the *defensor* met with only qualified success (Frakes 2001). However, the bishops could inhabit the awkward gap between central and local power with confidence, because their authority came from outside those structures and transcended them.

Within their cities, meanwhile, bishops presided over the reorientation of time-honored patterns of patronage. Unlike many other civic leaders, they retained the desire and the duty to minister to the needs of their communities. Imperial benefactions and privileges, combined with private donations, gave them the necessary means. By accepting responsibility for the population as a whole, and not merely for its citizen body, the bishops redefined the notion of the city community to embrace all of its members (Patlagean 1977; Brown 1992). The ideology of Christian philanthropy differed from that of classical munificence in its universal character, an advance that the customary idealization of curial government has tended to obscure. Its realization was nevertheless expressed not just in primary care for the poor and unfortunate, but in familiar and reassuringly solid monumental form. Religious building could be justified as making provision for the welfare of Christian communities in this world and the next, and it satisfied the social expectations of donors, public, and, not least, the bishops themselves. Ambrose warned against monumental extravagance even as he instigated a series of major building projects within Milan (*De Off. Ministr.* 2. 109–10; Krautheimer 1983: 77–81). The channeling of munificence through the Church meant that bishops became urban patrons *par excellence*, rivaled only in the provincial capitals by the governors. Having taken on this role, they tended in the fifth and sixth centuries to see it expand into a more comprehensive supervision of urban politics and monuments, largely with the encouragement of central government, but also in response to its failings. Bishops became linchpins of the otherwise informal political elites of the cities, and the very embodiment of urban status.

That transformation in political culture was paralleled by the emergence of a new late antique urban aesthetic, structured around two main types of public building: walls and churches. Many cities around the Mediterranean were already walled, either as a legacy of past defensive needs that often predated their incorporation into the Roman Empire or as expressions of their particular civic status within it (as colonies, for example). The military insecurity of the late empire brought some of those old wall circuits back into service, subject to appropriate modification and upgrading, or demanded the erection of new ones where none existed (Johnson 1983; Lewin 1991: 9–98). City walls have always carried both practical and symbolic resonance, and in Late Antiquity contemporaries had no difficulty in making a virtue out of what, in many regions, was fast becoming a necessity. Walls were "an adornment for peacetime, a requirement for wartime" (Cassiod. *Var.* 1. 29), and the logical consequence was that they became integral to contemporary conceptions of urbanism. When Procopius outlined Justinian's elevation of Caputvada, on the African coast, to civic status (*Aed.* 6. 8), he gave the building of its walls pride of place in the topographical transformation. At much the same time, Cassiodorus was deftly playing with contemporary expectations of settlement when expatiating upon the charms of Squillace (*Var.* 12. 15. 4–5), the city in Bruttium where his family's estates were concentrated. In the absence of walls, its residents had the best of both worlds – either rural city or urban villa – as they savored both the unimpeded view and the delicious local seafood. Fortifications were indeed unreliable guides to settlement categories, because walls were by no means exclusive to cities, while not every city had a wall. But their existence had become part of the rhetoric and, more often than not, the reality of late antique urbanism. Walls dominate the visual image of the city as portrayed in the *Notitia Dignitatum* or picked out in contemporary mosaics just as surely as they would have cast a long shadow over the daily lives of the majority of urban communities (Ehrensperger-Katz 1969).

If walls were not quite mandatory elements of the late antique urban landscape, churches and other religious establishments were universal. Every city needed a cathedral complex, typically including a number of churches and ancillary buildings, from which the bishop would perform his ministry. From the outset, this was usually located near the heart of the urban area or, if financial, cultural, or spatial constraints had dictated its initial establishment on the periphery, it might subsequently be transferred to a more central site. But this complex was only the core component of the christianization of urban space, as the new waves of state and private munificence orchestrated by the bishops swept over established urban landscapes, incrementally piling up more churches (sometimes of competing religious factions), monastic communities, hostels, and hospitals in their wake (Jaggi and Meier 1997). Basil of Caesarea in Cappadocia was unusual in that he concentrated his charitable foundations in one peripheral area, to the extent that he could be said to have created a "new city" alongside the old (Greg. Naz. *Or.* 48. 63; Sozom. *Hist. eccl.* 6. 34. 9). Most Christian builders operated within the constraints of existing urban layouts that they were obliged as well as eager to reshape. Those gradual changes within cities were matched, particularly in the west, by the more fundamental revolution taking place around their fringes in the cemeteries where, in accordance with Roman law, the dead lay separate from the living (see Rebillard, ch. 15). The recognition that some of the occupants of those tombs were holy meant that their resting places were enshrined within churches that could be every bit as architecturally elaborate as their urban counterparts. Christianity expanded the conception of the urban community to include the poor alongside the citizenry. It also extended the notion of urban space, establishing a suitably monumental setting for the saints in the suburbs, and incorporating them into the regular rhythms of urban life (Brown 1981).

Those twin dynamics of fortification and christianization will have simultaneously influenced the topographical development of the majority of cities in Late Antiquity, but their implications for the perception and the experience of urban space were inherently contradictory. Archaeological evidence has made it abundantly clear that a city's walled area cannot in itself serve as a reliable guide to the extent of urban settlement. In some cities, extramural occupation could be extensive, while in others the walled area might not be fully built up. In any event, the numerous and significant variables involved – particularly with regard to the chronology and extent of wall circuits, which are often hard to date closely or delineate precisely – mean that the relationship between walled area and extent of settlement has to be evaluated on a case-by-case basis. Even so, it can be broadly acknowledged that in the medium term the erection or maintenance of functioning defenses would have exercised a centripetal influence over urban populations. In cities where walls existed and security could not be guaranteed, it made sense to live within them.

The cult of the saints, by contrast, had a centrifugal effect. It regularly drew the community out to the suburbs for the practice of personal devotions or collective celebrations, and occasionally generated the development of subsidiary settlement around the most popular shrines, such as that of Felix at Nola (Paulinus, *Carm.* 28. 177). Such churches created a field of force around the city that could be seen, in conjunction with the more mundane protection afforded by the walls, as safeguarding its inhabitants. The emergence of a new Christian urban identity and topography also surmounted the physical limits imposed by fortification, most visibly when bishops united their congregations in processions through the city gates and out into the sanctified suburbs in fulfillment of the festal calendar proper to each city.

The physical processes of fortification and christianization were also very different in nature. Notwithstanding its scale and complexity, a functioning city wall is essentially a unitary structure, since its defensive function is vitiated by any single weakness within it. Its erection, restoration, or modification were generally matters for central government (*Dig.* 1. 8. 9), and major works were logistically or financially supported by the state; the provision of walls was an *opus imperium* (Modéran 1996). But the considerable effort of routine maintenance could require a substantial contribution from the local community in money, materials, or labor services, and naturally it was neglected until moments of crisis, often leaving the walls as dominant but dormant elements of the late antique urban experience. The creation of a Christian urban landscape in every city, on the other hand, was cumulative and essentially unplanned (Dagron 1977). Its topographical evolution took place within broadly consistent parameters, but was locally subject to a combination of random influences: the availability of space within the urban area, the distribution of holy tombs around its margins, and the patronage of private individuals. Some sort of liturgical order could subsequently be imposed upon this fortuitous and evolving pattern, but it had no prior spatial logic or integrity of its own.

Meanwhile, the emerging late antique urban landscape, dominated by walls and churches, was thrust up in an uneasy and often incoherent relationship with the architectural legacy of earlier centuries. In part, it was directly established at its expense, as redundant monuments were stripped of masonry and decoration that could be recycled for the building of their successors. The modern demolition of late antique city walls has often shown them to be packed with the *spolia* that now form the foundation of many a museum collection (such as that of the Musée Lapidaire in Narbonne). Substantial structures could sometimes be systematically dismantled; the stone footings of the circus at Arles, for example, were carted off wholesale around the middle of the sixth century (Sintès 1994: 162). More often, perhaps, such work was carried out piecemeal. In the same city, the priest Cyril's despoiling of the marble facings and the *proscaenium* of the theater for church-building purposes was painfully interrupted when a block slipped its ropes and shattered his foot (*V. Hil.* 20).

In the absence of explosives and bulldozers, such enterprises were clearly labor-intensive, and not without hazard. A more economical solution was to reuse the monuments themselves. Public buildings of all shapes and sizes were converted into churches (Caillet 1996), or subdivided into basic residential and industrial units, no longer misleadingly deemed "squatter occupation." Some types of monument, such as temples and entertainment buildings, were more obviously vulnerable to spoliation or adaptation, because they had become culturally redundant. The Christian state stepped up its suppression of organized forms of pagan worship from the late fourth century onward; it was easier, as Augustine observed, to close temples against idols than it was to change hearts (*Ep.* 232. 1). But, despite increasingly vociferous Christian opposition, the emperors were far less decisive in acting against traditional forms of public entertainment (Markus 1990: 107–21). As one of their most trenchant critics acerbically observed, their demise stemmed not from the collective moral transformation he desired, but from the withdrawal of the requisite funding (Salvian, *De Gub.* 6. 42–3). Shows and especially circus games remained integral to late antique urban culture, and provided periodic and volatile opportunities for popular political participation wherever imperial or, increasingly infrequently, private patronage could be found (Liebeschuetz 2001a: 203–20, 249–57; Whitby 2006). In most cities in the late antique west, however, such support was no longer forthcoming by the fifth century, except in the few centers where barbarian kings continued the tradition (Ward-Perkins 1984: 92–118). The provision of such entertainments petered out more gradually in the east, but here too the structures built to stage them became urban behemoths, colonized by housing, quarried for materials, or left to slow decay.

There was much more to the late antique urban transition, however, than the rationalization of those categories of public building rendered obsolete by cultural change. The forum was traditionally the space around which classical civic life revolved, and it often stood at the heart of the street layout. By the fifth century, however, its maintenance was becoming optional. Our texts are much less interested in this phenomenon than in the demise of temples or theaters, the fate of which was at the cutting edge of contemporary debates. But archaeological evidence reveals that in some cities the forum complex was equally expendable. Again in Arles, for example, the paving slabs of the forum were taken up, and the surrounding portico dismantled, in the first half of the fifth century; fragments of the latter were incorporated in the foundations of the beaten-earth floors of the shops or storerooms installed on the site (Heijmans 2004: 367–71). In Africa, despite indisputable evidence of late antique urban prosperity, forum zones in a number of cities were suffering neglect or being turned over to utilitarian functions from the decades around AD 400 (Potter 1995: 64–79). In the eastern Mediterranean, too, such areas begin losing their monumental character from the fifth century in major centers such as Athens or Ephesus (Foss 1980: 80–2; Frantz 1988: 79–116). In a further indication of their reduced importance, some *agorai*, such as those of Ephesus, were left outside newly built fortifications. The dating of the wall circuit there remains in doubt, but the *agora* at nearby Hierapolis was similarly excluded from defenses confirmed by excavation to have been built in the fifth century (Whittow 2001: 140–2).

The marginalization or deterioration in the monumental character of forum zones is not necessarily indicative of their abandonment; but it shows how urban layouts were being re-centered – sometimes to meet defensive imperatives, but more often around churches. Alternatively, the latter effect could be achieved without any change of focus. In cities from Aix-en-Provence to Ariassos in Pisidia, church complexes were being built directly upon the forum courtyard and its associated monuments in the course of the fifth century (Guyon et al. 1998: 293–8; Schulz 1992). It should be stressed that radical transformations of this nature are by no means universal and, even at the regional level, they are inconsistent in character and chronology. But the very idea that they were possible, even in provincial capitals, demonstrates the extent to which cultural expectations of urbanism were changing during Late Antiquity.

For the downgrading or dereliction of forum complexes is perhaps especially symptomatic of a more general disavowal of the classical urban values that have customarily been idealized in both past and present. The physical expressions of this late antique unraveling of the built environment are many and various, but include the aforementioned intrusion of occupation into public monuments and their interstices; the proliferation of smaller residential units, often created through the subdivision of such monuments or of substantial private houses (Saradi 1998); the use of simpler, shoddier building techniques and materials, or of worked stone recycled from demolished monuments (Deichmann 1975); the collapse of the zoning that had hitherto pushed artisanal activity to the margins of the urban area and the burial grounds beyond them (Wataghin Cantino 1999; Leone 2003); the gradual disintegration of urban space from a coherent entity into a series of disjointed fragments, creating the so-called *città ad isole* (Duval 1982; Brogiolo 1984); the insidious encroachment of structures into porticoes and streets, which might ultimately transform urban layouts (Kennedy 1985); and the decay and eventual failure of sophisticated systems of water supply and waste disposal (Ward-Perkins 1984: 119–54).

Those phenomena are perceptible, sooner or later and in diverse combinations, in most late antique cities for which archaeological evidence is available. They vary greatly in significance, and should ideally be examined individually, not least because in their more advanced stages, they exhibit the clear influence of reduced prosperity and technological involution (Ward-Perkins 2005). But that is scarcely apparent in many regions of the Mediterranean, particularly in the east, within the time frame of this study, and its contributory effects become visible only after most of those changes were well under way. This late antique urban transition was instigated not by any fundamental financial or social meltdown, but by the changed priorities and cultural preoccupations of urban elites and the communities they dominated. With all due caution, the initial phases of those developments can therefore be taken together as indications of an evolving and distinctively late antique conception of urbanism.

By and large, the authors of our texts offer little explicit recognition of urban decay. They move through the ruins without comment, taking pride and delight in Christian buildings or mighty walls, while showing scant regard or sentimental attachment to derelict monuments. For them, the new urbanism was as valid as the old, unless their rhetorical purpose specifically dictated the evocation of civic splendor along time-honored lines. The revealing exception lies in the law codes, where the condition of the classical monumental legacy was acknowledged as a serious problem. Two recurrent anxieties were already dominating imperial edicts "on public works" by the late fourth century (*Cod. Theod.* 15. 1). These directed first that provincial governors should concentrate their efforts on repairing existing public buildings instead of pursuing the far greater renown that came from erecting new ones, and second that any alienation of such monuments and spoliation of their materials should be effectively regulated (Janvier 1969; Alchermes 1994). A similar concern for urban decorum persisted under later regimes, both Roman and barbarian; it is especially and endearingly apparent in the efforts of the Ostrogoths at heritage management (Majorian, *Nov.* 4, AD 458; Cassiod. *Var.* 3. 29; 4. 24; 4. 30; Ward-Perkins 1984: 203–29). Even so, this was designed, like so much imperial and royal legislation, to limit serious abuses, not to reverse inexorable trends. It cost money to shore up centuries-old structures, and vigilance to protect them from intrusion and spoliation, and it brought little social capital. A proactive provincial governor might intervene, like Alexander of Osrhoene, who cleared the streets and colonnades of Edessa of garbage and tradesmen's stalls in AD 497/8, and thoughtfully provided a suggestion box for its inhabitants (Ps.-Joshua, *Chron.* 29). But we might doubt that all such officials were as zealous, or that they were present in the vast majority of cities.

That generally left the fate of the late antique urban landscape in the hands of the descendants of the decurions who had originally done much to create it. As we have seen, they were increasingly reluctant to discharge their time-honored obligations to their communities, and were ceasing to operate effectively in council as organs of local government. Collective regulation will always have been required to prevent the stallholder from extending his shop front out into the street, the artisan from bringing the risks of fire and pollution into the heart of the community, the humble citizen from building his home up against the solid walls of a public building, the builder from salvaging the choicer materials from a disused monument, and all and sundry from dumping their rubbish wherever they saw fit. The prevention of such opportunism had generally fallen to the city councils, and might therefore be assumed to have been a further casualty of their inertia.

The decline of formal authority structures within cities is a necessary but nevertheless insufficient explanation for the progressive deterioration of the urban infrastructure. The resident local elites can hardly have been hapless witnesses to the demise of classical urbanism. They retained sufficient coercive and financial power to preserve those elements of it that still seemed to them to be relevant, such as the street grids (wholly or in part) of many cities (Février 1974: 96–104; Ward-Perkins 1995). They took a pragmatic and utilitarian view of the remainder, presumably because they could live with many of the phenomena described above. In truth, the architectural priorities of the new civic leaders lay elsewhere, and often implicated them closely in urban transformation. Bishops and their benefactors were busily building a new Christian public landscape within, around, and out of the old. They had to work with the existing built environment, but they were not remotely in thrall to it.

In his formal oration in praise of Antioch, written some decades before his final disillusionment with its political culture, Libanius (*Or.* 11. 131) drew a flattering contrast between the enduring splendors of his home town and those cities that, "like retired veterans," were nostalgic for past glories. The image is evocative, but it was being overtaken by events. So far from shuffling off into a dignified senescence, most Mediterranean cities were shaken up and rejuvenated by a political and cultural transformation that entered a formative phase in the closing decades of the fourth century. In the west, its impact was distorted by the disintegration of imperial power; in the east, it ushered in a new burst of urban vitality and prosperity that, in conjunction with an economic boom, lasted into the sixth century and in some regions beyond. The outward form of cities was transformed in Late Antiquity, sometimes radically, and not always, it has been suggested, for the better, though we can hardly be unfamiliar with the juxtaposition of urban luxury and dereliction, or the conversion of redundant monumental architecture into myriad and hybrid spaces for living and working. Urban political culture had changed considerably, too, but with little impact upon the manifold functions of the cities as the organizing principles of late antique society, through which the relationship between central authorities and local populations was routinely maintained, or upon the bonds between cities and their dependent territories, which now acquired a spiritual as well as a social and economic dimension. When Procopius evoked the peculiar pride of the Romans in the city, there is no reason to think he was indulging in the contemporary fondness for anachronism. The Roman love of cities had found new forms of expression in Late Antiquity.

BIBLIOGRAPHICAL NOTE

The major monographs on late antique urbanism are Liebeschuetz 2001a and Claude 1969. Liebeschuetz 1992 and Ward-Perkins 1998 offer more concise but particularly wide-ranging overviews. The peerless analyses of Jones (1940; 1964: 712–66; 1971) remain fundamental, though only the second of these is specifically devoted to the late antique period. Laniado 2002 offers a cogent synthesis of the shift to urban government by notables, and Ward-Perkins 1984 a model survey of changing patterns of monumental patronage, with Di Segni 1995 and 1999 for the different chronology of such developments in the Near East.

The finest account of the late antique cities of a particular region is Lepelley 1979–81; a thought-provoking comparative regional approach to urbanism is taken by Wickham 2005: 591–692.

Much of the latest thinking in a field regularly refreshed by new archaeological evidence is best accessed through collections of essays, among which see Rich 1992; Brogiolo 1996; Christie and Loseby 1996; Lepelley 1996; Brogiolo and Ward-Perkins 1999; Brogiolo et al. 2000; Ripoll and Gurt 2000; Burns and Eadie 2001; Lavan 2001; and Krause and Witschel 2006. These vary in their emphases, but typically offer a mixture of case studies and thematic discussions.

Many of the major themes, such as christianization or the survival of classical urbanism, can also be pursued through the works cited in the text, among which Brown 1992 and Février 1974 are especially stimulating.

A few cities have been the object of what one might call urban biographies, particularly the great *métropoleis*; some of these works integrate the textual or the archaeological evidence, more often they favor one over the other. For Rome and Constantinople, left to one side in this chapter, the bibliography is vast. One might start with Dagron 1974; Mango 1990; Mango and Dagron 1995; Harris 1999; Curran 2000; and Witschel 2001. The rich evidence from Antioch is explored in the classic works of Petit 1955 and Liebeschuetz 1972. Haas 1997 does the same for Alexandria, but an up-to-date and thorough account of late antique Carthage is sorely needed. Among other profiles of individual Mediterranean cities in Late Antiquity (this list is by no means exhaustive) see Foss 1979, 1980; Spieser 1984; Roueché 1989; Raban and Holum 1996; Heijmans 2004; Sotinel 2005.

CHAPTER ELEVEN

The Archaeological Record: Problems of Interpretation

Olof Brandt

I shall not present here an introduction to the archaeology of Late Antiquity: rather, I wish to discuss how archaeology can be both a fundamental and a problematic source of historical evidence. I shall illustrate my discussion with examples taken mostly from the archaeology of late antique Rome and Ostia. But first, some remarks about the history of the discipline.

Classical, Christian, and Late Antique Archaeology

The archaeological exploration of Late Antiquity began in a scientific way in the nineteenth century, most often under the title of "Christian archaeology." Renaissance architects, especially in Italy, had been interested equally in pagan, civil, and early Christian buildings; but later tensions between Illuminism and Christianity in the eighteenth century – an Illuminism that sought for contemporary inspiration in the pre-Christian phases of Greek and Roman civilization – led to the development of a classical archaeology that was prepared to overlook the late antique and early Christian monuments. Interest in the latter developed more as a result of early nineteenth-century Romanticism and its passion for alternative cultures. The resulting Christian archaeology took its first steps together with the earliest archaeological exploration of Egyptian and Etruscan cultures. During the nineteenth century, Christian archaeology diverged from its classical counterpart, and the two increasingly separate disciplines divided antiquity between them. Theodor Mommsen, for example, published the non-Christian inscriptions of Rome in the sixth volume of the *Corpus inscriptionum Latinarum* (1876 onward), while his friend and colleague Giovanni Battista de

Rossi published the city's Christian inscriptions in the corresponding *Inscriptiones Christianae urbis Romae* (1857–88).

By 1900, separate international congresses of both classical and Christian archaeology began to be held. To concentrate on Christian archaeology was, of course, to limit one's approach to Late Antiquity; but the first serious studies of late antique topography were nevertheless developed within that discipline, many decades before the modern and more general interest in the archaeology of that period. Classical archaeology was more closely tied to the official culture of those modern states that had, like Greece and Italy, been created with ancient Greece and Rome as their models. That association often led to the destruction of late antique layers and phases of various sites, in order to "liberate" the classical phases represented by monuments like the Augustan Forum Romanum or the Acropolis in Athens. The tendency was even more marked in Egypt and Asia Minor, and compromised subsequent scientific access to Byzantine strata especially. Christian archaeology, on the other hand, inspired Christian renewal and *ressourcement*, especially in Catholic countries, and the Christian archaeology of Rome became a major source of inspiration for the renewal of the Catholic liturgy in the twentieth century.

Modern Method: Archaeology as History

As I say, both classical and Christian archaeology developed first as ways of going back to the sources of modern civilization. Archaeologists in that tradition aimed to uncover the original phases of political, civil, and religious architecture by removing later reconstructions and repairs. Excavation and renovation by classical archaeologists aimed at leaving important buildings and monuments visible in their original state at the center of modern cities. Little room was made for the preservation of traces of later life, even in those buildings themselves. During the twentieth century, however, archaeologists began to adopt methods that would allow them to disclose a development, a succession of events. Today, as a result, archaeology is seen not as a way of finding objects but of uncovering history. Indeed, archaeology is not so much a *source for* history as *a way of doing* history, albeit different from text-based history.

All study of the past is based, of course, on the belief that we can identify a succession of events accurately; but there are different ways of approaching that task, using different kinds of evidence and different methods. Events leave traces both in texts and in the physical remains investigated by archaeologists. Sometimes those traces corroborate each other; but sometimes they appear contradictory, or may survive only in one form, physical or textual; and sometimes there are no traces left at all, or at least not preserved. Archaeology always risks underestimating the importance of evidence that does not exist or that is still unknown. That is especially the case in the study of Greek and Roman civilization, where such an abundance of material has been preserved that it is easy to forget the monuments and other traces that we cannot see: in some cases they have not survived, but in others they are simply covered still by later phases.

Analysis and Synthesis

Modern archaeologists stress their right and duty to present the history they infer from their material, and do not expect anyone to interpret that material for them. The more traditional view was that archaeological specialists would collect and publish detailed evidence, which could then be interpreted by other scholars. In the nineteenth and early twentieth centuries, this view led to the production of huge bodies of different kinds of archaeological evidence (*Corpus inscriptionum*, *Corpus vasorum antiquorum*, *Corpus signorum*, and so on), and of site publications in large volumes, some of which still await the anticipated interpretation. Such publications are extremely expensive, and more recently their value has been questioned. Perhaps we should place that material on the Internet, producing in printed form only the interpretations and conclusions that follow a completed excavation or archaeological project. The chief point, however, is that only the specialist can master his evidence and his method well enough to use it to write history: his history; only trained archaeologists can fully understand, interpret, and explain the evidence from an excavation. It is in that sense that archaeologists have to see themselves as historians. Of course, it is challenging to relate archaeological evidence to texts. Textual historians do not always appreciate all the nuances of archaeological evidence; but it has to be said that many archaeologists treat texts with comparable superficiality. This problem will probably not be solved in the near future, not least because knowledge of classical languages is becoming the privilege of fewer and fewer specialists.

This fundamental shift toward an understanding of archaeology as a way of writing history was given further impetus by a methodological revolution introduced by Edward C. Harris in 1979 (see Harris 1989). For many decades, archaeologists had talked about "layers" on the one hand and "walls" on the other – "wall A," for example, or "layer 1C2" – which were then grouped together by being assigned to a specific historical period. That method is often associated with the name of Mortimer Wheeler. Harris simplified matters by talking about "units of stratification" or "stratigraphic units," which included both layers and walls, and were to be numbered in the same order as they are defined by the archaeologist. The true revolution, however, was Harris's decision to include what he called "interfaces" in the units of stratification. These interfaces could include cuts and holes on the site that defied tidy definition as either layers or walls (Harris 1989: 54). Layers, in other words, were only half the story, because the mass of the stratification is separated by the interfacial surfaces and contours. So, a layer and its interface were to be thought of as a single phenomenon, but other interfaces are created by the destruction of strata and not by their deposition. Harris introduced the notion of "interface" as an unambiguous word that would include not only the surfaces of layers but also such features as pits and ditches. These last had stratigraphic relations of their own, just like layers, and like layers they are numbered and put in the scheme of stratigraphic relations, what Harris called the "matrix." "The matrix," he says on his website, "is a new type of calendar, which allowed archaeologists for the first time, to *see* the stratigraphic sequences of complex sites" (www.harrismatrix.com).

Since a stratigraphic excavation removes layers in the order opposite to that in which they were deposited, it is necessary first to identify the layers (their boundaries and surfaces) and the relationship between them. Because of his clear distinction between analysis and synthesis (on which more shortly), Harris has offered archaeologists the chance of achieving new intellectual clarity. In the earlier method, the numbers or letters of layers and walls could be changed during the interpretation: scholars could adjust their opinion as to the period to which they should be assigned. According to the Harris method, the number of a unit of stratification is never changed and expresses no interpretation. Modern stratigraphic analysis thus has two distinct moments: the identification, definition, and numbering of the units, together with a judgment about the relationship between them – the analysis; and the process of then grouping them together as clues to actions and periods – the synthesis. Dating finds like coins, pottery, wall paintings, brick stamps, inscriptions, or graffiti found within a layer helps us also to date other units in the same position in the stratigraphic system, the matrix.

Among classical and late antique archaeologists, this stratigraphic method has been discussed with particular passion in Great Britain and Italy. Harris developed his matrix theory during an excavation in Winchester (1967–71). British evaluation has been particularly well expressed in the "Interpreting Stratigraphy" conferences held in York since 1993 (Roskams 2000; see also Harris et al. 1993). Italian archaeologist Andrea Carandini began using the method in Carthage in 1973, and in Italy at Settefinestre in 1976. In Rome, the method was introduced on a grand scale in 1981 during the excavation of the Crypta Balbi. As a result of that success, the method has now become standard in Italy – for example, in the excavations of the imperial fora begun in 1995. Italy was also the first country in which Harris's book was translated (1983). His method has been greeted with more skepticism in America; and in some other European countries, the Harris terminology has been simply superimposed upon what is still really the old method.

The Harris method was developed for use in excavations where the main approach was to remove one layer or unit at a time, beginning with the one created last. Recent discussion (Jones 2000) has focused on how the analysis can be applied to standing buildings. Here, the issue is more complex, because the units cannot usually be removed but only observed from outside, and the stratigraphic relationships observed between different parts of the same wall may reflect only the history of the surface of the wall, not that of its inner core. In recent years, however, an increasing number of buildings, and indeed large areas of cities, have been excavated according to the modern method. This makes it possible for the first time to date accurately both the foundation of a building and later reconstructions: either one identifies the foundation trench that cuts through earlier layers, and dates the material found in that layer, or one identifies traces of reuse, repair, and decay. One can see what a difference that makes, when one considers that, on sites like Ostia or North African cities, much information has been lost for ever, because the main objective of the archaeologists concerned was to uncover the walls of the buildings (and only of their earliest phase). The date of many churches and other important late antique buildings is still as a consequence rather uncertain, and will probably remain so. If only a small corner of a building has been left unexcavated, however, it is often possible to apply the modern method there, and gain a better understanding of the building's history. In the same way, new stratigraphic excavations in Ostia and the imperial fora at Rome have now thrown fresh light on earlier excavations in the same area. Where such advances have proved impossible, even a new stratigraphic analysis of a building's preserved remains can supply new information. According to the Harris method, earlier excavations are treated as negative units of stratification (interfaces): they have become just as much a part of the history of a monument or site as any other phase of destruction in other periods.

Example 1: Pottery and the End of Antiquity

Harris's method makes it possible to construct the relative chronology of a site by defining the stratigraphic relations between units within it. The establishment of an absolute chronology, however, usually depends on the presence of securely datable objects in any one layer. One such object is pottery. Its importance, for both classical and late antique archaeology, cannot be exaggerated. Pottery styles change like any other fashion and, although pots break easily, the resulting fragments are not destroyed. A layer usually contains, therefore, hundreds of shards that make it possible to relate that layer to a period, or even to an event. Pottery also tells us a lot about economy and trade. When studying the transport of grain, oil, and wine in Late Antiquity, we do not usually have at our disposal actual grain, oil, or wine: our deductions can be based only on the pottery within which those materials were carried or stored. Yet, in only a few places have large amounts of late antique and early medieval pottery from stratigraphic excavations been analyzed. Of particular importance in this regard is the pottery from the Crypta Balbi excavation in Rome, which, together with some other important excavations, presents us with the following picture (Panella and Saguì 2001; Romei 2004).

In the fourth and early fifth centuries, Rome established a particularly close trading relationship with Carthage, thanks to the growing status of Constantinople, which diverted to itself much of the Egyptian grain that had earlier been sent to Rome. From about AD 330 onward, Rome depended increasingly on grain from Tunisia, and the African economy reached a peak as a result. Indeed, in the same period, 90 percent of the fine tableware in Rome came from Tunisia.

Between AD 430 and 450, that situation began to change. After the Vandals had conquered North Africa (a victory completed by AD 439), the agricultural productivity of the eastern provinces had to supply Rome as well as Constantinople, despite Rome's now shrinking population. It is true that even the collapse of the Roman state in the west, traditionally dated to AD 476, did not bring the older pattern to an end, or at least not immediately. Recent analysis of pottery from modern stratigraphic excavations shows that, in addition to trade in food across the Mediterranean (which continued until the beginning of the seventh century), North African fine tableware was still dominant in Italy as late as AD 700. But there are signs of crisis. More common ware from Tunisia was gradually replaced by local Italian production. Similarly, while the proportion of grain, oil, and wine imported to Rome from the eastern Mediterranean steadily increased, North Africa remained an important source (although vegetables, milk, and eggs came from regional production).

Traces of that immense movement of food can be found in the large number of amphorae found in Rome. Recent excavations in the Crypta Balbi confirm the view that such imports, from both North Africa and the east, continued in the second half of the seventh century, even after the Arab conquest of Syria and Egypt. But the trade was less extensive than before, and valuable goods like high quality wines now constituted a prominent proportion of the total – imports for the elite. Then, in the eighth century, almost all the earlier amphora types disappear, and there is scarcely any evidence at all that food was imported, whether from North Africa or from the eastern Mediterranean. At the same time, the importation of not only finer tableware but also of more common ware is interrupted. There is no evidence in Rome that pottery was imported from North Africa after the Arab conquest of Carthage in AD 698. There are not even any eighth-century Islamic amphorae that suggest importation from areas now controlled by the Arabs, let alone from Byzantium. Recent archaeological evidence suggests, from the late fifth century, a corresponding dependence on wine from Campania. By the eighth century, most imports to Rome came from such places in the southern half of the peninsula. Although it is not always possible to distinguish between amphorae from Campania, Calabria, or Sicily, it is obvious that the circulation of goods in the eighth century was much more limited than before. Seventh-century vessels designed for transportation make up almost 50 percent of the total surviving pottery material: similar vessels from the eighth century make up only about 25 percent.

So, even in the seventh century, pottery imported to Italy from North Africa was very similar to that used in the first centuries of the empire. Despite the political and institutional changes that often get attention in handbooks, there is a clear continuity in material culture, and therefore in everyday life. Scholars may discuss whether the break in Mediterranean trade (and thus in material culture) occurred shortly before or shortly after AD 700; but, according to the pottery from the Crypta Balbi excavation and other similar excavations, that is more or less when we have to think of antiquity as ending, at least in Rome. The profound changes in material culture that resulted must reflect even deeper changes at the political, institutional, economic, and social levels (Panella and Saguì 2001: 815).

Example 2: Religion in the Late Antique City

It is not always easy to gain a complete picture of late antique cities (see, for a complementary treatment, Loseby, ch. 10). Churches provide us with much of our knowledge of late antique urbanism, because they are often the only late antique buildings still standing. During the first period of the archaeological exploration of Late Antiquity, a focus on the importance of the Christian religion yielded substantial results, but it has also led to a rather complicated alliance between archaeology and religion. For a long time, archaeological research on late antique cities concentrated on the traces of religious *activity*. Discussion took a great step forward when its focus was less on individual monuments and more on a broader topography of religious sites. Individual sites like Rome made an early contribution to the debate (Kraut-heimer 1980); but a topographical emphasis became more assured during the 1980s in, for example, the papers of the Eleventh International Congress of Christian Archaeology (Duval 1989a), where much of the discussion was concentrated on the relationship between bishops, cathedrals, and urban topography generally. Since the early 1990s, there has been an added interest in the more general secular topography of the fourth to seventh centuries (Rich 1992; Lavan 2001; Brands and Severin 2003). New excavations, especially in Israel and Jordan, have extended our knowledge even more. Regional studies have been made, as in the French series "Topographie chrétienne des cités de la Gaule."

Recent research has tended to stress, however, that it is not always easy to identify archaeologically the religious affiliation of an ancient city's inhabitants: even religious buildings and religious symbols on a building or within the city do not allow us to decide automatically what might have been the faith of its inhabitants. Ostia provides an eloquent example, which has been discussed recently by the Swiss art historian Beat Brenk (2003: 39–48).

Of the late antique constructions in Ostia, 90 percent are utilitarian, and it is impossible to know whether they were used or inhabited by pagans, Jews, or Chris-tians. Even deeply religious pagans, Jews, and Christians did not always take the trouble to put religious symbols in or on their buildings. The fourth century AD was a period of intense building activity – luxurious villas, baths, *nymphaea*, and (in Ostia) two big churches. One of the latter was the cathedral built by Constantine close to the Porta Laurentina, which has been excavated recently (Bauer et al. 2000; Bauer and Heinzelmann 2001). The other is the funerary basilica at Pianabella, outside the Porta Laurentina. The complete lack of religious symbols in private dwellings does not allow us, however, to posit a Christian quarter by the Porta Laurentina. Similarly, it has not been possible to identify a Jewish quarter around the synagogue built in the first century AD outside the Porta Marina.

The presence of "pagan" statues in private houses, on the other hand, does not mean that their inhabitants were pagans, but rather that those living in them shared the classical culture of their period. The inhabitants of the Domus of the Fortuna Annonaria, for example, cannot be thought of as pagan simply because of the presence of a statue of that symbolic divinity. Nor does the presence of Christian symbols always make it easy to understand the function of a building. A structure by the Decumanus, bearing an inscription that includes the Christian *chi-rho* symbol, was often identified as the cathedral of Constantine, until that church was found at the Porta Laurentina. Even then, it has continued to be thought of in recent interpret-ations as either the property of a Christian community (Gobbi 1998) or as a *domus* owned at least for some time by Christians (Brenk 2003: 41–3).

The inscription mentions the four rivers of Paradise – Geon, Fison, Tigris, and Eufrates. Brenk reads its last part *Tigrinianorum sumite fontes*, instead of an earlier reading *Christianorum sumite fontes.* The Tigriniani were a Roman family well known from fourth- and fifth-century inscriptions, and some of its members were indeed Christians. This particular inscription is found on the architrave above the entrance to a typical late antique *nymphaeum* (earlier interpreted as a baptistery). This, Brenk concludes, is the only *domus* in Ostia where it is certain that the inhabitants were Christians; but he also stresses that the otherwise small number of Christian monuments in the city does not allow us to draw any conclusions about the Christianization of its inhabitants (Brenk 2003: 48). The absence of Christian symbols in other *domus* does not allow us to conclude, for example (as Meiggs did: 1973: 401), that Christianity spread mostly among Ostia's poor.

Similar problems attach to public buildings, many of which were restored in the fourth century, and include the town's theater and some pagan temples. Although the emperor Theodosius prohibited pagan cults in AD 391, an inscription from the year AD 393/4 mentions the restoration of a temple of Hercules. This may indicate that both religions still lived side by side; but it may also indicate that some pagan temples were seen as monuments rather than as religious structures, and that they were repaired like any other public building (as suggested by *Cod. Theod.* 15. 1). The same thing happened in Rome itself: pagan temples at the Forum Romanum could be repaired even after the pagan cults were outlawed, because these buildings were symbols of the greatness of Rome's past (Bauer 1996: 128).

Example 3: The Roman *Tituli*

The importance of archaeological evidence that has *not* been found or identified, or has been destroyed, or has never existed is particularly evident in the case of the development of smaller Christian community centers or parishes. In the century or so after the development of early Christian archaeology in Rome, this was one of the questions most discussed. Although we know from written sources that there was an important Christian community in the city, no Christian cult places or churches from the period before the early fourth century, when the persecutions of the Christians ended, have been found inside the city walls. The first Christian church built in Rome that we know of was the cathedral, the Lateran basilica, called today San Giovanni in Laterano (Krautheimer 1977; De Blaauw 1996, 2001). According to the sixth-century *Liber Pontificalis* (Duchesne 1886: 172–5), this was built by the emperor Constantine soon after AD 312. There is no reason to doubt that, and contemporary sources from the fourth and fifth centuries go on to mention a growing number of smaller churches for local communities in the various quarters of Rome; churches that were known, at least from the fifth century onward, as *tituli* (Pietri 1989b).

The *Liber Pontificalis* states that some of these were founded in the fourth and fifth centuries; of others no textual trace remains. The *Liber* clearly used older material from the archives of the Roman church; but it presents a standardized and *a posteriori* picture that few people put faith in today – that is, that there were twenty-five *tituli*, and that they had already been created around AD 100 by Pope Evaristus, AD 96–108

(Duchesne 1886: 126). (The number twenty-five is given in the biography of Pope Marcellus, AD 308–9 (Duchesne 1886: 164).) On the contrary, this assertion is contradicted by material evidence. We know that the *tituli* could not have dated from the first century AD: those still standing today cannot possibly be dated earlier than the fourth century – not least because of the building techniques employed in their construction.

In 1918, Johann Peter Kirsch proposed a theory about how the *tituli* were created, and that theory has dominated discussion about these earliest Roman community centers ever since (Kirsch 1918: 117–37). He recognized that what the *Liber Pontificalis* said about Evaristus could not be true, and he believed that the establishment of the *tituli* was part of the reorganization of the Roman church after the end of the persecution of Valerian – that is, toward the middle of the third century, when the Roman church had so many members that it needed several buildings for liturgical celebrations. Kirsch also recognized that the foundation of a *titulus* did not always coincide with the construction of a regular church building. He knew of eight cases where private buildings of the second and third centuries had been found beneath Roman *titulus* churches, in particular San Martino ai Monti and Santi Giovanni e Paolo. His conclusion was that most Roman *tituli* originally *were* private houses. From the middle of the fourth century, regular church buildings were erected on top of these buildings, which he interpreted as *tituli* dating back to the third century. The names of these *tituli*, known from a Roman synod of AD 499 and in some cases already from fourth-century texts or inscriptions, repeat in many cases the names of the original owners of those houses. The *tituli* named after their founders (the dates of which are not mentioned in the literary sources) were mostly created before Constantine (Kirsch 1918: 133). The word *titulus* originally referred, therefore, to an inscription on the house that stated the name of the owner.

Archaeology does not contradict Kirsch's theory, but nor does it prove it (Guidobaldi 1989, 2000). The two cases to which Kirsch attached particular importance, the churches of San Martino ai Monti and Santi Giovanni e Paolo, are just as likely *not* to have been Christian community centers.

In San Martino ai Monti (Accorsi 2002), a Roman third-century hall has been interpreted as the original *titulus*, probably that of the priest Equitius or of Pope Sylvester, both of whom are mentioned in the *Liber Pontificalis* (in the biography of Pope Sylvester, AD 314–35 (1. 170–1, 186)); but no Christian traces of so early a date have been identified in the building.

The case of the church Santi Giovanni e Paolo is equally problematic (Krautheimer 1965; Brenk 1995, 2003). Nineteenth-century excavations beneath the floor of the church revealed a second-century building, rebuilt as a luxurious dwelling in the third century. In its last phase, in the early fourth century, it was decorated with Christian paintings: a praying figure (an *orans*) and a scene that almost certainly depicts a martyrdom – perhaps that of the John and Paul after whom the church was named. Literary sources mention, in relation to this site, not one but two *tituli*. One is the *titulus Pammachi*, probably named after the man who built the church (so this *titulus* has nothing to do with any earlier history). The other is called the *titulus Byzanti*, named after an otherwise unknown Byzantius, who might have played a part in creating a community center on the spot where the church was later erected. So, in this case, we have a fourth-century *titulus* replaced around AD 400 by a regular church building.

Kirsch's theory, however, that (fourth-century) churches were built on (third-century) house churches might be more justifiably applied to a later period, when (fifth-century) churches were built on top of (fourth-century) house churches. That would also fit with the more recent observation of Charles Pietri that the Latin word *titulus* (which normally does indeed mean inscription) cannot be found in contemporary sources with the meaning of a Christian community center before AD 377 (Pietri 1976: 90–6, 569–73; 1989b: 1043).

More recent research on the Roman house beneath Santi Giovanni e Paolo suggests, however, the need for an even more prudent approach. Brenk has argued convincingly (Brenk 1995; 2003: 82–113) that this house was no community center but rather a private dwelling, the owner of which became Christian in the early fourth century and decorated some of the rooms of his house with paintings alluding to his new faith. A century after Kirsch, there are still no traces of earlier Christian community centers beneath Roman churches.

Now there are different ways of dealing with the poverty of evidence from the first Christian centuries, especially the third century, when the Roman church had acquired a considerable number of members. One is to suppose that the *tituli* or similar organizations really did exist, but that they have left no traces. Another possibility is that the evidence has been destroyed, perhaps during the violent persecutions of Diocletian, who in AD 303 ordered the demolition of all Christian churches. A third way of approaching the situation is to compensate for the silence in the Christian third-century material by appealing to the patterns of Jewish communities in Rome in the same period.

The Jewish pattern in the third century seems to have been similar to that attributed to the Christians. Both communities buried their dead in catacombs, the great subterranean burial places outside Rome; burials that began for both communities around AD 200 (see Rebillard, ch. 15). But, exactly as in the case of the Christians, there are no archaeological traces of the places in Rome where the living Jews gathered in the third century. We do have, however, from that same century, many inscriptions from the Jewish catacombs, which give us a lot of information about how their communities were organized. They supply the titles of different functionaries in the synagogues, all of them mentioned also by name. There were at least eleven of these synagogues (Noy 1995), some named after the geographic origin of their members (Tripolitans), some after different parts of Rome (Calcaresians, Campesians, Siburesians), some after individuals (Agrippesians). Are we entitled to suppose that Christian communities of the same period were organized and identified in a similar way?

It is difficult, unfortunately, to date the Jewish inscriptions: they rarely specify a date explicitly. Their catacombs are also difficult to date, since they are not mentioned in other sources unlike the Christian catacombs, with their martyr graves, which are described in sixth-century pilgrim guides, the *itineraria*. So, it is hard to tell whether a Jewish inscription should be dated to the third or the fourth century. That does not mean, of course, that the third-century Jews of Rome were *not* divided into different communities. And it is understandable that, when we place side by side the Jewish inscriptions and the list of Christian *tituli* from AD 499, we are tempted to suppose that Christian and Jews were organized in similar ways – that is, in small, local communities. But it is important here to observe chronological differences, and to treat Late Antiquity not as a single unit but rather as a period that evolved at varying speeds and in varying directions. The Christian evidence for such local communities remains obstinately later than the Jewish – from the fourth century and later. The numerous third-century Christian inscriptions never mention local communities, not even in the funerary inscriptions of third-century priests or bishops. On the contrary, inscriptions mention local Christian communities only from the middle of the fourth century, when contemporary sources prove that the foundation of *tituli* had already begun.

Now it is difficult to reconcile even this complex picture with the one we gain from texts. Eusebius mentions (in relation to Pope Cornelius) forty-six Roman priests (*Hist. eccl.* 6. 43. 11). Optatus of Milevis mentions more than forty Christian *basilicae* in the city (*De schismate Donatistarum* 2. 4). If we accept Harnack's estimate that there were some 40,000 to 50,000 Christians in Rome in the late third and early fourth centuries (Harnack 1915: 255), this textual evidence might suggest that the church in the city was divided into some forty communities, each with around 1,000 members, and each presided over by its own priest. The archaeological and epigraphic evidence, on the other hand, points, as we have seen, to a more centralized organization, unlike the communities imagined by the *Liber Pontificalis* (and by many modern scholars) or created by Roman Jews. Yet, although texts and archaeology give different pictures, they must be in some way related to a single series of historical events. So, until a satisfactory way is found to reconcile the two sets of impressions, it would be wise to keep them both in mind. Neither can be taken exclusively for granted, since neither has been established as indubitably correct.

In any case, discussion in recent decades has moved to the fourth century: scholars now tend to think of the creation of the *tituli* as a fourth-century phenomenon. That the Christians of Rome were organized into *tituli* before the fourth century must be considered a legend, created largely by the sixth-century *Liber Pontificalis*. It is dangerous to take the preoccupations of one century as evidence for what happened in another. Indeed, one can go further: recent research (Guidobaldi 2000) suggests that the whole idea of the foundation of *tituli* emerges *only* in the sixth century. When Roman churches are first mentioned by contemporary Latin sources, there is no mention of *tituli*: the words used are *basilica*, *ecclesia*, or *dominicum*. Different words are likely to point to different functions and situations. In other words, Kirsch's chief error was to search in an earlier period for the answer to an entirely sixth-century question.

From the fourth century onward on, there was – not only in Rome but also in other large Mediterranean cities like Constantinople, Alexandria, and Carthage – more than one Christian basilica inside their walls (see the overviews of the four cities by Pietri, Dagron, Martin, and Ennabli in Duval 1989a). Archaeologists can date such buildings, telling us, for example, that the earliest preserved churches belong to the fourth century; but only texts can determine whether, on the one hand, there were actually corresponding *communities*, organized more or less like modern parish churches, as described for Alexandria around AD 375 by Epiphanius (*Adv. haeres.* 69. 1. 2–3; 2. 2), or whether they should be seen, on the other hand, as urban sanctuaries, the domain chiefly of the local bishop and subject to his authority (see further the treatment of bishops by Rita Lizzi Testa, ch. 35). A building's function – whether as the center of a community or as a bishop's personal domain – is rarely obvious from the site itself, and could change from period to period. Great prudence is necessary when using archaeology as a source for church organization.

Example 4: Architecture and Symbolism

Many late antique churches are still standing, allowing us to analyze their architecture and not just to construct the chronology of their foundation trenches, as is so often the case with other buildings demolished or abandoned centuries ago. The analysis of standing buildings is, however, problematic. It is particularly unacceptable to study a surviving late antique church as we find it today, with all its reconstructions and modern restorations, as if it is a work of art endowed with symbolic meaning. That kind of analysis, treating the building like sculpture, jumps over several fundamental steps.

We have to begin in a strictly formal way. We must first reconstruct the shape of a building at an identifiable moment in its life (which will often be its original phase). This step is carried out by applying the stratigraphic method I have already described. Then, we have to ask what kind of action that shape implies: one or many persons standing, sitting, or moving around? The use of water? Identifying such actions is possible, because although the form and decoration of buildings varied, late Roman architects used standardized techniques that were suited to the *actions* performed in or around those buildings. That standardized repertory of classical architecture might have depended exactly on the fact that the building was *not* considered a work of art in its own right, but rather a backdrop for human figures, either real or in the form of statues or mosaics. Only then can we take the third step, interpretation: what meaning did the ancient people themselves attribute to the actions performed in the building?

This emphasis on backdrop and action is particularly helpful when discussing octagonal baptisteries, which are plentiful from the fourth century onward, probably spreading from Rome to Milan, southern Gaul, and Asia Minor. The octagonal structure, the most monumental form of the baptistery, has been subjected to a great deal of symbolic interpretation. It is true that the church Fathers saw a symbolism in the number eight (Quacquarelli 1973). Similarities with both *mausolea* and baths have been seized upon as referring to the symbolic "death" that baptism evoked and to ritual purification (Styger 1933; Krautheimer 1993: 124–50), and it is true that Christian writers in earlier periods did apply that kind of interpretation to standing buildings. The connections were made and appealed to, however, *a posteriori*, and need not reflect the reasons for the choice of octagonal form in the first place, although they could have influenced the repetition and diffusion of the form, once it had been created. Octagonal halls, similar if not identical to those used as Christian baptisteries, were common in imperial Roman architecture, especially in the early fourth century (Brandt 2001, with bibliography). Many of them are found in baths, far beyond any Christian religious context. There is one in the mausoleum of Diocletian's palace in Split – the palace of the great persecutor. Such a hall, obviously, did not reflect any Christian symbolism: rather, it solved a practical problem – namely, how to focus the attention of those present on one particular spot, while permitting movement around it. Octagonal baptisteries were focused, therefore, on the pool in which ritual initiation took place. In contrast, the oblong shape of the standard Christian basilica was designed to accommodate the important processions and other movements that took place along the nave (Mathews 1962).

Ancient Christian texts may help us understand what was going on in the heads of late antique Christians, but they do not always disclose the motives behind architectural choices. Ambrose, in an inscription, provided a symbolic interpretation of the baptistery in Milan; but that inscription does not explain satisfactorily why the building looks something like a bath, something like a dining room, something like a vestibule, and something like a mausoleum, all at the same time. The sixth-century *Liber Pontificalis*, which provides detailed information about church foundations in Rome from the fourth to the sixth centuries, gives the numbers of columns and details of other decorations in precious materials, but says little about architectural forms. Baptisteries were the object of much investment and architectural refinement, and were a propaganda showcase for bishops and for the triumphant Church (Guyon 2000: 59; Wataghin Cantino et al. 2001: 243). The same is true of Eusebius' description of the Christian basilica in Tyre (*Hist. eccl.* 10. 4). He stresses the precious nature of the decoration and provides a symbolic interpretation of the building, but tells us very little about the reasons behind the choice of *form*. He presents his account rather as a proof of Christian triumph under imperial patronage. Constantine, who paid for the erection of the Church of the Holy Sepulchre in Jerusalem, ordered the use of precious materials and columns, but again, in his instructions to bishop Makarios and the bishop's architect Zenobios, had little to say about the building's shape (Euseb. *V. Const.* 3. 31, analyzed in Liverani 2003). Indeed, there is no text that explains how a discussion between a bishop and his architect might really determine the shape of a building. Also Procopius' famous description of the Hagia Sophia in Constantinople (*Aed.* 1. 1. 61–3) is an attempt to link the *form* of a building with its *effect*, not to explain the choices behind it.

BIBLIOGRAPHICAL NOTE

For modern archaeological method, see E. C. Harris 1989; Harris et al. 1993; and Carandini 1981. The relationship between modern archaeology and history has been discussed in Sauer 2004. For the history of Christian archaeology, see Frend 1996. Fundamental references for this field are the old but incredibly rich *Dictionnaire d'archéologie chrétienne et de liturgie*, the publications of the Pontificio Istituto di Archeologia Cristiana in Rome, like the *Rivista di archeologia cristiana* and the proceedings of the International Congresses of Christian Archaeology, and the publications of the Franz Joseph Dölger-Institut zur Erforschung der Spätantike in Bonn, like the *Reallexikon für Antike und Christentum* and the *Jahrbuch für Antike und Christentum*. The renewed interest in a general archaeological study of Late Antiquity has found expression in journals like *Antiquité Tardive* and at recent conferences on late antique archaeology (see Lavan 2001).

CHAPTER TWELVE

Inscribing Identity: The Latin Epigraphic Habit in Late Antiquity

Dennis E. Trout

Inscriptions often preserve unique images of late antique life and society; but, like the age itself, the epigraphic record resists most of the generalizations we would impose upon it (Heather 1997). Carved, painted, or scratched on stone, metal, and plaster, inscriptions may proclaim official policies or express imaginative realms never touched by imperial laws or conciliar canons. They may echo classical poets, reflect contemporary intellectual trends, or speak with voices seldom heard in the literature of the age. They may be elegantly carved on marble or crudely scribbled across a wall. In this chapter, I shall survey Late Antiquity's epigraphic landscape and examine some of the fundamental ways in which inscriptions often highlight the subtler textures of late antique and early medieval culture. I aim at breadth but still say too little on some topics. I single out certain texts as exemplary when others might have served equally well. I do contend, however, that nearly all late antique inscriptions, regardless of medium, message, and immediate ends, were deeply implicated in the fashioning of contemporary identities in an age of ever shifting boundaries (Brown 1971b).

Epigraphic Corpora and Epigraphic Curves

The fact that late Latin epigraphy was so long the close ally of Christian archaeology has broad implications for contemporary explorations of Late Antiquity's epigraphic legacy (see Brandt, ch. 11). Indeed, the modern discipline of Latin epigraphy emerged in the nineteenth century well before current conceptions of Late Antiquity as an age of creative cultural evolution began to take shape. From the outset, many post-Constantinian inscriptions were published and studied separately from the earlier texts that were typically deemed the true preserve of Romanists. This tendency is well illustrated by decisions made in mid-nineteenth-century Rome. The flood of inscriptions then pouring out of the catacombs was channeled into de Rossi's new *Inscriptiones christianae urbis Romae* (1857–1992, with further volumes projected for intra-mural inscriptions), while the city's hoard of other texts – including those of the *aetas Christiana* that the editors believed had not been inscribed *religionis Christianae causa* (*CIL* 6. 1, p. v) – were assigned to volumes vi (1876–) and xv (1891–) of Mommsen's equally young *Corpus Inscriptionum Latinarum* (Sandys 1927: 30–1; Bérard 2000: 111–17; Bodel 2001a: 159–65). Although various volumes of the *CIL* would randomly incorporate some recognizably Christian inscriptions (largely epitaphs), separate collections of Christian texts frequently appeared elsewhere. Consequently, regional corpora seldom sought to span the centuries from early to late antiquity (e.g., Le Blant 1856–65; Hübner 1871; see Bérard 2000). Finally, as the new Christian epigraphy inaugurated its own journals and developed its own handbooks (Marucchi 1910; Frend 1996: 76–86), it further removed itself from a Roman epigraphy also increasingly pursuing its own way (Sanders 1976: 133).

Certainly, many of the inscriptions associated, for example, with the extramural funerary areas of late antique Rome, as well as other cities and towns, do often form assemblies distinct in content, style, and age. At Rome itself, moreover, much of the work of discovery and the expense of publication of those texts was managed or assumed by the Commissione di Archeologia Sacra, approved by Pius IX in 1852 and dedicated to the systematic and scientific pursuit of its goals (Ferrua 1984; Giuliani 1994: 62–5). Nevertheless, the ghettoization of Late Antiquity's epigraphic heritage severely fragmented the discipline of Latin epigraphy and displaced many late antique inscriptions of all types away from their broader historical contexts. Historians were often stranded on either side of an academic divide and left to search out texts "cunningly concealed in the corpora and periodicals" (Jones 1964: vi, quoted in Handley 2003: 1). Not surprisingly, then, even a conscientious Roman epigraphist may still view "Christian epigraphy" as "virtually a field unto itself" (Bodel 2001a: xviii). This situation serves well neither Latin epigraphy nor the study of Late Antiquity, the true place of which, in the *longue durée* of Roman history, is now being vigorously debated once more (e.g., Swain and Edwards 2004; Ward-Perkins 2005).

Many recent studies, therefore, often transgress the boundaries set around late Latin inscriptions by earlier generations of scholars. Late Antiquity is now understood to have been an age of complex and often contested political, social, and religious change. At any given moment, the variety of cultural expressions within the bounds or former bounds of the empire was matched by the multiplicity of ties that linked every conception of the present to an image of its past. The fourth and fifth centuries especially, which saw both the reflowering of inscriptional culture in many regions of the empire and an intense remapping of the contours of identity, confound taxonomies drawn up on simplistic or predetermined religious lines. Similarly, the subsequent adoption of monumental writing in Latin by Vandals, Lombards, and other Germanic peoples signals the assimilation of those groups into a post-Roman world defined not only by Christian affiliations but also by association with even older Roman traditions of public literacy. Continuing to expand the horizons of epigraphic inquiry will further erode the barriers that have sometimes limited the kinds of questions scholars raise in the face of this rich resource.

One recent estimate places at 600,000 the number of all surviving Greek and Latin inscriptions produced between 800 BC and AD 700 (Bodel 2001b: 4). Latin inscriptions, numbering "250,000 or more," account for nearly half of this total (Saller and Shaw 1984). But those numbers also have a history. The fortuitous nature of preservation, together with the difficulty of assembling comprehensive data, still partially obscures the rhythm and scale of the production of inscribed monuments and objects across the centuries. Yet, one pattern appears incontestable: the manufacture of Latin inscriptions increased steadily from the first through the early third century, declined sharply in the later third century, and then began a new cycle of rise and fall from the fourth through the late seventh century (Randsborg 1991: 108–14; Durliat 1995b: 227–32; with one qualification for the third century at Forbis 1996: 101).

Our crude data, however, also hint at the relative vigor of the late antique phase of this phenomenon. The quantity of known late republican and early imperial Latin inscriptions still far surpasses the number of later Latin texts, conservatively estimated a decade ago at 50,000, or approximately one-fifth of all known Latin inscriptions (Galvao-Sobrinho 1995). This ratio may change as archaeologists and epigraphists continue their more intensive turn to the late antique material, and as updated corpora of late Latin inscriptions continue to appear, reconfiguring regional profiles (for Spain, see Handley 2003 and Kulikowski 2004; for Gaul, see Gauthier 1975 and Descombes 1985).

Moreover, the suspicion that the sixth and seventh centuries witnessed a rise in the proportion of more perishable *painted* inscriptions may, if justified, also redress the imbalance and smooth the (apparent) seventh- and eighth-century rupture between the Christian epigraphy of Late Antiquity and that of the Middle Ages (Durliat 1995b: 239). Nevertheless, the third-century hiatus remains stark and raises significant questions about the relationship between the epigraphic habits of the early empire and those motivating the comparatively limited "revival" that began in the fourth century.

It is now commonplace to insist that the steady rise in the total number of datable Latin inscriptions across the first two centuries AD reflects to some degree the romanization of regions increasingly subject to the influence of ideas emanating from Italy (MacMullen 1982). Scholars debate about the particular motives that inspired the epigraphic habit of those segments of the Roman or romanizing populations of the western provinces and Italy who then commissioned inscriptions (e.g., Meyer 1990; Cherry 1995; Woolf 1996). Some, indeed, prefer to emphasize the heterogeneity of Romanness in this period and the plurality of epigraphic impulses (Mattingly 2004; Mourtisen 2005). Most of those scholarly arguments, however, still assert a close link between the will to inscribe and the desire to assert identity and status within (or against) the structures of early imperial culture (Woolf 1998: 77–105; Kulikowski 2004: 36–7). It is also now widely accepted that epigraphic habits are "socially contingent" cultural practices, "which some people might embrace and others ignore" for reasons that only thick description can begin to reveal (Mourtisen 2005). Consequently, it must also be acknowledged that the epigraphic record of any period is an untrustworthy demographic sample, while the motives that inspired it may just as well have arisen from contestation as from consensus.

This early imperial debate has obvious implications for late Latin epigraphy. Whether personal or corporate, lay or clerical, late Latin inscriptions are similarly implicated in the identity politics of the late Roman and post-Roman worlds, and similarly contingent upon a host of social, religious, and political factors that go far beyond the mere ability to write and inscribe. Certainly, when the epigraphic impulse does (re)emerge in the fourth century, it displays distinct features. While many types of inscriptions continue to be carved – honorific texts, building dedications, imperial rescripts, and *elogia*, for example – funerary inscriptions now overwhelmingly dominate the record. Though epitaphs comprise slightly more than two-thirds of surviving *early* imperial Latin inscriptions (Saller and Shaw 1984), their percentage of the total increases sharply in Late Antiquity. This predominance is so pronounced that the rising regional curves of datable Christian funerary texts have been deemed an index of the new religion's arrival and growth in an area (Galvao-Sobrinho 1995). Though not all scholars agree that these regional epigraphic curves also plot rates of conversion (Handley 2003: 12–14), most do acknowledge that Late Antiquity's epigraphic signature is heavily epitaphic and flows from sources of inspiration that come to the fore with the fourth-century sea-changes in religious affiliation. Yet, it seems clear in general that these and other late Latin texts were more or less conscious participants in the ongoing (re)constructions of Romano-Christian personal and civic identity in the post-Constantinian centuries. Moreover, as new peoples moved into the provinces and former provinces of the western empire in Late Antiquity, some of them also discovered in Latin epigraphy an effective medium for articulating their own relationships to the Christian empire or the Church. The challenge facing the historian, then, is to identify the social contingencies lurking within and behind the epigraphic corpora and curves of Late Antiquity.

An Epigraphy of Christians

In the late summer of AD 359, the Roman senator Junius Bassus was buried at St. Peter's basilica on the Vatican hill. His body was laid to rest in a large double-register columnar marble sarcophagus. The facade of the sarcophagus displayed ten deeply cut tableaux depicting events from the Bible and the era of the apostles. Its lid, now badly damaged, presented on its right side a traditional "meal of the dead" and on the left a scene no longer identifiable. The sarcophagus also offered two inscriptions: one on the very upper edge of the sarcophagus box; the other, in verse, set in the center of the lid's forward-facing vertical field. The first identified Bassus as urban prefect and newly baptized at the time of his death on August 25, AD 359: *in ipsa praefectura urbi neofitus iit ad deum*. The second, of eight elegiac couplets now incomplete, praised his career and munificence, recalled his extraordinary public funeral, and asserted that death (*mors*) had not cheated him of further success but given him distinction far beyond any terrestrial honor. The verse epitaph, therefore, expressed in words the same pretensions as those signaled by the visual splendor of the sarcophagus's sculpting (*PLRE* i: 155; Malbon 1990; Alan Cameron 2002). Although inscribed sarcophagi have a long history at Rome – highlighted, for example, by those deposited in the late republican Tomb of the Scipios – Junius Bassus (or his heirs) used his to announce surprising claims about the afterlife, claims that reflected the new confidence that came with ritual incorporation into the community of Christian believers at Rome.

A generation later, another Roman aristocrat of high achievement was buried at St. Peter's. The ultra-wealthy Petronius Probus had been ordinary consul and four times praetorian prefect before he died in about AD 390 and was interred in a grand mausoleum snug against the apse of Constantine's church. Few at Rome then matched Probus in prestige. When it was discovered in the fifteenth century, his marble sarcophagus (a single-register columnar type) still contained remnants of the golden cloth that had adorned his corpse. Probus' sarcophagus bears no inscription, but his mausoleum itself was decorated with two lengthy verse inscriptions. Supremely self-confident epitaphs, the two poems echo both Virgil and Christian scripture to boast of Probus' earthly accomplishments and forecast his heavenly rewards. As with Junius Bassus, not death but eternal life – in this case to be enjoyed among the stars (*vivit et astra tenet*, his epitaph proclaimed) – was the proper reward for a *nobilis* like Probus (*PLRE* i: 736–40). Probus' claims appear bold enough when set against the more pessimistic background of early imperial epitaphs; but their immediate force emerges most vividly when read in conjunction with the highly conservative (literary) *elogia* of the earthbound Roman aristocrats celebrated by Probus' contemporary, the pagan senator Avianius Symmachus. Avianius' avowed model was the *Hebdomades* of the late republican writer Varro: Probus was tapping the rapidly rising stream of new Christian poetry and ideology (Trout 2001).

Both the sarcophagus of Junius Bassus and the mausoleum of Petronius Probus announced the claims of a particular segment of the fourth-century Roman elite, whose Christian affiliation did not directly induce them (as it did some of their Christian peers) to renounce the prerogatives of their class. As assemblies of words and images, these monuments were self-assured declarations within an increasingly strident debate over the value of wealth and secular achievements at a crucial moment when paganism was far from crushed but when Christian asceticism had increasingly powerful allies. Yet, while these grand funerary monuments are representative of some of the ways in which Christian epigraphy collaborated in the assertion of identity in a competitive atmosphere, they were, like Rome itself, atypical in other respects. Far more than half of the known Latin inscriptions of Late Antiquity come from this single city, where the tally of texts from the catacombs alone runs to 45,000 – 40,000 of them in Latin and the great majority of those post-Constantinian (Carletti 1986: 11). Furthermore, although aristocrats elsewhere were also sometimes buried in grand tombs and commemorated with verse epitaphs, the majority of extant funerary inscriptions in Italy and the provinces are far simpler.

In the mass of these relatively brief and humble epitaphs lurks a deeper social history. Third-century Christian epitaphs are relatively few; but even they suggest how early Christians used funerary epigraphy to demarcate communal identity. The great majority (82.9%) of the texts in an early third-century group (in Greek as well as Latin) from the catacomb of Priscilla on the Via Salaria Nova, for example, have been described as "neutral," avoiding explicit advertisement of religious allegiances (though some graves were marked by images of fish or anchors). Over the following decades, however, the Christian salutations seen in a minority of the texts from the catacomb of Priscilla, such as *pax* and *pax tibi*, as well as the eschatological expression *in pace*, become more common. In a group of inscriptions from the cemetery of Marcellinus and Peter on the Via Labicana, for example, dated to the later third century, half of the texts now signaled Christian affiliation, especially through the phrase *in pace* but also in the first appearances of the word *depositio*. In such language, as well as in the brevity of the earlier epitaphs, whose preference for a single name contrasted with contemporary non-Christian practice, it is possible to glimpse the desire of these Christians to proclaim the distinction and the collective cohesion of their community within an urban world characterized by countless religious and social opportunities (Carletti 1986: 12–15; 1988; Yasin 2005: 441–6).

The much larger number of surviving fourth- and fifth-century epitaphs highlights the variety of styles and formulae that emerged with the phenomenal post-Constantinian growth of Christianity. Not surprisingly, these more loquacious epitaphs continue to spotlight traditional values shared by Christians with their contemporaries – *innocentia* and *castitas*, for example. But other elements of praise also begin to appear or increase in incidence, perhaps as prescriptions for the living as much as descriptions of the dead. References to *caritas* or *amor pauperum* stress the Christian's social responsibility. Attributes such as faithfulness (*fidelis*) and obedience or humility (*servus Dei*) become prominent as terms of praise. Traditional images of death as sleep or repose are now made more specific with the tag *in pace*. The more frequent use of formulae of deposition (e.g., *depositus/a [in pace]*) accompanied by precise dates bears forceful witness to deeper shifts in thinking, for this practice reflects the Christian reconfiguration of death as a day of birth (*natalis*) into a new life that could be commemorated annually by those left behind. Indeed, although survivors still lament the loss of loved ones, solace is found in assurance of the victory over death won by Christ's followers. In these still relatively modest epitaphs, the familiar and the novel coalesce in the expression of ideals increasingly popular in this age (Charles Pietri 1983b: 1448–68).

These texts also reveal unintentionally the widening gap between the literary Latin of the formally educated and forms of the spoken language. They help us thereby to gauge the evolution of Vulgar (or demotic) Latin toward the Romance languages within the empire's former provinces. The definitive break in intelligibility between the spoken language and the far more conservative forms of literary Latin (i.e., late and then medieval Latin) may have come only in and after the eighth century;

but most aspects of demotic Latin had already evolved considerably during Late Antiquity. The changes are wholesale, spanning pronunciation, spelling, morphology, and syntax. As already evident in the texts just cited – in the case of *biba* (for *vivas*), for example – epitaphs offer clear examples of the exchange of labial *b* for *v* with the loss of a final consonant. Phonetic change is even more radical in the vowel system, where inscriptions reveal the disappearing distinction of many long and short vowels (for example, the frequent assimilation of short *i* and long *e*). Likewise, epigraphic texts signal the breakdown of the inflectional system, particularly in nominal morphology, and illustrate the increasing reliance on prepositional phrases to do the work of cases. Such changes in syntax as the replacement of accusative and infinitive constructions with subordinate clauses containing a finite verb and introduced by a conjunction (often *quod* or *quia*) are less evident in these short texts; but the often distinct evidence preserved on epitaphs may bring us closer than many literary texts to the Latin of Late Antiquity's non-elites (Rigg 1996; Herman 2000).

In the end, of course, epitaphs also bring us back to individuals. Thousands of the late antique dead are only names, but some graves are more forthcoming about the lives of their occupants. In the *basilichetta* of the Roman Catacomb of Commodilla, adjacent to a *memoria* of the saints Felix and Adauctus, a painted verse inscription in five elegiac couplets, probably of the mid sixth century, accompanies a large image of the deceased widow Turtura. The text (*Inscriptiones christianae urbis Romae*, ii: 6018) is the lament of a bereaved son. It highlights the marital fidelity of a maternal "turtle-dove" (*turtura*), who preserved her chastity for thirty-six years after her husband's death. Little is overtly "Christian" in the son's eulogy; but its words are part of the same large fresco panel that includes Turtura's portrait. Above the verses of an epitaph that centers on Turtura's life on earth, the saints Felix and Adauctus present the deceased *matrona* to an enthroned Madonna and Child (Deckers et al. 1994). This iconic panel, a "precocious example" of the rising cult of *Maria Regina* at Rome (Thunø 2003), conditioned every reading of the epitaph below it, just as the verses affected the viewer's response to the widowed mother's image. The classicizing lament draws emotional force from the portrait at the same time as the poem's consolatory tone is reinforced then obviated by the arresting image of Turtura's admission into a heavenly court unbounded by time. Many late antique epitaphs, in far simpler fashion, expressed similar hopes.

For many late antique Romans, death especially activated the will to inscribe, to set down in stone or plaster something about a life. The particular motives and contingencies behind every act of inscription surely vary across the centuries, as do the roles and proportions of tradition and innovation in the language of commemoration. The sarcophagus of Junius Bassus and the fresco of Turtura are separated by some two centuries of change. Though these two memorials are bound together by the verses that adorn them, they are distinguished by the historical events that divide the Rome of Constantine's sons from that of the popes of the Justinianic age. And yet, every Christian epitaph stills the social and religious cross currents of the moment. Despite epigraphy's inherent limitations as an index of late antique society and demography, inscribed late Latin funerary monuments nevertheless capture aspects of the age that might otherwise have slipped away.

Epigraphic Horizons

A good deal of Roman and late antique history is now based on an analysis of inscriptions. A regional assembly, such as that illustrating the vitality of urbanism in fourth-century North Africa (Lepelley 1979–81), may tell an unexpected story, while inscriptions in bulk often underpin quantitative or analytical studies (Bodel 2001b: 30–9). Fundamental investigations of the ancient economy rest as often on epigraphic evidence as upon the amphorae, bricks, and shipwrecks revealed by archaeology (Duncan-Jones 1974; Harris 1993). Studies of and debates about the age of Roman girls at marriage (Shaw 1987a) or the structure of the Roman family (Saller and Shaw 1984; Mann 1985; Martin 1996) rely heavily upon inscriptions analyzed in aggregate. Without the mass of more ordinary inscriptions, the lives of the urban lower classes would be even more poorly understood. Epigraphic evidence, for instance, makes it possible to talk more confidently about the working lives and self-representation of the servile, freed, and freeborn population of early imperial Rome, Pompeii, or Ostia (Joshel 1992; Mourtisen 2005), or about prostitution in the Roman world (McGinn 2004). And although consensus remains elusive, studies of literacy continue to marshal epigraphically informed arguments (Cooley 2002; Ward-Perkins 2005: 151–67).

Some of the studies just mentioned included among their data inscriptions from late as well as earlier antiquity (for example, Shaw 1987a). But recognition of the distinct features and qualities of late antique inscriptions has also encouraged investigations designed to take specific advantage of later texts. The more consistent inclusion of the precise time of the deceased's death in Christian epitaphs, for example, may make it possible to plot a "seasonal curve" for the cycle of mortality (excluding infant deaths) on display in this "data in bulk" (Shaw 1996). Furthermore, beyond revealing shifting patterns of nomenclature and epithets, epigraphy, together with archaeology, is a rich source of information about the late antique Jewish community in Rome. Though the majority of the epitaphs from Rome's Jewish catacombs preferred Greek to Latin, the naming (onomastic) practices, references to age at death, and propensity to advertise community-related offices in these epitaphs suggest that Jews interacted regularly with gentiles, while also maintaining their distinction among their pagan and Christian contemporaries (Rutgers 1995).

Similarly, the elite commemorative practices that persist into and beyond the fourth century remain the *sine qua non* of Roman prosopography. The dedicatory, honorific, and funerary inscriptions of the Roman aristocracy are fundamental to a reconstruction of the late empire's administrative structures as well as the career patterns, naming practices, and genealogical relationships of the Roman aristocracy. Thus, both a pioneering study of the urban prefects of Rome (Chastagnol 1962) and a more recent work on the administration of late Roman Italy (Cecconi 1994) rest as solidly on epigraphic as on literary foundations. Those foundations, in turn, have been shored up or undermined by pursuit of the principles of late Roman nomenclature, principles often deduced to an unavoidable degree from the epigraphic data itself (Kajanto 1966; Alan Cameron 1985b). Further rarified, these same inscriptions often undergird conclusions about the rate and nature of aristocratic conversion to Christianity in the fourth and fifth centuries (Salzman 2002), or reveal the competition and jockeying for status still endemic to this class (Niquet 2000).

Several examples can serve to illustrate the range and depth of the epigraphic horizons of Late Antiquity. The Casket of Proiecta is perhaps the most renowned item among the exquisite vessels and objects that comprise the Esquiline Treasure (Shelton 1981; Painter 2000). On the embossed and engraved lower front panel of this silver gilded box is depicted a young woman attended by servants as she dresses her hair before a mirror. Immediately above, on the front panel of the lid, is a depiction of Venus at her toilet, naked, seated on a shell, and attended by Centauro-tritons and Erotes, a "visual simile" of the real-life scene below it (Shelton 1981: 27). In the central panel on the top of the lid, encircled by a wreath held by two more Erotes, appear a husband and wife, suggesting the casket may originally have been a wedding gift. While these and the casket's remaining scenes of domestic and public life, especially the procession to the public baths that adorns the back panel of the lid, may evoke the fourth-century "world of elite women" (Elsner 1998: 40), it is the inscription running across the horizontal front rim of the lid – "Secundus and Proiecta, may you live in Christ (*vivatis in Chri[sto]*)" – that has made the object even more tantalizing. Proiecta's casket – with its conflation of erotic and mytho-logical imagery, its visual allusions to the mundane activities of its aristocratic female proprietor, and its exhortation to the Christian life – has taken a rightful place within modern debates about the aesthetic and artistic agenda, the compromises and the tensions, that accompanied the conversion of the Roman elite to Christianity in the mid and later fourth century (Kitzinger 1977; Alan Cameron 1985a; Shelton 1985).

Roughly from the same milieu, though quite different in length, medium, and function from the brief exhortation inscribed on Proiecta's casket, we have the complex story of *CIL* 6. 1. 1783. The inscription filled the base of a statue erected (or restored) in AD 431 in Rome's Forum of Trajan. The statue itself presumably represented Virius Nicomachus Flavianus, who is commemorated on the base, although he had died in disgrace more than three decades earlier at the Battle of the Frigidus River (AD 394). Indeed, *CIL* 6. 1. 1783, which apparently overwrote a previous inscription, announced the imperial rescue of Flavianus from the *damnatio memoriae* that had followed upon his miscalculated opposition to Theodosius I in the middle years of the AD 390s. Some contemporaries had quickly presented the Battle of the Frigidus, where Flavianus, portrayed as a conservative pagan, had supported the "usurper" Eugenius, as a new chapter in the story of Christianity's victory over Rome's traditional cults. The rehabilitation publicized in *CIL* 6. 1. 1783, then, which reprinted a florid letter of exculpation from Theodosius II and Valentinian III to the Roman senate, apparently testifies to the campaigns of revision and reconciliation then being waged to heal the wounds inflicted on the Roman aristocracy by the political and religious conflicts of the previous generation (Hedrick 2000). Exact interpretation of the amnesia and nostalgia that color *CIL* 6. 1. 1783 remains open to argument; but, as one of the few significant Latin "literary texts" of the AD 430s, this inscription must be part of any assessment of the cultural history of the Theodosian age – particularly because its publicly inscribed words, unlike those of Macrobius' nearly contemporary *Saturnalia*, were shared well beyond the confines of the literary salons and villas of the Roman elite.

To walk from the *domus* of Proiecta on the Esquiline to the Forum of Trajan is to move from essentially private to extremely public space. But the nature of public space itself was evolving in this period, as cityscape and countryside were transformed under the impetus of the social, religious, and political changes that accompanied christianization (see Loseby, ch. 10). New churches, *martyria*, and monastic foundations arose both in the suburbs and within the city walls. Alternative centers of civic and religious activity emerged as older ones declined. Moreover, as Christians redrew urban topography, public writing, formal and informal, spilled over from the temples, basilicas, and *fora* into new kinds of social space. Between the mid seventh and the mid ninth century, for example, far removed from the Rome of the Theodosian age, at least 165 texts were carved or scratched into the walls of the sanctuary of San Michele at Monte Sant'Angelo in the Apulian peninsula of Gargano (Carletti 1980; Everett 2003: 265–74). Several of the surviving inscriptions attest to official Lombard patronage of the sanctuary. One (Carletti 1980: no. 82) records the building activities of Duke Romoald I of Beneventum (AD 663–87); another (no. 44) apparently refers to Grimoald I (AD 647–71), as well as to Romoald, his son. The two texts were expertly carved and their lettering shows affinities with the Pavian epigraphy of the north (Carletti 1980: 24). Both have been seen as further evidence for a seventh-century royal program "to unite the Arian-Catholic divisions and help foster a sense of Lombard unity" (Everett 2003: 267). Similarly official, though somewhat more crudely carved, is an eight-line acclamation to the Roman saints Peter and Paul inscribed near one of the sanctuary's entrance ways, probably in the seventh century under the guidance of the site's patrons or administrators (Otranto 1980). Though interpretation of this text remains difficult, one thing seems clear: at early medieval San Michele, monumental writing in public space was still being enlisted to promote reconciliation and assert collective identity.

Yet, the great majority of the texts preserved at San Michele are not official pronouncements but pilgrims' graffiti (numbering 159). Most give only a name. Many appear to be autographs. Of the 168 men and fourteen women documented, ninety-seven have been identified on onomastic grounds as Germanic – primarily Lombards, but also Franks and Anglo-Saxons. Eighteen pilgrims identified themselves as presbyters (three of whom further self-identified as *peccatores*), one as a deacon, five as monks. Four are separately styled *peregrinus* (or *pelegrinus*). The high social rank of some of these visitors is indicated by the presence of ten *viri honesti* among the group. Twenty-three of the catalogued inscriptions also include variations on the acclamation "May you live in God [*biba in deo*]" (Carletti 1980: 18–24). Walls still attracted, as they had done for centuries, the personal testimonies of those who wished to memorialize their presence in that way, and who possessed a sufficient command of letters to write their names and a few standard phrases (Charles Pietri 1983b; Corbier 2005).

An exceptional natural catastrophe in first-century Campania has preserved unusually rich evidence at Pompeii for the allure of walls and the surfaces of public monuments in earlier Roman antiquity. Although the chances of survival are always especially slim for scratched, scrawled, or painted graffiti, a number of significant finds give a sense of what the pilgrims of San Michele could have learned from earlier late antique pilgrims. In the late third and early fourth century, visitors to the shrine of Peter and Paul on the Via Appia (soon to be the site of Constantine's Basilica Apostolorum) scratched their names, invocations, and prayers into a plastered red wall. "Peter and Paul, intercede [*petite*] for us" or "remember us [*in mente abeatis*]" appear frequently (*Inscriptiones christianae urbis Romae*, v. 12907–13096). The two apostles were glossed as "santi martyres" (v: 12955). These *tituli memoriales* recorded the fulfillment of vows and participation in meals (*refrigeria*) at the shrine (Charles Pietri 1983b: 1483–5; Donati 2000: nos. 107–8; Holloway 2004: 146–52). The assembly gives us privileged access to the ritual and social life unfolding around the tombs of the Roman martyrs in the decades before the first great wave of monumentalization overtook them.

Across Rome in the catacombs of Commodilla, a seventh-century fresco of St. Luke (roughly contemporary, therefore, with the earliest texts at San Michele) attracted thirty-seven graffiti. Again, many are simply names, often accompanied by *ego*, several denoting Lombards and Anglo-Saxons. Roughly a third also announced clerical rank while a few added *biba* or *biba in deo* – for example, "I, Petrus, may you live in God" (Carletti 1984–5). The same story can be read, at least by the early seventh century, at the small basilica *ad corpus* of the saints Marcellinus and Peter on the Via Labicana (Guyon 1987: 470–4). If more were known about the church of Minerve northwest of Narbonne in southern Gaul, similar devotional impulses might be identified behind some of the ninety-three names scribbled in the early Middle Ages on an altar table probably installed there in the fifth century by Rusticus, bishop of Narbonne (Le Blant 1856: no. 609; Marrou 1970: 345). Well into Late Antiquity, personal testimonies scrawled on walls and monuments continued to offer individuals a way of claiming affiliation with the "cultural milieu" of ancient pilgrimage and of identifying themselves with others of like mind and habit (Carletti 1995; Everett 2003: 271–2; but pessimism at Ward-Perkins 2005: 163–6). But, since pilgrimage may have been informed as much by contestation as by consensus, subtle reading may reveal fault-lines as well as commonality (Elsner 2005).

Finally, again roughly contemporary with the inscriptions and graffiti of San Michele, there are a number of inscribed, circular, animal-headed *fibulae* of south and central Italian origin. Luxury objects, far less elaborate than the casket of Proiecta but nevertheless expressing a comparable ethos, these silver and bronze clasps demonstrate the similarly persistent desire of late antique and early medieval men and women to customize personal items by inscription. One group of thirteen *fibulae* displays both names and acclamations (Salvatore 1977). The names, like Lucas and Aoderada, are presumably those of the owners. A typical acclamation reads *biba* or *bibas*, in one case expanded to *viva in D[e]o*. The phrase *D[ominu]s in nomine tuo* appears once. Although these *fibulae* and similar items raise questions about the relationship between workshops and clients and about levels of literacy in Lombard Italy, they nevertheless show that inscribed words remained, for some, crucial markers of personal status and corporate allegiance.

Though far removed in many ways from the Rome of Proiecta and Flavianus, both the mural inscriptions of San Michele and these inscribed *fibulae* attest to the persistence of familiar epigraphic impulses in early medieval Italy. Before returning to the Lombard states in the final section, however, we might first consider a further aspect of the relationship between communal identity and monumental texts already suggested by the inscriptions of San Michele.

Civic History and Public Memory

On a massive stone lintel (*limen*), Narbonne's fifth-century bishop, Rusticus, commemorated his reconstruction of the city's cathedral. A single line running the length of the cornice recorded the date when the lintel was set in place (*collokatum*): in the fourth year of the building project, during the sixth consulship of Valentinian Augustus, three days before the calends of December, in the nineteenth year of his own episcopate (November 29, AD 445). Below the cornice, in four columns filling the lintel's face, Rusticus advertised his genealogy and his *cursus honorum* and detailed his management of the project: he was the son and nephew of bishops and had been a monastic colleague and fellow presbyter at Marseille of that city's future bishop Venerius. The rebuilding, necessitated by a fire, had begun with the destruction of the old church's walls under the supervision of the presbyter Ursus and the deacon Hermes on the fifth day of the fifteenth year of Rusticus' episcopate, three days before the Ides of October (October 13, AD 441). The new foundations were in squared stone (*quadrata*) and, in the second year of the project, on October 9 (the anniversary of Rusticus' ordination), the apse had been completed under the management of the subdeacon Montanus. Financial backing came from Venerius, other bishops, and Marcellus, the praetorian prefect who had urged (*exegit*) Rusticus to undertake the task (*onus*) (Le Blant 1856: no. 617; Diehl 1961: no. 1806). The lintel is a remarkable document; but other stones elsewhere also announced Rusticus' benefactions (and ambitions): a lintel at an ancient church of St. Felix; a column dated precisely to the two hundred and sixty-sixth day of the seventeenth year of his episcopate (July 1, AD 444); an altar proclaiming *Orate pro me Rustico vestro*; and the previously noted graffiti-covered marble slab from Minerve (Le Blant 1856: no. 609), recording a project Rusticus had commissioned (*fieri fecit*) in the thirtieth year of his episcopate (Marrou 1970; Heinzelmann 1983: Rusticus 4; Durliat 1995a: 182). Rusticus' elaborate epigraphic dossier testifies to this combative bishop's efforts to anchor himself and his community to an inscribed identity amid the turmoil of a mid-fifth-century Narbonensis hedged in by Germanic kings (Mathisen 1989). The effort now appears masterfully shrewd. Connections to the empire were openly affirmed by naming the emperor, dating by consuls, and emphasizing the role of the praetorian prefecture. At the same time, Rusticus underscored those local sources of status and authority that were increasingly important, as the tide of empire receded from southern Gaul. Dating by reference to the years and days of his episcopate not only asserted Rusticus' personal authority but also promoted a local and more immediately relevant chronology linked to the episcopate of Narbonne. By recalling his own genealogy, his *cursus*, and his alliances with the region's other bishops, Rusticus advertised his claims to elite status and municipal authority at a time when so many other institutions of civic government had fallen into disuse. Similarly, his announcement of the *curae* exercised by members of the local clergy established them in like manner as benefactors of both city and church. Not surprisingly, of course, Rusticus' inscriptions also publicized his role as a builder of churches, now the key structures with which civic impresarios and patrons were redefining the late antique cityscape. Previously, the elite of Narbonne had associated themselves with the duovirate and had dedicated altars to Vulcan (*CIL* 12. 4338).

Not long after Rusticus set his name prominently over Narbonne's cathedral door, Perpetuus, bishop of Tours (AD 458/9–488/9), inscribed his in the apse of his new Basilica of St. Martin. It was not until the later fifth century that a suitable church finally rose over the tomb of the fourth-century bishop Martin. At his death in AD 397, Martin had been buried in a cemetery outside Tours's walls. Soon thereafter, his grave site, marked by a modest shrine, had emerged as the scene of spectacular miracles. Yet, only during the episcopate of the enterprising Perpetuus did Martin's relics receive the kind of lavish patronage that already distinguished the tombs of many local martyrs and saints (Gregory of Tours, *De virtutibus sancti Martini* 1. 6). Perpetuus' basilica, dedicated in AD 471 (but destroyed by the Normans in AD 997) has left few physical traces (Chevalier 1888; Lelong 1986), but twelve or thirteen texts inscribed on the church's walls were copied down some time before the year AD 559. Preserved together with a bundle of other documents related to the basilica and the cult of St. Martin, this epigraphic *syllogé* further attests to the way in which monumental writing contributed to the reinvention of civic history around the tombs of the saints in late Roman and Merovingian Gaul.

The inscriptions in prose and verse commissioned by Perpetuus, penned in part by eminent men of letters and set upon the church's walls, functioned in multiple ways to guide visitors to Martin's tomb. They encouraged the humility and purity of heart prerequisite to fulfillment of the vows that brought pilgrims to the basilica (5–7). They assured readers (and listeners) that Martin was present to welcome them, yet also resident in the starry "citadel [*arx*] of heaven" (5). They provided captions for the basilica's murals: a gospel scene of the widow's mites, Christ walking on the water, and an image of Jerusalem (8–10). A lengthy poem by Paulinus of Périgueux, who in those same years set to poetry Sulpicius Severus' influential *Life of Martin*, apparently glossed depictions of the living Martin's miracles, admonishing visitors to acknowledge the healings and exorcisms unfolding before their eyes: "Seek his protection; you do not knock at these doors in vain" (11). Martin's tomb was awash in words: the pilgrim, passing through the basilica's apsidal arch as if climbing Jacob's ladder (12; Gen. 28: 17), approached the "temple of God and the gateway to heaven [*vere templum dei est et porta coeli*]." Martin, confessor, martyr, and apostle, was wholly present at his grave, even while his soul rested in the hand of God (13–15). In the apse at the basilica's eastern end, beyond the holy Martin's tomb, a poem by Sidonius Apollinaris (16), *littérateur* and bishop of Clermont, advertised Perpetuus' patronage (Luce Pietri 1983: 372–405, 798–822, whose numeration is followed here; Gilardi 1983; Luce Pietri 1984, 1988; Pietri and Biarne 1987: 32–4; Van Dam 1993: 308–17, with English translations).

The dossier of Perpetuus illustrates well how words inscribed on a church's "very blocks and stones" (11. 6) might guide interpretation of the basilica complexes that were now often at the affective center of urban life and identity. Perpetuus' church arose in a Christian cemetery zone where Martin's grave had been one of many (Pietri and Biarne 1987: 26). Resplendent with marbles, mosaics, and glass, the basilica was now the scene of a series of annual vigils that included the anniversaries of Martin's elevation to the episcopate (July 4) and his *depositio* (November 11). Martin's tomb now attracted a constant stream of pilgrims. Wayfarers sought the saint's favor in matters of health and welfare. They squatted in the courtyards. They took home souvenirs and relics. Some surely scrawled messages recording their visits. Burial continued around the basilica and *ad sanctum*. Tours's bishops, with few exceptions, were now laid to privileged and protected rest near Martin, while other graves accumulated in the surrounding zones (Luce Pietri 1986; Van Dam 1993: 135). Gradually the area around the basilica became crowded with other structures: churches, monasteries, courtyards, and shrines. Indeed, by the time of Gregory, bishop of Tours AD 573–594, this suburban zone outrivaled the town as an attraction for visitors (Van Dam 1993: 128–35).

The image of Martin, whose life and immediate legacy had once been divisive, had slowly become central to the image of Tours. By the time of Perpetuus' episcopate, Paulinus of Périgueux could style Tours the "city of Martin" (*Vita* 5. 295). The same impulses were emerging elsewhere in the late Roman world. Churches and *martyria* decorated with inscriptions and images had already arisen in Milan, Vienne, Tarragona, Carthage, and many towns and cities. The roots of such behavior lay in the fourth century and led back to Rome. There, Christian cult and Christian leaders had quickly adopted the medium of monumental writing. In a city still resplendent with generations of inscribed private and imperial monuments, inscriptions adorned the first imperial churches of the city, soon decorated the subterranean tombs of the martyrs, and continued longer than in many other places in the Latin west to express the self-understanding of the lay and clerical communities of the city.

The fourth century had seen grand structures erected over the graves of the Roman martyrs and saints (Curran 2000: 90–115). At the Vatican basilica of St. Peter, a series of inscriptions, some in mosaic, announced the names of Constantine and other members of his family, linking them with the construction of the building and its cult (e.g., *Inscriptiones christianae urbis Romae*, ii: 4092–5; Holloway 2004: 77–84). Rome's bishops soon followed suit, in mosaic, on marble, and on liturgical objects (e.g., *Inscriptiones christianae urbis Romae*, ii: 4096–7). Still notable for their elegant script, the verse epigrams (*elogia*) of bishop Damasus (AD 366–84), praising the Roman martyrs and installed on marble tablets throughout the city's *martyria* and churches, harked back to the heroic age of the Roman church. As monumental texts, these *elogia* rescripted the civic history once promoted in other officially sanctioned "halls of fame" scattered throughout the city's public and imperial *fora*. For subsequent generations, these epigraphic poems provided the cornerstones for a revision of public memory that recast Rome as the city founded by Peter, Paul, and Lawrence

(Trout 2005). But throughout Late Antiquity, as the destination of pilgrims, Rome also educated others in the ways of Christian epigraphic culture: travelers returned home with those copies of the city's inscriptions that often form the core of the medieval *syllogae* (Everett 2003: 243–8). Over the course of several centuries, monumental writing remained prominent among the strategies by which late antique communities reestablished their corporate identities in a world of religious and social change. Moreover, epigraphy proved capable of defining, as well as weathering, some of the tumultuous transitions of the age.

Crossing Divides

Some time in the AD 540s, some seventy years after Perpetuus erected his basilica over the tomb of Martin, a new pilgrimage site arose on the northern outskirts of Carthage at Bir Ftouha. Recent excavations have revealed the plan and structures of this remarkable Byzantine period complex (Stevens et al. 2005). Within Bir Ftouha's buildings and peristyles, mosaic tomb inscriptions – those of the young Adeodatus and Gaudiosa, for example – decorated the floors, commemorating, as elsewhere in North Africa, the collective identity of those interred beneath (Ennabli 1991: no. 597; Stevens et al. 2005: 324–6, 332–3; Yasin 2005). Outside the basilica and around the main buildings, graves and epitaphs accumulated (Stevens et al. 2005: 571–6). The chancel area of the central basilica, stretching from the apse into the sanctuary and nave, protected at least sixteen privileged tombs (and perhaps twice that number). Though no surviving texts identify the saints honored at Bir Ftouha, there is little doubt that such inscriptions were once on display (Stevens et al. 2005: 43–7, 557–9). Epigraphic commemoration of the martyrs was by then deeply embedded in North African traditions of worship (Duval 1982): Donatist *memoriae martyrum* had dotted the countryside (Frend 1985) and even Augustine had composed verses for inscription (*Serm.* 319. 7 (Stephen); Duval 1982: 182–3 (Nabor)).

During the sixth century, however, the martyrs were also enmeshed in the political and religious confrontations introduced by the Vandal invasion and the Justinianic reconquest (Frend 2000). Traces of these conflicts still mark the epigraphic record. About a kilometer from the Bir Ftouha complex, for example, just outside Carthage at the fourth-century Basilica Maiorum (Mcidfa), an early sixth-century marble plaque (85 × 113 cm), apparently erected as part of a restoration of the church by the Arian Vandal kings and almost surely replacing earlier texts, celebrated the early third-century martyrs Perpetua, Felicitas, and their comrades (Duval 1982: 682–3, no. 6; Ennabli 1982: 7–8, no. 1; 1997: 132–5). Subsequently, inscriptions from the Byzantine period supplemented this Vandalic text (Ennabli 1982: nos. 2–3), as one shift apparently overwrote another. Meanwhile, in and around the basilica, burial continued as it had since the fourth century; and, though the epitaphs of the Vandal period are palaeographically distinct in their rough irregularity and are apparently fewer in number (Ennabli 1982: 23–5), they speak to the Germanic adaptation of epigraphic conventions.

It is tempting to look for history in such assemblies. At the Basilica Maiorum, for example, the recommemoration of Perpetua and Felicitas by the early sixth-century inscription just mentioned has been tied to the end of official persecution by the Vandals in AD 523 and the reopening of the church. Likewise, the later texts may be associated with a new phase of Byzantine rebuilding (Ennabli 1982: 23–5; 1997: 134–5). Similarly, Bir Ftouha's recent excavators suspect that the very construction of this newly founded basilica *ad corpus* "commemorated Carthage's official return to orthodoxy" – that is, Bir Ftouha "may have been a statement of orthodoxy, a celebration of the victory over Arianism" (Stevens et al. 2005: 574). In any case, it seems indisputable that the cult of the martyrs, sometimes rearticulated over time in a series of consecutive dedications, provided one durable element of continuity bridging late Roman and Byzantine North Africa.

Some two centuries after the construction of the Byzantine complex at Bir Ftouha, with Carthage's ragged remnants in Arab hands since AD 698, a "remarkable renewal in the use of epigraphy for the monumental display of text" blossomed in Lombard northern Italy. Rooted in and even consciously echoing the Roman past, whose monuments were still visible in the North Italian landscape, but bent toward the propagation of a new "court ideology," the epigraphic program associated with Liutprand (AD 712–44) now appears as a renaissance after the false starts of the seventh century (Petrucci 1995: 47–53; for what follows, Everett 2003: 235–76, preceding quotes 265, 251). Though the absolute number of extant eighth-century inscriptions (in stone or copies) is small by early imperial standards and the texts often present problems of dating and interpretation, the assembly testifies to royal, clerical, and monastic recognition of the social and political authority invested in inscribed words. Ornately carved, with stylized vegetal borders, the surviving verse epitaphs and building inscriptions of this "Liutprandian epigraphy" advertised the political pretensions, piety, and benevolence of the Lombard king, while underscoring the court's patronage of leading monastic and clerical institutions. They proclaimed peace, order, and prosperity; equated Liutprand with Solomon; and highlighted the Lombard king's commitment to literary culture. Favoring rhythmic meters that ran closer to the cadences of spoken Latin, the verse inscriptions of the period may even have been accessible to a relatively wide audience.

Although this rejuvenation of the epigraphic habit in eighth-century Lombardy also links Italy's epigraphic past with trends soon to be expressed in the inscriptions of the Pavese elite, Liutprand's "renaissance" may stand as our final example of epigraphy's recurrent appeal. The Latin epigraphic habit runs like a familiar thread through the history of the ancient and late antique world, sometimes brilliantly evoking local and imperial cultures, at other times nearly fading from view. The motives that underlie the impulse to write on durable surfaces are profoundly complex and arise out of social contingencies that vary with time, place, and social location. Not all who could inscribe did so, and in some times and places, it seems, very few cared to at all. Nevertheless, nearly all the epigraphic texts surveyed here can be read as statements about individual or collective identity. Consciously and unconsciously, they express contemporary attitudes and values. Moreover, because these words were often set out in public on permanent and semi-permanent surfaces, they themselves became part of the patrimony each age bequeathed to subsequent generations. Ancient epigraphic culture, therefore, and culture shaped by epigraphy, is deeply reflexive, ever bending back even as it looks forward.

BIBLIOGRAPHICAL NOTE

Various relevant corpora of inscriptions are referred to in the chapter but comprehensive coverage of the source material is most readily available in Bérard 2000. Bodel 2001b, though largely eschewing late antique material, is a solid introduction to the study of inscriptions as historical sources. Handley 2003 is both a recent survey of general questions and a set of perceptive arguments about how to approach the epigraphic data of one region, Gaul and Spain, in Late Antiquity. Many such studies are regional, for understandable reasons. Good examples of diverse but regionally based studies include Duval 1982 (North Africa), Carletti 1986 (Rome), and Everett 2003 (Lombard Italy). Herman 2000 is a sure-footed introduction to the value of inscriptions for the history of the Latin language. Galvao-Sobrinho 1995 begins a discussion about the meaning of the epigraphic curves that can be plotted across the regions and decades of Latin Late Antiquity. Hedrick 2000 and Trout 2005 suggest other ways in which inscriptions are implicated in the issues of identity formation and public memory to which this chapter has frequently returned. In the end, however, because epigraphy is foremost a medium of expression, exemplary treatments of inscriptions will be found in many of the best studies of the cultural panorama of Late Antiquity.

CHAPTER THIRTEEN

Gender and the Fall of Rome

Kate Cooper

Ancient historians record that, during the long siege of Rome by Alaric's Goths in AD 410, a lady of the highest Roman nobility finally opened the gates and simply invited the barbarians in. Whether she was moved by pity for the sufferers of famine and plague within the walls or by some more suspicious motive is unclear. In fact, historians were uncertain about the identity of the lady. Procopius (*Wars* 1. 2. 27) asserted that it was Anicia Faltonia Proba, while Zosimus (5. 38) suggested that the *augusta* Serena, widow of the generalissimo Stilicho, had intended to do so in AD 408, before she was executed by order of the Senate.

Though the status of the apocryphal story is dubious, it is almost certainly significant that, despite their many differences, Serena and Proba shared a number of characteristics. Both were matriarchs of dynasties at the pinnacle of Roman society, members of the group standing guard over the mores and values that defined what it was to be Roman. Serena was the niece and adopted daughter of Theodosius the Great, while Proba was the matriarch of the Senate's most distinguished dynasty. An inscription made by Proba's son and daughter-in-law celebrated her as "Anicia Faltonia Proba, trustee of the ancient *nobilitas*, pride of the Anician family, a model of the preservation and teaching of wifely virtue, descendant of consuls, mother of consuls" (*CIL* 6. 1. 1755, tr. Croke and Harries 1982: 116, amended). But, at the same time, both women were Christian, and both were known to be patronesses of the radical ascetic "fringe" in Rome, with Proba the grandmother of the celebrated virgin Demetrias, and Serena the protector of the wealthy eccentric Melania the Younger. Whether or not the story was true, it was alarming enough that it was thinkable. It was no small matter to suggest that a noble Roman *matrona* could be moved to undertake an act so contrary to the Roman values of solidarity, ferocity, and Stoic honor. The story reflects at worst a sense that these values were no longer held dear, and at best a suspicion of deviance among the class of women whose principal duty was to raise invincible and politically indispensable sons.

Gibbon famously argued that the Roman Empire fell because Christian ideas had compromised Roman manliness, and there is still life in the question implied. If one looks for ancient evidence to support Gibbon's hypothesis, one will certainly find it, not least because on this point Gibbon was merely a popularizer. The originator of the "Gibbon hypothesis" was none other than the eighteenth-century historian's preferred late Roman source, Zosimus, continuator of the *New History* of Eunapius of Sardis. Zosimus was no fan of Christianity in general, or of the empress Serena in particular. Writing during the reign of Anastasius (AD 498–518), he was the last of the great pagan historians. His view of Christianity, that it privileged the eccentricities of monks and women at a time when men of iron were called for, was the last in a long line of similar criticisms by pagan writers. There is no way of knowing how much this strategy of "blaming the Christians" was simply a continuation of an old theme, reaching back to Tacitus' account of the Roman fire of AD 64. In any event, the grand narratives of decline and fall on the one hand, and on the other of the rise of Christianity with its distinctive mores, have from the beginning been intertwined. For the historian of gender and the family, it is urgently necessary to understand how changing religious and gender ideals influenced the Roman ability to cope with challenging political and military circumstances.

After the death of Theodosius the Great in AD 395, both Roman and barbarian elites continued, for the most part, to marry and to reproduce as numerously as possible, even while a vocal minority began to live in ascetic communities. Scholars no longer accept a characterization of male ascetics as weak or neurotic. Ascetic virtue constituted a claim to authority (Rousseau 1978) recognizably couched in the language of Roman manliness (Leyser 1999), even if its terms were not acceptable to all parties (Francis 1995). If it was dangerous, it was dangerous because of the ferocious single-mindedness of ascetic practitioners, not because they were effeminate.

We can tell, from the fact that there was so much experimentation, that at least some influential late Romans were ready to identify and celebrate ascetic achievement as a third token of male prowess, alongside the winning of battles and the siring of vigorous sons. Some clearly perceived it as a means to enrich Roman men's collective ability to harness a godly impetus, while others saw the sometimes fiercely disruptive monks as a threat either to social order (McLynn 1992; Gaddis 2005) or to the recognition and encouragement of traditional Roman masculinity.

The present contribution will consider the rise of Christian ideas about gender, sexuality, and the family up to the death of Theodosius, and will then seek to reframe Gibbon's question, with specific reference to the fifth- and sixth-century crisis of the western empire. Both halves of the empire were affected by changing gender ideals, but the question has a particular urgency for the west in Late Antiquity since the west "fell" nearly a thousand years before the east – though AD 476 and 553, the "standard" dates for the "fall" of the western empire, are both problematic: the process they exemplify clearly happened in the fifth or sixth century (Croke 1983). We will suggest that ascetic virtue, in the west at least, seems to have pulled against the ideals of victorious and fertile Roman manliness as an invisible but powerful undertow, although the precise nature of its erosive influence is not yet known.

Gender and the "Decline and Fall"

Bryan Ward-Perkins has recently excoriated cultural historians for failing, with our talk of cultural "transformation" rather than "decline," to address the material devastation brought about by repeated war and a collapsing economy (Ward-Perkins 2005). There are two important points here for the historian of gender and family. First, that the developments in family and gender identity in Late Antiquity can be understood only with reference to what we know about the material reality of the period. The second, equally important, is that political, military, and economic "realities" often had cultural causes.

Peter Heather has argued that a crucial element in the fifth-century failure of the western empire was the "opting out" of landowners who, faced with a choice between vigorous barbarian warlords in the neighborhood and a distant Roman government whose armies might take months to arrive if they arrived at all, frequently made the self-interested decision to cast their lot with the local strong man in the hope that their own estates would be preserved (Heather 2005). Even the less well off could see opportunity in defection. We see this, for example, in the fifth-century historian Priscus of Panium, who described his surprise at meeting, during a diplomatic mission to Attila the Hun, a fellow Greek who had some years before been taken captive by the Hunnic chief Onegesius, and had subsequently neglected to return to the Romans, even when his freedom had been earned. In his view, the Romans could not match the package of low taxes and clean, honest living available among the Huns (Priscus, *Hist.*, fr. Blockley 1981: 268–73). Of course, this was a view straight out of Tacitus (Wolfram 1988), but it may still have been widely held: indeed, Priscus' Latin contemporary Salvian of Marseille makes a similar point (Salvian, *On the Government of God*, 5. 21–3, Lagarrigue 1975).

No military historian today would argue that the Romans were not in with a chance of defending the *limes* in the fifth and sixth centuries, had they made doing so their first priority. (On what follows, see also Gillett, Halsall, and Vanderspoel, chs. 26, 27, and 28, respectively.) Rather, it is widely agreed that the Romans squandered a considerable military advantage through what amounts to perpetual civil war in the repeated succession crises of the fifth century – even the comparatively stable fourth century saw lapses, such as the failure to capture the Gothic leader Alaric in AD 397, that can be attributed to the army's uncertainty over who was in command (Matthews 1975: 272). Modern scholarship suggests that, far from there being a continuous decline through the so-called "third-century crisis" across the fourth century into the sack of Rome and the eventual annexation of the western empire by Gothic kings in the fifth, the third and fourth centuries were characterized largely by prosperity and economic vitality. But, faced with threats from Persia and the Germanic peoples on the eastern and northern *limes* respectively, the Roman armies were repeatedly deployed to less than full advantage, or even led against one another, as emperors tried to insure that no one general became powerful enough to make a bid for the purple, while the generals attempted to crush one another's ambitions. A thousand self-interested decisions, many of them minor in themselves, amounted to a suicidal failure by Roman men to place the *salus populi romani* ahead of personal gain.

At the same time, the old techniques of accommodation and absorption of subject peoples were not functioning smoothly. The failure to settle Alaric's Goths on an amicable basis in the decades leading up to the sack of Rome in AD 410 is the classic example here, but there are countless others. If Rome failed to assimilate the Goths and Vandals as it had assimilated countless other subject peoples across a millennium of Mediterranean dominance, this was in essence a cultural failure as much as a military failure. The two critical tasks of empire, military victory and the coopting of non-Roman elites into the Roman hierarchy of power (see Ando 2000), both had a crucial cultural component. Each process involved a choreography of thousands of people who needed to fall into line quickly and efficiently – and to guide others in doing so – with a minimum of counter-productive input. The failure to stifle self-interest, where it did not coincide with duty, was essentially a cultural failure. But the Roman men in power after the death of Theodosius I in AD 395 seem to have been less bothered by failure than by the high cost of success. From the point of view of gender and family history, we may say that Roman mothers were no longer raising their sons to do their duty or to die trying.

Guy Halsall has breathed new life into Gibbon's view that the fall of the Roman Empire followed from a failure of Roman manliness, by calling attention to how the Later Roman Empire differed both from the early empire and from barbarian societies, in that the hierarchy of civil authority depended on a population of literate aristocrats without military experience, instead of requiring that civil authority be "earned" through military prowess. Thus in the *Notitia Dignitatum*, the Roman list of offices that has come down to us in its early fifth-century form, a disproportionate number of the regiments had "barbarian" names, alongside others bearing the names of ferocious animals, not because the soldiers were members of a barbarian people, but because certain peoples, like lions, were perceived as icons of masculine prowess (Halsall 2004). This meant that military power itself could slip away from being perceived as an intrinsically "Roman" virtue, even if the literati were raised on a diet of epic poetry and Roman military history.

A compelling alternative is offered by Peter Brown, who argued in *The Rise of Western Christendom* (Brown 2003) that the crisis of the fifth and sixth century was not caused by cultural factors at all, but was rather the inevitable outcome – long in reaching fruition – of the sheer implausibility of Roman military success, tensions that had been building ever since the Roman armies had pushed the frontier to its fullest expansion in the second century. On this view, Christianity can be understood as part of the solution – a new technology for establishing the bonds necessary to an ordered society – rather than part of the problem. This evocative hypothesis is in many ways compatible with Halsall's approach, in that it leaves open the question of how gender fits in. A far-reaching examination of the gender culture of the Roman civil bureaucracy is urgently called for, but such a task is beyond the scope of this chapter. I shall seek instead to establish initial terms of reference for understanding the role of gender in the fall of Rome, in the light of what we now know about Roman strategies for establishing hegemony and reciprocity; cultural strategies centered on religion, gender ideals, and the family.

Gender and Family from the Early Christian period to the Fifth and Sixth Centuries

For Late Antiquity, we need to understand both the role that the household played in the articulation of empire, and how the devolution of empire changed the terms of the household's social function. Historians of Late Antiquity and the early medieval period have yet fully to absorb the results of new work on Roman public men (Lendon 1997; Ando 2000; Barton 2001) and Roman households (Saller 1988; Wallace-Hadrill 1988; Laurence and Wallace-Hadrill 1997), which has centered on the negotiation of authority. The position of the Roman male at every level of society was utterly perilous and needed to be repeatedly reconfirmed through a choreography of competition and alliance-building. This is something that military historians have always known; but social historians, and especially gender historians, have yet entirely to shake themselves free of a notion of male power as gratuitous and absolute.

It is worth refreshing our memory about Lévi-Strauss's idea of the fundamental mechanisms of kinship networks. Here again, the emphasis is on the continuous renegotiation of relationships, which must be reciprocally recognized. Kinship is governed by relations in three modes: of consanguinity, through marriage (affinity), and of cohabitation (contiguity) (Lévi-Strauss 1969, 1987; Dumont 1980, 1983). What is critical to all three modes of relationship is the importance of symmetrical recognition – which is to say mutual acknowledgment of the legitimacy of the relationships of authority and accountability within the system (Gregory 1997). It is important that both sides of an alliance – or participants at all levels of a social subsystem – are included in the symmetry of mutual recognition, even if perfect consensus is elusive. Where asymmetrical recognition or rival cognitions are in play, the head of the hierarchy is perceived as less than fully successful in his or her role. Rival cognitions – alternative "readings" of events and alternative views of the motives and accountability of the key players – can undermine the legitimacy of the leadership to the point where the structure is untenable. (We shall return below to an idea of "rival cognitions" derived from Gregory's use of the concept.)

With the early stages of Christianization, we witness among other things the "pull" of alternative affiliations on the part of subordinate members of the household. Here, we see the destabilizing force of rival cognitions perfectly illustrated: through religious conversion, the "deviant" member gains access to a wider community of discourse, which can confirm him or her in resisting the expectations of the dominant culture. A text from North Africa, *The Martyrdom of Perpetua and Felicitas*, written at the turn of the second to third century, preserves the prison diary of the 22-year-old Christian martyr Vibia Perpetua. Included is an episode in which Perpetua attempts to explain to her father why she can no longer in honesty obey his paternal authority. What is important here is that both her status as a suspected criminal, and the equally serious matter of her repudiation of the bond of filial piety, were affirmed as acceptable and even exemplary by the Christian community of Carthage.

Christianity brought with it a distinctive new rhetoric of masculinity, and its initial diffusion among the Roman aristocracy in the fourth century had the effect of destabilizing the terms on which men of the ruling class could claim authority (Cooper 1992). Across our period, Romans and barbarians, pagans and Christians for the most part acknowledged a conceptual *lingua franca* of male prowess linking religion, sex, and gender to male military and political success. This culture of male prowess involved two principal modes of discerning the will and favor of the gods with regard to a man's claim to authority. The first was military. It goes without saying that an ability to win battles was a sign that the gods smiled on a man, while Diocletian and Constantine both showed that a god's power to grant victory would in turn govern his standing among mortals. The second sign of divine favor was a matter of fertility. To be survived by a hearty son, able to consolidate and perhaps extend one's dominance, was the crown of male military achievement. That this depended on factors beyond a man's own control, such as longevity and the right reproductive partner, made it all the more potent as a sign of divine favor.

The role of reproduction in this symbolic system was changing, however. Central here was the relative ranking of male ascetics and male householders. While men aspiring to public or military position continued to gamble on the production of healthy sons, the emerging ascetic establishment offered success in the discipline of sexual renunciation as an alternative token of divine favor (Cooper 1992). We still do not really know whether this third sign worked against the other two and contributed to the collapse of the symbolic system. An alternative structure such as the Church could strengthen or weaken a system depending on the other pressures bearing upon it.

Traditionally, both pagan and Christian communities had seen the biological household as a testing ground for male authority. The household was the key economic unit and, since the time of Plato, Greek thought had seen allegiance to the household as both a building block of civic identity and a source of temptation – the temptation to put the interests of one's own kin ahead of the common good (Cooper 1996; Gaca 2003). The household was not only a microcosm of the city: it was a potential source of disloyalty to the city. This is why household governance was such an effective measure of a man's abilities and accountability.

Christian attitudes to the biological family were ambivalent for entirely different reasons, however. A Christian tradition of tension between the biological family and the "family" of faith developed, and elaborated biblical hints that the end time would reverse or destroy the existing social order (Osiek 1996). The apostle Paul, it will be remembered, had expected the *eschaton* (the end of the world) to take place within his own lifetime, and had therefore discouraged his followers from making long-term plans for their private lives. In 1 Corinthians 7: 26–7, he says, "I think that, in view of the impending crisis, it is well for you to remain as you are. Are you bound to a wife? Do not seek to be free. Are you free from a wife? Do not seek a wife." For Paul, to be "bound to a wife" is to embrace, along with the hoped-for pleasures of conjugal life, anxieties and responsibilities that are likely to aggravate the distress and confusion of the coming *eschaton*.

Later generations, however, remembered Paul as the founder of a radical view of virginity. It is not difficult to see why, if one looks ahead a few lines in the same letter to the Corinthians:

> Yet those who marry will experience distress in this life, and I would spare you that. I mean, brothers and sisters, the appointed time has grown short; from now on, let even those who have wives be as though they had none, and those who mourn as though they were not mourning ... For the present form of this world is passing away. I want you to be free from anxieties. The unmarried man is anxious about the affairs of the Lord, how to please the Lord, but the married man is anxious about the affairs of the world, how to please his wife, and his interests are divided. (1 Cor. 7: 28–30, 32–4)

In fact, Paul's ideas here draw on a standard debate among pagan philosophers about whether a man committed to philosophy could afford to involve himself in the emotionally unbalancing business of raising children under social and medical conditions that forced even the rich to expect a low survival rate for their children in the face of infant and child mortality (Frier 1994). Clearly these words meant one thing in the context of an imminent end to the world, and another if those who embraced Paul's message had to wait, generation after generation, for an end that never seemed to come.

A generation later, the author of the gospel of John remembered Jesus as having challenged the claims of biological kinship by offering what might be called elective kinship through the medium of the Christian *ekklésia*. This version of the passion narrative records Jesus speaking from the cross to his mother, who stood vigil with her sister and Mary Magdalene: calling out to her and pointing to the beloved disciple, "he said to his mother, 'Woman, behold your son!' Then he said to the disciple, 'Behold your mother!' And from that hour the disciple took her to his own home" (John 19: 26–7). Though one can see here an incipient approach to communal care of women past child-bearing age, it must be remembered that Mary was understood by early Christian communities to be the mother of a surviving adult son, James.

Paul had also seen the Christian *ekklésia* as assuming responsibility for the widows and daughters who had no other protection. It was helpful if the moral standing of these women could be irreproachable, and it is very likely that the stringent disciplinary norms of these female communities were the basis for later ideals of the communal ascetic life. Our first evidence of a systematic approach to ascetic communities comes in a cluster of evidence from the second century. The most important sources are the Pastoral Epistles of the New Testament – a group of letters written in Paul's name by an anonymous Greek writer in second-century Asia Minor – and the late second-century Latin writer Tertullian of Carthage in North Africa. Both of these sources refer to unmarried women – virgins and widows – who were supported by the churches financially, and who seem to have lived communally. The Pastoral Epistles refer to an official list of widows in the community (1 Timothy 3: 9–10), which probably reflects an attempt to keep track of who received financial support from the churches, along with an acknowledgment that the women enrolled on the list of widows represented those churches in the eyes both of their communities and of outsiders (D. R. MacDonald 1983; M. Y. MacDonald 1996). It is likely that a church community's charitable foundations for unmarried women were the testing ground for its ideas about sexual renunciation. Communities of virgins seem to predate male monastic communities by at least a century (Lampe 1987; Elm 1994).

From as early as the second century, hagiographical sources began to link the idea of refusing marriage to the idea of withdrawing from the city in order to be tested; the composite would be central to ascetic literature. The *Apocryphal Acts of Paul*, for example, a novelistic second-century treatment of Paul's preaching career, contains a series of episodes known to modern scholarship as the *Acts of Paul and Thecla* (Hennecke and Schneemelcher 1963). These tell the story of how in Iconium, one of the cities of Asia Minor, a young woman named Thecla heard Paul's preaching and broke off her engagement to the eligible bachelor Thamyris, preferring instead to cut her hair short, disguise herself as a beardless young man, and follow Paul in his wanderings from city to city. This narrative tells us more about ancient Christian literature than it does about the women in Paul's entourage; but withdrawal from the common life of the ancient city was central to the Christian ideal of asceticism, whether this meant a geographic removal to rural areas such as the Egyptian desert, or simply a refusal to produce children to stand as heirs of one's name and fortune.

The theme of escape, so prevalent in early Christian literature cannot be understood, however, as an assertion of individualism per se, but rather as the election of a rival group as the vehicle for identity formation. Early Christian ideals of the relationship between the individual and his or her "relational matrix," whether a biological or an otherworldly family, is understood by Philip Esler, Bruce Malina, and others in light of the honor–shame culture of the ancient Mediterranean (Malina 1993; Esler 1994). Common in these discussions is what may be called a "dyadic" or "relational" notion of the self. On this view, identity was defined *through* group membership, rather than independently of it. Opposition to one group inevitably meant adherence to another. Any attempt to extract the individual from the relational matrix was always a flight *to* as well as a flight *from*. Even the heroic solitary was bound, in identity terms, to a community of like-minded souls.

Gender influenced the terms on which the individual could or could not be separated from the group, and one relational matrix could be substituted for another. This is partly because women and men occupied different positions in the hierarchy of the household, and the social meaning of their actions varied accordingly. At the same time, women (whether as loving mothers or vulnerable wives and daughters) stood as the symbol of the sometimes unwelcome bonds and duties of the biological household. Within the socially visible cast of characters of the Roman family, the aristocratic laywoman occupied a central, iconic place. In dynasty-based societies, female kin of high-status families are often accorded considerable symbolic value. From the early empire through the Byzantine period, women appear on coins as a symbol of concord (Holum 1982; Brubaker and Tobler 2000). Their role as icons of the family meant that when they were praised or denigrated it was often a way of speaking about wider social issues (Cooper 1992).

Did Women Have a "Decline and Fall"?

A further problem in the history of women is relevant to the wider issue of gender involving both "male" and "female" persons. Gender historians such as Julia Smith and Lisa Bitel have attempted to reframe Joan Kelly Scott's classic question, "Did women have a Renaissance?" in terms of the social and political transformation wrought by the end of antiquity (Smith 2000a). Given the fragmentary and indeed stereotypical nature of reference to women by ancient and early medieval sources (Bitel 2002), a satisfactory conclusion has yet to be posed. For the sake of clarity, we will consider the fall of the Roman Empire and the rise of Christianity as discrete events, since the relationship between the two is open to debate.

Where the fall of the Roman Empire is concerned, the first and most straightforward question is whether women fared better under Roman or barbarian law. It is well known that Roman law allowed dramatically greater scope to women as property-holders than did the Germanic law codes (Arjava 1996; Smith 2000a), thus allowing them to control resources that could be used in their own interest. It should further be argued that married women at least were better served by Roman family law than by Germanic law. In Roman law, a married woman remained legally independent of her husband, benefiting from protection by (and accountability to) her paternal kin, while Germanic systems assigned the *mundium* or jurisdiction of a woman to her husband, and thus left him as the unchallenged arbiter of her interests, with the power simply to suppress those interests when they did not coincide with his own (Johlen 1999). In structural terms, the interests of the wife "disappear" within those of the husband in the barbarian law codes, while in the Roman system she stands at the intersection of two competing spheres of interest, with scope to invoke the power of one kin group against the other. Whether this reflected a wider tendency to downplay protection of women's interests is not clear. The asymmetry between men and women's rights in marriage was compounded by the fact of polygamy, and complicated by a spectrum of reproductive relationships in which the marriage contract played a far less central role than in the Roman Empire.

There is evidence, of course, that elite barbarian women could make fluent use of their own version of warrior authority. The fifth-century writer Priscus again serves as a useful source, remarking on the hospitality he and his companion received during their embassy to the Huns from the sister-in-law of Attila, who ran her own village (Priscus, *Hist.*, fr. Blockley 1981: 260–1), and that Hereka, the mother of Attila's eldest son, presided over her own establishment (Priscus, *Hist.*, fr. Blockley 1981: 274–5). A woman's rise to this kind of status seems to have involved establishing a privileged relationship to feral menfolk, with the production of healthy sons serving as something like the female equivalent of male success in battle.

At the same time, this is where the emphasis on the decline of public systems (Ward-Perkins 2005) attracts the attention of the gender historian. As the Roman system of public justice ceased to function, those who could not defend themselves by force became increasingly vulnerable, although ecclesiastical courts or more informal mechanisms for adjudicating disputes were sometimes available. Access to public justice, even in the high empire, was patchy at best; but papyrus sources show that women did sometimes make use of the Roman legal system to deal, for example, with violence by men (see, for example, the affidavit against a violent husband preserved in *P. Oxy.* 903; Patricia Clark 1998).

Women and children were, of course, the paradigmatic vulnerable individuals, and the late Roman historians commented, as did the poets, on the brutal fates that sometimes befell them in the absence of enforceable norms of public order. The capture of Radegund during the destruction of the Thuringian royal family may be the most celebrated case of this vulnerability, due to its commemoration in *The Thuringian War*, a lament attributed somewhat uncertainly to Venantius Fortunatus (it is possible that the queen herself was its author). Another poem of Fortunatus, the lament for Galswinth, the wife of Radegund's stepson Chilperic and brutally murdered by him, echoes a theme of bridal vulnerability that stretches across the fifth and sixth centuries (Leo 1881; Roberts 2001).

While the decline of Roman law was on the whole a minus for women, the challenge to ancient religious ideals was less conclusively negative. The christianization of the Roman world made a difference to how women were imagined, and imagined themselves, not only because of the different "shape" of Christian ideas, but also because the cultural uncertainty accompanying the long "handover" between the two systems created opportunities for experimentation that might not have been open in a more successfully static system. The social tension around christianization created a window of opportunity through which individuals could renegotiate their standing and claim acceptance for eccentricity. Given their comparative vulnerability, women were far less likely than men to find hidden opportunities in military or political uncertainty, but *cultural* uncertainty could bring opportunities as well as disadvantages.

The tension between the biological family and the family of faith was especially significant for women, who had long stood as the representatives of the ethos of family life. In the uncertainty generated by this tension, new identity strategies became possible. Again, *The Martyrdom of Perpetua and Felicitas* gives a vivid account of what it was like to be part of a Christian community where awareness of rank and gender was suppressed in favor of the fragility of the body and the permanence of the otherworldly family. Even Perpetua's father, whose authority she would in normal circumstances be bound to honor according to both Roman and Christian norms, must bow to the greater claim of her calling to martyrdom. The inversion of the social hierarchy here reaches back to the eschatological paradox of the Beatitudes (Matt. 5: 1–12). But it would be a mistake to see women's religious views as intrinsically countercultural. Women's expressions of authority were often framed in socially conservative terms (Brubaker 1997). For the most part, the women at the pinnacle of the social order are the ones we know something about. These women tended to be fully in tune with – and in some respects in charge of – the social order as it was.

The women who stood high in the steep hierarchy of late Roman society were often extremely powerful by modern standards. While the empire lasted, there were real grounds for the complacency of these women with regard to their own role. We know ever more about the economic and political authority aristocratic women were able to exert in their own right, through jigsaw evidence preserved in inscriptions (Forbis 1990) or papyri (Rowlandson 1998). Scholars are only beginning to write the kind of composite or dynastic biography that can make sense of this fragmentary evidence (Kurdock 2003). Women were playing a crucial role as patronesses. Royal women were the obvious case in point: one thinks of Helen and the true cross, or of Constantina and the cult sites of the Roman martyrs (Brubaker 1997). But women of the senatorial aristocracy, too, were wielding enormous power. The women friends of St. Jerome, for example, should be seen as his patronesses, not his protégées (Rousseau 1995; Kurdock 2003). The fact that they did not play a clerical role is no longer seen as implying a lack of participation or authority: economic wherewithal and family standing could flow together in a powerful role as patron and arbiter (Elizabeth Clark 1990).

Women were certainly powerful as religious patrons, and their sensibilities were often dominant, sometimes to the dismay of the clergy. In the east, the empress Pulcheria fostered the Marian cult, at least in part because she believed that, like male emperors who had proposed themselves as the earthly counterparts of Jupiter or Christ, she as empress should stand as the avatar of an otherworldly power (Limberis 1994). A century later, Anicia Juliana built one of the great churches of Constantinople, St. Polyeuktos (Harrison 1989). Even for imperial women, there are important methodological problems here because of the fragmentary nature of the sources for women as historical agents (Brubaker 1997), but patterns are sometimes discernible.

The contribution of Roman women under Germanic rule can also be traced, particularly in the religious sphere. Some time around the beginning of the sixth century, for example, the aristocratic virgin Proba, probably a great-great-granddaughter of the Proba mentioned above, allowed the learned cleric Eugippius to use her library to compile a *florilegium* of the thought of the great North African father Augustine of Hippo: the result was the *Excerpta Augustini*, one of the standards of any medieval library. Another text from the same milieu, *Ad Gregoriam in palatio*, seems to be addressed to the mistress of a late fifth- or early sixth-century Italian aristocratic household (Daur 1992). *Ad Gregoriam* draws on the twin ideas of the ascent of the soul to heaven, made popular by Christian Neoplatonists such as Boethius, and the spiritual warfare between the forces of good and evil in the Christian soul (*psychomachia*), made popular in the monastic literature and in the poetry of Prudentius (AD 348–410). Both themes are linked in this text to the concrete problem of running the household, which emerges as a wonderfully heroic activity. *Ad Gregoriam in palatio* in fact reflects a wider genre of household manuals for the married Christian laity, a surprising number of which are preserved from the period (Cooper 2007). This may mean that the monastic libraries that preserved the texts foresaw a pastoral role for monks with respect to aristocratic families, or that lay readers were expected to make use of monastic collections in some cases at least. (It may also reflect the tendency of lay aristocrats to bequeath their personal libraries to monasteries.)

At the end of the sixth century, we see married women – aristocratic *matronae* as well as queens – collaborating with bishops in the care of the Italian communities faced by the Lombard invasion. Gregory the Great and his female correspondents consoled one another, and sent money and even blankets back and forth between Italy and Constantinople. Indeed, Gregory's friendship with Theodelinda, queen of the Lombards, was no accident, reflecting a tradition of popes and bishops corresponding and collaborating with the womenfolk of both Roman and barbarian rulers, without regard to lines of ethnic affiliation or the religious persuasion of the husband. At the same time, the *Epistulae Austrasiacae* (Gundlach 1892) reveal that across Europe, from Byzantium to Visigothic Spain, married women continued to serve a more traditional role, as the object of exchange in marriage allegiances aimed – unsuccessfully, as it turned out – at maintaining the fragile unity of the Mediterranean. But asceticism had opened an opportunity for women to side-step the roles assigned to them: again, we may think of Radegund who, after an unwilling marriage to her captor Chlothar, was able to embrace asceticism, initially by flight, and finally to live out her years as the foundress of an important monastery in Poitiers.

My suggestions about women's more perilous situation with the decline of Roman law and Roman public justice, and the attractiveness of religious institutions and networks as a venue for their activity, should not be taken as applying exclusively to women. Men, too, were made vulnerable by the same circumstances, and the fact that women were left more exposed to male brutality does not mean that men were not similarly exposed to the brutality of other men, or that there were not variations within each class. Christian networks and institutions offered an alternative "relational matrix" for both. The difference, of course, was that the terms on which men and women could hope to negotiate their place in the new dispensation diverged, with new emphasis on military accomplishment for men and reproductive accomplishment for women.

Conclusion

We return finally to the question, was Gibbon right to see a connection between the rise of Christianity and the fall of the empire? Did Christianity function as an escape valve that in fact fostered the values of Roman society by channeling nonparticipation into harmless channels, or did it sap the strength of Roman ideology by making nonparticipation seem less than an unthinkable crime?

A satisfying answer to the question is probably beyond reach, but a final fifth-century fertility episode offers an orientation. Shortly before the sack of Rome, the senatorial heiress Melania the Younger visited the *augusta* Serena to claim protection against relatives who wished to deprive her and her husband of their inheritance. Our source, Gerontius' *Life* of Melania (Gorce 1962; Elizabeth Clark 1984; Patrick Laurence 2002), is understandably impressionistic about why the relatives believed they had a legitimate claim. It is likely that they had called the urban prefect's attention to the fact that under Roman law, a parental gift could be revoked if the child heir failed in the duties of *pietas* with regard to the donor (Arjava 1996: 85). (That the urban prefect, who handled such cases, was involved seems to be implied by another somewhat confused reference in the *Life* to his persecution of Melania.) One of the specified offices of filial piety was of course the production of grandchildren. The vow of continence taken by both Melania and her husband Pinianus could thus disqualify them as heirs to their respective fortunes (Cooper 2005a). By closely associating Melania's renunciations with the devastation caused by Alaric – indeed, during the sack, his armies burned a Roman palace that she had not yet managed to sell off – the author of the *Life* wished to offer his readers a compelling sign of the transience of earthly fortunes and of the need to place one's hope in heaven. What is truly alarming in the story, from the perspective of traditional Roman values, is the idea that a member of the imperial family, the niece of Theodosius the Great, could be expected to obstruct the urban prefect in his attempt to exact the offices of piety from a Roman heir and to insure the production of a new generation of senators.

Serena's own daughters Maria and Thermantia were famously either unable or unwilling to bear sons. The consequences of this failure were far-reaching, since each sister in turn was married to the young emperor Honorius – Maria in AD 398 and Thermantia after the death of her sister. Each of the sisters having failed to provide a son, Honorius died childless in AD 423 and the succession passed to the 4-year-old Flavius Placidus Valentinianus, son of Serena's cousin Galla Placidia. More than one fifth-century author suspected Honorius of having taken a vow of continence (Holum 1982: 49). Whether his childlessness reflected the divine anathema of infertility or merely Christian eccentricity, it was equally devastating for the western empire. Like the apocryphal tale of the *matrona* opening the gates of Rome, or the episode of Serena's protection of Melania's vow of continence, the accusation against Honorius has the sound of a story designed to shock. A Roman emperor so far divorced from the values of Roman masculinity as to desire neither victories nor sons was unthinkable, and yet the unthinkable had seemingly come to pass.

If we can accept for the sake of argument that Christian communities played a socially destabilizing role by serving as a breeding ground for rival cognitions, we have yet to understand whether ascetic ideas in fact served to erode Roman ideas of legitimate male authority. In both the west and Byzantium, the Church reestablished itself during the seventh, eighth, and ninth centuries as the guardian of the Roman legacy, an institution in the service of legitimate public authority, whose critique of the ruling males was perceived as strengthening, rather than weakening, the social order. It goes without saying that gender ideas played a part in this process as well. But why were Frankish and Byzantine dynasties able to harness the power of Church as an instrument of legitimacy, where their predecessors in the West Roman Empire had not? Of course, Christian ideas and institutions were never monolithic, so the comparison is in some sense a false one. But we may also ask whether these more successful Christian empires tolerated rulers who underperformed as egregiously at their basic tasks of victory and succession as did those of the fifth-century west. Ultimately, rival cognitions were far less disturbing when God was smiling on the ruling house, the men were winning battles, and the women were producing an army of healthy sons.

BIBLIOGRAPHICAL NOTE

The cluster of topics from gender and sexuality to women and family have been unusually well served in recent scholarship. Stafford 1978, Holum 1982, Cameron 1989a, Elizabeth Clark 1990, and Nelson 1990 laid the methodological foundations for work in these fields, often responding explicitly to work on the construction of gender by scholars of other periods. Cameron 1989a, Cooper 1992, Elizabeth Clark 1998, Burrus 2001, and Brubaker 2004 offer a spectrum of strategies for coopting literary and critical theory into a "rhetoric of gender" approach to late antique texts. Smith 2000a, Bitel 2002, Halsall 2004, and Cooper 2005b offer recent historiographical overviews of different aspects of gender in Late Antiquity and the early Middle Ages.

CHAPTER FOURTEEN

Marriage and Family Relationships in the Late Roman West

Judith Evans-Grubbs

Over the past twenty-five years, scholarly interest in the study of the family in antiquity has grown dramatically. Scholarship of the 1980s focused on the family in the classical period but, more recently, attention has turned to Late Antiquity. There is a greater variety of relevant source material for this period than for earlier centuries: legal sources, funerary inscriptions (especially from Rome), papyri (less plentiful for the fourth century, but picking up again in the fifth and sixth centuries), letters, orations, and other literature, as well as abundant Christian writings: treatises, hagiographies, sermons, and the beginnings of canon law. Moreover, both legal and patristic sources evince a greater interest in those below the urban elite, because of an imperial desire to regulate the social orders and Christian concern for the poor and marginal. Women are more visible as well; although there are few extant writings by women, the new genre of saints' lives brings us the first full-length biographies of women in antiquity.

But, despite the variety and scope of the source material, there are serious drawbacks to its use for social history. A large proportion of the material is prescriptive, presenting norms, which we cannot assume were always followed. Documentary source material is very sparse, except for Egypt. And none of these writings, even the most modest funerary inscription, is entirely unselfconscious: all were written with an audience in mind, and all are to some degree tendentious. It would be disingenuous to use these sources to construct a straightforward, "factual" account of late Roman family relations.

In this chapter, I shall use instead personal narratives to map out some of the most striking features of family life in the late antique west. By "personal narratives," I mean primarily autobiographical writings, letters, and biographies by friends or relatives – most of them, necessarily, written by and for the literate elite. A focus on personal narratives rather than on laws or didactic texts allows one to pay more attention to the emotional responses of late antique men and women in their family relationships – or rather, the *representation* of these emotions in polished writings intended for publication. Although historians have been reluctant to talk about emotions in antiquity, recently there has been more willingness to consider the emotional life of ancient men and women by taking a microhistorical approach to individuals for whom we have a variety of documentation (Van Dam 2003a: 11–14).

Such an approach cannot lead to any quantifiable or universally valid conclusions. But it can offer a perspective on broader issues, like the impact of Christianity on the family in Late Antiquity, which is part of the much larger issue of the "christianization" of Roman society. Almost all of the material discussed here was in fact written by Christians, because Christians, with their interest in sexuality and in the tension between secular relationships and the Christian's relationship with God, had more to say about marriage and family relations than did non-Christians. The impact of Christian teachings on late Roman family life has been addressed by several recent studies (see bibliographical note below), which have stressed the continuity of pre-Christian mores rather than radical change, and have noted that changes arise from the interplay of social, military, political, and religious factors, and not from one cause only. At various points in this chapter I shall address the question of what "difference" Christianity made to family relationships and norms; but, as will be seen, there is no clear answer.

Displaying Family Feeling: Ausonius on His Kin

Decimus Magnus Ausonius, poet, teacher of rhetoric, and government official, was born around AD 310 in Bordeaux, came of age under the emperor Constantine, and died in the 390 s. He was at the center of social and political networks among the western senatorial aristocracy under the emperor Gratian, who rewarded his former tutor with the positions of quaestor, praetorian prefect, and consul (Matthews 1975: 56–87). Few of the momentous changes of the fourth century, however, are reflected in Ausonius' own voluminous literary output. His poetry focuses on the personal, whether he is writing about his family or his fellow teachers at Bordeaux, describing his daily activities (including a long prayer, one of the few references to his Christian faith) or the beauty of the Moselle river, or indulging in risqué epigrams and a sometimes obscene wedding *cento* (written at the request of Valentinian I).

Ausonius' family features frequently in his poetry, especially in the *Parentalia*, which commemorates the deceased members of his extended kin. Examination of the persons commemorated can tell us much about the family relationships of a wealthy member of the Gallic elite. The title *Parentalia* refers to the ancient (pre-Christian) religious celebration of the spirits of the dead, when offerings were made to deceased ancestors. Thirty poems commemorate a total of thirty-three people, fifteen females and eighteen males, including not only nuclear family, but also aunts, uncles, nephews, nieces, cousins, in-laws (*adfines*), and even great nieces and nephews. Both maternal and paternal kin are represented. This may be in part because the family of Ausonius' mother was more illustrious than that of his father, but it also demonstrates the importance of cognate as well as agnate kin, reflected in later Roman inheritance law, which gradually eroded the ancient preference for agnates (see Herlihy 1985: 6–7; Arjava 1996: 94–110). Relationships between some in-laws are as close as those between biological kin: for instance, Ausonius considered his sister Julia Dryadia's daughter-in-law as standing "in the place of a daughter" (Auson. *Parentalia* 16); and Dryadia was so close to her son-in-law that he qualified as a biological son rather than as an in-law (*Parentalia* 24).

Despite the richness of this evidence, the *Parentalia* is not a complete family record: the poems commemorate only *deceased* family and say little about those who are still living, however important they were to Ausonius. Thus we hear about the short-lived first husband of Ausonius' daughter (14), but the daughter's name is never mentioned, because she was still alive when he wrote. Nor did he commemorate all those relatives who died in infancy; he does mention four young children, but none was a newborn. Since the high mortality rate for children meant that about half of all born would die within ten years, mostly in infancy (Parkin 1992: 92–3), there would have been many more who died too soon for Ausonius to know them, perhaps even to know that they had existed.

Ausonius' parents take pride of place in the *Parentalia*, but do not receive the longest poems. Ausonius describes his mother in only the most generic terms, endowing her with all the traditional female virtues: she was *morigera* (an ancient term signifying a wife's willingness to mold her habits to those of her husband), known for her *pudicitia* (chastity) and "wool-working hands," a faithful wife and a good mother (*Parentalia* 2). The vagueness of this characterization may be due to the fact that Ausonius left Bordeaux at an early age to live with his mother's family in Toulouse. Indeed, he claims that his maternal grandmother, Aemilia Corinthia Maura, "trained me under her stern rule after I was snatched from the cradle and my mother's soft breasts" (*Parentalia* 5. 9–10); and his aunt Aemilia Dryadia "learned to become as a mother" to her "almost son" Ausonius (*Parentalia* 25). Ancient mortality meant that close relatives often played parental roles upon a parent's death, but Ausonius' parents were both alive and young when he was sent to his mother's family. There were other cases, however, where a grandmother took an active role in rearing grandchildren even during the parents' lifetime: Basil of Caesarea cites his father's mother Macrina as a formative influence in his life (*Ep.* 204, 223).

The *Parentalia* also has relatively little about Julius Ausonius, apart from his success as a modest doctor and his death at the advanced age of 88 (*Parentalia* 1). Elsewhere, Ausonius says more about his father. His earliest extant work, *Ad patrem de suscepto filio* ("To his father upon the raising of his son") was written upon the birth of Ausonius' first child, which he claimed had increased his feeling (*affectus*) for his own father, since it now arose not only from filial *pietas*, but also from the shared status of fatherhood. This sense of equality with his father also owed something to their respective ages: "for I am nearly equal to you in age and I could have the place of a brother" (*Ad patrem* 13–14). Apparently Julius Ausonius was only about twenty years older than his son, still in his teens when he married (Green 1991: 268). This is below the average age of male marriage in the early empire (Saller 1994: 25–42), but not so unusual for Late Antiquity, at least among the elite. On the other hand, the husband of Ausonius' niece was a contemporary of Ausonius himself, and therefore much older than his wife (*Parentalia* 24; Krause 1991: 543).

Many years later, after his father had died, Ausonius wrote a funeral elegy (Auson. *Epicedion in patrem*), spoken in the voice of Julius Ausonius and intended for inscription below his portrait (*imago*) in Ausonius' house. The *Epicedion* displays Ausonius' filial piety, opening with the words, "After God I have always venerated my father and have owed second-place reverence to my progenitor." Nor was his *pietas* confined to literary commemoration: he used his influence with Gratian to see that his father was made praetorian prefect of Illyricum (Matthews 1975: 69–71).

In the *Parentalia*, however, the more visible father figure is Ausonius' maternal uncle, Aemilius Magnus Arborius (*Parentalia* 3). Arborius was both "father and mother" to his nephew, not simply as a dominant male presence in the household of Ausonius' grandmother in Toulouse, but as a teacher and role model for the young Ausonius. A successful advocate in the courts of Gaul and Spain, Arborius was called to Constantinople to tutor a prince of the imperial family – as Ausonius himself was to be summoned to Trier to tutor the future emperor Gratian.

The fact that Arborius was Ausonius' teacher as well as his kinsman strengthened the affective ties between uncle and nephew. Indeed, like the *amicitia* between older men and their young protégés in the senatorial aristocracy, the teacher–pupil relationship was a nonbiological type of father–son relationship (Salzman 2002: 54; see Cribiore, ch. 16). Ausonius bonded with his students, particularly with the talented Meropius Pontius Paulinus (later of Nola), who was only about 7 when he became Ausonius' pupil. His deep affection for Paulinus was later to bring Ausonius grief when Paulinus converted to ascetic Christianity and broke epistolary ties (see below).

Ausonius also displays his paternal feelings for his own children. A poem to his son Hesperius describes Ausonius forlornly watching his son sail off into the distance, evoking echoes of Catullus' Ariadne or Virgil's Dido (Auson. *Pater ad filium*). Another poem was written on the occasion of his grandson's eighteenth birthday (Auson. *Genethliacos*; see also *Protrepticus* to his grandson). Ausonius even wrote a light-hearted piece about his foster daughter (*alumna*) Bissula, a Suebian given to him as war booty from an expedition with Valentinian I against the Alamanni. The nonbiological relationship between *alumni* and their fosterers is known from earlier imperial legal and epigraphic sources (Rawson 1986: 173–86; Nielsen 1987); it is rarer to find it commemorated in literature.

Like Roman funerary inscriptions, the *Parentalia* laments the deaths of young people "snatched" before their prime. Ausonius' talented younger brother, Avitianus, died before he had reached puberty. He receives a florid lament, punctuated by cries of "heu, heu!" from the bereaved Ausonius, who considered him "in love almost a son" (*Parentalia* 13). Paulinus and Dryadia, children of Ausonius' niece, both died in their early teens, Paulinus as an *ephebus* and Dryadia "seized from the place of her bridal bed" (23). His maternal aunt Aemilia Dryadia also died shortly after marriage (25). Untimely death similarly snatched away his sister-in-law's son, the "one and only hope of his mother." Like Paulinus, the youth was an *ephebus*, but he was "now already a husband, already in quick succession a father" (20). He must have married in his teens, like Ausonius' father. Another nephew, Pomponius Maximus Herculanus, who appears both in the *Parentalia* (17) and in Ausonius' poem commemorating the professors of Bordeaux (*Prof. Burd.* 11), was following in his uncle's footsteps in his studies (just as Ausonius had followed in those of Arborius). Full of promise he did not fulfill, Herculanus was involved in some youthful misbehavior that may have led to his death.

Also tragic were the deaths of very young children. Ausonius' grandson Pastor was killed by a tile thrown from the roof by a careless workman (*Parentalia* 11). His first-born son, "little Ausonius," died just as he was beginning to talk, and was buried with his grandfather (10). Two young girls are commemorated near the poem's end: Ausonius' paternal cousin Julia Idalia (28) and his older sister Aemilia Melania, whom he hardly remembered (29). Young children are more visible in the *Parentalia* than in most earlier classical literature, lending support to the conclusion of recent archaeological and epigraphic studies that late Roman society, at least in urban areas, commemorated the very young to a greater extent than that of earlier periods (Shaw 1991; Norman 2002, 2003). Whether this owes something to a new, "Christian" valuation of children or is "an adoption and further development of earlier Roman practices" (Rawson 2003: 284) remains a topic of debate.

One of the *Parentalia*'s longest and most emotionally charged poems commemorates Ausonius' wife, Attusia Lucana Sabina, who died at 27 after bearing three children, one of whom predeceased her (*Parentalia* 9). Ausonius, still a "youth" at the time of her death, had been mourning her for some thirty-six years, and claimed his grief had only increased over time, particularly as he observed the marriages of others. Elsewhere, in several short epigrams, Ausonius depicts his relationship with his wife in the language used by Augustan elegiac poets to describe definitely non-marital affairs with a mistress (Sklenár 2005). He did not remarry; indeed, while long-lived widows and widowers are much in evidence in Ausonius' family (Krause 1991: 541), there is only one attested remarriage, that of Ausonius' daughter (Étienne 1964: 25).

Other married couples appear in the *Parentalia*. Ausonius' parents share a tomb in death, just as they shared the marriage bed in life, and his mother, praised for her *pudicitia* and conjugal *fides*, embraces her husband's "gentle *manes*" even in death (*Parentalia* 2; see *Epicedion* 37–8). His sister, Julia Dryadia, had not only every *virtus* that a prudent woman could wish for but also many that the "stronger sex" would want. Having raised two sons and a daughter, she lived much of her sixty years in her father's household, where her dearest concern was "to know God and love her brother above all" (12). His sister-in-law was not only "noble, frugal, upright, pleasant, chaste (and) honourable," but also a smart and competent household manager, who took care of her own properties while her husband (who outlived her) cultivated a life of aristocratic *otium* (19). Pomponia Urbica, mother of Ausonius' son-in-law, was a woman of "famous family" and "ancient *mores*," devoted to her husband, who predeceased her (and with whom, Ausonius says, she would have gladly changed places in death). As it happened, she was not "tortured" by a long widowhood, dying soon after her husband (30).

Ausonius presents variations of the themes that appear repeatedly in Latin funerary inscriptions from the late republic to Late Antiquity (Treggiari 1991: 229–53; Evans-Grubbs 1995: 78–84) – not surprisingly, since his poems are literary epitaphs. Among the elite of Ausonius' time, commemorations by bereaved spouses also display a combination of sorrow at the death of loved ones and praise of their accomplishments (for men) or character (for women). This usage cuts across religious lines; indeed, it is often impossible to determine the religious affiliation of wealthy commemorands from their epitaphs (Evans-Grubbs 1995: 82–4). One of the longest and most famous late antique epitaphs is the joint monument of the pagan senator Vettius Agorius Praetextatus and Aconia Fabia Paulina, set up after Praetextatus' death in AD 384. On either side of a large marble base, Praetextatus addresses Paulina, praising her wifely virtues and religious piety: "Paulina, conscious of truth and chastity, devoted to the temples and friend of divinities, preferring her husband to herself (and) Rome to her husband, modest, faithful, of pure mind and body, kind to all, useful to the household gods" (*ILS* 1259). Paulina's address to Praetextatus is much longer, and recounts her good fortune in having such a husband and the many religious rites into which she was initiated under his sponsorship (see Kahlos 1994).

Ausonius differs from late antique commemorators on stone, however, in his attention to extended kin. Examination of thousands of epitaphs from the Latin west in the early empire reveals a strong preference for commemoration within the nuclear family (Saller and Shaw 1984), and this is even more the case in the Christian inscriptions of the fourth through sixth centuries (Shaw 1984b). There are changes in late Roman commemorative practice – not only a greater tendency to commemorate young children (see above) but also, in the Christian inscriptions of Rome, near parity between commemoration of females and of males, unlike in the earlier empire (Shaw 1991; 1996: 107). Moreover, "the public expression of personal sentiments in the valuation of the marital partner in funerary notices attenuates severely among the Christians. This pattern seems to be part of a long-term abandonment of expression of personal affective sentiments in favour of more abstract personal qualities that typify Christian funerary epitaphs" (Shaw 2002: 215). Of course, this is a change in commemorative practice, not necessarily a change in emotional response to the deceased or to death.

The Christian inscriptions largely derive from the lower strata of the urban population, especially of Rome (Shaw 1996: 108), and are extremely short and formulaic. Ausonius himself was a practicing Christian. But his eulogies of marital life have affinities not with the epitaphs of the common people of Rome, but with those of the senatorial elite, whatever their religious affiliation. He is more representative of his class than of his era or religion.

Alternative Households: Asceticism and the Family

In one respect, Christian ideals clearly departed from traditional Greco-Roman norms: whereas marriage (and often remarriage after widowhood or divorce) had been the lot of virtually all women, Christianity offered an alternative.

Two of Ausonius' aunts never married. Julia Cataphronia, his father's sister, lived sparingly until old age in "devoted virginity," and willed her (small) property to Ausonius (*Parentalia* 26). His mother's sister, Aemilia Hilaria, received the nickname "Hilarius" as a baby because she looked like a happy little boy. A doctor, like her brother-in-law, she remained a virgin for sixty-three years: "you always had a hatred of the feminine sex, and therefore a love of devoted virginity grew" (6. 7–8). She continued to live in her natal home, along with her mother and her brother Arborius, and also served as surrogate mother to Ausonius.

Scholars usually assume that *devota virginitas* denotes Christian dedication to holy virginity. Since Cataphronia and Hilaria would probably have reached their teens, and therefore marriageable age, in the early fourth century, they may have chosen permanent virginity even before Constantine's legalization of Christianity. Hilaria may have been motivated more by her distaste for sex and desire to pursue medicine than by spiritual promptings; one scholar even suggests she was a hermaphrodite, hence her boy's name (Green 1991: 310). Both women are examples of a new development in Late Antiquity: the choice of perpetual virginity (or, failing that, dedicated widowhood) and an ascetic, spiritual lifestyle.

The decision to remain unmarried for religious reasons was, ostensibly, a repudiation of the roles of wife and mother traditionally required of freeborn women of all social levels in ancient society. Men had always had more freedom of choice in marital matters, but they too were expected to marry and sire legitimate heirs. These social expectations were reinforced by laws of Augustus (31 BC–AD 14), mandating marriage and child-bearing for citizen males between 25 and 60 and for females between 20 and 50; noncompliance meant restriction of inheritance rights. In AD 320, Constantine rescinded the Augustan penalties on the unmarried and childless. His motives are debatable; there were few Christians practicing perpetual celibacy in the west at that time, and Constantine was probably more interested in courting the goodwill of the senatorial elite, who had always resented the Augustan laws, than in fostering Christian asceticism (Evans-Grubbs 1995: 103–39). But wealthy Christians who were ascetically inclined certainly benefited from his action, and removal of inheritance restrictions on the childless, along with imperial patronage of the now legalized religion, promoted the emergence of a well-documented group of aristocratic ascetics. They were few in number and did not represent the elite (or any class) as a whole; for the vast majority of the population, the age-old traditions of marriage and child-bearing continued (Arjava 1996: 257–66; Nathan 2000). Nevertheless, the phenomenon of Christian celibacy is of great importance for understanding late Roman family relationships.

Bereavement often provided the spur to recede from "the world." The senatorial aristocrat Antonia Melania married in her mid-teens, as was typical of elite females; lower-class women might marry somewhat later (Hopkins 1965; see Shaw 1987a). She had three children and several miscarriages, but at 21 lost her husband and two children within a year. She then entrusted her surviving son, Publicola, to God and a guardian and left Rome on pilgrimage, settling in Jerusalem and founding monasteries with her companion Rufinus. Melania did not see Publicola again until she returned to Italy more than twenty-five years later, by which time he was grown and had a daughter, the younger Melania, who became inspired by her grandmother's example (Palladius, *Historia Lausiaca* 46 and 61; Paulinus of Nola, *Ep.* 29. 9; Jer. *Ep.* 39. 5). Paula, another aristocrat, was left a widow with five children and turned to the ascetic life at Rome. She was encouraged by her friend Jerome, who led a spiritual study group of female ascetics until he had to leave Rome due to suspicion about his relationships with these women, especially Paula (Jer. *Ep.* 45; Kelly 1975: 91–115). Not long afterward, Paula left to join Jerome, and the two (like Melania and Rufinus) also founded joint monasteries, in their case in Bethlehem. Another noble member of Jerome's circle, Marcella, was widowed after only seven months of marriage. Her mother Albina, also a widow, was anxious that they find some protection, a realistic concern for widows in antiquity. She urged Marcella to accept the marriage offer of a wealthy and high-ranking older man. But Marcella refused, declaring that had she not preferred to dedicate herself to eternal chastity, she would have wanted a husband, not an inheritance (Jer. *Ep.* 127. 2).

The males who praise these women present bereavement as offering an opportunity for complete dedication to God, something the women had long desired. When Paula's husband died, Jerome says, "she lamented for him so much that she almost died herself, [but] she turned so much to service of the Lord, that she appeared to have desired his death" (*Ep.* 108. 5). Similarly, he claims that Melania, far from giving herself over to ostentatious mourning, laughed and said, "I will serve you more easily, Lord, since you have freed me from so great a burden" (*Ep.* 39. 5). The reality may have been somewhat different: grief and a desire to avoid society, especially pressures to remarry from well-meaning but insensitive relatives, were perhaps at least as influential in the women's decision as true religious calling (compare Van Dam 2003a: 103–13).

Biographies of early Christian ascetics also regularly assert that their subjects faced opposition from their families, who attempted to force them into traditional roles of marriage and procreation. Paulinus of Nola (*Ep.* 29. 9–10) defends Melania from the criticism that she abandoned her surviving son in Rome, insisting that she had handed the boy over to God in order to save him. Paulinus himself was criticized by his fellow nobles when he renounced his senatorial seat and sold his estates (Ambrose, *Ep.* 6. 27), and his former teacher Ausonius felt personally betrayed by Paulinus' rejection of their social and literary ties (Trout 1999: 68–84).

Melania's granddaughter, Melania the Younger, is depicted by her biographer Gerontius as facing continued familial opposition to the ascetic life she had desired since childhood. It was Melania's father, Valerius Publicola, whom the elder Melania had left in Rome twelve years earlier, and perhaps maternal abandonment had soured Publicola's own views on asceticism. He and his wife Albina (cousin of Jerome's friend Marcella) practiced a *modus vivendi* common in the fourth century: they were Christians, but did not break with traditional aristocratic values that stressed marriage, procreation, and family inheritance. Accordingly they arranged the marriage of their 13-year-old daughter Melania, allegedly "with much force" (*Vit. Melaniae* 1). The bridegroom, Valerius Pinianus, was a relative and only about seventeen himself, another example of teenage marriage for males. Marriage did not, however, free the younger Melania from her parents' scrutiny, for the couple lived with her parents – an unusual arrangement among wealthy Romans, since married children customarily set up a separate household (Hillner 2003: 137). Melania remained under paternal power (*patria potestas*), as did all Roman men and women until their *paterfamilias* either died or emancipated them (Arjava 1998). As long as he lived, the *paterfamilias* (either the father or, if still alive, the paternal grandfather) had control over his children's finances and could legally prevent them from selling or giving away anything they owned, particularly if he thought they were behaving irresponsibly. Publicola apparently threatened to take away the couple's property (presumably Melania's future inheritance) and give it to his other children (*Vit. Melaniae* 12), but in the end died repenting that he had tried to thwart their ascetic ambitions (7).

Some parents, however, were eager for the prestige and spiritual protection of a family virgin. Ausonius' nephew Magnus Arborius dedicated his daughter to virginity after she was miraculously cured of a quartan fever by a letter written by St. Martin of Tours (Sulpicius Severus, *Vit. Martini* 19). Paula's granddaughter was consecrated to virginity before she was even born (Jer. *Ep.* 107. 3), and Asella, another of Jerome's aristocratic friends, when she was scarcely more than 10. Not that Asella objected; on the contrary, by the time she was 12 she had adopted an ascetic regimen whose austerity dismayed even her parents (Jer. *Ep.* 24. 2). Asella was apparently the sister of Marcella, whose mother Albina was so anxious to have her remarry. Here we see a Roman "family strategy" at work; a family with more than one daughter might consider it socially and economically beneficial to establish marriage ties with other families, but also want to demonstrate their Christian piety – which could be equally beneficial (Sivan 1993; Arjava 1996: 164–7).

By the early fifth century, refusal of marriage and dedication to holy virginity could become an occasion for public celebration. On the verge of marriage, the young Anician heiress Demetrias announced her intention to remain a virgin. Her mother and grandmother supported her (her father was dead; one wonders if he would have agreed), allowing her to keep what would have been her dowry, which she promptly donated to the church. The aristocratic world was astounded; leading Christian ascetics were thrilled (August. *Ep.* 150; Jer. *Ep.* 130; Pelagius, *Ep. ad Demetriadem*).

Not all ecclesiastical or imperial authorities greeted this strategy with enthusiasm. Basil of Caesarea (*Ep.* 199. 18) complained that relatives, when they dedicated young girls who had no inclination for celibacy, acted simply to gain advantage for themselves. Augustine was consulted regarding a widow who had vowed her deathly ill baby to virginity in return for the girl's recovery. When the child revived, the mother wished to rescind the vow and dedicate herself to celibate widowhood instead (she wanted grandchildren). Augustine noted not only that she was essentially trying to cheat God by the substitution, but also that the choice of whether to marry or remain a virgin properly belonged to the girl, when she got older (*Ep.* 3*). In AD 458, the western emperor Majorian excoriated parents who consigned their minor daughters to perpetual virginity and disinherited them, which not only deprived the state of much needed manpower but also led the sex-deprived young women into "illicit allurements" (Majorian, *Nov.* 6, *praef.*).

Asceticism could have even more deleterious results for enthusiastic and impressionable young women. Paula's oldest daughter, Blesilla, was widowed before she turned 20. After a period devoted to worldly pleasures (understandable for a teenage widow), she was persuaded by her mother and Jerome to renounce the world, and threw herself wholeheartedly into mortification and scriptural study. Less than four months later, Blesilla was dead – a victim, critics claimed, of excessive fasting (she was probably severely anorexic, which can have fatal consequences). At Blesilla's funeral, Paula fainted, overcome with grief and guilt at her daughter's death. Blame fixed on her spiritual mentor Jerome, and people muttered that it was time to drive the "detestable race of monks" from Rome (Jer. *Ep.* 39). Such incidents only fueled resentment among nonascetics (Christian as much as pagan) and contributed to the unpopularity that led to Jerome's hasty departure the following year.

The desire on the part of both males and females to follow an ascetic lifestyle meant not only a rejection of marriage, but also the development of new styles of household. In the fourth century, women would pursue their holy calling in a familial setting. Indeed, family ties between adult women, especially mothers and daughters, were often strengthened, since daughters did not marry and leave home. Such close mother–daughter ties have been noted in Syriac hagiography, where "sacred bonding" reinforced both family ties and religious devotion (Harvey 1996), and can also be seen in accounts of elite ascetics. In Rome, for instance, Marcella lived with her mother Albina, gathering around herself like-minded ascetics, and corresponding with Jerome on matters of biblical interpretation. Another Albina, widowed mother of Melania the Younger, accompanied her daughter and son-in-law when they left Rome to pursue a life away from "the world," first in Sicily, then in North Africa, and finally in Jerusalem, where she died (*Vit. Melaniae* 41). Paula left her unmarried daughter Rufina and her young son, Toxotius, weeping on the dock when she followed Jerome to the Holy Land. But she took with her another daughter, Eustochium, already vowed to virginity, and the two lived together in the monastery Paula founded in Bethlehem, until her death in AD 404 (Jer. *Ep.* 108. 6).

Elite asceticism allowed wealthy women to maintain a comfortable lifestyle and interpersonal relationships while avoiding the more burdensome aspects of marriage. The inhabitants of these early monastic foundations might include former slaves of the founder, as in the *monasterion* built by the wealthy heiress Olympias in Constantinople, which housed Olympias and several of her female relatives along with fifty of her chambermaids (*Vit. Olympiadis* 6). In Bethlehem, Paula divided her virgins into "squadrons" comprising "nobles" and the "middle" and "lowest" classes; the three groups joined for prayers and psalm singing but worked and ate separately. Noblewomen could not keep their former attendants as companions, since that might lead to reminiscing about the old days (Jer. *Ep.* 108. 20); but class distinctions might be preserved intact, and traditional ideas of *noblesse oblige* carried over into the ascetic world. Melania the Younger founded male and female monasteries in North Africa, where she owned extensive properties even after her ascetic renunciations, and later in Jerusalem. In her repeated charitable benefactions, Melania was also indulging in time-honored aristocratic practices of euergetism and patronage.

In Cappadocia, Macrina, the sister of Basil of Caesarea and Gregory of Nyssa, refused another marriage after her fiancé died, remaining with her now widowed mother Emmelia and practicing domestic monasticism with their slave women and other virgins (Van Dam 2003a: 99–113; Rousseau 2005). These included girls rescued by Macrina after they had been "thrown along the roads in a time of famine" (*Vit. Macrinae* 26). They were "exposed" infants (*expositi*), abandoned at or shortly after birth because they were unwanted or because their mothers could not care for them. In Late Antiquity, both Christian writers and imperial laws condemn exposure (e.g., *Cod. Iust.* 8. 51. 2, AD 374; Basil of Caesarea, *Ep.* 199, canon 33). The change in attitude toward infant abandonment, which had been tolerated as a necessary evil in the classical period, is one area where Christian teachings appear to have made a difference in law and practice. Rescue of *expositi* was certainly not unknown in the classical period, but late Roman emperors positively encouraged it (*Cod. Theod.* 5. 9. 1, AD 331; 5. 9. 2, AD 412). Orphanages, first attested in the fifth-century east, as well as monastic institutions, provided a home for large numbers of abandoned children (Boswell 1988: 228–55; Miller 2003: 49–69, 152–61).

Other styles of household combined the new celibacy with traditional marriage. Some men and women lived with a member of the opposite sex, perhaps even sharing a bed, but (professedly) not engaging in sexual intercourse. Such "spiritual marriages" were repeatedly condemned by church authorities like John Chrysostom (Elizabeth A. Clark 1979: 158–248), who saw them as engendering scandal among pagans and unsuccessful imitation by other Christians. In AD 420, the emperor Honorius even forbade clerics to have any unrelated women living in their household, except the wife they had married before ordination (*Cod. Theod.* 16. 2. 44). But spiritual marriages remained popular well into the Middle Ages, because they combined ascetic celibacy with traditional gender roles, to the convenience of both partners. Women gained male protectors in a predatory world, and men received the housekeeping chores usually performed by a wife – apart from sexual services (Elm 1994: 46–51; Leyerle 2001). Nor should we discount the emotional fulfillment for both partners that derived from domestic intimacy (Elizabeth A. Clark 1979: 159).

While Christian leaders strongly discouraged cohabitation of unmarried celibate couples, they favored observance of celibacy by the legally married and even demanded it of clerics in major orders who were married at the time of ordination (Hunter 1999). Melania the Elder persuaded her niece Avita and Avita's husband Turcius Apronianus to live celibately (Palladius, *Hist. Laus.* 54); however, they already had a son and daughter. Again, bereavement might provide the impetus: Paulinus of Nola and his wife Therasia embraced marital celibacy after the death of their eight-day-old son, Celsus: "offspring long wished for but not granted to us, unworthy as we were to rejoice in a pious posterity," Paulinus says sadly (*Carm.* 31. 603–4). Not long before that, Paulinus' brother had died, apparently murdered (*Carm.* 21. 416–20; Trout 1999: 63–7). In AD 394, after Paulinus had publicly renounced his senatorial seat and had been ordained priest, he and Therasia moved to the shrine of St. Felix at Nola.

In a letter to two other drop-outs from secular society, Aper and Amanda, Paulinus praised their now chaste marriage. He was particularly impressed that Amanda was carrying on the "servitude" of managing the couple's rural estates and caring for their sons, allowing Aper, now an ordained priest, to devote himself to spiritual matters (Paulinus, *Ep.* 44). Paulinus borrowed heavily from a letter he himself had received from Augustine, in which the bishop of Hippo praised Therasia as a wife who did not lead her husband "to effeminacy or avarice ... but to continence and fortitude" (August. *Ep.* 27; see Cooper 1992: 156). Ambrose likewise rejoiced that Therasia had sold all *her* properties along with Paulinus, and was now content with her husband's "tiny plot of turf" (Ambrose, *Ep.* 6. 27). In an *epithalamium* (wedding poem) for Julian of Eclanum, Paulinus urged Julian and his bride Titia to maintain the "concord of virginity" themselves, or, failing that, to have children who would remain virgins (*Carm.* 25. 231–4). The traditional purpose of Roman marriage, to have children who would perpetuate the family and its property, has been turned upside down. Yet the ancient ideal of marital *concordia* remains.

The best-known example of a celibate couple is Melania the Younger and Pinianus. Early in their marriage, Melania had tried to persuade Pinianus to give up sex, but he wanted to wait until they had two children as heirs. This was a traditional sentiment among the property-conscious Roman elite; similarly, Jerome claims (*Ep.* 108. 4) that Paula had five children, despite her ascetic longings, because the first four were girls and her husband wanted to have a son. Melania had a daughter (who was immediately dedicated to virginity) and then gave birth prematurely to a son who died at birth; the older child died as well. Depressed and apparently close to death herself, Melania told Pinianus that he had to forgo any more children if he wanted her to live; after he agreed, she completely recovered (*Vit. Melaniae* 5–6). This episode epitomizes the couple's relationship throughout their lives: Melania was the dominant partner, and gradually prevailed upon Pinianus to follow the ascetic lifestyle she had always desired, despite his own preference for more worldly aristocratic pleasures. This reverses the traditional Roman marriage ideal, where the husband was to be the superior partner but was to esteem his wife and respect her contributions to the marriage.

Although Melania essentially used emotional blackmail to convince Pinianus to relinquish marital sex, he was willing to follow her lead. "Chaste marriage" could work only if both partners were committed to celibacy, as we see in a case handled by Augustine as bishop of Hippo (*Ep.* 262). Ecdicia and her husband had agreed to live celibately (they already had one son), but he broke his vow in an adulterous relationship. Ecdicia wrote to Augustine, expecting sympathy and advice, but the bishop was displeased when he learned that Ecdicia's husband had committed adultery in anger at her, after she gave her money as alms to wandering monks and changed her matron's dress for widow's weeds. To Augustine, Ecdicia's imprudence (he had doubts about the authenticity of the "monks") and contempt for her marriage were directly to blame for her husband's fall. She had not consulted her husband before disposing of her property, and had deprived their son of his future inheritance. If Ecdicia had wanted to use her property in this way, Augustine says, she should have "respectfully suggested" the idea to her husband and followed his authority as her "head" (see 1 Cor. 11).

Ecdicia assumed that her vow of celibacy enabled her to act like a true widow, and a childless widow at that. In giving her own money away, she was within her rights: legally, the property of each spouse remained separate during marriage, and only a wife's dowry would come into her husband's possession. But in practice, husbands and wives often administered their property in common, and husbands were expected to maintain supervision over not only the dowry but also other property legally belonging to their wives (Arjava 1996: 133–56). In neglecting her son's financial interests, moreover, Ecdicia went against both traditional Roman expectations that mothers should make their children heirs (Dixon 1988: 44–60) and contemporary Roman law, which regulated children's rights to *bona materna* (Arjava 1996: 94–105). And like Augustine, imperial law was suspicious of the motives of ecclesiastics who wheedled donations from wealthy women (Evans-Grubbs 2001: 225–34).

Ecdicia's case was not unique, as is shown by a letter from Augustine's theological opponent Pelagius to another woman who had vowed herself to chastity before consulting her husband (*Ad Celantiam*). The impetus for a celibate marriage may often have come from only one partner, with the other being "persuaded" reluctantly or not even consulted.

Wives and Concubines: Augustine and Marital Life

Aurelius Augustinus is the late antique individual who wrote the most about himself, and about whom the most has been written by others. More than any other early Christian writer, Augustine, who wrote extensively about marriage in treatises, letters, and sermons, has influenced the western view of the marital relationship. Without taking an overly "psycho-historical" approach, one can still suggest that Augustine's views were affected by his own experiences, known primarily from his most autobiographical work, the *Confessions*.

Augustine devotes several chapters of the *Confessions* to a biographical sketch of his mother Monica. This narrative of a North African woman from a Christian family far below the senatorial aristocracy (but far above the hand-to-mouth existence of most inhabitants of the empire) can be contrasted with the laudatory accounts of wealthy ascetic women like Melania the Younger and the friends of Jerome. The "life" of Monica is not objective reportage; it was written by the son who loved her deeply and was devastated at her death, despite his belief that such grief was inappropriate and displeasing to God (*Conf.* 9. 12. 29–33). Monica is portrayed as a "model *materfamilias*," using the "template of the ideal Roman mother, which Augustine modifies to incorporate his Christian and philosophic values" (Power 1996: 71). She appears as a strict, upright figure, dedicated to imparting moral values to her children and anxious for the spiritual and physical safety of her son. After Augustine's father Patricius died when Augustine was 16, Monica used her own funds to help her son pursue a career in rhetoric (*Conf.* 3. 4. 7), and eventually even arranged his marriage. In all this she conformed to the ideal of the good Roman mother of classical times (Dixon 1988). The embodiment of both traditional Roman and new Christian female virtues, she was greatly praised, "for she had been the wife of one man only, had returned the mutual service to her parents, had managed her own home dutifully and piously [*pie*], and had testimony to her good works" (*Conf.* 9. 9. 22).

Monica was married to Patricius "when she became nubile, at full age" (9. 9. 19), probably about 18. Patricius was not an easy husband, but Monica bore his infidelities patiently and was accommodating and agreeable, as befitted a Roman wife (Treggiari 1991: 238–41). She also hoped to bring him to Christianity, and this made her willing to tolerate his rough behavior, including the threat of violence. Augustine tells us how prudent and clever Monica was in handling the irascible Patricius, waiting until he cooled down before explaining whatever it was she had done to make him angry. Other wives, with "gentler" husbands but less adept at spousal management, bore the marks of blows on their faces and marveled that Monica was unscathed (*Conf.* 9. 9. 19). Augustine implies (though does not state outright) that Patricius did not beat Monica, but some scholars have assumed that he did (Shaw 1987b: 31–2; see Patricia Clark 1998: 114–15). Whatever Monica's own situation, wife beating was, in the society described by Augustine, an unexceptional, indeed expected, feature of domestic life.

Whether this marks a change from the classical period, and if so, whether that change is due to Christianity, is debatable (Arjava 1996: 130–2). In the classical period, however, a woman could escape an abusive husband by repudiating him, assuming that she had funds of her own (such as the dowry which she could reclaim after divorce) and a supportive natal family (Treggiari 1991: 435–82). This *does* change in Late Antiquity: legislation, from the time of Constantine onward, restricted the causes for which a spouse, particularly a wife, could divorce unilaterally. Although a law of Theodosius II allowed a wife to divorce her husband if he "afflict[s] her with whippings – which are inappropriate for freeborn women" (*Cod. Iust.* 5. 17. 8, AD 449), this applied only in the eastern empire and, at the time Monica's peers were experiencing their husbands' blows, divorce law was at its strictest. How much this legislation owes to Christian disapproval of divorce has also been debated by scholars (Bagnall 1987; Evans-Grubbs 1995: 225–60; Arjava 1996: 177–92). Imperial legislation probably had little impact, however; more influential were local mores, reinforced by the admonitions of Christian clergy that wives be submissive and endure beatings as well as infidelities and loss of money (Basil of Caesarea, *Ep.* 188. 9, but see Schroeder 2004 on John Chrysostom's condemnation of spousal abuse).

When wives whose husbands had abused them complained, Monica, "solemnly admonishing as if in jest," said that "from the time when they had heard those tablets, which are called matrimonial, read aloud, they ought to consider them as documents by which they had been made slaves, and therefore, mindful of their status, they ought not be prideful against their masters" (*Conf.* 9. 9. 19). Augustine often mentions such marriage contracts (*tabulae matrimoniales,* also called *tabulae nuptiales* or *dotales*), and clearly they were a regular feature of marriage arrangements in late Roman Africa (Hunter 2007). Only a small number of marriage contracts actually survive from the later empire, and none suggests that the wife was in the position of "slave" to her husband as "master." Although Augustine calls *tabulae matrimoniales* "documents of purchase," it is not clear that such phrasing actually appeared in marriage contracts of Augustine's day. It may be his own interpretation, illustrating how he "shifts the basis of power relationships" in marriage, from partners to master and slave (Power 1996: 122).

Documentation of marriage was optional in the classical period, and was used primarily to record dowry or other property transactions, or to make provisions for divorce. In Late Antiquity, documents took on new importance as proof that a union was a *iustum matrimonium* (a legitimate marriage) and came to be required in cases where disparity in the status of the partners might suggest that the woman was a concubine rather than a wife (Evans-Grubbs 2007). This was a distinction with which Augustine was personally familiar.

The mature, ascetic Augustine was to criticize his parents because they did not marry him off when he was 16, but rather allowed "the madness of lust" to reign (*Conf.* 2. 2. 4). They were, he claimed, only interested in making him an accomplished orator, which required further education without the responsibilities of marriage (although his father, noticing Augustine's sexual maturity, had rejoiced at the possibility of grandchildren). Instead, Augustine entered a long-term, quasi-marital relationship with a concubine, whom he never names. The union lasted thirteen years and resulted in a son named Adeodatus ("given by God"). It did not require paternal consent, as marriage would have, nor did it have the legal consequences of *iustum matrimonium*. Adeodatus was illegitimate, and did not have automatic inheritance rights from his father as a legitimate son or daughter would.

As bishop, Augustine condemned this relationship, and readers of the *Confessions* have taken him at his word and visualized *concubinatus* as a promiscuous and even adulterous relationship. But traditional Roman concubinage was an alternative, not a supplement, to legal marriage (Treggiari 1981). Unlike a wife, a concubine was not taken "for the purpose of procreating children" (the purpose of marriage stated in the marriage tablets Augustine so often cited), and concubines did not enjoy the social prestige (*dignitas*) accorded wives. Indeed, for the third-century jurist Ulpian (*Dig.* 32. 49. 4), that was the only real difference between the two, although other jurists cited marital intent (*affectio maritalis*) as an essential criterion for marriage (see 39. 5. 31, *praef.*; 25. 7. 4). Concubines were usually of lower status than the men with whom they lived, and legitimate marriage was either legally impossible or socially inadvisable. Ambitious young men who wanted to establish themselves before taking on the "burdens" of marriage might enter a monogamous but temporary relationship until they were ready to marry a woman who could offer more advantages. This was what Augustine, whose talents fitted him for a high-flying career in imperial government, chose to do (*Conf.* 4. 2. 2; Brown 1967a: 61–72).

Years later, aged 30, Augustine turned his thoughts to legal marriage. At his request, Monica found a suitable wife, although Augustine was perfectly capable of deciding for himself and did not need his mother's permission as he would his father's. Augustine describes the process of wife hunting in curiously impersonal terms: although Monica could not determine God's will, "Nevertheless, the matter was pursued and a girl was asked for, whose age was almost two years less than marriageable, and since she was pleasing, she was waited for" (*Conf.* 6. 13. 23). And the concubine had to go; it was poor form for a betrothed man to maintain a nonmarital relationship up to the wedding day. The separation was extremely traumatic for Augustine: "She with whom I was accustomed to sleep was torn from my side on the grounds of being an impediment to marriage" (*Conf.* 6. 15. 25). Marriage to the concubine was evidently never considered, despite Augustine's deep feelings for her, because career advancement was more important (Power 1996: 97–101; Shanzer 2002). Unable to remain celibate for two years, he took up with another woman in the interim.

Augustine's concubine returned to Africa, "vowing to you (God) that she would not know another man" (*Conf.* 6. 15. 25). Surprisingly, she left Adeodatus with Augustine. Although children born in *iustum matrimonium* came under their father's legal power and usually stayed with him after divorce, "natural" children had no *paterfamilias* and were their mother's responsibility. Perhaps the boy was particularly close to Augustine and to his grandmother Monica (who was living with them), or perhaps Augustine's concubine wished to make a new start back in Africa as a respectable, unmarried woman, and an illegitimate child would have complicated matters (Shanzer 2002: 174). We shall never know what would have happened to Adeodatus had Augustine married, since the boy died and Augustine broke his betrothal. But surely the family of a young, wealthy wife would have looked askance on her husband's bastard child.

Augustine's experience of concubinage informed his views on marriage and the relationship between men and women (Power 1996: 104–7; Shanzer 2002: 175). In *On the Good of Marriage*, after stating that the most important reason for marriage is "friendship" and the bonding of human society, Augustine follows the traditional Roman view that the purpose of marriage is procreation. However, he goes further by claiming that spouses who have sex for any other reason (i.e., concupiscence) are committing a sin, albeit venial. Augustine then addresses the question (which he says "is often asked") of whether monogamous cohabitation, undertaken for sex rather than procreation, can be called *conubium* (marriage). He concludes that it can, if the couple remain faithful to each other all their lives and do not try to prevent children (by contraception), even if they did not seek them in the first place. But if a man has a long-term sexual relationship with a woman, intending to repudiate her for another who would make a more suitable wife, "worthy because of her rank or her resources," he commits adultery with the first woman. And a woman who lived with a man faithfully and raised his children, knowing she was not his wife, also sins, although if she remains celibate after he has repudiated her, "I, indeed, would perhaps not easily call her an adulteress" (August. *De bono coniugali* 5). Many scholars have recognized that Augustine is referring to his own past conduct and condemning it.

In the late empire, the legal attitude toward nonmarital monogamy was becoming harsher, and laws made it more difficult for concubines and their children to receive anything under the will of their partners and husbands (Evans-Grubbs 1995: 277–304). The laws were aimed at strengthening social and legal distinctions between elite men and lower-ranking women rather than at repressing relationships perceived as immoral. But legal disfavor toward concubinage reinforced, and eventually blended with, the ecclesiastical attitude that marriage was to be undertaken solely to produce children. The ecclesiastical view was expressed by Pope Leo around AD 458, writing in response to the bishop of Narbonne (who had asked whether a cleric could marry his daughter to a man who had a concubine by whom he had children):

Not every woman joined to a man is the man's wife, since not every child is his father's heir. Moreover, the marriage pacts between freeborn persons are legitimate and between equals; the Lord decided this very thing long before the beginning of Roman law existed. Therefore a wife is one thing, a concubine another; just as a slavewoman is one thing, a free woman another. (Leo, *Ep.* 167, response 4)

Status distinctions, the hallmark of the Roman legal system, are here attributed to divine decision, "long before the beginning of Roman law." Despite the changes that Christian thinkers like Augustine brought to ideas of marriage and sexuality, some traditional Roman attitudes remained, now validated by religious teachings.

Epilogue: Family Feeling at the End of Antiquity

By the time Augustine died in AD 430, the empire had undergone momentous changes, and much of the west was no longer under Roman control: by AD 418, the Visigoths were established in southern Gaul, and in AD 429 the Vandals had entered Africa. How much impact such large-scale changes have on smaller units of society will depend, of course, on factors like region, class, and identification with the current regime; changes in family structure or ideologies do not necessarily coincide with changes in government or in legal or religious policies.

The *Eucharisticon* ("Hymn of Thanksgiving"), an autobiographical poem written in AD 459 at Marseille by the displaced Romano-Gallic aristocrat known as "Paulinus of Pella," provides a sense of both the endurance of traditional Roman ideals of family and the challenges brought by changing times. Paulinus, a grandson of Ausonius, was born in AD 376 in Macedonia, but moved west when a baby to his ancestral Bordeaux. His parents, overindulgent and concerned for his health, cut short his education and allowed him to fritter away his teens in the traditional aristocratic pursuits of hunting, riding, and seducing slave women. (He hastens to add that he avoided affairs with the unwilling, the free-born, and those who belonged to someone else, and although he sired at least one child, he never actually saw any of his slave offspring.) Unlike Augustine's parents, Paulinus' parents steered his sex drive into legitimate channels and arranged his marriage – against his will – at age 20, to a woman of good birth but small resources.

His most meaningful family bonds were with his parents. He repeatedly refers to his relationship with them in terms of *pietas* and the *pia cura* ("dutiful anxiety") they felt for him and he for them. His father died when Paulinus was 30. Barbarians had just entered Gaul, but the public disaster was "much lighter compared with my unrestrained grief for my deceased father, through whom both fatherland and home itself were dear to me; for we lived with lives joined together, performing our reciprocal duties with such faithful affection that our concord exceeded that of friends of the same age" (*Euch.* 240–5). His father's death also plunged Paulinus into a bitter dispute with his "difficult" (*indocilis*) brother over property his father had left to their mother. Paulinus took his mother's side, motivated by feelings of *pietas* as well as the justice of her cause.

Paulinus had at least three children who survived to adulthood. But his marriage was not happy. He wanted to become a monk, but God did not support this high ambition, since Paulinus had a household full of dependants to whom he owed *pietas*: "children, mother, mother-in-law, wife, along with a large herd of their slave women" (451–62). Apparently both widowed mothers were living with Paulinus and his wife, which must have strained domestic harmony. He also blamed his wife for preventing his return to Greece to escape the Gothic takeover in Gaul: "my difficult [*indocilis*] wife opposed yielding for our common advantage, refusing to sail from excessive fear; I did not think it at all right to drag her unwilling, and it would be equally wrong to leave her behind after taking away our children" (*Euch.* 485–9). Then, in short succession, his mother-in-law, mother, and wife died. He was angry at his wife for depriving him of the consolation of a shared old age (493–7) – a perverse, though common, way of expressing grief at the death of a loved one. Meanwhile, his sons, one of whom had become a priest, were trying their fortunes with the Gothic occupiers and so also had abandoned Paulinus; they both died untimely, apparently by violence. (A daughter had married and moved away earlier.)

When he wrote the *Eucharisticon* at the age of 83, Paulinus' fortunes were taking a turn for the better. But the poem as a whole is a litany of bereavement and missed opportunities. Through it all, Paulinus represents himself as behaving dutifully, though often unwillingly: obeying his parents, respecting his wife's wishes despite her unwifely disobedience, caring for dependent womenfolk instead of responding to an ascetic calling. And through it all, he periodically pauses to thank God for what he still had in a time of want and warfare. To a modern reader this relentless thanksgiving in the face of adversity appears almost ludicrous, and Paulinus presumably had ulterior motives for portraying himself as pious and honorable (McLynn 1995). But we should be more sympathetic. Paulinus was born on one side of antiquity and died on the other. He conducted himself as best he could in the most difficult of times, and he retained traditional "family values" while recognizing, and envying, the life of monasticism, which *pietas* prevented him from following. He looked to his Christian faith to provide a reason for his trials as well as comfort for having to endure them.

Indeed, the comfort provided by this faith was one of the biggest contributions Christianity made to family life. If any emotional response stands out in the biographical and autobiographical works discussed in this chapter, it is grief at the loss of a loved one – a parent, a child, a spouse, even a beloved concubine. Given the demographic patterns of antiquity, bereavement was an intrinsic part of family life; virtually everyone would have lost at least one close family member by the time he or she reached 30, and many, like Melania the Elder, would have lost several in short succession. Jerome claimed that Melania joyfully embraced the opportunity for an ascetic lifestyle presented by the deaths of her husband and children. One need not believe him, but it is easy to understand that dedication to God and pilgrimage to the holy places would have helped to relieve grief and to divert one's attention away from worldly sorrows.

Knowing that the loved one was living in eternal refreshment and no longer felt pain meant that excessive grief could even be sinful. As Paulinus of Nola told the bereaved parents of a child named Celsus (whose name recalled to Paulinus his own long-dead child of the same name): "Cease from sinning with many tears, I ask you, dutiful parents, so that *pietas* not become a fault. For it is an impious *pietas* to mourn a blessed soul and a harmful love to weep for one who is rejoicing in God" (*Carm.* 31. 43–6). This was a hard pill to swallow, as Paulinus well knew, but expectation of the resurrection and eternal bliss for those who believed and lived by Jesus' precepts suggested that some day lost loved ones could be recovered:

> Then we will be able to live as comrades with our own Celsus,
> and be parents of our sweet pledge forever.
>
> (*Carm.* 31. 631–2)

BIBLIOGRAPHICAL NOTE

Current scholarship on the family in Late Antiquity utilizes legal, epigraphic, and patristic sources, as well as evidence found in secular writers of the period. Evans-Grubbs 1995 and Arjava 1996 use primarily legal sources to compare late Roman legislation on women and marriage with classical law. Brent Shaw has analyzed the vast number of late Latin funerary inscriptions for evidence of demographic trends (see especially Shaw 1996 and 2002) and changes in attitudes toward women, children, and family relationships (Shaw 1984b, 1991, 2002). Shaw's landmark article, "The Family in Late Antiquity" (1987b), exploits the evidence of Augustine's sermons and letters as well as the *Confessions*. Augustine and other church Fathers are the focus of important work on gender and sexuality in Late Antiquity: see the work of Elizabeth A. Clark 1979, 1984, 1986; Elm 1994; Power 1996; Leyerle 2001; and Peter Brown's seminal *The Body and Society* (1988b). For an excellent survey of marriage practice and ideology in the early Christian west, see Reynolds 1994.

Relatively little work has been done on the family in late Roman Egypt, despite the existence of documentary evidence from papyri not available elsewhere. A noteworthy exception is Beaucamp's second volume (1992), and in her first (1990) she treats late imperial legislation on women.

Nathan 2000 presents a synthesis of the evidence and discussion of the most important issues in the study of the family in Late Antiquity. Another excellent synthesis, paying particular attention to women and gender issues, is Gillian Clark 1993.

Finally, one should note that Van Dam 2003a uses the extensive writings of the Cappadocian Fathers for a study that deliberately focuses on the emotional ties between Basil of Caesarea, his brother Gregory of Nyssa, their friend Gregory of Nazianzus, and their family members.

CHAPTER FIFTEEN

The Church, the Living, and the Dead

Éric Rebillard

In Late Antiquity, relations between the living and the dead were achieved for the most part without the intervention of church representatives. The role of the clergy as intermediaries between the living and the dead did not become exclusive before the twelfth century, when every Christian had to receive upon his death the *viaticum* – the Eucharist for the dying – in order to be admitted to the cemetery and benefit from the prayers offered by the Church for his remembrance. Medievalists have recently refined our understanding of the long and complex process through which, between the eighth and the twelfth centuries, death was not only christianized, but also clericalized (Paxton 1990; Lauwers 1997, 2005; Effros 2002). More often than not, Late Antiquity has been described as a period of transition, during which the clergy was trying to play an active role but was in no position to impose its will (Rush 1941; McLaughlin 1994: 28–30; Volp 2002). It is no surprise to find in late antique documents words that occur later, such as *viaticum* or *cimiterium* (Rebillard 1991, 1993), or to find in medieval documents references to and use of late antique sources. To deduce from these finds that the Christian ritual of death derives its origin from late antique Christianity would be, however, not only a methodological mistake but also a misreading and a misinterpretation of the late antique sources themselves. Such a deduction would also implicitly subscribe to what Patrick Geary (1994a: 90) has called a "conspiracy theory of ecclesiastical culture wrenching from the laity the major role in dealing with ancestors," as if church representatives waited until they had enough power to take over from the family all matters related to death and burial (as argued in Volp 2002). Such views seriously underestimate the role of the laity itself in the process of giving the primary role to the Church (Geary 1994a: 90; Lauwers 1997).

The description of the attempt by church representatives in Late Antiquity to christianize death is usually accompanied by a parallel description of the persistence of pagan practices. Ramsay MacMullen writes provocatively, "for hundreds of years, the pagan cult of the dead was a common part of Christianity"; and he therefore studies funerary practices under the heading of "assimilation" (MacMullen 1997: 111). He argues more generally that "religion" cannot be reduced to any creed, and that the Christianity promoted by the bishops did not exhaust the definition of the religion itself and did not succeed in suppressing other versions (158). It may be salutary to react against a tendency to envisage the practices inherited from the pagan past as pious instead of religious, as if denying their religious character could make them more commendable (for instance, Kotila 1992: 44–5). But such an interpretation underestimates the interaction between Christians generally and their bishops. We also understand better now what this modern account of a slow and difficult christianization process owes to the narratives of Augustine and some other fifth-century Christian writers, and for that very reason we should view the thesis with greater suspicion (Brown 1995).

In this chapter, therefore, I shall look at the role of the Church in the relations between the living and the dead in Late Antiquity on its own terms and for its own sake. To look at this issue will provide, I believe, some insight into the specific character of late antique Christianity. Church representatives in Late Antiquity did not pretend to control all aspects of the life of Christians. On the contrary, bishops and Christians negotiated very subtly the spheres where the Church might interfere. That death and burial was left under the control of the family will become clearer as we look at the rites performed before death, at funerals, at places of burial, and finally at ways of commemorating the dead.

Deathbed Rites

Our only evidence for the rites performed before death comes from the deathbed scenes of hagiography (Boglioni 1985). Composed by clerics, the hagiographical texts concentrated on fellow clerics and lay elites. They are valuable sources for determining what was thought desirable at the passing of a bishop or an ascetic, but they do not present an image of what happened at the death of the average Christian. Nor should they be read as normative texts: the saints were presented as exemplars, but no attempt was ever made to enforce an imitation of what was done at their deathbed.

Even beyond those limitations, one has to acknowledge the great variety of the ritual acts performed before death. The writers do not seem to have recognized any obvious norms, and they presented the choice of performing a precise rite more often than not as a personal one intimately linked to the saint's way of life. Martin, when he had to face the devil, chose several times during his life to lie down in sackcloth and ashes (Sulpicius Severus, *Ep.* 3. 14, with commentary in Fontaine 1967: 1322–4). Augustine asked for the penitential psalms to be copied and hung on the wall next to his bed, and he wept continuously while reading them (Possidius, *V. Aug.* 31. 1–2; Rebillard 1994: 213–14).

A modern reader cannot help being surprised by the relative absence of any mention of the *viaticum*, the giving of the Eucharist to the dying. The only clear example is that of Ambrose of Milan, in the life written by his deacon Paulinus in AD 411–13 (*V. Ambrosii*. 47. 3). One commentator concludes that in the fourth and fifth centuries, when the first hagiographical texts were composed, the reception of the *viaticum* was not thought of as a central moment of the deathbed scene (Boglioni 1985: 279). One should go further and ask whether there even was such a rite as the Eucharist for the dying in Late Antiquity. A critical review of the available evidence shows that, even though some clerics did receive the Eucharist just before dying or repeatedly in the days before death, it was not part of a regular ritual. The word *viaticum* appeared at this time only in the context of the help to be given to those who died while performing public penance (Rebillard 1991; 1994: 200–12 – not known to Volp 2002: 166–72, who reproduces the classical argument of Rush 1941 and 1974). The penitential context of the first regular use of *viaticum* provides important clues to the development of a Christian ritual of death that betrayed, during the early Carolingian period, a growing concern about salvation (Paxton 1990; Effros 2002: 201–4).

It has sometimes been suggested that, in Late Antiquity, baptism was the true ritual in advance of dying (Janssens 1981: 33; Saxer 1988: 424). There are a few examples of baptism delayed until late in adult life in the fourth and fifth centuries (some of them very famous, like Augustine or the Cappadocians), and even until death (as in the case of Constantine). It would be wrong, however, to imagine that most Christians waited until the last minute to be baptized. Thorough analysis of Augustine's preaching shows that the delay of baptism was not a pastoral issue in Africa in his time: as one might expect, he urges catechumens to receive baptism during Lent, but the rest of the time he does not distinguish them from other Christians in his sermons (Rebillard 1998). In any case, baptism was delayed until the last minute not as an aid in the process of dying, but as a way of avoiding sin after its reception.

Although arguments *e silentio* are not strong, it is worth noticing that we do not hear much about the pastoral duty of visiting the sick and the dying in early Christian sources. One can safely conclude that in Late Antiquity there was no Christian rite for the dying and that the presence of the clergy at the deathbed of Christians was at best optional.

Funerals

As there is no liturgical document before the eighth century, liturgists in the past have tried to reconstruct an early Christian ritual for funerals on the basis of fragments of texts from different geographic areas and periods. The result is obviously artificial, and we need not discuss such attempts. One source of evidence is hagiography, but I have already mentioned the risks in applying to the Christian population in general what is said about the clergy and the rich laity. Another source are the sermons in which bishops comment upon, usually critically, the practices of their flocks.

Let us consider the wake in the church: was it the usual practice in Late Antiquity? Macrina, the sister of Gregory of Nyssa, was brought to the church (Gregory of Nyssa, *V. Macrinae* 33). So was Ambrose, who died on Holy Saturday: his body was brought to the cathedral church, and the Easter vigil was his funeral wake (Paulinus, *V. Ambrosii* 48. 1). Paula was brought to the Church of the Savior, and the vigil held over her body lasted an entire week (Jerome, *Ep.* 108. 29. 1). These cases are obviously exceptional, and are presented as such in our sources. When one reads John Chrysostom's sermons, it becomes clear that for most Christians, at least in Antioch and Constantinople, the wake took place in the home of the deceased. He often criticizes Christians who mourn their deceased as pagans would (references in Rebillard 2003: 153–4; Rentinck 1970: 133–4; see Rush 1941: 179–81), and the context he envisages is clearly the household, with relatives and slaves present. Interestingly enough, it appears that some Christians not only asked for priests and chanters, very likely to have psalms and hymns sung during the wake, but also hired mourners, usually (according to Chrysostom) pagan women (*In Mat. hom.* 31. 3; *In ep. ad Hebraeos hom.* 4. 5). Even if he did not approve of such competition between the pagan mourning professionals and Christian chanters, the bishop never encouraged holding the wake in church. In his frequent criticisms of the traditional expenditure on funerals and burial, he points out that it runs counter to the Christian faith, but does not propose an alternative ritual. The involvement of the clergy in the funeral of a Christian, if they were called upon by the family, seems to have been limited to bringing ''philosophic consolation'' into the house of the deceased, and to some singing (*In Mat. Hom.* 31. 4).

The same picture can be drawn for Africa, from Augustine's sermons. The bishop of Hippo also repeatedly criticized the expenditure of his rich fellow Christians on funerals and burial (references in Saxer 1984: 153–6). He carefully explains, however, that, according to Scripture, caring for the dead is among the works of faith, although it provides no aid for the dead (*Sermo* 172. 2. 3). As such, it is the duty of the family to organize the funeral and burial; the Church has no say, except to encourage some moderation (Rebillard 2003: 152). Augustine never provides rules for a Christian ritual, nor does he picture the clergy at the home of the deceased. According to a canon from the Council of Hippo in AD 393, repeated in later councils in both Hippo and Carthage, some Christians wanted to bring the corpse of the deceased to the church immediately after death and expected the bishop to then celebrate the Eucharist. Interestingly, the canon forbids such a practice, arguing that the Eucharist cannot be celebrated in the presence of a corpse, and that the bishop can preside only if he is fasting. The recommended practice is, at least implicitly, to leave the corpse at home and to go to the church: if the bishop is fasting, he can celebrate the Eucharist; otherwise the family has to be content with prayers (*Concilium Hipponense* 4; see Rebillard 2003: 155–6). Reading this canon, one has the impression that the family took the initiative to involve the clergy in the funeral, not that the clergy attempted to impose its presence.

This is confirmed by other documents on the funerals of Christians. Scholars have striven to gather all the available information on the days that marked the mourning process and associated rites (Cumont 1918; Freistedt 1928; Vogel 1975). The collected evidence reveals that local practices varied greatly, and that it was the family's responsibility to ask for a eucharistic celebration, either at the grave or in the church, on the day of the burial or on the third, seventh, or ninth day. Commenting on Genesis 50: 10, where Joseph is said to have observed a mourning period of seven days, Augustine recommended that, instead of the period of nine days more generally observed by pagans (*magis in gentilium consuetudine*), Christians observe the same custom (*Quaestiones in Heptateuchum* 1. 172). The *Apostolic Constitutions*, which describe an ideal liturgy, follow the tradition of the ninth day like most of the eastern tradition and despite the Scriptures (8. 42. 1–3). The same variety of practice appears to have characterized the end of the mourning period on the thirtieth or fortieth day.

I believe that a useful distinction can be made between "Christian funerals" and the "funerals of Christians." The former did not exist in Late Antiquity: there was neither a Church-sanctioned ritual for death nor any attempt by the Church to impose uniformity. Family wishes and local traditions prevailed.

The Church and Christian Places of Burial

No one would deny that the Church had no control over the burial places of the vast majority of Christians in Late Antiquity. The involvement of the Church in the development of the first Christian cemeteries is a question that cannot be dealt with here. Whatever the exact role of the Roman church in the development of the catacombs, we do not know of any parallel in the rest of the empire (see the contributions in Fiocchi Nicolai and Guyon 2006).

Bishops developed places of burial for the poor as early as the third century, but they by no means replaced the local towns or cities in this responsibility. In Rome and Constantinople, the emperor delegated this task to the Church in exchange for tax exemptions (Rebillard 1999). The bishops' involvement in the burial of the poor, however, had more to do with the new style of urban leadership they were trying to impose (Brown 1992, 2002) than with a special concern for burial (Rebillard 2003: 130–41).

There is no late antique ecclesiastical regulation concerning who can be buried where, except when the burial is to be in a space controlled by the Church. This must be why, in a recently discovered sermon, Augustine explains why a catechumen cannot be buried where the Eucharist is celebrated. He was asked to intervene by a local bishop who had difficulty resisting the pressure of a family, rich local landowners, regarding the burial of their unbaptized son. It is difficult to assert positively that the family was trying to obtain for its son the privilege of a burial *ad sanctos*, in the close vicinity of the saints, as there is no allusion to saints or martyrs in the sermon; but it was clearly meant to be a privileged burial (*Sermo* 142 *augm.*; see Rebillard 1998). This short allocution is all the more precious because it is a unique document, opening a window on the expectations of the rich laity at the end of the fourth century and on the role they were ready to concede to the Church. Burial *ad sanctos*, however, was clearly a privilege reserved mainly for the clergy and for members of the lay nobility (Brown 1981; Duval and Picard 1986; Duval 1988).

Historians and archaeologists have increasingly dated the growth of parish cemeteries to later and later periods. The fourth and fifth centuries did see the development of "managed cemeteries," large areas of orderly rows of inhumation graves. They are no longer considered ethnic (mainly German) cemeteries, but we still lack an overview of their evolution (Young 1999; Effros 2003: 188–200). There was obvious control over the layout of graves, but nothing indicates that it was by the Church. Normally, no cult building was associated with these managed cemeteries, which were large and mainly urban. They were not abandoned until the end of the seventh century, and only then were they progressively replaced with burial areas linked to a church (Fixot and Zadora-Rio 1994).

There is a growing body of evidence regarding the role of the Church, or the absence of that role, in creating or managing Christian burial places; but a general account can still only be tentative.

The Commemoration of the Dead

The noninvolvement of the Church in the death and burial of Christians in Late Antiquity finds, if not an explanation, at least a plausible context in the complex relationship between the living and the dead. The usual picture is of fourth- and fifth-century bishops struggling against the cult of the dead, which they stigmatized as a pagan practice in which newly converted Christians indulged. We owe this picture largely to Augustine. In the letter in which he narrates his success in reforming the cult of the martyrs, he explains that, after the Peace of the Church, his predecessors had tolerated the customary eating and drinking on feast days because they did not want to discourage "a mass of pagans who wished to come to Christianity," and also that the time had now come to enforce proper Christian behavior for the feast of the martyrs (*Ep.* 29. 9). Peter Brown has already warned us about accepting as a historical truth this "piece of clerical euhemerism" (Brown 1981: 29): Augustine, who was addressing respectable Christian families, was only trying to shame them. Recently, Ramsay McMullen has also strongly reminded us how widely diffused those habits were, from at least the time when Christian funerary monuments can be identified as such (McMullen 1997: 110–11). What still needs to be emphasized and understood is that this struggle concerned the cult of the martyrs, not the cult of the ordinary dead.

It is important first to offer a description and an interpretation of the traditional cult of the dead in the Roman world. John Scheid (2005) has provided us with a thorough analysis of the available information. The feast for the dead, the *Parentalia*, was celebrated each year in February. Eight days after the official opening of the feast, on February 21 (*Feralia*), a sacrifice in holocaust was offered to the *Manes* of the deceased; it was followed by a banquet near the tomb. The food consumed at this banquet had to be brought from town, as there was no sharing of sacrificial food with the infernal deities unless a second sacrifice to the family deities (*Lares* and *Penates*) took place. The following day (February 22, *Caristia* or *Cara cognatio*), another banquet was held at home. Food and banquet were thus central elements in the traditional commemoration of the dead. They were the media through which the different statuses of the dead and of the living (and of their relations) were expressed. "As long as the family or the community celebrated the banquets of the *Parentalia* and the *parentationes*, the deceased survived as a member of this community, even if his place in it was not much to be envied" (Scheid 2005: 188). Thus, it is clear that the cessation of these rites would have meant abandoning the deceased to the definitive death of oblivion.

These rites are reconstructed from documents dated to the first and second centuries (Verg. *Aen.* 5. 64–5; Ov. *Fast.* 2. 533–4; inscriptions from Misenum: D'Arms 2000; see Scheid 2005: 320–3); but we have no reason to think that they changed much in the centuries that followed. In fact, Christian bishops mentioned the *Parentalia* and some associated rites throughout the fourth and fifth centuries, and even beyond. Christians, like their pagan parents and neighbors, celebrated funerary meals on, or near, the tombs of their dead. Archaeological evidence leaves no room for doubt on this matter (MacMullen 1997: 110–11).

The silence of the third-century Christian texts has sometimes been interpreted as a sign that early Christians did not take part in the traditional cult of the dead (Kotila 1992: 62–3; but see Rebillard 2005: 101–2). When Tertullian says that Christians do not sacrifice to the gods or give any food to the dead and that they do not eat from sacrifices or offerings to the dead (*De spectaculis* 28), he is prescribing what Christians *should* not do, not describing what they do not do. Archaeological evidence confirms that in the third century, at least in Rome, where we find the only monuments securely datable to this time, Christians celebrated funerary meals like their pagan relatives and neighbors (Février 1978). We have seen that the consumption of food near the tomb was not in fact directly linked to the sacrifice.

In the fourth century, bishops more regularly denounced funerary meals. In a sermon preached to newly baptized Christians (*c.* AD 360–80), Zeno of Verona includes among examples of forbidden sacrifices the meals on the tombs (*Tractatus* 1. 25. 6. 11). To justify their banqueting, some Christians were apparently mentioning the nearby tomb of a martyr. Zeno does not disguise his indignation. It is difficult to reconstruct the social context underlying such preaching but the sermon does provide evidence that, in the middle of the fourth century, some Christians in Verona continued the practice of funerary meals, and Zeno's moral reflections clearly indicate that prohibition would have been in vain. Gaudentius, bishop of Brescia in northern Italy at about the same time, adopted the same attitude. In a sermon also preached to the newly baptized (*Tractatus* 4. 14–15), he includes the *Parentalia* among a list of idolatrous practices and interrupts himself to explain why. He also chooses to insist that it is disrespectful to the dead to be drunk near their tombs. We know through a famous anecdote in the *Confessions* that Ambrose had forbidden the bringing of food and drink to the tombs of the martyrs in Milan. According to Augustine, Ambrose thought that the practice was too similar to the *Parentalia* (*Confessions* 6. 2. 2). That the prohibition concerned the tombs of the martyrs is confirmed by the fact that

Augustine's mother Monica (who was the immediate object of Ambrose's anxiety) had no family relatives buried in the city. In Africa, however, it was her custom to visit the tombs of her own dead and to "share" some wine with her parents. Ambrose himself does not comment on this prohibition among his extant texts: his only known allusion to the *Parentalia* is, like those of his Italian colleagues, a moral criticism of excessive drinking in honoring the dead (*De Helia et ieiunio* 17. 62). The issue was apparently more important for Augustine when he was writing the *Confessions* than it ever was for Ambrose (see McLynn 1994: 236).

Augustine's campaign back in Africa against these rites at the tombs of the martyrs is well known (documents in O'Donnell 1992, ii: 334–9; see Van der Meer 1962: 520–5; Saxer 1980: 141–7; Kotila 1992: 62–77). I want to emphasize that he makes a very clear distinction between the martyrs and the ordinary dead and does not forbid meals on the tombs of the latter. Like his Italian colleagues, he tries to convince the Christians to be moderate in their eating and drinking and to invite the poor to these meals so that they become an exercise in almsgiving and thus an aid to the dead (*Ep.* 22; see Rebillard 2005: 103). Other sermons (*Ennar. in Ps. 48*, sermo 1. 15; *Sermo* 361. 6. 6), preached long after the heat of his campaign against banquets at the feasts of the martyrs, show that, at least among his own flock, the practice of bringing food and drink to the tombs continued (see Rebillard 2005: 104–5). At the time of his reform, he explained why one should not forbid meals at the tombs of the ordinary dead: people believe that they are "a solace for the dead" and they do not want "the memory of their dead to be neglected" (*Ep.* 22. 1. 6).

Evidence from the east is scarce. In the *Apostolic Constitutions*, the members of the clergy are asked to drink moderately when they are invited to funerary banquets (8. 44). Gregory of Nazianzus has several epigrams against the gathering of drunkards on the tombs of the martyrs, but he does not allude to meals or food offerings for the ordinary dead (references in Mossay 1966: 244–6). Other bishops denounce feasts and banquets in moral terms, but not as practices against religion (Harl 1981). The lack of evidence prevents us from concluding that bishops in the east were less hostile to the traditional commemoration of the dead; but they surely did not forbid it.

According to Augustine, the true Christian commemoration of the dead was to be performed in the church (*Ep.* 22. 1. 6); but what was done exactly? There was no feast of the dead before the eleventh century, when the whole Church gradually adopted the feast of All Souls, instituted at Cluny by Odilo, and celebrated on November 2 (Lauwers 1996: 140–6). Joannes Belethus, a liturgist of the twelfth century, was struck by the fact that the festival of St. Peter's Chair, February 22, falls on the same date as the pagan festival of the *Caristia*, the familial banquet held at the grave of a dead relative (*Rationale divinorum officiorum* 83). Ancient and modern liturgists have tried to explain this coincidence as an attempt by the Church to substitute for the pagan festival of the dead a Christian one. No explanation, however, has been satisfactory, and it has now been proved that the Christian feast had no funerary character (Février 1977).

The Church regularly commemorated the dead among the intercessory prayers during the eucharistic service. It is sometimes said that the ancient Church made use of lists with the names of the dead, which were read during the eucharistic celebration. There is no convincing evidence of this before a late date, and I contend that the commemoration of the dead in Late Antiquity was, rather, general in character and anonymous. It is not necessary to review all the evidence here (see Rebillard 2003: 178–86), only the documents most discussed.

The testimony of Augustine for the African rite leaves no room for believing that the names of people were read aloud (Bishop 1912 had already made the point; see Rebillard 2003: 179–82, 2005: 106–7; *contra*, Saxer 1984: 162–5 and Klöckener 1992: 196–9). The only names read during the prayers were those of the living members of the clergy, some dead bishops, and the martyrs. The ordinary dead were mentioned under the general category of "those who have fallen asleep." In *On the Care for the Dead*, Augustine is explicit:

> The Church has undertaken to make those supplications [for the spirits of the dead] on behalf of all who die within the Christian and catholic community, even if they some-times take the form of a general commemoration, without names being mentioned, so that those who lack relatives or sons or any other acquaintance or friend ready for that task may nevertheless have them provided by the one faithful mother who is common to them all. (*De cura mort.* 4. 6)

According to Robert Taft (1991), the diptychs – the tablets on which the names of the dead were written – had been introduced in the east by the end of the fourth century. At first, the churches would have recorded the names of all the dead, and the deacon would have read their names during the intercessory prayers. The list was progressively restricted to official names, mainly of bishops, and their inclusion became a political issue. This last part of the story is well known and abundantly documented, and is especially true of the polemics surrounding the inclusion of the name of Chrysostom. The first part of Taft's reconstruction, however, is much less convincing. Among the documents he provides as support, the only unambiguous one is a rubric of the eucharistic prayer transmitted before AD 350 under the name of Serapion, bishop of Thmuis in Egypt (Johnson 1995).

The only other mention of a list of names appears in the description of the eucharistic liturgy in Cilicia by Theodore of Mopsuestia at the end of the fourth century. Before the consecration, the deacon reads from the tablets of the church the names of a few, living and dead; and "it is clear," says Theodore in his comment, "that in the few of them who are mentioned now all the living and the departed are mentioned" (*Catechetical Homilies* 15. 43, Mingana 1933: 94). These names were very likely the names of those who brought offerings and of the person for whom they offered, a well-known practice I shall comment upon later. Later in Theodore's commentary, there is in fact another mention of a commemoration of the dead, an anonymous and general one, included among the intercessory prayers (16. 14). There is positive evidence that other churches did not read the names of the dead (Antioch, Jerusalem, Constantinople: see Rebillard 2003: 182–6). Thus in the east as in the west, with perhaps the exception of Egypt, there was no reading of names, but a general and anonymous commemoration of the dead.

As I have just mentioned, it is possible that some more individual form of com-memoration in or by the Church did take place. According to a practice documented in both the west and the east, the names of the persons bringing the offerings and/or of the person on behalf of whom they brought them were mentioned in a special intercessory prayer at the beginning of the service. Tertullian thus mentions the duty of the widow to bring every year, on the anniversary of her husband's death, offerings on his behalf (*De exhortatione castitatis* 11. 1; *De monogamia* 10. 4). Cyprian makes a negative allusion to the practice in a letter where he discusses the case of a bishop who has been judged unworthy of such a commemoration (*Ep.* 1. 2. 1–2). In the fourth and fifth centuries, the practice is barely hinted at (Rebillard 2003: 176–7). A story told by Gregory of Tours, however, confirms that the practice was still prevalent at the end of the sixth century: he mentions a widow who, on behalf of her recently deceased husband, brings to the church every day an excellent wine from Gaza and eventually comes to realize that a subdeacon is substituting a worse one for it (*Gloria Confessorum* 64). In the East, the *Testamentum Domini* describes a liturgical installation at the entrance of the church for depositing the offerings and inscribing the offerers' names (1. 19), and Theodore, as we have seen, may allude to the practice. We can gather from these testimonies that the practice, even where attested, did not attract particular attention. In fact, every time the prayer of the dead is discussed, writers mention only the anonymous commemoration during the intercessory prayers at the Eucharist – which may suggest that it was precisely the anonymous character of the commemoration that was being questioned.

Some historians, in trying to outline the development of the medieval *missa specialis*, have put forward the hypothesis that communion was received privately at the tombs. The evidence is very tenuous. We know that the consecrated Eucharist could be kept on private premises, but we have no clear idea of the use made of it. We might wonder whether it was actually consumed or simply kept as a kind of prophylactic (Walker 1984). Both Ambrose and Augustine allude to the Eucharist in connection with a commemoration of the dead at the tombs. Their sense of a need to protect the *arcana*, however, the "secret mysteries" reserved to the baptized, forced them to be vague, which does not help us to understand what "Eucharist" might have meant in that context. Ambrose only says that Luke 9: 60, "let the dead bury their dead," can be understood in a prophetic sense: it was now prohibited to place on the tombs of the non-Christian dead what it had been acceptable in the past to place on the tombs of the elders (*In Lucam* 7. 43). Augustine refutes the understanding of Tobit 4: 17 as a reference to the *Parentalia*, arguing that the faithful know that can be done either "at the tombs of the dead" or "for the memory of the dead" – the Latin says rather ambiguously *erga memorias* (*Sermo* 361. 6. 6). I have found no similar allusion in the documents from the east. The evidence is not very convincing, and the most we can say is that the practice was not of great concern.

This lack of means for individual commemoration of the dead in the Church lies at the root of the numerous discussions about the prayer for the dead that were taking place both in the west and in the east during the fourth and the fifth centuries. If we look at the pastoral context of those discussions, it is apparent that they were not so much concerned with the efficacy of the prayers themselves as with the identity of the dead who could benefit from them. Both Augustine and John Chrysostom faced this pastoral problem, and they responded with the same answer: only baptized Christians not guilty of major sins can benefit from the prayers of the Church. While Augustine then insists on the limits imposed by the merits of the dead person, Chrysostom puts more emphasis on what other persons can do on their behalf. If Chrysostom gives more hope as to the help the dead can receive from the living, he clearly states that these hopes rely entirely on what the relatives care to do for their dead (Rebillard 2003: 189–97).

To define the boundaries of what the living could do for the dead was a capital issue in the creation of a Christian cult of the dead. The late antique Church, even if it had no single answer, was very cautious to state what those boundaries were. It did not forbid Christians to pray for those of their relatives who had died unbaptized or in sin, either personally or through intercessors like the poor or widows; but it gave no assurance about the outcome, any more than it did in the case of the non-Christian dead, and it left the care of the dead to the family. It is understandable, therefore, that the bishops, fearing to appear to be asking Christians to neglect their dead, did not turn them away from traditional forms of commemoration. In Late Antiquity, most of the dead who were still remembered were not Christian and therefore, according to church teaching, not saved; but Christians could cultivate their memory and still remain good Christians themselves. The memory of the dead and their salvation were two distinct matters, and only the second was a concern for the Church.

BIBLIOGRAPHICAL NOTE

Rush 1941 is still the only synthesis in English. It provides good access to the principal sources, but their interpretation is largely outdated. Toynbee 1971 is mainly concerned with the burial practices of pagans in the first three centuries, but also includes a few observations about Christians. Brown 1981 draws interesting parallels between the cult of the dead and the cult of the saints. MacMullen 1997 emphasizes the continuity between the Christian and the non-Christian cult of the dead. Effros 2002, though about the Merovingian world, describes the development of burial practices and beliefs since Late Antiquity.

PART III

Image and Word

Late Antiquity was a rhetorical age. The education of the governing and cultural elite was based on rhetoric, on the art of public speaking, whether political, forensic, or exhortatory (see Cribiore, ch. 16). Only a small number of people commanded a regular and assured income on the basis of their teaching rhetoric, but many more took private pupils, and many more again pursued careers in law or philosophical formation. The chapters in this section are devoted in part to this rhetorical tradition. There was a fine balance, frequently sought after and not infrequently achieved, between appreciating the wealth of literary forms and techniques inherited from Cicero, Quintilian, Demosthenes, or Menander and actually performing in public according to their canons of taste and skill. Although some could be criticized, even lampooned, for their facile, conceited, or merely greedy attachment to the power of words, it is remarkable how many public figures were also in a sense scholars, devoted to learned conversation, the writing of elegant letters and poetry, and the collection and emendation of literary texts.

The first two chapters in this section (Cribiore and Haines-Eitzen, chs. 16 and 17) describe in part the social settings within which rhetorical refinement was acquired, and trace indeed the ways in which rhetoric – both its learning and its practice – could create and sustain the very groups upon which its survival and dissemination depended. Rhetoric was part of the empire's organic structure. Two further chapters (Pollmann and Ebbeler, chs. 18 and 19) provide examples of the rhetorical discipline – forms in which words to some extent acquired the silence of the written page – namely, biblical commentary and letter-writing. The earlier chapter on inscriptions (Trout, ch. 12) has something of the same character. One begins to see the extent to which the various sections of this *Companion* unavoidably overlap, for letter writing was part of the communicative system described earlier (by both Leyerle and Sotinel, chs. 8 and 9), and biblical commentary was part of the "sacred" world to be examined in Part V (especially, perhaps, by Graumann, ch. 36). Here, however, the focus is on text as such. Finally, the intricacies of language itself, and the ways in which it changed over time, are examined in the two special contexts of Italy and Egypt (Burton and Choat, chs. 22 and 23 respectively). And one might note the element of intimacy in some of this activity – the revelation or disguise of self in letters, the construction of a public persona in inscriptions, the urgency of self-improvement in the study of virtue and etiquette – which adds a new layer to the humanity hinted at in the territorial analysis of the previous section.

But the late Roman speaker demanded a stage: there was a place for rhetoric as well as a form. This was a dramatic, a theatrical society, in which the spoken word was qualified or enhanced by a setting, whether it be a court of law, a philosophical seminar, the dramatic staging of imperial ceremony with its elaborate addresses full of praise and erudite allusion, or the ritual of temple or church in which extended prayer and detailed moral exhortation was presented against a backdrop of imagery and wealth. Almost every word that has come down to us was accompanied by gesture, movement, a symbolic choreography; was delivered in architectural spaces designed to stimulate incorporation or awe, reinforced by visual comment – statuary, fresco, mosaic, the very bricks and stones – which brought to bear either recollection of past glories or anticipation of achievements yet to come. In that sense history, too, was a pregnant text, placing the individual's life in a longer continuum that gave it dignity, both civic and religious, and made demands (see Woods, ch. 24).

To that extent, therefore, the visual – albeit silent, unspoken – was itself a set of words, a language with its own grammar, force, and familiar message. It was a language that became increasingly Christian (which anticipates observations made later in the volume by Lim, Lizzi Testa, and McLynn, chs. 33, 35, and 38 respectively). The "art" that we speak of here (Francis and Harley, chs. 20 and 21) was not a mere embellishment of the rhetorical culture: it was its mirror image, an echo of the voice of the age that took solid form in brush strokes and tesserae and in the very buildings that reflected back upon the eye and mind the impressions made first upon the ear. Some of this artistic wealth we now see only in museums, but an abundance still remains in its original setting, part of the "land" through which we are able to travel; and it needs almost to be listened to by the modern observer, so that one can gain a sense of the applause, the obeisance, the oratory and music that the art at once witnessed and inspired.

CHAPTER SIXTEEN

The Value of a Good Education: Libanius and Public Authority

Raffaella Cribiore

In AD 361 the sophist Libanius, teacher of rhetoric in Antioch (modern Antakya, in southern Turkey), wrote to the eminent philosopher Themistius to introduce one of his students, who was eager to study philosophy in Constantinople. Libanius assured the philosopher that his student, Julianus, had received a well-rounded education: "If you give a rhetorical display, he will applaud; if it is Plato and philosophy, he will be stimulated; if you lecture about the stars, he will show no idleness; and if you examine the poets, he will be serious about this lovely subject" (*Ep.* 667, ed. Foerster; all such references are henceforth numbered according to this edition). In a later letter regarding Julianus, Libanius insisted upon his vast culture, and introduced one more intellectual attainment, his knowledge of Latin (*Ep.* 1296). In AD 364 Libanius referred again to this former student in a long and eloquent letter (*Ep.* 1261). At that point, Julianus had attained the eminent position of *comes orientis* ("Count of the East"), and his young son was studying in Antioch. The sophist was triumphant on both accounts and celebrated Julianus' merits as a governor with a few lapidary phrases: "He believes that his duty is to render the cities happy; he is pleased if the sword lies idle; he embellishes the cities with buildings, worships the Muses, and in a trial never lets the guilty go unpunished."

This small dossier, a tiny fraction of the surviving 1,500 letters of Libanius, raises a number of questions that I will attempt to answer in what follows. Were all the students of this prominent sophist as accomplished as Julianus in their learning and careers? Did education show any sign of change in the fourth century? And was there a direct connection between rhetoric and power that made the possession of an advanced education an indispensable prerequisite for social and political advancement? The literary evidence from sophists such as Libanius and Himerius heavily emphasizes the connection between eloquence and success, but it is one-sided and needs to be counterbalanced by other sources when possible.

The School of Libanius

The works of Libanius (*c.* AD 314–93) are an ideal source for a study of change and continuity in fourth-century education. What we know about *paideia* in Late Antiquity derives from a range of literary and papyrological evidence; but only in the writings of Libanius does an actual rhetorical school, and the personalities of the students and teachers it comprised, emerge from the past. Medieval copyists preserved much of Libanius' voluminous literary production: sixty-four orations, fifty-one declamations, and 1,500 letters, besides the exercises and summaries of Demosthenes' speeches Libanius wrote for students. Many of his works have not yet appeared in translation, a situation that is perhaps in part due to the fact that Libanius' Greek is quite demanding. In the middle of the twentieth century, the school of Libanius attracted considerable attention. Peter Wolf in 1952, Paul Petit in 1956, and A.-J. Festugière in 1959 focused on Libanius' students and assistants, and looked at aspects of recruitment. Petit's work in particular was fundamental in establishing a list of the pupils of this sophist and clarifying their social and economic standing. He was strongly influenced, however, by the scholarly practices of the nineteenth and early twentieth centuries, and he looked at Libanius' works in a positivist spirit, as if they could be interpreted with complete objectivity. The outline he presented is weak in other respects, in spite of his lists of percentages and similar numerical details.

The most influential of Libanius' works has always been his *Autobiography.* He composed its first part (*Or.* 1. 1–155) in AD 374. The second part consists of bits and pieces of his personal journal that were added arbitrarily after his death. Incidentally, this second part, shapeless and pessimistic, has contributed to an image of Libanius as a choleric, dark, and paranoid character, different from the concerned teacher and intense man of letters that his correspondence and some other orations reveal. Libanius spent almost forty years as the official sophist of Antioch and received an imperial stipend, supplemented by students' fees (Kaster 1983). At that time, Antioch – together with Rome, Alexandria, and Constantinople – was one of the four major cities of the Roman world. Her population included Greeks, Romans, and Syrians, Jews, and Christians, and one could roughly distinguish between a Greek-speaking city and an Aramaic-speaking countryside. Libanius taught Greek rhetoric and did not know Latin.

Libanius' school included some assistant rhetors, whose principal function was to introduce students to the classical authors. He was anxious to maintain friendly relations with his assistants and appealed to the city council in an attempt to obtain more generous financial treatment for them (*Or.* 31), but he rarely alluded to them in his letters. Libanius *was* his school, which probably either disappeared or continued on a much reduced basis after his death. He ruled over a student population that reached eighty in the best years. In antiquity, there was no uniform rule about the age of admission to (or graduation from) a program of education at any level; but on average young men of the elite started studying rhetoric when they were about 14 or 15, after learning the rudiments of literacy from an elementary teacher and studying poetry and grammar under the tutelage of a grammarian. Girls, who sometimes had access to grammatical education, did not study rhetoric, which was seen as a preparation for a public life and career. In an age when most intellectuals had accepted Christianity, Libanius defended paganism. He admitted both Christian and pagan students to his classes, but his correspondence very rarely alludes to a student's religion, since his main allegiance was to rhetoric itself.

The evidence from Libanius and from other contemporary figures well schooled in rhetoric, such as Basil of Caesarea and Gregory of Nazianzus, shows that students frequently did not learn rhetoric from a single teacher. They started with a rhetor close to home, then moved to more prominent educational centers. For young men of the elite, the traditional boundaries between town, city, and metropolis did not exist. Gregory received his elementary instruction at Nazianzus and studied grammar and rhetoric at Caesarea. Even though this city in Cappadocia, which he called "the metropolis of the logoi" (*Or.* 43. 13), had legitimate claims to fame as a center for rhetoric, he considered it necessary to complete his education in Athens. Like Basil and Libanius, he remained in Greece for many years. Libanius' writings show that several trends affected school attendance. Students' mobility was not a new phenomenon, but seems to have become more common in the second part of the fourth century. The typical movement from smaller schools close to home to larger and more prestigious educational centers is perceptible in his letters. But while Libanius had to accept that reality, he wanted Antioch to be the culmination of the training of his students. He considered the fame of Athens as a center for rhetoric undeserved, and he aimed (albeit in vain) to dethrone her, putting Antioch in her place. On account of her past glories, Athens continued to be regarded as the ultimate educational destination, even though in the later fourth century she was no longer the vibrant place where the illustrious teachers described by Eunapius in the *Lives of the Sophists* held forth. Synesius felt obliged to visit the city in AD 399, because those who studied there continued to put on airs of superiority and behaved "like demigods amidst mules" (*Ep.* 56).

Students also frequently switched schools, and this was a perennial source of friction between students and their teachers. The problem of defection (*apostasis*) was apparently widespread, and was not confined to the end of the year. If we believe Libanius' late orations, it reached its climax in the 380s when, with some exaggeration, he complained of students leaving his school on a daily basis (*Or.* 43; *Ep.* 405. 8; *Or.* 36. 13; 1. 241–2; 3. 24; 34. 20; 62. 25). After a tour of other academic options, they supposedly returned to the place they started from; but then the cycle started again. In *Oration* 43 (*On the Agreements*), a speech addressed to other sophists in Antioch, Libanius tried to devise a remedy to target delinquent students. Yet, by making students' learning dependent on teachers' professionalism and proposing to submit the latter to parents' inspection, he must have alienated the other members of the teaching profession.

Libanius maintained that defections had been more rare in his own school days, and he considered the escalation of the phenomenon in Antioch as another manifestation of what he, in his old age, believed to be rampant disregard for traditional *paideia*. It is not easy to gain an objective view of the matter on the basis of his testimony alone. The orations of the sophist Himerius (*c.* AD 310–90), who taught in Athens, show that students' unrest was not confined to Antioch. Realistic details such as students' fights and classroom strife and discontent often appear amid Himerius' convoluted mythological and poetic allusions (*Or.* 18, 35, 38, 65, and especially 66). Late antique students of rhetoric seem to have been somewhat intolerant of a traditional, unchanging discipline, and wished to experiment. Himerius could offer them the fire of lyric poetry and the beauty of Pindar to imitate. Yet, his eloquence was heavy and lifeless (Kennedy 1983: 215–39; Barnes 1987). Libanius, enamored as he was of the classic models (Demosthenes in particular) and of his discipline, never doubted the intrinsic value of rhetoric, but he placed the blame for its diminished attraction on the changing times. The search for easy success, the lack of toleration of hard work, the desire to encapsulate learning in immediately digestible pills, and the increasing reliance on new subjects such as Latin and Roman law, all had an adverse effect on the number of those pursuing rhetorical studies.

Paul Petit's calculations of the length of attendance of students in Libanius' school need to be adjusted. When a letter shows that a young man was in Antioch in a certain year but the next letter that mentions him dates from many years later, one cannot suppose continuous attendance. Deaths in the family, illness, the geographic mobility of fathers, and other circumstances (besides *apostasis* per se) might interrupt schooling. A few years (two on average) would give a young man with good natural talent (*physis*) the ability to write, speak, and compose encomiastic orations. The student Albanius, the scion of a wealthy family of Ancyra in Galatia, provides a good example of how fruitful two years of rhetoric might be. Libanius said of him, "He is my student in the strictest sense of the word since he did not come to my teaching from another teacher nor did he have another after us. If his mother's crying and begging had not led him away from his studies before the time was right, he would now do what I do" (*Ep.* 1444). Once again, Libanius' dream that one of his "sons" (as he called his favorite students) could follow in his footsteps was shattered. Yet, he considered Albanius a complete success. This young man delivered a panegyric in praise of the powerful governor Modestus (*PLRE* i: Domitius Modestus 2), winning the admiration of a prominent orator, who took an interest in his work (*Ep.* 63). With the knowledge he had acquired, Albanius managed his patrimony, gained great wealth, undertook honorable civil service, and worked for the governor of Galatia, acquiring the reputation of a good orator. In writing to the governor (*Ep.* 834), Libanius urged him to continue to spur on Albanius and other students who were in his retinue, "so that no one may throw in our face the proverb of the one swallow" (which, according to the comic poet Cratinus, "could not make a spring"). The success of his pupils would silence those who objected that the training he offered was useless. To these "biting flies" he responded years later with *Oration* 62.

The Rival Studies

There is no doubt that toward the end of the fourth century the prestige of a rhetorical education was shaken and its monopoly was broken; but we should not lose sight of the fact that rhetoric was still alive and well in the fifth and sixth centuries and in later Byzantine society. Libanius' cries of despair in his late speeches need to be put in some perspective, and to do so, we need to rely on biographical data (Wintjes 2005). Old age, lingering depression, life circumstances, personal losses, lack of resilience, and inability to adapt to a changing social climate partially account for the dark view of the state of traditional *paideia* that emerges from his late orations. But when one juxtaposes his letters and his orations, it seems that the genre itself is one of the reasons for the obsessive pessimism that is prevalent in the speeches. In the fourth century, letters were preeminently vehicles of friendship (Thraede 1970: 125–46; White 1992; Van Dam 2003a: 136–8). Libanius' letters throw into relief his abiding love for his profession and his warm concern for his students; but the flight from Greek rhetoric and the decadence of *paideia* became the "hobby horses" that he rode in his late choleric speeches (Norman 2000: 89). A consideration of genre also helps us understand Libanius' apparently duplicitous attitude toward some public figures (for example, the official Proclus) to whom he addressed courteous letters but concerning whom he delivered (albeit to a small audience of friends) speeches inflamed with invective (*PLRE* i: Proclus 6; *Or.* 1. 212, 221–4; 10; 26; 27; 28; 42; Petit 1988: 205–11; Swain 2004: 385–90).

When we focus on the studies that rivaled rhetoric (shorthand writing, Latin, and Roman law), considerations of genre provide a helpful backdrop against which we can more realistically evaluate the apparently contradictory stances of Libanius' letters and orations. It is usually maintained that he was intolerant of all these disciplines and that his attitude hardened considerably as the years passed and they posed an ever greater threat to rhetoric (Liebeschuetz 1972: 242–55; Festugière 1959: 411); but one should attempt to reach a balanced view, even when the evidence is mostly one-sided. Shorthand writing became very popular under the emperor Constantius, who appointed notaries to high positions (*Or.* 42. 25; 18. 158–60; 62. 16; Petit 1955: 363–5; Cracco Ruggini 1987: 227–8; Heath 2004: 259–67). Julian stopped this practice: shorthand was revived but never regained its earlier predominance. The menace of shorthand continued to loom in Libanius' orations (even in the late *Or.* 62). Yet, he considered this skill useful for some of his students (*Ep.* 300 and 324) and for his cultivated secretary Thalassius (*Or.* 42). While shorthand writing was a technical skill that theoretically could accompany the study of rhetoric, Roman law and Latin posed a more direct threat to traditional Greek *paideia*, because students who pursued these studies in the hope of obtaining coveted positions in the administration shortened their rhetorical training.

Some Latin was necessary to enter a school of law, but how much? The so-called "Latin school exercises" show that students in Egypt attained only a reading know-ledge of the language (Cribiore, 2003–4). In a city such as Antioch, which was often the seat of the imperial court, it is possible that more Latin was necessary. Yet, I think that a veneer was sufficient in most cases. Governors could rely on scribes and on the few people in their retinues who knew that language; the philosopher The-mistius who became Constantinople's urban prefect did not know it (Vanderspoel 1995: 157–8). A good reading knowledge of Latin was necessary to enter a school of law, since legal texts were in this language in the fourth century; but an ability to write and speak accomplished prose was superfluous. We know that at least in the fifth century (and perhaps before) Greek summaries of Latin legal texts were in circulation to help students who had trouble with the language (Scheltema 1970: 12–16). I also doubt that classes in the renowned law school of Beirut were conducted in Latin, as is usually still maintained (Collinet 1925: 38–9, 211; Jolowicz 1952: 474; Rochette 1997: 168, 174; only Schulz 1946: 276 was against this assumption). The school served a mostly Greek student body, but the evidence on which that assumption rests (Gregory Thaumaturgus, *Oratio panegyrica in Origenem* 5. 57–62; Libanius, *Or.* 2. 44) is easily interpreted in a different way. No proof exists that Latin was the language of instruction in Beirut – a fact, moreover, that is a priori improbable. It is well known, in any case, that the increasing Hellenization of the imperial court culminated in AD 450, when Latin ceased to be the main language of court officials at Constantinople.

One wonders, therefore, how proficient in Latin the student Julianus, with whose dossier this discussion began, was. Libanius' words of praise in the letter to Themistius show that he was aware that some knowledge of that language might improve the general perception of a young man's accomplishments. Since, however, he did not know any Latin (like Themistius himself), any degree of knowledge of that language would have attracted his admiration. In spite of inveighing against the encroachment of Latin in his orations (*Or.* 58. 21–2, 24, 29–31; *Or.* 1. 255–6; 3. 24; 38. 6; 40. 5–6), Libanius realized that some training was necessary. He wrote letters to a former student and friend who resided in Rome, trying to attract him to Antioch to teach Latin at the school (*Ep.* 534, 539). He made a similar attempt to establish the teaching of law in Antioch, as other letters testify (*Ep.* 209, 433). Even though he did not succeed in bringing the rival studies to his city, his plans indicate that he was not blind to the reality that *paideia* was in a process of change but wished to make Antioch a self-sufficient educational center that could retain students for many years.

There are no indications that Libanius' pupil Julianus ever studied Roman law. Literary advocates trained only in Greek rhetoric could still achieve prominent positions. Yet, the predominance of technical advocates who knew Roman law became increasingly more evident in the second half of the fourth century. Libanius, whose ultimate wish was that his pupils choose an academic career, had to acknowledge that very few did, and that many considered rhetorical training as only a phase in their education (*Or.* 62). He sent letters of recommendation to professors of law for some young men who wanted to go to Beirut, but acutely resented it when his students hid their intentions and disappeared suddenly (*Ep.* 117, 533, 653, 1171, 1539). To reinforce the qualifications of their sons, some parents were ready to give them additional training in other subjects and places (Rome, Beirut, or Constantinople), but those parents who considered an education in rhetoric a sufficient qualification for careers as private and public advocates also tried to limit the length of their sons' rhetorical studies (e.g., *Ep.* 743, 1394).

The Prestige of Rhetoric

Libanius composed *Oration* 62 (*Against Critics of His Educational System*) in AD 382 (Norman 2000: 87–8) to rebut the accusation that very few of those he trained succeeded in the profession of advocacy and in the curial and imperial administration. His critics never questioned his ability as a rhetor but doubted that he could educate young men for successful careers. Libanius refuted them by citing the cases of a few outstanding pupils and denouncing the specific historical circumstances that caused rhetoric to be less highly prized than in the past. Rhetoric alone, moreover, could not assure material success without the help of Fortune, a deity in whom Libanius fervently believed. While it is likely that he did not fully convince his critics, he succeeded in presenting an image of himself as an educator who cared for the old (and neglected) values of honesty, personal commitment, and religious and social integrity. Throughout his work the practice of rhetoric and the worship of the traditional gods are linked according to the system of reforms that his beloved emperor Julian had intended but failed to achieve, and in which Libanius himself never ceased to believe. He wrote to Julian upon his arrival in Antioch in AD 362 that the emperor had brought back reverence for the gods and rhetoric: eloquence itself inspired him toward religious piety (*Or.* 13. 1).

When, in the 360 s, Libanius wrote spirited letters to his student Albanius, life had not yet dealt him the worst blows he was to suffer, and his faith in the material benefits of the training he offered was still intact. He told Albanius that rhetoric would be his ally in any profession he chose. Albanius was supposed to take advantage of the fact that a certain governor favored young men with an education because he "was nourished in the art of Hermes" and admitted to being a slave only to rhetoric's pleasures (*Ep.* 140). Besides providing an excellent training in the endurance of toil and discipline and a stimulating mental gymnastics (Cribiore 2001), what did this discipline offer? With time, Libanius became disillusioned and doubted that the connection between rhetoric and material power was as valid as it had been in the past. Yet, he never ceased proclaiming rhetoric's educational value. Rhetoric was not a dispensable adornment that titillated one's vanity and aroused admiration through its verbal fireworks. In a letter (*Ep.* 1261. 4), he asserted that it contributed to making a student "good and temperate" and had moral power. Those who, in the name of *paideia*, renounced less worthy pleasures to cultivate their minds were the truly valuable members of society. It is likely that Libanius' reluctance to praise prosperity and wealth (particularly when they were not achieved through education) contributed to his personal success with some of the young men in his following. By invoking the true glory and power that only knowledge could confer, he was able to appeal to the idealistic nature of some adolescents. His letters reveal numerous examples of the loyalty of pupils and their resentment when their families' priorities forced them to leave his school before they had completed their studies.

Rhetoric was valuable not only for moral and cultural reasons: it could, when historical circumstances were favorable, open the path to distinguished careers. Libanius maintained that rhetoric was able to reveal the right course of action (*Or.* 49. 32) by permitting correct understanding of any given issue. Eloquence was the product of understanding (*phronêsis*), but understanding was prompted by eloquence (*Or.* 12. 92). Education had the power to transform people from swine into human beings. Speaking of the education of the emperors Constantius and Constans, he reiterated that innate talent and knowledge of the art of ruling were not sufficient when eloquence was lacking (*Or.* 59. 33). Through rhetoric, a governor could become a "prophet" and forecast the future. Oracles predicted the future through inspiration, but orators foresaw future events by means of their intellect (*Or.* 23. 21). In AD 365, writing to a former student who was the son of an eminent governor but who was growing intellectually lax, Libanius pointed to the reasons Julius' father had acquired his position and to the wondrous quality of his tenure:

> When you were here, I both persuaded you and forced you to withstand the labours of rhetoric. I would not be able to do the latter now, since you are away, but I urge you to consider that education is the greatest of goods, and that none of the things that lead to it is heavy to bear. You would do this if you bore in mind the reason why your father governs and elicits admiration. You will find that those things do not derive from great wealth, physical beauty, and high birth, but are both the gifts of rhetoric. (*Ep.* 1335)

He reiterated the same concepts in a much later oration that he wrote to upbraid those students who had abandoned his school precipitously upon the occasion of the riots of AD 387 in Antioch (*Or.* 23. 21–2). By leaving the dangers of the city promptly (and perhaps rightly!), those young men had forgotten that "eloquence helps to conceal low birth, hides ugliness, and protects wealth." Dismissal of wealth and beauty figures throughout Libanius' work, but his position with respect to *eugeneia* (high birth) deserves a closer look. The youths who attended his school belonged to elite families, but some did not enjoy economic prosperity. When noble families that had fallen into disgrace for various reasons could not support their sons, the sophist tried to help by waiving tuition fees and asking benefactors for financial aid (*Ep.* 80, 319). In letters of recommendation, he also appealed on behalf of some poor young men in search of positions by asking governors to take into account their nobility and education rather than their financial means (*Ep.* 293. 2, addressed to Domitius Modestus). At a personal level, he was very proud of the nobility of his family and often bragged about it to the annoyance of others: he was convinced that few people were his equals by birth (*Or.* 2. 10–11). His financial means, however, did not correspond to the *eugeneia* of his family, which had lost much wealth at the beginning of the century. At the top of his scale of values, in any case, there was *paideia*. Rhetoric had the power to confer nobility on those who practiced it. Education could obliterate social barriers.

The Education of the Governors

In Antioch, governors represented Roman power. Their arrival was celebrated with solemn ceremonies in which all the population participated, and Libanius, as the official sophist of the city, delivered a panegyric. The multitude of letters he sent to various governors through the years to solicit favors for himself or for others testifies to the influence of these officials. At the same time, the effective power of these representatives of the emperor was curtailed (Cabouret 2002, 2004). They were present at the meetings of the city council, but their authority was limited, since the local potentates acted on their own initiative and made decisions. Likewise, as administrators of justice, they lived among the wealthiest and most influential citizens, though the mass of the population could have recourse to them in the face of abuses at the hands of the more powerful. Libanius' speeches and correspondence allow us to glimpse many facets of the governors' authority (their impotence included) and show what their power was, both in theory and in practice. Rhetoric enabled its practitioner to criticize and oppose the actions of "bad" governors. In AD 361, while urging the Antiochenes to remunerate his assistants fairly, Libanius pointed to this aspect of rhetoric, through which citizens were able to keep their city prosperous and independent. Eloquence had the ability "to overcome the irrational tendencies of governors through rational argument" (*Or.* 31. 7). In AD 374, Libanius referred to this combative side of eloquence at the very beginning of his *Autobiography* (*Or.* 1. 2). "My family," he says, "was one of the greatest in a great city, in education, wealth, provision of shows and games, and in that type of eloquence that confronts the excesses of governors." Throughout his work, he provided ample proof that he could exploit the adversarial potential of oratory.

Libanius' relations with governors were very uneven. He did not introduce himself to them but waited to be personally invited, and only then did he "honor" them with a visit. He defended himself from accusations of soliciting them incessantly, saying that he exercised the moral influence that derived from his cultural position in the city. His *Autobiography* shows to the full his ups and downs with governors, especially in its second part. Their mutual rapport was based on an appreciation of his rhetoric. He dismissed or considered plainly hostile the officials who did not attend his speeches, were literate only in Latin (like Festus in *Or.* 1. 156), or did not follow the advice he persisted in offering. "Bad" governors had a passion for the theater and the hippodrome and shunned the courts. They either refused to administer justice or had an amateurish approach to it and wasted time (*Or.* 33. 8–10). They also had people flogged and intervened in business that regarded only the city, filling the prisons. In sum, Libanius declared to the emperor Theodosius, "governors sent out to the provinces are murderers" (*Or.* 45. 3, written in AD 386). But there were also "good" governors, and Libanius lets us know several of them. It is easy to identify what these portraits have in common. The officials he approved of were those who appreciated his cultural appeal. One of them, for example, Strategius, who was called Musonianus for his love of the arts of the Muses (*PLRE* i: 611–12), was versed both in Greek and Latin and was instrumental in convincing the emperor to give the sophist gifts that increased his prestige and income. In AD 353, when governor of Achaea, Strategius made the professors of the University of Athens invite Libanius to teach there, an honor Libanius much appreciated but refused. A good education had to be the chief quality of a governor, since the manner in which an official governed was a direct reflection of his upbringing.

Libanius presented as an ignoramus any official he found ineffectual and untrustworthy. When he launched bitter, personal tirades against the incompetence and brutality of governors, he attacked their education first. Thus the bad outcome of Tisamenus' administration could have been predicted from the start (*PLRE* i:

916–17; *Or.* 33). This governor was of good lineage, and his grandfather had been a rhetor; but Tisamenus "participated in eloquence perforce and superficially, happily said goodbye to rhetoric and teachers, and turned to dancers." Likewise, in promoting the admission of his secretary Thalassius to the Senate of Constantinople, Libanius attributed the opposition of some senators to their lack of *paideia* (*Or.* 42. 11–13, 40). Thalassius was of lowly origin and was denigrated as a "sword maker" because (like Demosthenes!) he owned a sword factory. Libanius painted a flattering portrait of his character, culminating in Thalassius' devotion to studies and knowledge of philosophy. This oration contains "some of his choicest invective in character assassination" (Norman 2000: 147). We are told, on the one hand, that Optatus (who later became governor) manifested from the outset a pernicious disposition: he tried to avoid learning his letters by running away and hiding in a farmyard, and when brought back shunned education altogether. No wonder, therefore, that he turned to magic and tried to kill his brother and parents! Proclus, on the other hand, who came from a noble and cultivated family, appears in this oration as devoted to a life of pleasure and drunkenness. Libanius alleged that he was not proficient either in Greek or in Latin and did not know either rhetoric or Roman law.

If Libanius' relations with a certain governor turned sour over the years, he could not deny the education for which he had formerly praised him but could minimize and ridicule his attainments. Thus, for example, when Icarius (*PLRE* i: 455–6) succeeded Proclus as *comes orientis* in AD 384, Libanius was flattered by his admiration for his work: Icarius became "almost a son" to him. He presented the governor as a cultivated person who not only had the ability to compose orations and tried to improve the standing of orators, but also had received his office from the Muses as a recompense for his poetry (*Or.* 1. 255). After a honeymoon period, however, when Icarius supposedly became guilty of brutality and injustice, the sophist naturally ridiculed the poetry the latter composed to celebrate the emperor's deeds, and denounced its simplistic and excessively dramatic quality (*Or.* 28. 2).

When we try to look (through Libanius' lens) at the value late antique society placed on education in rhetoric, the picture seems quite uniform. In *Or.* 62. 46–8, for example, he presented with some disgust the success story of one Heliodorus (*PLRE* i: 411), a humble hawker of fish-pickle who became familiar with the law by paying attention to law suits and frequenting the courts, and who eventually began practicing oratory. Fame and wealth followed, especially when he delivered "the speeches that a man of his kind must make" at the palace, and he gained vast estates. This story, for which Libanius is the only witness and which he may have heard when he was a student in Athens, is remarkable. It was highly unusual for a complete ignoramus to achieve this kind of success. And why was Heliodorus able to become a governor in the end? "People held that he had been through the mill of oratory," said Libanius, referring to a common assumption that an education in rhetoric opened the door to power. Another example of eloquence providing a passport to office comes from the same speech (*Or.* 62. 63–9). The chief critic of Libanius' educational system was a supposedly ignorant governor who later achieved the rank of *honoratus*. He used his wealth to oppress families through usury with a complete lack of scruple and compassion, and was "more savage than the Cyclops, tearing the flesh from the starving."

If people objected that this fellow must have had an education because he delivered speeches, Libanius retorted that he bought them. Buying a speech on the market was reproachable, although sometimes excusable in a student; but entering the imperial service with the aid of speeches composed by others was dishonorable. Again, it is clear what prestige rhetoric carried, at least in Libanius' eyes.

Let us now look at another type of evidence, in the hope of gaining some perspective. The great epigrapher Louis Robert published a series of verse epigrams on stone that celebrated the attainments of governors (Robert 1948). Most of these Greek inscriptions can be dated from the end of the third to the fifth centuries, and were engraved on buildings, fountains, and statues. They can be distinguished from similar inscriptions belonging to the early Roman period mainly because they, unlike their predecessors, are in verse. The honorific character of these epigrams does not allow for disparaging comments of the sort that appear in Libanius' writings, but a comparison of the literary and epigraphic commendations reveals some surprises. The main themes of the epigrams are the justice and building programs of the governors. The theme of justice is almost omnipresent and appears in references to the officials' activities in the law courts and in the administration. Gregory of Nazianzus identified comparable traits when, in a letter to Olympius (Olympius 10, *PLRE* i: 646), he identified the main virtues of a governor. While he praised intelligence and courage, he pointed to integrity ("clean hands") and to the shunning of "unjust gold" as the *sine qua non* of good government (*Ep.* 140). The regular occurrence of the theme of justice in the inscriptions corresponds to an ideal and offers no testimony that respect for the law and personal integrity were customary marks of office. As Robert remarked, the celebration of these virtues is the counterpart of the complaints and accusations of the literary and legislative sources about the corruption of the courts and the misdeeds of governors. A second frequent theme in the metrical inscriptions is praise for the building activities of governors. Cities were grateful for the construction of walls, fountains, aqueducts, and baths that enhanced their beauty and improved their amenities, and the inscriptions underline the wondrous quality (*thauma*) and beauty of these ventures. Natural catastrophes such as earthquakes and tidal waves sometimes made the rebuilding and restoration imperative.

It is sometimes said that these inscriptions "combine justice with devotion to the Muses" (Brown 1992: 35), but one should notice that they almost never allude directly to the governors' *paideia*. The fact that sophists twice dedicated statues to magistrates and composed those epigrams is undoubtedly an indication of the latter's activities on behalf of education. These sophists celebrated a specific official's effort on behalf of rhetoric but did not point merely to the excellence of his education. The other metrical inscriptions testify to the predilection for poetry that was prevalent in Late Antiquity. The composers of these epigrams were probably not professional poets but individuals with a taste and an ability for poetry that were not uncommon. Alan Cameron (2004: 346) has pointed to the fact that writing classicizing hexameters and elegiacs was an easier task than composing prose in the style of Demosthenes and was a relatively popular activity. The governors must have appreciated these versified gifts through which they could be associated (at least indirectly) with the Muses. These epigrams, however, do not disclose that an accomplished rhetorical education was a prerequisite for office.

Let us turn once again to the evidence provided by the encomiastic orations of sophists, in order to compare their content with that of the inscriptions. The laudation of the respect of governors for justice is a permanent feature in these compositions, together with the celebration of their *paideia*. Like Libanius, Himerius extolled the justice of magistrates as an adjunct of their alliance with the Muses. He hailed the proconsul of Achaea, Cervonius, as "the eye of Justice and Law, the prophet of the Muses and Hermes" (*Or.* 38. 9). Justice and the Muses permeate the whole of *Oration* 48 in honor of Hermogenes, who was proconsul of Achaea after AD 337 and had devoted years to philosophy (*PLRE* i: 424–5). Himerius invited this "shoot and offspring of the Muses" not to neglect the Attic lecture rooms. A god had brought him to Greece so that eloquence could regain its youth. Hermogenes cultivated justice with persistence and often spent the whole day from morning to evening in the "temple of Dikê." The association of observance of the laws with cultivation of the Muses was irresistible.

The theme of the ideal governor's respect for justice is also a persistent motif in the works of Libanius. He recognized that governors should be allowed some authority, but contended that right alone should be the basis of it (*Or.* 50. 19). In *Oration* 62, when defending himself from the criticism that so few of his students attained office, he cited a few examples of success. Since it was unnecessary to insist on their culture, because their studies with him were the proof of it, Libanius focused on their incorruptibility and disregard for wealth. The passage on Andronicus, a beloved student who became involved with the revolt of Procopius in AD 365 and was executed by the Emperor Valens (*PLRE* i: 64–5), is a sorrowful encomium of his ability to purge the courts of abuses and of his administrative integrity and refusal of bribes. Andronicus' property was confiscated at his death, but the paucity of his possessions elicited the admiration of his opponents.

In a letter written to Andronicus when he was governor of Phoenicia (*Ep.* 216), Libanius praised the love and hard work he dedicated to Beirut, which he had embellished with buildings. In contrast to the composers of the epigrammatic inscriptions, Libanius was ambivalent with regard to the building activities of magistrates. In the letter mentioned at the beginning of this chapter (*Ep.* 1261), he also extolled this aspect of administration. He praised Proclus for his "constructions in the city, streets, colonnades, baths, and squares" (*Ep.* 852); and, in the oration written for Antioch, he admired the constant projects of her governors in making memorable additions to the city (*Or.* 11. 193). Yet, he generally felt that officials showed exaggerated love for the city through these expenditures, and ridiculed the extravagant colonnades built with lavish gold and stone by the governor of Syria, Florentius, in the 390s (*Or.* 46. 44). He criticized the efforts of Proclus to enlarge the *plethron*, one of the sites of Antioch's Olympic Games, on the grounds that such embellishments altered the religious character of the ceremonies (*Or.* 10). Libanius was aware that the reputations of governors depended in part on their building activities, but his priorities were elsewhere. Consider the beginning of a late letter to a student's father, Factinianus, governor of Pamphylia (*PLRE* i: 323): "This befits a man who knows how to govern: not tiles, stones, walls, paintings, and useless colonnades, but encouraging the education of his subjects and having good sense and the ability to speak" (*Ep.* 1012).

Drawing firm conclusions may be hazardous, since the evidence for a realistic evaluation of the effect of education on attaining administrative and political power is neither complete nor consistent. Peter Brown has remarked, "it is difficult to measure the exact relationship between the widespread expectation that governors should be cultivated persons and the political practice of the age" (Brown 1992: 38). Sophists attributed paramount importance to educational accomplishments because of their constant preoccupation with recruiting and promoting their profession. They could not be objective, because they looked at the world through the lens of their own passion for, and mastery of, rhetoric. Libanius proclaimed with conviction that his art was "his bride" (*Or.* 1. 54), and often advised his students to be diligent because rhetoric was going to open doors for them. But, when cornered by critics who asked him how many provinces he had administered through his pupils, he was forced to admit that "those who are going to be good governors need rhetoric, but obtaining a provincial governorship is no proof of its attainment" (*Or.* 62. 50). In my opinion, the lack of praise for rhetoric in late antique inscriptions for governors is indicative of the fact that a high level of education was not a strict requirement but only a secondary (albeit attractive) component of advancement. If we remember that the rhetorical training of most students was not very extended, it will be easier to gauge realistically how much rhetoric was needed for office. Most of the students of Libanius attended his school for a limited time and attained only a fraction of the competence in rhetoric and knowledge of the classics that their teacher had. Doubtless there were governors who possessed a very high degree of literary culture, but it is likely that a couple of years of rhetoric were sufficient for many others. In a short period of schooling, they were able to attain and project that veneer of cultural refinement that the governing class found desirable.

BIBLIOGRAPHICAL NOTE

In 1903–27, Richard Foerster produced the monumental (12 vols.) edition of Libanius' works (1903–27). A. F. Norman is responsible for most of the translations (see Norman 1969–77, 1992, 2000). Paul Petit (1988) and Pierre-Louis Malosse (2003) translated some orations, Bernadette Cabouret (2000) and Scott Bradbury (2004b) some of the letters. A. J. Festugière (1959) included in his study on education full or partial translations of several orations and of many of Libanius' letters.

Peter Wolf (1952) was the first to produce a study of Libanius' school, followed by Petit (1956). Both books are still useful. Peter Brown (1992) looked at the significance of a rhetorical education; Raffaella Cribiore studied Libanius' educational works (Cribiore 2001) and wrote on his letters of evaluation of students (Cribiore 2003).

Petit also produced an excellent study of Antioch (1955); and in 1972 Liebeschuetz published a comprehensive work on this city that, together with A. H. M. Jones (1973), is to be used as main reference.

CHAPTER SEVENTEEN

Textual Communities in Late Antique Christianity

Kim Haines-Eitzen

What was essential to a textual community was not a written version of a text, although that was sometimes present, but an individual, who, having mastered it, then utilized it for reforming a group's thought and action.

Stock 1983: 90

For I did not think that the information from books would help me as much as that from a living and surviving voice.

Papias, as recorded by Euseb. *Hist. eccl.* 3. 39

O people of the Book!

Qur'an 5: 15

It has often been assumed that Christianity was a "religion of the book" from its inception. Christians, of course, inherited a text-centeredness from Judaism: the use of the Hebrew Scriptures translated into Greek, the production of their own Scriptures, and the articulation of Christian doctrines in written form – such are the features that point toward Christianity as a "textual community." This view in its starkest form claims that "Christianity is an intellectual religion and cannot exist in a context of barbarism" (Marrou 1956: 421). However, recent scholarship has emphasized how the Hellenistic and late antique world was one dominated by orality or, at the very least, was a "culture of high residual orality which nevertheless communicated significantly by means of literary creations" (Achtemeier 1990: 3; see Ong 1982: 36). I shall focus here on the interplay of orality and literacy in early and late antique Christianity, and on how this is treated in modern scholarship; on the use of texts and the authority ascribed to texts by Christians in Late Antiquity; on early Christian attitudes toward education; and on what the form of early Christian books tells us about both the scribes who copied them and the communities who used (read or heard) them. Rather than the text-centeredness of early and late antique Christianity, I wish to point toward the dynamic interplay of the oral and the written that is embedded in Brian Stock's notion of "textual communities" – namely, those communities (broadly understood) that emerge, develop, or are sustained by their (primarily oral) engagement with and reflection on particular written texts.

Orality, Literacy, and Education

The starting point for nearly every discussion of orality and literacy in early Christianity is the statement made by Papias, bishop of Hierapolis in Asia Minor, as recorded by Eusebius. In the process of rehearsing the most important early Christian writers, Eusebius justifies Papias' claims to authority by quoting him as follows:

> And I shall not hesitate to append to the interpretations all that I ever learned well from the presbyters and remember well, for of their truth I am confident. For unlike most I did not rejoice in them who say much, but in them who teach the truth, nor in them who recount the commandments of others, but in them who repeated those given to the faith by the Lord and derived from truth itself; but if ever anyone came who had followed the presbyters, I inquired into the words of the presbyters, what Andrew or Peter or Philip or Thomas or James or John or Matthew, or any other of the Lord's disciples had said, and what Aristion and the presbyter John, the Lord's disciples, were saying. For I did not suppose that information from books would help me so much as the word of a living and surviving voice. (Euseb. *Hist. eccl.* 3. 39)

While some have taken Papias' claims to suggest something of a "cultural bias in favor of the oral over the written" (Achtemeier 1990: 10), others have argued that what is at stake is a preference for "first-hand information" rather than a denigration of the written word (Gamble 1995: 31). At the very least, this passage preserves something of an "oral residue" in the midst of a written text, highlighting the interplay between the oral and the written in Late Antiquity.

One way to approach that interplay is by assessing levels of literacy. The most important recent study of ancient literacy is that of William Harris, who draws on modern anthropological and sociological studies to demonstrate that the preconditions necessary for mass literacy did not exist, nor was there a forceful drive for widespread education in Greco-Roman antiquity. On this basis, Harris argues that "we must suppose that the majority of people were always illiterate" (Harris 1989: 13). Defining literacy as any ability to read or write, Harris estimates, more precisely, that at no point in the period from the invention of the Greek alphabet to the end of the Roman Empire did literacy exceed 10–15 percent of the entire population, women and slaves included. Such conclusions contrast markedly with older scholarship, which emphasized high levels of literacy (Harris 1989: 8–9) and, in the early Christian context, the bookish nature of the religion itself (Harnack 1912). More recently, scholars have recognized that Christians were like the broader inhabitants of the empire – largely illiterate (Gamble 1995: 6).

In part, disputes about the levels of literacy in antiquity and the interplay of the oral and the written have hinged on the nature of our evidence. If one reads ancient

Greek and Latin literature with an eye to educational practices, it is quite easy to gain the impression of widespread schooling and education (Fantham 1996). Studies, on the other hand, that have included the documentary evidence from Egypt (private letters, petitions, school exercises, and so forth) help us to construct a more nuanced picture of education in antiquity, for they provide "concrete details to supplement the rigid and idealized accounts of the literary sources" (Cribiore 2001: 246). Such studies force us to recognize the different stages of ancient education and how those stages were opportunities only for a small segment of the population – the elites. Recognizing the diverse social functions for which writing was needed, and the extent to which some cultures gave relatively greater emphasis to education in particular periods, scholars like Bowman and Woolf have adopted a more balanced standpoint, and avoid veering erratically between "the view of a literate elite narrowly defined by the limited spread of writing skills" and "any unrealistic notion of a broad, popular literacy in the ancient world" (Bowman and Woolf 1994: 10). It is important, moreover, to remember (and here we return again to the interplay of the oral and the written) that "in a world where most people were illiterate, literacy was desirable, but lack of education did not bring any stigma" (Cribiore 2001: 249).

Nowhere has the "bookish" character of early Christianity been more emphasized than in studies of the "catechetical school" in Alexandria. Perhaps influenced by idealistic views on the ancient Museum and Library at Alexandria and the literary remains of such Christian authors as Clement, Origen, and Eusebius, some scholars have imagined early Christian life in Alexandria as centered on two edifices – a catechetical school and a scriptorium – and have suggested that the Alexandrian text of early Christian Scriptures was copied, edited, studied, and interpreted within those structures. Take, for example, Metcalfe's highly idealized portrait of early Christianity in Alexandria, which is based entirely upon literary evidence: "classes of catechumens in which candidates for admission to the Church were indoctrinated, had long been customary ... [T]he Catechetical School at Alexandria was a real *studium generale*, the forerunner of the universities of Christian Europe" (Metcalfe 1920: 11–12). More recently, J. H. Ellen has claimed that "the Catechetical School continued and elaborated in an Hellenistic mode the scholarship of the Ancient Library of Alexandria in such detail that it must be concluded that the Catechetical School was an inheritor of that Library's role and heritage, either as a corollary institution or as the very continuation of the library and university center itself" (Ellen 1993: 29).

Such idealized imaginings of a "bookish" Christianity in its earliest stages, however, begins to fade when we look closely at the evidence for Christian catechetical instruction in the second and third centuries. Even our most educated and literary source from the period – the writings of Clement of Alexandria – suggest not a formalized Christian "school" but rather an emphasis on an oral form of instruction wherein the pedagogue is the divine *Logos*. The third-century writer Origen nowhere refers to a Christian educational system. Indeed, the earliest literature pertaining to catechetical instruction indicates repeatedly its oral nature: "and since knowledge springs up with illumination, shedding its beams around the mind, the moment we hear, we who were untaught become disciples" (Clement, *Paed.* 1. 6). Similarly, in the earliest stages of the *Apostolic Tradition*, learning involves hearing the word and not reading or studying (*Ap. Trad.* 16. 1–2; 35. 3). The only passage that suggests reading – "And if there is a day on which there is no Instruction let each one at home take a holy book and read in it sufficiently what seems profitable" (36. 1) – is found only in late Arabic, Ethiopic, and Sahidic versions of this text (dating from the fifth century at the earliest). Given the overwhelming portrait of oral learning and the limited accessibility to Christian Scriptures in this period (a point to which I shall return), it is a mistake to conclude from this passage that catechumens learned by reading, that Christians had some type of organized educational system in the second or third centuries, and that "portions of Scriptures were within the reach of all" (Easton 1962: 104).

Is it possible that Christianity, in fact, had a negative effect on ancient literacy levels? Such is the conclusion drawn by William Harris: "Christianity served to weaken the ancient reverence for humane *paideia* which had undoubtedly had some positive effects, over many centuries, on the general educational level of the more Greek and Hellenized inhabitants of the Empire" (Harris 1989: 321). Attitudes expressed by Tertullian, who claims that the teaching of schoolmasters borders on idolatry (*De Idol.* 10), may well have influenced wealthy Christians to withdraw their children from the Greco-Roman educational system. It is at the end of the fourth century, within the context of emergent monastic institutions, that we find the earliest statements about converts to Christianity being taught how to read – as, for example, in the Pachomian *Rules* (Rousseau 1985: 70). Likewise, it is in the fourth century that we find some "programs" of reading and education specifically aimed at women. In particular, our evidence for the education of Christian women indicates that monasticism permitted at least some women new opportunities for education: Jerome writes to Eustochium, "read constantly and learn as much as you can" (*Ep.* 22). Perhaps best known in this regard is Jerome's letter to Laeta on the education of her daughter, in which he outlines a program of reading (*Ep.* 107). The literary evidence for the elite Christian women of Late Antiquity suggests that any account of change in Late Antiquity should ask how women (in addition to men) combined "bookish reflection and high moral endeavour in the service of the new religion" (Rousseau 1995: 117).

The intersection of asceticism and books may well provide us with a way to reflect on how "textual communities" took shape in late ancient Christianity. We can think, for example, of the development of hagiography as the performance of piety: "writing was a vehicle for the expression of piety as well as a technology for its cultivation" (Krueger 2004: 4). Similarly, we can take numerous examples from our late antique literature that hark back to earlier uses of texts for shaping ethics: "By the time Augustine wrote, reading and writing had for some generations been united with oral habits in producing a 'technology' of self-reform, thereby opening a new chapter in the philosophy of the ascetic life that went back as far as Philo" (Stock 1996: 14). Any discussion of asceticism and textuality must account for both orality and literacy, for both the ways in which texts shaped the oral culture and the ways in which orality shaped the use of texts.

There is still much work to be done on Christianity, education, and literacy in Late Antiquity. What we can say for certain is that, throughout the period, literacy continued to remain a skill of the minority and orality and literacy continued to display a dynamic interplay. To illustrate this point briefly, and to come back to our notion of "textual communities," we can turn to one of the most paradigmatic stories from our sources: the story of Amoun of Nitria preserved in Palladius' *Lausiac History*. According to Palladius, Amoun was forced to marry against his wishes. After he and his wife had left the ceremony and were together in the bridal chamber, Amoun instructed his new wife: "The marriage which we have just gone through is not efficacious. We will do well if henceforth each of us sleeps alone so that we may please God by keeping our virginity intact." "And," continues Palladius, "he drew a small book from a fold in his cloak and read to her from the Apostle, from the Saviour Himself as it were, for she could not read. And to most of what he read he added comments from his own mind, and he kept instructing her about chastity and virginity, so that she was convinced by the grace of God" (Palladius, *Hist. Laus.* 8). The historicity of this story aside, it illuminates quite precisely the dynamic we should imagine: oral instruction for those who are illiterate by the reading and interpreting of texts by those who are literate. Such a story indicates, moreover, the role that texts came to play in late antique Christianity. For however we construe levels of literacy and the processes of instruction in Late Antiquity, we know for certain that Christian texts came to play an important role in the development of the religion itself.

Authority of the Written Word

The statements of Papias and limited levels of literacy notwithstanding, early Christians came to ascribe enormous authority to the written word. Of course, the attitudes of early Christians toward the written word are complex. On the one hand, from the very beginnings, the uneducated were welcomed and even praised. Among the earliest apostles, Peter and John were allegedly uneducated (Acts 4: 13). Traditionally, scholars have argued that early Christianity was a movement among the underprivileged and uneducated lower classes, but more recent studies have suggested that the socio-economic demographics of early Christianity were far more diverse (Meeks 1983: 51–3). Opponents of Christianity, such as Celsus, certainly criticize the movement for being composed of the ignorant and uneducated (Origen, *C. Cels.* 3. 44). Despite such claims, however, early in the development of Christianity, texts came to have a particular importance.

While Christianity was rooted first in the oral teachings of Jesus, the "words of the Lord" and "testimony of the apostles" became formulated as a fulfillment of the Jewish written Scriptures (Gamble 1985: 37). To be sure, we have from the outset a sense of a "scriptural consciousness" (Kraft 1996: 201) embedded in Christians' appeal to the Septuagint, the subsequent elevation of the gospels and Pauline letters to scriptural status, and the appeal to Scripture as authority from the second-century patristic writers onward. Moreover, if we consider the role that texts played in both the synagogues and house churches of earliest Christianity, as well as the more formal homiletic occasions in later Christianity, we see again the intersection of the oral and the written, the reading of Scriptures and their oral explication.

Alongside this "public" engagement with texts, the writings of commentators and heresiologists probably reached fewer but demonstrate no less significantly the authority attributed to written texts. Consider, for example, the earliest commentary on a New Testament book, the commentary of Heracleon on the gospel of John, written in the late second century. What is most striking about the commentary (and its refutation by Origen in the third century) is how the very words of Scripture, in addition to the theological claims drawn from them, are contested by different writers. The work of heresiologists such as Tertullian, Hipploytus, and Irenaeus was invariably rooted in arguments based on the very words of Scripture. It is, in fact, during the second century that the christological disputes come to play such an important role in the articulation of Christian identity. While some argued that Jesus was a man and not God (Adoptionists), others argued that Jesus was God and not a flesh-and-blood human being (Docetists) (Ehrman 1993: 4–11). Perhaps the most widely known "heretic" of the second century is Marcion, who acquired a substantial following. What is striking for our purposes is that Marcion appears to have derived his theology from a reading of particular *texts* – namely, the Pauline epistles and the gospel of Luke. He claimed, for example, that Paul clearly distinguished in Galatians between the gospel and Jewish law, and set the former over and against the latter. Marcion concluded that there must be two Gods: the God of the Old Testament, who created the universe, and the God proclaimed by Jesus as loving and merciful. Marcion rejected the Old Testament and any references to it in the Gospels and Pauline epistles. Moreover, he claimed that only a truncated version of Luke and the Pauline epistles were to be considered authoritative. The danger of Marcion for the church Fathers "can be inferred from the vigor with which they set about the refutation of [his] teaching" (Blackman 1948: 3). Tertullian alone wrote five volumes refuting the Marcionite "heresy." What is most striking for our purpose is the role played by texts in such disputes: authority (for both Marcion and Tertullian) derived from their interpretation of texts. In addition, Marcion's claims in relation to the canon of Scripture were to have an enormous impact on the response of other church Fathers.

The development of the Christian canon was prolonged. It was fueled and often directed by the doctrinal disputes of the second and third centuries. The first to respond to Marcion's "canon" was Irenaeus, who claimed that "it is not possible that the Gospels can be either more or fewer in number than they are" (*Adv. Haer.* 3. 11. 8). It is striking that this strong statement in favor of the four-gospel canon comes at precisely the time when Marcionism is flourishing (Campenhausen 1972: 203; Skeat 1992: 194–9). In the face of an "arch-heretic," then, Irenaeus has taken the first steps toward establishing "orthodoxy" in terms of texts that are to be considered authoritative; and, it is worth emphasizing, authoritativeness does not rest so much in the written nature of the gospels, but in the "orthodox" oral interpretation of them.

Contemporary with the writings of Irenaeus at the end of the second century are the first of our canonical lists. The Muratorian Canon (written possibly as early as

AD 190), appears to include the four gospels (Matthew, Mark, Luke, and John), the Acts of the Apostles, thirteen Pauline epistles, Jude, two Johannine epistles, the Wisdom of Solomon, and the Apocalypses of John and of Peter ("though some of us are not willing that the latter be read in church") (Metzger 1987: 194–201; Hahneman 1992). Eusebius, writing in the early fourth century, gives the list supported by Origen in his *Commentary on the Gospel of Matthew* (*Hist. eccl.* 6. 25) as well as his own list, which he divides into three categories: those that are universally accepted, those that are disputed, and those considered spurious (*Hist. eccl.* 3. 25). The first list that is identical to the one eventually adopted within the Christian church is found in Athanasius' Thirty-Ninth Festal letter, written in AD 367. Yet, while there was some degree of unanimity on the status of certain books by the early fifth century (namely, those on Athanasius' list), it was not until the sixteenth century that an official and binding pronouncement was made by the Roman Church (Gamble 1985: 45). Decisions about individual texts were made on the basis of claims about their apostolicity, their widespread use, their style, and, above all, their orthodoxy. All our evidence points, moreover, to a small minority of literate and highly educated patristic writers working to circumscribe the texts to be considered authoritative by the majority of Christians.

Debates over the canon of Scripture illuminate one of the central concerns of this chapter: the increasing importance attributed to texts – here to the question of *which* texts – over the course of Late Antiquity. Such debates were inextricably linked to debates over heresy and orthodoxy, which similarly engaged the small percentage of literate scholars and clergy, especially bishops, who worked to define "orthodoxy" in the face of "heresy." In such a situation, the power of literacy to define "right belief" for the majority of lay persons becomes apparent. The act of producing lists of authoritative written texts was a powerful instrument, involving "the domination of the non-literate segment of the population by the literate one, or even the less literate by the more" (Goody 1987: xv). To put it another way, an elite few collected and worked to canonize Scripture according to their ideal of "orthodoxy," and it was this collection of sacred writings that came to define the Church. The self-definition of the Church and its members was in part due to the formalization of a canon with restricted boundaries and ecclesiastical endorsement. This process has led Harry Gamble to argue that the movement toward creating a canon, which developed in the second century and persisted until the fifth century, "resulted in the articulation of Christian orthodoxy and the disenfranchisement of deviant interpretations" (Gamble 1985: 47).

But Gamble identifies only one side of the dialectic: just as the canon shaped "orthodoxy," so too "orthodoxy" shaped the canon. The arguments relating to the canon presented by church Fathers from the second to the fourth century illustrate only one of the ways in which texts had become a resource of power and authority. Like the canon, the formulation of credal statements sheds light both on the debates about interpretation, belief, and practice and on the ways in which those debates took shape within various "textual communities" in late antique Christianity. One should keep in mind that, until the early fourth century, those arguments were to a large extent arbitrary and decentralized: without the institutional support provided by Constantine's conversion, there could be no centralized mechanism for creating a uniform and universal Church. That has not prevented some scholars, however, from making claims about a centralized seat of power as early as the second century. Such arguments have depended in part on the physical form of early Christian books and it is to that subject that I now turn.

Christian Books: Form and Function

Among the most important sources for any exploration of the roles of texts in early and late antique Christianity are the material remains of early Christian books themselves. There are hundreds of papyrus and parchment fragments from identifiably Christian texts that can safely be dated to the period prior to the fifth century, and we have ostraka (texts written on pieces of pottery) containing scriptural texts. The papyrus and parchment fragments, some of which contain nearly complete books, provide a significant window onto how the form of Christian books intersected with their use. We can identify at least four different forms, which are not mutually exclusive: the "workaday" copies of the second and third centuries, the deluxe biblical codices of the fourth century and beyond, miniature books, and amulets. Each of those forms tells us something about the ways in which such works were produced, as well as about the use to which the books that contained them were put to.

Before turning to a brief description of book forms, it is worthwhile identifying the two features that have received most attention: the codex form and the use of the *nomina sacra*. It is curious that in the second century nearly all classical and Jewish literature continued to be copied on rolls. By contrast, nearly all the extant copies of identifiably Christian texts (both New Testament books and others) are codices, not rolls (Haines-Eitzen 2000: 95). Much attention has been given to this difference: some studies have argued that, because papyrus sheets used for codices could be written on both sides, codices were more economical to produce (Skeat 1982: 175); others have claimed that Christians used the codex form to distinguish their books from Jewish books (Roberts and Skeat 1987: 57); still others have pointed to the practical advantages of the codex form. That Christians came to adopt the codex form has suggested to some "a degree of organization, of conscious planning, and uniformity of practice" (Skeat 1969: 73), but that conclusion is not without problems, among them the fact that we have no secure evidence to support such a claim. Most striking is the shift in the distribution of codices in the fourth century, compared with rolls: "by the fifth century, at least if we may judge from the texts found in Egypt, the roll held barely 10% of the market; and by the sixth it had vanished for ever as a vehicle for literature" (Roberts and Skeat 1987: 75).

Another feature found in all extant copies of Christian texts is that of the *nomina sacra*: abbreviations – or contractions, to be more precise – of divine or sacred words such as *God, Lord, Jesus, Christ*, and – later – *mother, father, cross, son*, and so forth. In their most common form, the first and last letters of each word are written and a suprascript line is placed on top. While there may indeed have been some sense of "creed" embedded in the choice of which words to abbreviate, what is striking about the appearance of these abbreviations is the universal use of them in early Christian manuscripts but the lack of uniformity in their precise form (Haines-Eitzen 2000: 91–4). Some scholars have indeed argued that the *nomina sacra* indicate "that the treatment of the sacred names had been laid down by the Church at Jerusalem, probably before AD 70" (Roberts 1979: 46); but more recent studies have emphasized that the form of these contractions is far from uniform or standardized prior to the fourth century. Hence, appeals to some sort of centralized and controlled efforts to standardize the copying of early Christian texts prior to the fourth century are misleading (Haines-Eitzen 2000: 92).

We can now turn briefly to some forms of early Christian books, and see what we can learn from the forms regarding the uses.

"Workaday" copies

A combination of features found in most of the very earliest copies of Christian literature – those dated to the second or early third centuries – led Colin Roberts to identify them as "workaday" copies (Roberts 1979: 19). The handwriting lies somewhere between the careful and even bookhands normally employed for the copying of literature and the cursive and abbreviated hand used for the production of documents (contracts, receipts, petitions, and so forth). As with other literature, the script is continuous – in other words, there are very few, if any, breaks between words and very little marking even for paragraphs or sections. The quality of the papyrus used is neither particularly high nor particularly low. (The cost of papyrus in antiquity has been a subject of extensive scholarly debate: see Skeat 1995.) The use of "lectional aids," such as breathing marks, in some of the earliest copies may suggest "that most of these texts were intended for church use, to be read in public" (Roberts 1979: 22); but it is problematic to push this argument too far, since ancient reading practices in general were for the most part public (Knox 1968; Schenkeveld 1992: 130). One of the earliest references to the reading of Scriptures in the context of Christian gatherings on Sundays is found in Justin Martyr: "And on the day called Sunday all who live in cities or in the country gather together in one place, and the memoirs of the Apostles or the writings of the prophets are read, as long as time permits" (*Apology* 1. 67). The remark matches well the earliest papyrus remains, which stand in marked contrast with the deluxe copies that begin to appear in the fourth century.

Deluxe codices

It is in the fourth century that the great majuscule biblical manuscripts first appear – Codex Sinaiticus (fourth century), Codex Alexandrinus (fifth century), Codex Bezae (fifth century), and Codex Vaticanus (fourth century) being among the most important (Metzger 2005: 62–73). Much attention has been given to Eusebius' record of Contantine's request for fifty copies of Scripture: "I have thought it expedient to instruct your Prudence to order fifty copies of the sacred Scriptures, the provision and use of which you know to be most needful for the instruction of the church, to be written on prepared parchment in a legible manner, and in a convenient, portable form, by professional transcribers thoroughly practiced in their art" (*Vit. Const.* 36). Such a request may well indicate something of the resources available to Eusebius in fourth-century Caesarea. While we cannot ascertain whether the extant biblical majuscules from the fourth century were among those sent to Constantine, their features do suggest the use of highly trained scribes and a controlled process of correction. The handwriting is a clear, professional, and elegant bookhand; the quality of the materials used is particularly fine; and, where there are corrections, a number of different hands are employed. Moreover, the larger size of these copies when compared to the "workaday" copies may suggest more securely their use in liturgical services. The enormous shifts that take place in the fourth century certainly affected the production of early Christian texts as well as their use (Rapp 1991: 130).

Miniature books

There are extant some sixty miniature codices from antiquity, dated from the second to the seventh centuries. Eric Turner's listing of miniatures – which he defined as codices that are less than ten centimeters wide – included ten papyrus miniatures and forty-four parchment miniatures (Turner 1977: 29–30). More can now be added. One of the most striking features of these miniatures, when compared with the "workaday" copies, is that the variation in handwriting – especially the range of handwriting types, qualities, and skill – is far less wide, perhaps indicating that the production of miniatures required greater skill on the part of the scribe. It is also significant that the miniatures can be broken down into the following categories: twenty examples from the Old Testament (nine of which are from the book of Psalms), nine miniatures from apocryphal texts (especially from the apocryphal gospels and Acts), fourteen examples from various New Testament books, miscellaneous Christian examples, and non-Christian texts. While this list may not seem instructive at first glance, the fact that the most numerous miniatures contain portions of the book of Psalms may indicate something of the use of miniature codices. We know from literary sources, for example, that the Psalms in particular were considered important for private reading for new initiates, for desert monks trying to avoid temptation, and for girls trying to keep vows of celibacy (Burton-Christie 1993: 111–14). Moreover, the existence in miniature form of the apocryphal Acts – which have been connected to pilgrimages – may suggest a somewhat different liturgical and ritualistic use (Davies 2001: 145). Finally, the existence of such miniatures – some of which measure a mere four centimeters square – could well provide us with material evidence for the practices condemned by John Chrysostom: "Do you not see how women and little children suspend Gospels from their necks as a powerful amulet, and carry them about in all places wherever they go" (*Hom. ad pop. Ant.* 19. 14). This comment brings us to the last form of the early Christian book that I shall discuss here – namely, that of amulets inscribed with Christian Scriptures.

Amulets

Most of the extant amulets inscribed with Christian texts appear to date from the fourth century and later. As with the miniatures, a high percentage are inscribed with passages from the Psalms. The form of ancient amulets is quite varied, but we often find amulets inscribed on scraps of papyrus that are long and narrow. These were meant to be rolled up and then placed into a vial of some sort and hung around one's neck. Strikingly, the Christian ostraka become more common after Constantine; and these scraps of inscribed pottery often contain amuletic texts (in addition to passages from Scripture, prayers, or liturgical texts) (Judge and Pickering 1970: 4). That Christians used amulets should not surprise us, for they were part of a culture that used a variety of "magical" practices to insure safety or protection, to receive communication from the gods about the future, to obtain a cure of some sort, and so forth. Indeed, "the magical use of Christian texts was a function of the sanctity, authority, and . . . power attributed to the 'divine words' they contained" (Gamble 1995: 238). This notion of a text's "power" brings us back to the authority of the written word in early and late antique Christianity. Furthermore, the amulets take us beyond the binary of public or private use of texts, beyond even the binary of reading versus hearing early Christian texts: the use of miniature codices as amulets, as well as the use of amulets proper, suggest that in any discussion of early Christianity as a "textual community," we must include the early Christian book as a material witness to books as objects of inherent power.

Conclusions

Few would dispute that Christianity came to display a particular reverence for the written word – perhaps from its Jewish inception, or perhaps over time from the second to the fourth century. Such a claim does not require a return to an idealistic (and anachronistic) portrait of early Christianity as a "bookish" movement or a movement that either inherited or enabled widespread literacy. That literacy remained restricted to a very small elite throughout the ancient and late antique world seems now a given. Yet simultaneous with that restricted literacy, we have an increasing importance ascribed to texts. It serves us well to think of early Christianity as a "textual community," when we remember that a "textual community" in Brain Stock's sense retains a dynamic interplay of the oral and the written and requires not mass literacy but rather select literacy. By imagining such textual communities within which the oral and the written intertwine, we can find ready parallels to other textual communities in antiquity – for example, the producers, preservers, and interpreters of the Dead Sea Scrolls; the activities of Jewish synagogues and schools; the emergence of Rabbinic Judaism; and the philosophical "schools" of the Platonists, Epicureans, and Stoics (Snyder 2000). Likewise, the form of early Christian books themselves illuminates the various practices associated with hearing and reading by early Christians: books read aloud in liturgical settings, books carried in pilgrimages, books possibly used in homes for "private" reading, and books worn for protection – these are just a few of the ways in which we can imagine various Christians engaging with their Scriptures and becoming "textual communities."

BIBLIOGRAPHICAL NOTE

The best single volume that treats many of the issues raised in this essay, including literacy in early Christianity, the form and circulation of the early Christian book, and the uses of books in early Christianity generally is Gamble 1995. On the issue of literacy, Harris 1989 is invaluable, though much has been done since to refine his estimates of levels of literacy (as, for example, in Bowman and Woolf 1994). Ong 1982 has been enormously influential, and is especially worth reading for those interested in a comparative approach to the ideologies and implications of oral and literate cultures. Cribiore 2001 is an excellent and important study of educational practices in antiquity. While she treats only Egypt in depth, her evidence and conclusions have wider relevance. On early Christian books and their format, Roberts 1979 continues to be important, as does Skeat 1969. My own more recent study of the earliest Christian papyri has suggested some of the ways in which the form of these books suggests something of their production and transmission (Haines-Eitzen 2000). For those wishing to pursue the role of Scripture (or the role of books more generally) in early Christian asceticism, I recommend Burton-Christie 1993, which can be read alongside a more recent study that treats the practice of writing hagiography as one that enacts, or performs, piety (Krueger 2004).

CHAPTER EIGHTEEN

Exegesis without End: Forms, Methods, and Functions of Biblical Commentaries

Karla Pollmann

Consider another example, whosoever reads this: behold, what Scripture delivers, and the voice pronounces one only way, "In the Beginning God created heaven and earth." Is it not understood in manifold ways, not through any deceit of errors, but by various kinds of true senses? Thus does human offspring increase and multiply.

August. *Conf.* 13. 24. 36

Introduction

This Augustinian interpretation of God's commandment in Genesis 1: 28, "increase and multiply," as referring to the possibility of multiple interpretation ("exegesis") of the biblical text (O'Donnell 1992: 400–1; Müller 1998: 616, 625, 648), is remarkable in at least two ways. First, it confirms what one could call a general characteristic of the epoch of Late Antiquity, namely a strong rise not only in the production of new texts, but also in the renewed effort to interpret old ones. Second, it is a kind of *mise-en-abîme*, since the first chapters of Genesis – presumably the most interpreted texts of the Bible – are very fertile in generating multiple interpretations themselves. Augustine alone interpreted the text five times during his life (Taylor 1982, i: 1–7).

In this chapter, I shall, by way of example, concentrate on various commentaries that deal with Genesis in particular. Since Genesis can be understood as a foundation myth explaining the origins and nature of humankind and its relationship with God in the most fundamental way, and therefore as a book containing all principal theological questions *in nuce*, its interpretation allows exegetes potentially to tackle the entire spectrum of theological issues. The different ways in which the selected authors approached the text will illustrate this.

In Late Antiquity, generally speaking, a species of "globalization" took place, politically, because the empire had reached its widest expansion from east to west, and intellectually, because the educated elite, facing the rise and influence of new cultural forces, especially of Christianity, attempted to (re)establish some kind of identity. This led to the concentration on a past that was considered to be normative or "classical," and thus relevant in constituting the ingredients of contemporary identity: the pagans chose especially Homer (Richardson 1980) and Virgil (Murgia 2004) as their cultural Magna Charta, the Christians naturally the Bible (Young 1997: 285–99). Because of the gap in time between the writing and the reading of these texts, the late antique reader's ability to understand and explain them, and to provide background information, was seriously impeded. Commentaries were urgently needed, therefore, especially in the fourth and fifth centuries. These commentaries were not only helpful for educational and literary purposes; they could also be used by preachers for edification (*aedificatio*), in a liturgical setting. Indeed, commentaries themselves could be presented in the form of sermons. Apart from the specific didactic function of exegesis in a school context, interpretation permeated practically every other literary genre: poetry (Otten and Pollmann, forthcoming); legal and philosophical, especially Neoplatonic (Cürsgen 2002), treatises; and rhetorical forms, including homilies. In other words, we cannot confine the notion of "late antique exegesis" to the narrow intellectual genre of a learned commentary: it begins to pervade every mode of communication. Augustine makes this point in theoretical form in his hermeneutical handbook *De doctrina christiana*, where he emphasizes the universality of his Christian addressees and their interpretive activities (4. 18. 37; Pollmann 1996: 69–75).

Because of its essentially communicative, or mediating, function, exegesis establishes a bridge between the text and its readers in their mental and historical situations respectively. Thus, interpreters have to consider, and take into account, the context within which they intend their explanations to be effective, especially historical, social, personal, (church-)political, intellectual, educational, and (to a limited degree) economic. The context also governed their perception of the most suitable literary genre and their choice of an appropriate exegetical method. A broad spectrum of exegetical approaches existed in antiquity, originally deriving from grammar and rhetoric: a text could be analyzed according to *lectio* (correct pronunciation, intonation, and division of words), *emendatio* (textual criticism), *enarratio* (historical, mythological, and rhetorical commentary), and *iudicium* (judgment of authenticity and value) (Pollmann 2005: 206–7). Later, we have what came to be called the "fourfold sense of Scripture," justified by the unfathomable fecundity of Scripture: apart from a philological-literal analysis of the text, it included various possible figurative interpretations, namely a moralistic-psychological, an ecclesiastical-institutional, and a typological-eschatological analysis. Rarely were all four senses applied to the same passage, however, and exegetical terminology and approach could vary considerably (De Lubac 1998: 75–159); exegetical terms like *figura, allegoria, sensus spiritualis*, and so forth are neither univocal nor congruent with modern terminology (Young 1997: 186–213).

This broad spectrum of interpretive possibilities refutes any idea of exegetical naivety or lack of sophistication. On the contrary, practically all methods of interpretation practiced until our own time had already been established in antiquity and were adopted by the early Christians. Although they did not give the Bible a separate ontological status, these Christians were aware of the distinct quality of the biblical text, which was not meant to be a handbook for the natural sciences but the edifying word of God, instructing and guiding God's human creatures. Accordingly, ecclesiastical writers are not interested in finding scientific information in the Bible (Föllinger 1999: 256). This sharp distinction is particularly important when it comes to a potential discrepancy between human disciplines and the divine word, as for instance in Genesis (see below). The crucial difference between the ancient methods and the modern historical-critical ones is not their respective methodology – which is partly comparable – but their claim to a supra-individualistic objectivity and to historicity in a quasi-scientific sense (Casurella 1983: 135–6; Young 1997: 206–7; Metzdorf 2003: 243–62). Because of their rhetorical upbringing, (late) antique interpreters of texts were much more aware of the need to communicate convincingly to their communities what each text was about, which depended on a close interaction between exegete, text, and audience or readership (Young 1997: 265–84). Finally, the methods, forms, and functions of exegesis, which were very flexible in Late Antiquity, are markers of change and transition: their very presence and acknowledged importance characterize the period itself as lying between a "not anymore" and a "not yet," reflecting in its rich exegetical output a constant need for redefinition.

The following brief examples of commentary in prose will illustrate some of the features just mentioned. The reader is encouraged to use them as criteria when assessing texts from Late Antiquity that constitute or contain exegesis. The different issue of manuscript illuminations as "commentary" (Wittekind 2004) will not be taken into account here, nor will we consider the Jewish exegetical tradition (Najman and Newman 2004).

Basil and Ambrose on Genesis

Presumably during the Lent of AD 377 or 378 (Henke 2000: 15–16), Basil, bishop of Caesarea, delivered nine homilies on the six days of creation as told in Genesis 1: 1–26 (the so-called *Hexaemeron*, a term first used by the Jewish scholar Philo, 2. 197). In his *Apologia in Hexaemeron* (*PG* 44: 65), Gregory of Nyssa testifies to their success with both educated and (because of their simple style) illiterate listeners alike; but he also answers in the same work criticisms leveled against his brother's homilies, thus producing, as it were, exegesis of exegesis (Amand de Mendieta 1978: 349 n. 16, 351–4). In his line-by-line explanations, Basil does not want to interpret Genesis systematically as a Christian cosmogony but to demonstrate, by popularizing or "vulgarizing" (Amand de Mendieta 1978: 347) scientific knowledge of his day, its ethical function of instructing and edifying the human soul in the Christian faith. The parenetic sermon is the most suitable form for this purpose (Staritz 1931: 36–9). In general, he uses the literal sense to establish the authority of the Bible (*Hex.* 2. 5; 9. 1; Swift 1981: 318) and to demonstrate, against competing pagan and heretical views, that nature has been created by the trinitarian God for the benefit of humanity.

This enables him to allegorize these divinely originated natural phenomena, and to elucidate the didactic character of nature as a model or warning for human beings (Pollmann 2006: 190–3). This means that, for Basil, the principles that otherwise govern "reading" and "interpretation" govern in fact the very experience of "observation." The correct observation of natural phenomena can thus corroborate the right understanding of Scripture. Behind such reasoning lies an understanding of the created world as a "book" provided by God for humanity for didactic purposes: the will and purpose of the creator is discernible in the world created by him.

To illustrate this point, Basil sometimes integrates scientific knowledge about nature as it was held at his time. He explains, for instance, that the light of sun and moon is not part of their nature or substance but a quality or accidence (*Hex.* 6. 2), a distinction going back to Aristotle. He then uses this "scientific" fact to harmonize seemingly contradictory statements in the Bible. A bit later, however, he says that the phases of the moon remind us of the transience of everything worldly and of human fickleness (*Hex.* 6. 9). This moralizing interpretation is in no need of intermediary scientific corroboration.

Ambrose, bishop of Milan, came to know Basil's sermons through Eustathius' Latin translation (Amand de Mendieta and Rudberg 1958: xi–xvii). He composed, presumably in AD 389 (Henke 2000: 16), six sermons on Genesis 1: 1–26, based on Basil (Hier. *Ep.* 84. 7; Henke 2000: 17–22) and on other authors, delivering them (like Basil before him) during Lent that year. Ambrose's explanations are roughly twice as long as those of Basil, he is more generous in integrating the allegorical sense and, most importantly, he accentuates more strongly his skepticism about the power of the human intellect, stressing that divine intervention is indispensable to human understanding and salvation (Swift 1981: 319–23). His intentions, like those of Basil, are mainly pastoral, not speculative; he too sees nature as a symbol of human life. On occasion, however, he differs from Basil in his exegetical conclusions; and he is generally less dependent upon him than is sometimes assumed (Henke 2000: 28–9, 34–7, 423–9). For example, while Basil emphasizes the wisdom of God the creator, Ambrose highlights his power and activity (Staritz 1931: 39–41).

One instance will illustrate this in more detail. While dealing with Genesis 1: 24, Basil (*Hex.* 8. 4) and Ambrose (*Hex.* 5. 21) specify the bee as one of the "beasts of the earth." This is a typical example of the discursive exegesis of both writers, who digress considerably from the biblical text, where the bee is not mentioned explicitly. Both authors use the creation narrative as a framework to justify the moral edification of their respective congregations. Characteristically, Ambrose's explanations are much more extended, and he several times follows closely Virgil's remarks on bees in the fourth book of the *Georgics*. Both Basil and Ambrose extol the wholly positive qualities of bees, whose industriousness is already stated in Proverbs 6: 6 and 8, a passage quoted by both authors, who refer it to the bee (and not to the ant, as in the Hebrew original and in Ambros. *Hex.* 6. 4. 16). Basil makes the point that bees, although unreasoning creatures, even have a government – that is to say, they do things together, in an ordered fashion. They are governed by a king ordained by nature; he is the biggest and best of all bees and peaceful, since he does not use his sting. (In antiquity, the leader of the bees was thought to be of the male sex, and his gentleness was stressed, since he had a sting but did not use it: Arist. *Hist. an.* 5. 21; Basil, *Hex.* 8. 4; not in Verg. *G.* 4. Sen. *Clem.* 3. 17. 3 assumes that the king has no sting; Plin. *HN* 11. 17 offers both versions.) He, and the harmless bee in general, should serve as an example to Christians: "Listen, Christians, you to whom it is forbidden to 'recompense evil for evil' [Rom. 12: 17] and who are commanded 'to overcome evil with good' [Rom. 12: 21], take the bee for your model, which constructs its cells without injuring any one and without interfering with the goods of others" (Basil, *Hex.* 8. 4).

Ambrose differs from Basil in many details: he explicitly states that the idea of laws and customs common to all members of a citizen-body stems from the bees (Ambros. *Hex.* 5. 21. 66), an etiological claim not explicit in Basil. It makes all following statements much more directly relevant for his contemporary listeners. Bees also represent the virtue of virginity, since they do not copulate in order to procreate (Verg. *G.* 4. 198–201; Arist. *Hist. an.* 5. 21). In Ambrose, the king of the bees is ordained by the bees themselves, based on his superior qualities (*ipsae sibi regem ordinant … nam et praerogativam iudicii tenent*, *Hex.* 5. 21. 68). The bees live in a paradise-like state, since labor is enjoyment for them (*opus ipsum suave*, *Hex.* 5. 21. 69); they work for everything they own, and they do not rob others (ibid.). A Christian should use them as an example, since they are strong in wisdom and the love of virtue (*Hex.* 5. 21. 70). In Basil, by contrast, a complex discipline like geometry is reflected in the bees' ability to construct clever wax compartments to store the honey beneficial for humans: "See how the discoveries of geometry are mere by-works to the wise bee!" (*Hex.* 8. 4). Implicit in the statement is the conviction that nature embodies in its tiny creatures skills considered great human achievements. So the wonders of nature are exalted. Ambrose hints more explicitly at the creator behind these wonders, asking rhetorically, "Which architect taught the bees [*quis architectus eas docuit*]?" (*Hex.* 5. 21. 69).

Generally speaking, Ambrose is stylistically more ambitious than Basil and, by alluding repeatedly to Virgil and other classical authors, he tries to appeal to an educated audience, both to please them and to demonstrate how Scripture encompasses the teachings of the greatest Latin pagan writers. By romanizing, allegorizing, and dramatizing his Greek model, he intensifies the spiritualizing effect of his sermons for the simple listener as well (Henke 2000: 423–5).

Augustine on Genesis

From his *De Genesi contra Manichaeos* (his first exegetical commentary, written in AD 388/9) to *De Genesi ad litteram* (written between AD 401 and 415) and books 11 and 12 of *De civitate Dei* (written around AD 417), Augustine displays a remarkably sustained interest in struggling to understand correctly the beginning of Genesis (Staritz 1931: 153–7). Equally striking is the broad variety of genres he employs. We can identify at least five stages in his approach to the text. First, we have his antiheretical commentary against the Manichees, in which, to save the Old Testament from the Manichean accusation that it is both incorrect and obscene, he uses partly

Ambrose's allegorical method (Dulaey 2002: 276–85). Then there is the incomplete, literal commentary *De Genesi ad litteram liber unus imperfectus* (written in AD 393/4) and books 11 to 13 of the quasi-autobiographical *Confessions* (written around AD 400), in which he interprets Genesis, again in a mainly allegorical fashion, as an account of the culmination and fulfillment of a Christian life (Pollmann 2005: 217–18). In the complete commentary *De Genesi ad litteram*, he insists on a rigorous "literal" interpretation of the text. Finally, in the encyclopedic theology of universal history in *De civitate Dei*, he uses Genesis in books 11 and 12 as the template for expounding the beginning of history (and again favors a literal interpretation that can be properly understood only in the light of *De Genesi ad litteram*: Taylor 1982, i: 4).

Generally speaking, Augustine's strength, unlike Jerome's, does not lie in a close philological reading of the text. He often relies on the conclusions of others, and uses scriptural interpretation to prove or illustrate a preoccupying point of interest, be it the refutation of a heresy, the demonstration of a spiritual Christian life, or a historical-philosophical point. Let me illustrate more particularly the development outlined in the preceding paragraph.

In *De Genesi contra Manichaeos*, Augustine uses predominantly an allegorical method of interpretation against the Manichees, because this method is particularly suited to both refuting the Manichees' material dualism and proving the spirituality of God and the mutual interdependence of the Old and the New Testaments. Augustine's attitude is polemical and exegetically confident (for instance, in *De Gen. c. Man.* 1. 1. 1; 1. 2. 5; 1. 5. 9). This contrasts sharply with the *Liber imperfectus*, in which he repeatedly emphasizes that he feels very insecure, facing the difficult task of providing a sustained literal interpretation of Genesis. Already in the first chapter, he calls the random fashion of claiming an uncertain and dubious opinion (*temeritas adserendae incertae dubiaeque opinionis*) a great crime; a sentiment echoed, for instance, in chapter 8: "one must not confirm anything at random (*nihil ... temere adfirmandum*)." This lack of confidence explains why he abandoned the project (*Retract.* 1. 10. 1, although in 1. 18 he decides to preserve the fragmentary commentary as evidence of a certain stage in his intellectual development).

Although the exegetical *methods* in *De Genesi contra Manichaeos* and the *Liber imperfectus* are partly different, the individual *interpretations* often differ less, since even in *De Genesi contra Manichaeos* Augustine's approach is not always allegorical. Differences arise rather from the different contexts of the two commentaries: in the "orthodox" *Liber imperfectus*, Augustine integrates the Trinitarian dogma and treats all biblical passages relatively evenly in his exegesis; in *De Genesi contra Manichaeos*, on the other hand, he does not pay much attention to verses that are irrelevant for his antiheretical purpose. For example, in the commentary *contra Manichaeos* (1. 11. 17), commenting on Genesis 1: 6–8, Augustine says that he does not recall (*non memini*) that the Manichees used to criticize these verses; then he continues with a very brief literal(!) explanation that the firmament separates the invisible from the visible waters. He concludes by adding that this obscure matter has to be believed before it is understood (*antequam intellegatur, credenda est*). In *Liber imperfectus* 8–9, in contrast, his explanations of these verses are far more extensive, designed to demonstrate that the biblical account of God creating the firmament and separating the waters is compatible with pagan cosmological concepts. But here he is far more tentative in his argumentation, allowing for a plurality of opinions and urging his readers to be constantly aware of their human deficiency, which will never permit complete understanding of divine works (*Lib. imperf.* 9: *eligat quis quod potest; tantum ne aliquid temere atque incognitum pro cognito afferat memineritque se hominem de divinis operibus quantum permittitur quaerere*).

In books 11–13 of the *Confessions*, an interpretation of the first seven days of creation that moves from a literal to an allegorical exegesis (Müller 1998: 614) rounds off Augustine's quasi-autobiographical Christian portrait. The setting of the exegesis of Genesis in the *Confessions* is not a commentary in the narrow sense but is completely different in its interpretive focus. Scientific and cosmological aspects are less relevant, and Augustine concentrates rather on the existential relationship between human beings, who owe their existence to their creator, and God, the free and gracious creator of all nature. Thus, the three major theological issues dealt with in these books in connection with the interpretation of Genesis are the theology of grace, the human spiritual connection with God, and eschatology (Müller 1998: 619–20).

Augustine further develops these elements in *De Genesi ad litteram*, now by using predominantly the literal interpretive method (justified, for instance, in 8. 4. 8, 9. 11. 22, and 11. 1. 2), which represents an enormous intellectual and methodological progress since the *Liber imperfectus* of ten years earlier. Methodologically, *De Genesi ad litteram* is strongly influenced by Eustathius' Latin translation of Basil's *Hexaemeron*. In *Hex.* 3. 9 and 9. 1, Basil champions against Origen a literal interpretation of Genesis (Staritz 1931: 36; Vannier 1987: 376–7). Augustine has a notion of "literal" that is not immediately apparent to the modern reader: according to him, the literal meaning of a text explores or explains faithfully what really happened (*De Gen. ad litt.* 1. 1. 1). But, due to the specific quality of the narrative of the first chapters of Genesis, which tell about something that happens for the first time, the truest "literal" sense in that instance (as in some others) is the spiritual one (8. 1. 2). So, paradise has both a literal and a spiritual reality, since, in principle, Scripture can have a literal and a figurative meaning (8. 1. 1). In 4. 28. 45, Augustine explains that the literal sense is the truest sense of Scripture: "light" in Genesis 1: 3–4, for example, is neither material nor metaphorical light, but spiritual light, and therefore the spiritual understanding of this light reveals the true and appropriate "literal" meaning of the text. In other words, one has to consider carefully the differing contexts of different verses of Scripture and its purposes (10. 7. 12). Scripture does not provide, for example, an exhaustive guide to the nature of the soul (10. 10. 17).

In *De Genesi ad litteram*, Augustine starts from different exegetical premises than Basil and Ambrose to develop a much more nuanced, ambitious, and adequate way of coping exegetically with the specific nature of Genesis – which is neither myth nor purely historical narrative – and of taking into account the role of the reader (5. 6. 19) and the nature of the text which is silent regarding certain issues (5. 8. 23). In general, *De Genesi ad litteram* is directed at a more educated reader than is Basil's, and even Ambrose's, *Hexaemeron*. It aims at explaining how the works and laws of nature can be synthesized with a philosophical understanding of cause (the Stoic *rationes seminales*) and with the theological notion of God's foreknowledge (*De Gen. ad litt.* 6. 16. 27–8). Unlike Basil and Ambrose, Augustine uses the natural sciences only very rarely for moral edification: instead of claiming that thorns and other natural things unpleasant or dangerous to humanity acquired those qualities only after the Fall, he stresses that these creatures are dangerous to human beings precisely because of the *latter's* fallen state (3. 17. 26 to 3. 18. 28, and 8. 10. 21). For Augustine, characteristically, the disadvantages that follow upon the Fall are due entirely to humanity itself.

In *De Genesi ad litteram*, Augustine combines his previous three exegetical attempts, using the didactic genre of the line-by-line commentary – as in *De Genesi contra Manichaeos* and the *Liber imperfectus* – but combining it with rather contemplative digressions that remind one of the *Confessions*. Compared with the *De Genesi contra Manichaeos*, the mature approach of *De Genesi ad litteram* shows the widening of Augustine's outlook and his characteristic combination of various central theological issues. He explicitly corrects, at least once, the view he expressed in *De Genesi contra Manichaeos* (*De Gen. ad litt.* 8. 2. 5); but, as already in the *Liber imperfectus*, he combines a dogmatic analysis of the Trinity with the interpretation of the creation narrative. As, again, in the *Liber imperfectus*, he feels insecure, and eventually has to admit in *Retractationes* 1. 18 and 2. 24. 1 that this commentary raised more questions than it answered. But quite apart from this revocation of his earlier thought, he emphasizes quite frequently the fluidity and liminality of his interpretive results. Other people or later generations, he assumes, will be able to come up with something better (*De Gen. ad litt.* 1. 18. 37; 7. 28. 42–3; 9. 1. 1–2; 10. 18. 33). He believes, in other words, in intellectual progress, and sees exegesis as providing a necessary escape from human deficiency. Exegesis has to be, therefore, by its very nature, tentative and incomplete: it is governed by an eschatological suspense, a confidence that words and signs will disappear, when we see the true word, Jesus Christ (August. *In evang. Johan.*, *tract*. 35. 9).

In *De civitate Dei*, books 11 and 12, we have again a strikingly different context for Augustine's exegesis: namely, a gigantic attempt to describe the destined beginnings, progress, and end of the history of the world. Augustine uses symbolic-allegorical interpretations of various verses of Genesis to illustrate that the Scriptures are a means, although not the only one, to explain the origin of the world (O'Daly 1999: 136–7, 141–50).

Generally, Augustine is of the opinion that biblical exegesis is not really able to tell us anything fundamentally new: rather, it serves to educate in a moral and intellectual way (Fladerer 1999: 127–8). So, his aim as an exegete is relatively modest: his interpretation aims at finding the truth or at least at saying something tolerable about the Bible (*De Gen. ad litt.* 7. 1. 1; 10. 3. 4; similarly in *De civ. D.* 11. 19 and in his hermeneutical treatise *De doctr. chr.*, preface 9. 18).

John Philoponus on Genesis

John Philoponus, who had no knowledge of Augustine's work (Scholten 1996: 77–98), wrote between AD 546 and 560 (Scholten 1996: 56–76; 1997, i: 64–6)

De opificio mundi, a commentary on the first chapter of Genesis that stands in the tradition of the *Hexaemeron*. His commentary aims generally to prove that a cosmology built on the biblical narrative is compatible with, and even superior to, pagan scientific thinking (*Opif.* 1. 2). But, like his predecessors, John is also aware of the fact that Genesis is not a scientific textbook, but has the pastoral aim of leading human beings to God (Scholten 1997, i: 44–5, 62). Therefore he favors an allegorical interpretation, since a literal reading of Genesis easily supports a purely cosmological understanding of its message and leaves the reader ignorant of its theological dimension (Scholten 1997, i: 53–5; Fladerer 1999: 256).

Because of its systematic and detached approach to the biblical text, *De opificio mundi* has been called the first Christian scientific commentary on the six days of creation (Scholten 1997, i: 61). Philoponus' method has the following characteristics (Fladerer 1999: 391–8): each book of his commentary is structured, as it were, in a circular form, analogous themes being arranged in a symmetrical pattern. All biblical words are in principle homonymic: that is, they depend on the context, and the same word can express phenomena of both the material and the intelligible worlds, since those worlds are ontologically interrelated (e.g., *Opif.* 1. 42. 10–22). Thus Philoponus has the hermeneutical flexibility to shift between literal and allegorical interpretations, depending on whether he is working to avoid the criticism that Genesis is not compatible with the modern physics of his time. Following the pagan Hellenistic principle "to interpret Homer from Homer" (*Homerum ex Homero interpretari*), and in accordance with practically all Christian thinkers before him, he sees the Bible as a harmonious and organic whole, the overall message of which can help one to interpret individual passages in the text that are otherwise obscure or ambiguous. The aim is to avoid too close a literal reading.

Philoponus strongly emphasizes the importance of the ecclesiastical community's function: building on the exegetical tradition, it will always seek answers for new questions in the Bible, even if the biblical author has not explicitly given such answers (*Opif.* 28. 15; Fladerer 1999: 279–82). In order to establish Moses as the true prophet, therefore, Philoponus argues in part against a reading that follows Neoplatonic mysticism (*Opif.* 4. 17–20; Fladerer 1999: 345–8). In contrast to Basil, he never seeks to entertain his readers, but wants to prove the validity of the Genesis account at all levels of reality – although in doing so, he sometimes has specifically in mind antagonists like the Dyophysites (*Opif.* 6. 9–17; Fladerer 1999: 369–84).

In many ways, Philoponus' method is very modern, as are some of his general principles. So he says in 1. 18 that the figurative statements in Scripture have to be measured against the truth of reality: that is, he postulates the reconstruction first of a literal sense of the text. In 2. 13, and similarly in 3. 4, he emphasizes that it is not reasonable to investigate why God made creation as it is. This should not prevent us, however, from using sensual perception where appropriate, in order to understand the nature of the cosmos (3. 10; 4. 2). He also turns to the example of the bee, although he uses it differently from Basil and Ambrose. In *De opificio mundi* 6. 14, the bee is portrayed as a mindless creature that is nevertheless able to produce wax, honeycombs, and honey more magnificent and complex than anything made by a human artist. Moreover, like all animals, the bee is able to do this without being taught, whereas human beings constantly need instruction. In this respect, animals are closer to God than human beings (Pollmann 2006: 199).

Philoponus' exploration of the meaning of the Genesis text can be called philological. For example, based on philological arguments, he establishes his own critical version of the text of Genesis 1: 28 by comparing the relevant passages in the Septuagint, Aquila, Theodotion, and Symmachos (*Opif.* 7. 4). This method is already familiar from Origen's *Hexapla*. But, when Philoponus explores the meaning of an individual biblical word, not only does he look at the immediate context but he also compares other uses of the same word within the Bible. Thus in 6. 5–7, pondering the meaning and significance of the words *eikôn* and *homoiôsis* in Genesis 1: 26 – "Let us make a human being according to our image [*eikôn*] and likeness [*homoiôsis*]" (a much vexed question among early Christian thinkers) – he argues against Origen that *eikôn* does not refer to the Son but to the divine Trinity as a whole, illustrating his point by drawing on the Septuagint version of Genesis 9: 6, "I made man in the image of God" (6. 5; see also 6. 17). In 6. 8, similarly, he employs several parallels from the gospels and from Paul's letters to prove that there, as in Genesis 1: 26, *eikôn* and *homoiôsis* are used synonymously, referring to a good lifestyle that follows Christ's model. In 6. 1 and 6. 14, he identifies humanity's likeness to God as residing in the human, although he does not prove that explicitly, since here he adopts a notion accepted by Christians and pagans alike. In other places, he quotes various different opinions on the meaning of a word or verse and weighs them against each other in order to reach what he considers a sound conclusion – as, for instance, when he assesses the different possible meanings of *archê* (1. 3). He is also able to make a clear distinction between secure knowledge and speculation (Scholten 1997, i: 14).

So, in comparison with Augustine's diverse and multifunctional exegesis of Genesis, Philoponus is more single-minded. For him, exegesis is a valid tool that enables one to analyze the biblical text systematically; but its validity consists chiefly in its ability to penetrate and combine the different ways there are of looking at the world, including the cosmologies of pagan philosophy.

Conclusions

Early Christian biblical exegesis had first and foremost the function of clarifying obscure, difficult, or (at face value) contradictory passages of the text. Sometimes, exegetes also wished to demonstrate in what respect heresies or other dangerous inclinations were wrong. Finally, they wanted sometimes to square the certainties of their own experience or knowledge with the seemingly different certainties of the biblical text. In all instances, the exegetical results are closely connected with the individual author's position in relation to doctrine and church politics. As a result, the wealth of factual, ideological, and psychological information hidden in these commentaries will continue to be a rich source of research. These texts have so far received less scholarly attention than they deserve.

If asked, therefore, what sense there was in looking at late antique biblical commentaries, one could reply first that they make us aware of the fluidity, ephemerality, and contextuality of all interpretive principles and results, including our own, and second that our own view of the text can be enriched and differentiated by them (Eugene TeSelle in Gorday 1983: xiii–xvii). So, exegesis can never come to an end, since every generation needs its own explanations. Nor can it be restricted to one genre. Literary forms and exegetical terminology and method can be restricted only by the rule of faith, the *regula fidei* – that is, exegetical conclusions must not contradict axioms of the Christian faith.

One can conclude, therefore, that early Christian exegetes had a clear understanding of the specific quality of the biblical text, which was not to be seen exclusively or primarily as a report of historical fact but as God's word intended to communicate basic truths about human existence. In principle, therefore, a variety of literal and allegorical interpretations is permissible. Moreover, despite the later accorded authority of the so-called church Fathers (see Graumann, ch. 36), they themselves were very much aware of the transience and potential insufficiency of their attempts to explain Scripture. Later reception of their thought has sometimes overlooked this.

It is also striking that the rich variety of exegetical method is observable not only in the body of early Christian authors as a whole but also, at times, within the work of a single exegete, as the example of Augustine makes clear. But despite the variety of his exegetical writings on Genesis, Augustine's final goal is always the same – namely, to disclose God as the unchanging creator of the changing universe (August. *Retract.* 1. 10. 1). The function of exegesis is not so much to produce new results or dogmatic truths as to explain, illuminate, and communicate those truths to various kinds of readers who find it difficult to come to terms with the biblical text on their own. Thus, exegesis can be creative within a dogmatic framework that is nevertheless considered fixed. The stress within any one interpretation can be apologetic, polemical, personal, edifying, didactic-instructional, or a mixture of all these; but a plurality of exegetical opinions is also possible. Since the number of both exegetes and readers is potentially infinite, there are potentially infinite ways of giving that communication effect.

BIBLIOGRAPHICAL NOTE

For surveys of the history of textual interpretation, see, for the pagan tradition Coulter 1976, Lamberton 1986, and Obbink 2003; for Jewish and early Christian exegesis, including the Syriac tradition, Sæbø 1996; and solely for the early Christian tradition the comprehensive overview in Kannengiesser 2004, subdivided into "General Considerations" and "Historical Survey." For a list of commentaries on various biblical books written by ecclesiastical authors in Late Antiquity, see Stegmüller 1950 and Sieben 1991. Useful also is Allenbach et al. 1995–2000, listing biblical quotations in patristic literature. Sieben 1983 and Schneemelcher 1959 (chapter on "Patrum exegesis Veteris et Novi Testamenti") list secondary literature on the patristic exegesis of specific biblical passages. The methods, principles, forms, and functions of commentaries on ancient religious, scientific, and philosophical texts are compared in Most 1999, and those of individual biblical commentators in Gorday 1983. The history of commenting on a specific biblical motif is exemplified in Casurella 1983 and Metzdorf 2003. For the reception of patristic interpretive principles in later times, see Preus 1969.

CHAPTER NINETEEN

Tradition, Innovation, and Epistolary Mores

Jennifer Ebbeler

Letters are attested in Greco-Roman literature as early as Homer, when Bellerophon unwittingly delivered the *lygra sêmata* that ordered his own murder (*Il.* 6. 167–70; Rosenmeyer 2001: 39–44). Both Herodotus and Thucydides include letters in their historical narratives (Rosenmeyer 2001: 45–60); and letters have a role in several Euripidean plays (for instance, *Hippolytus* and *Iphigenia in Tauris*) as well as in Middle and New Comedy (Rosenmeyer 2001: 61–97). Collections of letters by Demosthenes, Plato, Aristotle, Isocrates, and Epicurus were known in antiquity. Though many (if not all) of the extant letters attributed to these authors are probably spurious, they testify to the pervasiveness of the letter-writing habit among Greeks living in the fifth and fourth century BC. The survival of numerous letters on papyrus from the Hellenistic period confirms that letter-writing played an essential role in the management of both private and more official matters. Indeed, by the third century BC, letters appear to have been used regularly by both Greeks and Romans to convey information or facilitate pleasant conversation *in absentia* (Cic. *Fam.* 2. 4. 1; Ambrose, *Ep.* 66. 1).

Authors could inscribe their letters on a variety of materials, including metal, lead, wax-coated wooden tablets, pottery fragments, animal skin, and papyrus. Acontius famously used an apple as the medium for his letter to Cydippe (Ovid, *Her.* 20; Kenney 1996: 15–18). A literate author with time on his hands might write his own letters. More typically, though, letters were dictated to an amanuensis (*librarius*, *servus ab epistulis*). If the author enjoyed a special relationship with the correspondent, he might personalize his letter with the addition of a postscript in his own hand. Because there was no centralized postal system for the delivery of private mail (the *cursus publicus* founded by Augustus was restricted to government business), most letter-writers relied on servants and traveling friends to act as messengers for their private correspondence (Nicholson 1994: 33–8). Letters were frequently lost or delayed. Postal problems were the rule, not the exception, in ancient letter exchanges. Common among extant collections are letters in which one correspondent reproaches the other for some delay in responding, for not writing at sufficient length, or for entrusting the letter to an unreliable carrier, that is, for failing to fulfill the obligations of his epistolary *officium*. It was the author's responsibility to find a reasonably efficient carrier who would deliver his letter in a timely manner (a period which could range anywhere from a few days to several months to a year, depending on the distance and terrain separating the correspondents). This was particularly true for letters with sensitive content. Nevertheless, correspondents could have little expectation of privacy and sometimes took steps to guard against interception (Nicholson 1994: 38–63).

In both classical and Late Antiquity, the messenger served as a stand-in for the letter's absent author and might even be expected to provide supplementary information or answer questions raised by the letter. Similarly, he might bring additional, extra-epistolary gifts (for example, consecrated bread, wine, produce, or books). His arrival at the addressee's locale might be greeted with great excitement, as the community anticipated the public reading of a letter from someone like Jerome or Augustine. The letter exchange, then, could be understood as a "historical event" that included the messenger's supplements to the written letter text (Conybeare 2000: 19–40). Messengers were not always mere bearers of a written message; they could and, in Late Antiquity, often did become, as Conybeare observes, participants in the performance of letter exchange.

Despite the documented prevalence of letter-writing and exchange from as early as the fifth century BC, the self-conscious composition, collection, and public circulation of one's letters is, so far as we can tell, unattested before Caesar's and Cicero's generation. This is not to say that that generation invented the letter collection. The letters of Demosthenes, Plato, and Isocrates, for instance, seem to have been compiled (and perhaps even composed) by later admirers. Similarly, certain pseudonymous, obviously fictional collections of letters may date to the Hellenistic period or earlier (Rosenmeyer 2001: 193–233).

But there is no indication that letters were composed with an eye toward collection and public circulation before the first century BC. Caesar, whose letters do not survive, may have prepared parts of his correspondence for public circulation (Ebbeler 2003: 12). Cicero's plans to publish a selection of his letters were cut short by his untimely death, but his letters were known in the years after his death and survive in abundance for modern readers (*Att.* 16. 5; Nicholson 1998: 63–105). Horace published a collection of hexameter letter poems, the *Epistulae*. Ovid and the Greek sophists Aelian, Alciphron, and Philostratus likewise experimented with the novel literary genre of the letter collection. The younger Seneca and the younger Pliny published collections of their prose letters as part of their literary *œuvre*; and a collection of letters from the correspondence of Fronto and Marcus Aurelius was known in antiquity and survives in fragmentary form.

Still, our most substantial evidence for Greek and Latin letter-writing and collection practices is late antique. Indeed, it would not be an exaggeration to characterize the period between AD 200 and 600 as the golden age of Greek and Latin letter-writing (Vessey 2005a: 74–5). A significant number of letters survive from various late antique writers, including Basil, Julian, Athanasius, Gregory of

Nyssa, Synesius, John Chrysostom, and the prolific Libanius; and in Latin, Ambrose, Ausonius, Symmachus, Paulinus, Jerome, and Augustine. The letters of Gregory the Great, Sidonius, Ruricius, Avitus, Cassiodorus, and Ennodius, as well as scattered letters from assorted bishops, scholars, emperors, and government bureaucrats remind us that the letter continued to be a popular literary form throughout Late Antiquity. In some cases, authors (for example, Gregory of Nazianzus, Jerome, and Sidonius) published a selection of their own letters; in others (for example, Symmachus and Augustine), they preserved copies of their letters in an archive, intending to publish some portion as a collection but leaving the laborious editorial work to others. In most cases, we cannot be sure of the process by which a collection of an author's letters was produced, though it is unlikely that this would have happened without some serious preservation efforts on the part of the author.

Until quite recently, the practice of late antique (and classical) prose letter-writing has not been an object of serious scholarly inquiry. This is not to say that the letters themselves were ignored. To the contrary, individual letters have proven to be a valuable historical source for biographers and prosopographers as well as social and cultural historians. Similarly, they have attracted the attention of New Testament scholars eager to explicate literary influences on the Pauline letters (J. L. White 1984; Stowers 1986: 17–26; Klauck 1998). These early studies, which focused on questions of typology as well as on the distinctions between "real" (private) and "literary" (public) letters, emphasized an atomistic rather than functional approach to ancient letters (Stowers 1986: 23). Little, if any, attention was paid to the literary and cultural practices that produced individual letters and governed their exchange, collection, and circulation. All letters, regardless of their transmission history, were treated as transparent windows into the world and personality of their author. Ancient rhetorical theorists like Demetrius, who insisted that letters reveal their author's soul, contributed to this misleading conception of the letter (*Eloc.* 227). In truth, most of our extant late antique letters, which survive because they were collected and frequently copied, are sophisticated textual performances intended to advertise their authors' literary skill to their contemporaries and posterity.

This is not to say that individual letters cannot be mined for important details about, for instance, the circulation of rural laborers in the late Roman west (Grey 2004) or late antique attitudes toward travel (Salzman 2004). Certainly, letters can be a valuable source of historical, biographical, and prosopographical information. They allow us revelatory glimpses into the lives of authors and their contemporaries. Still, as Raymond Van Dam reminds us, historians of all stripes must take into account the rhetoric of the epistolary genre, since "authors were concerned more about protocol than candor, more about form than substance and emotion" (Van Dam 2003a: 132). All social transactions, including letter exchange, are governed by a prescribed set of rules to which all participants are expected to adhere. In the case of elite letter exchange, this code of conduct included the expectations that a correspondent would write back, use reliable messengers, and employ conventional rhetoric. The scholarly interpretation of these letters demands that we go beyond literal reading to take into account these rules and their sophisticated manipulation by individual authors. Surviving ancient letters are not so much transparent windows as a reflective lens designed to distort as much as reveal.

The primary task for twenty-first-century scholars of Greek and Latin letter-writing of all periods is the identification and analysis of the letter's highly conventional idiom – the "rhetoric of epistolography," as we might call it – followed by a discussion of the creative manipulation of this idiom in specific instances. Andrew Cain's (2006) study of Jerome's manipulation of the reproach *topos* in his early correspondence exemplifies this rhetorically minded approach. Klaus Thraede's outstanding discussion of select epistolary *topoi* (Thraede 1970) is an essential starting place, but his observations could be substantially extended. The following discussion of epistolary censure illustrates the potential of this "rhetorical" approach for the interpretation of Augustine's famously difficult correspondence with Jerome.

Censure, Friendship, and Letter-Writing

Like so many other late antique literary practices with roots in the Greco-Roman world, letter-writing was characterized by notable continuities with classical tradition. In the manner of their classical predecessors, late antique letter-writers routinely described their correspondences as conversations *in absentia*. They lamented silence and reproached a correspondent who failed to respond quickly or substantially. They longed for an absent correspondent and protested the failings of the letter they received. They used conventional forms (for example, consolation, recommendation) and language (friendship, kinship). While the content of letters evolved to reflect contemporary sociohistorical circumstances, the forms and functions of individual letters (and collections of letters) remained remarkably consistent as the Roman Empire rose, converted to Christianity, and ultimately disintegrated.

Despite the overwhelmingly traditional forms and language of late antique letters, the influence of Christian ideology nevertheless produced some distinctive innovations on classical practice. Paulinus of Nola, for instance, reformulated the traditional notion that letters were an imperfect substitute for presence. Catherine Conybeare suggests that, as Paulinus theorized the matter, letters "become a crucial constitutive part of the expression of friendship ... Contact through letters – ideally, at any rate – comes to be considered as superior to the enjoyment of the physical presence of the friend" (Conybeare 2000: 67). The absent correspondent could be linked by analogy to the absent divine, allowing Paulinus to arrive at the brilliant, if idiosyncratic, conclusion that letter exchange, properly performed, was a sacramental act (Vessey 1993: 187). While the steady stream of traffic passing through Nola reminds us that Paulinus was generally spared the enactment of this "ideal" expression of Christian friendship, it is nonetheless significant that his radical Christianity (by late fourth-century standards) compelled him to theorize a new, specifically Christian, function for letter exchange.

Augustine's argument that frank censure is appropriate to a letter of friendship is another remarkable epistolary innovation. Both Pseudo-Demetrius, whose *Typoi*

Epistolikoi ("Letter Types") likely dates to some time after the second century AD, and Pseudo-Libanius include sample letters of censure in their epistolary treatises (Malherbe 1988: 35, 81). In basic terms, the addressee is urged to correct his errors and avoid further rebuke. In each case, however, the relationship between correspondents is assumed to be contentious rather than friendly. When Augustine incorporates censorious rhetoric into letters that purport to be friendly, he is conflating two apparently incompatible letter types and, it seems, hinting at the influence of the apostle Paul on his formulation of Christian friendship (L. M. White 2003: 307–8 explicates Paul's conflation of friendship and censure in the epistle to the Galatians).

As Augustine presents it in the *Confessions*, an essential feature of his conversion to Christianity was a new understanding of the Roman social institution of *amicitia*. When once his friendships were "a bright path" (*luminosus limes amicitiae*, 2. 2. 2) and his friends "the other half of my soul," now he understands that friendship between mortals is an "enormous lie" (*ingens fabula*, 4. 8. 13) because it leads to false belief (in this instance, Manichaeism). Yet Augustine does not altogether abandon the possibility of true friendship. Rather, he theorizes what he identifies as Christian friendship (*Christiana amicitia*; Carolinne White 1992: 189–90; Burt 1999: 57–76), that is, friendship inspired by love (*caritas*). For Augustine (and Paulinus), temporal friendship was a reflection of the devout Christian's love for God. All Christians are "friends" of one another; and there are no distinctions to be made within performances of friendship, since all men are equal in the eyes of God. Likewise, friendship is conceived of as reciprocal, involving both teaching and learning (*Conf.* 4. 8. 1–14; Carriker 1999: 128–31). Consequently, argued Augustine, the frank censure of faults in the friend (and the self) should be considered a normative feature of Christian friendship.

Of course, there is nothing uniquely Christian about such a conception. The role of self-disclosure and honest criticism in the rhetoric of friendship has a long history in classical philosophy, going back at least to the Cynics and Philodemus (Konstan 1997: 151; Fitzgerald 1996). Cicero observed that the occasional rebuke could be enormously beneficial to a friendship (*Off.* 1. 17. 58). The fourth-century pagan philosopher Themistius wrote a treatise on friendship (*Peri philias*), in which he argued that flattery had no place in true friendship (Konstan 1997: 153). This failure of sincerity, of "plain talking," he warned, posed a serious threat to all friendships, broadly conceived, in the Later Roman Empire. Ambrose likewise advocated the importance of self-disclosure and honest criticism in the third book of his *De officiis* (Konstan 1997: 150). Still, we might suspect that such endorsements of frank criticism worked better in theory than in practice. The rebuke of a friend was presumably a delicate matter, to be done in private so as to avoid public humiliation.

The distinctive feature of Augustine's use of censure in apparently friendly letters is his unwillingness to admit a difference between friendship itself and the letter exchange as a tool for managing a friendship. Letter exchange was central to the practice of friendship in imperial Roman culture. We might even say – as John Matthews has about Symmachus' letters – that letters are the textual remains of performed *amicitiae* (Matthews 1974: 62–5). Still, we must take care not to assume that the rules of friendship, writ large, can be applied without modification to the practice of letter exchange. Classical letter-writers, for instance, avoided anything smacking of direct censure. Cicero was not above the occasional indirect jab at a correspondent, but it was always carefully couched in impersonal, formulaic language. Similarly, Cicero's friends attempted to rouse him from his mourning following the death of his daughter by gently criticizing his excessive grief and neglect of social duties (Wilcox 2005). Pliny, who published an artfully arranged selection of his letters, generally highlighted his extreme deference toward his *amici* (Hoffer 1999: 10–13; Morello, forthcoming). When he censured Regulus' behavior, he did so indirectly and almost certainly post-mortem (Hoffer 1999: 55–9). Even in Late Antiquity, there was a clear expectation that any criticism of a correspondent ought to be circumspect and modulated. As the correspondence of Gregory of Nazianzus and Eusebius concerning Basil's strained relationship with Eusebius nevertheless illustrates, this expectation could be manipulated by a savvy writer.

Gregory had first become acquainted with Basil during his school days in Caesarea, and over the years the two had enjoyed a close, if complicated, friendship (Van Dam 2003a: 139–84). On several occasions, Gregory went out of his way to preserve good relations with Basil after some difficulty or period of separation. Given his strong commitment to the idea of friendship, Gregory was surely troubled by news of Basil's difficulties with Eusebius, particularly at a time when the Cappadocians desperately needed to present a united front to the external threat of Arianism. In pointed but not overly aggressive language, Gregory censured Eusebius' treatment of Basil and assured him that Basil would reciprocate any gesture of reconciliation (*Ep.* 16).

We might expect that such delicate and potentially embarrassing negotiations would be conducted either *viva voce* or through a trusted intermediary, yet Gregory instead opted for the far less secure, if more convenient, form of a letter. Eusebius' epistolary response is not extant, but two subsequent letters from Gregory suggest that his correspondent was not pleased by Gregory's methods. In one letter, Gregory defended himself from the accusation that he wrote "in an insolent spirit" (*Ep.* 17). In the second, he reminded Eusebius, "I was never meanly disposed towards your Reverence" and rationalized his behavior as the result of the impending Arian threat ("But if I had once been so mean and ignoble in my sentiments, yet the present time would not allow such feelings, neither the wild beasts which are attacking the Church, nor your own courage and manliness which so purely and genuinely fight for the Church," *Ep.* 18).

Gregory excused his blunt honesty by paraphrasing a familiar philosophical maxim: "It is the duty of a lofty soul to accept more readily the liberty of a friend than the flattery of an enemy" (*Ep.* 17). Of course, as Eusebius may have pointed out, the performance of friendship and the performance of letter exchange – though closely connected in antiquity – were not synonymous. It was one thing to offer a friend frank censure in private, quite another to commit it to a letter that could be lost, intercepted, or copied.

By recording his criticisms of Eusebius in a letter, Gregory forced his correspondent to respond. Considering the gravity of the crisis, Eusebius had little choice but to agree to Gregory's request. Had he refused, Eusebius would have risked public accusations of putting personal enmity above the welfare of the "orthodox" church.

He could not ignore Gregory's letter without risking the chance that Gregory would "accidentally" release his letter into public circulation, thereby revealing Eusebius' obstinacy. Even Gregory's effusive praise and conscious deference to Eusebius' superior episcopal status did not sufficiently assuage Eusebius' anger at being ambushed by a friend.

Left with no viable alternative, Eusebius apparently agreed to invite Basil to return to his post as priest at Caesarea. In a letter to Basil, Gregory informed his friend of his success and encouraged him to expect Eusebius' olive branch: "let us anticipate him then, either by going to him or by writing to him, or rather, by first writing and then going" (*Ep.* 19). Gregory encouraged Basil to announce his return with a letter so that Basil would be the first to construct the public narrative of his reconciliation with Eusebius. Having received such a letter, followed by a personal visit, Eusebius could not renege on his promise to Gregory without losing face.

In his letter to Eusebius, Gregory took care to avoid direct accusation and apologized for speaking whatever came to his mind, without the usual artifice (*Ep.* 16). The situation demanded that Gregory employ every available means to reconcile Eusebius to Basil, but he did his best to avoid direct censure. In other letters, Gregory reminded his correspondents that friendship imposed limits on criticism (*Ep.* 139. 2–3; 187. 2). Even when upset with a correspondent, Gregory was reluctant to put his censure in a letter (Van Dam 2003a: 137). In this respect, Gregory was typical of his age. Late antique letter-writers did not refrain from publicizing the faults of an enemy in treatises (*libri* or *libelli*) but were careful to avoid direct censure of friends in their letters (though they were not above censuring one friend in a letter to another friend!). Even if criticism was an important feature of ancient friendship more generally, it was avoided in the rather public form of a letter.

In this context, Augustine's importation of the censorious epistolary style into the traditional friendship letter is unusual. Where others, including Christians, avoided using letters for the blunt censure of friends, Augustine justifies his practice as an expression of Christian *caritas* and, especially, as a defense against heresy. His violation of traditional epistolary mores did not, however, go unchallenged. In the remainder of this chapter, I shall consider a striking example of this Augustinian epistolary innovation in his strained correspondence with Jerome. This rich letter exchange – one of the most extensive in Latin literature – has already been the subject of two extensive studies (Hennings 1994; Fürst 1999). I do not propose to undertake a comprehensive reading of the exchange, which must be understood in the broader context of Augustine's and Jerome's intersecting social networks. I simply want to analyze one aspect of this complicated set of texts: Augustine's introduction of censure to the "friendly" letter exchange and Jerome's resistance to what he perceived as a violation of epistolary decorum.

Raymond Van Dam has observed that "the greatest challenge to preserving a friendship was … alteration and innovation" (Van Dam 2003a: 138). The persistence of these long-distance relationships depended on predictability and close observance of traditional epistolary mores. Any violations generated suspicion and disrupted the smooth exchange of letters. Augustine defends his surprising behavior by explicitly characterizing his innovation as Christian. Taken together with my earlier observations about Paulinus' avant-garde epistolary views, we can see that, in the late fourth and early fifth centuries, there was some attempt by select Latin letter-writers to theorize a specifically Christian practice of letter-writing.

The Honeyed Sword

The letter exchange of Augustine and Jerome has been characterized as an instance of "two highly civilized men conducting with studied courtesy, a singularly rancorous correspondence. They approach each other with elaborate gestures of Christian humility. They show their claws, for an instant, in classical allusions, in quotations from the poets which the recipient would complete for himself. Neither will give an inch" (Brown 2000: 271). One of Jerome's modern biographers, J. N. D. Kelly, is less generous in his assessment of the correspondence's difficulties. Jerome, says Kelly, was "morbidly suspicious and ready to take offence" (Kelly 1975: 264). The correspondence, such as it was, endured on and off until Jerome's death in AD 420. Eighteen letters are extant, eleven of which (six by Augustine and five by Jerome) date to the tumultuous first phase of the epistolary relationship (Hennings 1994 and Fürst 1999 are useful for navigating the difficulties of chronology and content in the correspondence).

Augustine had a lot to gain by establishing a letter exchange with the famous translator of the Vulgate. "Jerome was nothing if not well-, if often acerbically, connected," remarks James O'Donnell, "and by coming into communication with Jerome Augustine was linking up with a 'textual community' of no small importance" (O'Donnell 1991: 14). By AD 394 Jerome had already networked with two well-connected North African Caecilianists – Aurelius and Alypius (Aug. *Ep.* 27*; 28). Augustine knew of these relationships and, we might imagine, wanted a part in the conversation. Jerome, on the other hand, probably had little sense of Augustine. If he had known anything of him in Rome (both were there in the early AD 380s), it was as an ambitious and talented but provincial North African Manichee looking for a career in the capital city. From Alypius and Aurelius he might have learned of Augustine's conversion and baptism into Ambrose's church in Milan. Given Jerome's feelings about Ambrose after his expulsion from Rome in AD 385, however, that particular connection would hardly have endeared Augustine to Jerome (McLynn 1994: 289).

Probably in AD 394 or 395 (the date is imprecise), Augustine composed a letter (*Ep.* 28) to Jerome, to be delivered by Profuturus, a long-time companion who had settled with him in Hippo. Augustine was not shy about introducing himself to influential men (for example, Hierus, Symmachus, and Ambrose) who might further his aspirations and enhance his reputation. Typically, someone in Augustine's position would ask a mutual acquaintance (Aurelius, Alypius) to mediate with a letter of introduction. In his initial letter to Jerome, however, Augustine suggests that such an introduction is unnecessary, both because he is familiar with Jerome's writings and because Alypius has described him in such detail: "Never has physical presence made anyone as well known to someone else as your peaceful joy and truly liberal pursuit of your studies in the Lord has made you known to me … After brother Alypius, now a most blessed bishop but then already worthy of the episcopacy, saw you and, returning here, was seen by me, I cannot deny that your physical presence was to a large extent impressed upon me by his report" (*Ep.* 28. 1. 1). In any case, continues Augustine, he and Alypius are essentially interchangeable: "For anyone who knows us may say of him and me that in body only, and not in mind, we are two, so great is the union of heart, so firm the intimate friendship subsisting between us." The overwhelmingly formulaic nature of Augustine's sentiments may well have led Jerome to conclude that this was a typical fan letter from a correspondent eager to flatter him and perhaps hoping to persuade him to send copies of his writings.

But this was no typical fan letter. Augustine presumes on his busy correspondent by forcing an unsolicited conversation: "I ought perhaps to write no more if I were willing to content myself with the style of a formal letter of introduction. But my mind overflows into conference with you concerning the studies with which we are occupied" (*Ep.* 28. 1. 1). Augustine specifically has in mind a textual conversation in the presence of the divine, permeated with the spirit of Christian *caritas*. In practice, such "conferences" with absent interlocutors frequently centered on the act of biblical interpretation – a subject of special interest to Augustine throughout the 390 s (Vessey 1993). Whereas Jerome adhered to his Origenist-influenced view that scriptural study was a "science" (*scientia*) best left to trained experts, Augustine believed that it was the purview of any believing Christian eager to learn (August. *De doctr. chr.*, prol. 1). In his letter exchange with Jerome, we find traces of the *Apologia contra Hieronymum* that Mark Vessey has uncovered in *De doctrina christiana* and the *Confessions* (Vessey 1993: 175–213).

Augustine concluded his letter of introduction to Jerome by questioning the scholar's translation methods and taking issue with his figural explication of Paul's rebuke of Peter in Galatians 2: 11–14. The meaning of this passage had long been debated. Jerome, by his own admission, had largely followed Origen and the Greek exegetes in his Latin commentary on Galatians (Plumer 2003: 33–53). Briefly, he suggested that the younger apostle's rebuke of Peter was a performance for the benefit of the erring Galatians. Augustine challenged this reading and argued that it undermined scriptural authority and introduced falsehood into the Scriptures (*Ep.* 28. 3. 4–5). The North African Caecilianist undoubtedly feared that Jerome would unwittingly offer his Manichaean opponents ammunition for their campaign against scriptural authority. Perhaps the immediacy of this threat to the Caecilianist Christians motivated Augustine to abandon traditional epistolary decorum and demand a retraction from Jerome, despite (rightly) fearing that he would be judged "burdensome and impudent" (28. 3. 5).

Augustine tried to model for Jerome the proper response to correction when he enclosed some unspecified writings and demanded that Jerome read them with "severe judgment" (28. 4. 6). Likewise, citing Scripture, he reminded Jerome that "the one who heals with his reproaches shows more love than a flatterer who anoints the head" (28. 4. 6). Augustine realized that he had broken the rules by importing censure into a letter that so explicitly invoked the codes of friendship letters, but hoped that he could excuse his misbehavior as normative in the context of Christian ideology. It can hardly be a coincidence that the letter's contents – a junior apostle's censure of a senior apostle – precisely mirrors Augustine's treatment of Jerome. Augustine implies that, just as Peter humbly accepted Paul's public rebuke, so should Jerome address his own errors in full view of the Christian literary community. The gaze of the Christian community is an essential aspect of Augustine's Pauline conception of correction. The more traditional Jerome, as we will see, did not share this outlook.

The letter's carrier, Profuturus, barely made it past the city gates of Hippo before he was conscripted as bishop of Cirta. There is no suggestion that he made arrangements for the letter to be conveyed to Bethlehem. A later letter from Augustine to Profuturus (*Ep.* 39) indicates that Profuturus was alive until at least the middle of AD 397 and that Augustine knew his messenger had been waylaid. Augustine would defend his lapse by claiming that Profuturus died shortly after becoming bishop (*Ep.* 71. 1. 2); the evidence nevertheless suggests that Augustine had ample time to arrange for another copy of the letter to be delivered. Instead, near the end of AD 397, he composed a new letter (*Ep.* 40) reiterating his disagreement with Jerome's interpretation of Galatians 2: 11–14. Augustine's choice of Paulus as carrier once again disappointed. Afraid of the dangers of a sea voyage, Paulus remained in Italy. To make matters worse, not only did Paulus fail to pass the letter on to another carrier – he even allowed it to circulate publicly around Italy as a book (*liber*) written against Jerome.

By labeling Augustine's text a *liber* (treatise, pamphlet), Jerome underscores his point that Augustine did not have a proper understanding of epistolary convention (*Ep.* 72.4). The *liber*, after all, was the traditional form for censure. *Ep.* 40 eventually made its way to Jerome, but only because a deacon, Sysinnius, made a copy (72. 1. 1). Augustine swiftly apologized for the misdirected letter and assured Jerome that the rumors of a *Liber contra Hieronymum* were false. Still, his unconventional behavior aroused Jerome's suspicions. That Jerome exhibited what has uncharitably been characterized as an "irascible refusal to be drawn into discussion" should not astonish us (Kelly 1975: 263). As far as Jerome was concerned, Augustine's letter was a "sword dripping with honey" (*litus melle gladius*, 72. 1. 2).

Jerome did eventually respond to Augustine's request for conversation, but pointedly refused to defend his interpretation of the Galatians passage. Instead, Jerome accused the North African of provoking him in order to parade his learning before the Christian elite: "But your wisdom well knows that everyone abounds in his own opinion and that it is puerile boasting to seek, as young men of old were in the habit of doing, fame for one's own name by finding fault with famous men" (*Ep.* 68. 2). In particular, Jerome is irritated that Augustine allowed his censures to become public knowledge. He suspects that this was not accidental: "Some of my close friends ... suggested to me that this had not been done by you in a guileless spirit, but seeking praise and celebrity and some smidgen of glory from other people, so that your reputation might grow at my expense and so that many men might know that you challenged me and that I was afraid of you" (*Ep.* 72. 1. 2; see Ebbeler, forthcoming, for a discussion of additional passages of this type). Finally, Jerome avers that Augustine's suspect behavior has undermined the possibility of friendship:

"true friendship can harbour no suspicion; a friend must speak to his friend as freely as to his second self" (*Ep.* 72. 1. 2). Jerome does not challenge the propriety of Augustine's epistolary censures per se. Rather, he takes issue with Augustine's motives for such a public form of rebuke, in the guise of a friendship letter.

Jerome's history of interpersonal difficulties has encouraged readers of the correspondence to fault him for its breakdown. His outrage is far more comprehensible when understood in the context of traditional epistolary mores (Cain 2006: 500–525 makes a similar argument for the interpretation of Jerome's early correspondence). Specifically, Jerome does not share the Augustinian conception of conference and correction. Like most classical and late antique letter-writers, Jerome believed that the censorious style should be limited to letters addressed to a despised rival. He agrees with Augustine that frankness and honesty are important to the practice of friendship; but he does not concur that it is therefore appropriate to censure a friend in a letter that could easily go astray.

The correspondence resumed only after Augustine soothed Jerome's wounded ego with effusive flattery (*Ep.* 73. 2. 5; 82. 2). Augustine nevertheless persisted in his assertion that censure was appropriate to a friendship letter. In an effort to persuade Jerome, he modeled for his correspondent the proper way to receive a well-meaning rebuke from a fellow Christian: "I also shall most thankfully receive your rebuke as a most friendly action even though the thing censured may be defensible and therefore should not have been censured. Or else I will acknowledge both your kindness and my fault and will be discovered, so far as the Lord allows me, grateful for the one and corrected in the other" (*Ep.* 73. 2. 3).

Whereas Jerome saw criticism and friendship as incompatible, even if acceptable in the general practice of late antique friendship, Augustine implicitly argued that, if the Christian community is a "society of friends," then there should be no distinction between the practice of friendship and the practice of letter exchange. To this end, he reminded Jerome of the standard philosophical aphorism, "our enemies who expose our faults are more useful than friends who are afraid to reprove us. For the former, in their angry recriminations, sometimes charge us with what we indeed require to correct; but the latter, through fear of destroying the sweetness of friendship, show less boldness on behalf of right than they ought" (73. 2. 4). David Konstan has demonstrated that Augustine's view of flattery was widespread among late antique friendship theorists, Christian and pagan alike (Konstan 1997: 153–6). This does not prevent Augustine from citing Scripture as his source (and implying that Jerome's resistance to correction is unchristian): "For I would hesitate to give the name of Christian to those friendships in which the common proverb, 'flattery makes friends and truth makes enemies"'is of more authority than the scriptural proverb "faithful are the wounds of a friend but the kisses of an enemy are deceitful'" (*Ep.* 82. 31).

In addition, by raising the specter of Rufinus, Augustine reminds Jerome (and the Christian community) of Jerome's most spectacular failed friendship. Formerly bosom friends, Jerome and Rufinus had a serious falling-out during the Origenist crisis (Clark 1992: 159–93). Where once Rufinus had been a favorite correspondent whose absence Jerome lamented, he was now the recipient of Jerome's literary vitriol, including the three-book *Apologia contra Rufinum*. Most painful to Jerome, however, was the extremely public demise of his friendship with Rufinus. When Augustine mentioned Rufinus ("Where is the friend who may not be feared as possibly a future enemy, if the breach that we deplore could arise between Jerome and Rufinus?" *Ep.* 73. 3. 6), he did so in a deliberate effort to destroy Jerome's credibility on the topic of Christian friendship.

Augustine concluded the letter by acknowledging that he and Jerome had different ideas regarding the role of correction in an epistolary friendship. He acknowledged Jerome's resistance in one final plea for productive discussion:

> If it is possible for us to examine and discuss anything by which our hearts may be nourished without any bitterness of discord, I entreat you to let us address ourselves to this task. But if it is not possible for either of us to point out what he may judge to demand correction in the other's writings without being suspected of envy and regarded as wounding friendship, let us, having regard for our spiritual life and health, leave such conference alone. (*Ep.* 73. 3. 9)

Of course, as Jerome realized, he could not continue to ignore Augustine's demands without serious risk to his scholarly reputation among his wealthy Gallic and Italian supporters (Kelly 1975: 269). Finally, nearly a decade after the composition of his *Letter* 28, Jerome responded with a detailed refutation of Augustine's challenge to his reading of Galatians 2: 11–14 (*Ep.* 75). The precisely argued letter was clearly intended for wide public circulation, despite Jerome's claim that he had dashed it off in three days (*Ep.* 75. 1. 1). In the end, Jerome complied with Augustine's request for public debate despite his (valid) suspicions that his correspondent had deliberately rewritten traditional epistolary mores to justify the inclusion of censure in a letter that purported to be friendly.

Augustine's introduction of censure into a friendship letter was not limited to his correspondence with Jerome. In his *Letter* 259, datable only to the episcopal period and addressed to a certain Cornelius who has been identified with Augustine's North African patron Romanianus, Augustine returned to the topic of public correction among fellow Christians. Romanianus, who had once shepherded Augustine's promising rhetorical career and remained on good terms with him even after Augustine's conversion in Milan, had asked the bishop of Hippo for a letter of consolation that praised the virtues of his now dead wife Cypriana. Augustine refused to comply, accusing Romanianus of seeking flattery rather than consolation (*Ep.* 259. 1). He inveighed against Romanianus' scandalous behavior (he had been dating other women) and urged him to correct his waywardness. As with Jerome, Augustine anticipated that Romanianus would feel abused. Consequently, he assured him that the censure was well-meaning and a product of their enduring friendship (259. 2). Indeed, Augustine reminded Romanianus, he had once corrected himself from the error of Manichaeism; there was nothing to deter Romanianus from correcting his own sexual deviancy.

Augustine even repeated the common argument that, among devout Christians who believed in resurrection and the promise of eternal life, letters of consolation were unnecessary. Romanianus should not grieve his dead wife but instead, should follow her example of chastity so that he might share in her salvation (259. 1, 5). In this way, Augustine figured his letter of censure as a substitute for a letter of consolation. The conflation of epistolary censure and consolation is attested as early as Cicero (Wilcox 2005); but Augustine put his own spin on the topic. Whereas Cicero's friends censured his excessive grief for Tullia by reminding him of his public duties, Augustine encouraged Romanianus to live as a committed Christian. By motivating Romanianus to correct his sins, Augustine enabled him to console himself in his grief for eternity – something that mere words could not do. Finally, Augustine offered his correspondent a deal: he would "sell" Romanianus a eulogy for Cypriana if Romanianus would commit to chastity (259. 4).

We have no idea how Romanianus responded to this rather unusual letter of consolation, but we might imagine that he was not pleased to have his former dependant scrutinizing his behavior. He may also have worried that Augustine's criticisms would cause him public humiliation, especially in light of Augustine's visibility as the bishop of Hippo. Romanianus, however, certainly knew Augustine well enough to be acquainted with his verbal tricks and may well have taken a certain pleasure in his protégé's audacity.

Inventing Christian Letters

Among Christian writers of the first three centuries, the letter was a popular literary form. Besides Paul's pastoral letters (some authentic, others probably later imitations), there survive letters from, inter alia, Ignatius, Polycarp, and Clement. In the Latin west, the North African Cyprian left behind a substantial epistolary corpus. His letters allowed him to maintain leadership over the Carthaginian church while in hiding during the third-century Decian persecution. Other bishops, presiding over far-flung churches, frequently resorted to letters to discuss questions of social or theological policy with their peers, while continuing to attend to the quotidian demands of their episcopal duties.

It should come as no surprise that these citizens of the Roman Empire, even if Christian, made use of a common Greco-Roman literary practice to communicate across time and space. As was also true for the letters of Cicero, Seneca, and Pliny, the content was adapted to suit the specific demands of the occasion; but the idiom, form, and function of these "early Christian" letters are remarkably similar to classical letters. It was not until the late fourth century, in the Latin west, that we see the first traces of a deliberate effort to theorize a specifically Christian epistolary practice that is distinct from the inherited classical tradition. Whereas earlier Christian letter-writers had merely appropriated the standard language and forms of traditional letter-writing, both Paulinus and Augustine attempted to reformulate the cultural function of letter exchange for the Christian community. Paulinus suggested, against standard convention, that letter exchange was actually preferable to *viva voce* conversation. Augustine's claim that letter exchange was an appropriate forum for the censure of friends precisely because it invited the gaze of the Christian community and encouraged the sinner's repentance was similarly revolutionary. Both Augustine and Paulinus reimagine the function of the letter exchange in the management of private, interpersonal relationships within the broader community to reflect tenets of Christian ideology. Still, their innovations to traditional epistolary practice should be seen as the exception rather than the rule. Most late antique letter-writers, particularly those in the Greek East, carefully adhered to traditional epistolary mores. This is not to say that Christian letters did not have a distinctive flavor; but their flavor was no more distinctive than the Stoic philosophical letters of Seneca or the studiously deferential letters of Pliny.

The term "Christian" is generally used to identify letters written by Christians or, more usually, with specifically Christian content. (For this reason, Ausonius' deliberately traditional letters are typically grouped with "pagan" letters, despite his probable status as a baptized Christian.) The argument I have presented here suggests that, in fact, the "Christian letter" was conceived as an innovative reformulation of traditional epistolary practice, designed to reflect the revolutionary implications of Christian theology: that friendship was a reflection of the individual's love for God – God as the absent presence, both here and not here – and a means of overcoming the dislocation of communities. The *epistula Christiana* was an invention of the late fourth century Latin west, and should be understood as part of a much larger movement led by certain "fundamentalist" converts (for example, Paulinus and Augustine), who were committed to the development of a uniquely Christian literary and artistic culture. Late antique letter-writing, like many other forms of artistic production in the period, was characterized by a complex interplay of tradition and innovation. While there emerged in this period an impulse to theorize a specifically Christian practice of letter-writing, it does not seem to have been widespread. Most late antique letter-writers, regardless of their religious identity, adhered to traditional epistolary protocol.

In recent years, studies of individual letter collections have demonstrated the value of uniting an awareness of historical context with sensitivity to the texts' profoundly literary nature (Zelzer 1989: 203–8; Conybeare 2000; Van Dam 2003a; Schröder 2007). Several such projects, focused on individual Greek and Latin letter collections (including Libanius, Jerome, Augustine, Symmachus, and Cassiodorus), are currently in preparation. As the fruits of these scholarly labors become widely available, our understanding of late antique letters will undoubtedly change dramatically. As well, these studies of individual letter collections should encourage more synthetic, diachronic studies of specific features of ancient letter-writing that reveal patterns of continuity and discontinuity across linguistic traditions, space, and time.

BIBLIOGRAPHICAL NOTE

There currently exists no monograph or collection of essays devoted exclusively to late antique letter-writing. For the student of the Later Roman Empire, the most useful surveys are Stowers 1986 and Zelzer 1997. Peter 1901 offers a standard overview of classical Latin letter-writing and its reception, but avoids a detailed discussion of explicitly Christian letter collections. Conybeare 2000 is an exemplary study of one late antique letter collection (for a less adventurous treatment of Jerome's letters see Conring 2001). Also instructive is Catherine Conybeare's textual "dialogue" with Mark Vessey on the topic of Augustine's letters to women (Vessey 2005a). Sogno 2006 includes useful discussion of Symmachus' letters; Schröder 2007 is indispensable for the study of Ennodius' letters. Mathisen 2001, treating Ruricius' letters and fifth-century epistolary culture in Gaul, is similarly profitable. Thraede 1970 traces the reception of key epistolary *topoi* throughout Late Antiquity. Bruggisser 1993 – a study on epistolary friendship in Symmachus' letters – is a useful entry point for exploring the relationship between letter-writing and friendship. Salzman 2004 and Bradbury 2004a extend the discussion to consider the function of letters in the creation of social networks (see also Mathisen 1981). Morello and Morrison (forthcoming) includes several essays devoted to aspects of late antique epistolary practice.

CHAPTER TWENTY

Visual and Verbal Representation: Image, Text, Person, and Power

James A. Francis

"A picture's worth a thousand words." This adage is so commonplace that we might not recognize that it says something fundamental about verbal and visual representation: the power of images to communicate directly and immediately is, at least potentially, vastly greater than the power of verbal description. It is paradoxical that this adage thrives in a culture that tends to be both highly literate and highly literal. The discursive precision of words remains for us the hallmark of certainty and truth, despite our saturation in electronic visual media. This points to a disorienting fact: how we see is not a physiological given, but a cultural process. Different cultures and historical periods can see, hear, and read differently than we do, and conceive and value these modes of perception differently.

Postmodern critics have effectively challenged the notion that texts are finished products and dominate the construction of meaning (for example, White 1987; Barthes 1988; Derrida 1988; Goldhill 1994; Elsner 1996), while, at the same time, contemporary art historians have emphasized the dynamic nature of seeing and being seen, the variety of ways of seeing, and the ability of images to convey multiple meanings (for example, Mitchell 1986, 1994; Bulloch et al. 1993; Elsner 1995; Belting 2003; relevant observations in Foucault 1983 and Bourdieu 1999). These methodological insights have opened up new ways of exploring the relationship between visual and verbal representation in general, and highlight the perceived interplay between image and text that was increasingly acknowledged during the second century AD in, for example, the works of Lucian and the Greek novels. In the light of this new understanding, I shall first describe how political and divine power were conceived and presented in Late Antiquity and how the human person was represented as image, and I shall then discuss in what manner early Christianity can be thought of as a visual culture. I shall suggest that the cultural passage into Late Antiquity is marked by a greater frequency and a more profound significance of visual conceptions and metaphors.

Classical Backgrounds

It is wise to establish first the relationship between late Roman art and its classical antecedents, since "the changes that came about in late antiquity can best be seen as a redistribution and re-orchestration of components that had already existed for centuries in the Mediterranean world" (Brown 1978: 8). What we would call "visuality" was an established concept in the Greco-Roman world. The complexity of the interrelation between visual and verbal expression was also well known, and its potential and paradox were exploited in the political imagery, philosophy, and literature of classical antiquity and the early empire.

Perhaps the most accessible manifestation of ancient visuality is political propaganda. This topic has received much scholarly attention (L'Orange 1947, 1953, 1965 [1958]; Alföldi 1970; Zanker 1988). In order to assert their legitimacy, Hellenistic kings frequently allowed themselves to be portrayed as gods or, more abstractly, as living representations of order itself – for example, as incarnations of *logos* (Chesnut 1978). Roman generals, in their solemn triumphal processions, were dressed to resemble the statue of Jupiter Optimus Maximus in the Capitoline temple. The victorious general was himself the image of an image; he was a living man who, by mimicking the visible image of a divinity, manifested his likeness to the actual and invisible god.

The idea that the statue of a god can both represent that god and be represented by a human being finds expression not only in sculpture and ritual but also in Greco-Roman literature. Vergil, for example, describes in *Aeneid* 1. 588–93 how Venus makes Aeneas appear like the statue of a god; and Artemidorus repeatedly explains that seeing the images of the gods in dreams is the same as dreaming of the gods themselves (1. 5; 2. 33, 35, 39). Platonic philosophers also have much to say about images and seeing; but their view is dichotomous. There is the critique of the arts and representation in Plato's *Republic*, where images as well as poetry are bad copies of bad copies, far removed from reality and truth (Pl. *Resp.* 377c–383c, 595a–608b). The *Symposium*, however, presents a more positive view, allowing for the ascent to the Idea of Beauty through the physically beautiful (Pl. *Symp.* 211c). Since it participates in the true and eternal Forms, the physical world can serve constructively as an image of ultimate reality, and is not simply a misleading or inadequate copy. It can contain a vestige of greater being. The *Timaeus* presents the natural cosmos as the perfect image of an eternal paradigm, a "moving image of eternity" (Pl. *Ti.* 29b, 37c–d), while in the *Laws* true images are linked to the realm of ideas through such principles as symmetry, number, and equality (Pl. *Leg.* 655c, 667d–e, 668e–669b). In later Platonism, *eikôn* becomes the technical term for a Platonic idea, an "incorporeal image." In the *Symposium*, Alcibiades begins his famous speech in praise of Socrates "by means of images" (*di' eikonôn*, Pl. *Symp.* 215a–c). The very word used, *eikôn*, can be translated "by means of similes" just as easily as "by means of images"; the two words are interchangeable even in English. Alcibiades then proceeds to liken his mentor to little figures of Silenus that hold within them images (*agalmata*) of the gods, so that Socrates becomes an image inside an image, an image that harbors a divinity within.

The notion that (visual) image and (verbal) simile are interchangeable also underlies the long-standing, classical literary *topos* of questioning which of the two types of portraiture known in classical and Late Antiquity – visual painting or sculpture on the one hand and verbal written biography on the other – conveys a truer and more complete likeness of the subject. Horace, for example, exalts the permanence of poetic memorial against the fragile portrait image (Hor. *Carm.* 4. 8); and Plutarch states that the fifth-century poet Simonides called the painting a silent poem and the poem a speaking painting (Plu. *Mor.* 346f).

In the later empire, the biographical element in both history and fiction becomes progressively more dominant; the portrait in words takes on a new character and emphasis. The elaborate hagiographical *Lives* of Apollonius, Plotinus, Constantine, and Antony are very different from, and perhaps more impelling than, the portraits we find in Suetonius or Plutarch (see Momigliano 1971; Syme 1971, 1980; Cox 1983; Edwards 1993; Edwards and Swain 1997; Hägg and Rousseau 2000). To be sure, collections of shorter *Lives* continue to be produced, as in the *Vitae sophistarum* of Philostratus and Eunapius and in Palladius' *Lausiac History* and the anonymous *Historia monachorum*; but the authors of these works are similarly inclined to turn biography into hagiography; either to divinize their subjects or to draw a spiritual portrait of them in words (see Miller 2000 and, more broadly, Frank 2000). Of course, Plutarch did foreshadow this development:

> For it is not Histories I am writing, but Lives. ... Accordingly, just as painters get the likenesses in their portraits from the face and the expression of the eyes, wherein the character shows itself ... so I must be permitted to devote myself rather to the signs of the soul in men, and by means of these to portray the life of each. (Plu. *Vit. Alex.* 1. 2–3)

A century or so later, Philostratus the Younger will say much the same thing about painters (Philostr. *Imag.*, *praef.*).

Porphyry combines the negative Platonic view of images with the *topos* of the verbal versus the visual portrait. He begins his *Life of Plotinus* by telling the reader that Plotinus objected to sitting for a painter or sculptor (Porph. *Plot.* 1). The reason he gave, according to Porphyry, was that it is bad enough to have to lug about the image (*eidôlon*) in which nature has encased us, without leaving behind an even longer-lasting image of that image (*eidôlou eidôlon*). This statement both echoes the *Republic* and substantiates Porphyry's rhetorical claim that his biography of Plotinus, the portrait in words, presents the true and lasting image of his master.

A characteristic genre in Late Antiquity was *ekphrasis*, commonly thought of today as the artistic verbal description of a work of art. Surviving ancient handbooks of rhetoric, however, do not define *ekphrasis* narrowly in terms of art, but rather as *vivid* description in general, *enargeia* – "bringing all before the eyes" through words, as Quintilian put it (Quint. *Inst.* 8. 3. 61–72, esp. 62) – and the models most frequently cited by later authors were the battle scenes in Homer (Elsner 1995: 24–6, citing Zanker 1988: 39). The essence and measure of success was precisely visuality – how well the words could conjure images in the mind's eye (see Fowler 1991; James and

Webb 1991; Heffernan 1993). *Ekphrasis* in the sense of describing art appears to have been developed in the second century AD by the writers of the Second Sophistic who, using its power to create mental pictures, set out to (re)create artistic images in words. In so doing, these literary artists explored and exploited the relation between word and image for their own literary purposes (Webb 1999).

Theories of Images and Seeing

Ancient sources consciously articulate concern with the concepts and dynamics of verbal and visual representation. But what can we make of all this? Here, contemporary art-historical scholarship and postmodern critical theory can aid in constructing an interpretative framework that accommodates itself to the concerns of the ancient writers. Within the past twenty years, a revolution has occurred in the discipline of art history. A detached focus on form and on the details of production has given way to an approach that sets art in the broader context of society and allows us to think more deeply about what it means to see and be seen. One dimension of this has been a fundamental revision of how to interpret visual artifacts. The goal in the past was often to establish the one meaning the artist "really" intended to transmit, a process that required not only leaving the visual frame in search of written evidence, but leaving the viewer behind as well. Viewers could not participate in the construction of meaning: they could only recognize what the artist intended. To suppose otherwise was simply wrong. As Jaś Elsner puts it, "This naturalist theory of art leads scholars into a debate of identifying and re-identifying figures and thereby tends to exclude the viewer. It deprives art of the many possibilities for additional creative and subversive interpretations which images inevitably evoke in different viewers and in different times" (Elsner 1995: 51).

Rather than interrogate images in isolation, therefore, we need to look more broadly at the viewing process itself – that is, the variety of ways in which an image can communicate and the variety of modes in which it can be seen, keeping in mind that viewing itself is culturally constructed. It is not enough to examine the visual artifacts of a period: we must also consider how seeing was conceived and what visual paradigms were employed; we must construct, in the words of Roland Barthes, a "history of looking" (Barthes 1982: 12).

We must also pay attention to the nature of visual communication and, concomitantly, to the drawbacks in supposing that an understanding of an image's meaning can depend upon intellectualization alone. David Freedberg has emphasized afresh the innate power of images to address the viewer directly and viscerally, bypassing cognitive processes with an intimate and even frightening effect. Images challenge and subvert our desire, rationality, and control. We repress what we find disturbing in them by ignoring it, explaining it away (symbolism is a handy tool in this), or insisting outright that we see something else (Freedberg 1989: 1–26, 74). We can also turn to Pierre Bourdieu and his critique of theoretical reason. Much of what he says about practice, anthropologists, and sociologists is directly applicable to images, art historians, and theologians. Both observer and theory are privileged, and the object of study is reduced to a code to be deciphered by an observer to uncover the "meaning" that the object "really" (and only) exists to express (Bourdieu 1999: 14–21, 27–9, 34–7; see also Jensen 2000: 6, 28, 32). Less abstractly and even more radically, it has become apparent that scholarly activity once viewed as "objective," such as the physical description of an image, can surreptitiously impose prescribed categories of meaning.

> Indeed even to *call* a scene, for example, "a satyr pursues a maenad" *rather* than "a maenad resists rape" is to engage in more than "mere" identification, not least because such acts of naming construct and imply a relationship between object and viewer. Naming is classing; and recognizing implies both a perceptual and an authoritative and authorizing gesture. The texts that are appended to works of art *change* how they are seen. (Goldhill and Osborne 1994: 4, emphasis original)

To describe is to interpret; and, since that interpretation is unavoidable, it must be recognized (see Burke 2001; Raab 2002).

But how can we let images "speak for themselves" without imposing our own intellectual, not to mention social or religious, agendas onto what we see? Here Susan Bordo offers a useful idea. In criticizing the Cartesian hierarchy of epistemological values, which marks each object off from the other and from the knower, Bordo suggests an alternative that she terms "sympathy." Sympathetic understanding of an object is achieved through "union" with it, or through "merging with" or "marrying" it. It allows a variety of meanings to unfold without coercion or excessively focused interrogation, and comes to understanding not from analysis of parts but from "placing oneself within" the full being of an object (Bordo 1987: 102–3).

Elsner takes a strikingly similar approach. He accounts for the transformation in style – from classical naturalism to the symbolic quality of late antique art – by describing a fundamental shift in viewing preferences, in the way in which images were seen to convey meaning. Since no mimetic representation can actually *be* that which it represents, a distinction that only becomes sharper the more closely the image resembles the model, the culture of the later empire cultivated an alternative to this actually deceptive character of naturalistic representation (fig. 20.1). This Elsner terms "sacred" or "mystic" viewing. Religious initiation transforms the world of ordinary assumptions and helps the viewer to discern the genuine, nonmaterial reality communicated through an image (Elsner 1995: 18–22, see also 4–7, 15–17, 88–124). He writes: "Mystic viewing is predicated upon the assumption that in mystic experience the dualism of subject and object can be transcended into a unity that is neither subject nor object and yet is simultaneously both." He further compares this concept with Plotinus' "super-intellection" (*hypernoēsis*), citing numerous passages in *Enneads* 6 (Elsner 1995: 90). At the same time, he is careful not to overdraw the distinction. There was never only one way of viewing images, even sacred images, in any period. A variety of modes of seeing coexisted side by side; the fundamental poles of naturalistic and mystic viewing are always present and intertwined. In this regard, the cultural transition into Late Antiquity is not a

Figure 20.1 Ancient *trompe l'oeil*. Panel from a cubiculum in the villa of P. Fannius at Boscoreale, Pompeii. 1st century BC. Metropolitan Museum of Art, New York/The Bridgeman Art Library.

wholesale change from one mode of viewing to another, but a shift of emphasis, a preference for and intensification of one particular mode of viewing and representation. The historical development of late antique art depended, therefore, on a broader view of how meaning is constructed; and the same dependence must characterize our own understanding of that development (Elsner 1995: 19–20).

Person and Power in Late Antiquity

Let us now turn specifically to the development of verbal and visual representation in the later empire, beginning in the second century AD. A number of literary works in this period are based on a visual premise, or play at the boundaries between the visual and verbal. For example, Longus' novel *Daphnis and Chloe* purports to be an immense *ekphrasis*, Achilles Tatius' *Leucippe and Clitophon* deluges the reader with mental images, while Apuleius' descriptively lush *Metamorphoses* (*The Golden Ass*) is based on a visual paradigm. Arguably the most powerful feat of *ekphrasis* in antiquity, the *Imagines* written by Philostratus the Elder, signals a new departure in literature, in which the boundaries between reader and text, text and image, image and viewer, and viewer and reader are broken down. Reading and viewing, subject and object merge together.

Philostratus presents a tour of an entire gallery, presented by him as real but most probably imaginary. Like a docent, the author leads the reader, represented in the text by a young boy eager to learn, from painting to painting, giving his interpretations and commenting on technique as he escorts the boy through the gallery. Intent on "looking" at the pictures and "hearing" the learned commentary, the reader is absorbed into the text and forgets that he or she *is* a reader. The paintings being viewed are actually words being read; the acts of reading and viewing are compounded, their boundaries blurred.

At the beginning of the work, Philostratus states that both poets and painters contribute to knowledge, since they both, through their observance of proportion and symmetry, partake of reason (*logos*) (Philostr. *Imag.* 1, *praef.*, echoing Plato in the *Laws*). In his first description – a painting of a scene from the *Iliad* – Philostratus instructs the boy to turn his eyes from the painting and, in order to understand its meaning, look only at the text upon which it is based (1. 1). He then proceeds to describe the painting with words and phrases from Homer. He tells the boy to "listen" to some paintings (1. 2, 5) and even to "smell" one (1. 6). As he proceeds, Philostratus begins to address the figures in the paintings as if they were present (1. 21). At one point, he asks the boy (that is, Philostratus asks the reader-viewer) to place himself within the painting in order to appreciate and understand it (2. 17). The reader, having become a viewer, now becomes part of the image being viewed (for discussion of this narrative technique, see Bowersock 1994a).

Experiments in verbal and visual representation were being deliberately and artistically pursued at the cutting edge of imperial high culture in the second century. The writers of the Second Sophistic played with the distinctions between the verbal and visual, while at the same time combining and conflating them in new and complex ways. At times they covertly bring their readers to a visual experience (or illusion) through their words, at others they call conscious attention to the interplay of word and image.

An eminent example of the latter is Lucian's *Eikones*, in which the author transforms a living person into an image. The work is an elaborate tribute to Panthea, mistress of the emperor Lucius Verus (AD 130–69). Words fail to do justice to her beauty, so Lucian engages in applied *ekphrasis*, describing the various parts and qualities of Panthea's body by pointing to their equivalents in great works of art: the brow from Praxiteles, the cheeks from Alcamenes, the blush of the cheeks from Polygnotus, and so on (Lucian, *Imag.* 6–7). Bit by bit, he transforms the living woman into a work of art.

From the very start, Lucian makes his audience play with the notion of image. He asks his readers to use words in order to "look" at a woman whom he has turned into a statue (Lucian, *Imag.* 1). At the same time, he reminds them of lookers who were themselves turned into stone (Lucian, *Imag.* 1). The *Eikones* begin with an allusion to a mythological Gorgon (a creature at the sight of which living people were turned into stone), continues with references to Niobe (who was turned into a statue by grief and remorse, after the gods had killed her children as a punishment for her pride), and then returns to a Gorgon (in this case, Medusa herself). To these examples, Lucian adds Panthea, whose beauty is so arresting that, at the sight of her, the viewer is stopped dead like a stone. The act of seeing and being seen transforms not only the viewed, but also the viewer into images. To underscore that point, the opening of the piece overflows with visual words such as "see," "seeing," "look," "looking," "notice," "vision," "spectacle," "appearance," "sight," and "image"; and by referring to the statue with the word *andrias*, he draws attention to the human exemplar of the image (Lucian, *Imag.* 1). Later, Lucian calls his finished verbal portrait an *eikón* upon which both his interlocutor and his reader will look (Lucian, *Imag.* 6, 15).

Just in case we might miss what is going on here, Lucian suddenly calls upon Homer and Pindar among his list of painters and uses poetry to describe Panthea's color (8), utterly conflating and confounding visual and verbal representation. The idea behind the *Eikones*, together with the other words Lucian chooses, and finally this introduction of poets into a list of artists, all drive home the intricate braiding of the verbal and the visual in what may appear at first glance to be a simple work. Panthea is finally likened to a divine image sent from the gods above (*diipetes*, 9) and this verbal portrait of her is itself called an *agalma*, a divine or cult statue (12). Lucian's interlocutor then complains that the woman has not been done justice, and proceeds to describe the virtues of her soul (15 and 16). He, however, will give each of these its own portrait, taken from the various genres of literature. With this, the strategy of the work is fully revealed as deliberate, highly sophisticated play on the visual and verbal. Panthea, having first been turned into an art museum now becomes a library; indeed, in her the two have become the same.

The representation of a living person as an image, which perhaps began as a literary conceit, becomes a fundamental mode of describing political and divine power. As already noted, images in the service of power were not new to Late Antiquity; but, as in literature, this dynamic was taken to a deeper level and used more widely and with greater force in that period. This connection is seen in the way H. P. L'Orange echoes Plutarch on the nature of biography quoted above. For L'Orange, imperial portraiture in the age of Constantine develops a stereometric abstraction, revealing "the inner and spiritual human being, the 'pneumatic personality,' so to speak in the language of that period. An 'abstract' or 'expressionistic' portrait, to use the modern term, comes to life" (L'Orange 1965 [1958]: 111). Such portraiture is, in his view, a "crystallization of imperial ideology," an "expression of *divina maiestas*, rather than a portrait of an individual man" (L'Orange 1965 [1958]: 124; see also Grabar 1968: 64–6).

There is great value in these insights, but this older view requires refinement. Though there is an obvious difference between classical and late antique art on the

Figure 20.2   Prima Porta Augustus. Vatican Museums. akg-images/Nimatallah.

general level, rigid definitions and dichotomies between naturalistic and hieratic art are misleading, and oversimplify the evidence. A comparison of two statues illustrates the point: the Prima Porta Augustus (from the first century BC; see fig. 20.2) and the Colossus of Barletta (early or mid fifth century AD, depending on which emperor one thinks is represented; see fig. 20.3). Both are imperial portraits in military dress; the naturalism of the one and the stiff, hieratic quality of the other seem at first glance obvious. But how truly naturalistic is the Augustus? He is far younger than he was in life at the time the statue was made. His bare feet, the cupid beneath him, and the allegories on his cuirass are all indications of divinity. Though naturalistic in some of its details, the image as a whole is far from realistic; it is in fact a portrayal of the *divina maiestas* of Augustus. The style of the Barletta statue is markedly different, though its message is virtually the same. This later statue cannot be called an abstract representation, as opposed to an individual portrait. The face is clearly that of an unidealized individual in the classical Roman tradition of realistic portrait busts. Although there is no agreement as to exactly which emperor is depicted (it is most

Figure 20.3 Bronze colossus of an emperor. 5th century AD. Barletta, Italy. Anderson/ Alinari Archives, Florence.

often thought of as Valentinian I, but may even be Marcian), it is beyond question that it represents an individual emperor. Naturalism does not preclude the portrayal of transcendent reality, nor does a hieratic style exclude realism and individuality. What distinguishes the two statues is not a matter of superficial appearance but is altogether more subtle and complex. The statue of Augustus is made to look like a living individual, while the individual presented at Barletta is presented unashamedly as a statue.

The latter mode of portraiture is also manifested in Ammianus' well-known description of Constantius' entry into Rome in 357. (On visuality in Ammianus, see MacMullen 1964b; Barnes 1998.) After depicting the cavalry preceding the emperor as "statues polished by the hand of Praxiteles, not men" (16. 10. 8), Ammianus describes Constantius himself:

> He both bent his rather short frame low upon entering the lofty gates and, as if his neck were in a brace holding his line of sight straight ahead, he turned his head neither right nor left; and as if he were an image of a man [*tamquam figmentum hominis*] he neither nodded when the wheel jolted, nor spat, nor wiped or rubbed his face or nose, or was ever even seen to move his hand. (16. 10. 10)

Constantius has no need to dress up like a statue as in a Roman triumph; he is a statue – paradoxically a statue of himself. His power is communicated and his greatness magnified by his static posture. The emperor's only movement is a ritual bending. In the compendious phrase of Bourdieu, "Bodily hexis is political mythology realized" (Bourdieu 1999: 69). Though Constantius makes a statement by acting as an image, his message must also be received by his audience. It is the people of Rome on one level, Ammianus on another, who "recognize" the image. Both image (Constantius) and viewer are enmeshed in a process of seeing and meaning to which both contribute. Imperial power is, in part, constructed by the dynamics of visuality. This may perhaps be one explanation for what should be a contradiction: a popular autocrat. Through their vision and recognition, spectators at some tacit level realize that they are constructing the power they see before them. Visuality can be a form of social contract.

This visual model of power also extends to the divine world – indeed, in one important respect, the divine even imitates the imperial image. Plotinus pursued the more positive estimation of images in Platonism. Citing as an example the "wise men of old" who made images (*agalmata*) in the hope of making the gods present among them, he speaks of how soul can be attracted to a sympathetic, that is imitative, image. This is possible because "the All, too, made every particular thing in imitation of the rational principles [*logous*] it possessed," so that each thing became a "rational principle in matter" of that which existed before matter (*Enn.* 4. 3. 11). God is an image maker, and the entire material universe is a representation. It is by such a process of mediation and representation that the sensible world is ultimately linked to divine being. This line of reasoning ushers in a new level of thinking about imaging the divine. Since for a Platonist, divine being is immaterial, invisible, and ineffable, the only way it can ever be seen is by means of an image. Furthermore such an image, as Plotinus indicates, has something of soul or life about it; it is a living image in some way. This mode of thought reaches an apex in the Christian doctrine of the Incarnation, as we shall see shortly. (See Barasch 1992: 63–104 for a synopsis of pagan and Christian sources.)

The relation between images and the divine also engaged the emperor Julian who, in his *Oration on the Mother of the Gods* (*Or.* 5), speaks of the image of the Phrygian goddess coming to Rome "no human thing, but really divine, not lifeless clay but something having life [or soul, *empnoun*] and divinity" (161a). Of course, Julian is no mere idol-worshiper. He makes clear that images of the gods are no more the gods themselves than images of the emperor are the emperor, but neither are they mere stones or wood. They are something in between that is constructed not by the artist but by the image and the viewer – as Julian endeavors to explain in a lengthy fragment dubbed *Letter to a Priest*:

> He therefore who loves the emperor delights to see the emperor's statue, and he who loves his son delights to see his son's statue, and he who loves his father delights to see his father's statue. It follows that he who loves the gods delights to gaze on the images [*agalmata*] of the gods, and their likenesses [*eikonas*], and he feels reverence and shudders with awe of the gods who look at him from the unseen world. (294c–d)

It is the viewer's relationship to the object, his or her recognition and reception of it and devotion to it, that changes the nature of the image itself. This "middle thing" between animistic idols and mere sculpture, what may perhaps be called the "sacred image," relies upon what the viewer brings to the viewing relationship. This is a "viewing relationship" in a literal sense: we look upon the images of the gods who, in turn, look upon us. Humans and gods are viewers seeing one another through the mediation of images. It might even be said that it is because the gods look at us that we can see them.

Even in the most philosophically refined circles, therefore, images (at least divine images) possessed a certain numinous quality; they were not reduced to mere symbols to be deciphered in an intellectual process. They possessed immediacy, force, power. Though images of the gods were not divine in themselves, they nevertheless shared in some way the nature and power of the being they represented. With this in mind, we can see the cultural and intellectual continuity common to both pagan and Christian thinkers regarding images and imaging. In all the attention that has been paid over the centuries to theology in the early Christological controversies, it is easy to forget that Christianity inherited from ages of pagan thought a wealth of concepts and language as to how divinity could be imaged. In the second and third centuries especially, there had been a flowering of apologetic writing concerning the images of the gods, represented by the works of Callistratus, Dio, Maximus of Tyre, Philostratus, Plotinus, and Porphyry (Bidez 1913: 143).

Ironically, while the pagan Julian hedges on the identification of image and archetype, the Christian bishop Athanasius shows himself possessed of no such qualms. In his *Third Oration against the Arians* (5), he offers an explanation of how the Son is the image of the Father:

> In the image [*eikón*] [of the emperor] there is the character [*eidos*] and the form [*morphê*] of the emperor, and in the emperor is that character which is in the image. For the emperor's likeness is exact in the image, so that the one gazing at the image sees the emperor in it, and again the one gazing at the emperor recognizes that he is the one in the image. And since the likeness does not at all differ, the image might say to one wishing to view the emperor after seeing the image: "I and the emperor are one; I am in him and he is in me. That which you see in me you behold in him, and what you look upon in him you behold in me" [cf. John 14. 9–11]. Therefore whoever adores the image also adores the emperor in it, for the image is his form [*morphê*] and character [*eidos*].

Athanasius frames this as a matter of imaging and representation, dramatically underscored by his comparison to the imperial icon. The material image of a living man operates in the same way as the living image of the incorporeal God. But Athanasius does not choose just any portrait to build his metaphor: he chooses the imperial portrait, an image that carries the power and shares the character and nature of the emperor (fig. 20.4). Basil (*De Spir. Sanct.* 18 (45)) and Ambrose (*Expos. in Psalm 118*, 10. 25) will later use a similar metaphor. This is a singularly potent image, indeed a "living" image; but what gives it its power, both in social reality and in rhetoric?

I would suggest that what people like Plotinus and Julian struggle to express, and what Athanasius simply asserts by comparison to a familiar reality in the Roman

Figure 20.4 Images of co-emperors displayed in icons and embroidery around an official, signifying effective imperial presence. Judgment of Pilate from the Rossano Gospels. Early 6th century AD, imitating a 5th-century model. ©1990. Photo Scala, Florence.

world, is what we would term the power inherent in the process of representation and viewing. Image and viewer forge a middle ground between animism and art, by constructing, so to speak, a universe of representation. Thus, the type of viewing at work here is an active, reciprocal relationship. An image comes into rapport with a viewer who, by means of his or her relation to the image, recognizes its power. Through this power relationship, both image and viewer construct the image's meaning.

Word and Image in Ancient Christianity

This discussion of image, text, and visuality has some very particular applications to early Christianity. As has been the case with intellectualism in art generally, a fundamental assumption has been that early Christian images represent theological

Figure 20.5   Wall painting of Orpheus and animals. 3rd century AD. Catacombs of Domitilla, Rome, Italy. Photo ©Held Collection/The Bridgeman Art Library.

statements and systems and that they exist to communicate those concepts to the viewer. They are traditionally interpreted by literal reference to Scripture, as if they could be no more than mere "illustrations" of a text. Certainly our current under-standing of the fluidity of pre-Constantinian Christianity should make us cautious in using as a guide to interpretation a canon or theology that was developed later. More fundamentally, we should question the assumption that theologies must predominate in anything considered Christian. It is clear that philosophically minded apologists (among numerous other writers) were concerned with theology; but what of those believers comfortable with the society and culture of the empire – those who, for example, could afford painted tombs? Did they have clear, articulated, and strongly held theological concepts, ones that would exclusively distinguish them from their non-Christian fellows? A good number of images in Roman Christian catacombs and tombs seem to indicate they did not. Scholars have had perennial difficulty in explaining the frequent presence of Orpheus (fig. 20.5), Dionysiac imagery (fig. 20.6), and even Hercules and Athena (fig. 20.7) in ostensibly Christian burial chambers (examples in Grabar 1968; Murray 1981; Finney 1994; Jensen 2000). The frequently nonnarrative, staccato presentation and the multivalent or ambivalent symbolism of this art challenge a discursive method of interpretation. Since Chris-tianity is a revealed religion, one with a divine authorizing text, it may be only common sense to read images in light of that text; but even so, did "read" and "text" mean the same thing for ancient Christians as they do for us (Gamble 1995: 30; Jensen 2000: 75–8)?

Figure 20.6   Dionysiac mosaic in Santa Costanza. Rome, Italy. ©1990. Photo Scala, Florence.

As Ramsay MacMullen has pointed out, in a world in which three-quarters of the population were illiterate, the knowledge and spread of Christianity, indeed of any religion, could not have been a matter of reading, at least not in the way we commonly understand it (MacMullen 1984: 21 and n. 14). Harry Gamble states categorically that "nothing remotely like mass literacy existed, nor could have existed, in Greco-Roman societies, because the forces and institutions required to foster it were absent." We cannot suppose that Christians differed in this respect from the general population, despite the importance of the revealed text, since "acquaintance with the scriptures did not require that all or even most Christians be individually capable of reading them and does not imply that they were" (Gamble 1995: 4–5, citing Harris 1989; see also Young 1997: 10–28; Haines-Eitzen 2000; Cribiore 2001). As Scripture itself indicates, Christianity was spread by preaching and, in its earliest period, bears more resemblance to an oral tradition or mythology than it does to our familiar form of literacy. The literary culture of antiquity was also itself profoundly oral in character. Authors wrote or dictated with an ear to the sound of their words and under the assumption that what they wrote would be audibly read both in public reading and in the ancient practice of reading aloud privately. As a result, "no ancient text is now read as it was intended to be unless it is also heard, that is, read aloud" (Gamble 1995: 204; see, for an example, August. *Conf.* 6. 3, though silent reading in antiquity was more common than has generally been thought: Burnyeat 1997; Gavrilov 1997). Hearing the text read aloud, particularly in the context of the liturgy, was the fundamental way in which all Christians appropriated

Figure 20.7 Wall painting of Hercules and Athena. Left-hand arcosolium, cubiculum N, Via Latina Catacomb. 4th century AD. Rome, Italy.

Scripture, not only the illiterate. Reading literature aloud was also a frequent form of cultured entertainment among the educated.

This point merits further discussion. John R. Clarke has recently questioned the prevailing view of widespread illiteracy in the Roman world, citing as evidence the bawdy and often witty graffiti that accompany wall paintings in taverns in Pompeii and Ostia (Clarke 2003: 271). These were clearly lower-class establishments, and getting the joke painted on the walls required the ability to read. The mere existence of such paintings suggests that at least basic literacy was common enough. That this question is raised by an art historian in the context of wall paintings illustrates well the inextricable link between the visual and verbal, in that paintings might be able to tell us something about literacy; but it also points to something else. It is a modern prejudice to assume that once people could read, they would somehow abandon orality and visuality in favor of the textual and literal; that reading trumps all other modes of reception and comprehension. It is as if an ancient Christian who learned to read would, as a result, suddenly turn into Martin Luther. Just as the acquisition of reading does not entail the end of aural or visual perception and comprehension, neither does it necessitate the end of the *primacy* of the aural and visual. In both medicine and philosophy, the "living voice" of the teacher was considered superior to books as a vehicle for imparting knowledge (Cribriore 2001: 145–6). Literate and educated persons can be as aurally and visually oriented as those who cannot read. The issue is one of culture, not education.

Texts appropriated through hearing do not possess the fixity of those assimilated and conceptualized according to modern practices of reading. As Frances Young contends, the scriptural text was itself "symbolic" of a greater and higher reality. Understood "sacramentally," Scripture was a "linguistic sign" that represented the reality to which it referred (Young 1997: 117–33). Similarly, Averil Cameron states: "Like visual art, early Christian discourse presented its audience with a series of images. The proclamation of the message was achieved by a technique of presenting the audience with a series of images through which it was thought possible to perceive an objective and higher truth" (Cameron 1991: 57). Given this understanding, we must be wary in establishing a literal, one-on-one correspondence between Christian images and Scripture. Robin Jensen draws the connection between this form of literacy and art:

> This explains why certain subjects were so often portrayed in abbreviated or unexpected ways. The viewer had already moved beyond the literal meaning of the narrative to its deeper messages. Christians would see for themselves, in pictorial form, the interpretations or symbolic associations they were regularly hearing in their weekly homilies and their baptismal catecheses. (Jensen 2000: 78)

The sacred text, because it was assimilated aurally, lent itself to visuality. The Christians responsible for such works as the catacomb paintings did not use images merely to illustrate their texts; nor did they use texts to justify their images. Rather, both these modes of expression and communication were grounded in a common experience of visuality in which, as with the writers of the Second Sophistic, the distinction between word and image tends to break down.

We have already discussed Bordo's concept of sympathetic understanding and Elsner's of mystic viewing. I would suggest these have a parallel in a concept and institution developed in the early church that was as alien to modern culture as ancient visuality: sacrament. The sacraments are effective signs. They both symbolize and are what they symbolize at the same time: water and grace, oil and the Holy Spirit, bread and body, wine and blood. In a manner analogous to the icon in later eastern Christianity, sacraments are both of this world and a gate to another. The ability to see beyond material reality to the transcendent is operative not only in the sacraments but also in the transformation of classical biography into late antique hagiography, where the human subject of the verbal portrait is transformed into a symbol, a saint. This type of viewing can also allow the object to transform the viewer. In the Eucharist especially, the viewer unites with the object and, by ingesting bread, is subsumed into the body of Christ:

> If mystic vision is the attainment of union with Christ beyond the distinction of subject and object, the eucharist is precisely the means by which such union may be achieved. ... By the late fifth century, the sacramental vision of Christian Neoplatonism revealed the liturgy and the eucharist to be operating in precisely the same way as sacred images. (Elsner 1995: 121)

Or, in the words of Robert Taft, Christian liturgy is a "living icon" (Taft 1997: 224). It also bears repeating that the liturgy was the privileged place for appropriating the Scriptures through oral reading, giving a sacramental, visual frame to the verbal revelation, which was understood sacramentally, as a verbal sign.

We can also suggest a further connection between images and the liturgy. Images decorate sacred spaces, places where religious actions are carried out – for example, burials in catacombs or worship in assembly halls. Images can reflect, enhance, or clarify the meaning of sacred acts. The images in the baptistery at Dura-Europos on the Parthian frontier (*c.* AD 230) present an example. Above the font as the center-piece of the room is a large mural of the Good Shepherd, conveying incorporation into his flock, the congregation, and care in this life unto salvation in the next (fig. 20.8). The frequency of this same image in the catacombs would point to fulfillment of this commitment in death. Similarly with the mural of three women (fig. 20.9): this is usually taken to refer to the Resurrection – to portray, in other words, the women at the tomb – but its significance may lie instead in the movement of the women itself. They are processing to meet their Lord, an action parallel to that of the baptizands, and perhaps of the entire congregation, approaching the font. Physical action rather than abstract thought can be the impetus behind image making.

But the transcendent element of liturgy and sacrament, that which is perceived by "mystic viewing," is only half the experience. Water, oil, bread, and wine remain visible and tangible; they do not disappear into the transcendent reality. If the eucharistic bread is not bread, it cannot be the body of Christ. The holy man and saint remain human; indeed, their sanctity would be meaningless if they were not human. What I would term "sacramental perception," embracing seeing, reading, and hearing, requires that the material, mundane, and historical be seen at the same time with their corresponding higher realities. It is a visual mode of understanding that comprehends in terms of "both and" instead of analyzing into "either or." In her survey of fourth-century eucharistic instructions, Georgia Frank discusses the predominance of visual metaphors and concludes:

> New experiences demanded new eyes. As this essay suggests, the "eyes of faith" stood for a variety of mental images and visual processes taught to new Christians as a way to receive the eucharistic bread and wine. Without erasing the evidence of the physical

Figure 20.8   The Good Shepherd. Wall painting from Dura-Europos. 3rd century AD. Dura-Europos Collection. Yale University Art Gallery.

Figure 20.9   Women at the Tomb(?). Wall painting from Dura-Europos. 3rd century AD. Dura-Europos Collection. Yale University Art Gallery.

senses, these visual strategies generated a host of mental images that would reframe the physical reception of the Eucharist. Rather than look away, neophytes were asked to look closer at the liturgy unfolding. (Frank 2001: 621)

The broad dynamics of liturgy and sacrament and the visuality inherent in them is, I would suggest, characteristic of visual and verbal representation and perception in Late Antiquity.

Conclusion

The issues we have been discussing find a dramatic culmination in the description of the death of St. Daniel the Stylite in his late fifth-century *Life*.

> But the people demanded that the holy man be shown to them before his burial, and in consequence an extraordinary tumult arose. For by the archbishop's orders the plank was stood upright – the body had been fixed to it so that it could not fall – and thus, like an icon, the holy man was displayed to all on every side; and for many hours the people all looked at him and also with cries and tears besought him to be an advocate with God on behalf of them all. (99, tr. Dawes and Baynes)

Like Constantius entering Rome, Daniel is transformed into an image of himself to magnify his power. In doing so, the archbishop reassures the crowd that Daniel's power will live on, so they beseech the saint in or on his icon – literally – to continue his work. Though the actual relic of the saint's body lies before them, they enhance its power by turning it into an image, adding the power of representation to the saint's power of intercession.

The visuality of the culture of the Later Roman Empire provides a vital context to understanding early Christianity. From the sophisticated and abstract experiments in verbal and visual representation of the literati to the visual appropriation of texts, Christianity was immersed in a culture characterized by ways of seeing and modes of representation significantly different from our own. It appears that a religion of the Word of God, Image of God, and Word made Flesh, one that developed a "firm commitment to the visible" (Rousseau 2002: 15), did not simply and fortuitously lend itself to this culture but rather was very much the product of it.

BIBLIOGRAPHICAL NOTE

Presenting a bibliographical guide can be difficult when dealing with an interdisciplinary topic. Some readers will have no previous experience, while others will possess expertise in some fields but not others. Here I suggest, in the limited space available, various fundamental and comprehensive works useful for those new to a given field. These should be considered good places to start but by no means a complete introduction.

With regard to images and art history, Elsner 1995 offers a good introduction not only to the period, but also to current trends and controversies in art history and the relation of image and text. This last topic is the particular focus of two fine volumes: Goldhill and Osborne 1994 and Elsner 1996, each containing a series of essays on specific topics. For those unsure of how to think about images and history, L'Orange 1965 [1958] offers a helpful model, though contemporary scholars will argue with some of his specific interpretations. Similarly, Burke 2001 offers a very useful and up-to-date discussion of the use of images as historical evidence, though not at all limited to antiquity. Those interested in the theoretical aspects of art history may consult Mitchell 1994 and Belting 2003. For those new to early Christian art, Jensen 2000 presents a very accessible introduction; Grabar 1968 remains the most comprehensive account, though now dated in a few respects. In the broader realm of Christianity and culture, Rousseau 2002 is very accessible with excellent bibliographical notes, while Averil Cameron 1991 offers a more conventional scholarly approach.

CHAPTER TWENTY-ONE

Christianity and the Transformation of Classical Art

Felicity Harley

In the study of the visual arts, as in all other areas of historical and cultural research, the centuries between classical antiquity and the high Middle Ages are no longer dismissed as years of decline and darkness, but are open to increasing diversity of appreciation and subtlety of analysis. Many of the principal theories regarding the development of western European art were, however, largely predicated on the assumed existence of a "dark age" prior to the revival of classical culture in the Renaissance. It is not surprising, therefore, that the journey from the latter viewpoint to the former has been a complex one for historians of art. Particularly challenging has been the dismantling of the view that the emergence and development of Christianity in the Mediterranean world presented one of the main threats to the survival of classical art.

The paradigm of decline and fall continues to unravel in late Roman scholarship (Ward-Perkins 2005). The disparaging undertones traditionally attached to the terms "medieval" and "Byzantine" have increasingly lost their currency in art-historical research (Elsner 1998) and there has been a renewed engagement with the art of the early Christians. This chapter will highlight the importance of continuing and refining that engagement by further exposing the very close relationship between late Roman art and early Christian iconography. Drawing on the example of the representation of the Crucifixion and using the Maskell ivories, I hope to demonstrate that the role of Christianity as the purveyor and transformer of the classical artistic heritage was a key factor in its ability to develop a pictorial language of its own. Hence the essential question of early Christian art may well be: how did artists utilize the comprehensive pictorial language of Roman art to illustrate the events described in the Holy Scriptures (Kessler 1976)? In answering that question, we increase our appreciation of Late Antiquity as a period of artistic innovation and experimentation, and so of creativity.

Christianity and the Making of the "Middle Ages"

In his *Commentari*, written in Florence *c.* 1450, the sculptor and goldsmith Lorenzo Ghiberti divided the history of art into three main epochs: the classical, medieval, and modern. As part of this radical partitioning between one historical period and another, Ghiberti put forward critical judgments about the value of the art that was produced in each. So, the perfection of the classical period was celebrated on the one hand, while the artistic integrity of Ghiberti's own "modern" period was endorsed and lauded on the other. The gulf intervening between the two was characterized by the artist as a regrettable period of decline. The ancient Greco-Roman models of artistic perfection were lost, preserved only in written descriptions by Pliny and Vitruvius (the sole surviving Roman authors on ancient art and architecture). Their revival in the modern period came at the hands of great artists like Raphael, who found natural prototypes for Christian heroes and stories in pagan themes and iconography. In the story of the dying hero Meleager, for instance, whose fated death was mourned by his companions but especially by his sorrowing mother, a model was found for the scene of the Deposition of Christ.

The notion of a long period of artistic decline between the classical and Renaissance periods was present in Florence a century earlier, as seen in Giovanni Boccaccio's mid-fourteenth-century collection of novellas, *The Decameron*. Drawing on an already established legend, Boccaccio portrayed Giotto as having brought back to light (*ritornata in luce*) that art of antiquity that for centuries had been buried (Day VI, Story 5, Falaschi 1998: 114–15). Yet, in explicitly portraying the years intervening between the classical and modern as an extended period of utter stagnation, it was Ghiberti who effectively gave the first categorical description of what was afterward called the "Middle Ages" (Buddensieg 1965: 44). And he posed the critical question: why had Roman art come to such a reprehensible end, only to be spectacularly revived in fifteenth-century Italy?

Ghiberti himself answered by locating a specific date and naming the culprits. The year was AD 312, the date of Constantine's conversion to Christianity. Although the Church would come to laud this as a critical moment in Christian history, Ghiberti and others saw the events of the fourth century as aesthetic apostasy:

> At the time of Emperor Constantine and Pope Sylvester, the Christian faith gained ascendancy. Idolatry being violently persecuted, all the statues and pictures, adorned with so much nobility as well as ancient and perfect dignity, were dismembered and mutilated; ... Since art was finished, the sanctuaries remained bare for about six hundred years. Then the Greeks made a very feeble beginning in the art of painting and practiced it with great clumsiness: they were as rude and clumsy in this age as the ancient [Greeks] had been competent in theirs. (Quoted in Panofsky 1960: 25)

For the history of Christian art, Ghiberti makes a new and pivotal point. Its novelty lies not in the ascription of guilt to early Christianity and the papacy for the collapse of antiquity – since the downfall of the art and literature of antiquity had already, by the middle of the twelfth century, been blamed on the sixth-century pope, Gregory the Great – but rather in Ghiberti's accusatory tone (Buddensieg 1965: 45–7). His voice of condemnation was to be adopted, along with the theory of Constantine's culpability, by other writers, artists, and commentators, including Leone Battista Alberti and the artist and historiographer of Renaissance Florence, Georgio Vasari.

Perhaps the most powerful accusation leveled against Christianity was that of the Nuremberg artist Albrecht Dürer, who, according to Gombrich, "saw himself both as a pupil of the Italian Renaissance and as its missionary" (Gombrich 1976: 112). In notes he made for the introduction to his *Treatise on Painting*, written in 1512, Dürer described the early Christians as "brutal oppressors of art" and as taking the visual arts for "black magic." In what can only be described as a personal and moving lament, Dürer wrote that had he been present in the time of Constantine, he would have addressed the early Christians thus:

> Oh my beloved holy Lords and Fathers! Do not, for the sake of the evil they can wreak, lamentably kill the noble inventions of art which have been gained by so much labour and sweat … Because the same proportions the heathens assigned to their idol Apollo, we shall use for Christ the Lord, the fairest of them all. (Quoted in Gombrich 1976: 114)

Dürer would have known the Apollo Belvedere, a marble sculpture possibly made in the reign of Hadrian (AD 117–38) and rediscovered just outside Rome in the late fifteenth century (now in the Belvedere Courtyard of the Musei Vaticani). The sculpture was revered throughout the Renaissance as epitomizing the ideal of classical antiquity. Dürer himself had used it as a model, borrowing the pose and reversing it for his representation of Adam in a 1504 engraving of *Adam and Eve*.

What Dürer may not have known was that the early Christians had themselves been influenced by classical representations of Apollo, and used them as models for Christ. This was demonstrated in April 1595, when an extraordinary white marble sarcophagus was discovered in the confessional of the old church of St. Peter in Rome during work undertaken by the then pope, Clement VII, for the erection of a new high altar (fig. 21.1). The large two-register column-sarcophagus survives as a truly magnificent piece of early Christian carving, remarkable not simply because of its superior quality (being highly polished and finely carved in a technically assured classical style) but also for its indication that the classical style was adopted in the fourth century for the expression of Christian subjects and emerging Christian iconographic types.

Following its excavation, the sarcophagus was displayed adjacent to the site in which it was discovered – that is, in the grottos of St. Peter, where it remained until 1936. It was included by Antonio Bosio in the group of forty-three sarcophagi that were exquisitely illustrated in his pioneering study of early Christian catacombs, *Roma sotteranea* (Bosio 1632, ii: 44–6). Given the active interest in the recovery of classical and late antique material culture within an elite stratum of Roman ecclesiastical society in seventeenth-century baroque Rome, the impact of the sarcophagus' discovery must have been profound.

The sarcophagus belonged to Junius Bassus, prefect of Rome in AD 359. At the center of its top register, the sculptor depicted Christ enthroned in glory. Portrayed as

Figure 21.1   Sarcophagus of Junius Bassus, c. AD 359. Marble. Detail. Museo Storico Artistico Tesoro, Basilica di San Pietro in Vaticano. akg-images/Erich Lessing.

a radiant youth, with curls of hair gently lapping about his face and at the base of his neck, this Christ-figure embodied those facial characteristics familiar to viewers as belonging to the divine Apollo, but simultaneously reminiscent of other types: idealized portraits of long-haired young men that had such Greek heroes as Achilles as their models, and – particularly popular in the later third century – romanticized images of pagan philosophers, who were recalled in literature as not only wise but also beautiful (Zanker 1996: 299). All of these thematic strands may be seen in the polished marble surface of Christ's cheek: turned slightly to the viewer, the smooth marble surface is contrasted with the woolly beards of both Peter and Paul, the disciples between whom the young Christ is seated.

The Christ-figure on the sarcophagus is presented to command the viewer's attention in other ways: with his left hand he clasps a scroll, attribute of his wisdom

Figure 21.2 Maskell Passion Ivories. c. AD 420–30. Italy. © The Trustees of the British Museum.

and authority; and with his right he serenely reaches forward to strike the ancient gesture of instruction (the lower limb now lost). Over the next centuries, countless other examples of this beardless, quietly poised but commanding Christ-figure would be found in various media, including fresco, sculpture, and mosaic, testifying to its wide use across the early Christian and medieval periods in a range of visual contexts. Indeed, it is this face (to be discussed further below) that *c.* AD 420–30 an ivory carver in Rome would choose to accompany the body of Christ shown triumphantly nailed to the cross in what is the earliest surviving depiction of the Crucifixion in a narrative context (fig. 21.2).

Early Christian Art Redefined

Our knowledge of early Christianity and its art has, of course, grown exponentially since Ghiberti's time; but certain assumptions about the beliefs and practices of the early Christians remain firmly entrenched in the mainstream of history – not least, the indefatigable theory of early Christian antipathy toward the visual arts. Both Greco-Roman culture itself and the formal structures of the earliest Christian communities developed in an image-rich environment. Images formed an integral part of daily life at all levels: the religious (relief and freestanding sculpture, votive figures, private amulets); the civic and political (mosaic, statuary, paintings, and coins); and everywhere in the personal and domestic spheres (from jewelry, seals, and clothing to furniture, pottery, and wall paintings within the home). Yet, for reasons that remain unclear, Christians were slow to utilize art as a means of expressing their own religious beliefs, embellishing their own rituals, or illustrating their own stories. Despite attempts to identify crosses or other symbols as clear visual marks of Christian faith in the first and second centuries, no unequivocally Christian works of art survive from before the third century (Spier 2007).

Can this apparent absence be attributed to antipathy? From surviving archaeological and literary evidence, the most that can presently be said about the origins of Christian art is that *c.* AD 200 there seems to have been an urge toward decoration among nascent Christian communities in various parts of the empire where Christianity had gained a foothold – not just in Rome, as was once assumed (Murray 1977 and 1982: 171; Finney 1994: 109; Weitzmann 1979: introduction). The earliest Christian art drew on pagan traditions for its technique and style, expressing itself in imagery that could include purely decorative motifs as well as typical pagan mythological figures. Hence iconographically the earliest phase of Christian art is often viewed as a recognizable subcategory of late Roman art, and is indeed often indistinguishable from contemporary pagan art (Jensen 2000: 15).

Even after the fourth century, clear identification of Christian art can be problematic, unless there is certainty about the context of discovery. It is not always possible to tell whether particular figures (the philosopher, the shepherd and the *orant*, for example) or symbols (the dove, the fish, even the cross) have a Christian significance. One perplexing example is the late fourth-century portrait of a man rendered in *opus sectile* in the hall of an opulent house excavated at the Porta Marina, Ostia (fig. 21.3). Found on a wall within a decorative program of apparently pagan imagery, including panels depicting animals in combat with circus lions, the identity of the man remains open to fervent debate. For, while important iconographic features might distinguish him as Christ – the nimbus, the beard, the raised right hand – these could also be the attributes of the philosopher in antiquity. The question remains open: is this Christ blessing a Christian congregation in a fourth-century meeting house in Ostia; or is the man a philosopher, making the gesture of instruction?

The early Christians were neither dismissive of the "noble inventions" of the ancients, nor hesitant in utilizing them for their own pictorial and educational needs. By comparing two images – a fragment from a Roman sarcophagus dated *c.* AD 280 (fig. 21.4) representing a Roman amateur philosopher (Zanker 1996: 277–8) and the similarly enthroned Christ at the center of the sarcophagus of Junius Bassus (fig. 21.1) – we are led to understand how a primary set of visual attributes could be used to indicate the leadership role of an individual and his learned status in the ancient world. A number of large and highly elaborate Roman sarcophagi from the later third century illustrate the extent to which certain individuals were publicly recognized as valuing intellectual pursuits and living according to the precepts of the ancient philosophers; and this fragment serves as a particularly fine example. Borrowing both the frontality used in imperial monuments for the representation of the

Figure 21.3 Christ/Philosopher. 3rd century AD. Opus sectile. Museo Ostiense, Ostia, Italy. akg-images/Erich Lessing.

emperor, and the visual symbolism associated with the philosopher, they illustrate the extent to which the inference of rigorous philosophical training had become essential in conveying the superior status and authority of the deceased. The prestige accorded to learning, especially philosophical learning, helped to convey the authority of the individual concerned. Christians needed to draw, and did draw, on this symbolism, to present their own leader in a recognizable guise: that of a figure who promised salvation through learning, but who also worked miracles.

Nor was this power confined to the temporal order. On the "amateur philosopher" sarcophagus, two muses flank the central figure, who, with a contemplative expression, pauses from reading the scroll open on his lap and turns his head away from the eye of the viewer to gaze intently into the distance. His feet are placed slightly askance, with scrolls accumulating at his side – a direct allusion to his intellectual pursuits and superiority. The feet of Christ on the Junius Bassus sarcophagus (fig. 21.1) are similarly parted and unevenly placed on either side of the head of the god Coelus, representing cosmic dominion. Christ is also enthroned, his own scroll folded and held in one hand so that he might make the gesture of instruction. His apostles stand looking at him with the same intent as the philosopher's muses. Christ is shown with the same thoughtful expression, his head turned slightly to the right; Peter and Paul might very well be an amalgam of muse and co-philosopher, Paul

Figure 21.4 Sarcophagus of Plotinus (so called). Late 3rd–4th century AD. Marble. Fragment. Museo Gregoriano Profano, Musei Vaticani. ©1990. Photo Scala, Florence.

shown clasping his own scroll. Christians were, in other words, remarkably astute in their appropriation of a visual language for their own ends.

In the fourteenth and fifteenth centuries, however, the age of Ghiberti and Dürer, the body of art that we now use to judge the interests and skills of the earliest Christian patrons and artists was still to be discovered and assembled. Early Christian marble sarcophagi, for instance, were not well known and rarely drawn, prior to the discoveries from the Vatican cemetery under St. Peter's in 1590–2. And although the Roman catacombs were discovered roughly a decade earlier, in 1578, illustrations of their ceiling and wall frescoes were not circulated until several decades later, by pioneering Christian archaeologist Antonio Bosio. While Bosio produced a folio of exquisitely detailed drawings (including one of the Junius Bassus sarcophagus), it was not published until 1632, three years after his death.

So, while Ghiberti's unfavorable assessment of "early Christian" art was, by contrast, limited to what is now categorized as early Byzantine art – that still much maligned and aesthetically discredited development of late antique style – we know that in Rome, at least, there were enough physical remnants of early Christianity to exert an influence on practicing artists in the late sixteenth century. In addition to the discovery and very public display of the Junius Bassus sarcophagus in 1595, there followed a decade of further archaeological discoveries associated with extensive excavations of early Christian monuments in Rome. Hence, many representations of Christ like the one on the Junius Bassus sarcophagus were known or at least available to artists working in Rome by the late sixteenth century.

Among these was Caravaggio, who appears to have held the type in his mind when working on his portrayal of the youthful, resurrected Christ in a painting of the *Supper at Emmaus* executed in Rome in 1601. Caravaggio seats the beardless Apollo-Christ at the center of the composition, behind a table, the long curls and smooth round cheeks of his youth still evident. The painter retains the original gesture that the Bassus Christ presumably once made, although now missing: the right arm extended and the hand raised in a gesture of instruction. Yet, Caravaggio takes the pose further than the Junius Bassus type, drawing the forearm out over the table to sanctify the food – a salient reminder that many iconographic developments and experimentations in later European art have their origins in the early Christian tradition as it emerged in the rich cultural crucible that was the Late Roman Empire.

Fading of the Dark Ages

Given the depth of hostility toward the early Christians in the beginnings of modern art-historical scholarship, it is difficult to fathom how a gradual overturning of the anti-Christian view was accomplished. Its persistence long after Vasari, in scholarly accounts of the fall of the Roman Empire, insured that early Christian art, in studies of artistic developments in western Europe, would be forcefully subsumed within the postclassical artistic morass that Ghiberti set so firmly aside as belonging to a middle or "dark" age. The reflections of Edward Gibbon and the more recent analysis of the Arch of Constantine by Bernard Berenson (1954) illustrate just how strong the "Dark Age" momentum was, and how firmly entrenched in scholarly opinion it has been (fig. 21.5; I shall discuss the Arch further below). It has taken a succession of scholars across several generations to loosen Ghiberti's period divisions and set the art of Late Antiquity into its own place, just as medieval and Byzantine art came only slowly to be valued in its own right. And it is this process of revising the significance of late antique and early Christian art that is itself worth briefly reviewing.

For late antique art specifically, this loosening began with a vibrant polemic conducted between two members of a "Vienna School" of art history, Alois Riegl (1858–1905) and Josef Strzygowski (1862–1941). Both scholars established new methods and patterns of interpreting Roman art and the so-called medieval and Byzantine art that emerged by the sixth century. Riegl, along with Franz Wickhoff (see Von Hartel and Wickhoff 1895) argued for the Roman origin of the late antique style (Riegl 1901). Strzygowski, on the other hand, argued that style changed in Late Antiquity as a result of Semitic or oriental influence (see Strzygowski 1901, which followed a dissertation on the iconography of the baptism of Christ, 1885, and a study of the Byzantine sources of Cimabue, 1888).

Their debate hinged on a shift of emphasis: the historical period between the late third century and the sixth could be read as an age of transformation of the classical heritage, as opposed to one of decline. One means of illustrating this was examination

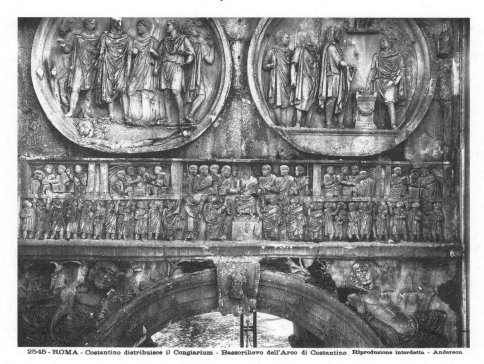

2545 - ROMA - Costantino distribuisce il Congiarium - Bassorilievo dell'Arco di Costantino. Riproduzione interdetta - Anderson

Figure 21.5 Arch of Constantine. c. AD 315. Detail: north facade, the *Congiarium*, or Distribution of Largess. Rome, Italy. Archivi Alinari, Florence.

of ancient religious images and myths and their continuing impact on post-antique visual and intellectual culture. This emerged at the turn of the twentieth century as one of the most important, but complex and potentially confusing, themes in writing the history of western civilization. The history of art in the late antique period was thus effectively established as an academic discipline in its own right, and "Late Antiquity" then first emerged as a clearly definable art-historical period (Elsner 2002). It was Ernst Kitzinger who introduced to an English-speaking audience the methods associated with this Vienna School, and continued to use them himself (Kitzinger 1955, 1977).

Elsewhere, almost contemporaneously with Riegl and Strzygowski, the careful exposure of a broader continuity of tradition, from antiquity through to its recovery in fifteenth-century Italy, was under way at the hands of cultural historian Aby Warburg (1866–1929) and his followers, including Fritz Saxl (1890–1948), Erwin Panofsky (1892–1968), and Edgar Wind (1900–71). Instead of the strenuous study of forms associated with the Vienna School, Warburg espoused the iconographic method. Pointing to the use of classical motifs and themes in representations of Christian subjects and to the repeated lapses into classical style that occurred across the Middle Ages, including the emperor Charlemagne's very deliberate revival (Weitzman 1979: 2), Warburg and his associates revealed that the pagan gods had survived, both in people's memory and in their imagination. They determined that an essential difference between the Middle Ages and the Renaissance resided in a general change in attitude toward antiquity: the former "accepted and developed rather than studied and restored the heritage of the past" (Panofsky 1955: 26). If this was accurate, the judgments of Ghiberti, Alberti, and Vasari were, at best, half-truths. Panofsky argued that they were right insofar as the attitude toward antiquity was changed in the Renaissance; but they were wrong in believing that there was a clear severance between classical antiquity and the Middle Ages (Panofsky 1955: 67–8).

As this scholarship gathered momentum, the traditional antithesis between cultur- ally stagnant Middle Ages and artistically brilliant Italian Renaissance began to diminish. In the introduction to his book *La Survivance des dieux antiques*, French scholar Jean Seznec was able to demonstrate that the "Dark Age" epithet was becoming less and less relevant (Seznec 1940). While Seznec had nurtured an interest in the visual arts, he had no professional training in art history. His singular achieve- ment was providing for a general audience a rich discussion of mythology in Late Antiquity and the Middle Ages, and an account of what became of the ancient gods after the fall of Rome and the rise of Christianity. Seznec's book is, essentially, a vibrant, elegantly written and indeed compelling synthesis of the work of Warburg, Saxl, and Panofsky. Translated into English thirteen years after its original publication in French, *La Survivance* became pivotal in the gradual overturning of "Dark Age" vocabulary more widely. It thereby made one of the most significant contributions to the understanding of the art of the Middle Ages and the Renaissance.

The title of Seznec's book – in its English translation, *The Survival of the Pagan Gods* – implied a new account of the relationship between early Christian art and classical antiquity. Was early Christianity in fact a conduit through which Greco- Roman ideals were passed to artists of subsequent generations, or was it the instru- ment that insured those ideals were lost? Following the methods established by his more prominent predecessors, Seznec examined the intellectual and imaginative lives of thinkers and artists in the ten centuries before the Renaissance. "The essential function of the visual image," he wrote, "which plays so important a part in this book, is the summing up of trends or currents of thought" (Seznec 1940, tr. Sessions 1953: 7). By his own admission, he selected and analyzed images mostly on the basis of their role as documents and witnesses, not on the basis of style or form. Iconog- raphy, he argued, serves as a constant auxiliary to the study of the history of ideas.

If, as Warburg, Saxl, Panofsky, Seznec and others had suggested, the traditional boundaries of art history could thus be pushed, just as the boundaries between the "megaperiods" (as Panofsky called them) within art history could be blurred, there were new possibilities for the definition of late antique art, for its study, and thus for the recognition of its broad significance in the understanding of western European art history. And that was certainly what Riegl, Stryzgowski, and successors had envisaged, each using his favored methods.

The Warburg-influenced study of the continuing impact of ancient religious images and myths on post-antique visual and intellectual culture was focused very little on early Christian art. Yet Saxl, who directed the Warburg Institute after Abby Warburg's death in 1929 and presided over its transfer to London in 1934, displayed a keen awareness of Christianity's importance in the transition of classical art into Late

Figure 21.6 Church of Santa Pudenziana: apse mosaic. Late 4th–early 5th century AD. Rome, Italy. akg-images/Andrea Jemolo.

Antiquity and the medieval period. In a lecture delivered at the Courtauld Institute in January 1944, four years after the publication of Seznec's book, Saxl took pains to emphasize the importance of beginning with the early Christian period in order to understand medieval art. The subject of his lecture was "Pagan and Jewish Elements in Early Christian Sculpture," a synthesis of the kind more commonly found today, and he highlighted the basic premise of German scholarship in this field: that there were bonds linking pagan and Christian art, the former essential to an understanding of the latter (Saxl 1957: 45–6).

Their successors in the field of early Christian art history drew on these insights, which included an observed connection between the post-Constantinian images of Christ and the iconography that developed in Roman imperial art of the fourth century for the representation of the emperor. We can return to the Arch of Constantine to see how this theory works: the hieratic presentation of the emperor amid his adoring retinue that we find in that frieze (fig. 21.5) is seen to influence near-contemporary images of Christ that emerged in the fourth century, particularly as they survive on sarcophagi. Within the same symmetrical composition, the same iconographic devices were used to denote Christ as the center (enthroned, elevated, and depicted on a larger scale), the same gestures of adoration taken from the emperor's subjects and given to the apostles. In mosaic (fig. 21.6) and in the minor arts too (fig. 21.7), the repetitive format of disciples lined uniformly on either side of

Figure 21.7   Engraved gem (intaglio). Mid-4th century AD. Carnelian. Syria(?). © The Trustees of the British Museum.

Christ to offer adoration could be adapted to a variety of other situations, as we shall see below.

The continuity with the classical tradition, explored through this evolutionary approach to iconography, was expressed in the 1977 exhibition and symposium organized by Kurt Weitzman (with Margaret Frazer) at the Metropolitan Museum of Art: "The Age of Spirituality: Late Antique and Early Christian Art, Third to Seventh Century." Weitzmann introduced the exhibition as follows:

> The transition from the dying classical to the rising and finally triumphant Christian culture was a complex process, extending over several centuries, in which the two coexisted and competed with each other. Christianity owed much of its ultimate success to the fact that it outgrew its Jewish heritage and adopted many elements from the very classical culture it had set out to dethrone. (Weitzmann 1979: xix)

Philosopher-Christ, Emperor-Christ

Within this increasing tendency to trace an evolutionary iconographical development from the earliest Christian images to later monumental art, there was a stress on how imperial imagery superseded iconography first seen in the catacombs, portraying Christ as philosopher and teacher. As I have already said, the gesture of instruction, made by the two figures on the far left of the "amateur philosopher" sarcophagus fragment (fig. 21.4) and by the Ostian man, was taken by the Christians and given to their teacher (for we assume this was the gesture made by Christ on the front of the Junius Bassus sarcophagus). In time, of course, it became a gesture of blessing: even in the apse of the church of Santa Pudenziana in Rome (fig. 21.6), where the scroll has become a codex, open to display specific text (the dedication of the church), the gesture implies something more than speech.

The identification of an evolving portrait type for Christ, from philosopher to emperor, was designed in part to explain the transition of Christian art from the catacombs to the basilicas where, in mosaics of the fourth century, Christ is clearly distinguished from his retinue by the use of various pictorial conventions, such as scale, strict frontality of presentation, expression (Christ looking directly at the viewer), posture, and dress (enthroned in regal, imperial fashion), all associated with imperial representations. That imagery was also taken to suggest that early Christian art and its iconography had an inextricable thematic relationship with Roman imperial iconographic schemes of victory and triumph (Grabar 1936; L'Orange 1965). But not all scholars have since agreed. The extent to which imperial prototypes were sought and used by early Christians became a point of particular contention with the publication of Thomas Mathews' forceful rejection of what he dubbed the *Kaisermystik* theory (Mathews 1993). Using the Santa Pudenziana apse mosaic as an example (fig. 21.6), Mathews argued that the late antique iconography of the philosopher, and with it the concept of the divine "holy man," received more emphasis in early Christian art than did the imperial imagery appealed to by Grabar and others.

While Mathews asserted a vital point about the multivalent nature of artistic influence on the representation of Christ, a point communicated in the "Age of Spirituality" exhibition and the symposium papers (Weitzmann 1979 and 1980), there should be no doubt about the influence of imperial iconography on early Christian art. This fact has been argued most cogently in more recent times by, among others, Paul Zanker. Through a meticulous study of sculpture in the ancient world, he has demonstrated that what we find on early Christian sarcophagi is in fact a highly nuanced blending of the received traditions of both imperial imagery and the iconography of the intellectual. Zanker argues that this blending had in fact begun on pagan Roman sarcophagi, but was continued by Christians for the depiction of Christ precisely because they needed a visual language that would express not simply the wisdom but also the divinity of the Son of God (Zanker 1996: 304–5). The Santa Pudenziana apse mosaic, dated to *c.* AD 390 and one of the earliest apses to be designed for a Roman church, in fact illustrates this very point.

If we look closely at the mosaic, we do find Christ enthroned, arrayed in golden garments, in a setting redolent of imperial splendor. Yet the attributes of throne and material riches are not merely indicative of imperial status, or peculiar to the pretensions of the later Roman emperors to universal dominion, as expressed in imperial art. Here is unmistakable evidence that, rather than a straightforward and intentional progression from philosopher to emperor (or a vacillation between the two), the philosopher type coexisted in Christian art of the fourth and fifth centuries alongside the new imperial image of Christ. The nimbus around the head of Christ might evoke the pagan gods, who were sometimes shown thus in Roman and late antique art, but so were philosophers (witness the Ostian man). What is new in the later period is the use of gesture: the gestures given to and the attitudes struck by Christ and each of the apostles in that mosaic are participatory in a way that they had not been before, and draw the viewer into the image in a way that the Constantinian friezes, for example, or those assemblies of the apostles around Christ on third-century sarcophagi or cata-comb frescoes, do not. That had not been their intention. But now, the distance between the protagonists of the Santa Pudenziana mosaic and the onlooker are energetically erased, and the congregation becomes part of the philosophical assem-bly, part of this celestial setting, and so beholders of the heavenly, enthroned Christ.

Toward a "Truly Religious" Christian Art

Saxl noted in his 1944 lecture that the earliest Christian works developed in pagan surroundings but that, by the fourth century, what he termed "truly religious" Christian groups of sculpture were created. He was referring to two groups of early Christian sarcophagi: those illustrating episodes from the Passion narratives; and those illustrating the institution of the Church, with the apostles pictured assembled around Christ, shown holding an open codex or scroll, instructing them in the new law. Both themes are presented in the apse at Santa Pudenziana: Christ is shown in the process of discourse, giving the law to the apostles, schooling them as they gather around him in what is probably intended to be a celestial setting, the heavenly Jerusalem, depicted by what are arguably Constantinian buildings in Jerusalem at the time. A glorious jeweled cross rises behind him, and the symbol of the sacrificial lamb was originally shown at his feet (Mathews 1993: fig. 72). This compositional type – Christ at the apex of his assembled apostles – could be experimented with easily, the central figure changed slightly without altering the general meaning of the scene.

The bulk of the evidence for such experimentation survives from sarcophagi, as Saxl was aware, and includes the series of so-called "star and wreath" sarcophagi – on the friezes of which the apostles approach the cross, bearing wreaths or raising their hands in veneration. A contemporary variant saw the cross replaced with the figure of Christ seated (as he is on the Junius Bassus sarcophagus and in the apse mosaic of Santa Pudenziana) or standing to deliver the new law, the *traditio legis*. An important example is now in the Musée Réattu, Arles, and is dated *c.* AD 380. It shows the apostles processing toward the cross, scrolls in hand, stars above their heads; and upon the cross the apostles Peter and Paul place a large victory wreath (Mathews 1993: fig. 126). The Pudenziana mosaic might in fact present a development of this theme for a public, monumental context, as opposed to a private, funerary one. Yet, experimentation with the compositional format and with the theme of celestial acclaim offered by the apostles either to the aniconic representation of Christ as victor (in the form of the triumphal cross) or to Christ himself, evidently took place in other contexts within the minor arts at an earlier date, and in unexpected ways. This is attested in the case of a rare carnelian gemstone, now in the British Museum, which can be dated to the middle of the fourth century (fig. 21.7), and about which more will be said below. Yet here we must note that with a small change to the central iconographic unit, the acclaim of Christ the philosopher or eternal ruler becomes the acclaim of the crucified but triumphant Christ – a defiant figure standing against his cross and depicted twice the size of his apostles.

In the fourth century, therefore, when new modes of visual narration were supposedly arising and thus facilitating the depiction of narrative stories in Christian art, it was often the old modes and pagan iconographic types that were reused and adapted to say something new. Particular compositional formats, such as the emperor flanked by his retinue and in the act of distributing largesse to his people, ultimately provided Christians with a key template for their own experimentation with the visual representation of Christ himself, with more complex theological themes, and even text-based subjects. Critically, this includes those subjects that previously, scholars have argued, were omitted from early Christian art, precisely because artists had no iconographic precedents for them. This is nowhere more evident than in the still controversial case of the Crucifixion, an image famously central to Christian devotion, yet strikingly rare in early Christian art. Indeed, the London Crucifixion gem furnishes a remarkably fine instance that illustrates definitively both continuity and change, both the survival of pagan iconography and the paradoxically concurrent emergence of Christian innovation.

The Case of the Crucifixion

The earliest extant example of a visual reference to the Crucifixion is the third-century wall *graffito*, excavated on the Palatine Hill, Rome, in 1856 (Harley 2007: 227, fig. 2). It depicts a man, with the head of a donkey, affixed to a cross and hailed by a man who stands in the foreground striking the standard Greco-Roman gesture of acclamation. An accompanying inscription reads "Alexamenos worships his God." The drawing is thus traditionally interpreted as a parody of the Christian worship of a crucified deity, and it has been used to forward the theory that Christians deliberately chose not to portray the Crucifixion. Interestingly, it has a literary counterpart in the image of Jesus erected in Carthage around AD 197, described by Tertullian, which confirms both that the early Christians were accused of worshiping an ass and that caricature images of Christianity and its tenets were being executed around the turn of the third century.

Certainly, as the preaching of Christ crucified by Paul attests, and as the discussions of the early church fathers illustrate, the early church was focused on the fact and soteriological significance of the Crucifixion. Although images of the Crucifixion are rare among extant material evidence from the early Christian material, there are three highly unconventional images that have survived on engraved gems (Harley 2007: 228–9, cat. nos. 55 and 56). Together with the Palatine *graffito*, the gems constitute a small but critical body of evidence testifying to the use of individual episodes from the Passion narrative as isolated images by the mid fourth century. One example is the carnelian intaglio in London, which is from the eastern part of the Roman Empire (possibly Syria), and was originally used as a personal seal (fig. 21.7).

The gem features a depiction of Christ nude, his arms stretched out below the *patibulum* of the cross, his head and feet turned in profile to the left but his body shown in strict frontality. Christ is flanked on either side by six diminutive apostles, who process toward him in the same ceremonious and symmetrical format as seen on the Arch of Constantine – where the figure of the emperor is also shown at the axis of the composition, in strict frontality. Above Christ's head is engraved the word ΙΧθΥC (*ichthys*), meaning "fish" in Greek but signifying in acrostic form "Jesus Christ, Son of God, Saviour" (*Iêsous Christos, theou uios, sôtêr*).

As I have noted, the composition utilizes pictorial devices familiar from late antique imperial art. Yet, the iconography bears a striking resemblance to those iconographic formats developed in the later fourth century for the acclamation of Christ, and specifically on the series of Roman "star and wreath" sarcophagi. As it is seen on the gem, therefore, the visual reference to the story of Christ's Crucifixion is made to suggest an interpretation of that story's significance, rather than its narration per se, the symbolism referring specifically to Christ's triumph and to the apostles as witnesses to his ministry. The iconography thus suggests a high degree of familiarity with the textual content of the Crucifixion story and its meaning within the early church. It also indicates a willingness to experiment with the visual expression of that knowledge at an earlier date than is still customarily acknowledged.

While episodes from the Passion narrative were developed for inclusion on a specific class of Christian sarcophagi between AD 340 and 370 (including the crowning with thorns, Pilate washing his hands of guilt, and Simon of Cyrene carrying the cross), the Crucifixion itself was not depicted (Harley 2006). The absence is particularly perplexing, both in light of the earlier representations that survive on the gemstones, including the London intaglio (fig. 21.7) – indicating that artists were capable of experimenting with the subject – and in view of the fact that the sarcophagi were probably created in the fourth century and later, after the conversion of Constantine and the end of Christian persecution. One possible explanation is that, while compositions as preserved on the London stone were realizable, the symbolic cross surmounted by a victory wreath – as found at the center of many "star and wreath" sarcophagi, evoking both the Crucifixion and Christ's triumph in the Resurrection – was in practice theologically preferable to a literal depiction of Christ crucified (Harley 2007: 227).

Only two representations of the crucifixion are known from the fifth century, most notably the panel that appears on the carved wooden doors of the church of Santa Sabina, Rome (*c.* AD 432; Harley 2007: 227, fig. 1). There, a bearded Christ stands crucified between two diminutive thieves against the backdrop of the walls of Jerusalem. The other image occurs on one of the four ivory panels that as a series, illustrate scenes of the Passion and Resurrection. These were once part of the private collection of the liturgical scholar William Maskell, and are among the most important minor art works to have survived from the early Christian period (fig. 21.2).

Probably made in Rome *c.* AD 420–30 in a workshop that was also producing consular diptychs for pagan customers, the so-called Maskell ivories are exquisitely carved in high relief with a sequential cycle of seven episodes; it is the first time in early Christian art that the Passion is represented as a cohesive passage from arrest to

Crucifixion, culminating in the Resurrection. Yet, the message asserted is not the suffering and death of Jesus but both his triumph and that of the Church. The ivories probably once constituted the four sides of a small box, perhaps commissioned and used by a wealthy individual or church community, either for the storage of a relic or as a container for the consecrated host. In craftsmanship and sophistication of design, they are an exceptionally fine example of the high standard of ivory carving achieved in Rome during the early fifth century.

If we look closely at the series, we discern the use of classical technique and style to illustrate an emergent Christian iconography, similar to that noted above in the case of the sarcophagus of Junius Bassus. The narrative reads across the four panels from left to right. It begins on the first panel with a depiction of Pilate washing his hands, Christ carrying his own cross (John 19: 17), and Peter denying Christ. Each episode draws on iconographic conventions developed for the representation of these particular episodes as self-contained stories on Passion sarcophagi. Yet here, a lucid passage from one event to the next is achieved through the deft placement of figures, careful direction of their gaze, and skillful use of gesture. The artist is thus capable of illustrating several pictorial elements within each episode to evoke both the fuller text and the wider significance of each event, without sacrificing pictorial coherence across the surface of the panel as a whole. The image of Christ, striding forward and carrying his own cross (John 19: 17) forms a striking and pivotal unit with the soldier who turns compassionately toward him, taking his shoulder with his right hand and ushering him forward with his left. The Latin cross, which symbolically dominates the center of this composition, is processional in size, but is of the same form (having flared ends) as the larger cross in the next panel, on which Jesus is shown nailed.

In the second relief, the suicide of Judas (Matt. 27: 5) is juxtaposed with a scene at the cross in what is a remarkable visual interpretation of Christ's death. The limpness of Judas' body (the neck broken, head cricked backwards, eyes closed, the flaccid hands and feet), is powerfully discordant with the vitality of Christ's taut body (the neck upright, head erect, eyes open, hands open, feet flexed firmly upward). As a result of the juxtaposition in this pictorial context, various dramatic tensions and paradoxes are explored by the artist. These cut across the image to articulate gracefully both of Christ's natures, the human and the divine: the nails and the lance, yet the open eyes and vibrancy of body; the human shape but divine appearance (muscled, yet nimbate); the demise of Judas and the new life forecast in the bird's nest in the tree and born of his betrayal; the coins symbolizing both the betrayal and the victory subsequently won on the cross.

Perhaps the most striking feature of the Crucifixion is the peculiar vigor conveyed by the artist in his representation of the youthful body of an apparently living and quiescent Jesus on the cross, flanked by his mother and John on one side, and a soldier on the other (John 19: 26–7). His eyes are wide open and looking intensely, yet his gaze is not directed at the viewer. Like the young Christ on the Junius Bassus sarcophagus, the head of this crucified Savior is turned fractionally to his right, so that he looks past the viewer and out of his physical condition on the cross. He is shown rigidly *en face*, as though standing defiantly against the cross and voluntarily unfolding his arms flat against the *patibulum*. His hands are stretched out and shown quite flat, unflinching at the nails penetrating the midst of the palms. His legs and feet are placed purposefully, side by side. A plain nimbus now encircles his head, as it does again in the fourth panel, emphatically pointing to the fact that Christ's indomitable divinity is shown forth on the cross and further revealed in the Resurrection.

The figures in this series conform to the rather stocky style associated with art of the Roman period and seen on the Arch of Constantine; and other pictorial elements betray the Roman artistic milieu in which these ivories were produced. They include, for example, the well-proportioned and somewhat idealized physique that the artist has carefully and quite explicitly portrayed: Jesus wears only the very narrow loincloth or *subligaculum*, shown pulled in around the waist to accentuate from side view the curve of the buttocks; the flesh creases of the groin are very deliberately rendered, as is the shapely musculature of his body. This is an athletic or heroic display of nudity of the kind understood in the Roman world as a mark of superior status – and, interestingly, seen in the earlier representation of the Crucifixion on the London gem (fig. 21.7). This interpretation is borne out in the juxtaposition of Jesus' strong, victorious, and semi-naked body with the fully clothed and unmistakably dead figure of Judas.

The third relief depicts just one scene and is dominated at its center by a sepulcher. Conventional early Christian iconography of the women visiting Christ's place of burial on Easter morning tends to follow the Gospel narratives in depicting them approaching the tomb, usually in the presence of an angel and sometimes watched by soldiers. Here, two grieving women are shown seated, wrapped in their *maphoria* (as Mary is at the Crucifixion scene) and hunched in sorrow, one on either side of the sepulcher. They face inward and are beautifully contrasted with the pair of sleeping soldiers depicted in the foreground, facing but leaning away from the tomb, sprawled out lazily on their shields and lances (both of which are broken). The doors of the tomb are ajar, one having burst open and splintered under the force of the Resurrection to reveal an empty strigillated Roman sarcophagus inside. There is further iconographic evidence here attesting both to the artist's knowledge of pictorial traditions in the funerary art of classical antiquity and to his ability in deftly modifying them in order to interpret specifically Christian stories. For example, Kötzsche has demonstrated that the hunched posture and introspective sorrow-filled mien of each woman, with hand raised either to chin or cheek, repeats the *topos* of the mourning female figure at the tomb (or grave) in the pagan tradition. Moreover, the iconography of the tomb with its doors open was one of the most common funerary motifs in Roman art, symbolizing the passage of the soul into the afterlife (Kötzsche 1994).

Finally, at the compositional axis of the fourth panel is the triumphant Christ, standing on a podium flanked by two disciples on either side. The open gesture made by his left arm is one of speech, from the same vocabulary as that hand sign we have noted in the representation of philosophers and of Christ. Yet here, it is a gesture impelled outward with the energy of the whole body, the palm now open and Christ shifting his weight onto his right foot to impel his arm upward above his head, as though engaged in active discourse with his disciples. Yet the movement has another function, being simultaneously a means of revealing the wound in his side to the diminutive figure of the doubting Thomas. Hence, amid the shift of drapery that occurs as Christ moves and raises his arm, the deliberate parting in his pallium cleverly provides a sliver of flat background against which the carefully modeled hand and pointed finger of Thomas can be set. The panel is thus a powerful evocation of both Thomas's skepticism, recounted in John 20: 24–8, and of Matthew 28: 16–20, where the risen Christ both commissions the apostles and faces doubters. Its composition is essentially a redaction and subtle adaptation of the Roman *traditio legis* iconography, in which Christ is shown handing the new law to the apostles – a version of which appears of course on the Junius Bassus sarcophagus. For this pictorial context, the customary attribute of the scroll or book must be dispensed with, and the left arm raised to expose the wound.

Conclusion

As these two case studies attest – the representations of the Crucifixion, and the Passion scenes on the Maskell ivories – the question of how late Roman artists utilized the pictorial language of Roman art to illustrate the events described in the Christian Bible remains key in appreciating the creativity that is to be found in the earliest Christian art. Certainly, Christian iconography begins as a recognizable subcategory of late Roman art, adopting stock pagan figures, motifs, and symbols. But something radically new also comes into existence. Just as the "darkness" of the Middle Ages gradually came to wane, so the influence of an illustrious art-historical tradition – interpreting the late Roman period as witnessing the termination of ancient culture (a tradition stretching from Boccaccio to Berenson) – has gradually come to recede.

BIBLIOGRAPHICAL NOTE

For a clear and incisive review of the emergence of late antique art history as a field of study, see Elsner 1998: together with an indispensable bibliographic essay, the book provides the most succinct and successfully integrated survey of the rise of Christian imagery and its continuity with the arts in the Roman Empire, giving an authoritative articulation of what is now the popular thesis: "that the dynamics that motivated the great cultural changes of Late Antiquity already existed within Roman culture, which had long been willing to redefine its present by freely interpreting its past" (Elsner 1998: 3). The catalog from the major 1977 exhibition "Age of Spirituality" (Weitzmann 1979), complemented by the volume of symposium papers (Weitzmann 1980), remain critical resources for studying the art of the Late Roman Empire and the emergence of Christianity, furnishing both seminal analyses of key individual artifacts and monuments and key composite statements about late antique art in general. The imperial, classical, secular, Jewish, and Christian realms into which the exhibition was divided were pioneering, yet controversial at the time. Their significance for the future direction of the field, however, is illustrated by subsequent critical assessment and by the refining of the relationship between those realms over the past thirty years. The fruits of this process are attested in the essays contained in the catalog *Picturing the*

Bible (Spier 2007): drawing on an unprecedented range of objects, it incorporates new historical research and archaeological discoveries. The clearer and deeper understanding of how Christians and Jews of Roman times illustrated their religious beliefs, what these images signified, and the depth of their relationship with Greco-Roman imagery, was made possible by the pioneering work of Murray (1981) and Finney (1994). The insightful work by Jensen (2000, with revised edition forthcoming) is the most accurate and accessible survey of early Christian art available in English.

CHAPTER TWENTY-TWO

The Discourse of Later Latin

Philip Burton

When did Latin become Late?

The history of language is, if anything, even less susceptible to periodization than other kinds of history. The practice of articulating history around key events, such as the conversion of Constantine or the removal of Romulus Augustulus, may play down the fact that these events were the outcome of historical processes lasting centuries, and that many people were doubtless either not aware of these events themselves, or did not feel that they had any particular bearing on their daily lives. Yet this practice continues, no doubt due to the value of these key events as a metonymy for the events leading up to them and the possibility of tracing their implications, however indirect, in later generations.

In tracing the history of a language, such events are much harder to identify. To take a familiar example, the loss of the second person pronoun *thou/thee/thy* in Standard English may be dated to a period around 1550–1650. But the forms remain in use in (increasingly) high literary language until the later nineteenth century, and are still current in many northern varieties of British English, besides being in residual use as a marker of community among Quakers (until recently at least – the difficulty in identifying a cut-off date to this use exemplifies the wider problem); to say nothing of the fact that such forms may still be heard regularly in other contexts, such as productions of Shakespeare, older liturgies, or Bible translations. In recent years linguists have found more and more evidence for a "bell curve" model of language change: specific innovations become common in small groups, spread rapidly through larger populations, then tail off, leaving remnants of the older, displaced forms in use among small groups of speakers. But the terms in which we have put the debate conceal other problems of describing language: to invoke – as we have – the concept of "Standard" English is to make some kind of judgment about the currency of a particular kind of language that would not necessarily be shared by all speakers of the language. And the distinction between "innovation" and "language change" is something that can be made only after the event; for instance, it is too early to say whether, a hundred years from now, the "high rise terminal" (the practice of ending a sentence on a rising tone, particularly associated with Australian and New Zealand English, and popularized in recent years among younger speakers) will be considered by linguists a "language change" in the proper sense.

The same historical and metahistorical questions confront the historian of the Latin language – the tendency toward periodization, the identification and labeling of the periods, and the extent to which contemporary Latin speakers would have been aware of (and agreed with) such distinctions – and the response of Latinists to these questions has varied. Let us take two distinguished examples from the last century. The editors of the *Oxford Latin Dictionary* set their limit at around AD 200, while allowing that this is "necessarily imprecise": they include the third-century jurists quoted in the sixth-century *Digest of Justinian*, but exclude (in parentheses) some significant second-century authors (Minucius Felix, Tertullian) on the ground of their religion: "(A proposal that the Dictionary should be extended to include Christian Latin had been finally rejected in 1951.)" The great Swedish linguist Einar Löfstedt (1959: 1–38) begins his intellectual testament with a lengthy discussion of the problem of periodization, yet even his magisterial account betrays doubts and inconsistencies: "In literature the great Roman tradition ends with Tacitus. Apuleius, born about 125, is already the representative of a different style; shifting, iridescent, borrowing freely from poetry, deliberately archaizing ... Whether we are to make Late Latin start with Apuleius ... or – perhaps more plausibly – to refer it to the age of Tertullian and the earliest martyrologies ... is a question of terminology rather than of substance." Yet, few Latinists would deny to Tacitus the "Apuleian" attributes of poetic borrowing and archaism; and if the starting point for later Latin is purely an arbitrary matter of terminology, how can one starting point be "more plausible" than another?

What emerges from this is a variety of nonlinguistic elements – such as confessional or aesthetic considerations – that tend to condition the identification of later Latin. Often these factors are implicitly linked to a wider sense that by the third century we are in the "late empire," and that therefore – somehow – people should be speaking "late Latin" (for further discussion, see Farrell 2001: 8–13, 85–94). Little would be gained by attempting to impose an alternative chronology or other organizing principle. But it may be worth while noting at the outset, first, the very early date of some "late Latin" phenomena and, second, the mismatch between ancient and modern terminologies, even if this means anticipating some aspects of our later discussion.

Consider, for instance, the famous epitaph on Lucius Scipio, consul in 259 BC:

> L. Cornelio L. f. Scipio | aidiles cosol cesor
> honc oino ploirume cosentiont R[omane]
> duonoro optumo fuise viro
> Luciom Scipione. filios Barbati
> consol censor aidilis hic fuet a[pud vos]

hec cepit Corsica Aleriaque urbe
dedet Tempestatebus aide mereto[d]

(*CIL* 1. 2 (2nd edn. 1918), fasc. 1. 8, 9, p. 379)

Lucius Cornelius Scipio, son of Lucius, aedile, consul, and censor. This man is agreed by most at Rome to have been the best man among the good: Lucius Scipio. The son of Scipio Barbatus, he was consul, censor, and aedile among you; he captured Corsica and the city of Aleria, and dedicated a temple to Storm-gods, as he should.   [This and all other translations my own.]

This is not the place for an exhaustive commentary on all the features of this text, many of which are indeed typical of earlier Latin rather than any later period. Some of them, however, deserve attention. The letter *n* is omitted before *s* in *cosol*, *cesor*, *cosentiont* (though not in the more "classical" *consol*, *censor*). We know from explicit statements in later authors that this was a genuine feature of ordinary pronunciation; but the classical habit of writing the *n* seems to have generated a spelling pronunciation in which the missing sound is restored (compare the variation between Italian *pensare* "to think" and *pesare* "to weigh," both from *pensare*). The final *m* is almost always omitted ("duonorum optumo fuise viro | Luciom Scipione" for classical "bonorum optimum fuisse virum | Lucium Scipionem"). The weakness of the final /m/ is well known, not least through its loss before initial vowels in later poetry; but this poetry also suggests a stronger pronunciation before consonants which is simply not attested here. Noteworthy is also the presence of the letter *e* in the unstressed syllables of *aidiles*, *fuet*, *dedet*, *Tempestatebus* where we would expect a short /i/ (classical *aedilis*, *fuit*, *dedit*, *Tempestatibus*); this too anticipates developments usually associated with the later language. What has happened is that the enormous interest (which we find in the first century BC) in standardizing the Latin language has imposed some very traditional patterns of orthography, effectively reversing, at least in formal educated speech, some very well-established speech habits. The same can be seen in the vocabulary of classical Latin, as compared to that found in earlier and later forms of the language. Thus modern Latin students are compelled to learn the highly irregular verb *ferre* "to carry" (perfect *tuli* "I carried," past participle *latus* "carried"). This verb is absent from the modern Romance languages, being completely displaced by reflexes of classical (and completely regular) *portare*, a verb that seems to have been mildly stigmatized in the classical language (rather like English *to get*, perhaps), while evidently remaining current in the popular speech. Another example often cited is the early Latin verb "to chat," *fabulari*; effectively absent from classical Latin, it resurfaces in the later language (as an archaism? or a vulgarism?) and goes on to give the Spanish and Portuguese verbs "to talk" (*hablar*, *falar*).

This phenomenon, sometimes known as the "classical gap," is one reason why speaking of "late Latin" is so problematic: so many "late" features appear so early. This in turn should lead us to consider the appropriateness of our terminology. There is rather a tendency to regard the phrase "late Latin" as referring to something whose existence and nature is not in doubt. In English, this tendency is reinforced by the convention of capitalizing the adjective; but Romance-speaking scholars also seem to have this inclination, even though the adjective in *latin tardif, latín tardío,* and so on, could be taken as qualifying rather than definitive. German *Spätlatein* has the same drawback as "late Latin." For this reason, it may be helpful to refer to "late" or "later" Latin, terms that are preferred here. They have their disadvantages: while "later" invites the question, "later than what?" (answer: earlier Latin), "late" suggests a language that is moribund, if not actually dead – a description which is highly questionable, and unlikely to occur to actual speakers of the language. But they are at least recognizably close to the familiar terminology, and can be used without making any tacit assumptions about the homogeneity of the language in question.

"Late Latin" in Late Antiquity

But how did real speakers of Latin characterize language change and nonclassical forms? To what extent were they aware of chronological change, and how did they react to it? Explicit statements about language change are found at least from the first century BC onward. Perhaps surprisingly, given the Roman affection for all things old, there is little evidence of a diehard reactionary attitude toward such change. Cicero criticizes those who give their /i/-sounds a value closer to that of /e/; they sound more like harvesters than orators, he says (*De or.* 3. 46). Varro reports how within recent memory the word *novissimus* ("newest," "latest") had come to mean "final," and the older word *aeditumus* ("temple-warden") had been replaced by *aedituus* (*Ling.* 6. 59; *Rust.* 1. 2). It is noteworthy, however, that he does not censure these innovations as such. Of the former he only says that it had been avoided by *some older* speakers on the basis that it was *too* modern; on the latter he comments with mild irony that a usage they had inherited from their fathers was now being "corrected" by "more up-to-date city types [*recentiores urbani*]." The third-century writer Aulus Gellius indeed has a lengthy discussion of the use of obsolete vocabulary as an ornament of rhetoric (*NA* 11. 7); he concludes that it is indicative of two serious faults, bad taste (*cacozêlia*) and adult education (*opsimathia*).

Gellius' comments are typical of the continuing interest in "correct" standards of Latinity. Scattered through the works of various Latin authors we find a range of expressions for sub- or nonstandard speech, most apparently calqued on Greek terms: *sermo rusticus* or *agrestis,* "country speech" (*lexis* or *dialectê agroecê*), opposed to *sermo urbanus* (*lexis asticê*); *sermo humilis,* "low speech" (*lexis tapeinê*), referring to the literary representation of current speech; *sermo plebeius/vulgaris/popularis/publicus,* "popular speech" (*lexis dêmoticê*); *sermo cottidianus,* "daily speech" (*lexis cathêmerinê*); *sermo peregrinus/extraneus/externus,* "foreign speech" (*lexis exôticê*). The exact sense of these terms in their individual context, however, is often frustratingly hard to pin down. The *sermo plebeius* set is a case in point; any of these descriptions may be intended as purely descriptive ("the way people talk") or evaluative ("the way ordinary people who don't know better talk"). Appeal to the Greek models does not always clarify matters, since these may be similarly ambiguous; as is the case, in fact, for *lexis dēmoticē*. Indeed, the Greek origin of much of the Latin sociolinguistic vocabulary is unhelpful, since the Greek vocabulary was itself devised to describe a situation in which one found a variety of local dialects and standards, as well as a diversity of political states – a situation very different to the linguistic and political homogeneity of the Roman Empire.

How do later authors view their position vis-à-vis the classical language? The rise in importance of the grammarian in both the east and the west is an index of the value attached to the correct use of language; successful grammarians could, on occasion, enjoy high-flying careers in their cities and in the wider empire (see Kaster 1988: 99–134). But what is particularly impressive is the general *absence* of awareness of what modern scholarship has regarded as "late Latin"; far more so than one might expect in a conservative and backward-looking literary culture. While there is an awareness of the fact of linguistic change, this seldom translates into an explicit preference for archaism; Servius, in his commentary on the *Aeneid*, repeatedly explains Virgilian uses as being "archaic" (*antiquus*), without commending them to his readers. In later authors expressions such as "debased Latin" or "the Latin of our day" or even "late Latin" are generally hard to find. Though the later grammarians are much concerned with "faults of language" (*vitia sermonis*), these tend to fall into the category of "barbarisms" or "solecisms" – strictly, errors involving individual words and groups of words respectively, though the terms sometimes overlap. Jerome (*c*. AD 340–420), himself a pupil of the great Roman grammarian Donatus, criticizes his ex-friend Rufinus for having used the verb *comparare* (Italian *comprare*, Spanish *comprar*) "to buy" rather than the classical *emere* (not found in Romance) (*Epistula adversus Rufinum* 2. 6; *PL* 23: 447–8); but he regards this purely as a barbarism, comparable to Rufinus' solecistic love of redundancy, rather than a neologism or even a lapse into popular use. Jerome similarly advises his correspondent Laeta to make sure her daughter Paula's education in Latin is not delayed too long, lest "her tongue be corrupted with a foreign accent [*peregrinus sonus*] and her ancestral language vitiated by extraneous faults [*externa vitia*]" (*Ep*. 107. 9). He is also concerned that she should not adopt the silly female habit of "cutting her words in half" (*dimidiata dicere verba*). But there is no criticism of "late" or "recent" usage.

Jerome's contemporary Augustine (AD 354–430) shows a notably more liberal attitude toward nonstandard language. Summarizing his own education, Augustine is scathing of those who avoid the barbarism of dropping the *h* in *homo*, "human" (a pronunciation current for centuries in informal speech), or of saying *inter hominibus*, "amongst humans" (for classical *inter homines*) – these are, he says, merely human laws, not the eternal commandments of God (August. *Conf*. 1. 18. 29). Likewise he defends the use in biblical translation of the plural *sanguines*, "bloods," even though Latin uses the word in the singular only, and of the nonclassical form *ossum*, "bone," for the classical *os*, on the grounds that the latter could be confused with the word *os* meaning "mouth"; African ears, he says, cannot distinguish between long and short vowels (August. *De doctrina Christiana* 4. 10. 24). Elsewhere, he famously defends his own barbarism of using the active form *faenerare*, "to lend on interest," on the ground that the "Latin" deponent *faenerari* was ambiguous, meaning also "to borrow" (August. *Enarrationes in Psalmos* 36. 6. 26). Yet this particular barbarism had been in good literary use since the first century AD.

Underlying Augustine's attitude is a profound awareness of the arbitrary and mutable character of all language; there is no reason why Christians, like any other group, should not have their own idiom. Ironically, this potentially anticlassical manifesto has as its intellectual substructure two key concepts in ancient linguistic thought, namely authority (that is, the practice of the great authors) and custom (the usage of the general community) – both normally associated with conservatism, if not mindless purism. Christian intellectuals were, in fact, quite frequently driven onto the defensive by the nonliterary character of the Latin Bible; but while Augustine's attitude is sometimes summed up in Gregory the Great's refusal to let the oracles of God be confined by the rules of Donatus, this formula by itself does not do justice to Augustine's complex and thoughtful position on the matter.

We have stressed so far the metalinguistic side of the debate. But historical linguistics is the description of specific, attested developments over time. A very brief summary of some of these may be in order (all treated much more fully in Herman 2000 and Väänänen 1981).

Developments in Later Latin

Sounds

1   Vowels

Classical Latin has a system of ten distinct vowels, namely long and short forms of /a/ /e/ /i/ /o/ /u/, plus the diphthongs /au/, /ae/, and (residually) /oe/. The fact that Latin has just five symbols for ten sounds means that changes can be hard to track; long and short /a/, for instance, fall together in a single sound, but this would appear only on the written record in poetry – which is in practice unlikely. Nonetheless, some "spelling mistakes" occur often enough for us to assume that they represent real changes in pronunciation. In stressed syllables, the most common among these are confusion between long /e/ and short /i/ (for instance, *sene* for *sine* "without"), and between long /o/ and short /u/ (*poto* for *puto* "I think"). Among the diphthongs, /au/ had the variant "rustic" pronunciation /o/ (the same as the inherited long /o/) from at least the age of Cicero, whose rival Publius Claudius Pulcer famously adopted the spelling *Clodius*. The sound /ae/ is monophthongized to /e/ (the same as the inherited short /e/) at some point early in the common era.

Vowels in unstressed syllables tended throughout the history of Latin to be less distinctly pronounced, and are often lost altogether, especially in the syllable after the main stress of the word; compare classical Latin *valde* "very much" from *valide*, *saeclum* "age" alongside *saeculum*, *repostus* "stored away" alongside *repositus*. This phenomenon, known as *syncope*, continues in later Latin, though not always predictably. Also unpredictable is the phenomenon of "vowel harmony," by which the vowel in one syllable is "harmonized" to that in an adjacent syllable: thus *passar* "sparrow" for *passer*, *carcar* "prison" for *carcer*, *balanx* "scales" for *bilanx*. In these cases, the presence of an /l/ or /r/ separating the syllables in question seems also to be a conditioning factor.

2 Consonants

The weakness of final /m/ in ante-classical and classical Latin has already been mentioned. Other nonclassical uses include the sporadic "voicing" of /p/ /t/ /c/ to /b/ /d/ /g/, when they occur between vowels (for instance, *pudet* for *putet* "s/he stinks"). The classical Latin /b/ and the classical /w/ (written as *u*) become very close, converging on a /v/ or /β/ sound; the forms *vibo/bivo/vivo/bibo* can all represent classical *bibo* "I drink" or *vivo* "I live." Final stop consonants are dropped, which gives forms like *vale* for *valet* "he can."

Consonant clusters tend to be simplified, sometimes with radical results; Old Latin *subvorsum* "turned upward" gives *sursum*, *sussu*, and ultimately *susu*. Some later texts show the beginnings of *palatalization*, by which the sequence of stop consonant plus the vowel /i/ gains the value of a stop plus affricate (for instance, *zabulus* for *diabolus* "devil," presumably representing a pronunciation /dz/ or similar). With every change, there is always the possibility of "hypercorrection," by which anxious scribes overcompensate for a mistake they are keen to avoid; for instance, *baptidiator* for *baptizator* "baptizer."

Morphology (word forms)

1 Nouns and adjectives

The weakness and eventual loss of the final /m/ had the effect of reducing the number of different case endings for most nouns and adjectives. This is most marked in the first declension, where the nominative, vocative, accusative, and ablative forms fell together as *puella* – identical after the loss of distinction between long and short vowels in word-final syllables. Now, given that the ablative case is most frequently found after prepositions, and given that most common classical Latin prepositions take one case only, the effect of this was a widespread loss of distinction in form between the accusative and ablative cases. This loss of distinction is sometimes called *formal syncretism*. To give a concrete example, in a classical Latin phrase such as *cum discipulo* ("with the student") the preposition is clearly taking the ablative case; but in the same phrase in later Latin it is far less transparently an ablative as opposed to an accusative. Alongside formal syncretism there is often *functional syncretism*, by which it is possible to express the same concept through two different constructions. "A pig from Epicurus' herd" may be expressed as *porcus gregis Epicuri*, *porcus ex grege Epicuri*, or (as Horace puts it) *Epicuri de grege porcus*. This construction is particularly interesting, since it shows how *de* plus ablative could easily take over from the classical genitive case, at first, as here, in partitive constructions, later in possessives. With this we may compare the syncretism between *ad* plus accusative and the dative case with verbs of saying (*dicere ad aliquem* "to say to someone" from Plautus onward) and as a marker of possession (*membra ad duos fratres* "the limbs of two brothers" for *duobus fratribus*, in a later funerary inscription).

Some classical declension patterns seem to cause particular difficulty and tend to be "regularized" in various ways. Nouns of the fifth declension are sometimes recruited to the first (compare the classical alternation between *duritia/durities* "hardness," or *materia/materies* "timber"); nouns of the fourth are sometimes recruited to the second (compare the alternating declension of classical *domus* "house"). Some third declension nouns and adjectives are remodeled through the addition of new suffixes: *ovicula* for *ovis* "sheep," *auricula* for *auris* "ear," *facula* for *fax* "torch." Neuter nouns are often either assimilated to the masculine, or have their plural ending *-a* reanalyzed as the basis for a new feminine singular (compare French *la feuille, la joie* from *folia, gaudia*).

2 Verbs

The later Latin verb is perhaps surprisingly stable, given the very different systems found in modern Romance. Take two of the major changes between Latin and Romance, namely the rise of future tense forms derived from *amare habet* "s/he will love" (for classical *amabit*), and of new perfect tense forms derived from *amatum habet* "s/he has loved" (alongside classical *amavit*). Both developments are adumbrated in the written record, but in no text of any length does either occur with any frequency.

Changes of morphology may, as with nouns, interact with the wider lexical system. Later Latin verbs are more likely to have preverbs, sometimes more than one: for instance, *superelevare* for (*e*)*levare* "to raise up," *adimplere* for (*im*)*plere* "to fill up," *exeligere* for (*se*)*ligere* or (*e*)*ligere* "to choose." The relatively irregular classical third conjugation tends to lose verbs in one of two ways: either by the spread of regular first conjugation intensive verbs built on the same root (such as *cantare* for *canere* "to sing," *pulsare* for *pellere* "to push," *iactare* for *iacere* "to throw"), or by gradual assimilation to the second and fourth declensions (such as *cupire* for *cupere* "to desire," *fugire* for *fugere* "to flee," *fervére* (second) for *férvere* (third)). All these tendencies are already visible in republican Latin. Indeed, it is likely that they are obscured in the record by the first-century standardization of Latin.

Lexis (vocabulary)

Some of the changes discussed under the heading of morphology have clear consequences for the later Latin lexicon. There is also a tendency for "popular" words, often with slightly different senses, to displace the more familiar classical alternatives. So, for instance, *caballus* "nag" is sometimes found in place of *equus* "horse" (compare French *cheval*, Italian *cavallo*), and *bucca* "cheek" in place of *os* "mouth" (French *bouche*, Italian *bocca*). But two general points should be noted. First, lexical change cannot always be described as a contest with eventual "winners" and "losers." What matters also is the degree of acceptance and currency the "winners" acquire. Some changes simply become part of the mainstream language; for instance, *urbs* is displaced by *civitas* (though *urbs* remains in use when reference is to Rome or Constantinople). Other changes retain something of a nonliterary air; *manducare* "to eat" (originally "to munch") is widely attested, but classical (*com*)*edere* also remains common (compare Spanish *comer*). Second, in each case it is important to consider the immediate context of each attestation of a "new" word or sense. It is often said, for instance, that *testa* replaces *caput* as the Latin word for "head," and that this is another slangy usage – originally "pot." But in classical Latin *testa* means "hard outer shell," and can be used of the human skull – a sense that fits well with at least some of the alleged examples of this development.

Sample Passages

How does all this work in practice? We may recall at this point Löfstedt's (1959) statement that Apuleius is the representative of a new *style* of Latin. Though Löfstedt himself did not pursue the matter, there is a difference between purely stylistic change and changes that affect the language as a whole. But in the absence of native speakers of later Latin, we can only rely on the written records that are still extant. Even though these are very diverse (useful anthologies in Rohlfs 1969; Väänänen 1981), the bulk of what survives has done so because of its literary merits or other intellectual interest. In short, surviving documents are likely to be untypical. The second-largest class of material, that of inscriptions, often reaches out to a wider social spectrum, but is itself often formulaic and conventional. For the linguist, then, there is always a tension between the desire for information on the language *as a whole* and the need to recognize in the record those features that are either *peculiar to the writer* or belong to a *generic mode of composition*. Before we consider a typical passage of "vulgar" Latin, let us look at a specimen of high artistic prose from Late Antiquity, Sulpicius Severus' *Life of Martin*, written around AD 400. In the quoted passage, the author, a Gallic aristocrat, describes Martin of Tours' monastery by the River Loire:

(3) aliquamdiu ergo adhaerenti ad ecclesiam cellula usus est: dein cum inquietudinem se frequentantium ferre non posset, duobus fere extra civitatem milibus monasterium sibi statuit. (4) qui locus tam secretus et remotus erat, ut eremi solitudinem non desideraret. ex uno enim latere praecisa montis excelsi rupe ambiebatur, reliquam planitiem Liger fluvius reducto paululum sinu clauserat: una tantum eademque arta admodum via adiri poterat. ipse ex lignis contextam cellulam habebat, multique ex fratribus in eundem modum: (5) plerique saxo superiecti montis cavato receptacula sibi fecerant. (*Vit. Martini* 10. 3–5)

(3) For some time he dwelt in a cell adjacent to the church; then, being unable to bear the tumult caused by the crowds that came to visit him, he established a monastery for himself about two miles out of town. (4) This place was so remote and sequestered that it lacked none of the solitude of the wilderness. On one side it was bounded by a sheer mountain wall. The flat ground on the other sides was locked within a small bend in the river Loire. It could be approached only by a single path, and a very narrow one at that. Martin himself had a cell made of raw timbers woven together, and many of the brothers had similar ones; (5) most, however, had made dens for themselves in the hollow formed by the overhanging mountainside.

At the level of individual words and constructions, there is very little that is distinctly "late" about Severus' Latinity. There are no biblical allusions, and only two distinctly Christian words, both Greek: *ecclesia* for "church" and *eremus* for "wilderness" (as the locus for spiritual struggle). All the word forms and constructions are in good classical order. In other respects, however, this passage exemplifies tendencies common to late antique artistic prose, whether Christian or not. Particularly notable is the highly patterned word order. Consider, for instance, the sequence *praecisa* (adjective 1) *montis* (noun 2) *excelsi* (adjective 2) *rupe* (noun 1); or *saxo* (noun 1) *superiecti* (adjective 2) *montis* (noun 2) *cavato* (adjective 1). In both cases, the patterning works in various ways: we have alternation of grammatical classes (adjective-noun-adjective-noun, noun-adjective-noun-adjective) alongside the so-called "enclosing" word order, the elements in agreement forming in either case a chiasmus (1–2–2–1). Such patterns, sometimes referred to as "tracery" – an image already laden with medieval associations – are common in poetry from the Augustan period onward. Despite their frequency in Horace, Virgil, Ovid, and the rest, however, their popularity in prose works is typical of the fourth century AD and later. The obvious artificiality of such writing raises serious questions about the relationship between such mannered prose and the spoken language.

Also noteworthy is the highly rhythmical character of the prose. Latin rhetorical prose writers often exploited various metrical patterns (known as *clausulae*) for the ending of a sentence or phrase; for instance, the cretic plus trochee pattern of — ∪ — | — ∪ (found here in *ferre non posset*), the double cretic of — ∪ — | — ∪ — (*paululum sinu clauserat*), the double trochee — ∪ | — ∪ (*desideraret*). There is nothing unclassical about these prose rhythms per se, which are common from the first century BC onward. But the rigor with which they are applied – and in a genre which traditionally avoided them – is another distinctly "late" feature. Jerome, in the critique of Rufinus quoted above, had censured him also for pursuing *clausulae* at the expense of accurate and logical expression.

Finally, this passage exemplifies the sort of intense intertextuality with classical Latin often cultivated in later writers. Compare Severus' description of Martin's monastery with the account by Sallust (around 86–35 BC) of the fortress by the river Muluccha in Numidia:

> Namque haud longe a flumine Muluccha, quod Iugurthae Bocchique regnum diiungebat, erat inter ceteram planitiem mons saxeus, mediocri castello satis patens, in immensum editus, uno perangusto aditu relicto; nam omnis natura uelut opere atque consulto praeceps ... iter castellanorum angustum admodum, utrimque praecisum ... (Sall. *Iug.* 92)

> Now, not far from the River Muluccha ... there was rocky mountain in the midst of a plain, big enough for a small fort, raised to an immeasurable altitude, with just one very narrow approach-road left; for the landscape was sheer as if so designed and built ... the defenders' path was narrow indeed, with sheer drops on either side ...

Severus' Sallustian is subtle and cumulative. No phrase is borrowed directly. Instead, we find the substitution of synonyms within a phrase (*reliquam planitiem* versus *ceteram planitiem, angusta admodum* versus *arta admodum*), and the use of related roots in different grammatical classes (*aditus* versus *adire, saxum* versus *saxeus*). Even the shared adjective *praecisus* occurs in different genders and cases. But there is no doubt that this *is* an imitation of the Sallustian passage and that the differences are likely to be deliberate and not the result of faulty memory. What is going on? It is tempting to suggest that Severus is trying to write an instant Christian classic, a work that will supplant Sallust as *the* historian read in the schools of his day. But if so, Severus' attempt would, from a literary point of view, be seriously flawed. Much of the pleasure in reading his works lies in tracing the ways in which he has adapted his models. What he writes is far from being a pastiche of Sallust (the patterned word order alone sees to that); rather, it is an idiom which depends for its effect on the ability of his readers to compare, contrast, and enjoy.

The use of earlier literature as intertext is, of course, nothing new, though it is something of a late antique fascination. Much of our knowledge of how Virgil used Ennius and his other Latin predecessors is derived from the account and excerpts given in the *Saturnalia* of Macrobius (first half of the fifth century AD). Often this technique involves overlaying images from two or more classical sources; for instance, Virgil's Golden Bough (*Aen.* 6. 136–44, 201–11) has some affinities with both the *moly* that grows on Circe's island (Hom. *Od.* 10. 298–306) and the magic "Drug of Prometheus" given to Jason by Medea (Ap. Rhod. *Argon.* 3. 843–57). But Christian authors such as Severus possess an additional set of literary models and intertexts in the Scriptures. Consider, for example, the following healing miracle of Martin:

> Eodem tempore Taetradii cuiusdam proconsularis viri servus daemonio correptus dolendo exitu cruciabatur: rogatus ergo Martinus ut ei manum imponeret deduci eum ad se iubet: sed nequam spiritus nullo proferri modo de cellula in qua erat potuit: ita in advenientes rabidis dentibus saeviebat. tum Taetradius ad genua beati viri advolvitur, orans ut ad domum in qua daemoniacus habebatur ipse descenderet. tum vero Martinus negare se profani et gentilis domum adire posse: nam Taetradius eo tempore adhuc gentilitatis errore implicitus tenebatur. spondet ergo se, si de puero daemon fuisset exactus, Christianum fore. ita Martinus imposita manu puero immundum ab eo spiritum eiecit. quo viso Taetradius dominum Iesum credidit, statimque catechumenus factus nec multo post baptizatus est, semperque Martinum salutis suae auctorem miro coluit affectu. (*Vit. Martini* 17)

At the same time, a slave belonging to Tetradius, a man of consular rank, was possessed by a demon and was being tortured to a grievous end. So Martin, summoned to lay hands on him, bade him be led to himself. But the evil spirit could in no way be brought forth from the cell in which he was, so rabidly did he gnash his teeth at those who approached him. Then Tetradius fell at the knees of the blessed hero, beseeching him to come in person to the house where the demoniac was being kept. Then Martin said he could not come to the house of a pagan and gentile – Tetradius being at this time still in the grip of the gentile fallacy. So he promised that if the demon were driven out of the boy, he would become a Christian. So Martin laid his hand on the boy and drove out the impure spirit. On seeing this, Tetradius believed in the Lord Jesus. He become a catechumen forthwith, and was baptized not long afterwards, and always revered Martin with wondrous fervor as the author of his salvation.

Severus' story draws heavily on elements from at least four gospel passages: Matthew 8: 5–13 (healing of the centurion's servant), Matthew 17: 14–17 (healing of a demoniac boy), Mark 9: 16–26 (Mark's version of the same story), and John 4: 46–50 (healing of the ruler's son). Severus' collage of these elements is typically subtle. In his account, Martin is *approached* (an element common to all four canonical gospels) by a *powerful* man (compare the "ruler" of John 4; contrast the others), who falls down *at/to his knees* (compare Matthew 17; contrast the others) and asks him to heal his *puer*, who may be his son but is probably his *house-boy* (compare Matthew 8, where the same ambiguity occurs; contrast the others). The *puer* in question is possessed by a *demon* (compare Matthew 17 and Mark 9; contrast the others); one effect of this is to make him *gnash his teeth* (compare Mark 9; contrast the others). Jesus is *asked* to *go down* to the house in question (compare John 4; contrast the others), but there is some question over *whether it is proper* for him to enter the house (compare Matthew 8; contrast the others). The heavy use of biblical allusions should not blind us to the fact that this is an eminently classical technique of writing.

For an example of something closer to popular speech, we turn to a very different sort of Christian Latin. Around AD 570, a man named Antoninus, from Piacenza, made a pilgrimage to the Holy Land. His account is preserved in a handful of ninth- and tenth-century manuscripts (itself a complicating factor: do they represent faithfully the sixth-century text, a copy of the sixth-century text using ninth-century conventions, or a more radical overhaul?). Here is Antoninus on Nazareth and Galilee:

> Deinde venimus in civitatem Nazareth in qua sunt multae virtutes. Ibi etiam sedit in sinagoga tomus in quo abcd habuit dominus inpositum. In qua etiam sinagoga posita est trabis ubi sedebat cum aliis infantibus. Quae trabis a christianis agitatur et sublevatur, iudaei vero nulla rerum ratione possunt agitare, sed nec permittit se foris tolli. Domus sanctae Mariae basilica est et multa ibi fiunt beneficia de vestimentis eius ... Provincia similis paradiso, in tritico et in frugis similis Aegypto, modica quidem, sed praecellit Aegyptum in vino et oleo et poma. Melium extra natura altum nimis, super statum hominis, talea grossa. (*Itinerarium Antonini Placentini* 5, *PL* 72: 900–1)

> Then we came to the city of Nazareth, where there are many miracles. There even resides in the synagogue a volume in which the Lord set down his alphabet. In the same synagogue there is also set a beam on which he used to sit with the other children. This beam can be shaken and lifted up by Christians, but in no wise in the world can Jews shake it, nor does it let itself be taken outside. Saint Mary's house is a church, and there many miracles come about through her clothing ... The province is like paradise, in wheat and produce like Egypt, small indeed, but it surpasses Egypt in wine and oil and fruit. The millet is preternaturally tall, above human stature, with a thick stem.

Before noting some of many nonclassical features of Antoninus' Latin, we should observe that he actually appears to be trying for an elevated style. Consider the recurrent use of the relative pronoun with the antecedent repeated (*sinagoga ... in qua etiam sinagoga; trabis ... quae trabis*), yet another stylistic tic of Rufinus ridiculed by Jerome; or the rather clumsy pretension of *nulla rerum ratione*, here translated "in no wise in the world." But for the most part, the language is distinctly postclassical. At the level of morphology (word forms), we may note the semi-Romance style use of *habere* plus the past participle (*habuit dominus inpositum*) to form a past tense, or the typical late use of *de* as a general purpose preposition marking origin or source (for *ex* or *ab*). The noun declensions show considerable change from the classical system. *Trabis*, for instance, has displaced the classical *trabs* (such so-called imparisyllabic nouns are frequently remodeled, even in the classical period). *Frugis* should, in classical terms, be *frugibus*, *poma* should be *pomis*, *natura* should be *naturam*. While manuscript variations make it impossible to reconstruct with certainty an original text, these readings are all at least plausible for the sixth century; collectively, they illustrate the loss of functional distinction between the classical ablative and accusative cases, at least after prepositions – the same tendency falsely corrected in Augustine's *inter hominibus*. At the level of vocabulary, there is the postclassical adjective *grossus*, "large" (French *gros*, Italian *grosso*), along with use of *civitas* for "city" already discussed. Several words have gained a new, specifically Christian sense: *virtus* now means "miracle" rather than classical "manliness, moral excellence," *basilica* "church," rather than "large public building." The case of *infans* is particularly interesting; in classical Latin "baby" (literally "nonspeaker"), it gains in Christian use the sense "young person," specifically "young believer," largely through its use in a single well-known Psalm verse (Ps. 8: 3).

We should not leave the subject, though, without striking a note of caution. It is all too easy to exaggerate the distinctly postclassical and nonliterary elements in such texts. The practice, freely followed here, of citing modern Romance data to illustrate the ultimate success of particular features may lead to a sort of teleological reading which risks excluding features that do not fit this pattern, while exaggerating those that may (but need not) be interpreted in this way. In the former category, we may note the entirely classical use of the synthetic passive forms (*agitatur*, *sublevatur*, *tolli*) – forms that are frequently found even in very "late" and "vulgar" forms, but that have completely dropped out of the Romance record. In the latter class, there is the use of *sedere* (or perhaps *sedire*) to mean "to reside, to be permanently" – a use that may be taken to resemble the Iberian Romance development of this verb (compare Spanish *ser* "to be permanently" from *sedere*). It is simply impossible to tell how Antoninus himself would have meant this verb, or what his readers would have understood by it.

When Will We Stop Speaking Latin?

Scholars have been for a long time fascinated by the question of when people stopped speaking Latin. Traditionally, arguments have proceeded along one of two lines. Some have proceeded by identifying those features that are distinctly "Latin" (as opposed to Romance) and trying to date when they disappeared from the living, spoken language; favorite candidates include the loss of the synthetic passive and future forms (*amabit*, *amatur*) and the breakdown of the classical five-case noun declension. Others have worked back from the modern situation of diverse Romance languages and tried to identify the first point at which it is possible to talk of a Latin continuum, in which an Apulian peasant, a soldier on the Rhine, and an aristocrat from Spain could expect to carry on a fairly comprehensible conversation in their everyday tongue. Each approach has its value, and its drawbacks. In the case of the first, it is clearly an important part of the historical linguist's task to identify and date key changes, even if (as with the example of the English *thou/thee/thy* considered above) the answers are not always clear-cut; developments are seldom just linear, and dialectal and sociolinguistic factors must always be considered. In the second approach, the implicit definition of a language may be reasonable and in line with our expectation from fieldwork on modern languages, but in practice it rests on some problematic assumptions about what constitutes comprehension and everyday language. It also involves playing down the fact that some very well-attested features of the theoretical reconstructed proto-Romance are simply not attested at all in Latin texts. Above all, neither approach is testable enough. Absolute scientific testability is rare in historical linguistics, and while linguists are generally prepared to make limited claims for the truth of quite specific claims (e.g., that the loss of final /m/ was already under way in the preclassical period, or that *edere* was being displaced by *manducare* in popular speech by the second century), the sheer level of fuzziness involved in big questions of this kind is too high for most modern scholars.

BIBLIOGRAPHICAL NOTE

Most traditional studies have acknowledged that in the spoken language, at least, the distinction between "late Latin" and "early Romance" is not an exact one. A more radical approach has been to question the validity of the distinction in relation to written texts as well. This school of thought, largely associated with Roger Wright (see Wright 2002), has stressed the ways in which written texts may be read differently over space and time. Shakespeare as staged in London today may sound very different from Shakespeare staged 400 years ago, or indeed from Shakespeare staged in Aberdeen or Adelaide today. By the same token, later Latin texts could have been read as something far closer to Romance vernaculars than has generally been assumed. Wright traces the distinction between "Latin" and "Romance" back to the "reformed" Latin pronunciation of the eighth-century English scholar Alcuin, with his insistence that within Charlemagne's empire written Latin texts should be pronounced letter by letter, as a foreign language – as it was pronounced in contemporary England, in fact. Thus the break between the written and the spoken language turns out to be the result of changes not in speech patterns, but in reading and writing practices. The good sense displayed by this approach, and the weight of evidence collected in its favor, has won it considerable support. Others claim that in its strong form this hypothesis would require an eighth-century clerk, coming across a Latin phrase such as *nautae mergebantur* ("the sailors were drowning"), to read it as *illi marinarii se annegavan* or similar.

Other trends in later Latin linguistics include a new concentration on specialized technical vocabularies, such as those of medicine or veterinary science. Particularly important examples are supplied by Jean André 1981, James Adams 1976, 2003, and David Langslow 2000. There has also been increasing emphasis on bilingualism and language contact in the late antique world (Adams again, and Frédérique Biville 1990–5). The divide between "literary" and "linguistic" studies has been eroded (largely thanks to Jacques Fontaine and Michael

Roberts: see Fontaine 1968, Roberts 1989), and useful work has been done on the pragmatics and rhetoric of later Latin. Much valuable material can be found in the proceedings of the triennial colloquium *Latin vulgaire – latin tardif*. To date, seven volumes of this series have appeared (from different publishers), edited (in order) by J. Herman, G. Calboli, M. Iliescu and W. Marxgut, L. Callebat, H. Petersmann and R. Kettemann, H. Solin et al., and C. Arias Abellán.

CHAPTER TWENTY-THREE

Language and Culture in Late Antique Egypt

Malcolm Choat

Late antique Egypt witnessed a linguistic and cultural change of some magnitude: the institution, in Coptic, of a new, fully articulated system of writing the Egyptian language. While the seeds of this innovation had been sown in the early Roman period, they reached fruition only as Late Antiquity dawned. A range of factors contributed to cultural change in late antique Egypt, many of which can be traced elsewhere in the Roman world. In Egypt itself, however, the survival of papyri allows us to observe the interaction between the dominant and native cultures at close quarters.

"Coptic" properly describes a stage in the writing of Egyptian; a stage in which the language was written in Greek characters, but with between six and eight additional letters derived from Demotic (the number depending on the dialect) for sounds not represented by the Greek alphabet. Freed from the confines of the deliberately archaizing Demotic script (and the conservative mentality that perpetuated it), and liberally including Greek loanwords, Coptic better represents contemporary spoken Egyptian.

During Late Antiquity, the Sahidic dialect of Coptic competed with a number of regional and so-called "vehicular" dialects – dialects that transcended a narrow locale – and emerged as the "classical" Coptic dialect (Kasser 1980–1; 1990). (Chief among the others were Bohairic, Fayumic, Mesokemic, Akhmimic, and Lycopolitan; see the respective entries in Atiya 1991, vol. viii.) Sahidic became both the primary literary dialect, and the pan-Egyptian vehicular dialect (a status its dialectal ancestor had probably acquired in the late Pharaonic and Persian periods: see Satzinger 1985), until superseded by Bohairic in the second millennium AD.

Late Antiquity in Egypt is often known, both academically and popularly, as the "Coptic period," the period when "Coptic culture" dominated. The term is also applied beyond late antique limits. But that vague designation raises numerous problems of definition. Is "Coptic culture" coterminous with the use of the Coptic script, or of the Egyptian language? Is it Christian culture, as manifested in Egypt through the Egyptian (Coptic) church, or is it, as most loosely (but not

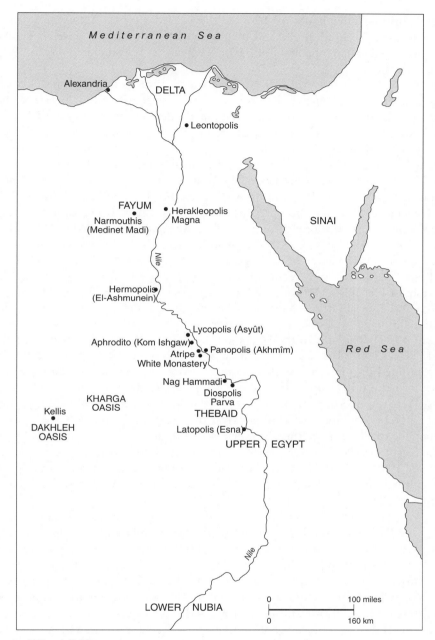

Map 4 "Coptic" Egypt.

uncommonly) applied, everything about Egypt from the late antique and early Byzantine periods? (See MacCoull 1993: ch. 1, 28–9; Clackson 2004.)

The words "Copt" and "Egyptian" are both linear descendants, through Arabic and Latin respectively, of the Greek *Aigyptios.* Applied by the Islamic rulers to the largely Christian inhabitants of *Misr* (as they called Egypt), Arabic *qibt* came to designate them both ethnically and religiously. Early Europeans travelers kept this meaning ("a Christian inhabitant of Egypt") when they transliterated *qibt* as "Copt" (or its equivalents).

Just as every *misry*, however, was not a *qibty* at the time modern Europeans reached Egypt, so, when the armies of the Prophet swept into the Byzantine province, many of its population would never have identified themselves as *Aigyptioi*. Many of them, indeed, were ethnically non-Egyptian, although a long process of Greco-Romanization had promoted a new type of Egyptian, conditioned by centuries of influence – and pressure – to participate in Hellenic language and culture.

Hellên, in Greek as well as in Coptic Christian discourse, was developing distinctly pejorative associations in Late Antiquity (Vinzent 1998: 34–5; Haas 2004: 217–18); but Hellenic culture was not in eclipse, nor was Greek being displaced as the preeminent literary medium: throughout Late Antiquity, a knowledge of Greek was essential (in the east), if one wished to gain full access to the contemporary cultural milieu, especally the level of state government (Bagnall 1993: 99–109). Recent scholarship has increasingly recognized that late antique Egypt saw a revision, not a rejection, of Hellenism (Fowden 1986; Bowersock 1990; Frankfurter 2000).

Even in the social settings most contested in religious terms, Hellenic culture lived on in pilgrimage and philosophy (Rémondon 1952; Wipszycka 1996: 63–105; Vinzent 1998). The sack of the Serapeum in AD 391 and the murder of Hypatia in AD 415 (Haas 1997: 161–3, 313–16) draw one's eye, but not enough to distract from the continued promotion of older traditions in both Hellenic and native-speaking circles into the fifth century (Van der Vliet 1993; Frankfurter 1998b; Montserrat 1998). Yet, the question of the survival of Hellenism and Greek culture in Egypt should not be confused with the survival of "paganism": religion was only one component of Hellenic culture (Bowersock 1990: 1–13). In the sunset of Roman rule in Egypt, people continued both to copy Greek classics to attain literacy in Greek (Cribiore 1999: 283; 2001: 24) and to read and imitate Homer as a way of displaying their cultural attainments (see especially Dioscorus of Aphrodito: MacCoull 1988; Fournet 1999).

The rise of Coptic must be seen in the context of a bilingual milieu established during the Ptolemaic and Roman periods. Functional and more developed bilingualism is evident throughout that era (Fewster 2002; see Bagnall 1993: 230–60; Dieleman 2005: 104–10) and provides a backdrop to the expressly bilingual activity of the earliest users of literary Coptic, Christian and otherwise. Explicit documentary evidence for bilingualism before the sixth century is more difficult to find, since it is largely restricted to "formulaic bilingualism" – that is to say, when a scribe appends to a letter in Greek appropriate Coptic formulae of greeting or farewell, or vice versa (e.g., Grenfell and Hunt 1901: no. 145; Bell 1924: no. 1921; and many of the letters from Kellis in Gardner et al. 1999: especially no. 22).

So, the "Coptic period" (if we need use the term at all: see Clackson 2004: 39–41) is best thought of as referring not to an ethnic or religious group but to the culture carried by the Coptic script and language from the third century onward. And we have to think in terms of a bilingual milieu, in which late antique Greek and Egyptian speakers participated in the rise of both an Egyptian expression of later Hellenism and a new manifestation of native Egyptian culture.

Coptic Texts from Late Antiquity

The first examples of what is traditionally recognized as Coptic appear in Christian contexts in the middle of the third century AD. A range of earlier, non-Christian experiments, however, helps us to place those Christian examples in a broader context (Quaegebeur 1982; Satzinger 1984; Pestman 1977: no. 11). Most important are examples of Egyptian transcribed into Greek characters dating from the first to the fourth centuries (principal texts listed in Satzinger 1991; see Dieleman 2005: 69–80 and, on issues of dependence, Kahle 1954, i: 252–6). Primarily intended to assist ritual pronunciation, these transcriptions are embedded, both as glosses and as more substantial sections, within a wider bilingual set of texts, popularly (although inaccurately) known as the "magical papyri" (and usually, until recently, as the "Greek magical papyri": see Dieleman 2005: 11–23). These manuals of ritual power are the product of an authentic Egyptian priestly milieu. Yet, they are articulated in a ritual vocabulary that includes Hellenic and even pan-Mediterranean elements, a syncretism reflected also in their multiple languages and scripts (Dieleman 2005). The common term for these pre-Christian transcription systems, "Old Coptic" (Satzinger 1991), exemplifies the distance frequently placed between them and "Coptic proper." While the distance is in many senses real, the evidence they supply cannot be excluded from our discussion without limiting the questions we can ask.

Early Christian literature in Coptic has been thoroughly discussed (e.g., Metzger 1977: 99–132; Orlandi 1986: 53–5; Wisse 1995; Smith 1998: 722–3), and it will suffice here to mention only the important points. The earliest texts (middle to late third century) are glosses and glossaries (Bell and Thompson 1925; Sanders and Schmidt 1927; Kenyon 1937), bearing witness to the tools by which Christianity was spreading through the *chóra*: translation into, and preaching in, Egyptian. The earliest full translations of the late third and early fourth centuries include canonical and apocryphal material with an (as yet not fully explained) emphasis on Old Testament texts (Kasser 1960; Diebner and Kasser 1989; Goehring 1990). While the translation of the Bible gathers pace and is completed and linguistically standardized in Sahidic at least by the end of the fourth century, traditions evolving on the edge of and alongside Christianity were also quick to employ the script. Notable are the "Gnostic library" found near Nag Hammadi (Robinson 1988: 1–26; Smith 1998: 730–3) and the Manichaean texts from Narmouthis and Kellis (modern Medinet Madi and Ismant el-Kharab; see Gardner and Lieu 1996; 2004: 35–45).

Few contemporary papyri bear witness to original Coptic productions in this period, but Epiphanius ascribes Coptic writings to Hieracas, an extreme ascetic based near Leontopolis under Diocletian (*Panarion* 67. 1. 3; see Goehring 1999), and later manuscripts survive of the letters and other writings of Pachomius and his first successors (Lefort 1956; Quecke 1975; see Orlandi 1986: 60–3). The Coptic fragments of the letters of Antony may also reflect their original language (Rubenson 1995; but see Lucchesi 2002: 561). Later in the fourth century, the preeminent Coptic author, Shenoute, begins a literary career stretching from the AD 380 s to his death in AD 465 (for the date, see Emmel 2002: 96–8). Many of his letters, sermons, catecheses, and other treatises are extant, and all in Coptic. They were collected in his "White" monastery across the river from Panopolis (Akhmîm), and transmitted in two parts, "Discourses" (*logoi*) and "Canons" (Emmel 2004; see Timbie 1986; Orlandi 1998: 133–5).

From the time of Shenoute onward, there stretches a tradition of textual production lasting nearly a millennium, until Coptic was superseded by Arabic. Apparently original compositions continue to appear in a limited range of genres; but they are as often as not spuriously attributed to earlier church luminaries (Orlandi 1991: 1456–8). They are complemented by a continuing and wide-ranging program of translation of patristic texts (Orlandi 1991: 1453–8; 1998: 135–7). Virtually no secular literature was ever produced in Coptic, and to a real extent no native literary culture ever developed outside a religious context. The millennia-old literary heritage of Egypt left its traces in Coptic texts (especially in "Gnostic," Hermetic, apocalyptic, and above all "magical" traditions: see Behlmer 1996) but was never absorbed into Coptic in any substantial form (Barns 1978: 20–1). Coptic literature does transmit elements of Hellenic culture, but even texts such as the "sayings of the philosophers" preserved in a White monastery manuscript (Till 1934) are transmitted within a Christian framework.

Early Coptic documents (as opposed to the literary texts discussed above) have received less attention. From the fourth and fifth centuries, some 200 codices or fragments thereof preserve literary texts in Coptic (the list in Kahle 1954, i: 269–74 is out of date but still useful). While this is far smaller than the number of literary productions in Greek from the same period (closer to 2,000), it still bears witness to a widely diffused program of literary production in Coptic.

Similar claims cannot be made for the use of Coptic for documents in Late Antiquity. Against over 5,000 documents of all sorts on papyrus in Greek from AD 284–451, fewer than 180 Coptic documents can be dated to that period with any confidence (including about sixty unpublished but certainly fourth-century documents from Kellis, noted here for statistical purposes only). While a still nascent understanding of Coptic paleography in this early period inhibits our understanding (Kasser 1991c), texts found in fourth-century archaeological context and those in more easily datable bilingual archives permit a sketch of the use of Coptic for documentary purposes in the period.

The record begins with the piece least representative, a single sherd from Kellis (the "old Coptic ostracon") that bears greetings and the opening of a short and perhaps incomplete letter (Gardner et al. 1999; Kasser 2004). Its archaeological context anchors it in the mid to late third century, and its orthography shows that it clearly predates the previously known earliest Coptic documents from the fourth century.

These come from the second quarter of the fourth century, and are written to a monastic leader at the Melitian monastery of Hathor in the Heracleopolite nome, Paieous (Bell 1924: nos. 1920–2; Crum 1927). A generation later (*c.* AD 350–60), one of his successors, Nepheros, also received letters in Coptic (Kramer and Shelton

1987: nos. 15–16; on the monastery and the Melitians see Hauben 2002). We should probably also date to the middle of the century the Christian letters in the binding of Nag Hammadi Codex VII, in which a monk named Sansnos is a prominent figure (Barns et al. 1981: Copt. 4–8, 15–18; see also Wipszycka 2000; Goehring 2001). These letters *may* come from the Diospolite area in the Thebaid near where the codices were found; no such uncertainty attaches to the documents from Kellis, found at the modern site (Ismant el-Kharab in the Dakhleh Oasis), in controlled archaeological context. This and internal indications date them to *c*. AD 350–80 (Gardner et al. 1999); those so far published include not only letters (nos. 11–43, 49–52), but also household accounts (nos. 44–8). They are largely the textual remains of the village's Manichaean community, and our understanding will be usefully augmented by those still to be published.

Toward the end of the fourth century come the letters sent to an Apa John, at least ten of which are in Coptic (Crum 1909: nos. 268–76, 396; for others see Van Minnen 1994; Zuckerman 1995 suggests that they are the papers of John of Lycopolis). Then, stretching from the fourth into the fifth centuries, there are the records of the Roman administrative center at Kysis (Douch) in the Khargeh Oasis. Hundreds of the ostraca found on this site are in Greek; but a small number are in Coptic. Although these are largely unpublished (described only in Cuvigny and Wagner 1986–92; Wagner 1999–2001; see also Choat and Gardner 2003; Bagnall et al. 2004), it seems that some of them at least overlap the genres represented in the Greek texts (overwhelmingly instructions for delivery of food and other products); one (Cuvigny and Wagner 1986–92: ii. no. 183) was sent by an *optio*.

With the Apa John and Kysis texts, we are at the turn of the fifth century. There we find not only a low point in papyrus survival in general (Habermann 1998), but also no prominent bilingual archives to locate a Coptic component in time, as with the fourth century assemblages discussed above. Without this assistance, few Coptic papyri can or have been dated specifically to the fifth century. Yet, the paleography is still poorly understood, and it is likely that at least some early-looking texts associated by purchase with the archive of Apa John and others among the forty-odd texts dated by paleography alone (some listed at Richter 2002: 20) come from the fifth century.

Learning Coptic

Such are the texts written in Coptic in Late Antiquity, but less is known about how people learned to write them. Heading into Late Antiquity, Greek education still flourished throughout Egypt in a variety of settings and fashions (Cribiore 2001; see the many school exercises in Harrauer and Sijpesteijn 1985; Cribiore 1996).

It is more difficult to locate and contextualize the beginnings of learning Coptic. Before the advent of Coptic, education in the Egyptian scripts was largely restricted to the Egyptian temples, and the use of them to priests (Tait 1992; Biedenkopf-Ziehner 1999: 24; Cribiore 2001: 22–3). Although the use of Demotic for documentary purposes had dramatically declined in the Roman period (Depauw 1997: 123–52), temple scriptoria continued to copy Egyptian literature, some into the third century (e.g., at Tebtunis: see Frandsen 1991; Frandsen and Ryholt 2000; Tait 1977; and near Thebes: Dieleman 2005: 40–4). Within the temple compound at Narmouthis, students in the second century practiced writing Greek, Egyptian, and, in some few cases, Egyptian in Greek characters (Gallo 1997; Bresciani et al. 1983; see also in general Zauzich 1983; Depauw 1997: 85–121; Frankfurter 1998b: 238–48; Hoffmann 2000).

Christian education in Coptic shows itself in the literary sources first in a monastic setting. The Pachomian *Rules* detail a rigid educational regime for postulants wishing to enter the monastery (*Rule* 140; see also *Rule* 49). The monastic evidence is usually given prominence in treatments of Coptic education, and it is tempting to seek for continuity between the temple and monastic educational systems, to parallel the continuity visible in the social roles of priests and monks (see esp. Frankfurter 1998b). Yet, while it is clear that Pachomius himself valued the learning of the Scriptures, the recitations he is pictured engaging in and encouraging (*Vit. Pachomii*, Bo 15; G[1] 24) are a long way from the organized schooling envisaged in the *Rules* (redacted later) (Rousseau 1999: 48–53, 70). Furthermore, the earliest Coptic school texts predate the encouragement of Coptic learning associated with the formation of the *koinobia*. We need to identify a milieu or a set of practices that stood between those two major promoters of written Egyptian.

This must be sought in the Coptic educational papyri themselves. These indicate in many cases an integration of Coptic into the standard Greco-Roman educational system, similar to the inclusion of Christian texts in Greek (Bucking 1997). A late third-century codex made of wooden tablets, probably from the Great Oasis, bears the texts routinely found in a Greek education setting: a paraphrase of the *Iliad*, fractions, conjugations, and declensions (Parsons 1970). Among these, the hand that wrote most of the codex also practiced writing a psalm in Coptic (Crum 1934). The hand is perhaps that of a confident student rather than a teacher, and bears the signs of having been copied from dictation. An educational papyrus codex from the Fayum that includes syllables and biblical passages executed entirely in Coptic was dated by its editor to the fourth century (Husselman 1947, with Kahle's concurrence on the date at 1954, i: 251; but see the caution at Hasitzka 1990: no. 207). Also from the Fayum comes a miniature bilingual exercise book from the fourth or fifth century consisting predominantly of the Psalms (Sanz 1946: no. 24: Henner et al. 1999: no. 42; in general, Cribiore 1999: 282).

Despite the best efforts of commentators (see especially the assumptions of Husselman 1947: 129, 133), none of these betrays an obvious monastic context in its form or provenance, especially the wooden codex. (The bilingual and possibly educational *ostracon*, purchased near the Theban monastic site of Deir el-Bahri, may be later than the date in the fourth century reported by Kortenbeutel and Böhlig 1935; see Hasitzka 1990: no. 196). Rather than being realized in an organized monastic program, the desire (or the need) to learn Coptic in the first century of its development (*c.* AD 250–350) seems to have generated diverse responses, dependent on circumstance. Some Christian teachers and students appended Coptic writing practice to their existing curricula; other groups may have integrated it into their religious instruction: in the middle of the fourth century a traveling Manichaean instructed his son by letter to "write a daily example, for I need you to write books here" (Gardner et al. 1999: no. 19).

The exact context of the last example is not known, but is likely to have been community based. If that is the case, to what extent did Christians combine their religious and scribal education in this way? It is tempting to cite the Alexandrian catechetical school alongside early Christian educational papyri, but the great theological establishment and its regional derivatives served different aims, and should not be given explanatory power here: reading – or at least learning – the Scriptures was of course the foundation of catechetical instruction; but it did not, at least in this early period, function as a substitute for a scribal education, nor was it intended to. The Pachomian practice of teaching reading as part of an initiation process (it could have been, for some novices, their first introduction to Christianity itself: Rousseau 1999: 71) may have helped to forge precisely a catechetical education that included the acquisition of more general skills; but it seems unwise to project that development back to the beginning of Late Antiquity.

Beyond this, a synthetic question suggests itself: to what degree did native Greek speakers learn Coptic? In most areas of society there would have been little impulse to do so: until the end of Byzantine rule, full articulation of family, daily, professional, and political life was possible in Greek (indeed, in the latter case, only in Greek). Yet, to pass into certain worlds one had to speak Egyptian. To visit a desert community and speak to a famous monk one could always engage an interpreter (note their ubiquity in monastic literature; e.g., *Vit. Antonii*, 72. 3, 74. 2, 77. 1; Palladius, *HL* 35. 5). But to live with and learn from such a monk, spoken Egyptian would have been a distinct advantage; the Pachomian texts in particular (e.g., *Vit. Pachomii*, G^1 94–5; Bo 89, 91), with others such as the *Life of Hilaria* (Drescher 1947: 75), clearly delineate the problem and the solutions, which ranged from the pilgrim or novice learning to speak Egyptian (the usual result) to the constant employment of interpreters recorded in the *Letter of Ammon* (e.g., *Ep. Amm.* 4, 5, 6, 22, 28, 29). Such procedures did not always depend, however, on learning to read and write Coptic. Nor do the educational papyri provide much support: while some of the educational material discussed above points in the direction of Greek speakers learning Coptic (note the apparent trouble with Demotic letters faced by the scribe of Crum 1934 – Lefort 1935; Cribiore 1999: 282 – and the deliberate use made of them by the scribe of Gardner et al. 1999: no. 10), the general impression is that the educational texts are largely those of Egyptian speakers learning Greek. During Late Antiquity at least, no rival Coptic education system developed, and high-level education (e.g., advanced exercises and grammar) continued to be possible only in Greek (Cribiore 1999). A group of people who could read and write *only* Coptic is not readily visible before the later Byzantine or Arab periods.

Contexts for the Use of Coptic in Late Antiquity

Among Coptic documents from the fourth and fifth centuries, personal letters dominate, with some few household accounts and lists (Gardner et al. 1999:

nos. 44–8; perhaps also Grenfell and Hunt 1901: no. 143 verso; Crum 1905: nos. 711, 1252; Hasitzka 2004: nos. 1035, 1037). That there are no dated Coptic texts in this period (the earliest that can be dated precisely come from AD 535/6: see MacCoull 1997; Richter 2002: 23–6; Worp 1990) illustrates well that Coptic was not used for any official or legally binding documentation until the sixth century. For most of Late Antiquity, vernacular Coptic remained a private tool.

The prominence of females in Coptic papyri, and of household concerns, reinforces that suggestion. Coptic seems to have particularly encouraged female written expression in Late Antiquity (Bagnall 2001; Cribiore 2001: 78). While the monastic archives are by their nature dominated by letters to men, the Kellis assemblage of forty-six Coptic texts includes four (and possibly five) letters composed by women, and no fewer than fourteen addressed to women. Female participation in the composition of at least some of the household accounts is also likely (Gardner et al. 1999: nos. 44–8; see also pp. 54–8, 253).

In this situation at least, women articulate their relationship with literacy primarily through Coptic. In Greek texts from the site, only one woman features as an addressee, and none as a letter-composer. When women write letters, they use Coptic, and their male relatives predominantly choose the native language when writing to them. This pattern is confirmed in letters dated later than the fourth century: while letters written by women in Greek decrease dramatically, their place is taken by compositions in Coptic, which women clearly preferred, once the option became available. Women took to the new script perhaps precisely because, in bilingual households throughout Greco-Roman Egypt, the native language dominated domestic life. The rise of Coptic merely allowed women to give written expression to this (so Bagnall 2001). More broadly, we may characterize a preference in some communities for conducting household and family communication in Coptic, extending into record-keeping in household industries where women were closely involved, such as the production of textiles.

Many have supposed that Coptic spread from educated areas in the valley to the hinterland and beyond. This supports the belief that literary usage came first, and that documentary usage was a consequence. Moreover, it is widely held that both were largely confined to a monastic setting in the early period. These well-rehearsed views provide a framework for wider considerations in those instances where new evidence and perspectives allow us to test those propositions further.

The attention to detail evident in the standardization of Coptic (among other factors) requires us to acknowledge that such standardization took place in an educated bilingual milieu (Bagnall 1993: 238, 253, 323). It was not a product of desert outposts or rural villages; rather, it was in the centers of literate culture (in particular the *poleis*) that decisive steps in translation and standardization were made. The papyrus record fails conspicuously, however, to confirm explicitly this interpretation of the rise of Coptic. Where we should see evidence for the use of Coptic in these large towns, few of the literary Coptic manuscripts can confidently be associated, through their find or purchase history, with an urban center, except for Panopolis (Gascou 1989; on the Bodmer papyri see Robinson 1990; Bagnall 1993: 103–4, with bibliography). Many of the letters found at Kellis were sent from the Nile valley, one explicitly from Hermopolis (Gardner et al. 1999: no. 26), but this cannot camouflage the noticeable lack of Coptic documents from the towns themselves, from some of which (e.g., Hermopolis) relatively vast caches of late antique documents are extant. Despite the growth of a class of Hellenized Egyptians, some of whom must have been involved in the propagation of Coptic, none of the well-known late antique "urban" papyrus archives have identifiable Coptic sections (for the archives see Montevecchi 1988: 257–9; together with that of Ammon, Willis and Maresch 1998), nor can many other early Coptic documents be securely associated with an urban setting (Bagnall 1993: 257).

The lack of Coptic papyri from the Nile *metropoleis* does not invalidate the argument for early development in an educated urban milieu, but rather underlines that linguistic choices are determined more by context and recipient than by location and scribe (Bagnall 1995: 20–1, with bibliography). The dearth of urban Coptic papyri reflects in part the nature of most papyrus archives, which are substantially records of their collector's relations with the state in one form or another, all necessarily conducted in Greek. At Kellis, this division between the public and private nature of the Greek documentation, as against the exclusively private nature of the Coptic texts, is noticeable (Clackson 2004: 38). Documentary use seems predominantly rural and village-based, but this may be a function of the addressees' location in and, in the case of the monastic assemblages, alongside villages. Letters can be sent from anywhere, including from the nome capitals down the Nile, as the Kellis letters demonstrate. But the vernacular use of Coptic in Late Antiquity still operated only in contexts where the writer and addressee were part of a (sometimes widely geographically dispersed) community where the use of Coptic was expected and unsurprising. Within the towns, it would appear that the Greco-Egyptian elites who assisted the rise of Coptic still expected to receive letters – and largely wrote their own – in Greek.

A progression from literature to documents is problematized by the "Old Coptic ostracon," which shows Coptic already in use for personal communications – at least among a restricted group of people – in the second half (or even the middle) of the third century. This piece may appear to exist in isolation, but formulaic continuities (see below) place it in a progression. Given the date of this text, however, we are not permitted to hold that this use of Coptic is necessarily a consequence of the earliest Christian Coptic texts, only just appearing in the valley and Fayum at this stage. It is still highly likely that literary texts (if non-Christian ritual texts may be included under this category) stand behind the rise of Coptic for letter-writing, but a direct relationship between this and the translation and distribution of the Coptic Bible seems too neat.

Monasticism and Coptic

Before the last decade of the twentieth century, a monastic context was overwhelmingly apparent in late antique Coptic documents. The majority of the Coptic documents from Kellis, however, are the product of a decidedly nonmonastic milieu (notwithstanding hints of a Manichaean monastery in the vicinity: Gardner 2000). They form part of a bilingual and multireligious record of a community's activities, and necessitate a wider explanation of the use of Coptic. Such will not invalidate the obvious importance to the growth of Coptic of the monastic movement. But it is important to recognize the degree to which we access much of this linguistic and cultural history through the collective memory of the Egyptian monastic tradition.

At certain points this tradition deviated dramatically from that preserved elsewhere in the Mediterranean. Athanasius was remembered in different ways within and outside Egypt: while the Greek tradition preserves the "historical" works of Athanasius (see Barnes 1993: 5–6), Coptic manuscripts (almost all from monastic libraries) preserve texts encouraging asceticism. Shenoute, arguably the most important monastic leader in late antique Egypt, is completely missing from the Greco-Roman monastic texts. He certainly made a conscious and thoroughgoing decision to write in Coptic, but that certainly did not shield him from visitors (Behlmer 1998; on his knowledge of Greek see Emmel 2002: 99; Bagnall 1993: 254, with n. 134). Foreign pilgrims may simply have preferred to write about the desert hermits who fired the imaginations of western readers.

Monasticism as an institution did not create Coptic, and monks were not the first to use it: their contribution to the educational heritage was to consolidate the language rather than to form it. But monasticism played a vital role in spreading and promoting Coptic by forging contacts between what would otherwise have been opposites: people travel up the Nile from Alexandria and beyond; residents of the Thebaid sail down to the capital; town dignitaries journey into rural areas to meet monks. The inhabitants of "the desert" made the city their own, bringing together the literate bilingualism of the city and the more functional bilingualism of the countryside.

Yet, for all this, the papyrus record demonstrates that an explanation for the growth of Coptic for everyday purposes must take note of a wider context. What may have linked monks with the Manichaeans at Kellis was the particular feature that they were scribal communities. On the available evidence, Kellis seems to have been a preeminent place of book production. Even if we lack literary texts associated with the fourth-century monastic archives, the "bookhands" in which many of the Coptic letters are written (see below) suggest a link with the production of books themselves. Such an explanation should not extend only to those who were part of the monastic communities, since that will not explain the preference displayed for Coptic by lay people in the orbit of monastic communities, who are clearly the authors of some of the letters to monks. It may be more profitable to conceive of these monasteries not as the contained loci of Coptic writing, but as the epicenter of textual footprints in the countryside which their own literary activity in Coptic, preaching in Egyptian, and social integration with the surrounding communities encouraged, but did not necessarily create.

"Coptic Egypt": Alternative Culture or New Fusion?

Coptic develops at the intersection of a number of cultural and linguistic axes: Christian and non-Christian, provincial and imperial, Greek and Egyptian, town and country, literary and documentary. A new culture arises along with the new script, but are we watching the creation of an alternative culture, or a new cultural fusion? To what degree was the rise of Coptic the product of a Christian milieu, and to what degree did it contribute to the rise of a native culture rival to that promoted at large within the Roman Empire?

Script, language, text, and text production form the primary witness to the continuities and contrasts that mark the rise of this culture. Contact between the syncretic ritual texts and the oldest Christian Coptic documents is evident at an orthographic, alphabetic, and dialectal level, particularly in the third century Bodmer manuscript of Proverbs (Kasser 1960; 1991a; 2004; on the dialect see Johnson 1976; Satzinger 1984). Yet, the language itself is closer to "Christian" Coptic than to "old Coptic" (Emmel 1992: 183).

Evolving Coptic scribal conventions reinforce the latter connection, and are closely linked with Christian scribal practice and modes of textual production. The latter is most noticeably characterized, from the earliest witnesses on, by an overwhelming preference for the codex format for texts on papyrus or parchment, and the practice of contracting important words (Lord, God, Jesus, Christ, etc.; see also Turner 1977; Roberts 1979: 26–48). Both of these practices almost immediately became standard for Coptic texts: virtually no Coptic texts are preserved on papyrus rolls, as used for previous Egyptian texts, and overwhelmingly for Greco-Roman literary texts (Kahle 1954, i: 275–7). *Nomina sacra*, as the abbreviated "sacred names" are known, appear already in early fourth-century Coptic texts, and are subsequently found in the Manichaean texts, many of the Nag Hammadi tractates, and Coptic magical texts.

At the level of epistolary formulae, however, other trajectories are visible. Coptic letters from the fourth and fifth centuries routinely begin with a characteristic "A is it who writes to B" cleft-sentence construction (so in the papyri, and always in Shenoute; see Biedenkopf-Ziehner 1983: 42–3). This is grammatically dissimilar to the way the Pauline and Catholic epistles are translated into Coptic; a trail does seem visible, however, back to the Kellis Old Coptic ostracon, and to the latest Demotic letters in the third century AD (Tait 1977: no. 22, with pp. 76 ff.). The latter are the compositions of Egyptian priests, and the Kellis ostracon dates from the period before we have firm evidence that the New Testament existed in Coptic translation. Below the level of sacred text, then, are the continuities of daily life.

The Egyptian priestly milieu presents itself at times as ambivalent or hostile toward Greek (whatever the realities; see Dieleman 2005: 1–10, 143–4). In a different way, the script of early Coptic documents yields an apparent agenda of differentiation from Greek. Many Coptic scribes in the fourth century eschewed the standard cursive scripts used for Greek documents, and persisted in writing Coptic documents in a type of handwriting more appropriate to a literary production (i.e., a "bookhand"; see MacCoull 1997). Where the same scribe writes Greek and Coptic side by side, a clear and conscious differentiation has been made (see, e.g., Grenfell and Hunt 1901: no. 145; see also Van Minnen 1995: 16). Even into the sixth and seventh centuries, some bilingual notaries, such as Paul, son of Megalos from the village This, used subtly different (although clearly related) styles of writing for Greek and Coptic. Dioscorus of Aphrodito himself employed one hand for Greek literary and Coptic documentary texts, and (on the whole) another, more cursive, hand for Greek documents (MacCoull 1995, 1997; on Dioscorus' literary output see now Fournet 1999). In the early period, this suggests a general acculturation to the milieu of copying literary texts, rather than a rejection of a "Greek" style of writing. But such did not function everywhere: at Kellis, a highly scribal community, Greek and Coptic documentary texts are frequently written in similar styles of hand (Gardner and Choat 2004). Evolution along pluralistic lines is again apparent.

Coptic reflects its proximity to the Egyptian vernacular in its wholesale adoption of Greek words; these would have been common in spoken Egyptian, but are infrequent in Demotic texts (Clarysse 1987; on ritual texts see Dieleman 2005: 110–20). But such tendencies do not always have to be seen as a clear delineation, a conscious setting off and restart; they may rather reflect pragmatic choices, and a desire to replicate the accessible and familiar *koinê* of the Greek Bible.

It is clear that a wider milieu than the Christian one was involved in the development and rise of Coptic. If it could not have spread without the Christian – and later monastic – impetus, vital groundwork had been laid by the wider Greco-Egyptian tradition, in particular the educated bilingual (and in particular biscribal) elements concentrated in the Egyptian priesthood. It need not necessarily be assumed that Christians were actively and successfully converting priests, but rather that in the third century they came to compete with the Egyptian priesthood for recruits among a certain section of society, the educated and bilingual Hellenized Egyptian elite. If exact historical circumstances are – perhaps deliberately – not recorded, the manuscripts themselves testify that the orbits of the Egyptian priesthood and Christianity intersected, allowing the transfer of ideas, techniques, and scripts.

That the rise of Coptic had a "nationalistic" element (Hopkins 1991: 146–7; MacMullen 1964a: 194–5) is difficult to prove, and alignment with the agendas of contemporary Christian schismatics and secular revolutionaries is hazardous (Wipszycka 1996: 9–61). It is tempting to seek empire-wide tendencies in the rise of provincial languages such as Coptic, Syriac, and the local languages of North Africa (e.g., MacMullen 1966). Outside the Near East, late antique evidence usually comes in the reports of onlookers who spoke (and wrote) Latin (on encounters between Latin and Punic see Brown 1968b; Adams 2003: 200–45). Only in Syria is the phenomenon sufficiently "literary" to allow the relationship with the hegemonic tongue (in that case Greek) to be tested.

In Egypt, the identification between expression in Coptic and an anti-imperial agenda belongs to the post-Chalcedonic period and is not fully manifested until the sixth century (Orlandi 1991: 1454–5). Schism and rebellion had their own, often quite specific, aims that frequently had little, if anything, to do with "Egyptian nationalism." Nor should Coptic be seen in the light of the latter. In its origins it was a diverse phenomenon, without an obvious center of gravity. The dialectal distribution of the early Christian manuscripts yields no natural geographic epicenter (Funk 1988; see also Kasser 1991b); nor is the preponderance of Sahidic necessarily an indication of a central program, but rather a testament to its dialectal neutrality and its preexisting vehicular status, particularly among the educated classes (Kahle 1954, i: 242–68; Satzinger 1985).

Center of the church in Egypt, home to Hellenized yet highly traditional Egyptians (Frankfurter 2000), and perhaps even the birthplace of the Sahidic dialect (Kahle 1954, i: 256–7; a more nuanced proposal in Satzinger 1985), Alexandria suggests itself as an appropriate melting pot in which transference of traditions and mutual interaction may have occurred. However, the climate of Egypt's Delta has robbed us of papyri with which we might test what role the inhabitants of the great metropolis played in the rise of Coptic. While some extrapolations, made in the face of that dearth of material, are thought-provoking (see esp. McBride 1989), it should be noted that, while much can be said about Athanasius' union of Alexandrian ecclesi-asticism and Upper Egyptian monasticism, evidence of the direct involvement of the archiepiscopal see in the rise of Coptic is scant, and there is no evidence (contra Lefort 1933) that Athanasius himself ever wrote or preached in Egyptian. The sheer dialectal diversity, and the early production of translations of texts of which Alexandrian theology would not necessarily have approved (see Orlandi 1991: 1451; 1998: 125–9), also indicates multiple emphases.

Coptic developed into a cultural revival, but it is difficult to discern such an intention among those who promoted it in the third and fourth centuries. Christians and like groups wished to provide texts for new converts; the Egyptian priests were clarifying and synthesizing their invocations. It was a cultural revival that revived not the millennia-old traditions of Egypt, but the written Egyptian word itself. Signifi-cantly, it did not perpetuate the "closed" nature of every previous Egyptian script: no guild had to be joined, no special social class born into: one had only to be able to read Greek and some few other characters. If this was a small portion of society, it was far higher than the portion of people who knew earlier Egyptian scripts in the Greco-Roman period.

Rather than a newly expressed cultural divide, the rise of Coptic enabled a linguistic fusion to match the cultural fusion that was late Roman Egypt. "Coptic culture" was not a separate entity to the dominant Mediterranean culture, which grew alongside and came to dominate Hellenic culture. Rather, it was a broad-based creation by the Greco-Egyptian culture that the Greek, Roman, and Egyptian worlds had bequeathed to Egypt. If Christians came to dominate the use of Coptic, it was largely because Christianity won a much wider battle, narrated elsewhere in this volume.

BIBLIOGRAPHICAL NOTE

A synthetic overview of the period is provided by Bagnall 1993, to which one should now add Bowman 1996 and Krause 1998. On Greek papyri, see Turner 1980, Montevecchi 1988, and Rupprecht 1994; on Coptic papyrology, Pernigotti 1995, Clackson 2004, and MacCoull 1995, 1997. Plenary reports to successive congresses of the International Association of Coptic Studies give up-to-date reviews of progress in Coptic studies (most recently, Immerzeel and Van der Vliet 2004; see also Emmel et al. 1999). On the Greco-Egyptian ritual texts ("magical papyri"), see Brashear 1995, Ritner 1995, and Dieleman 2005. The Greek and "old Coptic" texts are published in Preisendanz 1973–4; the Demotic more haphazardly (bibliography consolidated in Dieleman 2005). All are translated in Betz 1986 and Meyer et al. 1994.

Their historical and linguistic context is treated in Dieleman 2005, and the evolution of the Egyptian priesthood in Late Antiquity by Frankfurter 1998b. For Christianity in Egypt and the papyrological evidence in particular, see Wipszycka 1996, 1998, 2001; for catalogues of Coptic biblical papyri, Schüssler 1995– (see also Schmitz and Mink 1986–). Bibliography on the Nag Hammadi codices is collected in Scholer 1971 and 1997. On Manichaean texts, see Gardner and Lieu 2004: 35–45. Many remain unpublished: for recent progress, see the reports of R. van den Broeck and W.-P. Funk in Immerzeel and Van der Vliet 2004 and Emmel et al. 1999. Short treatments covering all aspects of Coptic language, literature, and history can be found in Atiya 1991 (see especially the specialized treatments of language and dialect in vol. viii), and many Coptic subjects are usefully treated in Helck and Westendorf 1975–92, especially vol. iii (1980). Orlandi (1986, 1991, 1998) provides in several places synthetic introductions to Coptic literature. A useful brief survey of Coptic is Emmel 1992; for a broader perspective, see Loprieno 1995. The classification of Coptic dialects is best treated by Funk (esp. 1988) and Kasser (1980–1; 1990). Education in Greco-Roman Egypt is fundamentally treated in Cribiore 2001 (see also 1999); see Biedenkopf-Ziehner 1999 for the earlier and later periods. Greek and bilingual exercises on papyrus are listed and discussed in Cribiore 1996; Coptic exercises in Hasitzka 1990. On Shenoute and his literary corpus, see now Emmel 2004, which is, despite its stated aims, much more than a codicological study.

CHAPTER TWENTY-FOUR

Late Antique Historiography: A Brief History of Time

David Woods

The production of complex literary narrative requires economic and physical security. In Late Antiquity, the economic and physical security that most of the inhabitants of the Roman Empire had enjoyed since the time of Augustus came to an end. It was for that reason that the period witnessed the rise and triumph of the chronicle as the primary vehicle for the transmission of historical knowledge. A chronicle was, in essence, a list of successive years, and included one or more brief notices concerning events that had occurred during each year. It differed little, either in content or in form, from the *annales maximi* that the *pontifex maximus* had kept at Rome during the republican period. Roman historiography ended, therefore, much as it began, and we are forced to rely upon various sparse chronicles for our knowledge of much of the period *c.* AD 300–750, particularly for events in the west.

Fortunately, the different political fortunes of the western and eastern halves of the Roman Empire insured that the production of complex historical narrative did not cease at the same time throughout the empire as a whole. The production of complex historical narrative in the west seems to have ceased with the work of Renatus Profuturus Frigeridus, whose history covered the period from *c.* AD 395 to 425. There was a long hiatus then, before the production of the next complex historical narratives by bishop Gregory of Tours (*c.* AD 538–94) and the English monk Bede (*c.* AD 673–735). Writing *c.* AD 594, Gregory produced his *Historiae Francorum* in ten books, which formally began with the creation of the world and ended with events in AD 591, although they focused mainly on the period after AD 573. He is our only source for the work of Frigeridus, which has not itself survived. Working *c.* AD 731, Bede produced his *Historia ecclesiastica gentis Anglorum* in five books, beginning with the first invasion of Britain by Julius Caesar in 55 BC and ending in AD 731, although he focused mainly on the period after AD 596. The works of Gregory and Bede are, however, the exceptions that prove the rule – namely, that the composition of complex historical narrative in the west ceased during the early fifth century. Furthermore, they are national histories, and did not preserve the wide-ranging geographical coverage of their classical ancestors.

In contrast (although not all their works have survived), a succession of eastern authors produced an almost continuous series of complex narratives in Greek, until Theophylact Simocatta composed *c.* AD 630 his account of the reign of the emperor Maurice (AD 582–602). The Arab invasions and successive civil wars then intervened to cause a relative literary dark age in the east also, so that the next surviving historical text in Greek is the *Breviarium* that Nicephorus, patriarch of Constantinople (AD 806–15), seems to have composed in the AD 780s, covering the period AD 602–769. For the most part, however, it reads like a series of confused and disjointed notes, with large gaps in its coverage. Even though the author eschews the strict form of a chronicle, the work is no better than the chronicles that he seems to have used as his main sources for much of the period.

As far as historiography was concerned, therefore, Late Antiquity was not a period of great innovation. Such innovations as did occur were forced by social and political change rather than by theoretical considerations. Nevertheless, two innovations stand out. The first was the invention of religious or church history. This is not to claim that the great historians of the classical period had entirely neglected religion in their works, or that they had been reluctant to impose their religious views upon their readers; but they had not focused so narrowly upon the history of one specific cult, nor had they been so relentless in their determination to reinterpret everything in accordance with their religious viewpoint.

The development that forced the invention of church history was the rise of Christianity and the religious tensions that accompanied this rise. It began as a form of apologetic against paganism – that is, a justification and defense of Christianity against its pagan critics – and continued in that vein into the early fifth century, when it was gradually transformed into an apologetic against rival Christian factions. Christian historians attempted to reply to two main pagan arguments against Christianity, the first being that it was a recent innovation, in contrast to the antiquity of the traditional religious and philosophical belief systems, and the second being that Christian atheism and immorality aroused the displeasure of the gods and so brought disaster on the wider population. It is arguable that the need to reply to the first inspired the development of the chronicle – an attempt to synchronize different chronological systems and prove thereby that Moses and the prophets of the Old Testament had lived long before the originators of Greek religion or philosophy – and that the need to reply to the second resulted in the development of the detailed church history – a demonstration of how the state prospered when the church prospered also. It is no accident that Bishop Eusebius of Caesarea, often known as the father of church history, actually devoted most of his career to the composition of apologetical works in a stricter sense, rather than to historical works (Kofsky 2000).

This is not to deny that other motivations may have been at play also, not least when paganism no longer posed a serious intellectual threat. Generally speaking, church histories served to prove that divine providence continued into the era of the writer, whether of Eusebius writing in the early fourth century or of one of his continuators subsequently; that God would protect his church, whether against pagan persecution (as in the pre-Constantinian era, or during the brief reigns of Julian "the Apostate," AD 360–3, and the western usurper Eugenius, AD 392–4) or against heretics (whether Marcion or Mani during the pre-Constantinian era or Arius and Nestorius during the subsequent period). As time progressed, the growing tendency to identify church and state meant that the military setbacks suffered by the empire – that is, the loss of the western half of the empire to various barbarian groups during the fifth century and the loss of much of the eastern half of the empire to the Arab invaders during the seventh – posed a new challenge to the Christian historian, all the more so in that those invaders had been either heretics or non-Christians. There were two possible responses, although they were not always distinguished clearly. In the midst of the crisis itself, the temptation was to interpret the defeats and massacres as preludes to the end of time and the Second Coming of Christ (Reinink 2002). In hindsight, when the situation had stabilized once more, the response was that God still cared for his people, but that he had allowed their enemies to triumph over them in order to punish them for their sins.

The second major innovation concerns the method of calculating the year, the chronological system one needs to adopt before one can write a history. The Romans had traditionally identified each year by the names of the two consuls who held office during that year. Since the first consuls had only held office in 509 BC, this system could not be used to refer to years before that date. Furthermore, the last private person to hold the office was Basilius in AD 541. Many people used regional dating systems that counted the years since the formation of the relevant Roman province or the refoundation of a local town; but these systems were clearly unsuited for use in any work designed to appeal to a broader readership (Meimaris 1992). Regnal dating was common, but the disintegration of the Roman Empire and the rise of various successor states in the west meant that historians used different systems of regnal dating according to whether they wrote in Gothic Spain, Frankish Gaul, or in the Eastern Roman Empire. This made it difficult to coordinate sources from different regions; but the secular nature of this system also proved unappealing, since the preservation and transmission of historical knowledge increasingly fell to the clergy, especially the bishops. Most chroniclers adopted as their main chronological system AM dating (*anno mundi*, "in the year of the universe"), which numbered the years from the creation of the universe (although several different systems were often used in parallel). There were several methods of calculating the initial year of creation in accordance with biblical data, so that the Alexandrian method dated it to 5500 BC (5492 BC in our Dionysian era) whereas the Byzantine method dated it to 5509 BC. AM dating predominated in the east, but AD dating (*anno domini*, "in the year of the Lord") eventually triumphed in the west. A Scythian monk at Rome, Dionysius Exiguus, used AD dating in the Easter table that he constructed in AD 525, and the spread of that table popularized his method, which numbered the years since the incarnation of Christ. It has recently been argued, however, that it was really Eusebius of Caesarea who had introduced this idea in his chronicle, and that Dionysius borrowed the idea from him without acknowledging this (McCarthy 2003). The most unusual system was developed in Ireland, where early medieval chroniclers distinguished one year from another by means of a kalend and ferial apparatus – that is, by identifying each year according to the day of the week on which January 1 fell. It has recently been argued that the anonymous author of the first Irish chronicle, the common ancestor of all the surviving Irish chronicles, continued an otherwise unattested translation by Rufinus of Aquileia of the chronicle of Eusebius, to which he had added this kalend and ferial system (McCarthy 2001). Hence Rufinus has been credited with this unusual system. It is more likely, however, that the kalend and ferial system was first used in a local Irish chronicle that had its origin in an Easter table and was then retrospectively applied to some version of Eusebius' chronicle when someone decided to convert this limited local chronicle into a universal history by joining the two texts together (Ó Cróinín 1983).

The lack of innovation during this period is revealed by the fact that many, if not most, of the surviving historical works were continuations of earlier works. This was true of both church histories and secular histories. Eventually, the production of complex narrative histories ceased altogether, and what remained were simply continuations of the chronicle of Eusebius. Even in the case of church history, most of the surviving texts aspire to be universal histories in the manner of Eusebius' *Church History* – but again, as continuations of that history. There were few, if any, attempts at regional or local history. The nearest one gets to this were the biographies of bishops or collections of biographies of successive bishops. The so-called *Historia Acephala* seems to have originated as a biography of Athanasius, bishop of Alexandria (AD 328–73); and the *Liber Pontificalis*, a collection of biographies of the popes that was probably first compiled in the fifth century and updated at regular intervals thereafter, while not strictly a history of the church at Rome, provides the skeleton of such.

Church Histories

Eusebius, bishop of Caesarea in Palestine (*c.* AD 314–39), composed a wide range of theological and apologetic works but was most famous for his historical works, as the result of which he is commonly hailed as the father of church history. Technically, he did not invent church history, since he had predecessors such as Sextus Julius Africanus, who wrote a five-book *Chronography* covering events from creation to AD 217, but he certainly reinvented it, so that it became more comprehensive in scope and more critical in matters of chronology.

The earliest of his three historical works was his chronicle, which consisted of two linked parts: a *Chronography*, which was a compendium of regnal and source lists nation by nation; and his *Chronicle Canons*, which was a complete chronology of world history, a synthesis of the material in the *Chronography* (Burgess 1999). In its final form, this chronology stretches from the birth of Abraham (2016 BC) to the beginning of the celebration of the twentieth anniversary of the accession of Constantine I in AD 325. Eusebius used three main chronological systems: years since the birth of Abraham, Olympiads, and regnal years. This work has not survived in its original Greek, but its content and format can be reconstructed from its preservation as part of four subsequent texts, the Latin translation and continuation that the monk Jerome composed at Constantinople in AD 381, an Armenian translation from *c.* AD 600, and two Syriac epitomes, one in the so-called *Chronicle of 724*, which was actually composed in AD 640, and the other in the *Chronicle of Zuqnin* (also called the *Chronicle of Pseudo-Dionysius*), which was composed in AD 775. Eusebius probably completed the first edition of his chronicle in AD 311, but revised and extended it in AD 314 and 325.

Eusebius' second historical work was his *Church History*, a detailed account of the history of the Christian church from the birth of Jesus Christ down to (in its final form) Constantine's defeat of his rival Licinius in AD 324. Eusebius seems to have produced four different editions of this work: a first edition in seven books, some time before Diocletian's persecution of the Christians in AD 303; a second edition in AD 314 after Maximinus' persecution of the Christians; a third edition in ten volumes in AD 315; and a final edition in AD 325 (Barnes 1980). The most noteworthy feature of this work, and one that distinguished it so greatly from traditional historical works, was that Eusebius did not hesitate to quote at length from a wide variety of earlier sources.

His final historical work was his *Life of Constantine*. He had not finished this by his death, so that one of his successors at Caesarea edited it and published it in his name shortly afterward. It consists of four books and defies easy classification, being a combination of panegyric and biography, but a religious biography rather than a biography in the strict classical sense (Averil Cameron 1997). Both his *Church History* and his *Life of Constantine* survive in the original Greek.

Several authors wrote continuations of Eusebius' *Church History*. The priest Rufinus produced at Aquileia *c.* AD 403 an abridged translation into Latin and a continuation of Eusebius' history until the death of the emperor Theodosius I (AD 379–95), but he found no continuator subsequently. In the Greek east, Philostorgius wrote a continuation of Eusebius' history in twelve books until the death of the usurper John in AD 425, but it has survived only as an epitome made by Photius, the patriarch of Constantinople (AD 858–67). Philostorgius' work is unique in that he wrote from an Arian perspective in defense of those theologians and emperors who were to be condemned as heretics by the other surviving continuators of Eusebius.

The first Greek continuation to survive in full was that by Socrates of Constantinople (Urbainczyk 1997). He wrote a church history in seven books from the accession of Constantine in AD 306 down to AD 439. His concern for the accuracy of his work reveals itself in several ways. He used an annotated consular list or chronicle to provide him with a series of precise dates for various events, concluded every book with a statement as to the length of time covered by that book, and dated the last events in most books according to the consulate and the Olympiad. More importantly, he reveals that he produced a second edition of his work when, as a result of reading the work of Bishop Athanasius of Alexandria, he discovered that one of his main sources, for his first and second books in particular – namely, the Latin church history of Rufinus of Aquileia – had contained several important chronological errors (Socrates, *Hist. eccl.* 2. 1). He probably wrote shortly after AD 439, and certainly before the death of Theodosius II in AD 450. He did so at the request of a "holy man of God" called Theodore, of whom nothing else is known. Our knowledge of Socrates himself derives entirely from his text, but he lets little slip about his identity. Later manuscripts describe him as a *scholasticus*, a lawyer, but nothing within the text itself supports this description. Insofar as he demonstrates an unusual degree of knowledge of, and sympathy toward, the Novatians, it has sometimes been argued that he was a member of this schismatic sect, but there is no firm proof either way. Socrates used a wide variety of sources, Christian and pagan, written and oral, and the scrupulous nature of his research reveals itself, for example, in his reference to two epic poems that remain unknown otherwise (Socrates, *Hist. eccl.* 3. 21. 14; 6. 6. 36).

The second Greek continuation of Eusebius' church history to survive in full is that by Sozomen. He composed a church history in nine books and, although he states in his preface that he would begin in AD 323 and end in AD 439, his narrative actually breaks off in AD 425. So, he probably died before he could complete the work. He dedicates it to Theodosius II. He also wrote an epitome in two books covering the period from the Ascension until the death of Licinius (Sozom. *Hist. eccl.* 1. 1). This had clearly been intended as an introduction to his main church history, but it has not survived. Although he used the history of Socrates as one of his main sources, he does not openly acknowledge this fact, and obviously wrote within a year or two of Socrates. Yet he also consulted afresh many of the same sources that Socrates had used. Furthermore, he consulted several new sources: legal texts, the secular history by Olympiodorus of Thebes, and the *Historia Lausiaca* by Palladius on the monks of Egypt.

The major differences between these two historians, Socrates and Sozomen, concern their style and their content. Sozomen adopts a more elevated and rhetorical style designed to appeal to a readership well versed in classical historiography. As to the content, he is more overtly polemical, as when he replies to the claims by pagan historians that Constantine I had his eldest son Crispus executed (Sozom. *Hist. eccl.* 1. 5). He also provides more information about his own life than does Socrates, so that we know that he was born into a Christian family near Bethela in Gaza, and that he came to Constantinople *c.* AD 426, where he worked as a lawyer.

The third continuation of Eusebius' church history to survive in full is that by Theodoret, bishop of Cyrrhus in Syria (AD 423–53). He composed a church history in five books from the defeat of Licinius in AD 324 down to the death of Bishop Theodotus of Antioch in AD 429. He also composed a wide range of theological works, a collection of letters, and his so-called *Religious History*, a collection of short biographies of the most famous monks of the deserts of Syria. He was born and reared at Antioch, and spent his whole life in Syria. He was very active in the ecclesiastical politics of his day and sought to defend Nestorius, bishop of Constantinople (AD 428–31), against the charge of heresy. The result was that in AD 449 the emperor ordered him confined within his own see, and he was twice condemned by church councils after his death. It is not certain whether he knew the works of Socrates or Sozomen, since his church history is very different. He reports events from an Antiochene perspective in contrast to their Constantinopolitan perspective, and he is far less concerned with precise chronology than either of them. He preserves a great deal of material unknown to either of his predecessors, but it is clear that he invented much of this, or relied on a source who had done so (Woods 2001a). His is by far the most unreliable and amateurish of the three histories, and he often seems more interested in pious propaganda than in a truthful report of the past.

The next church history in Greek to survive in full was that by the *scholasticus* Evagrius, composed *c.* AD 594 (Allen 1981). This was divided into six books and covered the period from the first Council of Ephesus in AD 431 down to the death of John, bishop of Jerusalem, in AD 594. Evagrius was born at Epiphania in Syria and spent most of his life as a lawyer in the service of Bishop Gregory of Antioch (AD 570–92). He writes, therefore, from an Antiochene perspective. He produced two other works, a collection of documents that had been issued in the name of Bishop Gregory, and a work that celebrated the birth of the emperor Maurice's eldest son in AD 584 (neither has survived). As a result, the emperor Tiberius Constantine (AD 578–82) granted him the rank of *quaestor*, while Maurice granted him the rank of prefect (Evagrius, *Hist. eccl.* 6. 24). In the preface to his history, Evagrius reveals that he saw himself continuing the work not only of Eusebius but also of Socrates, Sozomen, and Theodoret. He used a wide variety of different sources: the *acta* of the church councils, earlier church histories, the lives of holy men, and secular histories (even by pagans). One of his most important sources was the church history composed in Greek by Zechariah of Mitylene during the AD 490s, which seems to have covered events since the Council of Chalcedon in AD 451. Zechariah was a native of Gaza and practiced as a lawyer for a while at Constantinople before he was made bishop of Mitylene. Unfortunately, his work survives only in the form of an epitome by an anonymous Syriac author (now known as Pseudo-Zechariah), which continued down to AD 569. The most important secular source for the earlier part of Evagrius' history was the two-volume work (now lost) by Eustathius of Epiphaneia, covering the period from creation down to AD 503 (Evagrius, *Hist. eccl.* 5. 24). In the latter part of his history, his most important secular source was the *Wars* by Procopius of Caesarea (of whom more below). He also seems to have known and used the histories by the pagans Zosimus and Priscus of Panium, even though he had Eustathius for the same period, and (like Sozomen before him, but with an equal lack of success) he attempts to defend Constantine from the charges made against him by Zosimus (Evagrius, *Hist. eccl.* 3. 40–1). With Evagrius, unfortunately, the succession of continuators of the *Church History* of Eusebius reached its end.

Latin Secular Histories

In the field of secular historiography, the first complex narrative to survive from this period is the *Res gestae* composed in Latin by Ammianus Marcellinus *c.* AD 391. This work originally covered the period from the accession of the emperor Nerva (AD 96–8) to the repulsion of the Goths from Constantinople following the death of the emperor Valens (AD 364–78) at the battle of Hadrianople; but it does not survive in full. The surviving text commences with an account of the behavior of Gallus Caesar at Antioch in AD 353, although Ammianus occasionally refers back to his description of events during the earlier period. According to the transmitted book numbers, we possess the last eighteen books of a work that had originally consisted of thirty-one books; but it has recently been argued that the book numbers suffered corruption at an early stage in the transmission of this text, so that we actually possess the second eighteen books of a work that had consisted of thirty-six books (Barnes 1998: 20–31). Controversy also surrounds the career of the author. He describes himself as a former soldier and a Greek (31. 16. 9), and provides a great deal of information concerning his military career during the period AD 353–64, when he saw service in both the western and the eastern halves of the empire. He seems to have participated in the emperor Julian's ill-fated expedition against the Persians in AD 363, but his status subsequently remains something of a mystery. He was in Antioch during the treason trials there in AD 370, but seems to have moved to Rome by about AD 384. Nevertheless, his identification with the Antiochene Ammianus engaged in literary activity at Rome, to whom the rhetor Libanius addressed a letter in AD 392, remains improbable. While it is true that Ammianus spent much of his life in or about Antioch, he probably came from somewhere in Phoenicia (Barnes 1998: 54–64), perhaps Emesa (Woods 2003). While it is clear that Ammianus saw himself as a continuator of the work of Tacitus, whose *Historiae* had ended in AD 96, he did not follow his methodology or style very closely. His text contains many digressions more in keeping with the Greek historical tradition, the most noteworthy being his digressions on scientific matters such as earthquakes (17. 7. 9–14). He remains silent about the sources that he used for the surviving portion of his history, although one may assume that he supplemented his own memories with a variety of oral and written sources. Great controversy surrounds the relationship of his history to that by Eunapius of Sardis, since they were close contemporaries writing at the same time on the same subject matter; but the argument that Ammianus had access to a first edition of Eunapius' history has much to recommend it (Barnes 1978: 117–19). Otherwise, he probably used a variety of official reports, the writings of the emperor Julian, panegyrics, and letters. The accuracy and objectivity of Ammianus have been highly praised in the past, not least because his prejudices appeal so much to the modern academic. In fact, he is an anti-Christian polemicist, who allows his religious prejudice to distort much of what he reports (Barnes 1998: 79–94), although he is far more subtle in this than was Eunapius of Sardis. Furthermore, it is arguable that some of his apparent oral sources, such as the eunuch Eutherius, may have tailored their reminiscences to suit his obvious prejudices (Woods 1998). Hence, Ammianus' text is far more complex and difficult to use than might initially seem to be the case.

The only other substantial secular historical text to survive in Latin from this period was the collection of imperial biographies now known as the *Historia Augusta*. It consists of thirty biographies, although some are really collections of biographies, from Hadrian (AD 117–38) until Carinus (AD 283–5). It presents itself as having been written by six different historians working during the reigns of Diocletian and Constantine I; but it has long been accepted that it was probably written at Rome by one man shortly after AD 395. The fact that it contains several direct quotations from Aurelius Victor and Eutropius, that it betrays a knowledge of the history of

Ammianus Marcellinus, and that it seems to allude to several contemporary events such as the destruction of the Serapeum in AD 391 and the battle of Frigidus in AD 394, suffices to prove its late date (Syme 1968). It is not clear why the author of this text should have sought to conceal his date and identity, but the fictitious nature of much of the material that he reports, during the later biographies in particular, suggests that he designed the whole work as an academic hoax and that it was necessary to conceal his real date and identity as part of this hoax. It has been argued that he derived his authentic historical information from six main sources, four of whom can be identified by name: Marius Maximus, Herodian, Dexippus, and Eunapius. The remaining two are hypothetical sources, whose existence is deduced from the nature of the text and its relationship with other late Latin historical sources: a reliable Latin source that ended in AD 217, the author of which is sometimes misleadingly referred to as Ignotus by modern commentators, and another Latin source conventionally described as the *Kaisergeschichte*, which the author of the *Historia Augusta* seems to have shared with the authors of other Latin epitomes or brief histories composed during the late fourth century (on which more below; see Barnes 1978). The *Historia Augusta* preserves our most detailed surviving account of the period AD 238–85, but it is difficult to distinguish between the material that the author derived from a reliable source and the material he invented as part of his hoax.

As far as Latin historiography was concerned, the fourth century was otherwise very much the age of the epitome or brief history. This type of work represents an intermediate stage between the complex narrative history and the chronicle, and the popularity of such works during the late fourth century provides a telling insight into the social and political changes already afoot; changes that eventually saw the triumph of the chronicle as the primary vehicle for the transmission of historical knowledge. Writing *c.* AD 361, Sextus Aurelius Victor composed his *De Caesaribus*, a history of the emperors from 31 BC to AD 361 (Bird 1984). He was a career civil servant, who was appointed governor of Pannonia Secunda in AD 361 and prefect of Rome *c.* AD 388. Writing *c.* AD 369, Eutropius composed his *Breviarium*, a history of the Roman state from its mythical foundation by Romulus down to AD 364. He also was a career civil servant, who was *magister memoriae* in AD 369 and rose to become consul in AD 387. Next, writing *c.* AD 370, Festus composed his *Breviarium*, a history of the Roman state from the foundation of Rome to AD 364 once more, but it was only about a quarter of the length of Eutropius' text (Eadie 1967). He seems to have succeeded Eutropius as *magister menoriae* and rose to become proconsul of Asia by AD 372. Finally, an anonymous author composed the *Epitome de Caesaribus* shortly after AD 395, in which he summarized Roman history from 31 BC to AD 395. It is not clear what inspired these authors to write as they did, although Festus wrote in response to a direct request from the emperor Valens himself. It seems that the emperor felt that his work would serve some definite purpose, whether as a convenient educational tool for those ignorant of Roman history or as piece of propaganda designed to provide justification for an intended Persian campaign. In all cases, however, one suspects that the authors were motivated by a hope that the circulation of their work would enhance their reputation as men of learning and so prove them worthy of further promotion, rather than by a desire to prove a particular argument.

They all rely heavily on a common source, the *Kaisergeschichte* (or a continuation of the same down to AD 378). This was probably a comprehensive history of Rome from its origins to AD 358 rather than a history of the imperial period alone (Burgess 2005). The fact that so many ambitious men of relatively humble origin should have interrupted their busy careers in order to compose historical works provides a telling confirmation of the complaints by Ammianus Marcellinus (14. 6. 18; 18. 4. 14) that the senatorial elite, the great landed families whose members should have had both the time and the means to compose complex historical narrative in the manner of Tacitus or Cassius Dio, were no longer interested in such serious pastimes. Some senators did manage to bestir themselves, such as Virius Nicomachus Flavianus, consul in AD 394; but nothing is known about the nature of his *annales*, which may have been an epitome of republican history rather than a detailed original description of contemporary events (Hedrick 2000: 145–7).

Greek Secular Histories

Eunapius of Sardis composed the first secular narrative of this period in Greek, but it survives only in fragments (Blockley 1981: 1–26). The emperor Constantine Porphyrogenitus (AD 913–59) ordered the compilation of excerpts, the *Excerpta Historica*, arranged according to topic from a wide range of historical works, including that of Eunapius (Banchich 1985). The patriarch Photius preserves a description of Eunapius' history in his *Bibliotheca* (Phot. *Bibl.* 77), which reveals that it consisted of fourteen books and was intended as a continuation of the history by Dexippus. It began with the reign of Claudius II (AD 268–70) and concluded with the death of the empress Eudoxia in AD 404. Eunapius was a sophist and a staunch pagan, and Photius claims that he published two different editions of his history, the main difference being that he removed the more virulently anti-Christian comments from his second edition. He also published a second historical work, his *Lives of Philosophers and Sophists*. Fortunately, this survives in full and can be dated to AD 399. Since Eunapius refers several times in this to his earlier history, these references should help us to date the composition of the first edition of his history. Yet their interpretation remains controversial, so that it is not clear whether he had published the full text of the first edition by the time that Ammianus was writing his history about AD 391, or had merely published several installments of the full work by that date. The surviving fragments confirm that Eunapius was fiercely critical of leading Christian figures such as the emperors Constantine I and Theodosius I, while he praised those who sought to maintain traditional pagan religion.

The next author to compose a secular narrative in Greek seems to have been Olympiodorus, a pagan poet from Thebes in Egypt (Blockley 1981: 27–47). Again, his work survives only in fragments, most of them, again, preserved by Photius in his *Bibliotheca* (Phot. *Bibl.* 80). According to Photius, Olympiodorus composed his history in twenty-two books covering the period from the death of the western general Stilicho in AD 408 to the coronation of the emperor Valentinian III

(AD 425–55). The surprising feature of his work is that, despite being written in Greek, it is almost entirely concerned with events in the west.

The next author to consider is Priscus of Panium in Thrace (Blockley 1981: 48–70). He was a rhetor and sophist, who published a history in eight books apparently covering the period from the accession of Attila as king of the Huns in AD 434 to the death of the emperor Leo (AD 457–74). His interest in the relations between Byzantium and the Huns of Attila in particular, but also the relations between the Byzantines and other foreign peoples in general, is best explained by the fact that he seems to have served on several diplomatic missions, including one to Attila in AD 449. The *Excerpta Historica* of Constantine Porphyrogenitus preserve most of the fragments of his work. His history served as an important source for later authors such as Procopius and Evagrius.

Controversy surrounds the origin of Malchus and the range covered by his history, since Photius (*Bibl.* 78) and the *Suda* (a tenth-century lexicon) disagree with one another in these matters (Blockley 1981: 71–85). Photius states that Malchus was from Philadelphia in Syria, which is probably correct, given Malchus' Semitic name. The *Suda*, however, describes him as a Byzantine, which suggests that he spent most of his working life in Constantinople. Photius claims that Malchus wrote a history in seven books, beginning when the emperor Leo fell ill in AD 473 and ending with the murder of the western emperor Nepos (AD 474–80). The *Suda*, however, states that Malchus' history covered the period from the death of Constantine to the accession of Anastasius (apparently, therefore, from AD 337 to AD 491). However, since Photius also says that the seven books that he read show that Malchus had produced several books preceding them, and that he would have produced others also had he lived longer, the obvious suggestion is that Malchus published two different editions of his work. Again, the *Excerpta Historica* of Constantine Porphyrogenitus preserve most of the fragments of his work, although the *Suda* preserves several important fragments also.

The survival rate of the secular histories from the Greek east improves rapidly during the sixth century. Zosimus has left us his *New History* in six books. The work opens by summarizing events from the Trojan war until the reign of Probus (AD 276–82), but then resumes a more detailed narrative until it breaks off suddenly just before the sack of Rome in AD 410. The sudden ending suggests that he died before he could complete the work, and it remains unclear to what date he had actually intended to continue it. Photius reports that he was an *advocatus fisci* (Phot. *Bibl.* 98), and he seems to have lived during the early sixth century. Unfortunately, he did not produce any substantial original history, but seems merely to have epitomized the works of Dexippus, Eunapius, and Oympiodorus in turn, and to have conjoined the results. His importance, therefore, lies in his witness to these sources rather than in anything that he says himself. His stated purpose was to describe how the Romans had lost an empire in as short a time as they had gained it, and he blamed this loss squarely on the christianization of the state and the neglect of the traditional rites (Zos. *Hist. nova* 1. 1). It is not clear why he described his history as "new," but it may have been to emphasize the contrast between his task and that of Polybius of Megalopolis (d.118 BC), who had described how the Romans had originally won their empire.

The most important author of the sixth century was Procopius of Caesarea in Palestine (Averil Cameron 1985). He composed three historical works that focused on the reign of Justinian I (AD 527–65). His major work, the *Wars*, consisted of eight books when complete. The first seven books were divided geographically. Hence books 1–3 dealt with the Persian wars from AD 491 to 549, books 3–4 with the wars against the Vandals from AD 395 to 548, and books 5–7 with the Gothic wars from AD 475 to 550. The emphasis overall was on the progress of these wars under Justinian, especially his successful reconquest of Africa and most of Italy. Procopius probably completed these books by AD 550, but he added book 8 in AD 552, bringing his accounts of the wars in the various theaters up to that date. He also composed his *Buildings*, which cataloged and praised Justinian's building activities throughout the empire (excluding Italy). It has been variously dated between AD 552 and 560. Finally, he composed a *Secret History*, in which he savagely attacked Justinian and his wife Theodora, in complete contradiction of the praise lavished upon them in his other works. Its date is disputed, but it was probably written in AD 550. Procopius had firsthand knowledge of many of the events that he describes, since he served as an *assessor* on the staff of the most important general of the day, Belisarius, from AD 527 to 540, and accompanied him to the eastern frontier, Africa, and to Italy. He seems to have spent most of the rest of his life at Constantinople. The date of his death is unknown, but it has been argued that he died as early as AD 553 (Howard-Johnston 2000: 19–22). His classicizing style makes it difficult to determine what his religious views were and, while most accept that he was a conventional Christian, it has also been argued that he was a Platonist pagan (Kaldellis 2004).

Agathias continues the *Wars* of Procopius in five books covering the period AD 552–8 (Cameron 1970). He was born at Myrina in the province of Asia, but spent his adult life as a lawyer in Constantinople. He was a prolific poet, the author of nine books of erotic poetry in hexameters (*Daphniaca*, lost) as well as a collection of epigrams (*Cycle*), so that his decision to continue Procopius' history is surprising. It is no surprise, however, that the poet should turn out to be a dismal historian, who edits material to suit his moralizing tendencies and seems sometimes to use myth to supplement history, in a sort of intellectual challenge to his reader (Kaldellis 2003). He seems to have composed his history in the AD 570s, and to have intended to continue it much further, until the death of the Persian king Chosroes in AD 579 (Agathias, *Hist*. 4. 29), but his own death intervened. The *protector* Menander continued the history of Agathias from AD 558 until the fall of Sirmium to the Avars in AD 582 (Blockley 1985a). The *Suda* preserves a biographical fragment, but our knowledge of this author and his work derives mostly from the fragments preserved by Constantine Porphyrogenitus in the *Excerpta Historica*.

Finally, Theophylact Simocatta wrote a history in eight books concerning the reign of Maurice. His work survives in full, but he provides little information concerning himself. He seems to have been an Egyptian Christian and to have spent his adult life as a *scholasticus* at Constantinople. Three minor works by him survive also, revealing his interest in literature, natural philosophy, and theology as well as history. It has been argued that he contributed little new in his work, that he did not use oral sources in the way that he might have, and was generally content to combine a limited number of written sources into a larger narrative (Whitby 1988: 311–13).

Chronicles

Writing at Constantinople in AD 381, Jerome translated Eusebius' chronicle into Latin and supplemented it with material drawn from Suetonius and the *Kaisergeschichte*. He also continued it from AD 325 to the death of Valens in AD 378. Although Jerome specifically states that this was what he was doing, a comparison of his text with the Syriac *Chronicle of 724* and with that composed by Theophanes Confessor *c*. AD 814 reveals similarities that prove he shared with them a common source – namely, an earlier continuation of Eusebius' chronicle that proceeded down to AD 350 (Burgess 1999: 123–6; but in my opinion further). This highlights one of the most importance differences between the chronicle and the complex narrative history. The brevity and apparent simplicity of the chronicle encouraged its latest owner to add a few entries to it in order to bring it up to date. Hence a chronicle tended to grow as it circulated, and was recopied from one manuscript to another, until someone finally proceeded to compose a formal continuation of the original text for a more extended period but retained the anonymous intervening additions also.

The attractiveness of the chronicle format is amply illustrated by the number of different authors who attempted to write a continuation of Jerome's chronicle itself. Prosper abridged it and added the names of the consuls for each year from the death of Christ, before then continuing it until AD 433. Furthermore, he continued it twice more also, to AD 445, then to AD 455 (Muhlberger 1990). Again, the anonymous author of the so-called *Gallic Chronicle of 452*, who probably lived, to judge from the contents of his text, in the province of Viennensis in Gaul, continued Jerome's chronicle to AD 452 (Burgess 2001a). Similarly, Hydatius, bishop of Aquae Flaviae in Gallaecia (northern Portugal), discovered a copy of Jerome's chronicle, added Spanish era dates to its existing dating systems, and continued it from AD 379 to 468 (Burgess 1993). The anonymous author of the *Gallic Chronicle of 511* continued the chronicle of Jerome, or an epitome of it, to AD 511, and used Orosius, Hydatius, and the *Gallic Chronicle of 452* (in addition to other unknown sources) to assist him in this matter (Burgess 2001b). Finally, writing in Latin at Constantinople, Count Marcellinus continued Jerome's text, first down to AD 518 and then to 534 (Croke 2001: 20–35). Eventually, further continuators added to this first generation of continuations of Jerome's chronicle, and the process continued throughout the medieval period. Hence Victor, bishop of Tunnuna in Africa, continued the chronicle of Prosper until AD 567, while John of Biclaro, bishop of Gerona in Spain, continued the chronicle of Victor until AD 590 (Wolf 1990: 2–3). Then the anonymous author of the *Chronicle of 741* continued John of Biclaro until AD 741 at least, although the transmitted text breaks off in AD 724 (Hoyland 1997: 610–27). Sometimes the earliest sections of such continuations were severely abridged, but on other occasions they were left untouched.

The story in the east was no different. In addition to the anonymous continuation of Eusebius' chronicle that Jerome had used as the basis of his text, two early fifth-century Alexandrian monks, Panodorus and Annianus, composed revised editions and continuations of Eusebius according to their rather different calculations. Neither work has survived, but George Syncellus preserves scattered testimonies to their contents in the chronicle that he composed *c.* AD 810. The first Greek continuation to survive in large part at least is the chronicle of John Malalas. As it survives, it covers in eighteen books the period from creation to AD 563, where the main manuscript breaks off; but it had probably continued to the death of Justinian in AD 565. John seems to have composed a first edition at Antioch *c.* AD 532 and a second edition at Constantinople *c.* AD 565, although an anonymous continuator may also have been responsible for this alleged second edition (Croke 1990a: 17–22). The most noteworthy feature of Malalas' chronicle is that he composed it as continuous narrative rather than in the traditional tabular form; but he was not the first to do this. When the Spanish priest Orosius composed his *Historiarum adversus paganos libri VII* in AD 418, he converted much of Jerome's chronicle into narrative form also. The next Greek chronicle to survive almost in full is the *Paschal Chronicle*, which covered the period from creation to AD 630. Its anonymous author used a variety of sources, including a lost Arian history used also by Philostorgius, the chronicle of Count Marcellinus, and that of John Malalas; but he also drew on his own experience and on official records for the last period *c.* AD 602–30. As noted above, a gap then occurs until Nicephorus produced his *Breviarium* in the AD 780 s, although some activity continued in the regions conquered by the Arabs. Writing perhaps in Coptic *c.* AD 650, Bishop John of Nikiu in Egypt composed a continuation of the chronicle of John Malalas down to the Arab capture of Alexandria in AD 641 (Hoyland 1997: 152–6), while several anonymous authors composed continuations of Eusebius' chronicle into the seventh and eighth centuries in Syriac.

A final point requires emphasis. The evidence of chronicles is often much more complex, and unreliable, than may appear at first sight. Even if one can assume that the original author of a chronicle or section of a chronicle was perfectly informed about the events that he describes (which is never necessarily the case), the nature of the genre itself encouraged serious errors during the transmission of a chronicle, even at the earliest stage. First, the regnal or other chronological markers often shifted in their column so that they were no longer aligned against the notices to which they had originally referred. Second, chronicles were not self-correcting in the manner of complex narratives. A copyist who could not read a name at one place in a complex narrative could correct his reading of this name from its reoccurrence at other points in the same narrative. In contrast, notices in chronicles tended to be brief and isolated, so that a name usually occurred once only. The copyist simply had to make his best guess at what he thought the text had intended to say, and the results could be disastrous, especially when the copyist operated in a geographical or political context different to that of the original author. Hence it was probably the relatively unknown town of Boresis that revolted against Diocletian *c.* AD 293, not Busiris (Bowman 1984: 33–6), and the alleged name of the officer who began the persecution of Christians in the army *c.* AD 300, Veturius, is probably a corruption of the name of the legionary base where this persecution had begun, Betthorus (Woods 2001b). As for the fleet of UFOs that appeared in the skies over Ireland in AD 749, some skepticism is warranted (Woods 2000).

BIBLIOGRAPHICAL NOTE

Several different series combine to provide modern translations of most of the works cited above that have survived in full: Byzantina Australiensia (Zosimus, John Malalas); The Fathers of the Church (Orosius); Loeb Classical Library (Ammianus, Procopius, Bede); Nicene and Post-Nicene Fathers (Eusebius, Sozomen, Socrates, Theodoret); Liverpool Translated Texts (*Chronicon Paschale*, Eutropius, Evagrius, Irish chronicles, Isidore, John of Biclaro); Penguin Classics (Bede, Gregory of Tours), while Oxford University Press has published several important translations as monographs (*Consularia Constantinopolitana*, George Syncellus, Hydatius, Rufinus, Theophanes, Theophylact Simocatta). Modern editions of the Greek texts have slowly appeared in the series "Die Griechischen Christlichen Schriftsteller" (Eusebius, Philostorgius, Socrates, Sozomen, Theodoret, together with the Latin texts of Jerome and Rufinus), and in the "Corpus Fontium Historiae Byzantinae" (John Malalas, Nicephorus). Most of the Latin texts, especially the chronicles, can be found in the *Monumenta Germaniae historica*, while the Syriac texts are usually available in the *Corpus scriptorum Christianorum Orientalium*. Blockley 1981–3 provides text and translation of the more important fragmentary works. Two recent handbooks complement one another to provide a detailed treatment of most historical authors from the fourth to eighth centuries: Marasco 2003 and Hoyland 1997. Treadgold 2007 provides a detailed survey of every significant Byzantine historian from Eusebius of Caesarea to Theophylact Simocatta.

PART IV

Empire, Kingdom, and Beyond

At least two major developments have characterized the recent study of the Later Roman Empire. One has been to redefine, if not actually blur, the distinction between "Roman" and "barbarian" (notable here being the impact of Whittaker 1994 and the wealth of reflection generated in the "Shifting Frontiers" conferences – seven since 1995; and see Lee 1993; Mathisen and Sivan 1996; Pohl et al. 2001). Chapters here by Gillett (26), Halsall (27), and Vanderspoel (28) illustrate but also question the emphases that can result. There is, of course, a territorial dimension (more than hinted at already by Humphries (ch. 7) and Leyerle (ch. 8)), in that the "frontiers" of the Roman world are no longer seen as firm boundaries on a map (which was never a sound perception anyway) but rather as broad bands of country in which people subject (in varying degrees) to the writ of the emperor, whether fiscal or legal, mixed cautiously but extensively with people who might have seen themselves as allies but were essentially "free" (and therefore unpredictable and occasionally threatening). The mixing was to a considerable extent commercial, trade being to the advantage of both groups of people and vividly attested in the museum cases of the world; but there were political bargains struck – ad hoc squadrons of foreign horsemen for the Romans, and armed intervention against rivals for the barbarians. Well before the Goths crossed the Danube in the AD 380s and the *Völkerwanderung* truly began to impress itself on the Roman provinces, a shift in definition was also taking place, whereby individuals and groups essentially "foreign" to the Roman world began to think of themselves as Romans or committed to Roman values and customs, and (more rarely) Romans were ready to "defect" in some sense to a "barbarian" world, impelled by a thirst for adventure, a desire for profit, or a wish to escape personal or institutional pressures – their own crimes or failures, the burden of taxation, the ruthless hierarchies and competition of an autocratic and elitist society (the formal apparatus of which is revealed here by Humfress (ch. 25) and to some extent, in the next section, by Lim (ch. 33) and Gaddis (ch. 34); and see Honoré 1998; Harries 1999; Matthews 2000; Kelly 2004).

The other major development has been a more urgent and informed interest in "the east," which, in the late antique context, means all those areas that lay between the heartland of Roman culture and control and the centers of Persian power – the world of the Syriac-speaking peoples and of the Arabs that lived to their south. Contemporary circumstances, since the collapse of the Ottoman Empire (less than a century ago), the rise of Arab nationalism (if we can use so unitary a term), and the associated shift in the self-definition of Islam, have made this interest – political and economic as well as linguistic, historical, and cultural – both necessary and natural. It has been affected no doubt by "orientalism" and by a sense of superiority that has outlasted its imperialist self-justification; but it has led, nevertheless, to a powerful expansion of the western mind. But there has also been a more objective interest in these "oriental" cultures, seen on their own terms; an awareness of their some-times troubled but always intimate relations with the Greco-Roman world – relations that predated the rise of Islam – and of the wealth of those cultures themselves, in terms of their capacity to generate ideas that traveled beyond their immediate borders and to develop artistic and literary styles of great beauty and perception (leading examples: Bowersock 1983, 1990, 1994b; French and Lightfoot 1988; Millar 1993, 2002b; and Shahîd 1984a, 1989, 1995, with further volumes forthcoming; Howard-Johnston 2006). This is the world, and the field of inquiry, explored here by Drijvers (ch. 29), Shepardson (ch. 30), Cook (ch. 31), and Marsham (ch. 32).

One further consideration has to govern our analysis. Late Antiquity could be defined as the period in which stable ethnic identities (insofar as they ever existed), whether in Europe or in Asia (as those terms would then have been understood), underwent their most drastic revision since the closing decades of the Roman repub-lic (for a grand sweep, see Fowden 1993); a revision unequaled until our own "exploratory," imperial, and postimperial experience. (On ethnicity and identity generally, see Wolfram and Pohl 1990; Wood 1990, 1998; Miles 1999; Mitchell and Greatrex 2000; Geary 2002; Gillett 2002b; Goetz et al. 2003.) In the eastern sphere, we speak happily of Syrians and Arabs, even of Armenians, without always attending to their internal divisions (particularly notable in the Arab case) and their localized self-interest and tested loyalties vis-à-vis the greater powers to their east and west (factors most evident in the case of Syria and Armenia). There is a tendency to suppose that language by itself has a sufficient force when defining a people, an *ethnos* or *gens*. In the European sphere (where the observation applies as much to the Danube region as it does, say, to Gaul and the Rhine), vague terms like "Scythians" or "Alamanni" or apparently more precise labels like "Goth" or "Lombard" were all attempts to hold steady in the Roman mind, and to endow with a history (and hark back in this respect to Woods in the previous section (ch. 24), while noting Goffart 1980, 1988, 2006), groupings that were still in the process of being formed, and formed in a context of complex migration and varied patterns of negotiation, both among themselves and with Roman authorities, local and imperial. The very ability of a Goth, say, to think of himself as a Roman sprang from the fact that being a Goth in itself depended on a relationship already established with the Roman world (Wolfram 1988; Heather and Matthews 1991; Heather 1991, 1999). From there, it is easy and proper to move to a view that being a "Gallo-Roman" or an "African" or a "Copt" (see the particular example provided by Choat (ch. 23) in the previous section) demanded a constant adjustment, both in one's political relations and in one's sense of one's own past, that gave the "Roman" world itself a remarkably patchy and unstable character, dangerously disguised behind such terms as "province" or "local elites." This was indeed an age of "peoples" as much as of empires or kingdoms, with all the uncertainty and opportunism that implies (Goetz et al. 2003; and, for fundamental structural reflections, Hardt and Negri 2000).

CHAPTER TWENTY-FIVE

Law in Practice

Caroline Humfress

Introduction: Emperors and the Law in Late Antiquity

For in your time such an exchange of laws has been devised, like that which Homer, the Father of all virtue, describes between Glaucus and Diomedes when they exchanged dissimilar things between themselves: "Gold for bronze, the worth of a hundred oxen for nine." All this, we ordain, is to be in force for all future ages, to be observed by everyone: professors and students of the law, secretaries and the judges themselves.

Justinian, *Dig. Constitutio Omnem*, 11

In December AD 533, eight professors from the law schools of Beirut and Constantinople received an official letter (the *Constitutio Omnem*) drafted by the imperial bureaucrat Tribonian. This constitution heralded the final completion of the emperor Justinian's project to harmonize the sources, teaching, and practice of the Roman law of his day. In fewer than seven years, a millennium's worth of Roman legal development had been reformed and systematically reordered in a single *corpus* (body) of texts: the Justinianic *Code*, the *Institutes*, and the *Digest*. Justinian decreed that this legal *corpus* was to "be in force for all future ages" and, with the benefit of 1,500 years' worth of historical hindsight, we know that it has been (in one shape or another). The purpose of the *Constitutio Omnem*, however, was to instruct officially the Justinianic law professors in the use of the three new legal texts in their classrooms. Some of the professors had been involved in the drafting of the *Digest* text, but we can only guess at their reaction to the condensing of more than three million lines of classical jurisprudence into roughly 150,000 lines, one-twentieth of the original mass. The classical juristic opinions – from the late republic to the late third century – that did survive the purge were officially promulgated in the *Digest* as if they had been uttered from Justinian's own inspired mouth, "for we ascribe everything to ourselves, since it is from us that all their authority is derived" (*Dig. Const. Deo Auctore*, 6). Put simply, the *Digest* was intended to "replace the jurisconsults with the Emperor as the source of law" (Maas 2003: 17).

According to the final section of the *Constitutio Omnem*, however, Justinian had not replaced the classical Roman jurists, but had rather made an "exchange of laws." With a Hellenistic flourish, Tribonian compared this exchange to the unequal trade between the Homeric heroes Glaucus and Diomedes (Hom. *Il.* 6. 236). On the one hand, the completion of the *Digest* insured brevity in the sources of the law: "the worth of a hundred oxen for nine." On the other hand, classical jurisprudence had been exchanged for the law of the emperor Justinian: "gold for bronze." Ordinarily, of course, swapping gold for bronze would imply a bad deal. Yet in the *Iliad*, Glaucus and Diomedes made their unequal gift exchange as a mark of respect for the political friendship of their forefathers: the past governed their Homeric present. Similarly, the *Digest* was intended to showcase a gift exchange of laws between the classical juristic past and the Justinianic present, founded on ancestral ties that bind. To the sixth-century professors of Beirut and Constantinople, however, Justinian's *Digest* may well have seemed more like an imperial rip-off: no one was permitted to consult any jurisprudence outside of it, nor were legal experts allowed to produce any independent juristic commentary on it. The law professors could translate Latin passages from the *Digest* into Greek (presumably for teaching purposes), but this had to be in the same order and sequence as those in which the Roman words were written. Indexes were acceptable, but there were to be no attempts to sneak in any interpretive juristic glosses (Humfress 2005: 173). Homer's *Iliad* hints that Glaucus gave up his gold for bronze because Zeus had stolen his wits; the professional legal experts of the sixth century might have been tempted to agree.

When modern historians look at law in Late Antiquity, they see the emperor and his bureaucrats: "Once the monarchical principle of government had been fully established in the fourth century, the emperor or, as it might be, the central bureaucracy acting in his name was in sole control of the machinery of legislation" (Liebs 2000: 242). The dominant historical narrative is no longer necessarily one of decline (Honoré 2004), but it nonetheless tells a tale of how the emperors gradually reserved all legal authority and legitimacy to themselves. "The emperor, and his officials, now make the rules; they are the authority, as what happens in court increasingly comes to show" (Meyer 2004: 218). Under the principate, jurists had given independent legal advice to imperial officials. From at least the second century, they were also being absorbed into the bureaucracy as career professionals (Honoré 1994). The early third-century jurists Papinian and Ulpian, for example, both held the highest office of praetorian prefect. In the late fourth and fifth centuries, emperors – particularly eastern ones – may have deliberately promoted legal experts as the drafters of their constitutions, but the jurists' names are not recorded in this context (Honoré 1998). Nor do we have archives that were dedicated to recording the names of the countless *assessores* (legal advisers) who sat with late Roman magistrates. The relative anonymity of late Roman legal experts who acted as "civil servants" is frequently linked to a decline in the production of independent juristic writing in Late Antiquity. As Crook has stated, "Roman lawyers have been accustomed to exclaim not just at the . . . loss of creativity but at the diminished state in general of Roman jurisprudence after Ulpian and Modestinus – at its descent into handbook-knowledge and counting of authorities" (Crook 1995: 177). The significance of this "descent," however, should not be overestimated. By the early fourth century, the large-scale commentaries on Roman civil law, in its various branches, had already been written. Moreover, late Roman lawyers demonstrated considerable ingenuity in updating, glossing, reorganizing and even faking "existing" texts, even though Constantinian and Theodosian legislation had aimed at controlling that process (*Cod. Theod.* 1. 4. 1–3; also 9. 43. 1, which possibly should be joined to 1. 4. 1).

Late Roman emperors may have attempted to tighten their autocratic grip on the development of substantive legal principles (the rules that applied, for example, when late Roman citizens divided up their inheritances or contested possession of property or contracted obligations). Nonetheless, the substantive principles being developed were still fundamentally classical in their orientation. In AD 325, for instance, Constantine ruled in a concrete case that *veteris iuris definitio* (the rules of the old law) could be modified by the emperor out of consideration for equity and justice (*Cod. Theod.* 11. 39. 1) – thus incidentally proving that the old rules were still in force. The promulgation of the *Theodosian Code* in the fifth century did not make contemporary jurists redundant (they were needed to make sense of its imperial constitutions); nor, in its final form, did it attempt to do away with forensic arguments based on classical juristic opinions. In AD 473, a high-ranking official in Dalmatia sent a judicial report to the eastern emperor Leo, because he was unable to resolve a controversy between a woman and her brother: both parties supported their claim with many discordant jurisprudential and imperial texts. Having argued for the healthiness of diverse jurisprudential opinions, the emperor then decided to follow an opinion of the classical jurist Salvius Julianus (*Cod. Iust.* 6. 61. 5). Presumably similar concrete cases went some way to prompting the promulgation of Justinian's *Digest* exactly sixty years later. In sum, "Late Antiquity was an autocracy, but an autocracy founded on accumulated tradition, which was required to pay at least lip service to the rule of law" (Harries 1999: 25).

Formal legal procedure also fell increasingly within the limits of imperial control. In criminal law, the old *iudicia publica* (the "standing courts" established by statute) were replaced over the course of the principate with the inquisitorial processes of imperial officials. The criminal statutes of the late republic and early empire, however, still provided the basic categories of criminal offenses. In Roman civil law, the subtleties of the classical "formulary procedure" – with its two-stage proceedings, first before the praetor and then before a judge agreed upon by the litigants themselves – were dealt their final death knell by the emperor Constantius in AD 342 (*Cod. Iust.* 1. 57. 1). Civil cases in the late empire were heard – whether at Rome or in the provinces – under a single-stage procedure before the emperor or an imperial functionary (frequently referred to in modern discussions as *cognitio extra ordinem* or "extraordinary procedure"). Continuity within change, however, is also evident here: "Although *cognitio* was conceptually different from the formulary system, the differences between the two systems can be exaggerated" (Johnston 1999: 122). The concentration of formal legal processes in the hands of imperial officials did, however, pave the way for judicial appeals from one magistrate to another with a higher bureaucratic rank. Constantine appears to have been the first to formalize a new hierarchy of permanent appeal judges, with the emperor at the top (Chastagnol 1960: 131; and in general Pergami 2000). This change went hand in hand with the development of systematic rules of procedural evidence. While intended to streamline the judicial process, these developments inevitably created further delays and money-making opportunities for imperial bureaucratic officials. In sum, all of the above suggests a late antique legal culture in which, at the very least, appeals to imperial authority were given more weight than juristic expertise (Matthews 2000: 13). At worst, it suggests despotism masquerading as legal autocracy: "In theory legislation controlled the governed; in reality it darkened rather than defined their lives ... The Dominate transferred law from a discipline to a means of discipline" (MacMullen 1986a).

It was obviously in the interests of late Roman emperors to stress their legislative power. A typical preamble to an AD 458 constitution from the western empire ranks law-making alongside military prowess and reverence for religion as equal preservers of the Roman state – an irony perhaps not apparent to contemporaries until eighteen years later (*Nov. Majorian*, 6. 1, preamble). According to the Christian historian Orosius, the early fifth-century Gothic ruler Athaulf came to appreciate the centrality of legislative authority in the Roman Empire, "having discovered from long experience that the Goths, because of their unbridled barbarism, were utterly incapable of obeying laws" (Orosius, *Hist.* 7. 43). Codifications of law held out new possibilities for the articulation of imperial prestige (Matthews 2000: 1–54 details the complex circumstances behind the compilation of the *Codex Theodosianus*; for the background to the compilation of the *Codex Justinianus* see Humfress 2005). The *Codes* of Theodosius II (AD 438) and Justinian (AD 534) were not the first texts to collect together imperial constitutions and systematically edit them, but they were the first to bear the name of the emperor under whose auspices the codification was promulgated (Corcoran 2000: 25–42). Hence the impression given by both the *Codex Theodosianus* and the *Codex Justinianus* of self-assertive emperors, reaching out from a strong center (i.e., Constantinople) to regulate every waking hour of their subjects' lives – an impression admittedly strengthened by Theodosius II's rhetoric that "it is the function of imperial majesty to make wise provision even for those persons who have not yet been born" (*Nov. Theod.* 14. 1, preamble, AD 439), and Justinian's that "our subjects are our constant care, whether they are alive or dead" (*Nov. Iust.* 43, preamble, AD 537).

The visual images of late Roman emperors and magistrates, flanked by ceremonial inkstands and surrounded by written texts, are placed in sharp relief by the historian Priscus' equally stylized account of Attila the Hun's judicial technique: while on an embassy in AD 449 to a Hunnic camp north of the Danube, Priscus witnessed Attila coming out his house, swaggering and casting his eyes around, settling a few oral disputes and then going back inside again (Priscus, fr. Blockley 1983: 11. 2). At the extreme end of the spectrum reaching from the civilized to the barbarian, periodic raiding and invasion could suspend the Roman legal process altogether – as in AD 416, when a western constitution ruled that offences committed while fleeing the Vandals and the "disaster of barbarian devastation" should not be prosecuted

(*Cod. Theod.* 15. 14. 14). It may thus seem an ironic paradox that, if we did not possess a sixth-century "barbarian" law book (the so-called *Breviary of Alaric*), a significant proportion of the *Theodosian Code* itself would be lost to us today: we literally owe the survival of Books 2–5 to the Visigoths. "We might say that religion was not the only important factor in the cultural rapprochement between Goths and Romans. Law and the way it functioned in society apparently was another, and perhaps the other, important factor" (Sirks 1996: 155–6). A cultural shift in "barbarian" concepts of law-making may be identified among the "Franks," "Visigoths," and "Burgundians" of the late fifth and early sixth centuries (Wood 1993: 162–3; Charles-Edwards 2000: 271–87), but not among "Vandals" or "Huns."

Concentrating on Late Antiquity as the age of the codified law book is undoubtedly important, but it has the effect of placing the period at the beginning of a long march toward western legal rationalism and processes of modern state formation (see Stein 1999). That path seems to lead from the emperors' late antique *Codes* to Germany's *Bürgerliches Gesetzbuch* (1900) and beyond, via Prussia's *Allgemeines Landrecht* (1794), France's Napoleonic *Code Civil* (1804), and Austria's *Allgemeines Bürgerliches Gesetzbuch* (1811). In acknowledging the impact of Roman law on European political and legal thought, the historian of Late Antiquity faces certain methodological challenges. Can we, for example, speak of *Rechtstaat* or "the ideology of the rule of law" in AD 400 (Honoré 2004: 111), without importing ideas developed in specifically modern contexts – including debates over German nationhood, English parliamentary sovereignty, and American constitutionalism (discussed by Tamanaha 2004)? In any event, we need to cast our net wider in Late Antiquity itself, and think in terms of law as a set of social practices rather than as primarily the law of the emperor.

How to do Things with Laws in Late Antiquity

Late Roman law was bigger, in practice, than the emperors, the *quaestores* (who drafted imperial constitutions), and their texts. The imperial constitutions themselves point us outward, as their content reveals that late Roman law-making was still as reactive as it had been under the early empire (Honoré 1998: 133–4; Harries 1999: 47–53; Matthews 2000: 160–3; and, for the early empire, Millar 1977). Ammianus Marcellinus' portrayal of the emperor Julian at Ancyra showcases (intentionally) the expectation that the imperial government would be responsive: on leaving the city, Julian was beset by a huge mob, some demanding return of property of which they had been forcibly deprived, others complaining about conscription onto local town councils, others shouting accusations of high treason against opponents (Amm. Marc. 22. 9). That all seems reminiscent of Priscus' portrayal of Attila the Hun discussed above. In Julian's case, however, particular situations and concrete cases could prompt new imperial constitutions. A *Novel* issued by the emperor Justinian neatly sums up this activity: "It is our practice to seize the opportunity presented by cases coming before us to legislate on the point arising" (*Nov. Iust.* 108, preamble, AD 541).

Concrete cases could prompt imperial constitutions, as could pleas from interest groups and individuals. Harries identifies the latter process behind the texts collected in the *Theodosian Code*: "The *Code*, therefore, as a compendium of imperial responses to stimuli which were largely external, did not necessarily reflect the preferences of emperors, but the areas of late Roman life on which representations were most vigorously and repeatedly made" (Harries 1993: 15). Every imperial constitution thus has a "life cycle," which includes the specific circumstances that prompted the text, its official drafting in the palatine bureaus, and finally its promulgation and particular application (or lack thereof). One such "life cycle" is described in Mark the Deacon's *Life of Porphyry, Bishop of Gaza* (possibly to be read in the light of *Cod. Theod.* 15. 6. 1 and 2). Mark relates how he traveled on the instructions of Bishop Porphyry to the imperial court, to plead for the closure of "idolatrous temples" in the port of Maiuma. After seven days of hard effort attempting to make the right connections (both ecclesiastical and imperial), an imperial decree was granted. The decree was entrusted to a certain Hilarion, an adjutant from the bureau of the *magister officiorum* (the Master of the Palatine Offices). The same individual arrived in Gaza a couple of weeks later with a formal entourage, including two officers from the consular court and military guards. On his arrival in the city, Hilarion seized three municipal councillors, took oaths of surety from them, and promulgated the imperial constitution. Hilarion then supervised the overturning of idols and the closing of temples. Despite this centralized process of promulgating and enforcing the imperial text, Mark the Deacon claims that Hilarion was bribed with "a great sum of money" so that the temple of Marnas (Zeus) could continue to give oracles (Mark the Deacon, *Vit. Porph.* 26–7). Bribery of an imperial official is a crude mechanism for evading the emperor's commands; likewise simply burying the official text. In the late fourth century, the rhetor Libanius complains bitterly about an imperial constitution that was received and filed by municipal councillors in Antioch and never heard of again (Lib. *Or.* 48. 15–16).

A more subtle means of subverting imperial constitutions lay in applying rhetorical techniques of interpretation to them. Drafted only four months after the *Theodosian Code* came into effect, a constitution issued by Theodosius II clamps down on those who respect the letter of the law while evading its intention (not by any means a new concern, but one that perhaps had a new resonance for the imperial authorities after January 1, AD 439). The preamble to this constitution begins:

> There is no doubt that anyone who embraces the words of the law while contending against its spirit, is transgressing the law. Nor will he escape the penalties provided in the laws, by fraudulently pleading a perverse preference for the words above the sense of the law. (*Nov. Theod.* 9. 1, preamble)

Section 3 of the same *Novel* goes on to lay down a principle of extensive interpretation to be applied to all laws, "the ancient as well as the modern ones." This principle of interpretation is specifically designed to frustrate evasion and "oversubtle" constructions:

It shall be sufficient for the legislator merely to have prohibited what he does not wish to be done, and it shall be permitted to deduce the rest as if it were manifest in accordance with the intention [*voluntas*] of the law. So that, if those deeds which are outlawed by the law are in fact carried out, they are to be regarded as not just invalid [*inutile*] but as undone [*pro infectis*], even if the legislator stated merely that they were prohibited, and did not specifically rule that what was done should be regarded as invalid. But if anything followed out of, or because of, that which was done, against the law, in defiance of the prohibition written into the law, we pronounce that it too shall be null and void. (*Nov. Theod.* 9. 1, 3)

Of course, the rhetorical schools of the late empire, like those of the earlier period, taught precisely the techniques of interpretation that Theodosius II's *quaestor* was so keen to control and rein in. The author of a third-century rhetorical handbook, still being copied in the early sixth century, advises his students thus:

[We refute] laws either by an ambiguity and saying that not this but something else is signified, or, turning from the wording and examining the intent of the lawgiver, by concluding from what has been said that the subject is something else, or we ourselves bring up another law. (Anon. Seg. 3. 188, Dilts and Kennedy 1997: 53)

What the drafter of an imperial constitution sees as an obstreperous interpretive device is a rhetorical strategy to win the case for an advocate or litigant.

If we turn from the interpretation of imperial constitutions to the interpretation of legal instruments such as testamentary wills, we can begin to see how individuals handled Roman law, in practice, as a means to further their own ends and interests. In the west (in the middle of the fifth century), Valerian, bishop of Cimiez (formerly Cimelium, the Roman capital of the province of the Maritime Alps), paints a vividly rhetorical picture of forensic wrangling over wills and inheritances in the course of a homily against covetousness; while noting the homily's pastoral context, we should also remember that Valerian's description was deliberately designed to ring true for his immediate audience:

The corpse is not yet carried out, and already the true meaning of the will has been destroyed by an interpretation of law. One man is disputing about his father's signature; another is in despair over the person of a brother. One man affirms that the will is not confirmed by witnesses; another gives as a reason that the will is not consonant with the times. Thus the farm is at stake while the cases are argued. (Valerian, *Hom.* 20. 5, *PL* 52: 753D)

These forensic disputes, based on attacking the legal validity of the testamentary document, could also degenerate into outright fraudulent practices:

Look, when a will is brought out, immediately there is thought of falsehood. Someone asks, "Who heard the mute man speaking? What heir knew the dead man while he was making his dispositions?" What is worse, it is not hard for someone to find persons who are associated in his crime or bribed for a price. This miserable fellow imitates the

> signature of another's hand. Thus covetousness, by a pen frequently exercised in copying, often produces a document which the testator did not draw up. (ibid.)

Valerian implies that the same notaries who were employed to officially draw up valid legal instruments were also employed to forge signatures to those documents, when necessary.

All of the discussion above assumes access to the legal system – to public notaries, to legal officials in the cities, and perhaps to advocates and legal experts. As David Johnston argues, "in the end, the question whether a person enjoys a particular right comes down to whether he or she is able to enforce it in practice" (Johnston 1999: 112). This implies a certain social standing, patronage connections, and almost certainly cash. We should not underestimate, however, the extent to which local officials administered routine justice on a day-to-day basis. One official's daybook from Oxyrhynchus (*c.* AD 313) records twenty-eight days' worth of cases. During this time, the official had four Jove's days (Thursdays) off; had nothing to record for sixteen days; transferred one matter to another administrative official; released a body for burial; decided cases concerning property, liturgies, loans, and the opening of a will; and dealt with an inquiry about the driving-off of an ox and a deposition from a certain Asclepiades concerning an accusation that some baggage mules were not given their fodder (*P. Oxy* 54. 3741). Another local option was to lodge civil cases (illegally) before local military officers. It is easy to see how categories of "civil," "military," and "criminal" jurisdiction could become confused on the ground. A letter from the middle of the fourth century requests Flavius Abinnaeus – *praefectus alae* (commander of cavalry) stationed in a military fort in the Egyptian Fayûm – to aid a soldier and landowner in a nearby village, who has been robbed of his family possessions. The letter accuses the officials of the village, and asks Abinnaeus to arrest them all and then forward the case to "our Lord the Duke; for his function is to take vengeance on the perpetrators of such outrages" (Bell 1962: 102). Late Roman emperors, needless to say, attempted to control and regulate access to this alternative means of quick (and one assumes summary) justice.

In the higher imperial courts – those of the provincial governors or the praetorian prefects – only the social elite could either make the law work for them or disregard it altogether. The official papers of the late fourth-century urban prefect Symmachus record an extreme case of a Roman senator who was apparently "influenced neither by respect for rescripts, nor by the severity of laws, nor by loyalty to agreements, nor by regard for the law courts" (Symm. *Rel.* 31. 1, Barrow 1973: 169). Aspirant social climbers, however, were in a more tenuous position. John Chrysostom (patriarch of Constantinople, AD 398–404) observes that poor men who wish to be rich often get dragged into the courts of law, but no one ever drags the common mendicants into the law courts, "because they have come to the extreme of poverty" (John Chrysostom, *Hom. in Act. Apost.* 13). Those with nothing to lose do not appear in court, even as defendants. To borrow David Daube's memorable phrase and apply it to Late Antiquity, "the have-nots, the vast majority of citizens, were right out of it" (Daube 1969: 72). This is an important point, which I shall return to below. At the moment we should note in passing that, depending on the circumstances, the interests of the "haves" might include keeping the law and the lawyers at arm's length. According to the drafter of a Constantinian constitution, (elite) families were in the habit of making clandestine arrangements that either sidestepped the law or broke it outright. With a typical legislative distrust, the constitution states: "in the case of clandestine and domestic frauds anything you please can be easily devised in accordance with the opportunity of the situation, or that which has been actually done can be nullified" (*Cod. Theod.* 8. 12. 5, AD 333; Humfress 2006: 221).

Consuetudo (customary law) undoubtedly continued to play a significant part as a source of law in late antique disputes and legal arrangements, especially on a local level. However, as *consuetudo* "referred to law which was usually unwritten and which was agreed to by 'tacit consent'" (Harries 1999: 31), it is difficult for the historian to identify it in practice. One example comes (again) from Mark the Deacon's *Life of Porphyry*, in an incident where the citizens of Gaza attempted to uphold their customary law against Christians whom they suspected of undermining it (*Vit. Porph.* 22–5). With more than a hint of the theatrical, Mark describes how Barochas, a Christian, had been beaten to within an inch of his life outside the city walls of Gaza, while attempting to act as a debt collector for the church. Barochas was subsequently carried inside the walls, thus provoking a violent riot from the city's non-Christian population, who – believing Barochas to be dead – feared pollution from a corpse being brought inside the sacred boundary. By the following morning, the non-Christian citizens had mobilized the *defensor civitatis* (an imperially appointed minor city magistrate: see Frakes 2001), together with some public order officials and two chief municipal councillors, to interrogate the bishop of Gaza: "why have you brought a corpse into the city, seeing that the laws of our fathers forbid this?" (*Vit. Porph.* 25). The denouement to the affair comes with Barochas miraculously recovering his strength as the Christian "New Samson" (*Vit. Porph.* 25) and attacking the city's legal officials with a large chunk of wood. Alongside Mark's vivid (re)construction of late antique Gaza's religious fault-lines, we can gather a sense of how ancient customs and "the laws of [the] fathers" continued to be mobilized in a late fourth-century civic context.

The late antique period witnessed the growth of a new officially sanctioned system of legal practices, clustered around the concepts of a *lex Christiana* (law of the Christians) and a *ius ecclesiasticum* (custom of the Christian church). This development was not as coherent as the two terms imply. Eusebius tells us that the emperor Constantine "put his seal on the decrees of bishops made at synods, so that it would not be lawful for the rulers of provinces to annul what they had approved, since the priests of God were superior to any magistrate" (Euseb. *Vit. Const.* 4. 27. 2, Cameron and Hall 1999). Constantine thus created the possibility of an "independent" body of conciliar decisions, which would merge with various other strands of ecclesiastical law to form the canon law proper of the medieval period.

The idea that "priests of God" were superior (or at least equal) to an imperial magistrate resurfaces in two hotly debated Constantinian constitutions relating to the *episcopalis audientia* (bishop's hearing) and its official status (*Cod. Theod.* 1. 27. 1, AD 318(?), and *Const. Sirm* 1, AD 333). The bishops' ability to mediate in disputes between Christians certainly predates Constantine. It may even have received a boost in those provinces affected by the early third-century persecutions: according to Lactantius, Diocletian had commanded that altars were to be placed inside the magistrates' tribunals, so that each litigant had to offer incense to the gods before his case could be heard (Lactant. *De Mort. Pers.* 15). Leading bishops in the fourth and fifth centuries could still frame their hearings as alternatives to "secular" justice. Others chose to stress the authority that the apostles themselves had bestowed on Roman magistrates. An incident recorded by Basil of Caesarea, writing in the later fourth century, demonstrates the potential difficulties that an ecclesiastic could find himself in. A woman had been subjected to slanderous attacks by a man, but Basil tried to persuade her not to seek redress via the courts. The woman then accused Basil of wanting her to suffer a damaged reputation. Basil rather laconically concludes, "The decision I have come to in my own mind is not to surrender offenders to the magistrates; yet not to rescue those already in their custody, since it has long ago been declared by the apostle, that the magistrates should be a terror to them in their evil doings; for it is said 'he doesn't bear the sword in vain' [Rom. 13: 4]" (Basil of Caesarea, *Ep.* 289). The fact that this case may have encompassed "criminal" charges meant, presumably, that Basil could not opt to hear it officially himself – the Christian bishop's jurisdiction did not include criminal cases.

From Constantine onward, we know of judicial hearings taking place before bishops, in episcopal residences, inside churches, or in the public spaces in front of Christian basilicas (Lavan 2003: 325). At least some of these disputes were not related to the Christian *religio*; as Ambrose and Augustine both moaned, they concerned "gold and silver, farms and herds" (see Harries 1999: 204, 210). Some disputes also undoubtedly involved non-Christians. Whether bishops, however, had a legal authority beyond that granted to any officially appointed arbitrator is a complicated issue. Briefly, in AD 408 a western constitution confirmed the *iudicium episcopale* (the legal judgment of a bishop) after the model of official Roman arbitration, where both parties to the case had to agree to be bound by the judgment of their chosen arbitrator (*Cod. Theod.* 1. 27. 2). We should note, however, that this constitution does not necessarily imply that bishops had not also been granted a capacity to judge cases where both litigants did not agree to the hearing (i.e., non-arbitration cases). Ten years earlier, an eastern constitution had confirmed that Jews could choose "Jews or Patriarchs" as arbitrators in their civil suits, and that they could continue to refer matters concerning their *religio* to their customary (Jewish) laws. In all other cases, however, Jews had to "bring and defend all actions according to the Roman law" (*Cod. Theod.* 2. 1. 10) – a sure sign that, in practice, some (eastern) Jewish communities were hearing disputes that touched on Roman law in their own courts. In any event, by AD 530, the Christian *episcopalis audientia* had become such a successful legal venue that an imperial ceiling was put on fees and tips in church courts (*Cod. Iust.* 1. 4. 29).

While the *episcopalis audientia* has been the subject of modern scholarly interest (Selb 1967; Cimma 1989; Harries 1999: 191–211; and Lenski 2002), the role of *religio* as a guarantor of late Roman oaths and pacts has received less attention (Meyer 2004: 278–80 discusses written instruments, and Calore 1998a focuses on Justinianic officials). Yet this aspect of doing law is a telling indicator of changes in late antique society and culture. In the third century, the jurist Ulpian apparently gave his opinion that if an oath was tendered by a publicly forbidden *religio* it was "to be thought of as if no oath had been sworn" (*Dig.* 12. 2. 5. 3 = Ulpian, *Ad edictum*, 22). Presumably Christians were thereby excluded from swearing oaths on their *religio*, alongside other undesirables. In the fourth century, however, the custom of invoking the name of the Christian God as a guarantor to legal pacts became prevalent: a constitution of AD 395, issued by the emperor Arcadius at Constantinople, tacitly acknowledges this practice (*Cod. Theod.* 2. 9. 3 = *Cod. Iust.* 2. 4. 41). Given New Testament injunctions against swearing oaths, however, not all Christian bishops were happy with this procedural development. Also at Constantinople, John Chrysostom denounced the practice, undertaken by baptized and unbaptized individuals alike, of swearing oaths on copies of the gospel books placed on the church altar (John Chrysostom, *Hom. in Act. Apost.* 9). By comparison, Chrysostom's *Homily against the Jews* 1. 3 (preached at Antioch) claims to be an eyewitness account of an incident where a high-status woman was forced into a Jewish synagogue by a Christian (a pseudo-Christian, according to Chrysostom), "to make an oath about certain business matters which were in litigation." Apparently, the would-be kidnapper believed that oaths sworn in Jewish synagogues were to be feared more than those sworn elsewhere. Around the same time, late Roman Britons were putting their faith in the goddess Sulis (Minerva), swearing an oath at her sacred spring at Bath and requesting that any perjurer should pay the goddess "in his own blood" (*Tab. Sulis*, 94, Tomlin 1988: 226–7). Late antique Christian churches thus took their place alongside Jewish synagogues and sacred Roman shrines and temples, as places where individuals could seek god(s) to act as literal guarantors and enforcers of justice.

Seeking Justice

Whether "pagan" [*gentiles*] or Christian [*Christianus*], whether man or woman, whether boy or girl, whether slave or free, has stolen from me Annianus (son of) Matutina [?] six silver coins from my purse, you, lady goddess, are to exact [them] from him.

Tab. Sulis, 98, Tomlin 1988: 232–3

Late antique *defixiones* (curse tablets) stand in a long tradition of Greek and Roman social practices concerned with seeking justice (Versnel 1991; Gager 1992). The example given above, probably from the fourth century, was deposited in a sacred spring near Bath, Somerset (England). The individual who commissioned the curse tablet – or scratched the words onto the lead and folded it up himself – obviously believed that the *dea Sulis* had power over Christian and non-Christian thieves alike. A list of eighteen personal names is thoughtfully appended to the curse, to help the goddess in her task of identifying the culprit and recovering the stolen silver coins. As the editor of the Bath tablets astutely notes, "The tablets are petitions for justice, not magical spells ... it is the legalism of their language which strikes the reader more than its 'religiosity'" (Tomlin 1988: 63, 70). The Bath curse tablets are quite explicit in what they seek from the goddess Sulis: one states that a certain Docimedis has lost two gloves and asks that the thief responsible should lose their minds [*sic*] and eyes in the goddess' temple (*Tab. Sulis*, 5, Tomlin 1988: 114–15). Other late Roman examples seek the goddess' help in identifying a domestic burglar (*Tab. Sulis*, 99. 2–3, Tomlin 1988: 235); robbers of jewelry, clothing, and textiles (for example, *Tab. Sulis*, 10, Tomlin 1988: 122–3, and 97, Tomlin 1988: 230–1); and a possible plowshare stealer (*Tab. Sulis*, 31, Tomlin 1988: 148–9). Most of these tablets also seek restitution of the stolen goods, via the goddess. A further cache of British curse tablets, from Uley in Gloucestershire, record the theft of animals and farm implements and invoke the local deity Mercury (Tomlin 1993). In this "under-policed world" (Tomlin 1988: 70), both haves and have-nots took advantage of a cheap and immediate avenue of ("supernatural") justice.

John Gager notes that judicial cursing tablets, stretching in time from archaic Greece to Late Antiquity, cut across all social classes and are no respecters of gender (Gager 1992: 119). We can add to this the fact that "Christians" and "non-Christians" alike commissioned them. A made-to-order curse tablet from fourth- or fifth-century Egypt makes an appeal to the holy Christian martyrs on behalf of a woman named Theodora:

> I beg, I invoke, I pray to you, holy martyrs, I, Theodora, the injured party. I lodge this suit against Joor and his wife, throwing myself on your goodness, so that you may do as I would do with Joor and his wife: Beat them and bring them to naught. (*P. Michigan* 1523 lines 1–8, Meyer et al. 1994: 217–18)

The curse ends with the plea that the holy martyrs might speedily decide in Theodora's favor against her opponents, in a formulaic language highly reminiscent of contemporary petitions to imperial legal officials (for the latter see Gascou 2004). Some of the curse tablets also invoke biblical stories. In a seventh-century Coptic text, a widow appeals to the Christian God to bring quick judgment against a certain Shenoute, son of Panim: "You must strike him just as you struck 185,000 among the host of the Assyrians in a single night. You must bring upon him fever and chill and jaundice. You must make his enemies open their mouths" (*Munich Coptic papyrus* 5, Meyer et al. 1994: 188–9). With a neat twist to the idea of the intercession of Christian saints, the tablet closes with the instruction that it has to be buried with a corpse, which must then appeal day and night to the Lord, along with all the corpses lying around it, "all of them calling out, together, what is in this papyrus, until God hears and [brings] judgment on our behalf" (ibid.). Small wonder, we might conclude, that Augustine was intent on teaching his fifth-century audience that *daimones* ("demons," in a Judaeo-Christian context) are "in reality spirits whose only desire is to do harm, who are completely alien from any kind of justice" (August. *De civ. D.* 8. 22).

Some individuals in Late Antiquity also believed that special rites of "magical divination" could be employed to detect thieves and recover stolen property. For example, an undated papyrus gives a spell to catch thieves with the aid of the god Hermes and a host of other deities, involving the consumption of bread and cheese (*PGM* 5. 172–212, Betz 1986: 104). Curiously, a letter read out to the church synod at Ephesus in AD 449 accuses Sophronius, bishop of Constantia, of employing exactly such a spell in an attempt to recover a sum of stolen money. Far from appealing to Hermes, Bishop Sophronius, so the accusation reads, made the culprits swear on a gospel text before compelling them to complete a "bread and cheese" ordeal (Dickie 2001: 277). Accusations of "magical practices" should, of course, be viewed as symptomatic of social competition and conflict (Brown 1972b). However, while this type of justice may seem closer to early medieval dispute settlement than late Roman law, we should also note the existence of spells and curses that were specifically commissioned to interact with formal late Roman forensic proceedings.

Traditionally, curse tablets could also be commissioned to silence and "bind the tongues" of opponents in legal disputes. The second-century physician Galen adopts an attitude of intellectual superiority over those who would use spells and charms against their legal opponents, "so that they will be incapable of saying anything during the trial" (Galen "On the powers of all drugs," 12, quoted in Gager 1992: 120). The use of these forensic binding curses continued into Late Antiquity. The *Sepher ha-Razim*, a Hebrew collection of spells and curses copied in the late Roman period, includes a recipe for preparing a curse tablet to reverse bad fortune in a legal trial (Gager 1992: 117). Another remarkable papyrus, complete with drawing and *charaktēres* ("magical" signs), promises "an excellent charm for gaining victory in the courts, it works even against kings; no charm is greater" (*PGM* 36. 35–6, Betz 1986: 269). There are also late Roman apotropaic rituals aimed at protecting litigants against the magic of their opponents. A *lamella* (charm) that was meant to be worn on the body comes with a guarantee that anyone who carries it in court will stay undefeated. The "magical" words inscribed on this charm are three Homeric verses from Book 10 of the *Iliad*, intended to invoke the divine assistance of the gods (*PGM* 4. 2145–50 and 2160–5, Betz 1986: 76). Was Tribonian perhaps even remotely aware of this "magical" use of Homeric verses in legal contexts when he drafted his *Constitutio Omnem*?

There are also curse tablets aimed at cutting off disputes before they have had the chance to develop. A curse tablet of the third or fourth century makes a vivid request:

> Akeilios Phausteinos and Stephanos, my opponents in the matter concerning the slaves and concerning the private property and concerning the papers and concerning the things of which they might accuse me; ... concerning these matters may they neither think (about them) nor remember (them); and cool off their mind, their soul, and their passion, from today and from this very hour and for the entire time of (their) life. (Jordan, "Survey of Greek Defixiones," 179, quoted in Gager 1992: 144–5)

This type of tablet may have been especially useful in the context of mediation and arbitration. Finally, at the other end of the judicial process comes a spell known as "The Praise of Michael the Archangel," the ritual uses of which encompass jail breaks:

A person who is thrown in prison: Copy the power on sherds of a new jar. Throw them to him. They will force him out onto the street, by the will of god. (Heidelberg Kopt. 686, Meyer et al. 1994: 326–41 at 339)

According to the copyists of this spell, the Christian God could certainly move in mysterious ways.

Conclusion

Late Roman emperors professed for themselves an exclusive authority to make law, almost certainly at the expense of an independent juristic science. The codification projects of Theodosius II and Justinian embodied the imperial claim to regulate the lives of all their subjects, and this insistent bureaucratic rhetoric of autocracy was new in Late Antiquity. Moreover, the standardized legal process of *cognitio* placed judgment in the hands of officials whose mandate came ultimately from the emperor, and the bureaucratic hierarchy of such officials received firmer definition from Constantine onward. If we want to understand "law in practice," however, we have to go beyond the charmed circle of the emperor and his chosen officials.

Late Roman emperors did not, in general, sit down with their law books and ceremonial inkstands and spontaneously legislate. Imperial constitutions were typically reactive, as they had been under the early empire, issuing from individual or group petitions or from issues referred to the emperor by his bureaucrats. Further, the efficacy of legislation, once secured, was far from guaranteed; if not subverted by subtle legal interpretation, its enforcement could be thwarted through influence or fraudulent practice. Meanwhile, the routine administration of justice by local officials went on, accessed primarily by (and typically favoring) men of property. A letter of Theodoret, bishop of Cyrrhus in Syria in the early fifth century, is entirely convincing in its evocation of the attitude of have-nots to the Roman legal system:

Infants are scared of sorcerers, children of pedagogues and teachers, while grown men are especially thrown into a panic by judges, tribunals, heralds, beadles and those who execute the sentence, and if, in addition, they are poor, they are doubly fearful. (Theodoret, *Ep.* XXXVI, ed. Azéma 1955: 100–1)

Meanwhile, Late Antiquity was a formative period for a (very gradual) process that would eventually lead to the development of an independent canon law. One can only speculate on whether ecclesiastical justice was less socially discriminatory than Roman civil law.

There were two other important developments in legal practice in Late Antiquity that very likely affected a cross-section of the population (and did not please the most visible of the churches' leaders). The first was the procedural practice of swearing oaths by the name of the Christian God, and the second the invocation of the same in curse tablets or "magical" spells of one kind or another. Before we dismiss these practices as low-level superstition, we would do well to remember that in AD 530 the emperor Justinian ordered the placing of gospel books in every Roman law court where cases were heard according to Roman law (*Cod. Iust.* 3. 1. 14, 1–3). The presence of the holy gospel text was intended to guarantee the presence of God at every trial.

BIBLIOGRAPHICAL NOTE

The late Roman imperial constitutions are collected in the *Theodosian Code* (ed. Theodor Mommsen, *Theodosiani libri XVI cum constitutionibus Sirmondianis*, Berlin, Weidmann, 1905; tr. Pharr 1952) and the *Code of Justinian* (ed. Paul Krüger, *Corpus Iuris Civilis*, ii, Berlin, Weidmann, 1877). Justinian's *Novellae* are edited by Rudolf Schöll and Wilhelm Kroll, *Corpus Iuris Civilis*, iii, Berlin, Weidmann, 1895. Justinian's *Digest* is translated in four volumes in Watson 1985, which reproduces the edition of Mommsen and Krueger in parallel text. Matthews 2000 gives a full introduction to the complex compilation and transmission of the *Theodosian Code*, and elucidates as well the problems confronted by historians in its use. Charles-Edwards 2000 gives an excellent introduction to the so-called "barbarian *Codes*" of the successor states in the west.

Johnston 1999 focuses on classical Roman law, but is nonetheless essential background reading. Corcoran 1996 is a full and methodologically sophisticated study of the extant imperial legislation up to the year AD 324. A detailed analysis of late Roman constitutions from the Theodosian dynasty (AD 379–455) is provided by Honoré 1998. Liebs 2000 gives a concise overview of late Roman law and jurisprudence, as does Harries 1999, who also includes chapters on arbitration and dispute settlement. In general, the secondary literature is preoccupied with the emperors and codification. Meyer 2004, however, assesses late Roman legal culture through a focus on *tabulae* and notarial practices. The cursing tablets are discussed by Versnel 1991, Gager 1992, Meyer et al. 1994, and Tomlin 1988, 1993, although not with exclusive reference to Late Antiquity. Gagos and Van Minnen 1994 is a detailed study of a sixth-century family dispute, seen from the perspective of legal anthropology. The volumes produced by the Accademia Romanistica Costantiniana include detailed discussions of changes in late Roman legal practice (the monograph series is published by Giuffrè Editore, Milan; the Academy's conference proceedings by Edizioni Scientifiche Italiane, Naples). Finally, the website of the London "Projet Volterra" (www.ucl.ac.uk/history/volterra/), maintained by Simon Corcoran, is an excellent resource for late antique legal sources and further secondary literature.

CHAPTER TWENTY-SIX

The Mirror of Jordanes: Concepts of the Barbarian, Then and Now

Andrew Gillett

Barbarians are well-known figures in the late antique landscape, familiar for centuries before Late Antiquity began, either as a time period or as a field of study. Understanding the earlier history of barbarians, in modern scholarship as much as in ancient society, is essential for evaluating the late antique barbarian. Barbarians play key roles in several disciplines that have been tributary to what is now labeled Late Antiquity. In the old grand narratives of ancient and European history, barbarians are leading characters in the stories of the fall of Rome (as destructive outsiders) and in the origins of Europe (as forebears) – Janus-like figures who both usher out the old world of antiquity and ring in the new world of the Middle Ages. In church history, Alaric's sack of the city of Rome in AD 410 prompted Augustine to begin writing *The City of God*, and Clovis' acceptance of Nicene baptism insured religious uniformity in post-imperial western Europe – barbarians here acting as devices by which the Christian church was liberated from the weight of the Roman imperial past. More recently, research into late antique barbarian groups has been recast into the late twentieth-century terms of ethnicity, identity, and community. Much (though not all) of this recent work remains concerned with the barbarians who affected western Europe, traditionally *the* barbarians in classical and medieval studies, the actors of the "barbarian invasions" and the *Völkerwanderung*. A certain exceptionalism runs through both recent studies and their antecedents: among all the barbarian groups that interacted with the Late Roman Empire, the barbarians of the west are a particular case for study, because they generated future European states or cultures.

Neither the west nor Late Antiquity, however, has a monopoly on barbarians. Troublesome border peoples are shared with many other fields of ancient (and indeed modern) historical study, wherever major civilizations have abutted economically less complex societies: relations between Middle Kingdom Egypt and the Hyksos, and Han China and the Xiongnu, are prominent ancient examples. But, as a field of study, Late Antiquity shares most with its cognate discipline, Classics; not because the classical and postclassical worlds were partially coterminous, but because of their cultural continuity, seen best in the term "barbarian" itself. Greek in origin, used both by our late antique sources and by us, it bears within itself a potent set of concepts. This freighted term has been crucial to recent research on the classical world, which has placed ethnography and the concept of the barbarian at the center of our understanding of key aspects of ancient thought, literature, and politics. Its implications for the late antique world, however, are far from fully worked out.

Research on ethnicity and ethnography in classical studies has run parallel with work on Late Antiquity for some decades, with little contact or cross-pollination. Given the cultural indebtedness of the late antique world to its Hellenistic precursor, however, intersections between these fields of research are not only possible, but also profitable. This chapter aims to bring together some of the different approaches to the concept of the barbarian "now," and suggest some possible avenues for future research in this field. But it may be useful, in looking at the concept of the barbarian "then," in Late Antiquity and before, to begin with some examples of the varieties of this idea.

Late Antique Varieties of Ethnicity, Identity, and the Barbarian

The following list appears, with variants, in a number of Latin manuscripts:

The Weaknesses of Peoples	The Good Aspects of Peoples
The jealousy of the Jews	The Hebrews' foresight
The perfidy of the Persians	The Persians' constancy
The evasiveness of the Egyptians	The Egyptians' ingenuity
The deceit of the Greeks	The Greeks' wisdom
The savagery of the Saracens	The Romans' dignity
The fickleness of the Chaldeans	The Lombards' liberality
The inconsistency of the Africans	The Goths' soberness
The gluttony of the Gauls	The Chaldeans' wisdom
The bragging of the Lombards	The Africans' wit
The cruelty of the Huns	The Gauls' steadfastness
The uncleanliness of the Sueves	The Franks' fortitude
The ferocity of the Franks	The Saxons' perseverance
The stupidity of the Saxons	The Gascons' agility
The indulgence of the Gascons	The Scots' faithfulness
The lustfulness of the Scots	The Picts' broadmindedness
The inebriation of the Spaniards	The Spaniards' cleverness
The harshness of the Picts	The Britons' hospitality
The wrath of the Britons	
The squalor of the Slavs	

Source: *De proprietatibus gentium*, in *MGH*, *auct. antiquiss.* xi: 389–90.

This is one example of a small genre of such lists, some headed "The Qualities of Peoples." Reminiscent of similar catalogues used as a rhetorical trope by Roman poets including Statius and Sidonius Apollinaris, this text might have served a pragmatic function, a ready reference of variegated stereotypes forming part of an *ars poetica* (hence perhaps the intermittent tendency toward alliteration: "the ferocity of the Franks," "the Franks' fortitude") (Stat. *Achil.* 2. 133; Sid. Apoll. *Carm.* 23. 241–62, see *Ep.* 1. 2. 6; Dracontius, *Romulea* 5, *Proem.* 33–7). Echoes of this trope are heard in what we may call "ethnic rhetoric," arguments made, in a range of contexts, on the basis of the perceived natures of particular groups (e.g., Julian. *Contra Galilaeos* 115 *D*–131 *D*, 138 *B*; Salvian, *De gub.* 4. 14. 67). Noteworthy about the list here are its economy (each group is fixed by only one or two qualities) and its relative even-handedness (most groups are given both good and bad points, though perhaps this might be better understood as flexibility for different literary needs). Particularly striking is the unsystematic mixing of terms of identification we would consider as belonging to separate categories. The list captures no actual slice of time – it was added to cumulatively until at least Carolingian times – and past peoples, known from the Old Testament or other historical sources, stand alongside late antique and early medieval names (the same is true, for instance, for the examples in Sidonius). Names of classical Mediterranean political groupings (Greeks, Romans, perhaps Egyptians) appear next to peoples regarded as barbarians by the Hellenistic/Roman world (Huns, Lombards, Sueves, Franks). Most arresting is the juxtaposition of denominations based on geographic regions or Roman provinces (Gauls, Spaniards, Britons, Africans) alongside the term "Romans" (which all these provincials were for centuries) and names of barbarian peoples who settled in these same provinces (Franks, Sueves, Saxons, Saracens, respectively). What, if any, distinction there was between these overlapping categories is unclear. The compilers and users of this list recognized an eclectic range of properties as "identity markers" (in modern terminology), without privileging any one category of "ethnicity."

A similarly ecumenical acceptance of diverse and overlapping identity markers appears in a *Life* of an early fifth-century Gallic bishop, Orientius of Auch (*Vita (I) Orientii* 3 in *Acta Sanctorum*, Mai 1). Recounting the conflict between the army of the Western Roman Empire and the Gothic kingdom of southwestern Gaul in the 430s, the anonymous author describes the inhabitants of the latter alternatively as *Gothi*, *Getae*, and *Tolosani* – "Goths," "Getae," and "Toulousians" – terms referring, respectively, to "ethnic," literary, and civic contexts. The first name, "Goth," was the contemporary Roman term for what is now seen as the ethnicity of the ruling military elite of the federate kingdom in Aquitania. Once presumably a specific tribal name, in the fifth century *Gothi* represented not a true autonym but a Roman term of identification (as, indeed, it did in one of the earliest datable references to the term, Roman military lists of auxiliaries from the AD 240s reproduced in the inscription of the Sasanian shah Shapur I: (Greek inscription no. 6 in Huyse 1999, i: 25–6; see Potter 2004: 245 and 636 n. 122). It is an "ethnic" term only in a political sense. The second term used by the hagiographer, *Getae*, originally also had an "ethnic" sense, but appears here as a literary flourish. A tribal name of considerable antiquity, its last usage as an identifier of an actual group was in Roman times, when the emperor Trajan annexed the Getae of Dacia in AD 101–5 (a campaign commemorated by Trajan's column). By the late fourth century, all "Getic" identity had long since been assimilated into Roman provincialism, and Greco-Roman authors recycled the term as a purely literary, classicizing equivalent for the more recent term "Goth" (because of the orthographic similarity of the two words and the common, historical association with the Danubian regions). The third term, *Tolosani*, "Toulousians," designates citizenship of the south Gallic *civitas* of Toulouse. It had also, prior to the Roman conquest of Provence, been the name of a group, presumably an ethnic autonym, but had long since become a purely administrative and civic term for the town that served as a center of imperial administration in the province of Aquitania Secunda (Caes. *B Gall.* 1. 10; 3. 20; 7. 7). It is worth noting that, notwithstanding centuries of urbanization and demographic shifts, a member of a city in Late Antiquity was usually described not in a form such as *civis Tolosae* ("citizen of Toulouse") but with a "tribal" designation such as *Tolosanus*, much as we might say "a Parisian" or "a New Yorker," and with a similar lack of ethnic significance (see the ancient Greek practice of adding, as a second personal name, an adjectival form of one's hometown, called an *ethnica* in late classical Greek: Steph. Byz. *Ethnicae*). Unmindful of crossing categorical barriers, the author of the *Life* of Orientius employs political, classicizing, and civic terms for members of the Gothic kingdom, simultaneously and without distinction; they are terms taken from Roman administrative or literary usage, with only tenuous and often ahistorical connections to ethnic autonyms.

These examples suggest, first, how multiple registers of "identity" could coexist, their relevance dependent upon different circumstances. The coexistence of alternative categories of "ethnicity," and the possibility of selecting the category most appropriate to particular circumstances, has been described as "situationally constructed ethnicity"; this has been the topic of much recent discussion (Geary 1983; Amory 1997; Pohl 1998). As these examples indicate, however, categories of identity were not limited to equivalents of modern ethnicity; civic and geographic identifiers operated alongside ethnic terms, implying no apparent hierarchy (Murray 2002: 58–9). Given the overlapping categories of identity that operated concurrently, the modern term "ethnicity" seems increasingly to be an awkward anachronism. "Ancestry" has recently been proposed as a term better attuned to the premodern conceptions of the high Middle Ages, lacking deceptive pretensions to technical accuracy; it may also be more appropriate for Late Antiquity, and for the same reasons (McKee 2004: 38 n. 11).

Second, and perhaps more significantly, however, these texts indicate how unimportant what we call "ethnic" identity could be in Late Antiquity. Reducible to a poetic trope, it could be assimilated to the parochialism of Roman provincials. Foreign "ethnicities" might be suspect, but so too, at times, were provincial cliques within the Roman world (Matthews 1989b: 271–4; Sid. Apoll. *Epist.* 1. 7. 5; Ennodius, *Vita Epiphani* 53, 54). The terms of identification in the *Life* of Orientius do not represent perceived essential differences, just disparities of contingent circumstance. Throughout Late Antiquity, it was membership of a regional, political, or religious community, rather than of an "ethnicity," that was a motivating force to public behavior.

A far more substantial barrier between groups was the conceptual one contained in the Greek and Latin term *barbarus*, "barbarian." Whether one was a Gaul, a Frank, or an Isaurian mattered less than whether or not one was regarded as a barbarian, a categorization that was negotiable; in Late Antiquity, all three of the afore-named groups could be stood on either side of the "civilized/barbarian" ledger (Gauls: Julian. *Mis.* 359 *B*, *Contra Galilaeos* 116 *A*; Amm. Marc. 15. 12. 1–6; Franks: Sid. Apoll. *Epist.* 4. 17. 1–2; Isaurians: Burgess 1990; Elton 2000). We are wont, when seeing the term "barbarian" in a late antique context, to call to mind familiar passages such as the following: "wild nations are pressing upon the Roman empire and howling round about it everywhere, and treacherous barbarians, covered by natural positions, are assailing every frontier" (*De rebus bellicis* 6. 1, Thompson 1952: 113). This is an informative summary of one aspect of the concept of the barbarian in Late Antiquity. Like a hostile force of nature, these generic barbarians are proffered as a constant threat to the Roman Empire, the antithesis to the order of the Mediterranean world. Who these barbarians were is unimportant; tribal groups come and go, but barbarians are for ever. But this is not the only aspect of the concept of the barbarian that operated in antiquity. More casually, Jerome could dismiss the local languages of Dalmatia and Pannonia as "rustic and barbarian speech" (Jer. *Commentarii in Isaiam* 7. 19, *vers.* 5). The regions he denigrated had been Roman provinces for centuries; moreover, Jerome himself came from a small town on their border (Jer. *De vir. ill.* 135. 1). A "new man" made good in imperial administration and pontifical circles, Jerome distanced himself from his provincial origins by deployment of a divisive membrane, the concept of the barbarian.

The concept of the barbarian in Late Antiquity was not something newly formed by unique experience of the period, from a meeting between antagonistic cultures that were "Roman" and "Germanic" (or "Slavic" or "Arabic"). "The barbarian" was a fundamental part of the Hellenistic culture of Late Antiquity, and constituted considerably more than an objective figure of lesser cultural development. Late Roman historians used the term *barbarus* freely when discussing not only peoples of northern and central Europe, the North African hinterland, and Arabia, but also Sasanian Iran, the alternative empire in Late Antiquity, with claims (like Rome) to a millennium-long political and cultural tradition (e.g., Amm. Marc. 23. 5. 2; 24. 3. 4; Agathias 2. 28. 5 and 32. 3; Menander Protector, *frag.* 6. 2; Theophylact Simocatta 3. 7. 8, 11; Procopius introduces his narrative as "the history of the wars which Justinian, emperor of the Romans, waged against the barbarians of the East and of the West" (*Wars* 1. 1. 1)). The terminology of these Roman historians did not arise from any confusion about the complex level of Sasanian government or culture; each of these authors had good reason to be aware of the scale of Sasanian military organization, if nothing else. They chose their words accurately, for the term *barbarus* embraced what was grudgingly recognized as a peer civilization, as well as societies of warrior bands. In using the term, they deployed a badge of Hellenistic culture, a concept more or less unique to the ancient Mediterranean world. The Hellenistic background of this term weighs heavily on our picture of "barbarians" in Late Antiquity.

Greek, Hellenistic, and Roman Ethnography and Its Functions

"Barbarian" is a very old, Greek word. A compound form, *barbarophonus* ("speaking barbarian" or perhaps better "babbling") appears in Homer, though not the term *barbarus* itself (Hom. *Il.* 2. 867). In the *Iliad*, the archaic Hellenes confronted the Asiatic Trojans without the aid of a dichotomy of "us versus the barbarians" (Thuc. 1. 3. 3; Janse 2002: 332–8; J. Hall 2002: 111–17). It was in classical Athens of the fifth century BC that the term *barbarus* became commonly used, and whence it spread to become the dominant way of describing a foreigner, first in other Greek dialects and, later, in Latin (J. Hall 2002: 182–9). This blanket term applied not only to economically less developed neighbors of the Greeks, such as the Scythians, but also to civilizations the Greeks recognized as older, wiser, and more sophisticated – more "civilized" – than their own, including Achaemenid Persia and Late Period Egypt. The term "barbarian" applied not to a particular type of foreigner, but to the whole range of peoples the Greeks regarded as "outsiders." The term collapsed multiple possibilities of diversity into a single class of alienation, a sweeping conceptual categorization.

Early Roman culture appreciated the value of this term, as of so many other Greek concepts. Latin already had words for describing foreigners, strangers, or savages (terms such as *externus, peregrinus, ferus*), which continued to be used alongside the new borrowing. *Barbarus* was adopted by Romans not because of a lack of terms to describe these aspects of "outsiders" (as, e.g., philosophical terminology was imported from Greek into Latin in Roman republican times, or new ecclesiastical and theological terms in Late Antiquity, because of a lack of native equivalents for these concepts). The strong ideological associations of the Greek term conveyed more than the sum of these Latin terms. As part of the Roman appropriation of Hellenistic culture, *barbarus* was naturalized into Latin both as a word and as a package of concepts.

The conceptual compactness of *barbarus* comprised concepts ranging, in modern terms, from "non-native speaker" and "savage," to "decadent" and "Other." In most modern European languages, *barbarus* is glossed by a word that, though a derivative, has a narrower semantic range ("barbarian," *Barbar, barbare*, and so on). These false friends and our own familiarity with them can obscure not only the complexity of the original term, but also its cultural specificity. Middle Kingdom Egypt and Han China, mentioned above as *comparanda*, experienced a range of foreign confrontations and interactions, both with small tribal groups along their frontiers and with major civilizations of a complexity equivalent to their own. But the languages of neither ancient Egypt nor China developed a word equivalent to Greek *barbarus*, a blanket term for all foreign peoples, of both "inferior" and equivalent status, applicable also as a derogatory term within its own culture, as Jerome demonstrates above (Poo 2005: 38–48). Both Chinese and Egyptian cultures were very conscious of potentially threatening outsiders, but did not conceptualize the surrounding world by means of a term equivalent to *barbarus*. "The barbarian" was a specifically Hellenistic cultural construct.

The specificity of the Hellenistic term *barbarus* is all the more striking in view of its coexistence alongside other Greco-Roman practices for identifying alien peoples that, unlike *barbarus*, did have parallels in ancient Egypt and China. One habitual practice of Chinese sources was the transfer of a specific autonym, originally attached to one foreign group, onto others that were perceived as occupying similar categories, such as inhabiting the same geographic areas or sharing similar cultural qualities. These "transferred" names were preserved and used by Chinese writers, long after the historical existence of the original group (e.g., all western peoples were *Rong*, all nomads were *Hu*; Poo 2005: 38–48). Greco-Roman authors likewise generalized individual foreign autonyms into umbrella terms reused over centuries. Both *Scythii* and *Germani* were such "transferred" names, adopted in the classical period and enduring in Late Antiquity and beyond (Tac. *Germ.* 2. 3; see Rives 1999: 117–21; so too, apparently, was *Graeci*: J. Hall 2002: xix). Such generic titles simplified diversity: historically ("new" peoples could be understood as "old" ones), geographically (all lower Danubian peoples were Scythians), and taxonomically (all nomadic peoples beyond the Syrian desert were Saracens). *Gothi*, often synonymous with *Scythii*, was one of several late antique additions to such simplifying terms (Roman military lists of auxiliaries from the AD 240 s reproduced in the inscription of the Sasanian shah Shapur I: Greek inscription no. 6 in Huyse 1999, i: 25–6), where *Germani* and *Gothi* cover all European barbarian auxiliaries in the Roman army; Amm. Marc. 31, where terms applied to trans-Danubian groups, like *Theruingi* and *Greuthungi*, are collapsed into generic *Gothi* when describing events within Roman territory; Procop. *Wars* 3. 2. 2 and Agathias, *Histories* 1. 2. 1, 3. 3 for lists of "Gothic" peoples). These generalizing names provided terms for *types* of alien peoples, but lack the potent ideological function of the broader category *barbarus*.

In Greek, Hellenistic, and Roman societies, representation of "the barbarian" became a central element of cultural expression, embedded and elaborated in literary genres and visual motifs that we broadly label "ethnographic" (representations of foreign places, habits, culture, and history). Unlike "barbarian," "ethnography" is not an ancient term; it is a modern neologism, with Greek etymology but no actual existence in antiquity; "ethnography" was too fundamental an element in classical discourses to be identified, and thus restricted, by naming (see Dench 2005: 41–6). Ethnographic discourses permeated a spectrum of classical genres. In literary culture, "ethnic discourses" informed comic and tragic drama, history, geography, philosophy, and political theory (e.g., Ps.-Arist. *Rh. Al.* F658; Isoc. *Philippus* (*Or.* 5) 107; Long 1986; E. Hall 1989a, 1989b; Harrison 2000; J. Hall 2002: 175–8, 211–19). In visual media, works ranging from household utensils to pervasive governmental propaganda in numismatics featured images of "the barbarian" as an antitype or enemy of Hellenistic ideals (Pollitt 1986: 79–110; Cohen 2000; Ferris 2000; J. Hall 2002: 178–9). "Ethnographic" texts constituted major Greek and Roman literary and artistic monuments. Although barbarians were, by definition, liminal in ancient societies, the concept of the barbarian was central, not peripheral, to classical culture.

In the last two decades of classical studies, ethnographic conceptions have taken center stage in research on a range of key areas. Athenian literature, Panhellenism,

Hellenistic and Roman geography, and imperial "romanization" are all areas in which the concept of the barbarian has served as an explanatory model in the analysis of ancient thought and texts. Each of these areas shares a basic concern with that most characteristic theme of late twentieth-century research, identity. Each area also envisages our extant literary and visual texts not only as sources that illustrate Greco-Roman thought and belief, but also as being complicit in generating "identity and alterity," and the power relations that proceed from them. The *functions* of the classical concept of the barbarian, and of the texts which mediate it, has been a profitable field of study (see bibliographical note below).

The development of "Panhellenism" (or now "Hellenicity"; J. Hall 2002) – the subsuming of regional "Greek" communities, dialects, and cults under the single identity of *Hellenes* – is associated with the ethnographic bent of classical performative texts. Literary texts and their public performance are seen as fundamental to the construction of a unified classical Greek identity not only by scholars dealing primarily with the analysis of literary genres (primarily *historia* and drama; Hartog 1988, 2001; E. Hall 1989b), but also by those seeking to apply anthropological models of ethnicity to classical Greece (J. Hall 1997: 45–7; 2002: 172–220). A dominant model in current classical Greek studies sees classical Greek thought as fundamentally characterized by polarity: a structuring of the world around a series of mutually exclusive categories: male versus female, free versus slave, citizen versus alien, god versus mortal (Cartledge 2002). "Greek versus barbarian" (which should be understood as "Greek versus non-Greek") became one of these dichotomies, but not without the investment of cultural energy to cement it. In the wake of the Persian wars, Greek concepts and terminology were deployed in order to construct a single, unifying Panhellenic identity and – necessarily at the same time – also the concept of the barbarian as a single category for all foreign peoples. The multiplicity of regional Greek identities, and the great variety of peoples neighboring the Greek world, were collapsed into the simple polemical division of "Greek and barbarian." In this view, "ethnic" or political identity is therefore an oppositional construct, which only exists contrary to a single outside category, the Other.

Publicly presented texts were an important vehicle for this shift in thought. Prominent among extant examples are Greek comedies and tragedies (most obviously Aeschylus' *Persians*), and particularly Herodotus' *Histories* (E. Hall 1989b; Hartog 1988, 2001; Munson 2001). Ethnographic material was intrinsic to this font of the Greco-Roman historical tradition. Herodotus' narrative of political and military events (equivalent to the narrative style of later Thucydidean historiography) is more or less matched in length by his description of foreign peoples and lands (what we would call "ethnography" or, misleadingly, "digressions"). Both modes of description address the deeds and *mores* of barbarians.

The conception of the barbarian in Herodotus and other classical Athenian writers was not simplistic and one-dimensional, like our modern derivative words. Although Herodotus describes a range of non-Greek peoples – most importantly Egyptians, Scythians, and Persians – they all represent different aspects of one category, "the barbarian," schematized in such a way that together they form a cumulative pattern of "non-Greekness." The Egyptians are excessively submissive, the Scythians excessively aggressive, the Persians "soft" and suited to serve despotism; by contrast, the Greek is assertive, rational, and free. Herodotus does not tell the story of many different peoples but, as he says in his opening, of "Greeks and barbarians," of two classes only; both have multiple aspects (1. 1). Xenophon's varied portraits of the Achaemenid Persians (the dominant culture in the Mesopotamian and east Mediterranean world, against which Greek culture sought to define itself: Miller 1997; Burkert 2004), ranging from the Greeks' enemy to an idealized king in the person of Cyrus II, presents a comparable schema of aspects of the Other (Briant 2002; Cartledge 2002: 59–65; J. Hall 2002: 179–82). These multiple images of "the barbarian" facilitated the construction of a Greek self-portrait that was itself multifaceted.

The image of the barbarian could shade into the fantastic and the utopian, particularly in discussions of remote peoples (Evans 1999; see also Merrills 2004). Classical ethnography mixed the observable, the possible, and the bizarre (not always indifferently) in its accounts of "barbarian" peoples; verisimilitude and accountability were secondary to estrangement. (In Roman times, even as seemingly sober an author as Caesar concluded an ethnographic discussion with an account of improbable beasts: Caes., *B Gall.* 6. 26–8.) Distant "barbarians" could become models of moral virtue and religious piety, regrettably lost in the sophistication of the Mediterranean world (e.g., the fourth-century BC author Ephorus *apud* Strabo 7. 3. 9; Tac. *Germ.* 19–20; the third-century AD sophist Ael. *VH* 2. 31, cited in Potter 2004: 31; E. Hall 1989b: 211–23). Their virtue could be inculcated by philosophy, "alien wisdom" admired in the Mediterranean world, attributed not only to the ancient cultural centers of Mesopotamia and Egypt but also to northern European barbarians such as the Thracians and, in Late Antiquity, the Goths (e.g., the Getic Pythagorean Salmoxis/Zalmoxes: Hdt. 4. 94; Strabo 7. 3. 5; Diog. Laert. 1. 1; Julian. *Or.* 8. 244 A, *Caes.* 327 C–D; Jord. *Get.* 5. 39, see also 11. 67–72; *Suda,* s.v. "Zamolxis"; Hartog 1988: 84–111; E. Hall 1989b: 149–50).

The function of classical ethnography was not primarily descriptive but creative, to "articulate … a discourse of alterity" (J. Hall 2002: 176). In François Hartog's terms, ethnography is a "rhetoric of Otherness," concerned primarily not with reportage but with "difference and inversion." The "mirror of Herodotus" and of those who succeeded him in the writing of *historiae* is held up to their audiences as an aid to the construction of their own past and identity, emphasizing a contrast to the "barbarian" antitype (Hartog 1988: xxiii–iv, 212). Thucydidean narrative would be the most influential model for Roman and late antique classicizing historiographers, but Herodotean ethnographic "digressions" would nonetheless remain a standard element of *historia* (seen, e.g., in Ammianus Marcellinus' accounts not only of the Huns and Alani (31. 2), but also of the Persians (23. 6): Averil Cameron 1985: 37–8). The longevity of this discourse should not obscure its complexity or jade modern readers into dismissing reworkings of long-standing *topoi* as boilerplate; intertextual references themselves could communicate sophisticated messages (e.g., Claudian's portrait of Alaric in terms drawn from Roman representations of Hannibal: Dewar 1994). But more important was the ideological function of alienation performed by ethnography.

Though developed in the specific historical circumstances of fifth-century BC Athens, the concept of the barbarian was a cultural and political tool that, with adjustments, was transferable to Athens' cultural heirs in the Hellenistic and Roman periods. Attalus I of Pergamon (269–197 BC) presented himself as protector and avatar of Athenian culture in his monumental constructions, at Pergamon and Athens, celebrating his defeat of the barbarian Galatians (and playing down their Hellenistic, Seleucid allies: Pollitt 1986: 79–110; Marszal 2000). Classical Athenian public art had mythologized the Otherness of barbarians, most famously in the gigantomachy of the Parthenon, celebrating the defeat of the Achaemenid Persians with portrayals of vanquished giants and Amazons. The new, hyperrealistic, "baroque" style of the Attalid monuments, however, portrayed defeated barbarians as visually distinct from their victors in physiognomy and dress; hairstyle, clothing, ornament, and muscularity marked off the alien. These motifs became key elements of Hellenistic and Roman victory monuments down to the columns of Trajan and Marcus Aurelius in Rome, and the obelisk of Theodosius I and the column of Arcadius in Constantinople.

Roman culture consciously borrowed the oppositional concept of *barbarus* from Greek thought, and deployed it in a variety of ways to reinforce both Rome's membership of the Hellenistic cultural world and her own imperial status. From the third century BC, Rome's cultural alignment with the Hellenistic world was signaled by ideological adoption and internalization of the barbarian dichotomy, separating Roman "civilization" from the "primitivism" of other, unreconstructed parts of Italy (Dench 1995: 29–108; 2005: 96–117, 166–7). In turn, Roman imperial expansion was facilitated by exportation of the concept of the barbarian. In the western provinces annexed by Roman conquest, the same sharp divide between inclusion within the Hellenistic cultural world and exclusion among "the barbarians" provided an ideological scaffolding for "romanization," a contested term for the acceptance and appropriation by non-Romans of Hellenistic urban culture, modes of expression, and Roman self-identification. Provincial elites, like Romans before them, internalized Hellenistic cultural assumptions and their antitype, "the barbarian" (Woolf 1998: 48–76; Hingley 2005: 59–71). The concept of the barbarian was a powerful ideological tool: a membrane between participants and nonparticipants in Hellenistic culture, yet transferable between societies; able to be deployed both externally and within a society; and permeable by those who "bought into" its cultural assumptions (Dench 1995: 11–12).

Accompanying these broad ideological conceptions on their translation into Roman culture was the estranging function of literary and visual ethnographic texts. Genres and *topoi* need not, of course, remain fixed in their purposes; literary models can be exploited and turned to different ends. But Roman ethnographical writings followed the lead of their Greek and Hellenistic models, as the conservatism of Tacitus or Ammianus Marcellinus demonstrates (King 1987; Lund 1991). Ethnography, like the term *barbarus*, was naturalized into Latin literature because of its ideological value: the alienation of its subject.

It was not only *historia* that was transferred from the original Greek and Hellenistic to the later Roman practice: other complicit genres were subject to the same shift.

Geographia – a genre cognate with *historia*, and not necessarily very strictly distinguished from it (Clarke 1999: 1–76) – addressed the human inhabitants of lands as much as their topography; ethnography was fundamental also to this genre. *Geographia* too is increasingly seen in current scholarship as a literary rather than as a "scientific" genre, and for the most part ideologically motivated (Nicolet 1991; Romm 1992; Clarke 1999; for Late Antiquity: Lozovsky 2000; Merrills 2005; note that in Latin the term *chorographia* was more commonly used than *geographia*). As a genre, *geographia* received its greatest impetus at times of political expansion: in the wake of Alexander's conquests, and after the Roman consolidation of the Mediterranean basin. At these imperial moments (particularly under Rome), *geographia* served two contradictory yet complementary functions. By offering a systematic description of all known lands, it asserted "ecumenical claims," picturing the Roman Empire as coterminous with "the whole world" (Nicolet 1991: 29–56). At the same time, *geographia* was concerned to portray "the edges of the earth" – lands beyond Greco-Roman knowledge – as wild, alien, and dangerous; not just different from the Mediterranean world, but an other world, the reverse of the Greco-Roman *orbis*, the *antichthon*. Hostile and impassable borders closed off these Other worlds. The most insurmountable of these borders was Oceanus, *the* ocean, encircling the lands of the known world, a realm of chaos and monsters (Romm 1992: 21–3). *Geographia*, with its appropriation of the known world and demarcation from the unknown, provides a topographic aspect to ethnography's function of alienation.

Four points stand out from this digression into earlier antiquity. First, current scholarship sees the concept of the barbarian as central to the ideological foundations of classical societies, transferred from Athens to the Hellenistic and Roman thought-worlds. Second, this concept was a construct, an intellectual artifact of classical workmanship, not a neutral observation of the surrounding world. It served identifiable functions: to establish and reify oppositional categories. "Ethnography" was not essentially a descriptive genre, but a creative one – a genre intended to alienate its audience from its subject. Third, the ideological concepts of classical ethnography permeate our extant texts to a very high degree (formally in *historia* and *geographia*, more casually in other genres). And fourthly, these fundamentally structuralist and anthropological interpretations, neither new nor unique to classical studies, constitute a widely accepted interpretive framework within which by and large classical studies now operate.

Making Classical History into Barbarian Origins

These recent studies on ethnography in the classical world have sought to analyze the ideological nature and alienating function of ethnological texts, rather than to assess the historicity of their data, as a previous generation might have done (and with value: Momigliano 1971). By contrast, a major sector of research in Late Antiquity over the past two decades has undertaken a different project, seeking to deploy early medieval and Byzantine texts in order to reconstruct the self-identity and social dynamics of "barbarian" groups such as the Goths, Franks, Lombards, and others that bulk large in the history of Late Antiquity. This research continues the trajectory of one of Late Antiquity's tributary disciplines, the study of Germanic antiquity. Current approaches in this field are associated with the term "ethnogenesis," a word borrowed from mid-twentieth-century social sciences, referring to processes by which ethnic groups form (Wolfram 1981, 1988, 1994; Geary 1988, 1999, 2002; Pohl 1991, 1994). For a period in which "barbarians" take center stage – with "barbarian invasions" and "barbarian kingdoms" in "the barbarian west" – investigation into the self-identity of barbarian groups seems desirable: an opportunity to see nonclassical peoples in their own terms, and to extend to them the sort of examination previously undertaken for the literate cultures of the Mediterranean. This investigation features intellectual tools similar to those that configure the studies of the classical world outlined above. Group identity is analyzed as a construct manipulated by social elites in order to generate social and political cohesion, and identity is seen as oppositional, constantly defined and asserted against other competing identifiers. Texts are understood to serve ideological purposes, as communications of ideologies around which group identity can cohere (Pohl 1998; 1999).

Nevertheless, this project is not the same as that of the classical research discussed above. Greek and Roman constructs of self and Other can be examined through Greek and Roman sources. To identify the dynamics of self-identification among the barbarians of Late Antiquity, we also have Greek and Roman texts, only – not "barbarian" ones. We can look through Greco-Roman eyes to see how they perceived the Other and, therefore, themselves; we cannot do the same for the barbarians of Late Antiquity. Late antique ethnographic discourses, even when describing the barbarians who gained control of sections of the Roman Empire, remain Greco-Roman. There are, of course, differences between the ethnographic genres of earlier antiquity and the major relevant texts of Late Antiquity: primarily Christianity, which provided an additional register of conceptions of "ethnic" identity, with notions of divinely favored (and disfavored) peoples, an "ethnic" history stretching over millennia with periods of exile and wandering alternating with military and political glory, and extensive genealogies of royal houses. The deployment in recent research of late antique, Christian, Greco-Roman sources in order to reconstruct "barbarian" identities is problematic. These approaches do not simply trawl late antique texts in order to gather isolated fragments of data that report on barbarian groups, but see certain Latin works themselves as evidence for communications of identity-forming processes within those groups; Roman writings are appropriated as, essentially, ideological discourses of "Gothic" or other non-Mediterranean provenance, albeit preserved under strata of Judaeo-Christian and classical *topoi*.

Central to the "ethnogenesis" approach that seeks to reconstruct "barbarian" dynamics of identity is the text of Jordanes' *Getica*. The *Getica* is a short narrative written in Constantinople in the 550s, during the latter days of Justinian's war in Italy. It outlines a pseudo-history of the Goths over the previous 2,000 years, a history dominated by epic migration and royal dynasties. In "ethnogenesis" interpretations, the *Getica* is treated as a recension of genuine Gothic self-understanding, transmitted through one of several sources, known or putative: either the lost *Gothic History* of the Italian Cassiodorus, former bureaucrat to the crushed Ostrogothic regime, who is cited by Jordanes; or other, postulated lost

"Gothic" histories; or via hypothetical Gothic oral sources. It is not claimed to represent "real history," but rather is seen as a mythic narrative propagated by Gothic elites in order to generate ethnic unity through belief in a shared history and origins (Wolfram 1981; 1988; 1994). The text is not seen as preserving isolated "factual" elements of Gothic cultural provenance, scattered throughout a Greco-Roman literary work (as, e.g., Herodotus preserves isolated data about Scythian burial practices or royal Persian propaganda), but as replicating a coherent and articulated narrative, Gothic not classical in origin. The framework of the *Getica*, its migrations and dynasties, is understood as determined by the structure and key themes of an otherwise unreachable, oral ur-narrative cultivated by the Gothic elite. Though the Constantinopolitan Jordanes is belittled as a poor transmitter of this tradition, introducing many irrelevant classical clichés, the *Getica* is deployed as the residue of a barbarian "ethnic discourse" aimed at attracting adherence to Gothic group identity, in the face of competition both from other barbarian identifications and from Roman imperial allegiance. The evidence of Jordanes for the function of this "ethnic discourse" is fundamental for extrapolating the "ethnogenesis" model to other northern European barbarian tribes.

In this model, as in contemporary research on classical ethnography, a text serves to reify group identity. But the role of the text in this model is in fact diametrically opposite to the function of texts as understood in the current approaches to Greek and Roman writings discussed above. Current interpretations of Greco-Roman works understand classical ethnographic discourse as a communication within Greco-Roman society, functioning to alienate its audience from the object of its discussion, "the barbarian": Greek speaks to Greek about what makes the Scythians so different. Recent interpretations of Jordanes, however, see his text (or its postulated underlying ur-narrative) as a communication within the society of the object of discussion, the Goths, serving to reinforce group identity with the object: Goth speaks to Goth about what makes them Gothic. Classical ethnography seeks to repel, but ur-Jordanes seeks to consolidate. The "ethnogenesis" reading of the function of Jordanes' text (or of his sources) is at odds with the direction of the work of classical studies on the role of ethnographic texts as instruments of exclusion. The shared vocabulary of "constructing identity" conceals a more fundamental epistemological divergence.

There are practical stumbling blocks to this understanding of Jordanes as a recension of a "Gothic" ethnic ideology. The relationship between the extant text of the *Getica* and one known but lost source, Cassiodorus' *Gothic History*, is extremely problematic; the likelihood that Jordanes reflects Cassiodorus closely and consistently, or intended to, is not strong (Croke 1987; Christensen 2002: 127; Goffart 2005; Merrills 2005: 101–8). Hypotheses constructed on even earlier links in a hypothetical chain of lost sources are correspondingly more fragile. Interpretation of the *Getica* as a recension of an oral, Gothic tradition runs counter to the explicit statements of both Jordanes and Cassiodorus that they worked up their accounts of the Goths from written Greco-Roman sources, and that oral sources (i.e., Gothic traditions) were either contemptible or nonexistent (Cassiod. *Var.* 9. 4; Jord. *Get.* 38; Goffart 1988: 38–9, 86–7; Gillett 2000: 484–5). But the deeper concern with this model is epistemological: the nature of Jordanes as a source, a late Roman work appropriated as evidence for "Gothic" self-identification.

In fact, Jordanes' *Getica* looks very much like a classical ethnography, put together with more care and wit than is usually credited (see Merrills 2005: 115). Read in the light of current work in classical ethnography, Jordanes' text not only becomes more familiar, but also more informative of the circumstances of its composition, Justinian's Constantinople. The author exploits, from the outset, those features of classical ethnography that function to alienate the audience from his barbarous subject. The work commences with a geographic overview before proceeding to historical narration, a marriage of *geographia* and *historia* found not only in Herodotus but also in other Greek writings from the fourth century BC onward (Momigliano 1971: 58). The opening description of the northern islands of Britain and Scandza (whence the Goths are said to come) is a pot-boiler of Greco-Roman ethnographic *geographia*. Particularly prominent are the recurring references to Oceanus, the location of these islands. Impassable, sluggish, and hostile, Jordanes' Oceanus is the product of the long literary-geographic tradition in which Oceanus constituted the border between order and chaos (Jord. *Get.* 4–12, 16–18, esp. 5; Romm 1992: 11–26; see, on the literary role of islands, Merrills 2005: 164–5).

Jordanes' description of the tribes living in Scandza, neighbors to the "original" home of the Goths, is a systematic catalogue of ethnographic "barbarian" typologies, many already appearing in Herodotus: they live in lands where the laws of nature are turned upside down; they are pre-agrarian; they produce primitive primary goods, breeding horses and capturing animals for fur; and they exist, in multitudinous numbers, in a vast series of tribes that pressure one another like a long series of dominoes (Jord. *Get.* 19–24; see, e.g., Hdt. 4. 13; Gillett 2002b: 16 n. 32). The theme of migration, which provides one of the main narrative dynamics of the work (and a cornerstone to the early modern construct of the *Völkerwanderung*), derives from classical ethnographic writings, and is exploited in other late antique works (e.g., Hdt. 1. 16, 103; 4. 1. 11–12; and esp. 4. 13; Thuc. 1. 2. 12; Late Antiquity: Amm. Marc. 31. 3. 1; Priscus, fr. Blockley 1981: 40. 1). It evokes a key concept in classical ethnographic thinking: the hierarchy of autochthonic over migratory peoples, the latter inherently inferior (Loraux 2000; Dench 2005: 18–20, 96–101, 244; by contrast, some other late antique explanations of origins of barbarian groups saw them, more charitably, as new names for already existing aboriginal peoples: e.g., Agathias 1. 2. 1). Jordanes' short text includes frequent geographic digressions, and the author underscores the geographic-literary context within which he sets his depiction by citing an impressive array of geographic authors, including Ptolemy, Dio Chrysostom, Pomponius Mela, and Strabo, and snippets from writers in other genres who are often presented as if they also were geographers (Gillett 2000: 487–8).

Such features, consciously selected by the author and prominently displayed, signal that this sixth-century Byzantine text was intended to be understood in terms of the very long tradition of ethnographic *geographia* and *historia*, and that in doing so it exploits the potent, alienating conception of the barbarian Other. Jordanes stands in the company of many other late antique authors who adapted for their own purposes venerable Greco-Roman portraits of "barbarians" and other enemies of order: such as Claudian, who depicts Alaric as a new Hannibal; Synesius, who breezily transports rebellious Gothic soldiers back in time to an ancient Egypt culled from Plutarch; or the anonymous author of the romance-hagiography *Euphemia and the Goth*, who uses the stereotypically barbarian faithlessness of his villain as the pivot of the plot (Claud. *De bello Getico* 78–82; Dewar 1994; Synesius, *De providentia*; *Euphemia and the Goth*).

More specifically, Jordanes' ethnographic monograph (like his summary of Roman history, the *Romana*) was very much a part of contemporary literary activity in Justinian's Constantinople. In the early to mid sixth century, Constantinople and the eastern empire more generally witnessed the production of an impressive variety of texts with historical, geographical, and ethnographic interests that intersect with Jordanes (Amory 1997: 135–47; Goffart 2005; Merrills 2005: 129–30, 145, 162–7; on historical literature of the Justinianic period more generally, see Scott 1990; Wilson 1996: 55–6; Rapp 2005b). Perhaps most importantly, the historical narratives of Jordanes and Procopius not only overlap, inevitably given their subjects, but speak to each other, sometimes contradictorily, in a historiographic dialogue yet to be fully elucidated (Goffart 1988: 94–6). Other interactions or striking parallels are also evident: with the author Capito, who like Jordanes wrote both a breviary of Roman history and a history of an "ethnic" group within the empire, the Isaurians (Amory 1997: 136, 304–5); with the chronicler Marcellinus *comes*, who helped "manufacture" the east Roman assertion of AD 476 as the definitive end of the western Roman empire, and was followed in this by Jordanes (Croke 1983); with the ethnographic victory ideology espoused in Justinian's imperial titulature and legal rhetoric (Amory 1997: 140–1); with the attempt in the so-called *Frankish Table of Nations* to categorize contemporary barbarian peoples in terms drawn from classical ethnography (Goffart 1983); and more broadly with the geographical and "ethnological" interests of the *Cosmographia* of Julius Honorius, the *Christian Topography* of Cosmas Indicopleustes, and the *Ethnica* of Stephan of Byzantium. The range of points of contact between Jordanes and his contemporaries may, with further study, help triangulate his position within the debates of his time; together with the lively tradition of classical ethnography, they provide a potential matrix of interpretation for this often misconstrued text. Whatever the author's elusive purpose, the work is clearly a "mirror" not of barbarian but of Byzantine society and concerns.

Emphasizing the classicizing nature of Jordanes' text need not preclude the possibility that individual filaments of data genuinely of Gothic provenance may be preserved in the *Getica*, or in other late antique sources. Jordanes embellishes his text with a few items of Gothic vocabulary, just as Herodotus includes a smattering of Scythian, Persian, and Egyptian words (Waterfield and Dewald 1998: 742–4). But Herodotus does not represent a Scythian ideology, or Jordanes a Gothic one.

Approaching Late Antiquity, we need to be aware that large areas of the field have already been mapped in detail by earlier visitors, albeit that they knew the region by different names. Mindful of our debt to their pathfinding, we are nevertheless not obligated to adhere to their routes, or refrain from disturbing their markers. The habit in both past and current Germanicist scholarship of reading Greco-Roman sources as if they were "barbarian" ones obscures a genuine historical phenomenon: the vitality of classical conceptions of the barbarian and of ethnographic discourses in Late Antiquity, and consequently the scale of their impact on our perceptions of the period. Just as in earlier antiquity widely held ethnographic assumptions informed a variety of discourses ranging from drama to philosophy, so too in Late Antiquity the classical concept of the barbarian contributed to current thought and debate. Amid the religious disputes of the fourth century, Julian defended the reasonableness of polytheism on the basis of the varied inherent natures of different peoples; and Epiphanius of Salamis developed a schema of religious evolutionism, commencing after the Fall with "barbarism," in order to identify the origin of heresy (Julian. *Contra Galilaeos* 115 *D*–131 *D*; Epiph. *Adv. haeres.* 1. 1. 1–9). The moral diatribe of Salvian exploits the "qualities of peoples" literary tradition and the *topos* of barbarian simplistic virtue in castigating Roman decadence (Salvian, *De gub.* 4. 14. 67). The classical conception of the barbarian remained in Late Antiquity a ubiquitous and unquestioned intellectual resource, drawn upon reflexively.

The degree to which our vision of the barbarians of Late Antiquity is shaped by the tradition of Hellenistic ethnographic thought cannot be too heavily emphasized. The "Scandinavian origins" of Jordanes' Goths (and of their medieval imitators, Paul the Deacon's Lombards and Widukind's Saxons) derive from the classicizing milieu of Constantinople, not from barbarian cultural beliefs (Goffart 2005). The very names by which we think of barbarian groups, even if ultimately derived from genuine autonyms, have been reconstituted into Greco-Roman frameworks, as the pseudo-ethnic, administrative terminology used by the author of the *Life* of Orientius of Auch suggests. By contrast, our expectations of meeting ethnically proud Goths, Franks, and Lombards has been conditioned not by the force of late antique evidence but by the weight of five centuries of modern Eurocentric scholarship. The historical counterparts of these figures appear rather differently in our sources: as the pious Christians, avaricious landowners, and wily negotiators of Roman social and governmental structures who feature in the narratives of Gregory of Tours and Paul the Deacon, and in the transactions recorded by charters.

Several desiderata for future research have been mentioned in this discussion, and before concluding two more may be added. First, it would be healthy for study of the postimperial western kingdoms to be disturbed from its customary, Eurocentric context; the construct of Late Antiquity should facilitate this. The western "barbarian kingdoms" were not the only new states formed on or within the borders of the Roman Empire, combining "barbarian" rulership and Mediterranean culture. On its Syrian frontier, at roughly the same time, Rome dealt with the kingdoms of the Ghassanids and Lakhmids, ruled by Christian Arabic courts influenced culturally and politically by Hellenistic (and Iranian) culture (Shahîd 1984a, 1984b, 1989, 1995). Comparative studies of these western and eastern "provincial" or "transliminal" states, levering both away from their traditional scholarly contexts of medievalism and orientalism respectively, may well offer new insight not only into these kingdoms themselves, but into Late Antiquity more broadly; cultural dynamics are sometimes most tellingly revealed at peripheries.

Second, the energy of recent research into classical ethnography and its role in the social, political, and cultural dynamics of antiquity should be tapped by research on antiquity's heirs. In what ways and to what extent classical ethnography affected texts and thought in Late Antiquity is an open question. How widely were Herodotus and other ethnographical writers read in Late Antiquity? Some forty-six papyrus fragments of Herodotus from the Christian period are known, a respectable number indicating currency of his text (Clarysse et al.). References to Herodotus by late antique authors, writing in Greek and even in Latin, are dauntingly numerous (some 900 references by Greek authors between the second and seventh centuries AD are listed in the *Thesaurus linguae Graecae*). Many, perhaps most, will be mere name-dropping; nonetheless, the frequent citations attest consciousness of Herodotus as a weighty literary model and source of information, however outdated. A study of the late antique afterlife of Herodotus, and of the classical ethnographic tradition in general, has yet to be undertaken. Our understanding now of the concept of the barbarian then is yet to be enriched by appreciation of the force of the classical ethnographic tradition in Late Antiquity.

BIBLIOGRAPHICAL NOTE

At the time of writing, the following represented the major treatments of the theme.

For overviews of recent work on the concept of "the barbarian" in classical antiquity: Dench 1995; Cohen 2000; Malkin 2001; Cartledge 2002: 51–77; Harrison 2002; and see now Isaac 2004; Campbell 2006 (not available to me when this chapter was written). A useful index of the growth of this field is *OCD* 3rd edn.: 233, s.v. "barbarian"; there are no entries for this headword in the earlier editions. For similar approaches to other ancient societies: Poo 2005.

For Late Antiquity, essays on the concept of "the barbarian" include Dauge 1981; Chauvot 1998; Heather 1999. Important earlier approaches, sidelined by recent debate, include Reydellet 1981; Teillet 1984; and the English Marxist Thompson 1982. For historiographic discussion of earlier traditions: Goffart 1980: 3–39; 1989b; 1995; Halsall 1999; Nicolet 2003 (on French "Romanists" and "Germanists"); Pizarro 2003: 43–7 (on "Germanic antiquity").

Introductions to "ethnogenesis" approaches include: Wolfram 1981; 1988: 1–18; 1994; 1998; Pohl 1991; 1998; Geary 1988; 1999; 2002. There are several parallel or modified forms of this approach, not necessarily fully in agreement with each other, including Heather 1991; Amory 1997. The latter, the most valuable single contribution using this approach, embraces a range of methodologies and evidence. Critiques of "ethnogenesis" as an explanatory model are gathered in Gillett 2002b (essays by Bowlus, Gillett, Goffart, Kulikowski, and Murray; the latter is the fullest historiographic analysis of the model and its development from antecedents); see also Bowlus 1995; Goffart 1995; 2005; Gillett 2005. For Jordanes: Croke 1987; Goffart 1988: 20–111; 2005; 2006; Gillett 2000; Christensen 2002; Pizarro 2003: 47–51; Merrills 2005: 100–69.

Moving from the ideological construct of "the barbarian" to the underlying economic and military *realia* of Roman–barbarian relations: Whittaker 1994; 2004; Wells 1999; Burns 2003. For important new approaches to material evidence from European "barbarian" societies: Veit 1989; Halsall 1992; Brather 2002; 2004.

CHAPTER TWENTY-SEVEN

Beyond the Northern Frontiers

Guy Halsall

Introduction

From most discussions of the period, one could be forgiven for thinking that, to the people who lived beyond the northern frontiers of the Roman Empire, Late Antiquity was just something that happened to other people. Even in studies of the barbarian migrations, many of which (e.g., Heather 1996, 2005) espouse the sort of sharp historical break that the late antique periodization aimed to play down, the newcomers' homelands drop out of the picture as soon as the barbarians have moved. This, naturally, prevents any understanding of the period's relative continuities as surely as it precludes any real comprehension of the migrations themselves. This volume's inclusion of a brief survey of non-Roman northwestern Europe represents something of a break with tradition.

There are, however, some good reasons for this tradition. The concept of Late Antiquity came to prominence because of a desire to stress the continuities that transcended the "Fall of the Roman Empire" in both halves of the empire and to point out that economic, social, and other links between east and west persisted until the seventh century and sometimes beyond. This, inevitably, is a Romanocentric view, whether one is looking at the high politics of "476 and all that," the rise of the holy man, or Mediterranean economic structures. So, it is not surprising that the territories of northern *barbaricum* should play little part in the analysis. Furthermore, Late Antiquity has been, until quite recently, a subject explored more or less exclusively through the written record. The lands beyond the *limites* do not furnish us with written sources between the third and seventh century (or before and for some time afterward), so they are understandably excluded. Even art-historical approaches to the period have concentrated upon art of the classical tradition, and the recently developed late antique archaeology is, for reasons left unspecified, restricted to the lands of the empire and its southern and eastern neighbors. It remains puzzling why it should be more acceptable or thought less odd to talk of late antique Axum

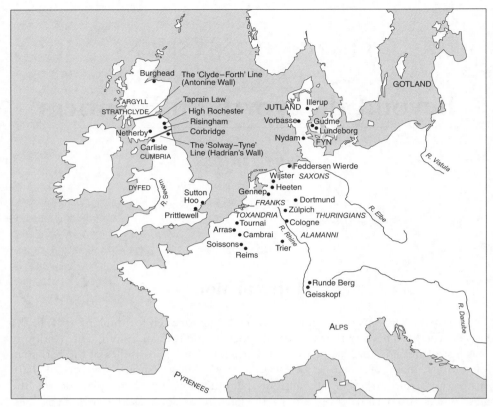

Map 5   Beyond the Northern Frontiers.

(e.g., Munro-Hay 1991) or late antique Persia than about late antique Ireland or Denmark. Either the "late antique problematic" is specific to the history of the empire and its inhabitants, in which case *all* non-Roman lands should be excluded, or (as sounds more reasonable) any and all territories that came into contact with Rome (and that therefore might or might not be affected by the west's political demise or the longer-term changes around the Mediterranean) should be understood as encompassed within the notion of Late Antiquity. This chapter explores the extent to which the features commonly understood to define Late Antiquity are visible east of the Rhine, north of Hadrian's Wall, and west of the Irish Sea (see Map 5). I shall concentrate on the regions between the Rhine and the Baltic, although important comparisons must be made with northern Britain and Ireland, and on the period between roughly AD 300 and 600. We shall encounter considerable variety. In some areas, the fifth century and the disintegration of the western empire had profound effects; in others, it did not. In all cases, however, the reasons for the extent of change or otherwise are to be sought in the nature of the links between the Roman state and the peoples beyond its northern frontiers. (These themes are explored in greater depth in Halsall 2007, especially chs. 4 and 12).

East of the Rhine

In the fourth century, the regions across the Rhine cannot be considered other than as an integral part of the Roman world, saturated by influences from the empire. It is difficult to see how this could have been otherwise after its inhabitants had been neighbors of an imperial superpower for several centuries. Archaeology shows regional differences in access to Roman goods. Close to the frontier, Roman material dominates find assemblages. At the site of Oespeler Bach near Dortmund, e.g., although this site was itself engaged in pottery production, Roman artifacts – finewares as well as jewelry, glass, and bronze vessels and weaponry – are found in great numbers (Brink-Kloke and Meurers-Balke 2003). Further into the heartland of Germania, however, access to Roman material was much more restricted so that in the third century, when society in some parts of the region had undergone some stress and reorganization, Roman wares were displayed in the lavish funeral rites of the elite (Todd 1987: 46–7, 49–52, 57, 71). The control of the trade routes between the empire and the Baltic – the amber routes – appears to have been important in the spread of political authority. If there was any third- and early fourth-century Gothic expansion up the Vistula and its tributaries and thence down the waterways to the Black Sea, though archaeology provides no prima facie support for the notion (Halsall 1999, 2007; Kulikowski 2007; contra, Heather 1996), then it was probably in a fashion reminiscent of the foundation of the Kievan Rus principality in the same region somewhat later. Political and military control of the waterways and the traffic moving along them, bearing goods that were important to the underpinning of prestige and authority, brought about the subscription of other local groups to a new regional hegemony. The Elbe formed another such economic artery, along which a number of groups moved, and acted in a similar fashion. A possible fourth-century expansion of the Saxon confederacy might have been made possible by the control of the lower Elbe. This would be particularly important in the fifth century.

Around the Baltic we can trace similar importance attached to the distribution of Roman material. Here the existence of a shorter sea route around the coast of northern Germany perhaps made access slightly easier than in the center of Germania. Some sites come into existence that graphically reveal the importance of controlling the supply of Roman material. These are, on the whole, little different, in terms of their scale, from other rural settlements, but distinguished by large quantities of imports. The most famous such site is that at Lundeborg on the island of Fyn, associated with a high-status inland site at Gudme (Nielsen et al. 1994), but an analogous site has also been located on the west of the Jutland peninsula at Dankirke (Hansen 1989). In these regions, study of the settlement patterns shows that access to Roman material was closely regulated by the elite occupants of these sites.

It is vital to stress that the impact of the empire upon Germania during the late Roman period far outweighed any influences in the other direction. Traditional historiographical perspectives have envisaged a deepening frontier zone, spreading further into Gaul from the *limes* (e.g., Whittaker 1994; Miller 1996), but this view is hard to sustain. If anything, the reverse is the case. Roman influences within Germania were strengthening all the time. The traditional view is essentially based upon a reading of a particular type of furnished burial that appears in northern Gaul in the late fourth century (for data see, classically, Böhme 1974). These burials are still frequently read as those of immigrant Germani, and the material culture found in them is therefore assumed to be "Germanic" (a hugely problematic term that I shall endeavor to avoid: Goffart 1980: 3–39 for justification). This reading is, however, riddled with empirical and logical flaws (Halsall 1992, 2000; Fehr 2002; Brather 2004). The burial rite itself and the material employed in the graves are overwhelmingly Roman in origin, refer to traditional Roman idioms of aristocratic power and, furthermore, have no precursors in *barbaricum* itself. Once this underpinning is removed, we can see that, rather than being evidence of influence spreading from *barbaricum* into Roman Germania and Gaul, this material further underlines the dominance of Roman Gaul over the lands east of the Rhine. Supposedly "Elbe-germanisch" items of jewellery are provincial Gallic productions exported into and later copied in *barbaricum* (Halsall 2000). This pattern of northern Gallic manufacture and export, as has long been known, can be seen in many other items. Argonne Ware ceramics are exported to Germania, as are bronze bowls from the Meuse valley, Rhineland glass, and so on. The north of Gaul was an economic unit largely separated from the more Mediterranean long-distance trade networks of the south, but it had its own hinterland beyond the Rhine (prefiguring by 300 years Pirenne's separation of northern Europe from the Mediterranean in the seventh century).

There is little or no other evidence of anything moving in the opposite direction, but that results at least partly from the nature of the archaeological record. There must have been perishable material – foodstuffs, raw materials, wool and cloth, and of course slaves – being traded with the Romans in return for their pottery, glass, and metalwork. Some settlements, and perhaps some barbarian rulers, prospered on the basis of the supply of, and exchange with, the armed forces on the Roman frontier. Nevertheless, in terms of the material culture used to create social identities and power, nothing – or very nearly so – was being used in northwestern provincial society that came from east of the Rhine. Given the Roman attitudes to barbarians, this is hardly surprising. Even in the military, where a case can be made that increasing importance was attached to "barbarian chic" (*Cod. Theod.* 14. 10. 1–2), it is hard to prove that the origins of supposedly barbarian items lay in trans-Rhenan reality rather than in Greco-Roman ethnography (Amory 1997: 27–32; Halsall 2007, ch. 3).

The empire's economic domination of *barbaricum* was part and parcel of its military and political hegemony. A standard means of hurting the people across the frontier was, after all, the restriction of markets. One reason for the attractiveness of Roman items among the peoples of Germania was precisely that it demonstrated a link with the mighty power to the south, where so many of them took service. Contexts of ritual display support this conclusion. In northwestern Germany, around the lower Elbe in the region dominated by the Saxon confederacy, Roman official belt-sets were much employed in cremation rituals (Böhme 1974). These were surely, as has long been supposed, brought back by Saxons who had served in the empire. At their funerals, public display was made of their links with Rome and the emperor. Slightly further north, inhumation began to be used by the local elites, probably, as has again been known for some time, because it made a conspicuous display of Romanness (Bemmann 1999; Kleemann 1999). At Fallward in lower Saxony, a lavish burial from the end of the fourth or the start of the fifth century has been found containing, as well as lavish goods and a boat, an intricately carved chair (Schön 1999). If this is not itself an import, its interest is only increased by the fact that it is decorated in the "chip-carved" technique associated primarily with official imperial belt-sets and other metalwork. Just beyond the Rhine frontier, in Alamannic territory, on the defended hill-forts that symbolized their power, local rulers had metalwork made to distribute to their followers (Steuer 1994). Interestingly, these were copies of Roman official metalwork. From the Rhine to the Baltic, social and political power was expressed in entirely Roman terms.

Two important points emerge from this discussion. The first is that there had clearly been much change in politics and society in Germania Magna since the days of Caesar and Tacitus, although the writings of these sources are still sometimes pressed into service in studying the fourth-century Germani (Wolfram 1997), in spite of the enormous problems of accepting them as accurate reportage even in their own day. Any similarities between Ammianus' brief accounts of the trans-Rhenan barbarians and those of Tacitus must be seen in the context of the former's desire to be seen as the latter's continuator. Some superficial similarities, such as Ammianus' account of bipartite kingship among the Burgundians, have been shown to result from his use, at that point, of an earlier source (Wood 1977). The second point, following on from the first, is that it is difficult to find in the fourth century anything that might look like a distinct, indigenous form of rulership between the Rhine and the Baltic. The empire was the fount of all ideas of political legitimacy, one of many reasons why postimperial western kingship should not be viewed as a "Germanic" barbarian introduction. One fourth-century Alamannic king even changed his son's name to Serapio, such was his infatuation with the empire (Amm. Marc. 16. 12. 25). More to the point, perhaps, Serapio himself does not appear to have minded being saddled with this unusual name. This might mean that there was less difficulty for Ammianus in translating non-Roman political terms and structures into Roman vocabulary than there had been for late republican and early imperial writers. Nevertheless, one must bear in mind that the gap between Roman model and the barbarian perception of it probably allowed for significant variation and creativity.

Survey of social and economic structures between the Rhine and the Baltic shows that there was diversity but also that the fourth century was, on the whole, a period of stability and increasing sociopolitical complexity. Throughout Germania settlements were growing and revealing more signs of central planning and of the fencing-off of individual properties. This can be seen at Wijster (Van Es 1967) and at Feddersen Wierde (Haarnagel 1979) as well as at rural settlements in Denmark and elsewhere in Scandinavia. The demarcation of individual plots has plausibly been read as evidence of a growing notion of private property. The sites at Wijster and Vorbasse (Hvass 1983) have suggested populations of about 200 people in their fourth-century phases. While minuscule compared with the great urban centers of the Mediterranean, there are signs that they were on a trend of development that might in time have led them to match the shrinking towns of the northwestern provinces.

The cemetery evidence also suggests stability, after a burst of lavish inhumations, generally taken to imply a brief moment of instability at the start of the fourth century. In most of this region, burials are fairly nondescript. In areas like lower Saxony, the norm is for large communal cremation cemeteries, which do not involve particularly lavish, competitive ritual displays. In the area inhabited by the Franks, the burial ritual is archaeologically invisible, presumably un-urned cremation burial or the ashes of the dead being scattered. In Denmark, although rites differed, the same picture emerges. Less attention was lavished upon burials of the fourth century than upon those of previous periods. Throughout Germania, the deaths of individuals within communities do not appear to have produced the stress within social relations that needed smoothing over by expensive funerary displays and gift-giving. This contrasts with evidence from periods before and, especially, immediately afterward (for the interpretation of burial ritual followed in this chapter, see Halsall 1995, 2003). The cemetery data thus accords well with that from the excavated settlements in suggesting social stability.

So too, perhaps, does the evidence from the votive bog deposits in Denmark and the far north of Germany at sites like Nydam, Ejsbøl and Illerup (Jørgensen et al. 2003), representing the "sacrifice" of *matériel* from defeated armies. The lavishness of these deposits increases during this period, as the wealth invested in burials diminishes. Whereas the display of grave goods was a mechanism for the creation or maintenance of individual families' status, these deposits were more of a communal rite. This did not make them egalitarian. The finds themselves suggest central organization. The objects disposed of were precisely those things that would normally have become booty, for the distribution of which war leaders were responsible. By disposing of large quantities of potential loot, presumably in a gift to the gods, the leader simultaneously demonstrated authority, removed from circulation objects that might have been used as gifts by others, and enhanced the value of those items that he *did* bestow upon his followers. The fourth-century bog-finds illustrate graphically the northern barbarian leaders' ability to raise substantial armed forces.

Other evidence points the same way. Just across the upper Rhine and Danube frontiers, Alamannic leaders demonstrated their power by constructing impressive hill-forts, the so-called *Höhensiedlungen*. The best-known of these is at the Runde Berg near Urach, a defended "princely" settlement occupied in the late Roman period. Although well known, we should not generalize from this site (Hoeper 1998). Others might have been simple refuges or cult centers. The Geisskopf near Freiburg im Breisgau, in addition to important terracing works that must have involved considerable labor and organization, yields evidence of the manufacture of Roman-influenced metalwork, presumably as badges of office, as noted earlier (Hoeper and Steuer 1999). Whatever their precise function, these sites made visible and permanent marks on the landscape, proclaiming a leader's control over manpower and other resources. New high-status sites, if not atop hills, are found in the Frankish territories. One, at Gennep (Heidinga 1994), lies just inside imperial territory and might represent the seat of a chieftain in some sort of treaty relationship with the empire. Another, at Heeten, has revealed organized iron working controlled by a fortified settlement (Groenewoudt and van Nie 1995; Verlinde and Erdrich 1998). It is unclear whether this iron working was geared toward exchange with the Roman frontier or reflected the manufacture of weapons and other goods, the distribution of which could be controlled by the local ruler. In addition to the high-status sites at Gudme and Dankirke mentioned above, elite settlements, sometimes fortified, are increasingly known in Scandinavia in the late Roman period.

While the absolute dominance of the region by Rome – by her ideas and her products – is manifest, archaeological data nevertheless make clear the gradually increasing social, economic, and political complexity of the fourth-century *barbaricum*. There was, however, crucial regional variation. The most impressive displays of regional power are found, first, in the geographic band closest to the frontier and, second, in that furthest away, in Scandinavia.

In the former region, the empire could and did maintain equilibrium among lesser leaders, through military and other direct action but also through the payment of diplomatic and other gifts. Nevertheless, one effect of those policies appears to have been to raise the stakes in barbarian politics: as is well known, over-kings rapidly acquired power when the Romans were distracted from their frontier policy (Heather 1994b). Such rulers could be and were employed in Roman civil wars, again increasing their power. As a result, the kings on the frontier appear to have established bases of power, which, though still insecure, could be built upon to create more impressive and lasting authority. By the late fourth century, some such frontier rulers, most notably the Alaman Macrianus, were proving difficult for the empire to deal with (Drinkwater 1997). In the more distant region, the Baltic, Rome had by contrast little ability to intervene actively in regional politics, and it was the much sought-after amber of the region that provided a valuable trading commodity, the control of which could bolster local authority.

In many ways the key area lay in between these two zones, where leaders appear to have been more dependent upon links with the Roman Empire. Roman artifacts were clearly very prestigious and their distribution an important means of cementing authority. Yet they could not be acquired as readily through exchange as in the frontier territories or those on the Baltic coast. They had to be acquired either through raiding or, more frequently, through the payment of diplomatic gifts by the Romans, who used these peoples, like the Burgundians, as a means of keeping the frontier rulers in check (Amm. Marc. 28. 5. 11). In these central areas, politics appear to have been much more fluid. The Romans were not aware of any large new confederacies in this area to match the Franks, Alamans, Saxons, or Goths that appeared on their frontiers in the third century. (The Saxons represent something of a special case, lying in many ways in this "middle band" of Germania yet also being located on one, albeit broad, frontier of the empire: the North Sea.) Instead, in the crucial intermediate band of *barbaricum* we continue to encounter the, probably smaller, groupings that had existed since the early Roman period, such as the Vandals, Longobards, and Burgundians.

These regional differences are of vital importance when we consider the dramas of the fifth century. These three bands of territory demonstrate (broadly) three trajectories of development and change. Closest to the frontier, the critical period around AD 400, which produced crisis in the northwestern provinces (see, e.g., Esmonde Cleary 1989), seems to have made little immediate difference. Change there comes in the mid fifth century and is especially associated with the growth of the Frankish kingdom in the sixth. By contrast, in the center of Germania, the events around AD 400 produced very important transformations. Some stability appears to have been created in the later fifth century, before the establishment of Merovingian hegemony brought more changes in the sixth. Finally, furthest away from the frontier, around the Baltic, a more gradual trajectory of change can be detected, though there are some interesting developments.

In the Alamannic and Frankish territories just across the Rhine frontier, settlements on the whole continued the trends discussed earlier. Indeed, in the Frankish areas on the lower Rhine, rural settlements experienced something of a boom at the end of the fourth century. The site at Gennep certainly underwent no decline. One type of change can be associated with the appearance of lavishly furnished inhumations, similar to those that appeared slightly earlier in northern Gaul (see above). These probably argue for some renegotiation of power in the area, but it is important to note again that the material and symbols deployed remain Roman in origin. Across the upper Rhine, Alamannic *Höhensiedlungen* continued to be occupied. Change here took place in the middle of the fifth century. A number of the hill-forts were abandoned and change took place in the region's burials, with the appearance, again, of more lavishly furnished inhumations. It is difficult to know how to read this data. One possibility is increasing political authority in Alamannia. The rulers, with power based in the remaining *Höhensiedlungen*, may have eroded the authority of more local leaders, producing competition within the latter's communities. This is suggested in the furnished burials. Alternatively, there might have been more widespread political crisis within the Alamannic territory, causing the abandonment of elite sites and general competition for local power. The former explanation is preferred here, mainly on the grounds of scattered evidence for expanding Alamannic power in the period, reaching into Noricum and even Champagne (Eugippius, *Life of Severinus of Noricum* 19. 1; 25. 3; 27. 1–2; 31. 4; *Life of Lupus of Troyes* 10: the similarity between these texts may stem from one author's dependence upon the other), and also because of Cassiodorus' reference to Clovis' troops having killed the king of the Alamans, the implication being that there was only one (Cassiod. *Var.* 2. 41).

Significant change took place in Alamannia in the early sixth century, plausibly associated with the Frankish king Clovis' subjugation of the area (though see Samson 1994). The *Höhensiedlungen* were abandoned and the furnished inhumation ritual was now employed by whole communities (rather than just by individual families, as had tended to be the case earlier) and in large cemeteries (many of which were founded at this time). Burials in this region are very lavish – much more so than in contemporary northern France or England. The death of local community members produced great tension in social relations, necessitating extreme displays of a family's ability to furnish a burial with the appropriate items. As elsewhere in the Frankish kingdoms (Halsall 1995: 262–70), there was significant change around AD 600. Local aristocratic families began to remove themselves from the large communal cemeteries for their burials. These took place in separate cemeteries, with the burials sometimes placed under mounds (a very similar phenomenon to that taking place in England at the same time and given particular expression in the famous burials at Sutton Hoo and at Prittlewell in Essex). These changes are most plausibly to be linked to an increase in the security of the elites' local preeminence (Halsall 1995: 262–70). Rural settlements also show more evidence of social stratification at this time (Damminger 1998).

The Frankish areas beyond the lower Rhine show similar developments, with the abandonment of earlier elite settlements, like Gennep, in the early sixth century (after late fifth-century decline), the introduction of furnished burial in communal cemeteries, more lavish burials than in the Merovingian heartlands, and similar transformations around the year AD 600. An interesting development is the introduction around AD 475 of metalwork decorated in a new polychrome style (sometimes referred to as the Flonheim-Gültlingen horizon), seen most famously in the burial of Childeric I in Tournai (Brulet 1997). The introduction of this style at precisely the time of the western empire's political demise must be important. It shows that people realized that a new political order was emerging, necessitating a new artistic vocabulary to display power (see Theuws and Alkemade 2000 for discussion).

In the intermediate band of trans-Rhenan *barbaricum*, change was much more dramatic around AD 400. It is significant that the invaders of AD 406/7 were largely from this region (especially if we add the Burgundians, who founded a kingdom on the middle Rhine in the great invasion's wake). The reasons for their irruption at this time have been variously explained. Heather (1995; now, at length, 2005) associates it with the "exogenous" impact of the Huns. It might be better understood in the context of the collapse of the important relationships between the empire and the heart of *barbaricum*. When the emperors retreated from the frontiers to Italy at the end of the fourth century, a close eye could no longer be kept upon frontier policy and the balancing of barbarian groups, as it had been in the fourth century. This caused political instability, in which emerging Hunnic power could furnish an alternative to the traditional backing of Rome, now no longer provided (Halsall 2007). It is unlikely that the Huns could have had the effects that they did have if this political context, within the empire and outside, had not existed. Be that as it may, the dramas of the period are manifest in bursts of lavishly furnished burials, such as the Niemberger Group in Thuringia, and a marked decline in the quality of local craftsmanship in that area (Schmidt 1983: 536).

In the Saxon regions, the early fifth century saw dramatic change. Many sites – settlements and cemeteries – were abandoned, and those that remained changed in nature. The last phase at Feddersen Wierde lacks the earlier period's planning, for example. The long *Wohnstallhäuser* (long houses incorporating byres for cattle as well as human living quarters) were replaced by smaller halls and ancillary *Grubenhäuser* (small tent-like huts built over a pit, sometimes floored over). Furnished inhumations were introduced. The interpretation of these changes, clearly indicating dramatic transformations in Saxon society, has not generally been sophisticated, tending to concentrate upon migration to England at the expense of other factors (abandonment may have been overestimated: Siegmund 2003: 81–3). They are better understood in a broader North Sea context. Settlement abandonment and change took place in a number of regions bordering that sea – the British lowlands, northern Gaul, and northern Germany (remember that fairly close links between northern Gaul and lower Saxony had existed in the fourth century) – yet migration cannot explain all of these changes. In all areas, new material culture and similar architectural repertoires appear in response. Although a role was surely played by the indisputable migration from Saxony to England, we would be better advised to see the exchange of ideas and influences as a two-way process across the North Sea. Another issue that needs to be considered is the break-up of the Saxon confederacy, possibly linked with the turmoil in *barbaricum* mentioned above. A number of peoples, not heard of since the early imperial period, reappear in our sources from the sixth century: Angles, Jutes, and Frisians. It seems likely that these levels of ethnicity, previously subsumed (as far as the Romans cared) within a confederate Saxon identity, came to the fore during the fifth-century changes.

Stability was apparently restored by the later fifth century. One reason was the emergence of a new power in the heart of Germania: the Thuringian kingdom. The Thuringians seem to have been one of those groups that prospered with Hunnic backing. They are recorded on Attila's side at the battle of Campus Mauriacus (AD 451), and the archaeological material that appears in the middle of the fifth century (which seems to be associated with their kingdom) shows some Hunnish influence (Schmidt 1983: 541). Not the least of these is the practice of skull deformation, whereby the skulls of small children were bound in order artificially to change their shape. Thuringian power seemingly spread along the trade artery of the Elbe valley. Thuringian material is found in lower Saxony and as far as the Rhine and upper Danube (matching the reference in the *Life of Severinus* to Thuringian warlords in that area: 27. 3; 31. 4), suggesting that people were subscribing to Thuringian lordship over much of the former trans-Rhenan *barbaricum*. Gregory of Tours believed that the Thuringian kingdom marched with those of the Franks on the lower and middle Rhine (Gregory of Tours, *Hist.* 2. 9 and 12). The Thuringian kingdom was destroyed by the Franks in the AD 530 s and their territories incorporated in the Merovingian hegemony, apparently under the rule of a duke. At about the same time, Slavic settlement in the area underlined the changes taking place.

Around the Baltic, the trajectory of development visible in the fourth century continues. The picture is of steadily increasing social stratification and political authority (Hedeager 1992). Some renegotiation of the bases of political power was apparently made necessary because of the breakdown of earlier patterns of trade with the western empire around AD 400. The Gudme site complex shows a change from the importance of control over imports through the port at Lundeborg to the manufacture of gold objects with religious significance. Again, the distribution of the latter was doubtless controlled by the rulers and provided them with a major means of underpinning their authority. Nevertheless, the settlement and cemetery evidence shows that this change was negotiated without undue stress. Trading links may have changed in emphasis, with greater importance given to the doubtless more sporadic links (both easier to control, perhaps, and more prestigious) down the amber routes to the eastern empire (Näsman 1998). The bog deposits become more token in character and die out completely by around AD 500. Clearly, there was no further need for this public, ritual underpinning of rulership. In the earlier sixth century, the trading station at Lundeborg was finally abandoned; the trading contacts of Denmark possibly switched back to the west. It has been suggested that some material culture, such as swastika brooches, is linked with the emergence of the Danes as the dominant group in the region (Hines 1998). This is also marked by the appearance of King Chlochilaich, who raided northern Francia in the early sixth century (Gregory of Tours, *Hist.* 3. 3). As well as possibly manifesting the change from eastern to western trading contacts mentioned above, it has been suggested that Chlochilaich's rivalry with the Merovingians might have been a component of the Italian Theoderic's foreign policy (Storms 1970 and Wood 1983 for different but compatible interpretations). Through our period, Denmark continued to develop toward the impressive royal power visible in the eighth century (of which the collapse around AD 800 was surely a key to the origins of the Viking age).

Similar changes to those taking place in Denmark can be seen in southern Sweden, and Norway also shows evidence of significant local political power in the form of a series of boathouses: the ships housed in them would require the manpower resources of a larger area to crew (Myrhe 1997). Changes took place in the mid sixth century, however, as artifacts take on different forms and designs, bringing in the "Vendel" period in Sweden (Lamm and Nordström 1983) and what has been known since the end of the nineteenth century, curiously, as the Merovingian period in Norway. The precise chronology of these changes is still debated, but it seems to have taken place in the middle quarters of the century. At the same time, a decorative style known as Style II appeared, which, it has been argued, relates to a new warrior elite (Høilund Nielsen 1997). In some areas, such as the island of Gotland off Sweden, these changes involved new local social structures (Rundqvist 2003). From the sixth century, Norway saw a significant expansion of the settlement pattern (Myhre 1992: 308). These sixth-century changes seem to make a suitable end point for this survey. The end of the Roman Empire did not produce dramatic transformations in Scandinavia, and does not seem to have affected drastically the general trajectory of social change; but it had some significant and interesting results nevertheless.

East of the Rhine, therefore, we encounter considerable variety in social, economic, and political developments. The impact of the collapse of the long-standing relationships with the empire differed between regions, but there were, regularly, other points at which significant restructuring of society and politics took place. There was too much regular change for one to be able to claim that, even in Scandinavia, Late Antiquity was a period characterized by long, fundamental continuities.

North of Hadrian's Wall

Some time probably in the third century, the Romans became aware of new confederacies, the Verturiones and Dicalydones, emerging north of Hadrian's Wall (Amm. Marc. 27. 8. 5). Roman authors generally refer to these peoples as *picti*, but this is clearly a Roman descriptive term ("painted men") rather than (at this date at least) a genuine indigenous ethnonym. This "Pictish" terminology has caused great confusion: when combined with our knowledge of seventh-century political geography, it has been taken to suggest that these "Picts" lived north of the Clyde-Forth line, with "Britons" like the Votadini between them and Hadrian's Wall. This seems very problematic. Roman writers use *picti* as a general description of anyone beyond the Wall, rhetorically employing the word to describe the reputation of an emperor reaching the ends of the earth (e.g., Claud. *Cons. Stil.* 54). Irish sources simply call the "Picts" *cruithne*, a Q-Celtic rendition of a P-Celtic word like *Pritani* (i.e., Britons), suggesting that "Picts" were undistinguishable from northern "Britons." It is ill judged to suppose either that the region between the Wall and the Forth was uniformly peaceable or that the fourth-century Roman campaigns against *picti* involved traversing a large swathe of tranquil "British" territory before "hostiles" were encountered. Comparison with the Rhine and Danube frontiers suggests that new large confederacies were formed *on* the frontier. That the Votadini of early Roman writers reemerge in the name of *Manau Gododdin* in the seventh is surely an analogue to the "disappearance" of the Angles, Jutes, and Frisians between the early Roman era and the postimperial period.

We can probably abandon the old idea of "Picts" and "Britons" divided along the Clyde-Forth line. Nevertheless, we can consider separately the region between the Wall and the firths of Clyde and Forth, on the one hand, and that to the north of those rivers, on the other, and see that the archaeology suggests dynamics at work in northern Britain similar to those operating east of the Rhine (Armit 1998; Edwards and Ralston 2003).

Just north of the Wall, the area's economy was a mixture of pastoral and arable farming. The souterrain, the characteristic rural settlement type of the early Roman period, died out at this time. The souterrains' large underground spaces have been interpreted most plausibly as for grain storage, and it might be that surplus was being directed to the leaders of the southernmost of the new Pictish confederacies. Unsurprisingly, Roman imports are commonest between the Solway–Tyne and Clyde–Forth, though never as common as in Germania Magna. The Romans had other links with elements of society north of the Wall. In the shadowy *barbarica conspiratio* of AD 367, the *areani* (often emended to *arcani*, i.e., spies) north of the frontier, were blamed for being derelict in their duty (Amm. Marc. 28. 3. 8).

Higher-status sites were generally less clearly fortified in the Roman period than had been the case earlier, but again this is a development that began too early to have a direct link with Roman military presence and intervention. The nature of their occupation has been debated (Close-Brooks 1987; Hill 1987; Armit and Ralston 2003: 180–2). Nevertheless, some socio-economic hierarchy can be reconstructed from these sites. It has been suggested that the presence of the Roman frontier brought some stability and prosperity to the region immediately to the north.

Further north, the famous brochs (towers) were no longer constructed, but many sites continued to be occupied in somewhat different form, with often cellular structures built into the rubble (Armit 1990, 2003; Ballin Smith and Banks 2002). This development, too, might relate to transformations in political structures. Another change in the northern region is an apparent shift toward an increasing focus upon dress and personal adornment at the expense of pottery, which becomes plainer in this period. This might relate to a situation in which status and gender was more clearly proclaimed through costume, possibly implying that marriage and descent had become more important because of a greater emphasis upon inherited property. Alternatively it could relate to a more fluid situation, wherein local standing was based on marriage alliances. Another explanation for changes in the later Roman period and after is a switch from kinship networks to clientship systems. The difference between kinship and clientship should not be overstated, however. Early medieval Irish society, after all, was based heavily on both. Such changes were probably also behind a slow move back toward investment in hill-forts. Burghead in Moray was occupied in the fourth century (Foster 1996: 43; Alcock 2003: 192–7). There is little evidence of close links with the empire, imports, while known, being much scarcer here.

On the whole, though the evidence is much more intractable than that for Germania, a broadly similar picture can be proposed, with areas close to the frontier showing comparable developments in social structure. A band behind this frontier zone, where contacts were much less common, can be suggested, just as it can in *barbaricum* east of the Rhine. These differences, as in Germania, explain the variations in the histories of the two regions, north and south of the Clyde-Firth line, in the fifth and sixth centuries. There is little or no evidence for any significant migration or any successful attempts to expand political power toward the south. (Gildas' reference to Pictish attacks, in his *De excidio Brittaniae*, is too rhetorical and too chronologically imprecise for any secure conclusions to be drawn in this regard: see Winterbottom 1978.)

One reason for this lack of expansion seems to have been instability in the regions just north of the Wall. Here, evidence of change is found in written and archaeological sources (see Lowe 1999 for survey). I suggest elsewhere (Halsall 2007) that the effective Roman frontier was withdrawn from the Wall in the AD 380s. At this time, the hill-fort of Traprain Law had its fortifications refurbished (Close-Brooks 1983). A famous treasure was deposited there, probably the result of raiding. Yet the burial of the treasure could relate to insecurity, and before long the site was abandoned. This region's inhabitants had had quite close ties with the empire and a stable society as a result. The retreat of the *limes* would have caused considerable instability, and probably the raiding described by Gildas. I propose that in this late fourth- and fifth-century stress the southernmost "Pictish" confederacy fragmented. This led to the reappearance of groups like the Votadini. Like those of the Angli and Frisians, apparently incorporated within the earlier Saxon confederation, this ethnic identity had been overlaid by a higher-level identity, especially in dealings with the Romans. When the larger group broke up in the turmoil around AD 400, these identities rose back to the surface. Other "British" polities appear in Strathclyde and further south in Cumbria, apparently straddling Hadrian's Wall (Rheged) by the time our earliest postimperial historical sources appear.

On the east coast, by the end of our period, that other symptom of social stress and local instability, furnished inhumation, had also appeared (Alcock 1987: 255–66). This is usually associated with "Anglian" settlement; indeed, Anglian was another of the competing political identities in the region. The formation of these Anglian polities north of Hadrian's Wall is, however, likely to have been a more interesting and complex process than the traditional view of English migration, conquest, and settlement allows. This was likely another consequence of the southern "Pictish" confederacy's fragmentation. All this doubtless makes unsurprising the failure of the southern *picti* to make much of a lasting inroad into the former provinces of Britain.

North of the Clyde-Forth, things seem to have been rather different. Fifth-century archaeological evidence is difficult to find (Foster 1992: 219). Nevertheless, important changes were clearly under way, although apparently not complete until the seventh century. They are most visible in the settlement pattern, where a trend had set in toward occupation and investment in the fortification of hill-forts. Some such sites are known from the fourth century, as mentioned, but the real upsurge in the use of such sites does not appear to have occurred until the fifth century and, usually, later. Transformations seem to have taken place in the nature of other settlements at about the same time, although the chronology is vague and, again, many changes do not appear to have been fully worked through until the seventh century or perhaps even later (Foster 1992: 221–8). The overall trend seems to be toward status in the settlement pattern being concentrated in defended high points, positioned somewhat on the margins of the principal farmed areas. This can be plausibly explained by a removal of political power from the immediate locality and kin network, although whether this means a shift from kinship to clientship is doubtful – at least when stated that simply (Driscoll 1988a, 1988b). There were also shifts in burial practice, such as the custom of interment under barrows and ultimately the appearance of "Class 1" symbol stones, probably as grave markers, although both are difficult to date (Driscoll 1988a, 1988b; Foster 1992: 228–33). With this apparent increase in investment in above-ground markers, the evident absence of grave goods is significant, further suggesting the steady establishment of a secure aristocracy in the areas north of the Forth. The Romans' general lack of interest in politics in the far north of Britain probably meant that the withdrawal of the frontier and the imperial crisis around AD 400 produced no significant results north of the Forth, and competition between rival chieftains for authority there continued as before. By the seventh century, this had resulted in the creation of large "Pictish" and Scottish polities. The end of any significant imperial involvement in north British politics from the late fourth century might have played some part in starting the series of events which eventually led to this situation but, overall, the fall of the west does not seem to have made very much difference to the inhabitants of the regions north of the Clyde and Forth. The northern confederation of *picti* apparently endured; by the time we have written sources again, in the seventh century, it seems to have become that referred to as the Kingdom of the Picts.

Mediterranean pottery is found on high-status sites around the Irish Sea (especially around the Severn estuary) in the fifth and sixth centuries. Known to British archaeologists as "A Ware" (African Red Slip and other Red Slip wares) and "B Ware" (various Mediterranean *amphorae*), these do not reach northern Britain, which appears only to be incorporated into long-distance trading networks from the seventh century (Lane 1994; Campbell 1996), again suggesting that whatever transformations were taking place among the "Picts" and their neighbors were not completed until after the end of the period. North British rulers were now keyed into long-distance exchange networks, and so could guarantee the safety of traders and control the production of whatever was exchanged in return for their wares. Overall, in Britain north of the Forth, the period AD 300–600 might, as in places like Denmark, be characterized as a period of gradual development and the growth of kingdoms.

West of the Irish Sea

As far as can be told from the archaeological record, the social and political structures that existed in Ireland at the start of the fourth century had endured for centuries. A largely pastoral economy existed within political units that were evidently quite large and based around important ritual sites. Political power appears to have been extensive in geographical terms, but comparatively weak (Harbison 1988). It is difficult to know anything about these political units, although they probably bear some relationship to the kingdoms that can dimly be seen fragmenting in the earliest, problematic Irish written sources relating to the sixth century (Ó Cróinín 1995: 41–62), and to those mentioned in the heroic cycles (though these sources link the kingdoms with sites known to be much earlier).

In the fourth century, Ireland began to be drawn into the Roman world. Although Roman imports are known from throughout the Roman period, they seem to change subtly in nature in the fourth century, perhaps indicating high-level political contacts rather than sporadic exchange, as earlier (Edwards 1990: 1–5; Freeman 2001; *Colloquium* 1976). Underlining this, perhaps, is the fact that as yet few Mediterranean finewares are found. The Irish Ogam script, which probably appeared in the late fourth century, was based upon the Latin alphabet, arguing for further cultural influences, and the Church began to take an interest in the island. St. Patrick himself is actually more difficult to date than often supposed and might just belong to the late fourth century (Ó Cróinín 1995: 23–7). If he did, it would perhaps make more sense of the references (in his *Apologia*) to his father's curial office. Irish mercenaries were also beginning to be employed in the Roman army, if the *Attecotti Seniores* and *Iuniores* attested in the *Notitia Dignitatum* are from Ireland rather than the Isles. It has been suggested that an Irish settlement in Wales was established under Magnus Maximus (Rance 2001). Such a settlement would have further facilitated contact between Ireland and the diocese of the *Britanniae* and migration across the Irish Sea.

From the fourth century, important changes began to take place within Irish society (Cooney 2000; Cooney and Grogan 1994). The centuries-old structures of the earlier Iron Age had, by the seventh century, been completely swept away. Dairy farming appears to have been introduced and changes in the nature of settlements also took place, probably in association with such socio-economic changes (see below). Although they have often been ascribed to the introduction of Christianity (technical language aside, there is little to choose between the explanations of Máire and Liam De Paor 1958 and Mytum 1992), the new religion seems to have been encompassed by these changes rather than to have been their cause. Some of the changes seem to begin too early, in the fourth century. Increasing contacts with the empire are likely to have played a part in initiating these changes.

However important, these were nevertheless fairly gradual and, as in northern Britain, took until the seventh century to be fully worked through.

In the archaeological record, the most important development was the appearance of small, defended sites, called cashels (if stone-built), raths (earth and timber) and crannogs (if on islands, often man-made). These have been well studied and have a wealth of information to give on early historic Irish society and economy (most recently, Stout 1997, 2000). They are so different from the previous settlements that they cannot but be interpreted as evidence of profound social change. Their enclosed nature must relate to new ideas of private property. Most would not keep out a large or determined enemy and some sites seem to be corrals rather than human habitations, connected to the rise of dairying noted above. These sites seem to be the material cultural signature of the society based upon cattle farming, clientship, and kindred, and upon the political hierarchy of small kingdoms, both of which emerged at this time. This sociopolitical turmoil also played a part in producing migration to Great Britain, especially Dyfed and Argyll. As noted, the latter migration is difficult to date (it has been postulated that the linguistic frontier between P-Celtic and Q-Celtic may have been located in Argyll long before the late antique period), and the migration to Wales might not have been significant before the sixth century. The evidence for movement (place names, stone monuments, and so on) is not susceptible to fine dating.

The introduction of Christianity, needless to say, brought new underpinnings of secular authority as well as novel religious forms of power. Monasteries, quite apart from representing new types, physically, of settlement and, institutionally, of land-ownership within Irish society, provided a religious life that was adapted to local conditions but provided different avenues through life for men and women (Bitel 1990; Harrington 2002). Christianity, furthermore, strengthened the ties between Ireland and the rest of Europe. By the seventh century, famously, Irish monks were playing a significant part in the religious life of the continent, in Great Britain and on the mainland. These contacts are also manifest in the way in which Ireland was, by the seventh century, incorporated into the long-distance exchange networks that were at this time reaching the north of Britain (see above). Similarly, though to a slightly lesser extent than in northern Britain, the fifth- and earlier sixth-century Mediterranean trading network had not really included the western shores of the Irish Sea.

Ireland, in sum, underwent a long period of important change, more gradual than that experienced in *barbaricum* east of the Rhine but, cumulatively, more revolutionary than that in northern Britain. The island's increasing contact with the empire in the fourth century probably played a major part in instigating these changes, but it is difficult, as in northern Britain, to see any dramatic breaks that can be linked with the crisis of the Roman Empire.

Conclusion

Only in Ireland, the far north of Britain, and Scandinavia can it be argued that the period between the fourth and seventh centuries saw a long trajectory of development that owed little to the political collapse of the Western Roman Empire. Elsewhere, the fifth century saw important changes that were dependent on the breakdown of the relationships that had existed between empire and *barbaricum* for centuries, and on the ending of the overarching political role model that was Rome. It may be that the nature and importance of those relationships meant that the fifth century was more traumatic north of the *limites* than within the provinces, and in some instances this is doubtless true, though the diversity of western social structures meant equally that some areas were every bit as badly hit as *barbaricum* (Halsall 2007). In many ways, Germanic-speaking *barbaricum* was, perhaps paradoxically, more integrally a part of the Roman Empire than many of the imperial provinces. If it is generally the case that the fifth century was more characterized by continuity than by change, then the attitude described at the start of this chapter is perfectly justified. For the northern barbarians, Late Antiquity *was* just something that happened to other people. None of that made the period between the fourth and seventh centuries any less important or dramatic.

BIBLIOGRAPHICAL NOTE

For the English reader, the archaeology of Germania is best introduced in the works of Malcolm Todd 1972 and 1987 (often reissued, sometimes with different titles), though the interpretive frameworks now look somewhat outdated. Peter Heather (1996: 63–84; 2005: 84–96) has provided briefer but more recent and very interesting overviews. A survey of the barbarian territories (in North Africa as well as the British Isles and mainland Europe), their relationships with the empire and the effects upon them of the Fall of Rome is found in Halsall 2007. Hamerow 2002 is very good on northern German rural settlement archaeology, though sadly more hesitant about social than about ethnic interpretations.

Myrhe 2003 is an excellent account of Scandinavian developments. A stimulating discussion of the social evolution of Iron Age Denmark, up to *c.* AD 700 can be found in Hedeager 1992. For the bog deposits of that region, one of the most important forms of evidence, one should consult the useful collection of essays edited by Jørgensen et al. 2003. The Gudme-Lundeborg complex on Fyn is the subject of much analysis, usually in English, particularly in Nielsen et al. 1994. This also contains discussion of other relevant aspects of southern Scandinavia in this era.

The areas further south (Saxon, Frankish, and Alamannic) are not as well treated in English-language literature, though there is useful material in Wood 1998 and Green and Siegmund 2003; and one should consult the overviews cited above. German readers can consult Capelle (1988) for a good introduction to Saxony, and the lavishly illustrated essays in Wieczorek et al. 1997 and Fuchs et al. 1997 for the Franks and Alamans respectively. For the Thuringians, see Schmidt 1987.

For Ireland, one should consult Harbison 1988 for the late Roman Iron Age and Edwards 1990 or Mytum 1992 for the period after the fifth century. Britain north of Hadrian's Wall is surveyed with estimable brevity and clarity in Foster 1996.

CHAPTER TWENTY-EIGHT

From Empire to Kingdoms in the Late Antique West

John Vanderspoel

One feature of the late Roman political landscape in the west is the presence of Roman *reges* or *reges Romanorum* governing areas once under the control of the empire. These men appeared at different times, in Africa, Britain, and Gaul, in circumstances that are surprisingly similar. Though they have received some individual attention, they have not been studied as a group in ways that enable us to assess what their collective appearance means for the process of transformation from empire to kingdoms. Yet the similarities in their emergence and in the attendant circumstances are worthy of examination, for this scrutiny reveals much about the workings of imperial collapse in these regions, and can lead to conclusions about the methods employed (largely unsuccessfully) by the late Roman imperial administration to avoid the inevitable, and even about the inevitability of the inevitable.

My subject here, therefore, is the rise of independent or semi-independent kingdoms in Roman or former Roman territory at the very fringes of the empire (see Map 5). The analysis of this period has often focused on invasion, defeat of Roman forces, absorption of Roman populations, cooperation with the existing elite, and on the kingdoms themselves – all valid approaches. Here, however, I address a different issue (with some recognition of those other factors): a transition in the nature of Roman power structures in three specific areas. Though intended to retain at least a minimal hold over these regions, the transition had the effect of becoming a stage in the demise of Roman authority. Because Ostrogoths in Italy, Visigoths in Spain, and Vandals in North Africa established themselves in ways quite different from the phenomenon explored here (despite some significant similarities), they will appear only casually below: I am concerned with a specific mechanism, not a complete picture of Roman losses of control in the west.

Let me begin with a crucial event: in AD 486, Clovis, the young recently installed king of the Salian Franks (who originated on the lower Rhine, but now inhabited parts of Belgica II), defeated a certain Syagrius at Soissons, also in what had been, and perhaps still was in some sense, that province. To the chagrin of scholars, Syagrius is one of the most shadowy figures of late antique administration in continental Europe. He was the son of the equally shadowy Aegidius. Gregory of Tours (AD 539–94) calls him *Romanorum rex* (Gregory of Tours, *Hist.* 2. 27). This has excited much speculation, with opinion divided basically along two lines (in various permutations): men like Syagrius were either usurpers or the equivalents of emperors (James 1988: 67; Fanning 1992) or (especially according to older scholarship) they represent a final effort of a Roman administrative structure to hold on to places like northern Gaul in the face of enemies from without and within (Dill 1926: 13). In some works (Geary 1988; O'Flynn 1983), Aegidius and Syagrius, as well as others like them, are regarded as more or less typical figures of the period: men who sought to generate powerful positions for themselves with all the means at their disposal, including the use of barbarians to govern Romans (whatever those terms might mean in this part of Europe in this period). They have sometimes been described as "warlords" (recently Whittaker 1994: 243–4 and MacGeorge 2002, but the concept is much older).

Aegidius, the father, was a native of Gaul, and had served in the military under Aëtius, Valentinian III's leading military commander from AD 434 to 454. He was appointed *magister utriusque militiae* ("master of both services") in Gaul, either by the Gallic emperor Avitus (AD 456–7) or, in the view of most scholars, by the emperor Majorian (AD 457–61; Mathisen 1979: 607–8), but the sources differ as to his exact title (MacGeorge 2002: 83). After Majorian was murdered in AD 461, Aegidius did not accept the new Ricimer-backed regime of Libius Severus (AD 461–5), nor was Ricimer, the *magister* controlling the imperial court from the reign of Avitus onward, able to control him. Aegidius did not give way to Agrippinus, the man who had been sent to relieve him (Demandt 1970: 690), and instead remained in his post until a treacherously inflicted death, by either poison or ambush, in AD 465.

His military career, conducted throughout Gaul, was sometimes distinguished, sometimes not. The most interesting aspect of that career is his relationship with the Salian Franks, who are said to have driven their king Childeric into exile among the Thuringians (or more likely the Tungri) *c.* AD 456 for pestering their daughters needlessly. According to Gregory, the Franks, now a significant part of the population of at least northern Belgica II and perhaps further south as well (James 1988), then "with one mind took Aegidius to themselves as king [*unanimiter regem adsiscunt*]" (Gregory of Tours, *Hist.* 2. 12). If Aegidius was indeed appointed *magister* by Majorian, who became emperor in AD 457, the date may pose a problem; but Majorian may have simply regularized a position that Aegidius had assumed on his own initiative at an earlier date (Harries 1994: 86), perhaps in the aftermath of the death of Aëtius (AD 454) and Valentinian III (AD 455). What interests us, however, is the significance of his "kingship." About eight years later, Childeric returned from exile and apparently governed with Aegidius, and then with Syagrius, as some sort of co-ruler. This development is unusual and variously interpreted, with most scholars rejecting the notion that Aegidius and Syagrius held in any literal sense kingship over the Franks. A command over combined forces is sometimes proposed as an explanation of Gregory's account (Harries 1994: 141).

Gregory gives the impression of being very careful in his effort to discover when the Franks *first* called their leaders "kings" (or, more accurately, when his Latin sources first do so): he complains that some historians had not given the topic any attention (Gregory of Tours, *Hist.* 2. 9; see MacGeorge 2002: 133–6). In retailing the early history of the Franks, Gregory states that their first leaders were not called kings (*reges*) at all, but *duces* (generals, leaders) or the like. Merovechus, the eponymous founder of the Merovingian dynasty (taken by Gregory to have been the father of Childeric and perhaps the son of Chlogio, to whom he was certainly related), may be seen as the first king. Some traditions credit Chlogio with that honor; and it was Chlogio who led the Franks into Roman territory from their original Toxandrian and lower Rhenish locations and established a presence at Tournai. In that case, Merovechus would have been the first to receive regal authority *within* Roman lands. (The emperor Julian had permitted the Salians to inhabit Toxandria in AD 358; but, at least from a Roman point of view, they may not have seemed a fully enough structured society to have kings.)

Now in some sense, the Salian Franks clearly banished Childeric, Merovechus' son, if only for a time; but they did not thereby reject kingship itself, and least of all the Merovingian line. As the career of Childeric's successor Clovis would subsequently reveal, intra- and inter-dynastic and intra- and inter-familial murder and assassination were not foreign concepts, and the Salians might easily have found another king among themselves, had they been so inclined. In other words, whatever title they gave to Aegidius during Childeric's exile, they were not suddenly revealing a disposition to become Roman like other inhabitants of Belgica II, or to become subjects of Roman rulers. While Gregory states that the Franks had taken Childeric's kingdom from him and were even ready to kill him for his misbehavior, their submission to Aegidius suggests that a possible compromise emerged, or simply that a story to explain Childeric's absence was spread abroad, either immediately or at the time of his return (MacGeorge 2002: 97).

As far as I know, one possible factor in Childeric's removal has not been considered – namely, his age. The date of his birth and his age at the time of his death in AD 481/2 are unknown (see Halsall 2001); but it is quite likely that he was young, though chosen king, in AD 456. Clovis, who replaced him in AD 481/2, was himself only about 15 years old. Clovis' mother Basina had been married to the Thuringian (Tungrian) ruler Bysinus, and it was at Bysinus' court that Childeric spent his period of exile. She then followed Childeric upon his return to Tournai and married him there. She is Childeric's only known wife, and he is not likely to have been of advanced years at the time. Similarly, the fact that Childeric was exiled for annoying the daughters of the Franks may hint at youth; his marriage some years later might have served to quiet any fears that his misbehavior might resume. The king's apparent youth is also the impression left by his seal-ring (Gregory of Tours, *Hist.* 2. 12). We do not know whether the artist created a portrait of an old king as a young man, or whether the seal had been in use for one year or twenty, but the portrait is that of a fairly young man. In sum, therefore, the Salian Franks may have feared for the security of a young representative of a newly established Merovingian line, and may have sent him off for safe keeping elsewhere in a desire to maintain their dynasty's independence from other Franks (to whom I shall turn in a moment). They may have looked to Aegidius and then to Syagrius for protection of their dynasty and their independence, during a period of fragility and insecurity engendered by their king's youth.

Some support for this may be garnered from campaigns of the Ripuarian Franks into Roman territory in AD 457, probably less than a year after Childeric's exile. In the wars, Aegidius lost both Cologne and Trier to the Ripuarians. The Salians may have had advance intelligence of what the Ripuarians were planning, and perhaps took the necessary steps to preserve both their king and themselves by applying to the (possibly self-appointed) Roman authority in the region. Whether Aegidius and Syagrius considered *themselves* kings is hard to determine – administrative succession of sons to their fathers' authority at the edges of empire is no longer unusual in this period – but, if we may trust Gregory's attempted precision in his use of the word *rex*, they may have thought of themselves in such terms. But, if kings, kings of whom? Concerning Aegidius, we have only Gregory's remark that the Franks chose him as their king (see above), and a few words in the Neustrian chronicle *Liber historiae Francorum* indicate that Syagrius succeeded to his father's "kingdom" (*in regnum eius resedit*, *Liber hist. Franc.* 8; see MacGeorge 2002: 133–6). (Actually, in the *Liber*, it is Aegidius who is described as *Romanorum rex*.) Most scholars, as I say, find true kingship difficult to accept; but, according to my suggestion immediately above, Aegidius' role may be closer to what we might term "regent" or, since it is less official, a guarantor of the Merovingian dynasty and of Salian security during Childeric's minority. With regard to the non-Frankish population, Aegidius was perhaps simply a *magister* who extended his term of office against the wishes of an empire incapable of dispossessing him. He could, of course, have been *magister* and guarantor at once, in respect to different populations.

By all accounts, Aegidius and the Salian Franks lived in relative harmony (though, for evidence of at least occasional disharmony, see MacGeorge 2002: 95–6). The position of Syagrius is more complicated. He was never given authority by what was left of imperial administration in Gaul, but simply succeeded his father (so Gregory: *reliquit filium Syagrium nomine*, *Hist.* 2. 18). No evidence survives to suggest that he was a *magister* or held any similar position. Fredegar (*Chron.* 3. 15) calls him *Romanorum patricius* (as opposed to *rex*), "patrician of [the] Romans," a title often enjoyed by late antique luminaries, barbarian and Roman. Fredegar's testimony is late and may be imprecise; but the term presumably implies rulership of some sort. The *Liber historiae Francorum*, as noted, states that Syagrius did succeed to a kingdom (the *regnum* of Aegidius), but stops short of calling him a king; Gregory, as noted above, calls him "king of [the] Romans," which presumably means the non-Franks in northern Gaul. We should not exclude the possibility that Gregory considers the Franks Romans – if not as citizens, perhaps as inhabitants of what was the Roman Empire. This would, however, imply that Syagrius actually became king of the Franks, a rather difficult view to hold. Presumably, Gregory did not consider him a usurper, for *rex* (assuming that Gregory is reliable) has an air of legitimacy; ancient writers tend to employ the terminology of tyranny for usurpers, and *rex* is rarely, if ever, used for a Roman who attempted to make himself emperor. To complicate the matter further, Syagrius might easily be seen, like his father, as a "regent" or guarantor – in his case, during Clovis' minority. But that does not solve the issue: Gregory mentions "Romans" specifically, and in any case this does not clarify Syagrius' title between the death of his father in AD 465 and that of Childeric in AD 481/2.

When Childeric returned, he no doubt resumed active kingship of the Salians and governed them alongside first Aegidius, then Syagrius. Is it not reasonable to think that, since these Romans, as I'll call them, and these Franks, as I'll call the others, governed more or less cooperatively in the same territory, both might have the same designation? Less clear is whether we have here true joint kingship or two kingdoms superimposed one on the other, with the same boundaries but governing different segments of the population. Or, since Syagrius governed from Soissons and Childeric from Tournai, do we have two kingdoms not superimposed one on the other? For reasons that will become clear eventually, collegiate rule, like the situation that obtained in Diocletian's tetrarchy, may best represent the situation, including occasional disputes. In any case, because the situation differs enough, it is probably not helpful to compare it with that of the Ostrogoths in Italy or the Visigoths in Aquitania and Spain. There, one king governed two population groups in different capacities (at any rate, Theoderic did), whereas in northern Gaul we have two rulers and two peoples occupying the same territory, with close ties between rulers and some rather unusual terminology for the Roman representatives. Some fourth-century experiences in Britain and North Africa offer similarities and are treated below. Aegidius and Syagrius or Childeric and Clovis may have had those other instances in mind.

As bishops will do in this period, Remigius of Reims adds complications. Not long after he succeeded Childeric, Clovis received a letter from him, congratulating him upon that event. Remigius writes:

> A great rumor has reached us that you have undertaken the command of Belgica Secunda. It is no surprise that you have begun just as your forefathers had always done ... the bestowal of your favor must be pure and honest, you must honor your bishops and must always incline yourself to their advice. As soon as you are in agreement with them your territory [or perhaps "rule': *provincia*] will prosper. (*Ep.* 2, Geary 1988: 82)

Thoughts upon this letter have divided historians. Many think that Remigius wrote at Clovis' accession in AD 481/2 (Wallace-Hadrill 1961: 166; James 1988: 65), but some suppose that a date after Clovis defeated Syagrius in AD 486 makes more sense. Dirk Henning, in a recent treatment (Henning 1999: 296), points out that both Childeric and Clovis ruled, before AD 486, from Tournai. Cambrai and perhaps Arras, both within Belgica II, were under the control of Frankish regional kings, but (according to Henning) the administration of Belgica II as a whole would have been, until AD 486, in the hands of Syagrius only. Moreover, Remigius' further remarks that Clovis should release captives and free them from the yoke of slavery presuppose (in Henning's view) a recent military victory.

These conclusions are not inevitable. Liberation of captives might happen at any time, and generosity of this nature at accession is hardly an unprecedented ploy to win favor. Second, we may wonder whether anyone had full and sole administrative control of all Belgica II at this time. If Aegidius and Syagrius were co-rulers with Childeric in a dyarchy, the succession of Clovis would give him full and equal authority at his accession and thus control of all Belgica – a control shared, to be sure, but a control full enough to be so expressed in panegyrical language. Of particular note is that neither the death of Aegidius nor that of Childeric seems to have excited thoughts of reestablishing sole rule on the part of the surviving ruler. There is no evidence that Childeric attempted to forestall the accession of Syagrius upon Aegidius' death, nor that Syagrius tried to prevent Clovis, then only 15 years old, from becoming king. In consequence, some kind of collegiate structure or dyarchy offers the best way of understanding the evidence for control by Clovis of all Belgica II at this period. I am not entirely convinced by John Drinkwater's suggestion (personal communication; and see MacGeorge 2002: 163) that Childeric and Clovis were subordinates of Aegidius and Syagrius. While that might be sufficient to explain Remigius' remark, at least as hyperbole, the issue of Syagrius as *Romanorum rex* is not thereby solved. Finally, the presence of regional rulers at Cambrai and perhaps Arras is specifically known from the reign of Clovis, who may well have left kinsman to protect his rear while he expanded southward, axing them later (in two cases, literally). Nothing is known of them before Clovis became king, though that does not mean they did not exist. Remigius' remark may have been more accurate in AD 481/2 than it would have been in AD 486, if the subordinate rulers were given their positions between AD 481/2 and AD 486. In any case, the fact that control over subordinate kings was described in hyperbolic language does not detract from the fact that it was the whole of Belgica II that was being controlled, and Henning's suggestions do not resolve the issues.

Briefly, the positive arguments for a date in AD 481/2 are as follows. Remigius refers to a rumor that Clovis had succeeded to the administration of Belgica II, using words that imply a smooth transition, like that from father to son. Surely he would have expressed himself differently had a recent military victory over Syagrius put Clovis in that position. The very reference to rumor suggests, though hardly compels, a view that this occurred some distance from Reims; Tournai, where Clovis succeeded his father, was farther from Reims than was Soissons. As for reference to honoring bishops and consequent good fortune, this may simply be pastoral advice, though of dubious utility, since the recipient was a pagan teenager (in Gregory's preconversion portrayal, though he may have been an Arian Christian: see Shanzer 1998). Alternatively, Remigius' remarks may be seen as an invitation, with the support of bishops, to eliminate Syagrius.

Even if the letter certainly dates to AD 481/2, Clovis certainly paid some attention to other bishops after his defeat of Syagrius. That victory was accompanied by the plundering of churches, one of which lost a vessel of great size to the marauders. An envoy of its bishop pleaded with Clovis for its return and was advised to travel to Soissons, where the spoils would be divided; if the vessel fell to the king's lot, he would return it. At the appointed hour, all the soldiers agreed to concede it to Clovis, except one who struck it with his ax, while shouting that the king was not entitled to anything that had not fallen to his lot. Clovis picked up the damaged vessel and handed it to the bishop's envoy without comment. The identity of the bishop is unknown, but Clovis was evidently willing to mollify a bishop on this occasion at least; we do not know his purpose, but gratitude for support or a desire not to antagonize are possibilities.

As the new Roman aristocracy of western Europe, filling roles traditionally played by the upper classes (Mathisen 1989, 1993; Brown 1992), the episcopate was not fully enamored of men like Aegidius or Syagrius, Roman functionaries who usurped or extended the powers granted to them at some cost to the authority of the bishops in their territories. For these late antique potentates were essentially local, and thus threatened the hegemony of bishops more than had earlier governors (even those of local origin), who had drawn their support from emperors and the imperial system. Indeed, these new potentates threatened episcopal autonomy more than even emperors did, particularly in Late Antiquity, when Gaul was more a place to rule than to visit. With the possible exception of the short-lived Avitus, Gratian in the AD 380s was the last emperor to visit northern Gaul as emperor – half a dozen or so usurpers notwithstanding, usurpers who in any case were usually of Gallic origin. All that being so, local aristocracies now in the persons of bishops might be favorably disposed to anyone, barbarian or not, who promised to rid their world of men like Aegidius and Syagrius. Even bishops recruited from places like Lérins soon regarded themselves as the appropriate local authority. Indeed, it has been suggested (Wallace-Hadrill 1961: 166) that Remigius was reminding the new king that the bishops did, in fact, control Belgica II. Whether this is true or not, I think it not unlikely that Remigius was inviting Clovis to bring about the downfall of Syagrius. For, in the absence of imperial authority, bishops preferred that there be no other Roman-based, Roman-originated authority but themselves: if not the state, then the Church. Barbarians were not Roman and, besides, the Visigothic experiment in Aquitania and Spain had not proved entirely disastrous. Alternatively, bishops may simply have employed the Franks as a force in their disputes with each other: perhaps Syagrius just got in the way. Incidentally, on this view, Gregory's perspective that the pagan Franks were acceptable because the Visigoths were heretics is far too simplistic as an explanation of fifth-century events: episcopal contests for authority transcended religious issues, except when the latter could be mobilized to generate political (and military) support. Though I cannot examine this here, Franks had by the AD 480s established themselves in places much deeper into Gaul than Tournai, Soissons, or Reims (see James 1988). Certainly not yet the majority of the population, Franks had become a significant element, with influence greater than their numbers might have led one to expect. For kings like Childeric and Clovis, support by both compatriots and bishops insured that Syagrius' reign had little chance of lasting long.

A year later, Clovis decided to review his troops. When he came to the man who had challenged him previously, he proclaimed that none had ever appeared with his weapons in such a poor state, seized the man's ax, and threw it to the ground. As the man bent down to pick it up, the king swung his own ax high and brought it down deep into the soldier's skull, shouting as he did so, "This is how you treated the vessel at Soissons." We may doubt whether the poor man heard the final syllables of Clovis' cry (and we need not wonder about the state of Frankish weapons from this point forward). Nor does Gregory overstate or exaggerate: "The man lying dead, he dismissed the rest, having put great fear of him into their hearts by his act." Why did Clovis hold his anger for a year? The stability of his throne was not in question, for he had been king five years and was already 20 years old. In AD 486, Clovis perhaps found it politic not to advertise close relations with the orthodox clergy; his men, if they were Arian Christians or pagans, might see this as a problem, and bishops might prefer not to have it guessed too readily, if they had indeed encouraged Clovis to dispose of Syagrius. Thus Clovis demurred, merely returning the vessel, and punished the challenge a year later.

The outcome of the engagement with Syagrius Gregory reports briefly: "when Clovis received [Syagrius] prisoner, he ordered him to be imprisoned; had him put to the sword in secret, while he took possession of his kingdom [*regnum*]" (Gregory of Tours, *Hist.* 2. 27; *regnum* also occurs in the *Liber. hist. Franc.* 9). The imprisonment and death we might take for granted, except that Syagrius was killed in secret. Perhaps this was the obvious way to deal with him. On the other hand, if Clovis and Syagrius did share a dyarchy, public execution or even public knowledge of Syagrius' death might induce thoughts of succession. More interesting is Gregory's last phrase: "he took possession of his kingdom." For herein lies an important interpretive theme. When a king is defeated by another, the latter takes the former's kingdom, even in a dyarchy (compare Constantine and Licinius). At the least, the winner had a right to dictate consequences. So too with an empire: a victor over an empire may choose its future direction. But an empire is harder to defeat than a kingdom. Were Syagrius an administrator on behalf of an empire, it could survive his defeat – indeed, might attempt to avenge him. As king of a kingdom, it was gone, if the victor wanted it that way. And so, because he was king over a part of Gaul that had once been Roman, Syagrius lost part of the empire to the Franks. We might argue for a while whether establishment of kingship, perhaps already with Aegidius, or its demise in AD 486 were the decisive factors. But that does not really matter: the establishment of a kingdom or personal fiefdom within Roman territory had serious consequences.

Let me move on now to Britain and Africa. Something similar (similar to events and policies in Gaul) appears to have happened in both places. Kings of Romans – that is, of inhabitants who were considered Romans – appear in Britain. I begin with Old King Cole. Genealogies make him an ancestor, rightly or wrongly, of many sixth-century kings in northern Britain. As Coelius or Coelestius, he was "apparently the source of constituted authority in northern Britain, the territory of the *dux Britanniarum*, at about the time when Roman rule ended, and may have been the last regularly appointed *dux*, who converted his command into an independent and hereditary kingdom" (*PLRE* ii: 304). Then we have Ambrosius Aurelianus, a leader of resistance to the Saxons, described by the sixth-century British writer Gildas as a *dux* rather than as a king, though his father is said to have worn the purple. What that means or who he was, scholars have not been able to decipher. We may add Vortigern, who bore as name or title the designation "superior ruler." All three figures are interesting, and the surviving records of their titles and careers are fraught with interpretive quagmires. Except for Old King Cole, however, they belong clearly to the sub-Roman period, after the emperor Honorius had told the Britons to fend for themselves in AD 410, and after Constantine III, at about the same time, had pulled troops from the island, together with what little was left of its administration, in order to fight his battles on the continent. But do we have, as in northern Gaul at the time of Aegidius and Syagrius, kings in a Britain that was still Roman, albeit at the fringes of the empire?

Here we move into the realm of the obscure. The so-called northern lists refer to four fiefdoms north of Hadrian's Wall. For some time, later kings and kingdoms draw from these fiefdoms their own authority and legitimacy. Almost certainly, the fiefdoms were established by the *comes* Theodosius in the late AD 360s or early AD 370s, when he reorganized Britain in the wake of the so-called "barbarian conspiracy" of AD 367 (Tomlin 1974; Blockley 1980; Salway 1981: 374–5). Among other things, he created a fifth province in Britain, Valentia. About its location there is disagreement; a preponderance of views favors the northwest in the area of Lancashire, but parts of Wales and bits of Scotland have been proposed. Ammianus Marcellinus (28. 3. 7) states that it was a lost province later restored to the empire, but not in immediate response to the "conspiracy."

The first volume of *PLRE* does not include the original owners of these fiefdoms, presumably because, in the eyes of the editors, they were not Roman administrators. Elsewhere, however, John Morris has discussed the relevant source material (Morris 1973a, 1973b). First, according to the lists, a Quintilianus Clemens, of Mediterranean origin, was given authority on the Clyde and established a dynasty that endured till the Norman Conquest. Second, a fellow named Paternus, son of a Tacitus, from Kent, was placed over the Votadini of the northeast coast; this line was later transferred to Wales. Third, Antonius Donatus is said to have been granted authority by Magnus Maximus, but this need not mean that he was without a fiefdom until the AD 380 s (when Maximus was variously emperor and usurper), for Maximus was an associate of the *comes* Theodosius and may have been acting on the latter's instructions; Donatus was handed territory in the southwest of Scotland. Fourth – less clear, due to a corrupt textual tradition – is the allocation of the northern Votadini (also called the Damnonii) to Catellius Decianus (originally from an island whose identity cannot be recovered); his authority reached beyond the Tweed and perhaps considerably further to the north. Though Morris does not say so, it seems that each of these four men was given authority over a people of Britain living north of the Wall. They were, as names and origins make clear, Romans, not native kings granted recognition. Almost certainly, father passed power to son, and whatever Theodosius' original intention or that of his emperor Valentinian I, these fiefdoms became kingdoms quickly. The rapid decline in imperial authority in northwestern Europe was largely responsible. Had imperial authority been more effective, the administrators might have been changed from time to time. We simply do not know, and ought not to presume.

Other evidence for kings in Britain in the last part of the fourth century does survive. A former king of the Alamannic Bucinobantes named Fraomarius was in AD 372 posted to Britain as tribune over an existing Alamannic unit (Amm. Marc. 29. 4. 7), perhaps in Wales. He is unlikely to have *founded* a kingdom in Britain itself, but he was at least a *former* king and now based in Britain. Ninian, missionary of Cumbria and Scotland, is, in Aelred's *Life*, a son of a Christian Cumbrian ruler probably headquartered at Carlisle. Little more is known and Aelred's treatment is somewhat fanciful, but Ninian's dates (he spent time on the continent, including a visit with Martin of Tours before the latter's death in AD 397) could suggest that his father's rule began in the AD 360s or AD 370s – precisely the time of Fraomarius, of the new province of Valentia, and of the fiefdoms of upper Northumbria and the Borders. Surely we have here a policy of Valentinian I carried out, perhaps even devised, by Theodosius. If Fraomarius was allocated to northern Wales, if Valentia was Lancashire, if Cumbria was entrusted to a king at Carlisle, then the western shores of northern Britain were being made secure, primarily against invasion from Ireland, but also against raids from the north. Even if the details are not correct, the security of the north was clearly a significant preoccupation in the late AD 360s and thereafter, with some regions handed to (semi-)independent individuals.

We do not know the origin of the Carlisle dynasty. Theodosius may have drawn his candidate from an hereditary ruling family among the Carvetii. Or perhaps the new ruler was formerly a Roman official, like the others. Later dynasties never regarded the Carlisle family as the source that justified their own authority – unless a thought that has crossed my mind is true: could that Cumbrian ruler be Old King Cole? Though the office of *dux Britanniarum* apparently existed to the end of the Roman period in Britain, Coelius may as easily have been a Cumbrian king as the last *dux*; perhaps he was both, at the same time or in sequence (as in the case of Masties, which I discuss below). A suitable time for a transformation of his position is the denuding of northern Britain's defenses by Magnus Maximus in prosecuting his grand design of becoming emperor in AD 383. This is possible chronologically. In any case, if the northwest was allocated as noted above, and if the north fell under the fiefdoms, what was a *dux* meant to do, anyway? Certainly, the east coast in broad terms did not fall under his authority, for that was charged to the Count of the Saxon Shore and the commander of the fleet in the North Sea. At best, Northumberland, or a part of it, south of the Wall, might come under his hegemony. The *Notitia dignitatum*, a late antique compilation describing provinces and their military officials and units, lists under the control of the *dux* units at Carlisle and Corbridge, at opposite ends of the Wall; but the *Notitia* is notoriously problematic (Mann 1976). Not one *dux* in Britain is known by name after AD 367. It is not impossible that the empire hoped at some point to restore Britain to its former state, and that therefore the *Notitia* reflects an ideal state of affairs or a previous situation. At any rate, whatever the truth about Fraomarius, or about Old King Cole, a monarchy almost certainly existed in Cumbria before the final removal of Roman forces from Britain.

The fiefdoms are located between the Hadrianic and Antonine walls, territory that the Romans regarded as theirs, despite an inability to hold it particularly well. A shadowy group called the *areani* (or *arcani*) caused much of the trouble in AD 367. A common view is that these agents betrayed Roman outposts to the enemy and that, to insure cooperation in the future, direct rule was instituted. Places north of Hadrian's Wall like Netherby, High Rochester, and Risingham were maintained until AD 367, but not later. Yet, if friendly rulers were appointed, why were the Wall defenses strengthened at precisely this period? In the aftermath of AD 367, Valentinian I and his advisers chose to hold what they could and to abandon the rest in a manner that gave scope for later recapture. The recovery of four provinces and the later addition of Valentia is a good example. Territory beyond the Wall was regarded as lost and defense was concentrated at the Wall and along the coasts. Hadrian's Wall became what it had never been and was never intended to be, the actual frontier. Meanwhile, peoples beyond it were given rulers of Roman origin as part of an overall system of defense and security. They were not client kingdoms, nor intended to be, but linked yet independent territories. There is not much difference, except this: as linked regions, they would be easier to reincorporate, if that ever became possible. That it never happened was not a fault of design, but a consequence of unforeseen developments, mainly the actions of Magnus Maximus, whose ambition induced him to remove forces that might have kept the fiefdoms from becoming kingdoms, and a *dux* from perhaps becoming Old King Cole.

Thus, we have four little territories that Romans had considered their own, first ruled by Roman officials then by kings, either the Roman officials or their descendants: not so different from the Gallic situation. There, the Roman Aegidius could not be ousted by the empire and transformed his rule from official to a kingship shared with the Franks. Once that happened, the area was lost, or was about to be. On the nature of these British territories, which I have so far neutrally persisted in calling fiefdoms, a little more can be said.

The point of departure is Africa, in the form of two inscriptions. The first (*L'Année Épigraphique* 1945: 97) is a funerary inscription for a Masties, who claims to have been a *dux* for sixty-seven years and *imperator* for forty. Some evidence suggests that he would not call himself emperor until the deposition of the last emperor Romulus Augustulus in AD 476 (*PLRE* ii: 949–50) – not a solid argument, given all the usurpers in Roman history, but perhaps not incorrect, and we might connect the assumption of the title with a revolt against the Vandals in the Aures mountains (*c.* AD 477). The inscription, which dates no earlier than AD 516 or AD 517, was found at Arris in these mountains. Masties claims to have been a good ruler, breaking trust with neither Romans nor Mauri (*neque fide(m) fregi neque de Romanos neque de Mauros*), and he believes that God has rewarded him for his efforts. Be that as it may, we seem to have here the same situation suggested above for Old King Cole: a *dux* became an independent ruler when the empire that had made him *dux* had become irrelevant. Though Masties calls himself *imperator* rather than *rex*, he clearly governed two populations, one of Romans, the other of Mauri: not so different from Aegidius as *rex Francorum* or Syagrius as *rex Romanorum* (which is what the sources say, though I have suggested that they were both *reges Romanorum et Francorum*, sharing their rule with others).

The second inscription (*CIL* 8. 9835) dates to AD 508, or rather to the year 469 of the province's era. In it, a ruler named Masuna has clearly ordered a camp to be built at Altava by sub-rulers. More interesting for present purposes, Masuna is identified as king of Moors and Romans (*reg(is) Masunae gent(ium) Maur(orum) et Romanor (um)*). The sub-rulers are called prefects and procurators, partly because the inscription is in Latin, but also because that is what they were still called, long after any Roman control of any part of Mauretania Caesariensis had ceased. Not even the

Notitia dignitatum speaks about Roman control of Mauretania Caesariensis or Mauretania Sitifensis after AD 375, and it is usually thought that Rome and these provinces parted company about that time.

In his still valuable treatment of Africa in the Vandal period, Christian Courtois points to the existence of eight native successor kingdoms in what had been Roman Africa (Courtois 1955). Because they occupied some of the same territory as the Romans had done, the subjects of these kings were of both Roman and native origin, in the sense that some ancestors of these subjects had possessed Roman citizenship and others had not. By analyzing all the miserable scraps of evidence, Courtois was able to locate these eight kingdoms. Alan Rushforth has since commented upon them, concentrating on two and drawing attention to a similar phenonemon at China's inner Asia frontier, in particular a cyclical process whereby the nomad became master of the former ruling inhabitants (Rushforth 2000). Rushforth also argues that these kingdoms, whose power bases he places outside the former boundaries of the empire, developed in the fifth and sixth centuries. The more usual view (e.g., Raven 1993: 205–6) is that the kingdoms were encroachments carved out of Vandal territory.

Given that Courtois is correct to see kingdoms of mixed native and Roman origin and that Rushforth is correct to see the existence of some of them in the fifth century, what was their actual origin? Courtois was inclined to consider them a late phenomenon, which rose like a multiplex phoenix from the ashes of empire. Rushforth treats mainly the empowerment of nomadic leaders, as the Roman Empire lost its ability to maintain effective control. I am not the first to suggest a coincidence that I will point to here, for John Morris noted it, though I will take it a step or two further. From AD 371 to AD 375, Africa was in a state of revolt, due largely to the ambitions of a local leader named Firmus. About AD 372, the most competent general of his day was posted to take charge. That general was the same Theodosius who had turned Britain around after the barbarian conspiracy.

In the course of a couple of years, Theodosius returned a semblance of stability to Africa. We know a little about how he did this, beyond the inevitable series of military campaigns. Ammianus Marcellinus (29. 5. 35) records that Theodosius put tried and true and loyal prefects in the frontier regions to govern the native peoples. Augustine (*Ep.* 199. 46) later notes that some barbarian peoples had been pacified, attached to the frontier and governed by prefects. There is little else, but it is enough. John Morris adduced these texts to suggest that the Romans placed over the four fiefdoms in Britain were also prefects. He must be correct, and I suggest that in both Britain and Africa the prefects handed power to sons and turned their fiefdoms, or prefectures as we now should call them, into kingdoms, because the empire could not force them to remain prefects. Presumably, Theodosius and Valentinian I did not regard these prefectures as parts of the empire that they had given away; at the minimum, they hoped to recover them later. Yet, once a weakening empire handed territory to prefects whom it could not control, independent kingdoms were almost inevitable. I believe this was a matter of choice in Britain and Africa, but probably undertaken less willingly in Gaul, for I would argue that the origins of Courtois's kingdoms lie in these African prefectures (see Whittaker 1994: 247–8, who makes the suggestion tentatively, and without the connection to Theodosius). The northern lists in Britain thus quite legitimately draw dynastic authority from the Roman Empire, for the empire had established the prefectures under legitimate prefects who, perhaps abusing their mandates, became kings and ancestors of dynasties.

It is not entirely clear whether Theodosius drew the frontiers back to a more defensible point in Africa, as he did in Britain by deciding that Hadrian's Wall was the frontier and not just the place where the empire would make a stand. A physical defense, the *fossatum Africae*, stood in parts of Africa. Probably dating to the reign of Hadrian and perhaps designed more to control the flow of nomadic peoples than to guard the frontier specifically, its course, where it existed, did not match the limits of Roman authority. Given that Valentinian I and his brother Valens were more involved than other emperors in building physical defenses, even on the Rhine/Danube frontier, it would not be surprising, in the context of the new role of Hadrian's Wall and these riverine defenses, to assign a new role for the physical defenses in Africa as well. Despite Rushforth's remarks, Courtois's kingdoms actually lay almost entirely inside what had been Roman jurisdiction, and line up along the frontier. The *fossatum* seems to have stood in the gaps between these kingdoms. Since it predates Theodosius, this suggests that prefectures were deliberately placed in gaps. In better times, Roman forces had guarded gaps and maintained the frontier. All this is far more interesting, and far more complicated, than I can pursue here, but it suggests that Theodosius pulled back further in Africa than in Britain, allocating even the Roman side of physical defenses to natives under Roman prefects. If so, and if my dating is correct, these kingdoms were not encroachments on Vandal lands. Instead, for the simple reason that the areas were no longer Roman when the invasion occurred in AD 429, the Vandals never took them over.

Three very different parts of the empire, therefore, designated by the empire as prefectures (or the sphere of a *magister*), all became kingdoms under native control in a similar manner. Though details differ, the prefects (or kings, if they had already become the latter) were either replaced by native rulers, possibly having shared power for a while first (as in Gaul), or simply became part of the people they or their ancestors had been appointed to govern as prefects. The process was not completely inevitable. In Dalmatia, a man named Marcellinus prevented emperors and barbarian rulers from gaining control of the region from about AD 454 to AD 468 (see *PLRE* ii: 708–9). He could have become another Aegidius, but did not; instead, he ended his life in Sicily, having fought on behalf of the empire to drive the Vandals from Sardinia. For most others, however, the temptations were too great.

We will never know whether Aegidius and Syagrius were inspired to transform a northern Gallic prefecture into a kingdom by the events nearly a century earlier in Britain and in Africa, but they may have been encouraged by the empire's failure to prevent it. Moreover, the existence of *reges Romanorum* in Britain and Africa suggests that Gregory could be correct in calling Syagrius a *rex Romanorum*. Other aspects of the British and African experience may also apply: just as the "barbarian conspiracy" and the revolt of Firmus occasioned specific responses in these areas, the assassination of Aëtius in AD 454 rendered northern Gaul defenseless, laying it even more open to the establishment of a Frankish kingdom in Belgica II, a process that had already begun. To counter this, an emperor appointed Aegidius as *magister* in a region he had perhaps already taken over as his fiefdom, but the latter cooperated more with Franks than with the empire and transformed his rule into something akin to the independent prefectures established in Britain and Africa nearly a century earlier. The Gallic experience may also shed some light on the British and African. At the very least, we have an inkling of how an independent ruler might first share power with a non-Roman population, then lose control to that population and its rulers.

I have focused in this chapter on the changing administrative structures in Africa, Britain, and northern Gaul, employing the combined evidence to suggest a common experience, at any rate in its broad outlines. Given limited space, I have only hinted at other aspects – the role of revolts, the issue of loyalty, the impact of the ecclesiastical establishment, the denuding of defenses at frontiers, and the establishment of peoples from outside the frontiers within the former borders of empire. These issues have been treated before (see especially Van Dam 1985; Mathisen 1989, 1993; Whittaker 1994; Rees 2002), but I hope to have shown at least that a comparative approach yields some valuable insights that a focus on a specific region or problem simply cannot generate. For, it seems, the actual administrative mechanism or process involved in transformation from empire to kingdoms is remarkably similar in some widely disparate areas.

BIBLIOGRAPHICAL NOTE

This essay draws its origins from a paper written in 2002 while I was on research leave at the University of Leicester and was presented, in various permutations, at Leicester, Nottingham, Reading, and Calgary in 2002 and 2003. For these oral presentations, I eschewed detailed discussion of scholarly disputes, and I have followed that procedure here: annotation is minimal and usually representative of a view rather than complete, but readers should understand that almost every detail is subject to various interpretations. I have made some attempt to signal differences of views where they may affect my wider theme of the similarities in the transformation of Africa, Britain, and northern Gaul.

The suggestion that Aegidius and Syagrius shared kingship with the Franks will no doubt be controversial. Readers should consult the volumes cited in the text and listed in the Bibliography for detailed treatments of the relevant issues and for alternative points of view; these volumes will contain further bibliography. Good overviews of the transformation of Gaul in Late Antiquity and the early medieval period may be found in Geary 1988 and Wood 1994, and the essays in Theuws and Nelson 2000 provide an overview on the ideology of power, which I have not addressed. Two recent books on Gregory of Tours, Heinzelmann 2001 and the collection of essays in Mitchell and Wood 2002, treat many aspects of a main source for Gaul in the Frankish period.

For Britain, the scholarship in English is vast. In addition to a couple of standard works (Salway 1981; Frere 1987), several historians concentrate on the late Roman period, offering different perspectives (Esmonde-Cleary 1989; Jones 1996; Dark 2002). Unfortunately, Africa has not received as much attention. Raven 1993 is the third edition of a book that has been a standard treatment since 1969, while Shaw 1995a and 1995b collect articles on Africa originally published in a variety of journals. For the late period, Courtois 1955 is still essential, while Clover 1993 is another collection of articles originally published elsewhere.

For a broader picture of the Roman Empire as a whole in this period, Moorhead 2001 and the very recent book by Heather 2006 offer very readable treatments; even more recent and also very readable is Mitchell 2007. On the issue of frontiers generally, Whittaker 1994 treats earlier times to Late Antiquity primarily from a social and economic perspective and offers much insight that may be read with profit as a complement to the emphasis on power structures in this essay.

CHAPTER TWENTY-NINE

Rome and the Sasanid Empire: Confrontation and Coexistence

Jan Willem Drijvers

The Sasanid Empire was for more than four centuries a formidable neighbor to Rome. The relations between the two superpowers of their time were character- ized by both antagonistic interaction and periods of friendly contact. Persian history itself has long been the domain of Orientalists; but, in recent times, the advantages of a multidisciplinary approach have encouraged historians of the Greco-Roman world to look beyond the boundaries of the Mediterranean region. The relationship between Greco-Roman civilization and neighboring cultures is receiving increasing attention. There has been a particular focus, sharpened by the growing interest in Late Antiquity, on relations between the Late Roman and Byzantine Empire on the one hand and the Sasanid on the other. A western perspective continues to dominate the study of those relations, and their exam- ination from the "other side" is still in its infancy (Wiesehöfer and Huyse 2006). Nevertheless, the key element to an understanding of the interaction between the superpowers is now more clearly recognized – namely, alternate confrontation and coexistence.

The relationship consisted partly of warfare, and much research has been, and still is, concentrated on the Roman–Persian wars. To emphasize war, however, is to place too much faith in the Greco-Roman sources, which like to deal with *topoi* that go back to Herodotus, and thus create a highly literary and tendentious image of Sasanian society. Those sources have rather less to say about the long periods of cooperation, which comprised active cultural, religious, economic, and diplomatic exchange. Only a careful reading of all available information makes it possible to sketch a more nuanced picture. I shall begin, therefore, with a brief description of the evidence that helps us to reconstruct a full account of the Roman–Persian relation- ship, and provide an overview of Sasanian society.

Sources

A variety of source material makes it possible to reconstruct Roman–Sasanian relations in Late Antiquity (Christensen 1944: 50–83; Frye 1984: 287–91; Schippmann 1990: 3–9; Wiesehöfer 2001: 153–64). But most of these sources are not without their problems: they are written from a specific perspective and unevenly distributed over the period. First of all, there are the Greco-Roman historiographic sources, foremost among them the works of Cassius Dio, Herodian, Ammianus Marcellinus, Procopius, and Agathias. These authors concentrate in particular on Roman–Persian warfare, and describe it almost exclusively from the Roman point of view. They tell us little, for instance, about Sasanian institutions and state structure. Historiographic sources of this kind are not available on the Sasanian side. The written materials we have are the impressive royal inscriptions such as the *Res gestae divi Saporis* in Naqsh-i Rustam (Huyse 1999). These inscriptions boast of accomplishments and victories of the Persian rulers Ardashir (AD 224–40), Shapur I (AD 240–72), and Narses (AD 293–302) and are very much of a propagandistic nature, but they also provide information on matters like the social and administrative structure of the Sasanian state. Unfortunately, these inscriptions are available only for the third century AD and have no analogues in later centuries. Other written sources for the history of the Sasanid Empire and its relations with Rome are the Syriac chronicles, the Armenian historians (e.g., Moses of Chorene) – Armenia had always had close connections with Persia as well as with Rome – and Arabic historians, foremost among them al-Tabari. Apart from religious texts, such as the *Avesta* – of which the earliest manuscript dates only from the thirteenth century – many texts written in Middle Persian on a variety of subjects, such as history, geography, didactics, astronomy, law, and etiquette, as well as novels and romances have been lost; only a fraction has been preserved in Arabic and New Persian translations. Most interesting for Roman–Persian relations is the Christian tradition. Martyr acts, chronicles, church histories, synodal decrees, and other sources inform us about the vicissitudes of the Christian communities in the Sasanid Empire: the persecutions, but also the relatively good relations with the authorities – in particular in the second half of the Sasanian period – as well as the many contacts with fellow believers in the Roman Empire. Manichaean texts are similar in kind. There is also other important material evidence: Sasanian rock reliefs; the architectural remains of cities, royal palaces, bridges, and Zoroastrian fire-temples, as well as seals, coins, and silver plates with royal (hunting) scenes (Ghirshman 1962). The *Book of Lords*, a kind of Iranian national history, holds a special place among the Sasanian sources (Yarshater 1983b). Compiled in the first half of the seventh century AD, it is mostly based on oral, legendary traditions and presents the Sasanian version of Iranian history.

Sasanian Society

Like the Late Roman Empire, the Sasanid Empire was a hierarchically organized and relatively centralized state. The heartland of the empire was Mesopotamia with its rich agricultural lands and many wealthy cities. Administratively, Sasanian society was divided into kingdoms and provinces, which in their turn were divided into smaller units, each of which was administrated by a variety of office-holders on behalf of the king. Politically and socially, Sasanian society was highly stratified (Christensen 1944: 97 ff.; Wiesehöfer 2001: 171 ff.), its social order similar to that of the contemporary Roman Empire. The "king of kings," the empire's ruler (whose status was divine), stood at the top of the hierarchical pyramid; his court was the center of royal power and administration (Wiesehöfer 2007). Just below came the prominent aristocratic clans and the local gentry, who assisted the king in administrating the empire and leading the armies. In the early Sasanian period, the power of these elites rested on lineage, the owning of land, and the holding of office. That, and their closeness to the king, sealed their partnership with him and determined the status of individual aristocrats and their families. This very partnership, however, shows the vulnerability of the monarch's power. He could not rule without the consent and support of the nobles in his realm. He needed their cooperation for governing the empire, collecting taxes, and recruiting armies. Enforcing his authority in his vast empire occupied the king permanently, and one may wonder how strong and effective that vaunted authority was in regions like the Iranian highlands and in the kingdoms and provinces on the outskirts of his empire. The administrative reforms of Khusro I (AD 531–79) addressed that problem by creating a new nobility. Its members were more dependent on the king for their position and influence, which made it easier to harness their support – something that Roman emperors continued to find difficult in relation to their own provincial elites.

The great mass of inhabitants of the Sasanid Empire consisted of farmers – freeholders or tenants. There must have been some sort of middle class – small office-holders, urban merchants – but information about them is scarce. Like every ancient civilization, Sasanian society had its slaves, mostly prisoners of war. Social differences were great, and upward social mobility was difficult to initiate or sustain. The generally good cooperation between the kings and the nobility made the Sasanid Empire an efficiently run state. Although the Sasanian institutions and administrative system are ill-documented, the large-scale foreign wars, the extensive line of defense works in the border region with the Roman Empire, the elaborate irrigation system in Mesopotamia, the development of new urban settlements, and the general infrastructure suggest a developed and efficient administrative apparatus on state and regional level. This apparatus was apparently able to deploy the necessary resources – for example, an advanced system of tax levy both in kind and money – and to plan and control large infrastructural projects (Christensen 1944: 97–140; Howard-Johnston 1995: 211 ff.; Rubin 2000: 654–6).

Warfare was one of the main activities of the Sasanid state. The Persian king was able to recruit a massive military manpower, which was vital for the survival of the empire and for his own success (Christensen 1944: 130–2, 206 ff.; Widengren 1976: 280 ff.; Schippmann 1990: 103–6; Wiesehöfer 2001: 197–9). Much of the state resources were spent on keeping up the military power and defense works. Because the Sasanian monarch did not have a standing army, he was dependent on the soldiers the nobles could furnish him. Only in the sixth century, under Khusro I, was a standing army introduced, consisting of elite cavalry units manned by young nobles. The *cataphracti*, the heavily armed cavalry in which the Sasanian nobility and men of rank served (Mielczarek 1993), was the backbone of the Sasanian army. The infantry was subordinate. The latter consisted of ordinary people (peasant soldiers) who were recruited when necessary. In addition to these forces, the Persian army also contained (mounted) archers. The supreme commander of the army was the king himself (Whitby 1994). It was natural for the king to make all strategic and tactical decisions, but – probably because of his divine status (Widengren 1965: 315) – he was not supposed to take part in the actual fighting. When the king did not command the army himself, his task was taken over by the Suren, the most important Persian nobleman after the king in the Persian hierarchy (Amm. Marc. 24. 2. 4). Various Persian grandees were in charge of contingents of the army. Whereas military success contributed considerably to the king's authority, failure on the battlefield was considered a sign of his weakness and could cause the nobility to withdraw their support. As is known, for instance, from Ammianus Marcellinus, the Sasanian military force impressed the Romans (Drijvers 2006: 54–7). They feared in particular the strength of the units of *cataphracti*; their approach alone, announced by the gleam and glittering of their iron armor, terrified the Roman soldiers (Amm. Marc. 25. 1. 1).

The Sasanid state was religiously diversified, and a variety of religions could be found within the boundaries of the empire: Judaism, Christianity, Manichaeism, Mazdakism, and others (Asmussen 1983; Neusner 1983: 913 ff.; Wiesehöfer 2001: 199–216). But the dualistic Zoroastrianism was the most widespread and had the greatest number of adherents (Duchesne-Guillemin 1983: 866 ff.). The class of Zoroastrian priests held high prominence at the court and in the empire. It has long been supposed that Zoroastrian religion was one of the fundamentals of Sasanian kingship and that Zoroastrianism was the empire's state cult, just as Christianity was the official state religion of the Late Roman Empire (Widengren 1965: 274 ff.; Winter and Dignas 2001: 230 ff.). Although all kings recognized and honored Ahura-Mazda, and Iran was "zoroastrianized" under the Sasanians as never before, as can be concluded from the great number of fire-temples that have been found and from the fact that the hierarchized Zoroastrian priesthood was a privileged social class in Sasanian society (Widengren 1965: 259–65), modern scholarship no longer accepts the idea of a Zoroastrian state church (Schippmann 1990: 92–8; Rubin 2000: 647–51; Wiesehöfer 2001: 199 ff.). That is not to say that, at times, there was not a close relationship between Sasanian kings and Zoroastrianism and its religious leaders, or that Sasanian kings did not support Zoroastrianism at the cost of the other religions and cults in their empire; but this relationship and support were not permanent over the whole period of the empire's existence, and Zoroastrianism never became the state-sponsored religious orthodoxy. The kings seem only to have sought support of the Zoroastrian priesthood and given Zoroastrianism a certain degree of domination over other religions in times of internal and political problems. At the end of the third century AD the Zoroastrian priest Kerdir managed to gain an unusually prominent position for himself and his religion, but apparently only because of the weakness of the kings of his time and their internal problems, resulting from military defeats against the Romans (Winter and Dignas 2001: 232–7). At times rulers and the Zoroastrian priesthood cooperated, in an alliance of convenience, in their persecution of religious minorities. These persecutions, such as those under

Shapur II (AD 309–79) against the Christians, were undertaken for political rather than religious reasons. There were, however, also long periods of religious open-mindedness in which Zoroastrians had to accept the existence of other religious groups and competitors within the Sasanid Empire.

Religion was a source of friction between the Romans and the Sasanians. Manichaeism – a religious movement of Persian origin – was seen as a pro-Persian fifth column in the Roman Empire (Brown 1969; Lieu 1992: 121–5). But Christianity in particular was a source of enmity, and religious-political issues had their influence on the relationship between the two states (Winter and Dignas 2001: 229 ff.). From Constantine the Great onward, the Roman emperors considered themselves the self-appointed patrons of Christians both inside and outside the boundaries of their realm, and therefore also of those living in Persia (Euseb. *Vit. Const.* 4. 9–13; Barnes 1985); and the Sasanians took this as interference in their internal affairs. The Sasanid Empire saw a gradual growth of the number of Christians in the cities in Mesopotamia (Labourt 1904; Asmussen 1983; Chaumont 1988; Jullien and Jullien 2002). The Sasanian authorities considered the Christians as a Roman vanguard that spied and transmitted (military) information to the Romans. Christians were particularly persecuted in times of Roman–Persian wars and had to pay higher taxes to fund the Sasanian war costs. Guarantees of tolerance toward Christians by the Sasanian authorities were usually included in peace agreements. The treaty of AD 562 between Khusro I and Justinian (AD 527–65) laid down that Christian inhabitants of the Sasanid Empire were allowed to build churches and to hold church services (Winter and Dignas 2001: 249). Nevertheless, there was no continuous suppression of Christianity in the Sasanid Empire, and there were kings who more than simply tolerated the Christian religion. Under Yazdgerd I (AD 399–421), Marutha of Maipherqat, bishop and envoy on behalf of the Roman Empire at the Sasanian court at the beginning of the fifth century AD, was not only able to obtain relief of persecution for the Persian Christians, but also allowed to lay down a new ecclesiastical, hierarchical organization for the Persian Christians under a recognized religious leader, the *katholikos* (patriarch) of Ctesiphon (Labourt 1904: 86–99; Asmussen 1983: 939–40; Blockley 1992: 54–5). When the Councils of Ephesus (AD 431) and Chalcedon (AD 451) condemned the teachings of Nestorius, the Sasanid Empire became a haven of refuge for many of its adherents in the eastern part of the Roman Empire, and they were able to establish their own church organization with the support of the Persian king (Winter and Dignas 2001: 55–6).

Confrontation

The Greco-Roman world has always had close contacts of a multifarious nature with the Near Eastern cultures. The Greeks and Macedonians had their interactions and confrontations with the Achaemenid Persians in the fifth and fourth centuries BC, and the Romans with the Parthians from the first century BC onward. A superpower on its eastern frontier was therefore not a new phenomenon for the Roman Empire. New was the fresh vigor of that superpower after the gradual weakening of the Parthian Empire in the second century AD (although the Parthians were still strong enough to defeat a Roman army at Nisibis in AD 217). The struggle for the Arsacid throne between the brothers Vologeses VI and Artabanus IV offered the Sasanians – local leaders in the region of Fars in southeastern Persia – the possibility to revolt, to replace the Arsacids, and to establish their power. Although much is unclear about the course of this revolt, it is generally accepted that it started in AD 205–6 and ended in AD 226 with the coronation of Ardashir as king of kings in the capital Ctesiphon (Christensen 1944: 84–96; Schippmann 1990: 10–17). From the beginning, the Sasanian policy toward Rome was aggressive. To sustain and legitimate their position as rulers over the empire, the Sasanian kings had to show their superiority toward internal rivals by successes and victories on the battlefield. Moreover, it is possible that the Sasanians presented themselves as heirs of the Achaemenids, with the intention of restoring the old Iranian kingdom, of which some of the eastern provinces of the Roman Empire had been a part (Whitby 1994: 234–5; Rubin 2000: 646–7; but see Yarshater 1971). Although Sasanian armies sometimes penetrated deep into Roman territory, and Roman armies reached the Persian heartland, warfare was chiefly focused on the rich and important cities in northern Mesopotamia that lay in the border region between the two empires (Isaac 1998a: 459). The desire to control Armenia, the buffer state between the two nations, made the area a constant scene of conflict.

The relations between the Sasanian and Roman Empires went through three main phases (Whitby 1988: 202–11). The first (AD 226–363) is characterized by an aggressive attitude toward Rome on the part of the Sasanians, by Rome's slow adaptation to its new aggressive neighbor, and by serious hostilities initiated from both sides. The second phase (AD 363–*c*.500) saw only a few conflicts, and is characterized by coexistence and cooperation. The third phase (*c.* AD 500–*c*.630) is marked by increasing mutual suspicion and warfare, but also by short periods of cooperation and understanding.

Shortly after he had come to power, Ardashir undertook several campaigns into Roman territory and captured the important cities of Nisibis, Carrhae, and Hatra; but the greatest successes were won by his son and successor Shapur I (Frye 1984: 296–303; Millar 1993: 159–67; Winter and Dignas 2001: 40–3). In AD 244, he defeated the Roman emperor Gordian, who possibly fell in that battle. In a devastating campaign in AD 253, Shapur ravaged northern Syria, took Hierapolis, managed to penetrate Roman territory as far as Antioch, and captured this third largest city of the Roman Empire (Downey 1961: 252–9). His third victory was even more humiliating for the Romans, since he not only defeated the emperor Valerian (AD 253–60) in a battle near Edessa (AD 260), but also took the emperor captive (Schippmann 1990: 23; Dodgeon and Lieu 1991: 57–65). Valerian was never to return and died in Sasanian captivity, possibly in the city of Gundeshapur ("the weapons of Shapur"), which was built with the manpower of the thousands of Romans Shapur had taken prisoner. After Shapur's death the Sasanid Empire suffered from a temporary weakness, of which the Romans were able to make use. Under the emperor Diocletian (AD 284–305), the defenses in the eastern frontier zone were reorganized and strengthened (Isaac 1992: 163 ff.). In AD 283, the Romans sacked the Sasanian capital Ctesiphon, and Diocletian's co-emperor Galerius (AD 293–311) won another great Roman victory. The subsequent peace treaty of AD 298/9 was very disadvantageous for the Sasanians: they lost considerable territory – the river Tigris would constitute the new border – and the Romans gained far-reaching influence in Mesopotamia, Armenia, and Iberia; important cities in northern Mesopotamia such as Nisibis were now within the boundaries of the Roman Empire (Blockley 1992: 5–7; Dodgeon and Lieu 1991: 125–35). From now on, Rome's posture toward the eastern neighbor was only defensive; but, out of dissatisfaction with the treaty of AD 298/9, the Persians revived their offensive policy again under Shapur II. In the later years of the reign of Constantine the Great (AD 306–37), whose universal christianizing policy undoubtedly fueled the aggressive Sasanian policy even more (Blockley 1992: 11), military intrusions into Roman territory were resumed, and continued under Constantius II (AD 337–61). In general, these military campaigns were of a small scale, and Shapur focused on regaining control of the cities in north Mesopotamia, which in these years were repeatedly besieged.

The character of warfare changed with the massive Roman expedition by the emperor Julian (AD 361–3) in AD 363. This expedition is very well documented, thanks to the historian Ammianus Marcellinus, who participated in it (Amm. Marc. 23–25. 3; Dodgeon and Lieu 1991: 230 ff.). The goals of the campaign are not entirely clear, but revenge for Shapur's aggression toward the Roman Empire was certainly one of them (Boeft 2002: 208). The Roman forces reached Ctesiphon, but then returned and were utterly defeated by the Persians in trying to reach Roman territory. Julian himself was killed in one of the battles with the enemy (Amm. Marc. 25. 3), and his successor Jovian (AD 363–4) was to make peace with Shapur. Rome had to give up the lands east of the Tigris and northeastern Mesopotamia, as well as various important cities, Nisibis among them (Blockley 1992: 24–30). This shameful treaty, as Ammianus calls it (25. 7. 13), restored the balance of power between the two empires, which had been distorted by the treaty of AD 298/9, and introduced a long period of relative peace and stability.

In spite of the invasions of the Sasanian kings deep into Roman territory, and Roman military expeditions into the Persian heartland, it seems never to have been the intention of either power to occupy captured territory outside of north Mesopotamia permanently; many military encounters were basically wars of plunder. Although it was possibly the Sasanians' intent to regain former Achaemenid holdings, and the Romans' official policy was intrinsically imperialistic, both superpowers were also ruled by realism and knew that neither would be able to incorporate and hold conquered territory on a permanent basis (Blockley 1992: 106–7, 121 ff.). At least after AD 363, each power remained intent upon keeping control of the territory that it thought of as its own, and upon preserving a balance of power.

The second phase saw a division of influence in Iberia (AD 370) and Armenia (AD 387), two other contested regions between Rome and Persia (Blockley 1992: 42–5); this seems only to have strengthened the stability between the two powers. Two short wars were fought (AD 421–2; 440–1), both, it seems, provoked by the Persians – for religious and financial motives, but also in order to make more secure the precarious position of their king, who had to prove himself in strife with Rome (Blockley 1992: 56–7, 61; Greatrex 1998: 13). Until the beginning of the sixth century tranquility dominated the relations between Rome and Persia. Both powers were occupied with other foes: the Sasanians with the Hephthalite Huns on their northeastern border, and the Romans with Huns, Goths, Vandals, and Isaurians. In the Huns, coming from north of the Caucasus, Rome and Persia had a common enemy. It is not clear whether there was an agreement between Rome and Persia about Rome's financial contribution to the maintenance of Persian defenses in the Caucasus against the Huns; but Rome's failure to make regular payments to the Persians, together with increasing mutual suspicion, are both at times put forward as reasons for the renewal of hostilities between the two superpowers at the beginning of the sixth century (Greatrex 1998: 14–17).

The third phase started with the renewal of the Sasanian expansion policy. Between AD 502 and 532, the Sasanians invaded Roman territory regularly and successfully. In AD 532, the so-called "Eternal Peace" was concluded (Greatrex 1998: 213 ff.), which, however, only held out shortly. Worried by the successes of Justinian I (527–65) in the west, the Sasanians attacked the Roman Empire again in AD 540, under Khusro I. Antioch was captured and its population deported to the Sasanid Empire (Procop. *Pers.* 2. 8. 1–35; 9. 14–18; Downey 1961: 542–4). As before, warfare was confined to Mesopotamia and Armenia. Neither the Persians nor the Romans, now led by Justinian's general Belisarius, were able to gain the upper hand. But in spite of several armistices, fighting regularly flared up again; formal peace was concluded only in AD 562 (Winter and Dignas 2001: 164–77). This peace was of short duration as well, and in AD 572, warfare was renewed (Whitby 1988: 219 ff.). This last long period of hostilities reached its climax during the reigns of Heraclius (AD 610–41) and Khusro II (AD 590–628). Initially, the Romans supported the latter against a usurper, but after regaining the Sasanian throne, he turned against them, proclaiming himself emperor over the Byzantine Empire. Due to internal weaknesses and strife over the imperial power in Constantinople, Khusro was able to conquer the eastern provinces of the Byzantine Empire (Schippmann 1990: 63 ff.; Winter and Dignas 2001: 136–40; Greatrex and Lieu 2002: 182–97). In particular, the fall of Jerusalem and the capture of the relics of the True Cross, the symbol par excellence of the Christian Byzantine Empire, may have been a tremendous shock to the Byzantines. Within a few years, however, Heraclius was able to reconquer the lost territory and, in AD 630, to return the Cross to Jerusalem (Drijvers 2002). At the beginning of the seventh century, the territory over which the Sasanians ruled came close to that of their Achaemenid predecessors; but their supremacy was short-lived. In the years AD 622–30, Heraclius brought about the downfall of the Sasanid Empire as a new Alexander (Howard-Johnston 1999). His reconquests led to anarchy in the Sasanid state, with some eight rulers in the years AD 628–32. When Yazdgerd III (AD 632–51) came to the throne, the empire was so weakened that it was unable to withstand the Muslim Arabs. In the years following the Sasanian defeat in the battle of Nihavand, in AD 642, the Muslims were able to conquer the Sasanid Empire and to occupy the territories over which Romans and Sasanians had fought for more than four centuries.

Coexistence and Exchange

Although warfare dominated the relationship between the Roman and Sasanid Empires for long periods, hostilities were definitely not the only component of Roman–Sasanian dealings; nor did they isolate the two states from each other. There was also a considerable amount of peaceful interaction, transcultural exchange, and acculturation (Garsoïan 1983). That interaction was greatly helped by the fact that there was no clear and fixed boundary between the two empires (Isaac 1992: 394–401) and that Mesopotamia constituted a permeable border zone. In this respect, the eastern frontier was no different from other border regions such as those on the Rhine and Danube (Whittaker 1994). Exchange of information, knowledge, and goods took place on a regular basis between those formally living on the Roman side and those on the Sasanian side. This exchange was facilitated by the fact that Syriac, a dialect of the Aramaic language, was the lingua franca, as well as by a culture shared in common on both sides of the frontier. The multicultural character of the border regions is well illustrated by Ammianus Marcellinus' story about Antoninus (18. 5). Antoninus was very well known in Mesopotamia; he had been a merchant and an accountant in the service of the Roman military commander of Mesopotamia, but had defected to the Persians with information on Roman military dispositions. Without difficulty, he was able to continue his life at the other side of the border and even to pursue a career in the service of the Persian king. Antonius was not a unique case. Ammianus (19. 9. 3–8) also mentions Cragausius, a prominent member of the elite of Nisibis, who also went over to the Persian side. Antonius and Cragausius are clearly examples of the adaptability that characterized social relations and conduct in this frontier zone between the two empires (Matthews 1989b: 68).

Exchange and cross-border transcultural contacts were diverse in nature: economic, diplomatic, cultural, and intellectual. Economic interchange between the states took place on a regular, though restricted, basis. The Romans were interested in luxury goods from India and China – silk, spices, incense, jewels, ivory – which reached the Roman Empire by the traditional routes over land such as the silk route, or via the ports located at the Persian Gulf. The tolls charged by the Sasanians seem to have been an important source of income for the Persian authorities. Rome was therefore keen on regulating and controlling trade and establishing trading centers on its own side of the border. The treaty of AD 298/9 made Nisibis the only place where the passage of goods between the Sasanid kingdom and the Roman Empire was allowed (Blockley 1992: 6), but in the fourth century commercial exchange was also authorized at the towns of Edessa, Batnae, Callinicum, and Artaxata (Winter and Dignas 2001: 211–12). Regulations on trade and the towns where commercial activities were allowed to take place were considered important by both sides, as, for example, a law from the *Justinianic Code* (sixth century AD) makes clear: former arrangements were reconfirmed, and the merchants who traded in places other than those mentioned in the law could face exile and the loss of their goods and wealth (*Cod. Iust.* 4. 63. 4). Apart from economic considerations, an important motive for restricting and controlling trade was to inhibit spying under the pretext of trade.

Marketplaces were ideal for gathering intelligence because of the mix of people that visited them, the information they carried, and the dissemination of news. Restriction of commerce was furthermore intended to prevent the export of contraband, more specifically iron and iron weapons, in which the Persians were particularly interested (Lee 1993: 63).

Throughout Late Antiquity, the two empires maintained diplomatic relations. There had always been diplomatic activity before, during, and after wars; but it seems that, in the fourth and fifth centuries, the notion developed that diplomacy could be used as an instrument in place of war (a notion that affected Rome's policy toward not only its eastern neighbor, but also the peoples on its northern borders). This perception of diplomacy probably arose from the belief of some Roman and Persian rulers that the two empires had to coexist (Blockley 1992: 151 ff.). Embassies and envoys regularly travelled between the courts in Constantinople and Ctesiphon to deliver messages, gather information, clarify interests, negotiate treaties, or pay respect on behalf of their ruler (Lee 1993: *passim*). The Roman emperor and his Persian counterpart respected each other, as appears, for instance, from correspondence between Constantius II and Shapur II in which they address each other as "brother" and Constantius even offers Shapur his friendship (Amm. Marc. 17. 5. 3–14; Blockley 1992: 115). This was definitely not empty politeness but a mutual recognition of sovereignty and equal rank as well as a clear wish for good relations and dialogue. At the beginning of the fifth century relations appear to have been extremely friendly, as may be concluded from the fact that the emperor Arcadius (AD 395–408) in his will made Yazdgerd I guardian of his infant son Theodosius, and charged him to preserve the throne for the boy. Yazdgerd gladly accepted this task and acquitted himself faithfully (Blockley 1992: 51 ff.). About a century later Justin I (AD 518–27) accepted the proposal by Kavad I (AD 488–96, 499–531) to adopt his son Khusro (Procop. *Pers.* 1. 11. 1–6). These instances show the mutual respect and the close, almost familial, relations that existed at times between the rulers of both superpowers.

In spite of efforts from both sides to keep up good relations and peaceful coexistence, military confrontation is part of the history of the relationship between both empires. Desertion and defection by both Persians and Romans seems to have been a fairly regular occurrence (Lee 1993: 65–6), as the above cases of Antoninus and Cragausius make clear. A consequence of warfare was also the capturing and deporting of war prisoners, both soldiers and civilians, on a large scale. Deportations as a consequence of war were a common phenomenon in antiquity. The Romans deported their Persian war prisoners mainly to Thrace, where they probably had to work as farm laborers (*Pan. Lat.* 8(5). 21. 1; Lib. *Or.* 9. 83 ff.; Lieu 1986: 487). The Roman authorities, who only occasionally deported civic populations from Persian cities, had no coherent plan for these captives of war, unlike the Sasanians, who settled them all over their empire. During the reigns of Shapur I and Shapur II in particular, deportation took place on a massive scale (Lieu 1986: 476–81, 495–9; Kettenhofen 1994). Complete populations of conquered Roman cities were transported to Persia, where they were often settled in newly founded cities, such as Bishapur or Gundeshapur, which were constructed with the labor of Roman prisoners. The sources relate that among the captives were many craftsmen, as well as architects and artisans. Their knowledge and skills were most welcome in the Sasanid Empire, and were used in large building projects such as cities, bridges, dams, roads, and royal palaces (Winter and Dignas 2001: 159–63). Roman influence is clearly recognizable in Sasanian architecture and art (Shahbazi 1990: 594), and even in city layout and daily life. Khusro I founded a new city which he called "Antioch of Khusro" and settled it with war prisoners he had made when he conquered Antioch. He allowed the new settlers to build *thermae* and even a race course; and, to make their life agreeable, he also had Roman musicians and charioteers deported to his Antioch (Procop. *Pers.* 2. 14. 1–4). The sources are silent about the human suffering resulting from these deportations.

The geographic and cultural setting of the Mesopotamian border region also provided great opportunities for intellectual exchange. Religion was often the driving force behind this. As observed above, the Sasanid Empire had a considerable Christian population, many of them captured Romans who were often Christian (Lieu 1986: 481–7; Jullien and Jullien 2002: 153 ff.). A great deal of interchange took place between the Christian communities in both empires (Matthews 1989a: 44–5; Lee 1993: 56–61). Christian pilgrims from Persia travelled to the holy sites in Palestine and the holy men in Egypt and the Syrian desert and visited monastic settlements. Border zone shrines, such as that of St. Sergius at Rustafa (Key Fowden 1999), were visited by Roman and Persian Christians alike, which again underlines the multicultural character of the frontier regions. Another motive for crossing the border was the desire for learning. In particular the schools of Edessa and Nisibis, famous for their theological learning and for their scholarship in rhetoric, philosophy, and literature, had a great number of Persians among their students (Hayes 1930; Vööbus 1965; Becker 2006). Cross-border travelling also reflected a wish to teach and proselytize. Most notably the Manichaeans came to the Roman Empire to spread their ideas (Brown 1969), but there were also miaphysite bishops who journeyed to Persia to fight those of dyophysite conviction. Learning, teaching, or the exchange of information were also a stimulus for the continuous interchange between the Jewish communities in both empires. Many Jewish scholars from Persia had been educated in Palestine, but Jewish academies in Babylonia also attracted Jews from the Roman Empire. In this way an intellectual academic climate was created that gave rise to such unique intellectual accomplishments as the Babylonian Talmud.

At least one Sasanian king appreciated cultural and intellectual interchange. Khusro I, a religiously tolerant ruler, was an intellectual, and open to influences from outside. He seems to have been devoted to Greco-Roman writers whose works he had translated into Persian. He also had a great interest in Greek philosophy and is said to have read Plato and Aristotle (Agathias 2. 28. 1–2; Rubin 1995; Wiesehöfer 2001: 216 ff.). His learning and tolerance became widely known in the Roman Empire as well. When, in AD 529, Justinian forbade pagans to teach philosophy and law, several Neoplatonic philosophers from the Academy in Athens are said to have gone to Ctesiphon, where they were well received by the learned king (Chuvin 1990: 135–41; Sheppard 2000: 841–2; Hartmann 2002). In his own empire, he stimulated education, which owed much to Byzantine learning (Shahbazi 1990: 593), in particular the study of law and medicine.

The periods of enmity and warfare did not isolate the two empires from each other. Through commerce, diplomacy, religion, desertion, and deportations there was a lively exchange of goods, information, and knowledge. Persian learning, architecture, and arts were clearly influenced by the contacts with the Roman Empire, while Rome, in its turn, was affected by the contacts with the east. Sasanian court rituals influenced Byzantine court ceremonial, and Persian influence can also be discerned, for instance, in architectural construction, form, and ornamentation, and in motifs in Byzantine art (Ghirshman 1962: 283 ff.; Shahbazi 1990: 594–5).

Image and Representation

Because of the multiple and multifaceted connections between the Roman and Sasanid Empires, each side knew a great deal about the other. Unfortunately, through lack of sources and the tendency to look at Roman–Persian relations from a western perspective, hardly anything is (yet) known about how the Sasanians perceived the Romans and their society. Through diplomacy and other contacts, however, they must at least have had knowledge of the way in which the Roman Empire was administratively, military, and socially organized; and through warfare, they must have been well acquainted with geographic and topographic conditions in the eastern Roman territories. Moreover, the shaping of an Iranian identity in Sasanian times – through, for instance, the composition of the *Book of Lords* – demanded the construction of a hostile "other" world. Rome was that other world and Persia's arch-enemy (Wiesehöfer 2005). The Sasanians felt superior to the Romans – obvious in the *Res Gestae Divi Saporis*. In this trilingual inscription, the Roman emperor is called the subordinate of the Sasanian king, and the Roman Empire considered a vassal state of the Sasanid state (Rubin 1998). The Sasanian rock reliefs express the same ideology in visual form: they show Roman emperors who kneel as suppliants before Persian kings. Even though the Sasanian rulers never abandoned their triumphal ideological presentation and image of the Roman Empire, reality demanded a more realistic approach, namely the treatment of the Roman emperors as their equals and the acknowledgment of the Roman Empire as a super power.

On the Roman side, the sources are more abundant. They give the impression that the Romans must have known something of, for example, Sasanian political and social institutions, the Persian army, Zoroastrianism, and the geographical situation of the western regions of the Sasanid Empire. Due to the Greco-Roman literary tradition, however, much factual and practical information was either not included in the sources or not presented as such. Geographical learning, for example, was predominantly literary in character, and geographical treatises contain relatively little concrete information. Ethnographical descriptions were still written in the Herodotean tradition, and according to these sources the customs of Sasanian Persians hardly differ from those of their Achaemenid predecessors.

Because they viewed other peoples through the inherited categories of classical ethnography, Roman sources portray their Persian neighbors (and, indeed, the northern "barbarians") in a negative light. Roman cultural prejudices and traditions went deep, and, judging from the available information, greater knowledge (or at least less ignorance) does not seem to have diminished estrangement. As a result, the Persians were characterized as the negative embodiment of Greco-Roman values. The Antiochene orator Libanius, an intellectual heavyweight, called the Persians barbarian and inhumane and compared them to wild beasts (*Or.* 15. 25–6). His contemporary Ammianus Marcellinus, who knew the Sasanians from his own experience and who was not averse to using the beast metaphor in characterizing all peoples outside the Roman Empire (Wiedemann 1986), never calls them barbarian (Chauvot 1998: 386 ff.); but nor does he present them in a favorable light. Ammianus, in his long digression on Persian geography and ethnography (23. 6), was not able to break loose from the portrayal of the Persians that Herodotus had given some eight centuries before. In his ethnographical account, Ammianus emphasizes the "otherness" of the Persians (Teitler 1999; Drijvers 2006). Persian national vices (as seen by Greeks and Romans) receive particularly close attention: sexual intemperance, cruelty, arrogance, effeminacy, violence, garrulity, constant domestic strife, and foreign wars. But Ammianus aspires at least to some sort of balanced picture since, apart from their vices, he also mentions the Persians' virtues: their avoidance of excessive eating and drinking, their moderation, and, above all, their military training and discipline, as well as their expertise in warfare. Ammianus, being a soldier himself, admired the Sasanian military qualities, although he criticizes the Persians for not always fighting in an organized way, for lacking endurance in battle, and for not being good in man-to-man combat. In general, he portrays the Persian king (Shapur II) in an unfavorable way. He is harsh and cruel, unrestrained in his greed, short-tempered and rude, treacherous and dishonest, and he suffers from uncontrolled rage. The Sasanian king is clearly portrayed as the opposite of Ammianus's ideal Roman emperor – philanthropic, just, moderate, mild, and gentle. Almost two centuries later, Procopius gave a similar picture of the Persian king (Khusro I); he shows hostility to Khusro and represents him as the denial of humanity (Averil Cameron 1985: 162–3; Brodka 1998; Börm 2007: 251–2). Some time later, Agathias holds similarly contemptuous views on the Persians and their (sexual) habits; he accuses the Sasanid kings of flaying people alive and of being wicked and abominable men (Cameron 1969: 121; Isaac 2004: 378–9). But Agathias as well as other Greco-Roman writers also showed some genuine interest in Sasanian religion and the – from the Roman point of view – peculiar burial customs of the Persians (e.g., Cameron 1969: 79–89).

In spite of frequent contacts, and the knowledge that east and west had about each other, there does not seem to have been a greater resulting empathy and understanding – not, at least, on the Roman side. Greco-Roman sources present on the whole a stereotypical and not very favorable image of the Sasanians. Sasanian society seems to have remained another world for the Romans, a world they did not always find easy to understand, about which they were prejudiced, and to which they felt superior.

Classical scholars have long studied the ancient Mediterranean civilizations, including the Late Roman Empire, as self-contained entities. The Persian Empire, outside their central area of inquiry, had been in general considered marginal, and had been left to study by Orientalists. New approaches in classical scholarship have led to an understanding of what novel insights can be gained by studying the interrelationships of civilizations. In studying the relationship between east and west, the artificiality of "Orientalism," first criticized in such terms by Edward Said (Said 1978), has put scholars fruitfully on their guard (although Said's argument is not without its problems and critics). The east, in our case the Sasanid Empire, was a Greco-Roman construct, as is clear from the Roman conception of Sasanian society. That society was seen as very much another and unfamiliar world, to which the Romans condescended; but Sasanian society was in reality more like late Roman society than the Romans themselves were probably inclined to admit. The Sasanians, who had almost certainly developed a corresponding ideology of superiority, had a similar attitude toward Roman society. In spite of the mental gulf that separated them, the east was very much a reality for the Romans, as was the west for the Sasanians. Wars were fought and diplomacy employed to preserve a balance of power between the two empires; but the authorities in both states also realized that they profited from peaceful economic, cultural, and intellectual exchange and that these friendly interactions were beneficial in upholding an acceptable equilibrium between them. Coexistence, just as much as confrontation, characterized the multifaceted and complicated relationship between the Roman and Sasanid Empires.

BIBLIOGRAPHICAL NOTE

For basic introductions to Sasanian history, see the various chapters in Yarshater 1983a, vol. ii, and relevant chapters in Schippmann 1990, Cameron and Garnsey 1998, Cameron et al. 2000, Wiesehöfer 2001, and Bowman et al. 2005. Sources in translation are provided in Dodgeon and Lieu 1991, in Winter and Dignas 2001 (and see Dignas and Winter 2007), and in Greatrex and Lieu 2002, all of which give references to relevant modern publications. For the relations and interchange between the two empires see, for example, Blockley 1992 and Lee 1993. On religious, in particular Christian, interchange between the two empires and Christianity in Iran see Chaumont 1988 and Jullien and Jullien 2002. On the Roman image of the Sasanians and their society, several contributions in Wiesehöfer and Huyse 2006 are very useful.

CHAPTER THIRTY

Syria, Syriac, Syrian: Negotiating East and West

Christine Shepardson

From Late Antiquity until now, eastern Roman Syria has conjured up exotic, "oriental" images for western writers. For those, then and now, accustomed to the known classics of the Greek east and the Latin west, the predominantly Greek-speaking Syrian city of Antioch has been a familiar landmark of ecclesiastical and political power, while the predominantly Syriac-speaking Syrian city of Edessa shimmers uncertainly on the edge of the unknown. Although they were both Syrians, the Greek-writing John Chrysostom (*c.* AD 347–407) stands solidly in conversation with his Greek and Latin contemporaries, while the Syriac-writing Ephrem (*c.* AD 306–73) has remained an obscure figure in western scholarship, shrouded behind the impenetrable veil of a language that never became a *sine qua non* of western erudition. Syria in Late Antiquity thus stands firmly planted between western distinctions of east from west – part of the Mediterranean world, but on its eastern periphery; partially Hellenized, but still adamantly Syrian. Syrian cities that produced predominantly Greek-speaking authors have for the most part remained influential to scholarship and, for that very reason, this chapter focuses primarily on Syriac-speaking Syria. The goal, however, will be to begin to bring these two overlapping Syrias back into conversation not only with each other, but with the larger Roman-Byzantine context to which they contributed. While the boundaries of "Late Antiquity" are notoriously flexible, I shall examine here the period from the end of Edessa's independent kingship and the growing political control of Rome in the third century AD to the region's conquest by Muslim armies from the Arabian Peninsula in the seventh. Both series of events mark significant political changes in Syria and had long-lasting effects on its culture.

From an overemphasis on the significance of Syriac's linguistic relation to Jesus' Aramaic to Peter Brown's flamboyant description of Syria as "notoriously the Wild and Woolly West of ascetic heresy" (Brown 1971a: 84), eastern Syria has played a colorful but caricatured role in western scholarship. It has traditionally emerged as alternately too "Jewish," too "pagan," or too "heretical" to be Christian by western standards of orthodoxy, while Syrians themselves were commonly described as too inferior, effeminately eastern, hedonistic, and morally suspect to be properly "Roman" (Juv. 3. 62–6; SHA, *M. Ant.*, *Verus*; Lucian, *Bis Accusatus* 27, 34; Liv. *Ab urbe condita* 38. 17; see Isaac 1998b, 2004). Contrary to that historical emphasis on difference, however, late antique Syria was integrally connected with its western neighbors – more so, in fact, than in the previous or following centuries. We must acknowledge Syria's relationship with the Roman and Byzantine Empires, neither denying its individuality nor making it so foreign that it does not have a place within the empire that was its home. Such an acknowledgment not only proves us more faithful to the primary sources, but also enriches our understanding of the period and of the broader empire. The example of Syria reminds us that places once dismissed as being so marginal that they were insignificant are in fact fundamental to a full understanding of the rhetoric and politics of Late Antiquity. At the same time, it demonstrates that even those individual places and people understood to be normative were also local and unique, tied to particular contexts. I attempt in this chapter to provide, therefore, an introduction to eastern Syria in Late Antiquity, while also demonstrating the advantages of restoring it to conversations about the empire as a whole. I shall not only begin to scrape away for westerners late antique Syria's sometimes misleadingly mysterious facade, but also provide the framework for a richer and more subtle reconstruction of the culture, theology, and politics of the Roman and early Byzantine Empires.

Confronting Caricatures, Identifying Influences

The third-century end of the Edessene kingship ushered in a new era for eastern Syria, but the developments, politics, and culture of the centuries that followed have meaning most directly in relation to what had come before. Likewise, modern caricatures of eastern Syria have not appeared out of thin air, but rely on earlier texts that continue to influence scholarship. For example, the portrayal of Syriac Christianity as a persistent "Jewish Christianity" that derived directly from Jewish apostles in Judea continues to mislead some scholars in their reading of Syriac texts, and in the comparisons they make between Syriac Christianity and its antecedents. Any discussion of late antique Syria, therefore, must first address some of the issues of earlier centuries, as they provide a necessary interpretative framework. A brief look at, first, Syria's linguistic and political history, and second its religious history, will highlight the importance of recognizing its cultural complexity.

1 Language and politics

Edessa, the urban center of Syriac-speaking Syria, was home to the kings who governed the surrounding area for several hundred years before Roman control. Although Antioch came under Roman rule in 64 BC with the creation of the Roman province of Syria, eastern Syria maintained its local kingship for much longer.

After the end of Seleucid control in the region in the second century BC, Edessene kings ruled under loose Parthian control. By AD 166, after ongoing power struggles between the Romans and Parthians for control of Edessa, the local ruler became officially tied to the Roman emperor through a treaty. In the late second century, Abgar VIII (Abgar the Great) even adopted the Latin name Lucius Aelius Aurelius Septimius, demonstrating his allegiance to Roman forces under Septimius Severus; and Abgar's son (Abgar IX) also added the name Severus to his own (Segal 2001: 14). Despite occasional skirmishes with Rome, especially under Trajan, and a few brief interregna, the dynasty continued to rule until AD 213/14, when Caracalla deposed Abgar IX and declared Edessa a Roman *colonia*. Although Rome allowed local kings to rule nominally in Edessa for a few more decades, by the AD 240s the monarchy had ended entirely, and the region remained clearly under Roman control. With its local kingship supported first by Parthia and then by Rome, Edessa lasted as a multilingual center long after the third century. In Late Antiquity it thus stood as a point of cultural interchange with lands to its east and west, with newly strengthened ties to the Roman Empire.

Other eastern Syrian towns have equally mottled political histories. Nisibis, for example, became a Roman *colonia* in AD 194, before the end of the Edessene kingship. As a politically significant border town between the Parthian (and then Persian) and Roman Empires, however, its affiliation was anything but stable. It was the victim of multiple sieges, including several Persian sieges under Shapur II in AD 338, 346, and 350. The death of the Roman emperor Julian in AD 363, and the consequent ceding of portions of eastern Syria to Persia, certainly did not mark the first time that Nisibis changed hands from one political power to another. So, eastern Syria of Late Antiquity inherited a complex variety of influences that set it apart from other Roman provinces. Since it was, however, the very process of establishing firm political connections with Rome that defines this part of Syria's history, it will serve scholars well to note its connections with Rome as much as its differences.

In addition to eastern Syria's changing political ties, its complex relationship to "Greek" thought and language has facilitated its isolation from studies of the Roman Empire. In the early twentieth century, F. C. Burkitt influenced decades of scholarship by describing Syriac Christianity as utterly separated from the Greek world (Burkitt 1904). While Robert Murray retracted his own similar claims, referring later to the "hybrid" context of Ephrem's fourth-century Syriac world (Murray 1982), many scholars still reveled in portraying Syriac Christianity as a "pure," unadulterated example of the "Semitic" Christianity that Jesus himself had initiated. More recently, Sebastian Brock began to temper this picture considerably, and now critical scholars such as Sidney Griffith, Ute Possekel, and Thomas Koonammakkal have argued definitively that, despite Ephrem's denunciation of "the poison of the Greeks" (Ephrem, *Hymns on Faith* 2. 24), he and late antique Syria were significantly influenced by both the language and the concepts of Greek philosophy (Griffith 1986, 1999a, 1999b; Koonammakkal 1994; Possekel 1999). Although Syriac was the predominant language under the Edessene kings and through Late Antiquity, Latin Edessene names (e.g., Severus, Aurelius, Augustina), local inscriptions in multiple languages, and coins in Syriac and Greek show that by Late Antiquity Edessa had been strongly influenced culturally and linguistically by the empire to its west (Segal 2001). Given the multilingual nature of the region and its political ties to Rome, scholars of Syria no longer imagine that it was sharply distinct from Hellenistic and Roman society and culture. In the fourth and fifth centuries, Syriac church leaders such as Ephrem and Rabbula demonstrated that Syriac Christians could even participate fully in the rhetorical construction of imperial orthodoxy that preoccupied their western counterparts.

2 *Religious variety in Roman Syria*

In addition to Syria's political separation from the west before and after Late Antiquity, much of the persistence of the otherness of eastern Syria relates to the history of Syriac Christianity, a history that in western scholarship has always provided an odd, unorthodox Other, as well as a tantalizing linguistic link to the words of Jesus. Thus, on the one hand scholars characterize Syriac Christianity as closely associated with the unorthodox followers of Mani, Marcion, and Bardaisan, while on the other hand they highlight its "Jewish-Christian" origins and hint that its Aramaic language and geographical proximity to Palestine allowed it to preserve a Christianity closer to the teachings of Jesus than those that developed in the wake of Paul and other Greek-speaking leaders. Along with strong pagan Syriac traditions surrounding such local divinities as Bêl and Nebo, and a strong emphasis on the apostle Thomas, this variety has perpetuated the image of eastern Syria as radically unlike its western neighbors. While it is of course undeniable that late antique Syria had local traditions, this was true for any given locale and should not obscure utterly the ways in which Syria also shared in the religious as well as the political culture of the Eastern Roman Empire. As with its politics and language, Syrian religion displays a significant uniqueness but also provides new bridges that allow scholars to reintegrate it into the broader Roman world.

Since both Nisibis and Edessa were important cities on the major trade routes that connected the Roman Empire with India and China, people and ideas (in a variety of languages) flowed through them (Harrak 2002). Within this bustling world of commerce, the second- and third-century teachings of Marcion, Mani, and Bardaisan flourished, as even the fourth-century writings of Ephrem show. Likewise, traditional religious practices in various forms continued to be a visible presence through the fourth century (Han Drijvers 1980, 1982). *The Syrian Goddess*, attributed to Lucian of Samosata, describes the cult of the goddess Atargatis in nearby Hieropolis, and the *Teaching of Addai* notes the many pagan temples (especially to Bêl and Nebo) in Edessa. Worship of these deities continued to thrive in Edessa at least until the strict fifth-century leadership of Bishop Rabbula (Blum 1969; Han Drijvers 1999).

Along with this rich mixture, eastern Syria had a significant population of Jews in Nisibis and Edessa in the early Christian period (Segal 1964; Neusner 1965; Han Drijvers 1985; Shepardson 2008). As mentioned, most scholars have, at least since the time of F. C. Baur, highlighted the continuing strength of Syrian Judaism and the "Jewish-Christian" nature of Syriac Christianity (Baur 1861). Using such early Christian texts as the *Didascalia*, the Pseudo-Clementine literature, and the legend of King

Abgar's correspondence with Jesus, many early scholars concluded that Christianity first arrived in Edessa as Aramaic "Jewish-Christianity" directly from Jewish apostles of Jesus (Burkitt 1904; Daniélou 1958; Vööbus 1958; Bauer 1996). More recent scholars agree that some Syriac Christian communities maintained more contact with contemporary Judaism than did many of their western counterparts, but also challenge earlier vocabulary and assumptions. Michael Weitzman's discussion of the Jewish origins of the Peshitta (the Syriac translation of the Old Testament), and many scholars' comparisons of Mesopotamian Jewish exegesis with Syriac Christian exegesis, demonstrate important points of connection (Tonneau 1955; Séd 1968; Hidal 1974; Kronholm 1978; Brock 1979, 1995; Weitzman 1992, 1999; Van Rompay 1997). Likewise, Gerard Rouwhorst's arguments – that early Syriac Christianity retained, until the fourth-century Council of Nicaea, traces of Jewish architecture and liturgical traditions, such as the presence of a bema, regular readings from both the Torah and the Prophets during the Eucharist, and perhaps the Quartodeciman practice of celebrating Easter on 14 Nisan, the date of the Jewish Passover) – demonstrate further the permeability of the categories "Jew" and "Christian" in late antique Syria (Rouwhorst 1989, 1997). Scholars should not, however, revert to the older stereotypes and labels implied by the term "Jewish-Christianity." The challenge mounted by recent scholarship against using this term in the Syrian context is persuasive, and one cannot interpret the data adduced as providing evidence that Syriac Christianity stood sharply outside the bounds of Roman Christianity. Indeed, the older terminology is inconsistent and sometimes historically inaccurate in its connotations (Taylor 1990; Mimouni 1994; Carleton Paget 1999).

Equally important, scholars have redressed another traditional argument, that at a certain moment "Christianity" parted ways with "Judaism" – a theory not only monolithic in itself, but also offering a supposedly stark contrast to the history of Syriac Christianity. As more recent work calls into question the suggested narrative of sharp and early separation (Becker and Reed 2003; Boyarin 2004), Syria's history no longer stands apart from the history of Christianity in general. This new configuration allows scholars to make useful connections, as between Ephrem's Syriac rhetoric and John Chrysostom's Greek anti-Judaizing texts from Antioch – a city that can hardly be characterized as "Jewish-Christian" or outside the bounds of orthodoxy (as Ephrem's eastern Syria routinely has been). It also demonstrates the degree to which the Syrian evidence helps us to revise misleading narratives of imperial uniformity.

Ephrem's Fourth-Century Syria

Having submitted to more direct Roman control in the third century, eastern Syria was thereafter subject to many of the same historical currents as the rest of the eastern empire: it experienced the growing influence of Christian groups, the vacillation of changing emperors' religious and political sympathies, and the rhetorical construction of an imperial Christian culture. As Christianity, and its struggle to define orthodoxy, became a powerful force in the empire, Syriac church leaders such as

Ephrem (*c.* AD 306–73) became active participants in Roman Christianity's development. Through the course of the fourth century, Christianity acquired an imperial voice, and Syriac Christians discovered thereby a way to connect their local communities with what they claimed to be universal tropes of "church" and "empire." While Syria maintained unique texts and practices, Ephrem tried to forge his community's singular self-understanding into a more general notion of imperial "orthodoxy." This was not, however, a case of simple substitution. Rather, the local identity and imperial "orthodoxy" were developing in creative conversation with each other. Fourth-century Syria cannot plausibly be understood without bridging the supposed chasm between Syrian religious discourse and contemporary discussions of Greek (and Latin) theology and politics. Historians have sometimes overlooked or underplayed local differences elsewhere in the empire, in order to allow a more vivid description of an imperial norm. In the case of Syria, the tendency has been reversed: normative aspects have too often been erased in order to highlight difference. We would benefit from a more tempered analysis, alert to the way in which imperial narratives of orthodoxy had to cope, face to face, with local difference.

Ephrem was a prolific writer and poet. His hymns, commentaries, and other writings not only tell us much of what we know about fourth-century Syriac Christianity, but also served as a model for later Syriac writers. They are an invaluable resource in a discussion of Syria's history, both for what his writings reflect about his own time and for how their poetic legacy influenced the writers of later centuries. They provide compelling evidence that fourth-century Syria showed both regional diversity and imperial Roman influence; and, as mentioned, Ephrem himself idealized the homogeneity of those characteristics, especially the bond between his own culture and his hope for a pro-Nicene Christian empire.

Late antique Syria would not be "Syrian" without its thriving religious diversity. Other late antique Roman cities displayed a comparable wealth of religious diversity; but the distinctive mix of Jews, Manichees, Marcionites, and Bardaisanites alongside other Christians and pagans made Syria unique. Eastern Syria's geographical location between Palestine and Babylon, and Syriac's linguistic relation to Aramaic (and Hebrew), created an environment in which Syriac Christianity, in eastern Syria and in Aphrahat's Persian home, developed a closer contact with contemporary Judaism than was possible in most other places. Ephrem's fourth-century texts share some exegetical motifs and strategies with those of his contemporary rabbinic counterparts, and his insistent anti-Judaizing pleas that his congregants flee from and not eat unleavened bread, suggest interaction, and even overlap, between some of those who attended his church and some of those who attended local synagogue festivals (Ephrem, *Hymns on Unleavened Bread* 19). Without connecting fourth-century Syriac Christianity with Baur's shadowy "Petrine" Jewish-Christianity, the visible local continuity and linguistic accessibility of Judaism does appear to have facilitated contact between some Syrian Christians and Jews. It was in response to precisely such associations that Ephrem deployed his imperial rhetoric, striving to link Syria with Greek Christian narratives of imperial orthodoxy (Griffith 1999b).

Other authors wrote against one or another of Ephrem's opponents: Augustine against the Manichees, for example (August. *C. Faustum*). But those opponents were gathered in a unique mix in the Syrian sphere, and were notably successful through the fourth century. Ephrem wrote vitriolic treatises against Mani, Marcion, and Bardaisan (*Discourses against Hypatius I–V*, *Against Marcion I–III*; *Against Bardaisan's "Domnus"*; *Against Mani*), and famously complained that "orthodox" Christians were called "Palûtians" after their early leader Palût, possibly because the name "Christian" already belonged to others (Ephrem, *Hymns against Heresies* 22. 5–6; Bauer 1996: 21–4). Just as Egypt was associated with Gnosticism, and fourth-century North African history was colored by the Donatist controversy, late antique Syria was home to Jews, Manichees, Marcionites, Bardaisanites, pagans, and pro-Nicene Christians. This complex amalgam highlights Syria's unique character, especially when combined with the textual distinctiveness of the Peshitta and the popularity, at least until Rabbula's episcopacy, of the *Diatessaron*, which was a harmonization of the New Testament gospels attributed to the Syrian Tatian.

But Syria's religious diversity marked it out as not only different from but also continuous with the eastern empire. Ephrem's writings against Arians, Anomeans, and Homoian Christians demonstrate his active engagement with precisely the opponents that other eastern pro-Nicene Christians addressed in the fourth century (for details, see Griffith 1986; Shepardson 2002, 2008). That Ephrem represented a Christianity that was comprehensible to contemporary Christian leaders who were themselves more firmly within (or in fact creating) "orthodoxy" is evident from the rapid translation of his works into Greek, from Epiphanius' reference to Ephrem within a few years of his death (Epiph. *Adv. haeres.* 51. 22. 7), and from Jerome's description of him not much later (Hieron. *De vir. ill.* 115). Christian authors such as Palladius, Sozomen, and Theodoret also wrote about Ephrem, demonstrating that knowledge of his Syriac writings and his life quickly spread across linguistic and geographical boundaries (Palladius, *Lausiac History* 40; Sozom. *Hist. eccl.* 3. 16; Theodoret, *Hist. eccl.* 4. 29). Ephrem helped to place Syria firmly within the empire, a factor to be taken into account if we are to acquire any persuasive understanding of Syriac particularities.

But as it transcended its own immediate context, Ephrem's Syriac Christianity still maintained a local flavor. This was particularly evident in its practice of asceticism. Asceticism was becoming popular throughout the empire, but varied locally nevertheless. Syria's ascetic history combined a growing list of severe forms of individual asceticism, such as that of Simeon the Stylite (d. AD 459), along with the history of a celibate community within the congregation. Early Syriac literature refers to the *bnay/bnât qyâmâ* (the sons/daughters of the covenant), a title that appears to have been connected with a vow of celibacy. Modifying Arthur Vööbus's suggestion that celibacy was a requirement for baptism in early Syriac Christianity (Vööbus 1951, 1961), Susan Ashbrook Harvey has recently shown both the limits of our knowledge about these covenanters and the uniqueness of the practices that they espoused, including Ephrem's famous female choirs (Harvey 2005).

This brief survey of Ephrem's career demonstrates the complex symbiosis that late antique Syria maintained with its western neighbors. The details of its religious diversity reflect a Syrian individuality, but Ephrem's pro-Nicene anti-Homoian arguments exemplify continuity with his Greek-speaking contemporaries. The covenanters form a particularly Syrian detail of early Christian asceticism, while the growth and influence of asceticism more generally show continuity with the rest of Roman Christianity. The Syriac language creates a regional distinctiveness, just as Berber does for North Africa and Coptic does for Egypt. The *Odes of Solomon*, the *Liber Graduum*, and Ephrem's poetry stand outside the Greek and Latin canon of church writings, and thus Syriac authors and the content of Syriac texts may appear foreign in the otherwise familiar Roman world. The overlay of Latin and Greek, however, as well as the early translation of texts and ideas to and from Syriac, creates some common ground. Ephrem's fourth-century Syria was delightfully unique but intelligible to, and in touch with, the larger Roman Empire. It is only by remembering both halves of this truth that we can begin to see both Syria and the Roman Empire more clearly.

Orthodoxy on the Eastern Edge: Ephesus, Chalcedon, and Beyond

Following eastern Syria's growing integration with the empire to its west, the late fourth century saw the birth of additional politicized theological controversies that would eventually etch a new fault-line between eastern Syria and the politically dominant forces of the early Byzantine Empire. Seventh-century military invasions from Persia and then from the Arabian Peninsula formalized this growing divide by severing Syria politically from the remainder of the Byzantine Empire. Thus, Late Antiquity begins and ends for Syria with a distinct political separation from the Greek-speaking empire to its west. Nonetheless, the intervening period itself is one in which Syria was deeply engaged with this empire, and to erase these centuries of connection or to fail to distinguish the different contours of its seventh-century separation from that of the third century would be to misrepresent radically the history of Syria as well as the history of the Roman Empire. Later Syriac Christian history can be understood only in conversation with Roman-Byzantine history. While late antique Syria was by no means exclusively Christian, and religious interactions are not the only components of Syrian history, the politics and society of Late Antiquity are radically intertwined with the history of Christianity, and a brief investigation of some of the empire's theological politics, brought to a head first at Ephesus and then at Chalcedon, offers an opportunity to demonstrate Syria's significant role in this history.

1 The Council of Ephesus and Syriac Christianity

The connection with imperial orthodoxy so persistently stressed in Ephrem's Syriac rhetoric was continued in the voice of Rabbula, bishop of Edessa (AD 411–35). By Rabbula's time, the controversy between pro-Nicene and Homoian theologies had waned, and attention had quickly centered on the arguments between Cyril of Alexandria and Nestorius, the deposed bishop of Constantinople, over the theological implications of calling Mary *theotokos* (the God-bearer). Nestorius' rejection of this term for Mary was grounded in his conviction that she could bear only the human and not the divine aspect of the Son. Nestorius was condemned at the ecumenical Council of Ephesus in AD 431, but the controversy was far from settled. Although the theology of the Greek-speaking Theodore of Mopsuestia (d. AD 428), formulated before the Council of Ephesus, differed from that of Nestorius, both emphasized the distinction of the human and divine aspects of the Son. That similarity allowed Rabbula, a strong supporter of Cyril's teachings and of the imperial orthodoxy of AD 431, to conflate the theologies of Nestorius and Theodore, thus condemning the latter after his death by association with the officially condemned Nestorius. Under Rabbula's influence, Syriac Christianity became sharply divided between those who followed Theodore's teachings and those who, like Rabbula, followed the Council of Ephesus in supporting Cyril. As under Ephrem, many Syriac Christians under Rabbula thus had a strong connection with imperial orthodoxy. Even though this association would not remain dominant in the coming decades, the fifth-century schism within Syriac Christianity between those who supported Theodore of Mopsuestia and those who with imperial sanction followed Cyril's teachings would never be healed.

In the later fifth century, the Persian Syriac Christian Narsai studied and then taught in Edessa and strongly supported Theodore's teachings. In the face of political opposition, Narsai and his followers moved in the late fifth century to teach in Nisibis. (For a broad discussion of the educational traditions thus established, see Becker 2006.) Once removed from the political pressure of Byzantine orthodoxy, Narsai's pro-Theodore Syriac Christianity flourished as orthodoxy within the Persian Empire. Inaccurately labeled "Nestorian" Christianity, due to the improper polemical conflation of Theodore's teachings with those of Nestorius, this form of Syriac Christianity survives to this day as the (Assyrian) Church of the East. Given its fifth-century displacement from the Byzantine Empire, it is small wonder that this form of Syriac Christianity has stood outside the purview of western scholarship. Within Late Antiquity, however, it remained a significant component of imperial political and theological history.

2 The Council of Chalcedon and Syriac Christianity

In the decades that followed the Council of Ephesus, political and ecclesiastical leaders struggled to articulate a clearer description of the human and divine aspects of the Son. In response to the condemnation of Nestorius, Eutyches, a monk in Constantinople, argued that in the act of the incarnation the Son's human and divine natures were so fully fused that they formed a single new nature. Those who supported Eutyches argued that this emphasis on one nature was the logical result of the condemnation of Nestorius' emphasis on two distinct aspects, one human and the other divine. Those who opposed Eutyches, however, argued that a fused new nature compromised the Son's full humanity, thus threatening the possibility of salvation. The one-nature teachings of Eutyches were condemned in AD 448 at a synod summoned by the bishop of Constantinople, then approved at the so-called "Robber Council" that met in Ephesus in AD 449 (the label "robber," *latrocinium*, was coined by Pope Leo), and then condemned again at the ecumenical Council of Chalcedon in AD 451. While this ecumenical council marked one more step in the formation of an imperial orthodoxy, it also resulted in a second theological schism within Syriac Christianity that would never be resolved. While few claimed the extreme (and condemned) one-nature teachings of Eutyches, the Syrian Orthodox Church of today is one of several (including the Coptic Church, the Armenian Church, and the Ethiopic Church) that reject the outcome of the Council of Chalcedon and maintain that a miaphysite (single nature) understanding of the Son is true Christian orthodoxy, consistent with earlier doctrine. (The once common term "monophysite" was coined as an insult against "one-nature" parties, and is for that reason now less favored.) Other Syriac Christians, known as Melkite (or Byzantine) Christians, because of their association with the Byzantine emperor, accepted the Council of Chalcedon's authority; a majority, however, sharply rejected the compromise that they thought the council represented.

This theological controversy, and the politics surrounding it, continued unabated in the eastern empire in the century that followed the Council of Chalcedon. Subsequent emperors alternately supported either side of the schism. The emperor Zeno, by his *Henotikon* of AD 482, made a further attempt to reconcile the two sides, and his successor Anastasius also offered support for the miaphysite Christians. As a result, miaphysite Christians in the late fifth and early sixth centuries were able to establish their own churches, monasteries, and episcopal structure, even though the majority of fifth- and sixth-century emperors supported the Council of Chalcedon. While in the end the emperor Justinian's attempts at compromise failed, the sporadic support granted to miaphysite leaders, including that attributed to the empress Theodora (d. AD 548), allowed the survival of a competing episcopacy in some of the major cities of the east, including Edessa. During the reign of Justinian and Theodora, Theodosius, the exiled miaphysite bishop of Alexandria, ordained Theodore as bishop of Bostra, the center of the miaphysite Ghassanid Arabs, and ordained Jacob Baradaeus bishop of Edessa. Even though the views of pro-Chalcedon Christians eventually triumphed as the imperial orthodoxy of the Byzantine Empire, this century of struggle allowed miaphysite Christians to survive as a minority within the empire until, in the seventh century, Persian and Arabian invasions divided the region politically from the Greek-speaking world. Although the surviving miaphysites have often been called "Jacobite" (after Jacob Baradaeus) as well as "monophysite," in most cases they reject both titles today in favor of "Syrian Orthodoxy."

When the Persians, under Khusro II, invaded the Byzantine Empire in the first decades of the seventh century, eastern Syria temporarily fell under Persian control. Although the Byzantine emperor Heraclius reclaimed this territory for Byzantium, much of the same territory was, within the decade following Khusro's deposition in AD 628, once again severed from Constantinople's control, this time by invading Muslim Arab armies. With Byzantium's loss of Damascus, Antioch, and Edessa in the late AD 630s, Syriac miaphysite Christians found themselves no longer "heretics" under a hostile Christian government, but a tolerated "people of the book" under Muslim rule. This historical happenstance had the dual result that miaphysite Syriac Christianity survived with less struggle in the following centuries than it might have faced had it remained within the Byzantine Empire, and that (like the Church of the East in Persia) it became in some significant ways non-Byzantine. That is not to suggest that the centuries of Greek influence disappeared, or that Syria became utterly cut off from the Greek-speaking world. As with the Church of the East, however, it does explain why Syriac language and history were not well preserved in the west.

Conclusion

The succession of seventh-century military conquests that politically separated Syria from Byzantine control also effectively changed Syria's role in our western histories, and buried the late antique period of interaction beneath centuries of perceived discontinuity and difference. Though bounded on either side by political ties that help to explain western history's idiosyncratic treatment of eastern Syria, the history of Late Antiquity reveals Syria to have been deeply involved in the largely familiar events of Roman and Byzantine history. We cannot add Syria to these narratives of Roman history, however, without also changing those very reconstructions, so that we take into account what scholars have until now largely understood to be the decidedly unorthodox (and sometimes un-Roman) history of eastern Syria. Whether in texts from the first or the twentieth century, Syria frequently emerges as an exotic Other, tantalizingly near yet unquestionably culturally distinct from the western authors' realm of the familiar. Late Antiquity itself, however, was a period in Syria's history during which its peoples not only adopted much from their western neighbors but also shared much in return. The story of fourth-century Syria disallows, for example, traditional narratives of "Christianity's" early clear separation from "Judaism," and scholars would lose vital information about fourth-century Christianity if they did not take Ephrem's pro-Nicene writings into account alongside those of his Greek contemporaries.

Western Syria, though not the focus of this chapter, was a region that helped to connect eastern Syria with the rest of the Roman Empire. While Greek was the predominant language of the major city of Roman Antioch, the smaller towns surrounding Antioch were predominantly Syriac-speaking, as Theodoret's visits to Syriac-speaking monks attest (Theodoret, *Historia religiosa*). Antioch is Greek, and therefore familiar, but it is also Syrian. Antioch served as an important point of linguistic and cultural contact as well as of textual, conceptual, and cultural translation that should make us consider more seriously its multilingual culture. Quick generalizations that Antioch was "Greek" while Edessa was "Syriac" base too much on the differences in the majority language and degrees of Hellenization in the two cities; but such generalities veil at the same time the overlapping culture that existed in both cities. The description of those commonalities will help us to rethink both the difference and the disconnectedness of the Syriac east and the all too easy separation of Syrian Antioch from that eastern Syriac world. Antioch was, on the one hand, a religious and political center, hosting emperors and ecclesiastical councils, and evangelized by the apostle Paul. On the other hand, Antioch remained within Syria, surrounded by Syriac-speaking ascetics, and troubled by Judaizing Christians in John Chrysostom's lifetime. By reconnecting late antique Antioch with Edessa, scholars will gain a more comprehensive image of Roman Syria, and will see better the diversity of what we call "Syrian" as well as the connections between what we distinguish as "Syriac" and "Greek."

Syria serves as an example of how late antique places and people were at once local and imperial. Scholars agree, for good reason, with late antique writers that the major cities of Alexandria, Rome, and Constantinople were more imperially influential than Edessa, and that the influence of authors such as Rabbula was more locally confined than that of Athanasius. Nonetheless, Ephrem adopted imperial pro-Nicene rhetoric even though he wrote in Syriac, and he is therefore valuable to discussions of fourth-century imperial politics and theological controversy, just as he is as he is to discussions of Syria. Major figures like John Chrysostom and Augustine were likewise local authors influenced by their contexts, but also became spokesmen for much larger Christian communities. The Syriac voices in what are thought of as the margins of the empire remind us how fruitful it can be to think also of traditional centers as uniquely local communities with individual particularities that persisted, as in Ephrem's Syria, despite a rhetorical veil of imperial normativity. In this sense, then, the apparent idiosyncrasies that have set Syria apart in traditional narratives become not the exception in Late Antiquity but the rule. By recognizing the ways in which Syria remained both "eastern" to its Greek and Latin counterparts and "western" in its Mediterranean connections, scholars can better reconstruct both Syria and the Roman-Byzantine Empire of which Syria was a part.

BIBLIOGRAPHICAL NOTE

Many of the foundational works on early Roman Syria no longer reflect the most recent scholarship in the field. The following nonetheless remain important starting points: Burkitt 1904, Vööbus 1951, Drijvers 1980, Segal 2001, Murray 2004. The numerous translations, original scholarship, and bibliographic resources of Sebastian Brock, perhaps the most notable western scholar of early Syriac Christianity, greatly enrich the field; see, for example, Brock 1997 and his regular contributions to *Hugoye: Journal of Syriac Studies*. While most of these earlier works focus on Christianity (with the exception of Drijvers), Millar 1993 and Ross 2001 present broader historical narratives.

Sidney Griffith's influential works demonstrate Syria's significant early ties with the Roman world (Griffith 1986, 1999b) and its later interactions with Islam (Griffith 2001). Possekel 1999 is a noteworthy contribution to the early conversation about the extent of Greek influence, linguistic and otherwise, in eastern Syria. Mimouni 1994, Rouwhorst 1997, Van Rompay 1997, and Weitzman 1999 provide influential arguments in the ongoing discussion of liturgical and scriptural connections between Jewish and Christian communities in the region. Susan Ashbrook Harvey's work on women in early Syriac Christianity expanded the field significantly (Harvey 2005, Brock and Harvey 1987).

Recent works (Becker 2006, Harvey 2006, Shepardson 2008) use a variety of contemporary methodological approaches and actively integrate scholarship on Roman Syria into broader academic conversations on Late Antiquity. The journal *Hugoye: Journal of Syriac Studies* and the online discussion lists associated with it provide valuable, accessible forums for scholarly discussion in the field of Syriac studies.

CHAPTER THIRTY-ONE

Syria and the Arabs

David Cook

Arabs, like most groups in the Middle East of Late Antiquity, were defined mostly by language. The terrain of Syria, enclosed as it is between the Mediterranean Sea on one side and the beginnings of the desert on the other, allowed for a considerable flow of nomadic and semi-nomadic peoples to move back and forth, especially in the extreme north around the area of Antioch, and the extreme south in Palestine. In general, the Greek-speaking population was strongest in the major cities (Antioch, Damascus, Jerusalem, and along the coast), while the Aramaic-speaking population (Jews, Samaritans, and others) predominated in the countryside and in smaller towns. In this latter region, semi-nomads speaking Arabic intermingled freely with the Aramaic-speaking population, raiding and trading intermittently.

Because many of the major towns of Syria existed either within an oasis surrounded by marginal land or deep desert, or proximate to such regions, there was no firm differentiation between the Hellenized city-dwellers, the Aramaic country-dwellers, and the (presumably) Arabic-speaking nomads. The earliest Arabic inscriptions that come from Syria use either an Aramaic dialect or the Greek script for the Arabic language, and the names of the people indicate a considerable blending of ethnicities (Hoyland 2001: 236–7). This blending remained a constant for the period under discussion. In genealogical tables derived from the Table of Nations (Gen. 10), there was usually a place for Arabs, or at least a note concerning the nomads of the Arabian Peninsula.

But not all of the peoples that would later be called Arabs were nomads. In general, those tribes closest to Syria were semi-nomadic and, while depending upon the camel for their subsistence, also raised other livestock such as sheep and goats, and were known for their skill with the horse (which cannot survive in the deep desert). In a number of marginal regions in present-day Israel (the Negev), Jordan, and Syria, either Arabs or their close relatives practiced dry farming and sold their goods at local markets or major hubs such as Jerusalem or Damascus. Trading routes from the southern desert of Arabia crossed this region, and the semi-nomads made their living by providing guides and protection to these caravans or, alternatively, by raiding and looting them.

It was due to this latter tendency of raiding and looting that there was such hostility towards the semi-nomads and nomads on the part of the settled population of Syria. In general, the sources present the Arabs as an unruly bunch, whose primary function in life was to destroy civilization or to test the faith of the believers. It is not unusual to find reflections of these negative attitudes in such early Muslim sources as the following:

> 'Abdallah b. Hawwala said: We were with the Messenger of God [Muhammad], and we complained to him about the poverty, the nakedness and the general lack of things. The Messenger of God said: "Take heart, because I am more worried about the plethora of things for you. This matter [of Islam] will continue until you have conquered the lands of Persia and the Byzantines and Himyar [Yemen]." Ibn Hawwala said: "O Messenger of God, who could possibly take Syria when the many-horned Byzantines [*al-rum dhat al-qurun*] are in it?" He said: "God will conquer it for you and appoint you as successors in it, until a group of them [the Byzantines] will be white-robed, with shaved necks, standing in service for a little black man [i.e., an Arab] – whatever he tells them to do, they do it. [This will happen] even though today there are men in it [Syria] who view you as more contemptible than the lice which inhabit the buttocks of camels." (al-Tabarani 1996, iii: 396)

Negative attitudes, however, were almost certainly not the whole truth. The settled population, the semi-nomads, and the nomads in Syria intermingled because of mutual economic necessity, because of intermarriage in many cases, and because of common beliefs (usually Christianity).

The Byzantine Empire and the Arabs

The relationship of the Byzantine Empire with the Arab population of Syria was federal in character (Shahîd 1989, 1995). Major tribes located along the settled regions of Syria-Palestine such as Salih, Tanukh, and Ghassan were allowed, even encouraged, to establish state-like entities whose function would be to police the semi-nomadic regions and to punish tribes in the deep desert whose raids could not be controlled. In addition, each of these federate tribes undertook to protect Syria-Palestine from the primary enemy: Sasanian Persia and its federate state, the Lakhmids (based in southern Iraq). Occasionally, the federate tribes were also allowed police functions within the territory of the empire, such as the suppression of the Samaritan revolt in AD 529.

There were tensions, however, between the Byzantines and their federates, especially the Ghassanids, whose capital south of Damascus was a major cultural center for northern Arabs. The primary tensions stemmed from the fact that the Ghassanids were strongly miaphysite (whereas the Byzantine emperors espoused orthodoxy). This sectarian adherence put the Ghassanid dynasty not only at odds with the distant capital of Constantinople, but more immediately with the strongly orthodox region of southern Palestine (centered on Jerusalem), which bordered their territory to the south.

But this tension, although occasionally leading to the Byzantines removing or exiling various Ghassanids rulers, was not such that the Ghassanids were actually moved to revolt or betray the trust placed in them. On the contrary, the Ghassanids fought on the side of the Byzantines very successfully against their perennial rivals in Iraq, the Lakhmids, despite the fact that the latter were also miaphysite (as well as a substantial percentage of the Christians in the Sasanian Empire), and are not known to have harbored traitorous leanings (Shahîd 1995: 439–40). During the Persian invasion of Syria and occupation (AD 612–28), the Ghassanids fought on the side of the Byzantines, and there exists circumstantial evidence that the Byzantines tried to reinstate them as federates during the brief period of Byzantine control (AD 628–36), after the Persians were defeated. In general, the federate relationship between the Arabs of Syria and the Byzantines was one of mutual benefit.

Not only that: there were positive social relations on the common level between Arabs and the many monks and anchorites in the region of Syria-Palestine. The Muslim literature, especially the ascetic literature that flourished during the eighth and ninth centuries, is replete with anecdotes that remind us of this positive reality:

> A [Arab] man passed by a monk and said: O monk, how [often] do you remember death? He said: I never lift my foot or put the other [down] without remembering that I am [as good as] dead. He said: And how is your [spiritual] striving? He said: I have never heard of anyone who has heard of paradise or hell without praying every hour. The man said: I pray and weep until my tears cause vegetables to grow. The monk said: If you laugh and confess your sins to God, you are better than if you weep while you are straying in your actions. Prayer of the erring [man] does not rise above him. The man said: Teach me. The monk said: You must practice asceticism in the world, and do not let its people influence you. (Ibn Abi Shayba 1979: 13. 491–2)

This type of anecdote could be multiplied hundreds of times. The monks lived close to the nomads and semi-nomads (as they continue to do today – for example, in the Monastery of St. Catherine at Mt. Sinai): the relationship was symbiotic and to the benefit of both sides.

Conquest of Syria by the Arabs/Muslims

The tribes deeper in the Arabian Desert did not necessarily share the cozy relationship between the Byzantines and the semi-nomads close to Syria. Inter-Arab rivalries, such as the one between the "northern" and "southern" tribes (descriptions that have no basis in the relative geographical distribution of these tribes), played a key role in undermining the Ghassanids, especially once the latter had been deprived of Byzantine support. With the rise of the Prophet Muhammad, the years following AD 629 were ones in which the fledgling Muslim community sought to expand its influence northward along the series of oasis caravan stops (Fadak, Khaybar, Dumat al-Jandal, etc.) that lead along the Hijaz up to Syria. This expansion was redoubled after the conquest of Mecca in AD 630, especially as a result of the conversion of the Umayyad family (closely related to Muhammad, but until that time his primary foes), which had traditional commercial ties to Syria.

These commercial ties were now linked together with the Islamic veneration for Jerusalem (the first direction for Muslim prayer) and insured that the Byzantines, who had recently reconquered Syria-Palestine from the Persians, would be attacked by the Muslims. There are other reasons for this attack, which commenced in AD 633, among them the fact that the usual pattern of intertribal raiding was banned by the appearance of Islam. There may have been other religious reasons for this attack as well, including possibly the feeling that the Byzantines (Romans) were responsible for the destruction of the Second Temple and the murder of the prophets (Jesus and John the Baptist) and should be made to answer for these actions.

For whatever reasons, the Byzantines were ill-equipped to repel the Muslim attack, small though it was. Having gone through the Byzantine–Sasanian war (AD 602–28), which effectively bled both empires white, and having previously canceled its alliance with the Ghassanids, which led to disaffection among the Arabs of Syria, the empire was at its weakest in AD 633. It had not had the opportunity to rebuild the defenses of the region of southern Syria-Palestine, or to reforge the alliances with local, Christian Arab tribes that could have defeated the Muslims.

Unfortunately, the sources concerning the Muslim conquest of Syria-Palestine (like many of the sources for early Islam) are so problematic and contradictory that it is difficult to establish the basic course of events. Nor do non-Muslim sources clarify the events to the extent we could wish, and there are apparently no surviving contemporary accounts of the conquest from either Muslims or non-Muslims. These facts open up the possibility that the Muslim accounts, which are designed to augment the fame of various personalities or tribes, or to prove that the conquest demonstrates the truth of Islam, are all unreliable. Scholars of Islamic history have not yet resolved this problem.

In the Muslim sources, we have initial probes by local Muslims by AD 633, designed mainly to achieve domination over the local Arab population, then the arrival of the noted commander Khalid b. al-Walid in AD 634 (Donner 1981: 112–27). Khalid almost immediately pushed the conquest forward, capturing Damascus in AD 635 after a series of battles in present-day northern Jordan (Ajnadayn, Fihl, etc.). The Byzantines returned, however, and reoccupied Damascus, chasing the Muslims to Yarmuk (on the present-day border between Syria and Jordan) where the former were decisively defeated in AD 636. During the next five years, the Muslims occupied most of Syria, up to the area of Antioch. Jerusalem was captured in AD 636, and the coast-lands were reduced by sieges during the years that followed.

For the most part, the Muslims in Syria during this period (and part of the Ummayad period that followed it) organized themselves along tribal lines and had their centers close to, but not inside, the major cities. The Arab centers close to Damascus – Jabiya (the old capital of the Ghassanids), Harasta, and Dariya (al-Khawlani 1989: 52–60) – were the major power base; but others existed in the region of the northern Negev (Lecker) and in the town of Hims (Emesa), which was the hub for conquest to the north. Ghassan, however, fell from importance, and the major tribes during the Umayyad period were Kalb (which had inhabited the desert to the east of Damascus) and Tanukh (which had formerly been the Byzantines' federate tribe). Throughout the early Umayyad period, these tribes were probably at least partially Christian, their full conversion to Islam being delayed until the beginning of the eighth century.

The northern region close to Hims became the hotbed for southern tribesmen who emigrated there in large numbers and stayed to fight the Byzantines (Madelung 1986). It is in this region, and further to the north in Antioch, that we find so much of the borderland ethos that was to become important in the development of the doctrine of *jihad*. During the latter part of the seventh century, the Byzantines (especially under Justinian II, AD 685–95 and 705–14) mounted a still mysterious guerrilla campaign using the Mardaites-Jarajima (Chalhoub 1999). These peoples, or groups, occupied the area of the northern Amanus Mountains, possibly as far south as the Lebanon Mountains, and terrorized the Muslims. Eventually, the Mardaites were withdrawn, as the result of a mutual agreement with the Byzantines.

The conquest of Syria by the Arabs occurred progressively over a fifty-year period, although most of the major conquests happened within the first fifteen years after AD 633. But the Byzantines were unwilling to give up this valuable and strategic province without a series of additional battles and attempts to reconquer it. Not until the end of the seventh century did the Byzantines actually acknowledge that Syria was lost to them for ever.

Importance of Syria to the Arabs/Muslims

Syria's importance to the Arabs and Muslims (at this period virtually all Muslims were Arab, but not all Arabs were Muslim) had a number of different sources. One has been discussed above: the religious importance accorded to Syria by Islam. Since Islam was seen as the final revelation, after a number of previous abrogated revelations (mostly at the hands of biblical prophets), it was important for Muslims to control territorially the region where most of those revelations occurred – that is, Syria. This control demonstrated to the outside world the truth of Islam as the final revelation, as well as God's favor upon it.

Most critical to that demonstration of God's favor was control of the city of Jerusalem. Starting shortly after the conquest of the city in AD 636, the Muslims began to revitalize the area of the former Temple Mount, which had probably lain fallow for some 500 years, since the destruction of the Second Temple (AD 70). At first, the Muslim project involved building a rude mosque into the southern retaining wall of the temple complex, but later focused on the bedrock exposed in the middle of the semi-rectangular platform. This rock was commonly held to have been the rock upon which Abraham was to have sacrificed his son Isaac (later, in the Muslim reinterpretation, Ishmael; Gen. 22), and possibly to have been the locality of the Holy of Holies during the time of the Second Temple (Elad 1995).

By the early Umayyad period the caliph 'Abd al-Malik (AD 685–705) sought to commemorate this tradition by building a Byzantine-style octagonal structure on top of the rock, called the Dome of the Rock (completed AD 691). Within a generation or two, this structure had acquired new Islamic significance, as it was attached to the story of the Prophet Muhammad's Night Journey and Ascension into heaven (*al-Isra' wa-l-mi'raj*; see Qur'an 17. 1–2). Given the fact that Jerusalem already had an aura of holiness about it, from the early period when it was the first direction of Muslim prayer, it was inevitable that it would become a center for pilgrimage as well. Other local holy sites such as the patriarchal tombs in Hebron also acquired Muslim significance, and, by the end of the Umayyad dynasty, various sites began to appear dedicated to holy figures said to have miraculous powers.

But for the Umayyads overall, whose capital was in the city of Damascus, the strategic importance of Syria itself cannot be underestimated. Their empire stretched from Spain and North Africa through Egypt to Iraq, Persia, and Central Asia. An empire of this breadth would be difficult to manage even today; during the seventh and eighth centuries, communication across and between such a wide range of territories required control over Syria, which stood literally at their heart. The Arabs also benefited from the fact that during the Umayyad period they were in control of the settled regions that were lusher and more bountiful than the marginal regions to which they were accustomed. They did not want to give them up at all. Apocalyptic traditions from the late Umayyad period reflect this reality:

> I [Kuhayl b. Harmala al-Namari] heard Abu Hurayra [the companion of Muhammad] say: How will it be for you when you are pushed out of it [Syria] village by village to the edge of the land called Hisma' of Judham [southern Jordan], where you will not receive either silver or gold, and neither Nabati, Greek, Jurjumi nor Mardaite will serve you. How will you be when you are pushed out of it village by village to the edge of the land called Hisma' of Judham? (Ibn 'Asakir 1995–8: 38. 426; al-Marwazi 1993: 286)

This fear was very real – understandably so, when one considers that the Mardaites-Jarajima did actually control much of the northern part of Syria until the end of the seventh century. Moreover, the most important enemies of the Umayyads were the Byzantines, and so control of Syria, close to the Byzantine border (usually just north of Antioch) was a strategic necessity. Thus, a combination of sacred and strategic factors made Syria extremely important to the early Muslims.

The Umayyad Dynasty in Syria and Egypt

The Umayyad dynasty took its legitimacy from the fact that it was among the close relatives of Muhammad (although, as I have said, most of its prominent personalities had opposed him during his lifetime) and that it avenged the assassination of its close relative the caliph 'Uthman in AD 656. Since the assassins were given refuge and in some cases high office by 'Uthman's successor, 'Ali b. Abi Talib (AD 656–61), the long-time governor of Syria-Palestine, Mu'awiya, had a good excuse to oppose and eventually to defeat him. The Umayyad dynasty made Damascus its center, although, true to its Arab heritage and marriage links, members of the extended family spent much of their time in the series of outlying settlements often called "the desert castles" (see below) and, toward the middle of the eighth century, moved their power bases progressively northward and eastward.

Conventionally, the Umayyad dynasty is divided into several periods: that of Mu'awiya and his son Yazid I (AD 661–83), called the Sufyanid period, and that of the Marwanid family (AD 683–747), comprising 'Abd al-Malik, his four sons and several other close relatives. In general, the Sufyanid period was noted for conquest and left a collective memory of wealth in the Arab tradition. For centuries after the fall of the Sufyanids, the figure of the Sufyani remained the focus of messianic expectations among Syrian Arabs.

But the more obvious conquests are associated with the early Marwanids, especially with 'Abd al-Malik and his son al-Walid I (AD 705–15), under whom the areas of North Africa and Spain, as well as most of the region of Central Asia were conquered. Both of these rulers were also well known for their monumental building projects, such as the Dome of the Rock in Jerusalem and the Umayyad Mosque in Damascus (as well as others scattered around the Muslim world). The tradition of conquest continued under the other three sons of 'Abd al-Malik, but increasingly the Arabs lacked the manpower to conquer further territories, or else the supply lines to distant battlefields were simply too long. A major attempt to conquer Constantinople, the capital of the Byzantine Empire, failed in AD 715–17. This reverse is reflected in some of the most popular apocalyptic traditions from Syria (especially Hims) concerning the future conquest of Constantinople, dating from that period:

> You will raid Constantinople three times: the first time you will meet with disaster and hardship, the second time there will be a peace between you and them – such that mosques will be built in Constantinople and you will raid behind Constantinople together with them, then they will go back on it [the peace agreement]. The third raid will be when God will conquer it with cries of *allahu akbar* [God is greater!], and it will be in three parts: one third will be destroyed, one third will be burned, and one third will be divided up and weighed out [as spoils]. (al-Marwazi 1993: 288)

This promised final conquest of Constantinople, however, the foremost desire of Syrian Muslims during the Umayyad period, never came about (at least for hundreds of years). In fact, the following years saw a series of reverses in the battlefield that Blankinship has rightly called "The End of the Jihad State" (Blankinship 1994). Hisham (AD 724–743), the last of the sons of 'Abd al-Malik to rule, was by sheer willpower able to keep the Umayyad state intact, even with the defeats that punctuated his reign. But the final group of Umayyad rulers (AD 743–7), mostly grandsons of 'Abd al-Malik, were unable to hold it together, and were overcome by the 'Abbasid revolution during the AD 740s.

The Umayyad dynasty is usually interpreted as a tribal Arab dynasty with little connection to Islam. Indeed, balancing the warring tribes in Syria, and especially in

Iraq, was a major part of the policy of any of their rulers. In general, this involved favoring tribes either from the "southern" or the "northern" Arabs. When one group was in favor, it usually suppressed or oppressed the other. For the most part, the Umayyads favored the southern tribes and brilliantly reworked the genealogy of a number of tribes of indistinct origins to assimilate them into the mostly southern oriented coalition they built in Syria. Tribal differences in Syria were kept to a minimum by severely curtailing which tribes could actually enter the province.

Many of these tribes were fiercely partisan, and some of their partisan propaganda has come down to us in the form of apocalyptic traditions, especially from Hims, where the dominant tribes were Yemenite (southern). They strongly opposed the official mosque, describing the people there as a "mixture" and as the mosque of Satan (the Christian church of St. Mary):

> There are three mosques in Hims: one belonging to Satan and his people – meaning Satan's – and a mosque belonging to God whose people are Satan's, and a mosque belonging to God whose people are God's. The Church of Mary and its people are the "mosque" belonging to Satan and Satan's people; as to the mosque belonging to God whose people are Satan's – [their] mosque and its people are a mixture of people, and the mosque belonging to God whose people are God's is the "mosque" of the Church of Zakariyya. Its people are Himyar and the people of Yemen gather in it. (al-Marwazi 1993: 255)

With this kind of atmosphere, it is not surprising that the Umayyads had difficulties controlling the disturbances between the northern and southern tribes in Syria.

It would be a mistake to say, however, that the Umayyads were entirely secular. It is true that the remains of their so-called desert castles bear frescoes that portray scenes of drinking and other un-Islamic activities. But in other, more formal ways, the Umayyads strongly supported Islam and made strenuous efforts not to be assimilated into the cultural sphere of the Christian Mediterranean basin. 'Abd al-Malik, for example, arabized the language of the administration, as well as turning away from the coinage minted by the Byzantines. His coins were the first to bear Islamic slogans and symbols. Until this occurred, there had been strong economic ties between the Byzantines and the Arabs of Syria:

> The Byzantine emperor wrote to 'Abd al-Malik b. Marwan: You have made new changes in the *qaratis* [coinage] – that which was never done previously. If you do not stop doing this, I will cause your prophet [Muhammad] to be cursed in everything that is done in my realm. 'Abd al-Malik was worried about this, and Da'ud b. Yazid b. Mu'awiya [grandson of the caliph Mu'awiya] entered in to him and saw him worried by what had arrived to him. He said: "Strike lesser dinars and dirhems than his dinars, and make the name of the Messenger of God clear on them so that you will not need what is being struck with him" so he ceased [being worried]; this was in the year 689–690. (Ibn 'Asakir 1995–8: 17. 195)

This break with the Byzantines was probably the most significant event in the entire Umayyad period, as it was essentially a declaration of cultural and economic independence from what had been until then the more dominant state bordering upon Syria to the north. It also indicates the religious nature of the Umayyad disagreement with the Byzantines, in which the issue of Muhammad's status as a prophet was of primary importance. The Umayyads took the title of "God's Caliph," meaning that they saw themselves as the viceregents of God on earth, and they exercised that authority by involving themselves in religious disputations (Crone and Hinds 1986). Thus, for them the war with the Byzantines was also one concerning religious authority.

Cultural Achievements of the Arabs in Syria

The Arabs in Syria were the cultural heirs of the Hellenistic civilization that had preceded them. Indeed, at the time of the Arab-Muslim conquest, there was no decisive break with that civilization. The Greek language continued to be employed in the court for some fifty years after that conquest, and even after that time it was still widely used. Byzantine artisans and architects planned and built the major buildings used by the Arabs, such as the Dome of the Rock in Jerusalem, the Umayyad Mosque in Damascus (formerly the Church of St. John), and the desert castles. Among these desert castles is the magnificent complex at Qasr al-Khayr al-Sharqi (to the north of Palmyra), where, on a large cultivated region, a palace was constructed. Although, in the past, these desert castles have been seen as locations for pleasure and for enjoying the desert life, today it is more common to see them as agricultural centers, as the Arabs continued the practice of dry farming in the marginal areas of the Negev and eastern Syria. Other locations, such as at Jericho, are more obviously palaces and contain magnificent mosaics.

The other major cultural achievement of the Arabs in Syria was poetry. Poetry was already a major factor in pre-Islamic Arabia, where it was used to express the gamut of emotions from love to vengeance to loss, as well as to commemorate important events and to praise or pillory important personalities. Because of the wealth and power of the Umayyads, their patronage was widely sought, and first class poets flourished at their various courts. Among these, the best known was al-Akhtal (d. *c.* AD 710), a Christian Arab whose *diwan* (collection of poems) is considered one of the finest. Many of his poems celebrate wine-bibbing, and are decidedly non-Islamic:

> We drank, and then we died the death of the Jahiliyya [pre-Islamic times], whose people have gone; they never knew Muhammad.
>
> Three days and when we returned to ourselves, it [the soul] came back to us. (al-Akhtal, nd.: 384)

Poems like this exist in abundance and demonstrate the blending of cultures at the nexus between Muslim, Arab, and Christian, since al-Akhtal had prestige among all three groups.

Christians, Jews, and Samaritans in Syria during the Umayyad Period

In all of these cultural achievements, the non-Muslim population played a key role, often providing much of the artisanship. During the Umayyad period, the vast bulk of the population was non-Muslim, and Islamization was probably delayed even among certain Arab tribes, such as Kalb and Ghassan, that had been historically Christian. This was much more the case in the settled regions, and especially in the larger cities, where Christianity was strongly identified with the Hellenistic heritage and seen as the higher culture.

During the early Umayyad period, Christians often held very high political office. The most noteworthy example is the family of St. John of Damascus, who was himself apparently a high official in the service of the Umayyads until the early eighth century. But his father al-Mansur (Sergius) is much better known; he served Mu'awiya and Yazid I as their primary minister, apparently without converting to Islam at all. (Some reports indicate that al-Mansur's grandfather was responsible for the surrender of Damascus to the Arabs in the AD 630 s, but this is uncertain.) It is interesting to note that St. John and other prominent Christians were orthodox; they did not serve the Umayyads because they had been persecuted by the Byzantines.

Not all Christians were as friendly to the Muslims as St. John and his circle. Toward the end of the seventh century, "The Apocalypse of Pseudo-Methodius" began to circulate, apparently written by a miaphysite (in northern Mesopotamia). This apocalypse reveals a considerable degree of hatred for the Muslims and a need to present their coming as a fulfillment of the signs of the apocalypse:

> This [the Arab-Muslim invasion] is the chastisement of which the Apostle [2 Thess. 2: 3] spoke: "The chastisement must come first, only then will that Man of Sin, the Son of Destruction, be revealed." This chastisement is not being sent only upon human beings, but upon everything that is on the face of the entire earth – on men, women, children, animals, cattle, birds. People will be tormented by that punishment – men, their wives, sons, daughters and possessions; the old who are weak, the sick and the strong, the poor along with the rich. For God called their forefather Ishmael "the wild ass of the wilderness" [Gen. 16: 12] ... For these barbarian tyrants are not men, but "children of desolation"; they set their faces towards desolation, and they are destroyers: they shall be sent for [or, to] devastation; they are destruction, and they shall issue forth for the destruction of everything. They are defiled, and they love defilement. At the time of their issuing forth from the wilderness they will snatch babies from their mothers' arms, dashing them against stones, as though they were unclean beasts. (*Apocalypse of Ps.-Methodius*, tr. Brock in Palmer 1993: 233–4)

Pseudo-Methodius reflects the negative feelings that some Christians had toward being ruled by Muslims, and he refutes to a large degree the claims that large numbers of Christians saw the conquests as a liberation (see also Hoyland 2001, who assembles a vast quantity of evidence along those lines).

There is very little information about Jews or Samaritans during the Umayyad period. We know from previous times that there were large communities of both groups in Palestine, and that Jews were compelled to settle along the coastal regions during the middle Umayyad period, but neither group attracted much attention. There was a close relationship, however, between the Jewish community of Jerusalem at least and the Dome of the Rock (the traditional site of the Second Temple, destroyed in AD 70), such that "the Jews would light [the candles] in Jerusalem (i.e. the Dome of the Rock) until 'Umar b. 'Abd al-'Aziz became ruler [AD 717–20], and he put them out, and made those from the *akhmas* [slaves] perform this task" (al-Wasiti 1979: 43–4).

In general, as long as they were not actively disloyal to the rulers, the Christian majority and the Jewish and Samaritan minorities did not have many difficulties with the Muslims in Syria during the Umayyad period. When there was some threat of disloyalty, then the Arabs often reacted in a harsh manner, massacring various Christian communities (like that of Hims) suspected of treachery. But for the most part, the harsh laws of the sharia upon Jews and Christians were far in the future, and there is not much substantial evidence that large numbers of them wanted the Byzantines to return.

Assessment of the Arabs in Syria and their Relationship to the Classical World

It would be incorrect to say that there was a cultural break at the time of the Arab-Muslim conquest, and yet, something did fundamentally change. The Arab-Muslims who conquered Syria were not like other various barbarian groups throughout the Mediterranean basin: they did not convert to Christianity (or even a heretical sect of it). They developed their own culture, based upon and incorporating large elements of the previous Hellenistic culture, but still distinctly Arab-Muslim. Although large numbers of settled Christians did not convert to Islam during the Umayyad period, by the end of the dynasty most of the nomadic and semi-nomadic Arabs were Muslims. By the middle of the Umayyad period, even the Ghassanids, so long the mainstay of Christianity in the region, were producing prominent Muslim scholars from their own ranks. Thus, even at that early period, the stage was set for the Islamization of Syria.

Other changes are apparent as well. The coastal cities, for example, clearly declined during the period of Umayyad rule, even though the Umayyads themselves made serious attempts to gain parity with the Byzantines on the sea (and defeated them a number of times). It was difficult to find Muslim populations willing to settle in coastal regions, and so non-Arabs (Jews, Persians, etc.) frequently had to be dragooned. Often, the Christian populations of the sea coasts were disloyal to the Muslims, and so had to be moved to the interior of Syria. There was a marked decline also in agriculture along the coastal regions from this period onward, in addition to the whole-scale abandonment of towns and villages that, especially in the north, was already in train when the Muslims arrived (Foss 1995; Schick 1995). But the major cities, such as Damascus and Jerusalem, saw a revival as a result of the close proximity of the government and the monumental building projects that took place in them. Even that revival, however, was brought to an end by the 'Abbasid revolution in AD 747, and Syria entered upon another period of more radical decline.

BIBLIOGRAPHICAL NOTE

The Umayyad period in Syria is severely underresearched. Virtually no Arabic sources from the Umayyad period itself survive; most of the contemporaneous Syriac and Greek sources are translated by Palmer 1993 and summarized by Hoyland 1997. The best available sources about Syria from the early 'Abbasid period are the two books on *jihad* and asceticism by 'Abdallah b. al-Mubarak (d. AD 797), and the apocalyptic book of Nu'aym b. Hammad al-Marwazi (d. AD 844). In addition to these meagre sources, there is the *History* of Abu Zur'a al-Dimashqi (written *c.* AD 894–5), problematic and spare, a few other minor historians from the ninth century, and then the mammoth (75-volume) *History of the City of Damascus* by Ibn 'Asakir (d. AD 1175 or 1176). The problem with using Ibn 'Asakir is not the quantity of information contained within it (which remains virtually untapped), but the lurking suspicion that much of it is back-projection, and there is little against which to test it. The archaeology of the early Muslim period in Syria remains in its infancy as well; the most important work today is done in Jordan and in the northern Negev. Many sites in Syria and Lebanon remain untouched (except by looters).

CHAPTER THIRTY-TWO

The Early Caliphate and the Inheritance of Late Antiquity (*c.* AD 610–*c.* AD 750)

Andrew Marsham

The rise of Islam turned the late antique Near East inside out. Rome and Sasanian Iran, who had faced one another across the "Fertile Crescent" of Syria and Mesopotamia for 400 years, were defeated in two decades of campaigning by Arab tribesmen in the AD 630s and 640s. The Roman Empire went on to lose all its African and Asian territories except Anatolia, while the Sasanian Empire was completely destroyed. Christianity, which had long been established as the religion of the Roman Empire and had been gaining ground in Iran, became the faith of a subject people, superseded by a new, Arabic revelation. Syria and Mesopotamia, which had been divided by the heavily fortified frontier between the two empires, became, from the AD 660s, the heartland of the new empire. It was here that the palaces and cities of the caliphs were founded, far from the new frontiers in Anatolia, North Africa, and Transoxiana (see Map 6).

This chapter traces the emergence of the first imperial Islamic state, which replaced the two late antique empires of the Near East. That is, it describes the history of the Islamic polity from Muhammad's first revelation in *c.* AD 610 until the fall of the Umayyad caliphate in AD 750. Viewed in the context of late antique history, two features of the development of this polity are particularly striking. The first is the importance of the inheritance of Iran. Although the Umayyad caliphs ruled from what had been Roman Syria, Iranian culture exerted an increasing influence on their court and administration. The 'Abbasid revolution of AD 750, which began in Khurasan and installed its new caliphs in Iraq, accelerated that development but did not begin it: Mesopotamia already possessed a cultural unity in which Iran was the dominant force, and the later Umayyad caliphs in Syria looked east for models of empire and monarchy. Constantinople was more distant than Ctesiphon, and both short-term events and the *longue durée* made Iran increasingly influential: the failure,

I am grateful to Simon Loseby, James Montgomery, and Chase Robinson for their helpful comments and criticisms. I am responsible for faults that remain.

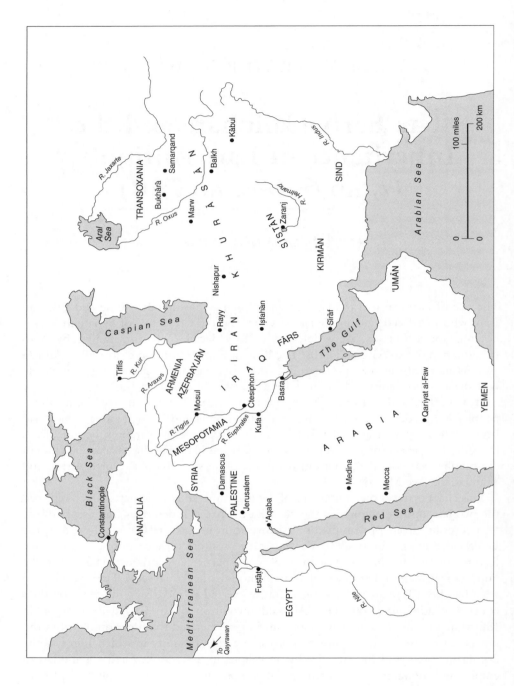

Map 6 The Islamic World in the Umayyad Period (AD 660–750).

first, of the Arab-Muslim siege of Constantinople in AD 717 ended serious attempts to absorb the Roman Empire in the way that the Sasanian Empire had been overwhelmed seventy years before; and second, economic prosperity in Iraq and the Persian Gulf began before the conquests and continued long after them.

The second distinctive feature of the early Islamic polity was the cultural resilience and self-confidence of the Arab-Muslims: the embryonic religion that they brought with them from the Arabian Peninsula influenced decisively the way in which they used the resources of the defeated late antique empires. This religion had come from the uplands of the Hijaz in west Arabia, on the margins of the late antique world. It shared much of biblical tradition with the conquered peoples' religions, but was distinct from them. In encounters with the indigenous populations of the empires, that distinctiveness was emphasized and developed, often through reference to an increasingly distant Arab past.

Any discussion of the place of the caliphate in Late Antiquity must therefore begin with the West Arabian origins of Islam; the relationship between the Hijaz and the late antique world is essential to an understanding of the origins and development of the Islamic polity. From there, we can pass to a discussion of the caliphate itself and its development into a quasi-imperial office, after the model of the Roman *basileus* and the Iranian *shahanshah*. Then, finally, we can elucidate the formation of the early Islamic state, and its relationship to the empires it replaced, by discussing its fiscal systems, its settlement patterns, and the social changes that occurred within it.

The Place of the Hijaz in the Late Antique World, and the Rise of Islam

Christianity was in the ascendant in late sixth-century Arabia. The Arab clients of the Roman and Sasanian Empires, who occupied the northern fringes of the Arabian Peninsula, were Christian, as was the southern kingdom of Himyar. Christianity was spreading along the coast of the Persian Gulf and was the religion of Ethiopia, across the Red Sea to the west. Faced with the appearance of a different monotheism in Mecca – a remote settlement in the desiccated uplands of the Hijaz, halfway up the western side of the peninsula – Orientalists have approached the phenomenon in one of two ways: either the Hijaz was such a remote pagan desert that Islam cannot have originated there in any form resembling what is known from sources that date from the eighth and ninth centuries – in which case the traditional narrative of Islam's origins requires significant revision – or the Hijaz was already in some ways part of the late antique (that is, the monotheist) world – in which case we have at least the beginnings of an explanation of its origins. The former interpretation depends primarily on the argument that the Arabic sources preserve little evidence for the seventh-century nature of Islam, and that even the Qur'an itself was produced not in seventh-century Arabia but in Mesopotamia during the eighth and ninth centuries. The literary analysis of Islamic scripture undertaken by John Wansbrough implies exactly that (Wansbrough 1978, 2004), and the historical implications have been taken up by scholars such as Suliman Bashear (Bashear 1997).

The revisionists' position has significant merits. The narrative of the origins of Islam is indeed extant only in very late sources (from the ninth and tenth centuries). Revisionist scholarship corrects the impression, conveyed by much of this later Islamic historical tradition, that "Islam" appeared in a fully developed, "classical" form in the seventh century. Complete rejection of the traditional narrative is, however, no longer tenable. Above all, there is mounting evidence that the Qur'an was indeed a product of early seventh-century Arabia (Donner 1998: 35–63): there is early (albeit fragmentary) documentary evidence for parts of it (Hoyland 1997: 687–703), and echoes of it are found in the demonstrably early "Constitution of Medina" (Serjeant 1978). Indeed, aspects of the Qur'an were obscure to many of its later interpreters (Crone 1994b), while, unlike the Bible, variant readings of the text are conspicuous by their absence. All this points to the Qur'an's formation as scripture during the early seventh century.

The Qur'an is religious prescription, not narrative history; but, as a text contemporaneous with the life of Muhammad, it provides evidence about the polemical religious environment in which he was preaching. With that context in mind, we must beware of mistaking rhetoric for reality and reconstructing history from it too literally (Hawting 1999). Furthermore, the exegesis that we might try to use to interpret it was produced over a century later in a milieu far removed from that of the Qur'an's origins. Nonetheless, it is evident from the Qur'an that Muhammad was engaged in polemical argument with Jews and Christians, among others, and that he saw himself as a reformer, in the tradition of the Jewish prophets and of Jesus. Muhammad's teaching was part of the religious tradition of the late antique world.

Exactly how Mecca and Medina fitted into that world is a problem that has yet to be solved satisfactorily. Apart from the Qur'an, and fragments of pre-Islamic poetry, our sources are late. The archaeology of Mecca and Medina is likely to remain unexplored for the foreseeable future (King 1995: 185, 187). However, the excavation of the town of Qariyat al-Faw has confirmed the existence of centers of mercantile activity, of the sort that Mecca and Medina are traditionally thought to have been (al-Ansary 1982). Qariyat al-Faw (*fl.* third to fifth centuries) undermined the revisionist notion that urbanism and long-distance trade could not have flourished in the more remote parts of the peninsula (Crone 1987). Indeed, a wider Arabian urban tradition can now be postulated (King 1995; Whitcomb 1996). It was suggested fifty years ago that the mercantile activity of the Hijaz might have been crucial to the emergence of Islam (Watt 1953), and this new archaeological evidence makes this an attractive proposition again. More recently, it has been suggested that the West Arabian economy may have been expanding in the sixth century, tying Mecca and Medina more closely into the wider late antique world (Conrad 2000: 696; Heck 2003). The presence of Persian terms for luxury goods in the Qur'an has long been recognized as evidence for connections with Sasanian Iran (Jeffery 1938; Montgomery 1995). Syriac loan words also suggest wider horizons (Luxenberg 2000). It is time to reconsider the mercantile language in which many of the Qur'an's key concepts are couched (Torrey 1892).

That Islam appeared after a century of intensifying imperial involvement in the Arabian Peninsula is unlikely to have been merely coincidental (Crone 1987: 245–50). Roman and Persian intervention undermined the dominance of the south Arabian kingdom of Himyar. That, and the decline of the great powers' clients in the north, may have left something of a power vacuum in the peninsula (Retsö 1993: 39–41). Two decades of war between Rome and Iran contributed to an apocalyptic atmosphere at the time of Muhammad's preaching, and the centrality of Jerusalem in the Islamic conquests is striking in the context of its prominence in the Roman–Persian war (Kister 1962; Drijvers 2002: 186–90). The Hijaz, on the margins of the two empires, lay outside their direct control, but was nevertheless connected to them culturally and economically. There had been a monotheist presence there for centuries: some Jews, during the diaspora that followed the destruction of the Second Temple, seem to have settled there (Stillman in Bearman et al. 1954–, xi: 239). In such a marginal zone, a holy man could preach unhindered by the established churches or state interference. As a result, the movement inspired by him could gain greater momentum there than was usual in groups inspired by desert eremites.

After the initial failure of his message in his home town of Mecca, Muhammad is said to have fled to Medina in AD 622, where a more receptive audience became the first Muslim community. The preservation in later sources of treaties between the members of that first Medinan community – the so-called "Constitution of Medina" – reveals that Muhammad deployed the traditional resources of West Arabian politics in founding a "theocratic community" (*umma*), in which he was to be the arbiter of disputes. Its language, and the language of Qur'anic verses that are related to it, echo earlier, pre-Islamic treaties (Serjeant 1978). In Muhammad's new polity, however, the stakes were raised by his monotheist message: salvation was the exclusive privilege of those who were members of the correct political community under a single leader (Crone 2004: 21–2).

That religious message gave a unity to the new polity without which its subsequent conquests are inexplicable. The notion of holy war in the Qur'an both fueled and explained the conquests, just as similar ideas had united Christian Armenians against Iran in the Roman–Persian war (Howard-Johnston 1999: 39–40; Robinson 2003: 126–7, 133). Of course, other factors were also critical to Muslim success: an Arabia linked to the wider world by trade may have benefited, like Viking Scandinavia, from crucial intelligence about when and where to strike; the two empires were weakened by decades of warfare; provincial populations were quick to make terms rather than fight; and the very success of the Arabs may have contributed to an apocalyptic sense that their success was inevitable (Hoyland 1997: 524). The *sine qua non*, however, was role of religion in binding together previously disparate tribes engaged in constant feuding and warfare (Donner 1981: 51–82). The religion that the tribesmen brought with them out of the desert exerted a determinative influence on how the inheritance of the two conquered empires was used.

The Caliphate and the Public
Expression of Authority

The death of the Prophet led to only a short-term crisis. His immediate successor, Abu Bakr (AD 632–4), successfully reestablished political control over the Arabian Peninsula, and he and his successor 'Umar (AD 634–44) then directed the energies of the tribes outward against the two empires to the north. There were two subsequent major crises over leadership in the following century, the *fitna*s ("trials" or "civil wars") of AD 656–61 and *c.* AD 683–92; but the assumption was maintained in both cases that a single person should lead the *umma* in religion and politics – an idea that gave to those conflicts a centripetal energy crucial to the survival of the "conquest society" as a united entity.

Many aspects of how the authority of the first caliphs was understood by those who followed them will remain obscure to us because of the lack of reliable early sources. The early caliphs became central figures in later "classical" Islamic doctrine, where polemic obscures all but their historical outlines. There are tantalizing glimpses of forgotten roles. 'Umar, for example, sometimes receives the title al-Faruq, an Aramaic word meaning "Redeemer," perhaps indicating a messianic role for the conqueror of Jerusalem (Bashear 1990). The caliphs' role as spiritual guides (*imam*s) seems to have been essential to their authority from the outset. "He who dies without an imam dies a pagan death," the Prophet is said to have stated (Crone 2004: 22). These early rulers are credited with using the titles *khalifa* ("caliph," "deputy," "successor") and *amir al-mu'minin* ("Commander of the Believers"). Although the first inscriptional attestations of these epithets are from AD 694 and AD 661 respectively (Miles 1952: 171; Hoyland 1997: 690–1), it seems likely that both were used much earlier than that: Adam and David are "caliphs" in the Qur'an (Q. 2. 30; Q. 38. 26); *amir* was a common epithet for a pre-Islamic tribal leader (Athamina 1999: 10).

A caliph could also be referred to as a *malik* ("king") and his authority as *mulk* ("kingship"). These more generic terms for authority were morally ambivalent, as they had been in pre-Islamic Arabian culture. The Bedouin poets had declared their hatred of kingship, fitting only for those who were prepared to pay tribute to rulers (Athamina 1998: 36–7). Mere temporal authority (that conferred by man, not by God) was often denounced and, while the Qur'an calls the prophets David and Solomon kings (Q. 2. 102, 251) and mentions Saul's divinely bestowed kingship (Q. 2. 247), it also declares that true "kingship" belongs only to God (Q. 20. 114). This tension between divinely inspired and earthly authority echoes the Hebrew Bible, which had exerted a profound influence on the conception of legitimate authority in the Christian Roman world (Dagron 2003: 48–53).

The caliphs' acquisition of the characteristics of late antique monarchs was facilitated not only by the presence in the Qur'an of ideas about authority analogous to those in the Hebrew Bible but also by the demands of ruling an extensive empire and by expectations about kingship among the conquered peoples. Islamic tradition attributes the transformation to Mu'awiya b. Abi Sufyan, the governor of Syria, who emerged victorious from the first civil war in AD 661 to become the first caliph to rule from Damascus rather than Medina. He was said to have declared himself the first "king" in Islam and to have accumulated the trappings of regal power: seals, bodyguards, palatial architecture, and formal audiences (Tab. ii: 205–6; Mas. v: 73–8). The shift of the political center from remote Medina to the former Roman provincial capital of Damascus must indeed have been decisive in this transformation, but the associated traditions are also shorthand for a more gradual process. One of Mu'awiya's rivals for the caliphate, the grandson of the Prophet, al-Hasan b. 'Ali, resided briefly at the Sasanian "White Palace" at Ctesiphon (Tab. ii: 1–2). Indeed, the civil war had been triggered when a clique angered at his autocratic, centralizing policies murdered the third caliph, 'Uthman (AD 644–56). The transformation of the office of leader of the new polity into something resembling a late antique monarch had begun before Mu'awiya and continued long after him.

After the conquests, all the caliphs deployed the resources of the defeated late antique empires to proclaim their legitimacy to three audiences: the conquered populations, their undefeated enemies, and their own Arab-Muslim following. Some media, like court poetry, were directed at quite specific (and sympathetic) audiences; others, like architecture and coinage, were less discriminate and had to speak to diverse interpreters. Different audiences assumed varying significance at different moments. In a Syriac chronicle from the AD 680s, we can see the impression made by Mu'awiya's royal ceremonial upon a hostile Christian observer living under Muslim rule (Palmer 1993: 31–2). Islamic historical tradition also preserves numerous stories that attribute the regal conduct of caliphs to the need to persuade Byzantine ambassadors of their power and authority: Mu'awiya built the palace of al-Khadra' (al-Rihâwî 1972: 35); 'Umar II retained the Great Mosque of Damascus (Flood 2001: 227).

Internal conflict, however, was the most important stimulus to the public expression of legitimate royal authority. Mu'awiya may have gained his reputation as the first king in part from his efforts to shore up his support in Syria during the first *fitna* (AD 656–61); there is certainly material evidence of his regal activities (Johns 2003: 418–24). The second *fitna* (AD 683–92) provoked a far more spectacular burst of creativity. The widespread adaptation of the Sasanian and Byzantine coinages to proclaim the legitimacy of rival Arab rulers dates from this period (Johns 2003: 426–33). The magnificent Dome of the Rock on the Temple Mount in Jerusalem was built by the eventual victor in the war, 'Abd al-Malik (685–705). It may have been constructed at a time when he did not control the Hijaz and required a rival shrine within his territory (Elad 1992).

'Abd al-Malik's victory in AD 692 allowed him and his successors to develop the administrative machinery of the new empire to a point where a far more extensive proclamation of their authority became possible, across all the provinces. The enunciation of royal power in the Umayyad caliphate had an experimental character. Initial adaptations of Byzantine and Sasanian images on coins were abandoned for issues that were purely epigraphic. Much of the original symbolic intent behind the Dome of the Rock was eventually forgotten. The most striking feature of this experimentation was that, although the forms in which royal power was expressed could not but be Roman and Sasanian, Arab-Muslim expectations determined their reconfiguration. Aniconism dominated religious contexts almost without exception. The Arabic script prevailed quickly over Greek and Persian in public contexts. For all that royal audiences and court culture came to resemble Sasanian practice (Grabar 1977; Hillenbrand 1981), caliphs never wore crowns or diadems, and the insignia of their authority were associated first and foremost with the Prophet. Such dramatic departures from late antique precedent indicate great cultural resilience and self-confidence. Caliphs' proclamations of their imperial authority had to be acceptable to the Arab-Muslims they ruled.

Taxation

The primary function of taxation in the early Islamic polity, as in the empires it replaced, was to fund the army. At first, the army and its dependants and the Islamic polity were coterminous: the Arab-Muslims lived off the wealth of their conquered territories. They were a minority of the population of the new empire, settled, for the most part, in separate, newly founded garrison cities (*amsar*, sing. *misr*), near the population centers of the conquered empires. Comparatively little tax was returned to the caliphal center: the governor (*amir*) of each *misr* was responsible for the distribution of tax to the tribal leaders billeted within the new town (Crone 1980: 30–1). Thus, at the highest level of government and administration, the conquests marked a complete break. The resources of the conquered populations now paid for the Muslim armies, not for Sasanian or Roman ones, and less tax left the provinces for the metropolis than it had under the defeated empires. Indeed, the fifty years between the conquests and the Marwanid caliphate (*c.* AD 640–*c.* AD 690) represent something of a hiatus in centralized state power, with local ad hoc agreements forming the financial basis of the new military class, and centralized efforts at gaining control of tax revenues having only limited effect.

At lower levels, the picture is more complicated: local tax collection systems within each province were usually retained, and collection was largely left to the indigenous authorities. There were, however, numerous exceptions to this pattern of continuity. It was disrupted where land ownership and administrative structures had changed because of the conquests (Donner 1981: 241); where agreements made at the time of the conquest superseded existing practice; where the Muslims expected more tax to be raised than previously; or where imperfect control over the conquered territory made tax-raising difficult (Robinson 2000: 39–44, 59–62). Furthermore, the Arab-Muslims may have brought taxation practices with them from the Arabian Peninsula, for pre-Islamic states there had levied taxes, as had the early Medinan polity (Lecker 2001).

The best evidence for taxation policies and related administrative practices comes from Egypt, where documentary evidence is abundant, thanks to the survival of numerous papyri. Much of this material remains to be edited, but these texts already serve as an important control in our interpretation of the ninth-century Islamic historical tradition, which sometimes preserves evidence of early practice, but more often presents inaccurate historical justifications for the contemporaneous fiscal situation. Earlier non-Muslim sources have likewise proved invaluable for an understanding both of Egypt and of other regions, because they also allow us to reconstruct "pre-classical" Islamic practice.

The creation of a system for paying the Arab-Muslim military is often ascribed in the Arabic sources to 'Umar I. He is said to have been responsible for the *diwan*s ("registers"), in which the names of those who had participated in the conquests were listed. *Diwans* were established in different conquered regions at different times and were inspired in part by practices in the first Islamic community at Medina in the AD 620s and 630s and in part by the administrative systems of the defeated empires (Morony 1984: 55–64; Morimoto 1994: 353, 364–5). In AD 640/1, 'Umar prohibited the Muslims from seizing land: they were told to rely instead on *'ata'* and *rizq* ("stipends" and "payments in kind") derived from taxation. In fact, this account of the matter probably simplifies a rather more ad hoc process that he was seeking to systematize and extend.

Early taxation arrangements were also improvised and local, depending upon agreements made with local elites as they surrendered to the Muslims. They often took the form of agreed "tribute" in money and kind, which was supplied through existing fiscal institutions (Morimoto 1981: 41–51, 60, 113–14; Morony 1984: 123). The amounts demanded in these agreements were often, at least initially, considerably higher than those that had been required by the Romans and Persians (Morimoto 1981: 113; Morony 1984: 102, 108). Modifications to the existing tax systems were also introduced. In Egypt, a Roman system based on the assessment of land was supplemented by a "personal" tax which, although often referred to as a "poll tax," probably resembled an income tax (Morimoto 1981: 82–91). Sasanian Iran also had a land tax and a "personal" tax, of which the latter had often been imposed on non-Persian, non-Magian, and noncombatant subjects. Both were adapted and developed to fit the needs of the Arab-Muslim rulers (Morony 1984: 99–111).

The Marwanid caliphs (AD 684–750) made repeated efforts to reorganize and regularize these ad hoc arrangements. Thus, in fiscal and administrative terms, the Marwanid period was both a return to the late antique pattern of effective centralized state power and a departure from it, in that state power was self-consciously Arab-Islamic. Taxation and administration were developed out of existing arrangements, but were run by Muslims who attempted to explain them in terms of an Islamic fiscal theory. Governors ceased to be concerned merely with the distribution of tax among their Arab-Muslim subjects and became more closely involved in the collection and administration of tax on behalf of a central caliphal authority that expected more surplus wealth to be sent back to Syria.

'Abd al-Malik decreed that Arabic was to be used in the tax bureaux (*dawawin al-kharaj*). Greek, Coptic, and Persian were previously the main languages in which the system had been administered in Egypt and Iraq (Morony 1984: 53; Morimoto 1994: 364–5). The evidence of the papyri indicates that Greek and Coptic often continued to be used in official documents into the beginning of the ninth century. It was simply impractical, presumably, to administer taxation without using the language of the subjects to be taxed (Morimoto 1994: 364–5). Nonetheless, Arabic does become more prevalent in administrative documents from this time (Grohmann 1934–74, iii: *passim*), just as non-Muslims became less prominent in the upper levels of the administration: the last Christian chief of the tax bureau in Egypt was an Athanasios, replaced in AD 705 or 706 (Morimoto 1981: 114); in Iraq, Persian converts occupied the same position, where non-Muslims had filled it previously (Morony 1984: 52–4, 206).

The Marwanid period also saw a series of censuses, cadastral surveys, and reforms aimed at increasing tax revenues and controlling population movement. These were not the first such efforts (Schick 1995: 168), but their intensity and effectiveness was of a different order to what had gone before. ʿAbd al-Malik's census (*taʿdil*) of AD 691 or 692 has left a distinct legacy in the Christian apocalyptic literature, where his efforts to wring more wealth out of Mesopotamia are "predicted" in Syriac texts of the late seventh and early eighth centuries. Those censuses were followed by two more under ʿAbd al-Malik's son and successor, al-Walid I (AD 705–15; Robinson 2000: 44–50). A similar process occurred in Egypt at the same time (Morimoto 1981: 114–15, 119–20, 122–3). Hisham (AD 724–43) also instituted a wide-ranging reform of taxation at the beginning of his reign (Morimoto 1981: 135). Marwanid success in raising tax was relative, however: they were far less successful than their ʿAbbasid successors (Robinson 2000: 49). Nonetheless, revenue did increase, and a greater proportion of it was expended at the center, increasingly in employing professional soldiers (Crone 1980: 37–8). At the same time, the conversion of non-Muslims eroded the clear fiscal distinction between the conquered populations and Arab-Muslims (Morimoto 1981: 127–34). Both the extension of state power and the taxation of all subjects marked something of a return to late antique fiscal patterns, albeit justified in Islamic language by its administrators.

Settlement Patterns and Social Change

Political and administrative change occurred at a pace different from that of social and economic processes. Conversion to Islam remained rare among the indigenous populations of the conquered territories: perhaps 10 percent of the urban population of Iran had converted by AD 750 (Bulliet 1979: 23). The figure may be taken as indicative for other regions. It might be expected to have been higher in areas like Syria that were conquered early and had large Arab populations, but what evidence there is suggests limited conversion even there (Schick 1995: 139–58). It is evident, meanwhile, that existing economic trends in Late Antiquity continued in the early Islamic period (Morony 2004), as did patterns of urban and rural settlement; the "classical" city had already begun to change before the coming of Islam (Kennedy 1985), and archaeology and field surveys do not suggest any dramatic "bedouiniza-tion" of the rural economy after the conquests (Gatier 1995; MacAdam 1995).

The most significant new departure was the foundation of the *amsar*, the new garrisons for the Arab-Muslim conquerors. Most of them eventually became genuine cities – indeed, many of them (such as Basra) have been continuously occupied down to the present. Although conversion to Islam did not have a great effect on the indigenous population, the comparatively small numbers of the Arab-Muslims meant that the converts had a significant impact on them. Many of the new Muslim "clients" (*mawali*, sing. *mawla*) settled in the *amsar*, where cultural interaction was already a significant influence on the development of Islam in the Marwanid period.

The foundation of the *amsar* reflected the importance of conquest and settlement in nascent Islam: emigration (*hijra*) and holy war (*jihad*) were the engines of the "conquest society" (Crone 1994a). These garrisons were the "houses of emigration" (*dur al-hijra*), and they became the administrative and political capitals of the conquered provinces. Thus, Basra (AD 635/6) and Kufa (AD 636–40) became the capitals of the two districts of Iraq, and al-Fustat (AD 642) became the capital of Egypt. As the conquests continued, the *misr* remained the pattern for new garrisons: Qayrawan became the capital of the Maghrib in AD 682, replacing an earlier nearby foundation of AD 654/5 (Sakly 2000: 57). An exception to this pattern was Syria, where garrisons were abandoned for settlement in existing towns, perhaps because of the presence of Arabs there.

The new foundations combined the urban traditions of the Arabian Peninsula with those of the conquered provinces. It has recently been proposed that all of them were based on the form of the late Roman quadrilateral Roman legionary fortress (Whitcomb 1995: 278–82). That may attribute too much weight to al-'Aqaba (a possible *misr* on the Red Sea, dating perhaps from the AD 640s or 650s) and to the evidence of later foundations in Syria, but literary evidence does indicate that the *amsar* in Iraq were also quadrilateral in layout (Wheatley 2001: 42–3). It is also striking that those garrisons are reported to have been established at the behest of 'Umar, the conqueror of Roman Syria (Wheatley 2001: 42, 45). Archaeology has confirmed the literary evidence that all the new foundations had a congregational mosque, with the house of the governor and the administrative buildings (such as the treasury) at their center. This architectural pattern was the chief material expression of the new religion and the focus of public life. Congregational prayers took place there, and the speeches and sermons of the commander (*amir*), who was also the prayer-leader (*imam*), were given there. The fundamental elements of that architectural arrangement were probably derived from the Hijaz and institutionalized under the first caliphs, in the era of the foundation of the *amsar* (Johns 1999: 86–8), although they also had analogues in the Roman and Iranian cities conquered by the Muslims.

Other elements of the new cities certainly came from pre-Islamic Arabia. The Arab-Muslims were settled in cantonments (*khitat*, sing. *khitta*) according to their tribal affiliations. Given that Mecca and Medina were only small settlements before Islam and that the Muslim conquerors were from tribes right across the peninsula, it seems likely that precedents should be sought outside the Hijaz, particularly in south Arabia (Whitcomb 1996).

It was in these new foundations, and in the places where Arab-Muslims settled in Syria, that early Islamic society developed. The advent of Islam suddenly and dramatically rearranged the power relationships of Late Antiquity. Previously dominant religious groups – Zoroastrians and Christians – were now subordinate, and Jews, already subordinate, had to come to an accommodation with the new faith. Other aspects of identity were also transformed: culture, language, and ethnicity became markers in new hierarchies. Many aspects of the process will probably remain opaque because of the late date of the sources. These tend to presuppose the existence of a "classical" Islam, underestimating the extent to which Islamic culture and dogma had been formed out of the encounter between the Arabs and the people of the defeated empires. One of the best hopes for reconstructing aspects of the early encounters between the Arab conquerors and the late antique populations lies in the *hadith* literature – the corpus of traditions about the actions of the Prophet and of early Muslims that had acquired the classical status of *sunna* ("normative practice") by the ninth century. Because these texts are compilations of material generated during the first two centuries, they contain traces of the negotiations that took place between the different communities in that period.

As in the successor states in the west during the fifth and sixth centuries, one of the major controversies in the Islamic world in the eighth century was the question of the legitimacy and desirability of mixed marriages (Bashear 1997: 118). Whereas only a poor sort of Roman would want to be like a Goth (the reputed sentiment of the Ostrogothic king Theodoric), many of the wealthiest Persians and Greeks wanted to affiliate themselves with the Arabs. There are plenty of *hadith*, therefore, linking the Persians to the Arab-Muslims through genealogies reaching back on both sides as far as Abraham, and in sayings such as, "the Persians are a band (related) to us, the people of the house (of the Prophet)" (Bashear 1997: 67–8). Attitudes among the Arab-Muslims were ambivalent, however, and the dominant theme of the *hadith* remains the superiority of the Arabs: "I am an Arab, the Qur'an is Arabic, and the speech of the people of Paradise is Arabic," said Muhammad (Bashear 1997: 56). Identities were also defined by cultic and cultural practices, and a great diversity of influences, exchanges, and negotiations are reflected in the *hadith* literature. "Persian" gestures like greeting by handshake received prophetic approval, but Arab-Muslim identity was mostly defined by difference – the wearing of silk and the kissing of hands were both unacceptable (Bashear 1997: 33–4). Religious material was borrowed and adapted, as the vast corpus of *Isra'iliyyat* literature confirms. Jewish and Christian material was also adapted and coopted into the interpretation of the Qur'an and the elaboration of Islamic traditions (Adang 1996).

The absence of a priestly class in Islam meant that the caliph could influence this formative process only through his provincial governors. There was no church hierarchy with which the state could make accommodations, as it had done in both Christian Rome and Zoroastrian Iran. In the event, the state's limited persuasive and coercive power meant that it failed to determine questions of Islamic orthodoxy in its own favor. The burst of creativity in public Islamic art and architecture that characterized the first decades of Marwanid rule faded with the collapse of the siege of AD 717 and, although the Sasanian-influenced architecture and ceremonial of the later Marwanids anticipated the style of the 'Abbasids who overthrew them, the brand of Islamic absolutism expressed in their chancery output and palace iconography failed to win acceptance. In the eastern cities, where the ferment of cultural interaction was most productive, ideas of orthodoxy and legitimacy were diverging from

Marwanid ones, a divergence fueled by resentment against what was perceived as foreign rule by Syrian Arabs. The trend culminated in the revolution of the mid eighth century and the installation of the 'Abbasid dynasty in AD 750.

Conclusions

In its perpetuation of a centralized, monotheist, and monarchical state, the caliphate was a direct inheritor of the legacy of Late Antiquity. Like the emperors of Rome and of Iran, the caliph claimed to be the representative of God on earth. Swift conquest meant that the institutions that underpinned an imperial state could be appropriated and maintained. Although the taxation system came to be explained in "Islamic" terms, its origins lay in the mechanisms of the Roman and Iranian fiscal administrations. The caliphate did not develop, however, into a simple calque on either Rome or Iran: a distinctive Islamic identity emerged from the encounter of the Arabs with the populations they conquered. This was because the Arab conquerors (or, at least, their leaders) already had a well-defined religious identity at the time of the conquests in the mid seventh century. The unique position of the Hijaz on the margins of the late antique world, beyond the direct control of the imperial powers but within a wider monotheist *koinê*, had allowed the formation of a distinctive, unifying religious ideology that was preserved by settlement apart from the established populations. The result did not resemble the "classical" Islam of the sources that survive from the ninth and tenth centuries. Nonetheless, the Qur'an does seem to have been brought out of Arabia, and with it ideas that limited the range of action of the Near East's new rulers. Ideology was not simply constructed by an "elite": rather, it supplied the context in which they made their claims to authority (albeit a context that they sought to influence). The abandonment of various Umayyad experiments, such as coins with images and the Dome of the Rock as a rival shrine to Mecca, is testament to how the nascent ideology of Islam limited the public expression of authority. Had Constantinople fallen, perhaps things would have been different. As it was, the failure of the siege of AD 717 seems to have increased the already important influence of Iran in administration and at the caliphal court. Iran was important in another sense, too: it was in the territories formerly ruled by the Sasanians that hostility to Syrian rule eventually proved to be beyond the Umayyads' control. The absence of a priestly class was a significant departure from the pattern of previous late antique polities – a departure of great importance for the subsequent development of the caliphate.

BIBLIOGRAPHICAL NOTE

In *The World of Late Antiquity*, Peter Brown (1971b) argued persuasively that the rise of Islam belonged, in some senses, to the history of Late Antiquity. Garth Fowden (1993) developed this argument further. A recent reassessment of the idea that Islam was part of the late antique world is found in Robinson 2003.

The best general narrative history of early Islam remains Kennedy 2004. On the Umayyad caliphate, see Hawting 2000. The place of Arabia in the late antique world and the origins of Islam remain controversial. Hawting 1999 is a recent, thought-provoking development of John Wansbrough's ideas (see Wansbrough 1978). Donner 1998 provides a less skeptical analysis.

The development of the political theory of the caliphate is covered by Crone 2004. Dagron 2003 provides a useful comparison with the situation in the Roman Empire. The administrative and fiscal history of the caliphate has received no such synthetic treatment. Morony 1984 focuses on the transition from Sasanian to Islamic rule and is magisterial in its scope. Robinson 2000 deals with Mesopotamia in detail. These volumes also treat some aspects of social change. Two studies that examine the encounter between the Arabs and the populations of the late antique world are Steven Wasserstrom 1995 and Bashear 1997.

PART V

The Sacred

Late Antiquity can often be made to seem coterminous with something like "Christian antiquity." The chapters in this section illustrate why that might be so, but also why the notion would be misplaced. It goes without saying that Christianity began long before "Late Antiquity" can be thought of as an applicable label; and it is equally possible to argue that the Roman world, in whatever sense one uses that term, was never "Christian" in any complete sense.

One used to talk about "the conversion of the Roman Empire to Christianity," as alluded to, for example, in the title of A. H. M. Jones's famous little book *Constantine and the Conversion of Europe* (Jones 1948), not to mention Merivale's Boyle Lectures of nearly a century before. The link with Constantine was not accidental: his personal "conversion," whatever its form, was taken to represent a change of religious allegiance throughout his empire. The change was slow, however, geographically patchy in its achievement, and scarcely widespread in the countryside for many centuries (see Map 7). Hence a preference for the language of "Christianity *and*" or (even better) "Christianity *in*" (Markus 1974; Chadwick 2001). Emphasis was to be on the *association* of Christianity with Rome, and the effect of that association on its own development – for example, famously, *Christianity and Classical Culture* (Cochrane 1940) or, more precisely, *Early Christian Thought and the Classical Tradition* (Chadwick 1966).

The "early" reference has its importance, for one might argue that Constantine presided over the closing stages of a Christianity that was superseded by models of piety and organization both novel and (in the eyes of some, both then and now) less true to its origins. Hence Robert Markus felt able to write about "the end of ancient Christianity" (Markus 1990), "Byzantine" or "medieval" Christianity being supposedly different (although Markus himself did not cast the debate in those terms). And, although the notion of "conversion" still has its value, even if we do not think of it in terms of some personal commitment or great awakening

Map 7 Major Christian Centers in Late Antiquity.

(see the splendid essays in Mills and Grafton 2003; and compare Nock 1933; also Fletcher 1997), we tend now to use terms like "christianization," although that is easier to recognize as an aspiration in certain sectors of late antique society than as a definable quality of that society itself (witness Brown 1992: "*towards* a Christian empire").

Gaddis (ch. 34), Lizzi Testa (ch. 35), Graumann (ch. 36), and Caner (ch. 39) make it clear in this section that an apparatus of power and clear traditions of thought and practice continued to characterize the Christian communities, even as they engaged with the new political dispensations made available to them by Constantine and his successors. But there is a dangerous tendency to privilege the Christian aspects of this story: for it is possible to argue that Judaism, for example, the seedbed of Christianity, and that range of cults and worldviews that we carelessly label "pagan" were themselves undergoing change, to the extent that we properly refer to late antique Judaism and late antique paganism (Koltun-Fromm and McLynn, chs. 37 and 38, respectively). They were becoming as "different" as Christianity, and one could toy with the notion of an "end" to "ancient" Judaism and "ancient" paganism. (Gnosticism, Mithraism, and Manichaeism – perhaps even Caner's monasticism – would also be parts of that story: Michael Williams 1996; Ulansey 1989 and Beck 2006; and Lieu 1985.)

But we have to carry our caution one step further yet. A great body of secondary literature informs us of the degree to which the Roman Empire was a "sacred" society, even apart from the presence of Christianity within it. In the eyes of pagan "persecutors," for example (Decius or Diocletian), it was as true as ever before that the Roman polity stood or fell in accordance with the favor of the gods, and that a sound worship of those gods was an essential guarantee, therefore, of the empire's stability. The point is that Christians said exactly the same thing: this was the basis of their supposition that the Roman Empire, as it seemed to be progressing from the end of the third century onward (the heyday of Eusebius and Lactantius), was indeed "God's empire" – the empire providentially foreseen by the "true," that is the Christian, God. The implication is, in other words, not that one religious party was losing and another winning, but that late Roman society as a whole was changing its mind about the proper relations between the divine and the human spheres. Notions of cult, of community and individual, of law and conscience, of authority and inspiration were all affected.

It is harder to untangle another web of change: the notion that not every department of life could be characterized as wholly sacral. Paradoxically, as the focus of worship shifted to a single God (a notion not by any means strange to pagan theorists), and as religious devotion and loyalty became more intense and interiorized, so some spheres of social activity acquired a more neutral or "secular" air. The "world," the *saeculum*, once given a Christian definition, could become either imperfect, incomplete, unfulfilled, or else untouched by the immediate influence of the creator, a zone of indifference, which might support or inhibit religious endeavor, not because of its inherent qualities but because of the motives of the agents who moved within it. It may be a mistake to suppose, therefore, that one species of sacrality was superseded by another. Rather, there developed an unresolved tension between, on the one hand, an optimistic eagerness to respect or transform or transcend the world of nature and, on the other, a gloomier sense of selfish, short-sighted, indulgent, or brutal ignorance of what that world was for. Since the tension could be played out even within the individual, tendencies latent in the earliest Christian reflections were given a new lease of life by the triumphs that supposedly rendered them irrelevant.

CHAPTER THIRTY-THREE

Christianization, Secularization, and the Transformation of Public Life

Richard Lim

Christianization has been a pivotal concept for understanding the transformations of the Roman world in Late Antiquity (Peter Brown 1993). Judged either positively or negatively in respect to its implications, few deny that the rise and later triumph of Christianity had a significant role to play in reshaping Greco-Roman culture and society. Scholars are nevertheless aware that its notional triumph never became complete, and therefore speak more in terms of a christianizing Roman Empire than a christianized Rome, a cautious approach that distantly echoes certain late antique Christians' lament that their own society failed to become more fully transformed by Christian values (MacMullen 1984). What was principally at issue was not whether Christianity could prevail against the worship of the traditional gods, for the defeat of so-called paganism was narrated in triumphalist Christian texts that documented instances of bans on public sacrifice and of the destruction of temples to the gods (Gregory 1986; Trombley 1993–4; Hahn 2004; see McLynn, ch. 38). Rather, scholars have focused on the late antique debate among Christians regarding what was pagan (a category that came to be understood as those beliefs and practices that could no longer be tolerated in a christianizing society), what was Christian, and what belonged to a "third" category that was neither fully pagan nor Christian (North 2005).

Indeed, a christianizing Roman society continued to accommodate social and cultural institutions that were not and could not be readily assimilated into the ambit of what many ecclesiastical figures regarded as the sanctified Christian world. One key aspect of traditional life that most persistently resisted christianization was the pervasive public spectacles, such as gladiatorial combats (*munera*), animal hunts (*venationes*), theatrical performances (*ludi scaenici*), and chariot races (*ludi circenses*), all of which took place within the great entertainment spaces of the ancient city. The culture of Roman games that was built around the amphitheater, theater, and hippodrome bore little resemblance to the idealized piety defined in normative Christian texts of the time. The negotiations that ensued among various late Roman elites regarding the status of public spectacles reveal salient disagreements regarding the very definition and scope of christianization. Demonized by some as unremittingly pagan practices, the culture of public spectacles came to be represented by other Christian figures as part of the *saeculum*, the unsanctified world, to which various values were ascribed (Markus 1970; 1998; French 1985). In this process, the category of the secular was developed into an autonomous discursive space that helped buffer select cultural practices, including Roman spectacles, from the claims of those who advocated a more thorough christianization of Roman society.

De-paganization and the Challenge of Roman Games

Eusebius of Caesarea, foremost champion of a triumphalist vision of Christianity, regarded Constantine's conversion in AD 312 as a definitive turning point in the history of salvation. Christ, through his suffering, death, and resurrection, had vanquished Satan, and yet for a long while the earthly realm remained under the latter's rule and that of his angels. The faith of Constantine, Eusebius' ideal prince, was supposed to have turned the Roman Empire into a fitting instrument of God's plan to effect the total triumph of Christianity. The emperor as *triumphator* represents a familiar Roman imperial image that was given a fresh face in the following manner: Constantine, according to Eusebius (*Vit. Const.* 3. 3), had commissioned numerous images that show himself bearing the Christogram and crushing the dragon-serpent underfoot. In short, he regarded Christ's triumph over Satan as the model for his earthly victory over the servants of the vanquished gods. For those who shared the Eusebian Constantine's vision of the defeat of the gods and their supporters as a form of *imitatio Christi*, christianization in the post-Constantinian age was merely a form of mopping up after the issue had already been decided.

As presented, this triumph was manifested first and foremost in the removal of the outward expressions of the old religion, such as sacrifice and cultic worship at shrines and temples. Putting an end to the blood sacrifice of animal victims thus became the singular goal of christianization (Barnes 1984; Bradbury 1994, 1995). While positions for and against the practice galvanized both sides of the debate regarding sacrifice, there was never any serious doubt in the mind of most Christians that blood sacrifice as such amounted to forbidden pagan idolatry. Along the same lines, the temples and shrines dedicated to the gods, which appeared as sacral places to their worshipers and as haunts of demons to Jews and Christians, were treated as an abominable aspect of pagan worship by a broad – but, surprisingly, by no means universal – consensus. Constantine's admirers underscored the fact that the first Christian emperor took decisive steps to abrogate or curtail these two most visible expressions of the old religion. Thus he was credited with a decree that outlawed blood sacrifice, the efficacy and scope of which remains open to debate, and was said to have declined to ascend the Capitol and enter the Temple of Iuppiter Optimus Maximus at the end of his triumphal procession in Rome, a clear break with centuries of Roman ritual tradition.

However, despite these and similar ostensibly robust gestures, hints abound that Constantine did not seek to institute many christianizing changes advocated by his fellow Christians. This has brought the nature of the emperor's religious outlook and even the authenticity of his conversion into question. The discussion of such matters has been treated fully and thoughtfully elsewhere, and requires no elaboration here (Van Dam 2003b). Whether Constantine acted as a "good Christian" has arguably served as a red herring for scholars over the generations. Rather than ask whether he deserved Eusebius' panegyrical praise of him as the ideal Christian prince on account of his staunch support of christianization, it is more historically relevant and accurate to ask what role Constantine – and his successors – played in negotiating and creating the categories of Christian, pagan, and secular.

As mentioned earlier, accounts of christianization have often been illustrated, on the one hand by enumerating the bans on sacrifices and the shutting down and destruction of temples, and on the other by the institution of Christian ritual practices and the building of ecclesiastical structures such as basilica churches. Seen as barometers of change, imperial interventions in such areas became the building blocks for the new narrative of religious transformation that is commonly associated with the story of christianization. Often left out is any acknowledgment that the imperial construction of paganism was focused mainly on the cultic worship of the gods and their divine statues through sacrifice (which drew on the normative early Christian definition of what is pagan) – a policy that effectively applied the label "religious" to selected traditional institutions and practices, while allowing others to be presented as "nonreligious" or secular. Whereas in the preceding period, the notion of sacrality and references to the gods permeated most aspects of life, the new construction of a "religious" sphere imposed sharp, distinct boundaries where they did not previously exist in the same manner. Such a perspective permitted the program of de-paganization to be narrowly construed as the deletion of offending divine statues, temples, and sacrifices.

This did little to alter the culture of public spectacles that *some* Christians wanted to regard as idolatrous, because reform in such an area was not widely regarded at the time as an aspect of christianization. While Constantine is alleged to have banned gladiatorial combats in AD 325, the report of this decree survives in only one source and, even if genuine, the law had in any case limited scope and effect (MacMullen 1986b). Gladiatorial *munera* in fact continued for well over a century, and their eventual disappearance may be better explained as due to social and economic causes, even to a change in fashion, rather than as a direct result of christianization (Ville 1960; Wiedemann 1995). Overall, Constantine's enacted measures had little or no transformative impact on the civic culture of ancient communities in general or on the culture of public spectacles in particular. If anything, the emperor did what he could to ensure the continued vitality of civic culture. In Rome itself, Constantine greatly embellished the Circus Maximus, to the delight of the citizens (Humphrey 1986: 126; Curran 2000: 84). He not only supported the shows but also helped establish them on a more solid footing by restructuring the obligations of senators to give games and by enrolling stage and other performers in hereditary professions, in order to bind them to "public service."

Overall, the so-called Constantinian Revolution had little immediate impact on the status of traditional spectacles. Such an observation need not have embarrassed even a fervent champion such as Eusebius, since his view of what christianization entailed did not materially include in its purview the culture of Roman shows. There was in fact a long-standing diversity of opinion on this issue within Christian communities. Pre-Constantinian Christians such as Minucius Felix (*Oct.* 37. 11) and Tertullian (*De spect. passim*) argued that all the public shows, be they games in the amphitheater, theater, or hippodrome, were inextricably tied to sacred rituals and therefore constituted pagan idolatry. Tertullian, in particular, offered a forensic response to counter the belief that Christians were not forbidden from attending the shows because the Scriptures do not refer to them at all: by using antiquarian and other arguments, he established an equation between attendance at the Roman spectacles and pagan idolatry. By making a case that the games were the *pompa diaboli*, he contended that (baptized) Christians who had vowed to forsake the devil's pomp could no more justify going to the theater than participating in a public sacrifice to the gods. Clearly, such an argument was needed only because many of Minucius Felix's and Tertullian's fellow Christians did not subscribe to the view that living a Christian life required abstinence from public spectacles. According to Tertullian (*De spect.* 3), some indeed refused to accept his identification of the shows with idolatry and, arguing that God was not offended by his own creation, asked for the authority of scriptural warrants (*scripturis auctoritatem*) before they would accept that the *spectacula* were forbidden to Christians. These men, according to Tertullian, carried on as though the public spectacles did not belong to the pagan sphere.

The anatomy of this pre-Constantinian Christian conversation highlights the extent to which arriving at the precise definition of what constituted objectionable pagan idolatry was by no means a straightforward exercise. Negotiations regarding the scope of christianization, particularly regarding whether it encompassed the culture surrounding the public spectacles, continued well into the late empire. The emperors' official bans on public sacrifice, and the elimination of the rite from the ceremonies surrounding the public spectacles, served to undercut some of Tertullian's most powerful arguments regarding the close connection between cult and spectacles.

In the post-Constantinian world, many Christians, including members of the aristocracy and imperial family, continued to sponsor and attend the shows. In short, the abolition of public spectacles was not generally regarded by the christianizing elite and the broader population as an integral goal of christianization (Lim 1994). Arguably, it took the rise of a Christian ascetic culture in the later fourth century to make the ending of public spectacles an avowed project of christianization. Since Tertullian's main argument that games were tantamount to idolatry gained little purchase, moralizing critiques against games (which philosophers had long offered) came into play. Tertullian himself invoked a stoicizing moral topos regarding the corrupting force of spectacles, a view that was articulated by, for instance, Seneca the Elder in his discourse on the adverse influence of crowds on the moral stance of an individual (Sen. *Ep.* 7). Later fourth-century Christian authors such as John

Chrysostom and Augustine of Hippo would further develop such a line of argument in discourses that criticized the morally corrupting effect that games had on those Christians who could not resist the temptation to attend them. Their line of attack, which again derived from Stoic critiques, focused on how the sounds and sight experienced at games enter the body through the senses and eventually work upon the soul in accordance with the ancient theory of emotions. By coupling this thesis with the Christian view regarding man's inability to resist evil without the aid of God, a theme particularly central to Augustine of Hippo's thinking in the *Confessions*, a lasting impression was formed that the continued "survival" of the Roman public spectacles in a christianizing empire was the result of recidivism, human weakness, and man's propensity to prefer the sins of the flesh.

Christianization thus came to be represented in textual sources from the later fourth century on as the remaking of society according to a Christian ethos inspired by the so-called desert ascetics. The effort to adapt such a strict moral code for the christianized population generally resulted in a *via media* that effectively universalized the ancient philosophers' worries about the dangers of living under the corruption of civilization. As everyone was now considered able and therefore also duty-bound to live a good life, the project of sanctification included as part of its brief the termination of Roman public spectacles that were thought to corrupt their spectators. The moral discourse preached by individuals such as John Chrysostom admitted of no middle ground, since a given aspect of life was either "in Christ" or it was not, and what was not in Christ properly belonged to the realm of Satan. In short, preachers such as Chrysostom would expand the project of christianization beyond the ban on sacrifices and attendance at temples to include the reform of morals and habits of everyday life (Leyerle 2001).

Urban spectacles such as gladiatorial combats, animal hunts, theatrical performances, and chariot races, long emblematic of Roman imperial civilization, were regarded by ascetic Christians as liabilities rather than assets and as stumbling blocks to Christian moral progress. Christianization, as articulated within this framework, required the reinvention of society and its mores according to the moral values upheld by martyrs and desert monks: "Ascetics competed with one another and with both churchmen and secular authorities for a specific prize – the authority to define, teach and exemplify in definitive form the virtues of the Christian religion, and to guarantee their observance and preservation" (Rousseau 2002: 256). According to this model, to christianize a Roman city would therefore have meant transforming it into a symbolic desert, a model of the heavenly Jerusalem. The new Christian community, saintly and pure, could have had no truck with the unruly and licentious culture of the ancient city.

Many aspects of traditional culture were thought to stand in the way of such a transformation, and none more so than that of Roman public entertainments. Some Christians even conceived of the *spectacula* as the devil's last-ditch effort to retard the christianization of Roman society. Thus the author of the *Life of Pelagia of Antioch* portrayed the mime actress Pelagia, with her charm and feminine guile, as Satan's final hope to ensnare unsuspecting Christians (Lim 2003). In this perceived role as a source of cultural resistance to christianization in the post-Constantinian age, the

Roman games came to be represented in many Christian works as the bulwark of the unchristianized, and indeed unchristianizable, *saeculum*.

Until very recently, the perspectives of Patristic authors such as John Chrysostom and Augustine have largely determined how scholars approach the question of changes in public life in Late Antiquity. At one level, the works of these writers offer an irresistible store of raw material for study, so that they are often mined for information regarding the *realia* of contemporary practices. On another level, the prestige of the Patristic figures and the voluminous quality of their works render the point of view contained therein a sympathetic lens – for certain modern readers at least – through which to view the social and cultural significance of public spectacles in Late Antiquity (Weismann 1972; Jürgens 1972). Every student of early Christianity who has to work with such highly filtered and sharply ideological texts faces this challenge: how can she find a way to use the texts to understand a given historical phenomenon without being unduly influenced by the perspectives that are bound up in the Patristic texts themselves? Some scholars have argued, for eminently persuasive reasons, that the highly ideological and rhetorical nature of such texts renders their employment as historical sources problematic, and that they are most appropriately used by a historian as texts that reveal particular modes of discursive representation (Clark 2004). I venture to suggest that historians should still be able to make use of Patristic texts to address questions in such a way as to move beyond their particular discursive frames, presumably having first come to an adequate understanding of what those frames are. In our case, a useful starting point is first to recognize that the anti-games writings of the likes of John Chrysostom and Augustine represent but one side of a complex set of past conversations, and then, second, to move to discover, as much as possible, the fuller contours of the ancient debate.

The ability to separate out the preacher's message and the points of view of his putative audience has been one of the major areas of advancement in the scholarship of early Christianity (MacMullen 1989; Klingshirn 1994; Rousseau 1998; Maxwell 2006). A similar principle may be introduced to guide one's approach in our case. Anyone seeking with an open mind to understand the reception of games in Late Antiquity will quickly come to the conclusion that many, if not most, Christians entertained views on the matter that were greatly at variance with those articulated in the celebrated Patristic writings. Many in fact did not accept the view that the games were forms of pagan idolatry or that their own Christian self-identities categorically required them to stop attending the shows of the theater, amphitheater, and hippodrome. Why did some Christians come to adopt the view that the games were not part of the objectionable tradition of Greco-Roman paganism? How indeed did the *ludi* and *munera* come to be desacralized or secularized?

Excursus: Desacralization and Secularization

Traditional Greco-Roman public spectacles boasted a plethora of associations with the worship of the gods, and not only on account of the rites of sacrifice and ritual processions of divine effigies that often preceded and closed the events. The idea that many institutions such as games were rooted in archaic sacred dramas and rites, which the ancient antiquarian lore helped to sustain, is now so widely accepted among scholars as to be a commonplace. The general underpinning theory is that historical societies typically develop from an archaic state, often preliterate, to a more modern form, often literate and urban; a supposition that informed the works of influential social thinkers such as Hegel, Marx, and Durkheim, as well as those of their innumerable modern followers. This development involved in turn a progressive desacralization or secularization, whereby a society's largely sacral vision of life was replaced by a more secular orientation (Dobbelaere 1981). The supposed shift from the sacred to the secular or profane underpins Max Weber's celebrated idea of *Entzauberung* or disenchantment, whereby an archaic, religiously oriented society gradually divests itself of its original belief that every aspect of life is suffused by the presence of the divine, and embraces in turn more individualistic and utilitarian (that is, more secular) values and outlook (Weber 1930; Flávio Pierucci 2000).

The notion of secularization as a necessary stage in the grand unfolding of history has informed and in turn been bolstered by the modern study of the development of European society. The changes whereby the cultural and institutional dominance of the Catholic Church came to be relaxed as a consequence of, among several factors, the rise of modern science and a sophisticated urban culture in the late medieval period, led to the emergence of a secular domain containing alternative forms of thought and practices that competed with the Christian church over the hearts, minds, and social habits of individuals within society (Luckmann 1967; Hammond 1985). Historians have since generalized this original European model of secularization in such a way as to suggest that it applies to all societies as part of their progress toward modernity. In this generic formulation, "secularization theory" refers to the historical process whereby a society, and specifically its nonpriestly power elite, develops an autonomous set of cultural forms and institutions that challenge the overall dominance of the priestly or religious elite and its control over the real and symbolic capital of a society (Lübbe 1965; Martin 1978; Marramao 1983).

Historians of religion have recently questioned whether "secularization" admits of a single definition or always displays unbroken continuity. According to Rodney Stark, for example, secularization should rather be regarded as just one element in the cyclical transformation of societies that undergo stages of desacralization (secularization) and sacralization (religious revivals) (Stark and Bainbridge 1985; Stark, 1996; Klutz 1998). Whereas earlier scholars have associated the notion of an immanent sacrality with the past and the secular with the present, the current, more nuanced approach posits that both sacralization and desacralization (as well as secularization) are dynamics that may be at play in any society at any given time (Butler 1990).

The allure of being able to assess, through the lens of desacralization and secularization, the stage of historical development that a given society happens to have reached at a certain time has even encouraged a few scholars to devise a set of metrics that gauges the presence or absence of particular attributes associated with religious and secular "normative orientations" (Fenn 1986). Here is where historical positivism becomes most strongly evident in the course of this ongoing scholarly discussion.

Yet all the already mentioned approaches not only accept a certain historical teleology but also the fundamental premise that the "sacred" and the "secular" represent essential givens and that they are real, even observable, states (Devisch 1973). But many societies in fact did not maintain a (strong) distinction between the two, and may even lack words that could allow the culture to conceptualize or mark the difference (Roosens 1963). Still, in the final analysis, the most substantial critique of these approaches has to do with their failure to give due consideration to the texts that represent (or do not represent) the distinctions between what is sacred and what is secular. References in texts to the "sacred" and the "secular," where they do appear, have to be read first and foremost as exercises in *moral* categorization rather than as transparent representations of the conceptual categories that historical actors employed.

Antiquarian texts that discuss the traditional origins of ideas and institutions of a given society are typically places where one finds a strong articulation of the idea that the archaic past is more religious or sacral and the putative present less so. Such a representation conforms to the ancient intellectual paradigm of progressive decline. Yet a historical theory that simply accepts this rhetoric of decline at face value fails to appreciate the politics at work in the representation of nostalgia and loss. Take, for instance, the use of Roman antiquarian texts in Tertullian's *On Spectacles* (Waszink 1948; Cortesi 1984). The Christian author drew freely on the learned representations of the *res antiqua* found in these earlier works, all of which seem to validate a strong temporal disjuncture between now and then, the present and the past. But Tertullian did so in a manner that precisely inverted the intellectual *Tendenz* of the original antiquarian works. In wanting to argue that all spectacles were and still remained firmly tied to the worship of the gods, he sought in fact to collapse the difference between now and then, past and present, at least where the sacrality of the games was concerned. How should a modern historian read Tertullian's work? It is clearly not advisable to read in it some kind of proof that there had been no desacralization of the games. But it is just as inadvisable to read this text, or any other text, as suggesting that there was desacralization. Texts function poorly as proof-texts in such instances.

Tertullian had not expected his fellow Christians to accept his argument readily. His heaping on of *recherché* references to antiquarian writings merely underscores how unrepresentative his work was of the general attitude among Christians who were his contemporaries. One might conclude that most Christians who attended the shows paid little attention to their history and were not at all inclined to believe that they had any religious (or cultic) associations at all. Yet textual sources simply do not allow us to form a sound judgment regarding the degree of desacralization or secularization of a given society. Literary traditions tend to generate their own narratives of change, and the dominant ancient literary ideology is that of decline and progressive decadence, which serves to reify the notion of a golden past. It is easy to be seduced into accepting such paradigms as descriptive rather than normative. But if we find Roman authors speaking of their own society as one that had been desacralized over time, it merely shows that such was the belief among the literary and literate elite. Whether indeed there had been desacralization in a broader historical sense is a question that could likely never be answered. Also, what some might characterize as desacralization can often just as easily be described by others as a shift in the religious imagination or the *loci* of the divine. Desacralization, then, has dubious value in historical analysis, save as an aspect of ancient and modern ideology. A literary representation that presents the past as past and another that renders the past as very much like the present, while they are diametrically opposite in character, have in common the quality of being ideological constructs that do not provide a single set of data from which a theory of desacralization, or religious change more generally, can be constructed.

Inventing the Secular in Late Antiquity

The secular, a notion that is now so firmly fixed in modern minds as to pass as a part of the natural order, was in Late Antiquity largely an unintended product of christianization. As such, it was a "betwixt and between" that was regarded as neither christianized nor pagan. Certainly the very label "pagan" was not itself unproblematic from a philological standpoint; in fact, it had to be gradually invented and made to fit the contours of what Christians imagined paganism to have been (O'Donnell 1971). As mentioned earlier, this process eventually led to an emerging consensus that saw the cultic worship of the gods as the core of paganism, and it was eventually to sacrifice, especially blood sacrifice, that the label was most fully applied.

Tertullian was only one Christian among many who voiced the opinion that almost every aspect of traditional Greco-Roman culture was pagan and hence ought to be rejected by Christians. But such sharply sectarian claims, made in a tutored rhetoric, simply helps underscore the fact that most Christians did not accept the view that all that was "old" was also "bad." Many indeed subscribed to the view that cultic practices such as sacrifice must go, but most other aspects of traditional culture, with appropriate reconfiguration, could be retained. In the process of negotiating between what among the "old" was bad and had to go and what was either good or at least neutral and hence could stay, late antique persons were engaged with each other over a vital debate regarding the nature and pace of christianization and, ultimately, the kind of society in which they wished to live. It was in this same process that the secular was to play a signal role as an enabling conceptual category in Late Antiquity.

How individuals and groups used the category of the secular in their mutual negotiations can be seen in several places. Earnest discussions, such as one finds in Basil of Caesarea's *Address to Young Men on the Right Use of Greek Literature* and Augustine of Hippo's *On Christian Doctrine*, regarding the value of traditional Greek and Roman literary classics in a christianizing culture, are too well known to require further treatment here (Rousseau 1994; Vessey et al. 1999). A similar dynamic can be discerned in the rival attempts to categorize particular physical spaces and objects. How the statues of the gods were treated in this period is most instructive (Curran

1994; James 1996). While many – probably even most – Jews and Christians long regarded such statues as demonic, others proposed that only certain statues, including cult statues found inside shrines and temples, were idols and hence subject to censure and destruction; others, such as those on public display, were in the latter view to be safeguarded and cherished as cultural artifacts, as neutral symbols of past achievements.

Christianization and Secularization as Cultural Claims

Historians of Late Antiquity rely on a limited corpus of surviving evidence for their interpretations of the past. Working strictly within the confines of this evidentiary corpus, they cannot hope to devise metrics for christianization, itself a form of sacralization, nor for secularization or desacralization, without having to contend with the problematic nature of their sources. While these processes will no doubt continue to function as favored categories in historical analysis, to come to a satisfactory understanding of each one, and of each in relation to the other, requires first the careful interpretation of textual strategies and deployment of forms of representation as historical acts. Here the historian would do well to take the "rhetorical turn," in order to grasp, through reading the surviving texts closely and contextually, the ideological claims put forward by those who were seeking to shape their worlds in accordance with their own beliefs and interests (Clark 2004). If we are to interpret secularization not as a large-scale historical development but as a set of discrete counter-claims (both written and read first and foremost in relation to the demands of christianization), we have to pay close attention to the strategies of textual representation that the ancient authors employed. To achieve this goal will require us to set aside the imperative of using past evidence to arrive at a master narrative of religious change in accordance with the model of "secularization theory." The reward in doing so will be a richer, more nuanced grasp of the historical challenges faced by individuals and communities in the past.

The latter approach depends largely on the survival of textual evidence, and the process whereby traditions are formed and texts transmitted clearly favors the entrenchment of select Patristic perspectives. This means that secularization and christianization tend to be approached exclusively from the points of view of select Christian writers. Possible balancing strategies include the practice of reading between the lines, trying to decide what the intended or historical audiences of works such as Tertullian's *On Spectacles*, John Chrysostom's sermons against the public shows, or Jacob of Sarugh's *Homilies against Spectacles* (Moss 1935) might themselves have thought or believed. But such ventures, critical as they are, are fraught with hermeneutical difficulties of the first order.

On the other hand, historians do occasionally have access to other texts that approach the issues in markedly different ways. One such corpus is the set of imperial laws that were codified under Theodosius II and Justinian. While the selection of laws for preservation and transmission was also determined by a process of tradition formation such as one finds in Christian texts, it reflects mainly the concerns of a nonecclesiastical elite in late antique society. While by the late fourth and early fifth century the emperors and imperial administrators had become mostly Christian in personal conviction and outlook, they sought in word and deed to validate a secular sphere whose qualities were significantly at odds with the ideals of Christian sanctity that were being preached from the pulpit at the time. Even as they incorporated christianizing language in the promulgation of some of their laws (Harries 1999; Matthews 2000), the overall effect of imperial legislation was not to place an ascetic imprint on society but rather to devise a middle way whereby many traditional institutions and practices that were deemed important to the common weal could be maintained even against the objections of critical Christian voices. It is in this context that the emperors and the political elite more generally played an active role in secularizing Roman public spectacles.

A devout Christian, Constantius II issued in AD 341 the decree of *cesset superstitio* or "Let *superstitio* cease!" (*Cod. Theod.* 16. 10. 3). As the emperor openly took the field against what was being presented as pagan superstition, others began to wonder which elements of traditional society would come to be so categorized. Some Christians clearly thought that the measure ought to bring about the demise of public spectacles, given the latter's association with the worship of the gods. But when the question was put before the emperor, he made it known that he believed the answer to be otherwise – namely, that the games were indeed secular in character. In a law to Catullinus, urban prefect of Rome AD 342–4 (who happened to be the father-in-law of the senator Praetextatus, a known worshiper of the traditional gods), Constantius II publicized the view that his AD 341 ban on *superstitio* was in no way to be applied to celebration of festivals and games. In the emperor's view, since the accompanying public sacrifice had already been taken out of the equation, traditional festivals and spectacles ought to be seen as having been sufficiently cleansed or desacralized as to be unobjectionable to Christians.

As if to underscore how far this principle might be extended, Constantius went on to explain that indeed those extramural temples associated with festivals and public spectacles or *voluptates* must be carefully preserved for that very reason:

> Although all superstitions must be completely eradicated, nevertheless, it is Our will that the buildings of the temples situated outside the walls shall remain untouched and uninjured. For since certain plays or spectacles of the circus or contests derive their origin from some of these temples, such structures shall not be torn down, since from them is provided the regular performance of long established amusements for the Roman people. (*Cod. Theod.* 16. 10. 3, tr. Pharr 1952: 472)

Through this and similar enactments, Christian emperors were actively seeking a way to establish a compromise position that would balance their own interests with the agenda of Christians who advocated a radical form of christianization. They reached the solution by placing the games and other aspects of traditional civic culture in a new and neutral category of the secular, defined as neither pagan nor Christian. Such a justification for public spectacles even enabled the emperors to include a plea to preserve the temples on account of the latter's traditional association with spectacles. Having desacralized the games by representing them as essential public services rather than sacral rites, the emperors were later able to use the imperative of offering spectacles to transform even otherwise objectionable temples into neutral cultural heritage sites that merited preservation rather than destruction.

An able ruler, Constantius was known to have adopted a pragmatic attitude toward the provision of games, at times checking excesses (*Cod. Theod.* 15. 12. 2), and also using them to forge a close connection with his favored subject populations, including the *plebs Romana*. Interaction with the people of Rome was particularly important during his *adventus* to Rome in AD 357, which culminated in chariot races in the Circus Maximus. Afterwards, the emperor thanked the people of the city for their warm reception by the gift of an obelisk that was installed there during the prefecture of Orfitus (Amm. Marc. 17. 4. 1).

Constantius thus demonstrated in practice how the notion that *panem et circenses* remained a vital element of Roman imperial ideology in the post-Constantinian world. His example was followed by other Christian rulers. In a law of AD 399, Arcadius and Honorius issued the following a law to a proconsul of Africa:

> Just as We have already abolished profane rites by a salutary law, so We do not allow the festal assemblies of citizens and the common pleasure of all to be abolished. Hence we decree that, according to ancient custom, amusements shall be furnished to the people, but without any sacrifice or any accursed superstition, and they be allowed to attend festal banquets, whenever public desires so demand. (*Cod. Theod.* 16. 10. 17, Pharr 1952: 475)

In the above examples, the imperial rationale for safeguarding spectacles was premised on the ban on public sacrifices that was the cornerstone of imperial de-paganization (Barnes 1984; Bradbury 1994, 1995). Severed from their moorings in ostensibly pagan cultic practices, the public shows could henceforth be represented as belonging to a secular sphere, that is, to the part of the Greco-Roman past that could be retained for the unfolding Christian present. The imperial imprimatur on the shows drew on the language of tradition, expedience, and public utility. The public games were deliberately referred to as *voluptates*, pleasures of the people, and their appeal to the people repeatedly cited as the chief reason why the elite continued to safeguard their availability. Thus the main justification for the games was that, while regrettable, they responded to the *voluptas spectandi* of the urban plebs so that, as *voluptates*, the shows constituted key elements of the essential *commoda* that it was the duty of the elite to provide to the people.

This effort to secularize public spectacles needs to be placed in the context of a broader project to define the meaning of pagan in the late Roman law codes (Salzman 1987; Hunt 1993). One example of this can be found in the process whereby the practice of the *ars magica* came to be associated with pagan idolatry, even as the traditional cultic practices of temple priests came to be linked with all other illegitimate "religious" practices such as divination, astrology, and the practice of magic (Sandwell 2005). When the pre-Constantinian Roman elite discourse clearly distinguished between state and civic cult and these latter marginalized practices, all of them became officially categorized henceforth as forms of condemned *superstitio*.

The strategic desacralization of the public spectacles also had important functions to perform among other segments of the Roman elite. The senator Symmachus the Elder, often regarded a defender of the ancient religious tradition as represented by his advocacy for the return of the Altar of Victory to the Roman senate house, came to articulate a position on games that was very similar to the one articulated by Christian Roman emperors. Symmachus' letters and official reports or *relationes* while urban prefect of Rome speak to the importance of the public spectacles in the life of the city and in the construction of relationships between the emperors, the senatorial aristocracy, and the people of Rome. The Christian emperors were then no longer interested in certain traditional forms of elite munificence such as the building of temples to the gods; they even began to allow local Christians to destroy certain rural temples. While in this respect, the emperors showed themselves resistant to the claims of tradition, as Symmachus discovered when his spirited fight for the return of the *ara Victoriae* came ultimately to naught, these same Christian rulers could be successfully asked to take part in a collaboration to provide the city with bread and circuses. Symmachus did not prevail in the partisan and divisive dispute over the restoration of the Altar of Victory to the *curia*. But he did win the imperial ear – to some extent – when, as urban prefect, he represented the people's wish for *panem et circenses* without overt reference to the religious connotation of the *ludi*:

> The Roman people looks for outstanding benefactions from your Divinities, but, my Lords Emperors, it now asks again for those which your Eternities voluntarily promised: for it regards them as owed. Not that it feels any doubt that they are to be rendered to it – for we can trust nothing with greater confidence than the undertaking of good emperors – but it does not wish, by not making an immediate demand, to give the impression of dissatisfaction with what is offered. And so it begs your Clemencies, after granting those subsidies [of food stuffs] which your generosity has made towards our sustenance, should furnish also the enjoyment of chariot races and dramatic performances to be held in the circus and in Pompey's theatre. The city delights in these entertainments and your promise has awakened anticipation. Every day messengers are awaited to confirm that these promised shows will soon arrive at the city; reports on charioteers and on horses are being collected; every conveyance, every ship is rumoured to have brought in theatrical artists. Nevertheless it is affection for your Perennities, not avidity for entertainment, that has whetted the longings of the populace. (Symmachus, *Relatio* 6, tr. Barrow 1973: 56–7)

By speaking of the Roman people's customary entitlement to shows but otherwise omitting references to the *res antiqua*, the traditional lore that could only underscore the association of the games to "pagan" religion, Symmachus was in effect desacralizing the shows so that religious partisanship no longer entered the equation when determining the allocation of resources for civic upkeep (Lim 1999).

Such examples, which can readily be multiplied, speak to the ways in which desacralization or secularization was invoked in the cause of advocacy. For the ruling elite in particular, secularization enabled a mode of constructive mutual engagement that transcended the claims of religious partisanship. By continuing to furnish both an occasion and an imperative for cooperation, it helped turn the otherwise fractious group into partners working toward a set of common goals.

Conclusion

The christianizing transformation of Roman society was something quite real and far-reaching. As a historically significant phenomenon it rightly continues to serve as a focus of scholarly investigations (Salzman 1999). Yet christianization can also be understood as a rhetorical and ideological strategy that was used by individuals in Late Antiquity. In this latter manifestation, it not only found expression in a set of discursive claims that individuals and groups drew upon to advocate particular changes but also gave rise to counter-rhetorics and forms of resistance that sought to palliate its radical and universal demands. I have tried here to present a picture of how christianization and secularization, in reference to the culture of Roman public spectacles, might be understood as historically meaningful discursive strategies that ancient persons employed in order to help shape the nature of the christianizing Roman society.

Extant literary texts from Patristic authors privilege the claims of christianization and help establish it as the master narrative for understanding the nature of social and cultural changes in this time. Only by reading between the lines and by examining alternative texts, such as imperial laws and writings by individuals like Symmachus the Elder, can scholars appreciate the quiet but determined support for the creation of the secular as a sanctuary into which particular elements of Roman culture could be placed for their own protection. Such a notion of the secular represents neither a neutral nor a residual category, but one that was actively cultivated by those individuals who proposed that Roman public spectacles were an indispensable part of communal and political life, and therefore merited preservation and support.

Secularization as a policy functioned both as a form of ideological representation and a statement regarding how resources, symbolic and physical, ought to be allocated. It was for many a direct riposte to the more radical claims of christianization. As the rise of Christianity began to reshape the civic and public cultures of cities, those who wished to resist the totalizing demands that other Christians made in the name of their common religion resorted to various means: some simply continued to attend and financially sponsor the games; others asked testily where in the Scriptures spectacles were prohibited, and insisted that in any event they were attending the shows only in order to seek relief from the cares of life; and still others argued that such shows belonged to the *saeculum* and as such were permissible to Christians. In various and subtle ways, the discourses and practices of secularizaton, which were much less visible in the historical record than those of christianization, helped create and sustain an autonomous sphere of action and beliefs – that of the *saeculum* – within the framework of a christianizing Roman society.

BIBLIOGRAPHICAL NOTE

The topics examined in this chapter do not fall easily within a single academic category. There exist many treatments of the Greco-Roman culture of public spectacles. Salzman's study of the Calendar of AD 354, offers a fine discussion of how the rise of Christianity created a parallel public culture (Salzman 1990). Many discussions of the impact that Christianity had on the culture of the games have focused on how it might have contributed to the demise of Roman gladiatorial combats. Ville 1960, MacMullen 1986b, and Wiedemann 1995 offer different perspectives on this nexus.

Many studies detail the Christian responses to the culture of public spectacles, often focusing on the sermons and works of a single author. Moss 1935, Jürgens 1972, and Weismann 1972, for example, are constructed both as Christian "Patristic" responses to the games and as studies of what "Patristics" tell us about particular ancient spectacles. More recently, Leyerle 2001 and Maxwell 2006 offer more nuanced historical approaches that suggest ways in which popular sermons against the spectacles may also be read as evidence for the cultural processes that led to the creation of a new Christian identity in Late Antiquity.

Christianization is an important topic that has greatly shaped modern research in Late Antiquity. Important approaches are laid out in MacMullen 1984, Peter Brown 1993, Klingshirn 1994, and Brown 1995. One aspect of christianization is the construction of paganism and pagans: see O'Donnell 1971, North 2005. Religious labels or categories were dynamic ones that were contested throughout Late Antiquity in a variety of arenas. On the definition of public blood sacrifice to the gods as the quintessential manifestation of paganism, see Barnes 1984, Bradbury 1994; on debates over the religious status of public statues, see Curran 1994, James 1996; on the classification of the *ars magica* and other forms of so-called *superstitio*, see Salzman 1987, Sandwell 2005; on christianization as de-paganization, see (among others) Rothaus 1996; and on christianization as a reconstitution of society in terms of the construction of time and space, see Salzman 1999, Curran 2000.

The concept of secularization as a historical process has been principally developed in reference to the major cultural shifts that occurred in early modern Europe: see Lübbe 1965. The classic formulation is that of Weber 1930. Modern interpreters in fields such as anthropology, historical sociology, and religious studies still actively apply and debate his propositions: see Devisch 1973; Martin 1978; Dobbelaere 1981; Hammond 1985; Stark and Bainbridge 1985; Fenn 1986; Stark 1996; Klutz 1998; Flávio Pierucci 2000.

On the construction of a secular sphere in Late Antiquity, see Markus 1970, 2006; Lim 1994. On reading secularization as more a rhetorical topos used in cultural and religious negotiations in Late Antiquity than as part of a grand historical process, see Lim 1999.

CHAPTER THIRTY-FOUR

The Political Church: Religion and the State

Michael Gaddis

Christians, as the late second-century author of the *Epistle to Diognetus* famously remarked, "dwell in the world, but are not of the world" (*Ep. ad Diognetum* 6). A formulation packing much into few words (compare John 17: 11–16), "in but not of" captures neatly the ongoing tension faced by the late antique Church as it struggled to reconcile the spiritual and the worldly. For the Church as an organization, implicated as it was in secular relations of power, such an ideal of detachment remained out of reach. By taking the Church as a political institution, I shall touch in this chapter on some of the ways in which patterns of behavior and habits of thought from secular politics and earthly society followed churchmen into the realm of the spiritual.

The emperor Constantine has traditionally taken a full measure of blame for dragging the Church into the worldly. But we must not overlook other dimensions of contact between secular and spiritual that were nearly as old as Christianity itself. Constantine aligned himself with a Church whose basic principles of hierarchy and structures of power had been in place for a long time (Rapp 2005a, arguing for continuity between the pre- and post-Constantinian eras). The offices of bishop and presbyter, the foundations of church government, were already well established by the middle of the second century, supported by the key doctrine of apostolic succession and by firm definitions of orthodoxy and heresy. By the third century, worries began to be voiced that certain bishops might be tempted to aggrandize their power at their colleagues' expense (see, e.g., Cyprian's remarks at the Seventh Council of Carthage, AD 256). In the fourth century, Constantine and his successors gave the leaders of the Church the means to pursue their rivalries on a much larger stage. Bishops could now employ the state's coercive powers against dissidents and rivals. From that point forward, the state was increasingly called upon to take sides and to settle disputes, as it found itself drawn deeper into the Church's internal conflicts (Gaddis 2005: *passim*).

While the emperor's role should not be denied its due weight, my focus here will instead be on what I call the "political Church." We must consider how the Church itself functioned as a polity – how it governed, regulated, and judged itself, and how its different authorities and centers of power related to one another. In so doing, it borrowed much from its external surroundings. Habits, discourses, and structures of power that had long pervaded the political and social culture of the Greco-Roman world found themselves transposed into the ecclesiastical realm and adapted to the government of the Church. Since constraints of space preclude a truly comprehensive treatment, I limit myself here to introducing several particular aspects of ecclesiastical politics that I believe deserve greater attention than they have yet received.

Honor and Dignity

Scholarship on premodern Mediterranean society has long emphasized the paramount importance of traditional concepts of "honor" and "shame" for understanding social relations, and particularly gender roles, at the level of the family or village society. A recent study (Lendon 1997) has postulated honor as a guiding paradigm for interpreting the workings of Roman imperial government and elite society. There has as yet been little significant study of "honor" in ecclesiastical usage, and much can be learned by an exploration of the ways in which honor-discourse insinuated itself into the politics of the late Roman Church.

For the bishops who shared in the government of the Church, authority and legitimacy rested upon common understandings of hierarchy, primacy, and deference, concepts articulated in the traditional secular language of honor and dignity. The interest here is less in how bishops operated within their own cities and congregations – the approach adopted in most of the ample scholarship on the role of the bishop that has appeared in recent years – but rather, how bishops related to each other through the larger power structures of the Church (on "primacy" among bishops see Daley 1993; and see Lizzi Testa, ch. 35). Both formal rules and informal mores governed their interactions. Expectations of reciprocal courtesy required bishops to give full faith and credit to the excommunications and disciplinary actions performed by their colleagues. Occasions for conflict arose when bishops failed to respect the judgments of their peers, by harboring or holding communion with persons excommunicated elsewhere (see, e.g., Nicaea canons 5, 16; Antioch canons 3, 6–8; Sardica canon 13; Chalcedon canons 11, 13, 20–1).

The pride of place held by bishops and leading churchmen coexisted uneasily with the admonitions to humility that dominated Christian moral and ascetic discourse. Dignity could all too easily shade into pride and arrogance when those entrusted with the guidance of the Church were tempted to power for its own sake rather than for the sake of the faith. Cyprian of Carthage, in the third century, warned against any man who would make himself a "bishop of bishops." Echoing the ancient secular fear of concentrating too much power in the hands of ambitious men, Cyprian castigated bishops who went beyond the proper boundaries of their own sees and sought to pursue dominion over the Church as a whole. He had in mind particularly his colleague the bishop of Rome, who even at this early date asserted a special primacy over the Church by virtue of his Petrine succession. Such concerns placed a sharp focus on the roles of individual churchmen, who would in later generations increasingly come to serve as power brokers and politicians as well as moral and spiritual leaders. The Church underscored its awareness of the problem in the numerous canons, regulations, and controversies regarding appropriate or inappropriate ordination, and in the often prohibited and often ignored rules against "translation," the promotion of bishops from one see to another (e.g., Nicaea canons 4, 6, 9, 15–16; Antioch canons 13, 21–2; Sardica canons 1–2; Chalcedon canons 2, 5–6, 10, 20). Ideologies of clerical duty, humility, and restraint coexisted uneasily with claims by particular bishops and sees – most notably Rome, but also leading eastern cities such as Alexandria and Constantinople – to special status within the Church. Accusations of corruption and misconduct, brought within the context of larger doctrinal and factional divisions and aired at regional and ecumenical synods, served to define and moderate the power of those who would behave as "tyrants" in the Church. Thus, the Council of Chalcedon made an example of the notorious Dioscorus of Alexandria, who was condemned more for his abusive actions at the Second Council of Ephesus (henceforward Ephesus II) than for doctrinal error (see Chalcedon, session 3, Price and Gaddis 2005, ii: 29–116; and more generally Gaddis 2005: chs. 7 and 8). The ecclesiology of late Roman Christianity was shaped by a profound tension: was the Church to be governed on a monarchical model, like the imperial state, or ought it to be guided by a more collegial paradigm of shared authority, exercised through conciliar action and canonical legislation?

In traditional social terms, of course, honor and shame were highly gendered – imposing very different rules upon men and women. As applied to the late antique Church, the qualities of honor and sources of dishonor show an intriguing mixture of both masculine and feminine characteristics. Male dignity often brought with it a certain brittleness, leaving its owners keenly sensitive to insult and easily provoked to anger. The maintenance of prestige required that challenges not go unanswered, demanding a firm and sometimes violent response. The honor of the Christian religion, and indeed that of God himself, could be offended by acts of sacrilege or words of blasphemy. Zealous Christians, driven by a "godly" anger, might use force to avenge these insults (Gaddis 2005: 179–91). There was, said Jerome, "no cruelty in defending God's honor" (Hieron. *Ep.* 109. 3).

Female honor, by contrast, tended to focus much more exclusively on sexual purity. Ecclesiastical discourse employed a highly sexualized language of loyalty and betrayal in its frequent invocation of "adultery" to describe heresy, apostasy, and other departures from true faith. Heretical teachers were "seducers," and women were thought especially susceptible to their blandishments (see, e.g., Burrus 1991; Lyman 1993; Knust 2005). Following normal patterns of subordination, the lay congregation was often described as "feminine" and thus in need of the fatherly guidance and protection of clergy. When the Church was imagined as a whole – the congregation as the collective "body of Christ" – defenders of the faith might invoke feminine imagery when it was subjected to outrage or violation. Athanasius used this strategy to characterize Arian mistreatment of consecrated virgins as symbolic of their violence against the true faith (e.g., *Encyclical Letter* 1; see Gaddis 2005: 83–7).

Alongside honor, of course, there must come a concept of "shame," deriving not from external attacks but rather from the conduct of the Church's own leaders. What were the sources of shame for the Church, and how were these handled? Christian authorities both secular and sacred repeatedly expressed the fear that pagans, Jews, and heretics would "laugh" and take heart at the spectacle of doctrinal disagreement or material corruption within the Church. Prior to the Council of Nicaea, Constantine had rebuked Alexander of Alexandria and his presbyter Arius for their unseemly and divisive doctrinal argument (Eusebius, *Vit. Const.* 2. 64–72 ; 3. 21, and Socrates, *Hist. Eccl.* 1. 6; also Millar 2004 on fear of Jewish laughter). The need to present a united and dignified face to those outside the Church, and thus facilitate their conversion, served as an argument to rebuke and control the behavior of those already within it.

As honor was due to individual bishops and clergy, so also and more importantly did it belong to the Church as an institution, and indeed to the Christian faith in the abstract. The honor of the institution could be put at risk by the misconduct of individual clerics, a problem not unique to the period. Augustine, arriving in the town of Fussala to deal with the scandal caused by the reprobate bishop Antoninus, whom he had himself recommended for the office, professed himself so ashamed that he could not look the townspeople in the eye (August. *Ep.* 20*. 15). But the primary concern of the North African church in this instance was to preserve its own institutional power, and the bishops bent over backward to preserve the dignity of the office to which Antoninus had been ordained, going to every possible length to allow him to retain the title and rank that he had dishonored by his behavior. But the normal tendency of the hierarchy to close ranks broke down in the face of doctrinal controversy and political rivalry. Most of our evidence for episcopal misconduct comes from accusations brought against bishops at synods dominated by their enemies (see charges against John Chrysostom at the Synod of the Oak, against Ibas of Edessa and others at the second session of Ephesus II (the so-called "Robber Council"), and against Dioscorus at Chalcedon's third session). Only in such a context – when doctrinal partisanship escalated into ecclesiastical "civil war" – would bishops be willing to set aside normal principles of order and entertain accusations brought by lesser clerics against their hierarchs.

Saving Face

The maintenance of honor, in the Church as in the broader culture, required considerable attention to the saving of face. Mistakes or policy changes, in ecclesiastical matters as in secular affairs, were not to be admitted or acknowledged, but rather concealed and finessed to the greatest extent possible. This imperative not only arose with respect to current authorities – individual bishops as well as institutions – but also implicated revered theologians and councils from the past. The "Fathers," on occasion, were found in retrospect to have been frustratingly imprecise or inconsistent in their choice of words when addressing particular doctrinal questions on which, long after their deaths, new controversies would underline the need for greater exactitude (see Graumann, ch. 36). The same fifth-century bishops who held up the Nicene Creed as a perfect standard of orthodoxy recognized that its authors – being unable to answer questions not yet asked – had failed to anticipate the controversies that would divide the Church in their own time. Ambiguity in Cyril's usage of key terms like *physis* ("nature") would later allow his writings to be invoked by both Monophysites and Dyophysite Chalcedonians in support of their respective Christological arguments (Gray 1997; Wessel 2004; Price and Gaddis 2005, i: 60–75).

An especially ticklish problem was posed by past emperors who had backed what in retrospect was judged to be the wrong side. This problem complicated the legacies of the fourth-century rulers Constantius and Valens, both of whom favored a moderate Homoian doctrinal position later remembered by Nicene orthodox tradition as "Arian" heresy. The same issue arose in the fifth century with respect to Theodosius II, whose backing of Dioscorus and of the violent Ephesus II in AD 449 had to be accounted for when his ecclesiastical policies, shortly after his death, were reversed at Chalcedon. Similar difficulties implicated later sovereigns in the course of the various doctrinal reversals of the late fifth and early sixth centuries (see generally Frend 1972; Grillmeier 1987; Meyendorff 1989). The emperor's complicity needed to be finessed or excused, and blame quietly displaced onto acceptable scapegoats such as the unpopular court eunuch Chrysaphius ("seduced by Chrysaphius": annotation by Rusticus in the Latin Acts, *ACO* 2. 3. 2: 347–8; Price and Gaddis 2005, iii: 188–92).

Defining orthodox doctrine necessarily required passing judgments upon persons, who earned condemnation or rehabilitation as they either clung to or backed away from teachings now judged incorrect. In most cases, timely repentance would resolve the problem. Several bishops who had been among the ringleaders at Ephesus II in AD 449 were allowed at Chalcedon to retain their offices after they abandoned Dioscorus and agreed to endorse the decrees of the new council (Juvenal of Jerusalem, Thalassius of Caesarea, and others: Chalcedon, session 1, 284–98, Price and Gaddis 2005, i: 188–90; and session 4, 14–18, Price and Gaddis 2005, ii: 147). At the same time, those whom the prior council had condemned as heretics (Theodoret of Cyrrhus, Ibas of Edessa, Eusebius of Dorylaeum, and, posthumously, Flavian of Constantinople) were restored to communion. More than 100 bishops who had attended and acclaimed the decisions of Ephesus II were also seated at Chalcedon, many of them admitting error and asking forgiveness. Among the architects of that infamous "Robber Council," only Dioscorus would remain condemned (Chalcedon, session 3, esp. 98–103, Price and Gaddis 2005, ii: 110–15).

Lesser clerics, monks, and laity might be forgiven for being "seduced" into heresy, if they invoked the necessary discourses of appeal and repentance in their petitions. By pronouncing an orthodox creed, those who had strayed could be restored to communion (e.g., repentant Quartodecimans from Lydia, at Ephesus I: Chalcedon, session 1, 918–43, Price and Gaddis 2005, i: 311–23). Humility and submission to authority were encouraged and rewarded. But obstinacy and defiant persistence in error – which in the all-important context of the faith could offer no clearer illustration of the sin of pride – brought anathema (e.g., the defiant monks Carosus and

Dorotheus, at Chalcedon, session 4, 63–116, Price and Gaddis 2005, ii: 153–63). Sometimes the tables might be turned: the archimandrite Eutyches, with the support of Dioscorus and his allies, brought about in AD 449 the condemnation of the bishops who had judged him in Constantinople in AD 448, because they had overreached in attempting to force him to accept the controversial formula "in two natures" (Chalcedon, session 1, esp. 484–551, 864–84, 943–64, Price and Gaddis 2005, i: 218–25, 271–92, 340–4; see discussion at i: 25–33).

The Conciliar Arena

Analysis of the conciliar acts offers the opportunity to explore the practices and strategies of contestation, persuasion, rhetoric, and resistance employed by both the council's architects and its critics. What gave a council its legitimacy, and what were the limits on what it could do? When bishops signed up to controversial statements of doctrine, on whose behalf did they speak, and by what right? Council participants not only claimed to hold authority over the whole Church, but also presumed to speak in the name of dead "fathers" and previous councils in asserting the right to interpret or "clarify" what their predecessors had meant. The bishops, as a group, appealed to hierarchical principle and apostolic authority – even though individual bishops could easily forfeit that position when they abused their office and fell into heresy. The engineered unanimity of conciliar pronouncements was believed, ideally, to reflect inspiration by the Holy Spirit.

The ample surviving documentation for the Councils of Ephesus and particularly Chalcedon allows us to look beneath the canons and definitions that constituted their final products and take a close look at the decision-making process in and around the councils themselves (for Chalcedon, see now Price and Gaddis 2005). The documentary acts preserve much information about the organization, procedure, and presidency of the conciliar assemblies. They illustrate the expression and suppression of opinion and debate, the operation of authority and processes of decision, across the different categories of issues with which the councils dealt – doctrinal definition, canonical legislation, and judicial adjudication. Though all met at the emperor's invitation, comparison of the Ephesian councils and Chalcedon illustrates very different models of procedure and presidency, the former dominated by the episcopal "tyranny" of Dioscorus of Alexandria and his allies, the latter held under tight imperial supervision. Where both Ephesian councils undertook the identification, denunciation, and exclusion of "Nestorian" heretics, Chalcedon emphasized instead the appearance of order and lawful procedure, and offered a centrist doctrinal formula, to which all were considered to have consented, whether they liked it or not (Gaddis 2005: ch. 8; Price and Gaddis 2005, i: 19–51). Nevertheless, these councils had much in common with one another and with most ecclesiastical synods. Their judgments, especially in matters of doctrine, were to be reached not by debate and majority vote but rather by a unanimous consensus that, when attained, would be taken as evidence of divine inspiration. Since arguments and differences of opinion were not to be aired in the public record, major decisions were typically reached behind the scenes by small groups of leading churchmen, before being presented to the assembled bishops for their acclamation (Chalcedon's Definition written by a select committee: session 2. 6; 5. 29, Price and Gaddis 2005, ii: 11, 200). The achievement of unanimity among hundreds of churchmen often required a considerable degree of pressure, applied with the support of the secular authorities or by the numerous and rowdy followers of the most powerful bishops. Ephesus II had been marred by explicit coercion, earning its reputation as a *latrocinium*, a lawless assembly disgraced by violence (Leo first coined the term: *Ep.* 95). Two years later, at Chalcedon, coercive pressure was considerably more measured and subtle – but nevertheless effective. Marcian first compelled the bishops to produce a new Definition of Faith, even though they saw no need for it (session 2. 2–7; 5. 2–8, Price and Gaddis 2005, ii: 9–11, 196–7) and then, when they produced a draft that did not satisfy the papal legates, ordered them to rewrite it (5. 9–29, Price and Gaddis 2005, ii: 197–201, with discussion at ii: 183–91).

Finding the Center

In the Christian empire, theological discourse and heresiological polemic followed in the long classical tradition of seeking a "middle way" between opposing extremes. Fourth-century Trinitarian controversy had been framed in terms of a contrast between Arian and Sabellian extremes. In the fifth century, conciliar authorities sought Christological truth between the opposite poles of Eutyches and Nestorius. This "three-term" model of orthodoxy as defined against multiple heresies contrasted with and coexisted alongside the more familiar "two-term" model, used in reference to single opponents, which set up a stark distinction between truth and falsehood. The use of "centrist" discourse in the context of the fifth century's controversies and conciliar pronouncements served to support broader political ideologies and strategies of ecclesiastical government. Emperors, in particular, tended to favor "centrist" strategies that privileged consensus and harmony above doctrinal exactitude. In this respect Zeno's *Henotikon* of the late fifth century, in its attempt to back away from the controversial issues raised at Chalcedon, followed in the tradition of those earlier fourth-century emperors who had endorsed the moderate Homoian position against both extreme Nicenes and extreme Arians. Where extremist discourse sought to sharpen distinctions, expose and denounce heretics, and provoke conflict, centrist discourse sought to blur boundaries, create consensus, and repress argument. Establishment authorities attempted to force compromise, create an appearance of unanimity, and enforce it by suppressing debate and by defining opponents not just as heretics but also as "extremists" and enemies of peace. These "extremists" could be singled out on more than one side, and used as contrasts to one's own "moderate" stance. Self-consciously centrist discourse seems to have been characteristic of the establishment, the party in power – whether in the state or within the Church itself – with the confidence to make distinctions more subtle than the purely binary while still maintaining a firm sense of its own superiority. Centrist paradigms supported governing authorities' propensity to explain and justify in disciplinary terms the coercive power they deployed to maintain religious unity (Gaddis 2005, esp. ch. 4).

In speaking of theological "moderation" and doctrinal "extremes," we should not take these terms as given, but rather remain aware of the ways in which conciliar authorities sought to define center and fringe. What degree of consensus needed to exist within the Church prior to the council, and to what extent was it created by the process of the council itself? What understandings and ideologies underlay the "consensus" they all claimed to prize? How paramount was its value, and how was it to be constructed? What was the permissible role in this process of emperors or secular officials? Of bishops? Of other religious figures such as monastic leaders or prominent "holy men"?

With these questions in mind, we may regard official creeds and conciliar definitions of faith as not only theological but also political and ecclesiological statements. The Chalcedonian Definition of Faith, which faced the difficult task simultaneously of expounding true doctrine and of explaining by what authority the assembled bishops dared to define it, devoted considerable space to answering charges of "innovation" and to arguing its fidelity to the Nicene Creed, even though much of its Christological teaching addressed issues that had not been considered at Nicaea (Chalcedon, session 5. 30–4, Price and Gaddis 2005, ii: 201–5, with discussion at 183–91). We find such apologia not only within the creeds and definitions themselves but also in the associated letters and proclamations made in the name of the council as a whole. The bishops at Chalcedon ended their synod with an "Address to Marcian" and a letter to Pope Leo, which both explained their condemnation of Dioscorus and defended their adoption of the Twenty-Eighth Canon over the opposition of the pope's legates (Price and Gaddis 2005, iii: 104–28, with discussion).

In its bold insistence that necessary clarification did not constitute impermissible innovation, Chalcedon's doctrinal product differed from other imperial initiatives that sought to sidestep controversies by imposing a simple prohibition on arguing the controversial term, in essence pretending that the divisive question had never been asked. With this rather optimistic approach, backers of the Homoian party in the fourth century, and of Zeno's *Henotikon* in the fifth, manufactured a centrist consensus that rested upon a fragile surface unanimity.

But the "center" itself was neither inflexible nor unchangeable. Imperial support, though not on its own sufficient to settle all argument, was certainly an essential precondition for consensus. Conciliar authority carried great weight, but even so it could be swayed by the emperor's expressed or implied preference. The death of Theodosius II in July of AD 450, and the subsequent accession of Marcian, swung the balance decisively against Dioscorus of Alexandria and the one-nature Christology that had prevailed at Ephesus II. At Chalcedon, more than 100 bishops who had attended and endorsed the decisions of the prior council now changed sides and repudiated their earlier pronouncements (for attendance numbers see Honigmann 1942–3; Price and Gaddis 2005, iii: 193–203).

Initially, Chalcedon seemed to command solid support within the episcopate, enjoying a more durable legitimacy than Ephesus II. In AD 457, when the emperor Leo circulated the *Codex Encyclius* in order to poll the bishops on their attitudes toward Chalcedon, the response was overwhelmingly positive. Only a few years later, however, equally large majorities of bishops followed the wishes of the new emperor Zeno and jumped aboard the more ambiguous position expressed in the *Henotikon* (see generally Frend 1972: 143–83; Meyendorff 1989: 187–202). It is impossible, of course, to discern to what degree this shift represented a genuine evolution in doctrinal stance rather than a simple response to political and institutional pressure. We may imagine that the great majority of bishops – hardly great theologians and polemicists like Cyril or Theodoret – were content to follow the dictates of higher authority. The problem, and the underlying cause of most ecclesiastical strife, lay in deciding which authorities were to be followed. Past creeds might be used to impeach current conciliar definitions, or teachings attributed to past Fathers set against the interpretations pronounced by contemporary leaders of the Church.

Those who were so minded had little difficulty in finding grounds for opposition to conciliar decisions. What if a present council seemed to contradict the truths expressed by councils past? The Nicene Trinitarian Creed, divisive and controversial in its own time, had by the early fifth century achieved a near-scriptural infallibility, codified in AD 431 when Ephesus I pronounced anathema against anyone who composed or taught a "different" faith from that of Nicaea ("seventh canon," quoted at Chalcedon, session 1. 943: Price and Gaddis 2005, i: 323). The Council of Chalcedon aroused considerable opposition and recrimination after the fact: did its elaborate Definition of Faith constitute necessary elaboration and explanation, or impermissible innovation? Arguments against the council made accusations of innovation and usurpation against apostolic and patristic authority. Critics questioned by what right the bishops at the council could decide matters of faith, how far were they authorized to go, and for whom they could claim to speak. As a constitution for the Christian Church, was the authority of the Nicene Creed to be taken in an "originalist" sense, limited to its strict wording and to the intentions of its early fourth-century authors, or was it rather to be understood as a "living" document within whose penumbras and emanations future councils might discover new answers to new questions never anticipated by its sainted authors?

The Written Record: The Conciliar Acts

The elaborate process of transcription, production, and circulation of the acts that formed the documentary record of the councils themselves became a subject of controversy (Price and Gaddis, 2005 i: 75–8). Council participants engaged in heated debates over accusations of forgery in the transcripts; debates that invoked broader questions of truth, falsehood, and the authority of the written word. The complex interaction of the acts' multiple layers of documentation, visible especially in the lengthy and convoluted first session of Chalcedon, shows us how the concerns of church leaders, charged with finding truth in authoritative Scriptures, converged with the legalistic and bureaucratic requirements of the late Roman imperial state to express a uniquely late antique obsession with textuality, and with the rigorous authentication of texts, as a basis for legitimate authority. Late Antiquity, broadly speaking, was an age in which great projects of codification and systematization were undertaken, in spheres ranging from secular law to religious doctrine, reflecting a broad-based cultural shift in favor of authoritative tradition and consensus (on law: Harries 1999; Humfress 2000 and ch. 25 in this volume; Matthews 2000; on religious and patristic authority: Gray 1989; Lim 1995). Late Roman Christianity, of course, was a religion that based itself very much upon the authority of the written word. In earlier centuries, the Church had assembled various sacred writings into an authoritative canon of Holy Scripture. In the fifth century, the decrees and credal statements of past councils, and the writings of certain long dead theologians, acquired an almost scriptural authority of their own. But the desire to find absolute truth in texts was tempered by the realization that copyists could be mistaken and manuscripts corrupted, scribes bribed, and transcripts doctored.

Scarcely had the council adjourned before Chalcedon itself became the subject of struggles to control its meaning and message. The hand of Theodoret of Cyrrhus – whom the bishops had only grudgingly rehabilitated from charges of "Nestorian" heresy – has been seen behind the "Address to Marcian," a document issued in the name of the council but probably composed shortly afterward, which attempted to place a more strongly Antiochene Dyophysite spin on the Definition of Faith than had been apparent during the council's recorded deliberations, which had tended instead to stress the Definition's consistency with Cyrillian and Alexandrian teaching (Price and Gaddis 2005, iii: 105–7, 111–20). The production and dissemination of the official Acts, the authoritative textual record of the council, was hardly a neutral process. Separate Greek and Latin versions of the Acts, compiled respectively by imperial and patriarchal staff in Constantinople, and by editors sympathetic to the papal position, reveal the competing agendas of their authors. The ongoing ecclesiastical rivalry between Rome and Constantinople shaped successive stages of editing, from the immediate aftermath of the council up through the time of Justinian a century later. Texts were arranged, or language omitted or altered, in support of arguments over the Twenty-Eighth Canon, or over how much weight ought to have been given to the authority of the pope's representatives at the council (Price and Gaddis 2005, i: 78–85). Monophysite opponents of Chalcedon, meanwhile, were alleged to have been responsible for deliberate mistranslations of Pope Leo's *Tome*, and of other writings, into Greek and Syriac, rewritten in order to conform them to the polemical caricature that attributed to him – and, by extension, to Chalcedon itself – a "Nestorian" division of Christ into two persons (Leo, *Ep.* 130, 131).

Much remains to be learned from careful study of the compilation and circulation of the conciliar acts, as well as the various documentary collections that often accompanied them (Chrysos 1990; Price and Gaddis 2005, i: 78–85; iii: 157–92). How did they circulate, who had access to them, in what manner were they copied, excerpted, or translated? For example, it remains a mystery how Nestorius – long since disgraced and condemned as a heretic, exiled in a remote corner of the Egyptian desert – managed to obtain full transcripts of the proceedings of Ephesus II, on which he commented at great length in his own *Bazaar of Heracleides*. The deepening cultural, political, and linguistic divisions of the fifth-century empire conspired to limit the ability of westerners to participate in theological debates that took place almost entirely in Greek. Language barriers generated constant headaches for the papal representatives, handicapped throughout the council by the necessity of speaking through interpreters. Back in Italy, translators were in short supply and important documents might sit unread for years, further complicating what were often delicate negotiations with Constantinople (see, e.g., Leo, *Ep.* 113 to Julian of Cos). Amazingly, more than a century would pass before a complete Latin edition of Chalcedon's proceedings would become available to westerners (Price and Gaddis 2005, i: 83–5). How easily and how accurately did eastern texts and knowledge about eastern developments reach Rome and the Latin west generally? These seemingly mundane considerations would hold great implications for the later evolution of the Greek and Latin churches.

Blessed Memory

Even as churchmen preached of eternity, they remained in a world shaped and transformed by the passage of time. As generations went by, eyewitnesses died and memories faded, even as traditions took shape and stories grew in the telling. Historical memory played a profoundly important role in shaping the traditions and sense of identity of the Church, as it evolved through the late antique centuries. Key events might look in the near term – in the perspective of those who witnessed, lived through, and were formed by them – very different from how they would appear in the recollections of more distant times.

Some councils aged well, looking decidedly better the further they receded into the past. Nicaea's exalted status in fifth-century debates would have seemed quite odd indeed to the Homoian bishops and emperors who had spent much of the fourth century distancing themselves from what they regarded as an extreme departure from the acceptable mainstream of Trinitarian teaching. By contrast, the several similar assemblies of bishops that had met in the mid fourth century to endorse Homoian or Homoiousian creeds gradually faded into obscurity, to be passed over when the firmly Nicene Church of later centuries built its doctrinal and ecclesiological identity around a select sequence of authoritative "ecumenical" councils (on fourth-century controversies see Brennecke 1988; Hanson 1988).

Posterity similarly held up revered deceased individuals – called, always, "of blessed memory" – as "Fathers of the Church." Men like Athanasius found themselves posthumously endowed by universal consensus with an exalted authority that could never have been imagined during their fiercely controversial lifetimes. The process repeated itself in the fifth century with Cyril of Alexandria, whose writings against Nestorius on the Incarnation would be used at Ephesus II and Chalcedon – less than a decade after his death in AD 444 – as touchstones of orthodoxy against which to judge the faith of others (Wessel 2004). What must it have been like for those of his contemporaries who lived through those years, especially old adversaries like Theodoret, who were now forced to join in acclaiming him (Theodoret: Chalcedon, session 8, Price and Gaddis 2005, ii: 250–7)? Ibas of Edessa fell victim in AD 449 to a new political correctness, finding himself condemned and deposed, among other reasons, on the basis of a decades-old letter in which he had sharply criticized the then living Cyril (*Letter to Mari*, read at Chalcedon, session 10. 137, Price and Gaddis 2005, ii: 295–8; Ibas' condemnation at Ephesus II, session 2, Flemming 1917: 6–68).

The counterpart to this sanctification, of course, was the designation of "heresiarchs," equally prominent in their notoriety. First and foremost came Nestorius, who played the same leading role in the heresiological demonology of the fifth century that Arius had in the fourth – even to the point of suffering a similarly miraculous and gruesome demise (Evagrius, *Hist. Eccl.* 1. 7; Zacharias, *Chron.* 3. 1). The secular Roman practice of *damnatio memoriae*, "condemnation of the memory" of despised rebels or tyrants (Hedrick 2000), found its ecclesiastical counterpart in the removal of the names of disfavored bishops from the diptychs regularly read in church. Constantinopolitan bishop Acacius' support of Zeno's *Henotikon* in AD 482 had led to a schism with Rome; in AD 518, communion was restored only after the new emperor Justin I acceded to the pope's demand that the name of the long-dead Acacius be stricken from the diptychs (Meyendorff 1989: 194–215). But in general, rather than erasing past heretics and tyrannical bishops from collective memory, the Church preferred instead to preserve their infamy, to hold them up as cautionary tales or as templates for the condemnation of future deviants.

The passage of time tended to clarify issues. Each new cycle of controversy resulted in further elaboration and refinement of orthodoxy as new questions were asked, debated, and – with varying degrees of finality – answered. Doctrinal statements, and those who uttered or wrote them, would in retrospect be judged as manifestly right or wrong. But in the Christian Roman Empire, theological debate could not take place in isolation from the political process. Bishops were now able to call upon the coercive powers of the secular arm to enforce their judgments, while emperors, firmly convinced that God held them responsible for maintaining the peace of the Church, sought to end disputes and create consensus by any means necessary (see generally Gaddis 2005, and Lizzi Testa, ch. 35). The application of political power to Church controversies served to consolidate and institutionalize the position of the favored faction and at the same time to marginalize its rivals much more effectively than would otherwise have been possible. Its consequence, then, was to make clearer the difference between winners and losers.

Conclusion: The Political Church

The blurring of the boundaries between the secular and the spiritual is a fundamental characteristic of this period (Markus 1990; Cameron 1995a; and see Lim, ch. 33).

Both state and society in Late Antiquity were profoundly if subtly shaped by discourses ultimately religious in origin, from the disciplinary paradigm of corrective force employed for the moral betterment of subjects that served to justify much of the state's violence, to the ascetic overtones that pervaded exhortations by both legislators and preachers. But the influence went both ways. Secular models of legitimacy and conflict, political virtues and vices, were transposed into the ecclesiastical sphere and applied to the government of the Church. This process can be seen, for example, in the application of the classical political category of "tyranny" to describe abuses of power by Christian bishops. Ecclesiastical writers, in defining the proper scope and exercise of ecclesiastical power, drew upon an ancient moral vocabulary of virtues and vices, the rights and wrongs of reason and emotion (see, e.g., Gregory the Great, *Pastoral Rule* 2. 9). Employing political discourses formerly used to praise and condemn the behavior of kings and emperors, Christian thinkers and leaders scrutinized themselves and their colleagues critically, as they weighed the dangers of pride, vanity, and ambition for an episcopacy caught between spiritual and worldly imperatives.

The government of the Church, both inside and outside the councils themselves, offered an arena in which clashing conceptions of ecclesiastical authority, and the proper boundaries between religious and secular spheres, could be contested. Late antique ideas on the relationship between Church and state, and on the nature of the Church itself, represented an ongoing struggle to define the proper boundaries between the spiritual and the worldly. Fifth- and sixth-century religious leaders were groping toward a constitution for Christendom, an ecclesiology that could embrace both the spiritual ideals of the Church and its necessary involvement with the powers and priorities of this world.

BIBLIOGRAPHICAL NOTE

A comprehensive introduction to ecclesiastical politics and the narrative of early church history can be found in Chadwick 2001. Young 1983 surveys the key authors and personalities of the fourth and early fifth centuries. With respect to secular politics, I have found several works to be particularly thought-provoking: Lendon 1997 on honor, Harries 1999 on law, Kelly 2004 on imperial government. I discuss in greater detail the use of violence and coercion in relations between church authorities and secular powers in Gaddis 2005. On the emperor's role in the Church, see now Dagron 2003. For the theology and political theory that informed Church–state relations in Late Antiquity, see Field 1998. Fundamental studies of the political and social role of the bishop include Brown 1992 and 2002; Drake 2000; and now Rapp 2005a. Lim 1995 is essential for understanding the means by which authority was defined and constructed within the fourth-century Church. Gray 1989 discusses the role of "the Fathers" as a source of doctrinal authority. The Christological controversies of the fifth century and their aftermath are thoroughly narrated in Frend 1972 and Meyendorff 1989. An essential resource for further theological and intellectual study is the exhaustive treatment of Grillmeier 1975, 1987, 1995–6. For the Council of Chalcedon, see now the translation, with extensive introduction and commentary, in Price and Gaddis 2005.

CHAPTER THIRTY-FIVE

The Late Antique Bishop: Image and Reality

Rita Lizzi Testa

But I ask myself, Why should a horse's bit be inscribed as "holy," if not to restrain the insolence of emperors, to curb the unrestrained boldness of tyrants?

Ambrose, *De obitu Theodosii* 50. 1–4

Jerome was very careful in commenting on Zechariah 14: 20 (which Ambrose here elucidated), and considered that the Ambrosian interpretation was "odd [*ridicula*]" (Jer. *Comm. in Zachariam* 3. 20). But it is well known that, fine exegete though he was, Jerome was not a subtle ideologist. When Ambrose decided, in AD 395, to end his funeral oration for Theodosius I with a digression on Constantine's mother Helena and her discovery of the true cross, the sense of what he meant escaped Jerome completely. Even at the beginning of the twentieth century, several authors considered that digression in bad taste, or even completely unrelated to the speech as a whole (Schanz 1904: 321–2; Laurand 1921: 349–50). The contrary is the case. If we restore the natural integrity of Ambrose's conclusion (Steidle 1978: 94), the significance of the account – of how Helena set a nail from the Crucifixion in Constantine's diadem and ordered another to be used in making a bit for the emperor's horse (Ambrose, *De obitu Theodosii* 48. 10–13) – now seems perfectly clear. "Thanks to her," said Ambrose in the same passage, "that day had dawned to which the prophet Zechariah had looked forward [14: 20], when the horse's harness would be inscribed 'holy to the Lord' [*in illo die erit, quod super frenum equi, sanctum domino omnipotenti*]." He pointed out to the young Honorius, Theodosius' western heir, that the only other reason (apart from dynastic right) that would earn him the principate was the submission of the emperor to the divine law (Consolino 1984: 176–7). In putting it that way, Ambrose placed the relationship between Church and state on a basis quite different from that which had governed Eusebius' attitude to Constantine.

Not many years before, in the east (AD 386), John Chrysostom – still only a presbyter in Antioch – did not refrain from using topical news of recent events in his comments on 2 Corinthians, and to direct scornful accusations against the Jews and the Gentiles. Constantine's mausoleum had been recently completed. His body had been solemnly laid to rest in the Apostoleion (the Church of the Holy Apostles) in Constantinople in AD 337, being given the position of Christ among the twelve pillars that represented the apostles. It had been relocated *c.* AD 359 in the Church of Saint Acacius, because of building work in the Church of the Holy Apostles. After AD 370, it was finally laid to rest close to that church (Dagron 1991: 407–14) – an opportune choice, declared Chrysostom, as it allowed dead emperors to act as "Doorkeepers of the Fisherman" (Ioh. Chrys. *In Epist. II ad Corint. Hom.* 26. 5; *Adversus Iudeos et gentiles* 9; Bonamente 1988: 133; Siniscalco 2000: 99–100).

Almost a century of good relations between empire and Church had not, therefore, passed in vain. At the end of the fourth century, it no longer seemed sensible to honor Constantine as "equal to the Apostles," as the intermediary between the King of Heaven and humanity on the earth, as the imitator of the Word Incarnate or *Logos* (Euseb. *Vit. Const.* 4. 71. 2; *Laus Constantini* 2. 3–5). So, during the reign of the pious Theodosius I (AD 379–95), while in the east Eusebius' political theology was seriously questioned (see also Gr. Naz. *C. Iulianum* 2 = *Or.* 5. 17), in the west Ambrose developed the theory of a necessary subordination of the emperor to the divine law and the dependence of his authority on God's intervention, so that only a true and proper faith could guarantee victorious permanence to power and its transmission to legitimate heirs (Ambrose, *De fide* 2. 16. 141).

It is significant that the same Fathers who would rethink the terms of the relationship between Church and empire (Gregory of Nazianzus, John Chrysostom, and Ambrose) drew virtually at the same time an ideal portrait of a bishop. Insisting on spiritual qualities and practical skills, they also indicated what should be the limits of a bishop's sphere of action in relation to the authority of citizens, of imperial functionaries, and of the emperor. But we are dealing here with two only apparently different aspects of a single process, because the unresolved tension between *imperium* (empire) and *sacerdotium* (priesthood) permeated the redefinition of the reciprocal roles of the Christian emperor and the bishop: each of them related to the divine and the holy; each of them related to the earthly structures that they both called upon to make that other relationship a reality.

The moment at which this new theorizing started to develop is revealing. As Ambrose was already suggesting, the two points of reference were Constantine the Great and Theodosius I. Some contemporaries believed that the latter, by declaring Christianity to be the sole religion of the Roman Empire, concluded the process started by Constantine when he had recognized the legality of that religion and conferred privileged status on its ministers. So, in studying the development of the figure of the late antique bishop, it is appropriate to broaden the chronological boundaries of the inquiry in order to evaluate how the Church had grown in the centuries preceding the Constantinian turning point. We have to take into consideration the many spiritual and temporal matters that the bishop had already had to deal with during the third century, and we cannot neglect the results of that process in the actual circumstances (which varied from region to region) and in the canonical codification of the fifth and sixth centuries (Rapp 2005a: 13). Nevertheless, the period between Constantine and Theodosius remains central and, as such, must be emphasized, in order to grasp how the figure of the late antique bishop developed as the result of a dynamic interaction of image and reality.

Many aspects of the process that supported the gradual rise of the bishop to become the center of the late antique city are by now well known. It is clear, for instance, that the responsibilities of the bishop grew – well before the final disruption of the western empire – within the vacuum of local power, well documented in many regions of the empire throughout the third century. In the same period, while the monarchical episcopate prevailed almost everywhere in the Church, bishops became the highest moral authority within the Christian communities, entrusted with manifold duties, not least the task of insuring the physical well-being of their congregations. Since he was expected to be inspired by the Holy Spirit, the bishop had to set an example of moral and virtuous conduct; he had to provide rules of behavior, and so was entitled to regulate the external comportment and internal balance of the faithful; above all, he was the guardian of the community chest and, as administrative officer, he managed those funds in order to support his own clergy and distribute the offerings for charity (Mazza 1993: 187–216).

Nevertheless, all those conditions would not have been sufficient to endow the bishop with the powers he came to exercise in the late antique city, had it not been for the revolutionary effect of Constantine's conversion. The consolidation of the Christian Church as an institution recognized by the state – an institutional change that deeply affected the structures of the empire – assured the final enhancement of the bishop's authority. Such a change also induced the most cultured and sensitive representatives of the ecclesiastical organization to define what kind of moral and spiritual identity a bishop ought to have in order to exercise his powers fully. This complex process was gradual, and reached different stages in different regions of the empire. It depended greatly on the interaction between certain variables: the political importance enjoyed by some cities that became episcopal sees; the lessening of local powers; and the personality of individual bishops. The foundation of such power, however, was already implicit in the status that Constantine had granted to the officiants of the Christian cult at the same moment in which Christianity was recognized as the lawful religion of the empire.

At the same time as proclaiming, soon after the defeat of Maxentius (AD 312), an end to persecution, and restitution to churches and individual Christians for damage to property, Constantine ordered the African proconsul Anullinus to support Caecilian, the bishop of Carthage, in the distribution among the clerics of his church of a sum of money that he, the emperor, had given, in order to provide his clergy with a salary in that difficult period following the persecutions. This step was taken in part under the influence of Ossius, bishop of Cordova. Constantine also decided to exempt clerics and bishops from the obligatory public liturgies, so that – as Cyprian of Carthage had suggested more than fifty years before (Cypr. *Ep.* 1. 1. 2) – secular problems would not distract them from celebrating that divine cult which, holier than all others, procured immense good fortune and benefit for the state (Euseb. *Hist. eccl.* 10. 7. 2). Such orders ratified the claim of Caecilian that he was the true bishop of the Christian community of Carthage, not Maiorinus – head of a schismatic group that in a few years would have Donatus as leader, giving rise to the Donatist movement (Maier 1987: 128–9; Duval 1989b); that he, Caecilian, was the only "Catholic," by virtue of his relationship with other communities, particularly the Christian congregation of Rome.

Later, after the defeat of Licinius (AD 324) and after a council of bishops at Nicaea had formulated a universal creed (AD 325), the privileges granted to Caecilian were extended to all Nicene churchmen in the empire. Once again, this generous gift of money was designed to assure at least a part of the monthly salary that every bishop, since the first half of the third century, had given his clergy, dipping into his personal patrimony as well as into the community funds (Schöllgen 1988). The distribution later took the form of corn, which, by imperial arrangement, each municipality had to provide every year to the ministers of the divine cult (Theod. *Hist. eccl.* 1. 11. 2–3; Soz. *Hist. eccl.* 5. 5. 2; *Cod. Iust.* 1. 2. 12 [November 12, AD 451, concerning *salaria* to be given from public funds in the form of foodstuffs]; Liebeschuetz 1997: 123; Wipszycka 1997; Lizzi Testa 2000b: 71–5). The exemption from all liturgies was specified through imperial rescripts (*Cod. Theod.* 16. 2. 1–2; 15. 5. 1), such as the exemption of the superior clergy from the *munera civilia* – that is, from the compulsory work that was required from individuals for the benefit of cities or of the state, such as the collection of taxes, the carrying and distribution of supplies to soldiers, maintenance of public buildings, and other similar tasks. These were all usually the responsibility of local citizens and proprietors, such as those inscribed in the *curia* (senate) of their original town (Lizzi Testa 2001a: 126).

Constantine granted other privileges to bishops: permission to travel by imperial post (the *cursus publicus*, usually enjoyed only by imperial officials) in order to attend ecclesiastical councils (a concession ratified by law only in AD 382: *Cod. Theod.* 12. 12. 9); *manumissio in ecclesia*, the right to notarize the manumission of slaves (prescribed by law in AD 316: *Cod. Iust.* 1. 13. 1; and again in AD 321: *Cod. Theod.* 4. 7. 1; see also *Cod. Theod.* 2. 8. 1; *Cod. Iust.* 3. 12. 2); the possibility of transferring pending cases from a municipal to an episcopal court (*audientia episcopalis*), provided that both parties agreed (*Cod. Theod.* 1. 27. 1 in AD 318 or 321; further developed in AD 333 by *Const. Sirmond.* 1, which allowed the transfer of a lawsuit from a municipal to an episcopal court at any time in the proceedings, and at the request of only one of the parties involved); and permission for anyone to bequeath whatever he wished to the "most holy and venerable council of the Catholic Church" (AD 321, *Cod. Theod.* 16. 2. 4).

None of those concessions was of such a sort as to absorb the episcopate into the imperial administrative apparatus, turning bishops into bureaucrats in the imperial service. This is clear from the titles of bishop, usually addressed with such adjectives as *gloriosissimus, reverentissimus, illustris, venerabilis*, which were honorary titles, unofficial and predicative, not formal and official like those applied to members of the imperial bureaucracy (Jerg 1970; Mazzarino 1974: 151–70, 171–82). The concessions simply permitted bishops to fulfill, publicly and with the support of imperial legislation, certain functions that they had already practiced in their congregations before the religious peace – conciliation as peacemakers; the redemption of slaves on the occasion of their baptism. Many became effective only over the next two centuries

(Rapp 2005a: 235–73) and thanks to the many bishops who pressured hostile and arrogant imperial functionaries into allowing them the patronage of their fellow citizens. There was the case, for example, of ecclesiastical asylum, which is first attested as a right in AD 343, guaranteed in the west in AD 409 (*Cod. Theod.* 16. 8. 19) but enforced by general law only in the first twenty years of the fifth century (*Cod. Iust.* 1. 12. 2). Bishops like Basil (Gr. Naz. *Or.* 43, 568), Ambrose (Paul. Med. *Vit. Ambr.* 34), John Chrysostom (*Hom. in Eutropium* 394), and Synesius (*Epp.* 42 and 72) fought hard for the freedom to exercise it (Lizzi 1987: 108–11).

What is more, those prerogatives would not have combined to favor the powers of bishops in the towns, had Constantine not first offered to Caecilian of Carthage and to his priests the sums of money already mentioned and exemption from *munera civilia*. Over the next fifty years, as economic difficulties increased, some emperors sought to limit those privileges, which had come to apply by then not just to a few officiants of the Catholic cult but to an increasing number of the Christian clergy. It was also felt necessary to offer different justifications for their continuation (*Cod. Theod.* 16. 2. 6, June 1, AD 329, Lizzi Testa 2001a: 133–5). Precautions were taken to avoid the recruitment of clergy that would compromise the functioning of a city (*Cod. Theod.* 12. 1. 59, 16. 2. 17, September 12, AD 364; 16. 2. 19, October 17, AD 370; 12. 1. 104, November 7, AD 383; and 12. 1. 99, April 18, AD 383). Despite this, the ministers of God were able to exercise sufficient pressure to preserve such immunities, which they judged to be more than simple fiscal concessions. Constantine's political and institutional reforms changed the system that had regulated social relations throughout the whole of ancient society, particularly his reform of *ordines*, which conferred senatorial rank on some who had previously held equestrian office. There was a shift implied in the customary relation between order and office. So, during the previous three centuries, belonging to a certain order (usually by birthright) was the main criterion for obtaining office; but, from the first decades of the fourth century, it was the fulfilling of the function that conferred the rank (Porena 2003: 391). We can recognize the change from a variety of indicators: from specific designation symbols (*insignia*), from titles, from some judicial privileges (such as freedom from trial by torture), and finally from the type of fiscal exemption granted. Even if a Christian priest was not integrated into the secular hierarchy, the social effects of this institutional change profoundly shaped his identity. Both salary and exemption, granted by virtue of the functions that bishops and clerics performed in their community, acted as status indicators. The sacerdotal status, with its privileges and public salary, brought it closer to the most eminent people of an imperial town: members of local senates who, having held office in public administration, were regarded as *primores* (the first) among citizens and distanced from simple *curiales* (Lizzi Testa 2001a: 130).

It is true that similar exemptions were a traditional privilege of some pagan priests (e.g., the Vestals) and that Constantine extended it to the religious leaders of the Jews (*Cod. Theod.* 16. 8. 2, November 29, AD 330; 16. 8. 4, December 1, AD 331; Linder 1987: 72–3, 132–8; De Giovanni 2001: 62). But for those people, the exemptions could never be taken for granted and were not of universal significance. When granting them to Christian priests, Constantine acted not simply out of generosity but for the common good, because he believed that the fortunes of the empire depended on the Christian religion. Christian clerics were therefore guaranteed privileged status under the law: they were no longer only figures within the Church but fulfilled a broader social function.

Such concessions had, however, unexpected consequences. In proclaiming the legality of the Christian Church, Constantine had been selective from the beginning. Only clerics in those parts of the Christian community that were declared Catholic were defined as Christian ministers (as was illustrated in the case of Caecilian and Maiorinus). This system had already been adopted by the Christian congregations in the third century, where bishops stopped payments to those clerics who had deviated from the true faith (Cypr. *Ep.* 34). Constantine now believed it would be useful to adopt the same strategy as an aid to imposing appropriate distinctions in cases of doctrinal dissent (*Cod. Theod.* 16. 2. 1; 16. 5. 1). On the basis of that criterion, and invoking his rights as arbiter of religious matters within his empire, Constantine started to manage the Donatist crisis (Euseb. *Hist. eccl.* 10. 5. 18–20), attempted to resolve the question of Arianism by calling the Council of Nicaea, and tried to bend a reluctant Athanasius to accept his commands (Barnes 1993). Subsequently, during the reign of Constantius II especially, the Church suffered the consequences of that overconfident interpretation of the relationship between *imperium* and *sacerdotium*, which was conceived without foreseeing how heavily the emperor could interfere in church affairs, even trying to influence its doctrinal choices. After the death of Constantine in AD 337, succession politics were both dramatic and cruel, resulting, during the following decade, in a precarious political balance, which in turn rekindled disputes within the Church. Constans was devoted to the Nicene cause; but Constantius II supported the moderate Arian party, denying the divinity of Christ and his identity in nature with the Father. He intervened against bishops of major sees who dared to dissent from the religious creed that had been formulated at the Councils of Arles and Milan (AD 353 and 355). Athanasius was removed from Alexandria, recalled, and then exiled again. Constantius, sole emperor after AD 353 (like Constantine after AD 324), was increasingly influenced by bishops of moderately Arian persuasion, and persecuted and exiled Nicene bishops – Dionysius of Milan, Eusebius of Vercelli, and Liberius of Rome (Pietri 1989a: 113–78). Bishops, standing outside the imperial hierarchy but strongly dependent on privileges granted by the emperor, could lose, therefore, both their autonomy and their social identity, if they lost imperial favor.

Emperors had become obsessed with safeguarding the unity of the empire by imposing doctrinal unity. The most dogged adversary of such a view, Lucifer of Cagliari, called the emperor of his day "the bishop of bishops [*episcopus episcoporum*]" (*De regibus apostaticis* 2). By allowing the split between different doctrines to grow, such emperors provoked a sort of moral laxity in the heads of major sees. The latter became inclined (with a few exceptions) to devise compromises and to seek a way of maintaining their sees without having to submit to imperial coercion. The emperor following Constantius, the pagan sympathizer Julian, was well aware of this. With his ascetic rigor, his utopian vision imbued with mysticism (hugely indebted, nevertheless, to the Christian culture that had pervaded society), he expressed a deep contempt for the spreading corruption of the Church. Yet, his moralizing impetus, paradoxically, was not so different from that which, within a short time, found new expression in the Church in the writings and episcopal careers of men like Basil of Caesarea, Gregory of Nazianzus, and Ambrose of Milan.

Other factors intervened to make the role of bishops within the Christian community both complex and problematical. In the second half of the fourth century, policies in favor of Christianity were realized through progressively more severe anti-pagan legislation. Suggested and supported by the religious advisers of the emperors, severe laws threatened divine and human sanctions against pagan ceremonies and practices (*Cod. Theod.* 16. 10. 2, 5, 7–11). The strong support given to the Nicene cause by Gratian and Theodosius I was translated into fierce moves against all the religious minorities that no Catholic leader could hope to absorb into the Church (*Cod. Theod.* 16. 5. 7, 9, 11). Furthermore, when he visited Rome in AD 357, Constantius had ordered the altar of Victory to be removed from the Senate chamber. It had been a civic and religious symbol of the fortune of the Roman Empire since the Augustan age and, over the next thirty years, the challenge to its acceptability provoked a conflict between the newly intolerant Christians and the conciliatory spirit of the last cultivated pagans of Rome. The great Symmachus, for example, had pleaded that "one cannot arrive at so great a mystery by a single path" (*uno itinere non potest perveniri ad tam grande secretum* (*Rel.* 3, 10)). In such a climate – when combined with the fact that, in choosing lower-level imperial functionaries, religious factors became more important and those who shared the faith of the emperors were favored in their careers – it was inevitable that the process of christianization should have gathered pace among the senatorial aristocracy (Salzman 2002: 34–5; Lizzi Testa 2004: 105–25).

That did not always mean an authentic and deep conversion. The subjects of bishops' homilies reflect with what difficulty they interacted with the new believers who came from the highest and richest classes. Involved in the political administration of the towns, they were used to looking for compromise and mediation, preferring dissimulation to direct speech. A bishop's ability to adapt his sermons to the social and cultural position of his audience was soon seen as crucial (Ambrose, *Ep.* 36. 5–7). It became a virtue, and was listed as the most important among other prerogatives recommended in treatises on correct episcopal behavior (Gr. Naz. *De fuga* 2. 28–9). The whole of the third part of Gregory the Great's *Pastoral Care*, dedicated to the issue of preaching, addresses the question of how to achieve this excellent episcopal ability (*Cur. past.* 3, preface; see Lizzi 1998: 81 n. 3; Rousseau 1998: 393; MacMullen 2003: 471–5).

The bishops could see that the faith of their fellow citizens, even though now openly declaring themselves Christian, was failing – a faith that implied doctrinal certainty, high moral behavior, and social commitment. They insisted, therefore, on specifically Christian duties: the shunning of crime, respect for widows, and contempt of avarice, arrogance, and fornication. They asked the faithful to adopt true humility in order to acquire virtue, not the semblance of humility (*virtutem, non speciem humilitatis*). Landowners were exhorted not to refuse to pay their servants (whether *operarii, mercenarii,* or *servi*: Ambrose, *Ep.* 36. 12; 31); not to wear them out as slaves till death – which would in any case accentuate a shortage of manpower already prevalent in territories such as northern Italy (Gaudentius of Brescia, *Tract.* 13. 21–2, 33). The rich were called upon to bestow hospitality upon troops requiring quarters (Ambrose, *Ep.* 62. 6), and to pay their due taxes (Maximus of Turin, *Sermo* 71. 3). They were asked not to become like "wolves for avarice," taking advantage of the other men's ruin during wartime, but to use their resources to ransom prisoners (Maximus, *Sermo* 18. 3). They should not abandon their land, if it were overrun by barbarians, escaping to their country houses (Maximus, *Sermo* 82. 2). They had to cooperate with the Church in eradicating superstition and paganism in the country-side (Maximus, *Sermo* 107. 1). And they should not enter into mixed marriages with barbarian or pagan women (Ambrose, *Ep.* 62. 2; 7; 34).

Besides those specific exhortations, there was an increasingly frequent and general tendency in episcopal sermons to attribute to the faithful a spiritual superiority in proportion to their high social status (Gaudentius, *Praefatio* 2). In fact, it made the teaching of the Christian message much easier among the higher classes of a town. Moreover, in emphasizing charity, some preachers readily attributed an expiatory and penitential value to the giving of alms (Maximus of Turin, *Sermo* 22. 1; 22a. 4). The emphasis placed on charity could even overshadow the importance of baptism – although Ambrose, for example, still considered baptism central to the experience of conversion: it had a distinctive value as an irrevocable choice, and it introduced the believer into a group marked by canons of excellence, preeminence, and perfection. A degree of moral tolerance, however, affected a bishop's view of the converted: associated with an ever growing intransigence toward religious minorities, that was the price that new Christian institutions had to pay in order to foster the growth of Christianity across an entire city. So, the power of the bishop within the city became proportional to his ability to come to terms with the acquisitive and contractual ethos of the highest and richest classes that were still at the head of the Roman cities (Lizzi 1989: 118–19).

Another factor that made the process of defining the role of the late antique bishop more complicated was the sudden acceleration of christianization. Since it was necessary to organize larger *plebes christianae,* more and more clerics and bishops were recruited. Constantius II did not hesitate to explain that his generous policy of fiscal immunities for the clergy was adopted "in order that the assembly of the churches [in itself, a striking allusion to the single nature of the Church within the empire] might be filled by a coming together of huge numbers of people" (*ut ecclesiarum coetus concursu populorum ingentium frequentetur* (*Cod. Theod.* 16. 2. 10)). Even when Valentinian I and Theodosius I returned to more reasonable concessions (Lizzi Testa 2001b: 194–202), the number of clergy increased, especially at the higher levels of the hierarchy, because in a large number of areas few sees had previously existed. What happened in northern Italy during Ambrose's episcopate (Lizzi Testa 2000a: 73–82) can be taken as an example of the organizational endeavors of the Church at a time when the Nicene group had the full support of an emperor like Theodosius I and the empire enjoyed a brief period of economic stability.

The increase in ecclesiastical personnel did not lower the social rank of bishops. A humble social background had never been an official obstacle – either then or in ensuing years – to a clerical appointment, episcopal or otherwise. Neither the normative texts of the Church nor the canons of councils provided any specific recommendations on that subject (Wischmeyer 1992: 101–4). There were a few instances when ecclesiastical officials came from very humble levels of society (including, as late as the fourth century, slaves). There were, by contrast, equally few instances of senatorial bishops, who began to make their appearance during the last twenty or so years of the fourth century, but included even then only a small percentage of the whole episcopate, varying from region to region and attested chiefly in Gaul in the fifth and sixth centuries (Sotinel 1997: 196). Otherwise, the chief source for the recruitment of deacons and bishops remained the curial class (Gilliard 1966, 1984; Eck 1978; Cracco Ruggini 1998a: 884–90). That must have been the case already when Constantine legalized the Catholic Church. It makes the best sense of the fiscal exemptions he granted, which clergy from a curial background would have appreciated the most. And throughout the fourth century, the curial origin of those at the highest levels of the ecclesiastical hierarchy was assured by the vitality of the curial class itself, which endured, at least in some regions, until the end of the fifth century. Besides, it was to just that class that Christian communities would almost always look when searching for an effective bishop – one likely to be not only a good shepherd but also a good patron, used to mixing with the great, to speaking and writing their language, and to understanding the intricacies of administration and law (Lepelley 1998: 29).

Churchmen soon felt, however, that the time had come to alter the pattern of recruitment at the higher levels of the hierarchy, since it seemed to be increasingly independent of religious faith and too acquiescent toward imperial authority. Church leaders continued to insure that legislation did not create too many obstacles to the ordination of *curiales* (Ambrose, *Ep.* 73). At the same time, new screening rules were brought in to guarantee the quality of ecclesiastical personnel: electoral rules were improved; the canons of councils insisted on sexual restraint, recommending continence, chastity, and celibacy; and training "seminaries" (in Cappadocia and northern Italy) were created for good ascetic-clerics. Even bishops like Basil and Ambrose did not dare to decide *ex auctoritate* (on their own authority) which candidates were best suited locally as deacons or bishops. A more theoretical model of priesthood was proposed, which stressed the many heavy tasks of the ministry and the risks of self-glorification. A single image of the ideal priest now defined his essential qualities: dedication of spirit, a thorough understanding of doctrine, an ability to interact with different sectors of the faithful, and exemplary behavior that would encourage the congregation to follow his teachings and pagans to recognize him as a worthy advocate (Lizzi 1998: 86).

The Christian literature of the previous three centuries had discussed, it is true, the nature and role of the ideal bishop. The letters of Ignatius of Antioch (AD 98–117), together with the *Apostolic Tradition* and the *Didascalia apostolorum* (both early third century), provide us with much information about the qualities expected of a bishop. He was regarded as a successor of the apostles and partook of the same Spirit as they had (*Apostolic Tradition* 2–3). His ministry was bestowed on him by an act of God's love, not because others wanted to appoint him or because he sought that distinction for himself (Ign. *Phld.* 1. 1–2). He needed to cultivate and display virtues that would give him the moral authority to lead the community (*Eph.* 6. 1; *Mg.* 3. 1; *Tr.* 2. 1; *Pol.* 6. 1), excluding unworthy members and readmitting them only after sincere repentance (*Didascalia apostolorum* 1929: 56, 104). And his practical attributes would make him a clever administrator (ibid. 32–3, 98–101). 1 Timothy 3: 1–7 lists the qualities required of a perfect bishop (and later on of deacons) and was used widely by Christian authors of the early period (Rapp 2005a: 6).

But it is easy to spot the differences between such earlier reflections and those that developed from the second half of the fourth century onward – as in Gregory of Nazianzus' *In Defense of His Flight*, John Chrysostom's *On the Priesthood*, and Ambrose's *On the Duties of the Clergy*, a tradition maintained in the treatise *On the Contemplative Life* (written in AD 497 by Julianus Pomerius, the teacher of Caesarius of Arles), and reaching forward to Gregory the Great's *Pastoral Care* a century later. In all those treatises, it is easy to detect an awareness of the public role demanded of a bishop and a determination to present his relationships with the emperor and his functionaries in terms of reciprocal autonomy. The evolution from treatise to treatise lay wholly within the Church. It began with the experience of the religious crisis brought about by Julian, moved from there to interference in doctrinal affairs by emperors like Constantius II and Valens, far from supportive of the Nicene party, and finally allowed that party to denounce such policies openly, during the reign of Theodosius I, as intolerable abuses. Several notable spokesmen, drawn from the leadership classes within the towns (Basil, Gregory of Nazianzus, John Chrysostom), and even from the senatorial class itself (Ambrose), transposed, in their configuration of the relationship between Church and empire, the ideological results of a centuries-old debate on the relationship between the imperial government and the Senate. In defining the new episcopal model, they were able to preserve the sense of Christianity's transcendent religiosity and of its aspiration toward spiritual perfection; but they infused the latter with the attributes and traditional qualities of the oldest Roman officials. Even within the Church, the authority and welfare of families with long and respectable pedigrees came once again to the fore (as is proven by hundreds of celebratory inscriptions), while on the other side a new "aristocracy of service" gathered strength, originally prompted by Constantine's institutional and political reforms.

Let us take as an example events in Milan when, in AD 386, Mercurinus Auxentius pretended that the building of a basilica for his congregation (the Arian community) had been supported by the court of Valentinian II and his mother Justina. Ambrose refused to appear before the imperial consistory to argue his contrary opinion (McLynn 1994: 179–80), and, in order to justify his courageous behavior, he quoted a decision of Valentinian I, which declared that bishops, not emperors, should judge other bishops on matters of faith (*haec enim verba rescripti sunt, hoc est sacerdotes de sacerdotibus voluit iudicare* (Ambrose, *Ep.* 75. 2)). It is impossible to question the existence of such a rescript. Even though it was not included in the *Theodosian Code*, we can already observe its application during Gratian's reign in the jurisdictional relationship between the bishop of Rome, provincial metropolitans, and other bishops (Lizzi Testa 2004: 175–6). It is symptomatic of how far ecclesiastics had gone in claiming an autonomous space for themselves vis-à-vis imperial authority.

In the new Theodosian climate, therefore, in order to avoid acquiescent submission to the imperial authorities, bishops realized that they had to acquire enough authority to compete with civic magistrates, with imperial functionaries, and even with the emperor. Only spiritual hegemony could guarantee that, which is exactly what the treatises on the priesthood express. In Greek examples of this kind of literature, the episcopal function is called *archê*, *hêgemonia*, *epistasia*, or *prostasia*, to show that these men exercised the same political patronage as was usually enjoyed by imperial functionaries. Indeed, the bishop was recognized as one kind of *exarchos* (leader) among other civic officials (Gr. Naz. *Or.* 2. 78; 3.7; Ioh. Chrys. *De Sacerd.* I. 3; II. 1, 2; III. 9, 10). In comparison to the Greek texts, the language of the Latin treatises is less forceful in its implications (even in Ambrose's *On the Duties of the Clergy*): the *episcopus* is *pastor, sacerdos, doctor, sanctus praedicator, praepositus, rector ecclesiae, princeps sacerdotii ipsius*. But in the works of Hilary of Poitiers, Eusebius of Vercelli, and of Ambrose himself, as in the deliberations of the councils directed by Damasus or inspired by Ambrose, the use of refined rhetorical *topoi* allowed the discussion of problems such as the right relationship between the bishop and the emperor, recognizing each of them as exercising equivalent power (Ambrose, *Ep.* 72. 13; 76. 19; 75. 10).

The new literary treatises, besides listing almost the same virtues as conferring both spiritual and temporal superiority, were careful to set out how those virtues should, in the case of churchmen, be displayed. In a society as formal as that of Late Antiquity, where relations among the members of the upper class (from which, for the most part, the authors of those treatises came) were regulated by a precise etiquette, much importance was given to exterior *habitus* and to its capacity to reveal the inner soul. Therefore it is not surprising that the perfect minister of God was asked to lead his public life "as if in some theatre" (*velut in quodam theatro* (Ambrose, *Ep. Extra coll.* 14. 71; compare Jer. *Ep.* 60. 14)). Since episcopal behavior was constantly subjected to other people's judgment, like that of any representative of the civil administration, our writers believed that a specific way of speaking, specific facial expressions, and a solemn comportment would reflect those inner qualities. Instructions were supplied about how to control anger before it flared up or how to repress it if it did so, when to speak and when to keep silent, how to avoid annoying others by raising one's voice (Ambrose, *De off.* 1. 90–7; 1. 5–13; 67; see Jer. *Ep.* 52. 5; 9; 15–16). Such behavior would adequately reflect the inner strength of a man who could control his passions with reason (*ratio*). And to show an outward, rational calm was a way of defending oneself against an adversary, be he heretic, pagan, or corrupt official (they were adept at describing all categories), such as might lie in wait ready to find fault with the minister of God on the basis of an uncontrolled gesture, a flushed face, or a single word spoken in anger (Ambrose, *De off.* 1. 105–15). The attitude of the priest at his ordination was also very important. Not seeking episcopal office, refusing it more than once, or even fleeing once ordained, he would truly express an indifference to power that revealed a nature most befitting to exercise it (Gr. Naz. *Or.* 2. 8; Ioh. Chrys. *De sacerd.* III. 10; see Synesius of Cyrene, *Ep.* 105).

Taken together, although they were written in different periods, the treatises we are discussing here give us a homogeneous image of the ideal bishop. That is partly because the writers shared a common social and cultural background: they came from the same elite, they had an aristocratic knowledge of appropriate behavior, they had learned the same rhetorical rules, and they clung to the same Stoic-Platonic traditions that Hellenistic Christianity had made its own. These authors, bearers of a systematic plan of moral life, also came from a social class used to managing political responsibilities in the city or the imperial administration, able to manage political power and to give it adequate ideological representation, and determined to further the assured development of the episcopal office, which included deciding what skills a bishop should have. The persistence of that social and cultural profile among churchmen is remarkable, even amid the crumbling of many public institutions. Gregory the Great, consecrated (albeit reluctantly) bishop of Rome in AD 590, wrote his manual for the training of priests, the *Pastoral Care*, entirely in the same spirit: as we have seen, it drew heavily upon earlier work by Gregory of Nazianzus, John Chrysostom, and Ambrose. In its own day, the work enjoyed instant popularity. Gregory sent copies to several bishops and priests, and even to the emperor Maurice in Constantinople, who wanted it translated into Greek. Gregory bequeathed to the Latin Middle Ages an argument for inner flight from an appointment with grave responsibilities, and both exemplified and analyzed the suffering provoked by tension between the active and the contemplative life. He reiterated the moral qualities and practical skills upon which the authors of the fourth century had built their model of the perfect priest-bishop, and he did so in a decisive period for the relationship between the Church and the empire.

All that effort of reflection and literary formulation was extremely effective in facilitating a gradual shift of major civic functions into the hands of new episcopal bureaucrats, who, during the fifth and sixth centuries in regions like Italy and Gaul, controlled resources well in excess of those accessible to individual wealthy citizens. The bishop, "nourisher" and "lover of the poor," protected in his own court this new constituency from abuse by the powerful – a constituency numbering many more than mere wretches or beggars. The "poor of Christ" was a rhetorical phrase used to embrace all citizens, and had a wider meaning than the traditional Roman *plebs* (Brown 2002: 45–6). During the reigns of the first barbarian kings, whether *curiales* abandoned their duties or continued to work alongside other civic institutions, the bishop was counted among the *primores* (first officials). He undertook to negotiate the entry of the new conquerors into his city. He pleaded for the defeated leaders. He was able to maintain the demographic profile of a city by, among other things, urging prominent figures to remain there, instead of fleeing to their country houses. A bishop could often cooperate with military leaders as well as civilian officials, alleviating through diplomacy the difficulties of a siege, ransoming prisoners, relieving famine, and obtaining remission of taxes (Liebeschuetz 1997: 113–14). By AD 409, the bishop was numbered among the most notable (the *honorati possessores* and *curiales*), who selected the *defensor civitatis* (*Cod. Iust.* 1. 55. 8). Emperor Anastasius included the bishop among those who chose officials charged with a city's corn supplies (the *sitónes*: *Cod. Iust.* 10. 27. 3), and made him responsible, with the *archôn* (the most important official), for the distribution of provisions to troops quartered near his town (*Cod. Iust.* 1. 4. 18). In accordance with Justinian's wishes, the bishop became, in AD 530, a member of the exclusive committee charged with checking on the operations of other civic administrators (*Cod. Iust.* 1. 4. 26).

So, alongside holy men and martyrs, bishops also began to be honored as wonder workers, and people celebrated on their tombs the cult of the saint bishop, the heavenly patron of his town. It was not felt necessary to find new reasons to justify this exalted notion of episcopal holiness. Already by the end of the fourth century, the bishop's superior virtue was enough to inspire the admiration of the faithful and the awe of his adversaries. It was this virtue that gave him the courage to challenge the officials of the empire. It conferred upon the bishop a sort of miraculous aura. Like a new Elisha, the prophet-shepherd, endowed with foresight and unarmed, he did all that he could against the enemies of his Church and country (Cracco Ruggini 2002). Very soon, therefore, Cyprian, Athanasius, Gregory the Wonderworker, Basil (Forlin Patrucco 1994), Acolius of Thessalonica, Eusebius of Vercelli (Lizzi 1994), Ambrose of Milan (Cracco Ruggini 1999) were venerated as bishop saints. Their saintliness was seen as based on a lifestyle that avoided solitary asceticism, conceived as an alternative to ministerial duty, and realized an attitude that Cicero had already praised as typical of Scipio Africanus: the *otium negotiosum* (the active quiet) of the great leaders of ancient Rome (Ambrose, *Ep.* 51. 5–7, 12; Cic. *Off.* 3. 1; *Rep.* 1. 17. 27). By the end of the fourth century, however, episcopal *otium* had become a kind of sublime meditation that guided the man who drew superior power from his contact with the divine. Even when such power was directed less to the perfection of self and more to helping the community, it was easy to see it as a hallmark of holiness (Lizzi 1994: 53–6).

So, the main characteristics of the late antique bishop were defined during the fourth century. The figure of the bishop revealed all the paradoxes of a civilization that purported to moderate the abuses and arrogance of absolute power with the values of the ancient *paideía* and of Roman *gravitas* (Brown 1992: 35–70). But that same civilization allowed charisma and holiness to absorb all those aspirations to a *democratizzazione* of culture (Mazzarino 1974: 74–98; 1984: 431–647; 1989: 63–4), which, since the third century, had marked the spiritual life as well the arts and the imperial economy (Giardina 2001; Salamito 2001: 174–8). This democratization of holiness was furthered by the fact that men of virtue characterized the periphery of the empire more than its center. No longer did emperors become saints: indeed, they were no longer automatically *divi* – such consecrations occurred only in a few cases and without much conviction, as in the case of poor Theodosius I (Bonamente 2002: 381). Only those thought of as *viri Dei* and ascetics were sanctified. So, the bishop, whom Constantine had made a public figure, confirming his vocation to devote great spiritual and practical talents to his congregation and to the faithful, in less than fifty years could be thought of as a saint, the patron saint of his city – provided that he was able to transform his *otium* of the spirit into an effective *negotium*.

BIBLIOGRAPHICAL NOTE

The study of the dynamic interaction between the construction of the episcopal figure and the reality of episcopal power has been relatively recent. For the east, see Lizzi 1987; for differences between east and west, see Rebillard and Sotinel 1998. The resulting impression owes much not only to new, but also to broader perspectives in the study of Christianity: the religious phenomena of Late Antiquity now share with institutional, political, and economic developments a central place in the historical analysis of the period. For crucial reflections, see Momigliano 1972; Brown 1982.

The study of bishops has thereby been associated with many other preoccupations: the study of women, of children, and of ethnic minorities; urban archaeology and monumental and funerary epigraphy; sociology, anthropology, and psychoanalysis. We take into account the understanding of human nature, private life, individual and collective *mentalités*, social etiquette, and the exercise of power outside the institutions of Church or empire (examples: Veyne 1985; Brown 1988b; and Giardina 1989). Meanwhile, study of the christianization of the empire now focuses on the emergence of a "dominant discourse" rather than (as used to be the case) on a "narrative of triumph": Cameron 1991.

The bishop, in this context, had to temper his religious ambitions by taking up in his own terms what were otherwise traditional roles. For civic leadership, see McLynn 1994; Cracco Ruggini 1998b; Lizzi Testa 2001a. For bishops and asceticism, see Rousseau 1978, 1994; Leyser 2000a. For the need to make one's stand even against emperors, still "the divine vortex of the earthly power," see Brown et al. 1982. For adaptation to audience, see Cunningham and Allen 1998. For "management" of the sacred more generally, see Brown 1981 and – specifically in relation to the management of the Church's financial resources – 2002.

Late antique bishops soon learned to juggle with those expectations and opportunities: see Sterk 2004; Rapp 2005a. The resulting "representation" was encapsulated, at least in the west, in Gregory the Great's *Pastoral Care*, and embedded thereafter in the thought-world of medieval Europe: Markus 1997; Elm 2003.

CHAPTER THIRTY-SIX

The Conduct of Theology and the "Fathers" of the Church

Thomas Graumann

Questions about the sources and norms of Christian teaching accompanied doctrinal deliberations in the churches from the start. From the early Middle Ages, certainly, it was taken for granted that the "Fathers" had some role to play in theological discourse, even if the actual weight given to their testimony in practice varied widely in different authors and at different times. In the sixteenth century, humanism and the Reformation brought the underlying question of theological norms and methods into sharper relief. For Erasmus, the ancient Church could provide models for necessary reform, and the texts of the Fathers offered guidance for the exposition of Scripture. Martin Luther, on the other hand, argued that the theology of the Fathers, far from being an exegetical or doctrinal yardstick, needed critical examination against the sole norm of Holy Scripture. As a reaction to the Reformation, the Council of Trent claimed the continuous tradition and the *consensus patrum* exclusively for the Roman Church. The following century saw intense controversy, between Protestant and Roman theologians on the one hand, and among Protestants themselves, whether Lutheran or Calvinist, on the other; all sides made polemical use of the Fathers. At the same time, more conciliatory-minded theologians repeatedly propagated the consensus of the Fathers as a sufficient basis for renewed communion between the denominations. However, the extent and very existence of such a doctrinal consensus in more distant periods was disputed, and fundamental disagreement over the norms of theological judgment remained insurmountable (Merkt 2001).

Today, many hopes are again placed in the common heritage of the Fathers, especially in modern ecumenical dialogues. Yet here, as in academia and the churches more widely, renewed contemporary interest in the heritage of the Fathers often lacks a considered hermeneutic of what exactly the nature and purpose of a recourse to the Fathers might be. Even the very concept of "the Fathers" frequently remains vague. Scholars commonly use the term "the Fathers" roughly as an equivalent to early Christian writers, or sometimes even more loosely as shorthand for the influential

Christian figures of the period. The notion of the Fathers no longer carries necessarily a specific sense of dignity and authority that sets them apart from other writers and thinkers. Yet in some Christian traditions, evoking the Fathers is still an iconic expression of a strong sense of ecclesiastical and cultural identity. Accordingly, participants in ecumenical dialogue need to be mindful of both the connection and the difference between, on the one hand, statements of identity and, on the other, assertions of normative truth claiming the support of the Fathers. Only then, as one attempts to identify either common ground or real difference, can a resort to the Fathers be more than ornamental, for many such deliberations are ultimately based on other principles.

The underlying difficulty in delineating the role and potential authority of the Fathers in theological discourse, and specifically in doctrinal definition, is shared, as we shall see, with the formation process of the notion in antiquity itself. A sense of Patristic authority emerged alongside a number of other newly developing forms of theological argumentation and decision-making in the fourth and fifth centuries; from the outset, it served as much to mark identity as to guide theological reasoning. The early evolution of the notion of Fathers and their role in theological discourse illustrates perfectly the intersection of, on the one hand, highly technical debates over norms and standards of doctrinal decision-making and, on the other, the quest for symbolic, unifying expressions of a common church identity (or, conversely, of the demarcation of internal boundaries).

As a consequence, future research in the reconstruction of Christian dogma and intellectual history of Late Antiquity will have to pay closer attention to the mechanisms, forms, and methods of theological discourse, and to its unspoken presuppositions. Disputes over the Fathers show that, as early as the fourth century, theological reasoning rested on, among other elements, received views of the history of the Church and its eminent representatives. Equally, elements of common piety, everyday assumptions about authority, the conditions for transmission of knowledge, and the circulation of documents, all played a role in what might seem purely doctrinal matters. And theologians of the time made deliberate use of received, often symbolic, images of their predecessors and the history of the Church, in order to bolster their authority or validate their thinking. In my view, this also means that neat distinctions between sources relating to the social history of the Church and sources of a primarily intellectual import are counterproductive. I want to move toward a deliberate and permanent historicizing of the concept of the Fathers – that is, to present in a historical light both the late antique rationales and purposes behind the very notion of the Fathers and the corpus of texts upon which it relies. Such an approach might also provide an antidote to the resolutely ahistorical – even antihistorical – readings of the Fathers that have become fashionable in some quarters.

Observations about the less formal and less technical expressions of Christian piety and belief need to be integrated into the task of construing a history of theological ideas, of identifying the main artery of doctrinal development and definition. This is in particular true of the ascetic and monastic traditions (see Caner, ch. 39). A stronger emphasis on their interaction with, and interest in, theology has only recently begun.

Cyril's exploration of patterns of authority in an address to monks (see below), deliberately echoing their present experience and the history of the ascetic movement, should alert us to the task of investigating more closely the possible resonance of those traditions in doctrinal writing. Equally, we need to take more strongly into account the role of other literature and public speech acts – homilies, exegetical exposition, and exhortation – in disseminating and popularizing technical discussion and in forging common identity as much as doctrinal allegiance.

Modes of Doctrinal Deliberation and Dispute in Late Antiquity

I shall concentrate in this chapter on the development of three distinctive features of doctrinal discourse in the fourth and fifth centuries: the increasing importance attached to councils, the strong emphasis placed on the coining of carefully worded creeds, and a growing interest in the Fathers and in the Christian literature of the past. The first two have their roots in earlier times, although they gained added significance and came into their own in the new era heralded by Constantine. The third idea, of Patristic authority, is, however, a relatively late and contested notion, even though it is inextricably linked to the other two. Attributing to the Fathers a role in theological discourse, therefore, marks a gradual change in theological style in the late fourth and fifth centuries, and symbolically encapsulates much of the distinct spirit of ecclesiastical self-awareness at the time.

There were already, at the turn of the fourth century, mechanisms in place to discuss and to rule on disciplinary or doctrinal differences. In polemical writing and exegetical commentary, the meaning of Scripture was expounded and questionable ideas put to the test. Eminent theologians tried to win over dissenters in public debate, and both local and regional gatherings of bishops and clergy (and lay people) ruled on custom and doctrine. Correspondence kept other churches informed of such decisions, and at times divergent practice and thinking sparked conflict between them. All those forms of engagement remained central in post-Constantinian times. The debates characteristic of the age could not remain unaffected, however, by the recently acquired status of the Church in the empire. Imperial favor toward, and involvement with, the Church gave differences of doctrine and discipline a new weight, and allowed for efforts toward their resolution on a new scale and with new means.

As a result, two – closely interrelated – elements initially gave a new focal point to doctrinal discussions. First, synods or councils, gatherings of large assemblies of bishops on a trans-regional or (ideally) empire-wide basis, became a distinct feature of the period. Second, the drafting and promulgation of creeds, precisely worded propositions of orthodoxy, evolved as a preferred form for the expression of doctrinal decision-making, and eventually also as a standard for future deliberations. The idea of Fathers as authoritative guides in those theological deliberations constituted a third element. While a strong sense of tradition had long prevailed, appealing to individual Fathers found acceptance only gradually and not without resistance.

The appeal to the Fathers often had only limited immediate doctrinal import. Claiming the inheritance of the great figures of the past expressed one's ecclesiastical self-awareness, achieved by rooting oneself in the history of the Church and associating with its well-known, symbolic figures.

Synods and Councils

Helped by imperial protection and benefaction, and frequently even by the direct prompting and invitation of imperial authorities, Christian bishops and theologians met more frequently than in previous times. These synods or councils brought face to face churchmen who were otherwise greatly removed from one another, in terms both of geography and of their local ecclesiastical cultures and theological traditions. The unprecedented scale of participation and geographical outreach provided opportunities not only to discuss a specific agenda of disciplinary or theological dispute, but also to deliver speeches and sermons and to read and discuss technical treatises on aspects of theology or exegesis. Forceful personalities clashed or formed alliances. In all this, synods created or aggravated doctrinal or personal conflict as much as they helped to solve it.

The council of Nicaea, convened by Constantine in AD 325, set the precedent for the increasing role of synods in theological discourse. It would eventually come to be regarded as the cornerstone of orthodoxy and the iconic expression of the self-identity of the Church in the Roman Empire. The council was instrumental in increasing the frequency of similar gatherings in future: it ruled that provincial synods should be held twice annually (canon 5). In addition to those regular provincial gatherings, many larger meetings (still ideally universal) were held during the following decades. Some were convened directly on the initiative of the emperor or emperors to solve conflict in the Church. The festive occasions associated with the anniversaries of emperors or with their grand building programs also provided frequent opportunities for bishops to come together and to discuss and determine doctrinal disagreement. The dedications of the Church of the Holy Sepulcher in Jerusalem (AD 336) and of the Great Church in Antioch (AD 341) are prime examples.

To the unsympathetic observer, the sight of scores of bishops traveling from one gathering to the next, and taking up much of the resources of public transport in the process, summed up the conflicts of the period (Amm. Marc. 21. 16. 18). But not all bishops were happy with the development. Gregory of Nazianzus, after a bad experience at the Council of Constantinople (AD 381), where he was ousted from the presidency, was scathing about them: no good ever came of a synod (*Ep.* 130. 1). Earlier, Athanasius poured contempt and ridicule over the many synods of his opponents, although he was content to see others held to his advantage. Synodal debates thus became one of the chief instruments in forging alliances, in identifying and contrasting varied theological suppositions, and in attempts at doctrinal decision-making.

Many treatises, often polemical, about the controversial theological issues of the time were written in the run-up to such synods and were designed to influence the deliberations. Other works tried to assert a specific interpretation of events now past, and to identify in their wake the real doctrinal import of conciliar statements. Sermons and addresses were delivered to disseminate major concepts. Even exegetical commentaries and homilies frequently had doctrinal problems in view, and sought to uncover the implications of scriptural passages for the discussions that ensued. Obviously, theological literature was not restricted to such discussions, and works on the Scriptures important in themselves, on religious practice and spirituality, and on many other themes, were also being produced. Yet even they often drew from the implications of doctrinal definition or, conversely, illustrated common presuppositions informing and motivating the more technical debates about doctrinal propositions and language. Hence, much of the Christian literature of the time needs to be interpreted in the context of a contemporary theological discourse, and the sequence of councils and synods provides a useful vantage point. Conciliar debates frequently summed up the discussions of previous literary exchanges and polemic. They brought opposing views to a head, vying for acceptance as orthodox. Synods proved valuable tools in clarifying difficult theological questions; but, in aiming to reach consensus over doctrinal differences and in ruling on disciplinary problems, they could seem equally to harden partisan loyalties, to perpetuate bickering, and even to spark fresh theological dissent. Sometimes, in bringing the best theological minds together, they could also assemble the worst ecclesiastical power mongers.

Creeds and Statements of Orthodoxy

The theological work undertaken by assemblies of bishops, and the kinds of reasoning used to deal with the topics under consideration, are, for the best part of the fourth century, difficult to assess in any detail. No acts of synods are extant before the Councils of Aquileia (AD 381) in the west and Ephesus (AD 431) in the east. If minutes were taken at Nicaea or Constantinople, they are lost. Discussions frequently resulted, however, in carefully worded statements of faith, and they have been preserved. They sum up the doctrinal positions of those gathered, who thereby laid claim to orthodoxy, and they occasionally reject explicitly opposing views. Frequently, these statements – *ektheseis*, or creeds – are obviously answering one another. Through allusions to and slight modification of what had been said by another (possibly rival) assembly, they enter into a dialogue or argument. Again, Nicaea set the precedent for this kind of creed-making. The church historian and scholar Eusebius, bishop of Caesarea in Palestine, presented to that assembly (if we can believe his account) a personal creed that was approved as orthodox (*Letter to the Church of Caesarea*, Opitz 1934: *Urkunden* 22. 24–6). At Constantine's instigation, however, a commission drafted a different statement, which would become known as the Nicene Creed. Eusebius insists that the controversial wording was discussed intensely and that he was reassured of the meaning of particular words and phrases before he agreed to sign (*Urkunden* 22. 9–13).

We learn of the work of similar drafting commissions as late as the Council of Chalcedon (AD 451), and of discussions behind closed doors that resulted in amendments and alterations until a final text was agreed upon. Most scholars now believe the so-called Nicene-Constantinopolitan Creed, associated with the Council of Constantinople of AD 381, to be such a draft (Ritter 1965: 189–91; Kelly 1972: 325–31). According to this view, it was used as a basis for discussion with a group of bishops who rejected the divinity of the Holy Spirit, but was not formally decreed after negotiations broke down and they walked out. Such creed-making, inextricably linked with the gathering of synods and councils, and indeed the very *genre* of a creed as such, became typical features of theological debate (Kinzig and Vinzent 1999).

Traditionally, the formation of creeds has been associated with their liturgical use at baptism, from which doctrinal expansions and precisions were supposedly derived. However, there is no evidence before the fourth century for the use of creeds at baptisms – that is, of declarations made by the candidates: rather, they answered basic questions about their belief with a simple "Yes." Formulae summing up orthodoxy had another *Sitz im Leben* and took another form. In the second and third centuries, summary statements of essential Christian teaching can be found in many writings. As the rule of faith, they set out key concepts that could be used to define the boundaries within which theological inquiry and exegetical exposition could legitimately be conducted. Crucially, however, the wording and structure of those formulae were fluid, and could be given different emphasis depending on the topic under discussion.

During the fourth century, by contrast, phrasing down to the last word became ever more decisive and divisive – so much so that later generations were baffled by the intense squabbling and heated argument displayed over what could seem at times only a single letter's difference: should the relationship between God the Father and the Son be defined as *homoousios* or *homoiousios*? The repeated efforts of synods to coin an exposition of faith that expressed a correct understanding of God and Christ in precise and definitive wording added a new dimension to theological discourse. Those efforts went hand in hand with pressure put upon individuals to assert their orthodoxy by signing such expositions or by making personal statements of a similar kind. Eusebius' statement at the Nicene Council was one of those professions of personal orthodoxy, as was a written supplication by Arius to Constantine (Socrates, *Hist. eccl.* 1. 26. 3; Opitz 1934: *Urkunden* 30), or the declaration demanded of Eunomius on the occasion of a synod in AD 383 (Eunomius, *Expositio fidei*), to name but a few. Many such statements have survived (collected in Hahn 1897), and it is likely that even more were drawn up at the time.

In their attempt to define doctrine in carefully phrased statements of belief, and in their insistence on specific technical language exclusively suited to express acceptable theological positions (or conversely, in their rejection of the technical language preferred by their opponents), churchmen focused their attention on the use of key words and the acceptance of certain documents. In the east, eventually, only one creed came to be used in liturgical contexts. Another, similarly exclusive, was developed in the west. The many other formulae of the time functioned exclusively in technical doctrinal controversy, as a test of the orthodoxy of bishops and theological specialists, an expression of the often fleeting agreement between them and of their party solidarity.

The Authority of the Nicene Council and Creed

The abundance of synods and the process of repeated creed-making helped, ironically, to create a sense of the unique authority of the Council of Nicaea and its creed. Over time, that creed came to be seen as a definitive statement of orthodoxy, rendering all further attempts at creedal definition superfluous. In the end, the council and its creed achieved such an elevated status that subsequent doctrinal clarification was presented as merely a commentary upon it. In the collective memory of the Church, Nicaea was remembered with reverence as a foundational event in the formation of the true, orthodox Church.

In the half-century of debate following the Council of Nicaea, some theologians became increasingly wary of the repeated rephrasing of doctrinal positions. Athanasius ridiculed his opponents' repeated efforts to define the faith in ever renewed formulae, calling them a perpetual reinvention of the Christian faith. He asked how any such formula could command the respect of future generations when its authors seemed to be constantly overturning the decisions and sentiments of their predecessors and continually changing their own minds (*De synodis*, 13. 2–4). In the face of such endeavors he, like others, began to claim the unalterable authority of the Nicene Council and Creed of AD 325. Initially, he had seen it as little more than a definitive juridical solution to the case of Arius. Gradually, he began to promote it as the only valid, and ultimately sufficient, exposition of Christian doctrine (Sieben 1979: 40–52). After his death, the process of systematic clarification and exposition of the council's teaching continued. Although its teaching was still controversial, it became ever more apparent that any resolution of differences could be based only on its acceptance in principle. Consequently, the Council of Constantinople (AD 381) declared that it wished merely to reiterate the Nicene faith, establishing it as the binding expression of orthodoxy (canon 1; see Socrates, *Hist. eccl.* 5. 8. 1, 14). By the time the next major doctrinal conflict arose, between Cyril of Alexandria and Nestorius of Constantinople, this status was beyond discussion. Both men, as a matter of course, used the creed as the starting point of their argument, and claimed simply to elucidate its teaching (Cyril, *Ep.* 4. 3; 17. 2–3; Nestorius, *Ep. ad Cyrillum* 2, *sermo* 14, 17). Formally at least, the Nicene Creed was the yardstick against which Cyril had his own and Nestorius' teachings tested at the Council of Ephesus (AD 431), making sure that the verdict could only be in his favor (Conc. Ephes. *Gesta*, 43–4, *ACO* 1. 1. 2, pp. 12–13). The eastern collections of canon law list a ruling of the assembly that decrees the sole authority of the Nicene Creed and forbids any future efforts to compose another (canon 7). The canon testifies to the supreme authority that the council and its creed had eventually achieved. Not only would the validity of doctrinal propositions by this time be measured against the creed as an authoritative norm in general, but theological reasoning would often also be based directly upon it. Theological treatises attempted an exegesis of the creed and interpreted its wording almost like Scripture. The canon asserting its sufficiency could, on the other hand, be used to circumvent demands for further doctrinal precision and to refuse theological judgment altogether (Eutyches at the *Synodos Endêmousa*, or Resident Synod, of

AD 448: Conc. Constant. *ACO* 2. 1. 1, no. 359). The Council of Chalcedon struggled with this apparent problem: while it reenacted the Ephesine prohibition, it found ways to allow for a renewed attempt at doctrinal definition. Pointing out precedence and referring to approved documents by select Fathers it modestly presented, implicitly at least, its own definitions as no more than a clarifying commentary upon the Nicene Creed (see below).

Still, while the creed had risen to such an elevated and indeed revered status by the early fifth century, a general theory of the authority of councils and of the creeds promulgated by them had not yet been formulated (Sieben 1979: 223–30, 263–9). The closest we come to a discussion of what constituted a council's authority is a *reductio ad absurdum* that Athanasius presents in order to refute criticism of Nicaea. His critics had unearthed an earlier condemnation of the word *homoousios*; this precedent appeared to invalidate the Nicene statements. Athanasius plays briefly with the idea that one might decide between synods on the basis of either priority in time or the participation of a larger number of churchmen, only to reject both alternatives as absurd. In fact, a contradiction between synods was unthinkable, just as much as a contradiction in Scripture: what was demanded, again as in the case of Scripture, was a harmonizing interpretation (*De synodis*, 45).

Immediately after Nicaea, Constantine had spoken of the assistance of the Holy Spirit in the council's decisions (Constantine, *Letter to the Churches*, in Socrates, *Hist. eccl.* 1. 9. 17–18, Opitz 1934: *Urkunden* 25. 8). Theologians and bishops seemed more reluctant initially to make such assertions. But later generations spoke with great reverence of the holy council and the holy Fathers gathered. By AD 431, when the Council of Ephesus looked back to it, such phrasing had long become common parlance. The idea of divine inspiration had also taken root; votes cast by the participants echoed it many times (Conc. Ephes. *Gesta*, 45; see also Cyril, *Ep.* 1. 5).

So, while the process of doctrinal interpretation and clarification continued, the desire for ever more subtle and precise definition, evident in the creed-making of the mid fourth century, slowly gave way to a sense of completeness and closure that would ultimately banish additional creeds. Commentary and the layering of documents, not renewed phrasing, became the preferred mode of doctrinal definition. From about the second half of the fourth century, concern with creed spilled over from the sphere of specialized debate to a wider audience and into liturgical and homiletical contexts. Catechetical instructions began to include explanations of the creed's central theological tenets, and its recitation became a feature in the context of preparation for baptism.

Fathers: Doctrine and Identity

With the growing reverence for the Nicene Council, the habit of calling and honoring its participants Fathers also emerged. Earlier theologians and participants in other councils were occasionally also referred to by this honorific title, and the earliest debate about the role of Fathers in theology was not related to the bishops of Nicaea at all. It took almost a century, and some intense if sporadic debate, before an argument from the Fathers, quoting their texts in support of one's position, was deemed acceptable and eventually even praiseworthy. The persuasiveness of such an argument relied heavily on the collective veneration of the eminent figures of recent church history and an accepted image of that history. Appealing to them was much more, and yet much less, than a vote of confidence in their theological reasoning. Read in the light of contemporary debates, the exact position advocated in their texts was often less important to those who quoted them than the general demonstration of continuity with the past, both in terms of doctrinal expression and, often more subtly and indirectly, in terms of a communal bond of a shared history and identity.

As early as the AD 350s and 360s, it had become customary in pro-Nicene groups to speak of Nicene Fathers. In this context, appealing to the Fathers was virtually synonymous with appealing to tradition in general, and the Nicene Fathers were increasingly considered by those groups to be the privileged exponents of that tradition. There remained, however, an uneasy tension between the appeal to the Fathers collectively and efforts to make use of individual authors and texts as doctrinal authorities. Once again, it was precisely the controversy over the Nicene Creed that brought this particular matter, as well as related wider questions of theological norms and authorities, ever more strongly to the fore.

As might be expected, all sides claimed to be repeating the biblical message and professed that Scripture was the source and yardstick of orthodoxy. With this provision in mind, Athanasius, writing some thirty years after the events, tells us how the orthodox at the Council of Nicaea tried to express their teaching in biblical terms and metaphors, but had to face the fact that those terms and metaphors remained vulnerable to divergent interpretation. Hence they resorted to technical, philosophical language (Athanasius, *Decret.*). His account answers critics of the creed, who attacked it as nonscriptural. With the same purpose in view, several of the formulae drafted by successive synods in the AD 340s and 350s tried to adhere scrupulously to biblical imagery and phrasing. Anti-Nicene groups eventually, with the political support of Constantius II, forbade any use of controversial nonbiblical terms such as *ousia* and *hypostasis* and their derivatives (Athanasius, *De synodis*, 8, 28, 30). In the eyes of Athanasius and other pro-Nicene theologians, this pious biblicism was but a disguise for heretical ideas. Resorting to exegesis alone proved in any case to be inconclusive, as Athanasius' report of the proceedings at Nicaea had already indicated. Both sides compiled in support of their respective views proof texts that could not simply be weighed against one another. Attempts to understand the biblical teaching about God and Christ in a more comprehensive and conceptual way, on the other hand, remained unconvincing, unless the governing theological principles were shared from the outset.

In this interpretive circle of dogmatic biblical exposition and proof-texting, it was not uncommon to seek support in the testimony of tradition. Again, that was an old strategy. In the second century, Irenaeus had claimed to follow genuine apostolic tradition, whereas his heretical opponents lacked it. Heresy could always be identified by its novelty, or traced back to roots outside the apostolic tradition (Irenaeus, *Adversus haereses*, 3. 1–5; Le Boulluec 1985). Not surprisingly, both Arius in a personal creed and his main opponent, Bishop Alexander, presented their respective teachings as entirely traditional (Arius, Opitz 1934: *Urkunden* 30. 5, and see 6. 2; Alexander, *Ep. ad Alexandrum, Urkunden* 14. 55). Athanasius subsequently took great pains to demonstrate that the Nicene Council expressed traditional doctrine and employed traditional phrasing precisely when it used terminology not found in Scripture. What was pronounced here had been handed down "from Fathers to Fathers" (Athanasius, *Decret.* 27. 4). Building on such reasoning, the council's teaching itself gradually became the quintessential expression of tradition in the eyes of its supporters.

Nevertheless, throughout the dispute, it remained imperative to demonstrate the biblical grounding of any teaching. Athanasius' defense of the Nicene Creed with reference to earlier Christian writers only supplemented his main argument that it summed up the meaning, if not the words, of biblical teaching. That was why he presented a version of the proceedings markedly different from the (equally partisan) report of Eusebius mentioned earlier. He underlines the orthodox efforts to bring forward biblical proof and criticizes the exegetical evasiveness of opponents. He saw no contradiction between the need to argue from Scripture, as from the principle norm of theology, and the supplementary recourse to tradition. He fought with his opponents on the common ground of an appreciation of past ecclesiastical writers. This line of thought, however, opened up a new front in the controversy, as we shall see.

By contrast, one of his earliest allies, Marcellus of Ancyra, drew the front line more sharply and insisted that scriptural exposition was the only acceptable theological method, denouncing any appeal to Fathers as heretical. He mounted a fierce attack on the Eusebians for the specific way in which they laid claim to tradition. He was careful not to criticize tradition in principle – a line of thought that his adversaries would not have accepted. Instead, he found his enemies guilty of a crucial hermeneutic error, over and above their exegetical flaws and logical mistakes. They valued the legacy and even specific passages of past authors to an extent that, for him, eclipsed scriptural authority (Marcellus, fr. 19, ed. Markus Vinzent, *Fragmente*). To expose these grave errors, he quoted from a number of his opponents' writings dating back to well before the Council of Nicaea: Asterius, one of their foremost thinkers, had claimed in a letter the supporting witness of the "wisest Fathers" (Asterius, fr. 5, ed. Vinzent, *Theologische Fragmente*). Paulinus, bishop of Tyre and another figurehead of the group, had elsewhere concluded his reasoning with quotations from Origen, thus suggesting that he had found in that author a definitive answer to the question in hand (Paulinus, in Opitz 1934: *Urkunden* 9; Marcellus, fr. 19). To Marcellus, this method of appealing to individual ecclesiastical writers as to potential authorities defined the group as a school similar to philosophical schools – *haireseis*. While the method as such was flawed, it also allowed tracing a genealogy of error, which led Marcellus to find in Origen and his usage of philosophical ideas the root of their misconceptions. His argument harks back to antiheretical stereotypes used since the second century: false teaching goes back to an individual originator and firmly places the group following his ideas outside the Church. Hence, quite apart from the specific propositions advanced, claiming individually named Fathers and quoting them as authorities is to Marcellus in itself a possible sign of heresy – that is, of teaching by the methods of the schools and of placing one's confidence in human resourcefulness rather than in the divine authority represented in Scripture (Marcellus, fr. 17–19).

In a furious counter-attack against Marcellus' allegations, Eusebius of Caesarea coined the term "Church Fathers" (*pateres ekklésiastikoi*: Eusebius, *Contra Marcellum*, 1. 4. 3). He applied it indiscriminately to all those censured by Marcellus, and did not feel the need to define the term. His defense includes theologians living as well as dead, those holding ecclesiastical and in particular episcopal office, as well as those who, like Asterius, had lapsed during persecution and were disqualified from office for life. It is safe to infer from this heterogeneous grouping that Eusebius was not looking for a specific sociological profile in identifying Fathers – a profile that would qualify someone to hold authority and to guard right teaching in the Church. Nor was he primarily interested in the voices of the past. Rather, his emphasis rests firmly on the adjective "ecclesiastical": by using the phrase "Church Father," he explicitly made the point that those concerned were primarily characterized and distinguished by their place *in* the Church. Being a Church Father was being a member of an in-group, and thus representing the true Church, whether past or present. According to this argument, therefore, the idea of Church Fathers was not primarily concerned with the doctrinal authority of individuals of the past, but served foremost as a litmus test for belonging to the true Church at present. Associating oneself with its leading representatives by extolling and claiming them as Fathers expressed a self-awareness grounded in a view of the history of the Church and articulated through genealogical language (Graumann 2002: 46–66, 85–7). What, to Marcellus, was indicative of narrowly defined, school-type allegiances and of an inappropriate theological method that went with it, was to Eusebius a means of avoiding the potential errors of any one individual's reasoning, and it assured and expressed the cohesion of the Church's social and intellectual life.

Using and Interpreting Fathers

In subsequent debates, the tension that can be felt in the confrontation between Marcellus and Eusebius resurfaced time and again. While appealing to tradition in general was considered acceptable, even praiseworthy, resorting to individual writers or texts could seem rather more problematic and created its own difficulties. For example, Athanasius' efforts to harness tradition in support of the Nicene Creed met with an antithetical interpretation of the legacy of those predecessors, turning them into Fathers of his opponents' own ideas. The legacy of the Alexandrian bishop Dionysius (d. AD 264/5) was especially a bone of contention. The Eusebians found in him support for subordinating the Son to the Father, while Athanasius tried to elicit his true opinion from a comparison of texts, and even managed to find his much favored keyword *homoousios* in a text from Dionysius' pen. Many modern scholars are skeptical of his find and some cautiously even suggest it to be his own interpolation

(Abramowski 1982). In any case, a decisive statement from a revered and eminent bishop of the past on a contentious matter was evidently considered to be a forceful argument on both sides. However, the theology of past writers was no less subject to divergent interpretation than Scripture and could be claimed in support of conflicting views. Moreover, the cause for which someone's legacy was mustered could turn the focus of criticism back onto him and even lead to posthumous condemnation, as is best illustrated by the fate of Origen, who was repeatedly criticized as self-contradictory, if not outright heretical.

Both aspects are well reflected in a compilation of quotes that Basil of Caesarea produces toward the end of his treatise on the Holy Spirit. Basil gives the best indication yet that, in addition to scriptural proof, the tradition and especially the liturgical life of the Church could help make a convincing case for a theological proposition. His quotes, consequently, serve primarily to illustrate the Church's custom in the past. They are little more than sources to ascertain that tradition. Hence, he is very cautious in introducing the writers he quotes, and differentiates subtly between their testimony to church custom and tradition and their personal merits and orthodoxy (*De spiritu sancto*, 72–4). A closer look reveals how little theological substance the passages bring to the argument. What bolsters his argument, rather, is the fact that an appeal to tradition in this wide sense, demonstrable through quotations from a range of authors and from different periods, is possible at all. Interestingly, the term Fathers is strictly avoided.

While Basil comes closest to theorizing the role of tradition in general, Athanasius before him is the only one who edges toward a systematic reflection about theological method in dealing with the seemingly ambivalent legacy of past authors. Conflicting claims to tradition evidently necessitated, for him, a proper method and hermeneutic of interpretation – of the Fathers as much as of Scripture. Simply taking separate and mutually contradictory phrases on their own merit rendered their legacy useless. His suggestions must seem circular to the modern interpreter. Presupposing the timeless and universal unity and coherence of the Church's teaching, any past author worthy of acceptance as an authority can only confirm present orthodoxy, if indeed he was orthodox himself. This, of course, Athanasius understands to be his own pro-Nicene position. The interpreter's task is to tease out the overarching harmony of thought in biblical teaching, tradition, and the contemporary teaching of the Church – or rather, of the group claiming to represent it. Nevertheless, he fleshes out this principle by applying the same philological tools used to interpret Scripture, deriving ultimately from the Alexandrian philological tradition. In this sense at least, he works to the standards of literary criticism in his day.

By contrast, appealing exclusively to the authority of an individual theologian remained to some extent heretical at the time. This is in particular visible in a group of Apollinarian writers, flourishing a little later than Basil, who fall back on a very specific, even narrow acknowledgment of Apollinaris as a Father, the only authority they were willing to follow in defining the nature of Christ (Lietzmann 1904: 274 (Polemon), 277 (Julian)). Interestingly, another group in their camp indicated their willingness to embrace a more mainstream view and their aspiration to be accepted back into a wider community by combining quotations from Apollinaris with those of Athanasius. By portraying themselves as the true descendants of both these Fathers, they made clear their self-image as churchmen and their sense of belonging as much as, if not more than, their Christological preferences (Graumann 2002: 183–200). In the same spirit, many of Apollinaris' own writings were, after his condemnation, circulated under the protection of (Pseudo-)Athanasian authorship – not without consequence for future doctrinal debate.

The Memory of Athanasius

These examples illustrate how the name "Athanasius," quite apart from his role in coalescing a coalition of pro-Nicene bishops and writers, had only a generation after his death become a potent symbol of mainstream church identity. What we see in our early example, the compilations of some Apollinarians, is even more evident in the aftermath of the Council of Ephesus in the fifth century. The schisms arising from it were healed by asserting a common identity derived from, and embodied in Athanasius (as he had by that time come to be perceived). Evoking his memory made it easier to lay mutual suspicions to rest and to tolerate different doctrinal emphasis and language within a shared sense of community (Graumann 2003).

It is no coincidence that it was precisely the memory of Athanasius that came to be harnessed to this effect. Despite occasional dismissals of the notion that historical precedent had any real value, he contributed eminently to a historical turn in theological discourse when, as we have seen, he was confronted with the specific use of historical argument by his adversaries. In addition to employing all the genres and techniques of polemical writing, he made frequent use of historical demonstration in his treatises. He wrote what we may call exercises in *Zeitgeschichte*, presenting his own partisan account of near contemporary events and embellishing his narrative with a score of relevant documents quoted or paraphrased at length (Athanasius, *Historia Arianorum* and *De synodis*). Both aspects, the historical presentation and the eagerness to include documents, marked a recent trend and, at the same time, helped promote this new style of discourse. Even more importantly, Athanasius' historical writing was instrumental in the creation of a stereotypical image of events that would form the perception of later generations. When the church historians of the fifth century looked back, they presented Athanasius as a heroic figure fighting against heresy. In doing so, they relied heavily on his texts and self-presentation. For his part, Athanasius himself had helped to create what became the dominant perception of fourth-century history, which eventually allowed privileged recourse to the iconic Athanasius, as he was remembered, as a way of expressing one's own ecclesiastical standing and self-identity in the fifth century.

The Fathers, the Creed, and Conciliar Theology

In the east, the historical turn in the conduct of theological debate was almost complete when Cyril and Nestorius engaged in fresh controversy from around

AD 429. Before we analyze its efficacy in the ensuing conflicts, it is worth noting that a parallel development, in my view unconnected, took place in the west around the same time (Maschio 1986; Rebillard 2000). First of all, the Donatist controversy was, certainly by the time Augustine began to engage in it, ever more concerned with the evaluation of past events and documents. To a great extent, this concern with the past was inherent in the subject matter: clarifying the origins of the schism was essential to any resolution of the conflict. At the same time, there were wider implications concerning the right of either side to claim the intellectual tradition of past authors, in particular Cyprian, and to muster their memory as a way of expressing an authentic North African Christian identity.

Similarly, Augustine's anti-Pelagian writings had to fend off appeals to the intellectual heritage of revered figures like Ambrose of Milan. Their particular pertinence arose from biographical overtones: the argument challenged Augustine with a view of his own past and tried to undermine his current self-image and presentation of doctrinal orthodoxy. In each case, presuppositions about emblematic figures of the past seem to be operative, similar to those we have sketched in the east. What makes them distinct, in my view, is that the historical or biographical problems underlying the issues debated were more real than imagined.

That was not the case in the conflict between Cyril and Nestorius. Cyril presented himself as the descendant of Athanasius, not primarily as one occupying the episcopal throne in Alexandria, but foremost as the principle guardian of orthodoxy. As well as arguing from the Nicene Creed, as we have seen, he bolstered his position by citations from Athanasius (Cyril, *Ep.* 1. 4). What is more, in attacking Nestorius, he resorted to a strategy that proved highly effective. He set out to promote his own orthodoxy as a humble follower in the footsteps of the Fathers and denounced Nestorius' heresy in turn as that of an arrogant critic of such Fathers and a detractor of tradition in general (Cyril, *Ep.* 11, 14; see also Conc. Ephes. *Gesta*, 60, no. 25, *ACO* 1. 1. 2, pp. 52–3). Less than a generation later, this polemical strategy had turned into historic knowledge for the church historian Socrates. He saw most of Nestorius' errors as the result of a distinct lack of familiarity with the writings of the Fathers (Socrates, *Hist. eccl.* 7. 32. 10). As guardian not only of proper Nicene teaching but also of the due respect for the Fathers in principle, Cyril was able to rally support from many quarters, not least from the monastic communities. The idea of the Fathers resonated with their experience of the ascetic struggle, usually begun under the close tutelage of a senior figure, which commended the virtues of humility and obedience. The implications of his self-styled image as another Athanasius, who had cultivated a close association with the great figures of the monastic tradition, were not lost on them. Waging a publicist war on Nestorius, Cyril appended extracts from such Fathers to his treatises (Cyril, *Arcad.* 10–19; *Apol. Orient.*), and such a compilation, virtually identical with his previous collections, features prominently in the Acts of the Council of Ephesus (Conc. Ephes. *Gesta*, 54, *ACO* 1. 1. 2, pp. 39–45), where he managed to have Nestorius condemned.

These Acts finally answered the question of how to conduct conciliar theology properly, and identified the norms according to which one might arrive at a doctrinal decision. If my reconstruction is correct (Graumann 2002: 385–93; see De Halleux

1993), they do not present us with a straightforward record, but are an elaborate piece of composition and redaction, produced by Cyril's chancery and distributed by his publicist machinery to great effect. This edited version of events presents an account of the meeting deposing Nestorius, held on June 22, AD 431, in which the testimony of the Fathers is awkwardly placed. The excerpts are introduced at a time when the decision-making process had, strictly speaking, already reached its goal. If we accept the presentation of the edited acts as an accurate representation of the sequence of events, the quotations, at this stage, could neither function any more as norms against which to judge Nestorius, nor help to establish a positive sense of traditional teaching. If they had a place in the proceedings and not merely in the published acts, their purpose remains shrouded. Their introduction by a team of redactors drawing up the documents seems to me more likely. The probable intentions of such an editorial addition become apparent when these acts are compared to those of a second meeting, held on July 22, AD 431, four weeks after the initial deposition of Nestorius. It is evident, here, that the acts are careful and deliberate compositions rather than transcriptions of proceedings, and the intentions and principles of organization are much clearer: the acts are composed to portray a prototype of theological procedure and decision-making in a synodal context. Much of the material used is identical to that of the earlier assembly, and in fact copied straight from it. What is new are the arrangement and the insertion of clarifying remarks about the purpose in particular of the appeal to the Fathers. The proceedings open this time, therefore, with a reading of the Nicene Creed, formally declared to be the norm of orthodoxy, and go on to emphasize the need to adhere to its meaning as much as its wording. Excerpts of the Fathers are then presented as authoritative guides precisely to the proper understanding of the creed. Only then is the inquiry made into the case at hand (Conc. Ephes. *Coll. Ath.* 73–6, *ACO* 1. 1. 7, pp. 88–96). This careful composition in a way addressed the questions left unanswered by the perhaps rather more perfunctory editorial process of the acts of the earlier meeting. Now the role of Fathers in doctrinal decision-making and its relation in particular to creedal definition, is outlined precisely and explicitly.

With this composition and the accompanying explanation of the proceedings, the compilers have arrived at a state of hermeneutic awareness. Their rationale has dominated the perception of an argument from the Fathers ever since. Its immediate consequences were visible in the Council of Chalcedon twenty years later. The council also testifies to the paradigmatic status Ephesus had achieved as a model council. In a similar fashion, the Council of Chalcedon produced a carefully composed, even more elaborate, document of its decision and the authorities on which it was based. It opens with the solemn endorsement of the Councils of Nicaea, Constantinople, and Ephesus, pointing to documents of the latter in particular. It then goes on to recite the Nicene and Constantinopolitan Creeds. After a repeated confirmation of the tradition of the Fathers represented in those creeds, and the acceptance of, in addition, a number of specified documents by Cyril and Pope Leo, it sets out its own formula as no more than an interpretive supplement to them: "following the holy Fathers." The formula concludes, yet again, with the assertion that its teaching was "handed down" through the "Symbol [i.e., the creed] of the Fathers," as well as by the Prophets and Jesus himself (Conc. Chalc. *Actio*, 5. 30–4; see also *Actio*, 6. 8, *ACO* 2. 1. 2, pp. 126–30, 141). Only this repeated appeal to Fathers enabled them to overcome the deep unease of many participants at the time against drawing up a new formula of faith. It is also the purest expression of a commonly held sense of the continuity and ultimate consistency in the Church's teaching, represented not least in the writings of eminent churchmen. Theological discourse could, legitimately at least, no longer operate outside a framework of deliberately resorting to the tradition of Fathers. Yet, despite such cautious and advised recourse to the tradition of councils and Fathers, the council's own validity and authority remained disputed for centuries. Much of the fight for and against its teaching took the form of ever growing compilations of *florilegia* of the Fathers, and of pondering over the acts and documents of previous debates. The rehearsing of those texts and of the Fathers in general became a predominant form of theological pursuit and inquiry. In the Byzantine Middle Ages, theology, albeit primarily still denoting the ongoing process of reflection on God, could at least for one author (Johannes Kyparissiotes) also mean the sum total of Scripture, the councils, and the Fathers (Podskalsky 1977: 30–1).

Conclusion

In Late Antiquity, over the course of a century and a half, theological inquiry and debate found new modes of expression that would have a lasting impact. Theology emerged as a specialized discipline with its own accepted methods and standards, reflecting on its past achievement, quoting from and commenting on authors and texts that were fast becoming classical in their field. In all this, the memory of the great figures of the past (foremost that of Athanasius), together with a contemporary revision of the Church's history, also served to construct the symbolic expression of leading churchmen's roles and self-awareness, and provided the means to project a communal sense of church identity. The conduct of theology at that time reminds us that the shaping of ecclesiastical identity and technical theological reflection go hand in hand and mutually stimulate each other. Any research in, as well as any contemporary appeal to, the Fathers will have to take that interaction seriously into account.

BIBLIOGRAPHICAL NOTE

For the use of the concept "Fathers" during the Reformation and in early modernity, see Merkt 2001 and the collections *Auctoritas patrum* (Grane et al. 1993, 1998). The form and style of theological discourse in Late Antiquity have attracted considerably less scholarly attention than the doctrinal questions concerned, despite many recent works on rhetoric. Aspects of theological writing and reasoning in general, set against the background of traditional pagan teaching and learning, are investigated in Studer 1998. The evolving of a conciliar theory, in particular with respect of Nicaea, is outlined in Sieben 1979. For an assessment of the decision-making at Nicaea and Ephesus, albeit very much limited in perspective and uncritical of the representation in the Acts, see Person 1978. Cyril's view of the Fathers, presented within categories of tradition predominant in western discussions and ultimately derived from Vincent of Lérins, is set out in Nacke 1964. For a more recent treatment, and an argument about the notion of Fathers specifically, see Graumann 2002, which also contains a detailed analysis of the course of events at Ephesus and their representation in the acts of the council.

CHAPTER THIRTY-SEVEN

Defining Sacred Boundaries: Jewish–Christian Relations

Naomi Koltun-Fromm

Jews, Christians, and Late Antiquity

Late antique Jewish–Christian relations defy easy categorization, for the simple reason that the terms "Jew," "Judaism," "Christian," and "Christianity" are equally difficult to define in relation to the period. Who was a Christian? Who was a Jew? The late antique world stretched from Persia to the Atlantic, from the northern European mountains to the arid African deserts. Each religious or ethnic community adopted its own ritual practices and theological frameworks that were affected by variations in geography, politics, culture, and history, and could vary greatly, even within the boundaries of a single city. Hence, there was no one prototypical late antique Christian or Jew, even though modern historians use those familiar terms "Jew" and "Christian," "Judaism" and "Christianity," as aids to describing what were in reality more complex phenomena. Jews and Christians accommodated themselves to their positions in society, their geographic location, and the surrounding cultures to such an extent that they were often not even recognizable as co-religionists to others who claimed also to be Jewish or Christian. Many scholars suggest that, while some Jews and some Gentiles did become Christians, the apparently monolithic or cohesive constructs "Judaism" and "Christianity" were developed only in the fourth century: they were not the product of first-century formative identities (Boyarin 2003: 78).

Jews existed, of course, before Christianity developed; but even they did not necessarily practice what we today call Judaism. To be a Jew in the period before the advent of Christianity meant to be a descendant of the Judean community, which was defined primarily as an ethnic group with a particular land, culture, cult, and history, not as a group set apart by its faith (Cohen 1999: 97–8). Affiliation by religious faith was a striking novelty introduced with the rise of Christianity, and carried with it a new category of identity (Schwartz 2001: 179–84; Boyarin 2003: 71). Prior to that, one's identity had been based on one's place of origin (e.g., Athens) or one's ethnic group (e.g., Judean).

Not only were they not easily defined: neither Judaism nor Christianity emerges fully formed. Some have argued (Boyarin 2004: 10) that Judaism evolved out of biblical religion as a reaction to, or at least simultaneously with, the development of Christianity (which was itself, of course, a product of the same amalgam of biblical traditions). In relation to that earlier phase, historians have labeled various in-between groups as "Jewish Christians"; but even that nomenclature can encompass a range of beliefs and practices. Those using the term refer by and large to ethnic Jews who believed that Jesus was their God's Messiah, even though they continued to identify themselves as Judeans or were descendants of Judeans; but the term can also refer to Gentile-born believers in Jesus who chose to follow biblically based Jewish laws and rituals, such as sabbath, dietary restrictions, and sacrifice.

How we determine what is "Jewish" and what is "Christian" can vary, moreover, from situation to situation and from text to text. Many of the texts that we think of as "Christian" or even "Jewish Christian" may be better understood as thoroughly Jewish (if we define our category "Jew" by late antique standards). The authors of Revelation and the *Ascension of Isaiah*, for instance, clearly saw themselves as members of self-defined Jewish prophetic or priestly groups in the biblical tradition. They show as much concern for the prerogatives associated with that identity as they do for Jesus' mission (Frankfurter 2003: 138). Moreover, even among those who profess faith in Jesus, we find differing theological interpretations of that faith. Jesus appears variously as a prophet, the Messiah, the *Logos*, or the Son of God. At times, those theological interpretations directly contradict one another. Finally, both Jews and Christians, as self-perceived heirs of biblical Israel, define themselves in terms of their relationship to God, the Holy One. Being holy or "owning" holiness, in some relation to the divine, often trumps any notion of Jewishness or Christianness.

So, when discussing Jews and Christians in Late Antiquity, we always have to ask, what *kind* of Jew or Christian are we dealing with? And while, to help us catalog our subjects, we can create lists of appropriate categories (follows Jewish law, believes Jesus was the Messiah, and so on), it is often better to observe how the subjects define themselves. Do they call themselves Jews or Christians? Priests or prophets? Do they label others as Jews or Christians? The often quoted gospel statement that the term "Christian" was first used at Antioch (Acts 11: 26) does not mean that from then on all who believed in Jesus understood themselves to be Christians, nor were they referred to as such by outsiders. Paul, for instance, rarely used the term "Christian," and usually referred to his readers as "holy ones." This notion of a holy people, once again, remains central to any discussion of Jewish–Christian relations in the late antique period. Even Aphrahat (Aphraates), a fourth-century Persian Christian, did not refer to himself or his readers just as Christians but, following Paul, labeled them "holy ones" as well. Likewise, those whom we might label "Jews" did not necessarily call themselves such, preferring "Judeans," "Galileans," "Israelites," or even "holy seeds." The Judeans whom we associate with the Dead Sea Scrolls, for instance, referred to themselves simply as the Yahad (the one community).

In the end, then, when discussing late antique Jewish–Christian relations, we have to sort out the similarities, differences, contacts, or influences between the many groups in Late Antiquity that claimed to be either Jewish or Christian, or that look Jewish or Christian from our modern vantage point. In addition, we have to investigate the various interactions (both harmonious and antagonistic) between those many groups. How did each define itself vis-à-vis other groups claiming the same or similar titles, lineage, history, or sacred space? Even when they constructed solid boundaries between themselves, which interactions continued and which were limited, avoided, or actively persecuted? What literary resources did they share, even unconsciously?

The literary and material culture of the late antique period enables us to answer those questions at least in part. The Mediterranean basin has supplied an abundance of archaeological remains, inscriptions, and artwork that attest to the lively culture that thrived in Late Antiquity, especially in its cities. Temples, synagogues, churches, and other buildings reveal traces of living communities. Inscriptions on walls, lintels, and mausoleums give us insight into the priorities of certain individuals, families, clans, and communities. Late antique Jews and Christians left written records of their lives, together with histories, theologies, philosophical musings, and stories (although many have been lost). Few of those records were written to answer the specific questions we are asking here: they were written for other purposes, thus making our task all the more difficult.

Among self-identifying Jews, we have the relatively early first-century writers Philo and Josephus, who attempted to delineate the various categories of contemporary Jews. The most comprehensive Jewish texts of the late antique period are, however, the rabbinic writings that record the ideals, theologies, and stories of what started as a radical minority in the first century but became the dominant force among Jews by the end of the late antique period. We have little record of what else late antique Jews might have written. The rabbis, for their part, composed their various tractates for themselves alone. Each text in its way collects rabbinic musings on the meaning and application of the biblical texts they hold sacred. Together, they comprise a corpus of law, lore, history, and theology, and are presented as notes to an inside conversation among the rabbis and their students.

Christian writers, on the other hand, wrote for an external as well as an internal audience. They attempted to support the faith, practice, and increasingly distinctive culture of their followers; but they also desired to attract outsiders to their way of life and faith. They created texts in many more genres – histories, collections of sermons, *apologiae*, and rhetorical and exegetical works. Some Christian writers were even more precise in their motives. They felt theologically compelled to deal with the fact that most Jews or Judeans did not accept the coming of Jesus as the fulfillment of biblical messianic prophecy. That Jewish "failing" provoked a new literary genre, particularly among Christians who would later be deemed "orthodox." No comparable genre exists within the late antique rabbinic corpus, although anti-Christian polemic (as well as polemic against nonrabbinic Jews) pervades the literature. The writers' purpose, on both sides, was often to persuade the Christian (or Jewish) laity to segregate themselves, in both place and attitude, from whatever the writers considered non-Christian (or non-Jewish). Yet, even the Christian *Adversus Judaeos* texts, while theologically motivated, were grounded in biblical exegesis; and the exegetical character of all this literature, Jewish and Christian, suggests that the writers had far more in common than might seem allowed by the distinctions they attempt to assert. They were all scholars, members of a late antique elite, who shared a great concern for the correct interpretation of Scripture and especially for the intellectual pursuit of truth as revealed through God's sacred Word. By the same token, their engagement in that literary exercise was one way, perhaps the primary way, of articulating their own senses of self (as compared with some competing "other"). And, as I have already hinted, and shall explain further below, that competition was often couched in the language of holiness.

The History of the Study of Late Antique Jewish–Christian Relations

Before venturing further, I wish to examine how modern scholars have reacted to those complexities. In attempting to reconstruct the history of late antique Jewish–Christian relations, they depend heavily on theologically driven writings, particularly the *Adversus Judaeos* literature. The modern history of the endeavor can be divided into three phases. In the earliest, "supersessionist" phase, epitomized by Adolf von Harnack's work, Christianity was thought of as springing onto the scene – almost fully formed – somewhere between AD 30 and 70. Judaism, considered to have become already ossified, ceased thereafter, according to the supersessionist account, to retain any vitality or to offer any challenge to the soon to be victorious Church. Nevertheless, many Christian leaders continued to worry about Jews and Judaism. They either composed tracts entitled *Adversus Judaeos*, or inserted diatribes against or arguments with Jews and Judaism within other writings, particularly exegetical treatises. Marcel Simon, writing a generation after Harnack, concludes from the same evidence not that Judaism ceased to function once Christianity was born, but rather that it continued to be a genuine and troublesome issue for the Church. On the basis of Simon's depiction of a vibrant Judaism and Jewish community flourishing alongside the growing Christian community, scholars developed another account of Jewish–Christian relations: one in which there was a "parting of the ways" (as it is often described) somewhere between AD 30 and the fourth century. According to this theory, either at the time of the destruction of the Jerusalem temple in AD 70 or perhaps after the second Jewish revolt (AD 132–5), Jews and Christians went their separate ways without any further interaction, mutual dependence, or mutual influence. Most scholars in the middle years of the twentieth century opted for a definitive parting of the ways at the second moment, the Jewish revolt in Palestine (also known as the Bar Kokhvah rebellion), when supposedly real Christians would have had to choose, as it was imagined, between their Messiah, Jesus, and the revolutionary war hero and erstwhile Messiah, Bar Kokhvah. (Nowadays, many scholars would question the very existence of a messianic figure in Bar Kokhvah's time.)

Other scholars in recent years have begun to rethink even the parting of the ways construct. Whether they emphasize further interaction despite the split, or question the notion of a parting altogether, they consider that the evidence, both archaeo-logical and literary (and especially the *Adversus Judaeos* literature), points to con-tinued interaction between Jews and Christians well into the late antique period. In addition, when one diversifies (as one must) one's classifications, it becomes harder to talk about partings: there are many more crossovers. Which community of Jews parted from which Christian group? When and where? As Paula Fredriksen argues (2003: 48), the very fact that the orthodox Christian Fathers, such as John Chry-sostom of Antioch, continued to rail against Jews and Judaism shows that they continued to perceive them as a particular threat. Moreover, other evidence indicates that the laity were less concerned about intermingling than were their leaders. In fact (particularly in urban settings such as Antioch), Jews, Christians, and pagans – however defined – freely mixed and interacted. They approached each other for medical help and magic potions; they attended each other's festivals and temple rites. Of course, it was that very intermingling that upset church Fathers like Chry-sostom; but it only serves to show us that people on the ground saw little reason to segregate themselves from their neighbors. Even the rabbinic texts testify to Jewish consultations with magicians and Christian doctors (Hirshman 1996: 114). The ambiguity of the archaeological evidence further illustrates the difficulties of trying to sort out the Jews from the Christians, particularly in urban settings.

Holy Communities and the Other

One fruitful way of getting at the issue of Jewish–Christian relations is to look at the way each community conceives of itself via-à-vis the Other (or Others, as it may be), especially in their exegetical writings. These Jewish and Christian groups revered in common the Hebrew Scriptures (which the Christians usually referred to as the Old Testament). Despite the rhetoric of competition I mentioned above – the rhetoric of polemic, possession, and dispossession (particularly from the Christian orthodox side) – an intellectual middle ground emerged among Jewish and Christian writers. Rabbis and Christian Fathers shared exegetical materials and methods even as they competed for the interpretive prize of sacred truth (Hirshman 1996: 118).

In order to demonstrate the nature of this shared literary milieu, I shall focus the rest of this chapter on the notion of a "holy people," on the biblical texts from which that notion is derived, and on a sampling of patristic and rabbinic exegetical texts that maneuver holiness into exclusively Jewish or Christian categories. Despite the label "polemical" that we often assign to these writings, I want to emphasize again that these exegetical texts share a common ideological battleground. Although late an-tique Christians may have perceived the Jews as opponents in a larger battle for salvation, they grappled in their exegetical writings with the same internal issue: how best to define their community boundaries (and the hierarchies within them) through a close reading of the Bible. I focus here on those instances where the boundaries were defined in terms of the holy people, for the notion of holiness pervades the biblical texts.

The pertinent Pentateuchal texts for this particular exegetical discussion present us with several different and often contradictory images of holiness. On one hand, holiness (*qeddusha* in biblical Hebrew) is limited to God and the things of God. Among the Israelites, only the priests are the holy people of God: the rest of Israel remains common. Other texts, however, allow just that – the sanctification of the nonpriestly Israelite. In this case, in what is known as the "holiness code" (Lev. 17–27), God calls upon *all* Israelites to make themselves holy. Collective obedience to the divine law gives the Israelite community access to God's holy emanations, or holy "wavelengths" that sanctify the obedient on contact. Yet another line of biblical argument claims that Israel is *already* holy, because God has chosen it to be the divine nation of priests and a holy people. But who had access to God's holiness in the *post*-biblical world? That was the ultimate question with which both Jews and Christians struggled in their exegetical works and theological musings, making parallel attempts to secure God's blessing exclusively for themselves.

Holy chosenness inspired many Christian writers to assert that the title "holy" had been divinely transferred from biblical Israelites or late antique Jews to the Christians; but the same biblical formulation provided fodder for many early Jewish attempts to define themselves as the exclusively holy community. The idea that one can sanctify oneself, however, whether by adopting behavior prescribed or by avoiding behavior proscribed, provoked other writers, both Jewish and Christian, to develop the "holiness code" line of thought. So, in the end, late antique exegetes capitalized primarily on two biblical paradigms of holiness. The first *ascribed* God-given holiness to Israel and its descendants; the second advocated a holiness *achieved*, something that an individual or community could attain or earn for themselves. Together, they allowed for the formation of a hierarchy of holiness within any one community *and* made clearer the boundaries between the communities themselves. It is through those constructs that we can make sense of one community's perceptions of the other, if not actually determine the nature and effect of the interactions between them.

Being Chosen, or Holiness Ascribed: The Christian Understanding

Many early Christian writers use the term "chosen" rather than "holy" to describe Israel. Yet, the notions are in essence the same. Someone who is holy, dedicated to God, is chosen from among others to belong to God. The status of being chosen brings with it easy, direct, and guaranteed access to God. So, when early Christian writers asserted that holiness was essential to salvation in the next life, they necessarily implied chosenness in some sense. Paul, in his letters, challenged the view of the Hebrew Bible on the *exclusive* holiness or chosenness of Israel: he never completely removed the Jews (as descendants of biblical Israel) from his salvific framework; but he certainly displaced them from its center. Thus, he allowed Gentiles into his new community of believers. Only those who accepted his message were "in" and hence "holy," whether originally Jew or Gentile. Paul's purpose, therefore, was to show that God had also thereby *chosen* the faithful Gentiles to replace the faithless among the Jews.

Those faithless Jews, nonetheless, remained at issue in Christian discourse, because, as witnesses to the Christ event and as relatives of and community members with Jesus, they should have seen the truth of his mission. History shows, from a Christian viewpoint, that most Jews did not. As a result of this failure, many Christian writers, furthering Paul's claims, argued that God replaced *all* of historical Israel with the Gentile believers who recognized Jesus' divinity, and who could be said in that sense to have been chosen.

Melito of Sardis

In his *Peri Pascha*, a paschal homily dated to the middle of the second century and most likely read at Quartodeciman midnight vigils, Melito claims that historical Israel (those descended from biblical Israel) did not live up to their name "Israel" – that is, they failed to recognize God when he appeared before them on earth in the form of Jesus. Melito plays here on the Hellenistic understanding of the Hebrew behind the name Israel, and translates it (as Philo does) as "seeing God." And, because that historical Israel (the Jews of Jesus' generation) failed to recognize God, God "unchose" them. Hence, Melito's Jewish contemporaries have no claim on God or on the title "Israel." He writes, "You forsook the Lord | you were not found by him | you did not accept the Lord | you were not pitied by him | you dashed down the Lord | you were dashed to the ground and you lie dead" (Melito, *Peri Pascha*, Hall, 99–100). Because first-century Israel refused to see God in Jesus (and Jesus in the God that they did worship), God left them for dead. In particular, Melito claims, their failure to recognize Jesus' divinity caused them to murder him – which provoked God to disinherit them. While Melito never makes any specific claim about a new divine choosing, he implies as much when he pronounces Jesus divine. All who believe Jesus is the God of Israel can claim to be true Israelites. Further-more, the Gentiles recognized what Israel failed to see. When Israel "cast the opposite vote against [its] Lord," this same Lord "the Gentiles worshipped | and the uncircumcised men admired | and foreigners glorified" (Hall, 92). So, the Gentile believers replace historical Israel as God's chosen nation and become the True and Holy Israel.

Justin Martyr

In his *Dialogue with Trypho*, written in the middle years of the second half of the second century, Justin has no problem elaborating in detail just how clearly things have changed since historical Israel rejoiced in God's favor. He devotes much of the work to marshaling text after biblical text in defense of his belief that Gentile Christians have finally and irreversibly replaced Israel. He writes, for instance, "But we Christians are not only a people, but a holy people ... 'And they shall call it a holy people, redeemed by the Lord' [Isa. 62: 12]. Wherefore, we are not a contemptible people, nor a tribe of barbarians, nor just any nation as the Carians or the Phrygians, but the chosen people of God who appeared to those who did not seek Him. 'Behold,' He said, 'I am God to a nation that has not called upon My name' [Isa. 65: 1]" (Justin, *Dial.* 119, *PG* 6. 752, Falls, 331–2). With support from Isaiah, Justin argues that the Israelites never had exclusive rights to holiness, for God called to other nations as well. He concludes, "For, just as he [Abraham] believed the voice of God, and was justified thereby, so have we believed the voice of God (which was spoken again to us by the Prophets and the Apostles of Christ) … Thus, God promised Abraham a religious and righteous nation of like faith, and a delight to the Father; but it is not you, 'in whom there is no faith' [Deut. 32: 20]" (Falls, 332). With greater exegetical force than Melito, Justin argues that God disinherited faithless Israel. Concurrently, God accepted and elevated the faithful Gentiles, declaring them to be the new divine holy people, and placing them in the direct lineage of Abraham, because like Abraham they listened to God. For those who complied with God's wishes and abandoned idolatry (among other sorts of bad behavior) thereby gained God's approval. As Justin remarks, "We have been led to God through this crucified Christ, and we are the true spiritual Israel, and the descendants of Juda, Jacob, Isaac, and Abraham" (*Dial.* 11, *PG* 6. 500, Falls, 165) The Christians obeyed, the Jews disobeyed. In one fell swoop, Justin dislodges the Jews from their historical moorings and replaces them completely with the Christians.

While Melito accused Jesus' contemporary Jews of not recognizing God in Jesus and thus being led to murder him, Justin admonished the biblical Israelites (from whom Jews claim descent) for failing to live up to the covenant God granted them. In particular, he attributed their complete and final downfall to their failure to worship only the one God. Justin framed his polemical treatise (probably fictitious) in philosophical garb. He and Trypho, Justin's Jewish partner in the dialogue, met in the marketplace and agreed to discuss the true meaning of the biblical texts. And while Justin wrote in a triumphant manner and Trypho listened politely (and even agreed at some points), to the outside listener they were simply conducting a philosophical discussion in which they agreed to disagree at the end. Most significant, it is clear that they both held the biblical text as sacred and felt compelled to interpret it correctly. Thus, Justin argued that Trypho had been misled by his teachers (sages of one sort or another, according to Justin) into believing, incorrectly, that the Jews retained God's favor and could proceed in following biblical law as if Jesus never existed. Trypho's teachers misinterpreted the true intent of the prophetic texts. This practice, Justin argued, leads nowhere, certainly not to salvation. Only those who truly understand the text can truly obey God (that is, accept Jesus as God's Messiah) and be holy; only they belong to God, only they live with God in the afterlife.

Aphrahat, the Persian Sage

Two centuries later and across cultural and geographic boundaries, the fourth-century Syriac Christian writer Aphrahat, "the Persian Sage," argued along similar theological and methodological lines. The Israelites, drawn to idolatry against their better judgment and certainly contrary to God's explicit instructions, eventually lost their special status as God's holy people. Aphrahat maintained that, while Judah and Israel, the two biblical nations of Israel, behaved like promiscuous, prostituting, and adulterous wives in the face of God's fidelity as a "husband," the "*people* who are from among the *peoples*," that is the Christians, "[are] the holy and faithful people [because they have] gone down and cling to the Lord" (Aphrahat, *Demonstrationes* 16. 3, *Pat. Syr.* i: 769. 18–20 (based on the Syriac of Hos. 11: 12); this and other such translations are my own). The Christians, because they listened to and followed God's instructions to abandon idolatry and other gods, earned the title "holy" in place of disobedient and idolatrous Judah and Israel. Aphrahat interpreted Hosea 11: 12 to mean that the Gentiles have "gone down" from their pride – their ignorance of God. In their humility, they acknowledged God, abandoned idolatry, and gained the title "holy."

Both Justin and Aphrahat, perhaps inspired by Paul, cite Deuteronomy 32: 21, "I shall provoke you with a people which is no people, and with a foolish people I shall anger you" (Aphrahat's version), in the cause of their supersessionist argument. Justin deploys the verse to support his contention that the faithful peoples replaced biblical Israel in God's favor; Aphrahat agrees, but argues further that the Christians, or the "people from among the peoples," because they abandoned their idolatry, and even provoked Israel, even in Aphrahat's day, to turn away from worshiping other gods. Nonetheless, both authors, together with Melito, construct their religious group identity as the chosen or holy people of God in contrast to Israel, the nation who previously claimed, but can claim no longer, to be the one and only holy people of God. The one holy community cannot define itself without redefining and demoting the other. Like siblings competing for their parent's favor, the Christian writers claim that although historical Israel may once have been God's favorite, the "people who are from among the peoples" superseded Israel to gain that privileged and holy status through their better conduct and greater obedience.

Being Chosen, or Holiness Ascribed: The Jewish Understanding

Early Jewish texts

From very early on, Jewish writers understood at least their part of the Jewish community to be "holy." Yet, they often used the term to differentiate among other Jewish groups claiming descent from the ancient Israelites. In the fourth century BC, for instance, Ezra called the returning Judeans a "holy seed" in order to distinguish them from those Judeans and northern Israelites who had remained in the land of Israel during the Babylonian exile. Only those who had experienced exile could claim to be truly holy. The author of the *Book of Jubilees* (second century BC) again differentiated between "good" and holy Israelites (those who marry other Israelites) and "bad" Israelites (those who marry outside the Israelite community). Similarly, the Yahad (the community that, until its destruction, lived at the Dead Sea) claimed holiness exclusively for itself and for anyone who followed their particular interpretation of Torah law. Although their emphases vary, all three groups maintained that a holy Israel continued to exist despite the failings of certain other descendants of ancient Israel.

Rabbinic texts

The early rabbis also created boundaries between themselves and others through the rhetoric of holiness. According to the *Mishnah* (Yev. 11. 2), a rabbinic Jew was "born into holiness." Nevertheless, the rabbis generally created more porous boundaries than their predecessors, allowing those born "out of holiness" to convert and to gain equal access to holiness. Moreover, in this rabbinic text, those "not born in holiness" (*qeddushah*) referred primarily to non-Jews, not nonconformist Jews. We can follow this line of thought further in the following *midrash* from *Midrash Tehillim* which describes Israel as a holy "item" of God (*qodesh visrael l'adonai*): "Oy to those who count heads … There is no head but Israel, as it says, 'when you take a census [head count of the people Israel]' [Exod. 30: 12], and there is no holy-one but Israel, as it says, 'Israel is a holy-item to God' [Jer. 2: 3]" (*Midrash Tehillim = Shoher Tov* 104. 1, ed. Buber, 439; my translation). Here, Israel is both the head (of all the other nations) and special – holy to God. The rabbinic authors interpret the census mentioned in Exodus 30 as a description of what Israel is rather than of what Israel needs to *do*, and they see it as parallel to Jeremiah's statement in 2: 3, "Israel is a holy-item of God." Israel is the head; hence, Israel is holy.

Despite the matter-of-factness of this citation, the same declaration of Israel's holiness is often embedded in a polemical statement about the permanent nature of that status – namely, despite Israel's sins, God did not take away their holiness. For instance, *Numbers Rabbah* 2. 15 compares God's indulgence of a sinful Israel to a king with a slovenly wife. Focusing on the same Jeremiah text (Israel is a holy-item), the rabbis extrapolate:

> This [verse] may be illustrated by another parable. A king took a wife and used to say of her, "There is none more beautiful, none more excellent, none more steady than she!" Her servant once came into the house and saw her looking disreputable, the house untidy, the beds not made. The servant said to her: "O that you could but hear how your husband praises you in public! The praise is not at all justified by this behaviour!" Then the servant thought to himself, "If he lavishes such praise on her when she is disreputable, how much more were she at her best!" So it was with the generation of Jeremiah. They sinned, yet He said to them, "I remember the devotion of your youth, *etcetera*" [Jer. 2: 2]. Jeremiah said to them, "O that you would but hear what He says concerning you: 'Go and cry in the ears of Jerusalem … I remember the devotion of your youth … Israel is a holy-item of God, *etcetera*.'" He argued: If He shows them such love when they sin, how much more when they do His bidding. (*Numbers Rabbah* 2. 15, tr. Judah J. Slotki in Freedman and Simon 1983, v: 49–50)

In this excerpt from a long winding set of *midrashim* purportedly commenting on Numbers 2: 32, the rabbis ruminate over Israel's relationship with God as expressed through the prophets, particularly Jeremiah. Wondering why God did not carry out his various threats to replace a rebellious Israel with another nation, they conclude that God is fundamentally unwilling or unable to do so. His consecration of Israel (Israel is a holy-item) cannot be undone. Even as Israel repeatedly sins, God repeatedly shows compassion and remembers Israel's "youth" (promises of good behavior and devotion) and forgives them. Because of God's undying love for, and commitment to, Israel, God continues to hope that Israel will be well behaved in the future, somewhat in the manner of the king who persists in praising his bedraggled and lazy wife in the hope that she will reform her behavior. The sentiment encourages the rabbis to believe that they too will find favor, prosperity, and a good life in the sight of God, while at the same time it undercuts Christian criticism – such as Justin's and Aphrahat's above – that Israel's rebelliousness and sinfulness eventually lead to God's rejecting of them in favor of the "peoples" who follow Jesus. Whether intentionally polemical or not, both Jewish and Christian writers depend on various biblically based notions of holiness or chosenness, in order to define, defend, and construct their community boundaries. In so doing, they also endow their individualized religious practices, faith, and the very existence of their distinct yet related communities with a stronger sense of purpose.

Holiness Achieved

In spite of their contribution to theories of ascribed holiness, the Hebrew biblical texts provide later readers with other methods of constructing the notion of a holy people. The levitical call to holiness lays itself open to alternative ways of being holy – ways that highlight human behavior rather than (or at least in addition to) God's choice. I want to focus now on types of holiness achieved, and in particular those that depend on sexual practices. The biblical texts link holiness and sexuality in various ways that later writers develop to suit their needs.

The Christian view

Paul, in his discourse on holiness achieved, reduces his understanding of the holy people to the level of community practices, particularly sexual behavior. In 1 Corinthians 6, for instance, he argues that the individual Christian, as a member of the larger community of believers, has become one (metaphorically) with the holy body of Christ, and is thereby holy by extension. Hence a believer must not defile his holy body with what Paul calls *porneia* (bad sexual behavior), for it will also necessarily pollute the whole community of believers, and by metaphorical extension the holy body of Christ of which they are jointly members. Without defining *porneia* in detail, Paul maintains in 1 Corinthians that there is holy behavior (avoiding *porneia*) and unholy behavior (indulging in *porneia*). While for Paul an individual's holiness depends first on faith, the community's holiness depends on its ability to monitor the sexual behavior of its members. In other passages, Paul suggests in the same way that a holy community differentiates itself from other nonholy communities by its behavior, particularly sexual behavior. 1 Thessalonians 4, for instance, distinguishes between holy Christian marriage and unholy Gentile marriage.

Turning to subsequent expressions of this notion – of holiness achieved through properly adjusted sexual behavior – we find new patterns of thought and argument evolving. The third-century Syriac *Acts of Judah Thomas*, for instance, assert that in order to be fully Christian one must sanctify oneself – that is to say, one has to pursue actively some sort of sanctifying behavior in order to become a Christian. Moreover, the Acts place holy sexual behavior above faith as the defining Christian characteristic. Real Christians achieve holiness by avoiding *porneia*. Yet the text goes even further: "holy sexual behavior" means either strict monogamy (one spouse for life) or full sexual abstinence. Paul's admonition to avoid certain "bad" forms of sexual behavior as an integral part of one's faith is, among some ascetically inclined Christian authors, displaced as the basis for achieving and maintaining Christian holiness by more restrictive sexual practices, even sexual renunciation.

This tendency to equate holiness with some sort of sexual behavior – be it chastity in marriage (that is, either monogamous marriage or sex for procreation only) or full sexual renunciation – can be found throughout the literature of the more ascetically inclined church Fathers (Clement, Origen, and Tertullian, to name but a few). They often attempted in their polemical works to defend or moderate what seemed to others culturally offensive positions. Yet, within communities already claiming chosenness, these exegetes' hermeneutics of achieved holiness also provided in the end alternative ways of enhancing their divinely sanctioned, ascribed holiness, resulting in the creation of a hierarchy within their respective communities that placed ascetics a notch or two above the rest of the laity.

Aphrahat, for instance, argues that, while God blesses both marriage and celibacy, he elevates celibacy over marriage. Aphrahat makes that argument by appealing to celibacy's holiness. He inherits thereby, within the Syrian tradition, the trend displayed in the *Acts of Judah Thomas*. The basic expression of his religious self-identity is not just holiness but *qaddishutha*, a technical term for total sexual renunciation, adopted by Aphrahat as his life's vocation. In *Demonstrationes* 18, entitled "Against the Jews concerning Virginity and Holiness," he argues that Moses' command, when Israel stood before Mount Sinai, that they should not "go near a woman" anticipated God's Sinaitic revelation. Crucial to his argument is his interpretation of the verb *qds* – which appears in Exodus 19: 10 and 14 and there describes the ritually purifying actions that the Israelites must undergo before they can attend upon God. Aphrahat, however, understands the verb to connote sanctification (a permanent status) rather than ritual purification (a temporary status). He argues further, "And if with Israel, that had sanctified itself for only three days, God spoke, how much better and more desirable are those who all their days are sanctified, alert, prepared and standing before God. Should not God all the more love them and his spirit dwell among them?" (*Demonstrationes* 18. 5, *Pat. Syr.* i: 830. 8–15)

Aphrahat suggests here that ritual acts of washing and temporary celibacy can sanctify rather than just ritually purify. And not only that: God, through Moses, commands the people to perform these acts in preparation for the greatest moment in their history, the divine revelation. As Aphrahat understands Exodus 19, before God can give Israel the covenant, Israel must sanctify itself through temporary sexual abstinence. He further argues that, if a whole community should choose to sanctify itself permanently through full sexual renunciation, would not God prefer them (that is to say, choose them) from among all other communities? Aphrahat places this particular exegetical reading within his polemic against the Jews. The Jews, he laments, claim an exclusive hold on holiness; a holiness achieved through their fulfilling of the divine laws, in particular the law to be fruitful and multiply. Aphrahat's counter-argument opposes this supposed Jewish belief on several fronts. First, he allows that some Christians do legitimately procreate (but this does not make them holy – they are already that by their faith). Second, and more important, he argues that those who do not procreate sanctify and further elevate themselves, because God commanded the Israelites to be celibate before Sinai and called that action "holy." Only celibate Christians have grasped the import of this command by adopting it as the basis of their religious vocation of "standing before God." Holiness is not only a sign of a whole community's chosenness, but also proof of divine approval for a community that follows God's "real" commandments to their logical conclusions. Aphrahat's celibates are holy not only because they understand that the command to "sanctify" in Exodus 19 implies sexual renunciation, but also because they, as opposed to the Jews, truly sanctify themselves – that is, fulfill the command of the holiness code in Leviticus by truly obeying God. Thus, the Jews misunderstand the biblical texts' import when they focus on the commandment to be fruitful and multiply as evidence of their obedience. As we shall see below, Aphrahat's Jews, whether fictitious or real, do not represent the theological stance of all fourth-century Mesopotamian Jews; but Aphrahat, certainly, and some rabbinic Jews understand the relationship between holiness and sexuality in strikingly similar ways.

Nevertheless, Aphrahat proves unable or unwilling to condemn marriage and procreation entirely. Rather, he and other like-minded Christian exegetes, in elevating celibacy above procreation, create a hierarchy of holiness within their communities. In *Demonstrationes* 16, Aphrahat argues that all Christians are holy in that they, as believing Gentiles, have displaced the disbelieving and particularly disobedient Israelites. Here he draws a line between holy (Christian) and unholy (Jews). In *Demonstrationes* 18, however, he draws a three-way division: Jews, procreating Christians, and celibate Christians. In arguing against Jewish claims based on a command to procreate, Aphrahat subdivides his own community into the holy faithful and the more holy celibate. The goal in the end is not to be "Christian" or "Jewish," but rather to exemplify holiness: belonging to God. And if you or your followers embody more holiness than others – all the better for you and your community. While Aphrahat argues that celibacy achieves holiness, some rabbis (as we shall see below) posit that other ascetic sexual practices could achieve similar results. Hence sexual abstinence cannot be seen as a strictly Christian category in the middle of the fourth century; nor can holiness be seen as a strictly Jewish one.

The Rabbinic view

In their own discussions concerning individually achieved holiness, the rabbis make two similar moves. Some agree with Aphrahat's reading of Exodus 19 – that the nature of Moses' call to temporary celibacy at Mt. Sinai is expressed by the word *qaddosh* (*Avot de Rabbi Natan* 2. 3; *Mekhilta Yitro Bahodesh* 3) and means "holy." But few, if any, rabbis would proceed to Aphrahat's conclusion that God prefers the celibate. The texts suggest rather that Moses needed to be celibate in order to serve God and Israel in the desert (although he did have two sons before that). He was special (that is, holier), as Deuteronomy 34: 10 notes: "and there has not arisen a prophet since in Israel like Moses whom the Lord knew face to face" (*Sifre* 103). Certain other rabbis, however, agree with Aphrahat's overall theory that certain ascetic practices (sexual and other) gain extra holiness for the practitioner. In this way, the rabbis also create a hierarchy: there is holy Israel and the more holy (more ascetic) rabbis – thus strengthening further their authoritative positions.

This final notion can be seen in the following exchange recorded under the names of two famous fourth-century rabbis:

> Abaye stated, "whosoever acts in accordance with the rulings of the Rabbis is called a holy man." Replied Rava to him, "Then he who does not act in accordance with the rulings of the Rabbis is not called a holy man, nor is he called a wicked man either." "Rather," said Rava, "sanctify yourself by that which is permitted to you." (Babylonian Talmud Yev. 20a; my translation)

These statements come at the end of a long discussion about the categories of holiness applicable to all Israelites. If some biblical texts refer only to priestly holiness, what are the rest of Israel? Based on other biblical texts that see holiness as resulting from following the commandments (the holiness code), the rabbis conclude that fulfilling the biblical commandments makes (or confirms) an Israelite (as) holy too. Hence, if all Israel is holy, then the priests must be more holy. Abaye further suggests that only Jews who follow rabbinic understandings of biblical law should be allowed to call themselves holy. Rava wonders, then, what of the nonconformist Jew? Is he no longer part of Israel? Rava, unlike Ezra or the author of the *Book of Jubilees*, does not wish to follow that line of inquiry. He clearly holds that all Israel is holy, whether they behave themselves or not (as was suggested in the rabbinic texts quoted above). So, he suggests instead, "sanctify yourself by that which is permitted to you" – that is, restrict yourself even in your permitted actions; in other words, be ascetically inclined. By limiting one's sexual activity, for instance, one moves oneself into a higher category of holiness – in the same way that God bestowed upon the priests a higher level of holiness among the other Israelites. Sexual limitation provides Aphrahat with similar mechanisms, and even some rabbis create extra avenues of individual spiritual achievement within a community's already delimited sacred boundaries.

For these late ancient authors, holiness was the prize of God's exclusive attention both ascribed and achieved. It afforded these Christian and Jewish exegetes several ways to define themselves, both as communities vis-à-vis competitors and internally as divided between the laity and those that would claim some religious authority. Melito and Justin Martyr diverted God's exclusive attention and gift of holiness from historic Israel to the growing Gentile Christian communities, in order to support their new-found faith. Aphrahat used sexuality within his discourse on holiness as a primary tool of community organization and self-awareness. The rabbis turned to the priestly precedence of internal hierarchy to create internal divisions of their own, based on individual sexual practices. All communities seeking access to God attempted to interpret the biblical notions of holiness to their exclusive advantage. In the end, these various hermeneutics of holiness – ascribed or achieved – became indispensable tools in Christian and Jewish exegetical hands for constructing internal and external community boundaries. Late antique Jewish–Christian relations can be defined then, in part, by how each community constructed its borders and divisions. The writings we have examined here demonstrate how hermeneutics of holiness aided these exegetes in their community-building projects in a world of competing claims on the truth of shared sacred texts. These groups did not aspire to be Jewish or Christian as much as they wished to claim God's holiness exclusively for themselves. Moreover, sexuality emerged for late ancient Jews and Christians as the shared criterion by which to measure their achievement of that ambition.

In conclusion, Jewish–Christian relations in the late antique period are not easily defined. Geography, politics, and cultural context helped in some small degree to determine the possible relationships between the many and variously configured Jewish and Christian communities around the Mediterranean basin and Near East. Material culture also provides some evidence of both hostility and harmonious contact between communities. Yet the literature, particularly the exegetical and polemical treatises, does most to open a window onto the complexities of constructing community boundaries between groups that in essence shared more cultural, religious, and literary resources than they were willing often to admit.

BIBLIOGRAPHICAL NOTE

Students who wish to start at the beginning should read both Harnack 1883 and Simon 1986. Others who wish to jump right into the contemporary debates would do well to start with Becker and Reed 2003. The introduction's bibliography is particularly useful. Other books of interest are: Sanders 1980–2; Rokeah 1982; Wilken 1983; Drijvers 1985; Segal 1986; Wilson 1995; Gregg and Urman 1996; Hirshman 1996; Cohen 1999; Porter and Pearson 2000; Boyarin 2004; Lieu 2004.

For greater ease of reference, I note the following editions and translations:
Aphraates, the Persian Sage (Aphrahat) (1894–1907), *Demonstrationes*, Syriac text and Latin tr. by John Parisot, in R. Graffin (ed.), *Patrologia Syriaca*, i: *Ab initiis usque ad annum 350*, 3 vols., Paris, Firmin-Didot.
Aphraates, the Persian Sage (Aphrahat) (1988–9), *Les Exposés*, 2 vols., French tr. by Marie-Joseph Pierre, Paris, Éditions du Cerf.

Avot de Rabbi Natan (1887), ed. S. Schechter, London, Nutt.

Justin Martyr (1948), *Dialogue with Trypho*. Text: *PG* 6. 471A–800D. English tr. by Thomas B. Falls, Washington, DC, Catholic University Press.

Mekhilta de-rabbi yishmael (1960), ed. H. S. Horoviz and I. Rabin, Jerusalem, Bamberger & Wahrman.

Melito of Sardis (1979), *On Pascha and Fragments*, ed. Stuart George Hall, Oxford, Clarendon Press; English tr. by Alistair Stewart-Sykes, *Melito of Sardis, On Pascha: with the Fragments of Melito and Other Material related to the Quartodecimans*, Crestwood, NY, St. Vladimir's Seminary Press, 2001.

Midrash Rabbah (Genesis–Deuteronomy Rabbah plus the five Scrolls) (1884–7), *Midrash Rabbah al Hamishah Humshe Torah ve-Hamesh Megillot*, 2 vols., Vilna, ha-almana veha-ahim rom; English tr. by H. Freedman and Maurice Simon, 10 vols., 3rd edn., London and New York, Soncino Press, 1983.

Midrash Tehillim (also called the *Shoher Tov*) (1891), ed. S. Buber, Vilna, Wittwe & Gebrüder Romm.

Mishnah: Shisha Sidrei Mishnah (1952–9), ed. Ch. Albeck, 6 vols., Jerusalem and Tel Aviv, Mosad Bialik/Dvir.

Sifre de-Be Rav (Sifre to Numbers) (1864), ed. M. Friedman (Ish Shalom), Vienna, Holzwarth.

Talmud, Babylonian (1882), *Talmud Bavli*, Prague, Landau; English tr. by I. Epstein, *The Babylonian Talmud in English*, London, Soncino Press, 1935–52.

CHAPTER THIRTY-EIGHT

Pagans in a Christian Empire

Neil McLynn

The title of this chapter invites trouble. The two fullest recent treatments of the theme, the one a lively narrative account (Chuvin 1990) and the other an extensive analytic survey (Trombley 1993–4), have both been subjected to severe criticism, the one for muddled sentimentality (O'Donnell 1990) and the other for incoherent arbitrariness (Mitchell 1995). Both books contain much of value, but the reviewers' strictures are solidly based. For such is the peculiar elusiveness of our evidence that *any* attempted retelling of the pagans' experiences from their own perspective will be vulnerable to the former complaint, and any comprehensive analytical scheme to the latter. This is a topic where modern critical techniques have dissolved old paradigms without yet establishing a usable replacement.

As a result, many recent treatments of the subject sound distinctly unsympathetic. Forty years ago, the traditionalist aristocrats of fourth-century Rome were credited with a brave rearguard defense of the symbols of their city's ancient greatness (Bloch 1963). Such views are now untenable, and the last pagans of Rome have been dismissed as spinelessly self-regarding (Cameron 1999). Whereas thirty years ago enthusiasts could still liken Emperor Julian's tragically unfulfilled promise to President Kennedy's (a comparison mildly deprecated by Browning 1975: xii), the dominant portrait is now of a quixotic fanatic, whose death occasioned a universal sigh of relief (Bowersock 1978). While modern studies have vindicated the coherence of Julian's philosophical and religious ideals (Athanassiadi 1992; Smith 1995), Julian the politician – the pagan ruler who sought to dismantle the Christian empire – still awaits his rehabilitation. The equivalent survey of our subject in the authoritative *Cambridge Ancient History* duly backs away from the Christian empire, finding its heroes instead in the stubborn philosophers who remained aloof from the hurly-burly of politics (Fowden 1998). Only in studies of the pre-Constantinian era does pagan society seem to come alive (Lane Fox 1986; MacMullen 1984); the pagans of our period are generally consigned to passivity, and even in the more sympathetic accounts (MacMullen 1997) remain on the receiving end of christianization.

The modest claim advanced in this chapter, that political and cultural space remained available throughout the fourth and even the fifth centuries for pagans to assert a religious identity, is therefore more controversial than it might initially seem.

The term "pagans" has itself become contentious. Certainly, none of the millions of Romans who still worshiped their fathers' gods when Constantine pledged his allegiance to Christ in AD 312 would have recognized the name. Nor indeed would their Christian neighbors, who still routinely applied the biblical label "Gentiles" to those who belonged neither to the Jewish Israel nor to their own. Paganism, with its implication of boorish rusticity, was a species identified a generation later, by Latin-speaking Christian taxonomists who revived an obsolete insult for their own rhetorical purposes (O'Donnell 1977); it would evolve as these purposes changed, but would remain a polemical tool. The only self-described pagan on record uses the term with exquisite irony (August. *Ep.* 234. 1). During the same fourth century, a rather different set of connotations would meanwhile be generated, as Greek-speaking Christians extracted from their Bibles a parallel category of "Hellenes"; complications ensued when some of those so labeled gleefully appropriated the title and confronted the Christians with its implications (Bowersock 1990).

But "paganism" has its uses, and no substitute succeeds better. For we are dealing with an artificial category: those who addressed their prayers to Zeus the all-highest, to Capitoline Jupiter, to Mithras, to Baal Ammon, to Serapis-Osiris, or to any combination of these, never felt the need for a collective name or identity. Well-intentioned modern efforts to provide a neutral substitute for derogatory Christian labels therefore risk creating a single religious community where none in fact existed; more dangerously, they serve to perpetuate the artificial boundary that Christian spokesmen conjured in order to separate their own Christian sheepfolds from the dangerous beasts roaming outside, a boundary that bore little relation to the complex interactions between the "faithful" and their multifariously unchristian neighbors. The recent fashion for the term "polytheist" is a good example of the complications that modern rebranding can create – for one of the most exciting areas of recent research in late antique religions has concerned the large numbers of non-Christians, extending far beyond a philosophically minded minority, who acknowledged a single all-powerful deity (Athanassiadi and Frede 1999; Barnes 2001).

"Paganism," by contrast, automatically generates its own scare quotes. The alarm is helpful, for nearly every reference in our sources serves a hostile agenda. The Christians invented paganism solely to measure it against their own religion; preachers kept it alive as a useful bogey, but its principal function was to suffer defeat. Much of the following will therefore pertain to the rhetorical tropes of the Christian empire, and will explore the messy realities – or at least the misty spectrum of possibilities – behind their smooth triumphalism. We must also listen closely on those occasions when pagans speak for themselves, not least because so much of what they say seems so irrelevant to what we feel they should be saying. Such evidence inevitably concentrates our attention on a tiny handful of the elite. But theirs was a significant minority, and if the vast majority of pagans, still the predominant element in the rural population in most provinces of the empire in AD 400, must remain beyond the scope of this short chapter, they remained equally beyond the reach of the legal framework of which the "Christian empire" was constructed.

Codifying Paganism: The Problem of the Theodosian Code

If Christian preachers invented paganism, imperial legislators defined it. And it is the imperial law codes that justify, above all, my using the term in this chapter, for it was as pagans that the Christian empire officially treated those who observed the traditional cults. In fact the word filtered only belatedly into legislative vocabulary (the earliest such usage occurring in AD 370: *Cod. Theod.* 16. 2. 18), but was firmly established by the early fifth century, when the editors of the *Theodosian Code* classified some twenty-five miscellaneous imperial pronouncements under the title "On Pagans, Sacrifices and Temples" (Delmaire and Rougé 2005). So important have these laws been in providing the basis for our narratives of pagan decline that we do well to recognize how intractable the editors evidently found their material. The section, the penultimate section of the whole *Code*, is a miscellany – an oddly jumbled conclusion to a book that otherwise organizes the institutions of Christianity and its deviations into crisply defined categories. The cumbersome title, bundling together (uniquely in the *Code*) people ("pagans"), actions ("sacrifices"), and places ("temples"), itself suggests the compilers' difficulty in imposing coherence. By the second quarter of the fifth century, all professional servants of the imperial regime could take for granted that the practice of paganism was a criminal monstrosity; the *Code* reflects their difficulties (like those the conscientious Pliny faced concerning the Christians over three centuries earlier) in discovering a basis for this.

The three terms in the title occur together in only two of the extracts preserved – since one is the last (*Cod. Theod.* 16. 10. 25), this might have suggested their heading to the editors. This method of organizing the material has had enormous consequences. The extracts chosen for inclusion, and indeed our own conception of late antique paganism, would have been quite different if, as might easily have happened, the compilers had decided to divide these measures between two separate chapters, "On Pagan Temples" and "On Pagan Sacrifices." Above all, it is thanks to the *Code* that we tend to think of pagan sacrifices and temples as intrinsically interrelated – and as clearly identifiable targets for effective repression. Hence the common interpretation of these laws as a creeping barrage, working inexorably toward the innermost citadels of paganism. And indeed the narrative that has been inferred from them seems plausible enough. Whatever restrictions were imposed by Constantine (according to this version) become positively repressive under his sons; a respite under the Valentinianic dynasty (Julian's legislation on this matter is naturally ignored) is followed by the definitive prohibition of public pagan ritual under Theodosius I, whose sons could cheerfully declare paganism extinct. Such is the commonly accepted trajectory. However, as the following sections will show, it has scant basis. Here again, the study of paganism has lagged behind recent scholarship on Christianity (in particular concerning the evolution and operation of the anti-heresy laws, which are to some extent parallel). A more nuanced reading of these laws would have important implications for our understanding of the people whose actions provoked them.

The Letter of the Law: Sacrifice

The most persistent theme in the legislation concerning pagans is that of sacrifice, which is central to fifteen of our twenty-five laws; but even here it is impossible to reconstruct a consistent picture. The very first surviving pronouncement on the subject (*Cod. Theod.* 16. 10. 2) refers back to a law of Constantine that does not survive, but was trumpeted also by Eusebius (Euseb. *Vit. Const.* 2. 45); fierce debate continues about what this might have involved (Barnes 1984; Errington 1988; Bradbury 1994). The debate is related to a wider lack of clarity that affects not only modern scholarship but also (in all probability) the ancient laws themselves. For, although sacrificial offerings were fundamental to all known pagan (as indeed they are to all Christian) cults (Dowden 2000: 168–88), they could mean many different things and take many different forms.

Only twice in the *Code* is there reference to what made sacrifices criminal; and both instances mention explicitly divination, and especially the seeking of information on the secrets of the imperial succession (*Cod. Theod.* 16. 10. 9 and 12). This is peculiar, since only a small fraction of attested sacrificial activity was ever intended for this purpose, and the law codes have an entirely separate heading, criminal magic, under which the laws dealing specifically with such behavior are collected (*Cod. Theod.* 9. 16). Although animal (if not indeed human) blood was traditionally thought to fuel "black" magic, and this was unproblematically illegal, the law codes seem careful (but not without some confusion) to keep the categories distinct: whatever was intrinsically illegal about sacrifices by the time of the *Code*, it was not any "magical" connotation (Sandwell 2005). The "classic" type of ancient sacrifice was immolation, the propitiatory slaughter of animals at public altars and the burning of their organs, a rite which, although hallowed by tradition, provoked particular horror among Christians and offered them a convenient target for disgusted polemic. They were not the only critics: Porphyry's *De abstinentia* suggests that pagan intellectuals themselves debated the gods' need for blood and burnt offerings (Porph. *Abst.* 2. 5–32; Gilhus 2006: 141–6). One of the tantalizing aspects of our subject is how little we know of the commitment of the "average" pagan to animal sacrifice. Julian's attempt to revive the practice of animal sacrifice, less than two generations after Constantine's triumph, seems to have stirred little enthusiasm (Amm. Marc. 22. 12. 6; 25. 4. 17; Bradbury 1995). However, the gods accepted a wide range of offerings, which could be made in any number of contexts – and throughout antiquity the overwhelming majority of sacrifices (both public and private) will have consisted of food, drink, decorations, or incense. These bloodless sacrifices were less vulnerable on grounds of taste, but had been used as a test against suspected Christians and therefore prompted memories of persecution.

Public sacrifices were traditionally incumbent upon magistrates, which makes it likely (although certainly not proven) that the new generation of overtly Christian officials promoted by Constantine were central to whatever regulation of sacrifice he might have imposed. Such a scenario leaves open a dizzying range of possibilities about the law's scope (from a redefinition of traditional obligations to perform blood sacrifices, to an attempt at total prohibition); nor, without further context, can we tell whether Constantius II's demand that the "insanity of sacrifices must cease" (*Cod. Theod.* 16. 10. 2) was directed at all sacrifices for all citizens, public blood sacrifices by public officials in their official capacity, or somewhere in between. But Constantius seems not to have made his point explicit, and legislative intentions were besides liable to be modified in practice – a judge could assume a narrower interpretation (refusing to hear cases except where animals had been slaughtered to assist sorcery), while an accuser could push for a broader one (haling a neighbor into court for sprinkling incense at a household altar). Our inability to establish any definite scope for the legislation of this period has encouraged the plausible suggestion that the government was deliberately equivocating (Salzman 1987). Significantly, the only penalties attested under the Constantinian dynasty were for sorcery – those crimes that the Theodosian codifiers would scrupulously relegate to a different category. It was still possible for government officials to bring heifers for slaughter at public altars, although this meant risking displeasure (Eunap. *VS* 491); prudent careerists would hesitate before displaying such bravado.

The residual taste for blood remained strongest, it would seem, among the elite of Rome itself, self-conscious heirs to a millennium of sanctified butchery. Their concerns are reflected in the puzzling evolution of the late antique *taurobolium*, from conventional animal sacrifice to a spectacular if still mysterious initiation ceremony involving bulls' blood; a transformation that apparently occurred during the early fourth century and that seems to have been designed specifically to provide opportunities for ritual animal slaughter without offending against the laws that now restricted it (McLynn 1996). The main significance of such behavior is to show how readily religious practices could be adapted to the legal situation. Senators of Rome protected their fortunes through canny deflection of occasional efficiency drives by the government; and in this case also, they seem to vault nimbly through a loophole. There was nothing furtive or defeatist about these initiations, which were conducted at the Phrygianum precinct directly adjacent to St. Peter's shrine on the Vatican; the proximity, an accident of historical topography rather than a deliberate provocation, usefully illustrates a theme that will become important in what follows, the capacity for apparently irreconcilable opposites to coexist.

The basis for the common view that all sacrifice was finally driven underground by Theodosius I is a cluster of three laws passed in AD 391–2, of which the first two prescribe penalties only for government officials who conducted sacrifices (*Cod. Theod.* 16. 10. 10–11). The third (*Cod. Theod.* 16. 10. 12, AD 392) casts the net much more widely, not only penalizing those who "should slaughter an innocent victim to insensate images" but also prohibiting the "more furtive pollution" involved in honoring the household Lar with fire, the personal Genius with wine, or the Penates with incense, or indeed with any form of candle-lighting, incense-offering, or garland-hanging. The language seems grimly specific: "But if any person should venerate, by placing incense before them, images made by the work of men ... or should bind a tree with fillets, or should erect an altar of turf that he has dug up ... he shall be punished, as one guilty of the violation of religion, by the forfeiture of that house or landholding in which it is proved that he served a pagan superstition." This law indeed covers new ground, explicitly including many specific forms of traditional observance under the rubric of sacrifice; however, the prime focus of the opening remarks is on the familiar target of divination, and a principal concern is again the behavior of public officials. We can only guess the context: the collapse of a prosecution, perhaps, because the offending sacrifice could not be traced to a public altar; or has a long frustrated Christian lobbyist finally succeeded in attaching his own cherished litany of outrages to an otherwise routine pronouncement? But there is no record that these clauses ever became the basis for any prosecution, let alone conviction. The enforcement procedures established in the law, which demanded vigilant collaboration between government officials and local magistrates, indicate the difficulties that faced any prosecutors, and the legislator clearly betrays his doubts about its likely efficacy (*Cod. Theod.* 16. 10. 12. 4). The law has been presumed significant largely because the editors of the *Code* decided to cite it so extensively (at far greater length than any previous one under this heading); they probably did so, however, not because of its contemporary significance but because they found there the fullest statement of the linkage between temples and sacrifice that gives this chapter such intellectual coherence as it possesses.

What, then, were the practical consequences of Theodosius' laws? We do not know. Even such alluring coincidences as the apparent end of the Roman *taurobolium*, the latest Phrygianum inscriptions being dated to AD 390, signify little. The new laws prescribed nothing to frighten a litigious tauroboliast. As we shall see in the following section, moreover, even apparently solid connections between imperial pronouncements and the repression of paganism can be deceptive.

Renegotiating Space: Temples

The AD 392 law mentions temples only as an afterthought – those caught sacrificing in public temples (rather than in their own homes) were to be fined, since there was no relevant property to confiscate (*Cod. Theod.* 16. 10. 12. 3). Previous references in the *Code* suggest that temples had become drawn into the scope of legislation as the sites where sacrifices were conducted (*Cod. Theod.* 16. 10. 4), and that the government attempted to neutralize them so that they could continue to host the various cultural and commercial activities with which they were associated. The eventual demolition of the temples seems a brusque afterthought: only in the last law in the chapter on pagans (*Cod. Theod.* 16. 10. 25, AD 435) are "all their groves, temples, shrines, if any still remain intact" consigned to destruction.

We tend, however, to attribute a larger significance to the temples, corresponding to their sheer visibility in the cityscape. Moreover, the physical traces of the vandalism that has scarred or shattered many pagan monuments are so impressive that they have been argued to amount to a wholesale "archaeology of religious hatred" (Sauer 2003; see Sauer 1996). Literary sources cataloguing the aggression of Christian iconoclasts have seemed to support the view that a campaign of systematic violence by Christian gangs, gathering momentum in the last quarter of the fourth century, inflicted fatal damage to the fabric of paganism (Fowden 1978): the Theodosian laws have thus been interpreted as a specious veil of legitimacy for a brutal populist assault.

And indeed, the temples *ought* to have been flashpoints, their mute presence a standing call to arms for zealous Christians, and a rallying point for pagans. But again the evidence fails to live up to our expectations. Eusebius crows over token actions by Constantine – three temples demolished and the treasuries of others plundered by a handful of roving commissioners, a command that temples be stripped of doors and roof cladding, and their idolatrous mystifications be exposed to public ridicule (Euseb. *Vit. Const.* 3. 54–8; see Cameron and Hall 1999: 301–5). But even Eusebius betrays the limited impact of this salutary humiliation: not only did the government lack both the resources and the certainty of purpose for a comprehensive crusade, but in a period when traditional civic services were being increasingly squeezed by the state, even token interventions by the central government might stir a patriotic resentment, which some local Christians might also share. With the temples, as with sacrifices, urban pagans thus had time to adjust to the Christian empire. Even if (as a law of AD 346 seems to command, although again context is lacking: *Cod. Theod.* 16. 10. 4) the temples were at some point and in some sense "closed" to the public, there is abundant evidence for their continued accessibility – one suspects that formal cult practices, which would imply government sponsorship, were forbidden, but (as with sacrifice) most ordinary temple activities could be redefined so as to escape any such ban. Nor should we foreshorten our perspectives. There was ample time to rethink the relationship between the gods and their temples during the several generations that elapsed while the Christian authorities gradually summoned up the political will to support the more drastic measures that some of their constituents demanded. This was a period, moreover, during which Christian leaders were seeking to contain a "privatization of the holy" (Brown 1982: 32–6); no such inhibitions were operative within the much looser institutional structures of paganism.

With temples, too, Theodosius I has been credited with a decisive shift in policy – for at the same time as he began issuing his laws restricting sacrifice, there occurred one of the most dramatic clashes on record between pagans and Christians. Zealous Christian crowds had occasionally destroyed temples previously; but the Serapeum of Alexandria was world-famous, a "treasure-house second only to the Capitol of Rome" (Amm. Marc. 22. 16. 12), and its destruction in AD 391 prompted the most extensive commentary we have of any such act, from the Christian historian Rufinus (*Hist. eccl.* 11. 22–30; see Thélamon 1981: 159–279). Rufinus seems to show the pagans swept helplessly away by a triumphant Christian tide. His account therefore deserves careful attention.

Rufinus minimizes a blatant provocation by the Alexandrian bishop Theophilus, who (according to the later historian Socrates: *Hist eccl.* 3. 2) had reopened a thirty-year-old wound by parading pagan images around the city; deliberate effort was needed to inflame intercommunal tensions. A band of militant pagans duly gratified Theophilus by organizing themselves, in response, into a terrorist militia. Their occupation of the Serapeum as their base recalls modern parallels, from India to Iraq (which might in turn suggest that the temple authorities were reluctant hosts); the kidnappings and ritual executions that followed also seem grimly familiar. But the most striking element in the episode, as reported by Rufinus, is the trust that these militants still placed in the emperor's justice. They defied the local authorities (who are plausibly alleged to have been complicit with the bishop: Eunap. *VS* 472), but after these had reported the stalemate to Theodosius, they joined the Christians for a solemn reading of the emperor's verdict. But they never heard it. So ominous did the opening paragraphs of Theodosius' letter sound, with their conventional flourish denouncing pagan superstition, that the pagans fled and the Christians then swept forward (thus Rufinus, carefully exculpating the latter of aggression) to ransack the temple and demolish the cult statue of Serapis. Rufinus helpfully supplies the contents of the letter, as if to reassure us that the destruction indeed accorded with the imperial will. The emperor granted impunity to the pagan extremists, whose victims had received compensation enough in their martyrs' crowns; he added, however, that "the cause and root of the discord, which had come from the defence of images, must be removed" (Rufinus, *Hist. eccl.* 11. 22). Like Rufinus himself, his readers have assumed that Theodosius had meant the statue of Serapis; however, the prominence of images in Socrates' converging account might suggest instead that the emperor had merely intended to sequestrate the statues that the Christians had used to provoke the original riot. Even in the most favorable possible circumstances, then, when a pagan temple had become the center of unequivocally criminal activity, it was no simple matter to mobilize official consent for repression.

Nor, perhaps, did the event have as much impact upon the pagans of Alexandria as Rufinus claims. He boasts casually of a rush of converts after the exposure of the frauds and crimes of the pagan establishment (*Hist. eccl.* 11. 24), but is much more concerned with those temple priests who happily discovered that their hieroglyphs had indeed prophesied Christ (*Hist. eccl.* 11. 29). Rufinus too readily credits these men with an ability to discard their past; during the same period, indeed, a mischievous pagan author at Rome could credit to Hadrian the claim that "those who worship Serapis are, in fact, Christians; and those who call themselves bishops of Christ are in fact priests of Serapis" (SHA Saturninus 8). Moreover, and more important, at least some Alexandrian pagans soon learned to live without the physical presence of Serapis. Their god was not destroyed by the brutish iconoclasts, but merely withdrew from a world that had proved itself unworthy of his beneficent presence (see Brown 1998: 635). Serapis' patient resignation recalls the Christian confessors, and pagans duly mocked the insensate fury of the persecutors who "made war on stones" (Eunap. *VS* 472).

Such divine quietism made no sense to contemporary Christians, and many modern scholars are equally unimpressed. But neither the pagans nor their gods necessarily felt obliged to fight the battles that we would have them fight. Our most circumstantial account of an officially sanctioned temple demolition thus shows Zeus and his minions at Gaza responding to the blow with whimpers rather than bangs; but, even if Mark the Deacon's narrative is treated as a genuine contemporary record (and controversy continues here), a close reading shows that it leaves the majority of the local pagans unaccounted for (Trombley 1993–4, i: 187–245). The temples were an adjunct to devotion rather than a prerequisite. Although some Christians certainly swallowed their own propaganda and believed that by smashing a cult statue they could expel the demon it represented, so freeing its deluded bondsmen from its thrall, we have no good evidence that those they thus rescued ever accepted this interpretation, and no reason to do so ourselves.

Pagan Survivors: Libanius, Symmachus, Ammianus

The age of Theodosius I is especially important for an analysis of our subject, because of the interlocking evidence that is available from different pagan sources. Libanius of Antioch, although he almost outlived Theodosius, was born a full generation earlier, just after Constantine's conversion; an ardent admirer of Julian, he long outlived his hero to die at the age of 80 in AD 393. A professional sophist, he was thoroughly immersed in the Homeric world that was his livelihood; he produced his long autobiography, a detailed record of his feuds with professional rivals and provincial governors, in AD 376, but successive updates take us deep into the reign of Theodosius.

Libanius has been comfortably incorporated into narratives of pagan decline, but also serves to illustrate how provisional any such narrative must remain. Conventional modern judgments have been based upon writings that are surprisingly difficult to contextualize. In old age, Libanius certainly strikes a note of elegiac bitterness, wearying his fellow citizens with his talk of the old days, when "sacrifices were many, and the temples were full of men doing sacrifice, and there were flutes and songs and garlands, and wealth in each temple, a bulwark for those in need" (*Or.* 2. 30). But he nowhere suggests that his religion had suffered defeat. His most celebrated commentary on the contemporary situation, *Oration* 30 ("On the Temples"), complains to Theodosius about the depredations of Christian monks, the harassment of those suspected of breaking the laws regulating sacrifice, and (above all) the involvement of an imperial official in the destruction of one particular temple. The text has become a standard source for the vulnerability of pagan cult sites under Theodosius I, when fanatical iconoclasts held high office (Petit 1951; Fowden 1978); although addressed to the emperor, it has been seen as devised initially as a fictive showpiece, in which Libanius vented his frustrations among like-minded friends and behind safely closed doors (Wiemer 1995: 123–9). However, such readings require us to stretch the obvious sense of the text, which can instead be treated as a serious (and possibly even successful) response to a single specific case, where a government official had overstepped the limits of the law (McLynn 2005: 111–17). Libanius paints a convincing picture of brutal Christian gangs and extortionist officials abusing their power; but this should be balanced by his belief in the possibility of redress. The *Autobiography*, moreover, nowhere suggests that Libanius' worldview was under serious strain. Although the additions take us in stages past the crucial dates in the standard chronology of antipagan repression, Libanius' world remains as full of gods as ever, their powers undiminished. Demeter enjoys the final word, unleashing famine upon Constantinople in a reenactment of the opening scene of the *Iliad* (*Or.* 1. 284–5).

The Roman senator Symmachus, a generation younger and significantly higher on the social scale, reached the consulship (and flattered Libanius with a letter) in the very year that Theodosius I issued the first of his sacrifice laws. His religious universe is more opaque than Libanius', for he left no autobiography to supply a framework for a letter collection whose chief characteristic is its "formal reticence" (Matthews 1974). But the letters show both Symmachus' diligence in attending to his gods and his easy facility in keeping both Christianity and obstreperous Christian correspondents in their proper places (Matthews 1986; McLynn 1994: 263–75). Symmachus, moreover, exhibits the same suave one-upmanship toward his pagan friends, not least toward the two most conspicuous figures in the supposed "pagan reaction," Nicomachus Flavianus and Agorius Praetextatus, both of whom are twitted for missing pontifical college meetings.

Symmachus earned his place in Christian historiography as a petitioner on behalf of the traditional cults of Rome, which had been deprived of their funding in AD 382. As city prefect in AD 384, Symmachus sent to Theodosius' colleague Valentinian II his third *Relatio* (official dispatch), which is often compared to Libanius' *Oration* 30, and similarly regarded as a forlorn plea for a cause long lost, "still haunted by the literary shades of Hannibal and the Senones" (Matthews 1975: 208). And indeed, Symmachus' petition was voted down in the imperial consistory, despite the care that he lavished on his prose and the publicity that he gave to an initiative that was presented as a formal embassy on behalf of the whole Senate. So oddly dissonant has the even, dispassionate tone sounded that Symmachus has even been reduced to merely a (perhaps reluctant) front man, providing sonorous phraseology for his more radically reactionary friends Praetextatus and Flavianus (O'Donnell 1979: 65–83) – the authentic "last pagans of Rome."

But we easily misread Symmachus. A wickedly deceitful framework has been constructed by Ambrose, bishop of Milan, who obtained a copy of the text and took full advantage of the opportunity to match Symmachus' effete elegance with the uncompromising muscularity of the new Christian order, in what has become a definitive diptych. Symmachus' petition, however, was not designed for any such contest; nor (more important) would the audience that most interested him ever have known it in this form. The "Altar of Victory Debate" is presented to us through the distinct manuscript tradition inspired by Ambrose, where Christian triumphalism has been packaged for internal consumption. Symmachus' collected *Relationes*, on the other hand, were published after the author's death, a private edition to be savored by his relations and admirers rather than a tawdry propaganda exercise, and with the third *Relatio* showcased as the jewel in a distinguished statesman's crown (Vera 1977); to these readers, such vulgar considerations as its effectiveness in influencing policy were immaterial.

We must ask whether this tradition might not reflect Symmachus' own perspectives. For this is a more curious text than is usually acknowledged. Uniquely in his

Relationes, Symmachus here leaves the emperor still uncertain after the first three sentences about what he was asking. Only after a long preamble does he request the restoration of "that religious position which long benefited the state"; he initially seems to identify this exclusively with the Altar of Victory in the senate house (*Rel.* 3. 3–7), and seems to mark his conclusion with his justly famous words on religious pluralism (8–10). However, he then resumes a passing remark concerning the Vestals (7), to introduce an elaborate plea that their privileges and allowances, and incidentally the emoluments of the pagan priests, be restored (11–19). Modern scholars have sought an argumentative coherence that the speech in fact lacks (Vera 1981: 19–20). Just as Theodosius' role in Libanius' *Oration* 30 has been understated, so here we might have overestimated Symmachus' concern to persuade Valentinian II. The text provides a compendium of the grievances of different Roman constituencies, who might reasonably be seen as Symmachus' primary intended audience; the prefect would thus be exercising patronage at Rome rather than fumbling for the levers of power at Milan. His high-sounding phrases certainly seem to have resonated locally, and would subsequently be echoed (somewhat to his eventual embarrassment) by the then academically detached teacher Augustine (*Rel.* 3. 10; August. *Soliloquia* 1. 13. 23, retracted at *Retract.* 1. 4. 3; see *De vera religione* 28. 51).

We must ask what Symmachus expected from the imperial government. The charge that he was driven by mercenary self-interest (Paschoud 1965) is now properly discredited; but hardly less fragile is the current interpretation that he was concerned for the formal validity of the traditional cults, which depended in turn upon their maintenance through public funds (Baynes 1955). Symmachus certainly never hints at such a consideration; and the senatorial class was already semi-detached from the imperial regime, and would comfortably survive its disappearance three generations later. Both Symmachus and his gods could therefore afford to shrug off an emperor's bad decisions. It was Ambrose of Milan who seized upon the narrowly political implications of the issue, and who moreover played the Altar of Victory card again a decade later (Ambrose, *Ep.* 57. 2) – thereby creating the caricature of a Symmachus obsessively preoccupied with turning back the clock. The effect was to make Symmachus appear a serial petitioner, repeating his plea in embassies sent to Gaul (according to Ambrose's biographer: Paulinus, *Vit. Ambrosii* 26) and to Theodosius (Quodvultdeus, *Liber Promissionum* 3. 41); Prudentius, too, portrays him as a clear and present danger to Honorius (Prudent. *C. Symm.* 2. 6–7, 760–1). These initiatives are phantoms, but they have shaped our assumptions. Instead, the most striking thing about Symmachus, as about Libanius, is how little the changes that loom so large in our narratives of "christianization" seem to have affected him; even the AD 384 petition is as invisible in his letters as is *Pro templis* in Libanius' autobiography. This has been interpreted as a lack of commitment to a "losing cause" (Cameron 1999: 112); but Symmachus seems blithely unaware that any such cause existed, and his perspectives deserve to be taken seriously.

Ammianus Marcellinus, the "former soldier and Greek" who published his history on the very eve of the destruction of the Serapeum, provides a link between Symmachus' Rome and Libanius' Antioch. Ammianus openly professes his paganism and makes Julian his hero, but describes a world where Christianity is thoroughly entrenched. He has been variously interpreted: as a robust secularist who consigned religion to his digressions (Matthews 1989b: 426–32); a genuine multiculturalist capable of doing justice to other religions (Hunt 1985); or else an embittered apostate haunted by his Christian past, who subtly but systematically denigrated his former fellow believers (Barnes 1998: 79–94). The most recent study of Ammianus' religiosity, however, presents a man concerned less with Christianity than with paganism, who created a cosmopolitan synthesis of traditional religious views, which brought coherence to the experience of his generation (Davies 2004: 226–85). And we look in vain, certainly, despite Ammianus' rich fund of indignation and gloom, for any sense of persecution or religious defeatism. Although the emperor's stern pronouncements on sacrifice were circulating through the empire, Ammianus could still quietly insist on the continuing applicability of a traditional religious framework, and could still assume that his views would find an audience.

All three of our pagans thus shared a capacity to accept the prescriptions imposed by the Christian empire, while leading comfortably unchristian lives within it. Their social status, of course, makes them entirely untypical of any pagan majority, but it exposed them more directly to the workings of the imperial machine. The contrast between the resolutely undramatic religiosity evoked in their works and the fulminations of contemporary legislation is therefore instructive.

Pagan Legacies: The Fifth Century

By the early fifth century, Ammianus, Symmachus, and Libanius were all dead, and with them ends a historiographical era. No subsequent pagan generation will seem fully alive or three-dimensional, a fact that has helped sustain the appearance of a decisive change with Theodosius I. But our perspectives are illusory. The vibrantly interconnected world that our three fourth-century witnesses inhabit is preserved for us only through the most fortunate of chances, with each of the texts upon which we depend preserved by only a handful of manuscripts (Vera 1977: 1003–6; Martin and Petit 1979: 36–92; Matthews 1989b: 477–8).

In fact, our three pagan exemplars each had his heirs, whom we glimpse navigating the challenges presented by the fifth century. The histories of Ammianus' fifth-century "classicizing" successors survive only in fragments, but Olympiodorus of Thebes would dedicate his overtly paganizing interpretation of his age to the pious Theodosius II, while a generation later Priscus of Panium and Malchus of Philadelphia apparently offered no clues to their allegiance (Blockley 1981: 59–60, 77). The current fashion is to accept both the latter as Christians, but their apparently deliberate refusal to present a now unequivocally Christian empire in its own Christian terms is significant. We have become accustomed to demanding solid proof of anti-Christianity from prospective pagans, while assuming unproblematic Christianity otherwise; of the various constraints that such a scheme imposes, perhaps the most insidious is the exclusion of any possibility that a minimal Christianity could be absorbed into a basically pagan outlook. Yet this was exactly the prospect that alarmed contemporary Christian leaders like Augustine (*Ep.* 232. 1; *De catechizandis rudibus* 7. 11). Our reluctance to accept pagan sympathies in historians like Priscus or Malchus, moreover, is conditioned largely by the exemplar of explicitly pagan historiography that we possess in one of their younger contemporaries, a public servant who produced in his retirement a history full of uninhibitedly vehement venom directed at the whole Christian project. But Zosimus' eccentricity arguably resides in his polemical tone rather than in his outlook – and he also represents continuity, a milieu where Eunapius (the fourth-century sophist who had pioneered the art of polemically anti-Christian historiography) and Olympiodorus were still available. Interesting questions remain concerning the religious implications of the secular literary tradition. Recent revisionist reinterpretation of the sixth-century historian Procopius as a cunningly coded pagan critic (Kaldellis 2004) unduly minimizes the abundant evidence for Procopius' comfortable accommodation to the Christian mainstream (Cameron 1985: 113–33), but it nevertheless suggests the potential for subversively unchristian currents to operate within this stream.

Symmachus' heirs in Rome also weathered the consolidation of Christianity peacefully – and the Roman aristocrats of the fifth century, although many of them accepted initiation into the Christian cult, remained much closer to Symmachus culturally than they ever came to Ambrose. This was the milieu that nurtured Macrobius, whose *Saturnalia* lovingly recreates the learned religiosity of Praetextatus, Symmachus, and their friends (Matthews 1975: 369–72). A century after the Altar of Victory controversy, a famous exchange between the pope of Rome and the Christian senator Andromachus illustrates the tenacity of the pagan past – and the dexterity of the Roman elite in maintaining its claim upon it. Our text, an open letter, dissects pitilessly these senators' possible excuses for their involvement in the Lupercalia, the venerable mid-February fertility festival whose central rite, a carnival of naked runners, was now performed by proxy, with "mean and ordinary" substitutes for the young nobles (*Adv. Andromachum* 16–17). This has been seen as a new stage of papal activism, a concerted campaign to eliminate anomalies (Markus 1990: 131–4; see Duval 1977); but the implied context deserves consideration. We have only one side of the argument, and the letter begins defensively – Andromachus has been complaining of a failure to police clerical wrongdoing (*Adv. Andromachum* 1–2); the Lupercalia thus serve rhetorically as a convenient glass house within which to confine this troublemaker. Did the ploy succeed? Most modern readers, concentrating on the stark choice with which the patrons of the Lupercalia are confronted – either to abandon their festival or face excommunication – have assumed a grudging surrender; but an intermediate outcome seems just as likely. Nor, just because Andromachus was a baptized Christian, need we assume that his patronage of the ceremonies (which of course had important social implications) was devoid of any religious significance. Rather, we might see the fifth-century Lupercalia as a descendant of the fourth-century *taurobolium*, another adaptation of traditional religiosity to suit the changing exigencies of the laws; the nobles of Rome were able to accept Christianity on their own terms, and exported their own values even into the ecclesiastical establishment (Salzman 2002: 200–19).

Here, once again, we fall easily into traps created by our own categories. It was easier to combine Christianity with other, apparently contradictory, allegiances than the ecclesiastical spokesmen from whom we tend to take our cues would wish, and disciplinary sanctions were in practice limited by the social power of the elite. Boethius' Lady Philosophy thus seems, a generation after the Lupercal controversy, to belong more to the salon of Macrobius' Praetextatus than to an Ambrosian church, but although a medieval monk might deplore the senator's refusal to seek consolation in his Christian faith, no contemporary pope could do so (Chadwick 1981: 247–53). Nor did papal authority extend to the Lady's less austerely cerebral cousins, the statues from the pagan past that continued to decorate senatorial palaces. Although recent commentators tend to present these as the safely desacralized objects of purely aesthetic appreciation (Stirling 2004: 22–8), this risks imposing an artificial boundary between two categories that had traditionally overlapped, and such judgments have depended heavily upon assumptions about the impact of anti-pagan legislation. Having overcome earlier tendencies to see all pagan images as symbols of anti-Christian defiance, we have perhaps become overhasty in denying them any numinous qualities. The serious archaeological investigation of domestic cult is still in its infancy (see Bakker 1994 for a painstaking analysis of the Ostian evidence); in general, the sphere of private worship – which includes the care of the dead, where, it is now emerging, the scope of institutional Christianity was far more limited than was previously thought (Rebillard 2003) – requires much fuller exploration than it has hitherto received (see MacMullen 1997: 61–5).

Meanwhile, Libanius' successors continued to inculcate the same classical texts, infused with the old gods, into each new generation of the elite. From some irresistibly vivid vignettes of clashes between pagan and Christian students in the classroom, where the Christians invariably not only prevail physically but also expose the emptiness of their opponents' claims (Zacharias of Mitylene, *Vit. Severi* 14–27; Chuvin 1990: 105–11), a Christian educational mainstream is easily inferred, one thoroughly inoculated against pagan textbooks by Basil of Caesarea's prescriptions. Much like pagan statuary, for example, that quintessential product of the late antique schoolroom, the vast Dionysiac epic by Nonnus of Panopolis has been stripped of any religious overtones by recent commentators (Liebeschuetz 1996). But there were teachers who continued to take their literary gods seriously, and it would be dangerous (given the intimacy of the ancient classroom) to deny them any influence over their pupils. We glimpse such teachers only fleetingly. Only after his promotion to court office, for example, did the Antiochene sophist Isocasius (to whom Theodoret, bishop of Cyrrhus, had cheerfully recommended pupils) face trial for his "Hellenism" (a trial occasioned, significantly, by an unrelated outbreak of rioting); his dignified bearing before his prosecutors earned him the sympathy of the crowd, who hauled him to the cathedral for instant catechesis and baptism (*Chron. Pasch.* s.a. 467). Only on the most mechanistic interpretation can this count as conversion. Isocasius' experience instead recalls the many narrow escapes of Libanius' career. Here again, then, a continuity can be observed from the fourth century to the fifth, despite the changed circumstances and the uncertainties that our fragmentary evidence creates: we do not know, for example, whether Isocasius was accused under a sorcery charge, as in the earlier period, or under a newly comprehensive formulation.

In Search of the Last Pagans

Fifty years before Isocasius' trial, the emperor Honorius could happily imagine that there were no pagans left at all (*Cod. Theod.* 16. 10. 22); some seventy years after it, Justinian's witchfinder-general, John of Ephesus, would find both the imperial court and Anatolian countryside riddled with them (Whitby 1991). Scholars have likewise tended to find in late antique paganism, perhaps more than in any other branch of the subject, what they were looking for. Conversion to Christianity and persecution by Christians are abundantly on record, and both have been energetically exploited; pagan decline and pagan survivals each has its careful monitors, who duly find their moribund corpse or their vital signs. John of Ephesus' missionary exploits among the backwoods villages of sixth-century Asia Minor have thus been interpreted to indicate either that paganism had already been confined to isolated pockets or that a robustly traditional rural culture continued to find its own forms of religious expression (Trombley 1985; Mitchell 1993, ii: 118–19). The present survey, with its repeated emphasis on the tricks of perspective that even our most familiar texts are apt to play, has likewise reflected its author's preoccupations.

A final example will bring together the various threads that have been interwoven through this chapter: the interplay between legislation and violence, the religious implications of classical rhetoric and civic patronage – and above all the impossibility of deriving more than provisional inferences from our sources. The small African town of Calama had erupted in violence in June AD 408; during the annual Bean Festival, dancers passing the city cathedral were accosted by clergymen and responded with a barrage of stones; when the bishop complained to an unsympathetic city council, the church was stoned again; a further complaint led to a full-scale assault, during which the cathedral was ransacked and a clergyman killed. The episode has been variously characterized, as proof that Calama had "not yet joined 'the Christian empire'" (MacMullen 1997: 41) or as an example of the "devastating" powers of retaliation available to local Christians (Harries 1999: 89). These powers are at issue in the correspondence that provides our evidence for the episode, between Augustine of Hippo, a near neighbor, and the local notable Nectarius (August. *Ep.* 90–1, 103–4). Augustine's painstaking itemization of the wrongdoing, in response to Nectarius' first appeal for Christian charity, indicates not only the social complexity of the issue, which evidently involved a triangular tension between the local bishop Possidius, the city council, and the festival crowd, but also the problems facing church leaders, even when they were confronting demonstrably criminal pagan activity. For Augustine's letter is clearly intended to pressurize the city bosses of Calama into conducting their own house-cleansing. As both he and Nectarius well knew, Christian bishops could gain little by taking responsibility for deploying the full sanctions of the law; Augustine's position was further complicated, it has recently been argued, by Possidius' unhelpful zeal in seeking redress from the imperial court (Hermanowicz 2004). The resumption of the exchange eight months later, with the question still pending, shows Nectarius still playing his hand most adroitly. Although he was Christian, Augustine had chosen to address him as a representative pagan; he responds in the same spirit, voicing the pagan perspective in a sympathetic but shrewd commentary upon Augustine's dilemma – and even offering himself as a possible "convert" (August. *Ep.* 103). Nectarius' paganism is thus at once a rhetorical device and also, since we must also assume that he was among the sponsors of the festival that had started the trouble, a living reality. This species of part-time paganism remains one of the least understood phenomena of our period, and offers rich potential for further study.

We do not know what subsequently happened at Calama. Our instinctive guesses, however, will reveal much concerning our assumptions about pagans, and about the Christian empire. The range of options that remain possible meanwhile offers a further reason why the investigation of these artificial pagans of Late Antiquity remains so fruitful. For us, no less than for the Christians who first invented them, the pagans are good to think with.

BIBLIOGRAPHICAL NOTE

An analytical overview of the subject is much needed. The narrative of Chuvin 1990 and the eastern case studies in Trombley 1993–4 meanwhile provide useful orientation, while there are further pointers and suggestive insights in Fowden 1998. Developments in Egypt, a crucial area neglected in this chapter, are brilliantly treated by Frankfurter 1998b, with implications relevant to other regions. For the endurance of pagan practice, see Harl 1990. The new framework for understanding religious legislation and its application in Humfress 2007 is of fundamental importance. Fresh perspectives on Libanius' cultural and religious milieu are available from Cribiore 2007 and Sandwell 2007; the broader question of paganism in educa-tion is incisively tackled in Watts 2006. The religiosity of Symmachus, among the topics to be reassessed in Alan Cameron's long awaited *The Last Pagans of Rome*, is judiciously contextual-ized in Sogno 2006. The case of Symmachus' friend Nicomachus Flavianus provides the starting point for Hedrick 2000, a penetrating study that ranges far beyond its advertised scope.

CHAPTER THIRTY-NINE

"Not of This World": The Invention of Monasticism

Daniel F. Caner

Christian monasticism was a late antique invention, and the last great social experiment to emerge from the ancient Mediterranean world. Its aim, like that of the Greek *polis* and various philosophical schools or religious communities before it, was to devise the ideal *politeia* – the regimen and circumstances – that would produce an ideal human being. What made the monastic movement different was its determination to define that ideal against the norms of "the world," so as to train practitioners to live "as true citizens of heaven, while dwelling on earth" (*History of the Monks of Egypt*, Prol. 5, tr. Russell 1981; see Philem. 3: 20). To modern observers, the asceticism and other-worldly concerns attributed to late antique monks have often seemed repellent, signaling a wrong turn in Christian history or a strange pathology within the Late Roman Empire itself. As E. R. Dodds once put it, "Where did all this madness come from?" (1965: 34). Yet, the very attempt to gain a transcendent existence gave monks a distinct place of honor in late antique society: "[They] eat from another table, are clothed differently, prefer different dialogue, and a different mentality. Because of this, they surpass all other men" (Ps.-Macarius, *Homily* 5.11, Maloney 1992).

In this chapter, I shall portray monasticism as a late antique profession that gained definition in part through concerted efforts to set monks apart, both physically and mentally, from "all other men" of the late Roman world. When speaking of "monasticism" or "the monastic movement," I am referring to a widespread phenomenon that initially had no common identity, founders, leaders, appearance, organization, or direction. Not until the late fourth and early fifth centuries did monastic history begin to be written or, rather, invented. Those responsible were all reformers, interested in promoting their own definitions of proper monasticism over alternative "types." Perhaps most influential in this regard was John Cassian (*c.* AD 360–435). Asked to provide instruction for a monastic community outside Marseille in the early fifth century, Cassian responded with a compendious survey of Egyptian monastic practices (the *Institutes* and *Conferences*), including a discussion of

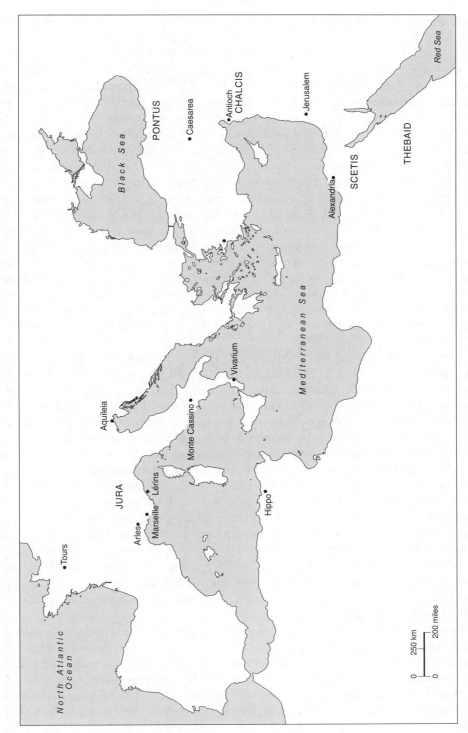

Map 8 The Ascetic World in Late Antiquity.

different monastic lifestyles and their origins. "In Egypt," he explained, "there are three types of monks. Two are very good, but the third is lukewarm and must be utterly avoided." The types that he favored were called *coenobites* and *anchorites*. Coenobites lived together in a community under the rule of an elder. According to Cassian, their type of monasticism went back to the apostolic community in Jerusalem, some of whose members sought out secluded places, "abandoning their towns and the company of those who believed that negligence ... was lawful for themselves and the church of God." Anchorites, on the other hand, lived alone, deeper in the desert, to which they withdrew after training in a *coenobium*; their type of monasticism was more recent, having originated with the Egyptian hermits Antony and Paul, whose desire for desert contemplation made them imitators, Cassian says, of John the Baptist. Then there was the third type of monk, whom he calls *sarabaites*. Emulating the renegades Ananias and Sapphira, who had refused to entrust all their property to the apostolic community in Acts 5: 1–11, these counterfeits took the name of monks without truly imitating them: refusing to submit to an elder's will, they lived as they pleased in their own homes, alone or in small groups of two or three; everything they did was for public acclaim. According to Cassian, this monastic lifestyle had come later than the other two, and was characteristic of those "compelled to this profession out of necessity." Though rare in Egypt, Cassian complains that this type of monasticism in his day prevailed nearly everywhere else (*Conférences* 18. 4. 2–8. 1, tr. Ramsey 1997).

This provides as good an introduction as any to the tendentious nature of early monastic history, as well as to its future trajectory. In Cassian's account we find all monastic possibilities reduced to three schematic types, each given its own scriptural genealogy, with coenobitic monasticism presented as the prototype; here physical isolation and obedience to an elder are put forth as defining features of true monasticism, with Egypt identified as home to monasticism in its purest forms. Such simplification immediately raises suspicion. Indeed, it is clear that Cassian, although an experienced monk, was influenced in writing his description of these monastic types by earlier literature, such as the introduction to monasticism that Jerome (*c.* AD 340–421) wrote for his protégé, the wealthy Roman virgin, Eustochium, in AD 384. It also contrasts Egyptian coenobites and anchorites against a third type of urban monk, here called *remnuoth*, whom Jerome describes as "a very inferior and despised type, though in our province [probably Italy], the chief, if not the only type": "Everything with them is an affectation: loose sleeves, big boots, clumsy dress, constant sighing, visiting virgins, disparaging the clergy, and when a feast day comes, they stuff themselves till they vomit" (*Ep.* 22. 34, tr. Wright 1954).

However, it was Cassian's own taxonomies that provided the introductory material in the sixth century for the so-called Benedictine Rule, which in turn would become the definitive monastic text in medieval Europe. This illustrates an important historical point: Christian monasticism gained its traditional categories and shape largely because of the circulation of such normative literature, which highly educated Greco-Roman monks produced for their late antique admirers. In early monastic history, as with early church history, it is often difficult to see beyond the authorized version that survives. Nevertheless, modern scholarship has helped reveal some of the original complexity of the early monastic movement in its late antique setting.

This has happened, first of all, through a critical examination of old sources and the discovery of new ones. Starting in the late nineteenth century, scholars began to apply the same analysis to early monastic texts that had already been applied to Old and New Testament literature. As a result, not only have old texts been restored to their original state, but surprising new relationships have been detected between some of them: for example, the discovery that certain heretical ("Messalian") teachings preserved in anti-heretical tracts actually derived from material that later tradition deemed orthodox (the Pseudo-Macarian homilies), or that a treatise associated with such teachings (the Pseudo-Macarian *Great Letter*) provided inspiration for, rather than derived from, a book by Gregory of Nyssa, one of orthodox monasticism's earliest recognized "Fathers" (Staats 1968; Fitschen 1998). Similar work on Syriac, Coptic, Georgian, Armenian, Ethiopic, and Arabic texts has familiarized us with lesser-known monastic traditions and their relation to Greco-Roman norms (e.g., Stewart 1991). Meanwhile, archaeology has yielded new information. Besides recovering hitherto unknown treatises, excavators in Egypt and Palestine have found archives that reveal much about early monastic terminology and interactions (e.g., Choat 2002), while fieldwork at monastic sites in Egypt (Evelyn-White 1932; Sauneron and Jacquet 1972; Guillaumont et al. 1991), Palestine (Hirschfeld 1992), Syria (Tchalenko 1953–8) and Italy (Hodges 1997) has laid bare their material culture and scale, as well as the proximity of most of them to the inhabited world.

But equally important are the new questions and approaches that modern scholars have brought to these sources. Adopting theoretical models from such disciplines as anthropology, sociology, literary criticism, and gender studies, historians have reconceptualized old material – for example, by interpreting monasticism in terms of the "rise of the Christian holy man" (Brown 1971a), or monastic history as the institutionalization of charisma (Elm 1994). Not only have these studies demonstrated the relevance of early monasticism to broader trends in Late Antiquity and beyond (including the articulation and control of power), but they have also made us recognize a broader range of organizational models and concerns (including those of women and gender: Clark 1986; Elm 1994; Krawiec 2002) within the early monastic movement itself. Common to most has been an effort to avoid using the oppositional categories imposed by normative tradition, such as monasticism/asceticism, desert/city, male/female, superior/inferior, or orthodox/heretical, but to make those categories and their creation a matter of historical investigation instead.

Such research has problematized the question of monastic origins in particular. Although we will never fully know why late antique Christians decided to embrace monasticism, we may assume that one of the earliest in Egypt to do so, Antony the Great (AD 251–356), spoke for many in writing that all who adopted monasticism had been inspired by a "Spirit of Repentance" (*metanoia*; see, e.g., Mark 1: 15; Matt. 3: 11) to "sanctify" themselves. That meant renouncing old habits and devoting themselves utterly to God's ways, necessitating various forms of self-alienation (*xeniteia*), such as God had first proposed to Abraham: "Go from your own country and your kindred and your father's house, to the land that I show you" (Gen. 12: 7; Antony,

Letter 1, tr. Rubenson 1995). The notions of *metanoia* and *xeniteia* underlie much of monastic thought and help explain many of the seemingly strange practices found in early monastic culture (Guillaumont 1968; Bitton-Ashkelony 1999; McNary-Zack 2000: 24–5). As Basil of Caesarea (*c.* AD 330–79) explained later in the fourth century, the "art of being well-pleasing to God" (i.e., monasticism) required initiates to "exile themselves, as it were, to another world in their habit of mind" – in other words, to recast their minds completely, renouncing all former preoccupations to become, like Jesus' disciples, "not of this world" (John 15: 19; *Longer Rules* 5, tr. Clarke 1925).

That said, it is no longer safe to say, as most textbooks do, that Christian monasticism began in Egypt, or with Antony the Great. Rather, its roots must be sought in the ascetic, philosophical, and penitential tendencies that bolstered nearly all forms of early Christianity (Brown 1988b: 205–9; O'Neill 1989). Already in the second century, Christian apologists from Palestine to North Africa had begun to extol those men and women whose sexual and material renunciations distinguished them from the rest in their communities. Although such behavior was standard in philosophical circles of the day, for Christians it was considered especially justified by scriptural passages in which Paul seemed to privilege celibacy above marriage (1 Cor. 7: 8–9), or where Jesus indicated that greater attainments would come from greater degrees of self-denial (e.g., "if you wish to be perfect, sell all your property" (Matt. 19: 21); see Matt. 4: 20; 19: 27; Acts 4: 34–5). Such utterances inspired, early on, a Christianity of "two ways":

> Two ways of life were thus given by the Lord to His Church. The one is above nature, and beyond common human living; it admits no marriage, childbearing, property, or the possession of wealth. ... The more human way prompts men to join in pure nuptials and produce children ... it allows them to have minds for farming, trade, and other more worldly interests. (Eusebius of Caesarea, *Proof of the Gospel* 1. 8, tr. Ferrar 1920)

While salvation was ultimately the goal for all, those who set their minds "beyond ... human living" sought assurance in a more immediate self-transformation. For Christian Platonists, like the Alexandrian priest and philosopher Origen (AD 185–254), that meant reducing distractions and looking inward, so as to liberate one's soul from the demonic passions that had infected human beings since the Fall (Brown 1988b: 160–77). Others found in the gospel descriptions of Jesus and his disciples a more obvious path to follow. Sometimes their imitation of Jesus led to an itinerant, "apostolic" lifestyle (Kretschmar 1964), but more often this was done by quietly focusing on prayer, abstinence, and scriptural recitations at church and home. Nowhere is such *imitatio Christi* more evident than in Syriac-speaking communities of the Near East, where Jesus was known as the great "Single One," or *iḥidaya* (the Syriac term used to translate "only-begotten" in John 1: 14; 3: 16; and elsewhere). Here, in every church, male and female lay persons who wished to imitate Jesus did so by consecrating themselves to a life of *iḥidayutha*, or "singleness" of body and mind. Collectively known as the "Sons and Daughters of the Covenant," such solitaries (*iḥidaye*) lived at home or with relatives, and were expected to set an example, "as a living icon of Paradise restored" for others in the communities that supported them (Gribomont 1965; Griffith 1995).

It has been proposed that the word *monachos*, "single one" or "solitary," was actually first coined in order to translate the Syriac term *ihidaya*, together with its Hebrew cognate *yahid*, into Greek (Morard 1973, 1975, 1980). Be that as it may, the earliest attested use of the word to designate a Christian ascetic is found in a papyrus petition from the Egyptian village of Karanis. Dated to June 6, AD 324, it cites an individual named "Isaac the monk" as one who helped a church deacon intervene in a dispute over a cow. This document is particularly interesting because it presents this first known monk as a familiar village figure. Indeed, it is apparent from allusions in other early fourth-century literature and papyri that the period after Constantine's conversion saw an increased prominence of Christian ascetics in cities and villages throughout the Roman Empire. Generally described as "renouncers" (*apotaktikoi*, a term suggesting renunciation of family property: see Luke 14: 33; Goehring 1999: 60–8), these lived alone or in groups either at home, in urban apartments, or on the fringe of villages and army camps. They represent not so much a new Christian movement, as a lifestyle of Christian singleness now left free to "go public" after the threat of persecution had passed. That is not to say that some did not seek further isolation in this early period. But the picture that emerges, especially from Egypt, is that of a Christian monasticism that originally was closely tied to urban or village society, and virtually identical with the "type" that Jerome and Cassian would later disparage as *remnuoth* or *sarabaite* counterfeits. Indeed, Isaac of Karanis may have been one such monk (Judge 1977; Goehring 1999: 20–6, 53–72; Choat 2002).

An interesting snapshot of monasticism as it looked in the eastern Mediterranean in the AD 370s is provided by Epiphanius of Salamis, a bishop on the island of Cyprus:

> Some of the church's monks live in the cities, but some reside in monasteries and retire far from the world. Some, if you please, see fit to wear their hair long as a custom of their own devising ... Many sleep on the ground, and others do not even wear shoes. Others wear sackcloth under their clothing ... It is inappropriate to appear in public wearing collars, as some prefer to ... Most are exercised in psalms and constant prayers, and in readings, and recitations by heart, of the holy scriptures. (Epiphanius of Salamis, *On the Faith* 23. 2–8, tr. Williams 1994)

It was out of this diverse and experimental background that monasticism evolved into a distinct profession or order (*taxis*), gradually becoming recognizable as such in the late fourth and early fifth centuries through the propagation of certain common assumptions, expectations, and goals. This happened unevenly from region to region, mostly by word of mouth, as disciples sought out experienced teachers or made up their own rules to follow, adapting Old and New Testament precedents. But no doubt the single most important step toward the standardization of monastic practice was its identification, early on, with physical isolation, and with the Egyptian desert in particular; and no doubt the main reason for that was the rapid dissemination of a single text, namely the *Life of Antony*. Written *c.* AD 357–62 by Athanasius, the embattled Nicene bishop of Alexandria, this describes how Antony the Great, portrayed as the illiterate son of a prosperous peasant family in Middle Egypt, renounced his inheritance after hearing the gospel passage read in church, "If you wish to be perfect, sell all your property, give to the poor, and come, follow me" (Matt. 19: 21). Antony first moved to the outskirts of town, where he apprenticed under some "serious" old men – local "renouncers," like those discussed above. Eventually, however, he decided to pursue greater degrees of withdrawal (*anachôr-ésis*), going farther and farther into the desert, until he finally reached a mountain near the Red Sea: "He was like someone who recognizes his own home: from that point on he considered the place his own." Before Antony, according to Athanasius, "no monk at all knew the remote desert"; but after him, "the desert was made a city by monks" (*Life of Antony* 3. 2, 14. 7, 50. 2, Vivian et al. 2003).

With the *Life of Antony*, Athanasius crafted the classic account of how the desert was won for Christian monasticism, making Antony its icon and Egypt its imaginative home (Brakke 1995; Stewart 2000). His biography also provided the first widely disseminated "rule": in Cappadocia in AD 380, Gregory of Nazianzus declared it "legislation for monastic life in narrative form" (*Or.* 21. 5), while John Chrysostom in the late 380 s, urged his congregations in Antioch to read it, since it would show even them exactly "what sort of life Christ's laws demand" (*Homily on Matthew* 8. 5). Indeed, Augustine says that hearing about Antony's renunciations in Italy in the summer of 386 had precipitated his own conversion (*Confessions* 8. 8. 19). Given this testimony, it is easy to forget that the *Life of Antony* might never have had such impact, had the death of the Arian emperor Valens on the battlefield in AD 378 not led to the accession of the pro-Nicene emperor, Theodosius I (AD 379–95), and, thus, to the promotion of Nicene Christianity, its literature and heroes. Exactly why monks began to populate deserted areas in large numbers remains an open question, admitting many answers (Heussi 1936: 53–69). It may have begun with Emperor Valens' anti-Nicene persecutions (Lenski 2004: 114–17); on the other hand, the fact that anchoretic solitaries in Syria were first called "mourners" (*avile*) and often wore chains suggests, at least for them, a penitential impetus (Henze 1999: 185–215). Yet it was Athanasius' image of Antony's withdrawal that informed subsequent monastic history, partly because it provided a simple framework for understanding a phenomenon that had already become visible around the empire (Goehring 1999: 73–88), partly because it plotted a trajectory, beyond the concourse of ordinary human beings, that met the concerns of many fourth- and early fifth-century readers.

Students of monastic history will note that the most influential monastic authors in this period were all either affiliated with episcopal leaders (e.g., Jerome with Pope Damasus, John Cassian with John Chrysostom) or were bishops themselves (Athanasius of Alexandria, Basil of Caesarea, Gregory of Nyssa, Gregory of Nazianzus, Augustine of Hippo, etc.). In addition, all were reared in late Roman *paideía*, the elite educational system that had traditionally regarded contemplative retirement as the *summum bonum humanum*. While this does not mean that they all held the same opinions (Augustine, for example, developed his own rather ambivalent ideas about the purpose of monasticism and ascetic practices: Lawless 1987; Markus 1990: 63–83), it did mean that all were inclined to define monasticism in terms of philosophical withdrawal – the improvement of one's soul through pursuit of tranquillity (*hesychia*) – and that the promotion of monasticism as such was closely related to episcopal concerns and patronage. We first see this in Basil's effort, as bishop of Caesarea (AD 370–9), to promote monasticism as a non-urban movement, inspired not only by the philosophic pleasures he had once enjoyed at his country retreat in Pontus (Rousseau 1994: 66–92), but also by the difficulties he later faced from urban monks opposed to his policies and appointees (Elm 1994: 211). Contentions with urban monks also plagued John Chrysostom as bishop of Constantinople (AD 398– 404); he responded by lavishing those who stayed in their monasteries with food and praise, while chastising those who appeared in the city for "insulting philosophy" (Sozomen, *Church History* 8. 3. 4, Hartranft 1989). Friction between church leaders and urban monks continued to escalate during the Christological controversies of the early fifth century, culminating with the fourth canon of the Council of Chalcedon (AD 451). This landmark canon distinguished monks who "sincerely and truly" adopted monasticism from those who moved "indiscriminately about the cities," forbidding any to leave their monastery without a bishop's permission: "Let them embrace tranquillity and attend to fasting and prayer alone, persevering in those places to which they have withdrawn." Thus, the bishops at Chalcedon made physical withdrawal the *sine qua non* of monastic practice throughout the empire, expressly so as to prevent monks from disturbing church or civic affairs.

Clearly one issue at stake in such encounters was the formal status of the monastic profession and the relation of monks to the church hierarchy, a relationship exacerbated by the readiness of some monastic leaders to speak out against local clerics and seek support from outside patrons. For these reasons alone, it is understandable why church authorities and their allies might prefer to define "true" monasticism in terms of physical withdrawal (Dagron 1970). Yet also at issue was a genuine debate over what it meant to be a monk. It is apparent that many considered their professional goal to be one of actively ministering to others (*diakonia*) as much as that of attaining tranquillity. For example, Pachomius, the reputed "founder" of coenobitic monasticism in Egypt, is said to have first become known through the services he provided to sick people in his village (Bohairic, *Life of Pachomius* 9; see McNary-Zack 2000: 32–3), while monastic leaders in Constantinople gained considerable prestige by providing guidance to the rich and welfare to the poor (Caner 2002: 190–241). An interesting critique of such activities is found in a short treatise ascribed to the monk Nilus of Ancyra (*fl. c.* AD 430), a contemporary of John Cassian and admirer of John Chrysostom. Nilus observes that "inexperienced people" typically admired monks who lived in cities among humans more than those who sought tranquillity on mountains or in caves. While Nilus concedes that showing compassion toward others was indeed dear to God, he contends that it was ultimately not conducive toward achieving one's own salvation. That required ridding the soul of contrary passions through vigilant introspection and prayer, something that was possible to achieve only in isolation. Cities were full of obvious distractions: besides women, there were the enticements of wealth and power. But the greatest peril arose simply from the fact that, in cities, one tended to practice virtue in plain sight of others. Consciously or not, those who remained "in the world" would pay attention to their spectators' concerns, and end up forgetting how to please God while trying to please people. Far safer, Nilus concludes, to retreat to the wilderness, where God alone would be watching (Nilus of Ancyra, *On the Superiority of Solitaries*, 1, 12, 15, 19, 26–7).

This "debate" is further illustrated in an early anecdote about three friends who became monks. Eventually the two who had opted to remain in their city – one tending the sick, the other settling disputes – became filled with a sense of failure. So, they went to visit the third, who had "sought quiet in solitude." He made them watch as he stirred a glass filled with water and dirt. Once the dirt had settled and they could see their image in it again, he remarked: "So it is with one who lives among men: He does not see his own sins because of the turmoil. But once at rest, especially in the desert, then he sees his sins" (*Sayings of the Fathers* 2. 16, Chadwick 1958). As this anecdote indicates, all agreed that care of the soul and detecting its sins were the primary goals of the monastic profession, and that such goals could be most easily achieved in quiet. But Nilus expresses an additional concern, one so basic to the psychology and formation of monasticism "proper" that it requires special attention here: the problem of vainglory, presented by Nilus in terms of "pleasing human beings" versus "pleasing God." Already the apostle Paul had warned "slaves of Christ" against directing their efforts toward "pleasing human beings" (*anthrôpareskia*) instead of their Master (Eph. 6: 6). Much danger followed from it. On one level, Nilus and others simply worried lest monks might seem no different from the rest of humanity, "with nothing left to distinguish them but their monastic garb," thereby jeopardizing the dignity of their profession (*Ascetic Discourse* 7; see Caner 2000). But *anthrôpareskia* summed up a more subtle danger, one noted by several writers of the period: not so much the deliberate pursuit of flattery, but rather an unconscious tendency of monks who lived among lay people to become "enslaved to human customs," and to measure themselves by standards human rather than divine. At risk was the monastic cast of mind: gradually, while trying to cope with ordinary human society, "it grows accustomed to complete neglect and forgetfulness of [God's] judgments, than which it could suffer no greater or more deadly evil" (Basil of Caesarea, *Longer Rules* 5–6, Clarke 1925).

Hence the conceptual importance of the desert in early monastic discourse, especially the Egyptian desert. Here was a place so alien that it seemed to hold great promise for permanent transformation: some of its earliest settlers become so acclimated to it that later monks were said to have found them living like Adam, naked among beasts, utterly ignorant of the outside "world" (e.g., *History of the Monks of Egypt* 10. 2). Pilgrims who came to the desert looking for such marvels did not leave disappointed. As Melania the Elder remarked of one Egyptian hermit in the late fourth century, "I found nothing of men in him at all" (Palladius, *Lausiac History*, Coptic version 10. 5, tr. Vivian 2004; Frank 2000). Yet, real change was hard won even there. Monks who tried to stay long at outposts like Kellia ("The Cells") and Shihêt (or Scetis, meaning "weigh the heart") soon learned why Egyptians traditionally considered the desert an abode of demons (Guillaumont 1975). It was at Kellia that the great monastic theorist, Evagrius of Pontus (AD 346–99), wrote his studies on the soul and its afflictions so as to help fellow monks withstand their temptations to return to "the world." Perhaps to the surprise of modern readers, greed and lust rank rather low on Evagrius' lists of deadly sins. The most serious demons of the desert were still those of vainglory and pride: at any moment, these could blind even the greatest ascetics, making them compete against other monks and, thus, lose sight of God's commandments, not unlike those who grew negligent by living "among men" (*Thoughts* 23, Sinkewicz 2003). Their failure became the stuff of desert drama. Palladius' *Lausiac History*, a description of monastic personalities of the Roman east, includes cautionary tales of desert loners whose ascetic extremism eventually broke them and drove them back to Egypt, where they roamed the taverns mad with pride, estranged not only from monks but from God.

As such literature illustrates, one challenge that monastic thinkers identified early on was how to maintain a healthy "fear of God" – that is, a religious mentality that kept one ever mindful of God's judgments, and therefore ever diligent in prayer and contrite in dealings with others. "The aim of the enemy," John Climacus would later write, "is to divert you from your mourning and ... fear of God" (*Ladder of Paradise* 6, Luibheid and Russell 1982). The need to foster the spirit of repentance by always keeping judgment day before one's eyes helps account for some of the more controversial ascetic practices of the day, such as growing long hair, wearing collars and chains, or standing on pillars. One monk, for example, was noted for keeping a stone in his mouth and a coil on his wrist, calling them the " 'irons' of his service." Just looking at the coil made him "suddenly turn ... and cry to God to deliver [him] from error" (John of Ephesus, *Lives of the Eastern Saints* 19, Brooks 1923–5). The fact that such artifices were often associated with solitaries living in or near villages suggests that they helped maintain an appropriate mindset among monks who lived far from a desert (Brown 1971a: 82–3). Indeed, some penitential practices may have been calculated precisely to attract scorn and reinforce a sense of compunction, analogous to fourth-century customs of placing the most egregious sinners in front of church gates to weep for their sins as "mourners" in public view: Augustine, for example, notes that some monks justified growing their hair provocatively long as a "degradation" assumed for their sins (*On the Work of Monks* 31. 39; Jerome, *Ep.* 22. 28; Basil of Caesarea, *Ep.* 199. 29). Precisely because they attracted so much attention, however, such practices were roundly criticized as "man-pleasing" and restricted to the confines of a monastery (*History of the Monks of Egypt* 8. 53; Rabbula of Edessa, *Rules for Monks* 5; John of Ephesus, *Lives of the Eastern Saints* 11, Brooks 1923–5). Egyptian desert tradition provided a different solution: "Put yourself under a man who fears God, and when you live with him, you will learn to fear God also" (*Sayings of the Fathers* 11. 23).

In this light we may better appreciate why John Cassian, who had apprenticed for fifteen years in Egypt (*c*. AD 385–400), emphasized obedience to an elder as a touchstone of true monastic practice. Perhaps the greatest legacy of the Egyptian desert experience was the recognition that no monk could go it alone: all needed to practice asceticism in consultation with experienced elders (Gould 1993: 26–106). This is reflected in the question-and-answer form of its wisdom literature, the "Sayings of the Fathers," as well as by many of its anecdotes:

> A brother who renounced the world and took the monk's habit immediately shut himself in a hermitage, saying: "I am a solitary." When the neighbouring elders heard of it, they

came and threw him out of his cell, and made him go round the cells of the brothers and do penance before them, saying, "Forgive me. I am no solitary, but have only just become a monk." (*Sayings of the Fathers* 10. 111)

Here we glimpse one method by which early monastic leaders sought to establish a *politeia* in the desert founded upon obedience and humility. In monastic thought, humility was considered the only ascetic attainment that the Devil could not subvert, and so a monk's ultimate defense against pride and vainglory. However, like fear of God (with which it was closely connected), it was considered an alien cast of mind that had to be learned (Burton-Christie 1993: 236–60). Hence the importance of obedience and service (*diakonia*) to an elder. By ministering to him, imitating him, confiding in him, and submitting to all of his demands (especially that of staying in one's cell), a novice would eventually attain a "real humility, which is not humble in word and outward appearance, but is deeply planted in the heart" (Dorotheus of Gaza, *On Renunciation*, Wheeler 1977; see Cassian, *Conferences* 18. 11). At the same time, the elder would put his own humility on trial by assuming his disciple's faults as his own, and by submitting to others for advice on particular problems. Developed in the heat of the fourth-century desert, this master–disciple relationship helped put a check on some of the more contentious aspects of anchoretic life, providing an intimate system of spiritual guidance that would eventually become incorporated into more complex communal institutions (Bitton-Ashkelony 1999).

Basil of Caesarea reached similar conclusions about the need for an elder in the formation of a monk – "for wherewith shall a man show humility, if he has no one in comparison with whom to show himself humble?" As far as we know, Basil was the first to explicitly prefer communal (i.e., coenobitic) monasticism to complete isolation. In his view, living in a sequestered community of "like-minded brothers" not only gave monks the opportunity to practice God's "commandments of love" while remaining withdrawn, but also imposed safeguards to prevent any from lapsing into worldly "habits of mind." The result was an incipient monastic hierarchy aimed at promoting an ever higher degree of humility. Indeed, many features of the communal *politeia* he prescribed, from its seating arrangements to its methods of correction, were justified in terms of the "proof of humility" they would afford (*Longer Rules* 7–8, 21, 35). Basil's sensitivity to the problem of vainglory may have arisen from his awareness that the monks he advised in fourth-century Cappadocia "seemed at times, to themselves and to others ... a radical and arcane élite" (Rousseau 1994: 205–7). But the main point for him (as for others) was that attaining "humility in the perfection of love" was considered the key to imitating Jesus and transcending "human" ways (Angstenberger 1997). Hence, all aspirants were to be tested by being assigned the lowliest chores, with those from "higher ranks of society" being given tasks especially "distasteful to worldlings" (Basil, *Longer Rules* 10).

Thus, we see a consensus emerging in normative monastic discourse of the fourth and early fifth centuries. Achieving a transcendent existence required not only withdrawal, fasting, and other physical disciplines, but also social training within a community that was deliberately structured to induce an abiding "contrition of heart, and humility of mind" (Basil, *Longer Rules* 8). Indeed, by the sixth century most monasteries seem to have instituted a system of apprenticeship that began with menial labor and progressed through several levels of more refined ministrations (as bakers, infirmarians, innkeepers, stewards, and so on) in a kind of inverse *cursus honorum* that culminated either in contemplative retirement, or monastic leadership (Zeisel 1975: 270–1).

This helps explain three further trends that become noticeable in the fifth and sixth centuries. First, coenobitic institutions do in fact become the norm: when anchorites are mentioned, they usually appear either as eccentrics, or as dependants attached to the local coenobium in which they had trained (Rousseau 2001). Second, such institutions became more directly bound to their regional church hierarchy; this happened in part because monasteries were viewed as dependable training grounds in obedience and doctrine, thereby suitably schooling candidates for church office (Escolan 1999; Sterk 2004). Finally, though all such institutions recognized an abbot's authority as absolute, some nevertheless developed cooperative forms of leadership "in which the charisma of the anchorites upheld the abbot's rule, each father reinforcing the authority of others" (Hevelone-Harper 2005: 47). The result was a balanced and deferential leadership structure that helped diffuse tensions within the community. That this leadership structure appears most fully in monasteries at Gaza (also the most fully documented monastic center of the sixth century) suggests that it was a legacy of earlier experiments at Kellia and Scetis, many of whose leaders had migrated to Palestine and Gaza in the early fifth century. It exemplifies, in any case, a collegial ideal that was otherwise rare in late Roman institutions, and perhaps explicable here only by a recognition that monastic authority needed to be grounded in demonstrative acts of humility and deference toward others (Hevelone-Harper 2005: 36, 47).

Noting the emphasis of early monastic texts on physical isolation, Karl Heussi argued long ago that monasticism differed from all other forms of Christian asceticism by requiring the creation of a *Sonderwelt*, an alternative environment that would help inhabitants attain a new relationship with their God (Heussi 1936: 53–4). As we have seen, that emphasis should not be taken for granted: it was partly the result of an early debate over exactly where and how monks might best perform the task of "pleasing God." Indeed, it is now apparent that many (if not most) lived closer to the world they had renounced than the *Life of Antony* and other normative texts of the period would imply, with their *Sonderwelt* often being demarcated by nothing more than a low wall or rock outcropping in a field (Wipszycka 1994; Goehring 1999: 39–52). In the final analysis, what set monks apart from lay society may not have been their physical withdrawal and austerities, so much as their commitment to acquiring and demonstrating an "other-worldly" humility. To appreciate that ideal, we must remember that it arose in a highly stratified society in which gradations of rank were constantly displayed, in which access to power was tightly controlled, where slaves cleared the streets for their masters' approach, and each person was imagined to look up at the emperor and think, "I would really like someone to give me something of that glory, majesty, and splendour" (Ps.-Macarius *Homily* 5.5, Maloney 1992). Their perceived indifference to such late Roman pomp not only made monks seem different from their contemporaries, but also made them more accessible, and professionally credible, to people in hope of their services. As one person explained in a letter to an Egyptian monk of the early fourth century, he knew that God would listen to him and his prayers because of his "glorious and revered *politeia*": for "you have renounced the boasting of the world, and the arrogance of the vainglorious" (Paphnutius archive, Bell 1924: 112).

BIBLIOGRAPHICAL NOTE

Modern introductions to late antique monasticism tend to be regional, with most focusing on the Roman east. Here the classic studies are Chitty 1966 and Vööbus 1958–88, which should be supplemented by Harvey 1990, Binns 1994, Patrich 1995, and Harmless 2004. For the relation of eastern monasticism to socio-economic structures of the East Roman Empire in general, see Patlagean 1977. The standard study of late antique monasticism in the west is Prinz 1965; see also Rousseau 1978, Markus 1990, and Leyser 2000a. For an overview of developments in both east and west, see Stewart 2000 and Rousseau 2001.

Bibliography

Only works cited by the contributors are listed here. Editions of primary sources are not included unless the editor or editors present additional reflections to which contributors refer. Translations of primary sources are acknowledged where necessary within the chapters themselves and are listed here under the translators' names. Conference proceedings and similar items are listed under their editors. Subsequent editions, reprints, and translations are often appended to the entry for the first edition.

Abramowski, Louise (1982), "Dionysius von Rom († 268) und Dionysius von Alexandrien († 264/5) in den arianischen Streitigkeiten des 4. Jahrhunderts," *Zeitschrift für Kirchengeschichte* 93: 240–72.

Abrams, Philip (1978), "Towns and Economic Growth: Some Theories and Problems," in Philip Abrams and E. A. Wrigley (eds.), *Towns in Societies: Essays in Economic History and Historical Sociology*, Cambridge, Cambridge University Press, pp. 9–33.

Accorsi, M. L. (2002), "Il complesso titolare dei SS. Silvestro e Martino ai Monti dal IV al IX secolo: Appunti di studio," in Guidobaldi and Guidobaldi (2002: 532–63).

Achtemeier, Paul J. (1990), "Omne Verbum Sonat: The New Testament and the Oral Environment of Late Western Antiquity," *Journal of Biblical Literature* 109: 3–27.

Adams, Colin (2001), " 'There and Back Again': Getting Around in Roman Egypt," in Adams and Laurence (2001: 138–66).

Adams, Colin, and Laurence, Ray (eds.) (2001), *Travel and Geography in the Roman Empire*, London, Routledge.

Adams, J. N. (1976), *The Text and Language of a Vulgar Latin Chronicle (Anonymus Valesianus II)*, London, Institute of Classical Studies.

Adams, J. N. (2003), *Bilingualism and the Latin Language*, Cambridge, Cambridge University Press.

Adams, J. N., Janse, Mark, and Swain, Simon (eds.) (2002), *Bilingualism in Ancient Society: Language Contact and the Written Text*, Oxford, Oxford University Press.

Adang, Camilla (1996), *Muslim Writers on Judaism and the Hebrew Bible from Ibn Rabban to Ibn Hazm*, Leiden, Brill.

Adler, William (1989), *Time Immemorial: Archaic History and Its Sources in Christian Chronography from Julius Africanus to George Syncellus*, Washington, DC, Dumbarton Oaks.

Afinogenov, D. E. (1995), "Patriarch Photius as Literary Theorist: Aspects of Innovation," *Byzantinoslavica* 56: 339–45.

Agapitos, Panagiotis A. (1998a), "Narrative, Rhetoric, and 'Drama' Rediscovered: Scholars and Poets in Byzantium interpret Heliodoros," in R. Hunter (ed.), *Studies in Heliodorus*, Cambridge, Cambridge Philological Society, pp. 125–56.

Agapitos, Panagiotis A. (1998b), "Teachers, Pupils and Imperial Power in Eleventh-Century Byzantium," in Too and Livingstone (1998: 170–91).

Agapitos, Panagiotis A. (2004), "Apo tên Persia stên Probêggia: Erôtikes diêgêseis sto hystero Byzantio," in E. Grammatikopoulou (ed.), *To Byzantio kai oi aparches tês Eurôpês*, Athens, National Hellenic Research Foundation, pp. 119–53.

Agapitos, Panagiotis A., and Reinsch, Dieter R. (eds.) (2000), *Der Roman im Byzanz der Komnenenzeit*, Referate des internationalen Symposiums an der Freien Universität Berlin, 3–6 April 1998, Frankfurt am Main, Beerenverlag.

Ahrweiler, Hélène (1966), *Byzance et la mer: la marine de guerre, la politique et les institutions maritimes de Byzance aux VIIe–XVe siècles*, Paris, Presses Universitaires de France.

al-Akhtal (nd.), *Diwan al-Akhtal*, ed. Majid Tarud, Beirut, Dar al-Jil.

Aland, B., Hahn, J., and Ronning, Chr. (eds.) (2003), *Literarische Konstituierung von Identifikationsfiguren in der Antike*, Tübingen, Mohr Siebeck.

Alchermes, Joseph (1994), "*Spolia* in Roman Cities of the Late Empire: Legislative Rationales and Architectural Reuse," *Dumbarton Oaks Papers* 48: 167–78.

Alcock, Leslie (1987), *Economy, Society and Warfare among the Britons and Saxons*, Cardiff, University of Wales Press.

Alcock, Leslie (1992), "Message from the Dark Side of the Moon: Western and Northern Britain in the Age of Sutton Hoo," in Carver (1992: 205–15).

Alcock, Leslie (2003), *Kings and Warriors, Craftsmen and Priests in Northern Britain, AD 550–850*, Edinburgh, Society of Antiquaries of Scotland.

Alföldi, Andreas (1970), *Die monarchische Repräsentation im römischen Kaiserreich*, Darmstadt, Wissenschaftliche Buchgesellschaft.

Allen, Pauline (1981), *Evagrius Scholasticus the Church Historian*, Louvain, Spicilegium Sacrum Lovaniense.

Allen, P. S. et al. (eds.) (1906–58), *Opus epistolarum Desiderii Erasmi Roterodami*, 12 vols., Oxford, Clarendon Press.

Allen, W. Sidney (1978), *Vox Latina: A Guide to the Pronunciation of Classical Latin*, 3rd edn., Cambridge, Cambridge University Press.

Allenbach, Jean et al. (eds.) (1995–2000), *Biblia Patristica: Index des citations et allusions biblique dans la littérature patristique*, 7 vols., Paris, Editions du CNRS.

Alston, Richard (2002), *The City in Roman and Byzantine Egypt*, London, Routledge.

Amand de Mendieta, Emmanuel (1978), "Les Neuf homélies de Basile de Césarée sur l'Hexaéméron: Recherches sur le genre littéraire, le but et l'élaboration de ces homélies," *Byzantion* 48: 337–68.

Amand de Mendieta, Emmanuel, and Rudberg, Stig Y. (eds.) (1958), *Eustathius: Ancienne version latine des neuf homélies sur l'Hexaéméron de Basile de Césarée*, Berlin, Akademie Verlag.

Amory, Patrick (1997), *People and Identity in Ostrogothic Italy, 489–554*, Cambridge, Cambridge University Press.

Ando, Clifford (2000), *Imperial Ideology and Provincial Loyalty in the Roman Empire*, Berkeley and Los Angeles, University of California Press.

Ando, Clifford (2001), "The Palladium and the Pentateuch: Towards a Sacred Topography of the Later Roman Empire," *Phoenix* 55: 369–410.

André, Jacques (1981), *Anonyme latin: Traité de physiognomie*, Paris, Les Belles Lettres.

Andreau, Jean, and Virlouvet, Catherine (eds.) (2002), *L'Information et la mer dans le monde antique*, Rome, École Française de Rome.

Angelidi, Christine G. (1991), "De Aelia Pulcheria Augusta Eiusque Fortuna," *Diptycha* 5: 251–69.

Angestenberger, Pius (1997), *Der reiche und der arme Christus: die Rezeptionsgeschichte von 2 Kor 8, 9 zwischen dem zweiten und dem sechsten Jahrhundert*, Bonn, Borengässer.

al-Ansary, Abdul Rahman (1982), *Qaryat al-Fau: A Portrait of Pre-Islamic Civilisation in Saudi Arabia*, London, Croom Helm.

Arce, Javier (1990), "El cursus publicus en la Hispania tardoromana," in *La red viaria en la Hispania romana*, Zaragoza, Institución Fernanco el Católico, pp. 35–40.

Arjava, Antti (1996), *Women and Law in Late Antiquity*, Oxford, Clarendon Press.

Arjava, Antti (1998), "Paternal Power in Late Antiquity," *Journal of Roman Studies* 88: 147–65.

Armit, Ian (ed.) (1990), *Beyond the Brochs: Changing Perspectives on the Later Iron Age in Atlantic Scotland*, Edinburgh, Edinburgh University Press.

Armit, Ian (1998), *Scotland's Hidden History*, Stroud and Charleston, SC, Tempus.

Armit, Ian (2003), *Towers in the North: The Brochs of Scotland*, Stroud and Charleston, SC, Tempus.

Armit, Ian, and Ralston, Ian B. M. (eds.) (2003), "The Iron Age," in Edwards and Ralston (2003: 168–93).

Asmussen, J. P. (1983), "Christians in Iran," in Yarshater (1983a, ii: 924–8)

Athamina, Khalil (1998), "The Tribal Kings in Pre-Islamic Arabia: A Study of the Epithet *malik* or *dhû-al-tâj* in Early Arabic Traditions," *al-Qantara* 19: 19–37.

Athamina, Khalil (1999), "The Pre-Islamic Roots of the Early Muslim Caliphate: The Emergence of Abû Bakr," *Der Islam* 76: 1–32.

Athanassiadi, Polymnia (1992), *Julian: An Intellectual Biography*, London and New York, Routledge.

Athanassiadi, Polymnia, and Frede, Michael (eds.) (1999), *Pagan Monotheism in Late Antiquity*, Oxford, Clarendon Press; New York, Oxford University Press.

Atiya, A. S. (ed.) (1991), *The Coptic Encyclopedia*, 8 vols., New York, Macmillan.

Austin, N. J. E., and Rankov, N. B. (1995), *Exploratio: Military and Political Intelligence in the Roman World from the Second Punic War to the Battle of Adrianople*, London, Routledge.

Backus, Irena (ed.) (1997), *The Reception of the Church Fathers in the West: Fom the Carolingians to the Maurists*, 2 vols., Leiden, Brill.

Backus, Irena (2003), *Historical Method and Confessional Identity in the Era of the Reformation (1378–1615)*, Leiden, Brill.

Bagnall, Roger S. (1987), "Church, State, and Divorce in Late Roman Egypt," in Robert E. Somerville and Karl-Ludwig Selig (eds.), *Florilegium Columbianum: Essays in Honor of Paul Oskar Kristeller*, New York, Italica Press, pp. 41–61.

Bagnall, Roger S. (1993), *Egypt in Late Antiquity*, Princeton, NJ, Princeton University Press.

Bagnall, Roger S. (1995), *Reading Papyri, Writing Ancient History*, London, Routledge.

Bagnall, Roger S. (2001), "Les Lettres privées des femmes: un choix de langue en Égypte byzantine," *Bulletin de la Classe des Lettres de l'Académie Royale de Belgique*, 6th ser. 12: 133–53.

Bagnall, Roger S., and Cribiore, Raffaella (eds.) (2006), *Women's Letters from Ancient Egypt, 300 BC–AD 800*, Ann Arbor, University of Michigan Press.

Bagnall, Roger S., and Frier, Bruce W. (eds.) (1994), *The Demography of Roman Egypt*, Cambridge, Cambridge University Press.

Bagnall, Roger S., Cameron, Alan, Schwartz, Seth R., and Worp, Klaas A. (1987), *Consuls of the Later Roman Empire*, Atlanta, GA, Scholars Press.

Bagnall, Roger S., Choat, Malcolm, and Gardner, Iain (2004), "O.Douch I 40," *Zeitschrift für Papyrologie und Epigraphik* 147: 205–7.

Baker, Derek (ed.) (1978), *Medieval Women*, Oxford, Blackwell.

Bakker, Jan Theo (1994), *Living and Working with the Gods: Studies of Evidence for Private Religion and Its Material Environment in the City of Ostia (100–500 AD)*, Amsterdam, Gieben.

Baldwin, Barry (1988), "Nicholas Mystikos on Roman History," *Byzantion* 58: 174–8.

Ball, Warwick (2000), *Rome in the East: The Transformation of an Empire*, London and New York, Routledge.

Ballin Smith, Beverley, and Banks, Iain (eds.) (2002), *In the Shadow of the Brochs: The Iron Age in Scotland*, Stroud and Charleston, SC, Tempus.

Banchich, Thomas (1985), "The Historical Fragments of Eunapius of Sardis," unpublished Ph.D. dissertation, State University of New York at Buffalo.

Banniard, Michel (1992), *Viva voce: communication écrite et communication orale du 4e au 9e siècle en Occident latin*, Paris, Institut des Etudes Augustiniennes.

Barasch, Moshe (1992), *Icon: Studies in the History of an Idea*, New York, New York University Press.

Barber, Charles (2002), *Figure and Likeness: On the Limits of Representation in Byzantine Iconoclasm*, Princeton, NJ, Princeton University Press.

Barfield, Thomas J. (1989), *The Perilous Frontier: Nomadic Empires and China*, Oxford and Cambridge, MA, Blackwell.

Barkan, Leonard (1999), *Unearthing the Past: Archaeology and Aesthetics in the Making of Renaissance Culture*, New Haven, CT, Yale University Press.

Barnes, Michel R., and Williams, Daniel H. (eds.) (1993), *Arianism after Arius: Essays on the Development of the Fourth-Century Trinitarian Conflicts*, Edinburgh, T. & T. Clark.

Barnes, Timothy D. (1978), *The Sources of the Historia Augusta*, Brussels, Latomus.

Barnes, Timothy D. (1980), "The Editions of Eusebius' *Ecclesiastical History*," *Greek, Roman, and Byzantine Studies* 21: 191–201.

Barnes, Timothy D. (1981), *Constantine and Eusebius*, Cambridge, MA, Harvard University Press.

Barnes, Timothy D. (1982), *The New Empire of Diocletian and Constantine*, Cambridge, MA, Harvard University Press.

Barnes, Timothy D. (1984), "Constantine's Prohibition of Pagan Sacrifice," *American Journal of Philology* 105: 69–72.

Barnes, Timothy D. (1985), "Constantine and the Christians of Persia," *Journal of Roman Studies* 75: 126–36.

Barnes, Timothy D. (1987), "Himerius and the Fourth Century," *Classical Philology* 82: 206–25.

Barnes, Timothy D. (1993), *Athanasius and Constantius: Theology and Politics in the Constantinian Empire*, Cambridge, MA, Harvard University Press.

Barnes, Timothy D. (1998), *Ammianus Marcellinus and the Representation of Historical Reality*, Ithaca, NY and London, Cornell University Press.

Barnes, Timothy D. (2001), "Monotheists All?" *Phoenix* 55: 142–62.

Barns, John W. B. (1978), *Egyptians and Greeks*, Brussels, Fondation Égyptologique Reine Élisabeth.

Barns, John W. B., Browne, G. M., and Shelton, J. C. (eds.) (1981), *Nag Hammadi Codices: Greek and Coptic Papyri from the Cartonnage of the Covers*, Leiden, Brill.

Barrow, R. H. (tr.) (1973), *Prefect and Emperor: The Relationes of Symmachus, AD 384, with translation and notes*, Oxford, Clarendon Press.

Barry, Terry (ed.) (2000), *A History of Settlement in Ireland*, London and New York, Routledge.

Barthes, Roland (1981), "The Discourse of History," *Comparative Criticism* 3: 7–20.

Barthes, Roland (1982), *Camera Lucida: Reflections on Photography*, tr. R. Howard, London, Cape.

Barthes, Roland (1988), *The Semiotic Challenge*, tr. R. Howard, New York, Hill & Wang.

Barton, Carlin (2001), *Roman Honor: The Fire in the Bones*, Berkeley and Los Angeles, University of California Press.

Bashear, Suliman (1990), "The Title 'Fârûq' and Its Association with 'Umar I'," *Studia Islamica* 72: 47–70.

Bashear, Suliman (1997), *Arabs and Others in Early Islam*, Princeton, NJ, Darwin Press.

Bass, George F. (ed.) (1972), *A History of Seafaring based on Underwater Archaeology*, New York, Walker & Co.

Basser, Herbert W. (2002), *Studies in Exegesis: Christian Critiques of Jewish Law and Rabbinic Responses, 70–300 CE*, Leiden, Brill.

Bassett, Sarah (2004), *The Urban Image of Late Antique Constantinople*, Cambridge, Cambridge University Press.

Bauer, Franz Alto (1996), *Stadt, Platz und Denkmal in der Spätantike: Untersuchungen zur Ausstattung des öffentlichen Raums in den spätantiken Städten Rom, Konstantinopel und Ephesos*, Mainz, von Zabern.

Bauer, Franz Alto, and Heinzelmann, M. (2001), "L'Église épiscopale d'Ostie," in Descoeudres (2001: 278–82).

Bauer, Franz Alto, Heinzelmann, M., Martin, A., and Schaub, A. (2000), "Ostia: ein urbanistisches Forschungsprojekt in den unausgregrabenen Bereichen des Stadtgebiets: Gabungskampagne 1999," *Römische Mitteilungen* 107: 375–415.

Bauer, Walter (1996), *Orthodoxy and Heresy in Earliest Christianity*, tr. Philadelphia Seminar on Christian Origins, Mifflintown, PA, Sigler Press.

Baur, F. C. (1861), *Kirchengeschichte der drei ersten Jahrhunderte*, Tübingen, Fues.

Baynes, Norman H. (1925), *The Byzantine Empire*, London, Thornton Butterworth.

Baynes, Norman H. (1926), *The Historia Augusta: Its Date and Purpose*, Oxford, Clarendon Press.

Baynes, Norman H. (1930), *Constantine the Great and the Christian Church*, Raleigh Lecture for 1929, London, H. Milford for the British Academy.

Baynes, Norman H. (1955), *Byzantine Studies and Other Essays*, London, University of London, Athlone Press.

Baynes, Norman H., and Moss, H. St. L. B. (eds.) (1948), *Byzantium: An Introduction to East Roman Civilization*, Oxford, Clarendon Press.

Bearman, P., Bianquis, Th., Bosworth, C. E., Van Donzel, E., and Heinrichs, W. P. (eds.) (1954–), *Encyclopaedia of Islâm*, 2nd edn., Leiden, Brill.

Beaton, Roderick (1996), *The Medieval Greek Romance*, London, Routledge.

Beaucamp, Joëlle (1990), *Le Statut de la femme à Byzance (4e–7e siècle)*, i: *Le droit impérial*, Paris, De Boccard.

Beaucamp, Joëlle (1992), *Le Statut de la femme à Byzance (4e–7e siècle)*, ii: *Les pratiques sociales*, Paris, De Boccard.

Becher, Matthias (ed.) (2004), *Der Dynastiewechsel von 751: Vorgeschichte, Legitimationsstrategien und Erinnerung*, Münster, Scriptorium.

Beck, Hans-Georg (1959), *Kirche und theologische Literatur im Byzantinischen Reich*, Munich, Beck.

Beck, Hans-Georg (1978), *Das byzantinische Jahrtausend*, Munich, Beck.

Beck, Roger (2006), *The Religion of the Mithras Cult in the Roman Empire: Mysteries of the Unconquered Sun*, Oxford and New York, Oxford University Press.

Becker, Adam (2006), *Fear of God and the Beginning of Wisdom: The School of Nisibis and Christian Scholastic Culture in Late Antique Mesopotamia*, Philadelphia, University of Pennsylvania Press.

Becker, Adam, and Reed, Annette Yoshiko (eds.) (2003), *The Ways that Never Parted: Jews and Christians in Late Antiquity and the Early Middle Ages*, Tübingen, Mohr Siebeck.

Behlmer, Heike (1996), "Ancient Egyptian Survivals in Coptic Literature," in Antonio Loprieno (ed.), *Ancient Egyptian Literature: History and Forms*, Leiden, Brill, pp. 567–90.

Behlmer, Heike (1998), "Visitors to Shenoute's Monastery," in Frankfurter (1998a: 341–71).

Behr, C.A. (tr.) (1973–), *Aristides in Four Volumes*, Cambridge, MA, Harvard University Press.

Behr, Charles A. (tr.) (1981–6), *P. Aelius Aristides: The Complete Works*, 2 vols., Leiden, Brill.

Bejczy, István (2001), *Erasmus and the Middle Ages: The Historical Consciousness of a Christian Humanist*, Leiden, Brill.

Bell, H. Idris (ed. and tr.) (1924), *Jews and Christians in Egypt: The Jewish Troubles in Alexandria and the Athanasian* Controversy, Illustrated by Texts from Greek Papyri in the British Museum, with three Coptic texts ed. by W. E. Crum, London, British Museum.

Bell, H. Idris, and Thompson, H. (1925), "A Greek–Coptic Glossary to Hosea and Amos," *Journal of Egyptian Archaeology* 11: 241–6.

Bell, H. Idris et al. (eds.) (1962), *The Abinnaeus Archive*, Oxford, Clarendon Press.

Belting, Hans (2003), *Art History after Modernism*, tr. C. Saltzwedel et al., Chicago, University of Chicago Press.

Bemmann, J. (1999), "Körpergräber der jungeren römischen Kaiserzeit und Völkerwanderungszeit aus Schleswig Holstein: zum Aufkommen einer neuen Bestattungssitte im überregionalen Vergleich," *Studien zur Sachsenforschung* 13: 5–45.

Béné, Charles (1969), *Érasme et saint Augustin ou Influence de saint Augustin sur l'humanisme d'Érasme*, Geneva, Droz.

Bentley, Jerry H. (1993), *Old World Encounters: Cross-Cultural Contacts and Exchanges in Pre-Modern Times*, Oxford and New York, Oxford University Press.

Bentley, M. (ed.) (1997), *Companion to Historiography*, London and New York, Routledge.

Bérard, François et al. (eds.) (2000), *Guide de l'épigraphiste: bibliographie choisie des épigraphies antiques et médiévales*, 3rd edn., Paris, Éditions Rue d'Ulm, with annual supplements at www.antiquite.ens.fr/guide-epigraphiste.html

Berenson, Bernard (1954), *The Arch of Constantine; or, The Decline of Form*, London, Chapman & Hall.

Berg, H. (ed.) (2003), *Method and Theory in the Study of Islamic Origins*, Leiden, Brill.

Bergvall, Åke (2001), *Augustinian Perspectives in the Renaissance*, Uppsala, Karlstad University.

Betz, Hans Dieter (ed.) (1986), *The Greek Magical Papyri in Translation, including the Demotic Spells*, Chicago, University of Chicago Press.

Bidez, Joseph (1913), *Vie de Porphyre: le Philosophe néo-platonicien*, Hildesheim, Olms.

Biedenkopf-Ziehner, Anneliese (1983), *Untersuchungen zum koptischen Briefformular unter Berücksichtigung ägyptischer und griechischer Parallelen*, Würzburg, Zauzich.

Biedenkopf-Ziehner, Anneliese (1999), "Kontinuität Ägyptischer Ausbildung und Bildung in Paganer und Christlicher Zeit," *Göttinger Miszellen* 173: 21–49.

Billanovich, Giuseppe (1954), *Un nuovo esempio delle scoperte e delle letture del Petrarca: l'"Eusebio-Girolamo-PseudoProspero"*, Krefeld, Scherpe.

Binns, J. W. (ed.) (1974), *Latin Literature of the Fourth Century*, London, Routledge.

Binns, John (1994), *Ascetics and Ambassadors of Christ: The Monasteries of Palestine, 314–631*, Oxford, Clarendon Press.

Bird, H. W. (1984), *Sextus Aurelius Victor: A Historiographical Study*, Liverpool, Francis Cairns.

Bischoff, Bernhard (1998–2004), *Katalog der festländischen Handschriften des neunten Jahrhunderts (mit Ausnahme der wisigotischen)*, part 1: *Aachen–Lambach*, part 2: *Laon–Paderborn*, Wiesbaden, Harrassowitz.

Bishop, Morris (tr.) (1966), *Letters from Petrarch*, Bloomington, Indiana University Press.

Bishop, W. C. (1912), "The African Rite," *Journal of Theological Studies* 13: 250–77.

Bitel, Lisa M. (1990), *Isle of the Saints: Monastic Settlement and Christian Community in Early Ireland*, Ithaca, NY, Cornell University Press.

Bitel, Lisa M. (2002), *Women in Early Medieval Europe, 400–1100*, Cambridge, Cambridge University Press.

Bitton-Ashkelony, Brouria (1999), "Penitence in Late Antique Monastic Literature," in Jan Assmann and Guy G. Stroumsa (eds.), *Transformations of the Inner Self in Ancient Religions*, Leiden, Brill, pp. 179–94.

Bivar, A. D. H. (1983), "The History of Eastern Iran," in Yarshater (1983a, i: 181–231).

Biville, Frédérique (1990–5), *Les Emprunts grecs en latin*, 2 vols., Louvain, Peeters.

Black, E. W. (1995), *Cursus Publicus: The Infrastructure of Government in Roman Britain*, Oxford, British Archaeological Reports.

Blackman, E. C. (1948), *Marcion and His Influence*, London, SPCK.

Blankinship, Khalid Yahya (1994), *The End of the Jihad State: The Reign of Hisham b. 'Abd al-Malik and the Collapse of the Umayyads*, Albany, State University of New York Press.

Bloch, Herbert (1963), "The Pagan Revival in the West at the End of the Fourth Century," in Momigliano (1963a: 193–218).

Blockley, R. C. (1980), "The Date of the 'Barbarian Conspiracy'," *Britannia* 11: 223–5.

Blockley, R. C. (1981–3), *The Fragmentary Classicising Historians of the Later Roman Empire: Eunapius, Olympiodorus, Priscus, and Malchus*, 2 vols., Liverpool, Francis Cairns.

Blockley, R. C. (ed.) (1985a), *The History of Menander the Guardsman: Introductory Essay, Text, Translation, and Historiographical Notes*, Liverpool, Francis Cairns.

Blockley, R. C. (ed.) (1985b), "Subsidies and Diplomacy: Rome and Persia in Late Antiquity," *Phoenix* 39: 62–74.

Blockley, R. C. (1992), *East Roman Foreign Policy: Formation and Conduct from Diocletian to Anastasius*, Leeds, Francis Cairns.

Blum, G. G. (1969), *Rabbula von Edessa: der Christ, der Bischof, der Theologe*, CSCO 300, Subsidia 34, Louvain, Secrétariat du CSCO.

Blum, Rudolf (1983), "Die Literaturverzeichnung im Altertum und Mittelalter: versuch einer Geschichte der Biobibliographie von den Anfängen bis zum Beginn der Neuzeit," *Archiv für Geschichte des Buchwesens* 24: 1–224.

Bodel, John (2001a) (ed.), *Epigraphic Evidence: Ancient History from Inscriptions*, London and New York, Routledge.

Bodel, John (2001b), "Epigraphy and the Ancient Historian," in Bodel (2001a: 1–56).

Boeft, J. den (1997), "Erasmus and the Church Fathers," in Backus (1997, ii: 537–626).

Boeft, J. den et al. (2002), *Philological and Historical Commentary on Ammianus Marcellinus XXIV*, Leiden, Brill.

Boesch Gajano, Sofia (2004a), *Gregorio Magno: Alle origini del Medioevo*, Rome, Viella.

Boesch Gajano, Sofia (2004b), "La memoria della santità: Gregorio Magno autore e oggetto di scritture agiografiche," *Gregorio Magno nel XIV centenario della morte*, Convegno internazionale, Roma, 22–25 Ottobre 2003, Rome, Accademia Nazionale dei Lincei, pp. 321–48.

Boglioni, Pierre (1985), "La Scène de la mort dans les premières hagiographies latines," in Couturier, Charron, and Durand (1985: 269–98).

Böhme, Horst Wolfgang (1974), *Germanische Grabfünde des 4. bis 5. Jahrhunderts zwischen untere Elbe und Loire: Studien zur Chronologie und Bevölkerungsgeschichte*, Munich, Beck.

Bolgar, R. R. (1954), *The Classical Heritage and Its Beneficiaries*, Cambridge, Cambridge University Press.

Bonamente, Giorgio (1988), "Apoteosi e imperatori cristiani," in Bonamente and Nestori (1988: 107–42).

Bonamente, Giorgio (2002), "Il ruolo del senato nella divinizzazione degli imperatori," in Carrié and Lizzi Testa (2002: 359–81).

Bonamente, Giorgio, and Nestori, Aldo (eds.) (1988), *I cristiani e l'impero nel IV secolo: Atti del Convegno sul Cristianesimo nel Mondo Antico (17–18 Dic. 1987)*, Macerata, Università degli Studi di Macerata.

Bond, Harold L. (1960), *The Literary Art of Edward Gibbon*, Oxford, Clarendon Press.

Bonnard, Georges (ed.) (1945), *Le Journal de Gibbon à Lausanne, 17 Août 1763–19 Avril 1764*, Lausanne, Librairie de l'Université.

Bonnard, Georges (ed.) (1961), *Gibbon's Journey from Geneva to Rome: His Journal from 20 April to 2 October 1764*, London, Thomas Nelson.

Bonnet, Corinne (2005), *Le "Grand atelier de la science": Franz Cumont et l'*Altertumswissenschaft, 2 vols., Brussels and Rome, Belgisch Historisch Instituut te Rome.

Bordo, Susan (1987), *The Flight to Objectivity: Essays on Cartesianism and Culture*, Albany, State University of New York Press.

Börm, Henning (2007), *Prokop und die Perser: Untersuchungen zu den römisch-sasanidischen Kontakten in der ausgehenden Spätantike*. Stuttgart, Steiner.

Børtnes, Jostein, and Hägg, Tomas (eds.) (2006), *Gregory of Nazianzus: Images and Reflections*, Copenhagen, Museum Tusculanum Press.

Bosio, Antonio (1632), *Roma sotteranea*, Rome, G. Facciotti.

Bosio, Luciano (1983), *La Tabula Peutingeriana: una descrizione pittorica del mondo antico*, Rimini, Maggioli Editore.

Boswell, John (1988), *The Kindness of Strangers: The Abandonment of Children in Western Europe from Late Antiquity to the Renaissance*, New York, Pantheon Press.

Bourdieu, Pierre (1999), *The Logic of Practice*, tr. R. Nice, Stanford, CA, Stanford University Press.

Bowersock, Glen W. (1978), *Julian the Apostate*, Cambridge, MA, Harvard University Press.

Bowersock, Glen W. (1983), *Roman Arabia*, Cambridge, MA, Harvard University Press.

Bowersock, Glen W. (1990), *Hellenism in Late Antiquity*, Ann Arbor, University of Michigan Press.

Bowersock, Glen W. (1994a), *Fiction as History: Nero to Julian*, Berkeley and Los Angeles, University of California Press.

Bowersock, Glen W. (1994b), *Studies on the Eastern Roman Empire*, Goldbach, Keip.

Bowersock, Glen W., Brown, Peter, and Grabar, Oleg (eds.) (1999), *Late Antiquity: A Guide to the Postclassical World*, Cambridge, MA and London, Belknap Press of Harvard University Press.

Bowes, Kim, and Kulikowski, Michael (eds.) (2005), *Hispania in Late Antiquity: Current Perspectives*, Leiden and Boston, MA, Brill.

Bowlus, Charles R. (1995), "Ethnogenesis Models and the Age of Migrations: A Critique," *Austrian History Yearbook* 26: 147–64.

Bowlus, Charles R. (2002), "Ethnogenesis: The Tyranny of a Concept," in Gillett (2002b: 241–56).

Bowman, Alan K. (1984), "Two Notes," *Bulletin of the American Society of Papyrologists* 21: 33–8.

Bowman, Alan K. (1996), *Egypt After the Pharaohs, 332 BC–AD 642: From Alexander to the Arab Conquest*, 2nd edn., London, British Museum.

Bowman, Alan K., and Woolf, Greg (eds.) (1994), *Literacy and Power in the Ancient World*, Cambridge, Cambridge University Press.

Bowman, Alan K., Garnsey, Peter, and Matthews, John (eds.) (2005), *Cambridge Ancient History*, xii: *The Crisis of Empire, AD 193–337*, Cambridge, Cambridge University Press.

Boyarin, Daniel (2003), "Semantic Differences; or, 'Judaism'/'Christianity'," in Becker and Reed (2003: 65–86).

Boyarin, Daniel (2004), *Border Lines: The Partition of Judaeo-Christianity*, Philadelphia, University of Pennsylvania Press.

Boyle, Marjorie O'Rourke (1977), *Erasmus on Language and Method in Theology*, Toronto, University of Toronto Press.

Bradbury, Scott (1994), "Constantine and the Problem of Anti-Pagan Legislation in the Fourth Century," *Classical Philology* 89: 120–39.

Bradbury, Scott (1995), "Julian's Pagan Revival and the Decline of 'Blood Sacrifice'," *Phoenix* 49: 331–56.

Bradbury, Scott (2004a), "Libanius's Letters as Evidence for Travel and Epistolary Networks among Greek Elites in the Fourth Century," in Ellis and Kidner (2004: 73–80).

Bradbury, Scott (tr.) (2004b), *Selected Letters of Libanius: From the Age of Constantius and Julian*, Liverpool, Liverpool University Press.

Brady, James F., and Olin, John C. (ed. and tr.) (1992), *Erasmus, Patristic Scholarship: The Edition of St. Jerome*, Collected Works of Erasmus 61, Toronto, University of Toronto Press.

Brakke, David (1995), *Athanasius and the Politics of Asceticism*, Oxford, Clarendon Press.

Brands, Gunnar, and Severin, Hans-Georg (eds.) (2003), *Die spätantike Stadt und ihre Christianisierung: Symposon von 14. bis 16. Februar 2000 in Halle/Saale*, Wiesbaden, Reichert.

Brandt, J. Rasmus, and Steen, O. (eds.) (2001), *Imperial Art as Christian Art, Christian Art as Imperial Art: Expression and Meaning in Art and Architecture from Constantine to Justinian*, Rome, Bardi Editore.

Brandt, J. Rasmus et al. (eds.) (2003), *Rome AD 300–800: Power and Symbol, Image and Reality*, Rome, Bardi Editore.

Brandt, Olof (2001), "Il battistero lateranense dell'imperatore Costantino e l'architettura contemporanea: come si crea un'architettura battesimale cristiana?" in Fleischer, Lund, and Nielsen (2001: 117–44).

Brashear, William (1995), "The Greek Magical Papyri: An Introduction and Survey: Annotated Bibliography (1928–1994)," *ANRW* 2. 18. 5: 3380–684.

Brather, Sebastian (2002), "Ethnic Identities as Constructions of Archaeology: The Case of the *Alamanni*," in Gillett (2002b: 149–75).

Brather, Sebastian (2004), *Ethnische Interpretationen in der Frühgeschichtlichen Archäologie: Geschichte, Grundlagen und Alternativen*, Berlin, de Gruyter.

Braudy, Leo (1970), *Narrative Form in History and Fiction: Hume, Fielding and Gibbon*, Princeton, NJ, Princeton University Press.

Bregman, Jay (1982), *Synesius of Cyrene, Philosopher-Bishop*, Berkeley and Los Angeles, University of California Press.

Brenk, Beat (1995), "Microstoria sotto la Chiesa dei SS Giovanni e Paolo: la cristianizzazione di una casa privata," *Rivista dell'Istituto Nazionale di Archeologia e Storia dell'Arte*, 3rd ser. 18: 169–206.

Brenk, Beat (2003), *Die Christianisierung der spätrömischen Welt: Stadt, Land, Haus, Kirche und Kloster in frühchristlicher Zeit*, Wiesbaden, Reichert.

Brenk, Beat (2005), *The Christianization of the Late Roman World: Cities, Churches, Synagogues, Palaces, Private Houses, and Monasteries in the Early Christian Period*, London, Pindar.

Brenk, Beat, Deckers, Johannes G., Effenberger, Arne, and Kötzsche-Breitenbruch, Lieselotte (eds.) (1996), *Innovation in der Spätantike: Kolloquium Basel 6. und 7. Mai 1994*, Wiesbaden, Reichert.

Brennecke, Hanns Christof (1988), *Studien zur Geschichte der Homöer: der Osten bis zum Ende der homöischen Reichskirche*, Tübingen, Mohr.

Bresciani, Edda, Pernigotti, Sergio, and Betrò, Maria C. (eds.) (1983), *Ostraka demotici da Narmuti*, i, Pisa, Giardini.

Briant, Pierre (2002), "History and Ideology: The Greeks and 'Persian Decadence'," tr. Antonia Nevill, in Harrison (2002: 193–210).

Brink-Kloke, H., and Meurers-Balke, J. (2003), "Siedlungen und Gräber am Oespeler Bach, Dortmund – eine Kulturlandschaft im Wandel der Zeiten," *Germania* 81: 47–146.

Brock, Sebastian (1979), "Jewish Traditions in Syriac Sources," *Journal of Jewish Studies* 30: 212–32.

Brock, Sebastian (1995), "A Palestinian Targum Feature in Syriac," *Journal of Jewish Studies* 46: 271–82.

Brock, Sebastian (1997), *A Brief Outline of Syriac Literature*, Baker Hill, Kootayam, St. Ephrem Ecumenical Research Institute.

Brock, Sebastian, and Harvey, Susan Ashbrook (1987), *Holy Women of the Syrian Orient*, Berkeley and Los Angeles, University of California Press.

Brodersen, Kai (2001), "The Presentation of Geographical Knowledge for Travel and Transport in the Roman World: *itineraria non tantum adnotata sed etiam picta*," in Adams and Laurence (2001: 7–21).

Brodka, D. (1998), "Das Bild der Perserkönigs Chosroes I. in den *Bella* des Prokopios von Kaisereia," *Classica Cracoviensia* 4: 115–24.

Brogiolo, Gian Pietro (1984), "La città tra tarda-antichità e medioevo," in Rolando Bussi and Alberto Molinari (eds.), *Archeologia urbana in Lombardia: valutazione dei depositi archeologici e inventario dei vincoli*, Modena, Panini, pp. 48–56.

Brogiolo, Gian Pietro (ed.) (1996), *Early Medieval Towns in the Western Mediterranean*, Mantua, Editrice S.A.P.

Brogiolo, Gian Pietro, and Ward-Perkins, Bryan (eds.) (1999), *The Idea and Ideal of the Town between Late Antiquity and the Early Middle Ages*, Leiden, Brill.

Brogiolo, Gian Pietro, Gauthier, Nancy, and Christie, Neil (eds.) (2000), *Towns and Their Territories between Late Antiquity and the Early Middle Ages*, Leiden, Brill.

Brooks, E. W. (ed. and tr.) (1923–5), *John of Ephesus: Lives of the Eastern Saints*, 3 vols., *Patrologia Orientalis* 17.1, 18.4, 19.2, Paris, Firmin-Didot.

Brown, John Seely, and Duguid, Paul (2000), *The Social Life of Information*, Boston, MA, Harvard Business School Press.

Brown, Peter (1967a), *Augustine of Hippo: A Biography*, London, Faber & Faber.

Brown, Peter (1967b), "The Later Roman Empire," *Economic History Review* 20 ("Essays in Bibliography and Criticism," 56): 327–43; repr. in Brown (1972a: 46–73).

Brown, Peter (1968a), "Approaches to the Religious Crisis of the Third Century A.D.," *English Historical Review* 83: 542–58; repr. in Brown (1972a: 74–93).

Brown, Peter (1968b), "Christianity and Local Culture in Late Roman Africa," *Journal of Roman Studies* 58: 85–95; repr. in Brown (1972a: 279–300).

Brown, Peter (1969), "The Diffusion of Manichaeism in the Roman Empire," *Journal of Roman Studies* 59: 92–103; repr. in Brown (1972a: 94–118).

Brown, Peter (1971a), "The Rise and Function of the Holy Man in Late Antiquity," *Journal of Roman Studies* 61: 80–101; repr. in Brown (1982: 103–52).

Brown, Peter (1971b), *The World of Late Antiquity: From Marcus Aurelius to Muhammad*, London, Thames & Hudson.

Brown, Peter (1972a), *Religion and Society in the Age of Saint Augustine*, London, Faber & Faber.

Brown, Peter (1972b), "Sorcery, Demons, and the Rise of Christianity," repr. in Brown (1972a: 119–46).

Brown, Peter (1978), *The Making of Late Antiquity*, Cambridge, MA, Harvard University Press.

Brown, Peter (1981), *The Cult of the Saints: Its Rise and Function in Latin Christianity*, Chicago, University of Chicago Press.

Brown, Peter (1982), *Society and the Holy in Late Antiquity*, Berkeley and Los Angeles, University of California Press.

Brown, Peter (1988a), "Arnoldo Dante Momigliano, 1908–1987," *Proceedings of the British Academy* 74: 405–42.

Brown, Peter (1988b), *The Body and Society: Men, Women and Sexual Renunciation in Early Christianity*, New York, Columbia University Press.

Brown, Peter (1992), *Power and Persuasion in Late Antiquity: Towards a Christian Empire*, Madison, University of Wisconsin Press.

Brown, Peter (1993), "The Problem of Christianization," *Proceedings of the British Academy* 82: 89–106.

Brown, Peter (1995), *Authority and the Sacred: Aspects of the Christianization of the Roman World*, Cambridge, Cambridge University Press.

Brown, Peter (1998), "Christianization," in Cameron and Garnsey (1998: 632–64).

Brown, Peter (2000), *Augustine of Hippo: A Biography*, Berkeley and Los Angeles, University of California Press.

Brown, Peter (2002), *Poverty and Leadership in the Later Roman Empire*, Hanover, NH, University Press of New England.

Brown, Peter (2003), *The Rise of Western Christendom: Triumph and Diversity, AD 200–1000*, 2nd edn., Oxford, Blackwell.

Brown, Peter et al. (1997), " 'The World of Late Antiquity' Revisited," *Symbolae Osloenses* 72: 5–90.

Brown, Peter, Cracco Ruggini, Lellia, and Mazza, Mario (1982), *Governanti e intellettuali: Popolo di Roma e popolo di Dio (I–VI secolo)*, Turin, Giappichelli.

Brown, T. S. (1993), "History as Myth: Medieval Perceptions of Venice's Roman and Byzantine Past," in R. Beaton and Ch. Roueché (eds.), *The Making of Byzantine History: Studies dedicated to Donald M. Nicol*, London, Variorum, pp. 145–57.

Browning, Robert (1975), *The Emperor Julian*, London, Weidenfeld & Nicolson.

Brubaker, Leslie (1997), "Memories of Helena: Patterns in Imperial Female Matronage in the Fourth and Fifth Centuries," in James (1997: 52–75).

Brubaker, Leslie (1999), *Vision and Meaning in Ninth-Century Byzantium: Image as Exegesis in the Homilies of Gregory of Nazianzus*, Cambridge, Cambridge University Press.

Brubaker, Leslie (2004), "Sex, Lies, and Textuality: The *Secret History* of Prokopios and the Rhetoric of Gender in Sixth-Century Byzantium," in Brubaker and Smith (2004: 83–101).

Brubaker, Leslie, and Haldon, John (2001), *Byzantium in the Iconoclast Era (ca. 680–850): The Sources. An Annotated Survey*, Aldershot, Ashgate.

Brubaker, Leslie, and Smith, Julia M. H. (eds.) (2004), *Gender in the Early Medieval World, East and West, 300–900*, Cambridge, Cambridge University Press.

Brubaker, Leslie, and Tobler, Helen (2000), "The Gender of Money: Byzantine Empresses on Coins (324–802)," in Stafford and Mulder-Bakker (2000: 572–94).

Bruggisser, Philippe (1993), *Symmaque ou le rituel épistolaire de l'amitié littéraire: recherches sur le premier livre de la correspondance*, Fribourg, Éditions Universitaires.

Brulet, R. (1997), "La Tombe de Childéric et la topographie funéraire de Tournai à la fin du Ve siècle," in Rouche (1997, i: 59–78).

Bruun, Patrick (1976), "Notes on the Transmission of Imperial Images in Late Antiquity," in *Studia Romana in honorem Petri Krarup Septuagenarii*, Odense, Odense University Press, pp. 122–31.

Bucking, Scott (1997), "Christian Educational Texts from Egypt: A Preliminary Inventory," in Bärbel Kramer et al. (eds.), *Akten des 21. Internationalen Papyrologenkongresses*, Stuttgart, Teubner, pp. 132–8.

Buddensieg, Tilmann (1965), "Gregory the Great, the Destroyer of Pagan Idols: The History of a Medieval Legend concerning the Decline of Ancient Art and Literature," *Journal of the Warburg and Courtauld Institutes* 28: 44–65.

Bulliet, Richard W. (1979), *Conversion to Islam in the Medieval Period: An Essay in Quantitative History*, Cambridge, MA and London, Harvard University Press.

Bulloch, Anthony et al. (eds.) (1993), *Images and Ideologies: Self-Definition in the Hellenistic World*, Berkeley and Los Angeles, University of California Press.

Burckhardt, Jacob (1853), *Die Zeit Constantins des Grossen*, Basel, Schweighausersche Verlagsbuchhandlung; tr. Moses Hadas, *The Age of Constantine the Great*, New York, Pantheon Books, 1949.

Burgess, Richard W. (1993), *The Chronicle of Hydatius and the Consularia Constantinopolitana*, Oxford, Clarendon Press.

Burgess, Richard W. (1999), *Studies in Eusebian and Post-Eusebian Chronography*, Stuttgart, Franz Steiner.

Burgess, Richard W. (2001a), "The Gallic Chronicle of 452: A New Critical Edition with a Brief Introduction," in Mathisen and Shanzer (2001: 52–84).

Burgess, Richard W. (2001b), "The Gallic Chronicle of 511: A New Critical Edition with a Brief Introduction," in Mathisen and Shanzer (2001: 85–100).

Burgess, Richard W. (2003), "The *Passio s. Artemii*, Philostorgius, and the Dates of the Invention and Translations of the Relics of Sts Andrew and Luke," *Analecta Bollandiana* 121: 5–36.

Burgess, Richard W. (2005), "A Common Source for Jerome, Eutropius, Festus, Ammianus, and the *Epitome de Caesaribus* between 358 and 378, along with Further Thoughts on the Date and Nature of the *Kaisergeschichte*," *Classical Philology* 100: 166–92.

Burgess, William D. (1990), "Isaurian Names and the Ethnic Identity of the Isaurians in Late Antiquity," *Ancient World* 21: 109–21.

Burke, Peter (1969), *The Renaissance Sense of the Past*, London, Edward Arnold.

Burke, Peter (2001), *Eyewitnessing: The Use of Images as Historical Evidence*, London, Reaktion Books; Ithaca, NY, Cornell University Press.

Burkert, Walter (2004), *Babylon, Memphis, Persepolis: Eastern Contexts of Greek Culture*, Cambridge, MA, Harvard University Press.

Burkitt, F. C. (1904), *Early Eastern Christianity*, London, John Murray.

Burns, Thomas S. (2003), *Rome and the Barbarians, 100 BC–AD 400*, Baltimore, MD, Johns Hopkins University Press.

Burns, Thomas S., and Eadie, John W. (eds.) (2001), *Urban Centers and Rural Contexts in Late Antiquity*, East Lansing, Michigan State University Press.

Burnyeat, Myles F. (1997), "Postscript on Silent Reading," *Classical Quarterly* 47: 74–6.

Burrus, Virginia (1991), "The Heretical Woman as Symbol in Alexander, Athanasius, Epiphanius and Jerome," *Harvard Theological Review* 84: 229–48.

Burrus, Virginia (2001), "Is Macrina a Woman? Gregory of Nyssa's Dialogue on the Soul and the Resurrection," in Ward (2001: 249–64).

Burt, Donald X. (1999), *Friendship and Society: An Introduction to Augustine's Practical Philosophy*, Grand Rapids, MI, Eerdmans.

Burton-Christie, Douglas (1993), *The Word in the Desert: Scripture and the Quest for Holiness in Early Christian Monasticism*, Oxford and New York, Oxford University Press.

Bury, J. B. (1889), *A History of the Later Roman Empire, from Arcadius to Irene, 395 AD to 800 AD*, London, Macmillan.

Bury, J. B. (1910), "The Constitution of the Later Roman Empire," Creighton Memorial Lecture, University College, London, 1909, Cambridge, Cambridge University Press.

Bury, J. B. (1912), *A History of the Eastern Roman Empire, from the Fall of Irene to the Accession of Basil I, AD 802–867*, London, Macmillan.

Bury, J. B. (1923), *History of the Later Roman Empire from the Death of Theodosius I to the Death of Justinian, AD 395 to AD 565*, London, Macmillan.

Bury, J. B. (1928), *The Invasion of Europe by the Barbarians*, London, Macmillan.

Butler, Jon (1990), *Awash in a Sea of Faith: Christianizing the American People*, Cambridge, MA, Harvard University Press.

Bynum, Carolyn W. (2001), *Metamorphosis and Identity*, New York, Zone Books.

Byzantine Books and Bookmen (1975), Dumbarton Oaks Colloquium, 1971, Washington, DC, Dumbarton Oaks.

Cabouret, Bernadette (tr.) (2000), *Libanius, Lettres aux hommes de son temps*, Paris, Les Belles Lettres.

Cabouret, Bernadette (2002), "Le Gouverneur au temps du Libanios, image et réalité," *Pallas* 60: 191–204.

Cabouret, Bernadette (2004), "Pouvoir municipal, pouvoir imperial à Antioche au IVe siècle," in Bernadette Cabouret, Pierre-Louis Gatier, and Catherine Saliou (eds.), *Antioche de Syrie: Histoire, images et traces de la ville antique*, Actes du colloque organisé à Lyon, Maison de l'Orient et de la Méditerranée, 4, 5, 6 Octobre 2001, Paris, De Boccard, 2004, pp. 117–42.

Caillet, J.-P. (1996), "La Transformation en églises d'édifices publics et de temples à la fin de l'Antiquité," in Lepelley (1996: 191–211).

Cain, Andrew (2006), "*Vox Clamantis in Deserto*: Rhetoric, Reproach, and the Forging of Ascetic Authority in Jerome's Letters from the Syrian Desert," *Journal of Theological Studies* 57: 500–25.

Calore, Antonello (1998a), " 'Iuro per deum omnipotentem . . .': il giuramento dei funzionari imperiali all'epoca di Giustiniano," in Calore (1998b: 107–26).

Calore, Antonello (ed.) (1998b), *Seminari di storia e di diritto*, ii: *Studi sul giuramento nel mondo antico*, Milan, Giuffré Editore.

Cameron, Alan (1985a), "The Date and the Owners of the Esquiline Treasure," *American Journal of Archaeology* 89: 135–45.

Cameron, Alan (1985b), "Polyonomy in the Late Roman Aristocracy: The Case of Petronius Probus," *Journal of Roman Studies* 75: 164–82.

Cameron, Alan (1999), "The Last Pagans of Rome," in Harris (1999: 109–21).

Cameron, Alan (2002), "The Funeral of Junius Bassus," *Zeitschrift für Papyrologie und Epigraphik* 139: 288–92.

Cameron, Alan (2004), "Poetry and Literary Culture in Late Antiquity," in Swain and Edwards (2004: 327–54).

Cameron, Averil (1969), "Agathias on the Sassanians," *Dumbarton Oaks Papers* 23: 67–183.

Cameron, Averil (1970), *Agathias*, Oxford, Clarendon Press.

Cameron, Averil (1985), *Procopius and the Sixth Century*, Berkeley and Los Angeles, University of California Press.

Cameron, Averil (1989a) (ed.), *History as Text: The Writing of Ancient History*, London, Duckworth.

Cameron, Averil (1989b), "Virginity as Metaphor: Women and the Rhetoric of Early Christianity," in Cameron (1989a: 184–205).

Cameron, Averil (1991), *Christianity and the Rhetoric of Empire: The Development of Christian Discourse*, Berkeley and Los Angeles, University of California Press.

Cameron, Averil (1995a), "Ascetic Closure and the End of Antiquity," in Wimbush and Valantasis (1995: 147–61).

Cameron, Averil (ed.) (1995b), *The Byzantine and Early Islamic Near East*, iii: *States, Resources and Armies*, Princeton, NJ, Darwin Press.

Cameron, Averil (1996), *Changing Cultures in Early Byzantium*, Aldershot, Variorum.

Cameron, Averil (1997), "Eusebius's *Vita Constantini* and the Construction of Constantine," in Edwards and Swain (1997: 145–74).

Cameron, Averil (2002), "The 'Long' Late Antiquity: A Late Twentieth-Century Model," in T. P. Wiseman (ed.), *Classics in Progress: Essays on Ancient Greece and Rome*, Oxford, Clarendon Press, pp. 165–91.

Cameron, Averil, and Garnsey, Peter (eds.) (1998), *Cambridge Ancient History*, xiii: *The Late Empire, A.D. 337–425*, Cambridge, Cambridge University Press.

Cameron, Averil, and Hall, Stuart (tr.) (1999), *Eusebius' Life of Constantine: Introduction, Translation and Commentary*, Oxford, Clarendon Press.

Cameron, Averil, and Herrin, Judith (1984), *Constantinople in the Early Eighth Century: The Parastaseis Syntomoi Chronikai*, Leiden, Brill.

Cameron, Averil, Ward-Perkins, Brian, and Whitby, Michael (eds.) (2000), *The Cambridge Ancient History*, xiv: *Late Antiquity: Empire and Successors, AD 425–600*, Cambridge, Cambridge University Press.

Campbell, Euan (1996), "Trade in the Dark Age West: A Peripheral Activity?" in Crawford (1996: 79–91).

Campbell, Gordon Lindsay (2006), *Strange Creatures: Anthropology in Antiquity*, London, Duckworth.

Campenhausen, Hans von (1972), *The Formation of the Christian Bible*, tr. J. A. Baker, Philadelphia, Fortress Press.

Camporeale, Salvatore I. (1972), *Lorenzo Valla: umanesimo e teologia*, Florence, Istituto Nazionale di Studi sul Rinascimento.

Camporeale, Salvatore I. (1993), "Renaissance Humanism and the Origins of Humanist Theology," in John W.O' Malley, Thomas M. Izbicki, and Gerald Christianson (eds.), *Humanity and Divinity in Renaissance and Reformation: Essays in Honor of Charles Trinkaus*, Leiden, Brill, pp. 101–24.

Camporeale, Salvatore I. (2002), *Lorenzo Valla: umanesimo, riforma e controriforma*, Rome, Istituto Nazionale di Studi sul Rinascimento.

Caner, Daniel F. (2000), "Nilus of Ancyra and the Promotion of a Monastic Elite," *Arethusa* 33: 401–10.

Caner, Daniel F. (2002), *Wandering, Begging Monks: Spiritual Authority and the Promotion of Monasticism in Late Antiquity*, Berkeley and Los Angeles, University of California Press.

Capdetrey, Laurent, and Nelis-Clément, Jocelyne (eds.) (2006), *La Circulation de l' information dans les états antiques*, Bordeaux, Ausonius.

Capelle, Torsten (1998), *Die Sachsen des frühen Mittelalters*, Stuttgart, Theiss.

Carandini, Andrea (1981), *Storie dalla terra: manuale dello scavo archeologico*, Bari, De Donato.

Carleton Paget, James (1999), "Jewish Christianity," in William Horbury, William D. Davies, and John Sturdy (eds.), *Cambridge History of Judaism*, iii: *The Early Roman Period*, Cambridge, Cambridge University Press, 1999, pp. 731–75.

Carletti, Carlo (1980), "Inscrizioni murali," in Carletti and Otranto (1980: 7–180).

Carletti, Carlo (1984–5), "I graffiti sull'affresco di S. Luca nel cimitero di Commodilla: Addenda et corrigenda," *Atti della Pontificia Accademia Romana di Archeologia, Rendiconti* 57: 129–43.

Carletti, Carlo (1986), *Iscrizioni cristiane di Roma: Testimonianze di vita cristiana (secoli III–VII)*, Florence, Nardini Editore.

Carletti, Carlo (1988), "Epigrafia cristiana, epigrafia dei cristiani: alle origini della terza età dell' epigrafia," in Donati (1988: 115–35).

Carletti, Carlo (1995), "*Viatores ad martyres*: Testimonianze scritte altomedievali nelle catacombe romane," in Cavallo and Mango (1995: 197–225).

Carletti, Carlo, and Otranto, Giorgio (eds.) (1980), *Il santuario di S. Michele sul Gargano dal IV al IX secolo, Contributo alla storia della Langobardia meridionale*, Bari, Edipuglia.

Carnochan, W. B. (1987), *Gibbon's Solitude: The Inward World of the Historian*, Stanford, CA, Stanford University Press.

Carrié, Jean-Michel (1999), "Agens in rebus," in Bowersock, Brown, and Grabar (1999: 278–9).

Carrié, Jean-Michel (2001), "Antiquité tardive et 'démocratisation de la culture'," *Antiquité Tardive* 9: 27–46.

Carrié, Jean-Michel, and Lizzi Testa, Rita (eds.) (2002), *Humana sapit: études d'Antiquité tardive offertes à Lellia Cracco Ruggini*, Turnhout, Brepols.

Carriker, Anne P. (1999), "Augustine's Frankness in his Dispute with Jerome over the Interpretation of Galatians 2:11–14," in Kreis and Tkacz (1999: 121–38).

Cartledge Paul (2002), *The Greeks: A Portrait of Self and Others*, 2nd edn., Oxford, Oxford University Press.

Carver, M. O. H. (ed.) (1992), *The Age of Sutton Hoo: The Seventh Century in North-Western Europe*, Woodbridge and Rochester, NY, Boydell Press.

Casey, P. J. (1994), *Carausius and Allectus: The British Usurpers*, New Haven, CT, Yale University Press.

Casson, Lionel (1969), "Shipping," in Carl Roebuck (ed.), *The Muses at Work: Arts, Crafts, and Professions in Ancient Greece and Rome*, Cambridge, MA, MIT Press, pp. 172–200.

Casson, Lionel (1971), *Ships and Seamanship in the Ancient World*, Princeton, NJ, Princeton University Press.

Casson, Lionel (1974), *Travel in the Ancient World*, Toronto, Hakkert; repr. Baltimore, MD, Johns Hopkins University Press, 1994.

Casson, Lionel (1988), "Transportation," in Michael Grant and Rachel Kitzingerin (eds.), *Civilization of the Ancient Mediterranean: Greece and Rome*, New York, Charles Scribner's Sons, pp. 353–65.

Castaldi, Lucia (2004), "Il *Registrum Epistularum* di Gregorio Magno," *Filologia Mediolatina* 11: 55–97.

Casurella, Anthony (1983), *The Johannine Paraclete in the Church Fathers: A Study in the History of Exegesis*, Tübingen, Mohr.

Cavallo, Guglielmo, and Mango, Cyril (eds.) (1995), *Epigrafia medievale greca e latina: ideologia e funzione*, Spoleto, Centro Italiano di Studi sull'Alto Medioevo.

Cavallo, Guglielmo et al. (eds.) (1991), *Scritture, libri e testi nelle aree provinciali de Bisanzio*, Spoleto, Centro Italiano di Studi sull'Alto Medioevo.

Cecconi, Giovanni (1994), *Governo imperiale e élites dirigenti nell'Italia tardoantica: problemi di storia politico-amministrativa (270–476 d.C.)*, Como, Edizioni New Press.

Certeau, Michel de (1984), *The Practice of Everyday Life*, tr. Steven Rendall, Berkeley and Los Angeles, University of California Press.

Chadwick, H. Munro (1912), *The Heroic Age*, Cambridge, Cambridge University Press.

Chadwick, Henry (1966), *Early Christian Thought and the Classical Tradition: Studies in Justin, Clement, and Origen*, Oxford and New York, Oxford University Press.

Chadwick, Henry (1981), *Boethius: The Consolations of Music, Logic, Theology, and Philosophy*, Oxford, Clarendon Press.

Chadwick, Henry (2001), *The Church in Ancient Society: From Galilee to Gregory the Great*, Oxford and New York, Oxford University Press.

Chadwick, Owen (1958), *Western Asceticism*, Philadelphia, Westminster Press.

Chakrabarti, K. (1996), "The Gupta Kingdom," in Litvinsky (1996a: 185–206).

Chalhoub, Georges (1999), *Recherches sur le Mardaites-Ǧarağima*, Jounieh, Université Saint-Espirit de Kaslik.

Charles-Edwards, Thomas (2000), "Law in the Western Kingdoms between the Fifth and the Seventh Century," in Cameron, Ward-Perkins, and Whitby (2000: 260–87).

Chastagnol, André (1960), *La Préfecture Urbaine à Rome sous le Bas-Empire*, Paris, Presses Universitaires de France.

Chastagnol, André (1962), *Les Fastes de la Préfecture de Rome au Bas-Empire*, Paris, Nouvelles Éditions Latines.

Chaumont, M.-L. (1988), *La Christianisation de l'Empire Iranien des origines aux grandes persécutions du IVe siècle*, Louvain, Peeters.

Chauvot, Alain (1988), "Guerre et diffusion des nouvelles au Bas-Empire," *Ktema* 13: 125–35.

Chauvot, Alain (1998), *Opinions romaines face aux barbares au IVe siècle ap. J.-C.*, Paris, Boccard.

Cherry, David (1995), "Re-Figuring the Roman Epigraphic Habit," *Ancient History Bulletin* 9: 143–56.

Chesnut, Glenn F. (1978), "The Ruler and the Logos in Neopythagorean, Middle Platonist, and Late Stoic Philosophy," *ANRW* 2. 16. 2: 1310–32.

Chevalier, C. (1888), *Les Fouilles de Saint-Martin de Tours*, Tours, Péricat.

Chevallier, Raymond (1976), *Roman Roads*, Berkeley and Los Angeles, University of California Press.

Chitty, Derwas (1966), *The Desert a City: An Introduction to the Study of Egyptian and Palestinian Monasticism under the Christian Empire*, Oxford, Blackwell.

Choat, Malcolm (2002), "The Development and Usage of Terms for 'Monk' in Late Antique Egypt," *Jahrbuch für Antike und Christentum* 45: 5–23.

Choat, Malcolm, and Gardner, Iain (2003), "O.Douch I 49," *Zeitschrift für Papyrologie und Epigraphik* 143: 143–6.

Christ, Karl (ed.) (1970), *Der Untergang des Römischen Reiches*, Darmstadt, Wissenschaftliche Buchgesellschaft.

Christ, Karl (1982), *Römische Geschichte und deutsche Geschichtswissenschaft*, Munich, Beck.

Christ, Karl (2006), *Klios Wandlungen: die deutsche Althistorie vom Neuhumanismus bis zur Gegenwart*, Munich, Beck.

Christensen, Arne Søby (2002), *Cassiodorus, Jordanes and the History of the Goths: Studies in a Migration Myth*, tr. Heidi Flegal, Copenhagen, Museum Tusculanum.

Christensen, Arthur E. E. (1944), *L'Iran sous les Sassanides*, 2nd edn., Copenhagen, Munksgaard.

Christian, David (1998), *A History of Russia, Central Asia, and Mongolia*, i: *Inner Eurasia from Prehistory to the Mongol Empire*, Oxford and Malden, MA, Blackwell.

Christie, Neil, and Loseby, Simon T. (eds.) (1996), *Towns in Transition: Urban Evolution in Late Antiquity and the Early Middle Ages*, Aldershot, Scolar Press.

Chrysos, Evangelos (1990), "Synodal Acta as Literary Products," in *L'Icône dans la théologie et l'art*, Études Théologiques de Chambésy 9, Chambésy-Genève, Centre Orthodoxe du Patriarchat Oecuménique, pp. 85–93.

Chrysos, Evangelos, and Schwarcz, Andreas (eds.) (1989), *Das Reich und die Barbaren*, Vienna, Böhlau.

Chrysos, Evangelos, and Wood, Ian (eds.) (1999), *East and West: Modes of Communication*, Leiden, Brill.

Chuvin, Pierre (1990), *A Chronicle of the Last Pagans*, tr. B. A. Archer, Cambridge, MA, Harvard University Press.

Cimma, Maria Rosa (1989), *L'episcopalis audientia nella costituzioni imperiali da Costantino a Giustiniano*, Turin, Giappichelli.

Clackson, Sarah (2004), "Papyrology and the Utilization of Coptic Sources," in Petra Sijpesteijn and Lennart Sundelin (eds.), *Papyrology and the History of Early Islamic Egypt*, Leiden, Brill, pp. 21–44.

Clark, Elizabeth A. (1979), *Jerome, Chrysostom, and Friends: Essays and Translations*, New York, Edwin Mellen.

Clark, Elizabeth A. (tr.) (1984), *The Life of Melania the Younger: Introduction, Translation, and Commentary*, New York, Edwin Mellen.

Clark, Elizabeth A. (1986), *Ascetic Piety and Women's Faith: Essays on Late Ancient Christianity*, Lewiston, NY, Edwin Mellen.

Clark, Elizabeth A. (1990), "Patrons not Priests: Gender and Power in Late Ancient Christianity," *Gender and History* 2: 253–73.

Clark, Elizabeth A. (1992), *The Origenist Controversy: The Cultural Construction of an Early Christian Debate*, Princeton, NJ, Princeton University Press.

Clark, Elizabeth A. (1998), "The Lady Vanishes: Dilemmas of a Feminist Historian After 'the Linguistic Turn'," *Church History* 67: 1–31.

Clark, Elizabeth A. (2004), *History, Theory, Text: Historians and the Linguistic Turn*, Cambridge, MA, Harvard University Press.

Clark, Gillian (1993), *Women in Late Antiquity: Pagan and Christian Lifestyles*, Oxford, Clarendon Press.

Clark, Patricia (1998), "Women, Slaves, and the Hierarchies of Domestic Violence: The Family of St. Augustine," in Joshel and Murnaghan (1998: 109–29).

Clarke John R. (2003), *Art in the Lives of Ordinary Romans: Visual Representation and Non-Elite Viewers in Italy, 100 BC–AD 315*, Berkeley and Los Angeles, University of California Press.

Clarke, Graeme (ed.) (1990), *Reading the Past in Late Antiquity*, Rushcutters Bay, NSW, Australian National University Press.

Clarke, K. (1999), *Between Geography and History: Hellenistic Constructions of the Roman World*, Oxford, Clarendon Press.

Clarke, W. K. L. (1925), *The Ascetic Works of Saint Basil*, New York, Macmillan.

Clarysse, Willy (1987), "Greek Loan-Words in Demotic," in S. P. Vleeming (ed.), *Aspects of Demotic Lexicography*, Acts of the Second International Conference for Demotic Studies, Leiden, September 19–21, 1984, Leuven, Peeters, pp. 9–33.

Clarysse, Willy et al., *Leuven Database of Ancient Books*, http://lbab.arts.kuleuvan.ac.be

Claude, Dietrich (1964), "Untersuchungen zum frühfrankischen Comitat," *Zeitschrift der Savigny-Stiftung für Rechtsgechichte, Germanistische Abteilung* 81: 1–79.

Claude, Dietrich (1969), *Die byzantinische Stadt im 6. Jahrhundert*, Munich, Beck.

Clausi, Benedetto (2000), *Ridar voce all'antico padre: l'edizione erasmiana delle Lettere di Gerolamo*, Soveria Mannelli, Rubbettino.

Close-Brooks, J. (1983), "Dr Bersu's Excavations at Traprain Law, 1947," in O'Connor and Clarke (1983: 206–23).

Close-Brooks, J. (1987), "Comment on Traprain Law," *Scottish Archaeological Review* 4: 92–4.

Clover, Frank M. (1993), *The Late Roman West and the Vandals*, Aldershot and Brookfield, VT, Variorum.

Clover, Frank M., and Humphreys, R. S. (eds.) (1989), *Tradition and Innovation in Late Antiquity*, Madison, University of Wisconsin Press,

Cochrane, Charles N. (1940), *Christianity and Classical Culture: A Study of Thought and Action from Augustus to Augustine*, Oxford, Clarendon Press.

Cochrane, Eric (1981), *Historians and Historiography in the Italian Renaissance*, Chicago, University of Chicago Press.

Coella, R. L., Gill, M. J., Jenkens, L. A., and Lamers, P. (eds.) (1997), *Pratum Romanum: Richard Krautheimer zum 100. Geburtstag*, Wiesbaden, Reichert.

Cohen, Beth (ed.) (2000), *Not the Classical Ideal: Athens and the Construction of the Other in Greek Art*, Leiden, Brill.

Cohen, J. M. (1957), *The Life of Teresa of Avila by Herself*, Harmondsworth, Penguin.

Cohen, Jeremy (ed.) (1991), *Essential Papers on Judaism and Christianity in Conflict: From Late Antiquity to the Reformation*, New York, New York University Press.

Cohen, Shaye (1999), *The Beginnings of Jewishness: Boundaries, Varieties and Uncertainties*, Berkeley and Los Angeles, University of California Press.

Coleman, Christopher B. (tr.) (1922), *The Treatise of Lorenzo Valla on the Donation of Constantine*, New Haven, CT, Yale University Press.

Collinet, Paul (1925), *Histoire de l'école de droit de Beyrouth*, Paris, L. Tenin.

Colloquium on Hiberno-Roman Relations and Material Remains (1976), Proceedings of the Royal Irish Academy 76, Dublin, Royal Irish Academy.

Connolly, Hugh (tr.) (1929), *Didascalia Apostolorum*, Oxford, Clarendon Press.

Conrad, Lawrence I. (2000), "The Arabs," in Cameron, Ward-Perkins, and Whitby (2000: 678–700).

Conring, Barbara (2001), *Hieronymus als Briefschreiber: ein Beitrag zur spätantiken Epistolographie*, Tübingen, Mohr Siebeck.

Consolino, Franca Ela (1984), "Il significato dell'inventio crucis nel de obitu Theodosii," *Annali della Facoltà di Lettere e Filosofia dell'Università di Siena* 5: 161–80.

Conybeare, Catherine (2000), *Paulinus Noster: Self and Symbols in the Letters of Paulinus of Nola*, Oxford, Oxford University Press.

Conybeare, Catherine (2005), "Spaces between Letters: Augustine's Correspondence with Women," in Olson and Kerby-Fulton (2005: 57–71).

Cook, Arthur Bernhard (1914–40), *Zeus: A Study of Ancient Religion*, 3 vols., Cambridge, Cambridge University Press.

Cooley, Alison E. (ed.) (2002), *Becoming Roman, Writing Latin? Literacy and Epigraphy in the Roman West*, Portsmouth, RI, Journal of Roman Archaeology.

Cooney, Gabriel (2000), "Reading a Landscape Manuscript: A Review of Progress in Prehistoric Settlement Studies in Ireland," in Barry (2000: 1–49).

Cooney, Gabriel, and Grogan, Eoin (1994), *Irish Prehistory: A Social Perspective*, Dublin, Wordwell.

Cooper, Kate (1992), "Insinuations of Womanly Influence: An Aspect of the Christianization of the Roman Aristocracy," *Journal of Roman Studies* 82: 150–64.

Cooper, Kate (1996), *The Virgin and the Bride: Idealized Womanhood in Late Antiquity*, Cambridge, MA, Harvard University Press.

Cooper, Kate (1999), "The Martyr, the *Matrona*, and the Bishop: The Matron Lucina and the Politics of Martyr Cult in Fifth- and Sixth-Century Rome," *Early Medieval Europe* 8: 219–317.

Cooper, Kate (2005a), "The Household and the Desert: Monastic and Biological Communities in the *Lives* of Melania the Younger," in Mulder-Bakker and Wogan-Browne (2005: 11–35).

Cooper, Kate (2005b), "The Virgin as Social Icon," in van Dijk and Nip (2005: 9–24).

Cooper, Kate (2007), *The Fall of the Roman Household*, Cambridge, Cambridge University Press.

Cooper, Kate, and Hillner, Julia (eds.) (2007), *Religion, Dynasty, and Patronage in Early Christian Rome, 300–900*, Cambridge, Cambridge University Press.

Cooper, Kate, and Leyser, Conrad (2000), "The Gender of Grace: Impotence, Servitude, and Manliness in the Fifth-Century West," *Gender and History* 12: 536–51.

Corbier, Mireille (2005), "Usage publique de l'écriture affiché à Rome," in A. Bresson, A.-M. Cocula, and C. Pébarthe (eds.), *L'Écriture publique du pouvoir*, Paris, Ausonius Éditions, pp. 183–93.

Corcoran, Simon (1996), *The Empire of the Tetrarchs: Imperial Proncouncements and Government, AD 284–324*, Oxford, Clarendon Press; New York, Oxford University Press; rev. edn., Oxford and New York, Clarendon Press, 2000.

Corradini, Richard (2006), "Die Annales Fuldenses: Identitätskonstruktionen im ostfränkischen Raum am Ende der Karolingerzeit," in Corradini et al. (2006).

Corradini, Richard, Meens, Rob, Pössel, Christina, and Shaw, Philip (eds.) (2006), *Texts and Identities in the Early Middle Ages*, Vienna, Österreichischen Akademie der Wissenschaft.

Cortesi, Alessandro (1984), "Varrone e Tertulliano," *Augustinianum* 24: 349–65.

Coşkun, Altay (2004), "Der *Comes* Romanus, der Heermeister Theodosius und die drei letzte Akte der 'Lepcis-Magna-Affair' (A. 373–377)," *Antiquité Tardive*, 12: 293–308.

Costambeys, Marios (2001), "Burial Topography and the Power of the Church in Fifth- and Sixth-Century Rome," *Proceedings of the British School at Rome* 69: 169–89.

Coulston, Jon (2001), "Transport and Travel on the Column of Trajan," in Adams and Laurence (2001: 106–37).

Coulter, J. A. (1976), *The Literary Microcosm: Theories of Interpretation of the Later Neoplatonists*, Leiden, Brill.

Courcelle, Pierre (1948), *Histoire littéraire des grandes invasions germaniques*, Paris, Hachette.

Courtois, Christian (1955), *Les Vandales et l'Afrique*, Paris, Arts et Métiers Graphiques.

Couturier, Guy, Charron, André, and Durand, Guy (eds.) (1985), *Essais sur la mort: travaux d'un séminaire de recherche sur la mort*, Montréal, Fides.

Cox, Patricia (1983), *Biography in Late Antiquity: A Quest for the Holy Man*, Berkeley and Los Angeles, University of California Press.

Cox Miller, Patricia (1993), "The Blazing Body: Ascetic Desire in Jerome's Letter to Eustochium," *Journal of Early Christian Studies* 1: 21–45.

Cracco Ruggini, Lellia (1987), "*Felix temporum reparatio*: realtà socio-economiche in movimento durante un ventennio di regno (Costanzo II Augusto, 337–361 D.C.)," *Entretiens sur l'Antiquité Classique* 34: 179–249.

Cracco Ruggini, Lellia (1988), "All'ombra di Momigliano: Peter Brown e la mutazione del tardoantico," *Rivista Storica Italiana* 100: 739–67.

Cracco Ruggini, Lellia (1998a), "La fisionomia sociale del clero e il consolidarsi delle istituzioni ecclesiastiche nel Norditalia (IV–VI secolo)," in *Morfologie sociali e culturali in Europa fra Tarda Antichità e Alto Medioevo (Spoleto, 3–9 Aprile 1997)*, Spoleto, Centro Italiano di Studi sull'Alto Medioevo, ii: 851–901.

Cracco Ruggini, Lellia (1998b), "Il 397: l'anno della morte di Ambrogio," in Pizzolato and Rizzi (1998: 5–29).

Cracco Ruggini, Lellia (1999), "Prêtre et foncionnaire: l'essor d'un modèle épiscopal aux IVe-Ve siècles," *Antiquité Tardive* 7: 175–86.

Cracco Ruggini, Lellia (2002), "Il profeta Eliseo, modello episcopale fra IV e V secolo," in Maritano (2002: 239–53).

Craddock, Patricia (ed.) (1972), *The English Essays of Edward Gibbon*, Oxford, Clarendon Press.

Craddock, Patricia (1982), *Young Edward Gibbon, Gentleman of Letters*, Baltimore, MD, Johns Hopkins University Press.

Craddock, Patricia (1987), *Edward Gibbon: A Reference Guide*, Boston, MA, G. K. Hall.

Craddock, Patricia (1989), *Edward Gibbon, Luminous Historian, 1772–1794*, Baltimore, MD, Johns Hopkins University Press.

Crawford, Barbara E. (ed.) (1994), *Scotland in Dark Age Europe*, St. Andrews, University of St. Andrews.

Crawford, Barbara E. (ed.) (1996), *Scotland in Dark Age Britain*, Aberdeen, Scottish Cultural Press.

Cribiore, Raffaella (1996), *Writing, Teachers, and Students in Graeco-Roman Egypt*, Atlanta, GA, Scholars Press.

Cribiore, Raffaella (1999), "Greek and Coptic Education in Late Antique Egypt," in Emmel et al. (1999, ii: 279–86).

Cribiore, Raffaella (2001), *Gymnastics of the Mind: Greek Education in Hellenistic and Roman Egypt*, Princeton, NJ, Princeton University Press.

Cribiore, Raffaella (2003), "Libanius's Letters of Evaluation of Students," in *L'Épistolographie et la poésie épigrammatique: projets actuel et questions de méthodologie. Actes de la 16e table ronde du XXe Congrès international des Études Byzantines, college de France, Sorbonne, Paris, 19–25 Août 2001*, Paris, Centre d'Études Byzantines, Néo-Helléniques et Sud-Est Européennes, École des Hautes Études en Sciences Sociales, pp. 11–20.

Cribiore, Raffaella (2003–4), "Latin Literacy in Egypt," *KODAI* 13/14: 111–18.

Cribiore, Raffaella (2007), *The School of Libanius in Late Antique Antioch*, Princeton, NJ, Princeton University Press.

Croke, Brian (1983), "A.D. 476: The Manufacture of a Turning Point," *Chiron* 13: 81–119.

Croke, Brian (1987), "Cassiodorus and the *Getica* of Jordanes," *Classical Philology* 82: 117–34.

Croke, Brian (1990a), "Malalas, the Man, and His Work," in Jeffreys, Croke, and Scott (1990: 1–26).

Croke, Brian (1990b), "Theodor Mommsen and the Later Roman Empire," *Chiron* 20: 159–89.

Croke, Brian (2001), *Count Marcellinus and His Chronicle*, Oxford, Oxford University Press.

Croke, Brian (2005), "Justinian's Constantinople," in Maas (2005: 60–86).

Croke, Brian, and Harries, Jill (1982), *Religious Conflict in Fourth-Century Rome: A Documentary Study*, Sydney, Sydney University Press.

Crone, Patricia (1980), *Slaves on Horses: The Evolution of the Islamic Polity*, Cambridge, Cambridge University Press.

Crone, Patricia (1987), *Meccan Trade and the Rise of Islam*, Cambridge, Cambridge University Press.

Crone, Patricia (1994a), "The First-Century Concept of *Hijra*," *Arabica* 41: 352–87.

Crone, Patricia (1994b), "Two Legal Problems Bearing on the Early History of the Qur'ân," *Jerusalem Studies in Arabic and Islam* 18: 1–37.

Crone, Patricia (2004), *Medieval Islamic Political Thought*, Edinburgh, Edinburgh University Press.

Crone, Patricia, and Hinds, Martin (1986), *God's Caliph: Religious Authority in the First Century of Islam*, Cambridge, Cambridge University Press.

Crook, John A. (1995), *Legal Advocacy in the Roman World*, Ithaca, NY, Cornell University Press.

Crum, Walter Ewing (ed.) (1905), *Catalogue of the Coptic Manuscripts in the British Museum*, London, British Museum.

Crum, Walter Ewing (ed.) (1909), *Catalogue of the Coptic Manuscripts in the Collection of the John Rylands Library*, Manchester, Manchester University Press.

Crum, Walter Ewing (1927), "Some Further Meletian Documents," *Journal of Egyptian Archaeology* 13: 19–26.

Crum, Walter Ewing (1934), "Un psaume en dialect d'Akhmim," in *Mélanges Maspero*, ii: *Orient grec, romain et byzantin*, Cairo, Institut Français d'Archéologie Orientale, pp. 73–6.

Cumont, Franz (1918), "La Triple commémoration des morts," *Comptes Rendus de l'Académie des Inscriptions et Belles-Lettres*, 278–94.

Cunliffe, Barry (2001), *Facing the Ocean: The Atlantic and Its Peoples*, Oxford and New York, Oxford University Press.

Cunningham, Mary B., and Allen, Pauline (eds.) (1998), *Preacher and Audience: Studies in Early Christian and Byzantine Homiletics*, Leiden, Brill.

Curran, John (1994), "Moving Statues in Late Antique Rome: Problems of Perspective," *Art History* 17: 46–68.

Curran, John (2000), *Pagan City and Christian Capital: Rome in the Fourth Century*, Oxford, Clarendon Press.

Cürsgen, Dirk (2002), *Die Rationalität des Mythischen: der philosophische Mythos bei Platon und seine Exegese im Neuplatonismus*, Berlin, de Gruyter.

Curta, Florin (2001), *The Making of the Slavs: History and Archaeology of the Lower Danube Region, c. 500–700*, Cambridge, Cambridge University Press.

Cutler, Anthony (1968), "The De Signis of Nicetas Choniates: A Reappraisal," *American Journal of Archaeology* 72: 113–18.

Cuvigny, Hélène, and Wagner, Guy (eds.) (1986–92), *Les Ostraca grecs de Douch (O. Douch)*, fasc. i–iii, Cairo, Institut Français d'Archéologie Orientale.

Dabrowa, E. (ed.) (1994), *The Roman and Byzantine Army in the East*, Krakow, Jagiellonian University Press.

Dabrowa, E. (ed.) (1998), *Ancient Iran and the Mediterranean World*, Krakow, Jagiellonian University Press.

Dagron, Gilbert (1970), "Les Moines et le ville: le monachisme à Constantinople jusqu'au concile de Chalcédoine (451)," *Travaux et Mémoires* 4: 229–76.

Dagron, Gilbert (1974), *Naissance d'une capitale: Constantinople et ses institutions de 330 à 431*, Paris, Presses Universitaires de France.

Dagron, Gilbert (1977), "Le Christianisme dans la ville byzantine," *Dumbarton Oaks Papers* 31: 1–25.

Dagron, Gilbert (1984), *Constantinople imaginaire: études sur le recueil de Patria*, Paris, Presses Universitaires de France.

Dagron, Gilbert (1989), "Constantinople: les sanctuaires et l'organisation de la vie religieuse," in Duval (1989a: 1069–85).

Dagron, Gilbert (1991), *Costantinopoli: Nascita di una capitale (330–451)*, tr. Aldo Serafini, Turin, Einaudi.

Dagron, Gilbert (2003), *Emperor and Priest: The Imperial Office in Byzantium*, tr. Jean Birrell, Cambridge, Cambridge University Press.

Daley, Brian E. (1991), *The Hope of the Early Church: A Handbook of Patristic Eschatology*, Cambridge: Cambridge University Press.

Daley, Brian E. (1993), "Position and Patronage in the Early Church: The Original Meaning of 'Primacy of Honour'," *Journal of Theological Studies* 44: 529–53.

Damminger, F. (1998), "Dwellings, Settlements and Settlement Patterns in Merovingian Southwest Germany and Adjacent Areas," in Wood (1998: 33–89).

Daniélou, Jean (1958), *Théologie du judéo-christianisme*, Paris, Desclée.

Dark, Ken (2002), *Britain and the End of the Roman Empire*, Stroud, Tempus.

D'Arms, John (2000), "Three New Inscriptions from the Collegium of the Augustales," *Journal of Roman Studies* 90: 126–44.

Daryaee, T. (2003), "The Persian Gulf in Late Antiquity," *Journal of World History* 14: 1–16.

Daube, David (1969), *Roman Law: Linguistic, Social and Philosophical Aspects*, Edinburgh, Edinburgh University Press.

Dauge, Yves (1981), *Le Barbare: recherches sur la conception romaine de la barbarie et de la civilisation*, Brussels, Latomus.

Daur, K.-M. (ed.) (1992), *Liber ad Gregoriam [Ad Gregoriam in palatio]*, CC, ser. lat. 25A, Turnhout, Brepols.

Davies, Jason P. (2004), *Rome's Religious History: Livy, Tacitus and Ammianus on Their Gods*, Cambridge, Cambridge University Press.

Davies, Stephen (2001), *The Cult of St. Thecla: A Tradition of Women's Piety in Late Antiquity*, Oxford, Oxford University Press.

Davies, Stevan L. (1980), *The Revolt of the Widows: The Social World of the Apocryphal Acts*, Carbondale, Southern Illinois University Press.

Dawes, Elizabeth, and Baynes, Norman H. (tr.) (1996), *Three Byzantine Saints*, Crestwood, NY, St. Vladimir's Seminary Press. First published Oxford, Blackwell, 1948.

De Blaauw, Sible (1996), "Das Fastigium der Lateranbasilika: schöpferische Innovation, Unikat oder Paradigma?" in Brenk et al. (1996: 53–65).

De Blaauw, Sible (2001), "Imperial Connotations in Roman Church Interiors: The Significance and Effect of the Lateran *fastigium*," in Brandt et al. (2001: 137–46).

Deckers, Johannes, Mietke, Gabriele, and Weiland, Albrecht (1994), *Die Katakombe 'Commodilla': Repertorium der Malereien*, 3 vols., Vatican City, Pontificio Istituto di Archeologia Cristiana.

De Giovanni, Lucio (2001), *Diritto romano tardoantico*, 5th edn., Naples, Jovene Editore.

De Halleux, André (1993), "La Première session du concile d' Éphèse (22 Juin 431)," *Ephemerides Theologicae Lovanienses* 69: 48–87.

Deichmann, Friedrich Wilhelm (1975), *Die Spolien in der spätantiken Architektur*, Munich, Bayrischen Akademie der Wissenschaften.

DeLaura, David J. (1969), *Hebrew and Hellene in Victorian England: Newman, Arnold, and Pater*, Austin, University of Texas Press.

Delehaye, Hippolyte (1910), "Les Premiers *Libelli miraculorum*," *Analecta Bollandiana* 22: 427–34.

D'Elia, Salvatore (1967), *Il Basso impero nella cultura moderna dal Quattrocento ad oggi*, Naples, Liguori.

Delmaire, Roland (1991), "Les 'lettres d'exil' de Jean Chrysostome: études de chronologie et de prosopographie," *Recherches Augustiniennes* 25: 71–180.

Delmaire, Roland, and Rougé, Jean (2005), *Les Lois religieuses des empereurs romains de Constantin à Théodose II (312–438)*, i: *Code Théodosien XVI*, Paris, Éditions du Cerf.

Delogu, Paolo (2002), *An Introduction to Medieval History*, tr. Matthew Moran, London, Duckworth.

De Lubac, Henri (1998), *Medieval Exegesis*, i: *The Four Senses of Scripture*, tr. Marc Sebanc, Grand Rapids, MI, Eerdmans.

Demandt, Alexander (1970), "Magister militum," *RE* suppl. 12: 553–790.

Demandt, Alexander (1984), *Der Fall Roms: die Auflösung des Römischen Reiches im Urteil der Nachwelt*, Munich, Beck.

Demoen, Kristoffel (1998), "The Theologian on Icons? Byzantine and Modern Claims and Distortions," *Byzantinische Zeitschrift* 91: 1–19.

Demoen, Kristoffel (2000), "Expliquer Homère par Homère: Nicéphore de Constantinople philologue et rhéteur," in *Corpus Nazianzenum*, viii/1: *Studia Nazianzenica*, ed. B. Coulie, *CC*, ser. Graec. 41, Turnhout, Brepols, pp. 147–73.

Demougin, Ségolène (1994), *La Mémoire perdue: à la recherche des archives oubliées, privées ou publiques, de la Rome antique*, Paris, Presses de la Sorbonne.

Dench, Emma (1995), *From Barbarians to New Men: Greek, Roman, and Modern Perceptions of People of the Central Apennines*, Oxford, Oxford University Press.

Dench, Emma (2005), *Romulus' Asylum: Roman Identities from the Age of Alexander to the Age of Hadrian*, Oxford, Oxford University Press.

Dennison, Walter, and Morey, Charles Rufus (1918), *Studies in East Christian and Roman Art*, London and New York, Macmillan.

Denny, Frederick M., and Taylor, Rodney L. (eds.) (1985), *The Holy Book in Comparative Perspective*, Columbia, University of South Carolina Press.

De Paor, Máire, and De Paor, Liam (1958), *Early Christian Ireland*, New York, Praeger.

Depauw, Mark (1994), "The Demotic Epistolary Formulae," *Egitto e vicino Oriente* 17: 87–94.

Depauw, Mark (1997), *A Companion to Demotic Studies*, Brussels, Fondation Égyptologique Reine Élisabeth.

Deroux, Carl (ed.) (1998), *Studies in Latin Literature and Roman History*, ix, Brussels, Latomus.

Derrida, Jacques (1988), *Limited Inc.*, Evanston, IL, Northwestern University Press.

De Ste Croix, G. E. M. (1981), *The Class Struggle in the Ancient Greek World from the Archaic Age to the Arab Conquests*, Ithaca, NY, Cornell University Press.

Descoeudres, Jean-Paul (ed.) (2001), *Ostia: port e porte de la Rome antique, Musée Rath Genève*, Geneva, Georg, Musée d'Art et d'Histoire.

Descombes, Françoise (1985), *Recueil des inscriptions chrétiennes de la Gaule*, xv: *Viennoise du Nord*, Paris, CNRS.

Devisch, Renaat (1973), "Le Problème de la sacralisation et de la désacralisation dans une religion traditionelle: essai d'une approche théorique," *Canadian Journal of African Studies* 7: 77–95.

Devos, P. (1964), "Le Mystérieux épisode final de la Vita Gregorii de Jean Diacre. Formose et sa fuite de Rome," *Analecta Bollandiana* 82: 356–81.

Dewar, Michael (1994), "Hannibal and Alaric in the Later Poems of Claudian," *Mnemosyne* 47: 349–72.

Dickie, Matthew W. (2001), *Magic and Magicians in the Greco-Roman World*, London and New York, Routledge.

Diebner, Bernd, and Kasser, Rodolphe (eds.) (1989), *Hamburger Papyrus bil. 1: Die alttestamentlichen Texte des Papyrus bilinguis 1 der Staats- und Universitätsbibliothek Hamburg*, Geneva, P. Cramer.

Diehl, Ernest (1961), *Inscriptiones Latinae Christianae Veteres*, 2nd edn., 3 vols., Berlin, Weidmann.

Dieleman, Jacco (2005), *Priests, Tongues, and Rites: The London-Leiden Magical Manuscripts and Translation in Egyptian Ritual (100–300 CE)*, Leiden, Brill.

Diesenberger, Maximilian (2005), "Rom als virtueller Raum der Märtyrer: zur gedanklichen Aneignung der Roma Suburbana in bayerischen Handschriften um 800," in Vavra (2005: 1–24).

Diesenberger, Maximilian (2006), "How Collections Shape the Texts: Rewriting and Rearranging Passions in Carolingian Bavaria," in Heinzelmann (2006: 195–224).

Diesenberger, Maximilian, and Niederkorn-Bruck, Meta (eds.) (forthcoming), *Hagiographische Handschriften im Mittelalter zwischen Wiederschrift und Niederschrift*, Vienna, Österreichischen Akademie der Wissenschaft.

Diesner, Hans J. (1968), "Zum vandalischen Post- und Verkehrswesen," *Philologus* 112: 282–7.

Dietz, Maribel (2005), *Wandering Monks, Virgins, and Pilgrims: Ascetic Travel in the Mediterranean World, A.D. 300–800*, University Park, Pennsylvania State University Press.

Dignas, Beate, and Winter, Engelbert (2007), *Rome and Persia in Late Antiquity: Neighbours and Rivals*, Cambridge, Cambridge University Press.

Dijkstra, Jitse, and van Dijk, Mathilde (eds.) (2006), *The Encroaching Desert: Egyptian Hagiography and the Medieval West*, Leiden, Brill.

Dilke, Oswald A. W. (1985), *Greek and Roman Maps*, Ithaca, NY, Cornell University Press.

Dill, Samuel (1899), *Roman Society in the Last Century of the Western Empire*, London, Macmillan.

Dill, Samuel (1926), *Roman Society in Gaul in the Merovingian Age*, London, Macmillan.

Dilts, Mervin R., and Kennedy, George A. (eds.) (1997), *Two Greek Rhetorical Treatises from the Roman Empire: Introduction, Text, and Translation of the Arts of Rhetoric Attributed to Anonymous Seguerianus and to Apsines of Gadara*, Leiden, Brill.

Di Paola, Lucietta (1999), *Viaggi, trasporti e istituzioni: studi sul cursus publicus*, Messina, Dipartimento di Scienze dell' Antichità dell'Università degli Studi di Messina.

Di Segni, Leah (1995), "The Involvement of Local, Municipal and Provincial Authorities in Urban Building in Late Antique Palestine and Arabia," in John H. Humphrey (ed.), *The Roman and Byzantine Near East: Some Recent Archaeological Research*, i, Ann Arbor, MI, Journal of Roman Archaeology, pp. 312–32.

Di Segni, Leah (1999), "Epigraphic Documentation on Building in the Provinces of Palaestina and Arabia, 4th–7th c.," in John H. Humphrey (ed.), *The Roman and Byzantine Near East: Some Recent Archaeological Research*, ii, Portsmouth, RI, Journal of Roman Archaeology, pp. 149–78.

Dixon, Suzanne (1988), *The Roman Mother*, Norman, University of Oklahoma Press.

Dobbelaere, Karel (1981), "Secularization: A Multi-Dimensional Concept," *Current Sociology* 29: 1–213.

Dobschütz, Ernst (ed.) (1912), *Das Decretum Gelasianum de libris recipiendis et non recipiendis*, Texte und Untersuchungen 38, Leipzig, Hinrichs.

Dodds, E. R. (1965), *Pagan and Christian in an Age of Anxiety: Some Aspects of Religious Experience from Marcus Aurelius to Constantine*, Cambridge, Cambridge University Press.

Dodgeon, Michael H., and Lieu, Samuel N. C. (1991), *The Roman Eastern Frontier and the Persian Wars A.D. 226–363: A Documentary History*, London, Routledge.

Dolbeau, François (ed.) (1996), *Augustin d'Hippo: vingt-six sermons au peuple d'Afrique*, Collection des Études Augustiniennes, Série Antiquité 147, Paris, Études Augustiniennes.

Donati, Angela (ed.) (1988), *La terza età dell' epigrafia*, Faenza, Fratelli Lega.

Donati, Angela (2000), *Pietro e Paolo: la storia, il culto, la memoria nei primi secoli*, Milan, Electa.

Donner, Fred M. (1981), *The Early Islamic Conquests*, Princeton, NJ, Princeton University Press.

Donner, Fred M. (1998), *Narratives of Islamic Origins: The Beginning of Islamic Historical Writing*, Princeton, NJ, Darwin Press.

Dopsch, Alfons (1918–20), *Wirtschaftliche und soziale Grundlagen der europäischen Kulturéntwicklung*, 2 vols., Vienna, Seidel, 2nd rev. edn., Vienna 1923–24.

Dowden, Ken (2000), *European Paganism: The Realities of Cult from Antiquity to the Middle Ages*, London, Routledge.

Downey, G. (1961), *A History of Antioch in Syria from Seleucus to the Arab Conquest*, Princeton, NJ, Princeton University Press.

Drake, Harold A. (2000), *Constantine and the Bishops: The Politics of Intolerance*, Baltimore, MD, Johns Hopkins University Press.

Drescher, J. (1947), *Three Coptic Legends*, Cairo, Imprimerie de l'Institut Français d'Archéologie Orientale.

Drijvers, H. J. W. (1980), *Cults and Beliefs at Edessa*, Leiden, Brill.

Drijvers, H. J. W. (1982), "The Persistence of Pagan Cults and Practices in Christian Syria," in Nina Garsoïan, Thomas Mathews, and Robert Thompson (eds.), *East of Byzantium: Syria and Armenia in the Formative Period*, Washington, DC, Dumbarton Oaks, pp. 35–43.

Drijvers, H. J. W. (1985), "Jews and Christians at Edessa," *Journal of Jewish Studies* 36: 88–102.

Drijvers, H. J. W. (1999), "Rabbula, Bishop of Edessa: Spiritual Authority and Secular Power," in Jan Willem Drijvers and John Watt (eds.), *Portraits of Spiritual Authority*, Leiden, Brill, pp. 139–54.

Drijvers, Jan Willem (2002), "Heraclius and the *Restitutio Crucis*: Notes on Symbolism and Ideology," in Reinink and Stolte (2002: 175–90).

Drijvers, Jan Willem (2006), "Ammianus Marcellinus' Image of Sasanian Society," in Wiesehöfer and Huyse (2006: 45–69).

Drijvers, Jan Willem, and Hunt, David (eds.) (1999), *The Late Roman World and Its Historian: Interpreting Ammianus Marcellinus*, London, Routledge.

Drinkwater, John F. (1987), *The Gallic Empire: Separatism and Continuity in the North-Western Provinces of the Roman Empire A.D. 260–274*, Wiesbaden, Steiner Verlag.

Drinkwater, John F. (1997), "Julian and the Franks and Valentinian I and the Alamanni: Ammianus on Roman–German relations," *Francia* 24: 1–16.

Drinkwater, John F., and Elton, Hugh (eds.) (1992), *Fifth-Century Gaul: A Crisis of Identity?* Cambridge, Cambridge University Press.

Driscoll, Stephen T. (1988a), "Power and Authority in Early Historic Scotland: Pictish Symbol Stones and Other Documents," in John Gledhill, Barbara Bender, and Mogens Trolle Larsen (eds.), *State and Society: The Emergence and Development of Social Hierarchy and Political Centralization*, London and Boston, MA, Unwin Hyman, pp. 215–36.

Driscoll, Stephen T. (1988b), "The Relationship between History and Archaeology: Artifacts, Documents and Power," in Driscoll and Nieke (1988: 162–87).

Driscoll, Stephen T., and Nieke, Margaret R. (eds.) (1988), *Power and Politics in Early Medieval Britain and Ireland*, Edinburgh, Edinburgh University Press.

Drobner, Hubertus R. (2000), "The Chronology of St. Augustine's *Sermones ad populum*," *Augustinian Studies* 31: 211–18.

Drobner, Hubertus R. (2003), "The Chronology of St. Augustine's *Sermones ad populum* II: Sermons 5 to 8," *Augustinian Studies* 34: 49–66.

Drobner, Hubertus R. (2004), "The Chronology of Augustine's *Sermones ad populum* III: On Christmas Day," *Augustinian Studies* 35: 43–53.

Duchesne, Louis (ed.) (1886), *Le Liber Pontificalis: Texte, introduction et commentaire*, Paris, Ernest Thorin.

Duchesne-Guillemin, J. (1983), "Zoroastrian Religion," in Yarshater (1983, ii: 866–908).

Dulaey, Martine (2002), "L'Apprentissage de l'exégèse biblique par Augustin: (I) Dans les années 386–389," *Revue des Etudes Augustiniennes* 48: 267–95.

Dumont, Louis (1980), *Homo Hierarchicus: The Caste System and Its Implications*, tr. Mark Sainsbury, Louis Dumont, and Basia Gulati, Chicago, Chicago University Press.

Dumont, Louis (1983), *Affinity as a Value: Marriage Alliance in South India, with Comparative Essays on Australia*, Chicago, Chicago University Press.

Duncan-Jones, Richard (1974), *The Economy of the Roman Empire: Quantitative Studies*, Cambridge, Cambridge University Press.

Duncan-Jones, Richard (1990), *Structure and Scale in the Roman Economy*, Cambridge and New York, Cambridge University Press.

Durliat, Jean (1995a), "Épigraphie et société: problèmes de méthode," in Cavallo and Mango (1995: 169–96).

Durliat, Jean (1995b), "Épigraphie chrétienne de langue latine," in Cavallo and Mango (1995: 227–66).

Dutton, Paul (1994), *The Politics of Dreaming in the Carolingian Empire*, Lincoln, University of Nebraska Press.

Duval, Noël (1982), "L'Urbanisme de Sufetula = Sbeitla en Tunisie," in *ANRW* 2. 10. 2: 596–632.

Duval, Noël (ed.) (1989a), *Actes du XI congrès international d'archéologie chrétienne: Lyon, Vienne, Grenoble, Genève et Aoste, 1986, 21–28 Septembre*, Vatican City, Pontificio Istituto di Archeologia Cristiana.

Duval, Noël (1989b), "Une nouvelle édition du Dossier du Donatisme avec traduction Française," *Revue des Études Augustiniennes* 35: 171–9.

Duval, Yves-Marie (1977), "Des Lupercales de Constantinople aux Lupercales de Rome," *Revue des Études Latines* 55: 222–70.

Duval, Yvette (1982), *Loca sanctorum Africae: le culte des martyres en Afrique du IVe au VIIe siècle*, 2 vols., Rome, École Française de Rome.

Duval, Yvette (1988), *Auprès des saints corps et âme: l'inhumation "ad sanctos" dans la chrétienté d'Orient et d'Occident du IIIe au VIIe siècle*, Paris, Études Augustiniennes.

Duval, Yvette, and Picard, J.-Ch. (eds.) (1986), *L'Inhumation privilégiée du IVe au VIIIe siècle en Occident*, Actes du colloque tenu à Créteil, 16–18 Mars 1984, Paris, Boccard.

Dyson, Stephen L. (2003), *The Roman Countryside*, London, Duckworth.

Eadie, John W. (1967), *The Breviarium of Festus: A Critical Edition with Historical Commentary*, London, Athlone Press.

Easton, Burton Scott (1962), *The Apostolic Tradition of Hippolytus*, Cambridge, Cambridge University Press.

Ebbeler, Jennifer (2003), "Caesar's Letters and the Ideology of Literary History," *Helios* 30: 3–19.

Ebbeler, Jennifer (forthcoming), "Mixed Messages: The Play of Epistolary Codes in Two Late Antique Latin Correspondences," in Morello and Morrison (forthcoming).

Eck, Werner (1978), "Der Einfluß der konstantinischen Wende auf die Auswahl der Bischöfe im 4. und 5. Jahrhundert," *Chiron* 8: 561–85.

Eck, Werner (1998), "Documenti amministrativi: pubblicazione e mezzo di autorappresentazione," in Paci (1998: 343–66).

Edwards, Kevin J., and Ralston, Ian B. M. (eds.) (2003), *Scotland After the Ice Age: Environment, Archaeology and History, 8000 BC–AD 1000*, Edinburgh, Edinburgh University Press.

Edwards, Mark J. (1993), "A Portrait of Plotinus," *Classical Quarterly* 43: 480–90.

Edwards, Mark J., and Swain, Simon (eds.) (1997), *Portraits: Biographical Representation in the Greek and Latin Literature of the Roman Empire*, Oxford, Clarendon Press; New York, Oxford University Press.

Edwards, Nancy (1990), *The Archaeology of Early Medieval Ireland*, Philadelphia, University of Pennsylvania Press.

Effros, Bonnie (2002), *Caring for Body and Soul: Burial and the Afterlife in the Merovingian World*, University Park, Pennsylvania State University Press.

Effros, Bonnie (2003), *Merovingian Mortuary Archaeology and the Making of the Early Middle Ages*, Berkeley and Los Angeles, University of California Press.

Efthymiadis, Stephanos (2000), "Eisagôgê," in *Phôtios patriarchês Kônstantinoupoleôs, Bibliothêkê, hosa tês historias anthologia: Eisagôgê-Metaphrasê-Scholia Stephanos Efthymiadês*, Athens, Ekdoseis Kanakê, pp. 7–44.

Egberts, A., Muhs, Brian, and Van der Vliet, Jacques (eds.) (2002), *Perspectives on Panopolis: An Egyptian Town from Alexander the Great to the Arab Conquest*, Leiden, Brill.

Egger, Christoph, and Weigl, Herwig (eds.) (2000), *Text–Schrift–Codex: quellenkundliche Arbeiten aus den Institut für Österreichische Geschichtsforschung*, Vienna, Oldenbourg.

Ehrensperger-Katz, I. (1969), "Les Représentations des villes fortifiés dans l'art paléochretien et leurs dérivés byzantines," *Cahiers Archéologiques* 19: 1–27.

Ehrman, Bart (1993), *The Orthodox Corruption of Scripture: The Effect of Early Christological Controversies on the Text of the New Testament*, Oxford, Oxford University Press.

Elad, Amikam (1992), "Why did 'Abd al-Malik Build the Dome of the Rock? A Re-examination of the Muslim Sources," in Raby and Johns (1992: 33–57).

Elad, Amikam (1995), *Medieval Jerusalem and Islamic Worship*, Leiden, Brill.

Ellen, J. H. (1993), *The Ancient Library of Alexandria and Early Christian Theological Development*, Claremont, CA, Institute for Antiquity and Christianity.

Ellis, Linda, and Kidner, Frank L. (eds.) (2004), *Travel, Communication and Geography in Late Antiquity: Sacred and Profane*, Aldershot, Ashgate.

Elm, Eva (2003), *Die Macht der Weisheit: das Bild des Bischofs in der Vita Augustini des Possidius und anderen spätantiken und frühmittelalterlichen Bischofsviten*, Leiden, Brill.

Elm, Susanna (1994), *"Virgins of God": The Making of Asceticism in Late Antiquity*, Oxford and New York, Oxford University Press.

Elm, Susanna (1998), "Introduction," *Journal of Early Christian Studies* 6: 343–51.

Elm, Susanna, Rebillard, Éric, and Romano, Antonella (eds.) (2000), *Orthodoxie, christianisme, histoire*, Rome, École Française de Rome.

Elsner, Jaś (1995), *Art and the Roman Viewer: The Transformation of Art from the Pagan World to Christianity*, Cambridge, Cambridge University Press.

Elsner, Jaś (1996), *Art and Text in Roman Culture*, Cambridge, Cambridge University Press.

Elsner, Jaś (1998), *Imperial Rome and Christian Triumph: The Art of the Roman Empire AD 100–450*, Oxford and New York, Oxford University Press.

Elsner, Jaś (2000), "The *Itinerarium Burdigalense*: Politics and Salvation in the Geography of Constantine's Empire," *Journal of Roman Studies* 90: 181–95.

Elsner, Jaś (2002), "The Birth of Late Antiquity: Riegl and Strzygowski in 1901," *Art History* 25: 358–79.

Elsner, Jaś (2005), "Piety and Passion: Contest and Consensus in the Audiences for Early Christian Pilgrimage," in Elsner and Rutherford (2005: 411–34).

Elsner, Jaś, and Rutherford, Ian (eds.) (2005), *Pilgrimage in Graeco-Roman and Early Christian Antiquity: Seeing the Gods*, Oxford and New York, Oxford University Press.

Elton, Hugh (1996), *Warfare in Roman Europe, AD 350–425*, Oxford, Clarendon Press.

Elton, Hugh (2000), "The Nature of the Sixth-Century Isaurians," in Mitchell and Greatrex (2000: 293–307).

Emmel, Stephen (1992), "Languages (Coptic)," in David N. Freedman, *The Anchor Bible Dictionary*, iv, New York, Doubleday, pp. 180–8.

Emmel, Stephen (2002), "From the Other Side of the Nile: Shenute and Panopolis," in Egberts, Muhs, and Van der Vliet (2002: 95–111).

Emmel, Stephen (2004), *Shenoute's Literary Corpus*, 2 vols., Louvain, Peeters.

Emmel, Stephen et al. (eds.) (1999), *Ägypten und Nubien in spätantiker und christlicher Zeit, Akten des 6. Internationalen Koptologenkongresses, Münster, 20.–26. Juli 1996*, 2 vols., Wiesbaden, Reichert.

Encyclopaedia of Islâm, 2nd edn., *see* Bearman et al.

Ennabli, Liliane (1982), *Les Inscriptions funéraires chrétiennes de Carthage*, ii: *La Basilique de Mcidfa*, Rome, École Française de Rome.

Ennabli, Liliane (1989), "Topographie chrétienne de Carthage: les régions ecclésiastiques," in Duval (1989a: 1087–101).

Ennabli, Liliane (1991), *Les Inscriptions funéraires chrétiennes de Carthage*, iii: *Carthage intra et extra muros*, Rome, École Française de Rome.

Ennabli, Liliane (1997), *Carthage: une métropole chrétienne du IVe à la fin du VIIe siècle*, Paris, CNRS.

Ensoli, Serena, and La Rocca, Eugenio (eds.) (2000), *Aurea Roma: dalla città pagana alla città cristiana*, Rome, Bretschneider.

Erasmus (1516), *Omnium operum divi Eusebii Hieronymi Stridonensis tomus primus*, Basel, Froben.

Errington, R. Malcolm (1988), "Constantine and the Pagans," *Greek, Roman, and Byzantine Studies* 29: 309–18.

Escolan, Philippe (1999), *Monachisme et église: le monachisme syrien du IVe au VIIe siècle: un ministère charismatique*, Paris, Beauchesne.

Esler, Philip (1994), *The First Christians in Their Social Worlds: Social-Scientific Approaches to New Testament Interpretation*, London, Routledge.

Esler, Philip F. (ed.) (2000), *The Early Christian World*, London, Routledge.

Esmonde Cleary, A. S. (1989), *The Ending of Roman Britain*, London, Batsford.

Étienne, R. (1964), "La Démographie de la famille d'Ausone," *Annales de Démographie Historique*, 1964: 15–25.

Evans, Rhiannon (1999), "Ethnography's Freak Show: The Grotesques at the Edges of the Roman Earth," *Ramus* 28: 54–73.

Evans-Grubbs, Judith (1995), *Law and Family in Late Antiquity: The Emperor Constantine's Marriage Legislation*, Oxford, Clarendon Press.

Evans-Grubbs, Judith (2001), "Virgins and Widows, Show-Girls and Whores: Late Roman Legislation on Women and Christianity," in Ralph W. Mathisen (ed.), *Law, Society, and Authority in Late Antiquity*, Oxford, Oxford University Press, pp. 220–41.

Evans-Grubbs, Judith (2002), *Women and the Law in the Roman Empire: A Sourcebook on Marriage, Divorce, and Widowhood*, London and New York, Routledge.

Evans-Grubbs, Judith (2007), "Marrying and Its Documentation in Later Roman Law," in Reynolds and Witte (2007: 43–94).

Evelyn-White, Hugh G. (1932), *The Monasteries of the Wadi'n Natrûn*, ii: *The History of the Monasteries of Nitria and Scetis*, New York, Metropolitan Museum of Art.

Everett, Nicholas (2003), *Literacy in Lombard Italy, c.568–774*, Cambridge, Cambridge University Press.

Falaschi, Enid (1998), "Giotto: The Literary Legend," in Andrew Ladis (ed.), *Giotto as a Historical and Literary Figure*, London and New York, Garland, pp. 109–35.

Fanning, S. (1992), "Emperors and Empire in Fifth-Century Gaul," in Drinkwater and Elton (1992: 288–97).

Fantham, Elaine (1996), *Roman Literary Culture from Cicero to Apuleius*, Baltimore, MD, Johns Hopkins University Press.

Farrell, Joseph (2001), *Latin Language and Latin Culture from Ancient to Modern Times*, Cambridge, Cambridge University Press.

Fehr, H. (2002), "*Volkstum* as Paradigm: Germanic People and Gallo-Romans in Early Medieval Archaeology since the 1930s," in Gillett (2002b: 177–200).

Feichtinger, Barbara, Lake, Stephen, and Seng, Helmut (eds.) (2006), *Körper und Seele: Aspekte spätantiker Anthropologie*, Munich, Saur.

Fenn, Richard (1986), "The Secularization of Values: An Analytical Framework for the Study of Secularization," *Journal for the Scientific Study of Religion* 8: 112–24.

Ferguson, Wallace K. (1948), *The Renaissance in Historical Thought: Five Centuries of Interpretation*, Cambridge, MA, Houghton Mifflin.

Ferrar, W. J. (tr.) (1920), Eusebius of Caesarea, *The Proof of the Gospel*, London, SPCK.

Ferris, I. M. (2000), *Enemies of Rome: Barbarians through Roman Eyes*, Stroud, Sutton.

Ferrua, Antonio (1984), "La pubblicazione delle iscrizioni cristiane antiche di Roma," *Archivum Historiae Pontificiae* 22: 357–67.

Festugière, A. J. (1959), *Antioche païenne et chrétienne*, Paris, De Boccard.

Février, P.-A. (1974), "Permanence et heritages de l'Antiquité dans la topographie des villes d'Occident durant le haut moyen âge," in *Topografia urbana e vita citadina sull'alto medioevo in Occidente: 26 Aprile–1 Maggio 1973*, Settimane di Studio del Centro Italiano di Studi sull'Alto Medioevo 21, Spoleto, Presso la sede del Centro, pp. 41–138.

Février, Paul-Albert (1977), "Natale Petri de cathedra," *Comptes Rendus de l'Académie des Inscriptions et Belles-Lettres*, 514–31.

Février, Paul-Albert (1978), "Le Culte des morts dans les communautés chrétiennes durant le IIIe siècle," in *Atti del IX Congresso Internazionale di archeologia cristiana, Roma, 21–27 Settembre 1975*, i: *I monumenti cristiani precostantiniani*, Vatican City, Pontificio Istituto di Archeologia Cristiana, pp. 211–74.

Fewster, Penelope (2002), "Bilingualism in Roman Egypt," in James N. Adams, Mark Janse, and Simon Swain (eds.), *Bilingualism in Ancient Society: Language Contact and the Written Text*, Oxford, Oxford University Press, pp. 220–45.

Field, Lester L., Jr. (1998), *Liberty, Dominion, and the Two Swords: On the Origins of Western Political Theology (180–398)*, Notre Dame, IN, University of Notre Dame Press.

Fincham, Garrick, Harrison, Geoff, Holland, Rene, and Revell, Louise (eds.) (2000), *TRAC 99: Proceedings of the Ninth Annual Theoretical Roman Archaeology Conference, Durham, April 1999*, Oxford, Oxbow Books.

Findlen, Paula (1998), "Possessing the Past: The Material World of the Italian Renaissance," *American Historical Review* 103: 83–114.

Finney, Paul C. (1994), *The Invisible God: The Earliest Christians on Art*, Oxford and New York, Oxford University Press.

Fiocchi Nicolai, Vincenzo, and Guyon, Jean (eds.) (2006), *Origine delle catacombe romane. Atti della giornata tematica dei Seminari di archeologia cristiana, Roma, 21 Marzo 2005*, Vatican City, Pontificio Istituto du Archeologia Cristiana.

Fitschen, Klaus (1998), *Messalianismus und Antimessalianismus: ein Beispiel ostkirchlicher Ketzergeschichte*, Göttingen, Vandenhoeck & Ruprecht.

Fitzgerald, John T. (ed.) (1996), *Friendship, Flattery, and Frankness of Speech: Studies on Friendship in the New Testament World*, Leiden, Brill.

Fitzgerald, John T., Olbricht, T. H., and White, L. M (eds.) (2003), *Early Christianity and Classical Culture: Comparative Studies in Honor of Abraham J. Malherbe*, Leiden, Brill.

Fixot, Michel, and Zadora-Rio, Elisabeth (eds.) (1994), *L'Environnement des églises et la topographie religieuse des campagnes médiévales, Actes du IIIe congrès international d'archéologie médiévale, Aix-En-Provence, 28–30 Septembre 1989*, Paris, Éditions de la Maison des Sciences de l'Homme.

Fladerer, Ludwig (1999), *Johannes Philoponos, "De opificio mundi": Spätantikes Sprachdenken und christliche Exegese*, Stuttgart, Teubner.

Flávio Pierucci, Antônio (2000), "Secularization in Max Weber: On Current Usefulness of Re-accessing that Old Meaning," *Brazilian Review of Social* Sciences, special issue 1: 129–58; originally pub. in *Revista Brasileira de Ciências Sociais* 13 (1998): 43–73.

Fleischer, Jens, Lund, John, and Nielsen, Marjatta (eds.) (2001), *Late Antiquity: Art in Context*, Copenhagen: Museum Tusculanum.

Flemming, Johannes (ed.) (1917), *Akten der Ephesinischen Synode vom Jahre 449, Syrisch*, tr. Georg Hoffmann, Berlin, Weidmann.

Fletcher, Ian (1979), *Decadence and the 1890s*, London, Edward Arnold.

Fletcher, Richard (1997), *The Barbarian Conversion: From Paganism to Christianity*, New York, Holt; London, Harper Collins.

Flood, Finbarr Barry (2001), *The Great Mosque of Damascus: Studies on the Meaning of an Umayyad Visual Culture*, Leiden, Brill.

Föllinger, Sabine (1999), "Biologie in der Spätantike," in Georg Wöhrle (ed.), *Geschichte der Mathematik und der Naturwissenschaften in der Antike*, i: *Biologie*, Stuttgart, Steiner, pp. 253–81.

Foltz, Richard C. (1999), *Religions of the Silk Road: Overland Trade and Cultural Exchange from Antiquity to the Fifteenth Century*, New York, St. Martin's Press.

Fontaine, Jacques (ed.) (1967), *Sulpice Sévère, Vie de Saint Martin*, 3 vols., Sources Chrétiennes 133–5, Paris, Éditions du Cerf.

Fontaine, Jacques (1968), *Aspects et problèmes de la prose d'art latine au IIIème siècle: la genèse des styles latins chrétiens*, Turin, Bottega d'Erasmo.

Fontaine, Jacques (1988), "Un sobriquet perfide de Damase: *matronarum auriscalpius*," in Porte (1988: 177–92).

Fontaine, Jacques, Gillet, R., and Pellistrandi, S. (eds.) (1986), *Grégoire le Grand, Colloque International sur Grégoire le Grand, Chantilly 1982*, Paris, Éditions du Cerf.

Forbes, Robert J. (1955), *Studies in Ancient Technology*, ii, Leiden, Brill.

Forbis, Elizabeth P. (1990), "Women's Public Image in Italian Honorary Inscriptions," *American Journal of Philology* 111: 493–512.

Forbis, Elizabeth P. (1996), *Municipal Virtues in the Roman Empire: The Evidence of Italian Honorary Inscriptions*, Stuttgart and Leipzig, Teubner.

Forlin Patrucco, Marcella (1994), "Modelli di santità e santità episcopale nel IV secolo: l'elaborazione dei padri cappadoci," in Giulia Barone, Marina Caffiero, and Francesco Scorza Barcellona (eds.), *Modelli di santità e modelli di comportamento: Contrasti, intersezioni, complementarità*, Turin, Rosenberg & Sellier, pp. 65–77.

Foss, Clive (1979), *Ephesus After Antiquity: A Late Antique, Byzantine and Turkish City*, Cambridge, Cambridge University Press.

Foss, Clive (1980), *Byzantine and Turkish Sardis*, Archaeological Exploration of Sardis 4, Cambridge, MA, Harvard University Press.

Foss, Clive (1995), "The Near Eastern Countryside in Late Antiquity: A Review Article," in John H. Humphrey (ed.), *The Roman and Byzantine Near East: Some Recent Archaeological Research*, Journal of Roman Archaeology Supplementary Series, Ann Arbor, MI, pp. 213–34.

Foster, Sally (1992), "The State of Pictland in the Age of Sutton Hoo," in Carver (1992: 217–34).

Foster, Sally (1996), *Picts, Gaels and Scots: Early Historic Scotland*, London, Batsford; Edinburgh, Historic Scotland.

Foucault, Michel (1972), *The Archaeology of Knowledge*, tr. A. M. Sheridan Smith, London, Tavistock.

Foucault, Michel (1983), *This is not a Pipe*, tr. J. Harkness, Berkeley and Los Angeles, University of California Press.

Fouracre, Paul (1995), "Carolingian Justice: The Rhetoric of Improvement and Contexts of Abuse," in *La giustizia nell'alto medioevo = Settimane di Studio* 42: 771–803.

Fouracre, Paul (1999), "The Origins of the Carolingian Attempt to Regulate the Cult of the Saints," in Howard-Johnston and Hayward (1999: 143–65).

Fournet, Jean-Luc (1999), *Hellénisme dans l'Égypte du VIe siècle: la bibliothèque et l'oeuvre de Dioscore d'Aphrodité*, Cairo, Institut Français d'Archéologie Orientale.

Fowden, Elizabeth Key (1999), *The Barbarian Plain: St. Sergius between Rome and Iran*, Berkeley and Los Angeles, University of California Press.

Fowden, Garth (1978), "Bishops and Temples in the Eastern Roman Empire, A.D. 320–435," *Journal of Theological Studies* 29: 53–78.

Fowden, Garth (1986), *The Egyptian Hermes: A Historical Approach to the Late Pagan Mind*, Cambridge, Cambridge University Press.

Fowden, Garth (1993), *Empire to Commonwealth: Consequences of Monotheism in Late Antiquity*, Princeton, NJ, Princeton University Press.

Fowden, Garth (1998), "Polytheist Religion and Philosophy," in Cameron and Garnsey (1998: 538–60).

Fowler, D. P. (1991), "Narrate and Describe: The Problem of Ekphrasis," *Journal of Roman Studies* 81: 25–35.

Frakes, Robert M. (2001), Contra potentium iniurias: *The* Defensor Civitatis *and Late Roman Justice*, Munich, Beck.

Francis, James A. (1995), *Subversive Virtue: Asceticism and Authority in the Second-Century Pagan World*, University Park, Pennsylvania State University Press.

Frandsen, P. J. (ed.) (1991), *The Carlsberg Papyri*, i: *Demotic Texts from the Collection*, Copenhagen, Carsten Niebuhr Institute.

Frandsen, P. J., and Ryholt, K. (eds.) (2000), *The Carlsberg Papyri*, iii: *A Miscellany of Demotic Texts and Studies*, Copenhagen, Carsten Niebuhr Institute.

Frank, Georgia (2000), *The Memory of the Eyes: Pilgrims to Living Saints in Christian Late Antiquity*, Berkeley and Los Angeles, University of California Press.

Frank, Georgia (2001), "Taste and See: The Eucharist and the Eyes of Faith in the Fourth Century," *Church History* 70: 619–43.

Frankfurter, David (ed.) (1998a), *Pilgrimage and Holy Space in Late Antique Egypt*, Leiden, Brill.

Frankfurter, David (1998b), *Religion in Roman Egypt: Assimilation and Resistance*, Princeton, NJ, Princeton University Press.

Frankfurter, David (2000), "The Consequences of Hellenism in Late Antique Egypt: Religious Worlds and Actors," *Archiv für Religionsgeschichte* 2: 162–94.

Frankfurter, David (2003), "Beyond 'Jewish Christianity': Continuing Religious Sub-cultures of the Second and Third Centuries and Their Documents," in Becker and Reed (2003: 131–44).

Franklin, Simon (1992), "Borrowed Time: Perceptions of the Past in Twelfth-Century Rus'," in Magdalino (1992: 157–71).

Frantz, Alison (1988), *Late Antiquity: AD 267–700*, Athenian Agora 24, Princeton, NJ, American School of Classical Studies at Athens.

Frayn, Joan M. (1984), *Sheep-Rearing and the Wool Trade in Italy during the Roman Period*, Liverpool, Francis Cairns.

Fredriksen, Paula (2003), "What 'Parting of the Ways'? Jews, Gentiles, and the Ancient Mediterranean City," in Becker and Reed (2003: 35–64).

Freedberg, David (1989), *The Power of Images: Studies in the History and Theory of Response*, Chicago, University of Chicago Press.

Freedman, H., and Simon, Maurice (eds.) (1983), *Midrash Rabbah*, v: *Numbers*, tr. Judah J. Slotki 3rd edn., London and New York, Soncino Press.

Freeman, Philip (2001), *Ireland and the Classical World*, Austin, University of Texas Press.

Freeman, Philip, and Kennedy, David (eds.) (1986), *The Defence of the Roman and Byzantine East*, 2 vols., Oxford, BAR.

Freistedt, E. (1928), *Altchristliche Totengedächtnistage und ihre Beziehung zum Jenseits-Glauben und Totenkultus der Antike*, Münster, Aschendorff.

French, D. H., and Lightfoot, C. S. (1988), *The Eastern Frontier of the Roman Empire*, Oxford, BAR.

French, Dorothy R. (1985), "Christian Emperors and Pagan Spectacles: The Secularization of the *ludi*, A.D. 382–525," unpublished Ph.D. dissertation, University of California, Berkeley.

Frend, W. H. C. (1972), *The Rise of the Monophysite Movement: Chapters in the History of the Church in the Fifth and Sixth Centuries*, London, Cambridge University Press.

Frend, W. H. C. (1985), *The Donatist Church: A Movement of Protest in Roman North Africa*, 3rd edn., Oxford, Clarendon Press.

Frend, W. H. C. (1996), *The Archaeology of Early Christianity*, Minneapolis, MN, Fortress Press.

Frend, W. H. C. (2000), "North African and Byzantine Saints in Byzantine North Africa," in *Romanité et cité chrétienne: permanences et mutations, intégration et exclusion du Ier au VIe siècle, Mélanges en l'honneur d'Yvette Duval*, Paris, De Boccard, pp. 319–33.

Frere, Sheppard S. (1987), *Britannia: A History of Roman Britain*, 3rd rev. edn., London and New York, Routledge & Kegan Paul.

Freud, Sigmund (1930), *Civilization and Its Discontents*, tr. Joan Riviere, London, Hogarth Press; New York, Cape & Smith.

Freund, Wilhelm (1957), *Modernus und andere Zeitbegriffe des Mittelalters*, Cologne, Böhlau.

Frier, Bruce W. (1994), "Natural Fertility and Family Limitation in Roman Marriage," *Classical Philology* 89: 318–33.

Frye, Richard N. (1984), *Handbuch der Altertumswissenschaft*, iii/7: *The History of Ancient Iran*, Munich, Beck.

Fubini, Riccardo (2003), *Humanism and Secularization: From Petrarch to Valla*, tr. Martha King, Durham, NC, Duke University Press.

Fuchs, R., Kempa, M., Redies, R., Theune-Großkopf, B., and Wais, A. (eds.) (1997), *Die Alamannen*, 2nd edn., Stuttgart, Theiss.

Funk, Wolf-Peter (1988), "Dialects Wanting Homes: A Numerical Approach to the Early Varieties of Coptic," in J. Fisiak (ed.), *Historical Dialectology, Regional and Social*, Berlin, de Gruyter, pp. 149–92.

Fürst, Alfons (1999), *Augustins Briefwechsel mit Hieronymus*, Münster, Aschendorffsche Verlagsbuchhandlung.

Gaca, Kathy L. (2003), *The Making of Fornication: Eros, Ethics, and Political Reform in Greek Philosophy and Early Christianity*, Berkeley and Los Angeles, University of California Press.

Gaddis, Michael (2005), *There is No Crime for Those who Have Christ: Religious Violence in the Christian Roman Empire*, Berkeley and Los Angeles, University of California Press.

Gaeta, Franco (1955), *Lorenzo Valla: Filologia e storia nell'umanesimo italiano*, Naples, Istituto Italiano per gli Studi Storici.

Gager, John (1992), *Curse Tablets and Binding Spells in the Ancient World*, Oxford, Oxford University Press.

Gagos, Traianos, and Van Minnen, Peter (1994), *Settling a Dispute: Toward a Legal Anthropology of Late Antique Egypt*, Ann Arbor, University of Michigan Press.

Gallo, Paolo (1997), *Ostraca demotici da Narmuti*, ii: *Ostraca demotici e ieratici dall'archivio bilingue di Narmouthis*, Pisa, ETS.

Galvao-Sobrinho, Carlos (1995), "Funerary Epigraphy and the Spread of Christianity in the West," *Athenaeum* 83: 431–62.

Gamble, Harry (1985), "Christianity: Scripture and Canon," in Denny and Taylor (1985: 36–62).

Gamble, Harry Y. (1995), *Books and Readers in the Early Church: A History of Early Christian Texts*, New Haven, CT, Yale University Press.

Ganshof, François-Louis (1928), "La Tractoria: contribution à l'étude des origines du droit de gîte," *Tijdschrift voor Rechtsgeschiedenis* 8: 69–91.

Ganz, David (1987), "The *Epitaphium Arsenii* and the Opposition to Louis the Pious," in Godman and Collins (1990: 537–50).

Ganz, David (1990), "On the History of Tironian Notes," in Peter Ganz (1990: 35–51).

Ganz, David (1995), "Book Production in the Carolingian Empire and the Spread of Caroline Minuscule," in McKitterick (1995: 786–808).

Ganz, David (2004), "The Study of Caroline Minuscule 1953–2004," *Archiv für Diplomatik* 50: 386–98.

Ganz, Peter (ed.) (1990), *Tironischen Noten*, Wiesbaden, Harrassowitz.

Gardner, Iain (1999), "An Old Coptic Ostracon from Ismant el-Kharab?" *Zeitschrift für Papyrologie und Epigraphik* 125: 195–200.

Gardner, Iain (2000), "He Has Gone to the Monastery," in R. E. Emmerick, W. Sundermann, and P. Zieme (eds.), *Studia Manichaica*, Berlin, Akademie Verlag, pp. 247–57.

Gardner, Iain, and Choat, Malcolm (2004), "Towards a Palaeography of Fourth Century Documentary Coptic," in M. Immerzeel and Jacques van der Vliet (eds.), *Coptic Studies on the Threshold of a New Millennium*, Proceedings of the Seventh International Congress of Coptic Studies, Leiden, August 27–September 2, 2000, 2 vols., i, Louvain, Peeters, pp. 501–9.

Gardner, Iain, and Lieu, Samuel (1996), "From Narmouthis (Medinet Madi) to Kellis (Ismant el-Kharab): Manichaean Documents from Roman Egypt," *Journal of Roman Studies* 86: 146–69.

Gardner, Iain, and Lieu, Samuel (eds.) (2004), *Manichaean Texts from the Roman Empire*, Cambridge, Cambridge University Press.

Gardner, Iain, Alcock, Anthony, and Funk, Wolf-Peter (eds.) (1999), *Coptic Documentary Texts from Kellis*, Oxford, Oxbow Books.

Garin, Eugenio (ed.) (1977), *Prosatori Latini del Quattrocento*, v, Turin, Einaudi.

Garnsey, Peter (1974), "Aspects of the Decline of the Urban Aristocracy in the Empire," in *ANRW* 2. 1: 229–52.

Garnsey, Peter (1998), *Cities, Peasants, and Food in Classical Antiquity: Essays in Social and Economic History*, ed. Walter Scheidel, Cambridge, Cambridge University Press.

Garnsey, Peter, and Humfress, Caroline (2001), *The Evolution of the Late Antique World*, Cambridge, Orchard Academic.

Garnsey, Peter, and Saller, Richard (1987), *The Roman Empire: Economy, Society, and Culture*, Berkeley and Los Angeles, University of California Press.

Garsoïan, Nina (1983), "Byzantium and the Sasanians," in Yarshater (1983, i: 568–92).

Garzya, Antonio (1985), "Visage de l'hellénisme dans le monde byzantin (IVe–XIIe siècles)," *Byzantion* 55: 463–82.

Gascou, Jean (1989), "Les Codices documentaires égyptiens," in Alain Blanchard (ed.), *Les Débuts du codex*, Actes de la journée d'étude organisée à Paris, 3 et 4-VII-1985, Turnhout, Brepols, pp. 71–101.

Gascou, Jean (2004), "Les Pétitions privées," in Denis Feissel and Jean Gascou (eds.), *La Pétition à Byzance*, Paris, Centre de Recherche d'Histoire et Civilisation de Byzance, pp. 93–103.

Gatier, Pierre-Louis (1995), "Villages du Proche-Orient protobyzantin (4ème–7ème s.): étude régionale," in King and Cameron (1995: 17–48).

Gauthier, Nancy (1975), *Recueil des inscriptions chrétiennes de la Gaule*, i: *Première Belgique*, Paris, CNRS.

Gauvard, Claude (2004), "Introduction," in Claire Bourdeau, Kouky Fianu, Claude Gauvard, and Michel Hébert (eds.), *Information et société en Occident à la fin du Moyen Âge*, Actes du colloque international tenu à l'Université du Québec à Montréal et à l'Université d'Ottawa (Mai 9–11, 2002), Paris, Publications de la Sorbonne, pp. 11–37.

Gavrilov, A. K. (1997), "Techniques of Reading in Classical Antiquity," *Classical Quarterly* 47: 56–73.

Geary, Patrick J. (1983), "Ethnic Identity as a Situational Construct in the Early Middle Ages," *Mitteilungen der Anthropologischen Gesellschaft in Wien* 113: 15–26.

Geary, Patrick J. (1988), *Before France and Germany: The Creation and Transformation of the Merovingian World*, London and New York, Oxford University Press.

Geary, Patrick J. (1990), *Furta Sacra: Theft of Relics in the Central Middle Ages*, Princeton, NJ, Princeton University Press.

Geary, Patrick J. (1994a), *Living with the Dead in the Middle Ages*, Ithaca, NY, Cornell University Press.

Geary, Patrick J. (1994b), *Phantoms of Remembrance: Memory and Oblivion at the End of the First Millennium*, Princeton, NJ, Princeton University Press.

Geary, Patrick J. (1999), "Barbarians and Ethnicity," in Bowersock, Brown, and Grabar (1999: 107–29).

Geary, Patrick J. (2002), *The Myth of Nations: The Medieval Origins of Europe*, Princeton, NJ, Princeton University Press.

Gelzer, Matthias (1963), *Kleine Schriften*, ii, Wiesbaden, Steiner.

Geuenich, Dieter (ed.) (1998), *Die Franken und die Alemannen bis zur "Schlacht bei Zülpich" (496/97)*, Berlin and New York, De Gruyter.

Ghirshman, R. (1962), *Iran: Parthes et Sassanides*, Paris, Gallimard.

Giamberardini, G. (2000), *S. Antonio abate, astro del deserto*, Cairo.

Giardina, Andrea (1977), *Aspetti della burocrazia nel Basso Impero*, Rome, Edizioni dell'-Ateneo e Bizzari.

Giardina, Andrea (ed.) (1989), *L'uomo romano*, Rome, Laterza.

Giardina, Andrea (1999), "Esplosione di tardoantico," *Studi Storici* 40: 157–80.

Giardina, Andrea (2001), "Conclusioni," in Gisella Cantino Wataghin and Jean-Michel Carrié (eds.), "Antiquité tardive et 'démocratisation de la culture': mise à l'épreuve du paradigme (Atti del Convegno di Vercelli, 14–15 giugno 2000)," *Antiquité Tardive* 9: 289–95.

Gibbon, Edward (1907), *Autobiography of Edward Gibbon as originally edited by Lord Sheffield*, intro. by J. B. Bury, London, Oxford University Press.

Gibbon, Edward (1984), *Memoirs of My Life*, ed. Betty Radice, NewYork, Penguin Classics.

Gibbon, Edward (1994), *The History of the Decline and Fall of the Roman Empire*, ed. David Womersley, 3 vols., London, Allen Lane.

Gibbon, Edward (2003), *The Decline and Fall of the Roman Empire*, ed. and abridged by Hans-Friedrich Mueller, New York, Modern Library.

Gilardi, Francis (1983), "The Sylloge Epigraphica Turonensis de S. Martino," unpublished dissertation, Catholic University of America.

Gilhus, Ingvild S. (2006), *Animals, Gods and Humans: Changing Attitudes to Animals in Greek, Roman and Early Christian Ideas*, Abingdon, Routledge.

Gillett, Andrew (2000), "Jordanes and Ablabius," in Carl Deroux (ed.), *Studies in Latin Literature and Roman History*, x, Brussels, Latomus, pp. 479–500.

Gillett, Andrew (2002a), "Was Ethnicity Politicized in the Earliest Medieval Kingdoms?" in Gillett (2002b: 85–121).

Gillett, Andrew (ed.) (2002b), *On Barbarian Identity: Critical Approaches to Identity in the Early Middle Ages*, Turnhout, Brepols.

Gillett, Andrew (2003), *Envoys and Political Communication in the Late Antique West, 411–533*, Cambridge, Cambridge University Press.

Gillett, Andrew (2005), "Ethnogenesis: A Contested Model of Early Medieval Europe," *History Compass* (forthcoming), www.history-compass.com

Gilliard, F. D. (1966), "The Social Origins of Bishops in the Fourth Century," unpublished Ph.D. dissertation, University of California, Berkeley.

Gilliard, F. D. (1984), "Senatorial Bishops in the Fourth Century," *Harvard Theological Review* 77: 153–75.

Giuliani, Raffaella (1994), "Catalogo della mostra," in *Giovanni Battista de Rossi e le cata-combe romane: mostra fotografica e documentaria in occasione del 1 Centenario della morte di Giovanni Battista de Rossi (1894–1994)*, Vatican City, Tipografia Vaticana.

Glover, T. R. (1901), *Life and Letters in the Fourth Century*, Cambridge, Cambridge University Press.

Gobbi, A. (1998), "Nuove osservazioni sulle fasi costruttuve della c.d. basilica cristiana di Ostia Antica," *Rivista di Archeologia Cristiana* 74: 455–84.

Godman, Peter, and Collins, Roger (eds.) (1990), *Charlemagne's Heir: New Perspectives on the Reign of Louis the Pious*, Oxford, Clarendon Press.

Goehring, James E. (ed.) (1990), *The Crosby-Schøyen Codex MS 193 in the Schøyen Collection*, Louvain, Peeters.

Goehring, James E. (1999), *Ascetics, Society and the Desert: Studies in Early Egyptian Monasticism*, Harrisburg, PA, Trinity Press International.

Goehring, James E. (2001), "The Provenance of the Nag Hammadi Codices Once More," *Studia Patristica* 35: 234–53.

Goetz, Hans-Werner, Jarnut, Jörg, and Pohl, Walter (eds.) (2003), *Regna and Gentes: The Relationship between Late Antique and Early Medieval Peoples and Kingdoms in the Transformation of the Roman World*, Leiden and Boston, MA, Brill.

Goez, Werner (1958), *Translatio imperii: ein Beitrag zur Geschichte des Geschichtsdenkens und der politischen Theorien im Mittelalter und in der frühen Neuzeit*, Tübingen, Mohr Siebeck.

Goez, Werner (1970), "Papa qui et episcopus: zum Selbstverständnis des Reformpapsttums im 11. Jahrhundert," *Archivum historiae pontificiae* 8: 27–59.

Goffart, Walter (1980), *Barbarians and Romans AD 418–585: The Techniques of Accommodation*, Princeton, NJ, Princeton University Press.

Goffart, Walter (1983), "The Supposedly 'Frankish' Table of Nations: An Edition and Study," *Frühmittelalterliche Studies* 17: 98–130; repr. in Goffart (1989b: 133–65).

Goffart, Walter (1988), *The Narrators of Barbarian History (AD 550–800): Jordanes, Gregory of Tours, Bede, and Paul the Deacon*, Princeton, NJ: Princeton University Press.

Goffart, Walter (1989a), "The Theme of 'The Barbarian Invasions' in Later Antique and Modern Historiography," in Chrysos and Schwarcz (1989: 87–107); repr. in Goffart (1989b: 111–32).

Goffart, Walter (1989b), *Rome's Fall and After*, London, Hambledon Press.

Goffart, Walter (1995), "Two Notes on Germanic Antiquity Today," *Traditio* 50: 9–30.

Goffart, Walter (2002), "Does the Distant Past Impinge on the Invasion Age Germans?' in Gillett (2002b: 21–37).

Goffart, Walter (2005), "Jordanes' *Getica* and the Disputed Authenticity of Gothic Origins from Scandinavia," *Speculum* 80: 379–98.

Goffart, Walter (2006), *Barbarian Tides: The Migration Age and the Later Roman Empire*, Philadelphia, University of Pennsylvania Press.

Goldhill, Simon (1986), *Reading Greek Tragedy*, Cambridge, Cambridge University Press.

Goldhill, Simon, and Osborne, Robin (eds.) (1994), *Art and Text in Ancient Greek Culture*, Cambridge, Cambridge University Press.

Gombrich, E. H. (1970), *Aby Warburg: An Intellectual Biography*, London, Warburg Institute.

Gombrich, E. H. (1976), *The Heritage of Appelles: Studies in the Art of the Renaissance*, Oxford, Phaidon.

Goodburn, R., and Bartholomew, P. (eds.) (1976), *Aspects of the Notitia Dignitatum*, Oxford, British Archaeological Reports.

Goody, Jack (1987), *The Interface between the Written and the Oral*, Cambridge, Cambridge University Press.

Gorce, Denys (ed.) (1962), *Vie de sainte Mélanie*, Sources Chrétiennes 90, Paris, Éditions du Cerf.

Gorday, Peter (1983), *Principles of Patristic Exegesis: Romans 9–11 in Origen, John Chrysostom, and Augustine*, New York, Mellen Press.

Gould, Graham (1993), *The Desert Fathers on Monastic Community*, Oxford, Clarendon Press.

Gouwens, Kenneth (1998), "Perceiving the Past: Renaissance Humanism After the 'Cognitive Turn'," *American Historical Review* 103: 55–82.

Grabar, André (1936), *L'Empereur dans l'art Byzantine: recherches sur l'art officiel de l'empire d'Orient*, Paris, Les Belles Lettres.

Grabar, André (1968), *Christian Iconography: A Study of Its Origins*, Princeton, NJ, Princeton University Press.

Grabar, André (1976), *Sculptures byzantines du moyen âge II (XIe–XIVe siècle)*, Paris, Dépositaire A. Maisonneuve.

Grabar, Oleg (1977), "Notes sur les cérémonies umayyades," in M. Rosen-Ayalon (ed.), *Studies in Memory of Gaston Wiet*, Jerusalem, Hebrew University of Jerusalem, pp. 51–60.

Graf, Fritz (2002), "Religionsgeschichte," in *Der Neue Pauly*, 15.2: *Rezeptions- und Wissenschaftsgeschichte*, Stuttgart, Metzler, pp. 679–99.

Grafton, Anthony (1992), "The Renaissance," in Richard Jenkyns (ed.), *The Legacy of Rome: A New Appraisal*, Oxford, Oxford University Press, pp. 97–123.

Grafton, Anthony (2001), *Bring Out Your Dead: The Past as Revelation*, Cambridge, MA, Harvard University Press.

Grane, Leif, Schindler, Alfred, and Wriedt, Markus (eds.) (1993), *Auctoritas patrum: zur Rezeption der Kirchenväter im 15. und 16. Jahrhundert*, Mainz, von Zabern.

Grane, Leif, Schindler, Alfred, and Wriedt, Markus (eds.) (1998), *Auctoritas patrum*, ii: *Neue Beiträge zur Rezeption der Kirchenväter im 15. und 16. Jahrhundert*, Mainz, von Zabern.

Graumann, Thomas (2002), *Die Kirche der Väter: Vätertheologie und Väterbeweis in den Kirchen des Ostens bis zum Konzil von Ephesus (431)*, Tübingen, Mohr Siebeck.

Graumann, Thomas (2003), "Kirchliche Identität und bischöfliche Selbstinszenierung: der Rückgriff auf 'Athanasius' bei der Überwindung des nachephesinischen Schismas und in Kyrills Propaganda," in Aland, Hahn, and Ronning (2003: 195–213).

Gray, Hannah H. (1965), "Valla's *Encomium of St. Thomas Aquinas* and the Humanist Conception of Christian Antiquity," in Heinz Bluhm (ed.), *Essays in History and Literature Presented by Fellows of the Newberry Library to Stanley Pargellis*, Chicago, Newberry Library, pp. 37–51.

Gray, Patrick T. R. (1989), "'The Select Fathers': Canonizing the Patristic Past," *Studia Patristica* 23: 21–36.

Gray, Patrick T. R. (1997), "Covering the Nakedness of Noah: Reconstruction and Denial in the Age of Justinian," *Byzantinische Forschungen* 24: 193–205.

Greatrex, Geoffrey (1998), *Rome and Persia at War, 502–532*, Leeds, Francis Cairns.

Greatrex, Geoffrey, and Lieu, Samuel N. C. (2002), *The Roman Eastern Frontier and the Persian Wars AD 363–630: A Narrative Sourcebook*, London, Routledge.

Green, Charles (1966), "The Purpose of the Early Horseshoe," *Antiquity* 40: 305–8.

Green, D. H., and Siegmund, F. (eds.) (2003), *The Continental Saxons from the Migration Period to the Tenth Century: An Ethnographic Perspective*, Woodbridge and Rochester, NY, Boydell Press.

Green, R. P. H. (ed.) (1991), *The Works of Ausonius*, Oxford, Clarendon Press.

Greene, Kevin (1986), *The Archaeology of the Roman Economy*, Berkeley and Los Angeles, University of California Press.

Greene, Thomas M. (1982), *The Light in Troy: Imitation and Discovery in Renaissance Poetry*, New Haven, CT, Yale University Press.

Gregg, Robert C., and Urman, Dan (1996), *Jews, Pagans, and Christians in the Golan Heights: Greek and Other Inscriptions of the Roman and Byzantine Eras*, Atlanta, GA, Scholars Press.

Gregorio magno e le origini dell'Europa (forthcoming), Florence, SISMEL, Galluzzo.

Gregory, Christopher A. (1997), *Savage Money: The Anthropology and Politics of Commodity Exchange*, Amsterdam, Harwood Academic Publishers.

Gregory, Timothy E. (1986), "The Survival of Paganism in Christian Greece," *American Journal of Philology* 107: 229–42.

Grenfell, Bernard P., and Hunt, Arthur S. (eds.) (1901), *The Amherst Papyri: Being an Account of the Greek Papyri in the Collection of the Right Hon. Lord Amherst of Hackney, F.S.A. at Didlington Hall, Norfolk*, ii: *Classical Fragments and Documents of the Ptolemaic, Roman and Byzantine Periods*, London, H. Frowde.

Grey, Cam (2004), "Letters of Recommendation and the Circulation of Rural Laborers in the Late Roman West," in Ellis and Kidner (2004: 25–40).

Gribomont, Jean (1965), "Le Monachisme au sein de l'Église en Syrie et en Cappadoce," *Studia Monastica* 7: 7–24.

Griffith, Sidney (1986), "Ephraem, the Deacon of Edessa, and the Church of the Empire," in Thomas Halton and Joseph Williman (eds.), *Diakonia: Studies in Honor of Robert T. Meyer*, Washington, DC, Catholic University of America Press, pp. 22–52.

Griffith, Sidney (1995), "Asceticism in the Church of Syria: The Hermeneutics of Early Syrian Monasticism," in Wimbush and Valantasis (1995: 220–45).

Griffith, Sidney (1998), "A Spiritual Father for the Whole Church: The Universal Appeal of St. Ephrem the Syrian," *Hugoye* 1/2, http://syrcom.cua.edu/Hugoye/vol1No2/HV1N2Griffith.html

Griffith, Sidney (1999a), "The Marks of the 'True Church' according to Ephraem's *Hymns against Heresies*," in G. J. Reinink and A. C. Klugkist (eds.), *After Bardaisan: Studies on Continuity and Change in Syriac Christianity in Honour of Professor Han J. W. Drijvers*, Louvain, Peeters, pp. 125–40.

Griffith, Sidney (1999b), "Setting Right the Church of Syria: Saint Ephraem's *Hymns against Heresies*," in William Klingshirn and Mark Vessey (eds.), *The Limits of Ancient Christianity: Essays on Late Antique Thought and Culture in Honor of R. A. Markus*, Ann Arbor, University of Michigan Press, pp. 97–114.

Griffith, Sidney (2001), " 'Melkites,' 'Jacobites' and the Christological Controversies in Arabic in third/ninth-century Syria," in David Thomas (ed.), *Syrian Christians under Islam: The First Thousand Years*, Boston, MA, Brill, pp. 9–55.

Grigoriadis, Iordanis (1998), *Linguistic and Literary Studies in the Epitomē historiōn of John Zonaras*, Thessaloniki, Kentron Vyzantinōn Ereunōn.

Grillmeier, Aloys (1975, 1987, 1995–6), *Christ in Christian Tradition*, 4 vols., London, Mowbray.

Groenewoudt, B. J., and van Nie, M. (1995), "Assessing the Scale and Organisation of Germanic Iron Production in Heeten, the Netherlands," *Journal of European Archaeology* 3: 187–215.

Grohmann, Adolf (1934–74), *Arabic Papyri in the Egyptian Library*, 6 vols., Cairo, Egyptian Library Press.

Gruen, Erich (ed.) (2005), *Cultural Borrowings and Ethnic Appropriations in Antiquity*, Stuttgart, Steiner.

Grünewald, Thomas (2004), *Bandits in the Roman Empire: Myth and Reality*, tr. John Drinkwater, London and New York, Routledge.

Guidobaldi, Federico (1989), "L'inserimento delle chiese titolari di Roma nel tessuto urbano preesistente: osservazioni ed implicazioni," in *Quaeritur inventus colitur: miscellanea in onore di padre Umberto Maria Fasola*, Vatican City, Pontificio Istituto di Archeologia Cristiana, pp. 381–96.

Guidobaldi, Federico (2000), "L'organizzazione dei tituli nello spazio urbano," in Pani Ermini (2000: 123–9).

Guidobaldi, Federico, and Guidobaldi, Alessandra Guiglia (eds.) (2002), *Ecclesiae Urbis*, Atti del congresso internazionale di studi sulle chiese di Roma (IV–X secolo), Roma, 4–10 Settembre 2000, Vatican City, Pontificio Istituto di Archeologia Cristiana.

Guillaumont, Antoine (1968), "Le Dépaysement comme forme d'ascèse dans le monachisme ancien," *Annuaire de l'École Pratique des Hautes Études, V section: Sciences Religieuses* 76: 31–58.

Guillaumont, Antoine (1975), "La Conception du désert chez les moines d'Egypte," *Revue d'Histoire des Religions* 181: 29–56.

Guillaumont, Antoine, Coquin, René-Georges, Weidmann, Denis, Grossmann, Peter, Partyka, Jan Stanislaw, and Rassart-Debergh, Marguerite (1991), "Kellia," in Atiyah (1991, v: 1396–406).

Gundlach, Wilhelm (ed.) (1892), *Epistulae Austrasiacae, MGH, epist.* 3 (*epist. Mer. et Kar. Aev.* 1), Berlin, Weidmann.

Guyon, Jean (1987), *Le Cimetière aux deux lauriers: recherches sur les catacombes romaines*, Rome, École Française de Rome

Guyon, Jean (2000), *Les Premiers baptistères des Gaules (IVe–VIIIe siècles)*, Rome, Unione Internazionale degli Istituti di Archaeologia, Storia e Storia dell'Arte in Roma.

Guyon, Jean et al. (1998), *Atlas topographique des villes de Gaule méridionale*, i: *Aix-en-Provence*, Montpellier, Editions de l'Association de la Revue Archéologique de Narbonnaise.

Gwynn, David M. (ed.) (forthcoming), *A. H. M. Jones and the Later Roman Empire*, Oxford, Oxford University Press.

Haarnagel, Werner (1979), *Die Grabung Feddersen Wierde: Methode, Hausbau, Siedlungs- und Wirtschaftsformen, sowie Sozialstruktur*, Wiesbaden, Steiner.

Haas, Christopher (1997), *Alexandria in Late Antiquity: Topography and Social Conflict*, Baltimore, MD, Johns Hopkins University Press.

Haas, Christopher (2004), "Hellenism and Opposition to Christianity in Alexandria," in William V. Harris and Giovanni Ruffini (eds.), *Ancient Alexandria between Egypt and Greece*, Leiden, Brill, 2004, pp. 217–29.

Habermann, Wolfgang (1998), "Zur chronologischen Verteilung der papyrologischen Zeugnisse," *Zeitschrift für Papyrologie und Epigraphik* 122: 144–60.

Hägg, Tomas, and Rousseau, Philip (eds.) (2000), *Greek Biography and Panegyric in Late Antiquity*, Berkeley and Los Angeles, University of California Press.

Hahn, August (1897), *Bibliothek der Symbole und Glaubensregeln der alten Kirche*, 4th rev. and expanded edn. by G. Ludwig Hahn, Breslau, Morgenstern.

Hahn, Johannes (2004), *Gewalt und religiöser Konflikt: Studien zu den Auseinandersetzungen zwischen Christen, Heiden und Juden im Osten des römischen Reiches (von Konstantin bis Theodosius II)*, Berlin, Akademie Verlag.

Hahneman, Geoffrey Mark (1992), *The Muratorian Fragment and the Development of the Canon*, Oxford, Clarendon Press.

Haines-Eitzen, Kim (2000), *Guardians of Letters: Literacy, Power, and the Transmitters of Early Christian Literature*, Oxford and New York, Oxford University Press.

Hall, Edith (1989a), "The Archer Scene in Aristophanes' Thesmophoriazusae," *Philologus* 133: 38–54.

Hall, Edith (1989b), *Inventing the Barbarian: Greek Self-Definition through Tragedy*, Oxford, Oxford University Press.

Hall, Jonathon (1997), *Ethnic Identity in Greek Antiquity*, Cambridge, Cambridge University Press.

Hall, Jonathon (2002), *Hellenicity: Between Ethnicity and Culture*, Chicago, University of Chicago Press.

Halperin, David M. (1992), "Plato and the Erotics of Narrativity," in J. C. Klagge and N. D. Smith (eds.), *Methods of Interpreting Plato and His Dialogues*, Oxford, Clarendon Press, pp. 93–129; also in R. Hexter and D. Selden (eds.), *Innovations of Antiquity*, New York, Routledge, pp. 95–126.

Halsall, Guy (1992), "The Origins of the *Reihengräberzivilisation*: Forty Years On," in Drinkwater and Elton (1992: 196–207).

Halsall, Guy (1995), *Settlement and Social Organization: The Merovingian Region of Metz*, Cambridge and New York, Cambridge University Press.

Halsall, Guy (1999), "Movers and Shakers: The Barbarians and the Fall of Rome," *Early Medieval Europe* 8: 131–45.

Halsall, Guy (2000), "Archaeology and the Late Roman Frontier in Northern Gaul: The so-called Föderatengräber Reconsidered," in Pohl and Reimitz (2000: 167–80).

Halsall, Guy (2001), "Childeric's Grave, Clovis' Succession, and the Origins of the Merovingian Kingdom," in Mathisen and Shanzer (2001: 116–33).

Halsall, Guy (2003), "Burial Writes: Graves, 'Texts' and Time in Early Merovingian Northern Gaul," in J. Jarnut and M. Wemhoff (eds.), *Erinnerungskultur im Bestattungsritual: Archäologisch-historisches Forum*, Munich, Fink, pp. 61–74.

Halsall, Guy (2004), "Gender and the End of Empire," *Journal of Medieval and Early Modern Studies* 34: 17–39.

Halsall, Guy (2007), *Barbarian Migrations and the Roman West, 376–568*, Cambridge and New York, Cambridge University Press.

Hamerow, Helena (2002), *Early Medieval Settlements: The Archaeology of Rural Communities in North-West Europe 400–900*, Oxford and New York, Oxford University Press.

Hammond, Philip E. (ed.) (1985), *The Sacred in a Secular Age*, Berkeley and Los Angeles, University of California Press.

Handley, Mark (2003), *Death, Society, and Culture: Inscriptions and Epitaphs in Gaul and Spain, AD 300–750*, BAR International Series 1135, Oxford, Archaeopress.

Hansen, H. J. (1989), "Dankirke: Affluence in Late Iron Age Denmark," in Randsborg (1989: 123–8).

Hanson, R. P. C. (1988), *The Search for the Christian Doctrine of God: The Arian Controversy 318–381*, Edinburgh, T. & T. Clark.

Harbison, Peter (1988), *Pre-Christian Ireland: From the First Settlers to the Early Celts*, London and New York, Thames & Hudson.

Hardt, Michael, and Negri, Antonio (2000), *Empire*, Cambridge, MA, Harvard University Press.

Hardy, E. G. (1925), *Christianity and the Roman Government: A Study in Imperial Administration*, London, Allen & Unwin.

Harl, Kenneth W. (1990), "Sacrifice and Pagan Belief in Fifth- and Sixth-Century Byzantium," *Past and Present* 128: 7–27.

Harl, Marguerite (1981), "La Dénonciation des festivités profanes dans le discours épiscopal et monastique, en orient chrétien, à la fin du IVe siècle," in *La Fête, pratique et discours: d'Alexandrie hellénistique à la mission de Besançon*, Paris, Belles Lettres, pp. 123–47.

Harley, Felicity (2006), "The Narration of Christ's Passion in Early Christian Art," in J. Burke et al. (eds.), *Byzantine Narrative: Papers in Honour of Roger Scott*, Melbourne, Australian Association for Byzantine Studies, pp. 221–32.

Harley, Felicity (2007), "The Crucifixion," in Spier (2007: 227–32).

Harley, J. B., and Woodward, David (eds.) (1987), *The History of Cartography: Cartography in Prehistoric, Ancient, and Medieval Europe and the Mediterranean*, Chicago, University of Chicago Press.

Harmless, William (2004), *Desert Christians: An Introduction to the Literature of Early Monasticism*, Oxford and New York, Oxford University Press.

Harnack, Adolf von (1883), "Die Altercatio Simonis Judaei et Theophili Christiani, nebst Untersuchugen über die antijudische Polemik in der alten Kirche," *Texte und Untersuchungen zur Geschichte der altchristlichen Literatur*, i/3, Leipzig, J. C. Hinrichs.

Harnack, Adolf von (1906), "The Present State of Research in Early Church History," in Adolf von Harnack, *Reden und Aufsätze*, ii, 2nd edn., Giessen, Töpelmann, pp. 217–35.

Harnack, Adolf von (1912), *Bible Reading in the Early Church*, New York, Putnam; London, Williams & Norgate.

Harnack, Adolf von (1915), *Die Mission und Ausbreitung des Christentums*, 2nd edn., Leipzig, J. C. Hinrichs.

Harrak, Amir (2002), "Trade Routes and the Christianization of the Near East," *Journal of the Canadian Society for Syriac Studies* 2: 46–61.

Harrauer, Hermann, and Sijpesteijn, Pieter (eds.) (1985), *Neue Texte aus dem antiken Unterricht*, Vienna, Hollinek.

Harries, Jill (1993), "The Background to the Code," in Harries and Wood (1993: 1–16).

Harries, Jill (1994), *Sidonius Apollinaris and the Fall of Rome, AD 407–485*, Oxford, Clarendon Press; New York, Oxford University Press.

Harries, Jill (1999), *Law and Empire in Late Antiquity*, Cambridge and New York, Cambridge University Press.

Harries, Jill, and Wood, Ian (eds.) (1993), *The Theodosian Code*, London, Duckworth; Ithaca, NY, Cornell University Press.

Harrington, Christina (2002), *Women in a Celtic Church: Ireland 450–1150*, Oxford and New York, Oxford University Press.

Harris, Edward C. (1989), *Principles of Archaeological Stratigraphy*, 2nd edn., London, Academic Press.

Harris, Edward C., Brown, Marley R., and Brown, Gregory J. (eds.) (1993), *Practices of Archaeological Stratigraphy*, London, Academic Press.

Harris, H. A. (1974), "Lubrication in Antiquity," *Greece and Rome* 21: 32–6.

Harris, William V. (1989), *Ancient Literacy*, Cambridge, MA, Harvard University Press.

Harris, William V. (ed.) (1993), *The Inscribed Economy: Production and Distribution in the Roman Empire in the Light of* instrumentum domesticum, Ann Arbor, University of Michigan Press.

Harris, William V. (ed.) (1999), *The Transformations of Urbs Roma in Late Antiquity*, Portsmouth, RI, Journal of Roman Archaeology.

Harris, William V. (ed.) (2005a), *Rethinking the Mediterranean*, Oxford and New York, Oxford University Press.

Harris, William V. (ed.) (2005b), *The Spread of Christianity in the First Four Centuries: Essays in Explanation*, Leiden and Boston, MA, Brill.

Harrison, Martin (1989), *A Temple for Byzantium: The Discovery and Excavation of Anicia Juliana's Palace-Church in Istanbul*, London, Harvey Miller.

Harrison, Thomas (2000), *The Emptiness of Asia: Aeschylus'* Persians *and the History of the Fifth Century*, London, Duckworth.

Harrison, Thomas (ed.) (2002), *Greeks and Barbarians*, Edinburgh, University of Edinburgh Press.

Hartmann, Günther (1929), *Photios' Literarästhetik*, Leipzig, Noske.

Hartmann, Udo (2002), "Geist im Exil: römische Philosophen am Hof der Sasaniden," in Monika Schuol, Udo Hartmann, and Andreas Luther (eds.), *Grenzüberschreitungen: Formen des Kontakts zwischen Orient und Okzident im Altertum*, Stuttgart, Steiner, pp. 123–60.

Hartog, François (1988). *The Mirror of Herodotus: The Representation of the Other in the Writing of History*, tr. Janet Lloyd, Berkeley and Los Angeles, University of California Press.

Hartog, François (2001), *Memories of Odysseus: Frontier Tales from Ancient Greece*, tr. Janet Lloyd, Edinburgh, University of Edinburgh Press.

Hartranft, Chester D. (tr.) (1989), *Sozomen: Church History*, in *A Select Library of Nicene and Post-Nicene Fathers*, ii, Grand Rapids, MI, Eerdmans.

Harvey, P. D. A. (1987), "Local and Regional Cartography in Medieval Europe," in Harley and Woodward (1987: 464–501).

Harvey, Susan Ashbrook (1990), *Asceticism and Society in Crisis: John of Ephesus and the "Lives of the Eastern Saints"*, Berkeley and Los Angeles, University of California Press.

Harvey, Susan Ashbrook (1996), "Sacred Bonding: Mothers and Daughters in Early Syriac Hagiography," *Journal of Early Christian Studies* 4: 27–56.

Harvey, Susan Ashbrook (2005), "Revisiting the Daughters of the Covenant: Women's Choirs and Sacred Song in Ancient Syriac Chrisitanity," *Hugoye* 8/2, http://syrcom.cua.edu/Hugoye/ Vol8No2/HV8N2Harvey.html

Harvey, Susan Ashbrook (2006), *Scenting Salvation: Ancient Christianity and the Olfactory Imagination*, Berkeley and Los Angeles, University of California Press.

Hasitzka, Monika R. M. (ed.) (1990), *Neue Texte und Dokumentation zum Koptisch-Unterricht*, Vienna, Hollinek.

Hasitzka, Monika R. M. (ed.) (2004), *Koptisches Sammelbuch*, ii, Vienna, Hollinek.

Hauben, Hans (2002), "Aurêlios Pageus, alias Apa Paiêous, et le monastère mélitien d'Hathor," *Ancient Society* 32: 337–52.

Hawting, Gerald R. (1999), *The Idea of Idolatry and the Emergence of Islam: From Polemic to History*, Cambridge, Cambridge University Press.

Hawting, Gerald R. (2000), *The First Dynasty of Islam: The Umayyad Caliphate AD 661–750*, 2nd edn., London and New York, Routledge.

Hayes, E. R. (1930), *L'École d'Édesse*, Paris, Les Presses Modernes.

Hayward, Paul (1999), "Demystifying the Role of Sanctity in Western Christendom," in Howard-Johnston and Hayward (1999: 115–42).

Head, Thomas (1990), *Hagiography and the Cult of the Saints: The Diocese of Orleans, 800–1200*, Cambridge, Cambridge University Press.

Heath, Malcolm (2004), *Menander: A Rhetor in Context*, Oxford, Oxford University Press.

Heather, Peter (1991), *Goths and Romans, 332–489*, Oxford, Clarendon Press.

Heather, Peter (1994a), "New Men for New Constantines? Creating an Imperial Elite in the Eastern Mediterranean," in Magdalino (1994: 11–33).

Heather, Peter (1994b), "State Formation in the First Millennium A.D.," in Crawford (1994: 47–70).

Heather, Peter (1995), "The Huns and the End of the Roman Empire in Western Europe," *English Historical Review* 110: 4–41.

Heather, Peter (1996), *The Goths*, Oxford and Cambridge, MA, Blackwell.

Heather, Peter (1997), "Late Antiquity and the Early Medieval West," in Bentley (1997: 69–87).

Heather, Peter (1998), "Senators and Senates," in Cameron and Garnsey (1998: 184–210).

Heather, Peter (1999), "The Barbarian in Late Antiquity: Image, Reality, and Transformation," in Miles (1999: 234–58).

Heather, Peter (2005), *The Fall of the Roman Empire: A New History*, London, Macmillan.

Heather, Peter (2006), *The Fall of the Roman Empire: A New History of Rome and the Barbarians*, New York, Oxford University Press.

Heather, Peter, and Matthews, John (1991), *The Goths in the Fourth Century*, Liverpool, Liverpool University Press.

Heck, G. W. (2003), " 'Arabia without Spices': An Alternative Hypothesis," *Journal of the American Oriental Society* 123: 547–76.

Hedeager, Lotte (1992), *Iron Age Societies: From Tribe to State in Northern Europe, 500 BC to 700 AD*, tr. John Hines, Oxford and Cambridge, MA, Blackwell.

Hedrick, Charles (2000), *History and Silence: Purge and Rehabilitation of Memory in Late Antiquity*, Austin, University of Texas Press.

Heffernan, James A. W. (1993), *The Museum of Words: The Poetics of Ekphrasis from Homer to Ashbery*, Chicago, University of Chicago Press.

Hefner, Robert W. (ed.) (1993), *Conversion to Christianity: Historical and Anthropological Perspectives on a Great Transformation*, Berkeley and Los Angeles, University of California Press.

Heidinga, H. A. (1994), "Frankish Settlement at Gennep: A Migration Period Settlement in the Dutch Meuse Area," in Nielsen, Randsborg, and Thrane (1994: 202–8).

Heijmans, Marc (2004), *Arles durant l'Antiquité tardive: de la duplex Arelas à l'urbs Genesii*, Rome, École Française de Rome.

Heinen, Heinz (1980), "Das Ende der alten Welt im Rahmen der Gesamtentwicklung der sowjetischen Althistorie," in Heinz Heinen (ed.), *Die Geschichte des Altertums im Spiegel der sowjetischen Forschung*, Darmstadt, Wissenschaftliche Buchgesellschaft, pp. 256–341.

Heinzelmann, Martin (1983), "Gallische Prosopographie: 260–527," *Francia* 10: 531–718.

Heinzelmann, Martin (2001), *Gregory of Tours: History and Society in the Sixth Century*, tr. Christopher Carroll, Cambridge and New York, Cambridge University Press.

Heinzelmann, Martin (ed.) (2006), *Livrets, collections et textes: études sur la tradition hagiographique latine*, Ostfildern, Thorbecke.

Helck, Wolfgang, and Westendorf, Wolfhart (eds.) (1975–92), *Lexikon der Ägyptologie*, 7 vols., Wiesbaden, Harrassowitz.

Henke, Reiner (2000), *Basilius und Ambrosius über das Sechstagewerk: eine vergleichende Studie*, Basel, Schwabe.

Hennecke, Edgar, and Schneemelcher, Wilhelm (1963), *New Testament Apocrypha*, ii: *Writings relating to the Acts of the Apostles and Related Texts*, Philadelphia, Westminster Press

Henner, Jutta, Förster, Hans, and Horak, Ulrike (eds.) (1999), *Christliches mit Feder und Faden: Christliches in Texten, Textilien und Alltagsgegenständen aus Ägypten*, Katalog zur

Sonderausstellung im Papyrusmuseum der Österreichischen Nationalbibliothek aus Anlass des 14. Internationalen Kongresses für Christliche Archäologie, Vienna, OVG.

Henning, Dirk (1999), *Periclitans res publica: Kaisertum und Eliten in der Krise des weströmischen Reiches 454/5–493 n. Chr.*, Stuttgart, Steiner.

Hennings, Ralph (1994), *Der Briefwechsel zwischen Augustinus und Hieronymus und ihr Streit um den Kanon des alten Testaments und die Auslegung von Gal. 2:11–14*, Leiden, Brill.

Henze, Matthias (1999), *The Madness of King Nebuchadnezzar: The Ancient Near Eastern Origins and Early History of Interpretation of Daniel 4*, Leiden, Brill, 1999.

Herlihy, David (1985), *Medieval Households*, Cambridge, MA, Harvard University Press.

Herman, József (1967), *Le Latin vulgaire*, Paris, Presses Universitaires de France.

Herman, József (2000), *Vulgar Latin*, tr. R. Wright, University Park, Pennsylvania State University Press.

Hermanowicz, Erika (2004), "Catholic Bishops and Appeals to the Imperial Court: A Legal Study of the Calama Riots in 408," *Journal of Early Christian Studies* 12: 483–523.

Herren, Michael W. (1988), *The Sacred Nectar of the Greeks: The Study of Greek in the West in the Early Middle Ages*, London, King's College.

Herzog, Reinhart (1987a), "Epochenerlebnis 'Revolution' und Epochenbewußtsein 'Spätantike': zur Genese einer historischen Epoche bei Chateaubriand," in Reinhart Herzog and Reinhart Koselleck (eds.), *Epochenschwelle und Epochenbewußtsein*, Munich, Fink, pp. 195–219.

Herzog, Reinhart (1987b), "'Wir leben in der Spätantike': eine Zeiterfahrung und ihre Impulse für die Forschung," Bamberg, Buchners; repr. in Peter Habermehl (ed.), *Spätantike: Studien zur römischen und lateinisch-christlichen Literatur*, Göttingen, Vandenhoeck & Ruprecht, 2002, pp. 321–48.

Herzog, Reinhart (ed.) (1989), *Handbuch der lateinischen Literatur der Antike*, v: *Restauration und Erneuerung 284–374 n. Chr.*, Munich, Beck.

Heuß, Alfred (1981), *Barthold Georg Niebuhrs wissenschaftliche Anfänge*, Göttingen, Vandenhoeck & Ruprecht.

Heussi, Karl (1936), *Der Ursprung des Mönchtums*, Tübingen, Mohr.

Hevelone-Harper, Jennifer L. (2005), *Disciples of the Desert: Monks, Laity, and Spiritual Authority in Sixth-Century Gaza*, Baltimore, MD, Johns Hopkins University Press.

Hidal, Sten (1974), *Interpretatio Syriaca: die Kommentare des Heiligen Ephräm des Syrers zu Genesis und Exodus mit besonderer Berücksichtigung ihrer auslegungsgeschichtlichen Stellung*, Coniectanea Biblica, Old Testament Series 6, Lund, Gleerup.

Hill, Edmund (2000), "Sermons III/11: Newly Discovered Sermons," in *The Works of Saint Augustine: A Translation for the Twenty-First Century*, New York, New City Press, pp. 13–17.

Hill, Peter (1987), "Traprain Law: The Votadini and the Romans," *Scottish Archaeological Review* 4: 85–91.

Hillenbrand, Robert (1981), "Islamic Art at the Crossroads: East versus West at Mshatta," in A. Daneshvari (ed.), *Essays in Islamic Art and Architecture in Honor of Katharina Otto-Dorn*, Malibu, CA, Undena Publications, pp. 63–86.

Hillner, Julia (2003), "*Domus*, Family and Inheritance: The Senatorial Family House in Late Antique Rome," *Journal of Roman Studies* 93: 129–45.

Hines, John (1998), "Culture Groups and Ethnic Groups in Northern Germany in and around the Migration Period," *Studien zur Sachsenforschung* 13: 219–32.

Hingley, Richard (2005), *Globalizing Roman Culture: Unity, Diversity and Empire*, London, Routledge.

Hirschfeld, Yizhar (1992), *The Judean Desert Monasteries in the Byzantine Period*, New Haven, CT, Yale University Press.

Hirshman, Marc (1996), *A Rivalry of Genius: Jewish and Christian Biblical Interpretation in Late Antiquity*, tr. B. Stein, Albany, NY, SUNY Press.

Hodges, Richard (1997), *Light in the Dark Age: The Rise and Fall of San Vincenzo al Volturno*, Ithaca, NY, Cornell University Press.

Hodges, Richard, and Bowden, William (eds.) (1998), *The Sixth Century: Production, Distribution, and Demand*, Leiden and Boston, MA, Brill.

Hoeper, M. (1998), "Die Höhensiedlungen der Alamannen und ihre Deutungsmöglichkeiten zwischen Fürstensitz, Heerlager, Rückzugsraum und Kultplatz," in Geuenich (1998: 325–48).

Hoeper, M., and Steuer, H. (1999), "Eine völkerwanderungszeitliche Höhenstation am Oberrhein: der Geißkopf bei Berghaupten, Ortenaukreis – Höhensiedlung, Militärlager oder Kultplatz?" *Germania* 77: 185–246.

Hoffer, Stanley E. (1999), *The Anxieties of Pliny the Younger*, Atlanta, GA, Scholars Press.

Hoffmann, Friedhelm (2000), *Ägypten: Kultur und Lebenswelt in griechisch-römischer Zeit: eine Darstellung nach den demotischen Quellen*, Berlin, Akademie Verlag.

Høilund Nielsen, Karen (1997), "Animal Art and the Weapon-Burial Rite – a Political Badge?" in Claus Kjeld Jensen and Karen Høilund Nielsen (eds.), *Burial and Society: The Chronological and Social Analysis of Archaeological Burial Data*, Aarhus and Oakville, CT, Aarhus University Press, pp. 129–48.

Holloway, R. Ross (2004), *Constantine and Rome*, New Haven, CT and London, Yale University Press.

Holum, Kenneth G. (1982), *Theodosian Empresses: Women and Imperial Dominion in Late Antiquity*, Berkeley and Los Angeles, University of California Press.

Hombert, Pierre-Marie (2000), *Nouvelles recherches de chronologie augustinienne*, Paris, Études Augustiniennes.

Honigmann, Ernest (1942–3), "The Original Lists of the Members of the Council of Nicaea, the Robber Synod and the Council of Chalcedon," *Byzantion* 16: 20–80.

Honoré, Tony (1994), *Emperors and Lawyers, with a Palingenesia of Third-Century Imperial Rescripts, 193–305 AD*, 2nd edn., Oxford, Oxford University Press.

Honoré, Tony (1998), *Law in the Crisis of Empire, 379–455 AD: The Theodosian Empire and Its Quaestors*, Oxford, Clarendon Press.

Honoré, Tony (2004), "Roman Law AD 200–400: From Cosmopolis to Rechtstaat?" in Swain and Edwards (2004: 109–32).

Hopkins, Keith (1965), "The Age of Roman Girls at Marriage," *Population Studies* 18: 309–27.

Hopkins, Keith (1991), "Conquest by Book," in M. Beard et al., *Literacy in the Roman World*, Ann Arbor, MI, Journal of Roman Archaeology, pp. 133–58.

Hopwood, Keith (1989), "Bandits, Elites, and Rural Order," in Wallace-Hadrill (1989: 171–87).

Horden, Peregrine, and Purcell, Nicholas (2000), *The Corrupting Sea: A Study of Mediterranean History*, Oxford and Malden, MA, Blackwell.

Howard-Johnston, James (1995), "The Two Great Powers in Late Antiquity: A Comparison," in Cameron (1995b: 157–226).

Howard-Johnston, James (1999), "Heraclius' Persian Campaigns and the Revival of the East Roman Empire, 622–630," *War in History* 6: 1–44.

Howard-Johnston, James (2000), "The Education and Expertise of Procopius," *Antiquité Tardive* 8: 19–30.

Howard-Johnston, James (2006), *East Rome, Sasanian Persia and the End of Antiquity: Historiographical and Historical Studies*, Abingdon and Williston, VT, Ashgate.

Howard-Johnston, James, and Hayward, Paul (eds.) (1999), *The Cult of the Saints in Late Antiquity and the Middle Ages: Essays on the Contribution of Peter Brown*, Oxford, Oxford University Press.

Howe, Nicholas (2005), "Anglo-Saxon England and the Postcolonial Void," in Ananya Jahanara Kabir and Deanne Williams (eds.), *Postcolonial Approaches to the European Middle Ages: Translating Cultures*, Cambridge, Cambridge University Press, pp. 25–47.

Hoyland, Robert G. (1997), *Seeing Islam as Others Saw It: A Survey and Evaluation of Christian, Jewish and Zoroastrian Writings on Early Islam*, Princeton, NJ, Darwin Press.

Hoyland, Robert G. (2001), *Arabia and the Arabs: From the Bronze Age to the Coming of Islam*, London and New York, Routledge.

Hübinger, P. A. (ed.) (1968), *Kulturbruch oder Kulturkontinuität im Übergang von der Antike zum Mittelalter*, Darmstadt, Wissenschaftliche Buchgesellschaft.

Hübinger, P. A. (ed.) (1969), *Zur Frage der Periodengrenze zwischen Altertum und Mittelalter*, Darmstadt, Wissenschaftliche Buchgesellschaft.

Hübner, Ernst (1871), *Inscriptiones Hispaniae Christianae*, Berlin, Reimer; repr. Hildesheim: Olms, 1975.

Humfress, Caroline (2000), "Roman Law, Forensic Argument, and the Formation of Christian Orthodoxy (III–VI Centuries)," in Elm, Rebillard, and Romano (2000: 125–47).

Humfress, Caroline (2005), "Law and Legal Practice in the Age of Justinian," in Maas (2005: 161–84).

Humfress, Caroline (2006), "Civil Law and Social Life," in Lenski (2006: 205–25).

Humfress, Caroline (2007), *Orthodoxy and the Courts in Late Antiquity*, Oxford, Oxford University Press.

Humphrey, John H. (1986), *Roman Circuses: Arenas for Chariot Racing*, Berkeley and Los Angeles, University of California Press.

Humphries, Mark (2000), "Italy, AD 425–605," in Cameron, Ward-Perkins, and Whitby (2000: 525–51).

Humphries, Mark (2007a), "From Emperor to Pope? Ceremonial, Space, and Authority in Rome from Constantine to Gregory the Great," in Cooper and Hillner (2007: 21–58).

Humphries, Mark (2007b), "International Relations," in Van Wees, Sabin, and Whitby (2007: 235–69).

Humphries, Mark (2007c), "A New Created World: Classical Geographical Texts and Christian Contexts in Late Antiquity," in Scourfield (2007: 33–67).

Hunger, Herbert (1978), *Handbuch der Altertumswissenschaft*, xii/5: *Die hochsprachliche profane Literatur der Byzantiner*, 2 vols., Munich, Beck.

Hunger, Herbert et al. (eds.) (1961), *Geschichte der Textüberlieferung der antiken und mittelalterlichen Literatur*, i, Zurich, Atlantis.

Hunt, E. David (1982), *Holy Land Pilgrimage in the Later Roman Empire AD 312–460*, Oxford, Clarendon Press.

Hunt, E. David (1985), "Christians and Christianity in Ammianus Marcellinus," *Classical Quarterly* 35: 186–200.

Hunt, E. David (1993), "Christianising the Roman Empire: The Evidence of the *Code*," in Harries and Wood (1993: 143–58).

Hunter, David (1987), "Resistance to the Virginal Ideal in Late Fourth Century Rome," *Theological Studies* 48: 45–64.

Hunter, David (1999), "Clerical Celibacy and the Veiling of Virgins: New Boundaries in Late Ancient Christianity," in Klingshirn and Vessey (1999: 139–52).

Hunter, David (2003), "Augustine and the Making of Marriage in Roman North Africa," *Journal of Early Christian Studies* 11: 63–85.

Hunter, David (2007), "Marrying and the *tabulae nuptiales* in Roman North Africa from Tertullian to Augustine," in Reynolds and Witte (2007: 95–113).

Husselman, Eleanor (1947), "A Bohairic School Text on Papyrus," *Journal of Near Eastern Studies* 6: 129–51.

Huyse, Philip (ed.) (1999), *Corpus Inscriptionum Iranicarum*, iii: *Pahlavi Inscriptions*, 1: *Die dreisprachige Inschrift Saburs I an der Ka'aba-i Zardust (ŠKZ)*, 2 vols., London, School of Oriental and African Studies.

Hvass, S. (1983), "Vorbasse: The Development of a Settlement through the First Millennium AD," *Journal of Danish Archaeology* 2: 127–36.

Ibn Abi Shayba, 'Abdallah b. Muhammad (1979), *Kitab al-musannaf*, Bombay, Dar al-Salafiyya.

Ibn 'Asakir al-Shafi'i, 'Ali b. al-Hasan b. Hibatallah (1995–8), *Ta'rikh madinat Dimashq*, ed. 'Ali Shibri, Beirut, Dar al-Fikr.

Immerzeel, M., and Van der Vliet, Jacques (eds.) (2004), *Coptic Studies on the Threshold of a New Millennium*, Proceedings of the Seventh International Congress of Coptic Studies, Leiden, August 27–September 2, 2000, 2 vols., Louvain, Peeters.

Inglebert, Hervé (2001), *Interpretatio Christiana: les mutations des savoirs (cosmographie, géographie, ethnographie, histoire) dans l'antiquité chrétienne 30–630 après J.-C.*, Paris, Études Augustiniennes.

Irmscher, Johannes (1973), "Der Hellenismus im Geschichtsverständnis der Byzantiner," in Pavel Oliva and Jan Burian (eds.), *Soziale Probleme im Hellenismus und im römischen Reich*, Akten der Konferenz (Liblice, 10–13 Oktober 1972), Prague, pp. 37–62.

Isaac, Benjamin (1984), "Bandits in Judaea and Arabia," *Harvard Studies in Classical Philology* 88: 197–203.

Isaac, Benjamin (1992), *The Limits of Empire: The Roman Army in the East*, rev. edn., Oxford, Clarendon Press.

Isaac, Benjamin (1998a), "The Eastern Frontier," in Cameron and Garnsey (1998: 437–60).

Isaac, Benjamin (1998b), "Orientals and Jews in the *Historia Augusta:* Fourth-Century Prejudice and Stereotypes," in Benjamin Isaac, *The Near East under Roman Rule: Selected Papers*, Leiden, Brill, pp. 268–82.

Isaac, Benjamin (2004), *The Invention of Racism in Classical Antiquity*, Princeton, NJ, Princeton University Press.

Isaac, Benjamin, and Roll, Israel (1982), *Roman Roads in Judea*, i: *The Legio–Scythopolis Road*, Oxford, BAR.

Jacks, Philip (1993), *The Antiquarian and the Myth of Antiquity: The Origins of Rome in Renaissance Thought*, Cambridge, Cambridge University Press.

Jacobs, Andrew S. (2004), *Remains of the Jews: The Holy Land and Christian Empire in Late Antiquity*, Stanford, CA, Stanford University Press.

Jaggi, C., and Meier, H.-R. (1997), " '. . . This Great Appetite for Church Building Still Needs Adequate Explanation': zum Kirchenbauboom am Ende der Spätantike," in Coella et al. (1997: 181–98).

James, Edward (1988), *The Franks*, Oxford and New York, Blackwell.

James, Edward (2001), *Britain in the First Millennium*, London, Arnold.

James, Liz (1996), " 'Pray not to Fall into Temptation and be on Your Guard': Pagan Statues in Christian Constantinople," *Gesta* 35: 12–20.

James, Liz (ed.) (1997), *Women, Men and Eunuchs: Gender in Byzantium*, London, Routledge.

James, Liz, and Webb, Ruth (1991), "To Understand Intimate Things and Enter Secret Places: Ekphrasis and Art in Byzantium," *Art History* 14: 3–41.

Janse, Mark (2002), "Aspects of Bilingualism in the History of Greek Language," in Adams, Janse, and Swain (2002: 332–91).

Janssens, Jos (1981), *Vita e morte del cristiano negli epitafi di Roma anteriori al sec. VII*, Rome, Università Gregoriana.

Janvier, Yves (1969), *La Législation du Bas-Empire romain sur les édifices publics*, Aix-en-Provence, La Pensée Universitaire.

Jardine, Lisa (1993), *Erasmus, Man of Letters: The Construction of Charisma in Print*, Princeton, NJ, Princeton University Press.

Jaritz, G., and Moreno-Riaño, G. (eds.) (2003), *Time and Eternity: The Medieval Discourse*, Turnhout, Brepols.

Jeffery, Arthur (1938), *The Foreign Vocabulary of the Qur'ân*, Baroda, Oriental Institute.

Jeffreys, Elizabeth M. (1979), "The Attitudes of Byzantine Chroniclers towards Ancient History," *Byzantion* 49: 199–238.

Jeffreys, Elizabeth, Croke, Brian, and Scott, Roger (eds.) (1990), *Studies in John Malalas*, Sydney, Australian Association for Byzantine Studies.

Jensen, Robin (2000), *Understanding Early Christian Art*, London and New York, Routledge.

Jerg, Ernst (1970), *Vir venerabilis: Untersuchungen zur Titulatur der Bischöfe in den ausserkirchlichen Texten der Spätantike als Beitrag zur Deutung ihrer öffentlichen Stellung*, Vienna, Herder.

Johlen, Monika (1999), *Die vermögensrechtliche Stellung der weströmischen Frau in der Spätantike: zur Fortgeltung des römischen Rechts in den Gotenreichen und im Burgunderreich*, Berlin, Duncker & Humblot.

Johns, Jeremy (1999), "The 'House of the Prophet' and the Concept of the Mosque," in Jeremy Johns (ed.), *Bayt al-Maqdis: Jerusalem and Early Islam*, Oxford, Oxford University Press, pp. 39–112.

Johns, Jeremy (2003), "Archaeology and the History of Early Islam: The First Seventy Years," *Journal of the Economic and Social History of the Orient* 46: 411–36.

Johnson, Janet (1976), "The Dialect of the Demotic Magical Papyrus of London and Leiden," in *Studies in Honor of George R. Hughes*, Chicago, Oriental Institute of the University of Chicago, pp. 105–32.

Johnson, Maxwell E. (1995), *The Prayers of Sarapion of Thmuis: A Literary, Liturgical and Theological Analysis*, Rome, Pontificio Istituto Orientale.

Johnson, Stephen (1983), *Late Roman Fortifications*, London, Batsford.

Johnston, David (1999), *Roman Law in Context*, Cambridge, Cambridge University Press.

Jolowicz, H. J. (1952), *Historical Introduction to the Study of Roman Law*, Cambridge, Cambridge University Press.

Jones, A. H. M. (1937), *The Cities of the Eastern Roman Provinces*, Oxford, Clarendon Press; 2nd edn., 1971.

Jones, A. H. M. (1940), *The Greek City from Alexander to Justinian*, Oxford, Clarendon Press.

Jones, A. H. M. (1948), *Constantine and the Conversion of Europe*, London, English Universities Press.

Jones, A. H. M. (1959), "Were Ancient Heresies National or Social Movements in Disguise?" *Journal of Theological Studies* 10: 280–86.

Jones, A. H. M. (1964), *The Later Roman Empire, 284–602: A Social, Economic and Administrative Survey*, 3 vols., Oxford, Blackwell; repr. in 2 vols., Oxford, Blackwell, 1973; Baltimore, MD, Johns Hopkins University Press, 1986.

Jones, A. H. M. (1966), *The Decline of the Ancient World*, London, Longman & Greens.

Jones, A. H. M. (1971), *Cities of the Eastern Roman Provinces*, 2nd edn., Oxford, Clarendon Press.

Jones, A. H. M. (1973), *The Later Roman Empire 284–602: A Social, Economic and Administrative Survey*, 2 vols., Oxford, Blackwell.

Jones, A. H. M., Martindale, J. R., and Morris, J. (1971), *The Prosopography of the Later Roman Empire*, i: *A.D. 260–395*, Cambridge, Cambridge University Press.

Jones, M. (2000), "The Stratigraphic Examination of Standing Buildings: Problems and Solutions," in Roskams (2000: 113–23).

Jones, Michael E. (1996), *The End of Roman Britain*, Ithaca, NY, Cornell University Press.

Jørgensen, L., Storgaard, B., and Gebauer Thomsen, L. (ed.) (2003), *The Spoils of Victory: The North in the Shadow of the Roman Empire*, Copenhagen, Nationalmuseets.

Joshel, Sandra (1992), *Work, Identity, and Legal Status at Rome: A Study of the Occupational Inscriptions*, Norman, OK and London, University of Oklahoma Press.

Joshel, Sandra R., and Murnaghan, Sheila (eds.) (1998), *Women and Slaves in Greco-Roman Culture: Differential Equations*, London and New York, Routledge.

Judge, E. A. (1977), "The Earliest Use of Monachos for 'Monk' (P.Coll. Youtie 77) and the Origins of Monasticism," *Jahrbuch für Antike und Christentum* 20: 72–89.

Judge, E. A., and Pickering, S. R. (1970), "Biblical Papyri Prior to Constantine: Some Cultural Implications of Their Physical Form," *Prudentia*, 10: 1–13.

Jullien, Christelle, and Jullien, Florence (2002), *Apôtres des confins: Processus missionnaires chrétiens dans l'empire Iranien*, Bures-sur-Yvette, Groupe pour l'Étude de la Civilisation du Moyen-Orient.

Jürgens, Heiko (1972), *Pompa diaboli: die lateinischen Kirchenväter und das antike Theater*, Stuttgart, Kohlhammer.

Kahle, Paul E. (1954), *Bala'izah: Coptic Texts from Deir el-Bala'izah in Upper Egypt*, 2 vols., Oxford, Oxford University Press.

Kahlos, Maijastina (1994), "Fabia Aconia Paulina and the Death of Praetextatus – Rhetoric and Ideals in Late Antiquity (*CIL* VI 1779)," *Arctos* 28: 13–25.

Kajanto, Iiro (1966), *Supernomina: A Study in Latin Epigraphy*, Helsinki, Societas Scientiarum Fennica.

Kaldellis, Anthony (2003), "Things Are Not What They are: Agathias *Mythistoricus* and the Last Laugh of Classical Culture," *Classical Quarterly* 53: 295–300.

Kaldellis, Anthony (2004), *Procopius of Caesarea: Tyranny, History, and Philosophy at the End of Antiquity*, Philadelphia, University of Pennsylvania Press.

Kannengiesser, Charles (2004), *Handbook of Patristic Exegesis: The Bible in Ancient Christianity*, 2 vols., Leiden, Brill.

Karkov, Catherine E., Wickham-Crowley, Kelly M., and Young, Bailey K. (eds.) (1999), *Spaces of the Living and the Dead: An Archaeological Dialogue*, Oxford, Oxbow Books.

Karpozilos, Apostolos (1997–2002), *Byzantinoi historikoi kai chronographoi*, i–ii, Athens, Ekdoseis Kanakê.

Kasser, Rodolphe (ed.) (1960), *Papyrus Bodmer VI: Livre des Proverbes*, Louvain, Secrétariat du CSCO.

Kasser, Rodolphe (1980–1), "Prolégomènes à un essai de classification systématique des dialectes et subdialectes coptes selon les critères de la phonétique," pts. 1 and 2, *Muséon* 93 (1980): 53–112, 237–97; 94 (1981): 91–152.

Kasser, Rodolphe (1990), "A Standard System of Sigla for Referring to the Dialects of Coptic," *Journal of Coptic Studies* 1: 141–51.

Kasser, Rodolphe (1991a), "Alphabets, Old Coptic," in Atiya (1991, viii: 41–5).

Kasser, Rodolphe (1991b), "Geography, Dialectal," in Atiya (1991, viii: 133–41).

Kasser, Rodolphe (1991c), "Paleography," in Atiya (1991, viii: 175–84).

Kasser, Rodolphe (2004), "Protodialectes coptes à systèmes alphabétiques de type vieux-copte," in Immerzeel and Van der Vliet (2004, i: 75–123).

Kaster, Robert A. (1983), "The Salaries of Libanius," *Chiron* 13: 37–59.

Kaster, Robert A. (1988), *Guardians of Language: The Grammarian and Society in Late Antiquity*, Berkeley and Los Angeles, University of California Press.

Kazhdan, Alexander (1987), "'Constantine imaginaire': Byzantine Legends of the Ninth Century about Constantine the Great," *Byzantion* 57: 196–250.

Kazhdan, Alexander (ed.) (1991), *The Oxford Dictionary of Byzantium*, New York, Oxford University Press.

Kazhdan, Alexander (1995), "Innovation in Byzantium," in A. R. Littlewood (ed.), *Originality in Byzantine Literature, Art and Music: A Collection of Essays*, Oxford, Oxbow Books, pp. 1–14.

Kazhdan, Alexander, with Sherry, Lee F., and Angelidi, Christine (1999), *A History of Byzantine Literature, 650–850*, Athens, National Hellenic Research Foundation Institute for Byzantine Research.

Kazhdan, Alexander, and Epstein, Ann Wharton (1985), *Change in Byzantine Culture in the Eleventh and Twelfth Centuries*, Berkeley and Los Angeles, University of California Press.

Kelley, Donald R. (1970), *Foundations of Modern Historical Scholarship: Language, Law and History in the French Renaissance*, New York, Columbia University Press.

Kelly, Christopher (2004), *Ruling the Later Roman Empire*, Cambridge, MA, Harvard University Press.

Kelly, J. N. D. (1972), *Early Christian Creeds*, 3rd edn., London, Longman.

Kelly, J. N. D. (1975), *Jerome: His Life, Writings, and Controversies*, London, Duckworth; New York, Harper & Row.

Kennedy, David (2000), "Zeugma," www.classics.uwa.edu.au/projects/zeugma

Kennedy, George A. (1983), *Greek Rhetoric under Christian Emperors*, Princeton, NJ, Princeton University Press.

Kennedy, Hugh N. (1985), "From *polis* to *madîna*: Urban Change in Late Antique and Early Islamic Syria," *Past and Present* 106: 3–27.

Kennedy, Hugh N. (2000), "Syria, Palestine and Mesopotamia," in Cameron, Ward-Perkins, and Whitby (2000: 588–611).

Kennedy, Hugh N. (2004), *The Prophet and the Age of the Caliphates*, 2nd edn., Harlow and New York, Pearson/Longman.

Kenney, E. J. (ed.) (1996), *Ovid Heroides XVI–XXI*, Cambridge, Cambridge University Press.

Kenyon, Frederick G. (ed.) (1937), *Chester Beatty Biblical Papyri*, vi: *Isaiah, Jeremiah, Ecclesiasticus*, London, Walker.

Ker, W. P. (1904), *The Dark Ages*, Edinburgh, Blackwood.

Kertzer, David, and Saller, Richard (eds.) (1991), *The Family in Italy from Antiquity to the Present*, New Haven, CT, Yale University Press.

Kessler, H. L. (1976), review of Yves Christe, *La Vision de Matthieu (Matth. XXIV–XXV): Origines et développement d'une image de la Seconde Parousie* (Paris, 1973), *Art Bulletin* 58: 121–3.

Kettenhofen, E. (1994), "Deportations," in Yarshater (1982–, vii/3: 297–308).

Key Fowden, Elizabeth (1999), *The Barbarian Plain: Saint Sergius between Rome and Iran*, Berkeley and Los Angeles, University of California Press.

al-Khawlani, 'Abd al-Jabbar (1989), *Ta'rikh Daraya*, ed. Sa'id al-Afghani, Benghazi, Manshurat Jami'at Benghazi.

King, Charles (1987), "The Veracity of Ammianus Marcellinus' Description of the Huns," *American Journal of Ancient History* 12: 77–95.

King, Geoffrey D. (1995), "Settlement in Western and Central Arabia and the Gulf in the Sixth–Eighth Centuries A.D.,", in King and Cameron (1995: 181–212).

King, Geoffrey D., and Cameron, Averil (eds.) (1995), *The Byzantine and Early Islamic Near East*, ii: *Land Use and Settlement Patterns*, Princeton, NJ, Darwin Press.

Kinzig, W., and Vinzent, M. (1999), "Recent Research on the Origin of the Creed," *Journal of Theological Studies* 50: 535–59.

Kirsch, Johann Peter (1918), *Die römischen Titelkirchen im Altertum*, Paderborn, Schöningh.

Kister, M. J. (1962), "'A Booth Like the Booth of Moses': A Study of an Early *hadîth*," *Bulletin of the School of Oriental and African Studies* 25: 150–5.

Kitzinger, Ernst (1955), *Early Medieval Art in the British Museum*, London, British Museum Publications.

Kitzinger, Ernst (1977), *Byzantine Art in the Making: Main Lines of Stylistic Development in Mediterranean Art, 3rd–7th Century*, Cambridge, MA, Harvard University Press.

Klauck, Hans-Josef (1998), *Die antike Briefliteratur und das Neue Testament: ein Lehr- und Arbeitsbuch*, Paderborn, Schöningh.

Kleberg, Tönnes (1957), *Hôtels, restaurants et cabarets dans l'antiquité romain: études historiques et philologiques*, Uppsala, Almqvist Wiksells.

Kleemann, J. (1999), "Zum Aufkommen der Körperbestattung in Niedersachsen," *Studien zur Sachsenforschung* 13: 253–62.

Klein, Kerwin L. (2000), "On the Emergence of Memory in Historical Discourse," *Representations* 69: 127–50.

Klingshirn, William E. (1994), *Caesarius of Arles: The Making of a Christian Community in Late Antique Gaul*, Cambridge, Cambridge University Press.

Klingshirn, William E., and Vessey, Mark (eds.) (1999), *The Limits of Ancient Christianity: Essays on Late Antique Thought and Culture in Honor of R. A. Markus*, Ann Arbor, University of Michigan Press.

Klöckener, Martin (1992), "Die *recitatio nominum* im Hochgebet nach Augustins Schriften," in A. Heinz and H. Rennings (eds.), *Gratias agamus: Studien zum eucharistischen Hochgebet*, Freiburg, Herder, pp. 183–210.

Klutz, Todd (1998), "The Rhetoric of Science in the *Rise of Christianity*: A Response to Rodney Stark's Sociological Account of Christianization," *Journal of Early Christian Studies* 6: 162–84.

Kneissl, Peter, and Losemann, Volker (1988), *Alte Geschichte und Wissenschaftsgeschichte: Festschrift für Karl Christ*, Darmstadt, Wissenschaftliche Buchgesellschaft.

Knox, Bernard M. W. (1968), "Silent Reading in Antiquity," *Greek, Roman, and Byzantine Studies* 9: 421–35.

Knust, Jennifer (2005), *Abandoned to Lust: Sexual Slander and Ancient Christianity*, New York, Columbia University Press.

Koder, Johannes (1991–2), "'Zeitenwenden': zur Periodisierungsfrage aus byzantinischer Sicht," *Byzantinische Zeitschrift* 84–5: 409–22.

Kofsky, Aryeh (2000), *Eusebius of Caesarea against Paganism*, Leiden, Brill.

Kolb, Anne (2000), *Transport und Nachrichtentransfer im Römischen Reich*, Berlin, Akademie Verlag.

Kolb, Anne (2001), "Transport and Communication in the Roman State: The *cursus publicus*," in Adams and Laurence (2001: 95–105).

Kondoleon, Christine (ed.) (2000), *Antioch: The Lost Ancient City*, Princeton, NJ, Princeton University Press; Worcester, MA, Worcester Art Museum.

Konstan, David (1997), *Friendship in the Classical World*, Cambridge, Cambridge University Press.

Koonammakkal, Thomas (1994), "St. Ephrem and Greek Wisdom," in René Lavenant (ed.), *VI Symposium Syriacum 1992*, Rome, Pontificio Istituto Orientale, pp. 168–76.

Kooper, E. (ed.) (2002), *The Medieval Chronicle*, ii, Amsterdam, Rodopi.

Kornemann, Ernst (1922), "Das Problem des Untergangs der antiken Welt," *Vergangenheit und Gegenwart* 12: 193–202, 241–54; repr. in Christ (1970: 201–27).

Kortenbeutel, Heinz, and Böhlig, Alexander (1935), "Ostrakon mit griechisch-koptischem Psalmentext," *Aegyptus* 15: 415–18.

Kotila, Heikki (1992), *Memoria Mortuorum: Commemoration of the Departed in Augustine*, Rome, Institutum Patristicum Augustinianum.

Kötting, Bernhard (1950), *Peregrinatio religiosa: Wallfahrten in der Antike und das Pilgerwesen in der alten Kirche*, Münster, Regensberg.

Kotula, T. (1974), "Snobisme municipal ou prospérité relative? Recherches sur le statut des villes nord-africaines sous le Bas-Empire romain," *Antiquités Africaines* 8: 111–31.

Kötzsche, Lieselotte (1994), "Die trauernden Frauen: zum Londoner Passionskästchen," in D. Buckton and T. A. Heslop (eds.), *Studies in Medieval Art and Architecture Presented to Peter Lasko*, Dover, NH, Alan Sutton; London, British Museum Publications, pp. 80–90.

Kraft, Robert (1996), "Scripture and Canon in Jewish Apocrypha and Pseudepigrapha," in Sæbø (1996: 199–216).

Kramer, Bärbel, and Shelton, John C. (eds.) (1987), *Das Archiv des Nepheros und verwandte Texte*, Mainz, von Zabern.

Krause, Jens-Uwe (1991), "Familien-und Haushaltsstrukturen im spätantiken Gallien," *Klio* 73: 537–62.

Krause, Jens-Uwe, and Witschel, Christian (eds.) (2006), *Die Stadt in der Spätantike: Niedergang oder Wandel?* Akten des internationalen Kolloquiums in München am 30. und 31. Mai 2003, Stuttgart, Franz Steiner.

Krause, Martin (ed.) (1998), *Ägypten in spätantik-christlicher Zeit: Einführung in die koptische Kultur*, Wiesbaden, Ludwig Reichert.

Krautheimer, Richard (1965), *Corpus basilicarum christianarum Romae. The Early Christian Basilicas of Rome (iv–ix cent.)*, iv, Vatican City, Pontificio Istituto di Archaeologia Cristiana.

Krautheimer, Richard (1977), *Corpus basilicarum christianarum Romae. The Early Christian Basilicas of Rome*, v, Vatican City, Pontificio Istituto di Archaeologia Cristiana.

Krautheimer, Richard (1980), *Rome: Profile of a City, 312–1308*, Princeton, NJ, Princeton University Press.

Krautheimer, Richard (1983), *Three Christian Capitals: Topography and Politics*, Berkeley and Los Angeles, University of California Press.

Krautheimer, Richard (1993), "Successi e fallimenti nell'architettura chiesastica tardoantica," in Richard Krautheimer, *Architettura sacra paleocristiana e medievale e altri saggi su Renascimento e Barocco*, Turin, Bollati Boringhieri, pp. 98–150.

Krawiec, Rebecca (2002), *Shenoute and the Women of the White Monastery: Egyptian Monasticism in Late Antiquity*, Oxford and New York, Oxford University Press.

Kreis, Douglas, and Tkacz, Catherine Brown (eds.) (1999), *Nova Doctrina Vetusque: Essays on Early Christianity in Honor of Fredric W. Schlatter, S.J.*, New York, Peter Lang.

Kretschmar, Georg (1964), "Ein Beitrag zur Frage nach dem Ursprung frühchristlicher Askese," *Zeitschrift für Theologie und Kirche* 61: 27–67.

Kronholm, Tryggve (1978), *Motifs from Genesis 1–11 in the Genuine Hymns of Ephrem the Syrian, with Particular Reference to the Influence of Jewish Exegetical Tradition*, Coniectanea Biblica Old Tesament Series 11, Lund, Gleerup.

Krueger, Derek (2004), *Writing and Holiness: The Practice of Authorship in the Early Christian East*, Philadelphia, University of Pennsylvania Press.

Kulikowski, Michael (2000), "Barbarians in Gaul: Usurpers in Britain," *Britannia* 31: 325–45.

Kulikowski, Michael (2002), "Nation versus Army: A Necessary Contrast?" in Gillett (2002b: 69–84).

Kulikowski, Michael (2004), *Late Roman Spain and Its Cities*, Baltimore, MD and London, Johns Hopkins University Press.

Kulikowski, Michael (2007), *Rome's Gothic Wars: From the Third Century to Alaric*, Cambridge and New York, Cambridge University Press.

Kurdock, Anne N. (2003), "The Anician Women: Patronage and Dynastic Strategy in a Late Roman Domus, 350 CE–600 CE," unpublished Ph.D. dissertation, University of Manchester.

Kustas, George L. (1953), "Photius' Idea of History," *Harvard Studies in Classical Philology* 61: 170–2.

Kustas, George L. (1962), "The Literary Criticism of Photius: A Christian Definition of Style," *Hellenika* 17: 132–69.

Kyriakidis, Stilpon (1961), *Eustazio di Tessalonica: la espugnazione di Tessalonica*, Palermo, Istituto Siciliano di Studi Bizantini e Neoellenici.

La Bonnardière, Anne-Marie (1965), *Recherches de chronologie augustinienne*, Paris, Études Augustiniennes.

Labourt, J. (1904), *Le Christianisme dans l'empire perse sous la dynastie Sassanide (224–632)*, Paris, Lecoffre.

Lagarrigue, Georges (ed. and tr.) (1975), *Salvien de Marseille: Oeuvres*, ii: *Du gouvernement de Dieu*, Paris, Éditions du Cerf.

Lamberton, R. (1986), *Homer the Theologian: Neoplatonist Allegorical Reading and the Growth of the Epic Tradition*, Berkeley and Los Angeles, University of California Press.

Lamm, J. P., and Nordström, H.-Å. (eds.) (1983), *Vendel Period Studies*, Transactions of the Boat-Grave Symposium, Stockholm, February 2–3, 1981 (Museum of National Antiquities, Stockholm, 2), Stockholm, Statens Historiska Museum.

Lampe, Peter (1987), *Die Stadtrömischen Christen in den ersten beiden Jahrhunderten*, Tübingen, J. C. B. Mohr; tr. Michael Steinhauser, *From Paul to Valentinus: Christians at Rome in the First Two Centuries*, London, T. & T. Clark, 2003.

Lane, A. (1994), "Trade, Gifts and Cultural Exchange in Dark Age Western Scotland," in Crawford (1994: 103–15).

Lane Fox, Robin (1986), *Pagans and Christians*, Harmondsworth, Viking.

Langslow, David (2000), *Medical Latin in the Roman Empire*, Oxford, Oxford University Press.

Laniado, Avshalom (2002), *Recherches sur les notables municipaux dans l'empire protobyzantin*, Paris, Association des Amis du Centre d'Histoire et Civilisation de Byzance.

Lardet, Pierre (2000), "La figure de Jérôme chez Lorenzo Valla," in Mariarosa Cortesi and Claudio Leonardi (eds.), *Tradizioni patristiche nell'umanesimo*, Atti del convegno … Firenze, 6–8 Febbraio 1997, Florence, SISMEL, pp. 211–30.

Laurand, Louis (1921), "L'Oraison funèbre de Théodose par saint Ambroise: discours prononcé et discours écrit," *Revue d'Histoire Ecclesiastique* 17: 349–50.

Laurence, Patrick (2002), *La Vie latine de sainte Mélanie: édition critique, traduction et commentaire*, Jerusalem, Franciscan Printing Press.

Laurence, Ray (1999), *The Roads of Roman Italy: Mobility and Cultural Change*, London, Routledge.

Laurence, Ray (2001), "The Creation of Geography: An Interpretation of Roman Britain," in Adams and Laurence (2001: 67–94).

Laurence, Ray (2004), "Milestones, Communications, and Political Stability," in Ellis and Kidner (2004: 41–58).

Laurence, Ray, and Wallace-Hadrill, Andrew (1997), *Domestic Space in the Roman World: Pompeii and Beyond*, Portsmouth, RI, Journal of Roman Archaeology.

Lauwers, Michel (1996), "La Sépulture des Patriarches (Genèse, 23): modèles scripturaires et pratiques sociales dans l'Occident médiéval ou Du bon usage d'un récit de fondation," *Studi Medievali* 37: 519–47.

Lauwers, Michel (1997), *La Mémoire des ancêtres, le souci des morts: morts, rites, et société au moyen age: diocèse de Liège, XIe–XIIIe siècles*, Paris, Beauchesne.

Lauwers, Michel (2005), *Naissance du cimetière: lieux sacrés et terre des morts dans l'Occident médiéval*, Paris, Aubier.

Lauxtermann, Marc D. (2003), *Byzantine Poetry from Pisides to Geometres: Texts and Contexts*, i, Vienna, Verlag der Österreichischen Akademie der Wissenschaften.

Lavan, Luke (ed.) (2001), *Recent Research in Late Antique Urbanism*, Portsmouth, RI, Journal of Roman Archaeology.

Lavan, Luke (2003), "The Political Topography of the Late Antique City: Activity Spaces in Practice," in Lavan and Bowden (2003: 314–37).

Lavan, Luke, and Bowden, William (eds.) (2003), *Theory and Practice in Late Antique Archaeology*, Leiden and Boston, MA, Brill.

Lawless, George (1987), *Augustine of Hippo and His Monastic Rule*, Oxford, Clarendon Press.

Le Blant, Edmond (ed.) (1856–65), *Inscriptions chrétiennes de la Gaule antérieures au VIIIe siècle*, 2 vols., Paris, L'Imprimerie Impériale.

Le Boulluec, Alain (1985), *La Notion d'hérésie dans la littérature greque, IIe–IIIe siècle*, Paris, Etudes Augustiniennes.

Lecker, Michael (1989), "The Estates of 'Amr b. al-'As in Palestine: Notes on a New Negev Arabic Inscription," *Bulletin of the School of Oriental and African Studies* 52: 24–37.

Lecker, Michael (2001), "Were Customs Dues Levied at the Time of the Prophet Muhammad?" *al-Qantara* 22: 19–43.

Leclercq, Jean (1957), *L'Amour des lettres et le désir de Dieu*, Paris, Éditions du Cerf.

Lee, A. D. (1993), *Information and Frontiers: Roman Foreign Relations in Late Antiquity*, Cambridge, Cambridge University Press.

Lefort, Louis-Theophile (1933), "S. Athanase Écrivain Copte," *Muséon* 46: 1–33.

Lefort, Louis-Theophile (1935), review of Crum (1934), *Muséon* 48: 234–5.

Lefort, Louis-Theophile (1956), *Oeuvres de S. Pachôme et de ses disciples*, Louvain, Secrétariat du CSCO.

Lehmann, Paul (1929), "Mittelalterliche Beinahmen und Ehrentitel," *Historisches Jahrbuch* 49: 215–39.

Lelong, Charles (1986), *La Basilique Saint-Martin de Tours*, Chambray-lès-Tours, CLD.

Lemerle, Paul (1986), *Byzantine Humanism, the First Phase: Notes and Remarks on Education and Culture in Byzantium from Its Origins to the 10th Century*, tr. Helen Lindsay and Ann Moffatt, Canberra, Australian Association for Byzantine Studies.

Le Nain de Tillemont, Louis Sébastien (1690–), *Histoire des empereurs*, 6 vols., Chez Charles Robustel; new edn. 1720–38.

Le Nain de Tillemont, Louis Sébastien (1693–1712), *Mémoires pour servir à l'histoire ecclésiastique des six premiers siècles*, 16 vols., Paris, Chez Charles Robustel.

Lendon, J. E. (1997), *Empire of Honour: The Art of Government in the Roman World*, Oxford, Clarendon Press; New York, Oxford University Press.

Lenski, Noel (2002), "Evidence for the Audientia episcopalis in the New Letters of Augustine," in Mathisen (2002: 83–97).

Lenski, Noel (2004), "Valens and the Monks: Cudgeling and Conscription as a Means of Social Control," *Dumbarton Oaks Papers* 58: 93–117.

Lenski, Noel (ed.) (2006), *The Cambridge Companion to the Age of Constantine*, Cambridge and New York, Cambridge University Press.

Leo, Friedrich (ed.) (1881), Venantius Fortunatus, *Carmina, MGH, auct. antiquiss.* 4.1, Berlin, Weidmann; tr. Judith George, *Venantius Fortunatus: Personal and Political Poems*, Liverpool, Liverpool University Press, 1995.

Leone, A. (2003), "Topographies of Production in North African Cities during the Vandal and Byzantine Periods," in Lavan and Bowden (2003: 257–87).

Lepelley, Claude (1979–81), *Les Cités de l'Afrique romaine au Bas-Empire*, 2 vols., Paris, Études Augustiniennes.

Lepelley, Claude (1983), "*Quot curiales, tot tyranni*: l'image du décurion oppresseur au Bas-Empire," in Edmond Frézouls (ed.), *Crise et redressement dans les provinces européennes de l'Empire (milieu du IIIe–milieu du IVe siècle ap. J.-C.)*, Actes du colloque de Strasbourg, Décembre 1981, Strasbourg, AECR, pp. 143–56.

Lepelley, Claude (1992), "Permanence de la cité classique et archaïsmes municipaux en Italie au Bas-Empire," in Michel Christol et al. (eds.), *Institutions, société et vie politique dans l'empire romain au IVe siècle ap. J.-C.*, Actes de la table ronde autour de l'œuvre d'André Chastagnol, Paris, 20–21 Janvier 1989, Rome, École Française de Rome, pp. 353–71.

Lepelley, Claude (ed.) (1996), *La Fin de la cité antique et le début de la cite médiévale*, Actes du colloque tenu à l'Université de Paris X-Nanterre, les 1, 2 et 3 Avril 1993, Bari, Edipuglia.

Lepelley, Claude (1998), "Le Patronat épiscopal aux IVe et Ve siècles: continuités et ruptures avec le patronat classique," in Rebillard and Sotinel (1998: 17–33).

Lévi-Strauss, Claude (1969), *The Elementary Structures of Kinship*, tr. James Harle Bell, ed. John Richard von Sturmer and Rodney Needham, Boston, MA, Beacon Press.

Lévi-Strauss, Claude (1987), *Anthropology and Myth: Lectures 1951–82*, tr. Roy Willis, Oxford, Blackwell.

Lewin, Ariel (1991), *Studi sulla città imperiale romana nell'oriente tardoantico*, Como, Edizioni New Press.

Lewis, Sian (1996), *News and Society in the Greek Polis*, London, Duckworth; Chapel Hill, University of North Carolina Press.

Leyerle, Blake (1996), "Landscape as Cartography in Early Christian Pilgrim Narratives," *Journal of the American Academy of Religion* 64: 119–43.

Leyerle, Blake (2001), *Theatrical Shows and Ascetic Lives: John Chrysostom's Attack on Spiritual Marriage*, Berkeley and Los Angeles, University of California Press.

Leyser, Conrad (1999), " 'This Sainted Isle': Panegyric, Nostalgia, and the Invention of 'Lerinian Monasticism'," in Klingshirn and Vessey (1999: 188–206).

Leyser, Conrad (2000a), *Authority and Asceticism from Augustine to Gregory the Great*, Oxford, Clarendon Press; New York, Oxford University Press.

Leyser, Conrad (2000b), "The Temptations of Cult: Roman Martyr Piety in the Age of Gregory the Great," *Early Medieval Europe* 9: 389–407.

Leyser, Conrad (2003), "Charisma in the Archives: Roman Monasteries and the Memory of Gregory the Great, c.870–c.940," in Pohl and de Rubeis (2003: 207–26).

Leyser, Conrad (2007), "'A Church in the House of the Saints': Property and Power in the *Passion of John and Paul*," in Cooper and Hillner (2007: 140–62).

Leyser, Conrad (forthcoming), "The Memory of Pope Gregory the Great in the Ninth Century: A Redating of the Interpolator's *Vita Gregorii* (*BHL* 3640)," in *Gregorio magno e le origini dell'Europa*.

Leyser, Henrietta (1984), *Hermits and the New Monasticism: A Study of Religious Communities in Western Europe, 1000–1150*, London, Macmillan,

Liebeschuetz, J. H. W. G. (1972), *Antioch: City and Imperial Administration in the Later Roman Empire*, Oxford, Clarendon Press.

Liebeschuetz, J. H. W. G. (1992), "The End of the Ancient City," in Rich (1992: 1–49).

Liebeschuetz, J. H. W. G. (1996), "The Use of Pagan Mythology in the Christian Empire with Particular Reference to the *Dionysiaca* of Nonnus," in Pauline Allen and Elizabeth Jeffreys (ed.), *The Sixth Century: End or Beginning?* Brisbane, Australian Association for Byzantine Studies, pp. 75–91.

Liebeschuetz, J. H. W. G. (1997), "The Rise of the Bishop in the Christian Roman Empire and the Successor Kingdoms," *Electrum* 1: 113–25.

Liebeschuetz, J. H. W. G. (2001a), *The Decline and Fall of the Roman City*, Oxford, Oxford University Press.

Liebeschuetz, J. H. W. G. (2001b), "Late Antiquity and the Concept of Decline," *Nottingham Medieval Studies* 45: 1–11.

Liebeschuetz, J. H. W. G. (2004), "The Birth of Late Antiquity," *Antiquité Tardive* 12: 253–61.

Liebs, Detlef (2000), "Roman Law," in Cameron, Ward-Perkins, and Whitby (2000: 238–59).

Lietzmann, Hans (1904), *Apollinaris von Laodicea und seine Schule*, Tübingen, Mohr.

Lieu, Judith (2004), *Christian Identity in the Jewish and Graeco-Roman World*, Oxford, Oxford University Press.

Lieu, Judith, North, John, and Rajak, Tessa (eds.) (1992), *The Jews among Pagans and Christians in the Roman Empire*, London, Routledge.

Lieu, Samuel N. C. (1985), *Manichaeism in the Later Roman Empire and Medieval China: A Historical Survey*, Manchester and Dover, NH, Manchester University Press.

Lieu, Samuel N. C. (1986), "Captives, Refugees and Exiles: A Study of Cross-Frontier Civilian Movements and Contacts between Rome and Persia from Valerian to Jovian," in Freeman and Kennedy (1986: 475–505).

Lieu, Samuel N. C. (1992), *Manichaeism in the Later Roman Empire and Medieval China*, 2nd edn. rev. and expanded, Tübingen, Mohr.

Lifshitz, Felice (2006), *The Name of the Saint: Martyrologies, Politics and Access to the Sacred in the European Early Middle Ages*, South Bend, IN, University of Notre Dame Press.

Lim, Richard (1994), "Consensus and Dissensus on Public Spectacles in Late Antiquity," *Byzantinische Forschungen* 21: 159–79.

Lim, Richard (1995), *Public Disputation, Power, and Social Order in Late Antiquity*, Berkeley and Los Angeles, University of California Press.

Lim, Richard (1999), "People as Power: Games, Munificence and Contested Topography," in Harris (1999: 265–81).

Lim, Richard (2003), "Converting the Un-Christianizable: The Baptism of Stage Performers in Late Antiquity," in Mills and Grafton (2003: 84–126).

Limberis, Vasiliki (1994), *Divine Heiress: The Virgin Mary and the Creation of Christian Constantinople*, London, Routledge.

Limor, Ora, and Stroumsa, Guy G. (eds.) (1996), *Contra Iudaeos: Ancient and Medieval Polemics between Christians and Jews*, Tübingen, Mohr Siebeck.

Linder, Amnon (1987), *The Jews in Roman Imperial Legislation*, Detroit, MI, Wayne State University Press.

Little, L. K. (2004), "Cypress Beams, Kufic Script, and Cut Stone: Rebuilding the Master Narrative of European History," *Speculum* 79: 909–28.

Litvinsky, B. A. (ed.) (1996a), *History of Civilizations of Central Asia*, iii: *The Crossroads of Civilizations AD 250 to 850*, Paris, UNESCO Publishing.

Litvinsky, B. A. (1996b), "The Hephthalite Empire," in Litvinsky (1996a: 135–62).

Liverani, Paolo (2003), "Progetto architettonico e percezione comune in età tardoantica," *Bulletin Antieke Beschaving* 78: 205–19.

Lizzi, Rita (1987), *Il potere episcopale nell' Oriente romano: Rappresentazione ideologica e realtà politica (IV–V secolo d.C.)*, Rome, Edizioni dell'Ateneo.

Lizzi, Rita (1989), *Vescovi e strutture ecclesiastiche nella città tardoantica: l'Italia Annonaria nel IV–V secolo d.C.*, Como, Edizioni New Press.

Lizzi, Rita (1990), "Ambrose's Contemporaries and the Christianization of Northern Italy," *Journal of Roman Studies* 80: 156–73.

Lizzi, Rita (1991), "La traduzione greca delle opere di Gregorio Magno: dalla Regula Pastoralis ai Dialogi," in *Gregorio Magno e il suo tempo*, XIX Incontro di studiosi dell'antichità cristiana in collaborazione con l'École Française de Rome (Roma 9–12 Maggio 1990), Rome, Institutum Patristicum Augustinianum, pp. 41–57.

Lizzi, Rita (1994), "Tra i classici e la Bibbia: l'*otium* come forma di santità episcopale," in Giulia Barone, Marina Caffiero, and Francesco Scorza Barcellona (eds.), *Modelli di santità e modelli di comportamento: Contrasti, intersezioni, complementarità*, Turin, Rosenberg & Sellier, pp. 43–64.

Lizzi, Rita (1998), "I vescovi e i potentes della terra: definizione e limite del ruolo episcopale nelle due partes imperii fra IV e V secolo d.C," in Rebillard and Sotinel (1998: 81–104).

Lizzi Testa, Rita (2000a), "Christianization and Conversion in Northern Italy," in Alan Kreider (ed.), *The Origins of Christendom in the West*, Edinburgh, T. &T. Clark, pp. 47–95.

Lizzi Testa, Rita (2000b), "Privilegi economici e definizione di status: il caso del vescovo tardoantico," *Rendiconti Morali dell' Accademia Nazionale dei Lincei*, 9th ser. 11: 55–103.

Lizzi Testa, Rita (2001a), "The Bishop, 'Vir Venerabilis': Fiscal Privileges and 'Status' Definition in Late Antiquity," *Studia Patristica* 34: 125–44.

Lizzi Testa, Rita (2001b), "Come e dove reclutare i chierici? I problemi del vescovo Agostino," in *L'adorabile vescovo di Ippona*, Convegno Interazionale (Paola, 24–25 Maggio 2000), ed. Franca Ela Consolino, Soveria Mannelli, Rubbettino, pp. 183–216.

Lizzi Testa, Rita (2004), *Senatori, popolo, papi: il governo di Roma al tempo dei Valentiniani*, Bari, Editrice Edipuglia.

Llewellyn, Peter (1974), "The Roman Church in the Seventh Century: The Legacy of Gregory I," *Journal of Ecclesiastical History* 25: 363–80.

Llewelyn, Stephen R., with Kearsley, R. A. (1994), *New Documents illustrating Early Christianity*, vii: *A Review of the Greek Inscriptions and Papyri published in 1982–1983*, North Ryde, NSW, Ancient History Documentary Research Centre, Macquarie University.

Llewelyn, Stephen R. (1995), "Sending Letters in the Ancient World: Paul and the Philippians," *Tyndale Bulletin* 46: 337–56.

Llewelyn, Stephen R. (1998), *New Documents illustrating Early Christianity*, viii: *A Review of the Greek Inscriptions and Papyri published in 1984–1985*, North Ryde, NSW, Ancient History Documentary Research Centre, Macquarie University; Grand Rapids, MI, Eerdmans.

Löfstedt, Einar (1959), *Late Latin*, Oslo, Aschehoug.

Long, J. (1996), "Two Sides of a Coin: Aurelian, Vaballathus, and Eastern Frontiers of the Early 270s," in Mathisen and Sivan (1996: 59–71).

Long, Timothy (1986), *Barbarians in Greek Comedy*, Carbondale, Southern Illinois University Press.

Loprieno, Antonio (1995), *Ancient Egyptian: A Linguistic Introduction*, Cambridge, Cambridge University Press.

L'Orange, H. P. (1947), *Apotheosis in Ancient Portraiture*, Cambridge, MA, Harvard University Press.

L'Orange, H. P. (1953), *Studies on the Iconography of Cosmic Kingship in the Ancient World*, Cambridge, MA, Harvard University Press.

L'Orange, H. P. (1965), *Art Forms and Civic Life in the Late Roman Empire*, tr. Knut Berg, Princeton, NJ, Princeton University Press; originally pub. in Norwegian, Oslo, Aschehoug, 1958.

L'Orange, H. P. (1982), *Studies on the Iconography of Cosmic Kingship in the Ancient World*, New Rochelle, NY, Caratzas; originally pub. in Norwegian, Oslo, Aschehoug, 1953.

Loraux, Nicole (2000), *Born of the Earth: Myth and Politics in Athens*, tr. Selina Stewart, Ithaca, NY, Cornell University Press.

Loseby, Simon T. (2000), "Power and Towns in Late Roman Britain and Early Anglo-Saxon England," in Ripoll and Gurt (2000: 319–70).

Loseby, Simon T. (2006), "Decline and Change in the Cities of Late Antique Gaul," in Krause and Witschel (2006: 67–104).

Lourdaux, W. (ed.) (1983), *Benedictine Culture*, Leiden, Leiden University Press.

Louth, Andrew (2006), "The Appeal to the Cappadocian Fathers and Dionysios the Areopagite in the Iconoclast Controversy," in Børtnes and Hägg (2006: 271–81).

Low, D. M. (ed.) (1929), *Gibbon's Journal to January 28th, 1763*, London, Chatto & Windus.

Lowe, Chris (1999), *Angels, Fools and Tyrants: Britons and Anglo-Saxons in Southern Scotland*, Edinburgh, Canongate.

Lowe, Elias Avery (1937–71), *Codices latini antiquiores: A Palaeographical Guide to Latin Manuscripts Prior to the Ninth Century*, Oxford, Clarendon Press.

Lozovsky, Natalia (2000), *The Earth is Our Book: Geographical Knowledge in the Latin West, ca. 400–1000*, Ann Arbor, University of Michigan Press.

Lübbe, Hermann (1965), *Säkularisierung: Geschichte eines ideenpolitischen Begriffs*, Freiburg and Munich, Karl Alber.

Lucchesi, Enzo (2002), review of Giamberardini (2000), *Bibliotheca Orientalis* 59: 558–65.

Luckmann, Thomas (1967), *The Invisible Religion: The Transformation of Symbols in Industrial Society*, New York, Macmillan.

Luibheid, Colm, and Russell, Norman (tr.) (1982), *John Climacus: The Ladder of Divine Ascent*, New York, Paulist Press.

Lund, A. A. (1991), "Zur Gesamtinterpretation der "Germania" des Tacitus," *ANRW* 2. 33. 2: 1857–988.

Luxenberg, Christoph (2000), *Die syro-aramäische Lesart des Koran: ein Beitrag zur Entschlüsselung der Koransprache*, Berlin, Das Arabische Buch.

Lyman, Rebecca (1993), "A Topography of Heresy: Mapping the Rhetorical Creation of Arianism," in Barnes and Williams (1993: 45–62).

Maas, Michael (1992), *John Lydus and the Roman Past: Antiquarianism and Politics in the Age of Justinian*, London, Routledge.

Maas, Michael (2003), *Exegesis and Empire in the Early Byzantine Mediterranean*, Tübingen, Mohr Siebeck.

Maas, Michael (ed.) (2005), *The Cambridge Companion to the Age of Justinian*, Cambridge and New York, Cambridge University Press.

MacAdam, Henry Innes (1995), "Settlements and Settlement Patterns in Northern and Central Transjordan, *ca* 550–*ca* 750," in King and Cameron (1995: 49–94).

McBride, Daniel R. (1989), "The Development of Coptic: Late-Pagan Language of Synthesis in Egypt," *Journal of the Society for the Study of Egyptian Antiquities* 19: 89–111.

McCarthy, Daniel (2001), "The Chronology and Sources of the Early Irish Annals," *Early Medieval Europe* 10: 323–41.

McCarthy, Daniel (2003), "The Emergence of *Anno Domini*," in Jaritz and Moreno-Riaño (2003: 31–53).

MacCormack, Sabine (1981), *Art and Ceremony in Late Antiquity*, Berkeley and Los Angeles, University of California Press.

McCormick, Michael (1986), *Eternal Victory: Triumphal Rulership in Late Antiquity, Byzantium, and the Early Medieval West*, Cambridge and New York, Cambridge University Press.

McCormick, Michael (2001), *Origins of the European Economy: Communications and Commerce AD 300–900*, Cambridge and New York, Cambridge University Press.

MacCoull, Leslie S. B. (1988), *Dioscorus of Aphrodito: His Work and His World*, Berkeley and Los Angeles, University of California Press.

MacCoull, Leslie S. B. (1993), *Coptic Perspectives on Late Antiquity*, Aldershot, Variorum.

MacCoull, Leslie S. B. (1995), "Further Notes on Interrelated Greek and Coptic Documents of the Sixth and Seventh Centuries," *Chronique d'Egypte* 70: 341–53.

MacCoull, Leslie S. B. (1997), "Dated and Datable Coptic Documentary Hands Before A.D. 700," *Muséon* 110: 349–66.

MacDonald, Dennis R. (1983), *The Legend and the Apostle: The Battle for Paul in Story and Canon*, Philadelphia, Westminster Press.

MacDonald, Margaret Y. (1996), *Early Christian Women and Pagan Opinion: The Power of the Hysterical Woman*, Cambridge, Cambridge University Press.

MacGeorge, Penny (2002), *Late Roman Warlords*, Oxford and New York, Oxford University Press.

McGinn, Thomas (2004), *The Economy of Prostitution in the Roman World: A Study of Social History and the Brothel*, Ann Arbor, University of Michigan Press.

McKee, Sally (2004), "Inherited Status and Slavery in Late Medieval Italy and Venetian Crete," *Past and Present* 182: 31–53.

McKitterick, Rosamond (1989), *The Carolingians and the Written Word*, Cambridge, Cambridge University Press.

McKitterick, Rosamond (ed.) (1995), *The New Cambridge Medieval History*, ii: *c.700–c.900*, Cambridge, Cambridge University Press.

McKitterick, Rosamond (2004), *History and Memory in the Carolingian World*, Cambridge, Cambridge University Press.

McLaughlin, Megan (1994), *Consorting with Saints: Prayer for the Dead in Early Medieval France*, Ithaca, NY, Cornell University Press.

McLynn, Neil (1992), "Christian Controversy and Violence in the Fourth Century," *Kodai* 3: 15–44.

McLynn, Neil (1994), *Ambrose of Milan: Church and Court in a Christian Capital*, Berkeley and Los Angeles, University of California Press.

McLynn, Neil (1995), "Paulinus the Impenitent," *Journal of Early Christian Studies* 3: 461–86.

McLynn, Neil (1996), "The Fourth-Century Taurobolium," *Phoenix* 50: 312–30.

McLynn, Neil (2005), " 'Genere Hispanus': Theodosius, Spain and Nicene Orthodoxy," in Bowes and Kulikowski (2005: 77–129).

MacMullen, Ramsay (1964a), "Nationalism in Roman Egypt," *Aegyptus* 44: 179–99.

MacMullen, Ramsay (1964b), "Some Pictures in Ammianus Marcellinus," *Art Bulletin* 46: 435–56.

MacMullen, Ramsay (1966), "Provincial Languages in the Roman Empire," *American Journal of Philology* 87: 1–17.

MacMullen, Ramsay (1976), *Roman Government's Response to Crisis, AD 235–337*, New Haven, CT, Yale University Press.

MacMullen, Ramsay (1982), "The Epigraphic Habit in the Roman Empire," *American Journal of Philology* 103: 233–46.

MacMullen, Ramsay (1984), *Christianizing the Roman Empire (AD 100–1400)*, New Haven, CT, Yale University Press.

MacMullen, Ramsay (1986a), "Judicial Savagery in the Later Roman Empire," *Chiron* 16: 147–66.

MacMullen, Ramsay (1986b), "What Difference did Christianity Make?" *Historia* 35: 322–43.

MacMullen, Ramsay (1989), "The Preacher's Audience (A.D. 350–400)," *Journal of Theological Studies* 40: 503–11.

MacMullen, Ramsay (1990), *Changes in the Roman Empire: Essays in the Ordinary*, Princeton, NJ, Princeton University Press.

MacMullen, Ramsay (1997), *Christianity and Paganism in the Fourth to Eighth Centuries*, New Haven, CT, Yale University Press.

MacMullen, Ramsay (2003), "Cultural and Political Changes in the Fourth and Fifth Centuries," *Historia* 52: 465–98.

McNary-Zack, Bernadette (2000), *Letters and Asceticism in Fourth-Century Egypt*, Lanham, MD, University of America Press.

Macrides, Ruth (1991), "Perception of the Past in the Twelfth-Century Canonists," in Oikonomides (1991: 589–99).

Macrides, Ruth, and Magdalino, Paul (1992), "The Fourth Kingdom and the Rhetoric of Hellenism," in Magdalino (1992: 117–56).

Madelung, Wilferd (1986), "Apocalyptic Prophecies in Hims during the Umayyad Age," *Journal of Semitic Studies* 41: 141–85.

Magdalino, Paul (1983), "Aspects of Twelfth-Century Byzantine Kaiserkritik," *Speculum* 58: 326–46.

Magdalino, Paul (ed.) (1992), *The Perception of the Past in Twelfth-Century Europe*, London, Hambledon Press.

Magdalino, Paul (ed.) (1994), *New Constantines: The Rhythm of Imperial Renewal in Byzantium, 4th–13th Centuries*, Aldershot, Variorum; Brookfield, VT, Ashgate.

Magdalino, Paul (1999), "The Distance of the Past in Early Medieval Byzantium (VII–X Centuries)," in *Ideologie e pratiche del reimpiego nell'alto medioevo*, Settimane di Studio del Centro Italiano di Studi sull'Alto Medioevo 46, pp. 115–47.

Magness, J. (2003), *The Archaeology of the Early Islamic Settlement in Palestine*, Winona Lake, IN, Eisenbrauns.

Maier, Jean Louis (1987), *Le Dossier du donatisme*, 2 vols, i/1: *Des origines à la mort de Constance II (303–361)*, Berlin, Akademie Verlag.

Malbon, Elizabeth Struthers (1990), *The Iconography of the Sarcophagus of Junius Bassus*, Princeton, NJ, Princeton University Press.

Malherbe, Abraham (1988), *Ancient Epistolary Theorists*, Atlanta, GA, Scholars Press.

Malina, Bruce J. (1993), *The New Testament World: Insights from Cultural Anthropology*, Louisville, KY, Westminster/John Knox Press.

Malkin, Irad (ed.) (2001), *Ancient Perceptions of Greek Ethnicity*, Cambridge, MA, Harvard University Press.

Malkin, Irad (ed.) (2005), *Mediterranean Paradigms and Classical Antiquity*, London, Routledge.

Maloney, George A. (ed. and tr.) (1992), *Ps.-Macarius: The Fifty Spiritual Homilies and the Great Letter*, New York, Paulist Press.

Malosse, Pierre-Louis (ed. and tr.) (2003), *Libanius, Discours*, iv: *Discours LIX*, Paris, Les Belles Lettres.

Mango, Cyril (1963), "Antique Statuary and the Byzantine Beholder," *Dumbarton Oaks Papers* 17: 53–75.

Mango, Cyril (1980), *Byzantium: The Empire of New Rome*, London, Weidenfeld & Nicolson.

Mango, Cyril (1986), "Epigrammes honorifiques, statues et portraits à Byzance," in B. Kremmydas, C. Maltezou, and N. M. Panagiotakis (eds.), *Aphierôma ston Niko Svorôno*, i, Rethymno, Panepistêmio Krêtês, pp. 23–35.

Mango, Cyril (1990), *Le Développement urbain de Constantinople (IVe–VIIe siècles)*, Paris, De Boccard.

Mango, Cyril, and Dagron, Gilbert (eds.) (1995), *Constantinople and Its Hinterland*, Papers from the Twenty-Seventh Spring Symposium of Byzantine Studies, Oxford, April 1993, Aldershot, Variorum.

Mann, J. C. (1976), "What was the *Notitia dignitatum* For?' in Goodburn and Bartholomew (1976: 1–9).

Mann, J. C. (1985), "Epigraphic Consciousness," *Journal of Roman Studies* 75: 204–6.

Mantello, F. A. C., and Rigg, A. G. (eds.) (1996), *Medieval Latin: An Introduction and Bibliographical Guide*, Washington, DC, Catholic University of America Press.

Marasco, G. (ed.) (2003), *Greek and Roman Historiography in Late Antiquity: Fourth to Sixth Century AD*, Leiden, Brill.

Marchand, Susan L. (1996), *Down from Olympus: Archaeology and Philhellenism in Germany, 1750–1970*, Princeton, NJ, Princeton University Press.

Marcone, Arnaldo (1998), "Late Roman Social Relations," in Cameron and Garnsey (1998: 338–70).

Marcone, Arnaldo (ed.) (1999), *Rostovtzeff e l'Italia*, Perugia, Università Degli Studi di Perugia.

Maritano, Mario (ed.) (2002), *Historiam perscrutari: Miscellanea di studi offerti al prof. Ottorino Pasquato*, Rome, Editrice LAS.

Markopoulos, Athanasios (2004), "New Evidence on the Date of Photios' Bibliotheca," in Athanasios Markopoulos, *History and Literature of Byzantium in the 9th–10th Centuries*, Aldershot, Variorum.

Markopoulos, Athanasios (2006), "Roman Antiquarianism: Aspects of the Roman Past in the Middle Byzantine Period (9th–11th c.)," in E. Jeffreys (ed.), *Proceedings of the 21st*

International Congress of Byzantine Studies: London 21–26 August 2006, i: Plenary Papers, Aldershot and Burlington, VT, Ashgate, pp. 277–97.

Markus, Robert A. (1970), *Saeculum: History and Society in the Theology of St Augustine*, Cambridge, Cambridge University Press.

Markus, Robert A. (1974), *Christianity in the Roman World*, New York, Scribner.

Markus, Robert A. (1986), "Gregory the Great's *rector* and His Genesis," in Fontaine, Gillet, and Pellistrandi (1986: 137–46).

Markus, Robert A. (1990), *The End of Ancient Christianity*, Cambridge and New York, Cambridge University Press.

Markus, Robert A. (1994), *Sacred and Secular: Studies on Augustine and Latin Christianity*, Aldershot, Variorum.

Markus, Robert A. (1997), *Gregory the Great and His World*, Cambridge, Cambridge University Press.

Markus, Robert A. (2006), *Christianity and the Secular*, Notre Dame, IN, University of Notre Dame Press.

Maróth M. (1979), "Le Siège de Nisibe en 350 ap. J.-Ch. d'après des sources syriennes," *Acta Antiqua Academiae Scientiarum Hungaricae* 27: 239–43.

Marramao, Giacomo (1983), *Potere e secolarizzazione: le categorie dell tempo*, Rome, Editori Riuniti.

Marrou, Henri-Irénée (1938), *Saint Augustin et la fin de la culture antique*, 2 vols., Paris, De Boccard.

Marrou, Henri-Irénée (1948), *Histoire de l'éducation dans l'antiquité*, Paris, Éditions du Seuil.

Marrou, Henri-Irénée (1949), "Retractatio," in *Saint Augustin et la fin de la culture antique*, 2nd edn., ii, Paris, De Boccard, pp. 623–713.

Marrou, Henri-Irénée (1956), *A History of Education in Antiquity*, tr. George Lamb, New York, Sheed & Ward.

Marrou, Henri-Irénée (1970), "Le Dossier épigraphique de l'évêque Rusticus de Narbonne," *Rivista di Archeologia Cristiana* 46: 331–49.

Marszal, John R. (2000), "Ubiquitous Barbarians: Representations of the Gauls at Pergamon and Elsewhere," in Nancy T. de Grummond and Brunhilde S. Ridgeway (eds.), *From Pergamon to Sperlonga: Sculpture and Context*, Berkeley and Los Angeles, University of California Press, pp. 191–233.

Martin, A. (1989), "Topographie et liturgie: le problème des 'paroisses' d'Alexandrie," in Duval (1989a: 1133–44).

Martin, Dale (1996), "The Construction of the Ancient Family: Methodological Considerations," *Journal of Roman Studies* 86: 40–60.

Martin, Dale, and Miller, Patricia Cox (eds.) (2005), *The Cultural Turn in Late Ancient Studies: Gender, Asceticism, and Historiography*, Durham, NC, Duke University Press.

Martin, David (1978), *A General Theory of Secularization*, New York, Harper & Row.

Martin, Jean, and Petit, Paul (1979), *Libanios, Autobiographie: Discours 1*, Paris, Les Belles Lettres.

Marucchi, Orazio (1910), *Epigrafia cristiana*, Milan, Hoepli.

al-Marwazi, Nu'aym b. Hammad (1993), *Kitab al-fitan*, ed. Suhayl Zakkar, Beirut, Dar al-Fikr.

Masai, François, and Vanderhoven, Hubert (1953), *La Règle du Maître: édition diplomatique des manuscrits latins 12205 et 12634 de Paris*, Brussels/Paris, Scriptorium.

Maschio, Giorgio (1986), "L'argumentatione patristica di S. Agostino nella prima fase della controversia Pelagiana (412–18)," *Augustinianum* 26: 459–79.

Mathews, Thomas (1993), *The Clash of Gods: A Reinterpretation of Early Christian Art*, Princeton, NJ, Princeton University Press.

Mathews, Thomas F. (1962), "An Early Roman Chancel Arrangement and Its Liturgical Functions," *Rivista di Archeologia Cristiana* 38: 73–95.

Mathisen, Ralph W. (1979), "Resistance and Reconciliation: Majorian and the Gallic Aristocracy after the Fall of Avitus," *Francia* 7: 597–627.

Mathisen, Ralph W. (1981), "Epistolography, Literary Circles and Family Ties in Late Roman Gaul," *Transactions and Proceedings of the American Philological Association* 111: 95–105.

Mathisen, Ralph W. (1989), *Ecclesiastical Factionalism and Religious Controversy in Fifth-Century Gaul*, Washington, DC, Catholic University of America Press.

Mathisen, Ralph W. (1993), *Roman Aristocrats in Barbarian Gaul: Strategies for Survival in an Age of Transition*, Austin, University of Texas Press.

Mathisen, Ralph W. (2001), "The Letters of Ruricius of Limoges and the Passage from Roman to Frankish Gaul," in Mathisen and Shanzer (2001: 101–15).

Mathisen, Ralph W. (ed.) (2002), *Law, Society and Authority in Late Antiquity*, Oxford, Oxford University Press.

Mathisen, Ralph W., and Shanzer, Danuta (eds.) (2001), *Society and Culture in Late Antique Gaul: Revisiting the Sources*, Aldershot, Ashgate.

Mathisen, Ralph W., and Sivan, Hagith S. (eds.) (1996), *Shifting Frontiers in Late Antiquity*, Aldershot and Brookfield, VT, Variorum.

Matthews, John (1974), "The Letters of Symmachus," in Binns (1974: 58–99).

Matthews, John (1975), *Western Aristocracies and Imperial Court, AD 364–425*, Oxford, Clarendon Press.

Matthews, John (1986), "Symmachus and His Enemies," in François Paschoud (ed.), *Colloque genevois sur Symmaque à l'occasion du mille-six-centième du conflit de l'autel de la Victoire*, Paris, Les Belles Lettres, pp. 163–75.

Matthews, John (1989a), "Hostages, Philosophers, Pilgrims and the Diffusion of Ideas in the Late Roman Mediterranean and Near East," in Clover and Humphreys (1989: 29–49).

Matthews, John (1989b), *The Roman Empire of Ammianus*, London, Duckworth; Baltimore, MD, Johns Hopkins University Press.

Matthews, John (1997), "Gibbon and the Later Roman Empire: Causes and Circumstances," in R. McKitterick and R. Quinault (eds.), *Edward Gibbon and Empire*, Cambridge, Cambridge University Press, pp. 12–33.

Matthews, John (2000), *Laying Down the Law: A Study of the Theodosian Code*, New Haven, CT, Yale University Press.

Mattingly, David (2004), "Being Roman: Expressing Identity in a Provincial Setting," *Journal of Roman Archaeology* 17: 5–25.

Mattingly, Harold (1967), *Christianity in the Roman Empire*, New York, W. W. Norton.

Maxwell, Jaclyn (2006), *Christianization and Communication in Late Antiquity: John Chrysostom and His Congregation in Antioch*, Cambridge, Cambridge University Press.

Mayer, A. (1911), "Psellos' Rede über den rhetorischen Charakter des Gregorios von Nazianz," *Byzantinische Zeitschrift* 20: 27–100.

Mayer, Wendy (1999), " 'Les Homélies de s. Jean Chrysostome en juillet 399': A Second Look at Pargoire's Sequence and the Chronology of the *Novæ homiliæ* (CPG 4441)," *Byzantinoslavica* 60: 273–303.

Mayer, Wendy (2006), "The Sequence and Provenance of John Chrysostom's Homilies *In illud: Si esurierit inimicus* (CPG 4375), *De mutatione nominum* (CPG 4372) and *In principium Actorum* (CPG 4371)," *Augustinianum* 46: 169–86.

Mazza, Mario (1993), "*Deposita pietatis:* problemi dell'organizzazione economica in comunità cristiane tra II e III secolo," in *Atti dell'Accademia Romanistica Costantiniana: IX Convegno Internazionale (Perugia-Spello 1989)*, Naples, Edizioni Scientifiche Italiane, pp. 187–216.

Mazzarino, Santo (1974), "La democratizzazione della cultura nel' basso impero" and "'Annunci' e 'Publica Laetitia': l'iscrizione romana di Fausto e altri testi," in *Antico, tardoantico ed erà costantiniana*, Bari, Dedalo libri, i: 74–98; 229–50.

Mazzarino, Santo (1984), *L'impero romano*, 3rd edn., Bari, Laterza.

Mazzarino, Santo (1989), *Storia sociale del vescovo Ambrogio*, Rome, Bretschneider.

Meeks, Wayne A. (1983), *The First Urban Christians: The Social World of the Apostle Paul*, New Haven, CT, Yale University Press.

Meier, Mischa (2003), "Das späte römische Kaiserreich ein 'Zwangsstaat'? Anmerkungen zu einer Forschungskontroverse," *Electrum* 9: 193–213.

Meiggs, Russell (1973), *Roman Ostia*, 2nd edn., Oxford, Clarendon Press.

Meimaris, Yiannis E. (1992), *Chronological Systems in Roman-Byzantine Palestine and Arabia*, Athens, National Hellenic Research Centre.

Mendels, D. (1986), "Greek and Roman History in the Bibliotheca of Photius: A Note," *Byzantion* 56: 196–206.

Menghin, Wilfried, Springer, Tobias, and Wamers, Egon (eds.) (1987), *Germanen, Hunnen und Awaren: Schätze der Völkerwanderungszeit*, Nuremberg, Verlag Germanisches Nationalmuseum.

Merkt, A. (2001), *Das patristische Prinzip*, Leiden, Brill.

Merrills, A. H. (2004), "Monks, Monsters, and Barbarians: Re-defining the African Periphery in Late Antiquity," *Journal of Early Christian Studies*, 12: 217–44.

Merrills, A. H. (2005), *History and Geography in Late Antiquity*, Cambridge, Cambridge University Press.

Metcalfe, W. (tr. and ed.) (1920), *Gregory Thaumaturgus: Address to Origen*, London and New York, Macmillan.

Metzdorf, Christina (2003), *Die Tempelaktion Jesu: patristische und historisch-kritische Exegese im Vergleich*, Tübingen, Mohr.

Metzger, Bruce (1977), *The Early Versions of the New Testament: Their Origins, Transmission, and Limitations*, Oxford, Clarendon Press.

Metzger, Bruce (1987), *The Canon of the New Testament: Its Origin, Development, and Significance*, Oxford, Clarendon Press.

Metzger, Bruce (2005), *The Text of the New Testament: Its Transmission, Corruption, and Restoration*, New York, Oxford University Press.

Meyendorff, John (1989), *Imperial Unity and Christian Divisions: The Church 450–680 AD*, Crestwood, NY, St. Vladimir's Seminary Press.

Meyer, Eduard (1884–1902), *Geschichte des Altertums*, 5 vols., Stuttgart, Cotta.

Meyer, Eduard (1910), *Geschichte des Altertums*, 3rd edn., i/1: *Einleitung*, Stuttgart, Cotta.

Meyer, Elizabeth A (1990), "Explaining the Epigraphic Pattern in the Roman Empire: The Evidence of Epitaphs," *Journal of Roman Studies* 80: 74–96.

Meyer, Elizabeth A. (2004), *Legitimacy and Law in the Roman World: Tabulae in Roman Belief and Practice*, Cambridge, Cambridge University Press.

Meyer, Marvin W., Smith, Richard, and Kelsey, Neil (eds.) (1994), *Ancient Christian Magic: Coptic Texts of Ritual Power*, Princeton, NJ, Princeton University Press; San Francisco, Harper.

Mielczarek, M. (1993), *Cataphracti and Clibanarii: Studies on the Heavy Armoured Cavalry of the Ancient World*, tr. Maria Abramowicz, Lódz, Oficyna Naukowa MS.

Miles, George C. (1952), "Mihrâb and 'Anazah: A Study in early Islamic Iconography," in George C. Miles (ed.), *Archaeologica Orientalia in Memoriam Ernst Herzfeld*, Locust Valley, NY, Augustin, pp. 156–71.

Miles, Richard (ed.) (1999), *Constructing Identities in Late Antiquity*, London and New York, Routledge.

Millar, Fergus (1968), "Local Languages in the Roman Empire: Libyan, Punic, and Latin in North Africa," *Journal of Roman Studies* 58: 125–51.

Millar, Fergus (1977), *The Emperor in the Roman World*, Ithaca, NY, Cornell University Press.

Millar, Fergus (1992), *The Emperor in the Roman World (27 BC–AD 337)*, 2nd edn., London, Duckworth.

Millar, Fergus (1993), *The Roman Near East, 31 B.C. – A.D. 337*, Cambridge, MA, Harvard University Press.

Millar, Fergus (1999), "The Greek East and Roman Law: The Dossier of M. Cn. Licinius Rufinus," *Journal of Roman Studies* 89: 90–108.

Millar, Fergus (2002a), "De la frontière au centre: la monarchie centralisée de Théodose II (408–450 ap. J.-C.)," in C. Moatti (ed.), *La Mobilité des personnes en Méditerranée de l'Antiquité à l'époque moderne: procédures et contrôles d'identification*, Rome, École Française de Rome, pp. 567–89.

Millar, Fergus (2002b), *Rome, the Greek World, and the East*, Chapel Hill, University of North Carolina Press.

Millar, Fergus (2004), "Christian Emperors, Christian Church and the Jews of the Diaspora in the Greek East, CE 379–450," *Journal of Jewish Studies* 55: 1–24.

Millar, Fergus (2006), *A Greek Roman Empire: Power and Belief under Theodosius II (408–450)*, Berkeley and Los Angeles, University of California Press.

Miller, D. H. (1996), "Frontier Societies and the Transition between Late Antiquity and the Middle Ages," in Mathisen and Sivan (1996: 158–71).

Miller, J. Innes (1969), *The Spice Trade of the Roman Empire: 29 BC to AD 641*, Oxford, Clarendon Press.

Miller, Margaret Christina (1997), *Athens and Persia in the Fifth Century B.C.: A Study in Cultural Receptivity*, Cambridge, Cambridge University Press.

Miller, Patricia Cox (2000), "Strategies of Representation in Collective Biography: Constructing the Subject as Holy," in Hägg and Rousseau (2000: 209–54).

Miller, Timothy (2003), *The Orphans of Byzantium: Child Welfare in the Christian Empire*, Washington, DC, Catholic University of America Press.

Mills, Kenneth, and Grafton, Anthony (eds.) (2003), *Conversion in Late Antiquity and the Early Middle Ages: Seeing and Believing*, Rochester, NY, University of Rochester Press.

Mimouni, Simon (1994), "Le Judéo-christianisme syriaque: mythe littéraire ou réalité historique?," in Lavenant (1994: 269–79).

Mingana, Alphonse (ed. and tr.) (1933), *Commentary of Theodore of Mopsuestia on the Lord's Prayer and on the Sacraments of Baptism and the Eucharist*, Cambridge, Heffer.

Mitchell, Kathleen, and Wood, Ian N. (eds.) (2002), *The World of Gregory of Tours*, Leiden and Boston, MA, Brill.

Mitchell, Stephen (1993), *Anatolia: Land, Men, and Gods in Asia Minor*, 2 vols., Oxford, Clarendon Press.

Mitchell, Stephen (1995), review of Trombley 1993–4, *Journal of Roman Studies* 85: 341–4.

Mitchell, Stephen (2000), "Ethnicity, Acculturation and Empire in Roman and Late Roman Asia Minor," in Mitchell and Greatrex (2000: 117–50).

Mitchell, Stephen (2007), *A History of the Later Roman Empire AD 284–641: The Transformation of the Ancient World*, Oxford, Blackwell.

Mitchell, Stephen, and Greatrex, Geoffrey (eds.) (2000), *Ethnicity and Culture in Late Antiquity*, London, Duckworth; Swansea, Classical Press of Wales.

Mitchell, W. J. T. (1986), *Iconology: Image, Text, Ideology*, Chicago, University of Chicago Press.

Mitchell, W. J. T. (1994), *Picture Theory: Essays in Verbal and Visual Representation*, Chicago, University of Chicago Press.

Moatti, Claudia (2006), "Translation, Migration, and Communication in the Roman Empire: Three Aspects of Movement in History," *Classical Antiquity* 25: 109–40.

Modéran, Yves (1996), "La Renaissance des cités dans l'Afrique du VIe siècle d'après une inscription récemment publiée," in Lepelley (1996: 85–114).

Mohrmann, Christine (1977), *Études sur le latin des chrétiens*, iv, Rome, Storia e Letteratura.

Momigliano, Arnaldo (ed.) (1963a), *The Conflict between Paganism and Christianity in the Fourth Century: Essays*, Oxford, Clarendon Press.

Momigliano, Arnaldo (1963b), "Introduction: Christianity and the Decline of the Roman Empire," in Arnaldo Momigliano (1963a: 1–16).

Momigliano, Arnaldo (1966a), "Gibbon's Contributions to Historical Method' (1954), in Momigliano (1966b: 40–55).

Momigliano, Arnaldo (1966b), *Studies in Historiography*, London, Weidenfeld & Nicolson; New York, Harper & Row.

Momigliano, Arnaldo (1969), *Quarto contributo alla storia degli studi classici e del mondo antico*, Rome, Storia e Letteratura.

Momigliano, Arnaldo (1971), *The Development of Greek Biography: Four Lectures*, Cambridge, MA, Harvard University Press.

Momigliano, Arnaldo (1972), "Popular Religious Beliefs and the Late Roman Historians," in G. J. Cuming and D. Baker (eds.), *Popular Belief and Practice*, Cambridge, Cambridge University Press, pp. 1–18; repr. in Momigliano (1975: 73–92).

Momigliano, Arnaldo (1975), *Quinto contributo alla storia degli studi classici e del mondo antico*, 2 vols., Rome, Storia e Letteratura.

Momigliano, Arnaldo (1980), "After Gibbon's *Decline and Fall*," in K. Weitzmann (ed.), *Age of Spirituality*, New York, Metropolitan Museum of Art, pp. 7–16.

Momigliano, Arnaldo (1982), *New Paths of Classicism in the Nineteenth Century*, Middletown, CT, Wesleyan University Press.

Momigliano, Arnaldo (1990), *The Classical Foundations of Modern Historiography*, Berkeley and Los Angeles, University of California Press.

Mommsen, Theodor (1942), "Petrarch's Conception of the 'Dark Ages'," *Speculum* 17: 226–42.

Montesquieu, Charles de Secondat, Baron de (1734), *Considérations sur les causes de la grandeur des Romains et de leur décadence*, Amsterdam, Chez Jacques Desbordes.

Montevecchi, Orsolina (1988), *La papirologia: ristampa riveduta e corretta con addenda*, Milan, Vita e Pensiero.

Montgomery, James (1995), "The Deserted Encampment in Ancient Arabic Poetry: A Nexus of Topical Comparisons," *Journal of Semitic Studies* 40: 283–316.

Montserrat, Dominic (1998), "Pilgrimage to the Shrine of SS Cyrus and John at Menouthis in Late Antiquity," in Frankfurter (1998a: 257–79).

Moorhead, John (2001), *The Roman Empire Divided 400–700*, Harlow and New York, Longman.

Moralee, Jason (2004), *"For Salvation's Sake": Provincial Loyalty, Personal Religion, and Epigraphic Production in the Roman and Late Antique Near East*, London and New York, Routledge.

Morard, F. E. (1973), "Monachos, moine: histoire du terme grec jusqu'au 4e siècle," *Freiburger Zeitschrift für Philosophie und Theologie* 20: 332–411.

Morard, F. E. (1975), "Monachus: une importatation sémitique en Égypte?" *Studia Patristica* 12: 242–6.

Morard, F. E. (1980), "Encore quelques réflexions sur Monachos," *Vigiliae Christianae* 34: 395–401.

Morello, Ruth (forthcoming), "Confidence, *invidia*, and Pliny's Epistolary Lessons," in Morello and Morrison (forthcoming).

Morello, Ruth, and Morrison, Andrew (eds.) (forthcoming), *Ancient Letters: Classical and Late Antique Epistolography*, Oxford, Oxford University Press.

Morey, Charles Rufus (1935), *Christian Art*, London and New York, Longmans, Green.

Morey, Charles Rufus (1942), *Early Christian Art: An Outline of the Evolution of Style and Iconography in Sculpture and Painting from Antiquity to the Eighth Century*, Princeton, NJ, Princeton University Press; London, Oxford University Press.

Morimoto, Kosei (1981), *The Fiscal Administration of Egypt in the Early Islamic Period*, Kyoto, Dohosha.

Morimoto, Kosei (1994), "The *Dîwân*s as Registers of the Arab Stipendiaries in Early Islamic Egypt," in R. Curiel and R. Gyselen (eds.), *Itinéraires d'Orient: Hommages à Claude Cahen*, Paris, Groupe pour l'étude de la civilisation du Moyen-Orient, pp. 353–66.

Morony, Michael G. (1984), *Iraq after the Muslim Conquest*, Princeton, NJ, Princeton University Press.

Morony, Michael G. (2004), "Economic Boundaries? Late Antiquity and Early Islam," *Journal of the Economic and Social History of the Orient* 47: 166–94.

Morris, John (1973a), *The Age of Arthur: A History of the British Isles from 350 to 650*, New York, Scribner.

Morris, John (1973b) (ed.), *Arthurian Sources*, London and Chichester, Phillimore.

Moss, Ann (2003), *Renaissance Truth and the Latin Language Turn*, Oxford, Oxford University Press.

Moss, C. (1935), "Jacob of Sarugh's *Homilies* on the Spectacles of the Theater," *Le Muséon* 48: 87–112.

Moss, H. St. L. B. (1935), *The Birth of the Middle Ages, 395–814*, Oxford, Clarendon Press.

Mossay, Justin (1966), *La Mort et l'au-delà dans saint Grégoire de Nazianze*, Louvain, Publications Universitaires de Louvain.

Mosshammer, A. A. (1998), "Roman History according to George the Syncellus," in Chr.-Fr. Collatz et al. (eds.), *Dissertatiunculae criticae: Festschrift für Günther Christian Hansen*, Würzburg, Königshausen & Neumann, pp. 377–93.

Most, Glenn (ed.) (1999), *Commentaries – Kommentare*, Göttingen, Vandenhoeck & Ruprecht.

Mostert, Marco (ed.) (1999), *New Approaches to Medieval Communication*, Turnhout, Brepols.

Mourtisen, Henrik (2005), "Freedmen and Decurions: Epitaphs and Social History in Imperial Italy," *Journal of Roman Studies* 95: 38–63.

Moxnes, Halvor (ed.) (1997), *Constructing Early Christian Families*, London, Routledge.

Muhlberger, Steven (1990), *The Fifth Century Chroniclers: Prosper, Hydatius, and the Gallic Chronicler of 452*, Leeds, Francis Cairns.

Muir, Richard (2000), *The New Reading the Landscape: Fieldwork in Landscape History*, Exeter, University of Exeter Press.

Mulder-Bakker, Anneke B., and Wogan-Browne, Jocelyn (eds.) (2005), *Household, Women and Christianities in Late Antiquity and the Middle Ages*, Turnhout, Brepols.

Müller, Christof (1998), "Confessiones 13: Der ewige Sabbat: Die eschatologische Ruhe als Zielpunkt der Heimkehr zu Gott," in Norbert Fischer and Cornelius Mayer (eds.), *Die Confessiones des Augustinus von Hippo*, Freiburg, Herder, pp. 603–52.

Mullett, Margaret, and Scott, Robert (eds.) (1981), *Byzantium and the Classical Tradition*, Birmingham, University of Birmingham.

Munier, Charles (1957), *Les Sources patristiques du droit de l'Église du VIIIe au XIIIe siècle*, Mulhouse, France, Salvator.

Munro-Hay, Stuart C. (1991), *Aksum: An African Civilisation of Late Antiquity*, Edinburgh, Edinburgh University Press.

Munson, Rosaria Vignolo (2001), *Telling Wonders: Ethnographic and Political Discourse in the Work of Herodotus*, Ann Arbor, University of Michigan Press.

Murgia, Charles (2004), "The Truth about Vergil's Commentators," in Roger Rees (ed.), *Romane memento: Vergil in the Fourth Century*, London, Duckworth, pp. 189–200.

Murray, Alexander Callander (2002), "Reinhard Wenskus on 'Ethnogenesis,' Ethnicity, and the Origins of the Franks," in Gillett (2002b: 39–68).

Murray, Robert (1967), "Ephrem Syrus," in *Catholic Dictionary of Theology*, ii, London and New York, Nelson, pp. 220–3.

Murray, Robert (1982), "The Characteristics of the Earliest Syriac Christianity," in Nina Garsoïan, Thomas Mathews, and Robert Thomson (eds.), *East of Byzantium: Syria and Armenia in the Formative Period*, Washington, DC, Dumbarton Oaks, pp. 3–16.

Murray, Robert (2004), *Symbols of Church and Kingdom: A Study in Early Syriac Tradition*; repr. Piscataway, NJ, Gorgias Press.

Murray, Sister Charles (1977), "Art and the Early Church," *Journal of Theological Studies* 28: 303–5.

Murray, Sister Charles (1981), *Rebirth and Afterlife: A Study of the Transmutation of Some Pagan Imagery in Early Christian Funerary Art*, Oxford, BAR.

Murray, Sister Charles (1982), "Early Christian Art and Archaeology," *Religion* 12: 167–73.

Musa, Mark (tr.) (1985), *Petrarch: Selections from the Canzoniere and Other Works*, Oxford, Oxford University Press.

Myhre, B. (1992), "The Royal Cemetery at Borre, Vestfold: A Norwegian Centre in a European Periphery," in Carver (1992: 301–13).

Myhre, B. (1997), "Boathouses and Naval Organisation," in Ann Nørgård Jørgensen and Birthe L. Clausen (eds.), *Military Aspects of Scandinavian Society in a European Perspective, AD 1–1300*, Copenhagen, National Museum, pp. 169–83.

Myhre, B. (2003), "The Iron Age," in K. Helle (ed.), *The Cambridge History of Scandinavia*, i: *From Prehistory to 1520*, Cambridge, Cambridge University Press, pp. 60–93.

Mynors, R. A. B., and Thomson, D. F. S. (tr.) (1974), *The Correspondence of Erasmus: Letters 1 to 141 (1484 to 1500)*, with annotations by Wallace K. Ferguson, Toronto, University of Toronto Press.

Mytum, Harold (1992), *The Origins of Early Christian Ireland*, London and New York, Routledge.

Nacke, Ewald (1964), "Das Zeugnis der Väter in der theologischen Beweisführung Cyrills von Alexandrien nach seinen Briefen und antinestorianischen Schriften," unpublished Ph.D. dissertation, Münster.

Najman, Hindy, and Newman, Judith H. (eds.) (2004), *The Idea of Biblical Interpretation: Essays in Honor of James L. Kugel*, Leiden, Brill.

Näsman, U. (1998), "The Justinianic Era of South Scandinavia: An Archaeological View," in Hodges and Bowden (1998: 255–78).

Nathan, Geoffrey (2000), *The Family in Late Antiquity: The Rise of Christianity and the Endurance of Tradition*, London, Routledge.

Naudet, Jérôme (1858), "De l'administration des postes chez les Romains," *Mémoires de l'Académie des Inscriptions et Belles Lettres* 23: 166–240.

Nedungatt, George (1973), "The Covenanters of the Early Syriac-Speaking Church," *Orientalia Christiana Periodica* 39: 191–225, 419–44.

Nelson, Janet (1990), "Women and the Word in the Earlier Middle Ages," in Sheils and Wood (1990: 53–78).

Nelson, Janet (1995), "Kingship and Royal Government," in McKitterick (1995: 383–430).

Nelson, Janet (1996), *The Frankish World, 750–900*, London, Hambledon.

Nelson, Janet (2002), "England and the Continent in the Ninth Century, i: Ends and Beginnings," *Transactions of the Royal Historical Society*, 5th ser. 12: 1–21.

Nelson, Janet (2006), "Charlemagne and the Paradoxes of Power," Reuter Lecture 2005, Southampton, Centre for Antiquity and the Middle Ages, University of Southampton.

Neusner, Jacob (1965), *A History of the Jews in Babylonia*, i: *The Parthian Period*, Leiden, Brill.

Neusner, Jacob (1983), "Jews in Iran," in Yarshater (1983a, ii: 909–23).

Nicholson, John (1994), "The Delivery and Confidentiality of Cicero's Letters," *Classical Journal* 90: 33–63.

Nicholson, John (1998), "The Survival of Cicero's Letters," in Deroux (1998: 63–105).

Nicolet, Claude (1991), *Space, Geography, and Politics in the Early Roman Empire*, tr. Hélène Leclerc, Ann Arbor, University of Michigan Press.

Nicolet, Claude (2003), *La Fabrique d'une nation: la France entre Rome et les Germains*, Paris, Perrin.

Nicolet, Claude, Ilbert, Robert, and Depaule, Jean-Charles (eds.) (2000), *Mégapoles méditerranéennes: géographie urbaine rétrospective*, Actes du colloque organisé par l'École Française de Rome et la Maison Méditerranéenne des Sciences de l'Homme, Rome, 8–11 Mai 1996, Rome, École Française de Rome.

Nielsen, Hanne Sigismund (1987), "*Alumnus*: A Term of Relation denoting Quasi-Adoption," *Classica et Medievalia* 38: 141–88.

Nielsen, P. O., Randsborg, K., and Thrane, H. (eds.) (1994), *The Archaeology of Gudme and Lundeborg*, Copenhagen, Akademisk Forlag.

Nilsson, Ingela (2006), "Discovering Literariness in the Past: Literature vs. History in the *Synopsis Chronike* of Konstantinos Manasses," in Odorico, Agapitos, and Hinterberger (2006: 15–31).

Nippel, Wilfried (1995), *Public Order in Ancient Rome*, Cambridge and New York, Cambridge University Press.

Nippel, Winfried (2000), "From Agrarian History to Cross-Cultural Comparison: Weber on Greco-Roman Antiquity," in Stephen Turner (ed.), *The Cambridge Companion to Max Weber*, Cambridge, Cambridge University Press, pp. 240–55.

Niquet, Heike (2000), *Monumenta virtutum titulique: senatorische Selbstdarstellung im spätantiken Rom im Spiegel der epigraphischen Denkmäler*, Stuttgart, Franz Steiner.

Noble, Thomas F. X. (ed.) (2006), *From Roman Provinces to Medieval Kingdoms*, London and New York, Routledge.

Nock, Arthur Darby (1933), *Conversion: The Old and the New in Religion from Alexander the Great to Augustine of Hippo*, London, Oxford University Press.

Nolhac, Pierre de (1907), *Petrarque et l'humanisme*, 2 vols., Paris, Honoré Champion.

Norman, A. F. (tr.) (1969–77), *Libanius, Selected Works*, 2 vols., Cambridge, MA, Harvard University Press.

Norman, A. F. (ed. and tr.) (1992), *Libanius, Autobiography and Selected Letters*, Cambridge, MA, Harvard University Press.

Norman, A. F. (tr.) (2000), *Antioch as a Centre of Hellenic Culture as Observed by Libanius*, Liverpool, Liverpool University Press.

Norman, Naomi (2002), "Death and Burial of Roman Children: The Case of the Yasmina Cemetery at Carthage, i: Setting the Stage," *Mortality* 7: 302–23.

Norman, Naomi (2003), "Death and Burial of Roman Children: The Case of the Yasmina Cemetery at Carthage, ii: The Archaeological Evidence," *Mortality* 8: 36–47.

North, John A. (2005), "Pagans, Polytheists at the Pendulum," in Harris (2005b: 125–43).

Norton, J. E. (1940), *A Bibliography of the Works of Edward Gibbon*, New York, Burt Franklin.

Noy, David (1995), *Jewish Inscriptions of Western Europe*, ii: *The City of Rome*, Cambridge, Cambridge University Press.

Obbink, Dirk D. (2003), "Allegory and Exegesis in the Derveni Papyrus: The Origin of Greek Scholarship," in G. R. Boys-Stones (ed.), *Metaphor, Allegory, and the Classical Tradition: Ancient Thought and Modern Revisions*, Oxford, Oxford University Press, pp. 177–88.

O'Connor, Anne, and Clarke, D. V. (eds.) (1983), *From the Stone Age to the 'Forty-Five: Studies Presented to R. B. K. Stevenson*, Edinburgh, John Donald; Atlantic Highlands, NJ, Humanities Press.

Ó Cróinín, Dáibhí (1983), "Early Irish Annals from Easter Tables: A Case Restated," *Peritia* 2: 74–86.

Ó Cróinín, Dáibhí (1995), *Early Medieval Ireland 400–1200*, London and New York, Longman.

O'Daly, Gerard (1999), *Augustine's* City of God: *A Reader's Guide*, Oxford, Oxford University Press.

O'Donnell, James J. (1971), " 'Paganus'," *Classical Folia* 31: 163–9.

O'Donnell, James J. (1979), "The Demise of Paganism," *Traditio* 35: 45–88.

O'Donnell, James J. (1990), review of Chuvin 1990, *Bryn Mawr Classical Review* 1: 3–4.

O'Donnell, James J. (1991), "The Authority of Augustine," *Augustinian Studies* 22: 7–35.

O'Donnell, James J. (1992), Augustine, *Confessions*, 3 vols., Oxford, Clarendon Press.

Odorico, Paolo, Agapitos, Panagiotis A., and Hinterberger, Martin (eds.) (2006), *L'Écriture de la mémoire: la littérarité de l'historiographie*, Paris, Centre d'Études Byzantines, Néo-Helléniques et Sud-Est Européennes, École des Hautes Études en Sciences Sociales.

O'Flynn, John Michael (1983), *Generalissimos of the Western Roman Empire*, Edmonton, University of Alberta Press.

Oikonomides, Nicolas (ed.) (1991), *Byzantium in the Twelfth Century: Canon Law, State and Society*, Athens, Hetaireia Vyzantinôn kai Metavyzantinôn Meletôn.

Oldelehr, Hermann (1977), *Seekrankheit in der Antike*, Düsseldorf, Triltsch.

Olson, Linda, and Kerby-Fulton, Kathryn (eds.) (2005), *Voices in Dialogue: Reading Women in the Middle Ages*, Notre Dame, IN, University of Notre Dame Press.

Olster, D. M. (1996), "From Periphery to Center: The Transformation of Late Roman Self-Definition in the Seventh Century," in Mathisen and Sivan (1996: 93–101).

O'Malley, John W. (1988), "Grammar and Rhetoric in the *Pietas* of Erasmus," *Journal of Medieval and Renaissance Studies* 18: 81–98.

O'Neill, J. C. (1989), "The Origins of Monasticism," in Williams (1989: 270–87).

Ong, Walter J. (1982), *Orality and Literacy: The Technologizing of the Word*, London and New York, Routledge.

Opitz, H. G. (ed.) (1934), *Athanasius Werke*, iii/1: *Urkunden zur Geschichte des arianischen Streites, 318–328*, Berlin and Leipzig: De Gruyter.

Orlandi, Tito (1986), "Coptic Literature," in Pearson and Goehring (1986: 51–81).

Orlandi, Tito (1991), "Coptic Literature," in Atiya (1991, v: 1450–60).

Orlandi, Tito (1998), "Koptische Literatur," in Krause (1998: 117–47).

Orth, Emil (1928), *Photiana*, Rhetorische Forschungen, i, Leipzig, R. Noske.

Orth, Emil (1929), *Die Stilkritik des Photios*, Leipzig, R. Noske.

Osiek, Carolyn (1996), "The Family in Early Christianity: 'Family Values' Revisited," *Catholic Biblical Quartery* 58: 1–24.

Osiek, Carolyn, and Balch, David (eds.) (1997), *Families in the New Testament World: Households and House Churches*, Louisville, KY, Westminster/John Knox Press.

Osiek, Carolyn, and Balch, David (eds.) (2003), *Early Christian Families in Context: An Interdisciplinary Dialogue*, Grand Rapids, MI, Eerdmans.

Osiek, Carolyn, and MacDonald, Margaret Y., with Tulloch, Janet H. (2005), *A Woman's Place: House Churches in Earliest Christianity*, Philadelphia, Fortress Press.

Otranto, Giorgio (1980), "L'iscrizione di Pietro e Paolo," in Carletti and Otranto (1980: 181–206).

Otten, Willemien, and Pollmann, Karla (eds.) (forthcoming), *Poetry and Exegesis: Forms of Interpretation in Early Christian Poetry*, Leiden, Brill.

Pabel, Hilmar M. (2004), "Credit, Paratexts, and Editorial Strategies in Erasmus of Rotterdam's Editions of Jerome," *Intersections: Yearbook for Early Modern Studies* 4: 217–56.

Paci, Gianfranco (ed.) (1998), *Epigrafia romana in area adriatica*, Actes de la IXe Rencontre franco-italienne sur l'épigraphie du monde romain, Macerata, 10–11 Novembre 1995, Pisa, Istituti Editoriali e Poligrafici Internazionali.

Painter, Kenneth (2000), "Cofanetto di Proiecta," in Ensoli and La Rocca (2000: 493–5).

Palmer, Andrew (ed. and tr.) (1993), *The Seventh Century in the West-Syrian Chronicles*, with additional material, translation, and notes by Sebastian Brock and Robert Hoyland, Liverpool, Liverpool University Press.

Panella, Clementina, and Saguì, Lucia (2001), "Consumo e produzione a Roma tra tardoantico e altomedievo: le merci, contesti," in *Roma nell'alto medioevo, 17 Aprile–1 Maggio, 2000*, Spoleto, Centro Italiano di Studi sull'Alto Medioevo, pp. 757–818.

Pani Ermini, Letizia (ed.) (2000), *Christiana loca: lo spazio cristiano nella Roma del primo millennio*, Rome, Palombi.

Panofsky, Erwin (1955), *Meaning in the Visual Arts: Papers in and on Art History*, Garden City, NY, Doubleday.

Panofsky, Erwin (1960), *Renaissance and Renascences in Western Art*, Stockholm, Almqvist & Wiksell.

Panofsky, Erwin, and Saxl, Fritz (1933), "Classical Mythology in Medieval Art," *Studies of the Metropolitan Museum* 4: 228–80.

Papaioannou, Stratis (2004), "Der Glasort des Textes: Selbstheit und Ontotypologie im byzantinischen Briefschreiben (10. und 11. Jh.)," in W. Hörandner, J. Koder, and M. Stassinopoulou (eds.), *Wiener Byzantinistik und Neogräzistik*, Beiträge zum Symposion Vierzig Jahre Institut für Byzantinistik und Neogräzistik der Universität Wien im Gedenken an Herbert Hunger (Wien, 4.–7. Dezember 2002), Vienna, Verlag der Österreichischen Akademie der Wissenschaften, pp. 324–36.

Papaioannou, Stratis (2006a), "Animate Statues: Aesthetics and Movement," in C. Barber and D. Jenkins (eds.), *Reading Michael Psellos*, Leiden, Brill, pp. 95–116.

Papaioannou, Stratis (2006b), "Gregory and the Constraint of Sameness," in Børtnes and Hägg (2006: 59–81).

Parker, S. Thomas (1986), *Romans and Saracens: A History of the Arabian Frontier*, Winona Lake, IN, Eisenbrauns.

Parkes, Malcolm (1992), *Pause and Effect: An Introduction to the History of Punctuation in the West*, Aldershot, Scholar Press.

Parkin, Tim P. (1992), *Demography and Roman Society*, Baltimore, MD, Johns Hopkins University Press.

Paroli, Lidia, and Vendittelli, Laura (eds.) (2004), *Roma dall'antichità al medioevo*, ii: *Contesti tardoantichi e altomedievali*, Milan, Electa.

Parsons, Peter (1970), "A School-Book from the Sayce Collection," *Zeitschrift für Papyrologie und Epigraphik* 6: 133–49.

Paschoud, François (1965), "Réflexions sur l'idéal religieux de Symmaque," *Historia* 14: 215–35.

Paschoud, François, and Szidat, Joachim (eds.) (1997), *Usurpationen in der Spätantike*, Stuttgart, Steiner.

Patlagean, Evelyne (1977), *Pauvreté économique et pauvreté sociale à Byzance, 4–7ème siècles*, Paris, Mouton.

Patrich, Joseph (1995), *Sabas, Leader of Palestinian Monasticism: A Comparative Study in Eastern Monasticism, Fourth to Seventh Centuries*, Washington, DC, Dumbarton Oaks.

Paxton, Frederick S. (1990), *Christianizing Death: The Creation of a Ritual Process in Early Medieval Europe*, Ithaca, NY, Cornell University Press.

Pearson, Birger A., and Goehring, James E. (eds.) (1986), *The Roots of Egyptian Christianity*, Philadelphia, Fortress Press.

Pergami, Federico (2000), *L'appello nella legislazione del tardo impero*, Accademia Romanistica Costantiniana, materiali per una palingenesi delle costituzioni tardo-imperiali, serie terza, 2, Milan, Giuffrè Editore.

Pernigotti, Sergio (1995), "Introduzione alla papirologia Copta," in Mario Capasso (ed.), *Atti del V Seminario internazionale di Papirologia: Lecce 27–29 Giugno 1994*, Lecce, Congedo, pp. 255–74.

Person, Ralf E. (1978), *The Mode of Theological Decision-Making at the Ecumenical Councils: An Inquiry into the Function of Scripture and Tradition at the Councils of Nicea and Ephesus*, Bern, Reinhardt.

Pestman, Pieter (ed.) (1977), *Recueil de textes démotiques et bilingues*, 3 vols., Leiden, Brill.

Peter, Hermann (1901), *Der Brief in der römischen Litteratur*, Leipzig, Teubner.

Petit, Paul (1951), "Sur la date du *Pro Templis*," *Byzantion* 21: 285–309.

Petit, Paul (1955), *Libanius et la vie muncipale à Antioche au IVe siècle après J.-C.*, Paris, P. Geuthner.

Petit, Paul (1956), *Les Étudiants de Libanius*, Paris, Nouvelles Éditions Latines.

Petit, Paul (tr.) (1988), *Libanius, Discours*, ii: *Discours II–X*, ed. Jean Martin, Paris, Les Belles Lettres.

Petrucci, Armando (1995), *Writers and Readers in Medieval Italy: Studies in the History of Written Culture*, ed. and tr. Charles Radding, New Haven, CT and London, Yale University Press.

Pfeiffer, Rudolf (1976), *History of Classical Scholarship from 1300 to 1850*, Oxford, Clarendon Press.

Pflaum, Henri (1940), "Le Cursus publicus sous le Haut-Empire romain," *Mémoires présentés par divers savants à l'Académie des Inscriptions et Belles-Lettres* 14: 189–390.

Pharr, Clyde et al. (tr.) (1952), *The Theodosian Code and Novels, and the Sirmondian Constititutions*, Princeton, NJ, Princeton University Press.

Phillips, Mark Salber (1996), "Reconsiderations on History and Antiquarianism: Arnaldo Momigliano and the Historiography of Eighteenth-Century Britain," *Journal of the History of Ideas* 57: 297–316.

Pietri, Charles (1976), *Roma christiana: recherches sur l'Église de Rome, son organisation, sa politique, son idéologie de Miltiade à Sixte III (311–440)*, Rome, Bibliothèque des Écoles Françaises d'Athènes et de Rome.

Pietri, Charles (1983a), "Graffiti," in Pietri (1997: 1469–90).

Pietri, Charles (1983b), "Inscriptions funéraires latines," in Pietri (1997: 1407–68).

Pietri, Charles (1989a), "La Politique de Constance II: un premier 'césaropapisme' ou l'*imitatio Constantini?*" in *L'Église et l'Empire au IVe siècle*, Vandœuvres, Fondation Hardt, pp. 113–78; repr. in Pietri (1997: 281–346).

Pietri, Charles (1989b), "Régions ecclésiastiques et paroisses romaines," in Duval (1989a: 1035–62).

Pietri, Charles (1997), *Christiana respublica: éléments d'une enquête sur le christianisme antique*, 3 vols., Rome, École Française de Rome.

Pietri, Luce (1983), *La Ville de Tours du IVe au Vie siècle: naissance d'une cité chrétienne*, Rome, École Française de Rome.

Pietri, Luce (1984), "Une nouvelle édition de la sylloge martinienne de Tours," *Francia* 12: 621–31.

Pietri, Luce (1986), "Les Sépultures privilégiées en Gaule d'après les sources littéraires," in Duval and Picard (1986: 133–42).

Pietri, Luce (1988), "Pagina in pariete reserata: épigraphie et architecture religieuse," in Donati 1988: 137–57.

Pietri, Luce, and Biarne, Jacques (1987), *Province ecclésiastique de Tours (Lugdunensis Tertia)*, Topographie chrétienne des cités de la Gaule des origins au milieu du VIIIe siècle 5, Paris, De Boccard.

Piganiol, André (1947), *L'Empire chrétien (325–395)*, Paris, Presses Universitaires de France; 2nd edn., ed. André Chastagnol, 1972.

Pilsworth, Clare (forthcoming), "Vile Scraps: 'Booklet' Style Manuscripts and the Transmission and Use of the Italian Martyr Narratives in Early Medieval Europe," in Diesenberger and Niederkorn-Bruck (forthcoming).

Pirenne, Henri (1937), *Mahomet et Charlemagne*, Paris, Alcan; Brussels, Nouvelle Société d'Éditions.

Pizarro, Joaquín Martínez (2003), "Ethnic and National History ca. 500–1000," in Deborah Mauskopf Deliyannis (ed.), *Historiography in the Middle Ages*, Leiden, Brill, pp. 43–87.

Pizzolato, Luigi F., and Rizzi, Marco (eds.) (1998), "*Nec timeo mori*," Atti del Congresso Internazionale di Studi Ambrosiani nel XVI Centenario della morte di sant'Ambrogio (Milano, 4–11 Aprile 1997), Milan, Vita e Pensiero.

Plumer, Eric (2003), *Augustine's Commentary on Galatians*, Oxford, Oxford University Press.

Pocock, J. G. A. (1996), "Classical and Civil History: The Transformation of Humanism," *Cromohs* 1: 1–34, www.cromohs.unifi.it/1_96/pocock.html

Pocock, J. G. A. (1999a), *Barbarism and Religion*, i: *The Enlightenments of Edward Gibbon*, Cambridge, Cambridge University Press.

Pocock, J. G. A. (1999b), *Barbarism and Religion*, ii: *Narratives of Civil Government*, Cambridge, Cambridge University Press.

Pocock, J. G. A. (2003), *Barbarism and Religion*, iii: *The First Decline and Fall*, Cambridge, Cambridge University Press.

Pocock, J. G. A. (2005), *Barbarism and Religion*, iv: *Barbarians, Savages and Empires*, Cambridge, Cambridge University Press.

Podskalsky, Gerhard (1977), *Theologie und Philosophie in Byzanz: der Streit um die theologische Methodik in der spätbyzantinischen Geistesgeschichte (14.–15. Jh.), seine systematischen Grundlagen und seine historische Entwicklung*, Munich, Beck.

Pohl, Walter (1991), "Conceptions of Ethnicity in Early Medieval Studies," *Archaeologia Polona* 29: 39–49; repr. in Lester R. Little and Barbara Rosenwein (eds.), *Debating the Middle Ages: Issues and Readings*, Malden, MA, Blackwell, 1998, pp. 15–24.

Pohl, Walter (1994), "Tradition, Ethnogenese, und literarische Gestaltung: eine Zwischenbilanz," in K. Brunner and B. Merta (eds.), *Ethnogenese und Überliefung: Angewandte Methoden der Frühmittelalterforschung*, Vienna, Oldenbourg, pp. 9–26.

Pohl, Walter (ed.) (1997), *Kingdoms of the Empire: The Integration of Barbarians in Late Antiquity*, Leiden and New York, Brill.

Pohl, Walter (1998), "Introduction: Strategies of Distinction," in Pohl and Reimitz (1998: 1–15.

Pohl, Walter (1999), "Social Language, Identities, and the Control of Discourse," in Chrysos and Wood (1999: 127–41).

Pohl, Walter (2001), *Werkstätte der Erinnerung: Montecassino und die Gestaltung der langobardischen Vergangenheit*, Vienna, Oldenbourg.

Pohl, Walter, and de Rubeis, Flavia (eds.) (2003), *Le scritture dai monasteri*, Secondo seminario internazionale di studio "I monasteri nell'alto medioevo," Rome, Institutum Romanum Finlandiae.

Pohl, Walter, and Reimitz, Helmut (eds.) (1998), *Strategies of Distinction: The Construction of Ethnic Communities, 300–800*, Leiden, Brill.

Pohl, Walter, and Reimitz, Helmut (eds.) (2000), *Grenze und Differenz im früheren Mittelalter*, Vienna, Österreichischen Akademie der Wissenschaften.

Pohl, Walter, Wood, Ian, and Reimitz, Helmut (eds.) (2001), *The Transformation of Frontiers from Late Antiquity to the Carolingians*, Leiden and Boston, MA, Brill.

Polge, Henri (1967), "L'Amélioration de l'attelage a-t-elle réellement fait reculer le servage?" *Journal des Savants* 1967: 5–42.

Pollitt, J. J. (1986), *Art in the Hellenistic Age*, Cambridge, Cambridge University Press.

Pollmann, Karla (1996), *Doctrina Christiana: Untersuchungen zu den Anfängen christlicher Hermeneutik mit besonderer Berücksichtigung von Augustinus, De doctrina christiana*, Fribourg, Universitätsverlag.

Pollmann, Karla (2005), "Augustine's Hermeneutics as a Universal Discipline?" in Pollmann and Vessey (2005: 206–31).

Pollmann, Karla (2006), "Wann ist der Mensch ein Mensch? Anthropologie und Kulturentstehung in spätantiken Autoren," in Feichtinger, Lake, and Seng (2006: 181–206).

Pollmann, Karla, and Vessey, Mark (eds.) (2005), *Augustine and the Disciplines: From Cassiciacum to Confessions*, Oxford, Oxford University Press.

Pontikos, Ilias N. (ed.) (1992), *Anonymi Miscellanea Philosophica: A Miscellany in the Tradition of Michael Psellos (Codex Baroccianus Graecus 131)*, Athens, Academy of Athens.

Poo, Mu-chou (2005), *Enemies of Civilization: Attitudes toward Foreigners in Ancient Mesopotamia, Egypt, and China*, Albany, State University of New York Press.

Porena, Pierfrancesco (2003), *Le origini della prefettura del pretorio tardoantica*, Rome, Bretschneider.

Porte, Danielle (ed.) (1988), *Hommages à Henri le Bonniec: res sacrae*, Brussels: Latomus.

Porter, Roy (1988), *Edward Gibbon: Making History*, London, Weidenfeld & Nicolson.

Porter, S. E., and Pearson, B. W. R. (2000), *Jewish–Christian Relations through the Centuries*, Sheffield, Sheffield Academic Press.

Possekel, Ute (1999), *Evidence of Greek Philosophical Concepts in the Writings of Ephrem the Syrian*, Louvain, Peeters.

Potter, David S. (2004), *The Roman Empire at Bay*, AD *180–395*, London, Routledge.

Potter, Timothy W. (1995), *Towns in Late Antiquity: Iol Caesarea and Its Context*, Oxford, Oxbow Books.

Potts, Daniel T. (1990), *The Arabian Gulf in Antiquity*, ii: *From Alexander the Great to the Coming of Islam*, Oxford, Clarendon Press.

Poulin, Jean-Claude (2006), "Les Libelli dans l'édition hagiographique avant le XIIe siècle," in Heinzelmann (2006: 15–193).

Poulter, Andrew G. (1992), "The Use and Abuse of Urbanism in the Danubian Provinces during the Later Roman Empire," in Rich (1992: 99–135).

Power, Kim (1996), *Veiled Desire: Augustine on Women*, New York, Continuum Press.

Pradels, Wendy, Brändle, Rudolf, and Heimgartner, Martin (2002), "The Sequence and Dating of the Series of John Chrysostom's Eight Discourses *Adversus Iudaeos*," *Zeitschrift für Antikes Christentum* 6: 90–116.

Preisendanz, Karl (1973–4), *Papyri Graecae Magicae: die griechischen Zauberpapyri*, 2 vols., Stuttgart, Teubner.

Preus, James S. (1969), *From Shadow to Promise: Old Testament Interpretation from Augustine to the Young Luther*, Cambridge, MA, Harvard University Press.

Price, Richard, and Gaddis, Michael (2005), *The Acts of the Council of Chalcedon*, 3 vols., Liverpool, Liverpool University Press.

Prinz, Friedrich (1965), *Frühes Mönchtum in Frankenreich: Kultur und Gesellschaft in Gallien, den Rheinlanden und Bayern am Beispiel der monastischen Entwicklung (4. bis 8. Jahrhundert)*, Munich and Vienna, Oldenbourg.

Quacquarelli, Antonio (1973), *L'ogdoade patristica e i suoi riflessi nella liturgia e nei monumenti*, Bari, Adriatica.

Quaegebeur, Jean (1982), "De la préhistoire de l'écriture copte," *Orientalia Lovaniensia Periodica* 131: 125–36.

Quecke, Hans (1975), *Die Briefe Pachoms: griech. Text d. Hs. W. 145 d. Chester Beatty Library: Anh., Die kopt. Fragmente u. Zitate d. Pachombriefe*, Regensburg, Pustet.

Quillen, Carol E (1998), *Rereading the Renaissance: Petrarch, Augustine, and the Language of Humanism*, Ann Arbor, University of Michigan Press.

Raab, T. K. (2002), Review of Burke (2001), *Journal of Interdisciplinary History* 33: 88–9.

Raban, Avner, and Holum, Kenneth G. (1996), *Caesarea Maritima: A Retrospective after Two Millenia*, Leiden, Brill.

Rabe, Hugo (ed.) (1931), *Prolegomenon sylloge*, Leipzig, Teubner.

Rabil, Albert, Jr (1988a), "Petrarch, Augustine, and the Classical Tradition," in Rabil (1988b, i: 95–114).

Rabil, Albert, Jr. (ed.) (1988b), *Renaissance Humanism: Foundations, Forms, and Legacy*, 3 vols., Philadelphia, University of Pennsylvania Press.

Raby, J., and Johns, J. (eds.) (1992), *Bayt al-Maqdis: 'Abd al-Malik's Jerusalem*, Oxford, Oxford University Press.

Ramsay, A. M. (1925), "The Speed of the Roman Imperial Post," *Journal of Roman Studies* 15: 60–74.

Ramsay, William M. (1904), "Roads and Travel (in NT)," in J. Hastings (ed.), *Dictionary of the Bible*, extra vol., Edinburgh, T. & T. Clark, pp. 375–402.

Ramsey, Boniface (tr.) (1997), *John Cassian: Conferences*, Ancient Christian Writers 57, New York, Paulist Press.

Rance, P. (2001), "Attacotti, Déisi and Magnus Maximus: The Case for Irish Federates in Late Roman Britain," *Britannia* 32: 243–70.

Randsborg, Klavs (ed.) (1989), *The Birth of Europe: Archaeology and Social Development in the First Millenium A.D.*, Rome, Bretschneider.

Randsborg, Klavs (1991), *The First Millennium AD in Europe and the Mediterranean: An Archaeological Essay*, Cambridge, Cambridge University Press.

Rapp, Claudia (1991), "Christians and Their Manuscripts in the Greek East in the Fourth Century," in Cavallo et al. (1991: 127–48).

Rapp, Claudia (2005a), *Holy Bishops in Late Antiquity: The Nature of Christian Leadership in an Age of Transition*, Berkeley and Los Angeles, University of California Press.

Rapp, Claudia (2005b), "Literary Culture under Justinian," in Maas (2005: 376–97).

Raven, Susan (1993), *Rome in Africa*, 3rd edn., London and New York, Routledge.

Rawson, Beryl (1986), "Children in the Roman *Familia*," in Beryl Rawson (ed.), *The Family in Ancient Rome: New Perspectives*, Ithaca, NY, Cornell University Press, pp. 170–200.

Rawson, Beryl (2003), "Death, Burial, and Commemoration of Children in Roman Italy," in David Balch and Carolyn Osiek (eds.), *Early Christian Families in Context: An Interdisciplinary Dialogue*, Grand Rapids, MI, Eerdmans, pp. 277–97.

Rebenich, Stefan (1997a), "Mommsen, Harnack und die Prosopographie der Spätantike," *Studia Patristica* 29: 109–18.

Rebenich, Stefan (1997b), *Theodor Mommsen und Adolf Harnack: Wissenschaft und Politik im Berlin des ausgehenden 19. Jahrhunderts*, Berlin, De Gruyter.

Rebenich, Stefan (1999), "Die Altertumswissenschaften und die Kirchenväterkommission an der Akademie: Theodor Mommsen und Adolf Harnack," in Jürgen Kocka (ed.), *Die Königlich Preußische Akademie der Wissenschaften zu Berlin im Kaiserreich*, Berlin, Akademie, pp. 199–233.

Rebenich, Stefan (2000a), "Historismus," in *Der Neue Pauly*, xiv: Rezeptions- und Wissenschaftsgeschichte, Stuttgart, Metzler, pp. 469–85.

Rebenich, Stefan (2000b), "Otto Seeck und die Notwendigkeit, Alte Geschichte zu lehren," in William M. Calder III et al. (eds.), *Wilamowitz in Greifswald*, Akten der Tagung zum 150. Geburtstag Ulrich von Wilamowitz-Moellendorffs in Greifswald, 19.–22. Dezember 1998, Hildesheim, Olms, pp. 262–98.

Rebenich, Stefan (2001), "Der alte Meergreis, die Rose von Jericho und ein höchst vortrefflicher Schwiegersohn: Mommsen, Harnack und Wilamowitz," in K. Nowak and O. G. Oexle (eds.), *Adolf von Harnack: Theologe, Historiker, Wissenschaftspolitiker*, Göttingen, Vandenhoeck & Ruprecht, pp. 39–69.

Rebenich, Stefan (2002), *Theodor Mommsen: eine Biographie*, Munich, Beck.

Rebillard, Éric (1991), "La Naissance du viatique: se préparer à mourir en Italie et en Gaule au Ve siècle," *Médiévales* 20: 99–108.

Rebillard, Éric (1993), "KOIMHTHRION et COEMETERIUM: Tombe, tombe sainte, nécropole," *Mélanges de l'École Française de Rome, Antiquité* 105: 975–1001.

Rebillard, Éric (1994), In hora mortis: évolution de la pastorale chrétienne de la mort aux IVe et Ve siècles dans l'Occident latin, Rome, École Française de Rome.

Rebillard, Éric (1998), "La Figure du catéchumène et le problème du délai du baptême dans la pastorale d'Augustin," in G. Madec (ed.), *Augustin prédicateur (395–411)*, Actes du colloque international de Chantilly (5–7 Septembre 1996), Paris, Institut d'Études Augustiniennes, pp. 285–92.

Rebillard, Éric (1999), "Les Formes de l'assistance funéraire dans l'Empire romain et leur évolution dans l'Antiquité tardive," *Antiquité Tardive* 7: 269–82.

Rebillard, Éric (2000), "A New Style of Argument in Christian Polemic: Augustine and the Use of Patristic Citations," *Journal of Early Christian Studies* 8: 559–78.

Rebillard, Éric (2003), *Religion et sépulture: l'église, les vivants et les morts dans l'antiquité tardive (IIIe–Ve siècles)*, Paris, Éditions de l'École des Hautes Études en Sciences Sociales.

Rebillard, Éric (2005), "Nec deserere memorias suorum: Augustine and the Family-Based Commemoration of the Dead," *Augustinian Studies* 36: 99–111.

Rebillard, Éric, and Sotinel, Claire (eds.) (1998), *L'Évêque dans la cité du IVe au Ve siècle: image et autorité*, Actes de la table ronde organisée par l'Istituto Patristico Augustinianum et l'École Française de Rome (1er–2 Déc. 1995), Rome, École Française de Rome.

Rees, Roger (2002), *Layers of Loyalty in Latin Panegyric, AD 289–307*, Oxford and New York, Oxford University Press.

Reimitz, Helmut (2000a), "Grenzen und Grenzüberschreitungen im karolingischen Mitteleuropa," in Pohl and Reimitz (2000: 105–66).

Reimitz, Helmut (2000b), "Ein karolingisches Geschichtsbuch aus Saint-Amand: der Codex Vindobonensis palat. 473," in Egger and Weigel (2000: 34–90).

Reimitz, Helmut (2004), "Der Weg zum Königtum in den historiographischen Kompendien der Karolingerzeit' in Becher (2004: 277–320).

Reincke, G. (1935), "Nachrichtenwesen," in Pauly-Wissowa, *Real-Encyclopädie*, xvi, Stuttgart, Metzler, pp. 1496–541.

Reinink, Gerrit J. (2002), "Paideia: God's Design in World History according to the East Syrian Monk John Bar Penkaye," in Kooper (2002: 190–8).

Reinink, Gerrit J., and Stolte, Bernard H. (eds.) (2002), *The Reign of Heraclius (610–641): Crisis and Confrontation*, Louvain, Peeters.

Reinsch, Dieter R. (2002), "*Historia ancilla litterarum*? Zum literarischen Geschmack in der Komnenenzeit: das Beispiel der *Synopsis Chronikê* des Konstantinos Manasses," in Paolo Odorico and Panagiotis A. Agapitos (eds.), *Pour une "nouvelle" histoire de la littérature byzantine*, Paris, Centre d'Études Byzantines, Néo-Helléniques et Sud-Est Européennes, École des Hautes Études en Sciences Sociales, pp. 81–94.

Remensnyder, Amy (1994), *Remembering Kings Past: Monastic Foundation Legends in Medieval Southern France*, Ithaca, NY, Cornell University Press.

Rémondon, Roger (1952), "L'Égypte et la suprême résistance au christianisme (Ve–VIIe siècles)," *Bulletin de l'Institut français d'Archéologie orientale* 51: 63–78.

Rémondon, Roger (1964), *La Crise de l'Empire romain, de Marc Aurèle à Anastase*, Paris, Presses Universitaires de France.

Rentinck, Pietro (1970), *La cura pastorale in Antiochia nel IV secolo*, Rome, Università Gregoriana, 1970.

Retsö, Jan (1993), "The Road to Yarmuk: The Arabs and the Fall of Roman Power in the Middle East," in Rydén and Rosenqvist (1993: 31–41).

Reydellet, Marc (1981), *La Royauté dans la littérature latine de Sidoine Apollinaire à Isidore de Séville*, Rome, École Française de Rome.

Reynolds, L. D., and N. G. Wilson (1991), *Scribes and Scholars: A Guide to the Transmission of Greek and Latin Literature*, 3rd edn., Oxford, Clarendon Press.

Reynolds, Lyndon (ed.) (1983), *Text and Transmission*, Oxford, Oxford University Press.

Reynolds, Philip L. (1994), *Marriage in the Western Church: The Christianization of Marriage during the Patristic and Early Medieval Periods*, Leiden, Brill.

Reynolds, Philip L., and Witte, John, Jr. (eds.) (2007), *To Have and to Hold: Marrying and Its Documentation in Western Christendom, 400–1600*, Cambridge, Cambridge University Press.

Rice, Eugene F., Jr (1985), *Saint Jerome in the Renaissance*, Baltimore, MD, Johns Hopkins University Press.

Rice, Eugene F., Jr (1988), "The Renaissance Idea of Christian Antiquity: Humanist Patristic Scholarship," in Rabil (1988b, i: 17–28).

Rich, John (ed.) (1992), *The City in Late Antiquity*, London, Routledge.

Richardson, Nicholas J. (1980), "Literary Criticism in the Exegetical Scholia to the *Iliad*: A Sketch," *Classical Quarterly* 30: 265–87.

Riché, Pierre (2003), *Henri-Irénée Marrou: historien engagé*, Paris, Éditions du Cerf.

Richter, Tonio Sebastian (2002), *Rechtssemantik und forensische Rhetorik: Untersuchungen zu Wortschatz, Stil und Grammatik der Sprache koptischer Rechtsurkunden*, Leipzig, Wodtke & Stegbauer.

Riegl, Alois (1901), *Spätrömische Kunstindustrie*, Vienna, Österreichisches Archäologisches Institut; tr. Rolf Winkes, *Late Roman Art Industry*, Rome, Bretschneider, 1985.

Rigg, A. G. (1996), "Medieval Latin Philology: Introduction," in Mantello and Rigg (1996: 71–8).

al-Rihâwî, "Abd al-Qâdir (1972), "Qusûr al-Hukkâm fi Dimashq 1," *Les Annales Archéologiques Arabes Syriennes* 22: 31–70.

Ripoll, Gisela, and Gurt, Joseph M. (eds.) (2000), *Sedes regiae (ann. 400–800)*, Barcelona, Reial Acadèmia de Bones Lletres.

Ritner, Robert K. (1995), "Egyptian Magical Practice under the Roman Empire: The Demotic Spells and Their Religious Context," *ANRW* 2. 18. 5: 3333–79.

Ritter, Adolf Martin (1965), *Das Konzil von Konstantinopel und sein Symbol: Studien zur Geschichte und Theologie des II. Ökumenischen Konzils*, Göttingen, Vandenhoeck & Ruprecht.

Rives, James B. (1995), *Religion and Authority in Roman Carthage from Augustus to Constantine*, Oxford, Clarendon Press.

Rives, James B. (tr.) (1999), *Tacitus: Germania*, Oxford, Clarendon Press.

Robert, Louis (1948), "Epigrammes relatives à des gouverneurs," *Hellenica* 4: 35–114.

Roberts, Colin H. (1979), *Manuscript, Society and Belief in Early Christian Egypt*, London, Oxford University Press for British Academy.

Roberts, Colin H., and Skeat, T. C. (1987), *The Birth of the Codex*, London, Oxford University Press for British Academy.

Roberts, Michael (1989), *The Jeweled Style: Poetry and Poetics in Late Antiquity*, London and Ithaca, NY, Cornell University Press.

Roberts, Michael (2001), "Fortunatus' Elegy on the Death of Galswintha (*Carm.* 6.5)," in Mathisen and Shanzer (2001: 298–312).

Robinson, Chase F. (2000), *Empire and Elites after the Muslim Conquest: The Transformation of Northern Mesopotamia*, Cambridge, Cambridge University Press.

Robinson, Chase F. (2003), "Reconstructing Early Islam: Truth and Consequences," in Berg (2003: 101–34).

Robinson, James M. (ed.) (1988), *The Nag Hammadi Library in English*, San Francisco, Harper & Row.

Robinson, James M. (1990), *The Pachomian Monastic Library at the Chester Beatty Library and the Bibliothèque Bodmer*, Claremont, Institute for Antiquity and Christianity.

Rochette, Bruno (1997), *Le Latin dans le monde grec*, Brussels, Latomus.

Rohlfs, Gerhard (1969), *Sermo Latinus Vulgaris: vulgarlateinisches Lesebuch*, 3rd edn., Tübingen, Niemeyer.

Roilos, Panagiotis (2005), *Amphoteroglossia: A Poetics of the Twelfth-Century Medieval Greek Novel*, Washington, DC and Cambridge, MA, Center for Hellenic Studies and Harvard University Press.

Rokeah, David (1982), *Jews, Pagans and Christians in Conflict*, Leiden, Brill.

Romei, D. (2004), "Produzione e circolazione dei manufatti ceramici a Roma nell'alto medioevo," in Paroli and Vendittelli (2004: 278–311).

Romm, James S. (1992), *The Edges of the Earth in Ancient Thought*, Princeton, NJ, Princeton University Press.

Roosens, Eugeen (1963), "Monde Yaka et développement économique communitaire," *Cahiers économiques et sociaux* 1: 5–6.

Rosenmeyer, Patricia (2001), *Ancient Epistolary Fictions: The Letter in Greek Literature*, Cambridge, Cambridge University Press.

Roskams, Steve (ed.) (2000), *Interpreting Stratigraphy: Site Evaluation, Recording Procedures, and Stratigraphic Analysis*, Papers Presented to the Interpreting Stratigraphy Conferences 1993–1997, Oxford, Archaeopress.

Ross, Steven (2001), *Roman Edessa: Politics and Culture on the Eastern Fringes of the Roman Empire, 114–242 CE*, London, Routledge.

Rostovtzeff, Michael (1926), *The Social and Economic History of the Roman Empire*, Oxford, Clarendon Press.

Rothaus, Richard (1996), "Christianization and De-paganization: The Late Antique Creation of a Conceptual Frontier," in Ralph W. Mathisen and Hagith Sivan (eds.), *Shifting Frontiers in Late Antiquity*, Aldershot, Ashgate, pp. 299–308.

Rouche, Michel (ed.) (1997), *Clovis: Histoire et Mémoire*, 2 vols., Actes du colloque international d'histoire de Reims, Paris, Presses de l'Université de Paris-Sorbonne.

Roueché, Charlotte (1989), *Aphrodisias in Late Antiquity*, London, Society for the Promotion of Roman Studies.

Rougé, Jean (1966), *Recherches sur l'organisation du commerce maritime en Méditerranée sous l'Empire romain*, Paris, SEVPEN.

Rougé, Jean (1975), *La Marine dans l'Antiquité*, Paris, Presses Universitaires de France; tr. Susan Frazer, *Ships and Fleets of the Ancient Mediterranean*, Middletown, CT, Wesleyan University Press, 1981.

Rouse, Mary A., and Rouse, Richard H. (1991), *Authentic Witnesses: Approaches to Medieval Texts and Manuscripts*, Notre Dame, IN, University of Notre Dame Press.

Rousseau, Philip (1978), *Ascetics, Authority, and the Church in the Age of Jerome and Cassian*, Oxford, Oxford University Press.

Rousseau, Philip (1985), *Pachomius: The Making of a Community in Fourth-Century Egypt*, Berkeley and Los Angeles, University of California Press.

Rousseau, Philip (1994), *Basil of Caesarea*, Berkeley and Los Angeles, University of California Press.

Rousseau, Philip (1995), "'Learned Women' and the Development of a Christian Culture in Late Antiquity," *Symbolae Osloenses* 70: 116–47.

Rousseau, Philip (1998), "'The Preacher's Audience': A More Optimistic View," in T. W. Hillard, R. A. Kearsley, C. E. V. Nixon, and A. M. Nobbs (eds.), *Ancient History in a Modern*

University, ii: *Early Christianity, Late Antiquity and Beyond*, Grand Rapids, MI: Eerdmans, pp. 391–400.

Rousseau, Philip (1999), *Pachomius: The Making of a Community in Fourth-Century Egypt*, 2nd edn., Berkeley and Los Angeles, University of California Press.

Rousseau, Philip (2001), "Monasticism," in Cameron, Ward-Perkins, and Whitby (2001: 745–80).

Rousseau, Philip (2002), *The Early Christian Centuries*, London, Longman.

Rousseau, Philip (2005), "The Pious Household and the Virgin Chorus: Reflections on Gregory of Nyssa's Life of Macrina," *Journal of Early Christian Studies* 13: 165–86.

Rouwhorst, G. (1989), *Les Hymnes pascales d'Ephrem de Nisibe: analyse théologique et recherche sur l'évolution de la fête pascale chrétienne à Nisibe et à Edesse et dans quelques églises voisines au quatrième siècle*, 2 vols., Leiden, Brill.

Rouwhorst, G. (1997), "Jewish Liturgical Traditions in Early Syriac Christianity," *Vigiliae Christianae* 51: 74–82.

Rowlandson, Jane (ed.) (1998), *Women and Society in Greek and Roman Egypt: A Sourcebook*, Cambridge, Cambridge University Press.

Rubenson, Samuel (1995), *The Letters of St. Antony: Monasticism and the Making of a Saint*, Minneapolis, MN, Fortress Press.

Rubin, Ze'ev (1995), "The Reforms of Khusro Anushirwan," in Cameron (1995b: 227–97).

Rubin, Ze'ev (1998), "The Roman Empire in the Res Gestae Divi Saporis: The Mediterranean World in Sasanian Propaganda," in Dabrowa (1998: 177–85).

Rubin, Ze'ev (2000), "The Sasanid Monarchy," in Cameron, Ward-Perkins, and Whitby (2000: 638–61).

Rummel, Erika (1986), *Erasmus' Annotations on the New Testament: From Philologist to Theologian*, Toronto, University of Toronto Press.

Rummel, Erika (1995), *The Humanist-Scholastic Debate in the Renaissance and Reformation*, Cambridge, MA, Harvard University Press.

Rundkvist, Martin (2003), *Barshalder 2: Studies of Late Iron Age Gotland*, Stockholm, Stockholm University.

Rupprecht, Hans-Albert (1994), *Kleine Einführung in die Papyruskunde*, Darmstadt, Wissenschaftliche Buchgesellschaft.

Rush, Alfred Clement (1941), *Death and Burial in Christian Antiquity*, Washington, DC, Catholic University of America Press.

Rush, Alfred Clement (1974), "The Eucharist: The Sacrament of the Dying in Christian Antiquity," *Jurist* 34: 10–35.

Rushforth, A. (2000), "From Periphery to Core in the Late Antique Mauretania," in Fincham et al. (2000: 99–103).

Russell, Norman (tr.) (1981), *The Lives of the Desert Fathers: The* Historia monachorum in Aegypto, London, Mowbray; Kalamazoo, MI, Cistercian Publications.

Rutgers, Leonard (1995), *The Jews in Late Ancient Rome: Evidence of Cultural Interaction in the Roman Diapora*, Leiden, Boston, MA, and Cologne, Brill.

Rydén, L., and Rosenqvist, J. O. (eds.) (1993), *Aspects of Late Antiquity and Early Byzantium*, Istanbul, Swedish Research Institute in Istanbul.

Sæbø, Magne (ed.) (1996), *Hebrew Bible/Old Testament: The History of Its Interpretation*, i/1: *Antiquity*, Göttingen, Vandenhoeck & Ruprecht.

Said, Edward W. (1978), *Orientalism*, New York, Pantheon Books.

Sakly, Mondher (2000), "Kairouan," in J.-C. Garcin, J.-L. Arnaud, and S. Denoix (eds.), *Grandes villes méditerranéennes du monde Musulman médieval*, Rome, École Française de Rome, pp. 57–85.

Salama, Pierre (1987), *Bornes milliaires d'Afrique proconsulaire: un panorama historique du Bas Empire romain*, Rome, École Française de Rome.

Salamito, Jean-Marie (2001), "Aspects aristocratiques et aspects populaires de l'être-chrétien aux IIIe et IVe siècles," in "Antiquité tardive et 'démocratisation de la culture': mise à l'épreuve du paradigme (Atti del Convegno di Vercelli, 14–15 Giugno 2000)," *Antiquité Tardive* 9: 165–78.

Salamon, Maciej (ed.) (1991), *Paganism in the Later Roman Empire and in Byzantium*, Krakow, Towarzystwo Autorów i Wydawców Prac Naukowych "Universitas."

Saller, Richard (1988), "Pietas, Obligation and Authority in the Roman Family,' in Kneissl and Losemann (1988: 393–410).

Saller, Richard (1994), *Patriarchy, Property, and Death in the Roman Family*, Cambridge, Cambridge University Press.

Saller, Richard, and Shaw, Brent (1984), "Tombstones and Family Relations in the Principate: Civilians, Soldiers, and Slaves," *Journal of Roman Studies* 74: 124–56.

Salvatore, Mariarosaria (1977), "Fibule con iscrizione dall'Italia meridionale," *Vetera Christianorum* 14: 339–57.

Salway, Benet (2001), "Travel, *Itineraria* and *Tabellaria*," in Adams and Laurence (2001: 22–66).

Salway, Peter (1981), *Roman Britain*, Oxford, Clarendon Press; New York, Oxford University Press.

Salzman, Michele Renee (1987), " 'Superstitio' in the Codex Theodosianus and the Persecution of Pagans," *Vigiliae Christianae* 41: 172–88.

Salzman, Michele Renee (1990), *On Roman Time: The Codex Calendar of 354 and the Rhythms of Urban Life in Late Antiquity*, Berkeley and Los Angeles, University of California Press.

Salzman, Michele Renee (1999), "The Christianization of Sacred Time and Sacred Space," in Harris (1999: 123–34).

Salzman, Michele Renee (2002), *The Making of a Christian Aristocracy: Social and Religious Change in the Western Roman Empire*, Cambridge MA, Harvard University Press.

Salzman, Michele Renee (2004), "Travel and Communication in the Letters of Symmachus," in Ellis and Kidner (2004: 81–94).

Samson, R. (1994), "The End of Alamannic Princely Forts and the Supposed Merovingian Hegemony," *Journal of European Archaeology* 2: 341–60.

Sanders, E. P. (ed.) (1980–2), *Jewish and Christian Self-Definition*, 3 vols., Philadelphia, Fortress Press.

Sanders, Gabriel (1976), "Les Chrétiens face à l'épigraphie funéraire latine," in Sanders (1991: 131–53).

Sanders, Gabriel (1991), *Lapides memores: païens et chrétiens face à la mort: le témoignage de l'épigraphie funéraire latine*, ed. Angela Donati, Dorothy Pikhaus, and Marc Van Uytfanghe, Faenza, Fratelli Lega.

Sanders, Henry A., and Schmidt, Carl (eds.) (1927), *The Minor Prophets in the Freer Collection and the Berlin Fragment of Genesis*, New York, Macmillan.

Sandwell, Isabella (2005), "Outlawing 'Magic' or Outlawing 'Religion'? Libanius and the Theodosian Code as Evidence for Legislation against 'Pagan' Practices," in Harris (2005b: 87–123).

Sandwell, Isabella (2007), *Identity and Religious Interaction in Fourth Century Antioch*, Cambridge, Cambridge University Press.

Sandys, John Edwin (1927), *Latin Epigraphy: An Introduction to the Study of Latin Inscriptions*, 2nd edn. rev. by S. G. Campbell, Cambridge, Cambridge University Press.

Sansterre, Jean-Marie (ed.) (2004), *L'Autorité du passé dans les sociétés médiévales*, Brussels, Institut Historique Belge de Rome.

Sanz, Peter, ed. (1946), *Griechische literarische Papyri christlichen Inhaltes*, i: *Biblica, Väterschriften und Verwandtes*, Baden bei Wien, Rohrer.

Saradi, Heleni (1998), "Privatisation and Subdivision of Urban Properties in the Early Byzantine Centuries," *Bulletin of the American Society of Papyrologists* 35: 17–43.

Saradi, Heleni (2000), "Perceptions and Literary Interpretations of Statues and the Image of Constantinople," *Byzantiaka* 20: 37–77.

Satzinger, Helmut (1984), "Die altkoptischen Texte als Zeugnisse der Beziehungen zwischen Ägyptern und Griechen," in Peter Nagel (ed.), *Graeco-Coptica: Griechen und Kopten im byzantinischen Ägypten*, Halle, Martin-Luther-Universität, pp. 137–46.

Satzinger, Helmut (1985), "On the Spread of the Sahidic Dialect," in Tito Orlandi and Frederik Wisse (eds.), *Acts of the Second International Congress of Coptic Studies*, Rome, CIM, pp. 307–12.

Satzinger, Helmut (1991), "Old Coptic," in Atiya (1991, viii: 169–75).

Sauer, Eberhard W. (1996), *The End of Paganism in the North-Western Provinces of the Roman Empire: The Example of the Mithras Cult*, Oxford, Tempus Reparatum.

Sauer, Eberhard W. (2003), *The Archaeology of Religious Hatred in the Roman and Early Medieval World*, Stroud, Tempus.

Sauer, Eberhard W. (ed.) (2004), *Archaeology and Ancient History: Breaking Down the Boundaries*, London, Routledge.

Sauneron S., and Jacquet, J. (1972), *Les Ermitages chrétiens du désert d'Esna*, 4 vols., Cairo, Institut Français d'Archéologie Orientale du Caire.

Sawyer, P. H., and Wood, I. N. (eds.) (1977), *Early Medieval Kingship*, Leeds, University of Leeds Press.

Saxer, Victor (1980), *Morts, martyrs, reliques en Afrique chrétienne aux premiers siècles: les témoignages de Tertullien, Cyprien et Augustin à la lumière de l'archéologie africaine*, Paris, Beauchesne.

Saxer, Victor (1984), *Vie liturgique et quotidienne à Carthage vers le milieu du IIIe siècle: le témoignage de saint Cyprien et de ses contemporains d'Afrique*, 2nd edn., Vatican City, Pontificio Istituto di Archeologia Cristiana.

Saxer, Victor (1988), *Les Rites de l'initiation chrétienne du IIe au VIe siècle: esquisse historique et signification d'après leurs principaux témoins*, Spoleto, Centro Italiano di Studi sull'Alto Medioevo.

Saxl, Fritz (1957), *Lectures*, 2 vols., London, Warburg Institute.

Schanz, Martin (1904), *Geschichte der römischen Litteratur bis zum Gesetzgebungswerk des Kaisers Justinian*, iv/1, Munich, Beck.

Scheid, John (2005), *Quand faire, c'est croire: les rites sacrificiels des Romains*, Paris, Aubier.

Scheltema, H. J. (1970), *L'Enseignement de droit des antécesseurs*, Leiden, Brill.

Schenkeveld, Dirk (1992), "Prose Usages of AKOUEIN 'To Read'," *Classical Quarterly* 42: 129–41.

Schiavone, Aldo (2000), *The End of the Past: Ancient Rome and Modern West*, tr. Margery J. Schneider, Cambridge, MA, Harvard University Press.

Schick, Robert (1995), *The Christian Communities of Palestine from Byzantine to Islamic Rule: A Historical and Archaeological Survey*, Princeton, NJ, Darwin Press.

Schiffman, Lawrence H. (1985), *Who was a Jew? Rabbinic and Halakhic Perspectives on the Jewish-Christian Schism*, Hoboken, NJ, KTAV Publishing House.

Schippmann, K. (1990), *Grundzüge der Geschichte des sasanidischen Reiches*, Darmstadt, Wissenschaftliche Buchgesellschaft.

Schmidt, B. (1983), "Die Thüringer," in Bruno Krüger et al. (eds.), *Die Germanen: Geschichte und Kultur der germanischen Stämme in Mitteleuropa: ein Handbuch in zwei Bänden*, ii: *Die Stämme und Stammesverbände in der Zeit vom 3. Jahrhundert bis zur Herausbildung der politschen Vorherrschaft der Franken*, Berlin, Akademie Verlag, pp. 502–48.

Schmidt, B. (1987), "Das Königreich der Thüringer und seine Provinzen," in Menghin, Springer, and Wamers (1987: 471–80).

Schmitz, Franz-Jürgen, and Mink, Gerd (1986–), *Liste der koptischen Handschriften des Neuen Testaments*, Berlin, De Gruyter.

Schneemelcher, Wilhelm et al. (eds.) (1959–), *Bibliographia Patristica: Internationale patristische Bibliographie*, Berlin, De Gruyter.

Scholer, David M. (1971), *Nag Hammadi Bibliography, 1948–1969*, Leiden, Brill.

Scholer, David M. (1997), *Nag Hammadi Bibliography, 1970–1994*, Leiden, Brill.

Schöllgen, Georg (1988), *Die Anfänge der Professionalisierung des Klerus und das kirchliche Amt in der syrischen Didaskalie*, Münster, Aschendorff.

Schöllgen, Georg (1993), "Franz Joseph Dölger und die Entstehung des Forschungsprogramms 'Antike und Christentum'," *Jahrbuch für Antike und Christentum* 36: 7–23.

Scholten, Clemens (1996), *Antike Naturphilosophie und christliche Kosmologie in der Schrift "De opificio mundi" des Johannes Philoponus*, Berlin, De Gruyter.

Scholten, Clemens (tr. and intro.) (1997), *Johannes Philoponus, De opificio mundi – Über die Erschaffung der Welt*, 3 vols., Freiburg, Herder.

Scholz, Sebastian (1992), *Transmigration und Translation: Studien zum Bistumswechsel von der Spätantike bis zum Hohen Mittelalter*, Cologne, Böhlau.

Schön, Matthias D. (1999), *Feddersen Wierde, Fallward, Flögeln: Archäologie im Museum Burg Bederkesa, Landkreis Cuxhaven*, Bremerhaven, Landkreis Cuxhaven.

Schröder, Bianca (2007), *Bildung und Briefe im 6. Jahrhundert: Studien zum Mailänder Diakon Magnus Felix Ennodius*, Berlin, De Gruyter.

Schroeder, Joy (2004), "John Chrysostom's Critique of Spousal Violence," *Journal of Early Christian Studies* 12: 413–42.

Schulz, Armin (1992), "Ariassos: eine hellenistisch-römische Stadt in Pisidien," in Elmar Schwertheim (ed.), *Forschungen in Pisidien*, Bonn, Habelt, pp. 29–41.

Schulz, Fritz (1946), *History of Roman Legal Science*, Oxford, Clarendon Press.

Schüssler, Karlheinz (1995–), *Biblia Coptica: die koptischen Bibeltexte*, Wiesbaden, Harrassowitz.

Schwartz, Seth (2001), *Imperialism and Jewish Society, 200 B.C.E. to 640 C.E.*, Princeton, NJ, Princeton University Press.

Scott, Roger (1990), "Malalas and His Contemporaries," in Jeffreys, Croke, and Scott (1990: 67–85).

Scourfield, J. H. D. (ed.) (2007), *Texts and Culture in Late Antiquity: Inheritance, Authority, and Change*, Swansea, Classical Press of Wales.

Séd, N. (1968), "Les Hymnes sur le paradis de saint Ephrem et les traditions juives," *Muséon* 81: 455–501.

Seeck, Otto (1897–1920), *Geschichte des Untergangs der antiken Welt*, 6 vols., Berlin, Siemenroth & Troschl.

Seeck, Otto (1901), "Cursus publicus," in Pauly-Wissowa, *Real Encyclopädie*, iv, Stuttgart, Metzler, pp. 1846–63.

Segal, Alan F. (1986), *Rebecca's Children: Judaism and Christianity in the Roman World*, Cambridge, MA, Harvard University Press.

Segal, J. B. (1964), "The Jews of North Mesopotamia," in J. M. Grintz and J. Liver (eds.), *Sepher Segal*, Jerusalem, Kiryat Sepher, pp. 32–63.

Segal, J. B. (2001), *Edessa, "The Blessed City"*; repr. Piscataway, NJ, Gorgias Press.

Selb, Walter (1967), "Episcopalis audientia von der Zeit Konstantins bis zur Nov. XXXV Valentinians III," *Zeitschrift der Savigny-Stiftung für Rechtsgeschichte, Romanistische Abteilung* 84: 162–217.

Semmler, Josef (1983), "Benedictus II: una regula - una consuetudo," in Lourdaux (1983: 1–49).

Serjeant, Robert B. (1978), "The *Sunna Jâmi'a*: Pacts with the Yathrib Jews and the Tahrîm of Yathrib: Analysis and Translation of the Documents Comprised in the so-called 'Constitution of Medina'," *Bulletin of the School of Oriental and African Studies* 41: 1–42.

Setz, Wofram (1975), *Lorenzo Vallas Schrift gegen die konstantinische Schenkung*, Tübingen, Max Niemeyer.

Setzer, Claudia (1994), *Jewish Responses to Early Christians: History and Polemics, 30–150 C.E.*, Minneapolis, MN, Fortress Press.

Ševčenko, Ihor (1992), "The Search for the Past in Byzantium around the Year 800," *Dumbarton Oaks Papers* 46: 279–93.

Seznec, Jean (1940), *La Survivance des dieux antiques: essai sur le role de la tradition mythologique dans l'humanisme et dans l'art de la Renaissance*, London, Warburg Institute; tr. Barbara F. Sessions, *The Survival of the Pagan Gods*, New York, Pantheon Books, 1953.

Shahbazi, S. A. (1990), "Byzantine–Iranian Relations," in Yarshater (1982–, iv: 588–99).

Shahîd, Irfan (1984a), *Byzantium and the Arabs in the Fourth Century*, Washington, DC, Dumbarton Oaks.

Shahîd, Irfan (1984b), *Rome and the Arabs: A Prolegomenon to the Study of Byzantium and the Arabs*, Washington, DC, Dumbarton Oaks.

Shahîd, Irfan (1989), *Byzantium and the Arabs in the Fifth Century*, Washington, DC, Dumbarton Oaks.

Shahîd, Irfan (1995), *Byzantium and the Arabs in the Sixth Century*, Washington, DC, Dumbarton Oaks.

Shanzer, Danuta (1998), "Dating the Baptism of Cloves: The Bishop of Vienne vs. the Bishop of Tours," *Early Medieval Europe* 7: 29–57.

Shanzer, Danuta (2002), "*Avulsa a latere meo*: Augustine's Spare Rib: Confessions 6.15.25," *Journal of Roman Studies* 92: 157–76.

Shanzer, Danuta (2005), "Augustine's Disciplines: *Silent diutius Musa Varronis?*" in Pollmann and Vessey (2005: 69–112).

Sharpe, Richard (2003), *Titulus: Identifying Medieval Latin Texts: An Evidence-Based Approach*, Turnhout, Brepols.

Shaw, Brent (1984a), "Bandits in the Roman Empire," *Past and Present* 105: 3–52.

Shaw, Brent (1984b), "Latin Funerary Epigraphy and Family Life in the Later Roman Empire," *Historia* 33: 457–95.

Shaw, Brent (1987a), "The Age of Roman Girls at Marriage: Some Reconsiderations," *Journal of Roman Studies* 77: 30–46.

Shaw, Brent (1987b), "The Family in Late Antiquity: The Experience of Augustine," *Past and Present* 115: 3–51.

Shaw, Brent (1991), "The Cultural Meaning of Death: Age and Gender in the Roman Family," in Kertzer and Saller (1991: 66–90).

Shaw, Brent (1995a), *Environment and Society in Roman North Africa: Studies in History and Archaeology*, Aldershot and Brookfield, VT, Variorum.

Shaw, Brent (1995b), *Rulers, Nomads, and Christians in Roman North Africa*, Aldershot and Brookfield, VT, Variorum.

Shaw, Brent (1996), "Seasons of Death: Aspects of Mortality in Imperial Rome," *Journal of Roman Studies* 86: 100–38.

Shaw, Brent (2002), " 'With Whom I Lived': Measuring Roman Marriage," *Ancient Society* 32: 195–242.

Sheils, W. J., and Wood, Diana (eds.) (1990), *Women in the Church*, Oxford, Blackwell.

Shelton, Kathleen (1981), *The Esquiline Treasure*, London, British Museum Publications.

Shelton, Kathleen (1985), "The Esquiline Treasure: The Nature of the Evidence," *American Journal of Archaeology* 89: 147–55.

Shepardson, Christine (2002), " 'Exchanging Reed for Reed': Mapping Contemporary Heretics onto Biblical Jews in Ephrem's Hymns on Faith," *Hugoye* 5/1, http://syrcom. cua.edu/hugoye/Vol5No1/HV5N1Shepardson.html

Shepardson, Christine (2008), *Anti-Judaism and Christian Orthodoxy: Ephrem's Hymns in Fourth-Century Syria*, Washington, DC, Catholic University of America Press.

Sheppard, Anne (2000), "Philosophy and Philosophical Schools," in Cameron, Ward-Perkins, and Whitby (2000: 835–54).

Sherk, Robert K. (1974), "Roman Geographical Exploration and Military Maps," *ANRW* 2. 1: 534–62.

Shipley, Graham, and Salmon, John (eds.) (1996), *Human Landscapes in Classical Antiquity: Environment and Culture*, London and New York, Routledge.

Sider, Robert D. (1978), Tertullian, *On the Shows*: An Analysis," *Journal of Theological Studies* n.s. 29: 339–65.

Sider, Robert (1998), "Erasmus and Ancient Christian Writers: The Search for Authenticity," in John Petruccione (ed.), *Nova et Vetera: Patristic Studies in Honor of Thomas Patrick Halton*, Washington, DC, Catholic University of America Press, pp. 235–54.

Sieben, Hermann Josef (1979), *Die Konzilsidee der alten Kirche*, Paderborn, Schöningh.

Sieben, Hermann Josef (1983), *Exegesis Patrum: saggio bibliografico sull'esegesi biblica dei Padri della Chiesa*, Rome, Institutum Augustinianum.

Sieben, Hermann Josef (1991), *Kirchenväterhomilien zum Neuen Testament*, Steenbrugge, In Abbatia S. Petri; The Hague, Nijhoff.

Siegmund, F. (2003), "Social Relations among the Old Saxons," in Green and Siegmund (2003: 77–95).

Simon, Marcel (1986), *Verus Israel: A Study of the Relations between Christians and Jews in the Roman Empire (135–425)*, tr. H. McKeating, Oxford, Oxford University Press; translation of *Verus Israel: étude sur les relations entre chrétiens et juifs dans l'Empire romain, 135–425*, Paris, De Boccard, 1948.

Siniscalco, Paolo (2000), "Gli imperatori romani e il cristianesimo nel IV secolo," in Jean Gaudemet, Paolo Siniscalco, and Gian Luigi Falchi (eds.), *Legislazione imperiale e religione nel IV secolo*, Rome, Institutum Patristicum Augustinianum, pp. 67–120.

Sinkewicz, Robert E. (tr.) (2003), *Evagrius of Pontus: The Greek Ascetic Corpus*, Oxford, Oxford University Press.

Sinor, D. (1990), "The Hun Period," in D. Sinor (ed.), *The Cambridge History of Early Inner Asia*, Cambridge, Cambridge University Press, pp. 177–205.

Sintès, C. (1994), "La Réutilisation des espaces publics à Arles: un témoignage de la fin de l'Antiquité," *Antiquité Tardive* 2: 181–92.

Sirks, A. J. Boudewijn (1996), "Shifting Frontiers in the Law: Romans, Provincials and Barbarians," in Mathisen and Sivan (1996: 146–57).

Sivan, Hagith (1993), "On Hymens and Holiness in Late Antiquity," *Jahrbuch für Antike und Christentum* 36: 81–93.

Skeat, T. C. (1969), "Early Christian Book-Production: Papyri and Manuscripts," in G. W. H. Lampe (ed.), *The Cambridge History of the Bible*, ii, Cambridge, Cambridge University Press, pp. 54–79.

Skeat, T. C. (1992), "Irenaeus and the Four-Gospel Canon," *Novum Testamentum* 34: 194–9.

Skeat, T. C. (1995), "Was Papyrus Regarded as 'Cheap' or 'Expensive' in the Ancient World?" *Aegyptus* 75: 75–93.

Sklenár, R. (2005), "Ausonius's Elegiac Wife: Epigram 20 and the Traditions of Latin Love Poetry," *Classical Journal* 101: 51–62.

ŠKZ (or *Res gestae divi Saporis*), *see* Huyse 1999.

Smith, Julia M. H. (2000a), "Did Women have a Transformation of the Roman World?" *Gender and History* 12: 552–71.

Smith, Julia M. H. (ed.) (2000b), *Early Medieval Rome and the Christian West: Essays in Honour of Donald A. Bullough*, Leiden, Brill.

Smith, Julia M. H. (2000c), "Old Saints, New Cults: Roman Relics in Carolingian Francia," in Smith (2000b: 317–39).

Smith, Mark (1998), "Coptic Literature, 311–425," in Cameron and Garnsey (1998: 720–35).

Smith, Rowland (1995), *Julian's Gods: Religion and Philosophy in the Thought and Action of Julian the Apostate*, London and New York, Routledge.

Snyder, H. Gregory (2000), *Teachers and Texts in the Ancient World: Philosophers, Jews and Christians*, London and New York, Routledge.

Sodini, J.-P. et al. (1980), "Déhès (Syrie du Nord), Campagnes I–III (1976–1978), Recherches sur l'habitat rural," *Syria* 57: 1–303.

Sogno, Cristiana (2006), *Q. Aurelius Symmachus: A Political Biography*, Ann Arbor, University of Michigan Press.

Sommar, Mary (2002), "Hincmar of Reims and the Canon Law of Episcopal Translation," *Catholic Historical Review* 88: 429–45.

Sorlin, I. (1973), "La Diffusion et la transmission de la littérature chronographique byzantine en Russie prémongole du XIe au XIIIe siècle," *Travaux et Mémoires* 5: 385–408.

Sotinel, Claire (1997), "Le Recrutement des évêques en Italie aux IVe et Ve siècles: Essai d'enquête prosopographique," in *Vescovi e Pastori in epoca teodosiana*, XXV Incontro di studiosi dell'antichità cristiana (Roma 8–11 Maggio 1996), Rome, Institutum Patristicum Augustinianum, pp. 192–202.

Sotinel, Claire (2004), "How were Bishops Informed? Information Transmission across the Adriatic Sea in Late Antiquity," in Ellis and Kidner (2004: 63–72).

Sotinel, Claire (2005), *Identité civique et christianisme: Aquilée du IIIe au VIe siècle*, Rome, École Française de Rome.

Sotinel, Claire (forthcoming), "La Circulation de l'information entre les Églises," in L. Capdetrey (ed.), *Information et structures de pouvoir*, Bordeaux, Ausonius.

Speck, Paul (1998), "Byzantium: Cultural Suicide?" in L. Brubaker (ed.), *Byzantium in the Ninth Century: Dead or Alive?* Aldershot and Brookfield, VT, Ashgate, pp. 73–84.

Spence, Sarah (1996), *Texts and the Self in the Twelfth Century*, Cambridge, Cambridge University Press.

Spengler, Oswald (1918–22), *Der Untergang des Abendlandes: Umrisse einer Morphologie der Weltgeschichte*, 2 vols., i (1918): *Gestalt und Wirklichkeit*; ii (1922): *Welthistorische Perspektiven*, Vienna, Braumüller; Munich, Beck; tr. Charles Francis Atkinson, *The Decline of the West*, 2 vols., London, Allen & Unwin, 1926–8.

Spiegel, Gabrielle M. (1983), "Genealogy: Form and Function in Medieval Historical Narrative," *History and Theory* 22: 43–53.

Spiegel, Gabrielle M. (1993), *Romancing the Past: The Rise of Vernacular Prose Historiography in Thirteenth Century France*, Berkeley and Los Angeles, University of California Press.

Spiegel, Gabrielle M. (1994), review of Magdalino (1992), *Speculum* 69: 1218–20.

Spier, Jeffrey (ed.) (2007), *Picturing the Bible: The Earliest Christian Art*, New Haven, CT, Yale University Press.

Spieser, Jean-Michel (1984), *Thessalonique et ses monuments du IVe au VIe siècle: contribution à l'étude d'une ville paléochrétienne*, Paris, De Boccard.

Spurr, David (2001), *The Rhetoric of Empire*, 5th edn., Durham, NC, Duke University Press.

Staats, Reinhart (1968), *Gregor von Nyssa und die Messalianer*, Berlin, De Gruyter.

Stafford, Pauline (1978), "Sons and Mothers: Family Politics in the Early Middle Ages," in Baker (1978: 79–100).

Stafford, Pauline, and Mulder-Bakker, Anneke B. (eds.) (2000), *Gendering the Middle Ages*, Oxford, Blackwell.

Stancliffe, Clare (1983), *St. Martin and His Hagiographer: History and Miracle in Sulpicius Severus*, Oxford, Clarendon Press.

Staritz, Katharina (1931), *Augustins Schöpfungsglaube dargestellt nach seinen Genesisauslegungen*, Breslau, Verlag Wilhelm Gottlob Korn.

Stark, Rodney (1996), *The Rise of Christianity: A Sociologist Reconsiders History*, Princeton, NJ, Princeton University Press.

Stark, Rodney, and Bainbridge, William S. (1985), *The Future of Religion: Secularization, Revival and Cult Formation*, Berkeley and Los Angeles, University of California Press.

Stegmüller, Friedrich (1950–), *Repertorium biblicum medii aevi*, 11 vols., Madrid, Consejo Superior de Investigaciones Cientificas.

Steidle, Wolf (1978), "Die Leichenrede des Ambrosius für Kaiser Theodosius und die Helena-Legende," *Vigiliae Christianae* 32: 94–112.

Stein, Ernst (1919), *Studien zur Geschichte des byzantinischen Reiches, vornehmlich unter den Kaisern Justinus II und Tiberius Constantinus*, Stuttgart, Metzler.

Stein, Ernst (1928), *Geschichte des spätrömischen Reiches*, Vienna, Seidel.

Stein, Ernst (1949–59), *Histoire du Bas-Empire*, i: *De l'état romain a l'état byzantin (284–476)*, ii: *De la disparition de l'Empire d'Occident à la mort de Justinien (476–565)*, tr. Jean-Rémy Palanque, Paris, Desclée de Brouwer.

Stein, Peter (1999), *Roman Law in European History*, Cambridge, Cambridge University Press.

Stephens, Mitchell (1997), *A History of News*, Fort Worth, PA and San Diego, CA, Harcourt Brace.

Sterk, Andrea (2004), *Renouncing the World yet Leading the Church: The Monk-Bishop in Late Antiquity*, Cambridge, MA, Harvard University Press.

Steuer, Heiko (1994), "Handwerk auf spätantiken Höhensiedlungen des 4/5. Jahrhunderts in Südwestdeutschland," in Nielsen, Randsborg, and Thrane (1994: 128–44).

Stevens, C. E. (1933), *Sidonius Apollinaris and His Age*, Oxford, Clarendon Press.

Stevens, Susan T., Kalinowski, Angela V., and vanderLeest, Hans (2005), *Bir Ftouha: A Pilgrimage Church Complex at Carthage*, Portsmouth, RI, Journal of Roman Archaeology.

Stewart, Columba (1991), *"Working the Earth of the Heart": The Messalian Controversy in History, Texts, and Language to A.D. 431*, Oxford, Oxford University Press.

Stewart, Columba (2000), "Monasticism," in Esler (2000: 344–67).

Stinger, Charles L. (1977), *Humanism and the Church Fathers: Ambrogio Traversari (1386–1439) and Christian Antiquity in the Italian Renaissance*, Albany, State University of New York Press.

Stinger, Charles L. (1997), "Italian Renaissance Learning and the Church Fathers," in Backus (1997, ii: 473–510).

Stirling, Lea (2004), *The Learned Collector: Mythological Statuettes and Classical Taste in Late Antique Gaul*, Ann Arbor, University of Michigan Press.

Stock, Brian (1983), *The Implications of Literacy: Written Language and Models of Interpretation in the Eleventh and Twelfth Centuries*, Princeton, NJ, Princeton University Press.

Stock, Brian (1996), *Augustine the Reader: Meditation, Self-Knowledge, and the Ethics of Interpretation*, Cambridge, MA, Harvard University Press.

Stock, Brian (2001), *After Augustine: The Meditative Reader and the Text*, Philadelphia, University of Pennsylvania Press.

Stoffel, Pascal (1994), *Über die Staatspost, die Ochsengespanne und die requirierten Ochsengespanne: eine Darstellung des römischen Postwesens auf Grund der Gesetze des* Codex Thedosianus *und des* Codex Iustinianus, Frankfurt am Main, Lang.

Stolte, B. (1991), "The Past in Legal Argument in the Byzantine Canonists of the Twelfth-Century," in Oikonomides (1991: 199–210).

Storms, G. (1970), "The Significance of Hygelac's Raid," *Nottingham Medieval Studies* 14: 3–26.

Stout, Matthew (1997), *The Irish Ringfort*, Dublin, Four Courts Press.

Stout, Matthew (2000), "Early Christian Ireland: Settlement and Environment," in Barry (2000: 81–109).

Stowers, Stanley K. (1986), *Letter Writing in Greco-Roman Antiquity*, Philadelphia, Westminster Press.

Straw, Carole, and Lim, Richard (eds.) (2004), *The Past before Us: The Challenge of Historiographies of Late Antiquity*, Turnhout, Brepols.

Strzygowski, Josef (1888), *Cimabue und Rom: Funde und Forschungen zur Kunstgeschichte und zur Topographie der Stadt Rom*, Vienna, Hölder.

Strzygowski, Josef (1901), *Orient oder Rom: Beiträge zur Geschichte de spätantiken und frühchristlichen Kunst*, Leipzig, J. C. Hinrichs'sche Buchhandlung.

Studer, Basil (1998), *Schola Christiana: die Theologie zwischen Nizäa (325) und Chalcedon (451)*, Paderborn, Schöningh.

Styger, Paul (1933), "Nymphäen, Mausoleen, Baptisterien: Probleme der Architekturgeschichte," *Architectura* 1: 50–5.

Sullivan, Richard (1989), "The Carolingian Age: Reflections on Its Place in the History of the Middle Ages," *Speculum* 64: 267–306.

Swain, Simon (2004), "Sophists and Emperors: The Case of Libanius," in Swain and Edwards (2004: 355–400).

Swain, Simon, and Edwards, Mark (eds.) (2004), *Approaching Late Antiquity: The Transformation from Early to Late Empire*, Oxford and New York, Oxford University Press.

Swift, Louis J. (1981), "Basil and Ambrose on the Six Days of Creation," *Augustinianum* 21: 317–28.

Syme, Ronald (1968), *Ammianus and the Historia Augusta*, Oxford, Clarendon Press.

Syme, Ronald (1971), *Emperors and Biography: Studies in the* Historia Augusta, Oxford, Clarendon Press.

Syme, Ronald (1980), "Biographers of the Caesars," *Museum Helveticum* 37: 104–28; repr. in E. Badian (ed.), *Roman Papers*, iii, Oxford, Clarendon Press, pp. 1251–75.

al-Tabarani, Sulayman b. Ahmad (1996), *Musnad al-Shamiyyin*, ed. Hamdi 'Abd al-Majid al-Silafi, 4 vols., Beirut, Mu'assasat al-Risala.

Taft, Robert F. (1991), *A History of the Liturgy of St. John Chrysostom*, iv: *The Diptychs*, Rome, Pontifical Oriental Institute.

Taft, Robert F. (1997), *Beyond East and West: Problems in Liturgical Understanding*, 2nd edn., Rome, Pontifical Oriental Institute.

Tait, William John (ed.) (1977), *Papyri from Tebtunis in Egyptian and Greek*, London, Egypt Exploration Society.

Tait, William John (1992), "Demotic Literature and Egyptian Society," in Janet H. Johnson (ed.), *Life in a Multi-Cultural Society: Egypt from Cambyses to Constantine and Beyond*, Chicago, Oriental Institute of the University of Chicago, pp. 303–10.

Tamanaha, Brian Z. (2004), *On the Rule of Law: History, Politics, Theory*, Cambridge and New York, Cambridge University Press.

Tate, G. (1992), *Les Campagnes de la Syrie du Nord du IIe au VIIe siècle*, i, Paris, Geuthner.

Taylor, Joan E. (1990), "The Phenomenon of Early Jewish-Christianity: Reality or Scholarly Invention?" *Vigiliae Christianae* 44: 313–34.

Taylor, John H. (tr.) (1982), *Augustine: The Literal Meaning of Genesis*, 2 vols., New York, Newman Press.

Tchalenko, G. (1953–8), *Villages antiques de la Syrie du nord: le massif du Bélus à l'époque romaine*, 3 vols., Paris, Geuthner.

Teillet, Suzanne (1984), *Des Goths à la nation gothique: les origines de l'idée de nation en Occident du Ve au VIIe siècle*, Paris, Les Belles Lettres.

Teitler, H. C. (1999), "*Visa vel lecta*? Ammianus on Persia and the Persians," in Drijvers and Hunt (1999: 216–23).

Thélamon, Françoise (1981), *Païens et chrétiens au IVe siècle: l'apport de l'*Histoire ecclésiastique *de Rufin d'Aquilée*, Paris, Études Augustiniennes.

Theuws, Frans, and Alkemade, M. (2000), "A Kind of Mirror for Men: Sword Depositions in Late Antique Northern Gaul," in Theuws and Nelson (2000: 401–76).

Theuws, Frans, and Nelson, Janet L. (eds.) (2000), *Rituals of Power: From Late Antiquity to the Early Middle Ages*, Leiden, Brill.

Thompson, E. A. (1952), *A Roman Reformer and Inventor, being a New Text of the Treatise* De rebus bellicis, Oxford, Clarendon Press.

Thompson, E. A. (1982), *Romans and Barbarians: The Decline of the Western Empire*, Madison, University of Wisconsin Press.

Thomson, R. W. (2000), "Armenia in the Fifth and Sixth Century," in Cameron, Ward-Perkins, and Whitby (2000: 662–77).

Thraede, Klaus (1970), *Grundzüge griechisch-römischer Brieftopik*, Munich, Beck.

Thunø, Erik (2003), "The Cult of the Virgin, Icons, and Relics in Early Medieval Rome," in Brandt et al. (2003: 79–98).

Till, Walter C. (1934), "Griechische Philosphen bei den Kopten," in *Mélanges Maspero*, ii: *Orient grec, romain et byzantin*, Cairo, Institut Français d'Archéologie Orientale, pp. 165–75.

Timbie, Janet (1986), "The State of Research on the Career of Shenoute of Atripe," in Pearson and Goehring (1986: 258–70).

Todd, M. (1998), "The Germanic Peoples," in Cameron and Garnsey (1998: 461–86).

Todd, Malcolm (1972), *Everyday Life of the Barbarians: Goths, Franks and Vandals*, London, Batsford; New York, G. P. Putnam's Sons.

Todd, Malcolm (1987), *The Northern Barbarians, 100 BC–AD 300*, rev. edn., Oxford and New York, Blackwell.

Tomlin, Roger S. O. (1974), "The Date of the 'Barbarian Conspiracy'," *Britannia* 5: 303–9.

Tomlin, Roger S. O. (1988), "The Curse Tablets," in Barry Cunliffe (ed.), *The Temple of Sulis Minerva at Bath*, ii: *The Finds from the Sacred Spring*, Oxford, Oxford University Committee for Archaeology, pp. 59–280.

Tomlin, Roger S. O. (1993), "The Inscribed Lead Tablets," in Ann Woodward and Peter Leach (eds.), *The Uley Shrines: Excavation of a Ritual Complex on West Hill, Uley, Gloucestershire, 1977–79*, London, English Heritage Archaeological Reports, pp. 113–26.

Tonneau, R.-M. (1955), "Moïse dans la tradition syrienne," in H. Cazelles et al. (eds.), *Moïse, l'homme de l'Alliance*, Paris, Desclée, pp. 242–54.

Too, Y. L., and Livingstone, N. (eds.) (1998), *Pedagogy and Power: Rhetorics of Ancient Learning*, Cambridge, Cambridge University Press.

Torrey, Charles C. (1892), *The Commercial-Theological Terms of the Koran*, Leiden, Brill.

Toynbee, J. M. C. (1971), *Death and Burial in the Roman World*, Ithaca, Cornell University Press; pb edn. Baltimore, Johns Hopkins University Press, 1993.

Treadgold, Warren T. (1980), *The Nature of the Bibliotheca of Photius*, Washington, DC, Dumbarton Oaks Center for Byzantine Studies.

Treadgold, Warren T. (2007), *The Early Byzantine Historians*, Basingstoke, Palgrave Macmillan.

Treggiari, Susan (1981), "Concubinae," *Papers of the British School at Rome* 49: 59–81.

Treggiari, Susan (1991), *Roman Marriage: Iusti Coniuges from the Time of Cicero to the Time of Ulpian*, Oxford, Clarendon Press.

Trilling, James (1987), "Late Antique and Sub-Antique, or the 'Decline of Form' Reconsidered," *Dumbarton Oaks Papers* 41: 469–76.

Trinkaus, Charles (1970), *"In Our Image and Likeness": Humanity and Divinity in Italian Renaissance Thought*, 2 vols., London, Constable.

Troeltsch, Ernst (1925), "Aufsätze zur Geistesgeschichte und Religionssoziologie," in *Gesammelte Schriften*, iv, Tübingen, Mohr.

Trombley, Frank R. (1985), "Paganism in the Greek World at the End of Antiquity: The Case of Rural Anatolia and Greece," *Harvard Theological Review* 78: 327–52.

Trombley, Frank R. (1993–4), *Hellenic Religion and Christianization, c.370–529*, 2 vols., Leiden and New York, Brill.

Trombley, Frank R. and Watt, John W. (tr.) (2000), *The Chronicle of Pseudo-Joshua the Stylite*, Liverpool, Liverpool University Press.

Trout, Dennis (1999), *Paulinus of Nola: Life, Letters, and Poems*, Berkeley and Los Angeles, University of California Press.

Trout, Dennis (2001), "The Verse Epitaph(s) of Petronius Probus: Competitive Commemoration in Late-Fourth-Century Rome," *New England Classical Journal* 28: 157–76.

Trout, Dennis (2005), "Damasus and the Invention of Early Christian Rome," in Martin and Miller (2005: 298–315).

Turcan-Verkerk, Anne Marie (forthcoming), "Gregorio magno negli inventari di biblioteche medievali prima del sec. XIII," in *Gregorio magno e le origini dell'Europa*, Florence, SISMEL-Galluzzo.

Turner, Eric G. (1977), *The Typology of the Early Codex*, Philadelphia, University of Pennsylvania Press.

Turner, Eric G. (1980), *Greek Papyri: An Introduction*, 2nd edn., Oxford, Oxford University Press.

Ulansey, David (1989), *The Origins of the Mithraic Mysteries: Cosmology and Salvation in the Ancient World*, New York, Oxford University Press.

Ullman, B. L. (ed.) (1928), *Sicconis Polentoni scriptorum illustrium linguae latinae libri XVIII*, Rome, American Academy in Rome.

Ullman, B. L. (1955), *Studies in the Italian Renaissance*, Rome, Edizioni di Storia e Letteratura.

Urbainczyk, Theresa (1997), *Socrates of Constantinople: Historian of Church and State*, Ann Arbor, University of Michigan Press.

Väänänen, Veiko (1981), *Le Latin vulgaire*, 3rd edn., Paris, Klincksieck.

Van Creveld, Martin (1985), *Command in War*, Cambridge, MA, Harvard University Press.

Van Dam, Raymond (1985), *Leadership and Community in Late Antique Gaul*, Berkeley and Los Angeles, University of California Press.

Van Dam, Raymond (1993), *Saints and Their Miracles in Late Antique Gaul*, Princeton, NJ, Princeton University Press.

Van Dam, Raymond (2002), *Kingdom of Snow: Roman Rule and Greek Culture in Cappadocia*, Philadelphia, University of Pennsylvania Press.

Van Dam, Raymond (2003a), *Families and Friends in Late Roman Cappadocia*, Philadelphia, University of Pennsylvania Press.

Van Dam, Raymond (2003b), "The Many Conversions of the Emperor Constantine," in Mills and Grafton (2003: 127–51).

Van der Meer, Frederik (1962), *Augustine the Bishop: The Life and Work of a Father of the Church*, London, Sheed & Ward.

Vanderspoel, John (1995), *Themistius and the Imperial Court: Oratory, Civic Duty, and Paideia from Constantius to Theodosius*, Ann Arbor, University of Michigan Press.

Van der Vliet, Jacques (1993), "Spätantikes Heidentum im Ägypten im Spiegel der koptischen Literatur," in *Begegnung von Heidentum und Christentum im spätantiken Ägypten*, Riggisberg, Abegg-Stifftung, pp. 99–130.

van Dijk, Mathilde, and Nip, Renée (eds.) (2005), *Saints, Scholars, and Politicians: Gender as a Tool in Medieval Studies*, Leiden, Brill.

Van Doorninck, Frederick (1972), "Byzantium, Mistress of the Sea: 330–641," in Bass (1972: 133–58).

Van Es, W. A. (1967), *Wijster: A Native Village beyond the Imperial Frontier, 150–425 A.D.*, Groningen, Wolters.

Van Minnen, Peter (1994), "The Roots of Egyptian Christianity," *Archiv für Papyrusforschung und verwandte Gebiete* 40: 71–85.

Van Minnen, Peter (1995), "The Earliest Account of a Martyrdom in Coptic," *Analecta Bollandiana* 113: 13–38.

Vannier, Marie-Anne (1987), "Le Rôle de l'hexaéméron dans l'interprétation augustinienne de la création," *Revue des sciences philosophiques et théologiques* 71: 537–47.

Van Rompay, Lucas (1997), "Antiochene Biblical Interpretation: Greek and Syriac," in Judith Frishman and Lucas van Rompay (eds.), The Book of Genesis *in Jewish and Oriental Christian Interpretation*, Louvain, Peeters, pp. 103–23.

Van Wees, H., Sabin, P., and Whitby, L. M. (eds.) (2007), *The Cambridge History of Greek and Roman Warfare*, ii: *Rome from the Late Republic to the Late Empire*, Cambridge, Cambridge University Press.

Vasari, Giorgio (1987), *Lives of the Artists: A Selection*, tr. George Bull, Harmondsworth, Penguin.

Vavra, Elizabeth (2005), *Virtuelle Räume, Raumwahrnehmung und Raumvorstellung im Mittelalter*, Berlin, Akademie Verlag.

Veit, Ulrich (1989), "Ethnic Concepts in German Prehistory: A Case Study on the Relationship between Cultural Identity and Archaeological Objectivity," in Stephen Shennan (ed.), *Archaeological Approaches to Cultural Identity*, London, Unwin Hyman, pp. 35–56.

Vera, Domenico (1977), "Sulle edizioni antiche delle Relationes di Simmaco," *Latomus* 36: 1003–36.

Vera, Domenico (1981), *Commento storico alle Relationes di Quinto Aurelio Simmaco*, Pisa, Giardini.

Verlinde, A. D., and Erdrich, M. (1998), "Eine germanische Siedlung der späten Kaiserzeit mit umwehrter Anlage und umfangreicher Eisenindustrie in Heeten, Province Overijssel, Niederlande," *Germania* 76: 693–719.

Versnel, Henk S. (1991), "Beyond Cursing: The Appeal to Justice in Judicial Prayer," in Christopher A. Faraone and Dirk Obbink (eds.), *Magica Hiera*, Oxford and New York, Oxford University Press, pp. 60–106.

Vessey, Mark (1988), "Ideas of Christian Writing in Late Roman Gaul," unpublished D.Phil. dissertation, University of Oxford.

Vessey, Mark (1993), "Conference and Confession: Literary Pragmatics in Augustine's 'Apologia contra Hieronymum'," *Journal of Early Christian Studies* 1: 175–213.

Vessey, Mark (1998), "The Demise of the Christian Writer and the Remaking of 'Late Antiquity': From H.-I. Marrou's Saint Augustine (1938) to Peter Brown's Holy Man (1983)," *Journal of Early Christian Studies* 6: 377–411.

Vessey, Mark (2004), "Latin Literary History after Saint Jerome: The *Scriptorum illustrium latinae linguae libri* of Sicco Polenton," *Neulateinisches Jahrbuch* 6: 303–11.

Vessey, Mark (2005a), "Response to Catherine Conybeare: Women of Letters?," in Olson and Kerby-Fulton (2005: 73–96).

Vessey, Mark (2005b), "*Vera et Aeterna Monumenta*: Jerome's Catalogue of Christian Writers and the Premises of Erasmian Humanism," in Günter Frank, Thomas Leinkauf, and Markus Wriedt (eds.), *Die Patristik in der Frühen Neuzeit: die Relektüre der Kirchenväter in den Wissenschaften des 15. bis 18. Jahrhunderts*, Stuttgart, Frommann-Holzboog, pp. 351–75.

Vessey, Mark (intro.), and Halporn, James (tr.) (2004), *Cassiodorus: Institutions of Divine and Secular Learning, and On the Soul*, Liverpool, Liverpool University Press.

Vessey, Mark, Pollmann, Karla, and Fitzgerald, Allan D. (eds.) (1999), *History, Apocalypse, and the Secular Imagination: New Essays on Augustine's* City of God, Bowling Green, OH, Philosophy Documentation Center.

Veyne, Paul (1976), *Le Pain et le cirque: sociologie historique d'un pluralisme politique*, Paris, Seuil.

Veyne, Paul (1985), "L'Empire romain," in Philippe Ariès and George Duby (eds.), *Histoire de la vie privée*, i: *De l'empire romain à l'an mil*, Paris, Seuil, pp. 19–223.

Vidier, Alexandre (1965), *L'Historiographie à saint Benoît sur Loire et les miracles de saint Benoît*, Paris, Picard.

Ville, Georges (1960), "Les Jeux des gladiateurs dans l'empire chrétien," *Mélanges de l'Ecole Française de Rome* 72: 273–335.

Vinzent, Markus (1998), "Das 'heidnische' Ägypten im 5. Jahrhundert," in J. van Oort and D. Wyrwa (eds.), *Heiden und Christen im 5. Jahrhundert*, Leuven, Peeters, pp. 32–65.

Vitiello, M. (2004), "Teoderico a Roma: politica, amministrazione e propaganda nell'*adventus* dell'anno 500 (Considerazioni sull' 'Anonimo Valesiano II')," *Historia* 53: 73–120.

Vivian, Tim (tr.) (2004), *Four Desert Fathers: Pambo, Evagrius, Macarius of Egypt, and Macarius of Alexandria: Coptic Texts relating to the Lausiac History of Palladius*, Crestwood, NY, St. Vladimir's Seminary Press.

Vivian, Tim, Athanassakis, Apostolos N., and Greer, Rowan A. (tr.) (2003), Athanasius of Alexandria, *The Life of Antony*, Cistercian Studies Series 202, Kalamazoo, MI, Cistercian Publications.

Vogel, C. (1975), "L'Environnement cultuel du défunt durant la période paléochrétienne," in *La Maladie et la mort du chrétien dans la liturgie*, Conférences Saint-Serge, XXI Semaine d'Études Liturgiques, Paris, 1–4 Juillet, 1974, Rome, Edizioni Liturgiche, pp. 381–413.

Volp, Ulrich (2002), *Tod und Ritual in den christlichen Gemeinden der Antike*, Leiden, Brill.

Von Hartel, Wilhelm, and Wickhoff, Franz (eds.) (1895), *Die Wiener Genesis*, Vienna, Tempsky.

Vööbus, Arthur (1951), *Celibacy: A Requirement for Admission to Baptism in the Early Syrian Church*, Stockholm, Estonian Theological Society in Exile.

Vööbus, Arthur (1958), *Literary Critical and Historical Studies in Ephrem the Syrian*, Stockholm, Estonian Theological Society in Exile.

Vööbus, Arthur (1958–88), *A History of Asceticism in the Syrian Orient*, 3 vols., Louvain, Secrétariat du CSCO.

Vööbus, Arthur (1961), "The Institution of the behai qeiama and benat quiama in the ancient Syrian Church," *Church History* 30: 19–27.

Vööbus, Arthur (1965), *The School of Nisibis*, Louvain, Peeters.

Vryonis, Spyros (ed.) (1978), *The "Past" in Medieval and Modern Greek Culture*, Malibu, CA, Undena Publications.

Wagner, Guy (ed.) (1999–2001), *Les Ostraca grecs de Douch (O. Douch)*, iv–v (356–639), Cairo, Institut Français d'Archéologie Orientale.

Wailes, Stephen (2001), "Flesh and Spirit in the Plays of Hrosvitha of Gandersheim," *Speculum* 76: 1–27.

Walker, Andrew D. (1993), "Enargeia and the Spectator in Greek Historiography," *Transactions of the American Philological Association* 123: 353–77.

Walker, J. H. (1984), "Further Notes on Reservation Practice and Eucharistic Devotion: The Contribution of the Early Church at Rome," *Ephemerides Liturgicae* 98: 392–404.

Wallace-Hadrill, Andrew (1988), "The Social Structure of the Roman House," *Papers of the British School at Rome* 56: 43–97.

Wallace-Hadrill, Andrew (ed.) (1989), *Patronage in Ancient Society*, London and New York, Routledge.

Wallace-Hadrill, J. M. (1961), *The Long-Haired Kings and Other Studies in Frankish History*, London, Methuen.

Walmsley, Alan (2007), "Economic Developments and the Nature of Settlement in the Towns and Countryside of Syria–Palestine, ca. 565–800 CE," *Dumbarton Oaks Papers* 61: 319–52.

Wansbrough, John (1978), *The Sectarian Milieu: Content and Composition of Islamic Salvation History*, Oxford, Oxford University Press.

Wansbrough, John (2004), *Qur'anic Studies: Sources and Methods of Scriptural Interpretation*, with foreword, translations, and expanded notes by Andrew Rippin, new edn., Amherst, MA, Prometheus Books.

Warburg, Aby (1999), "Dürer and Italian Antiquity," in *The Renewal of Pagan Antiquity: Contributions to the Cultural History of the European Renaissance*, tr. David Britt, intro. by Kurt W. Forster, Los Angeles, Getty Research Institute for the History of Art and the Humanities, pp. 553–8.

Ward, Graham (ed.) (2001), *The Companion to Postmodern Theology*, Oxford, Blackwell.

Ward-Perkins, Bryan (1984), *From Classical Antiquity to the Middle Ages: Urban Public Building in Northern and Central Italy, AD 300–850*, Oxford, Oxford University Press.

Ward-Perkins, Bryan (1995), "Can the Survival of an Ancient Town-Plan be Used as Evidence of Dark-Age Urban Life?," in Guiliana Cavalieri Manasse and Elisabetta Roffia (eds.),

Splendida civitas nostra: studi archeologici in onore di Antonio Frova, Rome, Quasar, pp. 223–9.

Ward-Perkins, Bryan (1998), "The Cities," in Cameron and Garnsey (1998: 371–410).

Ward-Perkins, Bryan (2005), *The Fall of Rome and the End of Civilization*, Oxford and New York, Oxford University Press.

al-Wasiti, Muhammad b. Ahmad (1979), *Fada'il al-Bayt al-Maqdis*, ed. Isaac Hasson, Jerusalem, Magnes Press.

Wasserstrom, Steven (1995), *Between Muslim and Jew: The Problem of Symbiosis under Early Islam*, Princeton, NJ, Princeton University Press.

Waswo, Richard (1987), *Language and Meaning in the Renaissance*, Princeton, NJ, Princeton University Press.

Waszink, Jan H. (1948), "Varro, Livy and Tertullian on the History of Dramatic Art," *Vigiliae Christianae* 2: 224–42.

Wataghin Cantino, Gisella (1999), "The Ideology of Urban Burials," in Brogiolo and Ward-Perkins (1999: 147–80).

Wataghin Cantino, Gisella, Trinci Cecchelli, Margherita, and Pani Ermini, Letizia (2001), "L'edificio battesimale nel tessuto della città tardoantica e altomedievale in Italia," in *L'edificio battesimale in Italia: Aspetti e problemi*, Atti dell'VIII Congresso nazionale di archeologia cristiana, Genova, Sarzana, Albenga, Finale Ligure, Ventimiglia 21–26 Settembre 1998, Bordighera, Istituto Internazionale di Studi Liguri, v: 230–65.

Waterfield, Robin (tr.), and Dewald, Carolyn (1998), *Herodotus: The Histories*, Oxford, Oxford University Press.

Watson, Alan et al. (tr.) (1985), *The Digest (Pandecta) of Justinian*, Philadelphia, University of Pennsylvania Press.

Watt, W. Montgomery (1953), *Muhammad at Mecca*, Oxford, Clarendon Press.

Watts, Edward J. (2004), "Student Travel to Intellectual Centers: What Was the Attraction?" in Ellis and Kidner (2004: 13–23).

Watts, Edward J. (2006), *City and School in Late Antique Athens and Alexandria*, Berkeley and Los Angeles, University of California Press.

Webb, Ruth (1999), "Ekphrasis Ancient and Modern: The Invention of a Genre," *Word and Image* 15: 7–18.

Weber, Alison (1990), *Teresa of Avila and the Rhetoric of Femininity*, Princeton, NJ, Princeton University Press.

Weber, Max (1930), *The Protestant Ethic and the Spirit of Capitalism*, tr. Talcott Parsons, London, Allen & Unwin.

Weber, Max (1988), "Agrarverhältnisse im Altertum," and "Die sozialen Gründe des Untergangs der antiken Kultur," in *Gesammelte Aufsätze zur Sozial- und Wirtschaftsgeschichte*, ed. Marianne Weber, Tübingen, Mohr, pp. 1–288, 289–311.

Weismann, Werner (1972), *Kirche und Schauspiele: die Schauspiele im Urteil der lateinischen Kirchenväter unter besonderer Berücksichtigung von Augustin*, Würzburg, Augustinus.

Weiss, Roberto (1969), *The Renaissance Discovery of Classical Antiquity*, Oxford, Blackwell.

Weitzman, Michael P. (1992), "From Judaism to Christianity: The Syriac version of the Hebrew Bible," in Judith Lieu, John North, and Tessa Rajak (eds.), *The Jews among Pagans and Christians in the Roman Empire*, London, Routledge, pp. 147–73.

Weitzman, Michael P. (1999), *The Syriac Version of the Old Testament: An Introduction*, Cambridge, Cambridge University Press.

Weitzmann, Kurt (ed.) (1979), *The Age of Spirituality: Late Antique and Early Christian Art, Third to Seventh Century*, New York, Metropolitan Museum of Art.

Weitzmann, Kurt (ed.) (1980), *Age of Spirituality: A Symposium*, New York, Metropolitan Museum of Art; Princeton, NJ, Princeton University Press.

Wells, Peter (1999), *The Barbarians Speak: How the Conquered Peoples Shaped Roman Europe*, Princeton, NJ, Princeton University Press.

Wessel, Susan (2004), *Cyril of Alexandria and the Nestorian Controversy: The Making of a Saint and of a Heretic*, Oxford, Oxford University Press.

Wheatley, Paul (2001), *The Places where Men Pray Together: Cities in Islamic Lands, Seventh through Tenth Centuries*, Chicago and London, University of Chicago Press.

Wheeler, Eric P. (tr.) (1977), *Dorotheos of Gaza: Discourse and Sayings*, Cistercian Studies 33, Kalamazoo, MI, Cistercian Press.

Whitby, Michael (1988), *The Emperor Maurice and His Historian: Theophylact Simocatta on Persian and Balkan Warfare*, Oxford, Clarendon Press.

Whitby, Michael (1991), "John of Ephesus and the Pagans: Pagan Survivals in the Sixth Century," in Salamon (1991: 111–31).

Whitby, Michael (1994), "The Persian King at War," in Dabrowa (1994: 227–63).

Whitby, Michael (2006), "Factions, Bishops, Violence, and Urban Decline," in Krause and Witschel (2006: 441–61).

Whitcomb, Donald (1995), "The Misr of Ayla: New Evidence for the Early Islamic City," in K. 'Amr, F. Zayadine, and M. Zaghloul (eds.), *Studies in the History and Archaeology of Jordan*, v: *Art and Technology through the Ages*, Amman, Department of Antquities, pp. 277–88.

Whitcomb, Donald (1996), "Urbanism in Arabia," *Arabian Archaeology and Epigraphy* 7: 38–51.

White, Carolinne (1992), *Christian Friendship in the Fourth Century*, Cambridge, Cambridge University Press.

White, Hayden V. (1973), *Metahistory: The Historical Imagination in Nineteenth-Century Europe*, Baltimore, MD, Johns Hopkins University Press.

White, Hayden V. (1987), *The Content of the Form: Narrative Discourse and Historical Representation*, Baltimore, MD, Johns Hopkins University Press.

White, John L. (1984), "New Testament Epistolary Literature in the Framework of Ancient Epistolography," *ANRW* 2. 25. 2: 1730–56.

White, John L. (1986), *Light from Ancient Letters*, Philadelphia, Fortress Press.

White, Kenneth D. (1984), *Greek and Roman Technology*, Ithaca, NY, Cornell University Press.

White, L. M. (2003), "Rhetoric and Reality in Galatians: Framing the Social Demands of Friendship," in Fitzgerald, Olbricht, and White (2003: 307–49).

Whittaker, C. R. (1994), *Frontiers of the Roman Empire: A Social and Economic Study*, Baltimore, MD, Johns Hopkins University Press.

Whittaker, C. R. (2004), *Rome and Its Frontiers: The Dynamics of Empire*, London, Routledge.

Whittow, Mark (1990), "Ruling the Late Roman and Early Byzantine City: A Continuous History," *Past and Present* 129: 3–29.

Whittow, Mark (2001), "Recent Research on the Late Antique City in Asia Minor: The Second Half of the Sixth Century Revisited," in Lavan 2001: 137–53.

Wickham, Chris (2005), *Framing the Early Middle Ages: Europe and the Mediterranean, 400–800*, Oxford, Oxford University Press.

Widengren, G. (1965), *Die Religionen Irans*, Stuttgart, Kohlhammer.

Widengren, G. (1976), "Iran, der grosse Gegner Roms: Königsgewalt, Feudalismus, Militär-wesen," in *ANRW* 2.9.1: 219–306.

Wieczorek, A., Périn, P., von Welck, K., and Menghin, Wilfried (eds.) (1997), *Die Franken: Wegbereiter Europas. Vor 1500 Jahren, König Chlodwig und seine Erben*, 2nd edn., Mainz, von Zabern.

Wiedemann, T. E. J. (1986), "Between Men and Beasts: Barbarians in Ammianus Marcellinus," in I. S. Moxon, J. D. Smart, and A. J. Woodman (eds.), *Past Perspectives: Studies in Greek and Roman Historical Writing*, Cambridge, Cambridge University Press, pp. 189–201.

Wiedemann, T. E. J. (1995), "Das Ende der römischen Gladiatorenspiele," *Nikephorus* 8: 145–59.

Wiemer, Hans-Ulrich (1995), "Die Rangstellung des Sophisten Libanios unter den Kaisern Julian, Valens und Theodosius. Mit einem Anhang über Abfassung und Verbreitung von Libanios' Rede 'Für die Tempel' (Or. XXX)," *Chiron* 25: 89–130.

Wiesehöfer, Josef (2001), *Ancient Persia*, London and New York, Tauris.

Wiesehöfer, Josef (2005), "Rūm as Enemy of Iran," in Gruen (2005: 105–20).

Wiesehöfer, Josef (2007), "King, Court and Royal Representation in the Sasanian Empire," in A. J. S. Spawforth (ed.), *Court and Court Society in Ancient Monarchies*, Cambridge, Cambridge University Press, pp. 58–81.

Wiesehöfer, Josef, and Huyse, Ph. (eds.) (2006), *Ērān und Anērān: Studien zu den Beziehungen zwischen dem Sasanidenreich und der Mittelmeerwelt*, Stuttgart, Steiner.

Wilcox, Amanda (2005), "Sympathetic Rivals: Consolation in Cicero's Letters," *American Journal of Philology* 126: 237–55.

Wilken, Robert L. (1983), *John Chrysostom and the Jews: Rhetoric and Reality in the Late Fourth Century*, Berkeley and Los Angeles, University of California Press.

Wilken, Robert L. (1992), *The Land Called Holy: Palestine in Christian History and Thought*, New Haven, CT, Yale University Press.

Williams, Frank (tr.) (1994), *The* Panarion *of Epiphanius of Salamis: Books II and III (Sects 47–80, De Fide)*, Leiden, Brill.

Williams, Michael Allen (1996), *Rethinking "Gnosticism": An Argument for Dismantling a Dubious Category*, Princeton, NJ, Princeton University Press.

Williams, Rowan (ed.) (1989), *The Making of Orthodoxy: Essays in Honour of Henry Chadwick*, Cambridge, Cambridge University Press.

Willis, William H., and Maresch, Klaus (eds.) (1998), *The Archive of Ammon Scholasticus of Panopolis*, i: *The Legacy of Harpocration*, Opladen, Westdeutscher Verlag.

Wilson, Nigel G. (1978), "A Byzantine Miscellany: Ms. Barocci 131 Described," *Jahrbuch der Österreichischen Byzantinistik* 27: 158–79.

Wilson, Nigel G. (1996), *Scholars of Byzantium*, 2nd edn., London, Duckworth.

Wilson, S. G. (1995), *Related Strangers: Jews and Christian 70–170 C.E.*, Minneapolis, MN, Fortress Press.

Wimbush, Vincent L., and Valantasis, Richard (eds.) (1995), *Asceticism*, Oxford and New York, Oxford University Press.

Winkler, John. J. (1990), *The Constraints of Desire: The Anthropology of Sex and Gender in Ancient Greece*, New York, Routledge.

Winter, Engelbert, and Dignas, Beate (2001), *Rom und das Perserreich: Zwei Weltmächte zwischen Konfrontation und Koexistenz*, Berlin, Akademie Verlag.

Winterbottom, M. (ed. and tr.) (1978), *Gildas:* The Ruin of Britain *and Other Works*, Chichester, Phillimore.

Wintjes, Jorit (2005), *Das Leben des Libanius*, Rahden, Leidorf.

Wipszycka, Ewa (1994), "Le Monachisme égyptien et les villes," *Travaux et Mémoires* 12: 1–44.

Wipszycka, Ewa (1996), "Le Nationalisme a-t-il existé dans l'Égypte byzantine?' and "La Christianisation de l'Égypte aux IVe-VIe siècles: Aspects sociaux et ethniques," in *Études sur le christianisme dans l'Égypte de l'antiquité tardive*, Rome, Institutum Patristicum Augustinianum, pp. 9–61, 63–105.

Wipszycka, Ewa (1997), "La sovvenzione costantiniana in favore del clero," *Rendiconti Morali dell' Accademia Nazionale dei Lincei*, 9th ser. 8: 483–98.

Wipszycka, Ewa (1998), "I papiri documentari e la storia del cristianesimo in Egitto," in G. Cavallo et al. (eds.), *Scrivere libri e documenti nel mondo antico*, Mostra di papiri della Biblioteca Medicea Laurenziana, Firenze, 25 Agosto–25 Settembre 1998, Florence, Gonnelli, pp. 67–78.

Wipszycka, Ewa (2000), "The Nag Hammadi Library and the Monks: A Papyrologist's Point of View," *Journal of Juristic Papyrology* 30: 179–91.

Wipszycka, Ewa (2001), "Les Papyrus documentaires concernant l'Église d'avant le tournant constantinien: un bilan des vingt dernières années," in Isabella Andorlini et al. (eds.), *Atti del XXII Congresso Internazionale di Papirologia. Firenze, 23–29 Agosto 1998*, ii, Firenze, Istituto Papirologico G. Vitelli, pp. 1307–30.

Wischmeyer, W. (1992), *Von Golgatha zum Ponte Molle: Studien zur Sozialgeschichte der Kirche im dritten Jahrhundert*, Göttingen, Vandenhoeck & Ruprecht.

Wisse, F. (1995), "The Coptic Versions of the New Testament," in Bart D. Ehrman and M. W. Holmes (eds.), *The Text of the New Testament in Contemporary Research: Essays on the Status Quaestionis. A Volume in Honor of Bruce M. Metzger*, Grand Rapids, MI, Eerdmans, pp. 131–41.

Witschel, Christian (2001), "Rom und die Städte Italiens in Spätantike und Frühmittelalter," *Bonner Jahrbücher* 201: 113–62.

Witt, Ronald G. (2000), *In the Footsteps of the Ancients: The Origins of Humanism from Lovato to Bruni*, Leiden, Brill.

Wittekind, Susanne (2004), "Die Illustration von Augustinustexten im Mittelalter," in Wilhelm Geerlings and Christian Schulze (eds.), *Der Kommentar in Antike und Mittelalter*, ii: *Neue Beiträge zu seiner Erforschung*, Leiden, Brill, pp. 101–27.

Wolf, Kenneth Baxter (tr.) (1990), *Conquerors and Chroniclers of Early Medieval Spain*, Liverpool, Liverpool University Press; 2nd edn., 1999.

Wolf, Peter (1952), *Vom Schulwesen der Spätantike: Studien zu Libanius*, Baden-Baden, Verlag für Kunst und Wissenschaft.

Wolfram, Herwig (1981), "Gothic History and Historical Ethnography," *Journal of Medieval History* 7: 309–19.

Wolfram, Herwig (1988), *History of the Goths*, tr. Thomas J. Dunlap, Berkeley and Los Angeles, University of California Press.

Wolfram, Herwig (1994), "*Origo et religio*: Ethnic Traditions and Literature in Early Medieval Texts," *Early Medieval Europe* 3: 19–38.

Wolfram, Herwig (1997), *The Roman Empire and Its Germanic Peoples*, Berkeley and Los Angeles, University of California Press.

Wolfram, Herwig (1998), "Typen der Ethnogenese: ein Versuch," in Geuenich (1998: 608–27).

Wolfram, Herwig, and Pohl, Walter (eds.) (1990), *Typen der Ethnogenese unter besonderer Berücksichtigung der Bayern*, 2 vols., Vienna, Verlag der Österreichischen Akademie der Wissenschaften.

Womersley, David (1988), *The Transformation of The Decline and Fall of the Roman Empire*, Cambridge, Cambridge University Press.

Womersley, David (2002), *Gibbon and the "Watchmen of the Holy City": The Historian and His Reputation, 1776–1815*, Oxford, Clarendon Press.

Wood, Ian (1977), "Kings, Kingdoms and Consent," in Sawyer and Wood (1977: 6–29).

Wood, Ian (1983), *The Merovingian North Sea*, Alingsås, Viktoria Bokförlag.

Wood, Ian (1990), "Ethnicity and the Ethnogenesis of the Burgundians," in Wolfram and Pohl (1990, i: 53–69).

Wood, Ian (1993), "The Code in Merovingian Gaul," in Harries and Wood (1993: 161–77).

Wood, Ian (1994), *The Merovingian Kingdoms, 450–751*, London, Longman.

Wood, Ian (ed.) (1998), *Franks and Alamanni in the Merovingian Period: An Ethnographic Perspective*, Woodbridge and Rochester, NY, Boydell Press.

Wood, Ian (2001), *The Missionary Life: Saints and the Evangelization of Europe, 400–1050*, Harlow, Longman.

Woods, David (1991), "The Date of the Translation of the Relics of SS. Luke and Andrew to Constantinople," *Vigiliae Christianae* 45: 286–92.

Woods, David (1998), "Ammianus and Eutherius," *Acta Classica* 41: 110–18.

Woods, David (2000), "On 'Ships in the Air' in 749," *Peritia* 14: 429–30.

Woods, David (2001a), "Dating Basil of Caesarea's Correspondence with Arintheus and His Widow," *Studia Patristica* 37: 301–7.

Woods, David (2001b), "'Veturius' and the Beginning of the Diocletianic Persecution," *Mnemosyne* 54: 587–91.

Woods, David (2003), "Ammianus Marcellinus and Bishop Eusebius of Emesa," *Journal of Theological Studies* 54: 585–91.

Woolf, Greg (1992), "Imperialism, Empire and the Integration of the Roman Economy," *World Archaeology* 23: 283–93.

Woolf, Greg (1996), "Monumental Writing and the Expansion of Roman Society in the Early Roman Empire," *Journal of Roman Studies* 86: 22–39.

Woolf, Greg (1998), *Becoming Roman: The Origins of Provincial Civilization in Gaul*, Cambridge, Cambridge University Press.

Worp, Klass A. (1990), "A Forgotten Coptic Inscription from the Monastery of Epiphanius: Some Remarks on Dated Coptic Documents from the Pre-Conquest Period," *Analecta Papyrologica* 2: 139–43.

Wright, F. A. (tr.) (1954), *Select Letters of Saint Jerome*, Loeb Classical Library, Cambridge, MA, Harvard University Press.

Wright, Roger (1982), *Late Latin and Early Romance in Spain and Carolingian France*, Liverpool, Francis Cairns.

Wright, Roger (2002), *A Sociophilological Study of Late Latin*, Utrecht, Brepols.

Yarbrough, Anne (1976), "Christianisation in the Fourth Century: The Example of Roman Women," *Church History* 45: 149–64.

Yarshater, Ehsan (1971), "Were the Sasanians Heirs to the Achaemenids?," in *La Persia nel Medioevo*, Atti del Convegno Internazionale (Roma, 31 Marzo–5 Aprile 1970), Accademia Nazionale dei Lincei, Quaderno, 160, Rome, pp. 517–31.

Yarshater, Ehsan (ed.) (1982–), *Encyclopaedia Iranica*, 14 vols., London and Boston, Routledge & Kegan Paul.

Yarshater, Ehsan (ed.) (1983a), *The Cambridge History of Iran*, iii: *The Seleucid, Parthian and Sasanian Periods*, 2 vols. Cambridge, Cambridge University Press.

Yarshater, Ehsan (1983b), "Iranian National History," in Yarshater (1983a, i: 359–477).

Yasin, Ann Marie (2005), "Funerary Monuments and Collective Identity: From Roman Family to Christian Identity," *Art Bulletin* 87: 433–56.

Yeo, Cedric A. (1946), "Land and Sea Transportation in Imperial Italy," *Transactions of the American Philological Association* 77: 221–44.

Young, Bailey (1999), "The Myth of the Pagan Cemetery," in Karkov, Wickham-Crowley, and Young (1999: 61–85).

Young, Frances M. (1983), *From Nicaea to Chalcedon: A Guide to the Literature and Its Background*, Philadelphia, Fortress Press.

Young, Frances M. (1997), *Biblical Exegesis and the Formation of Christian Culture*, Cambridge, Cambridge University Press.

Zanker, Paul (1983), *Provinzielle Kaiserporträts: zur Rezeption der Selbstdarstellung des Princeps*, Munich, Bayerische Akademie der Wissenschaften.

Zanker, Paul (1988), *The Power of Images in Age of Augustus*, Ann Arbor, University of Michigan Press.

Zanker, Paul (1996), *The Mask of Socrates: The Image of the Intellectual in Antiquity*, tr. Alan Shapiro, Berkeley and Los Angeles, University of California Press.

Zauzich, Karl-Theodor (1983), "Demotische Texte römischer Zeit," in G. Grimm, H. Heinen, and E. Winter (eds.), *Das römisch-byzantinishche Ägypten*, Akten des internationalen Symposiums 26.–30. September 1978 in Trier, Mainz, von Zabern, pp. 77–80.

Zeisel, William M. (1975), "An Economic Survey of the Early Byzantine Church," unpublished Ph.D. dissertation, Rutgers University.

Zeitlin, Froma I. (1996), *Playing the Other: Gender and Society in Classical Greek Literature*, Chicago, University of Chicago Press.

Zelzer, Klaus (1989), "Von Benedikt zu Hildemar: zu Textgestalt und Textgeschichte der Regula Benedicti auf ihrem Weg zur Alleingeltung," *Frühmittelalterliche Studien* 23: 112–30.

Zelzer, Michaela (1989), "Plinius Christianus: Ambrosius als Epistolograph," *Studia Patristica* 23: 203–8.

Zelzer, Michaela (1997), "Die Briefliteratur," in L. J. Engels and Heinz Hofman (eds.), *Neues Handbuch der Literaturwissenschaft*, iv, Wiesbaden, AULA Verlag.

Ziolkowski, Jan M. (1996), "Towards a History of Medieval Latin Literature," in F. A. C. Mantello and A. G. Rigg (eds.), *Medieval Latin: An Introduction and Bibliographical Guide*, Washington, DC, Catholic University of America Press, pp. 505–31.

Zuckerman, Constantine (1995), "The Hapless Recruit Psois and the Mighty Anchorite, Apa John," *Bulletin of the American Society of Papyrologists* 32: 183–94.

Index

Bold text indicates pages where the subject is treated as a main topic.